USA
THE ROUGH GUIDE

KT-562-347

written and researched by
Samantha Cook, Jamie Jensen,
Tim Perry and Greg Ward

additional contributions by
Deborah Bosley, Martin Dunford, Donald Hutera,
Jack Holland and Mick Sinclair

edited by
Greg Ward

THE ROUGH GUIDES

CONTENTS

Introduction x

PART THREE   CONTEXTS   951

HELP US UPDATE

Much hard work has gone into ensuring that this second edition of the *Rough Guide to the USA* is comprehensive and accurate. However, from the moment of publication things will, of course, change. Prices rise, opening hours alter, restaurants and hotels close, and new ones appear.

A crucial element in the monumental task of keeping this book up to date is the response we get from readers. Please write and let us know if you spot anything that is no longer true, if you feel we have omitted anything that deserves inclusion, or if you have any comments on our information or the way it is presented. We are happy to send a copy of any *Rough Guide* to the writers of the best letters. Among those whose letters were invaluable this time around were Hugh Bayley, Walter Blake, R M Boynton, Mark Carubia, Anthony Clements, Anna Crago, Denise Cripps & Martin Conway, William Culbert, Daniel Czaran, Sarah Donatantonio, Alison Duckham, Kathleen Elliott, Neil Elton, Dr C J Evans, Stephanie Grimm, Carol Hamilton, Renate Herz, Grahaeme Hesp, Tim Hill, Diane Ionta, Jacqueline Jackson, Helen Jibson, Sam Johnson, Mr & Mrs D M Kingsley, G F Kirby, Brian MacDonald, Matt McAllester, Giuditta Merli, Kristine Michaels, Charlotte Morgan, Paul Morris, Conxi Pareras, Simon & Jill Parkinson, F H Pedley, Joanne Philpot, Victoria Pittard, Matthew Price, Stefan Sanders, Mrs E Savory, Fiona Sharp, Rob Sherwin, J D Smith, Nick Snowdon, Kerry Sumner, Richard Ulyett, Philip von Simson, Margaret Vyle, Mrs S M Webb, Glenn West, Andy White, Sarah Wilson, Egbert Wolf, and Mark Woodhead.

We also welcome correspondence from the owners of any establishments reviewed in this book, with news of updated prices or facilities, and will send researchers to those who are not mentioned and feel that they should be.

Please mark letters "Rough Guide USA Update" and send to:

Rough Guides, 1 Mercer Street, London WC2H 9QJ,
or Rough Guides, 375 Hudson Street, 4th Floor, New York, NY 10014.

THANKS TO EVERYONE

This book could never have been written without the assistance of the many people across the United States who gave us their unstinting help:

Becky Aleshire, Ronda Allen, Sandy Anacker, Carol Ann Anderson, Jane Andrade, Carla Andrews, Bonnie Barness, Frank Bauer and John Davis Jr (and Murphy), Jim and Doris Begnaud, Doug Bell, Susan Bell, J Ray Bennison, Amy Blyth, Kim Booth, Becky Bovell, Barb Bowman, Lindy Boyes, Jeannine Breshears, Colin Brodie, Dan Brown, W Patrick Brown, Barbara Campbell, Linda Carlson, Mark Cestari, Anne Chadwick, Anita Clark, Mary Kay Cline, Marcia Cobun, Cynthia Collyer, Shirley Condiff, Dorothy Coyle, Tom Crain, Marygael Cullen, Tim Culver, Jane DeBlieux, Phyllis Delfitt, Mary Denis, Judy Draucker, Maureen Droz, Andrea Ernst, E J Farhood, Celeste Fenger, Tamara Ferguson, Beryl Fishbone, Emelyn Flythe, Gwen Fullbrook, Robert Gibbons, Jane Gillespie, Rich Grant, Nancy Gray, Evelyn Hall, Lucinda Hampton, Mark Hancock, Robert Hanna, Tyler Hardeman, Jennifer Harsh, Doris Harty, Bob Hastings, Shelly Helmerick, John Hickenlooper, Kathy Hildre, Chuck Hillestad, Pamela Hoedel, Karen Howard, Melinda Huntley, Dana Johnson, Amy Jonak, Donna Jung, Keith Kaminski, Jim Karras, Connie Kenney, Tom King, Karen Koser, Kurt Kosmowski, Rosetta Stone Land, Denise Lattery, Shelly Lau, Blair Learn, David Lee, Joyce Lee, Bob Levine, Cheryl Lewis, Jim Lovejoy, Stephen Martin, Jutta Matalka, John McIlhenny, Sharon McKeague, Ellen McMahon, Susan Middleton, Nancy Miller, Anne Mohon, Tania Moore, Kevin Morrissey, Kathleen Myers, Mary Novotny, Timothy Olsen, Jerry Olson, Joe O'Mealy, Jeff Osborn, Jim Pape, Ann Parthé, Carol Pasternak, Mary Pepitone, Tracy Potter, Rob Powers, Craig Pugsley, Anne-Marie Quagliaroli, Susan Ricciardi, Mike Robertson, Wendy Roe, Karon Rogers, Rudy, Cindy Sanders, Linda Sauer, Jennifer Schmits, Mary Schmitz, Ray Shepard, Kay and Peter Shumway, Halli Simmins, Ami Simpson, Georgia Smith, Nancy Smith, Vivian Stanley, Gully Stanford, Jackie Stewart, Tom Stilz, Susan Stoney, Kelly Strenge, Carla Sullivan, Ruth Birch Sykes, Bob Sylvia, Christine Szalay, Betty Szerencse, Sandy Torres, Joan van Otheren, Jackie Voight, Bonnie V'Soske, Mark Waldo, Christy Walker, Ellen Wein, Don Wick, Marty Willett, Floyd Williams Jr.

LIST OF MAPS

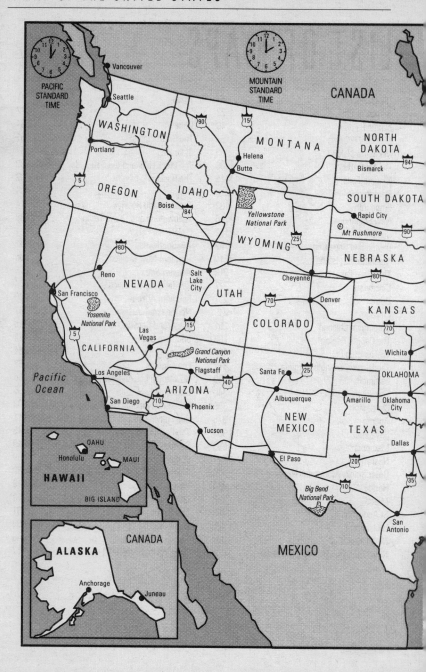

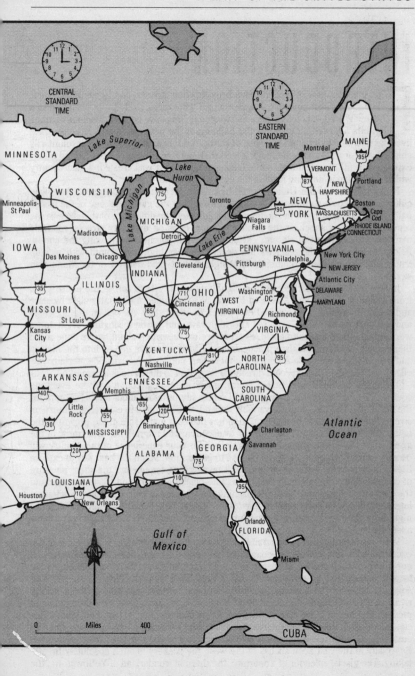

INTRODUCTION

For five centuries, travellers have brought their dreams and hopes to America. For the earliest pioneers, it was a virgin wilderness ready to be shaped into a "New World", a potential paradise wasted on its native peoples. Millions of immigrants followed, to share in the building of the new nation and to better their lives, far from the hidebound societies of Europe and Asia; the slaves, too, involuntarily shipped over from Africa, eventually joined them as free citizens. As the United States expanded to fill the continent, something genuinely new was created: a vast country which took pride in defining itself in the eyes of the world.

Every traveller in the United States has some idea of what to expect. American culture has become so thoroughly shared throughout the globe that one of the principal joys of getting to know the country is not so much the difference of the place as the repeated delicious shock of the familiar. Yellow taxis on busy city streets; roadside mailboxes straight out of *Peanuts* cartoons; wooden porches overlooking the cotton-fields; tumbleweed rolling across the desert; endless highways dotted with pick-up trucks and chrome-plated diners; the first sight of the Grand Canyon, or the Manhattan skyline.

In this book, we've picked out the highlights for travellers across the entire USA, from Maine to Hawaii, and Alaska to Florida. We've divided the country state by state and region by region, and covered every area of every state. As well as the big cities and national parks, we've explored the highways and byways, singling out detours worth making and places to avoid. Everywhere we've written about, we've done more than simply provide up-to-date practicalities for visitors: we've delved into the history and people who have made America what it is. Our hope is to inform and entertain travellers, and to point in unexpected directions as well as to the obvious landmarks.

Travelling in the United States is extremely easy; in a country where everyone seems to be forever on the move, there's rarely any problem about finding a room for the night, and you can almost invariably depend on being able to eat well and inexpensively. The development of transportation has played a major role in the growth of the nation; the railroad opened the way for transcontinental migrations, while most of the great cities have been shaped by the automobile. Your experience of the country will be very much flavored by how you choose to get around. Much the best way to explore the country is to drive your own vehicle: it takes a long time before the sheer pleasure of cruising down the interstate, with the radio playing country and western music and the signs to Chicago and Nashville flashing past, begins to pall. Car rental is an absolute bargain, every main road is lined with budget motels charging around $30 per night for a good room, and, whatever Americans may say, the price of gasoline remains absurdly low.

We have also detailed public transportation options everywhere; with the aid of the excellent-value nationwide rail, coach and air passes, foreign visitors in particular can get wherever they choose. However, if you do travel this way, there's a real temptation to see America as a succession of big **cities**. True enough, **New York** and **Los Angeles** have an exhilarating dynamism and excitement, and among their worthy rivals are **New Orleans**, the flamboyant home of jazz; **Chicago**, at the cutting edge of modern architecture; and **San Francisco**, on its beautiful Pacific bay. Few other cities can quite match this level of interest, however, and following a heavily urban itinerary cuts you off from the astonishing **landscapes** that make the USA truly distinctive. Especially in the vast open spaces of the west, the scenery is often absolutely breathtaking. The glacial splendor of **Yosemite**, the thermal wonderland of **Yellowstone**, the awesome red-rock **canyons** of Arizona and Utah, and the spectacular **Rocky Mountains** are among many of the treasures preserved and protected in the splendid national park system. Once you reach such places, the potential for **hiking** and **camping** is magnificent – the United States possesses wildernesses in a sense that Europe simply doesn't – but it's usually essential to have a car to get near them.

Above all, travellers can enjoy the sheer thrill of experiencing American popular culture in the places where it began. Place names from rock'n'roll songs spring into life; panoramas straight out of Hollywood movies spread across the horizon. For **music** fans, the chance to hear country music in Nashville or rhythm and blues in New Orleans, or to visit Elvis in Memphis, verges on a religious experience; readers brought up on the **books** of Mark Twain can ride a paddle-wheeler on the Mississippi; **moviegoers** can live out their Western fantasies in the Utah desert.

The United States is all too often dismissed, even by its own inhabitants, as a land almost devoid of **history**. Though mainstream America tends to trace its roots back to the Pilgrims and Puritans of New England – an area which to European sensibilities can seem somewhat twee – the rest of the continent has an even longer past, stretching back way beyond the French culture of Louisiana and the Spanish presence in California to the majestic cliff palaces built by the Anasazi in the Southwest a thousand years ago. There are also any number of fascinating strands to America's post-revolutionary history – relics of the Gold Rush in California, of the Civil Rights years in the South, or of the Civil War anywhere east of the Mississippi.

Though we've had to structure this book regionally, the most invigorating expeditions are those which take in more than one area. You do not, however, have to cross the entire continent from shore to shore in order to appreciate its amazing diversity, or to be impressed by the way in which such an extraordinary range of topography and people has been melded into one nation. It would take forever to see the whole place, and the more time you spend on the road the less time you'll have to savor the small-town pleasures and backroads oddities that may well provide your strongest memories. It doesn't take long to realize that there is no such thing as a typical American person, any more than there is a typical American landscape, but there can be few places where strangers can feel so confident of a warm reception.

PART ONE

THE
BASICS

GETTING THERE FROM BRITAIN AND EUROPE

Non-stop flights to **Los Angeles** from London take ten or eleven hours; the London–**Miami** flight takes eight hours, while flying time to **New York** is seven or so hours. Following winds ensure that return flights are always an hour or two shorter than outward journeys. One-stop direct flights to destinations beyond the East Coast obviously add time to the journey, but can work out cheaper than non-stop flights. Because of the time difference between Europe and the US, flights usually leave Britain in mid-morning, while flights back from the US tend to arrive in Britain early in the morning.

Over twenty US cities are accessible by non-stop flights from the UK (see p.4). At these "gateway cities", airport hubs for US air carriers, you can connect with extensive networks of domestic flights on into the rest of the country. "Direct" services (which may land once or twice on the way, but are called direct if they keep the same flight number throughout their journey) fly from Britain to nearly every other major US city.

FARES AND AIRLINES

Britain remains one of the best places in Europe to obtain flight bargains, though **fares** vary widely according to season, availability and the current level of inter-airline competition. The chart below will give you a broad idea of typical rates available from the operators listed on p.5.

The comments that follow can only act as a general guide, so be sure to shop around carefully for the best offers by checking the travel ads in

SAMPLE AIR FARES FROM BRITAIN

The prices given below (in £ sterling) are a general indication of the (minimum) transatlantic air fares obtainable from specialist companies in 1994. Each airline decides the exact dates of its seasons.

	LOW Nov 1–Dec 11, Dec 25–Mar 14		SHOULDER Mar 15–Jun 14, Sep 16–Oct 31		HIGH Jun 15–Sep 15, Dec 12–Dec 24	
From **London** to	one-way	return	one-way	return	one-way	return
New York	126	199	158	294	189	363
Boston	126	220	158	298	189	363
Washington	126	219	158	298	189	357
Miami	142	258	161	322	207	413
Denver	160	303	198	322	225	431
Chicago	147	274	184	357	213	409
Houston	157	274	195	282	230	412
Seattle	162	293	205	362	225	431
Los Angeles	157	299	193	357	225	449
San Francisco	157	293	193	357	225	429
From **Manchester** to						
New York	156	219	214	322	259	413
Chicago	232	368	265	418	294	469
Los Angeles	219	317	295	466	362	582

NON-STOP FLIGHTS TO THE US FROM BRITAIN

FROM LONDON
(Heathrow or Gatwick)

Atlanta *British Airways, Delta*

Baltimore *British Airways*

Boston *American Airlines, British Airways, Northwest, Virgin Atlantic*

Charlotte *British Airways*

Chicago *American Airlines, British Airways*

Cincinnati *Delta*

Dallas/Fort Worth *American Airlines, British Airways*

Denver *Continental*

Detroit *Delta*

Houston *British Airways, Continental*

Los Angeles *Air New Zealand, American Airlines, British Airways, United, Virgin Atlantic*

Miami *American Airlines, British Airways, Delta, Virgin Atlantic*

Minneapolis *Northwest*

Nashville *American Airlines*

New York *Air India, American Airlines, British Airways, Continental, Kuwait Air, United, Virgin Atlantic*

Orlando *British Airways, Virgin Atlantic*

Philadelphia *British Airways*

Raleigh/Durham *American Airlines*

St Louis *TWA*

San Francisco *British Airways, United, Virgin*

Seattle *British Airways, United*

Washington DC *British Airways, United*

FROM MANCHESTER

Atlanta *Delta*

Chicago *American Airlines*

New York *American Airlines, British Airways*

FROM GLASGOW

Boston *Northwest*

Chicago *American Airlines*

New York *British Airways*

AIRLINES

Air India	☎071/493 4050	**Icelandair**	☎071/388 5599
Air New Zealand	☎071/741 2299	**Northwest**	☎0293/561000
American Airlines	☎081/572 5555	**TWA**	☎071/439 0707
British Airways	☎081/897 4000	**United**	☎081/990 9900
Continental	☎0800/776464	**USAir**	☎0800/777333
Delta	☎0800/414767	**Virgin Atlantic**	☎0293/747747

Toll-free phone numbers for airlines **in the United States** are listed on p.26.

the Sunday papers and, in London, scouring *Time Out*, *City Limits* and the *Evening Standard*. Giveaway magazines aimed at young travellers, like *TNT*, are also useful resources.

Stand-by deals are few and far between, and don't give great savings: in general you're better off with an **Apex** ticket. The conditions on these are pretty standard whoever you fly with – seats must be booked 21 days or more in advance, and you must stay for a minimum of seven nights; tickets are normally valid for up to six months. Some airlines also do a less expensive **Super-Apex** ticket, which can be up to £100 cheaper than an ordinary Apex but often must be booked thirty days in advance and is only valid for up to 21 days; usually, it's also non-refundable or changeable. With an **open-jaw** ticket you can fly into one city and out of another; fares are calculated by halving the return fares to each destination and adding the two figures together. This makes a convenient

option for those who want a fly-drive holiday (see opposite).

Generally, the most expensive time to fly is **high season**, roughly between June and August and around Christmas. May and September are slightly less pricey, and the rest of the year is considered low season and cheaper still. Remember, however, that high season in the UK can sometimes be the least costly and crowded season at your destination. For example, South Florida and New Orleans are both unbearably hot – almost swampy – in the summer, so the extra you might spend on a summer flight can be more than compensated for by low prices once you're on the ground. Keep an eye out for slack season bargains, and, additionally, make sure to check the exact dates of the seasons with your operator or airline; you might be able to make major savings by shifting your departure date by a week – or even a day. **Weekend rates** for all flights tend to be £30–50 more expensive than those in the week.

Whenever you're travelling, the competition between carriers is such that it's always worth phoning the **airlines** direct to check on **current deals** they may be offering, which will often undercut even the Apex fares.

Once in the US, a **Visiting US Airpass** (VUSA) can be a good idea if you want to see a lot of the country. These are only available to non-US residents, and must be bought before reaching the States (see p.25).

AGENTS AND CHARTER FLIGHTS

For an overview of the various offers, and unofficially discounted tickets, go straight to an **agent** specializing in low-cost flights (we've listed some below). Especially if you're under 26 or a student, they may be able to knock up to fifty percent off the regular Apex fares when there are no special airline deals, thus bringing prices to the East Coast down as low as £200 return.

The same agents also offer cut-price seats on **charter flights**. These are particularly good value if you're travelling from a British city other than London, although they tend to be limited to the summer season, be restricted to so-called "holiday destinations" and have fixed departure and return dates. Brochures are available in most high street travel agents, or contact the specialists direct.

COURIER FLIGHTS

It is possible for those on a very tight budget to travel as **couriers**. Most of the major courier firms offer opportunities to travel for up to fifty percent off the cheapest fare (as low as £150–200

return to New York, or £200 return to the West Coast) in return for delivering a package. There'll be someone to check you in and to meet you at your destination, which minimizes any red-tape hassle. However, you'll have to travel light, with only a cabin-bag, and accept tight restrictions on travel dates – stays of more than a fortnight are rare. For phone numbers, see below or check the Yellow Pages.

PACKAGES

Packages – fly-drive, flight/accommodation deals and guided tours (or a combination of all three) – can work out cheaper than arranging the same trip yourself, especially for a short-term stay. To take a typical example, a return flight plus middle-range midtown hotel accommodation for three nights in New York City costs around £350 per person. Drawbacks include the loss of flexibility and the fact that you'll probably be made to stay in hotels in the mid-range to expensive bracket, even though less expensive accommodation is almost always readily available.

High street travel agents have plenty of brochures and information about the various combinations available. Most charter deals from agents include accommodation along with the flight. Prices are based on two or more people travelling together; and this can be such a bargain that even if you do end up paying for a hotel room, which, of course, you don't have to use, it may still be cheaper than the standard fare. Flight-only deals do turn up at the last minute to fill unused seats; scan high street travel agents for the latest offers.

FLIGHT AGENTS IN BRITAIN

Low Cost Flight Agents

Campus Travel
52 Grosvenor Gdns, London SW1 ☎071/730 2101
Also many other branches around the country.

Council Travel
28A Poland St, London W1 ☎071/437 7767

STA Travel
86 Old Brompton Rd, London SW7 ☎071/937 9971
Offices nationwide.

Travel Cuts
295 Regent St, London W1 ☎071/637 3161

Specialist Flight Operators

Globespan	☎0737/773171
Unijet	☎0444/458181
Travel Express	☎0273/835095
Jetsave	☎0342/322771

Major Courier Firms

CTS Ltd	☎071/351 0300
DHL	☎081/890 9393
Polo Express	☎081/759 5383

SPECIALIST HOLIDAY OPERATORS

Airtours
Helmshore, Rossendale
Lancs BB4 4NB ☎0706/260000

AmeriCan Adventures
45 High St, Tunbridge Wells
Kent TN1 1XL ☎0892/511894

Bon Voyage
18 Bellevue Rd, Southampton
Hants SO1 2AY ☎0703/330332

British Airways Holidays
Atlantic House, Hazelwick Ave, Three Bridges
Crawley, West Sussex RH10 1NP ☎0293/572704

Contiki Travel
Wells House, 15 Elmfield Rd
Bromley, Kent BR1 1LS ☎081/290 6422

Destination USA
41–45 Goswell Rd
London EC1V 7EH ☎071/253 2000

Enterprise
Groundstar House, London Rd
Crawley, West Sussex RH10 2HB ☎0293/560777

Explore Worldwide
I Frederick St, Aldershot
Hants GU11 1LQ ☎0252/319448

Green Tortoise
PO Box 24459
San Francisco, CA 94124 ☎415/821-0803

Greyhound
Sussex House, London Rd
East Grinstead, West Sussex RH19 ☎0342/317317

Premier
Westbrook, Milton Rd
Cambridge CB4 1YQ ☎0223/355977

Sierra Club
c/o Outings Dept, 730 Polk St
San Francisco, CA 94110 ☎415/776-2211

Thomson
Greater London House, Hampstead Rd
London NW1 7SD ☎071/387 6534

Top Deck
131 Earls Court Rd
London SW5 ☎071/244 8641

TransAmerica
3A Gatwick Metro Centre, Balcombe Rd
Horley, Surrey RH6 9GA ☎0293/774441

Trek America
Trek House, The Bullring
Deddington, Oxford OX15 0TT ☎0869/38777

Unijet
"Sandrocks", Rocky Lane, Haywards Heath
West Sussex RH16 4RH ☎0444/459191

Virgin Holidays
The Galleria, Station Rd
Crawley, West Sussex RH10 1WW ☎0293/617181

FLY-DRIVE

Fly-drive deals, which give cut-rate (sometimes free) car rental when buying a transatlantic ticket from an airline or tour operator, are always cheaper than renting on the spot and give great value if you intend to do a lot of driving. On the other hand, you'll probably have to pay more for the flight than if you booked it through a discount agent. Competition between airlines (especially *Northwest* and *TWA*) and tour operators means that it's well worth phoning to check on current special promotions.

Northwest Flydrive, PO Box 45, Bexhill-on-Sea, East Sussex TN40 1PY (☎0424/224400), offers excellent deals for not much more than an ordinary Apex fare; for example, a return flight to Boston and a week's car rental costs less than £300 per person in low season. Several of the companies listed in the box above offer similar packages. However, there will often be little to choose between them; the most important deter-

mining factors are the current strength of the dollar against the pound, and your destination in the US. Florida, California and Hawaii usually offer the lowest rates, starting at around £65 per week for a small family saloon, and working up to £150 per week for an estate. Watch out for hidden extras, such as local taxes, "drop-off" charges, which can be as much as a week's rental, and Collision Damage Waiver insurance (see p.26). Remember, too, that while you can drive in the States with a British licence, there can be problems renting vehicles if you're under 25. For complete car-rental and driveaway details, see "Getting Around" (p.26).

FLIGHT AND ACCOMMODATION DEALS

There are no end of **flight and accommodation** packages to all the major American cities; although you can do things cheaper independently, you won't be able to do the same things cheaper. *STA Travel* (see p.5) offers "City

Packages" using hostel accommodation (not available in every US city) for around $15 per night plus airfare. Among the many tour operators which offer more costly deals, *Virgin Holidays* are about the least expensive: for example, seven nights in San Francisco plus return flight costs around £600–700 per person, and the same deal in a Florida destination, with car rental included, can be as low as £300. Pre-booked accommodation schemes, under which you buy vouchers for use in a specific group of hotels, are not normally good value – see p.36.

TOURING AND ADVENTURE PACKAGES

A simple and exciting way to see a chunk of America's Great Outdoors, without being hassled by too many practical considerations, is to take a specialist **touring and adventure package**, which includes transport, accommodation, food and a guide. Some of the more adventurous carry small groups around on minibuses and use a combination of budget hotels and camping (equipment, except sleeping bag, is provided). Most also have a food kitty of maybe £25 per week, with many meals cooked and eaten communally, although there's plenty of time to leave the group and do your own thing.

TrekAmerica is one UK-based company to offer such deals; a typical package would be ten days in California and the "Wild West" for £400 or so excluding flights. Other operators are listed on p.6. You'll find more details on *Green Tortoise* on p.24, and the *Sierra Club* on p.39.

FROM IRELAND

The cheapest flights **from Ireland** – if you're under 26 or a student – are available from *USIT*.

Student-only fares to **New York** or **Boston** go for around IR£400 return, while fares to **Chicago** and **San Francisco** are about IR£450. Ordinary Apex fares are roughly IR£150 higher. You can get to **Florida** and the East Coast via London on *Northwest* for around IR£420 return. *Aer Lingus* has occasional special offers to gateway cities, with services from Dublin and Shannon to Florida via New York from IR£500. *Delta* flies to Florida, via Atlanta, for the same fare. Flights from Shannon may be IR£15 or so cheaper than those from Dublin.

USIT can be contacted at Aston Quay, O'Connell Bridge, Dublin 2 (☎01/778117), while *Aer Lingus* is at 41 Upper O'Connell St, Dublin 1 (☎01/377 777 or 01/370191).

FROM EUROPE

It is generally far cheaper to fly non-stop to the States – especially the West Coast – from London than any other European city. However, for the best deals to New York from Brussels and Paris, contact **Nouvelles Frontières**, 66 boulevard St-Michel, Paris (☎46.34.55.30) and 21 rue de La Violette (Grand Place), Brussels (☎02/511 8013). Their London branch is at 1–2 Hanover St, W1 (☎071/629 7772).

Other options are the cut-price charter flights occasionally offered from major European cities; ask at your nearest travel agent for details. In West Germany, look for deals which *United* may be offering from Frankfurt, their continental hub since taking over *Pan Am*'s routes. The cheapest deals from all continental Europe are with *Icelandair*, which flies from Luxembourg to Baltimore, Chicago, Detroit, New York and Orlando.

GETTING THERE FROM AUSTRALASIA

Other than charter deals, seasonal bargains and all-in packages which may be on offer from high street travel agents, the cheapest flights from Australasia to the US are available from the specialists listed below.

From **Australia**, the best current offer to **Los Angeles** is on *Air New Zealand* – AU$1290, from Melbourne, Sydney, Brisbane, Adelaide and Cairns – while **San Francisco** is reachable for $1320 on *Qantas* from the same set of cities. *Northwest* has the lowest price to **Miami**, charging AU$1760 for flights from Melbourne, Sydney, Brisbane and Canberra.

From **New Zealand**, a return to **Los Angeles** costs around NZ$1550 from *STA*, flying on *Qantas* or *Air France*, and **San Francisco** is $1599 on *Air France*. **Miami** on *United Airlines* was NZ$2279 at the time of writing (single NZ$1464). All flights are from **Auckland**.

With any of the American carriers, you can continue on to **New York** for around US$170 on top of the fare to the West Coast. Most flights stop off in Honolulu, Hawaii; you can usually stay over for as long as you like for no extra charge.

AIRLINES AND AGENTS IN AUSTRALASIA

Air New Zealand
Air New Zealand House
Queen St, Auckland ☎09/357-3000

Anywhere Travel
345 Anzac Parade, Kingsford
Sydney ☎02/663-0411

Brisbane Discount Travel
360 Queen St, Brisbane ☎07/229-9211

British Airways
64 Castlereagh St
Sydney, NSW ☎02/258-3300
Dilworth Building
Queen St/Customs St
Auckland ☎09/367-7500

Budget Travel
PO Box 505, Auckland ☎09/309-4313

Flight Centres
Circular Quay, Sydney ☎02/241-2422
Bourke St, Melbourne ☎03/650-2899
205–225 Queen St, Auckland ☎09/309-6171
152 Hereford St, Christchurch ☎03/379-7145
50–52 Willis St, Wellington ☎04/472-8101

Northwest
309 Kent St, Level 13
Sydney NSW ☎02/290-4455

Passport Travel
320b Glenferrie Rd, Malvern
Melbourne ☎03/824-7183

Qantas
Qantas International Centre, International Square
Sydney, NSW ☎02/236-3636

STA Travel
209 King St, New Town
Sydney, NSW 2000 ☎02/519-9866
256 Flinders St, Melbourne ☎03/347-4711
10 High St, Auckland ☎09/309-9723
233 Cuba St, Wellington ☎04/385-0561

Thai International Airways
Kensington Swan Building
22 Fanshawe St, Auckland ☎09/377-0268

Topdeck Travel
45 Grenfell St, Adelaide ☎08/410-1110

Tymtro Travel
Wallaceway Shopping Centre
Chatswood, Sydney ☎02/411-1222

United
5th Floor, 10 Barrack St
Sydney NSW ☎02/237-8888
7 City Rd, Auckland ☎09/379-3800

ENTRY REQUIREMENTS FOR FOREIGN VISITORS

Prospective visitors from Ireland, Australia, New Zealand, and all other parts of the world require a valid passport and a **non-immigrant visitor's visa**. To obtain a visa, fill in the application form available at most travel agents and send it with a full passport to the nearest US Embassy or Consulate. Visas are not issued to convicted criminals and anybody who owns up to being a communist, fascist or drug dealer.

IMMIGRATION CONTROLS

The standard immigration regulations apply to all visitors, whether or not they are using the Visa Waiver Scheme.

During the flight, you'll be handed an **immigration form** (and a customs declaration: see below), which must be given up at immigration control once you land. The form requires details of where you are staying on your first night (if you don't know, write "touring") and the date you intend to **leave** the US. You should be able to prove that you have enough money to support yourself while in the US – anyone revealing the slightest intention of working while in the country is likely to be refused admission – and may experience difficulties if you admit to being HIV positive or having AIDS. You stand the best chance of a problem-free entry if you happen to be English-speaking, white, well dressed, and polite to the officials.

Part of the immigration form will be attached to your passport, where it must stay until you leave, when an immigration or airline official will detach it.

VISAS

Under the Visa Waiver Scheme, designed to speed up lengthy immigration procedures, British citizens visiting the United States for a period of less than ninety days only need a **full UK passport** (not a British Visitor's Passport) and a **visa waiver form**. This will be provided either by your travel agency, or by the airline during check-in, or on the plane, and must be presented to immigration on arrival. The same form can be used by citizens of most European countries, provided their passports are up-to-date, and covers entry across the land borders with Canada and Mexico as well as by air.

Canadian Visitors

Canadian citizens are in a particularly privileged position when it comes to crossing the border into the US. For a brief excursion, you do not necessarily need even a passport, just some form of ID; if you're obviously setting off on a longer trip, you should carry a passport, and if you plan to stay for more than ninety days you need a visa too.

Bear in mind that if you cross into the States in your car, trunks and passenger compartments are subject to spot searches by US Customs personnel, though this sort of surveillance is likely to decrease as remaining tariff barriers fall over the next few years. Remember, too, that Canadians are legally barred from seeking gainful employment in the US.

CUSTOMS

Customs officers will relieve you of your customs declaration and check whether you're carrying any fresh foods. You'll also be asked if you've visited a farm in the last month: if you have, you could well lose your shoes. The **duty-free allowance** if you're over 17 is 200 cigarettes and 100 cigars and, if you're over 21, a liter of spirits.

As well as foods and anything agricultural, it's prohibited to carry into the country any articles from Vietnam, North Korea, Kampuchea or Cuba, obscene publications, lottery tickets, chocolate liqueurs or pre-Columbian artefacts. Anyone

US EMBASSY AND CONSULATES IN CANADA

Embassy:
100 Wellington St, Ottawa, ON K1P 5T1 ☎613/238-5335

Consulates:

Suite 1050, 615 Macleod Trail
Calgary, AB ☎403/266-8962

Suite 910, Cogswell Tower, Scotia Square
Halifax, NS ☎902/429-2480

Complex Desjardins, South Tower
Montréal, PQ ☎514/281-1468

2 Place Terrace Dufferin
Québec City, PQ ☎418/692-2095

360 University Ave
Toronto, ON ☎416/595-1700

1095 West Pender St
Vancouver, BC ☎604/685-4311

US EMBASSIES AND CONSULATES ELSEWHERE

UK

5 Upper Grosvenor St
London W1 ☎071/499 9000

3 Regent Terrace
Edinburgh EH7 5BW ☎031/556 8315

Queens House, 14 Queen St
Belfast BT1 6EQ ☎0232/328239

Australia
Moonhah Place
Canberra ☎62/270 5000

Denmark
Dag Hammerskjöld Allé 24
2100 Copenhagen ☎31/ 42 31 44

Ireland
42 Elgin Rd, Ballsbridge
Dublin ☎01/687122

Netherlands
Museumplein 19
Amsterdam ☎020/310 9209

New Zealand
29 Fitzherbert Terrace, Thorndon
Wellington ☎4/722 068

Norway
Drammensveien 18
Oslo ☎22 44 85 50

Sweden
Strandvägen 101
Stockholm ☎08/783 5300

FOREIGN EMBASSIES AND CONSULATES IN THE US

Great Britain
Embassy:
3100 Massachusetts Ave NW
Washington DC 20008
☎202/462-1340

Consulates:
33 N Dearborn St
Chicago, IL 60602
☎312/346-1810

3701 Wilshire Blvd, #312
Los Angeles, CA 90010
☎213/385-7381

1001 S Bayshore Drive, #2110
Miami, FL 33131
☎305/374-1522

845 Third Ave
New York, NY 10022
☎212/745-0200

1 Sansome St, #850
San Francisco, CA 94104
☎415/981-3030

Australia
1601 Massachusetts Ave NW
Washington DC 20036-2273
☎202/797-3000

Canada
501 Pennsylvania Ave NW
Washington DC 20001
☎202/682-1740

Denmark
3200 Whitehaven St NW
Washington DC 20008
☎202/234-4300

France
4101 Reservoir Rd NW
Washington DC 20007
☎202/944-6000

Germany
4645 Reservoir Rd NW
Washington DC 20007
☎202/298-4000

Ireland
2234 Massachusetts Ave NW
Washington DC 20008
☎202/462-3939

Netherlands
4200 Linnean Ave NW
Washington DC 20008
☎202/244-5300

New Zealand
37 Observatory Circle NW
Washington DC 20008
☎202/328-4800

Norway
2720 34th St NW
Washington DC 20008
☎202/333-6000

Sweden
600 New Hampshire Ave NW,
#1200
Washington DC 20037
☎202/944-5600

caught carrying drugs into the country will not only face prosecution but be entered in the records as an undesirable and probably denied entry for all time.

EXTENSIONS

The date stamped on your passport is the latest you're legally allowed to stay. Leaving a few days later may not matter, especially if you're heading home, but more than a week or so can result in a protracted, rather unpleasant, interrogation from officials which may cause you to miss your flight. Overstaying may also cause you to be turned away next time you try to enter the US.

To get an extension before your time is up, apply at the nearest **US Immigration and Naturalization Service** (INS) office (their address will be under the Federal Government Offices listings at the front of the phone book). They will assume that you're working illegally and it's up to you to convince them otherwise. Do this by providing evidence of ample finances, and, if you can, bring along an upstanding American citizen to vouch for you. You'll also have to explain why you didn't plan for the extra time initially.

WORK AND STUDY

Anyone planning an extended legal stay in the United States should apply for a special working visa at any American Embassy before setting off. Different types of visas are issued, depending on your skills and length of stay, but unless you've got relatives (parents or children over 21) or a prospective employer to sponsor you, your chances are at best slim.

Illegal work is nothing like as easy to find as it used to be, now that the government has introduced fines of up to $10,000 for companies caught employing anyone without the legal right to work in the US. Even in the traditionally more casual establishments like restaurants and bars, things have really tightened up, and if you do find work it's likely to be of the less visible, poorly paid kind – washer-up instead of waiter.

Students have the best chance of prolonging their stay in the US. One way is to get on to an Exchange Visitor Programme, for which participants are given a J-1 visa that entitles them to accept paid summer employment and apply for a social security number. However, you should note that most of these visas are issued for jobs in American **summer camps**, which aren't everybody's idea of a good time; they fly you over, and after a summer's work you end up with around $500 and a month to blow it in. If you live in Britain and are interested, contact *BUNAC* (16 Bowling Green Lane, London EC1; ☎071/251 3472), or *Camp America* (37 Queens' Gate, London SW7; ☎071/589 3223). If you want to **study** at an American university, apply to that institution directly; if they accept you, you're more or less entitled to unlimited visas so long as you remain enrolled in full-time education.

INSURANCE, HEALTH AND PERSONAL SAFETY

INSURANCE

Though not compulsory, **travel insurance** is *essential* for **foreign travellers**. The US has no national health system and you can lose an arm and a leg (so to speak) having even minor medical treatment. Insurance policies can be bought through any high street travel agent or insurance broker, though the cheapest are generally *Endsleigh*, which charges around £35 for three weeks to cover life, limb and luggage (with a 25 percent reduction if you choose to forgo luggage insurance). Their forms are available from most youth/student travel offices (though their policies are open to all), or direct from 97–107 Southampton Row, London WC1 (☎071/436 4451). Another good option in Britain is *Touropa*, 52 Grosvenor Gardens, London SW1W 0NP (☎071/730 2101). Elsewhere in the world, get in touch with your nearest *STA* or *Travel Cuts* office (addresses on p.5 and p.8).

On all policies, read the small print to ensure the cover includes a sensible amount for medical expenses – this should be at least £1,000,000, which will cover the cost of an air ambulance to fly you home in the event of serious injury or hospitalization.

American travellers should find that their **health insurance** should cover any health charges or costs; if you don't have any you can get adequate coverage either from a travel agent's insurance plan or from specialist travel insurance companies such as *The Travelers*. If you are unable to use a phone or if the practitioner requires immediate payment, save all the **forms** to support a claim for subsequent reimbursal.

Remember also that time limits may apply when making claims after the fact, so promptness in contacting your insurer is highly advisable.

Not surprisingly, however, few if any American health insurance plans cover against **theft** while travelling, though most **renter's or homeowner's insurance** policies will cover you for up to $500 while on the road.

HEALTH ADVICE FOR FOREIGN TRAVELLERS

If you have a serious **accident** while in the US, emergency medical services will get to you quickly and charge you later. For emergencies or ambulances, dial ☎911 (or whatever variant may be on the information plate of the pay phone).

Should you need to see a **doctor**, lists can be found in the Yellow Pages under "Clinics" or "Physicians and Surgeons". A basic consultation fee is $50–75, payable in advance. Medications aren't cheap either – keep all your receipts for later claims on your insurance policy.

Many **minor ailments** can be remedied using the fabulous array of potions and lotions available in **drugstores**. Foreign visitors should bear in mind that many pills available over the counter at home need a prescription in the US – most codeine-based painkillers, for example – and that local brand names can be confusing; ask for advice at the **pharmacy** in any drugstore.

Travellers from Europe do not require **inoculations** to enter the US.

CRIME AND PERSONAL SAFETY

No one could pretend that America is trouble-free, although away from the urban centers, crime is often remarkably low-key. Even the lawless reputation of New York, Detroit or Los Angeles is far in excess of the truth, and most parts of these cities, by day at least, are fairly safe; at night, though, quite a few areas are completely off-limits. All the major tourist areas and the main nightlife zones in cities are invariably brightly lit and well policed. By being careful, planning ahead and taking good care of your possessions, you should, generally speaking, have few real problems.

Foreign visitors tend to report that the police are helpful and obliging when things go wrong, although they'll be less sympathetic if they think you brought the trouble on yourself through carelessness.

MUGGING AND THEFT

The biggest problem for most travellers is the threat of **mugging**. It's impossible to give hard and fast rules about what to do if you're confronted by a mugger. Whether to run, scream or fight depends on the situation – but most locals would just hand over their money.

Of course, the best thing is simply to avoid being mugged, and a few basic rules are worth remembering: *don't* flash money around; *don't* peer at your map (or this book) at every street corner, thereby announcing that you're a lost stranger; even if you're terrified or drunk (or both), *don't* appear so; avoid dark streets, especially ones you can't see the end of; and in the early hours stick to the roadside edge of the pavement so it's easier to run into the road to attract attention. If you have to ask for directions, choose your target carefully. Another idea is to carry a wad of cash, perhaps $50 or so, separate from the bulk of your holdings so that if you do get confronted you can hand over something of value without it costing you everything.

If the worst happens and your assailant is toting a gun or (more likely) a knife, try to stay calm: remember that he (for this is generally a male pursuit) is probably scared, too. Keep still, don't make any sudden movements – and hand over your money. When he's gone, you should, despite your shock, try to find a phone and dial ☎911 (the nationwide emergency number), or hail a cab and ask the driver to take you to the nearest police station. Here, report the theft and get a reference number on the report to claim insurance and travellers' check refunds. If you're in a big city, ring the local *Travelers Aid* (their numbers are listed in the phone book) for sympathy and practical advice. For specific advice for women in case of mugging or attack, see p.33.

Another potential source of trouble is having your **hotel room burgled**. Always store valuables in the hotel safe when you go out; when inside keep your door locked and don't open it to anyone you are suspicious of; if they claim to be hotel staff and you don't believe them, call reception on the room phone to check.

Needless to say, having bags snatched which contain travel documents can be a big headache, none more so for foreign travellers than **losing**

your passport. If the worst happens, go to the nearest Consulate and get them to issue you a **temporary passport**, basically a sheet of paper saying you've reported the loss, which will get you out of America and back home.

CAR CRIME

Crimes committed against tourists driving **rented cars**, especially in Florida, have garnered headlines around the world in recent years. In major urbanized areas, any car you rent should have nothing on it – such as a particular licence plate – that makes it easy to spot as a rental car. When driving, under no circumstances stop in any unlit or seemingly deserted urban area – and especially not if someone is waving you down and suggesting that there is something wrong with your car. Similarly, if you are "accidentally" rammed by the driver behind, do not stop immediately but drive on to the nearest well-lit, busy area and phone the emergency number (☎911) for assistance. Keep your doors locked and windows never more than slightly open. Do not open your door or window if someone approaches your car on the pretext of asking directions. Hide any valuables out of sight, preferably locked in the boot or in the glove compartment (any valuables you don't need for your journey should be left in your hotel safe).

COSTS, MONEY AND BANKS

To help with planning your vacation, this book contains detailed price information for lodging and eating throughout the United States. Unless otherwise stated, the hotel price codes given (explained on p.35) are for the cheapest double room in high season, exclusive of any local taxes which may apply, while meal prices include food only and not drinks or tip. For museums and similar attractions, the prices we quote are for adults; you can assume that children get in half-price. Naturally, as time passes after the publication of the book, you should make allowances for inflation.

Even when the exchange rate is at its least advantageous (see below), most western European visitors find virtually everything – accommodation, food, petrol, cameras, clothes and more – to be better value in the US than it is at home. However, if you're used to travelling in the less expensive countries of Europe, let alone

in the rest of the world, you shouldn't expect to scrape by on the same minuscule budget once you're in the US. You should also be prepared for regional variances; most New York prices, for example, are well above those in rural America.

Accommodation is likely to be your biggest single expense. Few hotel or motel rooms in cities cost under $35 – it would be more usual to pay something like $55 – and rates in rural areas are little cheaper. Although hostels offering dorm beds – usually for $10 to $15 – are reasonably common, they're by no means everywhere, and in any case they save little money for two or more people travelling together. Camping, of course, is cheap, ranging from free to perhaps $18 per night, but is rarely practical in or around the big cities.

As for **food**, fifteen dollars a day is enough to get an adequate life-support diet, while for a daily total of around $30 you can dine pretty well. Beyond this, everything hinges on how much sightseeing, taxi-taking, drinking and socializing you do. Much of any of these – especially in a major city – and you're likely to be getting through upwards of $50 a day.

The rates for **travelling** around using buses, trains and even planes, may look cheap on paper, but the distances involved are so great that costs soon mount up. For a group of two or more, renting a **car** can be a very good investment, not least because it will enable you to stay in the ubiquitous budget motels along the interstates instead of expensive city-center hotels.

In almost every state, **sales tax**, at rates varying up to eight percent, is added to virtually everything you buy in shops, but it isn't part of the marked price (for more details, see p.56).

MONEY: A NOTE FOR FOREIGN TRAVELLERS

Regular upheaval in the world money markets causes the relative value of the **US dollar** against the currencies of the rest of the world to vary considerably. Generally speaking, one **pound sterling** will buy between $1.40 and $1.80; one **Canadian dollar** is worth between 76¢ and $1; one **Australian dollar** is worth between 67¢ and 88¢; and one **New Zealand dollar** is worth between 55¢ and 72¢.

Bills and Coins

US currency comes in **bills** worth $1, $5, $10, $20, $50 and $100, plus various larger (and rarer) denominations. Confusingly, all are the same size and same green color, making it necessary to check each bill carefully. The dollar is made up of 100 cents in **coins** of 1 cent (known as a **penny**), 5 cents (a **nickel**), 10 cents (a **dime**) and 25 cents (a **quarter**). Very occasionally you might come across **JFK half-dollars** (50¢), **Susan B Anthony dollar coins**, or a **two-dollar bill**. Change (quarters are the most useful) is needed for buses, vending machines and telephones, so always carry plenty.

Emergency phone numbers to call if your checks and/or credit cards are stolen are on p.13.

TRAVELLERS' CHECKS

US dollar travellers' checks are the best way to carry money, for both American and foreign visitors; they offer the great security of knowing that lost or stolen checks will be replaced. You should have no problem using the better-known checks, such as *American Express* and *Visa*, in shops, restaurants and gas stations (don't be put off by "no checks" signs, which only refer to personal checks). Be sure to have plenty of the $10 and $20 denominations for everyday transactions.

Banks are generally open from 10am until 4pm Monday to Thursday, and 10am to 6pm on Friday, although the trend is towards longer opening hours. Until recently, banks were organized along state lines, so even the largest US banks only had branches in a single state. This is rapidly changing, but it can still be an awkward task to keep track of who's who. Most major banks change dollar travellers' checks for their face value (not that there's much point doing this – and some charge for the privilege, so ask before you do), and **change foreign travellers' checks and currency**. Exchange bureaux, always found at airports, tend to charge less commission: *Thomas Cook* or *American Express* are the biggest names. Rarely, if ever, do hotels change foreign currency.

PLASTIC MONEY AND CASH MACHINES

If you don't already have a **credit card**, you should think seriously about getting one before you set off. For many services, it's simply taken for granted that you'll be paying with plastic. When renting a car (or even a bike) or checking into a hotel you may well be asked to show a credit card to establish your creditworthiness – even if you intend to settle the bill in cash. **Visa**, **Mastercard** (known elsewhere as **Access**), **Diners Club**, **Discover** and **American Express** are the most widely used.

With *Mastercard* or *Visa* it is also possible to **withdraw cash** at any bank displaying relevant stickers, or from appropriate automatic teller machines (**ATMs**). *Diners Club* cards can be used to cash personal checks at *Citibank* branches. *American Express* cards can only get cash, or buy travellers' checks, at *American Express* offices (check the Yellow Pages) or from the travellers' check dispensers at most major airports. Most **Canadian** credit cards issued by hometown banks will be honored in the US.

American holders of ATM cards are likely to discover that their cards work in the machines of certain banks in other states (check with your bank before you leave home). Not only is this method of financing safer, but at around only a dollar per transaction it's economical as well.

Most major credit cards issued by **foreign banks** are accepted in the US, as well as cash-dispensing cards linked to international networks such as *Cirrus* and *Plus* – once again, check before you set off, as otherwise the machine may simply gobble up your plastic friend. Overseas visitors should also bear in mind that fluctuating exchange rates may result in spending more (or less) than expected when the item eventually shows up on a statement.

Each of the two main networks operates a toll-free line to let customers know the location of their nearest ATM; *Plus System* is ☎1-800/THE-PLUS, *Cirrus* is ☎1-800/4CI-RRUS.

EMERGENCIES

Assuming you know someone who is prepared to send you money in a crisis, the quickest way is to have them cash to the nearest **Western Union** office (information on ☎1-800/325-6000 in the US, or ☎0800/833833 in the UK) and have it instantaneously **wired** to the office nearest you, subject to the deduction of ten percent commission. **Thomas Cook** provides a similar service.

It's a bit less expensive to get a bank to transfer cash by cable, while if you have a few days' leeway, sending a postal money order, which is exchangeable at any post office, through the mail is cheaper still. The equivalent for foreign travellers is the **international money order**, for which you need to allow up to seven days in the international air mail before arrival. An ordinary check sent from overseas takes 2–3 weeks to clear.

Foreign travellers in difficulties have the final option of throwing themselves on the mercy of their nearest national **Consulate** (see p.10), who will – in worst cases only – repatriate you, but will never, under any circumstances, lend you money.

TELEPHONES, TIME ZONES AND THE US MAIL

Visitors from overseas tend to be impressed by the speed and efficiency of communications in the US (with the exception of the US mail, which is incredibly slow and careless). In rural areas you may find it slightly frustrating just getting to the nearest public phone – which may be many miles away – but in general keeping in touch is easy.

TELEPHONES

US **telephones** are run by a huge variety of local companies, many of which were hived off from the previous *Bell System* monopoly – the successor to which is the nationwide *AT&T* network.

Public telephones invariably work, and in cities at any rate can be found everywhere – on street corners, in railway and bus stations, hotel lobbies, bars and restaurants. They take 25¢, 10¢ and 5¢ coins. The cost of a **local call** from a public phone (generally within the same area code) varies, from a minimum of 20¢ – when necessary, a voice comes on the line telling you to pay more.

Some numbers covered by the same area code are considered so far apart that calls between them count as **non-local** (*zone calls*). These cost much more and sometimes require you to dial 1 before the seven-digit number. Pricier still are **long-distance calls** (ie to a different area code), for which you'll need plenty of change. Non-local calls and long-distance calls are much less expensive if made between 6pm and 8am, and calls from **private phones** are always much cheaper than those from public phones. Detailed rates are listed at the front of the **telephone directory** (the White Pages, a copious source of information on many matters).

Making telephone calls from **hotel rooms** is usually more expensive than from a payphone, though some budget hotels offer free local calls

---

USEFUL NUMBERS

Emergencies ☎911; ask for the appropriate emergency service: fire, police or ambulance

Long-distance
  directory information ☎1 (Area Code)/555-1212

Directory enquiries
  for toll-free numbers   ☎1-800/555-1212

INTERNATIONAL TELEPHONE CALLS

International calls can be dialled direct from private or (more expensively) public phones. You can get assistance from the **international operator** (☎1-800/874-4000), who may also interrupt every three minutes asking for more money, and call you back for any money still owed immediately after you hang up. The **lowest rates** for international calls to Europe are between 6pm and 7am, when a direct-dialled three-minute call will cost roughly $5.

In **Britain**, it's possible to obtain a free **BT Chargecard** (☎0800/800 838), using which all calls from overseas can be charged to your quarterly domestic account. To use these cards in the US, or to make a **collect call** (to "reverse the charges"), contact the local operator: *AT&T* ☎1-800/445-5667; *MCI* ☎1-800/444-2162; or *Sprint* ☎1-800/800-0008.

The telephone code to dial **TO the US** from the outside world (excluding Canada) is 1.

To make international calls **FROM the US**, dial 011 followed by the country code:

Australia 61	**Germany** 49	**Netherlands** 31	**Sweden** 46
Denmark 45	**Ireland** 353	**New Zealand** 64	**United Kingdom** 44

TELEPHONE AREA CODES WITHIN THE US

Alabama (AL) 205
Alaska (AK) 907
Arizona (AZ) 602
Arkansas (AR) 501

California (CA)
Los Angeles 213
West Los Angeles 310
Orange County 714
San Francisco 415
East Bay 510
Monterey & San Jose 408
Riverside 909
Pasadena 818
Santa Barbara 805
San Diego & eastern California 619
Wine Country & North Coast 707
Sacramento & northeastern California 916
Colorado (CO)
Denver & northern Colorado 303
Colorado Springs 719
Connecticut (CT) 203

Delaware (DE) 302

Florida (FL)
Miami & Fort Lauderdale 305
Orlando 407
Tampa 813
Jacksonville & Tallahassee 904

Georgia (GA)
Atlanta 404
Northern Georgia 706
Savannah 912

Hawaii (HI) 808

Idaho (ID) 208
Illinois (IL)
Chicago 312
Peoria 309
Springfield 217
Centralia 618
Indiana (IN)
Indianapolis 317
South Bend 219
Southern Indiana 812
Iowa (IA)
Des Moines 515
Dubuque 319
Council Bluffs 712

Kansas (KS)
Kansas City & east Kansas 913
Dodge City & Wichita 316
Kentucky (KY)
Louisville 502
Covington 606

Louisiana (LA)
New Orleans 504
The rest 318

Maine (ME) 207
Maryland (MD)
Frederick 301
Baltimore 410
Massachusetts (MA)
Boston 617
Eastern Massachusetts 508
Western Massachusetts 413
Michigan (MI)
Detroit 313
Lansing 517
Grand Rapids 616
Minnesota (MN)
Minneapolis 612
Rochester 507
Duluth 218
Mississippi (MS) 601
Missouri (MO)
Kansas City 816
St Louis 314
Springfield 417
Montana (MT) 406

Nebraska (NE)
Omaha and the east 402
Western Nebraska 308
Nevada (NV) 702
New Hampshire (NH) 603
New Jersey (NJ)
Princeton & the coast 609
Newark 201
Central New Jersey 908
New Mexico (NM) 505
New York (NY)
Manhattan & the Bronx 212
Brooklyn & Queens 718
Long Island 516
Hudson Valley 914
Buffalo & Rochester 716
Syracuse 315
Albany 518
Binghampton 607
North Carolina (NC)
Charlotte 704
Central North Carolina 910
Raleigh 919

North Dakota (ND) 701

Ohio (OH)
Southern & central Ohio 614
Cleveland 216
Cincinnati 513
Toledo & Lake Erie Islands 419
Oklahoma (OK)
Oklahoma City & west 405
Eastern Oklahoma 918
Oregon (OR) 503

Pennsylvania (PA)
Philadelphia 215
Eastern Pennsylvania 610
Harrisburg & central Pennsylvania 717
Pittsburgh & southwest 412
Altoona & the north 814

Rhode Island (RI) 401

South Carolina (SC) 803
South Dakota (SD) 605

Tennessee (TN)
Memphis 901
Nashville 615
Texas (TX)
Central Texas & Austin 512
Dallas 214
West Texas 915
Houston 713
Fort Worth 817
The Panhandle 806
Paris 903
Galveston 409

Utah (UT) 801

Vermont (VT) 802
Virginia (VA)
Richmond 804
Lexington 703

Washington (WA)
Seattle 206
Eastern Washington 509
Washington DC (DC) 202
West Virginia (WV) 304
Wisconsin (WI)
Milwaukee 414
Madison 608
Northeastern Wisconsin 906
Northwestern Wisconsin 715
Wyoming (WY) 307

from rooms – ask when you check in. An increasing number of phones accept **credit cards**, while anyone who holds a credit card issued by an American bank can obtain an **AT&T charge card** (information on ☎1-800/874-4000 ext 359).

Many government agencies, car rental firms, hotels and so on have **toll-free numbers**, which always have the prefix ☎1-800. From within the US, you can dial any number which starts with those digits free of charge. Phone numbers with the prefix ☎1-900 are pay-per-call lines, generally quite expensive and almost always involving either sports or phone sex.

The US has around 100 **area codes** – three-digit numbers which must precede the seven-figure number if you're calling from abroad or from a region with a different code. In this book, we've highlighted the local area codes at appropriate moments in the text, and they're also listed in the box on p.17. On any specific number we give, we've only included the area code if it's not clear from the text which one you should use, or if a given phone number lies outside the region currently being described.

US MAIL

Post offices are usually open Monday to Friday from 9am until 5pm, and Saturday from 9am to noon, and there are blue **mail boxes** on many street corners. Ordinary **mail within the US** costs 29¢ for a letter weighing up to an ounce; addresses must include the **zip code**, as well as the sender's address on the envelope. **Air mail** between the US and Europe generally takes about a week. Postcards cost 40¢, aerograms are 45¢, while letters weighing up to half an ounce (a single thin sheet) are 50¢.

The last line of the address is made up of an abbreviation denoting the state (California is "CA", Texas is "TX", for example, though you can spell it in full if you're unsure; see the list in the phone codes box) and a five-figure number – the **zip code** – denoting the local post office. (The additional four digits you will sometimes see appended to zip codes are not essential.) Letters which don't carry the zip code are liable to get lost or at least delayed; if you don't know it, phone books carry a list for their service area, and post offices – even in Britain – have directories.

Letters can be sent c/o **General Delivery** (what's known elsewhere as **poste restante**) to the one relevant post office in each city (which we've listed in the *Guide*), but *must* include the zip code and will only be held for thirty days before being returned to sender – so make sure there's a return address on the envelope. If you're receiving mail at someone else's address, it should include "c/o" and the regular occupant's name; otherwise it, too, is likely to be returned.

Rules on sending **parcels** are very rigid: packages must be in special containers bought from post offices and sealed according to their instructions, which are given at the start of the Yellow Pages. To send anything out of the country, you'll need a green **customs declaration form**, available from a post office.

TELEGRAMS AND FAXES

To send a **telegram** (sometimes called a *wire*), don't go to a post office but to a *Western Union* office (listed in the Yellow Pages). Credit card holders can dictate messages over the phone. **International telegrams** cost slightly less than the cheapest international phone call: one sent in the morning from the US should arrive at its overseas destination the following day. For domestic telegrams ask for a **mailgram**, which will be delivered to any address in the country the next morning.

Public **fax** machines, which may require your credit card to be "swiped" through an attached device, are found at photocopy centers and, occasionally, bookstores.

TIME ZONES

The continental USA is so big that it spreads over four different time zones, plus another one for Alaska and Hawaii; these are shown on the map at the start of this book. The **Eastern** zone, which covers the area inland to the Great Lakes and the Appalachian mountains, is five hours behind Greenwich Mean Time; so 10am London time is 5am in New York City. The **Central** zone, starting at Chicago and spreading west to Texas and the Great Plains, is an hour behind the east; the **Mountain** zone covers the Rocky Mountains and the Southwest states and is two behind the East Coast, seven behind Britain; and the **Pacific** zone includes the three coastal states and Nevada and is three hours behind New York, eight behind London. **Alaska** is another two hours behind the **Pacific** zone, as is Hawaii.

INFORMATION AND MAPS

The most useful source of information on the United States is the wide range of free maps, leaflets and brochures distributed by each of the various State Tourist Offices. The box on the next two pages contains a full list; write well in advance of your departure, and be as specific as possible about your interests.

The USTTA – United States Travel and Tourism Administration – has offices all over the world, usually in US embassies and consulates. These serve mainly as clearing houses, stocking vast quantities of printed material, but are unable to help with specific queries. In Britain, you can only contact them by telephone, on ☎071/495 4466 (Mon–Fri 10am–4pm).

As you travel around the country, you'll come across state-run **Welcome Centers**, usually along the main highways close to the state borders, which dispense all sorts of information. In the more heavily touristed states, these centers often have piles of discount coupons for cut-price accommodation and food.

Visitor centers in most large towns provide details on the area (typically open Mon–Fri 9am–5pm, Sat 9am–1pm, they're often known as the "Convention and Visitors Bureau", or CVB). **Chambers of Commerce**, designed to promote local business interests, also hold local maps and information. Most communities have **free newspapers** carrying entertainment listings.

MAPS

The **free maps** issued by each state are usually fine for general driving and route planning. To get hold of one, either write to the office directly or stop by any visitor center. *Rand McNally* produces good commercial maps, bound together in their *Rand McNally Road Atlas*, which also covers Mexico and Canada, or printed separately for each state. For something more detailed, say for **hiking** purposes, camping shops generally have a good selection, and park ranger stations in national parks, state parks and wilderness areas all sell good-quality local hiking maps for $1 to $3.

The *American Automobile Association* (*AAA;* toll-free ☎1-800/336-4357), based at 1000 AAA Drive, Heathrow, Florida 32746, provides free maps and assistance to its members, and to British members of the *AA* and *RAC*.

MAP AND TRAVEL BOOK SUPPLIERS

UK

Daunt Books, 83 Marylebone High St
London W1 ☎071/224 2295
Stanford's, 12–14 Long Acre
London WC2E 9LP ☎071/836 1321
The Travellers' Bookshop, 25 Cecil Court
London WC2N 4EZ ☎071/836 9132

CANADA

Open Air Books & Maps, 25 Toronto St
Toronto, ON M5R 2C1 ☎416/363 0719

AUSTRALIA

The Travel Bookshop, 20 Bridge St
Sydney, NSW 2000 ☎02/241 3554

UNITED STATES

The Complete Traveler, 199 Madison Ave
New York, NY 10016 ☎212/685-9007
The Complete Traveler, 3207 Filmore St
San Francisco, CA 92123 ☎415/923-1511
Elliot Bay Book Company, 101 S Main St
Seattle, WA 98104 ☎206/624-6600
Rand McNally, 150 E 52nd St
New York, NY 10022 ☎212/758-7488
Rand McNally, 595 Market St
San Francisco, CA 94105 ☎415/777-3131
The Savvy Traveller, 50 E Washington St
Chicago, IL 60602 ☎312/263-2100
Traveler's Bookstore, 22 W 52nd St
New York, NY 10019 ☎212/664-0995

STATE TOURIST OFFICES

Alabama
Alabama Bureau of Tourism &
 Travel
532 South Perry St
Montgomery AL 36104
☎205/242-4169
☎1-800/ALABAMA

Alaska
Alaska Division of Tourism
PO Box 11081, Juneau AK 99811
☎907/465-2010

Arizona
Arizona Office of Tourism
1100 W Washington St
Phoenix AZ 85007
☎602/542-TOUR

Arkansas
Arkansas Dept of Parks & Tourism
One Capitol Mall
Little Rock AR 72201
☎501/682-7777
☎1-800/628-8725

California
California Office of Tourism
Suite 1600, 801 K St
Sacramento CA 95814
☎916/322-2881
☎1-800/862-2543

Colorado
Colorado Tourism Board
1625 Broadway, Suite 1700
☎303/ 592-5510
☎1-800/433-2656

Connecticut
Connecticut State Information
 Bureau
165 Capital Ave
Hartford CT 06106
☎203/842-2200
☎1-800/282-6863

Delaware
Delaware State Tourism Office
99 Kings Hwy, Box 1401
Dover DE 19903
☎302/736-4271
☎1-800/441-8846

Florida
Florida Division of Tourism
126 Van Buren St
Tallahassee FL 32399-2000
☎904/487-1407

Georgia
Georgia Dept of Industry, Trade &
 Tourism
285 Peachtree Center Ave NE
Suite 1100
Marquis Two Tower
Atlanta GA 30303-1232
☎404/656-3545

Hawaii
Hawaii Visitors Bureau
Waikiki Business Plaza
2270 Kalakaua Ave
Honolulu HI 96815
☎808/923-1811

Idaho
Idaho Travel Council
700 W State St
Rm 108, State Capitol Building
Boise ID 83720
☎208/334-2470
☎1-800/635-7820

Illinois
Illinois Office of Tourism
620 E Adams St
Springfield IL 62701
☎217/782-7500

Indiana
Indiana Division of Tourism
1 N Capitol Ave #700
Indianapolis IN 46204
☎317/232-8860
☎1-800/289-6646 in-state

Iowa
Iowa Division of Tourism
200 E Grand Ave
Des Moines IA 50309
☎515/281-3100

Kansas
Kansas Dept of Economic
 Development
Travel & Tourism Division
400 SW Eighth St
Topeka KS 66603-3450
☎913/296-2009

Kentucky
Kentucky Dept of Travel
 Development
2200 Capital Plaza Tower
500 Mero St
Frankfort KY 40601
☎502/564-4930
☎1-800/225-8747

Louisiana
Louisiana Office of Tourism
Box 94291
Baton Rouge LA 70804-9291
☎504/342-8146
☎1-800/334-8626

Maine
Maine Publicity Bureau
97 Winthrop St
Hallowell ME 04347
☎207/582-9300

Maryland
Maryland Office of Tourism
217 E Redwood St
Baltimore MD 21202
☎301/333-6611
☎1-800/543-1036

Massachusetts
Massachusetts Division of Tourism
100 Cambridge St
Boston MA 02202
☎617/727-3201
☎1-800/632-8038

Michigan
Michigan Travel Bureau
333 S Capitol Ave
Lansing MI 48909
☎517/373-1220
☎1-800/543-2937

Minnesota
Minnesota Office of Tourism
100 Metro Square
121 Seventh Place E
St Paul MN 55101
☎612/296-5029
☎1-800/657-3700

Mississippi
Mississippi Division of Tourism
PO Box 1705
Ocean Springs MS 39564
☎601/359-3297
☎1-800/927-6378

Missouri
Missouri Division of Tourism
PO Box 1055
Jefferson City MO 65102
☎341/751-4133

Montana
Montana Dept of Commerce
1424 Ninth Ave
Helena MT 59620-0401
☎406/444-2564
☎1-800/541-1447

STATE TOURIST OFFICES

Nebraska
Nebraska Division of Tourism
PO Box 94666
Lincoln NE 68509
☎402/471-3796
☎1-800/228-4307

Nevada
Nevada Commission on Tourism
5151 S Carson St
Carson City NV 89710
☎702/687-4322

New Hampshire
New Hampshire Office of Travel
105 Loudon Rd, PO Box 856
Concord NH 03301
☎603/271-2666
☎1-800/262-6660

New Jersey
New Jersey Division of Travel &
  Tourism
20 West State St
Trenton NJ 08625-0826
☎609/292-2470

New Mexico
New Mexico State Tourism
PO Box 20003
Santa Fe NM 87503-20003
☎505/827-0291
☎1-800/505-2040

New York City
New York City CVB
2 Columbus Circle
New York NY 10019
☎212/397-8222

New York State
New York Division of Tourism
1 Commerce Plaza
Albany NY 12445
☎518/474-4116
☎1-800/225-5697

North Carolina
North Carolina Travel & Tourism
430 N Salisbury St
Raleigh NC 27611
☎919/733-4171
☎1-800/VISIT-NC

North Dakota
North Dakota Tourism Division
Liberty Memorial Building
Bismarck ND 58505
☎1-800/437-2077 national
☎1-800/472-2100 in-state

Ohio
Ohio Office of Travel & Tourism
Box 1001, Columbus OH 43216
☎614/466-8844

Oklahoma
Oklahoma Tourism & Recreation
500 Will Rogers Building
Oklahoma City OK 73105
☎405/521-2409
☎1-800/652-6552

Oregon
Oregon Tourism Division
775 Summer Street NE
Salem OR 97310
☎503/378-3451
☎1-800/547-7842

Pennsylvania
Pennsylvania Bureau of Travel
416 Forum Building
Harrisburg PA 17120
☎717/787-5453
☎1-800/237-4363

Rhode Island
Rhode Island Dept of Economic
  Development
7 Jackson Walkway
Providence RI 02903
☎401/277-2601
☎1-800/556-2484

South Carolina
South Carolina Dept of Parks,
  Recreation & Tourism
1205 Pendleton St #522
Columbia SC 29201
☎803/734-0122

South Dakota
South Dakota Dept of Tourism
711 Wells Ave
Pierre SD 57501
☎605/773-3301
☎1-800/843-1930 national
☎1-800/952-2217 in-state

Tennessee
Tennessee Dept of Tourism
PO Box 23170
Nashville TN 37202
☎615/741-2158

Texas
Texas Dept of Commerce, Tourism
  Division
Box 12008
Austin TX 78711
☎512/463-9191

Utah
Utah Travel Council
Council Hall
Capitol Hill
Salt Lake City UT 84114
☎801/538-1030

Vermont
Vermont Travel Division
134 State St
Montpelier VT 05602
☎802/828-3236

Virginia
Virginia Division of Tourism
Bell Tower, Capital Square
101 N Ninth St
Richmond VA 23219
☎804/786-4484
☎1-800/847-4882

Washington
Washington State Tourism
  Development Division
101 General Administration
  Building, AX-13
Olympia WA 98504-0613
☎206/753-5600

Washington DC
Washington Convention & Visitors
  Association
1212 New York Ave Suite 600
Washington DC 20005
☎202/789-7000

West Virginia
Travel West Virginia
State Capitol Complex
2101 Washington St
E Charleston WV 25305
☎304/348-2286
☎1-800/CALL-WVA

Wisconsin
Wisconsin Tourism
  Development
123 West Washington Ave
PO Box 7970
Madison WI 53707
☎608/266-6797
☎1-800/432-TRIP national
☎1-800/372-2737 in-state

Wyoming
Wyoming Division of Tourism
I-25 at College Drive
Cheyenne WY 82002
☎307/777-7777
☎1-800/225-5996

GETTING AROUND

Distances in the US are so great that it's essential to think carefully in advance about how you plan to get from place to place. Your choice of transport will have a crucial impact on your trip. *Amtrak* provides a skeletal but often scenic rail service, and there are usually good bus links between the major cities – though *Greyhound*, the mainstay of the US bus network, is in deep financial trouble and services are subject to sudden changes. Things are only liable to get difficult in isolated rural areas – and even here, by adroit forward planning, you'll usually be able to reach the main points of interest without too much trouble by using local buses and charter services, as detailed state-by-state throughout this book.

It has to be said, however, that things are always easier if you have a **car**. Many of the most worthwhile and memorable destinations in the United States are far removed from the cities. Even if a bus or train can take you to the general vicinity of one of the great National Parks, for example, it can be nearly impossible to explore the area without your own vehicle. For that matter, the cities themselves can be so vast, and so heavily car oriented, that the lack of a car can seriously impair your enjoyment.

BY TRAIN

Travelling by **rail** is not all that viable a way of getting from A to B, though if you have the time it can be a pleasant and relaxing experience. As you will see from our map, the *Amtrak* system isn't at all comprehensive – such popular destinations as Nashville and Santa Fe, and even some entire states, are missed out altogether. What's more, the cross-country routes tend to be served by one or at most two trains per day, so in large areas of the nation the only train of the day

> At the end of the introduction to each individual state in this book, a "**Getting Around**" section summarizes local transportation options.

passes through at 3 or 4 in the morning. That said, the train is by far the most comfortable way to go, and especially on long-distance rides it can be a great way to meet people.

For any one specific journey, the train can be more expensive than taking a *Greyhound* or even a plane – the standard fare from New York to Los Angeles, for example, is around $300 one-way – though special deals, especially in the off-peak seasons, bring the cost of a coast-to-coast round-trip down to well under $350 (closer to $250 at certain times). In addition to these, *Amtrak*'s **All Aboard America** fares, allowing three stopovers en route, are available by region (Florida, for some reason, is excluded). Foreign travellers can benefit from the passes detailed on p.25.

Always **reserve** as far in advance as possible (on ☎1-800/USA-RAIL); all passengers must have seats, and some trains, especially between major East Coast cities, are booked solid. Supplements are also payable, for **sleeping compartments** (which cost around $100 per night for one or two people, including three full meals), and for the plush *Metroliner* carriages, for example. Even standard *Amtrak* carriages are surprisingly spacious, and there are additional dining cars and lounge cars (with full bars and sometimes glass-domed 360° viewing compartments).

Beautiful East Coast *Amtrak* rides include the Hudson River Valley north of New York City (on the *Adirondack* route among others); along the Potomac River at Harpers Ferry, West Virginia (on the *Capitol Limited* out of Washington DC); and the New River gorge (on the *Cardinal*). In the West the sights only get bigger and better: the *California Zephyr*, between Chicago and San Francisco, follows a stunning route up and over the Rockies west of Denver, rivalled a day later by the towering Sierra Nevada, while the *Coast*

> For all information on *Amtrak* **fares and schedules** in the US, use the toll-free number
> ☎**1-800/USA-RAIL**
> Do not phone individual stations.

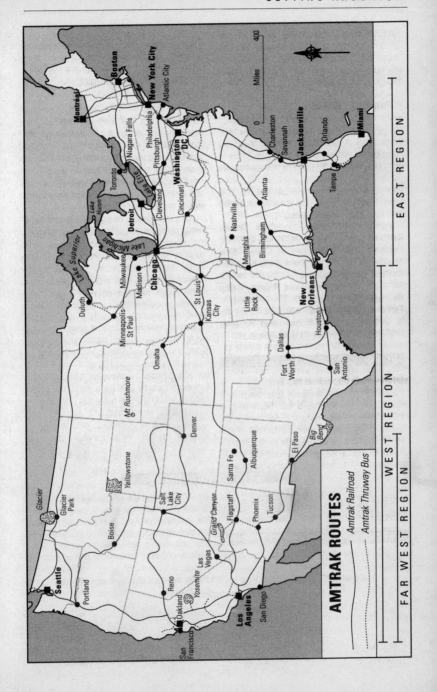

AMTRAK ROUTES

—— Amtrak Railroad
‑ ‑ ‑ Amtrak Thruway Bus

EAST REGION

WEST REGION

FAR WEST REGION

Boston
Montreal
New York City
Atlantic City
Niagara Falls
Philadelphia
Pittsburgh
Washington DC
Toronto
Cincinnati
Cleveland
Detroit
Charleston
Savannah
Jacksonville
Orlando
Miami
Tampa
Atlanta
Nashville
Memphis
Birmingham
New Orleans
Milwaukee
Madison
Chicago
St Louis
Kansas City
Little Rock
Duluth
Minneapolis St Paul
Omaha
Dallas
Fort Worth
Houston
San Antonio
Mt Rushmore
Denver
Albuquerque
Santa Fe
El Paso
Big Bend
Yellowstone
Salt Lake City
Grand Canyon
Flagstaff
Phoenix
Tucson
Glacier
Glacier Park
Boise
Las Vegas
Reno
Yosemite
Oakland
San Francisco
Los Angeles
San Diego
Seattle
Portland

Lake Superior
Lake Michigan
Lake Huron
Lake Erie

Miles
0   400

Starlight gives unsurpassed views of the California coast on its journey between San Luis Obispo and Santa Barbara. Try to make sure when you book your journey that the train passes through during daylight hours.

HISTORIC RAILROADS

While *Amtrak* has a monopoly on long-distance rail travel, a number of **historic** or **scenic railways**, some of them steam-powered or running along narrow-gauge mining tracks, do much to bring back the glory days of train travel. Many are purely tourist attractions, doing a full circuit through beautiful countryside in two or three hours, though some can drop you off in otherwise hard-to-reach wilderness areas.

Popular lines include the **Cass Scenic Railroad** in West Virginia (☎304/456-4300); the **Cumbres and Toltec** line in Chama, New Mexico (☎505/756-2151); **Durango & Silverton Narrow Gauge Railroad** in Colorado (☎303/247-2733); the **Big Trees and Roaring Camp Railroad** in Santa Cruz (☎408/335-4400) and the **Fort Bragg–Willitts** line (☎707/964-6371), both in California; and the **Mount Hood Railroad** (☎503/386-3556) outside Portland, Oregon.

BY BUS

If you're travelling on your own, and making a lot of stops, **buses** are by far the cheapest way to get around. The main long-distance service is *Greyhound*, which links all major cities and many smaller towns. Out in the country, buses are fairly scarce, sometimes appearing only once a day, and here you'll need to plot your route with

> *Greyhound*'s nationwide **toll-free information service** can give you routes and times, plus phone numbers and addresses of local terminals:
>
> ☎1-800/231-2222

care. But along the main highways, buses run around the clock to a fairly full timetable, stopping only for meal breaks (almost always fast-food dives) and driver change-overs. *Greyhound* buses are slightly less uncomfortable than you might expect, too, and it's feasible to save on a night's accommodation by travelling overnight and sleeping on the bus – though you may not feel up to much the next day.

To avoid possible hassle, lone female travellers in particular should take care to sit as near to the driver as possible, and to arrive during daylight hours – many bus stations are in fairly dodgy areas. It used to be that any sizeable community would have a *Greyhound* station; in some places the post office or a gas station doubles as the bus stop and ticket office, and in many others bus service has been cancelled altogether. All seats are on a first-come, first-served basis; there are no reservations, and if a bus is full you may be forced to wait until the next one – sometimes overnight or longer.

Fares average 10¢ a mile, which can add up quickly – for example, $49 from Los Angeles to San Francisco one-way. For long-trip travel riding the bus costs about the same as the train; considering the time (75 hours coast-to-coast, if you eat and sleep on the bus) it's not that much cheaper than flying. However, the bus is the best deal if

---

GREEN TORTOISE

One alternative to Long-Distance Bus Hell is the slightly counter-cultural *Green Tortoise*, whose buses, furnished with foam cushions, bunks, fridges and rock music, ply the major cities of the West Coast, running between Los Angeles, San Francisco and Seattle. In summer, they also cross the country to New York and Boston, transcontinental trips which amount to mini-tours of the nation, taking around a dozen days (at a current cost of around $249, not including food), and allowing plenty of stops for hiking, river-rafting, and hot springs. Other *Green Tortoise* trips include excursions to the major national parks (in 17 days for $399), and north to Alaska.

Main Office: PO Box 24459, San Francisco, CA 94124; ☎415/821-0803 or ☎1-800/227-4766.

Seat Reservation Numbers

Boston	☎617/265-8533	San Francisco	☎415/821-0803
Eugene	☎503/937-3603	Santa Barbara	☎805/569-1884
Los Angeles	☎310/392-1990	Santa Cruz	☎408/462-6437
New York	☎212/431-3348	Seattle	☎206/324-7433
Portland	☎503/225-0310	Vancouver	☎604/732-5153

ADVANCE PLANNING FOR OVERSEAS TRAVELLERS

Amtrak Rail Passes

Overseas travellers have a choice of the following **rail passes**, covering the areas shown on our map; the **Coastal Pass** permits unlimited train travel on the east and west coasts, but not between the two.

	15-day (June–Aug)	15-day (Sept–May)	30-day (June–Aug)	30-day (Sept–May)
East or **Far West**	$178	$158	$229	$209
West	$228	$188	$289	$259
Coastal	–	–	$199	$179
National	$308	$208	$389	$309

On production of a passport issued outside the US or Canada, the passes can be bought at *Amtrak* stations in the US. In the **UK**, you can buy them from *Destination Marketing*, 2 Cinnamon Row, York Place, London SW11 3TW (☎071/978 5212); in **Ireland**, contact *Eurotrain* (☎01/741 777); in **Australia**, *Walshes World* (☎02/232 7499); and in **New Zealand**, *Atlantic & Pacific* (☎071/978 5212).

Greyhound Ameripasses

Foreign visitors intending to travel virtually every day by bus (which is unlikely), or to venture further around the US, can buy a *Greyhound* **Ameripass**, offering unlimited travel within a set time limit, before leaving home: most travel agents can oblige. In the UK, they cost £50 (4-day), £85 (7-day), £125 (15-day) or £170 (30-day). *Greyhound*'s office is at Sussex House, London Road, East Grinstead, West Sussex RH19 1LD (☎0342/317317). Extensions can be bought in the US for the dollar equivalent of £12 a day.

The first time you use your pass, it will be dated by the ticket clerk (which becomes the commencement date of the ticket), and your destination is written on a page which the driver will tear out and keep as you board the bus. Repeat this procedure for every subsequent journey.

Air passes

All the main American airlines (and *British Airways* in conjunction with *USAir*) offer **air passes** for visitors who plan to fly a lot within the US: these have to be bought in advance, and in the UK are usually sold with the proviso that you cross the Atlantic with the relevant airline. All the deals are broadly similar, involving the purchase of at least three **coupons** (for around £160; around £55 for each additional coupon), each valid for a flight of any duration in the US.

The **Visit USA** scheme entitles foreign travellers to a 30 percent discount on any full-priced US domestic fare, provided you buy the ticket before you leave home. This is only a wise choice for travel in regions where fares are low anyway; flights within Florida, for example, are very expensive.

you plan to visit a lot of places: *Greyhound*'s **Ameripasses** for domestic travellers are good for unlimited travel nationwide for 7 days ($250), 14 days ($350) and 30 days ($450); the reduced rates for foreign travellers are on p.25.

Greyhound produces a condensed **timetable** of major country-wide routes, but do not distribute it to travellers; to plan your route, pick up the free route-by-route timetables from larger stations.

BY PLANE

Don't be too misled by the scenes from Hollywood movies in which characters stroll into large airports and casually buy cross-country air tickets; that kind of plane travel is outrageously expensive – $1000 for a one-way flight is not unheard of. However, if you plan ahead, **air** travel can work out reasonably cheap, as well obviously as being the quickest way to get around. Indeed, it can cost less than the train – especially if you take into account how much you save not having to pay for food and drink while on the move – and only a little more than the bus. Currently, the cheapest **coast-to-coast** airline ($159 New York–California) is *Tower Air* (see p.26). Flying can also make sense for relatively short local hops, turning a full day's cross-desert $25 bus journey, for example, into a quick and scenic $50 flight of under an hour. We mention such options wherever appropriate.

Any good **travel agent**, especially student and youth-oriented travel ones like *Council Travel* and *STA*, can usually get you a much better deal than the airlines themselves. Phone the airlines to find out routes and schedules, then buy your ticket using the **Fare Assurance Program**, which processes all the ticket options to find the cheapest fare, taking into account the requirements of individual travellers. One agent using the service

TOLL-FREE AIRLINE NUMBERS IN THE US

Air Canada	☎1-800/776-3000	KLM	☎1-800/374-7747
Aer Lingus	☎1-800/223-6537	Lufthansa	☎1-800/645-3880
Air France	☎1-800/237-2747	Mesa	☎1-800/933-6372
Alitalia	☎1-800/223-5730	Northwest Airlines	☎1-800/225-2525
American Airlines	☎1-800/433-7300	SAS	☎1-800/221-2350
America West	☎1-800/247-5692	Southwest	☎1-800/435-9792
British Airways	☎1-800/247-9297	Swissair	☎1-800/221-4750
Canadian	☎1-800/426-7000	Tower Air	☎1-800/221-2500
Continental Airlines	☎1-800/231-0856	Trans World Airlines	☎1-800/221-2000
Delta	☎1-800/221-1212	United Airlines	☎1-800/241-6522
Iberia	☎1-800/772-4642	US Air	☎1-800/428-4322
Icelandair	☎1-800/223-5500	Virgin Atlantic	☎1-800/862-8621

is *Travel Avenue* (☎1-800/333-3335). Few stand-by fares are available, and the best discounts are usually offered on tickets booked and paid for at least two weeks in advance, which are almost always non-refundable and hard to change.

BY CAR

For many people, the concept of cruising down the highway, preferably in an open-top convertible with the radio blaring, is one of the main reasons to set out on a tour of the US. The romantic images of countless road movies, from *Bonnie and Clyde* to *Thelma and Louise*, are not far from the truth, though you don't have to embark on a wild spree of drink, drugs, crime and murder to enjoy driving across America. Apart from anything else, a car makes it possible to choose your own itinerary and to explore the wide-open landscapes that may well provide your most enduring memories of the continent.

Driving in the **cities**, on the other hand, is not exactly fun, but places tend to be so large that a car is by far the most convenient way to negotiate your way around, especially as public transit is all but non-existent outside the major metropolises. Many cities, especially in the west, have grown up and assumed their present shape since cars were invented, sprawling for so many miles in all directions – Los Angeles and Houston are classic examples – that your hotel may be fifteen or twenty miles from the sights you came to see, or perhaps simply on the other side of a freeway which there's no way of crossing on foot. Only on the East Coast, and perhaps Chicago, are the main attractions and facilities concentrated within walking distance of each other. Even in smaller towns the motels may be six miles or more out

along the interstate, and the restaurants in a brand-new shopping mall on the far side of town.

Drivers wishing to **rent** cars are supposed to have held their licences for at least one year (though this is rarely checked); people under 25 years old may encounter problems, and will probably get lumbered with a higher than normal insurance premium. Car rental companies (listed opposite) will also expect you to have a credit card; if you don't have one they may let you leave a hefty **deposit** (at least $200) but don't count on it. The likeliest tactic for getting a good deal is to phone the major firms' toll-free 800 numbers and ask for their best rate – most will try to beat the offers of their competitors, so it's worth haggling.

In general the lowest rates are available at the airport branches – $149 a week for a subcompact is a fairly standard budget rate. Always be sure to get free unlimited mileage, and be aware that leaving the car in a different city to the one in which you rent it will incur a **drop-off charge** that can be as much as $200 or more. Also, don't automatically go for the cheapest rate, as there's a big difference in quality of cars from company to company; industry leaders like *Hertz* and *Avis* tend to have newer, lower-mileage cars, often with air-conditioning and stereo cassette decks as standard equipment – no small consideration on a 2000-mile desert drive.

Alternatively, various **local** companies rent out new – and not so new (try *Rent-a-Heap* or *Rent-a-Wreck*) – vehicles. They are certainly cheaper than the big chains if you just want to spin around a city for a day, but free mileage is not included, so they work out far more costly for long-distance travel. Addresses and phone numbers are documented in the Yellow Pages.

CAR RENTAL COMPANIES

In the US

Alamo	☎1-800/327-9633	**National**	☎1-800/227-7368
Avis	☎1-800/722-1333	**Payless**	☎1-800/729-5377
Budget	☎1-800/527-0700	**Rent-a-Wreck**	☎1-800/535-1391
Dollar	☎1-800/421-6868	**Snappy**	☎1-800/669-4800
Enterprise	☎1-800/325-8007	**Thrifty**	☎1-800/367-2277
Hertz	☎1-800/654-3131	**Value**	☎1-800/468-2583

In the UK

Alamo	☎0800/272 200	**Europcar**	☎081/950 5050
Avis	☎081/848 8733	**Hertz**	☎081/679 1799
Budget	☎0800/181 181	**Holiday Autos**	☎071/491 1111

Driving for Foreigners

UK nationals can **drive** in the US on a full UK driving licence (International Driving Permits are not always regarded as sufficient). Fly-drive deals are good value if you want to **rent** a car (see p.6), though you can save up to 60 percent simply by booking in advance with a major firm. If you choose not to pay until you arrive, be sure you take a written confirmation of the price with you. Remember that it's safer not to rent a car straight off a long transatlantic flight; and that standard rental cars have **automatic transmissions**.

It's also easier and cheaper to book **RVs** in advance from Britain. Most travel agents who specialize in the US can arrange RV rental, and usually do it cheaper if you book a flight through them as well. A price of £400 for a five-berth van for two weeks is fairly typical.

American Driving Terms

Antenna	Aerial	*Parking brake*	Hand brake
Divided highway	Dual carriageway	*Parking lot*	Car park
Fender	Bumper/Car wing	*Speed zone*	Area where speed limit decreases
Freeway	Limited access motorway	*Stickshift*	Gear stick/manual transmission
Gas(oline)	Petrol	*Trunk*	Boot
Hood	Bonnet	*Turn-out*	Lay-by
No standing	No parking or stopping	*Windshield*	Windscreen

When you rent a car, read the small print carefully for details on **Collision Damage Waiver (CDW)**, sometimes called Liability Damage Waiver (LDW), a form of insurance which often isn't included in the initial rental charge but is well worth considering. This specifically covers the car that you are driving yourself – you are in any case insured for damage to other vehicles. At $9 to $13 a day, it can add substantially to the total cost, but without it you're liable for every scratch to the car – even those that aren't your fault. Some credit card companies (*AMEX* for example) offer automatic CDW coverage to anyone using their card; read the fine print beforehand in any case.

Increasing numbers of states (New York for one) are requiring that this insurance be included in the weekly rental rate, and are regulating the amounts charged to cut down on rental car company profiteering; companies are also becoming more particular about checking up on the driving records of would-be renters and refusing to rent to high-risk drivers.

If you **break down** in a rented car, there'll be an emergency number pinned to the dashboard. Otherwise you should sit tight and wait for the highway patrol or state police, who cruise by regularly. Raising your car hood is recognized as a call for assistance, although women travelling alone should be wary of doing this. Another tip, for women especially, is to rent a **mobile telephone** from the car rental agency – you often only have to pay a nominal amount until you actually use it, and in larger cities they increasingly

Disabled Travellers

Specific information on public transportation and car rental for travellers with disabilities can be found on p.30.

Driving Distances In Miles

The distances shown on this chart represent the total mileages between selected cities and National Parks in the US and Canada. They are calculated according to the shortest available route by road, and are thus higher than figures obtained by drawing a straight line on a map.

	Albuquerque NM	Atlanta GA	Boston MA	Chicago IL	Dallas TX	Denver CO	Grand Canyon NP AZ	Great Smoky Mtns NP	Las Vegas NV	Los Angeles CA	Memphis TN	Miami FL	Nashville TN	New Orleans LA	New York NY	Orlando FL	St Louis MO	Salt Lake City UT	San Francisco CA	Seattle WA	Washington DC	Yellowstone NP WY	Yosemite NP CA	Montréal Canada	Toronto Canada
Albuquerque NM																									
Atlanta GA	1404																								
Boston MA	2220	1108																							
Chicago IL	1312	708	994																						
Dallas TX	644	822	1753	921																					
Denver CO	437	1430	1998	1021	784																				
Grand Canyon NP AZ	407	1818	2627	1732	1051	708																			
Great Smoky Mtns NP	1457	177	917	585	905	1385	1831																		
Las Vegas NV	586	1979	2752	1780	1230	758	283	2036																	
Los Angeles CA	811	2191	3017	2048	1399	1031	555	2254	272																
Memphis TN	1010	382	1341	537	454	1043	1416	450	1603	1807															
Miami FL	1970	663	1520	1397	1343	2107	2499	614	2570	2716	997														
Nashville TN	1225	246	1092	466	659	1184	1610	221	1811	2011	209	910													
New Orleans LA	1157	480	1507	919	517	1277	1548	622	1732	1858	393	860	532												
New York NY	1997	854	208	809	1559	1794	2401	706	2572	2794	1102	1335	900	1334											
Orlando FL	1741	426	1301	1147	1098	1879	2271	614	2350	2429	776	229	688	648	1092										
St Louis MO	1042	565	1207	289	655	863	1449	522	1620	1836	283	1226	321	698	976	1004									
Salt Lake City UT	604	1934	2376	1417	1257	534	534	1910	419	691	1551	2566	1775	1703	2189	2337	1362								
San Francisco CA	1109	2483	3128	2173	1752	1255	954	2592	570	387	2116	3093	2278	2325	2930	2871	2118	752							
Seattle WA	1453	2625	3016	2052	2131	1341	1213	2630	1180	1134	2317	3303	2590	2442	2841	3088	2135	848	810						
Washington DC	1849	618	448	709	1307	1616	2304	469	2420	2646	854	1057	659	1099	237	856	862	2048	2843	2721					
Yellowstone NP WY	973	1944	2382	1388	1343	563	755	1907	809	1081	1604	2568	1712	1840	2213	2432	1385	390	958	827	2081				
Yosemite NP CA	971	2375	2961	2021	1634	1000	641	2384	358	348	1946	2928	2184	2096	2777	2708	1863	558	182	928	2616	1003			
Montréal Canada	2131	1199	310	847	1770	1824	2542	1035	2583	2855	1315	1649	1112	1651	382	1462	1101	2225	2959	2714	607	2009	2644		
Toronto Canada	1787	1011	609	515	1435	1492	2198	807	2251	2523	956	1494	776	1307	516	1346	749	1910	2823	2564	571	2303	2938	344	
Vancouver Canada	1590	2756	3155	2176	2234	1484	1357	2774	1322	1278	2461	3447	2566	2734	2943	3232	2191	990	954	144	2887	971	1072	3014	2820

come built in to the car, but having a phone can be reassuring at least, and a potential lifesaver should something go terribly wrong (see p.13).

DRIVEAWAYS

One variation on renting is a **driveaway**, whereby you drive a car from one place to another on behalf of the owner, paying only for the gasoline you use. The same rules as for renting apply, but look the car over before you take it, as you'll be lumbered with any repair costs, and a large fuel bill if the vehicle's a big drinker. Most driveaway companies want a personal reference from someone either in the town you're leaving or in the car's eventual destination, and it makes obvious sense to get in touch in advance, to spare yourself a week's wait for a car to turn up. The most common routes are between the coasts, although there's a fair chance of finding something that needs shifting to where you want to go. You needn't drive flat out, although four hundred miles a day is expected. Look under "Automobile Transporters" in the Yellow Pages and phone around for current offers; or try one of the ninety branches of *Auto Driveaway,* based at 310 S Michigan Ave in Chicago (☎312/341-1900).

RENTING AN RV

Besides cars, Recreational Vehicles or *RVs* – those huge juggernauts that rumble down the highway complete with multiple bedrooms, bathrooms and kitchens – can be rented from around $400 per week (plus mileage charges) for a basic camper on the back of a pickup truck. Though good for groups or families travelling together, these can be unwieldy on the road. Also, rental outlets are not as common as you might expect, as people tend to own their RVs. On top of the rental fees, take into account the cost of gas (some RVs do twelve miles to the gallon or less) and any drop-off charges, in case you plan to do a one-way trip across the country. Also, it is rarely legal simply to pull up in an RV and spend the night at the roadside; you are expected to stay in designated parks that cost up to $20 per night.

The *Recreational Vehicle Rental Association*, 3251 Old Lee Highway, Fairfax VA 22030 (☎703/591-7130 or 1-800/336-0355), publishes a newsletter and a directory of rental firms. A couple of the larger companies offering RV rentals are *Cruise America* (☎1-800/327-7799) and *Go! Vacations* (☎1-800/845-9888).

BY BIKE

In general, **cycling** is a cheap and healthy method of getting around all the big **cities**, some of which have cycle lanes and local buses equipped to carry bikes (strapped to the outside). *Greyhound* will take bikes (so long as they're in a box), and *Amtrak* charges $5 every time you board with one. In **country areas**, roads are usually well maintained and with wide shoulders. A number of companies organize multiday cycle tours, either camping out or staying in country inns; we've mentioned local firms where appropriate. The biggest of the nationwide organizations is the non-profit *Bikecentennial* (PO Box 8308, Missoula MT 59807; ☎406/721-1776), founded in 1974 as part of the national bicentennial celebrations, to promote transcontinental cycle trips. It publishes maps ($6.95 each) of several 400-mile routes, detailing campgrounds, motels, restaurants, bike shops and sites of interest. Many individual states issue their own cycling guides; contact the tourist offices listed on pp.20–21. **Backroads Bicycle Tours**, 1516 Fifth Street, Berkeley CA 94704 (☎510/527-1555 or 1-800/462-2848), and the *AYH* hostelling group (see p.37) also arrange group tours.

For more casual riding, bikes can be **rented** for $15 to $30 per day, or at discounted weekly rates, from outlets which are usually found close to beaches, university campuses, or simply in areas that are good for cycling, although rates in heavily touristed areas can be much higher. Local visitor centers should have details. Before setting out on a **long-distance cycling** trip, you'll need a good-quality, multispeed bike, panniers, tools and spares, maps, padded shorts, a **helmet** (not a legal obligation but a very good idea), and a route avoiding interstates (on which cycling is unpleasant and usually illegal). Of **problems** you'll encounter, the main one is traffic – RVs driven by buffoons who can't judge their width, and huge eighteen-wheelers (or in the western states, logging trucks) which scream past and create intense back-draughts capable of pulling you out into the middle of the road.

DISABLED TRAVELLERS

By international standards, the US is exceptionally accommodating for travellers with mobility problems or other physical disabilities. All public buildings have to be wheelchair accessible and provide suitable toilet facilities, almost all street corners have dropped kerbs, and most public transit systems have such facilities as subways with elevators, and buses that "kneel" to let people board.

Most states provide information for disabled travellers – contact the tourism departments on pp.20–21. Among **national organizations** are **SATH**, the **Society for the Advance-ment of Travel for the Handicapped** (345 Fifth Ave #610, New York, NY 10016; ☎212/447-7284), a non-profit travel-industry grouping which includes travel agents, tour operators, hotel and airline management, and people with disabilities. They will pass on any enquiry to the appropriate member; allow plenty of time for a response. **Mobility International USA** (PO Box 3551, Eugene, OR 97403; ☎503/343-1248) answers transport queries and operates an exchange programme for disabled people.

Larger **hotels,** including most *Holiday Inns,* have at least one or two suites designed specifically for their disabled guests, and the entire *Red Roof* chain of motels (☎1-800/843-7663) is accessible to travellers with disabilities.

The **Golden Access Passport**, issued without charge to permanently disabled US citizens, gives free lifetime admission to all National Parks. *Easy Access to National Parks*, by Wendy Roth and Michael Tompane ($15), details every National Park for people with disabilities, senior citizens and families with children. It's published by the Sierra Club, 730 Polk St, San Francisco CA 94110 (☎415/776-2211). *Disabled Outdoors* (2052 W 23rd St, Chicago IL 60608; ☎708/358-4160) is a quarterly magazine specializing in facilities for disabled travellers who wish to explore the great outdoors; their friendly office serves as a clearinghouse for all related information.

Others include *Travel for the Disabled* ($14.95), *Wheelchair Vagabond* ($9.95) and *Directory for Travel Agencies for the Disabled* ($19.95), all produced by *Twin Peaks Press*, PO Box 129, Vancouver WA 98666 (☎1-800/637-2256 or 206/694-2462).

GETTING AROUND

Most **airlines**, transatlantic and within the US, do whatever they can to ease your journey, and will usually let attendants of more seriously disabled people accompany them at no extra charge. The Americans with Disabilities Act 1990 obliged all air carriers to make the majority of their services accessible to travellers with disabilities within five to nine years.

Almost every *Amtrak* **train** includes one or more coaches with accommodation for handicapped passengers. Guide dogs travel free and may accompany blind, deaf or disabled passengers in the carriage. Be sure to give 24 hours' notice. Hearing-impaired passengers can get information on ☎1-800/523-6590.

Greyhound, however, is not to be recommended. Buses are not equipped with lifts for wheelchairs, though staff will assist with boarding (intercity carriers are required by law to do this), and the "Helping Hand" scheme offers two-for-the-price-of-one tickets to passengers unable to travel alone (carry a doctor's certificate).

The *American Public Transit Association*, 1201 New York Avenue, Suite 400, Washington DC 20005 (☎202/898-4000), provides information about the accessibility of **public transit** in cities.

The *American Automobile Association* (see p.19) produces the *Handicapped Driver's Mobility Guide* for **disabled drivers** (available from *Quantum-Precision Inc*, 225 Broadway, Suite 3404, New York NY 10007). The larger car rental companies provide cars with hand-controls at no extra charge, though only on their full-size (ie most expensive) models; reserve well in advance.

TOUR OPERATORS

Many tour companies cater for disabled travellers or arrange disabled group tours. The *Handicapped Travel Division* of the *National Tour Association*, 546 East Main St, PO Box 3071, Lexington KY 40596 (☎606/253-1036), can put you in touch. National companies include *Wings on Wheels*, 4114 198th St SW Suite 13, Lynnwood WA 98036 (☎1-800/435-2288 or 206/776-1184), *Whole Persons Tours*, PO Box 1084, Bayonne NJ 07002 (☎201/858-3400), and *Directions Unlimited*, 720 N Bedford Rd, Bedford Hills NY 10507 (☎1-800/533-5343 or 914/241-1700).

SENIOR TRAVELLERS

For many senior citizens, retirement brings the opportunity to explore the world in a style and at a pace that is the envy of younger travellers. As well as the obvious advantages of being free to travel during the quieter, more congenial and less expensive seasons, and for longer periods, anyone over the age of 62 can enjoy the tremendous variety of discounts on offer to those who can produce suitable ID. Both *Amtrak* and *Greyhound*, for example, offer (smallish) percentage reductions on fares to older passengers.

Any US citizen or permanent resident aged 62 or over is entitled to free admission for life to all National Parks, monuments and historic sites, using a **Golden Age Passport**, which can be issued free at any such site. This free admission applies to all accompanying travellers in the same car – a welcome encouragement to families to travel together. It also gives you a fifty percent reduction on park user fees such as camping charges.

The *American Association of Retired Persons*, 601 E St NW, Washington DC 20049 (☎1-800/227-7737 or 202/434-2277), membership of which is open to US residents aged 50 or over for an annual fee of $8, organizes group travel for senior citizens and can provide discounts on accommodation and vehicle rental. The *National Council of Senior Citizens*, 1331 F St NW, Washington DC 20004 (☎202/347-8800), is a similar organization with a yearly membership fee of $15.

TRAVELLING WITH CHILDREN

Travelling with kids in the United States is relatively problem-free; children are readily accepted – indeed welcomed – in public places across the country.

Hotels and motels are well used to them, most state and national parks organize children's activities, every town or city has clean and safe playgrounds – and of course Disneyland in Los Angeles, and Disney World in Florida, are the ultimate in kids' entertainment.

Restaurants make considerable efforts to encourage parents in with their offspring. All the national chains offer bolster chairs and a special kids' menu, packed with huge, excellent-value (if not necessarily healthy) meals – cheeseburger and fries for 99¢, and so on.

Virtually all museums and tourist attractions offer reduced rates for kids. Most large cities have natural history museums or aquariums, and quite a few have hands-on children's museums.

State tourist bureaux can provide specific information, and various guidebooks have been written for parents travelling with children – such

as *California With Kids* ($14.95) and *The Candy Apple – NY With Kids* ($12.95), both published by Prentice Hall, and the very helpful *Trouble Free Travel with Children* ($6.95), available through Publishers Group West. Each of John Muir Publications' *Kidding Around* series covers the history and sights of a major US city.

GETTING AROUND

Children under two years old **fly** free on domestic routes, and for 10 percent of the adult fare on international flights – though that doesn't mean they get a seat, let alone frequent-flier miles. When aged from 2 to 12 they are usually entitled to half-price tickets.

Travelling **by bus** may be the cheapest way to go, but it's also the most uncomfortable for kids. Under-2s travel (on your lap) for free; ages 2 to 4 are charged 10 percent of the adult fare, as are any toddlers who take up a seat. Children under 12 years old are charged half the standard fare.

Even if you discount the romance of the railroad, **taking the train** is by far the best option for long journeys – not only does everyone get to enjoy the scenery, but you can get up and walk around, relieving pent-up energy. Most cross-country trains have sleeping compartments, which may be quite expensive but are likely to be seen as a great adventure. Children's discounts are much the same as for bus or plane travel.

Most families choose to travel **by car**; if you're hoping to enjoy a driving vacation with your kids, it's essential to plan ahead. Don't set yourself unrealistic targets; pack plenty of sensible snacks and drinks; plan to stop (ie don't make your kids make you stop) every couple of hours; arrive at your destination well before sunset; and avoid travelling through big cities during rush hour. Also, it can be a good idea to give an older child some responsibility for route-finding – having someone "play navigator" is good fun, educational and often a real help to the driver. If you're doing a fly-drive vacation, note that when **renting a car** the company is legally obliged to provide free car seats for kids.

Recreational Vehicles (RVs) are also a good option for family travel, combining the convenience of built-in kitchens and bedrooms with freedom of the road (see "Getting Around" on p.29).

Lost and Found

Wherever you are, be sure to keep track of one another – it's no less terrifying for a child to be lost at Disneyland than it is for him or her to go missing at the mall. Whenever possible agree a meeting place *before* you get lost, and it's not a bad idea, especially for younger children, to attach some sort of wearable ID card.

Another good idea is to tell your kids to stay where they are, and not to wander; if *you* get lost, you'll have a much easier time finding each other if you're not all running around anxiously.

WOMEN TRAVELLERS

Women's support centers, bookstores, bars and organizations across the country provide testimony to the continuing, and widespread, commitment to female self-determination in the US.

Practically speaking, a woman **travelling alone** in America is not usually made to feel conspicuous, or liable to attract unwelcome attention. The **cities** can feel a whole lot safer than you might expect from recurrent media images of demented urban jungles, simply because there are so many people about. But as with anywhere, particular care has to be taken at night: walking through unlit, empty streets is never a good idea, and if there's no bus service, take cabs. It's true that women who look confident are less likely to encounter trouble – those who stand around looking lost and a bit scared are prime targets.

In the major urban centers, provided you listen to advice and stick to the better parts of town, going into **bars** and clubs alone should pose few problems: there's generally a pretty healthy attitude towards women who do so and your privacy will be respected. Gay and lesbian bars are usually a trouble-free and welcoming alternative.

However, **small towns** tend not to be blessed with the same liberal or indifferent attitudes toward lone women travellers. People seem to jump immediately to the conclusion that your car has broken down, or that you've suffered some terrible tragedy; in fact, you may get fed up with well-meant offers of help. If your **vehicle breaks down** in a country area, walk to the nearest house or town for help; on interstate highways or heavily travelled roads, wait in the car for a police or highway patrol car to arrive. One increasingly available option is to rent a portable telephone with your car, for a small additional charge – a potential lifesaver.

Rape statistics are outrageously high, and it goes without saying that you should *never* **hitch** alone – this is widely interpreted as an invitation for trouble, and there's no shortage of weirdos to give it. Similarly, if you have a car, be careful who you pick up: just because you're in the driving seat doesn't mean you're safe. Avoid travelling at night by public transport – deserted bus stations, if not actually threatening, will do little to make you feel secure – and where possible you should team up with a fellow traveller. There really is security in numbers. On *Greyhound* buses, follow the example of other lone women and sit as near to the front – and the driver – as possible. Should disaster strike, all major towns have some kind of rape counselling service; if not, the local sheriff's office will make adequate arrangements for you to get help, counselling, and, if necessary, get you home.

A central group protests women's issues; lobbying by the National Organization for Women (featuring Gloria Steinem and Betty Friedan) has done much to effect positive legislation. NOW branches, listed in local phone directories, can provide referrals for specific concerns such as rape crisis centers and counselling services, feminist bookstores, and lesbian bars. Principal offices include 15 W 18th St, 9th Floor, New York NY 10011; 425 13th St NW, Washington DC 20004; and 3543 18th St, San Francisco CA 94110.

The annual *Index/Directory of Women's Media* (published by the Women's Institute for the Freedom of the Press, 3306 Ross Place NW, Washington DC 20008; ☎202/966-7793), lists women's publishers, bookstores, theater groups, news services and media organizations, and more, throughout the country.

Further back-up material can be found in *Places of Interest to Women* ($8; Ferrari Publications, PO Box 35575, Phoenix AZ; ☎602/863-2408), an annual guide for women travelling in the US, Canada, the Caribbean and Mexico.

GAY AND LESBIAN TRAVELLERS

The gay scene in America is huge, albeit heavily concentrated in the major cities. San Francisco, where between a quarter and a third of the voting population is reckoned to be gay or lesbian, is probably the premier gay city of the world; New York runs a close second, and up and down both coasts gay men and women enjoy the kind of visibility and influence those in other places can only dream about. Gay politicians, and even police officers, are more than a novelty, and representation at every level is for real. Resources, facilities and organizations are endless.

However, head into the heartland and life more than looks like the Fifties – away from large cities homosexuals are still oppressed and commonly reviled, and gay travellers would regrettably be well advised to watch their step to avoid hassles and possible aggression.

Ghettoization is no longer the self-defensive manoeuvre it used to be, but virtually every major city has its own sizeable, predominantly gay area – **Christopher Street** in New York City, Los Angeles' **West Hollywood**, San Francisco's **Castro** district, Houston's **Montrose**, Seattle's **Capitol Hill**, and so on.

However, although gay life exploded into the public eye in the Seventies, in the face of the AIDS pandemic the energies of gay men and women have been directed to the protection of existing rights and to increasing support and help for victims of the disease. Activist groups like ACT-UP (the AIDS Coalition To Unleash Power)

and Queer Nation hold sit-ins (and kiss-ins) as part of continuing efforts to maintain a high profile in the face of increasing intolerance and isolation.

Things change as quickly in the gay and lesbian (and emerging bisexual) scene as they do everywhere else, but we've tried to give an overview of local **resources**, **bars** and **clubs** in each of the major cities.

Of national **publications** to look out for, most of which are available from any good bookstore, by far the best are the range produced by Bob Damron in San Francisco (PO Box 422258, San Francisco CA 94142; ☎1-800/462-6654 or 415/255-0404). These include the Address Book, a pocket-sized yearbook full of listings of hotels, bars, clubs and resources for gay men, costing $15; the Women's Traveller, which provides similar listings for lesbians ($11); and the Road Atlas, which shows lodging and entertainment in major cities ($14).

Gay Yellow Pages (PO Box 292, Village Station, New York NY 10014; ☎212/674-0120; $12) is also a valuable resource. The Advocate (Liberation Publications, 6922 Hollywood Blvd, Los Angeles CA 90028; $2.95) is a bimonthly national gay news magazine, with features, general info and classified ads (not to be confused with Advocate Men, which is a soft-porn magazine).

Another useful lesbian publication is Gaia's Guide (132 W 24th St, New York NY 10014; $6.95), a yearly international directory with a lot of US information.

ACCOMMODATION

Accommodation costs form a significant proportion of the expenses for any traveller exploring the United States – in part, at least, because the standards of comfort and service are so dependably high.

If you're on your own, it's possible to pare down what you pay by sleeping in dormitory-style hostels, where a bed usually costs between $6 and $14. However, with basic room prices away from the major cities tending to start at around $30 per night, groups of two or more will find it little more expensive to stay in the far more abundant motels and hotels. Many hotels will set up a third single bed for around $10 on top of the regular price, reducing costs for three people sharing. On the other hand, the lone traveller will have a hard time of it: "singles" are usually double rooms at an only slightly reduced rate.

Wherever you stay, you'll be expected to **pay in advance**, at least for the first night and perhaps for further nights too, particularly if it's high season and the hotel's expecting to be busy. Payment can be in cash or in dollar travellers' checks, though it's more common to give a credit card imprint and sign for everything when you leave. **Reservations** are only held until 5pm or 6pm unless you've told the hotel you'll be arriving late. Most of the larger chains have an advance booking form in their brochures and will make reservations at another of their premises for you; alternately you can take advantage of the toll-free phone numbers of the national organizations (listed overleaf) that handle bookings for properties across the country.

Since inexpensive beds tend to be taken up quickly, always **reserve in advance** if possible in the cities. In major cities **campgrounds** tend to be on the outskirts if they exist at all, but there are excellent opportunities for camping in the many parks and natural areas all over the US – see the "Outdoors" section beginning on p.38 for an overview.

HOTELS AND MOTELS

It is consistently easy to find a basic hotel room in the United States. Drivers approaching any significant town are confronted by endless lines of motels along the highway, with prominent neon signs flashing their rates. Along the major cross-country routes the choice is phenomenal. In every town mentioned in this book we have recommended particular establishments, but you can also assume that there are a whole lot more

---

ACCOMMODATION PRICE CODES

Throughout this book, accommodation prices have been graded with the symbols below, according to the cost of the least expensive double room throughout most of the year.

However, with the exception of the budget interstate motels, there's rarely such a thing as a set rate for a room. A basic motel in a seaside or mountain resort may double its prices according to the season, while a big-city hotel which charges $200 per room during the week will often slash its tariff at the weekend when all the business types have gone home. As the high and low seasons for tourists vary widely across the country, astute planning can save a lot of money. Watch out also for local events – ranging from big spectacles such as Mardi Gras in New Orleans, through Spring Break in Myrtle Beach or Palm Springs, down to college football games – which can raise rates far above normal.

Only where we explicitly say so do these room rates include local taxes.

①	up to $30	④	$60–80	⑦	$130–180
②	$30–45	⑤	$80–100	⑧	$180+
③	$45–60	⑥	$100–130		

NATIONAL HOTEL, HOSTEL AND MOTEL CHAINS

Most of the hotel and lodging chains listed below publish handy free directories (with maps and illustrations) of their properties. Although we have indicated typical room rates (using the codes explained on p.35), bear in mind that the location of a particular hotel or motel has a huge impact on the price.

American Youth Hostel Association (①)	☎202/783-6161	**ITT Sheraton** (⑤ and up)	☎1-800/325-3535
		La Quinta Inns (④)	☎1-800/531-5900
Best Western (③–⑥)	☎1-800/528-1234	**Marriott Hotels** (⑥ and up)	☎1-800/228-9290
Budgetel (③)	☎1-800/428-3438	**Motel 6** (②)	☎505/891-6161
Comfort Inns (④–⑤)	☎1-800/221-2222	**Ramada Inns** (④ and up)	☎1-800/272-6232
Courtyard by Marriott (⑤)	☎1-800/321-2211	**Red Carpet Inns** (②)	☎1-800/251-1962
Days Inn (④–⑤)	☎1-800/325-2525	**Red Roof Inns** (②–③)	☎1-800/848-7878
Econolodge (②)	☎1-800/446-6900	**Scottish Inns** (②)	☎1-800/251-1962
Embassy Suites Hotels (⑥)	☎1-800/362-2779	**Select Inns** (②)	☎1-800/641-1000
Fairfield Inns (③)	☎1-800/228-2800	**Sleep Inns** (③)	☎1-800/221-2222
Friendship Inns (③)	☎1-800/424-4777	**Stouffer Hotels** (⑤ and up)	☎1-800/468-3571
Hallmark Inns (③)	☎1-800/251-3294	**Susse Chalet** (②–③)	☎1-800/524-2538
Hampton Inns (④)	☎1-800/426-7866	**Super 8 Motels** (②–③)	☎1-800/800-8000
Hilton Hotels (⑤ and up)	☎1-800/445-8667	**Travelodge** (②)	☎1-800/255-3050
Holiday Inns (⑤ and up)	☎1-800/465-4329	**Sonesta** (⑤ and up)	☎1-800/766-3782
Howard Johnson (③–④)	☎1-800/654-2000	**YMCA** (①)	☎1-800/922-9622

we haven't got the space to list. Only where there is a genuine shortage of accommodation have we explicitly said so.

Hotels and **motels** are essentially the same thing, although motels tend to be located beside the main roads away from city centers – and thus are much more accessible to drivers. The budget ones are pretty basic affairs, but in general there's a uniform standard of comfort everywhere

---

Hotel Discount Vouchers

For the benefit of overseas travellers, many of the higher-rung hotel chains offer **pre-paid discount vouchers**, which in theory save you money if you're prepared to pay in advance. To take advantage of such schemes, British travellers must purchase the vouchers in the UK, at a usual cost of between £30 and £60 per night for a minimum of two people sharing. However, it's hard to think of a good reason to buy them; you may save a nominal amount on the fixed rates, but better-value accommodation is not exactly difficult to find in the US, and you may well regret the inflexibility imposed upon your travels. Most UK travel agents will have details of the various voucher schemes; the cheapest is the "Go As You Please" deal offered by *Days Inn* (☎0483/440480 in Britain).

– double rooms with bathroom, TV and phone – and you don't get a much better deal by paying, say, $50 instead of $35. Over $50, the room and its fittings simply get bigger and more luxurious, and there'll probably be a swimming pool which guests can use for free. Paying over $100 brings you into the decadent realms of the en-suite jacuzzi. Not many budget hotels or motels bother to compete with the ubiquitous diners and offer **breakfast**, although there's a trend towards providing free self-service coffee and sticky buns.

During **off-peak periods** many motels and hotels struggle to fill their rooms, and it's worth **haggling** to get a few dollars off the asking price. Staying in the same place for more than one night will bring further reductions. Additionally, pick up the many **discount coupons** which fill tourist information offices. Read the small print, though: what appears to be an amazingly cheap room rate sometimes turns out to be a per-person charge for two people sharing and limited to midweek.

When it's worth blowing a whole lot of cash on somewhere really atmospheric we've said as much. The most upscale establishments have all manner of services which may appear to be free, but for which you will be expected to **tip** in a style commensurate with the hotel's status – ie *big*.

BED AND BREAKFAST

Over the last decade or so, **bed and breakfast** has become an ever more popular option, often as a luxurious alternative to conventional hotels, if not necessarily any more expensive. Sometimes a B&B may just be a couple of furnished rooms in someone's home, and even the larger establishments tend to have no more than ten rooms, without TV and phone but often laden with flowers, stuffed cushions and an almost over-contrived homely atmosphere.

The price you pay for a B&B – which varies from $40 to $200 – always includes a huge and wholesome breakfast (sometimes a buffet on a sideboard, but more often a full-blown cooked meal). The crucial determining factor is whether or not each room has an en-suite bathroom; most B&Bs feel obliged to provide private bath facilities, although that can damage the authenticity of a fine old house. Those that do tend to cost between $60 and $80 per night for a double. At the top end of the price spectrum, the distinction between a "hotel" and a "bed and breakfast inn" may amount to no more than that the B&B is owned by a private individual rather than a chain.

In many areas, B&Bs have grouped together to form central **booking agencies**, making it much easier to find a room at short notice; we've given addresses for these where appropriate.

Ys AND YOUTH HOSTELS

Although hostel-type accommodation is not as plentiful in the US as it is in Europe and elsewhere, provision for backpackers and low-budget travellers is on the increase. Aside from the odd private hostel in the larger cities, there are three basic kinds of hostel: YMCA/YWCA hostels (known as "*Y's*"), which offer mixed-sex or, in a few cases, women-only accommodation, the official *AYH/Hostelling International* network, and the growing AAIH (*American Association of Independent Hostel*) organization.

Prices in **YMCAs** range from around $12 for a dormitory bed to $20–35 for a single or double room. Y's offering accommodation (and not all do, many being basically health clubs) are often in older buildings in less than ideal neighborhoods, but facilities can include a gymnasium, a swimming pool, and an inexpensive cafeteria.

Most of the roughly 120 regular *AYH* youth hostels are in popular hiking areas, with a few in the big cities, ski resorts and tourist centers. They

For advice on **camping**, see the "Outdoors" section beginning on p.38.

usually have a limited check-in time, and some operate strict daytime lockouts. Rates range between $6 and $14 per night; non-members, and those without an *AYH Hostelling International* card, pay a few dollars extra.

The thirty hostels in the **AAIH** group are usually a little less expensive than their *AYH* counterparts, and have fewer rules. The quality is not as consistent; some can be quite poor, others absolutely wonderful. **Unaffiliated hostels** tend to be found in the larger cities. Their independent status may be due to a failure to come up to the *AYH*'s (fairly rigid) criteria, but often it's simply because the owners prefer not to be tied down by *AYH* regulations. Standards range from downright unsafe to excellent; naturally, we've included the latter in this book.

Especially in high season, it's advisable to **reserve ahead** by writing to the relevant hostel and enclosing a deposit. Some hostels will allow you to use a **sleeping bag**, though officially *AYH* affiliates should insist on a **sheet sleeping bag**. The maximum stay is often restricted to three days, though this rule is often ignored if there's space. Few hostels provide meals but most have **cooking** facilities. Many impose a curfew, as well as a ban on alcohol, drugs and smoking.

All the information in this book was accurate at the time of going to press; however, youth hostels are often shoestring organizations, prone to changing address or closing down altogether. Similarly, new ones appear each year; check the noticeboards of other hostels for news.

The *Hostel Handbook for the USA and Canada*, produced each May, lists over four hundred hostels and is available for $1 plus postage from Jim Williams, *Sugar Hill House International House Hostel*, 722 Saint Nicholas Ave, New York, NY 10031 (☎212/926-7030). The official *AYH/ Hostelling International Handbook* can be picked up from affiliated hostels or direct from the *AYH National Office*, PO Box 37613, Washington DC 20013-7613 (☎202/783-6161).

Overseas travellers will find a comprehensive list of hostels in the *International Youth Hostel Handbook*. In the UK, it's available from the **Youth Hostel Association** headquarters/shop, at 14 Southampton St, London WC2 (☎071/836 1036), where you can also buy a year's *IYHF* membership for £9 (under-18s £3).

OUTDOORS

The United States is scattered with fabulous backcountry and wilderness areas, coated by dense forests, cut by deep canyons and capped by great mountains. Even the heavily populated East Coast has its share of open space, notably along the Appalachian Trail, which winds from Mount Katahdin in Maine to the Blue Ridge Mountains of Tennessee – some two thousand miles of untramelled forest. In order to experience the full breath-taking sweep of America's wide-open stretches, however, head west to the Rockies, to the red-rock deserts of the Southwest, or right across the continent to the amazing wild spaces of the West Coast states. The shoreline itself, however, is often disappointingly hard to access, with a high proportion firmly under private ownership.

Protected backcountry areas fall into a number of potentially confusing categories, especially as the various federal, state and local jurisdictions do not necessarily reflect any hierarchy of beauty. **National Parks** are federally controlled areas of great natural beauty and/or historical significance: places like **Yellowstone**, with its teeming geysers and wildlife, **Yosemite**, with its towering granite walls, or the **Grand Canyon**. Don't blithely expect to tour such parks on foot; it can be done, of course, but they are huge places, and you can't just turn up and stroll around. (Yellowstone, for example, is bigger than the states of Delaware and Rhode Island combined.) **National monuments** tend to be outstanding geological features (such as Devil's Tower, Wyoming), covering

smaller areas than National Parks and not having quite the same facilities or broad tourist appeal; National seashores, lakeshores and so on are self-explanatory. The tracts of **national forest** that often surround National Parks are also federally administered, but are much less protected, and usually allow some limited logging and other land-based industry – ski resorts more often than strip mines, fortunately.

If you plan to visit more than a couple of such sites, all of which charge an admission fee per carload (between $3 and $10), buy a *Golden Eagle* **pass**, which gives unlimited access to (almost) any National Park or monument, and costs $25 for a calendar year. Special free passes are available for disabled travellers and senior citizens – see p.30 and p.31 respectively.

State parks, operated by the individual states, tend to focus on sites of geological or historical importance. Various government departments administer a whole range of wildlife refuges, national scenic rivers, recreation areas and the like – such administration consisting basically of leaving the natural landscape alone. The **Bureau of Land Management (BLM)** has the largest holdings of all, most of it open rangeland, such as in Nevada and Utah, but also including some enticingly out-of-the-way reaches.

Any of the above areas will have at least basic facilities for **camping**. In general, the better-known a place is, the more likely it will be to have some semblance of the comforts of home, with shops and petrol stations and lodges – all of which are handy but tend to detract from the natural splendor. It's usually possible to set off on trails and camp out overnight.

CAMPING AND BACKPACKING

If your time and money are limited, but you want to get a feel for the wilderness, one of the best options is to tour around by car, camping out at night and cooking your own meals (either on a camp stove or an open fire). If you don't fancy roughing it all the way, there is also a wide selection of public and commercially run **camp-grounds** in or very near areas of great beauty. Every state produces comprehensive lists of the campgrounds in its state parks; there are far too many to mention them all in this book.

In California, the **Sierra Club**, c/o Outings Dept, 730 Polk St, San Francisco CA 94110 (☎415/776-2211), offers a range of backcountry hikes into otherwise barely accessible parts of the High Sierra wilderness, with food and guide provided. The tours are summer-only, cost around $300 for a fortnight and are heavily subscribed, making it essential to book at least three months in advance. You'll also have to pay about $40 to join the club.

Campgrounds range from the primitive (a flat piece of ground that may or may not have a water tap, and may charge nothing at all) to some which are more like open-air hotels, with shops, restaurants and washing facilities, and nightly rates of around $15. The family-oriented **KOA** network publishes an annual directory of its campgrounds all over the country (*Kampgrounds of America*, Billings, MT 59114-0558; ☎406/248-7444), but lone or budget travellers will probably not appreciate their commercial atmosphere. As well as plenty of campgrounds, there are plenty of people intending to use them: take special care plotting your route if you're camping during public holidays or the high season. By contrast, basic campgrounds in isolated areas may well be completely empty whatever time of year you're there, and if there's any charge at all you'll be expected to pay by leaving the money in the bin provided.

Half of the land in the US is in the public domain; if you're backpacking, you can **camp** in the gaping **wilderness areas** and **deserts** pretty much anywhere you want. In certain areas, including the backcountry reaches of most National Parks, you need a **Wilderness Permit** (either free or $1) issued by the nearest park rangers' office. Before you set off on anything more than a half-day hike, and whenever you're headed for anywhere at all isolated, be sure to inform the ranger of your plans, and ask for weather conditions and relevant information. Carry sufficient food and drink to cover emergencies, as well as all the necessary equipment and maps.

When **camping rough**, check that fires are permitted before you start one; even if they are, try to use a campstove in preference to local materials – in some places firewood is scarce, although you may be allowed to use deadwood. In wilderness areas, try to camp on previously used sites. Where there are no toilets, **bury human waste** at least four inches into the ground and a hundred feet from the nearest water supply and campground. **Burn rubbish**, and what you can't burn, carry away. One very serious problem is *Giardia*, a water-borne bacteria causing an intestinal disease, of which the symptoms are chronic diarrhoea, abdominal cramps, fatigue and loss of weight. Treatment at that stage is essential; much better to avoid catching it in the first place. **Never drink** from rivers and streams, however clear and inviting they may look (you never know what unspeakable acts people – or animals – further upstream have performed in them); **water** that doesn't come from a tap should be boiled for at least five minutes, or cleansed with an iodine-based purifier (such as *Potable Aqua*) or a *Giardia*-rated filter, available from any camping or sports store.

Hiking at **lower elevations** should present few problems, though the thick swarms of **mosquitoes** you're likely to encounter near any body of water can drive you crazy; *DEET* and *Avon Skin-so-soft* handcream are two fairly reliable repellents. **Ticks** – tiny beetles that plunge their heads into your skin and swell up – are another hazard. They sometimes leave their heads inside, causing blood clots or infections, so get advice from a park ranger if you've been bitten. Beware, too, of **poison oak**, an allergenic shrub that grows all over the western states, usually among oak trees. Its leaves come in groups of three and are distinguished by prominent veins and shiny surfaces. If you come into contact with this, wash your skin (with soap and cold water) and clothes as soon as possible – and don't scratch: the only way to ease the itching is to smother yourself in calamine lotion or to take regular dips in the sea. In serious cases, hospital emergency rooms can give antihistamine or adrenaline jabs.

MOUNTAIN HIKES

Hiking at **higher elevations**, as in the 14,000ft peaks of the Rockies or California's Sierra Nevada, and certainly in Alaska, you need to take especial care: late snows are common, even into July, and in spring there's a real danger of avalanches, not to mention meltwaters making otherwise simple stream crossings hazardous. Altitude sickness, brought on by the depletion of oxygen in the atmosphere, can affect even the fittest of athletes. Take it easy for the first few days you go above seven thousand feet; drink lots of water, avoid alcohol, eat plenty of carbohydrates, and protect yourself from the increased power of the sun.

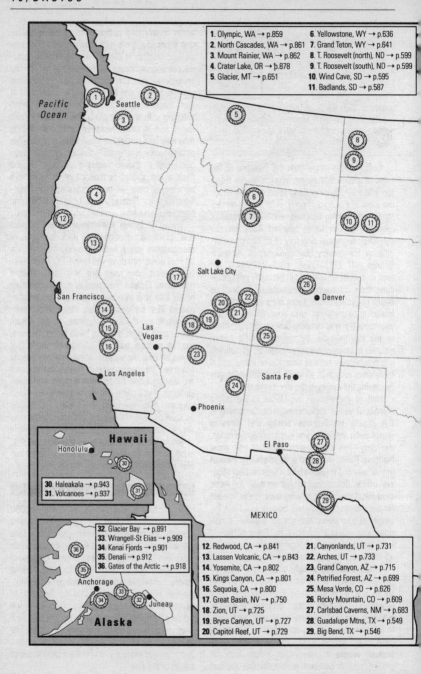

1. Olympic, WA → p.859
2. North Cascades, WA → p.861
3. Mount Rainier, WA → p.862
4. Crater Lake, OR → p.878
5. Glacier, MT → p.651
6. Yellowstone, WY → p.636
7. Grand Teton, WY → p.641
8. T. Roosevelt (north), ND → p.599
9. T. Roosevelt (south), ND → p.599
10. Wind Cave, SD → p.595
11. Badlands, SD → p.587

30. Haleakala → p.943
31. Volcanoes → p.937

32. Glacier Bay → p.891
33. Wrangell-St Elias → p.909
34. Kenai Fjords → p.901
35. Denali → p.912
36. Gates of the Arctic → p.918

12. Redwood, CA → p.841
13. Lassen Volcanic, CA → p.843
14. Yosemite, CA → p.802
15. Kings Canyon, CA → p.801
16. Sequoia, CA → p.800
17. Great Basin, NV → p.750
18. Zion, UT → p.725
19. Bryce Canyon, UT → p.727
20. Capitol Reef, UT → p.729
21. Canyonlands, UT → p.731
22. Arches, UT → p.733
23. Grand Canyon, AZ → p.715
24. Petrified Forest, AZ → p.699
25. Mesa Verde, CO → p.626
26. Rocky Mountain, CO → p.609
27. Carlsbad Caverns, NM → p.683
28. Guadalupe Mtns, TX → p.549
29. Big Bend, TX → p.546

Pacific Ocean

Seattle

Salt Lake City

Denver

San Francisco

Las Vegas

Los Angeles

Santa Fe

Phoenix

El Paso

MEXICO

Hawaii

Honolulu

Alaska

Anchorage

Juneau

US NATIONAL PARKS

For a detailed description of each park see the page indicated

0   Miles   400

Boston

Detroit

Chicago

New York City

Washington
DC

St Louis

Nashville

Memphis

Atlanta

Atlantic
Ocean

Houston   New Orleans

Gulf of
Mexico

Miami

37. Voyageurs, MN → p.284
38. Isle Royale, MI → p.243
39. Acadia, ME → p.210
40. Mammoth Cave, KY → p.396
41. Great Smoky Mtns, TN → p.364, 415

42. Shenandoah, VA → p.320
43. Hot Springs, AR → p.436
44. Everglades, FL → p.478
45. Biscayne, FL → p.448

DESERT HIKES

If you plan to hike in the **desert**, the crucial thing is to *think*. Tell somebody where you are going, and write down all pertinent information, including your expected time of return. Carry an extra two days' food and water and never go anywhere without a map. Try and cover most of your ground early morning: the midday heat is too debilitating, and you shouldn't even think about it when the mercury goes over 90°F (temperatures in California's Death Valley, for example, can reach 136°F). If you get lost, find some shade and wait. As long as you've registered, the rangers will eventually come and fetch you.

Not only can you anticipate battling with incredible heat, but at high elevations at night you should also be prepared for below-freezing temperatures. At any time of year, you'll stay cooler during the day if you wear full-length sleeves and trousers: shorts and a vest will expose you to far too much sun – something you won't be aware of until it's too late. A wide-brimmed hat and a pair of good sunglasses will spare you the blinding headaches that can result from the desert light. You may also have to contend with **flash floods**, which can appear from nowhere: an innocent-looking dark cloud can turn a dry wash into a raging river. Never camp in a dry wash, and don't attempt to cross flooded areas until the water has receded.

You can never drink enough **liquid** in the desert: the body loses up to a gallon every day and even when you're not thirsty you should keep drinking. Before setting off on any expedition, whether on foot or in a car, *two* gallons of water per person should be prepared. Waiting for thirst, dizziness, nausea or other signs of dehydration before doing anything can be dangerous. If you notice any of these symptoms, or feel weak and have stopped sweating, it's time to get to the doctor. Watch your alcohol intake, too: if you must booze during the day, compensate heavily with pints of water between each drink.

When **driving** in the desert, you should always take along an emergency pack with flares, a first-aid and snakebite kit, matches and a compass. A shovel, tyre pump and extra petrol are always a good idea.

If the car's engine overheats, don't turn it off; instead, try to cool the engine quickly by turning the front end towards the wind. Carefully pour some water on the front of the radiator, and turn the air-conditioning off and heating up full blast. In an emergency, never panic and leave the car: you'll be harder to find wandering around alone.

ADVENTURE TRAVEL

The opportunities for active travelling in the US are all but endless, from whitewater rafting down the Colorado River, to mountain biking in the volcanic Cascades, canoeing down the headwaters of the Mississippi River, horse riding in the Big Bend on the Rio Grande in Texas, and Big Wall rock-climbing on the sheer granite monoliths of Yosemite Valley.

While an exhaustive listing of the possibilities could fill another volume of this book, certain places have an especially high concentration of adventure opportunities, such as Moab UT (p.735) or New Hampshire's White Mountains (p.192). All through the book, we recommend guides, outfitters, and local adventure tour operators.

WILDLIFE

It's crucial in the backcountry to watch out for bears, deer, moose, mountain lions and rattlesnakes, and the effect your presence can have on their environment.

Other than in a National Park, you're highly unlikely to encounter a **bear**. Even there, it's rare to stumble across one in the wilderness. If you do, don't try to run, just back away slowly. As friendly as they appear, they are *wild* animals. Most fundamentally, they will be after your food, which should be stored in airtight containers when camping. Ideally, you should hang both food and garbage from a high branch (too weak to support the weight of a bear) some distance from your camp. Never attempt to feed bears (frequently they'll beg, but once fed will become aggressive in their demands for more), and never get between a mother and her young. Young animals are cute; irate mothers are not.

Particularly in the deserts, there's a danger of being bitten or stung by various **poisonous creatures**. You'll soon know if this happens. Current medical thinking rejects the concept of cutting yourself open and attempting to suck out venom; whether snake, scorpion or spider is responsible, you should apply a cold compress to the wound, constrict the area with a tourniquet to prevent the spread of venom, drink lots of water and bring your temperature down by resting in a shady area. Stay as calm as possible and seek medical help **immediately**.

FOOD AND DRINK

"Junk food" may be America's most enduring contribution to the modern culinary world, but most travellers find the sheer variety – and, for the most part, quality – of the foods available around the United States quite staggering.

Whether it's for basic sustenance or for a special social occasion, most Americans love to dine out, and it's not too much of an exaggeration to say that you can eat whatever you want, whenever you want. Along all the highways and on every main street, restaurants, fast-food places and coffeeshops try to out-do one another with flashing neon signs as well as bargains and special offers.

For **quick snacks**, many delis sell ready-cooked meals for a couple of dollars, as well as salads, sandwiches and filled bagels. Street stands provide hot dogs, burgers, tacos or slices of pizza for around $1, and most shopping malls hold a range of ethnic fast-food stalls, often pricier than their equivalent outside.

REGIONAL SPECIALTIES

While the predictable enormous steaks, burgers, piles of ribs or half a chicken, served up with salads, cooked vegetables and bread, are found everywhere, visitors are encouraged to explore the many diverse regional and ethnic cuisines around the country. Beef is especially prominent in the midwest and Texas, while **fish and seafood** dominate the menus in Florida, Louisiana, around the Chesapeake Bay, and in the

Pacific Northwest. **Shellfish**, such as the highly rated dungeness crab – smoother and creamier than the average crab – and the Chesapeake's unique soft-shell crab, highly spiced and eaten whole, is popular too. Maine lobsters and *steamers* (clams), eaten alone or mixed up in a chowder, are a great reason to visit New England.

Cajun food, which originated in the bayous of Louisiana as a way of using up leftovers, is centered on red beans and rice, enlivened with unusual seafood like crawfish and catfish and always highly spiced. The often-misunderstood distinction between Cajun and **Creole** cooking is explained in our "Louisiana" chapter, on p.495. It's rarely inexpensive, outside New Orleans and the Mississippi Delta, and its current cachet has pushed prices up tremendously.

Southern American cooking – also known as "soul food" – is not always easy to find away from the South, but is well worth seeking out. You may not fancy eating bland **grits** for breakfast (ground white corn served hot, mixed with butter) but full meals can be delicious, and incredibly filling. Vegetables such as **collard greens**, **black-eyed peas**, fried **eggplant** and **okra** (a principal ingredient of the Cajun gumbo) are added to staples such as fried chicken, roast beef, and **hogjaw** – meat from the mouth of a pig. **Chitterlings** (or chitlins) are a delicacy

---

Coping as a Vegetarian

In the big cities at least, being a **vegetarian** in the United States presents few problems. Cholesterol-fearing Americans are turning to healthfoods in a big way, and most towns of any size boast a wholefood or vegetarian café, while the ubiquitous Mexican restaurants tend to include at least one vegetarian item on their menus. However, don't be too surprised in rural areas if you find yourself restricted to a diet of eggs, cheese sandwiches (you might have to ask them to leave the ham out), salads and pizza. In the southeast, most soulfood cafés offer great-value vegetable plates (four different vegetables, including potatoes) for $2 to $4, but these are often cooked with pork fat. Similarly, baked beans, and the nutritious-sounding red beans and rice, usually contain bits of diced pork. None of the major fast-food chains includes a vegetarian burger on its menu, but the Mexicanesque *Taco Bell* sells meatless tostadas and burritos.

AMERICAN FOOD TERMS FOR OVERSEAS VISITORS

A la mode	With ice cream
Au jus	Meat served with a gravy made from its own juices
Biscuit	Similar to a scone, eaten as an accompaniment to a meal
BLT	Bacon, lettuce and tomato toasted sandwich
Broiled	Grilled
Brownie	A fudgy, filling chocolate cake
Burrito	Folded *tortilla* stuffed with refried beans or beef and grated cheese
Caesar salad	Cos lettuce in egg dressing with anchovy paste, olives and lemon served with garlic croutons and parmesan cheese
Calf fries	Deep-fried calfs' testicles
Check	Bill
Chips	Potato crisps
Chitterlings	Pigs' intestines
Cilantro	Coriander
Clam chowder	A thick soup made with clams and other seafood
Club sandwich	Large, overstuffed sandwich
Cookie	Sweet biscuit
Crawfish (also crayfish)	Crustacean, resembling a baby lobster
Eggs:	
sunny side up	fried on one side only
over	flipped over to stiffen the yolk
over easy	flipped for a few seconds only
Eggplant	Aubergine
Enchiladas	Soft *tortillas* filled with meat and cheese or chili and baked
English muffin	Toasted bread roll, like a crumpet
Fajitas	Soft *taco*-like flour *tortilla* stuffed with shrimp, chicken or beef
Frank	Frankfurter (hot dog)
(French) fries	Chips
Frijoles	Refried beans, ie mashed fried pinto beans
Gravy	White lard-like sauce poured over biscuits for breakfast
Grits	Southern breakfast item of ground white corn, served hot with butter
Gumbo	Thick Cajun soup of seafood, chicken and vegetables, named for the Bantu word for okra
Half-and-half	Half cream, half milk
Hash browns	Fried chopped or grated potato
Hero	French-bread sandwich
Hoagie	Another French-bread sandwich
Hot cakes	Pancakes
Home fries	Thick-cut fried potatoes

Jambalaya	A sort of Cajun paella, containing seafood, chicken, sausage and vegetables
Jello	Jelly
Jelly	Jam
Kalua pork	Hawaiian pig, roasted whole in an underground oven
Muffuletta	Italian French-bread sandwich, served in Louisiana
Muffin	Small cake made with bran and/ or fruit and other sweeteners
Nachos	Tortilla chips with melted cheese
Navajo taco	Frybread covered with beans
Pecan pie	Pastry shell filled with pecan nuts and syrupy goo
Po'Boy	Southern equivalent of a sub sandwich, often filled with deep-fried seafood
Poi	Tasteless Hawaiian paste made from *taro* root
Popsicle	Ice lolly
Pretzels	Savory circles of glazed pastry
Quahog	Large clam, served in New England
Salsa	Chilis, tomato, onion and cilantro, in varying degrees of spiciness
Sashimi	Thinly sliced raw fish eaten with soy sauce and *wasabi*
Seltzer	Fizzy/soda water
Sherbet	Sorbet
Shrimp	Prawns
Soda	Generic term for any soft drink
Squash	Marrow
Steamers	Steamed clams, served with butter
Sub	French-bread sandwich
Sushi	Japanese specialty; raw fish wrapped with rice in seaweed
Tab	Bill
Tacos	Folded, fried *tortillas*, stuffed with chicken, beef, etc
Tamales	Corn meal dough with meat and chili, baked in a corn husk
Tempura	Seafood and vegetables deep fried in batter
Teriyaki	Chicken or beef, marinated in soy sauce and grilled
To go	Take-away
Tortillas	Maize dough pancakes used in most Mexican dishes
Waldorf salad	Celery, chopped apple and walnuts served on lettuce leaves with mayonnaise
Zucchini	Courgettes

prepared from the innards of a pig. Meat dishes are usually accompanied by **cornbread** to soak up the thick gravy poured over everything; with fried fish, you'll often get **hush puppies** – fried corn balls with tiny bits of chopped onion.

By contrast, a more high-style innovation, **California cuisine**, is geared towards health and aesthetics. Raved about by foodies, it's basically a development of French *nouvelle cuisine*, utilizing the wide mix of fresh, locally available ingredients. The theory is to eat only what you need, and what your body can process. Vegetables are harvested before maturity and steamed to preserve both vitamins and flavor. Seafood comes from oyster farms and the catches of small-time fishers, and what little meat there is tends to be from animals reared on organic farms. The result is small but beautifully presented portions, and high, high prices: not unusually $50 a head (or much more) for a full dinner with wine; the minimum you'll need for a sample is $15, which will buy a couple of appetizers.

A spin-off from California cuisine is the so-called New New Mexican or **Santa Fe-style** food, again emphasizing ultra-fresh and unusual ingredients, and spiced to reflect the Spanish and Mexican heritage of the Southwest desert region.

Although technically ethnic, **Mexican** food is so common it often seems like an indigenous cuisine, especially in Southern California. In Texas, **Tex-Mex** food is a somewhat less spicy local version, whose distinguishing dish is beef and bean *chili con carne*. Day or night, this is the cheapest type of food to eat: even a full dinner with a few drinks will rarely be over $10 anywhere except in the most upmarket establishment.

Mexican food in the States is different from that found in Mexico, making more use of fresh meats and vegetables, but the essentials are the same: lots of rice and pinto beans, often served refried (ie boiled, mashed and fried), with variations on the **tortilla**, a very thin corndough or flour pancake that can be wrapped around the food and eaten by hand (a **burrito**); folded, fried and filled (a **taco**); rolled, filled and baked in sauce (an **enchilada**); or fried flat and topped with a stack of food (a **tostada**). Meals are usually served with complimentary **nachos** (chips) and a hot **salsa** dip. The **chile relleno** is a good vegetarian option – a green pepper stuffed with cheese, dipped in egg batter and fried.

Local variations are endless. Many farming and ranching regions – Nevada in particular – have a surprising number of **Basque** restaurants; the **Amish** communities of Pennsylvania have their own traditions; and **Portuguese** restaurants, dating from whaling days, abound in New England. **Chinese** food is everywhere, and can often be as cheap as Mexican; **Japanese** is much more rare, more expensive and fashionable, especially on the coasts – sushi is worshipped by some Californians. **Italian** food is popular, but can be expensive once you leave the simple pastas and explore the exotic pizza toppings or the specialist Italian regional cooking catching on fast in the major cities. **French** food, too, is available, though always pricey, the cuisine of social climbers and power-lunchers and rarely found outside the larger cities. **Thai**, **Korean** and **Indonesian** food is similarly city-based, though usually cheaper. **Indian** restaurants, on the other hand, are thin on the ground just about everywhere except New York – although as Indian cuisine catches on the situation is gradually changing for the better, with a sprinkling of moderately priced Southern Indian food outlets.

DRINKING

Across the country, bars and cocktail lounges are pretty true to their *Cheers*-celebrated popular image: long dimly lit counters with a few punters perched on stools before a bartender-cum-guru, and tables and booths for those who don't want to join in the drunken bar-side debates. New York, Baltimore, Chicago, New Orleans and San Francisco are the consummate boozing towns, but almost anywhere, men, at any rate, shouldn't have to search very hard for a comfortable place to drink.

To **buy and consume alcohol** in the US, you need to be 21, and could well be asked for ID even if you look much older. Mormon Utah has the most byzantine restrictions, while many other states have prohibitions about selling alcohol on Sunday, during elections, or – in the case of various counties in the Midwest – at all, ever. The famous **distilleries** of Tennessee and Kentucky, including *Jack Daniels* (see p.413), can be visited – though maddeningly, several are in "dry" counties so they don't offer samples. A few states – Vermont, Oklahoma, and, once more, Utah – restrict the alcohol content in beer to just 3.2 percent, half the usual strength. In more liberal areas, alcohol can be bought and drunk any time between 6am and 2am, seven days a week (New Orleans is a law unto itself, with certain bars open 24 hours and a far from rigid policy on ID).

Though for the most part American **beer** is limited to fizzy and tasteless national brands like *Budweiser, Miller* and *Coors*, there are alterna-tives: on the East Coast look out for Boston-based *Samuel Adams* or *New Amsterdam Bitter,* not to mention the budget-beer-turned-style-accessory *Rolling Rock.* The Texan brand *Lone Star* has its dedicated followers; out in California, the full-bodied, San Francisco-brewed *Anchor Steam* beer is available all over, while the rarer *Red Tail Ale* is among the finest brews in the country.

Of especial interest to travellers, **micro-breweries** and **brewpubs** are springing up all over the western US, in which you can drink excellent beers, brewed on the premises and often not available anywhere else. These are usually friendly and welcoming places, and almost all serve a wide range of good-value, hearty **food** to help soak up the drink.

As for **wine** and wineries, you'll find details of tours and tastings for visitors scattered throughout the book, for example in California on p.838, Texas on p.543, Ohio on p.224, and even Hawaii on p.945.

SPORTS

Besides being good fun, catching a baseball game at Chicago's Wrigley Field on a summer afternoon, or joining in with the screaming throngs at an Oilers game in Houston, can give an unforgettable sense of the peculiar characters inhabiting the various cities and towns around the US. Professional sports almost always put on the most spectacular shows, but big games between college rivals, minor league baseball games — even Friday-night high-school football — provide an easy and enjoyable way to get on intimate terms with a place.

Baseball, because the teams play so many games — 162 in total, usually five or so a week throughout the summer — is probably the easiest sport to catch when travelling. The stadiums — such as Wrigley Field, Boston's Fenway Park, LA's glamorous Dodger Stadium, or Baltimore's evocative new Camden Yards — are great places to spend time. It's also among the cheapest (at around $7 a seat), and tickets are usually easy to come by.

Pro football is quite the opposite — tickets are exorbitantly expensive and almost impossible to get (if the team is any good) — and most games are played in anonymous municipal bunkers; you'll do better stopping in a bar and watching it on TV. **College football** is a whole lot better and more exciting, with chanting crowds, cheerleaders, and cheaper tickets; while New Year's Day games such as the Rose Bowl or the Cotton Bowl are all but impossible to see in the flesh, big games like Nebraska vs. Oklahoma, Michigan vs. Ohio State, or Notre Dame vs. anybody are not to be missed if you're anywhere near where they're played.

Basketball, on both the college and pro level, also focuses local attention and emotions. We've listed the major league teams for all three sports in the box overleaf; local tourist offices can also help with schedules and ticket information.

The **Kentucky Derby**, held in Louisville on the first Saturday in May (see p.394), is the biggest event in the **horse racing** calendar.

SKIING

Skiing is the biggest mass-market participant sport, and downhill resorts can be found all over

---

SKIING: HOW TO SAVE MONEY

Especially in the Rocky Mountains, the US features some of the best ski terrain in the world, but without careful planning a ski vacation can be horribly expensive. In addition to the tips listed below, phone (toll-free) or write in advance to resorts for brochures, and when you get there, scan local newspapers for money-saving offers.

Visit during early or late season to take advantage of lower accommodation rates.

The more people in your party, the more money you save on lodgings. For groups of four to six, a condo unit costs much less than a standard motel.

Before setting a date, ask the resort about package deals including flights, rooms and ski passes. This is the no-fuss and often highly economical way to book a ski vacation.

Shop around for the best boot and ski rentals — prices often vary enormously.

Purchase advance sale lift tickets; for example, gas stations and supermarkets in Colorado offer savings of around thirty percent on ski-slope rates.

If you have to buy tickets at the resort, save money by purchasing multiday tickets.

If you're an absolute beginner, look out for resorts that offer free "never-ever" lessons with the purchase of a lift ticket.

Finish your day's skiing in time to take advantage of happy hours and dining specials, which usually last from 4pm until 7pm.

PRO SPORTS INFORMATION

BASEBALL

Major League Baseball ☎212/339-7800
National League ☎212/339-7700

Atlanta Braves	☎404/522-7630	*Montreal Expos*	☎514/253-3434
Chicago Cubs	☎312/404-2827	New York Mets	☎718/507-6387
Cincinnati Reds	☎513/421-4510	Philadelphia Phillies	☎215/463-6000
Colorado Rockies	☎303/292-0200	Pittsburgh Pirates	☎412/323-5000
Florida Marlins	☎305/623-6100	St Louis Cardinals	☎314/421-3060
Houston Astros	☎713/799-9500	San Diego Padres	☎619/283-4494
Los Angeles Dodgers	☎213/224-1500	San Francisco Giants	☎415/468-3700

American League ☎212/339-7600

Baltimore Orioles	☎410/685-9800	Milwaukee Brewers	☎414/933-4114
Boston Red Sox	☎617/267-9440	Minnesota Twins	☎612/375-1366
California Angels	☎714/937-7200	New York Yankees	☎212/293-4300
Chicago White Sox	☎312/924-1000	Oakland Athletics	☎510/638-4900
Cleveland Indians	☎216/861-1200	Seattle Mariners	☎206/628-3555
Detroit Tigers	☎313/962-4000	Texas Rangers	☎817/273-5222
Kansas City Royals	☎816/921-2200	*Toronto Blue Jays*	☎416/341-1000

BASKETBALL

National Basketball Association (NBA) ☎212/826-7000

Atlanta Hawks	☎404/827-3800	Milwaukee Bucks	☎414/227-0500
Boston Celtics	☎617/523-6050	Minnesota Timberwolves	☎612/673-1600
Charlotte Hornets	☎704/357-0252	New Jersey Nets	☎201/935-8888
Chicago Bulls	☎312/943-5800	New York Knicks	☎212/465-6499
Cleveland Cavaliers	☎216/659-9100	Orlando Magic	☎407/649-3200
Dallas Mavericks	☎214/748-1808	Philadelphia 76ers	☎215/339-7600
Denver Nuggets	☎303/893-6700	Phoenix Suns	☎602/379-7900
Detroit Pistons	☎313/377-0100	Portland Trailblazers	☎503/234-9291
Golden State Warriors	☎510/638-6300	Sacramento Kings	☎916/928-0000
Houston Rockets	☎713/627-0600	San Antonio Spurs	☎512/554-7787
Indiana Pacers	☎317/263-2100	Seattle Supersonics	☎206/281-5800
Los Angeles Clippers	☎213/748-8000	Utah Jazz	☎801/325-2500
Los Angeles Lakers	☎310/419-3100	Washington Bullets	☎301/773-2255
Miami Heat	☎305/577-4328		

FOOTBALL

National Football League (NFL) ☎212/758-1500

Atlanta Falcons	☎404/945-1111	Miami Dolphins	☎305/620-2578
Buffalo Bills	☎716/649-0015	Minnesota Vikings	☎612/333-8828
Chicago Bears	☎312/663-5100	New England Patriots	☎508/543-1776
Cincinnati Bengals	☎513/621-3550	New Orleans Saints	☎504/522-2600
Cleveland Browns	☎216/696-3800	New York Giants	☎201/935-8222
Dallas Cowboys	☎214/556-9900	New York Jets	☎516/538-7200
Denver Broncos	☎303/649-9000	Philadelphia Eagles	☎215/463-5500
Detroit Lions	☎313/335-4151	Phoenix Cardinals	☎602/379-0102
Green Bay Packers	☎414/496-5700	Pittsburgh Steelers	☎412/323-1200
Houston Oilers	☎713/797-9100	San Diego Chargers	☎619/280-2121
Indianapolis Colts	☎317/297-7000	San Francisco 49ers	☎415/468-2249
Kansas City Chiefs	☎816/924-9300	Seattle Seahawks	☎206/827-9766
Los Angeles Raiders	☎310/322-5901	Tampa Bay Buccaneers	☎813/870-2700
Los Angeles Rams	☎714/937-6767	Washington Redskins	☎202/546-2222

the US. The eastern resorts of Vermont and New York State, however, pale by comparison with those of the Rockies, such as Vail and Aspen in Colorado, and the Californian Sierra Nevada. You can usually rent equipment for about $15 per day, and expect to pay another $20 to $45 a day for lift tickets.

A cheaper option is **cross-country skiing**, or ski-touring. Backcountry ski lodges dot mountainous areas along both coasts and in the Rockies, offering a range of rustic accommodation, equipment rental and lessons, from as little as $10 a day for skis, boots and poles, up to about $100 for an all-inclusive weekend tour.

THE WORLD CUP

Soccer fans around the globe were shocked by the decision to hold the 1994 **World Cup** – the world's largest single-sport event – in the United States. This is a country where "football" very definitely means the grid-iron variety, and soccer has been reported as ranking below big-wheel truck-racing in national popularity. The abortive early-Eighties experiment when teams such as the New York Cosmos hired over-the-hill megastars such as Pele, Cruyff and Beckenbauer has long since foundered, and professional participation is confined to a barely watched indoor league.

However, over eleven million Americans now play soccer regularly, there are firm plans to begin a new professional league in 1995, and US players such as John Harkes and Kasey Keller have made significant names for themselves in Europe. No one expects the home team to lift the trophy – the USA's two previous World Cup final appearances in 1950 and 1990 bore little fruit – although their 2–0 thrashing of once-mighty England in 1993 gave some hint of promise.

All indications are that the 52-game tournament, which holders Germany kick off in Chicago on June 17, will be a glitzy well-organized affair. It will also herald a soccer "first", with games played indoors (on natural grass) at Detroit's impressive Pontiac Silverdome. For the **First Round**, the 24 teams are divided into six groups of four, in which each side plays the other three once. The top two sides from each group, along with the four best third-place teams, progress to the "**Round of 16**", to commence the more conventional, and exciting, system of knock-out games. From here on in, if a game is tied after ninety minutes, thirty minutes of overtime is played (not the "sudden-death" overtime employed in NFL football games); if there is still no winner, the game is decided by penalty kicks. The championship continues through **Quarterfinals** and **Semifinals** to the **World Cup Final** itself, played in Los Angeles' Rose Bowl on July 17.

The World Cup is likely to place great stress on accommodation and facilities in each of the nine host cities, and indications are that a trip to the games could be an expensive affair. The vast majority of match **tickets** have been sold in advance or allocated to tour companies, and few if any tickets may be available for popular individual matches – the "scalpers" may be in for a good time. **Prices** range from $55 in the First Round to $500 for the later stages; *World Cup Ticketing* in LA (☎310/843-2011) will sell any remaining tickets; other alternatives include booking a package trip through the *National Tour Association* (☎606/253-1036). Foreign visitors should reserve through an operator in their own country.

The two dozen competing nations are all that remain, after two years of gruelling qualifying games, of an original line-up of 141; notable absentees include England – indeed all four British teams – and France. The participating countries are USA (as hosts), Germany (as champions, having won in Italy in 1990), Italy, Switzerland, Norway, Holland, Spain, Ireland, Belgium, Romania, Russia, Greece, Sweden, Bulgaria, Mexico, Colombia, Argentina, Brazil, Bolivia, Nigeria, Morocco, Cameroon, South Korea, and Saudi Arabia.

City	Game Date
Boston/Foxboro	**June** 21, 23, 25, 30; **July** 5, 9
Chicago	**June** 17, 21, 26, 27; **July** 2
Dallas	**June** 17, 21, 27, 30; **July** 3, 9
Detroit	**June** 18, 22, 24, 28
Los Angeles	**June** 18, 19, 22, 26; **July** 3, 13, 16, 17
New York/E Rutherford, NJ	**June** 18, 23, 25, 28; **July** 5, 10, 13
Orlando	**June** 19, 24, 25, 29; **July** 4
San Francisco	**June** 20, 24, 26, 28; **July** 4, 10
Washington DC	**June** 19, 20, 28, 29; **July** 2

ENTERTAINMENT AND MEDIA

Even first-time visitors touring the United States are liable to find themselves travelling through a landscape that is already intensely familiar, where the place names come from classic rock 'n' roll songs and the wide-open spaces seem straight out of Hollywood westerns. In fact exploring the reality behind the glamorous media images – and experiencing at first hand the mighty entertainment industry responsible for so many preconceptions – are two of the greatest pleasures of getting to know America.

Whether you want to follow in the footsteps of Bob Dylan in north-country Minnesota or Robert Johnson in Mississippi, see Woody Allen's Manhattan or JR's Dallas, there's nowhere like the USA for living out musical and movie fantasies. Mickey Mouse and Dolly Parton have their own theme parks, the buffalo still roam the Great Plains, Route 66 still winds from Chicago to LA, and Elvis still lives in Graceland.

MUSIC

Music fans make pilgrimages from all over the world to the cities that spawned jazz, blues, country, soul and rap. No country devotee could fail to enjoy the rhinestone glitter, halls of fame, honkytonks and stars' homes of **Nashville**, while **Memphis**, the home of Sun, Stax and the Reverend Al Green, and **Chicago** are the prime destinations for live blues. The party town of **New Orleans**, with its legendary Bourbon Street, boasts an unrivalled jazz and r'n'b scene; hard-

core rock fans head for **Los Angeles**, **Boston**, or **Seattle**. Not everywhere lives up to the myth, however; Motown fans, for example, may well be disappointed by Detroit.

The musical excitement is by no means confined to the big cities. Travel through rural Appalachia and you may find ensembles of backwoods **fiddlers**; the otherwise sleepy bayous of southern Louisiana are enlivened by the footstomping **Cajun** and **zydeco** sounds; and the little jook-joints of Mississippi Delta hamlets enrapture **blues** purists. The influence of **country** music extends well beyond Tennessee; the south, particularly Texas, is awash with unpretentious honky-tonk bars, and the cowboy bars of southern Wyoming play nothing but good old c'n'w. Towns as far flung as **Bakersfield**, California, with its gutsy honky-tonk style, and tiny but more mainstream **Branson**, Missouri, boast almost as many live country venues as Nashville.

Today's rock and soul superstars may play virtually all their gigs in huge 30,000-seater stadiums, but there are innumerable smaller venues where you can see the latest up-and-coming groups. College towns in particular play a major role in introducing new artists to wider audiences, and you shouldn't pass through **Ann Arbor**, Michigan, **Austin**, Texas (also the home of progressive country music) or **Athens**, Georgia (where REM and the B-52s come from) without checking on what's going on.

CINEMA AND THEATER

Foreign visitors who want to be ahead of the crowds back home should take in a film or two while in the States; Hollywood **movies** are generally on show three to six months before they reach the rest of the world. Most cities have good cinemas downtown, though in smaller places you often have to make your way out to the multiscreen venues in the malls on the edge of town. Sadly, you don't come across many drive-ins these days.

Theater is very hit and miss in the big cities. The international reputation of New York's Broadway theaters is generally well deserved but it costs a small fortune to get a seat even for most of the Off-Broadway productions. The larger college towns tend to feature well-funded performances of Shakespeare and the usual canon, while throughout the country – in Minneapolis, for example – local companies provide their own stimulating alternatives.

Every major town and city has at least one **comedy club**. Standards vary enormously; in some, sexist xenophobes pander to the basest of prejudices; in others the material is fresh, incisive and above all funny. We've listed the best venues, though as ever you should consult the local entertainment weeklies.

NEWSPAPERS

Due mainly to its vast size, the US had no national **newspaper** (aside from the staid financial *Wall Street Journal* and the tacky sex-and-scandal weekly, the *National Enquirer*) until the arrival of the color *USA Today* a few years back. Most Americans still prefer their newspapers grainy, inky and local. Every large town has at least one morning and/or evening paper, generally excellent at covering its own area but relying on agencies for foreign – and even national – reports.

One good thing most newspapers share is their low cost – normally 25¢ to 40¢, with the enormous Sunday editions selling for $1 to $1.25. Newspapers are sold from vending machines on street corners; outside big cities, newsagents are very rare.

Every community of any size has at least a few **free newspapers**, found in street distribution bins or in shops and cafes. These can be handy sources for bar, restaurant and nightlife information, and we've mentioned the most useful titles in the relevant cities.

TELEVISION

For low-budget travellers, watching cable **television** in an anonymous motel room may well be the predominant form of entertainment.

American TV can be quite insanely addictive; it certainly comes in quantity, and the quality of the best of it can keep you watching indefinitely. With perhaps thirty-odd channels to choose from, there's always something to grab your attention. The schedules are packed with sycophantic chat shows, outrageous quizzes and banal sitcoms, persistently interrupted by commercials. As for **news** coverage, local reports are comprehensive: a couple of hours each night, usually from 5pm until 6pm and 10pm until 11pm. The hour of national and international news which normally

follows tends to be much less thorough, and world events which don't directly affect the US barely get a look-in.

Cable TV is widely found in motels and hotels, although sometimes you have to pay a couple of dollars to watch it. Most cable stations are no better than the major networks (*ABC, CBS* and *NBC*), though some of the more specialized channels are consistently interesting. The *ARTS* channel broadcasts enjoyable, if po-faced, arts features, imported TV plays and the like. *CNN* (*Cable Network News*) offers round-the-clock news, *HBO* (*Home Box Office*) shows recent big-bucks movies, *AMC* (*American Movie Company*) shows old black-and-white films, and *ESPN* exclusively covers sport. Finally, there's *MTV* (*Music Television*), which, with the exception of its slots on rap, heavy metal and the like, is wearingly mainstream.

Other cable channels – each major city has at least a dozen – are even more narrowcast. You'll frequently find Japanese soaps and earnest half-hour interviews with people claiming to have come back from the dead. Soccer fans should scan the Spanish-language channels, which often show matches from Europe and South America.

Many major sporting occasions are transmitted on a pay-per-view basis. To watch events like world heavyweight boxing bouts you may have to pay as much as $40, either to your motel or to a bar that's putting on a live screening.

RADIO

Radio stations are even more abundant than TV channels, and the majority, again, stick to a bland commercial format. Except for news and chat, stations on the **AM** band are best avoided in favor of **FM**, in particular the nationally funded public and college stations, found between 88 and 92 FM. These provide diverse and listenable programming, be it bizarre underground rock or obscure theater, and they're also good sources for local nightlife news.

Though the large cities boast good specialist **music** stations, for most of the time you'll probably have to resort to skipping up and down the frequencies, between re-run Eagles tracks, country and western tunes, fire-and-brimstone Bible thumpers and crazed phone-ins. Driving through rural areas can be frustrating; for hundreds of miles you might only be able to receive one or two (very dull) stations. It's not usual for car rental firms to equip their vehicles with cassette players.

FESTIVALS AND PUBLIC HOLIDAYS

Someone, somewhere is always celebrating something in the USA, although apart from national holidays, few festivities are shared throughout the country. Instead, there is a disparate multitude of local events: art and craft shows, county fairs, ethnic celebrations, music festivals, rodeos, sandcastle building competitions, and many others of every hue and shade.

The box opposite contains a selection of the best of the local festivals covered in this book. In addition, tourist offices for each state (see pp.20–21) can provide full lists, or you can just phone the visitor center in a particular region ahead of your arrival and ask what's coming up. Certain festivities, such as **Mardi Gras** in New Orleans (p.498), are well worth planning your vacation around; obviously other people will have the same idea, and visiting during these times requires an extra amount of advance effort.

PUBLIC HOLIDAYS

The biggest and most all-American of the **national festivals and holidays** is **Independence Day**, on the Fourth of July, when the entire country grinds to a standstill as people get drunk, salute the flag and partake of firework displays, marches, beauty pageants and more, all in commemoration of the signing of the Declaration of Independence in 1776. **Halloween** (October 31) lacks any such patriotic overtones, and is not a public holiday despite being one of the most popular yearly flings. Traditionally, kids run around the streets banging on doors demanding "trick or treat", and being given pieces of candy. These days that sort of activity is mostly confined to rural and suburban areas, while in bigger cities Halloween has grown into a massive gay celebration: in West Hollywood in LA, in New York's Greenwich Village and San Francisco's Castro district, the night is marked by mass cross-dressing, huge block parties and general licentiousness. More sedate is **Thanksgiving Day**, on the last Thursday in November. The third big event of the year is essentially a domestic affair, when relatives return to the familial nest to stuff themselves with roast turkey, and (supposedly) fondly recall the first harvest of the Pilgrims in Massachusetts – though in fact Thanksgiving was already a national holiday before anyone thought to make that connection.

On the national **public holidays** listed below, shops, banks and offices are liable to be closed all day. Many states also have their own additional holidays, and in some places Good Friday is a half-day holiday. The traditional summer season for tourism runs from Memorial Day to Labor Day; some tourist attractions are only open during that period.

January 1 **New Year's Day**

January 15 **Martin Luther King's Birthday**

Third Monday in February **President's Day**

Easter Monday

Last Monday in May **Memorial Day**

July 4 **Independence Day**

First Monday in September **Labor Day**

Second Monday in October **Columbus Day**

November 11 **Veterans' Day**

Last Thursday in November **Thanksgiving Day**

December 25 **Christmas Day**

ANNUAL FESTIVALS AND EVENTS

For further details of the selected festivals and events listed below, including more precise dates, see the relevant page of the guide, or contact the local authorities direct. The state tourist boards listed on pp.20–21 can provide fuller calendars for each area.

JANUARY

Aspen CO: Winterskol	→ p.620
Elko NV: Cowboy Poetry Gathering	→ p.751
St Paul MN: Winter Carnival	→ p.277

FEBRUARY

Cordova AK: Iceworm Festival	→ p.908
Daytona Beach FL: Daytona 500 Race	→ p.460
Fort Worden WA: Hot Jazz Festival	→ p.858
Picuris Pueblo NM: Buffalo Dance	→ p.669

MARCH

Butte MT: St Patrick's Day	→ p.647
Fairbanks AK: Ice Festival	→ p.914
Los Angeles CA: Academy Awards	→ p.784
New Orleans LA: Mardi Gras	→ p.498
also elsewhere in Louisiana	→ p.505

APRIL

Boston MA: Patriot's Day – Marathon	→ p.161
Lafayette LA: Festival International de	
Louisiane	→ p.505
New Orleans LA: French Quarter Festival and	
Jazz & Heritage Festival (into May)	→ p.498
Sanctuario de Chimayo NM: Easter	
Pilgrimage	→ p.670

MAY

Black Mountain NC: Folk Festival	→ p.364
Breaux Bridge LA: Crawfish Festival	→ p.505
Charleston WV: Vandalia Festival of	
Appalachian Culture	→ p.328
Denver CO: Capitol Hill Peoples' Fair	→ p.608
Flagstaff AZ: Zuni Crafts Show	→ p.700
Honokaa HI: Western Week	→ p.933
Indianapolis IN: Indianapolis 500 Race	→ p.246
Los Angeles CA: Cinco de Mayo (May 5)	→ p.784
Louisville KY: Kentucky Derby	→ p.394
Memphis TN: Memphis in May, including	
Barbecue Cook-Out	→ p.405
San Antonio TX: International	
Conjunto Festival	→ p.525

JUNE

Fort Worth TX: Chisholm Trail Round Up	→ p.540
Hardin MT: Little Bighorn Days	→ p.645
Nashville TN: Fan Fair	→ p.412
Shreveport LA: Good Times Festival	→ p.510
Telluride CO: Bluegrass Festival	→ p.625

JULY

Blowing Rock NC: Highland Games	→ p.362
Cheyenne WY: Cheyenne Frontier Days	→ p.629
Elkins WV: Augusta Festival of	
Appalachian Culture (into Aug)	→ p.326

Elko NV: National Basque Festival	→ p.751
Fairbanks AK: Eskimo/Indian Olympics	→ p.915
Flagstaff AZ: Hopi Crafts Show	→ p.700
Navajo Crafts Show (into Aug)	→ p.700
Fort Totten ND: Pow-wow and Rodeo	→ p.598
Milwaukee WI: Great Circus Parade	→ p.276
Minneapolis MN: Aquatennial	→ p.279
Nambe Pueblo NM: Ceremonial Dance	→ p.669
Philadelphia PA: Freedom Fest	→ p.125
Riverblues	→ p.125
San Ildefonso Pueblo NM: Festival of	
Pueblo Arts & Crafts	→ p.669
St Paul MN: Taste of Minnesota	→ p.279
Talkeetna AK: Moose Dropping Festival	→ p.911
Traverse City MI: Cherry Festival	→ p.240

AUGUST

Asheville NC: Mountain Dance &	
Folk Festival	→ p.364
Gallup NM: Inter-Tribal Indian Ceremonial	→ p.683
Memphis TN: Anniversary of Elvis' Death	→ p.404
Newport RI: Folk & Jazz Festivals	→ p.180
San Antonio TX: Texas Folklife Festival	→ p.525
Santa Fe NM: Indian Market	→ p.671
Sturgis SD: Motorcycle Rally & Races	→ p.591

SEPTEMBER

Fort Worth TX: Pioneer Days	→ p.540
Greenville MS: Delta Blues Festival	→ p.428
Lafayette LA: Festivals Acadiens	→ p.505
Los Angeles CA: LA's Birthday (Sept 4)	→ p.784
LA County Fair	→ p.784
Lubbock TX: Panhandle South Plains Fair	→ p.543
Monterey CA: Monterey Jazz Festival	→ p.796
Opelousas LA: Zydeco Festival	→ p.505
Pendleton OR: Pendelton Round-Up	→ p.880
Santa Fe NM: Fiesta de Santa Fe	→ p.671
Savannah GA: Jazz Festival	→ p.387
Tulsa OK: Chili Cookoff & Bluegrass Festival	→ p.555

OCTOBER

Albuquerque NM: Hot-Air Balloon Rally	→ p.679
Charleston SC: Moja Arts Festival	→ p.371
Custer State Park SD: Round Up of Bison	→ p.594
Globe AZ: Apache Days	→ p.698
Helena AR: Blues Festival	→ p.434
Opelousas LA: Louisiana Yambilee	→ p.505
Tombstone AZ: Helldorado Days	→ p.694
Tuba City AZ: Western Navajo Fair	→ p.714

NOVEMBER

Tesuque Pueblo NM: Corn Dance	→ p.669

CLIMATE AND WHEN TO GO

The climate of the United States is characterized by wide variations, not just from region to region and season to season, but also day to day and even hour to hour. Even setting aside the exceptionally far-flung states of Alaska and Hawaii, the main body of the US is subject to dramatically shifting weather patterns, most notably produced by westerly winds sweeping across the continent from the Pacific.

It is of course possible to make certain generalizations. Temperatures tend to rise the further south you go, and to fall the higher you climb, while the climate along either coast is, on the whole, milder and more equable than inland.

Starting a brief survey of the nation's weather in the east, the **Northeast**, from Maine down to Washington DC, experiences relatively low precipitation as a rule, but temperatures can range from bitterly cold in winter to stiflingly hot (made worse by humidity) in the short summer. Further south, summers get warmer and longer. Though **Florida**'s air temperatures are not necessarily dramatically high in summer, being kept down by the proximity of the sea both east and west, it's warm and sunny enough in winter to attract visitors from all over the country.

The **Great Plains**, which for climatic purposes can be said to extend from the Appalachians to the Rockies, are alternately exposed to icy Arctic winds streaming down from Canada, and humid tropical airflows from the

Caribbean and the Gulf of Mexico. Winters in the north, around the Great Lakes, can be abjectly cold, with driving winds and freezing rain. It can freeze or even snow in winter as far south as the Gulf of Mexico, though spring and fall get progressively longer and milder further south through the Plains. Summer is much the wettest season in the **South** as a whole, the time when thunderstorms are most likely to strike. One or two **hurricanes** each year rage across Florida and/or the **Southeastern** states, from obscure origins somewhere in the Gulf of Mexico on the way to extinction out in the Atlantic. **Tornadoes** (or "twisters") are usually a much more local phenomenon, tending to cut a narrow swath of destruction in the wake of violent spring or summer thunderstorms. Average rainfall dwindles to lower and lower levels the further west you head across the plains.

Temperatures in the **Rockies** correlate closely with altitude; beyond the mountains in the south lie the extensive arid and inhospitable deserts of the **Southwest**, much of which lies in the rainshadow of the Californian ranges. In cities such as Las Vegas and Phoenix, the mercury regularly soars above 100°, though the atmosphere is not usually humid enough to be as ennervating as that might sound.

Once across the barrier of the Cascade mountains, the fertile **Pacific Northwest** is the only region of the country where winter is the wettest season, and throughout the year the European-style climate is wet, mild, and seldom hot. **Californian** weather more or less lives up to the popular idyllic image, though the climate is markedly hotter and drier in the south than the north, and there's enough snow to make the mountains a major skiing destination. There are also noteworthy local variations. **San Francisco** is kept milder and colder than the immediately surrounding district by the propensity of the Bay Area to attract sea fogs, while the basin of **Los Angeles** is prone to fill up with smog, trapping pollution and fog beneath a layer of warm air.

For daily **weather forecasts**, detailed enough to satisfy the greatest obsessive, tune in to TV's 24-hour *Weather Channel*.

AVERAGE TEMPERATURES (°F) AND RAINFALL

		Jan	Feb	March	April	May	June	July	Aug	Sept	Oct	Nov	Dec
Anchorage	av. max temp	19	27	33	44	54	62	65	64	57	43	30	20
	av. min temp	5	9	13	27	36	44	49	47	39	29	15	6
	days of rain	7	6	5	4	5	6	10	15	14	12	7	6
Atlanta	av. max temp	51	54	62	71	79	86	87	86	82	72	61	52
	av. min temp	35	37	43	51	60	67	70	69	64	54	43	37
	days of rain	12	11	11	10	10	11	13	12	8	7	8	11
Boston	av. max temp	36	37	43	54	66	75	80	78	71	62	49	40
	av. min temp	20	21	28	38	49	58	63	62	55	46	35	25
	days of rain	12	10	12	11	11	10	10	10	9	9	10	11
Chicago	av. max temp	32	34	43	55	65	75	81	79	73	61	47	36
	av. min temp	18	20	29	40	50	60	66	65	58	47	34	23
	days of rain	11	10	12	11	12	11	9	9	9	9	10	11
Honolulu	av. max temp	76	76	77	78	80	81	82	83	83	82	80	78
	av. min temp	69	67	67	68	70	72	73	74	74	72	70	69
	days of rain	14	11	13	12	11	12	14	13	13	13	13	15
Las Vegas	av. max temp	60	67	72	81	89	99	103	102	95	84	71	61
	av. min temp	29	34	39	45	52	61	68	66	57	47	36	30
	days of rain	2	2	2	1	1	1	2	2	1	1	1	2
Los Angeles	av. max temp	65	66	67	70	72	76	81	82	81	76	73	67
	av. min temp	46	47	48	50	53	56	60	60	58	54	50	47
	days of rain	6	6	6	4	2	1	0	0	1	2	3	6
Miami	av. max temp	74	75	78	80	84	86	88	88	87	83	78	76
	av. min temp	61	61	64	67	71	74	76	76	75	72	66	62
	days of rain	9	6	7	7	12	13	15	15	18	16	10	7
Nashville	av. max temp	47	50	59	69	78	86	89	88	82	72	58	49
	av. min temp	31	33	40	49	58	67	70	68	62	50	40	33
	days of rain	12	11	12	11	11	11	11	9	8	7	9	11
New Orleans	av. max temp	62	65	71	77	83	88	90	90	86	79	70	64
	av. min temp	47	50	55	61	68	74	76	76	73	64	55	48
	days of rain	10	12	9	7	8	13	15	14	10	7	7	10
New York City	av. max temp	37	38	45	57	68	77	82	80	79	69	51	41
	av. min temp	24	24	30	42	53	60	66	66	60	49	37	29
	days of rain	12	10	12	11	11	10	12	10	9	9	9	10
San Francisco	av. max temp	55	59	61	62	63	66	65	65	69	68	63	57
	av. min temp	45	47	48	49	51	52	53	53	55	54	51	47
	days of rain	11	11	10	6	4	2	0	0	2	4	7	10
Seattle	av. max temp	45	48	52	58	64	69	72	73	67	59	51	47
	av. min temp	36	37	39	43	47	52	54	55	52	47	41	38
	days of rain	18	16	16	13	12	9	4	5	8	13	17	19
Washington DC	av. max temp	42	44	53	64	75	83	87	84	78	67	55	45
	av. min temp	27	28	35	44	54	63	68	66	59	48	38	29
	days of rain	11	10	12	11	12	11	11	11	8	8	9	10

To convert °F to °C, subtract 32 and multiply by 5/9

DIRECTORY

ADDRESSES Generally speaking, roads in built-up areas in the United States are laid out on a grid system, creating "blocks" of buildings. The first one or two digits of a specific address refer to the block, which will be numbered in sequence from a central point, usually downtown; for example, 620 S Cedar Avenue will be six blocks south of downtown. It is crucial, therefore, to take note of components such as "NW" or "SE" in addresses; 3620 SW Washington Boulevard will be a very long way indeed from 3620 NE Washington Boulevard.

AIRPORT TAX This is invariably included in the price of your ticket.

CIGARETTES AND SMOKING The country which first gave tobacco to the world is now probably the most concerned about its detrimental effects on health, with smoking now severely frowned upon. It's possible to spend a month in the US without ever smelling tobacco; most cinemas are non-smoking, restaurants are usually divided into non-smoking and smoking sections, and smoking is universally forbidden on public transport – including almost all domestic airline flights. Work places, too, tend to be smoke-free zones, so employees are reduced to smoking on the street outside.

DATES In the American style, the date 1.8.95 means not August 1 but January 8.

ELECTRICITY 110V AC. All plugs are two-pronged and rather insubstantial. Some travel plug adapters don't fit American sockets.

FLOORS The *first* floor in the US is what would be the ground floor in Britain; the *second* floor would be the first floor, and so on.

ID Should be carried at all times. Two pieces should suffice, one of which should have a photo: a passport and credit card(s) are your best bets.

MEASUREMENTS AND SIZES The US has yet to go metric, so measurements are in inches, feet, yards and miles; weight in ounces, pounds and tons. American pints and gallons are about four-fifths of Imperial ones. Clothing sizes are always two figures less what they would be in Britain – a British women's size 12 is a US size 10 – while British shoe sizes are 1½ below American ones.

TAX Be warned that **sales tax** is added to virtually everything you buy in a shop, but isn't part of the marked price. The actual rate varies from place to place: in New York and parts of California it's over 8 percent, while other states – Alaska, Delaware, Montana and Oregon – have no sales tax at all. **Hotel tax** will add 5 to 10 percent to most bills.

TEMPERATURES Always given in Fahrenheit.

TIME ZONES See p.18.

TIPPING Many first-time visitors to the US think of tipping as a potential source of huge embarrassment. It's nothing of the sort; tipping is universally expected, and you quickly learn to tip without a second thought. You really shouldn't depart a bar or restaurant without leaving a tip of *at least* 15 percent (unless the service is utterly disgusting). The whole system of service is predicated on tipping; not to do so causes a great deal of resentment, and a short paypacket for the waiter or waitress at the end of the week. About the same amount should be added to taxi fares – and round them up to the nearest 50¢ or dollar. A hotel porter who has lugged your suitcases up several flights of stairs should get $3 to $5. When paying by credit or charge card, you're expected to add the tip to the total bill before filling in the amount and signing.

VIDEOS The standard format used for video cassettes in the US is different from that used in Britain. You cannot buy videos in the US compatible with a video camera bought in Britain.

PART TWO

THE

GUIDE

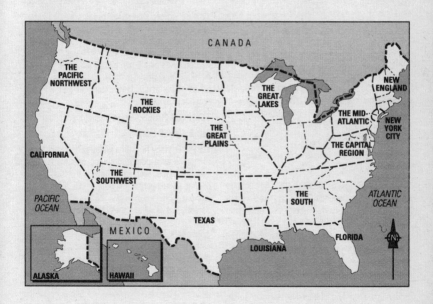

CHAPTER ONE

NEW YORK CITY

New York City is one of the most sensationally exciting cities to visit in the world. You may not think so at first – for the place is nothing short of mad, epitomizing the faults of modern America. But spend even a few days here and the adrenalin takes hold. Walking through the canyon-like city streets, eyes forever drawn upwards by the soaring architecture, *is* an experience, the buildings like icons to the modern age. And despite all the hype, the movie-image sentimentality, the island of **Manhattan** is massively romantic. Whether it's the flickering lights of the midtown skyscrapers, the 4am half-life in Greenwich Village, or just wasting the morning on the Staten Island Ferry, you would have to be made of stone not to be moved by it all.

New York is not a conventionally pleasing city – or for that matter conventional in any respect. The divisions between rich and poor in Manhattan could hardly be more extreme, and the city's problems are increasing. New York suffers from a spectacular case of urban blight, as you are made constantly aware; indeed, in a perverse way, these tangible and potent contrasts give New York much of its excitement.

The city does have more straightforward pleasures, such as its different **ethnic neighborhoods** in Lower Manhattan, from Chinatown to the Jewish Lower East Side, the arty concentrations of SoHo and TriBeCa, Greenwich and East Village; its **architecture** (the whole city reads like an illustrated history of modern design); and its **art**, over which you can spend weeks in the Metropolitan and Modern Art museums and countless smaller collections. And there is, of course, the opportunity to consume. You can **eat** anything, cooked in any style; **drink** in any kind of company; sit through any amount of **movies**. The established arts – **dance, theater, music** – are superbly catered for, and New York's **clubs** are varied and exciting. As for **shops**, the choice in this heartland of the great capitalist dream is almost numbingly exhaustive.

History

The first European to see Manhattan Island, then inhabited by the Algonquin, was the Italian navigator Verrazano, in 1524. Dutch settlers established the settlement of **New Amsterdam** exactly one hundred years later; its first governor, Peter Minuit, was the man who "bought" the whole island for a handful of trinkets, though considering the Indians he actually paid were not locals, but were only passing through, they might be said to have got the better of the deal. The colony was surrounded by a strong defensive wall – today's Wall Street follows its course – but by the time the British laid claim to the area in 1664, the heavy-handed rule of governor **Peter Stuyvesant** had so alienated its inhabitants that control was handed over without a fight.

Renamed New York, the city prospered and grew, and by the time of the Revolution, its population had reached 33,000. The impetus given by the opening of Erie Canal in 1825, facilitating trade far inland, further spurred it towards becoming the economic powerhouse of the nation, the base later in the century of **financiers** such as Cornelius Vanderbilt and J Pierpont Morgan. The **Statue of Liberty** arrived in 1886, a symbol of the city's role as the gateway for generations of immigrants, while the early twentieth century saw the sudden proliferation of Manhattan's extraordinary **skyscrapers**, which cast New York as the city of the future in the eyes of an astonished world.

Arrival, Information and Getting Around

New York City is served by two **international airports**: most flights use **John F Kennedy (JFK)** (☎718/656-4520) in Queens, but some *Virgin* and *Continental* flights touch down at **Newark** (☎908/961-2000) in New Jersey. In addition, some **domestic** arrivals come in at **La Guardia** (☎718/533-3400), also in Queens. From all the airports, the cheapest and most straightforward way into Manhattan is by **bus**.

From **JFK**, *Carey* buses run to the Port Authority Bus Terminal and Grand Central Station in Manhattan (every 30min, 5am–12.30am, journey time 45–75 min; $11; ☎718/632-0500). The alternative bus/subway link (☎718/330-1234) costs just $1.50: take the shuttle bus (labelled "Long-term parking") to Howard Beach station on the #A subway line, a ninety-minute train ride from central Manhattan (every 20min, 6am–1am).

Olympia Trails buses take up to forty minutes to get from **Newark** to Manhattan, where they stop at the World Trade Center, Grand Central and Penn stations ($7; every 20min, 6.15am–midnight; ☎201/964-6233). *New Jersey Transit* buses also run to the Port Authority Terminal ($7; every 15–30min, day and night; ☎201/762-5100).

Carey buses (see above) from **La Guardia** take 45 minutes to Grand Central ($8.50; every 30min, 6.45am–midnight) and Port Authority ($8.50; 7.30am–10pm). *Carey* also links **JFK and La Guardia**, taking 45 minutes ($9.50; every 30min, 6am–11pm).

Taxis are pricey from all the airports; reckon on paying $20 from La Guardia, $30-plus from JFK, $40 or more from Newark. **Car and minibus services** can also be costly *from* the airports, but prices from Manhattan *to* the airports are around $12 per person to La Guardia, $15 to JFK, $18 to Newark (*Gray Line Air Shuttles*; ☎757-6840). For **general information** on getting to and from the airports, call ☎1-800/AIR RIDE.

Greyhound buses (☎635-0800) pull in to New York at the Port Authority Bus Terminal, 41st St and Eighth Ave (☎564-8484). **Trains** come in at either **Grand Central Terminal**, 42nd St and Park Ave (☎532-4900), which takes arrivals from the Hudson Valley, the north and west US and Canada, or **Penn Station**, at Seventh Ave and 33rd St (☎868-8970), which serves Long Island and New Jersey. Trains from Boston, Chicago, Washington and Florida may arrive at either station.

Information

The best place for information is the **New York Convention and Visitors Bureau** at 2 Columbus Circle (Mon–Fri 9am–6pm, Sat & Sun 10am–6pm; ☎397-8222). They have up-to-date leaflets on what's going on, bus and subway maps, and details of accommodation – though they can't actually book anything.

The main Manhattan **post office** is at 421 Eighth Ave, between W 31st and 33rd streets (Mon–Sat 24hr for important services; zip code 10001).

City Transit

Few cities equal New York for sheer street-level stimulation, and **walking** is the most exciting method of exploring. However, it's also exhausting, and you'll need to use some other form of **public transportation**. The fastest way to get from A to B in Manhattan and the boroughs is the dirty, noisy, and intimidating – but reasonably efficient – **subway**. Each train and route is identified by a number or letter; the majority of routes run uptown or downtown, following the great avenues, rather than crosstown. The subway is open 24 hours a day, but most routes operate at certain times only. Every journey, whether on the **express** lines, which stop only at major stations, or the **locals**,

Unless otherwise specified, all telephone numbers in this chapter share **area code** ☎212.

which stop at them all, costs $1.50, bought in the form of a **token** from station booths, or from any branch of *McDonalds*, and also valid on the buses. There's no discount for buying several. Subway and bus maps can be obtained from token booths, or from the concourse office at Grand Central. At night always try to use the crowded center cars, and while you're waiting, keep to the area marked in yellow where you can be seen by the booth attendants. By day the whole train is safe, at least in theory.

New York's **bus system** is a lot simpler than the subway, and fairly frequent. Its one disadvantage is that it can be extremely slow – in peak hours almost down to walking pace. Buses stop every two or three blocks, at five- to ten-minute intervals. Anywhere in Manhattan the fare is $1.50, payable on entry with either a subway token or with the correct change – but not pennies or dollar bills. Ask for a transfer if you need to change buses anywhere along your journey, valid for an hour from boarding.

Taxis are reasonably priced and the best way to get around in the evening, but their drivers don't always know their way around terribly well and often speak little English.

Guided Tours

Grayline is the biggest operator of guided **bus** tours, with two terminals in midtown Manhattan: on Eighth Ave between 53rd and 54th streets (☎397-2600), and at 166 West 46th St (☎354-5122). Half-day tours, taking in the main sights of Manhattan, go for around $27, and a full day costs $39, bookable through any travel agent.

The **Circle Line Ferry** takes three hours to sail right round Manhattan from Pier 83 at the far west end of 42nd Street, taking in everything from soaring views of Lower Manhattan to the bleaker stretches of Harlem, with a commentary and on-board bar ($16; March–Dec with varying regularity; ☎563-3200). The **Staten Island Ferry** (see p.85) lays on a staggering panorama of the downtown skyline for just 50¢.

Island Helicopter, at the far eastern end of East 34th St (☎683-4575), and *Liberty Helicopter Tours*, at the western end of 30th St, near the Jacob Javits Convention Center (☎465-8905), offer **helicopter** flights from around $40 upwards.

The City

New York City comprises the central island of Manhattan along with four outer boroughs – Brooklyn, Queens, the Bronx and Staten Island. **Manhattan**, to many, is New York; certainly, this where you're likely to spend most time, and to stay. The island is broadly divided into three districts: **Downtown** (below 14th St); **Midtown** (from 14th St up as far as Central Park); and **Upper Manhattan** (north of Central Park). The southern (downtown) part of Manhattan was first to be settled, which means that its streets have names and are somewhat randomly arranged. Uptown, above Houston Street on the east side, 14th Street on the west, the streets are numbered and follow a grid pattern, the numbers increasing as you move north.

Fifth Avenue, the greatest of the main avenues, cuts along the east side of Central Park and serves as a dividing line between east streets (the "East Side") and west streets ("the West Side"). House numbers increase as you walk away to either side; numbers on avenues increase as you move north. It's useful also to know that traffic on **odd**-numbered streets runs from east to west, and on **even**-numbered streets from west to east, though major crosstown streets run in both directions. Apart from Park, Broadway, and Eleventh Avenue, which are two-way, avenues run in alternate directions.

Manhattan is a hard act to follow, and the four **outer boroughs** – **Brooklyn**, **Queens**, **the Bronx** and **Staten Island** – inevitably pale in comparison, being essentially residential, with fewer specific sights. However, Brooklyn Heights is one of the city's most beautiful neighborhoods, and both the faded resort of Coney Island, also in Brooklyn, and nearby Brighton Beach, deserve a trip out on the subway; the Staten Island Ferry is worth a trip in its own right.

Lower Manhattan

LOWER MANHATTAN harbors its extremes in close proximity. For some it's the most spectacular, most glamorous skyline in the world, for others a run-down and seedy home. But whatever your perspective, it is undeniably archetypal New York, encompassing Greenwich Village and the East Village, Chinatown and Little Italy, and, at the skyscraper heart of things, the corporate monoliths of the Financial District.

The **Statue of Liberty** is the obvious focus – not so much for the vaunted symbol (though this is hard to ignore) as for the views of southern Manhattan. This lower part of the island begins with the shoreline **Financial District** – Wall Street at its center – and then drifts, within half a mile, into the first of the city's ethnic districts: bustling, insular **Chinatown**, fast expanding into adjacent **Little Italy**. Over to the west, the onetime industrial areas of **SoHo** and **TriBeCa** are now up-and-coming residential blocks, home to Manhattan's (alternative) art scene. Further north come the traditionally politicized/literary **Greenwich Village** (touristy now but fun) and the **East Village**, which has taken on much of Greenwich's alternative mantle. All of this makes for enjoyable walking and café browsing. Walk beyond, though, into the **Lower East Side**, and the riches fade fast – the very real poverty quite unhidden and not a little threatening.

The Statue of Liberty and Ellis Island

The tip of Manhattan island, and the enclosing shores of New Jersey, Staten Island and Brooklyn, form the broad expanse of **New York Harbor**, one of the finest natural harbors in the world, stretching as far as the Verrazano Narrows – the narrow neck of land between Staten Island and Long Island. It's possible to appreciate it by simply gazing out from the promenade on Battery Park. But to get the best views of the classic skyline, you should really take to the water. You can do this on the Staten Island Ferry, but the islands in the bay are far more compelling.

Ferries, run by *Circle Line*, go to both the Statue of Liberty and Ellis Island from the pier in Battery Park (sailings every half-hour in summer, roughly Mon–Fri 9.15am–3.30pm, Sat & Sun 9.15am–4.30pm; tickets from Castle Clinton, $6 round-trip). If you take the last ferry, it's not possible to visit both islands, so it's best to try and leave as early as possible, and avoid the queues (which can be very long in high season, and at weekends). Each island deserves a couple of hours at least, and Liberty Island makes a pleasant place to spend an entire afternoon.

The **STATUE OF LIBERTY**, torch in hand and clutching a stone tablet, has for a century acted as a figurehead for the American Dream, with probably the most immediately recognizable profile in existence. Depicting Liberty throwing off her shackles and holding a beacon to light the world, it was the creation of the French sculptor Frédéric Auguste Bartholdi, crafted a hundred years after the American Revolution in recogni-

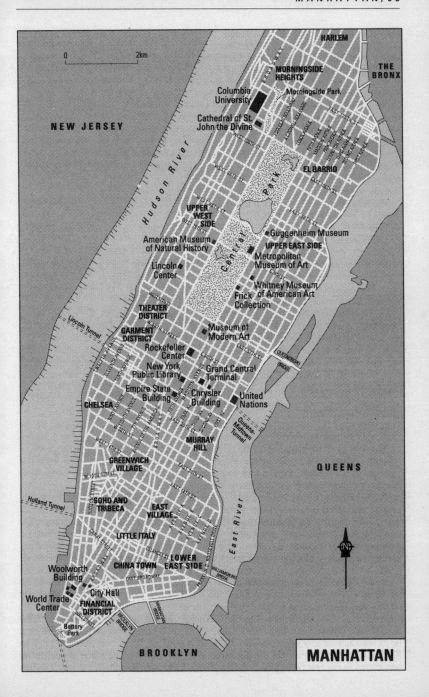

0   2km

HARLEM

MORNINGSIDE HEIGHTS

Columbia University

Morningside Park

NEW JERSEY

Cathedral of St. John the Divine

WEST 110TH ST.

EL BARRIO

WEST 96TH ST.

EAST 96TH ST.

Hudson River

UPPER WEST SIDE

WEST 72ND ST.

Guggenheim Museum

American Museum of Natural History

UPPER EAST SIDE

Central Park

Lincoln Center

Metropolitan Museum of Art

Whitney Museum of American Art

Frick Collection

THEATER DISTRICT

Museum of Modern Art

GARMENT DISTRICT

Rockefeller Center

New York Public Library

Grand Central Terminal

QUEENSBORO BRIDGE

Lincoln Tunnel

Empire State Building

Chrysler Building

United Nations

CHELSEA

Queens-Midtown Tunnel

MURRAY HILL

GREENWICH VILLAGE

WEST 10TH STREET

QUEENS

Holland Tunnel

SOHO AND TRIBECA

EAST VILLAGE

LITTLE ITALY

East River

LOWER EAST SIDE

CHINA TOWN

EAST BROADWAY

WILLIAMSBURG BRIDGE

Woolworth Building

World Trade Center

City Hall

FINANCIAL DISTRICT

MANHATTAN BRIDGE

Battery Park

BROOKLYN BRIDGE

BROOKLYN

MANHATTAN

THE BRONX

tion of fraternity between the French and American people (though he originally intended it for Alexandria in Egypt). Liberty, which consists of thin copper sheets bolted together and supported by an iron framework designed by Gustave Eiffel, was built in Paris between 1874 and 1884. Bartholdi enlarged his original terracotta model through four successive versions – one of which stands beside the Seine in Paris – to its present size. It was formally dedicated by President Cleveland on October 28 1886. You can climb up to the crown, though the cramped stairway to the torch sadly remains closed to the public. Don't be surprised if you have to wait an hour to ascend; while you do so, you can always enjoy Liberty Park's views of the Lower Manhattan skyline.

Just across the water, a few minutes by ferry, sits **ELLIS ISLAND**, the first stop for over twelve million prospective immigrants. Originally known as Gibbet Island by the English (who used it for punishing unfortunate pirates), it became an immigration station in 1894, mainly to handle the massive influx from southern and eastern Europe. It remained open until 1954, when it was left to fall into atmospheric ruin.

The immigrants who arrived at Ellis Island were all steerage class passengers; richer voyagers were processed at their leisure on board ship. Most families arrived hungry and penniless; con men preyed from all sides, stealing their baggage as it was checked and offering rip-off exchange rates for whatever money they had managed to bring. Each family was split up, men sent to one area, women and children to another, while a series of checks weeded out the undesirables and the infirm. Steamship carriers were obliged to return any immigrants not accepted to their original port, but according to official records only two percent were ever rejected, and many of those jumped into the sea and tried to swim to Manhattan rather than face going home.

By the time of its closure, Ellis Island was a formidable complex, the island having been expanded by fresh landfill. In the turretted central building, films and tapes in the ambitious **Museum of Immigration** try hard to recapture the spirit of the place. The huge vaulted Registry Room has been left bare, but for a couple of inspectors' desks, and gives on to a series of suitably institutional interview rooms and white-tiled corridors. Each is illustrated by the recorded voices of those who passed through Ellis Island, along with photographs, small artefacts, and informative explanatory text.

The Financial District

The skyline of Manhattan's **FINANCIAL DISTRICT** is the one you see in all the movies – dramatic skyscrapers crammed into the southern tip of the island and framed by the monumental elegance of the Brooklyn Bridge. At the heart of the nation's wheeler-dealing, this is the place where Manhattan began, though precious few leftovers of those days remain, shunted out by big corporations eager to boost their images with headquarters at the right addresses.

The wooden wall built by the Dutch at the edge of their small settlement, to protect it from pro-British settlers to the north, gives the narrow canyon of **Wall Street** its name. Here, behind the thin neoclassical mask of the **New York Stock Exchange**, the purse strings of the world are pulled – a process you can view from the **visitors' gallery** (Mon–Fri 9.15am–4pm; free) and have explained by way of a glib introductory film and a small exhibition. The **Federal Hall National Memorial**, at Wall Street's head, looks a little foolish surrounded by skyscrapers. The building was once the Customs House, but the exhibition inside (Mon–Fri 9am–5pm; free) relates the headier days of 1789, when George Washington was sworn in as president from a balcony on this site. Washington's statue stands, very properly, on the steps outside the daintily rotunded hall. At Wall Street's other end, **Trinity Church** (guided tours daily at 2pm) is an ironic onlooker to the street's dealings, a knobbly neo-Gothic structure that went up in 1846 and for fifty years was the city's tallest building. It's got much of the air of an English church, especially in the sheltered graveyard, the resting place of such early luminaries as the first Secretary to the Treasury, Alexander Hamilton.

Broadway comes to a gentle end at the **Bowling Green**, an oval of turf used for the game by eighteenth-century colonial Brits on a lease of "one peppercorn per year". Earlier still the green was the site of one of Manhattan's more memorable business deals, when Peter Minuit, first director general of the Dutch colony of New Amsterdam, bought the whole island from the Indians for a handful of baubles worth 60 guilders (about $25). Today the green is a spot for office people picnicking in the shadow of Cass Gilbert's **US Customs House**, an heroic monument to New York the port. Four statues at the front represent the four continents (sculpted by Daniel Chester French, who also created the Lincoln Memorial in Washington DC) and the twelve near the top personify the world's commercial centers, all fixed in homage to the maritime market. From the fall of 1994, the Customs House will contain the superb collection of the Museum of the American Indian (see p.81).

Lower Manhattan lets out its breath in **Battery Park**, where the nineteenth-century **Castle Clinton** (daily 9am–5pm) once protected the southern tip of Manhattan and now sells ferry tickets to the Statue of Liberty and Ellis Island. North up Water Street, at Pearl and Broad, the partially reconstructed **Fraunces Tavern** (Mon–Fri 10am–4pm, Sun noon–5pm; free Mon–Fri 10am–noon, otherwise $2.50), was where on December 4 1783, with the British conclusively beaten, a weeping George Washington took leave of his assembled officers, intent on returning to rural life in Virginia. The second floor re-creates the simple colonial dining room where this took place – all probably as genuine as the relics of Washington's teeth and hair in the adjacent museum.

Further up Water Street, at the eastern end of Fulton Street, the renovated **South Street Seaport** was formerly New York's sailship port, from where Robert Fulton started a ferry service to Brooklyn. Trade eventually moved elsewhere, and the blocks of warehouses and ship's chandlers were left to rot. Regular guided tours of the Seaport run from the visitor center at 207 Water St, but the best place to start looking around is the so-called **Museum Block**, where upmarket shops lurk behind Water Street's hotchpotch of Greek Revival and Italianate facades. You might also look in on the **Fulton Fish Market**, a tatty building that wears its eighty years as the city's wholesale outlet with no pretensions. If you can manage it, the time to be here is around 5am (organized tours run each first & third Thurs; $10, reservations required; ☎669-9416) when buyers' lorries park up beneath the highway to collect the catches – invigorating stuff, and a twilight world that may not be around much longer. The adjacent **Pier 17 Pavilion**, a complex of restaurants and shops, could be one nail in its coffin. Next door, around piers 15 and 16, is the **South Street Museum** (daily 10am–5pm; $6), a collection of nimble sailships and chubby ferries.

From just about anywhere in the seaport you can see the much-loved **Brooklyn Bridge**. Now just one of several spans across the East River, it was in its day a technological quantum leap. It towered over the low brick structures around and for twenty years after it opened in 1883 was the world's largest suspension bridge, the first to use steel cables and for many more the longest single span. It didn't go up without difficulties. John Augustus Roebling, its architect and engineer, crushed his foot taking measurements for the piers and died of gangrene three weeks later; his son Washington took over only to be crippled by the bends from working in an insecure underwater caisson, and subsequently directed the work from his sick bed overlooking the site.

Wherever you are in Lower Manhattan, the twin towers of the **World Trade Center** (which is in fact a five-building complex) dominate the landscape. Spirited down to a tenth of their size they wouldn't get a second glance. But the fact is they're *big*, undeniably and frighteningly so, and a walk across the plaza below in summer makes your head reel (it's closed in winter, as icicles falling from the towers can kill). The towers were in fact quickly surpassed as the world's tallest building by the Sears Tower in Chicago, and were half empty for several years. Despite the damage wrought by the explosive device of February 26 1993, which killed six people and seemed briefly to threaten the destruction of the entire building, the Center is full and successful, and has become one of the emblems of the city itself. With courage, a trip to the 107th floor **observation deck** of Two World Trade Center (daily 9.30am–9.30pm; $4) gives a mind-blowing view from a height of 1350 feet; and from the open-air rooftop promenade the silent panorama is more dramatic still – even Jersey City looks exciting. As you timidly edge your way around, ponder the fact that one Philippe Petit once walked a tightrope between the two towers – nerve indeed.

Across from the World Trade Center on Vesey Street and Broadway, **St Paul's Chapel** comes from a very different order of things. It's the oldest church in Manhattan, dating from 1766 – eighty years earlier than Trinity Church and almost prehistoric by New York standards.

City Hall Park and the Civic Center

Immediately north of St Paul's Chapel, Broadway and Park Row form the apex of **City Hall Park**, a noisy, pigeon-splattered triangle of green with Cass Gilbert's 1913 **Woolworth Building** as a venerable onlooker. For many, this is New York's definitive skyscraper, its soaring lines fringed with Gothic decoration. The famous lobby is a real must. Frank Woolworth made his fortune from "five and dime" stores, and true to his philosophy he paid cash for his skyscraper. The whimsical reliefs at each corner of the lobby show him doing just that, counting out the money in nickels and dimes. Facing him in caricature are the architect (medievally clutching a model of his building), renting agent and builder. Within, vaulted ceilings ooze honey-gold mosaics, and even the mailboxes are magnificent.

At the top of the park, marking the beginning of the **CIVIC CENTER** and its incoherent jumble of municipal offices and courts, stands **City Hall** (Mon–Fri 10am–4pm), completed in 1812. After the city's 1927 feting of returned aviator Charles Lindbergh, it became the traditional finishing point for Broadway tickertape parades, as given for triumphant baseball stars, astronauts, and, more recently, returned Iranian hostages. Inside it's an elegant meeting of arrogance and authority, with the sweeping spiral staircase delivering you to the precise geometry of the **Governor's Room** and the self-important rooms that formerly contained the **Board of Estimates Chamber**.

If City Hall is the acceptable face of municipal bureaucracy, the **Tweed Courthouse** behind is a reminder of a seamier underbelly. William Marcy "Boss" Tweed worked his way from nowhere to become chairman of the Democratic Central Committee at Tammany Hall in 1856, and manipulated the city's revenues through his own and his supporters' pockets. For a while his grip strangled all dissent, until a political cartoonist, Thomas Nast, and the editor of the *New York Times* (who'd refused a half-million-dollar bribe to keep quiet) turned public opinion against him. With suitable irony Tweed died in 1878 in Ludlow Street jail – which he'd had built as Commissioner of Public Works.

Chinatown and Little Italy

A short stroll north from Civic Center, **CHINATOWN** is Manhattan's most thriving ethnic neighborhood, over recent years pushing its boundaries north across Canal Street into Little Italy, and east as far as the fringes of the Lower East Side. It has close on 100,000 residents (about half of New York's Chinese population), seven Chinese newspapers, around 150 restaurants and over 300 garment factories.

The Chinese began to arrive in the mid-nineteenth century. Most had previously worked out west, building railways and digging gold mines, and few intended to stay: their idea was simply to make a nest-egg and retire to a life of leisure with their families (99 percent were men) back in China. Some did go back, but on the whole the big money took rather longer to accumulate than expected, and so Chinatown took shape as a permanent settlement. Budget restaurants boomed, thanks in part to working women who had no time to cook and bought food to take home. **Mott Street** is the main thoroughfare and the streets around – Canal, Pell, Bayard, Doyers and Bowery – host a positive glut of restaurants, tea and rice shops and grocers.

On the other side of Canal Street, **LITTLE ITALY** is light years away from the solid ethnic enclave of old. Originally settled by the huge nineteenth-century influx of Italian immigrants, it is encroached upon a little more each year by Chinatown; few Italians live here and the restaurants (of which there are plenty) tend to have valet-parking and high prices. However, some original delis and bakeries do survive, and you can still indulge yourself with a cappuccino and pastry. September's **Festa di San Gennaro** is a wild splurge to celebrate the saint's day, when Italians from all over the city turn up and **Mulberry Street**, the main strip, is transformed by street stalls and numerous fast-snack outlets. Of the **restaurants**, *Umberto's Clam House* on Mulberry Street remains most famed, not for the food but as the scene of a vicious gangland murder in 1972, when Joe "Crazy Joey" Gallo was shot dead while celebrating his birthday with his wife and daughter. The bullet holes from the slaying are still visible in the windows.

SoHo and TriBeCa

Since the mid-1960s, **SOHO**, the grid of streets that runs *So*uth of *Ho*uston Street, has meant **art**. Squashed between the Financial District and Greenwich Village to the north, it had long been a wasteland of manufacturers and wholesalers, but as the Village declined in hipness, SoHo was suddenly "in". Its loft spaces were ideal for low-rental studios, and galleries quickly attracted the city's art crowd, boutiques and restaurants following close behind. Gentrification soon followed, and what remains is a mix of chi-chi antique, art and clothes shops and high living, although no amount of gloss can cover up SoHo's quintessential appearance of dark alleys and shabby factories, fronted by some of the best cast-iron facades in America.

The technique of **cast-iron architecture** originated as a way of assembling buildings quickly and inexpensively, with iron beams rather than heavy walls carrying the weight of the floors. The result was the removal of load-bearing walls, greater space for windows, and, most noticeably, decorative facades. Almost any style or whim could be cast in iron and pinned to a building, and architects indulged themselves in Baroque balustrades, forests of Renaissance columns and all the effusion of the French Second Empire to glorify SoHo's sweatshops. Have a look at 72–76 Greene St, a neat extravagance whose Corinthian portico stretches the whole five storeys, all in painted metal, and at the strongly composed elaborations of its sister building at nos 28–30. At the northeast corner of Broome St and Broadway the magnificent **Haughwout Building** is perhaps the ultimate in the genre, with rhythmically repeated motifs of colonnaded arches framed behind taller columns in a thin sliver of a Venetian palace.

TRIBECA, the *Tri*angle *Be*low *Ca*nal Street, retains a lived-in, worked-in feel. Less a triangle than a crumpled rectangle – the area bounded by Canal and Chambers streets, Broadway and the Hudson – its spacious industrial buildings house the apartments of TriBeCa's new gentry.

Greenwich Village

If you're a New Yorker, it's fashionable to dismiss **GREENWICH VILLAGE** (or simply "the Village"). And it's true that while the bohemian image endures well enough if you don't actually live in New York, it's a tag that has long since lost genuine currency. However, the Village is still exciting, and to a great extent still sports the attractions that brought people here in the first place. Though quiet and residential, it has a busy street life that lasts later than any other part of the city; there are more restaurants per head than anywhere else, and bars, while never inexpensive, clutter every corner. Indeed there are few better initiations into the city's life, especially at night.

Greenwich Village grew up as a rural retreat from the early and frenetic nucleus of New York City, given impetus during the yellow fever epidemic of 1822, when it served as a refuge from the infected streets downtown. Refined Federal and Greek Revival terraces lured some of the city's highest society names, and later proved a fertile hunting ground for struggling artists and intellectuals. By the turn of the century Greenwich Village was on its way to becoming New York's Left Bank.

The natural center of the Village, **Washington Square** is not exactly elegant, but it does retain its northern edging of red-brick rowhouses – the "solid, honorable dwellings" of Henry James' eponymous novel – and Stanford White's imposing **Triumphal Arch**, built in 1892 to commemorate the centenary of George Washington's inauguration. It's also the heart of the truly urban campus of New York University. As soon as the weather gets warm, the park becomes sports field, dance floor, drug den and social club, boiling over with life as frisbees fly, skateboards flip and boom boxes crash through the urgent cries of dope peddlers and the studied patrols of police cars.

Follow **Macdougal Street** south and you hit **Bleecker Street** – Greenwich Village's Main Street, packed with shops, bars, people and restaurants. This junction is also the area's best-known meeting place, a vibrant corner whose mock-European sidewalk cafés have been literary hang-outs since the start of this century. Turning right takes you through the hubbub of Village life, stretching up **Sixth Avenue** to the unmistakable nineteenth-century bulk of the **Jefferson Market Courthouse**, voted fifth most beautiful building in America in 1885 and now serving as the local public library. Cut through from here to **Seventh Avenue**, off which **Bedford Street** represents one of the Village's quietest and most desirable corners. Nearby, **Christopher Street** joins Seventh at **Sheridan Square**, site of the **Stonewall** gay bar where a 1969 police raid precipitated a siege which lasted the best part of an hour. If not a victory for their rights, it was the first time that gay men had stood up to the police *en masse*, and as such represents a turning point in their struggle, formally instigating the Gay Rights movement and remembered by the annual **Gay Pride march** held on the last Sunday in June.

The East Village

The **EAST VILLAGE** is quite different in look and feel to its western counterpart, Greenwich Village. Once, like the Lower East Side proper which it abuts, a refuge of immigrants, and always solidly working-class, it became home to New York's nonconformist fringe in the earlier part of this century. Much later the East Village became the New York haunt of the Beats – Kerouac, Burroughs, Ginsberg *et al* – who would get together at Alan Ginsberg's house on East Seventh Street for declamatory readings. Later, Andy Warhol debuted the Velvet Underground; the Fillmore East played host to every band under the sun; and Richard Hell proclaimed himself the inventor of punk rock. Perhaps inevitably, a lot has changed over the last decade, thanks in part to escalating rents. The East Village isn't the hotbed of creativity it once was, but St Mark's Place is still one of Lower Manhattan's more vibrant strips, even if the thrift shops and panhandlers and political hustlers have given way to a range of ritzy boutiques.

Though it's hard to believe now, **Astor Place**, at the western end of St Mark's Place, was in the 1830s one of the city's most desirable neighborhoods. Undistinguished-looking Lafayette Street was home to such wealthy names as John Jacob Astor himself, one of New York's most hideously greedy tycoons. The Astor Place **subway station**, in the middle of the junction, discreetly remembers the man on the platforms, its colored reliefs of beavers recalling Astor's first big killings – in the fur trade.

The Lower East Side

South of Tompkins Square, the **LOWER EAST SIDE** began life towards the end of the last century as an insular slum for over half a million Jewish immigrants. Since then it has become considerably depopulated, and the slum-dwellers are now largely Puerto Rican rather than Jewish; but otherwise little has visibly changed. The area retains a Jewish feel, and if outsiders come here at all it's either to **eat** or for the bargain **shop-**

ping. You can get just about anything cut-price in the stores, especially on Sunday mornings when Orchard Street is filled with stalls and stores selling off hats, clothes and designer labels for hefty discounts. When you've finished shopping, the **Lower East Side Tenement Museum**, 97 Orchard St (Tues–Fri 11am–4pm, Sun 10am–5pm; suggested donation $3), housed in a former tenement building, provides the lowdown on the neighborhood's immigrant past and present.

To the west, the **Bowery** spears up as far as Cooper Square on the edge of the East Village. This wide thoroughfare has gone through many changes over the years: it took its name from "Bouwerie", the Dutch word for farm, when it was the city's main agricultural supplier; later, in the closing decades of the last century, it was flanked by music halls, theaters, hotels and middle-market restaurants, drawing people from all parts of Manhattan. Currently it's a skid row for the homeless, flanked by a demoralizing line of boarded-up shops and long-stay hotels near which few New Yorkers venture of their own accord, although it's rarely all that dangerous. The one – bizarre – focus is the **Bowery Savings Bank** on the corner of Grand Street. Designed by Stanford White in 1894, it rises out of the neighborhood's debris like a god, much as does its sister bank on 42nd Street, a shrine to the virtue of thrift.

Midtown Manhattan

MIDTOWN MANHATTAN is in many ways the center of the city. Most of the hotels are here, and it's where you're most likely to arrive – at Penn or Grand Central Station, or the Port Authority. New York's most glamorous (and most expensive) street, **Fifth Avenue**, cuts through its heart, with the theater strip of **Broadway**, an increasingly disreputable neighbor, just to the west for much of the way. The character of midtown undergoes a radical transformation depending on which side of Fifth you find yourself. Fifth and **east** holds the corporate businesses and big prestige skyscrapers – the Chrysler, the Empire State, the Seagram. **West** of Fifth Avenue, and in particular west of Broadway, the area takes a dive. The **Theater District** is these days more than a little sleazy, although **Times Square**, the traditional center of sex shows and petty crime, has recently undergone a multimillion-dollar clean-up. **The Garment District** has a certain throwback interest as a nineteenth-century foil to the corporate skyscrapers across the way, but the residential districts are frankly dull: **Chelsea** is long established but downbeat; **Clinton**, further up the west side, is gentrifying slowly but is still rough down by the West Side Highway.

Fifth Avenue and East: Union Square to 42nd Street

Downtown Manhattan ends with 14th Street, which slices across from the housing projects of the east side to the cut-price shops and eventually the meat-packing warehouses on the banks of the Hudson. In the middle, **Union Square** was until the mid-1980s a seedy haunt of dope pushing and street violence, but it's much more inviting now, the spill of shallow steps enticing you in to stroll the paths, feed the squirrels, and gaze at its array of statuary. The stretch of **Broadway** north of here used to be known as "Ladies' Mile" for its fancy stores and boutiques, but despite a few sculpted facades and curvy lintels, it's now hard to imagine as an upmarket shopping mall. Turn right on East 20th Street for **Theodore Roosevelt's Birthplace** at no 28 (Wed–Sun 9am–5pm; $1) – or at least a reconstruction of it: a grim brownstone mansion that boasts a few rooms with their original furnishings, some of Teddy's hunting trophies and a small gallery documenting the president's life. Past here Manhattan's clutter breaks into the ordered open space of **Gramercy Park**, a former swamp reclaimed in 1831 that is one of the city's best squares, its center tidily planted and, most noticeably, completely empty for much of the day – principally because the only people who can gain access are those rich enough to live here.

Broadway and Fifth Avenue meet at **Madison Square**, by day a maelstrom of dodging cars and cabs, but with a monumentality and neat seclusion that Union Square has long since lost. Most notable among the grand structures that surround it is the **Flatiron Building**, set cheekily on a triangular plot of land on the square's southern side, the city's first true skyscraper, hung on a steel frame in 1902 with its full twenty storeys dwarfing all the other structures around. Its tapered structure creates unusual wind currents at ground level, and years ago police officers were posted to prevent men gathering to watch the wind raise the skirts of women passing on 23rd Street. The cry they gave to warn off voyeurs – "23 Skidoo!" – has passed into the language.

Further up Fifth Avenue is New York's prime **shopping territory**, home to the heavyweight department stores. Overshadowing them all is the **Empire State Building**, on what has always been a prime site. A potent symbol of New York since its completion in 1931, after just two years in the making, its 102 storeys and 1472 feet – toe to TV mast – make it the world's third tallest building; but the height is deceptive, rising in stately tiers with steady panache. Inside, its basement is an underground marbled shopping precinct, finished everywhere with delicate Deco touches. The first elevator towards the top takes you to the 86th floor, summit of the building before the radio and TV mast was added. The views from the outside walkways here are as stunning as you'd expect – better than the World Trade Center because Manhattan spreads on all sides. If you're feeling brave, and can stand the queues for the small single elevator, go up to the Empire State's last reachable zenith, a small cylinder at the foot of the TV mast (part of a hare-brained scheme to erect a mooring post for airships – a plan subsequently abandoned after some local VIPs almost got swept away by the wind). You can't go outside and the extra sixteen storeys don't really add a great deal to the view, but you will at least have been to the top (daily 9.30am–midnight; $3.50).

East of the Empire State lies **MURRAY HILL**, a residential district formerly dominated by the crusty old financier J P Morgan and his offspring. The **Pierpont Morgan Library**, 29 E 36th St (Tues–Sat 10.30am–5pm, Sun 1–5pm, closed Sun in July & Aug; suggested donation $5), is a gracious Italian-style nest built in 1917 and feathered with the fruits of the Morgans' magpie-ish trips to Europe. Its two main rooms are reached along a corridor lined with Rembrandt prints. The first, the **West Room**, remains much as it looked when Morgan's study, with a carved sixteenth-century Italian ceiling, paintings by Memling and Perugino, and a custom-carved desk. Through a domed and pillared hallway lies the **East Room** or library, a sumptuous three-tiered cocoon of rare books, autographed musical manuscripts and trinkets culled from European households and churches. A changing exhibit holds original manuscripts by Mahler (the museum has the world's largest collection of his work); a Gutenburg Bible from 1455 (one of eleven surviving); and literary relics ranging from the letters of Vasari and George Washington to works by Keats and Dickens.

North up Fifth Avenue, on the corner of **42nd Street**, stands the Beaux Arts **New York Public Library** (free guided tours Mon–Sat at 11am & 2pm). Trotsky worked in the large coffered Reading Room at the back of the building on and off during his brief sojourn in New York, just prior to the 1917 Revolution, having been introduced to the place by his friend Bukharin, who was bowled over by a library you could use so late in the evening. The opening times are less impressive now, but the library still boasts one of the five largest collections of books in the world. East down 42nd Street looms the huge bulk of **Grand Central Station**, constructed around a basic iron frame but clothed with a Beaux Arts skin. The most spectacular aspect of the building is its size, now cowed by the soaring airplane wing of the Met Life building behind but still no less impressive in the main station **concourse** – one of the world's most imposing open spaces, 470ft long and 150ft high, the barrel-vaulted ceiling speckled like a Baroque church with a painted representation of the winter night sky, its 2500 stars shown back to front: "As God would have seen them", the painter is reputed to have remarked. It's a pity about the broad billboards which obscure the enormous windows, but stand in the middle and you realize that Grand Central represents a time when stations were seen as appropriate dwarfing preludes to great cities.

For the best view of the concourse, climb up to the catwalks which span the sixty-feet-high windows on the Vanderbilt Avenue side; then explore the terminal's more esoteric reaches. The **Oyster Bar** in its vaulted bowels – one of the city's most highly regarded seafood restaurants – is crammed every lunchtime. You can stand on opposite sides of any of the vaulted spaces here and hold a conversation just by whispering, an acoustic fluke that makes this the loudest place in town.

Across the street, the **Bowery Savings Bank** echoes Grand Central's grandeur, extravagantly lauding the shibboleths of sound investment and savings. A Roman-style basilica, the floor is paved with mosaics, each column is fashioned from a different kind of marble, and bronze bas-reliefs on the elevator doors show bank employees hard at work. The more famous **Chrysler Building**, across Lexington Avenue, has equal style. This was for a short while the world's tallest building, and since the rediscovery of Art Deco has become Manhattan's best loved, its car-motif friezes, jutting gargoyles and arched stainless-steel pinnacle giving the solemn midtown skyline a welcome touch of fun. Chrysler moved out some time ago, and for a while the building was left to degenerate by a company that didn't wholly appreciate its spirited silliness, but a new owner has pledged to keep it lovingly intact. The lobby, once a car showroom, is for the moment all you can see, its opulently inlaid elevators, walls covered in African marble and murals showing airplanes, machines and brawny builders who worked on the tower.

At the eastern end of 42nd Street, you can descend to the **United Nations** complex. Guided tours leave from the monumental General Assembly lobby (every 30min, 9.15am–4.45pm; $6.50), taking in the conference chambers of the UN and its constituent parts. Foremost among these is the General Assembly Chamber itself, expanded a few years back to accommodate up to 179 delegations, but not yet completely filled.

THE SKYSCRAPERS OF NEW YORK

Along with Chicago and Hong Kong, Manhattan holds one of the world's greatest concentrations of **skyscrapers**. In fact there are only two main clusters, but they set the tone for the city – the **Financial District**, where the narrow streets and tall buildings form lightless canyons, and **midtown Manhattan**, where the big skyscrapers, flanking the wide central avenues between the Thirties and the Sixties, compete for height and prestige.

New York's first generally recognized skyscraper was the **Flatiron Building** on Madison Square, designed in 1902, which made the most of the new iron-frame technique of construction. A few years later, in 1913, the city clinched the title of the world's tallest building with the sixty-storey **Woolworth Building** on Broadway, later going on to produce such landmarks as the **Chrysler** and **Empire State** buildings and, more recently, the **World Trade Center** – though the latter has since been dwarfed by Chicago's Sears Tower. Styles over the years have been influenced by stringent zoning laws. At first skyscrapers were sheer vertical monsters, maximizing the floor space with no regard to the effect on neighboring buildings – more often than not, thrown into shade. The authorities came up with the concept of "air rights", putting a restriction on how high a building could be before it had to be set back from its base. This forced skyscrapers to be designed in a series of steps – seen at its most elegant in the Empire State Building, which has no less than ten steps. The pattern is repeated all over the city.

Due to the pressure on space in Manhattan's narrow confines, and the price of real estate, which makes the speculatory building of office blocks so potentially lucrative, the skyscrapers continue to rise, and some steel frame is always slowly rising somewhere in the city. There seems to be almost no limit to the heights envisaged in the future, and even in times of recession skyscrapers remain the "machines for making money" that Le Corbusier originally proclaimed them to be.

The West Side: Chelsea, the Garment District and Times Square

Few visitors bother with Chelsea and the Garment District, the two areas that fill the West Side between 14th and 42nd streets. **CHELSEA** took shape in 1830 when its owner, Charles Clarke Moore, laid out his land for sale in broad lots. Enough remains to indicate Chelsea's middle-class suburban origins, though in fact the area never quite achieved the desirability it sought. Instead, Manhattan's chic residential focus leap-frogged dreary Chelsea, stuck between the ritziness of Fifth Avenue and the poverty of Hell's Kitchen, straight to the East 40s and 50s.

During the nineteenth century the area was a center of New York's theater district. Nothing remains of that now, but the hotel which put up all the actors, writers and bohemian hangers-on – the **Chelsea Hotel** – remains a New York landmark, with a down-at-heel Edwardian grandeur all of its own. Mark Twain and Tennessee Williams lived here, Brendan Behan and Dylan Thomas staggered in and out during their New York visits, and in 1951 Jack Kerouac, armed with a customized typewriter (and a lot of Benzedrine) typed the first draft of *On the Road* non-stop onto a 120ft roll of paper. In the 1960s Andy Warhol and his doomed protégé Edie Sedgwick holed up here and made the film *Chelsea Girls* in (sort of) homage; and most recently Sid Vicious stabbed Nancy Spungen to death in their suite, a few months before his own pathetic life ended with an overdose of heroin. It also inspired Joni Mitchell to write *Chelsea Morning* – which in turned inspired Bill and Hillary Clinton in naming their daughter. A few streets north, Sixth Avenue collides with Broadway at **Greeley Square**, an overblown name for a trashy triangle celebrating Horace Greeley, founder of the *Tribune* newspaper, and known for his rallying call to "Go West, young man!". His paper no longer exists and his square looks ready to disintegrate at any moment. Across the way is **Macy's**, the self-proclaimed largest department store in the world, with some two million square feet of floor space and around $5 million turnover a day.

In a way this part of Broadway is the storefront to the **GARMENT DISTRICT**, a loosely defined patch between 34th and 42nd streets and Sixth and Eighth avenues that produces around three-quarters of all the women's and children's clothes in America – you'd never believe it, as the outlets are strictly wholesale with no need to woo customers. The dominant landmark is the **Pennsylvania Station** and **Madison Square Garden** complex, a combined box and drum structure that swallows up millions of commuters in its train station below and accommodates the *Knicks* basketball and *Rangers* hockey teams up top. The original Penn Station, demolished to make way for this, is now hailed as a lost masterpiece, which reworked the ideas of the Roman Baths of Caracalla to awesome effect: "Through it one entered the city like a god . . . . One scuttles in now like a rat", mourned one observer. Immediately behind Penn Station, the same architects – McKim, Mead and White – were responsible for the **General Post Office**. The old joke is that it had to be this big to fit in the sonorous inscription above the columns – "Neither snow nor rain nor heat nor gloom of night stays these couriers from the swift completion of their appointed rounds." The Post Office moved out of the building in 1993; suggestions that it may be utilized as a new entrance to Penn Station remain speculative, though the plans, involving the construction of a massive steel arch in its center, are certainly spectacular.

Further up, the **Port Authority Terminal Building** at 40th St and Eighth Ave serves as an appropriately unpleasant signal for the squalid stretch of **42nd Street** beyond, a strip of prostitution and petty vice best missed altogether – as is most of Eighth Avenue north of 42nd. **Times Square**, beyond, was in its excess and brashness for years a distillation of the city itself, an increasingly sleazy, sometimes dangerous area that has recently undergone a massive clean-up. Almost all of the peep shows and sex shops have gone, replaced by new office blocks and safely sanitized cinemas and electrical stores. Much of the danger and a lot of the feel have gone too, but you should still be careful in the streets off the square, at least at night.

Further north, the **Equitable Center**, 757 Seventh Ave, houses Roy Lichtenstein's 68ft *Mural with Blue Brush Stroke*, which pokes you in the eye as you enter, and Thomas Hart Benton's *America Today* murals, a magnificent portrayal of ordinary American life in the days before the Depression. Otherwise **Carnegie Hall**, an overblown and fussy warehouse-like venue for opera and concert at 154 West 57th St, is the thing to see. Tchaikovsky conducted the programme on opening night and Mahler, Rachmaninov, Toscanini, Frank Sinatra and Judy Garland played here; it's dropped in status since Lincoln Center opened, but the superb acoustics still ensure full houses most of the year (tours Mon, Tues & Thurs at 11.30am, 2pm and 3pm; $6).

A block east, **Sixth Avenue** is properly named "Avenue of the Americas", though no New Yorker ever calls it this and the only manifestation are the flags of Central and South American countries. If nothing else Sixth's distinction is its width, a result of the Elevated Railway that once ran along here, now replaced by the Sixth Avenue subway. In its day the Sixth Avenue "El" marked the borderline between respectability to the east and vice to the west, and it still separates the glamorous strips of Fifth, Madison and Park avenues from the less salubrious western districts. One odd quirky corner is **Diamond Row** on West 47th Street, between Fifth and Sixth avenues, a short strip of shops chockful of expensive stones and jewellery, managed by ultra-Orthodox Hasidic Jews. Further up, Sixth Avenue is solidly corporate, especially between 47th and 50th streets, where the towers of **Rockefeller Center Extension** don't have the romance of their predecessor (see below) but do possess some of its monumentality – although across the avenue at 49th Street, the **Radio City Music Hall** is the last word in 1930s luxury. The staircase is regally resplendent with the world's largest chandeliers, the murals from the men's toilets are now in the Museum of Modern Art and the huge auditorium looks like an extravagant scalloped shell or a vast sunset. To explore, take a tour from the lobby (Mon–Sat 10.15am–4.45pm, Sun 11.15am–4.45pm; $8).

Fifth Avenue and East: 42nd Street to Central Park

Fifth Avenue, bowling ahead from 42nd Street, has been a great strip for as long as New York has been a great city. Its very name evokes wealth and opulence; all that considers itself suave and cosmopolitan ends up here, and the stores showcase New York's most conspicuous consumerism. That the shopping is beyond the means of most people needn't put you off, for Fifth Avenue has some of the city's best architecture; the boutiques and stores are just the icing on the cake.

At the heart of Fifth Avenue's glamour, **Rockefeller Center**, built between 1932 and 1940 by John D Rockefeller, son of the oil magnate, is one of the finest pieces of urban planning anywhere: office space with cafés, a theater, underground concourses and rooftop gardens work together with a rare intelligence and grace. It's a combination that shows every other city-center shopping mall the way; Cyril Connolly's snide description of it as "that sinister Stonehenge of Economic Man" was way off the mark. The **GE Building** here rises 850 feet, its monumental lines matching the scale of Manhattan itself, though softened by symmetrical setbacks. Down below, the **Lower Plaza** holds a sunken restaurant in summer, linked visually to the downward flow of the building by Paul Manship's sparkling *Prometheus*; in winter it becomes an ice rink, allowing skaters to show off their skills to passing shoppers. Inside is no less impressive, with José Maria Sert's murals, *American Progress* and *Time*, a little faded but eagerly in tune with the Thirties Deco ambience – presumably more so than the original paintings by Diego Rivera, which were removed by John D's son Nelson when the artist refused to scrap a panel glorifying Lenin. A leaflet available from the lobby desk details a **self-guided tour** of the center; you can't get right to the top, but a cocktail in the *Rainbow Room* restaurant on the 65th floor gives Manhattan's best skyscraper view, especially at night. Among the GE Building's many offices are the **NBC Studios** (one-hour tours leave regularly, daily 9.30am–4.30pm, reservations in the foyer; $8). If you're a TV freak, pick up a (free) ticket for a **show recording** from the mezzanine lobby or out on the street. The most popular tickets evaporate before 9am.

Almost opposite Rockefeller Center, **St Patrick's Cathedral**, designed by James Renwick and completed in 1888, seems the result of a painstaking academic tour of the Gothic cathedrals of Europe – perfect in detail, but lifeless in spirit, with a sterility made all the more striking by the glass-black **Olympic Tower** next door, an exclusive apartment block where residents include Jackie Onassis. Across Fifth Avenue, the **Museum of Television and Radio**, exactly one block south of MoMa at 25 W 52nd St (Tues–Sat noon–5pm; suggested donation $4), is an archive of American TV and radio broadcasts, whose excellent card reference system allows you to trace 1950s comedies, old newsreels and other oddities.

Continuing north, the **Trump Tower** at 57th Street is the last word in Fifth Avenue opulence, with an outrageously over-the-top atrium, filled with designer stores, that is just short of repellent. Perfumed air, polished marble panelling and a five-storey waterfall are calculated to knock you senseless with expensive good taste. But the building is clever, a neat little outdoor garden is squeezed high in a corner, and each of the 230 apartments above the atrium gets views in three directions.

The next big avenue east, **Park Avenue**, was said in 1929 to be the place "where wealth is so swollen that it almost bursts". Things haven't changed much: corporate headquarters jostle in triumphal procession, pushed apart by Park's broad avenue. It's one of the city's most awesome sights, culminating in the high altar of the delicate, energetic **New York Central Building** (now the Helmsley Building), with its lewdly excessive Rococo lobby. In its day it formed a skilled punctuation mark to the avenue, but its thunder was stolen in 1963 by the **Met Life Building** that looms behind. Former headquarters of the (now defunct) airline Pan Am, the building has a profile meant to suggest an aircraft wing, and the blue-grey mass certainly adds drama to the cityscape, but it robs Park Avenue of the views south it deserves. Another black mark was the rooftop helipad, closed in the 1970s after a helicopter undercarriage collapsed shortly after landing, killing four people who had just got off and injuring several people on the ground.

Wherever you placed it, the solid mass of the **Waldorf Astoria Hotel** (between 49th and 50th) would hold its own, a resplendent statement of Art Deco elegance. Crouching behind, the contrasting **St Bartholomew's Church** is a low-slung Byzantine hybrid that adds immeasurably to the street, giving the lumbering skyscrapers a much-needed sense of scale. The spikey-topped **General Electric Building** behind seems like a wild extension of the church, its slender shaft rising to a meshed crown of abstract sparks and lightning strokes that symbolizes the radio waves used by its original occupier, RCA. The lobby (entrance at 570 Lexington) is yet another Deco delight. Among all this it's difficult at first to see the originality of the **Seagram Building** between 52nd and 53rd. Designed by Mies Van der Rohe with Philip Johnson and built in 1958, this was the seminal curtain-wall skyscraper, the floors supported internally, allowing a skin of smoky glass and whisky-bronze metal (*Seagram* are distillers), now weathered to a dull black. Every interior detail down to the fixtures and lettering on the mailboxes was specially designed. It was the supreme example of Modernist reason, and its opening caused a wave of approval. The plaza, an open forecourt designed to set the building apart from its neighbors, was such a success as a public space that the city revised the zoning laws to encourage other high-rise builders to supply plazas – the result being the windswept anti-people places now found all over Manhattan.

A block east, the chisel-topped **Citicorp Center** on **Lexington Avenue** (between 53rd and 54th) was finished in 1979 and is now one of Manhattan's most conspicuous landmarks. The slanted roof was designed to house solar panels and provide power, but the idea was ahead of the technology and Citicorp had to content itself with adopting the distinctive top as a corporate logo.

The Museum of Modern Art

11 W 53rd St. Subway #E or #F to Fifth Ave–53rd St. Fri–Tues 11am–6pm, Thurs 11am–9pm. $7.50, students $4.50,Thurs 5–9pm pay what you wish.

Instigated in 1929, moved to its present permanent home ten years later, and in the mid-1980s extensively updated in a steel pipe and glass renovation that doubled its gallery space, **The Museum of Modern Art** (MoMA) offers probably the finest and most complete account of late nineteenth- and twentieth-century art you're likely to find. It covers every medium – illustration and design, architecture and photography – but focuses primarily on painting and sculpture, divided between pre-war work on the first floor, and post-war stuff on the second.

The first-floor galleries kick off with the Impressionists. Cézanne's 1885 *Bather* leads on to Gauguin, Seurat, and Van Gogh – represented by *Starry Night*. In the third room are paintings by the Belgian James Ensor, Redon and Bonnard. Then come galleries of works by the major Cubist painters, including Picasso's *Demoiselles d'Avignon of 1907*, a revolutionary clash of tones and planes said to be the heralder (and initial arbiter) of Cubist principles. A room off to the left holds Monet's *Water Lilies*, stirring attempts to abstract color and form. Later rooms encapsulate entire periods and movements: after Chagall, Kirchner's *Dresden* and *Berlin* street scenes dominate a gallery devoted to the glaring realities of the German Expressionists; the whirring abstractions of Boccioni are the mainstay of another, devoted to the Futurists' paeans to the industrial age; and a further room takes in the work of De Stijl, following Mondrian's development from early limp Cubist pieces to works like *Broadway Boogie Woogie*. Beyond here Matisse has a large room to himself, centering on the *Dancers* of 1909, and then come paintings by Klee, swirling canvases by Kandinsky, and late works by Braque and Picasso. In contrast, further on are the brooding skies of de Chirico, a room containing works by Miro, and a handful of dreamlike paintings by Dali, Magritte and Delvaux.

The second painting and sculpture gallery continues chronologically, perhaps inevitably with a more American slant, taking in the gloomy canvases of Edward Hopper and work by the artists of the New York School – Pollock and de Kooning – along with the more ordered efforts of Rothko and Barnett Newman and the later works of Matisse – mainly paper cutouts such as the bold blue shapes of his *Swimming Pool*, which the ageing artist made to decorate the walls of his apartment in Nice. Pop Art pieces include Jasper Johns' *Flag* and works by Robert Rauschenberg and Claes Oldenburg.

Upper Manhattan

UPPER MANHATTAN begins above 57th Street, where the prosperity of midtown gives way abruptly to the smug domesticity of the Upper East and West sides. People come to **Central Park** in between, the city's back garden, to play, jog, and, in summer, to escape midtown's crowds in a particularly intelligent piece of urban landscaping.

The **Upper East Side** is at its most opulent in the mansions of **Fifth** and **Madison avenues**, today taken over by the Metropolitan and other great museums of "Museum Mile". **The Upper West Side** is less refined, though its Lincoln Center hosts New York's most prestigious arts performances. It is again predominantly residential, well heeled on its southern fringe, especially along Columbus Avenue, but less so as you move north to its top end, marked at the edge by the monolithic Cathedral of St John the Divine and Columbia University – the last gasp of Manhattan's wealth which is creeping ever further into the streets of **Harlem**. Further north is the city's least expected museum, the medieval arts collection of **The Cloisters**.

Central Park

"All radiant in the magic atmosphere of art and taste." So enthused *Harper's* magazine on the opening of **Central Park** in 1876, and though it's hard to be quite so jubilant about the place today, few New Yorkers could imagine life without it. Whether you're into jogging, baseball, boating, botany or just plain walking, or even if you rarely go near the place, there's no question that Central Park is what makes New York a just-about-bearable place to live.

The poet and newspaper editor William Cullen Bryant had the idea for an open public space back in 1844, and spent seven years trying to persuade City Hall to carry it out. Eventually 840 desolate and swampy acres north of the city limits, then occupied by a shantytown of squatters, were set aside. The two architects commissioned to design the landscape, Frederick Olmsted and Calvert Vaux, planned to create a rural paradise, a complete illusion of the countryside bang in the heart of Manhattan – even then growing at a fantastic rate. Today, in spite of the advent of motorized traffic, the sense of disorderly nature they intended largely survives, although the skyline has changed greatly and much of the open space has been turned into asphalted play-ground. Lately, too, the success of Central Park has been its downfall, for as the crowds have become thicker, so the park has become more difficult to keep up to scratch; its lawns have become muddied, the gardens weary-looking and patchy, and the quieter reaches, which the architects imagined a haven of peace and solitude, sites of muggings and attacks. To their credit, the authorities have since 1980 mounted a determined assault on all these evils, renovating large portions, upping the park's policing, and greening it at the expense of softball pitches and basketball nets.

Much the best way to explore is to rent a **bicycle** (roughly $6 an hour) from either the *Loeb Boathouse* or *Metro Bicycles* (Lexington at 88th St). **On foot**, there's little chance of getting lost, but to know exactly where you are, find the nearest lamppost: the first two figures signify the number of the nearest street. After dark it's verging on suicidal to enter on foot. If you want to see the buildings of Central Park West lit up, à la Woody Allen's *Manhattan*, one option is to fork out for a **carriage ride**, as hawked along Central Park South, between Fifth and Sixth avenues. However, these are widely opposed as being cruel to the animals, and generally incompetent, and also cost around $25 per half-hour.

Most things of interest lie in the southern reaches of the park. Near Grand Army Plaza is Central Park **Zoo**, which tries to keep caging to a minimum and the animals as close to the viewer as possible (April–Oct Mon–Fri 10am–5pm, Sat & Sun 10am–5.30pm; Nov–March Mon–Sun 10am–4.30pm; $1). Beyond here, the **Dairy**, once a ranch building intended to provide milk for nursing mothers, is now the park's **visitor center** (Tues–Sun 11am–4pm), giving out free leaflets and maps, selling books and putting on exhibitions. Nearby, the **Wollman Rink** is a lovely place to skate (Mon 9am–5pm, Tues–Thurs 10am–9.30pm, Fri–Sun 10am–11pm; $5 plus $2.50 for skates) in winter. The most obvious route onwards is north up the formal **Mall** to the **Bandshell**, and the terrace and sculpted birds and animals of the **Bethesda Fountain**. To your left, **Cherry Hill Fountain** once provided a turnaround point for carriages, and has excellent views of the **Lake**, sprawling across the heart of Central Park. Rent a **boat** from the **Loeb Boathouse** on the eastern bank (April–Oct daily 9am–6pm; $20 deposit, $10 per hour), or cross the water by the elegant cast-iron **Bow Bridge** and delve into the wild woods of **The Ramble**, on the far side of which stands the mock citadel of **Belvedere Castle**, which sometimes hosts small exhibitions.

The Metropolitan Museum of Art

Fifth Ave at 82nd St. Tues–Thurs & Sun 9.30am–5.15pm, Fri & Sat 9.30am–8.45pm. Suggested donation $6, $3 for students, includes admission to the Cloisters on same day.

Jutting into the park from the east is one of the great art museums of the world, the **Metropolitan Museum of Art** (usually, simply the "Met"). Its all-embracing collection amounts to over three-and-a-half-million works of art, spanning not just America and Europe but also China, Africa, the Far East, and the Classical and Islamic worlds. You could spend weeks in here and still not see everything, and the choice of works which follows is inevitably selective in the extreme.

If you're obliged to make just one visit, head first for the **European Painting** galleries. Of the **early Flemish and Netherlandish paintings**, the best are by Jan van Eyck, who is generally attributed with having started the tradition of North European realism, and Rogier van der Weyden, whose *Christ Appearing to His Mother* is one of his most beautiful works. Later canvases include Brueghel's *Harvesters*, part of the series of twelve paintings that included his familiar Christmas-card *Hunters in the Snow*. Cutting left at this point brings you to the Spanish paintings and the very different landscape of El Greco's extraordinary *View of Toledo*, and Velazquez's *Portrait of Juan de Parej* – "All the rest are art, this alone is truth", remarked a critic of this somber portrait when it was first exhibited. The **Italian Renaissance** is less spectacularly represented but a worthy selection includes an early *Madonna and Child Enthroned with Saints* by Raphael, a late Botticelli and Fra Filippo Lippi's *Madonna and Child Enthroned with Two Angels*. The culmination of the European Galleries is the **Dutch paintings** section, dominated by the major works of Rembrandt, Vermeer and Hals. Vermeer, genius of the domestic interior, is represented by five works, most haunting of which is the *Portrait of a Young Woman*, and there are some fine portraits by Rembrandt – a beautiful painting of his common-law wife, *Hendrike Stoffjels*, painted three years before her early death, and a superb *Self-Portrait* from 1660, the year he was declared bankrupt.

The **nineteenth-century galleries** house a startling array of **Impressionist and Post-Impressionist** art, beginning with Edouard Manet, the movement's most influential precursor, and his striking *Woman with a Parrot*. The prolific Monet is represented by his *Rouen Cathedral*, the *Houses of Parliament from the Thames* and *Poplars* – in which you can detect the beginnings of his final phase of near-Abstract Impressionism. Courbet's *Young Ladies from the Village* constitutes a virtual manifesto of his idea of realism; nearby is his own superbly erotic *Woman with a Parrot*, along with a vaguely macabre casting of Degas' *Little Dancer*, complete with real tutu, bodice and shoes.

Tacked on to the rear of the Met in 1975 to house the collection of banker Robert Lehman, the **Lehman Pavilion** fills the gaps in the Met's **Italian Renaissance** paintings, most notably with a small Botticelli *Annunciation* and a sculptural *Madonna and Child* by Giovanni Bellini. There are also works from the **Northern Renaissance**, notably Hans Holbein the Younger's *Portrait of Erasmus of Rotterdam* and Rembrandt's *Portrait of Gerard de Lairesse*. By all accounts de Lairesse was disliked for his luxurious tastes and unpleasant character, but mainly for his face, which had been ravaged by congenital syphilis. Boldly colored canvases such as *Reclining Nude* by Suzanne Valadon – largely neglected today, or remembered simply as a model for Toulouse-Lautrec, Renoir and Degas – show her originality and influence on her son, Utrillo, whom she taught to paint as an attempt to wean him off drink and drugs. Utrillo's *Rue Ravignon* stands besides his mother's painting.

Housed over two floors in the **Lila Acheson Wallace Wing**, the Met's compact **twentieth-century collection** features paintings such as Picasso's *Portrait of Gertrude Stein* alongside works by Klee, Matisse, Braque and Klimt, and post-war pieces such as Pollock's masterly *Autumn Rhythm (Number 30)*, Thomas Hart Benton's rural idyll of *July Hay*, R B Kitaj's *John Ford on His Deathbed*, and Andy Warhol's final *Self-Portrait*, along with works by Max Beckmann, Roy Lichtenstein and Gilbert and George.

The **American Wing**, in the northwest corner of the Met, is virtually a museum in its own right, with furnished historical rooms, starting with the Early Colonial period and the Hart room of around 1674, and ending with Frank Lloyd Wright's *Room from the Little House, Minneapolis*, originally windowed on all four sides, in key with Wright's concept of minimizing interior–exterior division. **American paintings** include the nineteenth-century canvases of William Sidney Mount, who depicted genre scenes on his native Long Island, and the landscape artists of the Hudson Valley School – Thomas

Cole and his pupil Frederick Church. Winslow Homer is allowed a gallery to himself, while later rooms bring the Met's American art into the twentieth century with work by Thomas Eakin, William Merritt Chase, and John Singer Sargent, whose *Portrait of Madam X* was one of the most famous pictures of its day, exhibited at the 1884 Paris salon and considered so improper that Sargent had to leave the city.

The Met's **Medieval Galleries** are no less exhaustive, with displays of sumptuous Byzantine metalwork and jewellery donated by J P Morgan and a main sculpture hall piled high with religious statuary and carvings, as well as later period rooms – panelled Tudor bedrooms, florid Rococo boudoirs and salons from France, and an entire Renaissance patio from Velez Blanco in Spain. The **Egyptian rooms** also have as much to see – huge statuary, smaller sculptural pieces and jewellery – although the most prominent exhibit is the **Temple of Dendur**, housed in its own huge gallery, designed to give hints and symbols of its original site on the banks of the Nile. Built by the Emperor Augustus in 15 BC as an attempt to placate a local chieftain, the temple was moved here as a gift of the Egyptian people during the construction of the Aswan High Dam – it would otherwise have been drowned.

The Upper East Side

A two-square-mile grid, scored with the great avenues of Madison, Park and Lexington, the **Upper East Side** has wealth as its defining characteristic, as you'll appreciate if you've seen any of the many Woody Allen movies set here. **Fifth Avenue** up here has been the patrician face of Manhattan since the opening of Central Park attracted the Carnegies, Astors and Whitneys to migrate north and build fashionable residences. **Grand Army Plaza**, at the junction of Central Park South and Fifth Avenue, serves as the introduction, flanked by the extended chateau of the swanky **Plaza Hotel**. Fifth Avenue's wall continues with Henry Clay Frick's house at 70th St, marginally less ostentatious than its neighbors and now the tranquil home of the **Frick Collection** (Tues–Sat 10am–6pm, Sun 1–6pm; $3), the first of many prestigious museums in the area. The Frick is perhaps the most enjoyable of the big New York galleries, made up of the art treasures hoarded by Frick during his years as probably the most ruthless of New York's robber barons. The legacy of his self-aggrandizement is a revealing glimpse of the sumptuous life enjoyed by New York's big industrialists. The collection includes paintings by Reynolds, Hogarth, Gainsborough's *St James's Park* – "Watteau far outdone", wrote a critic at the time – and Bellini's *St Francis*, which suggests his vision of Christ by means of pervading light, a bent tree and an enraptured stare. El Greco's *St Jerome*, above the fireplace, reproachfully surveys the riches all around, and looks out to the South Hall, where one of Boucher's very intimate depictions of his wife hangs near an early Vermeer, *Officer and Laughing Girl*. In the opposite direction are the Library's British works, most notably one of Constable's Salisbury Cathedral series, and the North Hall holds an engaging and sensitive portrait of the Comtesse de Haussonville by Ingres. But the West Gallery holds Frick's greatest prizes: two Turners, views of Cologne and Dieppe; Van Dyck's informal portraits of Frans Snyders and his wife – two paintings only reunited when Frick purchased them; and a set of piercing self-portraits by Rembrandt, along with the enigmatic *Polish Rider* (although serious doubt has recently been thrown on its authenticity). A tiny room on the other side of the West Gallery houses an exquisite set of Limoges enamels and a collection of small-scale paintings that includes a *Virgin and Child* by Jan van Eyck.

The **Guggenheim Museum**, further up Fifth Avenue past the Met at 89th St (Fri–Wed 10am–8pm; closed Thurs; $7), is better known for the building than its collection. This purpose-built structure, designed by Frank Lloyd Wright, caused a storm of controversy when it was unveiled in 1959. Even now, though the years have given it a certain respectability, no one seems to have quite made up their mind, as demonstrated by the recent furore over what turned out to be a highly successful extension.

Much of the building is still given over to temporary exhibitions, but the permanent collection includes work by Chagall, Leger, the major Cubists, and, most completely, Kandinsky. The new extension allows a much greater part of the museum's collection to be on rotational display. Additionally, the small rotunda contains late nineteenth-century paintings, not least the exquisite Degas *Dancers* and other Post-Impressionists, Van Gogh's *Mountains at St Remy* and some sensitive early Picassos.

East of here, the **Whitney Museum of American Art**, 945 Madison Ave at 75th St (Wed & Fri–Sun 11am–6pm, Thurs 1–8pm; $6, free Thurs 6–8pm), brings things up-to-date, a pre-eminent collection of twentieth-century American art and a superb exhibition locale that every other year mounts the Whitney biennial show of contemporary American art. When that's not on, you can view the somewhat arbitrary Highlights of the Permanent Collection, arranged by both chronology and theme. It's particularly strong on Edward Hopper: *Early Sun Morning* is typical, a bleak urban landscape. The Abstract Expressionists are prominent too, with great works by high priests Pollock and de Kooning, leading on to Rothko and the Color Field painters, and the later Pop Art works of Warhol, Johns and Oldenburg.

The Upper West Side

North of 59th Street, midtown Manhattan's tawdry west side becomes less commercial, fading after Lincoln Center into a residential area of mixed charms. This is the **Upper West Side**, these days one of the city's most desirable addresses, though unlike its counterpart to the east of the park a neighborhood whose typical resident would be hard to pin down. There's no shortage of money, but it has to co-exist alongside slum areas that have been little affected by any shifts in status.

Broadway sheers north from Columbus Circle to **Lincoln Center for the Performing Arts**, a marble assembly of buildings put up in the early 1960s on the site of some of the city's worst slums. Home to the Metropolitan Opera and the New York Philharmonic, as well as a host of other smaller companies – see p.94 – this is worth seeing even if you don't catch a performance (**tours** leave daily on the hour 10am–5pm; phone first, ☎769-7020 or 875-5350; $7.75). At the center of the complex, the **Metropolitan Opera House** is a rather overdone building, but an impressive one nonetheless, with murals by Marc Chagall behind each of its high front windows. On the left, *Le Triomphe de la Musique* is cast with a variety of well-known performers, landmarks snipped from the New York skyline and a portrait of Sir Rudolph Bing, the man who ran the Met for more than three decades, garbed as a gypsy. The other mural, *Les Sources de la Musique*, is reminiscent of Chagall's renowned Met production of *The Magic Flute*: the god of music strums a lyre while a Tree of Life, Verdi and Wagner all float down the Hudson River.

A block east from Columbus Avenue, the most famous of the monumental apartment blocks of **Central Park West** is the **Dakota Building**, a grandiose Renaissance-style mansion built in the late nineteenth century to persuade wealthy New Yorkers that life in an apartment could be just as luxurious as in a private house. Over the years, big-time tenants have included Lauren Bacall and Leonard Bernstein, and not so long ago the building was used as the setting for Polanski's film *Rosemary's Baby*. Most people now know the building as the former home of **John Lennon** – and (still) of his wife Yoko Ono, who owns a number of the apartments. It was outside the Dakota, on the night of December 8 1980, that Lennon was murdered – shot by a man who professed to be one of his greatest admirers. Fans may want to light a stick of incense for Lennon across the road in **Strawberry Fields**, a section of Central Park which has been restored and maintained in his memory through an endowment by Yoko Ono; trees and shrubs were donated by a number of countries as a gesture towards world peace.

North up Central Park West, the often-overlooked **New York Historical Society** at 77th St (Tues–Sun 10am–5pm; $3, Tues pay what you wish) is more a museum of

American than of New York history, with a collection that includes the paintings of James Audubon, the Harlem artist and naturalist who specialized in lovingly detailed watercolors of birds, a broad sweep of nineteenth-century American portraiture (including the picture of Alexander Hamilton that found its way onto the $10 bill) and Hudson River School landscapes (among them Thomas Cole's fantastically pompous Course of Empire series), and a glittering display of Tiffany glass, providing an excellent all-round view of Louis Tiffany's attempts "to provide good art for American homes".

Two blocks away, the **American Museum of Natural History** (Sun–Thurs 10am–5.45pm, Fri & Sat 10am–8.45pm; suggested donation $4, Planetarium $5) claims to be the largest museum of any kind in the world, filling four blocks with its strange architectural mélange of heavy neoclassical and rustic Romanesque styles. It houses intelligently mounted artefacts from Asia and Africa, sandwiched between dusty dioramas of the two continents' mammals. The wilting dinosaurs on the fourth floor are currently out of sight; all side galleries are being refurbished, and will progressively reopen between April 1994 and 1996. However, the **Hall of Meteorites** holds some strikingly beautiful crystals, not least the *Star of India*, the largest blue sapphire ever found, and the adjacent **Hayden Planetarium** (Mon–Fri 12.30–4.45pm, Sat 10am–5.45pm, Sun noon–5.45pm) has various astronomical displays and gadgetry, assorted celebrities relating an impassioned tale of space endeavor, and stages a soporific history of the universe (narrator Vincent Price) in the theater.

The Upper West Side's second best address after Central Park West is **Riverside Drive**, which weaves its way up the western fringe of Manhattan island, flanked by palatial townhouses put up in the early part of this century by those not quite rich enough to compete with the folks down on Fifth Avenue, and by **Riverside Park**, landscaped in 1873 by Frederick Olmsted of Central Park fame. It makes the most pleasant route up to the prestigious **Columbia University**, whose campus fills seven blocks between Amsterdam and Broadway, and boasts a set of precincts laid out by McKim, Mead and White in grand Beaux Arts style. Regular guided **tours** start from the information office on the corner of 116th St and Broadway.

On the eastern side of the Columbia precincts, the **Cathedral Church of St John the Divine** rises out of the burned-out tenements, dumped cars and hustlers of the southern fringes of Harlem with a sure, solid kind of majesty – far from finished but already one of New York's main tourist hot spots. A curious mixture of Romanesque and Gothic styles, the church was begun in 1892, but stopped with the outbreak of war in 1939 and has only resumed recently, fraught with funding difficulties and controversy. St John's is intended as very much a community church, housing a soup kitchen and shelter for the homeless, studios for graphics and sculpture, a gymnasium, and a (planned) amphitheater for drama and concerts. The construction itself is being undertaken by local blacks trained by English stonemasons. Only two-thirds of the cathedral is finished, and completion isn't due until around 2050, when it will be the largest cathedral structure in the world, its floor space – at 600ft long and at the transepts 320ft wide – big enough to swallow both the cathedrals of Notre Dame and Chartres whole.

Harlem, El Barrio and the North

HARLEM is the side of Manhattan that few visitors bother to see. Home of a culturally and historically – if not economically – rich **black** community, Harlem is still a focus of black activism. It has its share of racial tension, and poverty, unemployment and attendant crime mean that foreign visitors, especially whites, can be soft targets for trouble. Harlem's flavor may be changing with seeping gentrification from the Upper West Side, but, thanks in part to a near-total lack of federal and municipal support, it is an extremely self-reliant community, worth seeing if you can. Though it's unlikely you'll be hassled in daytime, 125th St, 145th St, Convent Ave and Malcolm X Blvd (formerly Lenox Ave) are the safest areas; at night, stick to the clubs.

Harlem's **sights** are very spread out; it's not a bad idea to get acquainted with the area via a **guided tour** (see p.61), and follow that up with further trips. **125th Street** between Broadway and Fifth Avenue is its working center, a flattened expanse spiked with the occasional skyscraper. No 253 is the famous **Apollo Theater** – not much from the outside, but for many years the center of black entertainment in New York and northeastern America. Almost all the great figures of jazz and blues played here; **James Brown** recorded his seminal *Live At The Apollo* album in 1962.

Close by, **Adam Clayton Powell Jr Boulevard** pushes north, a broad and busy thoroughfare named after the 1930s minister who helped to force the white-owned stores of Harlem to employ the blacks on whom their economic survival depended. Powell later became the first black on the city council, then New York's first black representative at Congress, a career which came to an embittered end in 1967, when amid rumors of the misuse of public funds he was excluded from Congress by majority vote. This failed to diminish his standing in Harlem, where voters twice re-elected him before his death in 1972. A block east, the **Schomburg Center for Research in Black Culture**, 515 Malcolm X Blvd at 135th St (Mon–Wed 10am–8pm, Fri 10am–6pm), has thought-provoking displays on black history. Just north at 132 West 138th St, the **Abyssinian Baptist Church** was where Powell preached, and a small **museum** inside records his life (minus the scandal). The church is also famed for its revival-style Sunday morning services and a gospel choir of gut-busting vivacity. Cross over to 138th Street between Powell and Eighth, and you're in what many consider the finest, most articulate block of row houses in Manhattan – **Strivers' Row** – commissioned during the 1890s housing boom and taking in designs by three sets of architects. Within the burgeoning black community of the turn of the century this came to be *the* desirable place for ambitious professionals to reside; hence its nickname.

From Park Avenue to the East River, Spanish Harlem, or **EL BARRIO**, dips down as far as East 96th Street to collide head on with the affluence of the Upper East Side. The center of a large Puerto Rican community, it is quite different from Harlem – the streets are dirtier, the atmosphere more intimidating. In the early 1950s the government's "Operation Bootstrap" policy offered Puerto Ricans incentives to emigrate to the US. But the occupants have had little opportunity to evolve Latino culture in any meaningful way, and the only space where cultural roots are in evidence is **La Marqueta** on Park Ave between 111th and 116th, a five-block street market of tropical produce, sinister-looking meats and much shouting, and the **Museo del Barrio** at Fifth Ave and 104th St (Wed–Sun 11am–5pm; suggested donation $2), a showcase of Latin art and culture. Close by, the **Museum of the City of New York**, on the corner of 103rd St (Wed–Sat 10am–5pm, Sun 1–5pm; suggested donation $5), might also grab your interest, with a competent rundown on the history of the city from Dutch times to the present day; it also runs Sunday walking tours of various New York neighborhoods.

North of Harlem, but easily reached from the #1 train to 157th and Broadway or the #A to 155th or 163rd, **Audubon Terrace** at 155th and Broadway is a weird, clumsy nineteenth-century complex of museums dolled up as Beaux Arts temples, the best of which is the **Museum of the American Indian** (Tues–Sat 10am–5pm, Sun 1–5pm. $3, students $2), a fascinating assembly of artefacts from almost every tribe native to the Americas (scheduled to move to the Custom House in Lower Manhattan in late 1994; see p.65). Highlights include assorted scalps, the personal knick-knacks of Sitting Bull and Geronimo, shrunken human figures from Ecuador and some amazing Inuit scrimshaw. A very reasonable museum shop sells various authentic items.

The **Morris-Jumel Mansion**, within walking distance on 160th St between Amsterdam and Edgecombe (Tues–Sun 10am–4pm; $2), is another uptown surprise, its proud Georgian outlines faced with a later Federal portico. Built as a rural retreat in 1765 by Colonel Roger Morris, it was briefly Washington's headquarters before falling into the hands of the British. Later, wine merchant Stephen Jumel bought the mansion and refurbished it for his wife Eliza, formerly a prostitute and his mistress. When Jumel died in 1832, Eliza married ex-Vice President Aaron Burr, twenty years her senior. The marriage lasted six months before old Burr upped and left, to die on the day of their divorce. Eliza battled on to the age of 91, and on the top floor of the house you'll find her obituary, a magnificently fictionalized account of a "scandalous" life.

From most western stretches of Washington Heights you get a glimpse of the **George Washington Bridge** that links Manhattan to New Jersey, a dazzling concoction of metalwork and graceful lines. **The Cloisters** in Fort Tryon Park houses the pick of the Metropolitan Museum's medieval collection (March–Oct Tues–Sun 9.30am– 5.15pm, Nov–Feb Tues–Sun 9.30am–4.45pm; suggested donation $6; $3 students, includes the Met on same day) – also reachable by hourly direct shuttle bus from the Met (June, July & Aug, Fri & Sat; $5). The collection is the handiwork of collectors George Barnard and John D Rockefeller, who spent the early years of this century shipping over all they could buy of medieval Europe. Among its larger artefacts are a monumental Romanesque Hall made up of French remnants and a frescoed Spanish Fuentiduena Chapel, both thirteenth-century and cornering on the prettiest of the four sets of cloisters here, from St Guilhelm from thirteenth-century France. At the center of the museum is the Cuxa cloister from a twelfth-century Benedictine monastery in the French Pyrenees, whose capitals are brilliant peasant art, carved with weird, self- devouring grotesque creatures. Among smaller sculpture, the Early Gothic Hall houses a memorably tender *Virgin and Child*, carved in England in the fourteenth century. Tapestries on show include the spectacular *Unicorn Tapestries*. Campin's *Merode Altarpiece*, housed in its own antechamber, depicts the Annunciation in a typical Flemish interior of the day, beyond which life goes on in a fifteenth-century market square, perhaps Campin's native Tournai. The amazing downstairs Treasury houses the *Belles Heures de Jean, Duc de Berry* – perhaps the greatest of all medieval Books of Hours, executed by the Limburg Brothers with dazzling genre miniatures of seasonal life – and the twelfth-century altar cross from Bury St Edmunds in England, a mass of tiny expressive characters from biblical stories.

The Outer Boroughs

Most visitors to New York don't stray off Manhattan. But if you're staying a while, you might choose to investigate the **outer boroughs**. **Brooklyn** is certainly worth a trip out, primarily for the salubrious neighborhood of Brooklyn Heights just across the East River, bucolic Prospect Park and the Brooklyn Botanical Garden, and the Brooklyn Museum. For inveterate nostalgics, Coney Island and its Russian neighbor, Brighton Beach, lie at the far end of the subway line. Few indeed make it to **Queens**, though it holds the bustling Greek community of Astoria and the new Museum of the Moving Image. **Staten Island** boasts a couple of unusual museums, and the ferry ride is fun in itself. Even the **Bronx**, renowned for the desolate and bleak environs of its southern reaches, has the city's largest **zoo** and another glorious **botanical garden**.

Brooklyn

If it were still a separate city, **BROOKLYN** would be the fourth largest in the US, but until as recently as the early 1800s it was no more than a group of autonomous towns and villages distinct from the already thriving Manhattan. Robert Fulton's steamship service across the water first changed the shape of Brooklyn, starting with the establishment of a leafy retreat at Brooklyn Heights. What really transformed things, though, was the opening of the Brooklyn Bridge. Thereafter development spread deeper inland, as housing was needed to service a more commercialized Manhattan. By the turn of the century, Brooklyn was fully established as part of New York City, and its fate as Manhattan's perennial kid brother was sealed.

Brooklyn Heights, now one of New York City's most beautiful neighborhoods, has little in common with the rest of the borough – a peaceful, tree-lined enclave originally settled by financiers from Wall Street across the water and today still very exclusive. There isn't much to see as you wander its perfectly preserved terraces and breathe in the air of civilized calm, but students of urban architecture can have a field day. The obvious place to begin a tour is the so-called **Esplanade**, with its fine views of Lower Manhattan across the water, east of which **Pierrepoint and Montague streets** are the Heights' main arteries, studded with delightful – and fantastic – brownstones.

Further into Brooklyn, Flatbush Avenue leads up to **Grand Army Plaza**, a grandiose junction laid out by Calvert and Vaux late in the nineteenth century as a dramatic approach to their new Prospect Park just behind. The triumphal **Soldiers and Sailors' Memorial Arch** was added thirty years later, topped with a fiery sculpture of Victory in tribute to the Northern triumph in the Civil War. **Prospect Park** itself was landscaped in the early 1890s, and remains for the most part remarkably bucolic – far more so than Central Park – as does the adjacent **Brooklyn Botanic Garden** (April–Sept Tues–Fri 8am–6pm, Sat & Sun 10am–4pm; Oct–March Tues–Fri 8am–4.30pm, Sat & Sun 10am–4.30pm) – one of the most enticing park spaces in the city, smaller and more immediately likeable than its more celebrated rival in the Bronx. Behind, the **Brooklyn Museum**, 220 Eastern Parkway (Wed–Sun 10am–5pm; $4), though doomed to stand perpetually in the shadow of the Met, is a major museum and a good reason in itself for forsaking Manhattan for an afternoon, with five demanding floors of miscellaneous artefacts. Highlights include the ethnographic department on the ground floor, with arts and applied arts from Oceania and the Americas, the Classical and Egyptian antiquities on the second floor, and the evocative American Period Rooms on the fourth floor. Be sure, too, to look in on the top-story American and European Picture Galleries, where the eighteenth-century portraits include one of George Washington by Gilbert Stuart. Pastoral canvases by William Sidney Mount, alongside the heavily romantic Hudson River School and paintings by Eastman Johnson (such as the curious *Not at Home*) and John Singer Sargent, lead up to twentieth-century work by Charles Sheeler and Georgia O'Keeffe. European artists featured include Degas, Cézanne, Toulouse-Lautrec, Monet, and Dufy. The gift shop sells ethnic items from around the world at reasonable prices.

Generations of working-class New Yorkers came to relax at one of Brooklyn's furthest points, **Coney Island**, reachable direct from Manhattan on the #B, #D, F# or #N subway lines. At its height it was visited by 100,000 people a day; now, however, it's one of the city's poorest districts, and not a little threatening. The amusement park is peeling and run-down, and until recently the boardwalk was cracked and broken – although if you like run-down seaside resorts there's no better place on earth. The beach at least is beautiful, a broad swath of golden sand. The **New York Aquarium** on the boardwalk opened in 1896 and is still going strong, displaying fish and invertebrates from the world over in its darkened halls, along with frequent open-air shows of marine mammals (daily 10am–4.45pm; summer Sat & Sun 10am–7pm; $5.75).

Further along, **Brighton Beach**, or "Little Odessa", is home to the country's largest community of Russian emigrés – around 20,000, who arrived in the 1970s – and a long-established and now largely elderly Jewish population. Livelier than Coney Island, it's also more prosperous, especially along its main drag, **Brighton Beach Avenue**, which runs underneath the el in a hotchpotch of food shops and appetizing restaurants.

The Bronx

Though everyone has a horror story about the **BRONX**, as long as you avoid its seriously decayed southern reaches it's not much different from any other New York borough, and has proved less vulnerable to the racial tensions that have surfaced elsewhere during the Eighties. The borough developed – and has since declined – more quickly than any other part of the city. First settled in the seventeenth century by the

Swedish Jonas Bronk, like Brooklyn it only became part of the city proper at the turn of the last century. From 1900 onwards things moved fast, and the Bronx became one of the most sought-after residential areas of the city, its main thoroughfare, **Grand Concourse**, becoming edged with increasingly luxurious Art Deco apartment blocks – many of which, though greatly run-down, still stand.

The **Bronx Zoo** (Mon–Sat 10am–5pm, Sun 10am–5.30pm; Fri–Mon $4.75, otherwise a donation) is accessible either by its main gate on Fordham Road or by a second entrance on Bronx Park South. This last is the entrance to use if you come directly here by subway (to East Tremont Ave). Even if you don't like zoos, the largest urban zoo in the US is better than most, and one of the first to realize that animals both looked and felt better out in the open. Its Wild Asia exhibit is an almost forty-acre wilderness through which tigers, elephants and deer roam relatively free, viewable from a monorail (May–Oct; $1.25). Look in also on the World of Darkness, which holds nocturnal species, and the simulation of a Himalayan mountain area, holding endangered species such as the giant panda and snow leopard. Across the road from the zoo's main entrance is the back turnstile of the **New York Botanical Gardens** (Tues–Sun 10am–5pm, last admission 4pm) which in parts is as wild as anything you're likely to see upstate. West of their main entrance, the **Poe Cottage** (Wed–Fri 9am–5pm, Sat 10am–4pm, Sun 1–5pm; $1) is a tiny white clapboard shack that was Edgar Allan Poe's home for the last three, unhappy years of his life, which saw his wife's death and very little writing beyond the short, touching poem, *Annabel Lee*. Poe left the cottage for the last time in 1849 to secure backing for his long-running dream – his own literary magazine – but got entangled in the election furore in Baltimore, disappeared, and was eventually found delirious in the street; he died in hospital a few days later. What actually happened no one knows, and the house, with its few meager furnishings spread thinly through half a dozen rooms, tells you little more about the man.

Queens

Of the four outer boroughs, **QUEENS**, named after the wife of Charles II of England, is the most consistently ignored. Though considerably more accessible than Staten Island, a great deal larger than Brooklyn, and immeasurably safer than the Bronx, it is simply not seen as a desirable place to live. People who live in Queens, the thinking seems to run, are either excruciatingly dull or just can't afford to live anywhere else.

Which belittles its role as one of the rare places where post-war immigrants could buy their own homes and establish their own communities. **Astoria**, for example, holds the largest concentration of Greeks outside Greece itself (Melbourne included). It has a long **film-making** tradition: *Paramount* had its studios here until it was lured away by Hollywood's reliable weather. Astoria was left empty and disused by all except the US Army, until Hollywood's stranglehold on the industry finally weakened. The new studios here – not open to the public – now rank as the country's fourth largest and are set for a major expansion. The **Museum of the Moving Image** in the old Paramount complex at 34–31 35th St near Broadway (Tues–Fri noon–4pm, Sat & Sun noon–6pm; $5) is devoted to the history of film, video and TV. In addition to viewing posters and kitsch movie souvenirs from the Thirties and Forties, you can listen in on directors explaining sequences from famous movies; watch fun short films made up of well-known clips; add your own sound effects to movies; and view original sets and costumes. A wonderful, mock-Egyptian pastiche of a 1920s movie theater shows kids' movies and TV classics.

If you're really keen on exploring Queens, the **Queens Museum**, at Flushing Meadows-Corona Park (Tues–Fri 10am–5pm, Sun noon–5pm; $3), is another possible target. Its one permanent item is an 18,000-square-foot model of the five boroughs of New York City, spectacularly lit, constantly updated and originally conceived for the 1964 World's Fair by Robert Moses. Great fun if you know the city well, and useful orientation if you don't. Take the subway #7 to Willets Point–Shea Stadium.

Staten Island

Until 1964 **STATEN ISLAND** was isolated – getting to it meant a ferry trip or long ride through New Jersey, and commuting into town was almost an eccentricity. The opening of the Verrazano Narrows Bridge changed things; upwardly mobile Brooklynites found inexpensive property on the island and swarmed over the bridge to buy their parcel of suburbia. Today Staten Island has swollen to accommodate dense residential neighborhoods amid the rambling greenery, endless backwaters of neat look-don't-touch homes; and residents pining for a lost sense of isolation voted in November 1993 to begin the long process of divorcing their borough from New York City altogether.

The **Staten Island Ferry** sails around the clock from Battery Park, with half-hourly departures between 9.30am and 4pm, giving great wide-angled views of the city for just 50¢ return. The ferry terminal quickly dispels any romance, but it's easy to escape to the adjoining bus station and catch the #74 bus to the **Jacques Marchais Center of Tibetan Art** at 338 Lighthouse Ave (May–Sept Wed–Sun 1–5pm; April, Oct, Nov, Fri–Sun 1–5pm; call ☎718/987-3478 for details of additional summer hours; $3). Jacques Marchais was the alias of Jacqueline Kleber, a New York art dealer who reckoned she'd get on better with a French name. She assembled the largest collection of Tibetan art in the western world and housed it in a hillside "Buddhist temple". The exhibition is small enough to be accessible, with magnificent bronze Bodhisattvas, fearsome deities in union with each other, musical instruments, costumes and decorations from Tibet. During the first or second week of October it hosts a **harvest festival**: Tibetan monks in saffron robes perform the traditional ceremonies, and Tibetan food and crafts are sold.

Back on the main Richmond Road, a short walk leads to the **Richmondstown Restoration** (Wed–Fri 10am–5pm, Sat & Sun 1–5pm; $2, students $1.50), where a dozen or so old buildings have been transplanted from their original sites and grafted on to the eighteenth-century village of Richmond. Half-hourly tours negotiate the best of these – including the oldest elementary school in the country, a picture-book general store, and the atmospheric Guyon-Lake-Tyson House of 1740 – and craftspeople use old techniques to weave cloth and fire kilns. It's all carried off to picturesque and ungimmicky effect in rustic surroundings, a mere twelve miles from downtown Manhattan.

Accommodation

Prices for **accommodation** in New York are well above the norm for the US as a whole; a decent $50 hotel room should be regarded as extraordinarily good value, and **budget** hotels and motels barely exist. If you're just here for a few days, you may well be away from your lodgings for all your waking hours, anyway, so spending $100 on a bed doesn't make all that much sense. On the other hand, a lot of high-standard accommodation is of course available, and if you pay that bit more you can stay in a much more central location. Getting yourself a room with a **TV** is also a definite plus; New York's cable stations have to be seen to be believed.

Hostels

Chelsea Center Hostel, 511 W 20th St (☎243-4922). Small, clean and safe private downtown hostel, with prices from $18 in winter, $20 in summer. Reservations essential in high season. ①.

International House – Sugar Hill, 722 St Nicholas Ave, NY 10031 (☎926-7030). Noisy but adequate dorms in friendly, well-run hostel. $12 per night, no curfew, no chores and no lock-out. Way up on border of Harlem and Washington Heights, opposite 145th St subway station. ①.

International Youth Hostel, 891 Amsterdam Ave at 103rd St (☎932-2300). Dorms $20 per night (on-the-spot IYHA membership $25), plus restaurant, travel shop and theater. Phone in advance. ①.

Vanderbilt YMCA, 224 E 47th St (☎755-2410). Smaller and quieter than its handy midtown Manhattan location, just five minutes' walk from Grand Central Station, might suggest. Inexpensive restaurant, swimming pool, gym and laundromat. ③.

ACCOMMODATION PRICE CODES

All accommodation prices in this book have been coded using the symbols below. Prices are for the least expensive double rooms in each establishment, and in this section include New York State tax at 14.25% or 19.25%, City tax at 6% and occupancy tax of $2. Note that hotels *never* include taxes when quoting dollar rates.

For a full explanation see p.35 in *Basics*.

①	up to $30	④	$60–80	⑦	$130–180
②	$30–45	⑤	$80–100	⑧	$180+
③	$45–60	⑥	$100–130		

Newark YMWCA, 600 Broad St, Newark, New Jersey 07102 (☎201/624-8900). A major cost-cutting option if you don't mind not being based on Manhattan. Basic. It has a gym and swimming pool and costs $25 per person per night, $85 per week. Ten minutes' walk from Newark's Penn Station, for frequent PATH and NJ Transit trains to Manhattan ($1), and reasonably close to the airport. ①.

Bed and Breakfast

Bed and breakfast – staying in a New Yorker's spare room or subletting an apartment – is an increasingly popular (and inexpensive) option. Normally arranged through an agency, such as those listed below, rates run at about $75 for a double, or $100 a night for a studio apartment. It is essential to book well in advance.

Bed and Breakfast in Manhattan, PO Box 533 NYC, NY 10150-0533 (☎472-2528). Rooms in hosted ④–⑤ and unhosted apartments ⑤–⑧.

Bed and Breakfast Network of New York, Suite 602, 134 W 32nd St, NY 10001 (☎645-8134). Write at least a month in advance. Hosted doubles ⑤, unhosted accommodation ⑤–⑧.

Colby International, 139 Round Hey, Liverpool L28 1RG, England (☎703/551-5005 or, in UK, 051/ 220-5848). Guaranteed B&B accommodation, which can be arranged from the UK. Reserve at least a fortnight ahead in high season. Excellent-value doubles ④ and studios ⑤.

Urban Ventures, PO Box 426, New York NY 10024. Personal callers welcome at Suite 1412, 38 W 32nd St (☎594-5650). No minimum stay, and you can book up until the last minute. Budget doubles ④, "comfort range" rooms ⑤, unhosted apartments ⑥.

Hotels

Most of New York's **hotels** are in midtown Manhattan – a good enough location, though you may well travel downtown for food and nightlife. **Booking ahead** is very strongly advised; at certain times of the year – Christmas and early summer particularly – everything is likely to be full. Phone the hotels direct, or contact a **booking service** to reserve rooms at no extra charge, such as *Meegan's* (☎718/995-9292 or 1-800/221-1235), *CRS* (☎1-800/950-0232; fax 305/274-1357), *The Room Exchange*, 450 Seventh Ave NY 10123 (☎760-1000), or *Express Reservations* (☎1-800/356-1123).

Aberdeen, 17 W 32nd, NY 10001 (☎736-1600). Rather spartan rooms, but in a good location just off Fifth Ave. Complimentary continental breakfast is served in the lobby, under chandeliers. ⑤.

Algonquin, 59 W 44th St, NY 10036 (☎840-6800). New York's classic literary hang-out. Decor remains little changed, though the bedrooms have been refurbished to good effect. ⑧.

Ameritania, 230 W 54th, NY 10019 (☎247-5000). Opened in 1992. The best value of the city's inexpensive hotels. Brand-new, well-furnished rooms with marble bathroom, cable TV. Restaurant and pizza parlor off the high-tech, neon-lit lobby. ⑤ if you mention *Rough Guides*; normal rates ⑥–⑦.

Best Western President, 234 W 48th St, NY 10036 (☎246-8800). Solid, reasonably priced hotel, offering small, recently renovated rooms and free continental breakfast. ⑤–⑦.

Carlton Arms, 160 E 25th St, NY 10010 (☎684-8337). The city's latest bohemian hang-out, with eclectic interior decor by would-be artists, and very few comforts (though more expensive rooms have en-suite bath). Check it out before you commit yourself. ③/④.

Chelsea, 222 W 23rd St, NY 10011 (☎243-3700). One of New York's most noted landmarks, an ageing neo-Gothic building with a notorious past (see p.72). Avoid the older rooms; ask for a renovated one with wood floors, log-burning fireplaces, and plenty of space for a few extra friends. ⑨.

Chelsea Inn, 46 W 17th St, NY 10011 (☎645-8989). Nicely situated in the heart of Chelsea, not too far from the Village. ⑨ with bath shared with one other guest room; studio with bathroom ⑥.

Chelsea Pines Inn, 317 West 14th St (☎929-1023). Well-priced gay-oriented hotel housed in an old brownstone. Clean, comfortable, attractively furnished rooms. ③–⑤.

Esplanade, 305 West End Ave, NY 10023 (☎874-5000). Low prices but smart decor in a quieter residential area within reach of midtown's attractions. ⑨.

Excelsior, 45 W 81st St (☎362-9200). Old-fashioned hotel across from Natural History Museum in the heart of lively Columbus Avenue. Decent-sized rooms, and good four-person suites. ⑤–⑥.

Gorham, 136 W 55th St, NY 10019 (☎245-1800). Excellent-value midtown hotel, handy for Central Park and with jacuzzis, cable TV and self-service kitchen in every room. ⑦.

Gramercy Park, 2 Lexington Ave, NY 10010 (☎475-4320). Pleasant enough hotel, where residents get a key to the adjacent private park. A mixture of newly renovated and tatty rooms. ⑦; weekends ⑥.

Malibu Studios, 2688 Broadway at W 103rd St, NY 10025 (☎222-2954). Probably the best-value budget accommodation in the city. A fair way out at the Morningside Heights end of the Upper West Side, but next to 103rd St stop on #1 subway line, and within walking distance of restaurants and nightlife. Mention *Rough Guides* and you get a discount for 3 or more nights paid upfront. ③.

Mansfield, 12 W 44th St, NY 10036 (☎944-6050). Value alternative to the nearby *Algonquin* and *Royalton*. Better-than-average rooms (some triples and quads), with luxuries like thermo-vapor whirlpools and steambaths. Good deli off the lobby, and there's a steakhouse on the premises. ⑨.

Milburn, 242 W 76th St (☎362-1006). Welcoming and well-situated hotel which has recently been renovated in very gracious style. Doubles and large two-room suites. ⑥.

Morgans, 237 Madison Ave, NY 10016 (☎686-0300). The chic creation of the instigators of *Studio 54* and the *Palladium* nightclub. The black-white-grey decor is starting to look self-consciously 1980s and a little passé, but you get a jacuzzi, a great stereo system and cable TV in your room .⑧.

New York Bed and Breakfast, 134 W 119th St (☎666-0559). Lovely old brownstone with nice and very inexpensive double rooms. The only drawback is the location, way uptown in El Barrio. ③.

Paramount, 235 W 46th St, NY 10036 (☎764-5500). Former budget hotel renovated by the *Morgans/Royalton* crew. One of the hippest places in town to stay, popular with a pop and media crowd, who come to enjoy a Philippe Starck interior and to be waited on by sleek young things. ⑧.

Penn Plaza, 215 W 34th, NY 10001 (☎947-5050). Budget hotel in a slightly sleazy location opposite Penn Station; decent rooms with and without bath. ③/⑤.

Pickwick Arms, 230 E 51st St, NY 10022 (☎355-0300). Thoroughly pleasant budget hotel, and one of the best deals in this part of midtown. All 400 rooms are air-conditioned, with cable TV, direct dial phones and room service. Open-air roof deck with stunning views, and *Torremolino's* restaurant. ⑥.

Remington, 129 W 46th St, NY 10036 (☎221-2600). Spotless, if a little tacky, central hotel near Times Square. Service is brusque and efficient; all rooms have air-conditioning and cable TV. ④–⑤.

Royalton, 44 W 44th St, NY 10036 (☎869-4400). Attempting to capture the market for the discerning style-person, with more Philippe Starck interiors. It aims to be the *Algonquin* of the 1990s, and is as much a power-lunch venue for NYC's media and publishing set as a place to stay. ⑧.

Salisbury, 123 W 57th, NY 10019 (☎246-1300). Good service, large rooms with kitchenettes. ⑥–⑦.

Southgate Tower, 371 Seventh Ave NY 10001 (☎563-1800). Way over on the western edge of midtown. If you come for a week or two, stay in one of the big, fully equipped suites. ⑦.

Wales, 1295 Madison Ave, NY 10128 (☎876-6000). Almost in Spanish Harlem, though very definitely Upper East Side in feel. Excellent prices for the lovingly-restored accommodation. ⑦.

Washington Square, 103 Waverley Place, NY 10011 (☎777-9515). Bang in the heart of Greenwich Village, and a stone's throw from the NYU campus. Don't be deceived by the posh-looking lobby – the rooms are what you'd expect for the price, and the staff are surly. ⑥.

Webster Apartments, 419 W 34th St, NY 10001 (☎967-9000 or 1-800/242-7909). Nice women-only residences, in unexciting location but with unusual extras: several lounges with piano or stereo, a leafy private garden and plant-filled roof terrace. Rooms are all singles, at $35 per night B&B, with shared bathrooms on each floor. Weekly rates include two meals a day; all prices before taxes.

Wolcott, 4 W 31st St, NY 10001 (☎268-2900). Surprisingly relaxing budget hotel, with a gilded, ornamented lobby and more than adequate rooms. Economical single rates, plus triples and quads. ③–④.

Eating

There isn't anything you can't **eat** in New York. The city has more restaurants per head than anywhere else in the States, and many New Yorkers not only eat out often but take their food incredibly seriously, obsessed with new cuisines, new dishes and new restaurants. Certain areas are pockets of ethnic restaurants: **Chinatown** (including Vietnamese) below Canal Street; **Little Italy** just to the north; **Little India**, Sixth St east of Bowery; **Little Brazil**, 46th St between Fifth and Sixth avenues. On the **Upper West Side**, quite a few places offer the surprising combination of Cuban and Chinese.

Lower Manhattan

Anjelica, 300 E 12th St (☎228-2909). Good-quality vegetarian with daily specials. Low-priced, too. Patronized by an artistic and fashion crowd.

Brother's Bar-B-Q, 228 W Houston St (☎727-2775). Downbeat SoHo diner serving some of the best barbecue food east of the Mississippi.

Café Le Figaro, 184 Bleecker St (☎677-1100). Former Beat hang-out during the Fifties; the ersatz Left Bank at its finest. Good views of Bleecker Street, and excellent snacks and meals.

Caliente Cab Co, 61 Seventh Ave at Bleecker St (☎243-8517). Popular Tex-Mex restaurant with good happy hour and weekend brunch bargains.

Caribe, 117 Perry St (☎255-9191). Loud and usually crowded Caribbean restaurant filled with a leafy jungle decor serving spicy food and wild tropical cocktails. A fun night out.

Cent' Anni, 50 Carmine St (☎989-9494). Small Village place. Delicious, well- priced Florentine food.

Corner Bistro, 331 W Fourth St (☎242-9502). Dingy pub with cavernous cubicles and healthy servings of burgers, etc, for reasonable prices. Long-standing West Village literary haunt.

The Cupping Room Café, 359 W Broadway (☎925-2898). Quaint place, serving good wholesome food with occasional jazz and the odd tarot or palm reader. The brunches are best. Recommended.

El Faro, 823 Greenwich St (☎929-8210). Dark, lively Spanish restaurant. You can't go wrong with the paella or the seafood in green sauce. Moderate prices too, and you can share most main dishes.

Empire Diner, 210 Tenth Ave (☎243-2736). Chrome-spangled Art Deco beauty, average diner food.

Florent, 69 Gansevoort St (☎989-5779). Ultra-fashionable bistro on the edge of the meat-packing district that serves good French food, either à la carte or from a *prix fixe* menu ($16.95).

Japonica, 90 University Place (☎243-7752). Some of the freshest sushi in the city, at very reasonable prices. Sat and Sun brunch deals are excellent at around $12 a head.

Jerry's, 101 Prince St (☎966-9464). American-French restaurant with an upscale diner atmosphere that's one of SoHo's trendier spots. Casual and good for people-watching. Moderate prices.

John's Pizzeria, 278 Bleecker St (☎243-1680); 408 E 64th St (☎935-2895); and 48 W 65th St (☎721-7001). No slices, no takeouts, but great thin-crust pizzas. Be prepared to queue.

Katz's, 205 E Houston St (☎254-2246). Wisecracking Lower East Side deli serving archetypal NYC pastrami and corned beef. Best known as the scene of the faked orgasm in *When Harry Met Sally*.

Life Café, 343 E 10th St (☎477-8791). Peaceful East Village haunt on Tompkins Square that hosts sporadic concerts. All sandwiches, Tex-Mex or vegetarian – around $6–8.

Little Mushroom Café, 183 W 10th (☎242-1058). Fish, pasta and omelettes, $5–12. One of the least expensive places along this stretch of the Village. Bring your own booze from the deli opposite.

Lupe's East LA Diner, 110 Sixth Ave (☎966-1326). Very laid-back hole-in-the-wall restaurant serving great beer and burritos. Good fun, and inexpensive.

Nice Restaurant, 35 E Broadway (☎406-9776). Vast, packed restaurant, great for dim sum.

Royal Canadian Pancake Restaurant, 145 Hudson St (☎219-3038). Vast, delicious pancakes; fillings range from lager through white chocolate to berries and bananas. Perfect for Sunday brunch.

Second Avenue Deli, 156 Second Ave (☎677-0606). East Village deli serving marvellous burgers, pastrami and other goodies in ebullient, snap-happy style.

Whole Wheat'n'Wild Berries, 57 W 10th St (☎677-3410). Gourmet health food and vegetarian specials, including fresh fish, pasta dishes, salads and homemade soups.

Yonah Schimmel's, 137 E Houston St (☎477-2858). Home-baked knishes and wonderful bagels.

Midtown Manhattan

The Ballroom, 253 W 28th St (☎244-3005). Long-established Chelsea tapas bar, good both for snacks and for a full feed. Also one of the city's classiest comedy spots.

Carnegie Deli, 854 Seventh Ave (☎757-2245). The most generously stuffed sandwiches in the city.

Genroku Sushi, 365 Fifth Ave (☎947-7940). Sushi and other Japanese-Chinese food. You pick what you fancy off a moving conveyor belt.

Hourglass Tavern, 373 W 46th St (☎265-2060). Tiny midtown French place. Excellent-value two-course menu for just $11.50. You're supposed to leave when the hourglass above your table is empty.

Landmark Tavern, 626 Eleventh Ave (☎757-8595). Long-established Irish bar/restaurant popular with the midtown yuppie crowd. Good food, and huge portions.

Lox Around the Clock, 676 Sixth Ave (☎691-3535). Blintzes, bagels and, of course, lox, in a trendy, noisy environment. Good for brunch. Open 24 hours.

Oyster Bar, Grand Central Terminal (☎490-6650). Wonderfully atmospheric old place, down in the vaulted dungeons of Grand Central, where midtown office workers break for lunch (see p.70). Clam chowder with bread is around $3 – great bowls of pan-roast oysters or clams more like $10.

Trattoria del'Arte, 900 Seventh Ave (☎245-9800). Airy Italian restaurant, with excellent service. Great crispy pizzas and imaginative pasta for around $15, and mouthwatering antipasto bar. Book.

Uncle Vanya, 315 W 54th St (☎262-0542). White Russian delicacies, moderately priced.

Upper Manhattan

All State Café, 250 W 72nd St (☎874-7883). Interesting mixture of American and French food in a popular Upper West Side hang-out. Get here early to be sure of a place.

Asmara, 951 Amsterdam Ave (☎749-9614). Very inexpensive African restaurant serving assorted curried meat dishes, along with a few vegetarian alternatives, eaten with chapati-like *injera* bread.

Brother Jimmy's BBQ, 1461 First Ave (☎545-RIBS). Casual, fun barbecue restaurant whose motto is "Pig Out!" Quite a happening bar scene too.

La Caridad, 2199 Broadway (☎874-2780). Upper West Side institution, doling out plentiful and inexpensive Cuban-Chinese food. Bring your own beer, and don't expect polite service.

Carmine's, 2450 Broadway (☎362-2200). Decent home-style Southern Italian food, in mountainous portions, at a large and loud Upper West Side place. Be ready to wait; only large groups can book.

Dock's Oyster Bar, 2427 Broadway (☎724-5588) and 633 Third Ave (☎986-8080). Uptown restaurants with ultra-freshest seafood. The Upper West Side one is a bit homelier – both can be noisy.

Ecco-la, 1660 Third Ave (☎860-5609). Unique pasta combinations at very moderate prices make this place one of the Upper East Side's most popular Italians. If you don't mind waiting, a real find.

Flor de Mayo, 2651 Broadway (☎630-5520) and 171 Third Ave (☎472-0600). Very inexpensive, very popular Cuban-Chinese restaurant with coffeeshop decor, though not much for vegetarians.

Genoa, 271 Amsterdam Ave (☎787-1094). Small and very authentic Italian restaurant. Inexpensive, dark and always crowded. Expect to queue for a table.

Malaga, 406 E 73rd St (☎737-7659). Intimate local Spanish restaurant with good, wholesome food.

Mme Romaine de Lyon, 29 E 61st St (☎758-2422). The place for omelettes: they've got 550 on the lunch menu and dinner features an expanded non-omelette menu.

New Wave Coffee Shop, 937 Madison Ave (☎734-2467). Standard coffeeshop known as a venue for celebrities. Nice and inexpensive if you've just blitzed in the nearby designer clothing emporia.

Ollie's, 2315 Broadway (☎362-3712); 2957 Broadway (☎932-3300); and 200 W 44th St (☎921-5988). Downscale Upper West Side Chinese café with marvellous noodles.

Pig Heaven, 1540 Second Ave (☎744-4333). Good-value Chinese restaurant decorated with images of pigs. Not surprisingly, the accent is on pork.

Poiret, 474 Columbus Ave (☎724-6880). A trendy – and reasonably inexpensive – French bistro with excellent food and outside seating in summer. A nice place for brunch too.

Third World Café, 700 W 125th St (☎749-8199). Harlem restaurant serving a jumble of Cajun, Indian and Caribbean cuisine. Fun atmosphere, low prices, fantastic food.

Vince & Eddie's, 70 W 68th St (☎721-0068). Slightly pseudo-country-style restaurant serving home-cooking like granny used to make – hearty, wholesome, and delicious.

West Side Storey, 700 Columbus Ave (☎749-1900). A wide range of standard American food, and ultra-friendly management. $8–12 for a main course.

Drinking

New York's best **bars** are in **lower Manhattan** – Greenwich Village, the East Village and SoHo. The **midtown** places tend to be geared to an after-hours office crowd and (with a few exceptions) are pricey and rather dull; **uptown,** the Upper West Side at least, between 60th and 85th streets along Amsterdam and Columbus avenues, has several good places to drink. Most of the bars listed below serve food of some kind.

Lower

Broome Street Bar, 363 West Broadway (☎925-2086). A popular and long-established local haunt, now more restaurant than bar, serving reasonably priced burgers and salads in a dimly lit setting.

Cedar Tavern, 82 University Place (☎929-9089). Legendary Fifties Beat meeting point. Cozy place, with well-priced drinks and inexpensive food served in summer in their covered roof garden.

Chumley's, 86 Bedford St (☎675-4449). Atmospheric former speakeasy with a good choice of beers and food from around $8. Arrive before 9pm to be sure of one of the battered tables.

Downtown Beirut, 158 First Ave (☎777-9011). Mega-sleaze East Village punk bar with music, live and recorded. Jukebox vintage 1977–79.

Fanelli, 94 Prince St (☎226-9412). SoHo's oldest bar, cozy and informal. Food from $5.

Grassroots Tavern, 20 St Mark's Place (☎475-9443). Basement bar at the center of the East Village hum: not expensive, and with a good oldies jukebox and two dartboards.

Jeremy's Alehouse, 254 Front St (☎964-3537). South Street Seaport area bar serving well-priced pint mugs of beer and excellent fish, as well as burgers.

La Jumelle, 55 Grand St (☎941-9551). Trendy, youthful, and normally very crowded SoHo bar.

McSorley's, 15 E Seventh St (☎473-9148). New York City's longest-established bar – male-only until just over a decade ago. Looks like a saloon, and serves nothing but strong ale.

Sugar Reef, 93 Second Ave (☎477-8754). High-spirited East Village bar. 40 different varieties of rum, and Caribbean food.

Vazac's, 108 Ave B (☎473-8840). Known as "Seven and B", on the corner of Tompkins Square. East Village hang-out used as a sleazy set in films and commercials – most famously in *Crocodile Dundee*.

White Horse Tavern, 567 Hudson St (☎243-9260). Convivial, inexpensive Village bar where Dylan Thomas supped his last. Excellent jukebox.

Midtown

The Coffee Shop, 29 Union Square West (☎243-7969). Former coffeeshop turned trendy bar and restaurant. Vaguely Caribbean-style food in the noisy adjacent restaurant, and bar grub too.

Live Bait, 14 E 23rd St (☎353-2400). Cajun bar/restaurant run by the same people as the *Coffee Shop* (above), and popular with the after-office crowd. Not the place for a quiet drink.

Mumbles, 603 Second Ave (☎889-0750). Casual, friendly and cozy sports bar. Mixed local crowd.

Murphy's, 977 Second Ave (☎751-5400). Irish bar which attracts the midtown singles set. Drinks are costly but food less so – a rare and useful standby in this part of town.

Old Town Bar and Restaurant, 45 E 18th St (☎473-8874). Atmospheric bar popular with publishing types, models and photographers from the surrounding Flatiron district.

PJ Clarke's, 915 Third Ave (☎759-1650). Legendary spit-and-sawdust alehouse with a not-so-cheap restaurant out the back. You may recognize it as the location of *The Lost Weekend*.

Upper

Augie's, 2751 Broadway (☎864-9834). Downbeat, unpretentious Broadway bar favored by local jazz fans for its live music from 10pm.

Border Café, 244 E 79th St (☎535-4347). Friendly neighborhood hang-out good for satisfying cravings for frozen margaritas. Down to earth despite its upscale location.

Buckaroo's Bar & Rotisserie, First Ave and 74th St (☎861-8844). *The* place to mingle with thirtysomethingish Upper East Siders. Fruity drinks, including jello-shots, and well-priced food.

Ruby's River Road Café & Bar, 1754 Second Ave (☎348-2328). Home of the famous jello-shots (shots of liquor made with different colored jello), and a fun bar with a Cajun café in the back.

Rusty's, 1271 Third Ave (☎861-4518). Small bar, good for burgers and brew, that's run by an ex Mets baseball player and is packed with sporting paraphernalia.

The Saloon, 1920 Broadway (☎874-1500). Large bar/restaurant with a vast menu. Bonuses include outside seating and waiters serving on roller skates. Good for brunch.

Gay and Lesbian Bars

Crazy Nanny's, 21 Seventh Ave (☎366-6312). Yuppie-orientated, rather stylish lesbian bar.

Marie's Crisis, 59 Grove St (☎243-9323). Well-known cabaret/piano bar popular with gay men and featuring old-time singing sessions on Friday and Saturday nights. Often packed, always fun.

The Monster, 80 Grove St (☎924-3558). Large, campy bar with a drag cabaret, piano and video.

Pandora's, 70 Grove St (☎242-1408). Formerly known as the *Grove Club*, this is a legendary lesbian dive – small, tacky and overpriced but with a devoted following.

South Dakota, 405 Third Ave (☎684-8376). Male-oriented, extremely friendly, excellent food.

Spike, 120 11th Ave (☎243-9688). Highly popular leather bar.

The Tunnel Bar, 116 First Ave (☎777-9232). Caters to a younger, more activist gay male crowd.

Ty's, 114 Christopher St (☎741-9641). Relaxed but convivial gay men's bar.

Nightlife and Entertainment

Considering New York's everyday energy and diversity, its **music scene** can be disappointing. Excellent traditional and contemporary **jazz** is still concentrated in Greenwich Village, and you'll find a scattering of blues, Latin American and hip hop. But straight **rock music** is something of a write-off – at least as far as originality goes. Admission **prices** vary, but most jazz clubs have a hefty **cover** ($10–12.50) and a **minimum** charge for food and drinks; rock venues ask from nothing to around $15.

With **nightclubs**, New York is more in its element, although the city's clublife is an amorphous creature; the name DJs remain the same, but venues shift around according to the whims of fashion. Musically **house** holds sway at the moment – with the emphasis on the deep, vocal style that's always been popular in the city – but Latin Freestyle, dance hall reggae and rap all retain interest. The hippest time to club is during the week; only out-of-towners would dream of clubbing at weekends, when prices are in any case much more expensive. Nothing gets going much before midnight; there's no point turning up earlier. All venues tend to be strict about demanding **ID**.

New York Magazine carries good **what's on listings**, though the *Village Voice* is better for things downtown and anything vaguely "alternative". The Sunday *New York Times Weekly Guide* is also good, especially for mainstream events: on Friday, the paper's *Weekend* section lists "ticket availability" of the major shows. Specific Broadway listings can be found in the widely available free *Official Broadway Theater Guide*, while *The Paper* specializes in club and disco information.

The Big Performance Venues

Madison Square Garden, between Seventh and Eighth aves, W 31st–33rd St (☎465-6741). New York's principal large stage plays host to big rock acts. Not the most soulful place to see a band.

Radio City Music Hall, Sixth Ave and 50th St (☎247-4777). Not as prestigious a venue as it used to be, although the building itself still has the same sense of a great occasion.

Rock and Pop Venues

The Bottom Line, 15 W Fourth St (☎228-6300). Regular venue for established name bands. Cabaret setup, with tables crowding out any suggestion of a dance floor. $15–25.

CBGB, 315 Bowery (☎982-4052). Deliberately sleazy, and despite a relative demise in influence still a great place to see (if not actually listen to) a band. $5–10.

Dan Lynch's, 221 Second Ave (☎677-0911). Blues and r'n'b bands from 10pm. $5 at weekends.

Continental Club, 25 Third Ave (☎529-6924). Bargain beer and loud alternative rock. $3 and up.

The Grand, 76 E 13th St (☎505-0090). Long-established club and venue with a minimalist interior and live bands most nights of the week. $15+.

Irving Plaza, 17 Irving Place (☎249-8870). Excellent, intimate rock, jazz and folk showcase. $10–25.

Lone Star Café Roadhouse, 240 W 52nd St (☎245-2950). One of the city's better live venues, with all sorts of nightly acts, low-priced drinks and good food. $5–25.

Manny's Car Wash, 1558 Third Ave (☎369-2583). Smoky, Chicago-style blues bar with a small dance floor and and reasonable prices. Shows from 9.15pm. Covers range from $3 to $25.

Marquee, 547 W 21 St (☎929-3257). Supposedly a sister club to its London namesake, the *Marquee* presents a mixture of blues, rock and, especially, new British bands. Admission $10–20.

Nightingale Bar, Second Ave at 13th St (☎473-9398). Blues and new wave bands nightly.

North River Bar, 145 Hudson St (☎226-9411). Down-to-earth TriBeCa bar that books regular live – mostly rock – bands. Try the shots served in test tubes.

SOB's ("Sounds of Brazil"), 204 Varick St (☎243-4940). Lively club/restaurant, with regular jazz, salsa-tinged and World Music acts. Two performances a night. $5–20.

Tramps, 54 W 21st St (☎727-7788). Blues and new wave bands almost nightly, from 9pm (weekends additional show at midnight). $5–20.

Wetlands, 161 Hudson St (☎966-4225). A self-proclaimed "ecosaloon" that books regular live bands – particularly reggae – and circulates petitions among the punters. Very Sixties. $6–15.

Jazz Venues

The Blue Note, 131 W Third St (☎475-8592). Big names mainly and with high prices – but good music and atmosphere. $5 drinks minimum plus $15–45 cover per table, $10 if you sit at the bar.

Bradley's, 70 University Place (☎228-6440). Neighborhood bar, good for catching big names jamming in unexpected combinations. $8 minimum at the tables; $5–10 cover, free Mon & Tues.

Condon's, 117 E 15th St (☎254-0960). Big-name venue. Cover $12.50, and a two-drink minimum. Although the sound is good the view is very restricted.

Fat Tuesday's, 190 Third Ave (☎533-7902). Small and atmospheric jazz venue. $7.50–12.50.

Greene Street Café, 101 Greene St (☎925-2415). Converted warehouse, with odd acoustics but excellent bands. Best inexpensive seats are on the balcony. $5 cover + $5 minimum.

The Knitting Factory, 47 E Houston St (☎219-3055). Small, vibrant club hosting regular live jazz and avant-garde rock. Entrance $5–10.

Sweet Basil, 88 Seventh Ave (☎242-1785). Major jazz spot. $15 cover and a $6 minimum at the tables ($12 at the bar including a drink).

Village Gate, Bleecker St at Thompson (☎475-5120). One of New York's oldest jazz clubs and still one of the best. Monday salsa nights are the current highlight, well worth the $10 entrance.

Village Vanguard, 178 Seventh Ave (☎255-4037). Jazz landmark that still lays on a regular diet of big names. Admission around $10; $5 drink minimum at weekends.

Clubs and Discos

Island Club, 285 W Broadway (☎226-4598). Wed, Thurs and Sun hard-core reggae music, Fri and Sat salsa and Latin-edged sounds. Admission $5–10.

Jackie 60, *Bar Room 432*, 432 W 14th St (☎366-5680). Would-be bohemians, artists and cross-dressers cavort to beats provided by Johnny Dynell and David Morales. Poetry readings, too. $5.

Limelight, 660 Sixth Ave (☎807-7850). Long-established club now enjoying something of a renaissance after a lean period, particularly for its UK-influenced Thurs night sessions. Admission $18.

Mission, 531 E Fifth St, between aves A and B (☎473-9096). East Village club specializing in goth, punk and new wave music. Thurs–Sat, from 10pm; admission is $6 and drinks are inexpensive.

Muze, 28–30 Tenth Ave (☎691-6262). Four floors of hip hop and ragga. $8–15.

Palladium, 126 E 14th St (☎473-7171). Biggest of the New York clubs. Amazing dance floor, light and sound system in an enormous old theater. No-nonsense dancing without the posing. $15–20.

Red Zone, 440 W 54th St (☎582-2222). Popular place for heavy-duty dance music, catering to a young, mainly Latin crowd. David Morales plays on Sat.

Save the Robots, Ave C (no phone). East Village club that gets going when the others are winding down. Thurs–Sat 4am–8am. $10.

Shelter, 157 Hudson St (☎677-2582). A lethal mixture of deep house and disco classics for a mainly black crowd. Great atmosphere, with the emphasis on serious dancing. Sat is gay night.

Soul Kitchen, at the Supper club, 240 W 47th St (☎921-1940). Classic funk and soul spun by Frankie Jackson. No unaccompanied men. Men $10, women $5.

Sound Factory, 530 W 27th St (☎643-0728). Currently NYC's best clubbing experience, though not for the faint-hearted, with the deepest house and the hardest garage. No alcohol. $20.

Comedy Clubs

Caroline's Comedy Club, 1626 Broadway (☎757-4100). Glitzy room that books some of the best acts in town. Two-drink minimum. $2–17.50 cover during the week, $5 or $17.50 at weekends.

Catch a Rising Star, 1487 First Ave (☎794-1906). New talent showcase twice nightly, three times on Saturday. Two-drink minimum, cover $6–12.

Comic Strip, 1568 Second Ave (☎861-9386). Famed showcase for stand-up comics and young singers going for the big time. Nightly shows from 9pm, two shows at weekends. Cover $8–12.

Dangerfield's, 1118 First Ave (☎593-1650). New talent showcase run by the established comedian Rodney Dangerfield. Cover $12–15.

Don't Tell Mama, 343 W 46th St (☎757-0788). Lively, convivial piano bar and cabaret featuring rising stars. Shows at 8pm and 10pm. Two-drink minimum, cover $6–15.

Duplex, 61 Christopher St (☎255-5438). Village cabaret popular with gays. Two-drink minimum. Cover $12. The rowdy piano bar downstairs is also worth catching.

Improvisation, 358 W 44th St (☎765-8268). New comic and singing talent, mostly improvised. Shows at 9pm during the week; two shows on Fri, three on Sat. Cover $11.

Stand Up New York, 236 W 78th St (☎595-0850). Upper West Side club that's a forum for established acts. Nightly shows, two, sometimes three, at weekends. Two-drink minimum, cover $7–12.

Theater

New York is one of the great **theater** centers of the world. You can find just about any kind of production here, from lavish, over-the-top musicals to experimental productions in converted garages. Venues are referred to as **Broadway**, **Off Broadway**, or **Off-Off Broadway**, representing a descending order of ticket price, production polish, elegance and comfort – but don't necessarily have much to do with the address.

Broadway offerings consist primarily of large-scale musicals, comedies and dramas with big-name actors, with the occasional classic and one-person show. **Off Broadway** theaters tend to combine high production qualities with a greater willingness to experiment. Off Broadway is social and political drama, satire, ethnic plays and repertory: in short, anything that Broadway wouldn't consider a sure-fire money-spinner. **Off-Off Broadway** is the fringe – drama on a shoestring, perhaps on sensitive or uncommercial subjects. Most Broadway theaters are located just east or west of Broadway between 40th and 52nd streets; Off and Off-Off Broadway theaters are sprinkled throughout Manhattan, with a concentration in the East and West Villages, Chelsea, and several in the 40s and 50s west of the Broadway Theater District.

Nowhere are regular **tickets** inexpensive on Broadway; Off Broadway prices have risen recently too, to as much as $40 in some cases: in general, expect to pay upwards of $15 Off Broadway and $10 Off-Off. These prices can, however, be cut considerably if you can wait in line on the day of the performance at the **TKTS** booth in Times Square (Mon–Sat 3–8pm, 10am–2pm for Wed & Sat matinees), where at least one pair of tickets for every performance of every Broadway and Off Broadway show is available at half price (plus a $2.50 ticket service charge). There's another *TKTS* booth in the lobby of 2 World Trade Center. Both take cash or travellers' checks only.

Twofer discount coupons are available in either of the New York CVBs, as well as many shops, banks, restaurants and hotel lobbies. The days are long gone when they really did offer two-for-the-price-of-one, but they still entitle two people to a hefty discount. Unlike *TKTS*, twofers make it possible to book ahead, though don't expect to find coupons for the latest shows.

LINCOLN CENTER

Lincoln Center, on Broadway at 64th St, is New York's powerhouse of highbrow art. Each of its major auditoria is in active use through the year.

The New York State Theater (☎870-5770). Home for six months of the year to the *New York City Ballet* – considered by many to be the greatest dance company in existence – this more accessible venue is also where the *New York City Opera* plays David to the Met's Goliath. Seats go for less than half the Met's prices, and standing room tickets are available if a performance sells out.

The Avery Fisher Hall (☎875-5030). The permanent base of Zubin Mehta's *New York Philharmonic*, and a temporary one to visiting orchestras and soloists. Tickets $12–50.

The Metropolitan Opera House (☎362-6000). Hosts the *Metropolitan Opera Company* from September until late April, and the *American Ballet Theater* early May to July. Tickets are outrageously expensive and difficult to get hold of. Last-minute cancellations and standing-room tickets can in theory be picked up from the box office, but lines form the night before any significant occasion.

The Alice Tully Hall (☎875-5050). Smaller venue used by chamber orchestras, string quartets and instrumentalists. Prices similar to those in the Avery Fisher Hall.

If you're prepared to pay **full price** you can, of course, either go directly to the theater, or *Tickets Central*, 406 West 42nd St (daily 1–8pm; ☎279-4200). Also *Ticketron* (☎1-800/SOLD OUT) books seats for those with credit cards for a $2.50 charge.

Classical Music, Opera and Dance

New Yorkers take serious music seriously. Long queues form for anything popular, many concerts sell out, and on summer evenings a quarter of a million people may turn up in Central Park for free performances by the New York Philharmonic. Half-price **tickets**, on a day-to-day basis only, are available from the **Music & Dance Booth** in Bryant Park on Fifth Ave and 42nd St (Tues–Sun noon–3pm & 4–7pm; ☎382-2323).

Besides Lincoln Center (see box), the most important venue is **Carnegie Hall**, 154 W 57th St (☎247-7800), where the greatest names from all schools of music have performed. The acoustics remain superb, and a patching-up operation is under way to amend years of structural neglect and restore the place to its former glory.

As for **dance**, for which Lincoln Center once again serves as showcase, a number of other venues regularly host events. The **Brooklyn Academy of Music** (or BAM), 30 Lafayette St, Brooklyn (☎718/636-4100), is America's oldest performing arts academy and one of the most daring producers in New York – definitely worth crossing the river for. Five resident dance troupes at the **City Center**, 131 W 55th St (☎581-1212), include America's two undisputed choreographic giants, the *Merce Cunningham Dance Company* and the *Paul Taylor Dance Company*, as well as the *Joffrey* and *Dance Theatre of Harlem*. At the most important mid-sized dance space in Manhattan, the **Joyce Theater**, 175 Eighth Ave (☎242-0800), the *Eliot Feld Ballet* is in residence.

Film

Revival cinemas are increasingly giving way to multi-screen "plexes", but some alternatives still exist.

Angelika Film Center, Houston and Mercer streets (☎995-2000). Latest non-Hollywood offerings and European art-house movies.

Anthology Film Archives, 32–34 Second Ave (☎505-5181). Shows many films you thought you'd never have the chance to see again.

Biograph, 225 W 57th St (☎582-4582). Revival house featuring all your favorite movie classics.

Museum of the Moving Image, 35th Ave and 36th St, Queens (☎718/784-0077). Foreign and avant-garde films.

Theatre 80 St Marks, 80 St Mark's Place (☎254-7400). Classic movies. Don't miss the mini-*Grauman's Chinese Theater* (see p.769) collection of star footprints and autographs in the pavement.

Gay and Lesbian New York

Gay refugees from all over America and the world come to New York, home to a large **lesbian** or **gay** population. **Greenwich Village** is the traditional and most established gay neighborhood, but the **East Village**, too, has a growing scene, especially for younger, more politically active gays and lesbians. Other promising locales include the **East 20s and 30s**, **Chelsea**, and the **Upper West Side**. Gay and lesbian **bars** are listed on p.91. For more information get hold of the **Gayellow Pages** ($11.95), available from the bookstores below. Up-to-the-minute news can be found in *HomoXtra* (*HX*), a provocative free listings magazine, or the monthly lesbian/feminist *Sappho's Isle*.

Resources

Community Health Project, 208 W 13th St (☎675-3559). Low-priced gay clinic .

A Different Light Bookstore, 548 Hudson St (☎989-4850). Excellent selections of gay and lesbian publications. Open late throughout the week, and often hosts book-signing parties and readings.

Gay & Lesbian Visitors' Center, 135 W 20th St (☎1-800/395-2315 or 463-9030). A full travel service for visitors to NYC, including hotel and entertainment reservations, plus guided tours.

Gay Switchboard (daily 10.30am–midnight; ☎777-1800). Help and what's on information.

Lesbian and Gay Community Services Center, 208 W 13th St (☎627-1398). Umbrella group and meeting space for over eighty gay organizations, which holds regular social events.

Lesbian Switchboard (Mon–Fri 6–10pm; ☎741-2610). *The* place to phone for information on events, happenings and contacts in the New York community.

The Oscar Wilde Memorial Bookshop, 15 Christopher St (☎255-8097). The first gay bookstore in the US. Unbeatable.

Shopping

New York is the consumer capital of the world. You can **shop** for every possible taste, creed or perversity, in any combination and at any time of day or night – and, in the markets of Greenwich Village for example, it can be extraordinarily cheap as well as phenomenally expensive. **Midtown Manhattan** is mainstream territory, with its department stores, big-name clothes designers and branches of the larger chains; **downtown** plays host to a wide variety of more offbeat stores. **Uptown**, the Upper East Side is uncompromisingly upmarket, while the funkier **Upper West Side** has an array of off-the-wall stores to compare with anything SoHo or the Village can offer.

Overseas visitors looking for bargain rates on **electrical goods** should head for the discount stores on Seventh Avenue, a little north of Times Square in the 50s; for **cameras**, try midtown from 30th and 50th streets between Park and Seventh avenues.

Department Stores

Bloomingdale's, 1000 Third Ave (☎355-5900). Perhaps Manhattan's most famous department store, packed with designer clothiers, perfume concessions and the like.

Macy's, Broadway at 34th St (☎695-4400). The largest department store in the world; two buildings, two million square feet of floor space, ten floors, and around $5m gross turnover every day.

Saks Fifth Avenue, 611 Fifth Ave (☎753-4000). Although *Saks* remains virtually synonymous with style, it has also updated itself to carry the merchandise of all the big designers.

Books

Brentano's, 597 Fifth Ave (☎826-2450). Housed in the fine old *Scribner's* bookstore, and continuing that shop's tradition of good service and stock in elegant surroundings.

Complete Traveller, 199 Madison Ave (☎679-4339). Manhattan's premier travel bookshop, excellently stocked, secondhand and new.

Endicott Booksellers, 450 Columbus Ave (☎787-6300). Venerable store with a wonderful range.

Gotham Book Mart, 41 W 47th St (☎719-4448). Literary bookstore, good on drama and theater.

Rizzoli, 31 W 57th St (☎759-2424); 200 Vesey St (☎385-1400); and 454a W Broadway (☎674-1616). Manhattan branches of Italian store, with a good selection of foreign newspapers and magazines.

Strand Bookstore, 828 Broadway (☎473-1452). Gigantic place, one of the few surviving secondhand stores in an area that used to be full of them. Also offers half-price review copies.

Records

Dayton's, 799 Broadway (☎254-5084). Rare records, old review copies, deleted soundtracks.

Footlight Records, 113 E 12th St (☎533-1572). *The* place for show music of all kinds.

The Golden Disc, 239 Bleecker St (☎255-7899). Jazz, rock oldies, blues and gospel.

House of Oldies, 35 Carmine St (☎243-0500). What the name says – oldies but goldies of all kinds.

Second Coming, 235 Sullivan St (☎228-1313). Heavy metal and hard-core punk.

Sounds, 16 St Mark's Place (☎677-2727). New and used records.

Vinyl Mania, 41 Carmine St (☎463-1720). Where DJs go for the newest, rarest releases.

Out from the City: Long Island

The state of New York extends five hundred miles west of Manhattan, to Niagara Falls on the Canadian border – a vast area covered in Chapter Two of this book. However, **Long Island**, which unfurls east of the city for 125 miles of lush farmland and broad sandy beaches, is best seen as an excursion of perhaps a few days from the metropolis. Its western end includes the urban boroughs of Brooklyn and Queens, but further east, the settlements begin to thin out and the countryside can get surprisingly remote. The **north** and **south shores** differ greatly – the former more immediately beautiful, its cliffs topped with luxurious mansions and estates, while the South Shore is fringed by almost continuous sand, interspersed with holiday resorts such as **Jones Beach** and gay-oriented **Fire Island**. At its far end Long Island splits in two, the **North Fork** retaining a marked rural aspect while the **South Fork**, much of which is known as **The Hamptons**, has long been an enclave of New York's richest and finest.

The quickest way to reach Long Island is via the reliable if rather grubby **Long Island Railroad** from Penn Station (☎718/454-LIRR), though numerous **bus services** (operated by major companies and the **Hampton Jitney**, ☎212/895-9336) cover most destinations. **Parking permits** for Long Island's **beaches** are issued only to local residents; on the whole it works out less expensive to head down to the beach on foot.

The **area code** for Long Island is ☎516.

The South Shore and Fire Island

Long Island's **SOUTH SHORE** merges gently with the wild Atlantic, shallow, open and slicked with slithers of creamy sand and luscious duney beaches such as **Long Beach** and **Jones Beach**. These get less crowded the further east you go; once you get as far as **Gilgo** or **Oak Beach**, or cross the water to **Robert Moses State Park** on the western tip of Fire Island, you can find whatever solitude you want. **Ocean Parkway** leads along the narrow offshore strand from Jones Beach to **Captree**, a good base for whale-watching expeditions (☎785-1600), before crossing back to **Bay Shore**, a dull town which serves as a **ferry** terminal for Fire Island ($4). This way you bypass the sprawling mess of **Amityville**, famous for its "horror" of a decade or so ago. The house on the hill, from which a family were driven by some mysterious supernatural force, still stands.

Fire Island

FIRE ISLAND, a slim spit of land parallel to the South Shore, is in many ways a microcosm of New York City. On summer weekends half of Manhattan seems to be holed up in its tiny settlements. It's primarily a **gay** resort: young gays make for **Cherry Grove**; older and wealthier ones for **Fire Island Pines**; **Kismet** is the hang-out of older Jews, **Ocean Bay Park** yuppie and jappie; while **Point O Woods** is the most exclusive of the lot. The **season** is as rigidly defined as the people. Memorial Day onwards Fire Island hums with activity and is swamped with crowds, though it's always possible to escape for gorgeous wild walks along the sand; after Labor Day, the weather may still be very warm, but the throngs diminish dramatically.

Most ferries dock at trendy **Ocean Beach**, where trippers pile up groceries on trolleys (cars are forbidden) and set off for their vacation pads. All **accommodation** should be booked in advance; options include *Jerry's*, 620 Bay Walk, Ocean Beach (☎583-8870; ③), which doubles its rates at weekends, and *Flynn's*, in nearby Ocean Bay Park (☎583-8000; ④), which has doubles from $60. *Giovanni's*, opposite the ferry terminal, is the best and most convivial place to **eat** for under $5; on weekends, *Flynn's*, and *Leo's* on Bay Walk, are good for riotous boozing and eating.

The North Shore and North Fork

Along the rugged **NORTH SHORE**, Long Island drops to the sea in a series of bluffs, coves and wooded headlands. The expressway beyond Queens leads straight onto the **Gold Coast**, where **Great Neck** was F Scott Fitzgerald's *West Egg* in *The Great Gatsby*, home of Gatsby himself. Some of this real estate is so expensive that no one can afford to live here. The motley European-style buildings, at **Sands Point**, on the sharp tip of the next peninsula, were once owned by the Guggenheims; they now house a museum (May–Oct Sat–Wed 10am–5pm; $1). The 209 acres of unkempt parkland offer great views over what Fitzgerald called "the most domesticated body of salt water in the Western hemisphere, the great barnyard of Long Island Sound".

Sagamore Hill, on the coast road six miles beyond Glen Cove, is the heavily touristed former country retreat where **Teddy Roosevelt** lived for thirty-odd years (May–Oct daily 9.30am–5pm, Nov–April 9.30am–4.30pm; $1). Its 23 rooms are adorned everywhere by the great man's trophies, sprouting horns from walls or grinning toothily up from the firesides. The **Old Orchard Museum** near the parking lot recounts Teddy's political and personal life, but the real reason to come is to stroll in the gorgeous grounds, where springy lawns drop to Oyster Bay and the sea.

Nearby **Cold Spring Harbor** grew up as a whaling port, and retains some of its looks. A fully equipped whaleboat and a 400-piece assembly of scrimshaw work help its **Whaling Museum** (Tues–Sun 11am–5pm) to recapture that era. The **Vanderbilt Mansion** just outside Centerport (April–Oct Tues–Sat 10am–4pm, Sun noon–5pm; Nov–March Tues–Sun noon–4pm; $1) displays the dubious taste typical of Vanderbilt residences. In the style of a Baroque Spanish palace, it's heavily ornate both outside and in, with marble-encased galleries, swirling staircases and gaudy fireplaces.

On the less touristed **North Fork** – once an independent colony – the scenery has something of the feel of New England at its wildest. In **Greenport**, its most picturesque town, a clutter of narrow streets and alleys lead down to a harbor pierced by the masts of visiting yachts. Plentiful **accommodation** includes the *Bartlett House*, 503 Front St (☎477-0371; ④). Regular 15-minute **ferries** connect with Shelter Island and the South Fork; others cross to New London, Connecticut, described on p.183 (summer, 6 daily, last leaves 2pm; 90-min trip; foot passengers $8 one-way, $12 day-return).

The South Fork

The US holds few wealthier quarters than the small towns of Long Island's **SOUTH FORK**, where huge palaces lurk in the trees or stand boldly on the flats behind the dunes. Nowhere is consumption as deliberately conspicuous as in **The Hamptons** – among the oldest communities in the state, settled by restless New Englanders in the mid-1650s, but relatively isolated until the rich began to turn up in their motor cars.

Southampton

Long association with the smart set has left **SOUTHAMPTON** unashamedly twee. Its streets are lined with galleries and clothes and jewellery stores, but the nearby beaches are superb. The **visitor center** at 76 Main St (daily 9am–5pm) has lists of B&Bs, such as the *Hill Guest House*, 535 Hill St (May–Oct; ☎283-9889; ④). *Joe's*, 23 Hill St, does pizzas and pasta at low prices, and *Barrister's* on Main St has marvellous soft-shell crabs.

Sag Harbor

Historic **SAG HARBOR**, once a harbor second only to that of New York, was designated first Port of Entry to the New Country by George Washington. The **Whaling Museum** on Main St (mid-May–Sept, Mon–Sat 10am–5pm, Sun 1–5pm) commemorates the town's brief whaling days with guns and scrimshaw. Nearby the **Whaler's Presbyterian Church** is crenellated with jutting rows of whale blubber spades, and beautifully reliefed memorials in **Oakland Cemetery** commemorate young whalers.

In summer, the windmill where John Steinbeck once lived serves as a **visitor center**. Only the *Baron's Cove Inn* (☎725-2100; winter ③, summer ⑥) has **rooms**, but the elegantly curving Main Street abounds in reasonably priced restaurants.

Montauk

Blustery, wind-battered **MONTAUK**, beyond Amagansett on the furthest tip of Long Island, never quite made it as a resort; plans to develop it were shattered by the Wall Street Crash of 1929. This unattractive town now provides access to the rocky wilds of **Montauk Point**, whose rare beauty figures in all the tourist brochures. A **lighthouse** forms an almost symbolic finale to this stretch of the American coast.

Motels in the town center offer fairly priced rooms; rates at the *Oceanside Beach Resort* (☎668-9825; ②–⑤), on the junction of the Old Montauk Hwy and Main St, vary seasonally. *The Lobster Roll* on the Highway serves excellent fresh fish and seafood.

CHAPTER TWO

THE MID-ATLANTIC

The three Mid-Atlantic states – **NEW YORK, PENNSYLVANIA** and **NEW JERSEY** – stand at the heart of the most populated and industrialized corner of the US. Although dominated in the popular imagination by the grey smokestacks of New Jersey, and the coal fields and steel factories of Pennsylvania, as they stretch far from the coast to the north and west these states also encompass lakes, forests and rolling green countryside, and, in places, expanses of virtual wilderness.

European settlement was characterized by considerable shifts and turns: the **Dutch**, who arrived in the 1620s, were methodically squeezed out by the **English**, who in turn fought off the **French** challenge to secure control of the region by the mid-eighteenth century. The Native American population, including the **Iroquois Confederacy** and Lenni Lenape, had sided with the French against the English, and were soon confined to reservations or pushed north into Canada. At first the economy depended on the fur trade, though by the 1730s English **Quakers**, along with **Amish** and **Mennonites** from Germany and a few Presbyterian Irish, had made farming a significant force, their holdings extending to the western limits of Pennsylvania and New York.

All three states were important during the **Revolution**: over half the battles were fought here, including major American victories at **Trenton** and **Princeton** in New Jersey. Upstate New York was geographically crucial, as the British forces knew that control of the Hudson River would effectively divide New England from the other colonies, and the long winter spent at **Valley Forge** outside Philadelphia turned the rag-tag Continental Army into a well-organized force.

After the Revolution industry became the region's prime economic force, with **mill towns** springing up along the numerous rivers. By the mid-1850s the large **coal fields** of northeast Pennsylvania were powering the smoky steel mills of Pittsburgh, and the discovery of high-grade **crude oil** in 1859 marked the beginning of the automobile age. Though still significant, especially around New York City, heavy industry has now by and large been replaced by tourism as the economic engine.

Although many travellers to the East Coast may not consider venturing much further than New York City itself – covered in Chapter One of this book, together with Long Island – the region is much more than just an overspill of the Big Apple, whatever chauvinistic city-dwellers might say. Each state has its own personality. **Upstate New York** is for outdoor-lovers: the wooded **Catskill Mountains** line the Hudson River (which Henry James claimed was "in the geography of the ideal"), the imposing **Adirondack Mountains** spread over a quarter of the state, and the **Finger Lakes** region offers a pastoral alternative to the industrial Erie Canal cities along I-90. In the

---

ACCOMMODATION PRICE CODES

All accommodation prices in this book have been coded using the symbols below. Note that prices are for the least expensive double rooms in each establishment. For a full explanation see p.35 in *Basics*.

①	up to $30	④	$60–80	⑦	$130–180
②	$30–45	⑤	$80–100	⑧	$180+
③	$45–60	⑥	$100–130		

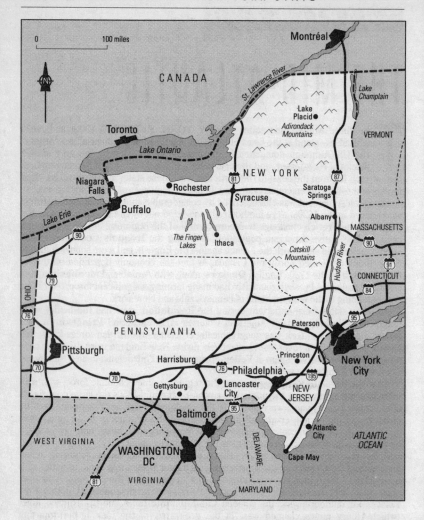

northwest corner of the state, on the Canadian border, are the awesome **Niagara Falls**. **Pennsylvania** is best known for the fertile "**Pennsylvania Dutch**" country and the two great cities of **Philadelphia** and **Pittsburgh**. **New Jersey**, often pictured as one great industrial carbuncle, offers shameless tourist pleasures along the shore: day-trippers in their millions flock to the Boardwalk and gambling casinos of **Atlantic City**.

The entire region is well covered by **public transportation**, with New York's JFK and New Jersey's Newark airports acting as important international gateways, and New York's La Guardia Airport serving domestic flights. *Amtrak* **trains** run Northeast Corridor routes north–south through New York, New Jersey and Pennsylvania, while the *New Jersey Transit* rail and bus network serves all of New Jersey, extending from Atlantic City west to Philadelphia and north to Manhattan. *Greyhound* **buses** follow the major interstates, with a few subsidiary lines running to more out-of-the-way places.

NEW YORK STATE

However much the tourist authorities try to encourage visitors, the large and rambling state of **NEW YORK** remains inevitably in the shadow of America's most celebrated city. The words "New York" bring to mind soaring skyscrapers and congested streets, not the 50,000 square miles of rolling dairy farmland, colonial villages, workaday towns, lakes, waterfalls, and towering mountains that spread north and west from New York City and constitute **upstate New York**. Their strongest appeal is to the outdoor fanatic. Just an hour's drive north of Manhattan, the valley of the **Hudson River**, with the moody **Catskill Mountains** rising stealthily from the west bank, offers a brief respite from the intensity of the city. Much wilder and more rugged are the peaks of the vast **Adirondack Mountains** further north – far beyond the scope of a casual excursion, but holding some of the country's most enticing scenery. To the west, the central portion of the state is occupied by the slender **Finger Lakes** and endless miles of dairy farms and vineyards. Few of the cities hold much of interest, but the smaller towns like Ivy League **Ithaca** can be quite charming for a day or two, while the venerable spa town of **Saratoga Springs** attracts thousands of punters during the August racing season.

In the seventeenth and eighteenth centuries, as nation-molding political and military battles were taking place, semi-feudal **Dutch land-owning dynasties** such as the Van Rensselaers held sway upstate. Their control over tens of thousands of tenant farmers was barely affected by the transference of colonial power from Holland to Britain, or even by American independence. Only with the completion of the **Erie Canal** in 1825, linking New York City with the Great Lakes, did the interior start to open up; improved opportunities for trade enabled canal-side cities like **Rochester**, **Syracuse** and especially **Buffalo** to undergo massive expansion. On the other hand, this industrial and agricultural growth in the hinterland served, inevitably, to increase the financial standing of the Wall Street capitalists, and the story of the past century and a half has been one of consistent political and economic domination of New York City over New York State.

Getting Around New York State

Greyhound and *Adirondack Trailways* **buses** run to all the major towns, while *Amtrak* operates an inconvenient **train** service along a beautiful route through the Hudson Valley to the state capital, Albany; from there trains continue north to Montreal via the Adirondacks, and west along the Erie Canal to Buffalo and Niagara Falls. Many bus and train **stations** are several miles out from the town centers; the necessary walking can be unpleasant in the muggy heat of summer (not to mention the freezing winter).

Car rental in and around New York City is expensive, and restricted to drivers over 25 years of age; lower rates can be found by taking public transportation away from the metropolitan area. Be aware as well that the New York State Thruway (I-95 and I-87) is a **toll road**, which adds up to around $15 end-to-end. **Flying**, at as little as $150 round-trip New York to Buffalo, is not that expensive, but by the time you get out to JFK or La Guardia you might just as well be on your way upstate. **Cycling** is best enjoyed as a means of exploring small areas such as the Finger Lakes or Catskills, and if you have a lot of time you may want to consider hiring a **canal boat** and cruising the Erie or Champlain canals; contact the state tourist office (see p.21) for details on either of these options, and for general information on visiting New York.

The Hudson Valley and the Catskills

To the average commuter, the **Hudson River** is just an inconvenient barrier en route to New Jersey. However, you only need to travel a few miles north of Manhattan before the valley takes on a Rhine-like charm, with prodigious historic homes, such as those

> The **area code** for the lower Hudson Valley is ☎914.

of the Roosevelt, Vanderbilt and van Cortland families, rising from its steep and thickly wooded banks. A little further on come the forests of the **Catskill Mountains**, whose brilliant fall colors rival anything to be seen in New England. Few of the valley towns, including the large but lackluster state capital of **Albany**, hold much to attract the visitor, though it's worth calling in – if just for old times' sake – at the New Agey village of **Woodstock**, nestled among the Catskills.

The Lower Hudson Valley

A mere 25 miles north of central New York City, leafy **TARRYTOWN** was the original setting for Washington Irving's tales of *Rip Van Winkle* and *The Legend of Sleepy Hollow*. In 1835 the author rebuilt a farm cottage just south of town on West Sunnyside Lane (off US-9) which he named **Sunnyside**: "a little old-fashioned stone mansion, all made up of gable ends, and as full of angles and corners as an old cocked hat". Tours squeeze around its cozy rooms, enjoyable even if you've never read a word of Irving (April–Dec, Wed–Mon 10am–5pm; March, Sat & Sun 10am–5pm; $5). It's also worth looking around the neighboring village of **LYNDHURST**, where the spikily crenellated Lyndhurst Castle is as dapper a piece of nineteenth-century Gothic revivalism as you'll find (May–Oct, Tues–Sun 10am–5pm; Nov, Jan & March, Sat & Sun 10am–5pm; $5).

About ten miles north of Tarrytown along US-9, the town of **OSSINING** holds two impressive mid-Victorian creations: one is a huge bridge carrying the **Old Croton Aqueduct**, New York City's first water supply; the other, just south of town, is **Sing Sing Prison,** which for over 150 years has been the place where New York City criminals get sent "up the river".

The West Bank and Catskill Mountains

Rising above the west bank of the Hudson River, the magnificent crests of the **Catskills**, cloaked with maple and beech which turn orange, ocher and gold each fall, have a rich and absorbing beauty. This dislocated branch of the Appalachians is inspiring country, filled with amenities – campgrounds, hiking, floating, fishing and, especially, skiing. To enjoy it to the full, venture onto the trails; the mountains are so tightly packed that good roadside overlooks are rare.

West Point

The first real place of interest on the west bank of the Hudson is the United States Military Academy at **WEST POINT**, which Congress established in 1802 after it realized that the ragged troops who had won the Revolutionary War had been knocked into shape almost exclusively by European officers. Homegrown skills had to be cultivated in case foreign help wasn't so readily forthcoming again. Since then, West Point has provided the military training for US Army generals Grant, Lee, MacArthur, Eisenhower, Patton and Schwarzkopf, to name but a famous few. Today, four-thousand-odd candidates on a tough four-year course fill the smart showpiece campus, which protectively overlooks the Hudson from a wide, strategic bluff. The free **West Point Museum** (daily 10.30am–4.15pm) shows trophies of war including a pistol that belonged to Hitler and, disturbingly, the pin from the Nagasaki bomb. There may be little mention of Vietnam, but no doubt a full Desert Storm exhibit will be unveiled shortly, which should delight the crowds drawn by the stirring patriotism embodied in the Parade Ground drilling. The **visitor center** (daily; 8.30am–4.15pm; ☎938-2638) can provide a schedule of parades, at their most frequent in spring and fall.

Kingston

Of the various towns on the fringes of the mountains, **KINGSTON** is one of the most pleasant and convenient places to stop. An agreeable mix of well-preserved old houses and neat little business premises line **Green** and **Crown** streets at the center of town, much of which dates from the late eighteenth century, when Kingston played a vital political and military role in the fight for American independence.

It's very easy to reach – it's just off I-87, and *Adirondack Trailways* buses heading north from New York City stop ten minutes' walk from the center – and if you want to **stay** the large *Holiday Inn*, 503 Washington Ave (☎338-0400; ④), is probably the best option, complete with sauna, pool and games area, though its rates rise on summer weekends; the *Super 8 Motel*, 487 Washington Ave (☎333-3078; ③), costs a little less. The *Market Basket Deli*, 308 Wall St (☎338-2755), serves fresh breads and bagels, and *Dallas Hot Wieners*, 51 North St, has cheap burgers. Further **food and drink** options can be found across the river in Rhinebeck (see p.104).

Woodstock

West from Kingston, Hwy-28 meanders into the Catskills, looping past the lovely Ashokan Reservoir where Hwy-375 branches off to **WOODSTOCK**. The village, carved out of the lush deciduous woodlands and cut by fast-rushing creeks, was not actually the venue of the famed **psychedelic picnic** of August 1969 – that was some sixty miles southwest in Bethel, where a monument at Herd and West Shore roads marks the site on Max Yasgur's farm. However, Woodstock has enjoyed a bohemian reputation since the foundation in 1902 of the Byrdcliffe arts colony, and during the 1960s, it was a favorite stomping ground for the likes of Dylan, Hendrix and Van Morrison. It still bears signs of its **hippie** past – shops sell tie-dyed T-shirts and crystals, and there's even the occasional commune – but in the cafés you're more likely to bump into a successful Manhattanite who owns a second home here than a long-haired beatnik (not that those two categories are necessarily mutually exclusive).

Woodstock's best **accommodation** is the *Twin Gables Guest House* (☎679-9479; ②) at 77 Tinker St, in the center of the village. If this is full, as is often the case, the higher rates at *Pinecrest Lodge* on Country Club Lane get a cabin and breakfast (☎679-2814; ④). *Duey's*, 50 Mill Hill Rd (☎679-9593), and *Misty's* on the village green can provide filling, inexpensive **meals**. To savor a little nostalgia, sample the New Age atmosphere at the *Tinker Street Café*, 59 Tinker St, or the *Joyous Lake* on Mill Hill Rd (☎679-9300); both feature live bands at the weekend. Several **buses** each day take two-and-a-half hours to reach Woodstock from New York City's Port Authority Bus Terminal (*Adirondack Trailways*; ☎212/947-5300). Sturdy **bikes** can be rented from *Overlook Mountain Bikes*, 93 Tinker St (☎679-2122).

For more **information** tune into the local radio station, WDST (100.1 FM), pick up the *Woodstock Times* or phone the Chamber of Commerce (☎679-6234).

On through Catskill Park

As you continue along Hwy-28, the picturesque hamlet of **PHOENICIA**, in a hollow to the right of the road, is an ideal place to rent mountain bikes and rafts. You can also catch the circular **Catskill Mountain Railroad** (summer & fall; ☎688-7400) through scenic Esopus Creek. A few miles further west, Hwy-49A affords a good vista of the rambling Catskills from the parking lot of the Belleayre ski resort. The *AYH Hostel*, Bonnieview Ave, Pine Hill (☎254-4200), provides a bed for $10 ($12 in winter).

The return route to I-90 along Hwy-23A includes a breathtaking view of the dramatic **gorge** between the villages of Hunter and Catskill, along with the area's premier **ski runs** on Hunter Mountain. This is not a cheap place to be during the main November to Easter skiing season; daily lift passes cost over $30 and the least expensive rooms start at $75. The resort's chairlifts also run during the summer ($5; ☎518/263-4223).

The East Bank

HYDE PARK, set on a peaceful plateau on the east bank of the Hudson twenty miles south of Kingston, is not an especially attractive town, but is worth a stop for the homes of **Franklin D** and **Eleanor Roosevelt**. Well signposted off US-9, the house where the "New Deal" president was born and spent much of his adult life now holds a good **museum** (daily 9am–5pm; $4) with extensive photos and artefacts, including the specially adapted car he drove after being struck down by polio in 1921, and the letter from Einstein that led to the development of the atomic bomb.

FDR lies buried in the rose garden, beside his wife (and distant cousin) Eleanor, a gifted and influential Democratic politician without whose help his career might well not have survived his long bouts of illness. She broke away from the tradition that the president's wife should merely serve as a hostess at society functions, by playing a prominent role in the New Deal programmes, touring the country and reporting to FDR on the living conditions of the poor. After FDR's death in 1945 she moved to the nearby cottage, **Val-Kill**, from where she carried on her work as chair of the United Nations Human Rights Commission, receiving dignitaries such as Tito, Nehru, Khrushchev and John F Kennedy until her death in 1962. Shuttle buses leave the FDR house every half-hour for free **tours** (April–Oct daily 9am–5pm).

Admission to the Roosevelt homes also gets you into the Beaux Arts **Vanderbilt Mansion**. A three-mile-long clifftop **path** along the Hudson from the Roosevelt winds up at this virtual palace – believe it or not, the smallest of the family's residences – which was built for Frederick, a grandson of railroad baron Cornelius. The furnishings are quite garish, but the parklike grounds are very pretty (April–Oct, daily 9am–5pm; Nov–March, Thurs–Mon 9am–5pm).

Apart from these historic homes Hyde Park has one huge tourist draw, the excellent public dining rooms of the **Culinary Institute of America**, the largest and most prestigious cooking school in the country. Housed in a huge Gothic-style red-brick castle along US-9, south of Hyde Park, the various restaurants – ranging from the family-oriented *Coppola's* to the four-star *American Bounty* and *Escoffier* rooms – have trained some of America's best chefs; for reservations, phone (☎471-6608).

Beyond Hyde Park US-9 cuts slightly inland from the Hudson, passing through a number of sleepy towns on its way north toward Albany. **RHINEBECK**, six miles north of Hyde Park, is the first and most worthwhile of these, holding a number of good restaurants as well as America's oldest hotel. The white colonial *Beekman Arms*, in the center of town at Mill and Market, has been hosting and feeding travellers in its warm wood-panelled dining room since 1766 (☎876-7077; ④). Other good places to eat include the all-American *Foster's Coachhouse Tavern,* half a block up Mill St, and the pricier but very authentic French *Le Petit Bistro* at 8 E Market St (☎876-7400). Rhinebeck is also home to the New Agey **Omega Institute**, which runs a wide range of self-improvement workshops at a large campus east of town; find out more at their very pleasant bookshop, 22 E Market St (☎876-5701).

The other good stop on the East Bank of the Hudson is **Olana**, the hilltop home of noted landscape artist **Frederick Church**. High above a bend in the river, across the bridge from the town of Catskill, the quirky but very attractive house rises in an odd blend of Persian and Moorish motifs; obligatory (and very popular) guided **tours** (April–Aug Wed–Sat 10am–4pm, Sept & Oct Wed–Sun noon–4pm; $3) take in the bric-a-brac clogged rooms as well as a number of his picturesque paintings.

Albany

Founded by Dutch fur trappers in the early seventeenth century, **ALBANY** made its money by controlling trade along the Erie Canal, and its reputation by being capital of

The **area code** for Albany and the Adirondacks is ☎518.

the state. It's not an unpleasant town, just rather boring, with its contemporary character almost exclusively shaped by political and bureaucratic affairs.

A good place to start a tour is the **Quackenbush House**, the city's oldest building, built along the river in 1736 and now serving as part of the **Albany Urban Culture Park**. The modern **visitor center** next door at Broadway and Clinton (daily 10am–4pm; ☎434-5132) has free maps and occasional guided **tours** of the downtown area, as well as engaging displays tracing Albany's history, with a special emphasis on the impact of the Erie Canal. It also has maps describing driving tours of the surrounding area, taking in a still-functioning flight of **locks** from the original canal along with the impressive industrial legacy of **Troy**, across the Hudson.

Uphill from the waterfront, piercing like an arrowhead into downtown Albany, Nelson A Rockefeller's **Empire State Plaza** went up in the Sixties and Seventies, replacing 98 acres of nineteenth-century buildings (and displacing hundreds of Albanian families) with a complex that includes a subterranean retail arcade, lined with impressive modern art. The view from the **Corning Tower** observation deck (daily 9am–4pm; free) seems designed to make you feel like the conqueror of an invaded territory, looking out beyond the twisting Hudson to the Adirondack foothills, the Catskills and the Massachusetts Berkshires. It also peers down on the neighboring Performing Arts Center – known locally as "The Egg" – which adds the only curves to the Plaza's harsh angularity.

The **New York State Museum** (daily 10am–5pm; free) reclines one level down at the south end of the plaza, revealing everything you could want to know about New York State in imaginative if static tableaux. The excellent section on New York City is better than anything in Manhattan itself, with histories of immigration and skyscraper construction, storefronts and trolley cars along with the original set of *Sesame Street*.

The most engaging part of Albany is the few blocks west of the plaza, stretching between Washington and Madison avenues to the open green spaces of **Washington Park**, laid out by Frederick Law Olmsted. The **Albany Institute of History and Art**, 125 Washington Ave, has a good range of Hudson River School paintings, and the neighborhood is full of the same sort of nineteenth-century brick-built homes Rockefeller had pulled down.

Practicalities

Arrive by *Greyhound* (☎434-0121) or *Trailways* (☎436-9651) and it's a short hilly walk to the heart of downtown; come in by *Amtrak* (☎465-9971) and you face a two-mile bus ride (☎482-8822) across the river. If you intend to stay the night, bear in mind that downtown lodging is not particularly cheap. Suburban chain motels start at $40; the *Econolodge*, 300 Broadway (☎434-4111; ④), is more central. A small **youth hostel** offers budget rates at 46 Elm St (☎434-4963; ①).

The one exceptionally nice place to stay is the *Mansion Hill Inn*, 115 Philip St (☎465-2038 or ☎1-800/477-8171; ⑤), a B&B in a restored home just down the hill from Governor Cuomo's mansion; it's also a fine restaurant. Other good **places to eat** include *Jack's Oyster House*, 42 State St (☎465-8854), and the Indonesian *Yono's*, 289 Hamilton Ave (☎436-7747). **Lark Street**, a few blocks west of the plaza, has a number of low-priced places like *Sonny's Fish Fry*, at no 254, and *El Loco*, on the corner of Lark and Madison.

The college town of **Troy**, across the river, has a number of lively spots, but Albany itself gets pretty quiet after dark; if there's nothing on at The Egg, check out the *Half Moon Café*, 154 Madison Ave (☎436-0329), which hosts a good range of mostly acoustic folk, jazz and bluegrass.

North through the Adirondacks

Mountaineers, skiers and dedicated hikers form the majority of visitors to the vast northern region between Albany and the Canadian border. Outdoor pursuits are certainly the main attractions in the rugged wilderness of the **Adirondack Mountains**, though a few small resorts, especially the former Winter Olympic venue of **Lake Placid**, have a bit of life to offer, and the elegant spa town of **Saratoga Springs** nestles invitingly in the delicate countryside of the southern foothills.

Saratoga Springs

For well over a century, **SARATOGA SPRINGS**, just 42 miles north of Albany on I-87, was very much the place to be seen for the northeast's richest and most glittering names. At first, the town's curative waters were the main attraction; then John Morrisey, an Irish boxer, transformed things by opening a **racecourse** and **casino** during the 1860s. The Morgans, Vanderbilts and Whitneys all had houses in the town at one time, and Diamond Jim Brady was one of the most ostentatious visitors.

Saratoga Springs retains the feel of an exclusive vintage resort during the August racing season, but for the rest of the summer it is accessible, affordable and fun. **Broadway**, the main axis, takes in just about every aspect of the modern town from the ugly motel signs to the Gothic and Renaissance residential palaces on the northern tip of downtown; most of the town's many good bars are here or in the few blocks just east.

The carefully cultivated **Congress Park**, off South Broadway, laid out for the *curistes*, remains a shady retreat from the bustle of the town center. Three of the original mineral springs still flow up to the surface here, funnelled out into drinking fountains (it's tepid and salty, but some people swear by it). Also here is the original **casino**, which when built formed part of a whole city block; it now houses a small historical **museum** (July & Aug daily 9.30am–4.30pm, otherwise Wed–Sun 1–4pm; $2).

The **racetrack** (post time 1pm; $5; ☎641-4700) still functions in the same old ultraformal manner, enforcing strict dress codes for all meetings, but there's no such pretension at the **harness track** on nearby Crescent Ave (evening meetings several times a week, May–Nov; $2). If you can't get to either, visit the array of paintings, trophies and audio-visual displays at the **National Museum of Racing and Thoroughbred Hall of Fame** on Union Ave at Ludlow St (Mon–Sat 10am–4.30pm, Sun noon–4.30pm; $3).

On the southern edge of town, green **Saratoga State Park** presents opportunities to swim in great old Victorian pools, picnic, hike or even bathe in one of two bathhouses (around $12; ☎584-2011). The **Saratoga Performing Arts Center** here (☎587-3330) was built during the Sixties in a successful attempt to revive the town's fortunes. As well as being home to the New York City Opera in June, the New York City Ballet in July and the Philadelphia Orchestra in August, it hosts the "Newport Jazz Festival – Saratoga" in late June and promotes rock concerts by big-name stars.

Practicalities

Central Saratoga Springs is easily explored on foot. **Accommodation** is only a problem during August's race meeting, when prices can more than double. Central budget motels include the *Spa Motel*, 73 Ballston Ave (☎587-5280; ③) and the *Turf and Spa*, 140 Broadway (☎584-2550 or ☎1-800/972-1779; ③). The lavishly restored landmark *Adelphi Hotel*, 365 Broadway (☎587-4688; ④) and the *Sheraton*, a little further north at 534 Broadway (☎584-4000; ⑤), are nicer and more characterful. The **Chamber of Commerce**, 494 Broadway (☎584-3255), has full lists, with prices.

Eating is also easy. One longtime favorite is the soul food at *Hattie's Chicken Shack*, 45 Phila St (☎584-4790), where lunches cost under $5 and huge dinners are $10; another good bet is *Wheat Fields*, 440 Broadway (☎587-0534), with good salads and pastas on an outdoor patio. There's usually good Irish music at the *Parting Glass Pub*, 40 Lake Ave (☎583-1916). *Nine Maple Avenue*, logically enough at 9 Maple Ave (☎583-2582), offers live jazz and blues until 1am, and the folksy *Caffe Lena*, 47 Phila St (Thurs–Sun only; ☎583-0022) – which was where Don McLean first inflicted *American Pie* on the world – still pulls in the crowds.

The Adirondacks

Covering a larger area than Connecticut and Rhode Island combined, the **Adirondacks** have until recent decades been the almost exclusive preserve of loggers, fur-trappers and a few select New York millionaires who really knew how to get away from it all (E L Doctorow's novels *Loon Lake* and *Billy Bathgate* both describe the bucolic retreats of Manhattan mobsters). For sheer grandeur, the region is hard to beat. Forty-three peaks stretch to over 4000 feet; in summer the purple-green mountains span far into the distance in shaggy tiers, in fall the trees form a woozy russet-red kaleidoscope.

Though *Trailways* buses serve the area, you'll find it hard going without a **car**. General information can be had from the state tourist office (see p.21, or phone ☎1-800/487-6867), or the Welcome Center along I-87 south of Lake George (☎761-6366 or ☎1-800/365-1050). The *Adirondack Mountain Club* (*ADK*), PO Box 3055, Lake George 12845 (☎668-4447), or the Adirondack Park **visitor center** in Paul Smiths, north of Saranac Lake (☎327-3000), can provide details on hiking and camping.

Lake George

Though the undulating scenery around **LAKE GEORGE**, 25 miles up I-87 from Saratoga Springs, is pleasant, the "village" itself is overrun with cheap souvenir shops catering to the thousands of tourists who come here in search of a quick taste of the Adirondacks. The numerous sightseeing cruises, hot-air balloon rides and other diversions now on offer, here and in neighboring Glens Falls, obscure the natural splendor, as well as the region's considerable history. James Fenimore Cooper's *Last of the Mohicans* was based upon the Battle of **Fort William Henry** which was fought here between the British and the French in 1757, but the replica fort (daily 9am–10pm in summer, otherwise 10am–5pm; $7), along the lakeshore on Canada Street in the center of town, does little to evoke the era when this was the distant frontier.

Blue Mountain Lake

While Lake George and the eastern fringes of the Adirondacks in general hold little to compete with the interior, an hour's drive northwest along Hwy-28 takes you past the headwaters of the Hudson River to the tiny resort of **BLUE MOUNTAIN LAKE**. A handful of **motels** and lakeside **cabins** are available for rent, and you can swim at the pretty little **beach** that fronts the village center. **Sagamore Lodge**, about fifteen miles west, in the woods above Raquette Lake, is the sole survivor of the many "Great Camps" which wealthy easterners constructed in the Adirondacks around the turn of the century. Not to be confused with the four-star *Sagamore Resort* on Lake George, it was a summer home of the **Vanderbilts**, basically a huge and luxurious log cabin in which they entertained illustrious guests – including Hoagie Carmichael, who supposedly wrote *Stardust* while driving the four-mile dirt road that leads up to the house. The still-intact house and grounds are now used as a conference and educational center, and for cross-country skiing in winter; call for details of summer art and photography **classes**, or to reserve a place on a guided **tour** (daily 10am & 1.30pm; $6; ☎315/354-5311).

Just north of Blue Mountain Lake on Hwy-30, the twenty-building **Adirondack Museum** (mid-June to mid-Oct, daily 9.30am–5.30pm; $6) has exhibits on aspects of regional life including art, sports, mining and wildlife, but is perhaps most memorable for its grand views out over the lake and surrounding mountains.

Lake Placid and Saranac Lake

The winter sports center of **LAKE PLACID**, twice the proud host of the Winter Olympics, lies thirty miles west of I-87 on Hwy-73. Throughout the year, the self-guided **Olympic Tour** takes in such sites as the bobsleigh run, ski jump (via chairlift) and a white-knuckle eight-mile drive up the sharply rising Whiteface Mountain toll road ($15 all-in; ☎1-800/44-PLACID). **John Brown's Farm and Grave**, on Hwy-73 outside the village, was where the famous abolitionist brought his family in 1849 to aid a small colony of black farmers and conceived his kamikaze battle to end slavery. The house is less interesting than his story (see p.324), but at least it's free (late May to late Oct, Wed–Sat 10am–5pm, Sun 1–5pm). In summer, there are **boat trips** on Lake Placid ($6; ☎523-9704); good **mountain bikes**, and maps of local trails, are available from the very helpful *Adirondack Adventure Tours*, 126 Main St (☎523-1475).

A scatter of economical **motels** can be found on Wilmington Road – try the *Cobble Mountain Lodge* (☎523-2040; ③) or *Hi-Ridge Motel* (☎523-3938; ③). *Leslie's*, 99 Main St (523-4279) has excellent pastries, coffees and teas, while the cozy *Artist's Café*, 1 Main St (☎523-9493), provides filling lunches. For dinner or a drink, try the *Black Bear*, 157 Main St (☎523-9886).

While Lake Placid is the place to go for skiing and other winter sports, the neighboring community of **SARANAC LAKE** is in many ways a more attractive place to spend time. The tranquil (and easily accessible) lakeshore is lined by lovely gingerbread cottages, most of them built during the late 1800s when this was a popular middle-class retreat. Robert Louis Stevenson spent the winter of 1888 in a small cottage, now preserved as a **museum**; contact the **Chamber of Commerce**, 30 Main St (☎891-1990 or ☎1-800/347-1992) for details and directions. Saranac Lake is still a rather quiet year-round resort, the main attraction for budget travellers being the large, $12-a-night **youth hostel,** housed in the grand old *Hotel Saranac* at 101 Main St (☎891-2200). *Mountain Mist Custard*, on Hwy-86 on the east side of town, has good burgers and great **ice creams**, which you can eat in the lakeside park right next door.

The Thousand Islands

Beyond the Adirondacks, on the broad St Lawrence River that forms the border with Canada, are 1800 barely populated hunks of earth known as the **Thousand Islands**. They share their name with a salad dressing because one turn-of-the-century visitor – George Boldt, president of New York's *Waldorf-Astoria Hotel* – is said to have asked the steward on his yacht to concoct something different for a special luncheon. The resultant pink goo is now famous the world over.

From both **Alexandria Bay** and the smaller fishing port of **Clayton**, boat excursions set out to explore the waterway; the tiny craft are all but swamped by the passing huge cargo ships, larger than many of the islands. For departure times, contact *Empire* (☎315/482-9511) or *Uncle Sam's Tours* (☎315/686-3511).

The Finger Lakes

At the heart of the state, southwest of Syracuse on the far side of the Catskills from New York City, are the eleven **Finger Lakes**, narrow channels gouged out by glaciers which have left tell-tale signs in the form of drumlins, steep gorges and any number of waterfalls. With the exception of well-to-do **Ithaca** and tiny **Skaneatles**, few towns compete with the lakeshore scenery, but the area as a whole is a relaxing place to spend some time, particularly if you enjoy sampling **wine**: it comes as a surprise to many people, but the Finger Lakes region, and much of upstate New York, produce a number of good vintages.

Skaneatles and Seneca Falls

SKANEATLES (pronounced *Skinny-Atlas*), crouching at the neck of Skaneatles Lake, is perhaps the prettiest Finger Lakes town. It's also the best place to go swimming in the Finger Lakes region: just a block from the town center, and lined by huge resort homes, the appealing bay sports a **beach** and a marina where you can take boat trips and rent water sport equipment. **Accommodation** is sparse, but the handful of motels includes the *Hi-Way Host*, 834 W Genessee St (☎716/685-7633; ②), while the *Sherwood Inn* (☎716/685-3405; ④), overlooking the lake, is not as expensive as it looks. It also has a good restaurant; cheaper but still scrumptious meals can be had at the ever-popular *Doug's Fish Fry*, 8 Jordan St (☎716/685-3288).

At **SENECA FALLS**, just west of the northern tip of Cayuga Lake, Elizabeth Cady Stanton and a few colleagues planned and held the first Women's Rights Convention in 1848 – 72 years before the Nineteenth Amendment gave all US women the vote. On the site of the **Wesleyan Chapel**, 126 Fall St, where the first campaign meeting was held, the National Park Service recently opened the **Women's Rights Visitors Center** (daily, 9am–5pm), setting the early women's movement in its historical context. The center also has details of a **walking tour** that takes in the small museum at the Cady Stanton house and passes the (privately owned) former home of **Amelia Bloomer**, whose crusade to urge women out of their cumbrous undergarments won her a place in the dictionary. A block east of the visitor center, the **National Women's Hall of Fame** (May–Oct, daily 9.30am–5pm; Nov–April, Wed–Sat 10am–4pm & Sun noon–4pm; $3 suggested donation), at 76 Fall St, where over 100 women have been honoured for their efforts in fields such as humanitarianism, sports and the arts, makes an interesting stop.

The town itself is a blend of old mills and different-styled homes, tucked away among the mature trees. If you want to stop over, the best **place to stay** is the *Guion House* B&B, at 32 Cayuga St (☎716/568-8129; ④). **Eat** at one of the cafés along Fall Street, or try the dining room of the *Gould Hotel* (☎716/568-5801), at Fall and State.

Hwy-89 south of Seneca Falls has been dubbed the **Cayuga Wine Trail**, with dozens of small wineries operating along the west shore of the largest of the Finger Lakes. One of the best is the *Lucas Vineyard* (☎716/532-4825).

Ithaca

Cayuga Lake comes to a halt at its southern end at picturesque **ITHACA**, piled like a diminutive San Francisco high above the lakeshore and culminating in the towers, sweeping lawns and shaded parks of the Ivy League **Cornell University**. On campus, the boxy, I M Pei-designed Herbert F Johnson **Museum of Art** (Tues–Sat 10am–5pm; free) merits a visit more for its fifth-floor view of the town and lake than for the unspectacular collection of Asian and contemporary art. The pick of the countless **waterfalls** within a few miles of town is the slender 210ft **Taughannock Falls** off Hwy-89, which has a swimming beach close at hand.

Greyhound and other **buses** operate out of the terminal at W State and N Fulton (☎607/272-1313). Inexpensive **places to stay** are few and far between; try the cramped *Hillside Inn*, 518 Stewart Ave (☎607/273-6864; ③) or the *Elmshade Guest House*, 402 S Albany St (☎607/273-1707; ③), or the *Econolodge*, 2303 Triphammer Rd (☎607/257-1400; ②), on Hwy-13 north of town.

Ithaca boasts two top-rated vegetarian **restaurants** – *Cabbagetown Café*, 404 Eddy St (☎607/273-2847), and the inventive *Moosewood*, 108 E Green St (☎607/273-9610), of cookbook fame, in DeWitt Mall in the central vehicle-free **Commons**. A block away, *Just a Taste*, 416 N Aurora St, is a lively wine-and-tapas bar, while *The Mad Café*, State and Aurora at the east end of the Commons, offers "freedom of espresso" along with comfy booths and excellent fresh baked goods. Numerous cheap student-oriented places to eat include *Oliver's Deli*, 415 College Ave. For news of the lively music scene – and gigs at the *Haunt*, 114 W Green St (☎607/273-3355) – check out the free *Ithaca Times*.

Corning

Forty miles southwest of Ithaca, world-famous Steuben Glass has been manufactured in the otherwise undistinguished town of **CORNING** since Frederick Carder started making his characteristic Art Nouveau pieces in 1903. The excellent **Museum of Glass** in the Corning Glass Center traces its history from ancient heads and amulets to modern sculptures and paperweights. Also in the complex, where glass is omnipresent in mirrors and motifs, are the Hall of Science and Technology, full of push-button exhibits, and the Steuben Glass factory itself, where every stage of the production process can be viewed from behind (glass) screens (daily 9am–5pm; $6).

The **Rockwell Museum**, ten minutes' stroll away at Cedar St and Denison Parkway, has more glass, plus antique toys and a strong collection of western art (summer Mon–Fri 9am–7pm, Sat 9am–5pm, Sun noon–5pm, shorter hours rest of year; $3).

Toward Niagara Falls: the Erie Canal Towns

The fertile farming country stretching from **Albany** at the head of the Hudson to **Buffalo** on Lake Erie, along the route of **Erie Canal**, comprises the agricultural heartland of New York State. The eastern parts – also known as **Central Leatherstocking**, after the protective leggings worn by the area's first settlers – are well off the conventional tourist trails. Unless you want to check out one of the specialist sports museums, such as the Baseball Hall of Fame at **Cooperstown**, it's best passed by.

With the captivating exception of **Niagara Falls**, one of the continent's biggest crowdpullers, there's little to see in the northwest reaches of New York State. Standing out from the mostly flat farmland, the industrial giants of **Rochester**, **Syracuse** and **Buffalo** each possesses a couple of worthy museums, but are best approached as bases for seeing the surrounding area (Buffalo, for example, is a good base for Niagara Falls).

Cooperstown

Seventy miles west of Albany, sitting gracefully on the wooded banks of tranquil Otsego Lake, is the almost aggressively pretty village of **COOPERSTOWN**, christened "Glimmerglass" by novelist James Fenimore Cooper, son of the town's founder. The fact that baseball is said to have originated here on Doubleday Field is commemorated by the inspired and spacious **National Baseball Hall of Fame**, on Main Street. Everything is displayed in such an attention-grabbing manner that even if you know nothing about the game it's difficult to remain uninterested. Babe Ruth gets a whole display to himself while more of the greats are shown in action in photographs and videos (daily; May–Oct 9am–9pm; Nov–April 9am–5pm; $6).

Cooperstown is a pleasant community; it's worth taking a stroll around, or swimming from the beach at Glimmerglass State Park. Except for the **youth hostel** ($5 for AYH members; ☎607/293-7324; ①), **accommodation** is expensive; the *Lake View* on Hwy-80 (☎607/547-9740; ⑤) is one of the cheapest motels. *Obie's Brot und Bier*, 46 Pioneer Alley (☎607/547-5601), sells cheap sandwiches with a Germanic influence.

Canastota

Just before Syracuse, at exit 34 from I-90, nondescript **CANASTOTA** is the home of the **International Boxing Hall of Fame**. Canastota's links with boxing go back to early in the last century, and this ten-thousand-strong village has produced two post-war world champions: Carmen Basilio, who took away the middleweight crown of Sugar Ray Robinson in an epic 1958 encounter, and Billy Backus, a welterweight title-holder during the early Seventies. All the greats are represented in the two-room museum, whether by picture, dressing-gown, mouthpiece, handwraps, gloves or bronze fist impressions, and there's a selection of big-fight videos (daily 9am–5pm; $3).

Syracuse

A lively but largely unattractive modern city, busy **SYRACUSE** made its name first for the production of salt and, more importantly, for its central position on the Erie Canal. Despite a population nudging half a million, there's little to see, though the presence of Syracuse University gives downtown an active and youthful feel. The redevelopment of **Armory Square**, around Franklin and Fayette streets, as an area of specialty shops, galleries and cafés has gone some way toward adding character to the city center, but the city still feels dominated by the highways and railroads that slice through it.

The **Erie Canal Museum** (Tues–Sun 10am–5pm; $1), housed in one of the few surviving canal-era buildings, an 1850s weighing station at 318 E Erie Blvd, tells the story of the long battle between politicians and taxpayers before work on the canal began in 1810. The waterway was designed to link the Great Lakes with New York City via the Hudson, so cutting hefty transportation costs – which it did by an average of ninety percent. At first, however, not everyone was in favor, critics speaking of a "big ditch" in which "would be buried the treasure of the state". The project eventually took fifteen years and one thousand lives, and went three million dollars over budget, but it spawned America's first generation of engineers, and after it opened in 1825 prosperous towns arose alongside the canal almost overnight. Erie Boulevard itself was created by filling in the old canal bed, and the industrial surroundings do little to evoke the era, though the reconstructed **canal boat** inside the museum is definitely worth a look.

Practicalities

Good-value **rooms** can be found in downtown's *Comfort Inn,* 454 James St (☎315/425-0015; ③), and the fairly central *Downing International AYH Hostel,* 535 Oak St (☎315/472-5788; ①), has $8 dorm beds. *Niko's,* 135 Water St (☎315/475-7000), serves standard cheap **food,** while the nearby, slightly more healthy, *Pastabilities,* 311 S Franklin St (☎315/474-1153), is also reasonable. Student numbers ensure a lively **music** scene; consult the resourceful *Syracuse New Times* freesheet for details.

Rochester

In contrast to its sprawling suburbs, downtown **ROCHESTER** is a salubrious place, with its central office-block area bordered by well-heeled mansions on spacious boulevards. High-tech companies such as *Bausch & Lomb* and *Xerox* have brought capital to the city, but by far the most conspicuous names on view are those of **Kodak** and its founder, George Eastman. Legacies throughout the metropolitan area include Kodak Park, the *Eastman Theater,* and above all the **International Museum of Photography** at George Eastman House, two miles from downtown at 900 East Ave. A first-rate exhibition of photographic history ranges from unbelievably clear Civil War prints to modern experimental works, and the twentieth-century gallery forms an A to Z of modern greats: Ansel Adams, Cartier-Bresson, Steiglitz, Weston and lots more. Upstairs is the fun, hands-on Discovery Room, plus cabinets of unusual **cameras**. Nonetheless, with Kodak cash behind it, you would expect the museum to be much bigger; a visit will leave most people thirsting for more and frustrated that a large part is given over to research and storage rather than exhibition space (Tues–Sat 10am–5pm, Sun 1–5pm; $4).

Assorted domestic artefacts collected by another wealthy former resident, Margaret Woodbury Strong (1897–1969), are gathered in the **Strong Museum** on Manhattan Square. With everything from stuffed toys to porcelain plates and Shaker furniture, it is seen by many as an over-the-top souvenir hypermarkét, but afficionados of Victoriana will have a field day. Of more general interest are the well-presented temporary exhibits

The **area code** for Rochester, Buffalo, and the Niagara region is ☎716.

looking at American consumer society (Mon–Sat 10am–5pm, Sun 1–5pm; $3). Another place worth a look is the self-proclaimed "World's Largest Music Store", the **House of Guitars** at 645 Titus Ave. Besides having six floors full of instruments and sound equipment, it also has millions of new and used albums, tapes and CDs.

Practicalities

Amtrak and *Greyhound* drop off at 320 Central Ave near downtown, served by *RTS* buses (☎654-0200). **Accommodation** is nowhere inexpensive. Downtown choices include the *Holiday Inn*, 120 E Main St (☎546-6400; ⑤) and the excellent *428 Mt Vernon* B&B (☎271-0792; ⑤) at the entrance to lush Highland Park, one mile north. Among budget options in the south of the city, near the I-90 Thruway, is the *Red Roof Inn*, 4820 W Henrietta Rd, off I-90 exit 46 (☎359-1100; ②).

Popular **places to eat** in the fairly lively downtown include *Aladdin's*, 141 State St (☎546-4320), serving inexpensive Middle Eastern food, the pub-style *Old Toad*, 277 Alexander St (☎232-2626), where British staff serve beer and cheap meals, and *Café Crème de la Crème*, 295 Alexander St (☎263-3580), whose magnificent pastries and creative entrees don't cost the earth. To quench a thirst, keep an eye out for the local soft drink *Jolt*, which tastes like a normal cola but packs a big wallop of caffeine.

Out from Rochester

The **Lake Ontario State Parkway** is a quiet, scenic way of driving to Niagara Falls from Rochester, taking about an hour longer than the standard route along I-90 via Buffalo. The parkway starts eight miles from downtown at the end of Lake Avenue, near the popular **Ontario Beach Park**. This short golden strand, overlooked by exclusive holiday homes, is a real poseur's paradise; you may well feel self-conscious if your shades don't match up to the ubiquitous (locally manufactured) *Ray-Bans*.

If big crowds and the churning noise of speedboats are not your thing, head twenty miles along the parkway to the more secluded **Hamlin Beach State Park** ($3 per car). The parkway passes through few towns, and the best place to stop for refreshments is the small and attractive Point Breeze harbor, ten miles on from Hamlin.

Buffalo

As I-90 sweeps down into the state's second largest city, **BUFFALO**, downtown looms up in a cluster of Art Deco spires and glass box skyscrapers – Manhattan in miniature on Lake Erie. The city's early twentieth-century prosperity is reflected in such architecturally significant structures as the towering 1928 **City Hall** (the tallest in the country), and the deep red terracotta relief of Louis Sullivan's **Guaranty Building** on Church Street, as well as major buildings by H H Richardson, Eliel Saarinen and Frank Lloyd Wright. However, the dereliction of the immediate environs suggests this may now be the beginning of the Rust Belt. Buffalo has set aside memories of the boom years – when the massive **grain elevators** that line the Erie waterfront were busy 24 hours a day – and in the wake of the new NAFTA treaty now looks to Canada for its economic future.

That Buffalo's wealthy merchants were a cultured lot is also apparent in the excellent **Albright-Knox Art Gallery** (Tues–Sat 11am–5pm, Sun noon–5pm; donation), 1285 Elmwood Ave, two miles north of downtown amid the green spaces of the F L Olmsted-designed Delaware Park. One of the top modern collections in the world, it's especially strong on recent American and European art: the Color Field painters, Abstract Expressionism, Pop, Op and Kinetic Art, with Pollock, Rothko and Rauschenberg among the names. Other highlights include thirty large paintings by Clyfford Still, and a fine selection of pieces by earlier artists such as Matisse, Picasso and Monet.

In between downtown and Delaware Park is **Allentown**, Buffalo's most bohemian quarter, its leafy streets lined by lovely Victorian homes as well as numerous good cafés, bars and restaurants. Allen Street between Main and Elmwood holds some of the best; the area around Theatre Place downtown is also good (see below).

Being a staunchly blue-collar city, Buffalo loves its professional **sports** teams: football's *Bills* (☎649-0015), ice hockey's *Sabres* (☎856-7300) and baseball's *Bisons* (☎846-2003), who as the top farm team for the Pittsburgh Pirates attract over a million fans per season to downtown's very pleasant Pilot Field stadium.

The **Lake Erie shoreline** west of Buffalo is lined by numerous beaches where **windsurfers** skim across the water and do flips in the waves, while to the south, in the town of Orchard Park, the **Bicycling Museum** (Fri–Mon 11am–5pm; $4.50) holds over two hundred antique bikes and engaging displays of cycling memorabilia.

Practicalities

Greyhound (☎855-7511), *Metro Bus* and *Metro Rail*, the city's new tramway (both ☎855-7211), all operate from the downtown depot at Ellicott and Church. To get to **Niagara Falls**, take bus #40 (hourly 7am–10pm; one-hour journey; $1.70). *Amtrak* **trains** to and from Niagara Falls stop nearby at 75 Exchange St; all others stop in the eastern suburb of Depew, eight miles from town but close to the **airport** (☎632-3115). There's a helpful **visitor center** at 107 Delaware Ave (☎852-0511 or ☎1-800/BUF-FALO).

The one moderately priced **place to stay** downtown – except for the *YWCA*, 245 North St (☎884-4761; ①), where women pay $7 a night – is the *Hotel Lenox*, 140 North St (☎884-1700 or ☎1-800/82-LENOX; ③), with reduced rates for students). The *Holiday Inn*, 620 Delaware Ave (☎886-2121; ④) is a safe bet, while the *Hilton*, 120 Church St (☎845-5100; ⑤), gives you free use of its extensive health club.

The city's specialty of **buffalo** (spicy chicken) **wings** with blue cheese dressing is said to have been invented at the *Anchor Bar*, 1047 Main St (☎886-8920), where lunch costs around $6; at night they sometimes have live jazz. For snacks, the cheap food stalls and tiny Polish cafés of ancient **Broadway Market**, 999 Broadway, are well worth perusing. Good restaurants include the upscale *Beau Fleuve*, 150 Theatre Place (☎885-3029), and hearty *Hemingway's*, 492 Pearl St (☎852-1937). Among the liveliest of Allentown's bars and cafés are *Topic: Coffee*, 224 Allen St, for espresso and a bagel; *Nietzsche's*, 248 Allen St, for beers and live music; and *Colter Bay*, at Allen and Delaware. Downtown the late-night hot spot *Calumet Arts Café*, 56 W Chippewa St (☎855-2220), has very good food and drinks. Further listings are given in *Art Voice*, a biweekly freesheet.

Niagara Falls

Every second, over half a million gallons of water explode over the knife-edge **NIAGARA FALLS**, right on the border with Canada some twenty miles north of Buffalo on I-190. This awesome spectacle is made even more so by the variety of methods laid on to help you get closer: boats, catwalks, observation towers and helicopters all push as near to the curtain of gushing water as they dare. At night the falls are lit up, and the colored waters tumble dramatically into blackness, while in winter the whole scene changes as the falls freeze to form gigantic razor-tipped icicles.

Many visitors will, however, find the whole experience a bit too gimmicky; no commercial opening has been left unexploited in the attempt to extract cash from tourists (Oscar Wilde quipped that he would have been more impressed if the falls ran upwards; at least no one's tried that yet). Don't expect too much; neither the small city of **Niagara Falls**, still a smelly, shabby industrial eyesore despite recent efforts to spruce it up, nor the more developed tinsel town of **Niagara, Canada,** is a place to savor in any way. Once you've seen the falls, from as many different angles as you can manage, there's no real point in sticking around, and you'll have a better time heading on to Buffalo (or Rochester, or anywhere . . .) rather than trying to rustle up some fun here.

The Falls

Niagara Falls comprises three distinct cataracts. The tallest are the **American** and **Bridal Veil** falls on the American side, separated by tiny Luna Island and plunging over jagged rocks in a 180ft drop; the broad **Horseshoe Falls** which curve their way over to Canada are probably the most impressive. They date back a mere twelve thousand years, when the retreat of melting glaciers allowed water trapped in Lake Erie to gush north to Lake Ontario. Back then the falls were seven miles downriver, but constant erosion has cut them back to their present site. The falls are colorfully lit-up at night, and many say they're most beautiful in winter, when the grounds are covered in snow and the waters turn to ice.

The best views on the American side are from the **Prospect Point Observation Tower** (daily; 25¢), and from the area at its base where the water rushes past; Terrapin Point on **Goat Island** in the middle of the river has similar views of Horseshoe Falls. The nineteenth-century tightrope-walker Blondin crossed the Niagara repeatedly near here, and even carried passengers across on his back; other suicidal fools over the years have taken the plunge in barrels. One survivor among the many fatalities was the Englishman Bobby Leach, who went over in a steel barrel in July 1911 and had to spend the rest of the year in hospital. That practice has since been banned, for reasons which become self-evident when you approach the towering cascade on the not-to-be-missed **Maid of the Mist** boat trip from the foot of the observation tower (summer, Mon–Fri 10am–5pm; Sat & Sun 10am–6pm; $7; ☎284-4233). From Goat Island, the **Cave of the Winds** tour leads down to the base of the falls by elevator to within almost touching distance of the water (mid-May–late Oct; $3.50). Alternatively it's a twenty-minute walk across the **Rainbow Bridge** to the Canadian side (25¢ each way; bring ID, and check with US Immigration officials *before* heading across), where you get an arguably better view, bigger crowds and even more tawdry commercialism.

As you look on in awe, reflect that you're seeing about half the volume of water – the rest is diverted to hydro-electric power stations. The full story of this engineering feat is related at the free **Niagara Power Project Visitors Center** in nearby Lewiston (daily; ☎285-3211). With your own transportation it's also possible to trace the inhospitable Niagara Gorge two miles along the dramatic Robert Moses Parkway to the **Whirlpool Rapids**, a violent maelstrom swollen by broken trees and other flotsam. Ten miles east of Niagara Falls, the town of **LOCKPORT** takes its name from the series of locks that raise and lower boats some 65 feet at the western end of the Erie Canal. You can see the impressive flight of locks from the Pine Street Bridge, or up close on canal boat **tours** (May–Nov daily at 12.30 & 3pm; $8; ☎693-3260).

Arrival and Information

Amtrak **trains**, en route between New York and Toronto, stop a long two miles from downtown at 55 Dick Rd. If you arrive at the **bus station** (☎285-9391), on Fourth and Niagara, you're next door to the official **Welcome Center** (☎285-2400). The countless other places in town that claim to be visitor centers are in fact just fronts for tour companies hoping to entice you on one of their overpriced trips.

Arriving **by car**, follow the signs to the main parking lot, which is right next to the falls and costs $3. Local *Metro Transit System* **buses** run to all areas of the city and to Buffalo (bus #40; $1.70 each way). To send the obligatory postcards, you'll need the **post office** at 615 Main St (Mon–Fri 8.30am–5pm, Sat 9am–noon; ☎285-7561).

Accommodation

Places to stay in central Niagara can work out quite expensive if you don't plan ahead or shop around, but US-62, east of Hwy-190, is lined with dozens of motels charging from $30. Many of these are pretty tacky, targetting the thousands of honeymoon

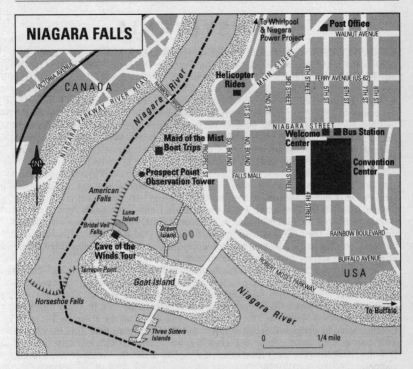

couples who come here every year (despite Wilde's assertion that the falls "must be one of the earliest if not keenest disappointments of American married life"). As the falls are under an hour's drive, both **Rochester** and **Buffalo** make better bases.

The closest place to **camp** is seven miles from downtown at the **Niagara Falls Campground & Lodging**, 2405 Niagara Falls Blvd in Wheatfield (☎731-3434), for $15 a night.

All Tucked Inn B&B, 574 3rd St (☎282-0919). Cozy, unpretentious B&B. ③.

Budget Inns, 492 Main St (☎285-8366). No-frills downtown motel. ③.

Days Inn Falls View, 201 Rainbow Blvd (☎285-9321 or ☎1-800/876-3297). Landmark hotel with grand lobby but rather plain rooms. The rates fluctuate, dropping dramatically off-season. ③.

Frontier AYH Hostel, 1101 Ferry Ave (☎282-3700). Friendly, well-run hostel with around forty beds at $10 ($14 non-members). Facilities include showers, kitchen and TV lounge. Preference is given to AYH members and it's advisable to book ahead in summer. ①.

Eating

Though most of the **eating options** in Niagara Falls are fast-food joints of indifferent quality, there are a few decent local bars and restaurants – with some better places over in Canada.

Arterial Restaurant, 314 Niagara St. Tasty burgers for under $2 and generous portions of spicy chicken wings at $3 make this an excellent downtown alternative to the fast-food emporia.

The Bakery and Ports of Call Restaurant, 3004 Niagara St (☎282-9498). A bit out of the way but a wide variety of European dishes for $10–20. The bar is good for a quiet drink.

Cataract House Restaurant, 225 Rainbow Mall (☎282-5635). Posh-looking Greek restaurant. Kebab, pizza and sandwich lunches for around $5, and a slightly more expensive dinner menu.

PENNSYLVANIA

PENNSYLVANIA, which but for a small stretch on Lake Erie is the only landlocked state in the northeast, was explored by the Dutch in the early 1600s, settled by the Swedes forty years later, and claimed by the British in 1664. Charles II of England, who owed a debt to the Penn family, rid himself of the potentially troublesome young **William Penn**, an enthusiastic advocate of religious freedom, by granting him land in the colony in 1682. Penn Jr immediately established a "holy experiment" of "brotherly" love and tolerance, naming the state for his father and setting a good example by signing a peaceful cohabitation treaty with the Native Americans. Most of the early agricultural settlers were religious refugees: Quakers like Penn himself, Mennonites from Germany and Switzerland, and Irish Catholics.

"The keystone state" was crucial in the development of the US. Politicians and thinkers like **Benjamin Franklin** congregated in Philadelphia – home of both the Declaration of Independence and the Constitution – and were prominent in articulating the ideas behind the Revolution. Later, the battle in Gettysburg, south Pennsylvania – best remembered for Abraham Lincoln's immortal **Gettysburg Address** – marked a turning point in the Civil War. Pennsylvania was also vital industrially; Pittsburgh, in the west, was the world's leading steel producer in the nineteenth century, and nearly all the nation's anthracite coal is still mined here.

The two great urban centers of Philadelphia and Pittsburgh, both lively and vibrant tourist destinations, are at opposite ends of the state. The three hundred miles between them, though predominantly agricultural, are topographically diverse. There are over one hundred state parks, with green rolling countryside in the east, brooding forests in the west, and in the northeast, the rivers, lakes and valleys of the Poconos. Lancaster County, home to traditional Amish farmers, and the Gettysburg battlefield both heave with busloads of day-trippers, and even the unexciting chocolate-factory town of Hershey, minutes away from Harrisburg, the capital, draws thousands of cocoa-loving visitors.

Getting Around Pennsylvania

Although to appreciate the less-populated stretches of Pennsylvania you really need a car, public transportation is adequate if you organize yourself carefully. Both I-76 (the Pennsylvania Turnpike) and I-80 sweep right the way across to Ohio, nearly five hundred miles east to west. US-30 (the Lincoln Highway) also runs east–west between Philadelphia and Pittsburgh, past Lancaster City, York and Gettysburg, while the prettiest north–south route is US-15, from Maryland to New York State, which follows the Susquehanna River for about fifty miles.

Amtrak crosses daily from Philadelphia to Pittsburgh, stopping at Lancaster City, Harrisburg and other smaller towns. Greyhound covers all the major cities and some small towns not served by rail, but its routes can be circuitous – check arrival times when buying your ticket, especially if you need to make a connection.

Philadelphia

The original capital of the nation, **PHILADELPHIA** was laid out by William Penn, Jr in 1682, on a grid system that was to provide the pattern for most American cities. It was envisaged as a "greene countrie towne", and today, for all its historical and cultural significance, it still manages to retain a certain quaintness. Just a few blocks away from the noise, crowds, heat and dust of downtown, shady cobbled alleys stand lined with red-brick Colonial houses, while the peace and quiet of huge Fairmount Park make it easy to forget you're in a major metropolis.

Settled by **Quakers**, Philadelphia prospered swiftly on the back of trade and commerce, and by the 1750s had become the second largest city in the British Empire. Economic power fuelled strong Revolutionary feeling, and the city was the capital during the **War of Independence** (but for nine months under British occupation in 1777–78). It also served as the US capital until 1800, while Washington DC was being built. The **Declaration of Independence** was written, signed and first publicly read here in 1776, as was the **US Constitution** ten years later. Philadelphia was also a hotbed of new ideas in the arts and sciences, as epitomized by the scientist, philosopher, statesman, inventor and printer **Benjamin Franklin**.

Philadelphia, which translated from Greek means "City of Brotherly Love", is in fact one of the most **ethnically mixed** US cities, with substantial communities of Italians, Irish, eastern Europeans and Asians living side by side among the majority black population. Many of the city's **black** residents are descendants of the migrants who flocked here after the Civil War when, like Chicago, Philadelphia was seen as a mecca of tolerance and liberalism. More recently, it voted in the nation's first black mayor, and has the country's best museum dedicated to African-American history and culture. On the downside, Philadelphia is also the place where, as part of a huge police effort to dislodge the separatist black group MOVE, a bomb dropped from a helicopter set fire to entire city blocks, killing women and children and leaving many hundreds homeless.

Once known as Filthydelphia, and the butt of endless derision from W C Fields in the Thirties (as in his famous epitaph: "On the whole, I'd rather be in Philadelphia"), the city underwent a remarkable resurgence preparing for the nation's bicentennial celebrations in 1976. Philadelphia's strength today is its great energy – fuelled by history, strong cultural institutions, and an impressive new downtown convention center – grounded in its many staunchly traditional neighborhoods, especially Italian South Philadelphia.

Arrival, Information and Getting Around

Philadelphia's **International Airport** (☎492-3181) is eight miles southwest of the city off I-95. Taxis into town cost around $20 (try *United Cabs*, ☎625-2811), and the South East Pennsylvania Transit Authority (*SEPTA*) runs **trains** every thirty minutes (6am–midnight; $4) to three downtown destinations: 30th Street near the university, Suburban Station near City Hall, and Market East, adjacent to the *Greyhound* terminal at 1001 Filbert St (☎931-4000). The very grand 30th Street *Amtrak* station, the second busiest in the US, is just across the Schuylkill River in the university area (*Amtrak* passengers can transfer downtown on *SEPTA* for free), opposite the city's main (24-hour) **post office** at 30th and Market (zip code 19104).

The excellent **visitor center**, 1525 JFK Blvd (☎636-1666) at the Penn Center subway station in the heart of downtown, supplies a wealth of interesting information and helps with accommodation (daily 9am–5pm, 9am–6pm in the summer); another visitor center can be found at Third and Chestnut in Independence National Historic Park (INHP), near the Liberty Bell (daily 9am–5pm; ☎597-8974).

City Transportation
SEPTA (☎574-7800) runs an extensive **bus** system (6.30am–1am) and a **subway**. The most useful subway lines cross the city east–west (Market–Frankford line) and north–south (Broad Street line); the handiest **bus** route is #76, which runs from Penn's Landing and the Independence Hall area out Market Street past City Hall to the museums and Fairmount Park and costs only 50¢. All other bus and subway services require exact fares of $1.50; **day passes**, which are also good for a ride to or from the airport, go for $5.

The **area code** for Philadelphia is ☎215.

City Tours

American Trolley Tours cruise the historic area in fake streetcars on three-hour narrated jaunts ($14); you'd do much better to get a map and wander around on your own. The most worthwhile guided **walking tours** are offered by the *Foundation for Architecture* (☎569-3187, ☎569-TOUR for taped information); *Candlelight Tours* through the hidden gardens and courtyards of Society Hill leave from the *City Tavern* (May–Oct, Thurs–Sat, 6.30pm; $5; ☎735-3123). *Gray Line* **coach tours** (☎569-3666; from $13.50) range from three-hour historical tours to all-day bashes and trips to Pennsylvania Dutch Country.

The City

Philadelphia stretches for about two miles from the Schuylkill (pronounced *Schoolkill*) River on the west to the Delaware on the east; the urban area extends for many miles to the north and south, but everything you're likely to want to see is right in the central swath. The city's central districts are compact, walkable and readily accessible from each other; Penn's sensibly planned grid system makes for easy sightseeing.

Independence Hall National Park

Any tour of Philadelphia should start with **Independence National Historic Park**, or **INHP**, "America's most historic square mile", which covers a mere four blocks just west of the Delaware River between Walnut and Arch, but can take more than a day to explore in full. The solid red-brick buildings here, not all of which are open to the public, epitomize the Georgian (and after the Revolution, Federalist) obsession with balance and symmetry. Free **tours** set off from the rear of the east wing of Independence Hall, the single most important site.

It's best to reach **Independence Hall** early, to avoid the hordes of tourists. Built in 1732 as the Pennsylvania State House, this was where the Declaration of Independence was prepared and signed and, after the pealing of the Liberty Bell, given its first public reading on July 8 1776. Today, in the room in which Jefferson *et al.* drafted and signed the United States Constitution, you can see George Washington's high-backed chair with the half-sun on the back – Franklin, in optimistic spirit, called it "the rising sun".

The **Liberty Bell** itself hung in Independence Hall from 1753, ringing to herald vital announcements such as victories and defeats in the Revolutionary War. Stories as to how it received its famous crack vary; one tells that it occurred while tolling the funeral of Chief Justice Marshall in 1835. Whatever the truth, it rang publicly for the very last time on George Washington's birthday in 1846.

Later in the century, the bell's inscription from Leviticus, advocating liberty "throughout all the land unto all the inhabitants", made it an anti-slavery symbol for the New England abolitionists – the first to call it the Liberty Bell. After the Civil War the silent bell was adopted as a symbol of reconciliation and embarked on a national rail tour. The well-travelled and somewhat lumpen icon now rests at eye level in a purpose-built concrete-and-glass **pavilion** on Market Street between Fifth and Sixth; reverent groups are herded through, given a speedy talk, and invited to take photos from a respectful, cordoned-off distance.

Next door to Independence Hall, **Congress Hall**, built in 1787 as the Philadelphia county courthouse, on Sixth and Chestnut, is where members of the new United States Congress first took their places, and where all the patterns for today's government were established. The US Supreme Court sat from 1791 until 1800 in **Old City Hall**, on the other side of Independence Hall on Fifth and Chestnut (daily 9am–5pm; free).

In 1774, delegates of the first Continental Congress – predecessor of the US Congress – chose defiantly to meet at **Carpenter's Hall**, 320 Chestnut St, rather than the more commodious State House, to air their grievances against the English king. Today the building exhibits early tools and furniture (Tues–Sun 10am–4pm). Directly

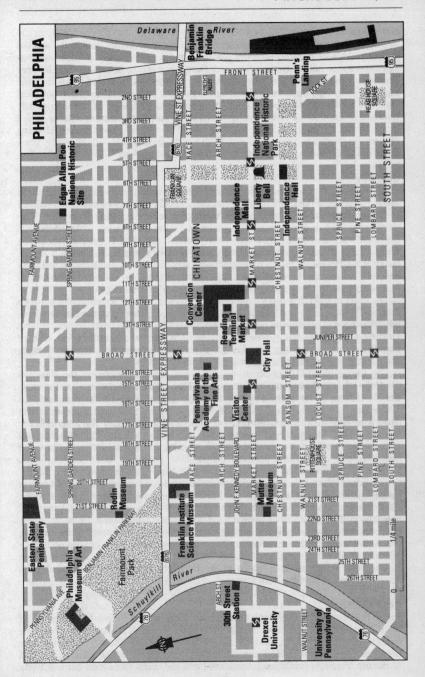

north, **Franklin Court**, 313 Market St, is a tribute, on the site of his home, to Benjamin Franklin. The house no longer stands, but steel frames outline the original structure. An underground museum has dial-a-quote recordings of his pithy sayings and musings of his contemporaries, and there's a working printshop. The **B Free Franklin Post Office**, 316 Market St, sells stamps and includes a small postal museum (daily 9am–5pm; free). Other buildings in the park include the **Philosophical Hall**, 104 S Fifth St, still used today by the nation's first philosophical debating society (founded by Franklin). The building is closed to the public, but features a statue of Ben in intellectual mode, garbed in a fetching toga. The original **Free Quaker Meeting House**, two blocks north of Market at Fifth and Arch, was built in 1783 by the small group of Quakers who actually fought in the Revolutionary War.

Olde City

INHP runs north into **Olde City**, Philadelphia's earliest commercial area, above Market Street near the riverfront. Washington, Franklin and Betsy Ross all worshipped at **Christ Church**, on Second St just north of Market St. Dating from 1727, it is surrounded by the gravestones of signatories to the Declaration of Independence (Mon–Sat 9am–5pm, Sun 1–5pm; free). The church's official burial ground, two blocks west at Fifth and Arch, includes **Benjamin Franklin's grave**. At 239 Arch St, the **Betsy Ross House**, by means of unimpressive wax dummies, salutes the woman credited with making the first American flag. There's a gift shop and shady **garden**, an oasis away from the busy streets outside (Tues–Sun 10am–5pm; free).

The claim of **Elfreth's Alley** – a pretty little cobbled way off Second Street between Arch and Race – to be the "oldest street in the United States" is somewhat nebulous, but it has been in continuous residential use since 1727, and its thirty houses, notable for their wrought-iron gates, water pumps, wooden shutters and attic rooms, all date from the eighteenth century. Number 126 is a small **museum** with household goods and a quaint overgrown back garden (daily 10am–4pm; free).

The area north of Market Street also holds two excellent museums: the **National Museum of American-Jewish History**, 55 N Fifth St, which is dedicated to the experiences of Jews in the States and includes a synagogue (Mon–Thurs 10am–5pm, Fri 10am–3pm, Sun noon–5pm; $1.75), and the emotive and politically informed **Afro-American Historical and Cultural Museum**, Seventh and Arch. The latter tells the stories of the thousands of blacks who migrated north to Philadelphia after Reconstruction and in the early twentieth century. As well as lectures, films and concerts, there are photos, personal memorabilia, poems by black poet Langston Hughes and a Billie Holiday soundtrack (Tues–Sat 10am–5pm, Sun noon–6pm; $3.50).

The **Edgar Allan Poe House** (daily 9am–5pm; free), 523 N Seventh St just north of Spring Garden St, is the only one of five Philadelphia houses Poe lived in that survives; it's also where he wrote *The Black Cat* in 1843. The stripped-down walls and bare wood floors do little to evoke Poe's presence (plans to restore the house are as yet unfulfilled, and for now it looks like a building site), but the staff in the small **museum** adjacent to the house can answer most any Poe-related questions. If you're keen on literary pilgrimages, you might also want to visit the grave of another key figure of American letters, **Walt Whitman**; he's buried in the Harleigh Cemetery, on Haddon Avenue across the river in Camden, New Jersey.

Penn's Landing

Just to the east of Olde City along the Delaware River, where William Penn stepped off in 1682, spreads the huge and heavily industrialized port of Philadelphia. Along the port's southern reaches, on the river side of the I-95 freeway, the old docklands have been renovated as part of the **Penn's Landing** development, which includes the Port of History Museum, exhibiting international arts and crafts (Wed–Sun 10am–4.30pm;

$2), and a variety of historical ships including the flagship *USS Olympia* and World War II submarine *Becuna* (both daily 10am–5pm; $3), and the three-masted Portuguese Tall Ship *Gazela*, built in 1883 (while in port Sat & Sun 12.30–5.30pm; donation). All along the riverfront promenade are food stalls, landscaped pools and fountains, regular outdoor concerts and festivals. A **ferry** crosses the Delaware ($2 each way) to the new **New Jersey State Aquarium** (daily 9.30am–5.30pm; $8.50) – good for kids but otherwise eminently missable.

Society Hill

Society Hill, an elegant residential area west of the Delaware and directly south of INHP, spreads itself between Walnut and Lombard streets. Though it is indeed Philadelphia's high society who live here now, the area was named for its first inhabitants, the Free Society of Traders – a rather more fun-loving bunch than the strict Quakers who lived to the north. After falling into disrepair, the Hill itself was flattened in the early 1970s to provide a building site for the huge condominium development near the waterfront, but the rest of the neighborhood has been restored to form one of the city's most picturesque districts: cobbled gaslit streets are lined with immaculately kept Colonial, Federal and Georgian homes, and markers everywhere point out the area's rich history. One of the few buildings open to the public is the **Hill Keith Physick House**, 321 S Fourth St, home to "the Father of American Surgery" and filled with eighteenth- and nineteenth-century decorative arts (Tues–Sat 10am–4pm, Sun 1–4pm; $3).

Center City

Center City, Philadelphia's main business and commercial area, stretches from Eighth Street west to the Schuylkill River, dominated by the endearing baroque wedding cake of **City Hall** and its 37ft bronze statue of Penn. Before ascending thirty storeys to the observation deck at Penn's feet, check out the quirky sculptures and carvings around the building, including the cats and mice in the south entry. A couple of blocks north, the **Pennsylvania Academy of the Fine Arts** (Tues–Sat 10am–5pm, Sun 11am–5pm; $5, free Sat 10am–1pm), housed in an elaborate, multicolored Victorian pile at Broad and Cherry, exhibits three hundred years of American art including works by Mary Cassatt and Thomas Eakins.

Beginning at Eighth Street, **Chinatown**, marked by a forty-foot oriental gate, has some of the best budget food in the city. Another good bet is the lively, century-old **Reading Terminal Market**, a block from City Hall on 12th St (see "Eating" on p.124 for specific recommendations). The new, $500-million **Convention Center**, which opened next door in 1993, signals major changes for this once dodgy area, as flashy hotels replace the once derelict shops and offices.

Rittenhouse Square

Grassy **Rittenhouse Square**, one of Penn's original city squares, is in one of the most fashionable areas in town. On one side it borders chic Walnut Street, on the other, a residential area of solid brownstones with beautifully carved doors and windows. The red-brick 1860 **Rosenbach Museum**, 2010 Delancey Place, holds over thirty thousand rare books and James Joyce's original hand-scrawled manuscripts of *Ulysses* (Tues–Sun 11am–4pm, last tour 2.45pm; $1.50). On summer evenings there are free outdoor jazz and r'n'b concerts in the square itself.

Three blocks northwest from the square, the **Mutter Museum** (Tues–Fri 10am–4pm; $1 donation), 19 S 22nd St in the College of Physicians (between Chestnut and Market), is definitely not for the squeamish. Filled with weird pathological and **medical oddities** including sickeningly lifelike wax models of tumors and infections alongside closets full of skeletons, syphilitic skulls, pickled internal organs and the death cast of a pair of Siamese twins, it's unique to say the least.

The Museums

The mile-long Benjamin Franklin Parkway, known as **Museum Row** – or, less convincingly, as "America's Champs-Elysees" – sweeps northwest from City Hall to the colossal Museum of Art in **Fairmount Park**, an area of countryside annexed by the city in the nineteenth century. Spanning nine hundred scenic acres on both sides of the Schuylkill River, this is the world's largest landscaped city park, with jogging, biking and hiking trails, endless streams and trees, early American homes, an all-wars memorial to the state's black soldiers, and a **zoo**, 3400 Girard Ave (Mon–Fri 9.30am–5pm, Sat–Sun until 6pm; $5.75, free on Mon Dec–Feb). In the late 1960s, local residents **Muhammad Ali** and **Joe Frazier** all but brought the city to a standstill with the announcement one afternoon that they were heading for Fairmount for an informal slug-out.

Sylvester Stallone later immortalized the steps of the **Philadelphia Museum of Art** (Tues & Thurs–Sun 10am–5pm, Wed 10am–9pm; $5, free Sun 10am–1pm), 26th St and Franklin Parkway, by running up them in the film *Rocky*, but he missed out on a real treat inside: one of the finest collections in the US, with a twelfth-century French cloister, Renaissance art, a complete **Robert Adam** interior from a 1765 house in London's Berkeley Square, Pennsylvania Dutch crafts and **Shaker furniture**, a strong **Impressionist** collection and the world's most extensive gathering of the works of **Marcel Duchamp**. The entire museum has been undergoing reorganization for the past few years, so it can be difficult to find your way around, but it's still among Philly's most worthwhile stops.

A statue of Stallone as Rocky stood for a while on the steps, but the museum authorities shunted it away as soon as discreetly possible, considering it to be out of keeping with the general theme of their decor. Statuary addicts may find some consolation for that loss in the exquisite **Rodin Museum**, a few blocks away at Franklin Parkway and 22nd St. Marble-walled, and set in a shady garden with a green pool, it holds the largest collection of Rodin's Impressionistic sculptures and casts outside Paris, including *The Thinker*, the *Burghers of Calais* and the *Gates of Hell* (Tues–Sun 10am–5pm; $1). Among rare books at the Free Library of Philadelphia, 19th and Vine, are cuneiform tablets from 3000 BC, medieval manuscripts, first editions of Dickens and Poe, and such intriguing titles as the 1807 *Inquiry into the Conduct of the Princess of Wales* (Mon–Fri 9am–5pm, tours at 11am; free).

Over the road in the vast **Franklin Institute Science Museum** (daily 9.30am–5pm), are a **Planetarium** ($6), the four-storey **OMNIVERSE movie theater** ($7), and the **Futures Center** (also open Wed–Sun until 9pm; $6) – a state-of-the-art facility filled with entertaining high-tech gadgets like a hugely popular machine on which you can see (disappointingly hazy) images of your face aged by 25 years. A **combination ticket** ($14.50) covers admission to all three. Continuing the educational theme, the nearby **Academy of Natural Sciences** exhibits dinosaurs, mummies and gems (Mon–Fri 10am–4.30pm, Sat & Sun 10am–5pm; $5.50).

Eastern State Penitentiary

One of Philadelphia's most significant historic sites stands, all but forgotten, just a short walk from the Fairmount Park museums. The **Eastern State Penitentiary**, whose gloomy Gothic fortifications fill an entire block of the residential neighborhood along Fairmount Avenue at 22nd Street, embodies an almost complete history of attitudes toward crime and punishment in the US. Since it opened in 1829, the Quaker-inspired prison's efforts to rehabilitate inmates rather than punish them attracted visitors from around the world; when Charles Dickens came to America in 1842, he wanted to see two things, this prison and Niagara Falls. Though it underwent substantial changes in its 140-year history, and has slowly decayed since its final closure in 1970, the bulk of the Panopticon-style radial prison survives, and preservationists have recently embarked on a major restoration programme. Because many of the buildings are in a perilous state, the prison is open only for **guided tours** (reserve on ☎546-0532), which point out its many novel architectural features, as well as the cell where Al Capone cooled his heels and the cell block where Tina Turner filmed a music video.

West Philadelphia

Across the Schuylkill River, **West Philadelphia** is home to the Ivy League **University of Pennsylvania**, where Franklin established the country's first medical school. The compact campus blends into fairly gritty urban areas, but has a few good museums: the small **Institute of Contemporary Art**, 36th and Sansom, with cutting-edge travelling exhibitions in an airy white space (Tues & Thurs–Sun 10am–5pm, Wed 10am–7pm; $2, free on Wed); the **University Museum of Archeology and Anthropology**, 33rd and Spruce (Sept–June, Tues–Sat 10am–4.30pm, Sun 1–5pm; $3); and the galleries inside the newly restored **Fine Arts Library** (Mon–Sat 9am–5pm; free), 34th and Walnut, which has an exceptional collection of architectural drawings and models.

South Philadelphia

South Philadelphia, center of Philadelphia's black community since the Civil War, is also home to many of the city's Italians; opera singer **Mario Lanza** (who has his own museum at 416 Queen St) and pop stars Fabian and Chubby Checker grew up here. It's also where to come for an authentic – and very messy – **cheesesteak**, and to rummage through the wonderful **Italian Market**, which runs along Ninth Street south from Christian Street. One of the last surviving urban markets in the US, the wooden market stalls that have stood here for generations are packed to overflowing with bargain-basement flowers, fabrics, secondhand Levis, live seafood, and fragrant olive oils.

South Street, the original boundary of the city, is now Philadelphia's main **nightlife** district, with dozens of cafés, bars, restaurants and nightclubs lined up along the few blocks west from Front Street. During the day you can wander amongst the many good book, record and clothing **shops** (the *Book Trader*, 501 South St, is open daily until midnight), and it's lively almost every night – on summer weekends it can be impossible to move for the crowds.

Accommodation

Philadelphia's luxury downtown hotels are prohibitively expensive, though many do bargain **weekend packages**. The visitor center is a great resource for accommodation discounts. **B&Bs** are a good option, but often need to be arranged in advance. *B&B Center City*, 1804 Pine St (☎735-1137), has rooms throughout the city for rates between $40 and $85 per night.

Bank Street Hostel, 32 S Bank St (☎922-0222 or 1-800/392-HOST). Friendly, central hostel with good facilities (fully air-conditioned) and public spaces. Beds $14, closed 10am–4.30pm. ①.

Chamounix Mansion International AYH Hostel, West Fairmount Park (☎878-3676). Quaker country estate in a gorgeous park setting, but a bit of a trek from downtown. Midnight curfew, closed 11am–4pm and in winter; beds $10 members, $13 non-members. ①.

Comfort Inn, 100 N Delaware Ave (☎627-7900). High-rise hotel in a great location near Penn's Landing; rates include continental breakfast. ⑤.

International House, 3701 Chestnut St (☎387-5125). Student-only rooms adjacent to University of Pennsylvania. ③.

Penn's View Inn, 14 N Front St (☎922-7600). Modern, clean and comfortable rooms between the river, Olde City and Independence Hall. ⑤.

Ramada Inn, 501 N 22nd St (☎568-8300). North of the Franklin Parkway, near the museums and Fairmount Park. ④.

Shippen Way Inn, 418 Bainbridge St (☎627-7266). Newly renovated, family-run B&B a block from South St. ④.

Thomas Bond House, 129 S Second St (☎923-8523). Twelve-room 1769 B&B near INHP. ⑤.

Eating

Eating out in Philadelphia is a real treat; try Chinatown, Reading Terminal Market and the Italian Market for ethnic food, South Street for trendy and reasonably priced restaurants, and the ubiquitous street stands for **soft pretzels** with mustard (around 50¢). The South Philly **cheesesteak** varies from joint to joint around town, though logically enough some of the best are to be found in the Italian cafés around Ninth and Passyunk in South Philadelphia. And remember: a cheesesteak is hot, a **hoagie** is not.

Alyan's, 603 S Fourth St (☎922-3553). Small Middle Eastern restaurant off South St. Dinner from $7. Bring your own bottle.

City Tavern, Second and Walnut (☎923-6059). Reconstructed 1773 tavern in INHP, familiar to the city's founders, and called by John Adams "the most genteel tavern in America". Costumed staff serve "olde style" food (pasties, turkey rarebit) to a harpsichord accompaniment, but the prices, sadly, are historically inaccurate – from about $16 for dinner. Lunch is cheaper.

Delilah's, Reading Terminal Market, 12th and Spruce (☎574-0929). Superb soul food, scatty service. Nigerian stew with cornbread $4.75, beans and rice $3.50.

Diner on the Square, 1839 Spruce St (☎735-5787). 24hr diner off Rittenhouse Square serving staple foods (including a good cheesesteak) from $4 and with a circular soda- and ice-cream bar.

Lee's Hoagies, 44 S 17th St (☎564-1264). Downtown lunch place; a thousand variations on a single theme. The regular hoagies (from $3.75) are giant; the giants (from $7.50), truly gargantuan.

Montserrat, 623 South St (☎627-4224). Wide variety of fresh healthy food, with a vegetarian emphasis, served inside or on a large deck overlooking the South Street parade.

Serrano, 20 S Second St (☎928-0770). Intimate Olde City café. International home-cooking – comfort food from around the world. Diners get preferred seating at the *Tin Angel* folk club (see opposite).

South Street Diner, 140 South St (☎627-5258). Huge menu with Greek and Italian specialties from $5.25. Seven days, 24hr.

White Dog Café, 3420 Sansom St (☎386-9224). Trendy, creative food in an antique-filled room near the universities. Arty, student crowd, dinners cost $12–25.

Drinking

A trail of theme bars has sprung up along Penn's Landing and the Delaware River, but by far the most popular place for bar-hopping is **South Street; Second Street** in the Olde City also has a few good places. Philly's few cafés are spread around the city; South Street and Second Street again have the densest concentrations.

BeatHaus, 12th and Ellsworth (☎465-6106). "Where Art Lives" – late-night South Philly coffee bar with jazz, folk and spoken word performances.

Borgia Café, 406 S Second St (☎574-0414). Live jazz, plus food.

Dickens Inn, 421 S Second St (☎928-9307). English-style pub in Head House Square, with three large bars and over 60 different single malt whiskies.

Irish Pub, 1123 Walnut St (☎568-5603). Good music and atmosphere near Rittenhouse Square.

The Khyber Pass, 56 S Second St (☎440-9683). Philly's oldest and most congenial bar, with huge range of beers; it's also a good place to hear local bands (see opposite).

Last Drop Coffeehouse, 1300 Pine St (☎893-0434). Trendy new café, with Philly's best espresso.

Who's on Third, 700 S Third St (☎625-2835). Irish pub just below South St. Happy hour 7–9pm.

Woody's Pub, 202 S 13th St (☎545-1893). Friendly downtown beer bar that's a popular haunt of Phily's gay community.

Nightlife and Entertainment

Few reminders are left of the 1970s "Philly Sound"; stars like Patti LaBelle, the O'Jays and Harold *If You Don't Love Me By Now* Melvin and the Blue Notes have waned, though their legacy is readily apparent in the smooth vocals of contemporary artists like Boyz II Men. The world-famous **Philadelphia Orchestra** performs at the grand

Academy of Music on Broad St (☎893-1930), modelled after Milan's La Scala; nose-bleed seats cost just $2 on the day, and they give free summer concerts at the Mann Music Center in Fairmount Park (☎567-0707). Philadelphia's other great strength is its **theater** scene: small theaters abound. Check the **listings** in Friday's free *City Paper*, or call the 24-hour **event hotline** (☎574-1200). *TIXSTOP*, in the visitor center, offers half-price standby tickets (Tues–Thurs 11.30am–3.30pm, Fri & Sat 11.30am–5pm).

Annual events in Philadelphia include the week-long *Freedom Fest* around the Fourth of July, and the superb *Riverblues* weekend festival on the Delaware River, at the end of July, which features top-name blues artists.

Chestnut Cabaret, 3801 Chestnut St (☎382-1201). Wide range of once and soon-to-be big name rock and blues performers.

Katmandu, Pier 25, N Delaware Ave (☎629-7400). World music in "exotic" surroundings just north of the decidedly unexotic Franklin Bridge. Bar and nightly outdoor barbecue.

The Khyber Pass, 56 S Second St (☎440-9683). Small rock venue with a gargoyle-lined wooden bar, bluesy jukebox and casual young clientele. Cover $2–6 when bands are playing.

Painted Bride Art Center, 230 Vine St (☎925-9914). Art gallery with live folk, jazz, poetry performances after dark.

Theater of Living Arts, 334 South St (☎922-1011). Converted movie palace that's the best place to catch "alternative" rock bands.

Tin Angel, 20 S Second St (☎928-0770). Intimate upstairs bar and coffeehouse, featuring top local and nationally known singer-songwriters.

Trocadero, Tenth and Arch (☎923-ROCK). Trendy downtown dance club with occasional live bands. Cover varies, ID essential.

Central Pennsylvania

Central Pennsylvania, cut north to south by the broad **Susquehanna River**, has no major cities, although it holds the state capital, **Harrisburg**, and the Civil War site of **Gettysburg** at its southern border. Its assorted landscapes are sparsely populated, from the rolling Amish farmlands of **Lancaster County** in the southeast to the mighty northern forests of the "Grand Canyon of Pennsylvania" around **Williamsport**, which reveals the legacy of its great nineteenth-century lumber wealth in mansion-lined streets. **Johnstown**, beyond the dramatic Allegheny Mountains in the west, is a tough survivor, subject of many folk songs for its tragic history of floods (the most destructive in 1889 when the South Fork Dam, ten miles east, collapsed and killed over two thousand in ten minutes; the most recent happened in 1977). Northeastern Pennsylvania is also hard-rock **coal mining** country, remembered in cities like **Scranton** by a number of museums, preserved mines, blast furnaces and the country's largest remaining stock of coal-fired railroad machinery at **Steamtown USA National Historic Site**.

Lancaster County – Pennsylvania Dutch Country

Lancaster County, fifty miles west of Philadelphia, stretches for about 45 miles from Churchtown in the east to the Susquehanna River in the west. Although Lancaster City, ten miles east of the river, was US capital for a day in September 1777, the region is famed more for its preponderance of agricultural religious communities, known collectively as the **Pennsylvania Dutch** (a mistaken derivation of *Deutsch*, or German).

An extremely touristy place, even before it was brought to international fame by the movie *Witness*, Lancaster County has maintained its natural beauty in the face of encroaching commercialization. It is a region of gentle countryside and fertile farm-

The **area code** for central Pennsylvania is ☎717.

THE PENNSYLVANIA DUTCH

The people now known as the Pennsylvania Dutch originated as **Anabaptists** in sixteenth-century Switzerland, under the leadership of Menno Simons. His unorthodox advocacy of adult baptism and literal interpretation of the Bible led to the order's persecution. Invited by William Penn to settle in Lancaster County in the 1720s, today the twenty thousand or so Pennsylvania Dutch include the "plain" Old Order **Amish** (a strict order who originally broke away from Simons in 1693) and freer-living **Mennonites**, as well as the "fancy" **Lutheran** groups (distinguished by the colorful circular "hex" signs on their barns). The Amish are the best known, the men with their wide-brimmed straw hats and beards (but no "military" moustaches), the women in bonnets, plain dresses (with no fripperies like buttons), and aprons. Shunning electricity and any exposure to the corrupting influence of the outside world, the Amish power their farms with generators, and travel (at roughly ten miles per hour) in handmade horse-drawn buggies. For all their insularity, the Amish are very friendly and helpful; resist the temptation to photograph them, however, as the making of "graven images" offends their beliefs.

lands, mule-drawn ploughs, tiny roadside bake shops crammed with jams and pies, Amish children wending on old-fashioned scooters to and from their one-room schoolhouses, and flower-filled, immaculate farmhouses. However, attempting to live a simple life away from the pressures of the outside world has proved too much for many Pennsylvania Dutch. A few (mainly Mennonites) have succumbed to commercial need by offering rides in their buggies and meals in their homes. Members of the stricter orders in particular have moved away from ceaseless intrusions of privacy – as well as soaring land prices – to less touristed Ohio and Iowa.

Arrival and Information

The Pennsylvania Turnpike sweeps across the north of the region, but most activity is concentrated further south near the east–west US-30. *Greyhound* arrives in Lancaster City at 22 W Clay St (daily 7am–5.15pm; ☎387-4861), *Amtrak* at 53 McGovern Ave. The bustling **Pennsylvania Dutch Visitors Bureau**, just off US-30 at 501 Greenfield Rd, provides orientation and advice on accommodation (daily 8.30am–5pm; ☎299-8901). In Lancaster City itself, the small **visitor center** at 100 S Queen St downtown in the Southern Farmers' Market has maps for self-guided walking tours (April–Oct Mon–Fri 8.30am–5pm, Sat 10am–3pm, Sun 9am–3pm; ☎392-1776). It organizes guided tours on weekdays at 10am and 1.30pm, and on Sundays at 1.30pm, costing $3.

Visitors keen to learn about Pennsylvania Dutch culture should head to the excellent **People's Place**, Main St, Intercourse, 11 miles east of Lancaster City, which has a well-stocked bookshop, an informative if sentimental slide show, an Amish world museum, and the film *Hazel's People*, plus quilts and artwork (April–Oct Mon–Sat 9.30am–9.30pm, Nov–March 9.30am–4pm). The **Mennonite Information Center**, 2209 Millstream Rd off US-30, organizes lodging with Mennonite families. Call at least two hours ahead for a guide to come with you for a two-hour, $16.50, tour in your car (April–Oct Mon–Sat 9.30am–9.30pm, Nov–March 9.30am–4.30pm; ☎299-0954).

Getting Around

Winding country lanes weave through Pennsylvania Dutch country, passing small villages with eccentric-sounding names such as **Intercourse** (source of many droll postcards, but simply named for its location on the junction of two main roads). Although a car will get you to the quieter back roads the tour buses miss, it's more fun to **ride a bike**. Only then can you feel the benefits of all that pure fresh air – and it shows more consideration for the horse-drawn buggies with which you share the road. *Lancaster Bicycle Touring*, 41 Greenfield Rd (☎394-8475), rents bikes by the day or hour.

For those without transportation, *Red Rose Transit*, 47 N Queen St in Lancaster City (☎397-4246), runs an extensive **bus** and **trolley** system. *Amish Country Tours*, on US-340 between Bird-in-Hand and Intercourse, do four-hour farmlands tours ($19) and limited-number "VIP" tours which stop at Amish properties – a rare opportunity to talk to the people rather than merely gawp at them ($29.95; ☎392-8622). *Ed's Buggy Rides*, US-896, north of Strasburg, are lolloping three-mile countryside excursions for $6 (☎687-0360).

Touring Pennsylvania Dutch Country

Though useful for a general overview and historical insights, the "authentic" Amish attractions of Lancaster County – farms, homes, villages and so on – are all much of a muchness. It's far more satisfying just to explore the countryside for yourself. Here, among the streams with their wooden covered bridges and fields striped with corn, alfalfa and tobacco, the reality hits you – these aren't just actors re-creating an ancient lifestyle, but a living, working community. There's no guarantee as to what you'll see; on Sunday, for example, there are no quilt sales or bake shops, and the men don't work the fields, but there may well be a large gathering of buggies outside one of the farms, indicating an Amish church service (in High German), or a "visiting day".

Among the widely spread formal "attractions", the **Ephrata Cloister**, 632 W Main St, Ephrata (on US-272 and 322) re-creates the eighteenth-century settlement of German Protestant celibates that acted, amongst other things, as an early publishing and printing center (Mon–Sat 9am–5pm, Sun noon–5pm; $4). Further south, about three miles northeast of Lancaster City, the **Landis Valley Museum**, 2451 Kissell Hill Rd, is a living history museum of rural life (Tues–Sat 9am–5pm, Sun noon–5pm; $7).

In Lancaster City itself, a stolid red-brick town with treelined avenues, the **Heritage Center Museum**, Penn Square, exhibits Lancaster folk art, including wagons and rifles, ancient fraktur calligraphy, wooden toys, weathervanes and quilts (May–Dec Mon–Sat 10am–4pm; free). At **Strasburg**, a mixture of tourist tweeness and historical authenticity southeast of Lancaster City on US-896, the **Strasburg Railroad** gives 45-minute round-trip rides in original steam trains through patchwork farmland to Paradise (daily; $6.50; ☎687-7522). Disappointingly, **Paradise** itself holds no heavenly delights, but there are some good views on the way (if little that couldn't be seen by bike or car), and the train makes regular picnic stops. The oldest building in the county, the **Hans Herr House**, 1849 Hans Herr Drive, Willow St, five miles south of downtown Lancaster City off US-222, is a 1719 Mennonite church with a pretty garden and orchard, a medieval German facade and exhibits of early farm life (April–Dec Mon–Sat 9am–4pm; $3).

Lancaster County Accommodation

Accommodation options in Pennsylvania Dutch country range from reasonably priced **hotels** in and around Lancaster City, through **farm vacations** (ask at the Pennsylvania Dutch CVB) to campgrounds. *White Oak Campgrounds*, 372 White Oak Rd, Quarryville, four miles north of Strasburg, overlooks the heart of the Dutch farmlands and hosts a quaint auction on Saturdays (reservations recommended; $12; ☎687-6207).

Brunswick Hotel, Chestnut and Queen (☎397-4801). Seventies-style luxury hotel in the center of downtown Lancaster City, with spacious comfortable rooms. ②.

Countryside Motel, 134 Hartman Bridge Rd (☎687-8431). Six miles east of Lancaster City on Hwy-896. ①.

Dingledein House, 1105 E King St (☎293-1723). Friendly B&B close to Lancaster City. Only four rooms, so call ahead. Rates include a huge country breakfast. ④.

Lancaster Travelodge, 2101 Columbia Ave, US-462 (☎397-4201). Standard lodging two miles south of downtown Lancaster. Slightly higher prices at weekends. ③.

Patchwork Inn, 2319 Old Philadelphia Pike (☎293-9078). Nineteenth-century farm between Lancaster City and Smoketown. ④.

Red Caboose Motel, Paradise Lane, Strasburg (☎687-6646). Quirky accommodation in converted train cabooses. ③.

Lancaster County Eating and Nightlife

Lancaster County **food** is delicious: Germanic, organic, and served in vast quantities. There are no Amish-owned restaurants, but Amish roadside stalls sell fresh homemade root beer, jams, pickles, breads and pies. The huge "all-you-can-eat" **tourist restaurants** on US-30 and US-340 may look off-putting, all pseudo-rusticism with costumed waitresses, but most serve excellent meals (for around $13.50), "family-style" – you share long tables and limitless mountains of fried chicken, sauerkraut, noodles, pickles, cottage cheese and apple butter, corn, hickory-smoked ham, *schnitz, knepp*, apple dumplings and shoo-fly pie with crowds of other tourists. None stays open later than 8pm.

Rural Lancaster County, where people get up at the crack of dawn, is not known for its wild **nightlife** – or any nightlife for that matter; even the streets of Lancaster City are strangely quiet after dark. Options are not totally limited to early nights or cable TV, however; a couple of good – and very friendly – bars are worth exploring downtown. The *Fulton Opera House*, 12 N Prince St (☎397-7425), is a plush red and gold restored Victorian theater, hosting dance, plays and special events.

Central Market, Penn Square, Lancaster City. Fresh farm produce and sandwiches. Tues & Fri 6am–4.30pm, Sat 6am–2pm.

Family Style Restaurant, 2323 E Lincoln Hwy (☎393-2323). The only "family-style" restaurant open on Sunday, and one of the few to serve alcohol. Also does breakfast.

Good'n'Plenty, East Brook Rd, US-896, Smoketown (☎394-7111). Not Amish-owned, but Amish women cook and serve food in the best of the family-style restaurants. Open Mon–Sat until 8pm.

Lancaster Dispensing Co, 33–35 N Market St, Lancaster City (☎299-4602). Downtown Lancaster's trendiest and friendliest bar. Live weekend jazz and blues, plus chili, burgers and sandwiches.

Molly's Pub, 53 E Chestnut St, Lancaster City (☎396-0225). Neighborhood bar with lively atmosphere and good burgers. Closed Sun.

Tom Paine's Grog House and Restaurant, 317 N Queen St, Lancaster City (☎393-3671). One of the more expensive restaurants, with an ancient candlelit wooden bar where Revolutionary War tactics were whispered and plotted. Closed Sun.

Harrisburg and Hershey

HARRISBURG, Pennsylvania's capital, lies on the Susquehanna River thirty or so miles northwest of Lancaster City. As you approach, the tower blocks of the skyline appear to lurk miserably on the horizon, but once you arrive it's a surprisingly attractive city, lined with many shuttered colonial buildings and well complemented by its kitsch Chocolatetown neighbor **Hershey**. Harrisburg is also known as the site of **Three Mile Island** nuclear facility, which stands along the river on the east side of town.

Harrisburg's ornate **capitol** at Third and State is undeniably beautiful; at its dedication in 1906, Theodore Roosevelt called it "the handsomest building I ever saw". Italian Renaissance in style, it has a dome modelled after St Peter's in Rome (Mon–Sat 9am–4pm; free). The complex includes the archeological and military artefacts, decorative arts, tools and machinery exhibited in the free **State Museum of Pennsylvania**, a cylindrical building at Third and North (Tues–Sat 9am–5pm, Sun noon–5pm).

One of the nicer ways to spend a Harrisburg afternoon is to cross the Susquehanna along the Walnut Street footbridge and stroll through **City Island**, a waterfront development that, as well as offering vast sports facilities (including a family-filled concrete beach, a baseball stadium and a football ground), gives good views across to downtown, shady picnic areas and riverboat rides, and hosts regular festivals and concerts.

HERSHEY, ten miles east, is by no means the "sweetest place on earth" – whatever the brochures may say. This sober small town, built in 1903 by candy magnate Milton S Hershey for his chocolate factory, does, however, have streets named Chocolate and Cocoa Avenue, streetlamps in the shape of Hershey's chocolate kisses, and air rich with the smell of cocoa. The excessive **Hershey Chocolate World** (daily 9am–6.45pm) offers a free mini-train ride through a simulated chocolate factory (accompanied by sugary piped warblings of *It's a chocolate, chocolate world*). Those not content with the free sample given out at the end can guzzle in the vast gift and souvenir shops and cafés.

Hersheypark, which began in 1907 as a picnic ground for Hershey factory workers, is now a huge **amusement park** with roller coasters and sundry other rides (mid-May–Sept daily, hours vary; $21.95). The adjacent **Hershey Museum of American Life** has exhibits on the Pennsylvania Dutch and tells the story of Hershey himself, the man who started it all (daily 10am–5pm; $1.25).

Practicalities

Amtrak **trains** share the central new station at Fourth and Chestnut with *Greyhound* (☎232-4251), who also stop in Hershey at 337 W Chocolate St (☎397-4861). Harrisburg's **visitor center** at 114 Walnut St (☎232-1377) provides maps and a downtown **walking tour**. **Hotels** on the outskirts of town, aimed towards business travellers, are pricey (but considerably cheaper at weekends). *Quality Inn Riverfront*, 525 S Front St (☎233-1611; ③), is in downtown Harrisburg; alternatives include the *Fairway*, 1034 E Chocolate Ave (☎533-5179; ④), in Hershey, and the *Chocolatetown Motel* (March–Oct only; ☎533-2330; ④), a mile further down the road at 1806 Chocolate Ave.

Cheap **restaurants** line Second Street in downtown Harrisburg, the very best being *Zephyr Express*, 400 N Second St, which serves superb gourmet pasta from $5 in a lively chrome Art Deco setting (☎257-1328). The popular *Roberto's Pizza*, 340 N Second St, does juicy slices and subs from $1.50 (☎234-6633), and *Kick'n Chicken Café*, 900 N Third St, has good spicy chicken from around $3 (☎236-1930).

Gettysburg

The attractive small town of **GETTYSBURG**, thirty miles south of Harrisburg near the Maryland border, gained tragic notoriety in July 1863 for the cataclysmic **Civil War** battle in which fifty thousand men died. There were more casualties during these three days than in any American battle before or since – a full third of those who fought were killed or wounded – and entire regiments were wiped out when the tide finally turned against the South.

Four months later, on November 19, Abraham Lincoln delivered his **Gettysburg Address** at the dedication of the National Cemetery. His two-minute speech, in memory of all the soldiers who died, is acknowledged as one of the most powerful orations in American history. Lincoln himself was convinced that it was a "flat failure", and prefaced his remarks with the words "the world will little note nor long remember what we say here . . ."; you'll be muttering it in your sleep by the time you leave.

Gettysburg, by far the most baldly **commercialized** of all the Civil War sites, is overwhelmingly geared towards **tourism**, relentlessly replaying the minutest details of the battle. Fortunately it is perfectly feasible to avoid the crowds and commercial overkill and explore for yourself the rolling hills of the battlefield (now a national park) and the tidy town streets with their shuttered historic houses.

Arrival, Information and Getting Around

Greyhound (☎334-7064) makes two stops daily to and from Philadelphia outside the Gettysburg College on Carlisle St. From here it's a short walk to the extremely helpful **Gettysburg Travel Council**, 35 Carlisle St, housed in the tiny historic train depot where Lincoln disembarked in November 1863 (☎334-6274).

Though the town is small, and easy to walk around, a car helps when touring the huge battlefield. There are no taxis, but **bikes** can be rented in the battleground at 610 Taneytown Rd (April–Oct; from $2 per hour to $16 per day; ☎334-1258). Two-hour *Battlefield Bus Tours*, running through the town and making two stops in the battlefield, depart from 778 Baltimore St (daily, every thirty minutes; $9.75; ☎334-6296).

The Battleground

It takes most of a day to see the 3500-acre **Gettysburg National Military Park**, which surrounds the town (daily 6am–10pm; free). The **visitor center** on Taneytown Rd (daily 8am–6pm; ☎334-1124) doubles as the best **museum** with guns, uniforms, surgical and musical instruments, tents and flags, as well as touching photos of the 1938 Joint Soldiers Reunion. A thirty-minute – and painstakingly thorough – electric map show ($2) plots the intricacies of the battle; you can pick up details of a self-guided **driving route** or a **guide** will join you in your car for a personalized two-hour tour ($17.50).

A short walk away, the **Cyclorama Center** holds a 356ft circular painting of **Pickett's Charge**, the suicidal Confederate thrust across open wheat fields in broad daylight, and is accompanied by a recitation of the Gettysburg Address (daily 9am–5pm; $2). The earliest existing draft of the Address (not, as commonly believed, scrawled on the back of an envelope), sits in a hallowed cabinet in a dark room on the lower storey. If you're dissatisfied with mere representations of the battlefield, the unsightly **National Tower** opposite the visitor center gives views of the real thing from 300ft observation decks (summer daily 9am–7.30pm, winter 9am–6pm; $3.75). The battlegrounds themselves, golden fields reminiscent of an English country landscape, are peaceful now except for the names – **Valley of Death**, **Bloody Run**, **Cemetery Hill**. Uncanny statues of key figures stand at appropriate points and heavy stone monuments honor different regiments.

The Town

Pick just a couple of the numerous museums in town and follow the Travel Council's fourteen-block downtown walking tour for a sense of the history of the place. The **National Civil War Wax Museum** (daily 9am–9pm; $3.95), 297 Steinwehr Ave, shows, using dreadful dummies, the lead-up to the Civil War, the Underground Railroad for escapee slaves, abolitionist John Brown, and the famous Southern belle spies Rose Greenhow and Belle Boyd. Across the National Cemetery in the battlefield, there are yet more dummies in the **Hall of Presidents and their First Ladies**, 504 Baltimore St, complete with pearls of presidential wisdom and stirring patriotic music (daily, summer 9am–9pm, off-season 9am–5pm; $4). The only civilian to die in the battle, twenty-year-old Jennie Wade, was killed by a stray bullet as she made bread for the Union troops in her sister's kitchen. The **Jennie Wade House**, next to the Gettysburg Tour Center on Baltimore St, looks exactly as it did on July 3 1863, with bullet holes in the front door and on the bedpost, an artillery shell hole ripped through the wall adjoining the neighbor's house, and a macabre model of Jennie's corpse lying under a sheet in the cellar (daily 9am–10pm, 9am–5pm off-season; $2.95).

President Eisenhower, who retired to Gettysburg, is commemorated to the west of the park at the **Eisenhower National Historic Site**, where his Georgian-style mansion holds an array of memorabilia. The site is only accessible on shuttle bus tours from the National Park visitor center (daily 8.30am–4.15pm; $2.25).

Accommodation

There are plenty of lodgings in Gettysburg itself; choose from B&Bs, luxury motels and a very good hostel.

AYH Gettysburg International Hostel, 27 Chambersburg St (☎334-1020). Historic Civil War building in the center of downtown. Excellent value at $10 for non-members. ①.

Farnsworth House Inn, 401 Baltimore St (☎334-8838). An 1810 townhouse, used as Union HQ in the war and still riddled with bullet holes. Four rooms, with breakfast, afternoon tea and ghost stories in the cellar. ④.

Heritage Motor Lodge, 64 Steinwehr Ave (☎334-9281). Between downtown and the battlefield. ③.

Howard Johnson Lodge, 301 Steinwehr Ave (☎334-1181). Directly opposite the entrance to the battleground. ④.

Eating and Nightlife

Evenings in Gettysburg tend to be quiet; the tour buses have gone home and many people choose to drink in their hotel bars. However, there are some good **restaurants**, many in historically important buildings, and for those still hungry for battle trivia, James Getty, an Abe Lincoln lookalike, gives summer evening performances, answering questions and recounting "memories" of his life, at the *Conflict Theater*, 213 Steinwehr Ave (Mon–Thurs 8pm; $5; ☎334-8003).

Dobbin House Tavern, 89 Steinwehr Ave (☎334-2100). The oldest house in the city, dating from 1776 and once an underground slave hideout. Lunch from $6, candlelit dinners more expensive. Food veers between Pennsylvania Dutch and early American.

Dutch Cupboard, 523 Baltimore St (☎334-6227). Sturdy Pennsylvania Dutch cooking (meatloaf, *snitz und knepp*, chicken and noodles, shoo-fly pie) in simple setting, from $3 for lunch, $8 dinner.

Tavern in the Village, 619 Baltimore St (☎334-5648). Gourmet sandwiches, happy hour 6–8pm.

Western Pennsylvania

Western Pennsylvania, a key point for frontier trade and an important thoroughfare to the west, was the focus of the fighting between English and French in the seven-year French and Indian War for colonial and maritime power (1756–63). It grew to industrial prominence in the nineteenth century, with the exploitation of its coal resources gathering pace after the Civil War, and the opening of the world's first oil well at Titusville (now Drake Well Memorial Park) in northwestern Pennsylvania in 1859.

Today, tourism in western Pennsylvania, like the now-quiet coal and steel industries, is concentrated around the surprisingly appealing city of **Pittsburgh**. If you're looking for a more rural experience, however, the lush **Allegheny National Forest** in the north, twenty miles from I-80, is a great place to explore. The summer-only Kinzua Point Information Center on Hwy-59 (☎726-1291) can provide details on campgrounds and trails.

Pittsburgh

The vibrant ten-block district, known as the "Golden Triangle", at the heart of downtown **PITTSBURGH** stands at the confluence of the Monongahela, Allegheny and Ohio rivers, once bitterly fought over as the gateway to the west. The French built Fort Duquesne on the site in 1754, only for it to be destroyed four years later by the British, who replaced it with **Fort Pitt**. Industry began with the development of iron foundries in the early 1800s, and by the time of the Civil War Pittsburgh was producing half of the iron and one third of the glass in the US. Soon after Pittsburgh became the world's leading producer of steel, thanks to the vigorous expansion programmes of **Andrew Carnegie** – who, by 1870, was the richest man in the world.

Although transformed by two so-called "renaissances" since the Fifties, Pittsburgh still can't quite shake off its grimy Victorian reputation as dirty and polluted. The first face-lift involved large-scale demolition which freed up much of the downtown waterfront, but all-out yuppification has been kept in check by the student population and the small-town feel of the older ethnic neighborhoods to the north and south. Pittsburgh today, with one of the lowest crime rates in the country, has been rated America's most liveable city, and these days resilience and enthusiasm fill the air rather than coal fumes, and sleek architecture and green parks supplant smokestacks and slums.

Each of Pittsburgh's close-knit neighborhoods – the **South Side** and **Mount Washington**, across the Monongahela River from the **Golden Triangle** downtown, the **North Side** across the Allegheny River, and **Oakland**, the university area in the east – attests in its own way to the city's history and its resurgence. Easily accessible from each other, they retain individual identities while remaining part of a proud whole.

The **area code** for Pittsburgh and southwestern Pennsylvania is ☎412.

Arrival and Information

Greyhound (☎391-2300) pulls in at Eleventh St and Liberty Ave downtown, across from *Amtrak*. From the airport, 15 miles west, the *Airline Transport Company* (☎665-8115) runs **shuttles** downtown (daily 5am–10pm; $9) and to Oakland (daily 7am–8pm).

Pittsburgh has two main **visitor centers**: downtown on Liberty Ave, adjacent to the Gateway Center (Mon–Fri 9.30am–5pm, Sat & Sun 9.30am–3pm; ☎281-9222), and in Oakland at Forbes Ave on the University of Pittsburgh campus (Tues–Sun 10am–4pm; ☎624-4660). The main **post office** is at Seventh and Grant (Mon–Fri 7am–6pm, Sat 7am–2.30pm; ☎642-4472; zip code 15230).

Getting Around

Though Pittsburgh is a city of distinct districts, transportation between them is simple. **Buses** through town ($1.15), the Monongahela trolley incline to Mount Washington (daily until late; $1) and a small "*T*" **subway** system (free downtown, 75¢ to cross the river to the South Side) are all run by PAT (☎231-5707). Useful routes run to Oakland and Shady Side along the **East Busway**, avoiding the traffic-clogged city streets. For **taxis**, call *Yellow Cabs* (☎665-8100). *Gray Line* (☎741-2720) runs city and area tours.

Downtown: the Golden Triangle

The *New York Times* once described Pittsburgh as "the only city with an entrance", and the view of the **Golden Triangle** skyline on emerging from the tunnel on the Fort Pitt Bridge is undeniably breathtaking. Surrounded by water and fronted with a huge fountain, Pittsburgh's downtown pays tribute both to its coal-grimed past and sunny future. In the core of the original city, the Triangle's imaginative contemporary architecture stands comfortably next to Gothic churches and red-brick warehouses. Philip Johnson's magnificent postmodern concoction, the black-glass Gothic **PPG Place** complex, looms incongruously over the old **Market Square**, lined with historic restaurants and shops. More recent history is apparent on the faded buildings along Liberty Avenue, with Forties and Fifties fronts left in peace during successive face-lifts.

Point State Park, at the peak of the Triangle, is where it all began, the site of five different forts during the French and Indian War. This popular gathering area has a 150ft fountain with a pool, as well as great views of port activity and across to the colorful old buildings on verdant Mount Washington. The **Fort Pitt Museum** (Tues–Sat 9am–5pm, Sun noon–5pm; $3), 101 Commonwealth Place in the park, was once England's largest North American fort; now its exhibits include dioramas, scale models and reconstructions of three forts. Opposite, the 1764 Fort Pitt Blockhouse is the oldest structure in the city, a look-out of sandstone and rough brick.

Northeast of downtown along Penn Avenue, the **Strip District** is an anarchic early-morning market with wholesale outlets and fresh produce stalls, popular with bargain hunters and good for cheap breakfasts. Guided **walking tours** detail the history and development of the area (☎276-0908).

South Side

In the nineteenth century, 400ft **Mount Washington**, across the Monongahela River, was the site of most of the city's coal mines. No longer dominated by belching steel mills and industry, the South Side, banked by the green "mountain", is an area of many churches, colorful houses nestling in steep hills, and old neighborhoods. These days only two survive of the twelve cable cars which, at the height of steel production, used to carry coal up the trolley inclines. The 1877 **Duquesne Incline**, from 1197 W Carson St to 1220 Grandview Ave, is the most interesting for its small museum of Pittsburgh

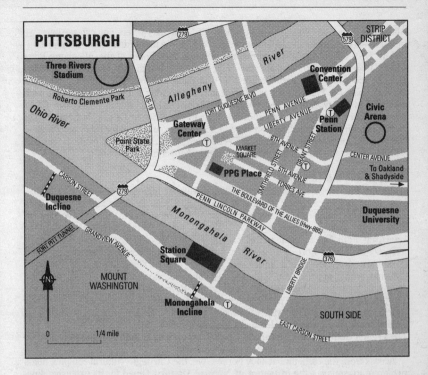

history in the waiting room at the top; old photos of the city show workers struggling blindly through the streets in pitch-black midday smog (daily until 1am; $1). The outdoor observation platform is a prime spot for **views** over the Golden Triangle to the hills on the horizon; the prospect is absolutely awesome after dark. Not surprisingly, many (expensive) bars and restaurants here take advantage of the vista.

South Side's new gentility begins with red-brick **Station Square**, a complex of renovated railroad warehouses filled with restaurants and shops. Its showpiece is the beautiful stained glass and marble of the *Grand Concourse* restaurant, filling the huge waiting room of the old *Pittsburgh and Lake Erie* train station. Old cars and steam train memorabilia in the **Transportation Museum** in Bessemer Court illuminate the story of western Pennsylvania's railroads (summer daily noon–8pm, winter noon–6pm; $1).

Along the banks of the Monongahela at the foot of Mount Washington, East Carson Street is the main drag of the lively mixed residential and commercial **South Side**, where a longstanding community of Polish and Ukrainian steelworkers has gradually absorbed an offbeat mix of cafés, bars and bookstores. Onion-domed churches stand alongside thrift stores and galleries, and the narrow backstreets are lined by brick-built rowhouses. This is also one of Pittsburgh's prime **nightlife** centers.

North Side

Revitalization on the **North Side**, annexed by Pittsburgh only in 1907, centers around the intriguingly named **Mexican War Streets** on the northern edge of Allegheny Commons. In this unevenly restored tree-lined area of nineteenth-century grey brick and limestone terraces, old families, descendants of German and Scandinavian immigrants, live in an uneasy truce alongside young professionals. The **Pittsburgh Aviary**,

Allegheny Commons West, is a huge indoor bird sanctuary where you can see over two hundred species, including foul-mouthed parrots, in free flight (daily 9am–4.30pm; $2).

The **USS Requin**, a 1945 submarine, bobs on the shores of the Allegheny River (daily 10am–6pm; $2), outside the huge new state-of-the-art **Carnegie Science Center**, most of whose exhibits are aimed at children more than adults. One, "The Works", explores Pittsburgh's past by means of a working foundry. It also holds such wonders as the world's largest cockroach (from Florida), and an impressive IMAX movie theater. **Three Rivers Stadium**, next to the Science Center, is home to the Pittsburgh Pirates baseball and Steelers football teams, and open for hour-long "behind the scenes" tours when no games are scheduled; if you come for a game, be sure to climb up to the top levels for a grand panorama of downtown Pittsburgh.

Oakland and the East Side

Oakland, Pittsburgh's university area (dotted with the mansions of wealthy industrialists), today houses a strong mixture of Italian and Greek families. Sights concentrate around the campuses of **Carnegie-Mellon University** and the **University of Pittsburgh** (always known as "Pitt"). The 42-storey Gothic-revival **Cathedral of Learning**, Fifth Ave at Bigelow Blvd, called by Frank Lloyd Wright "the world's largest *Keep Off the Grass* sign", is a university building with a difference: over twenty classrooms are furnished with antiques and specially crafted items donated by the city's different ethnic groups, from Lithuanian through Chinese to Irish. These beautiful rooms, far more interesting than they may sound, have been used by students since the Thirties; all are open to the public except the exotic Syria-Lebanon room and the Early American room, complete with trap door and secret passage, which are shown on guided tours only (tape-recorded tours Mon–Sat 9am–4.30pm, Sun 11am–4.30pm; $2). The French Gothic **Heinz Memorial Chapel**, on campus at Fifth Ave and Bellefield St, is notable for its long, skinny, stained glass windows.

Across from the cathedral at 4400 Forbes Ave, the **Carnegie** cultural complex holds two great museums – the **Museum of Natural History**, famed for its extensive dinosaur relics and sparkling gems, and the **Museum of Art**, with Impressionist, Post-Impressionist and American regional art, as well as an excellent modern collection (Tues–Thurs & Sat 10am–5pm, Fri 10am–9pm, Sun 1–5pm; $5, Fri 3–9pm half-price). Schenley Park nearby includes the colorful flower gardens of **Phipps Conservatory** (June–Aug Mon–Fri 9am–5pm, Sept–May Mon–Fri 9am–5pm & 7–9pm; $3).

If you're coming to the East Side from downtown, be sure to avoid the area along Centre Avenue known as **"The Hill"**; this is one of Pittsburgh's most deprived and dangerous districts, especially after dark. Cab drivers avoid it, but as it neighbors the college precincts tourists can easily stumble into it.

Shady Side, on the eastern fringes of Oakland, is an upmarket student district with a villagey feel, especially along Walnut Street. The **Pittsburgh Center for the Arts**, at 6300 Fifth Ave in Mellon Park, showcases innovative Pittsburgh art in various media (Tues & Thurs–Sat 10am–5pm, Wed 10am–8pm, Sun noon–4pm; free).

Further east, the small **Frick Art Museum**, 7227 Reynolds St, has on show Italian, Flemish and French art from the fifteenth to the nineteenth centuries; its collection of decorative art includes two of Marie Antoinette's chairs (Tues–Sat 10am–5.30pm, Sun noon–6pm; free). On the same grounds, **Clayton** is a mansion furnished exactly as it was when industrialist Henry Clay Frick lived there. Obligatory guided **tours** (Wed–Sat 10am–5.30pm, Sun noon–6pm; $5) walk you around the house pointing out the various late-Victorian decorative touches, as well as the bed where Frick recovered after being stabbed by an anarchist during the bitter Homestead Steel Strike. Frick and most of his family are buried, under tons of protective concrete and steel, just south of the family home, on the highest hill in **Homestead Cemetery**, which also holds the tombs of H J Heinz (of the catsup and baked beans fortune) and sundry Mellons.

Accommodation

Pittsburgh's **hotels** are expensive, although weekend packages at luxury downtown hotels can bring rooms down to $75. Oakland has a couple of reasonably priced business hotels and some student accommodation, and the *Pittsburgh B&B Registry*, 2190 Ben Franklin Drive (☎367-8080), has details of rooms from $45.

Carnegie-Mellon University, 1060 Morewood St (☎268-2939). College dorm rooms in Oakland, available during the summer for $25, with a $5 reduction for students. Office hours 8am–5pm. ①.

Howard Johnson, 3401 Blvd of the Allies (☎683-6100). One of the best deals in Oakland. ④.

Point Park College Youth Hostel (AYH), 201 Wood St (☎392-3824). The best deal for budget travellers; clean dorms and good views for $10. June–Sept only, eight blocks from *Greyhound*. ①.

The Priory, 614 Pressley St (☎231-3338). Recently restored 1880s inn, originally built to house travelling Benedictine monks and now offering North Side's nicest B&B. ④.

Pittsburgh Vista, 1000 Penn Ave (☎281-3700). Flashy downtown tower, with pool and gym. ⑦.

Red Roof Inn, 6404 Stubenville Pike, route 60 (☎787-7870). Standard doubles near the airport. ③.

University Inn, Forbes Ave at McKee Place (☎683-6000). Luxury Oakland hotel. ⑤.

Eating

Eating downtown can prove expensive, but there are good neighborhood Italian and eastern European places along and around **Carson Street** on the South Side. Station Square and Mount Washington cater to a more upmarket crowd, while **Oakland** is, as you might expect, home to an array of cheap student hang-outs.

Clark Bar and Grill, 503 Martindale St (☎231-5720). Boisterous burger bar that reaches fever pitch just before Pirates and Steelers games – Three Rivers Stadium is just across the street.

1902 Landmark Tavern, 24 Market Square (☎471-1902). Pricey for dinner, but oysters at the city's oldest oyster bar in the center of downtown go for $7–10.

Grandview Saloon, 1212 Grandview Ave (☎431-1400). Cheap, relaxed Mount Washington restaurant, usually packed with a young crowd. Huge plates of pasta. Arrive early for a table with a view.

Great Scot, 413 Craig St (☎683-1450). Dark publike restaurant round the corner from the Carnegie.

Mallorca, 2228 E Carson St (☎488-1818). Excellent *paella* and Mediterranean dishes on South Side.

South Shore Diner, 1728 E Carson St (☎431-9292). Unpretentious diner on hip South Side street.

Star of India, 412 Craig St (☎681-5700). Functional Indian restaurant in Oakland.

Suzie's Greek Specialties, 1704 Shady Ave (☎422-8066). Homemade Greek dishes including fish and seafood. Good lunchtime sandwiches from $4, with dinner from $9.

Nightlife and Entertainment

With its recent cultural resurgence, Pittsburgh's **nightlife** has soared upmarket, dominated by the performing arts. The nationally regarded *City Theater*, 57 S 13th St (☎431-4900), puts on groundbreaking productions in a converted South Side church; *TIX* booth, 209 Ninth St (☎391-8353), offers half-price theater and concert **tickets** on the day. Jazz fans should check out the South Side and Shady Side districts.

In Pittsburgh, a free newsweekly, has extensive **listings**, as do the *City Paper* and the sexier *Pittsburgh Beat*. There's also a 24-hour Activities Line (☎391-6840).

Balcony, 5520 Walnut St (☎687-0110). Shady Side jazz club. No cover charge, excellent food.

Beehive Coffeehouse, 3807 Forbes Ave (☎488-HIVE). Pittsburgh's liveliest late-night coffeehouse, drawing a young, artsy-alternative crowd. Also at 1327 E Carson St on the South Side.

Metropol, 1600 Smallman St (☎261-4512). Huge, very popular, Strip District warehouse dance club.

Peter's Pub, 116 Oakland Ave (☎681-7465). Rowdy student bar in Oakland (a dodgy area at night).

James Street Tavern, 422 Foreland Ave (☎323-2222). An expensive place to eat, well out on the North Side, but they put on good live jazz in the downstairs bar at weekends.

Nick's Fat City, 1601 E Carson St (☎481-6880). South Side hot spot for playing pool or listening to the usually good live bands. Happy hour 10pm–midnight.

Pittsburgh Sports Garden Bar, 1 Station Square Drive East (☎281-1511). Massive sports bar on the South Side.

NEW JERSEY

The long skinny state of **NEW JERSEY**, squashed between Philadelphia and New York on the Atlantic coast, suffers a severe image problem. Most travellers only see "the Garden State" from the stupendously ugly New Jersey Turnpike toll road, which, heavy with truck traffic, cuts through a landscape of grey smokestacks and industrial estates. Even the songs of **Bruce Springsteen**, Asbury Park's golden boy, paint his home state as a gritty **urban wasteland** of empty lots, grey highways, lost dreams and blue-collar tragedy. In reality, the majority of the refineries and factories hug a mere fifteen-mile-wide swath along the turnpike, but bleak cities like **Newark**, home to the major airport, and **Trenton**, the capital, do little to improve the look of the place.

The Dutch, who had snatched New Jersey from the peaceful Lenni Lenape Indians, turned the land over to the English in the 1660s. During the **Revolution** a battle was fought at **Princeton**, and George Washington spent two bleak winters at **Morristown**. When the **Civil War** came, the state's obvious industrial future ensured that despite its border location along the Mason-Dixon line, it fought with the Union.

There's more to New Jersey than factories and pollution. Both Thomas Paine and Walt Whitman wrote of their years here with fond nostalgia; the **northwest corner** near the **Delaware Water Gap** is traced with picturesque lakes, streams and woodlands, while the **Atlantic shore** offers many attractive resorts.

Getting Around New Jersey

With a car, New Jersey is easily accessible from New York City, via I-95, while the **New Jersey Turnpike** (a $4 toll road) sweeps from the northeast down to Philadelphia. The **Garden State Parkway** runs parallel to the Atlantic from New York to Cape May (with a 35¢ toll every twenty miles), and gives easy access to the shoreline resorts. One nice route in the north of the state is US-29, from Trenton along the Delaware River.

Newark International Airport (☎201/961-2000) is the fastest-growing gateway to the US, served by all the major international carriers and popular for its convenient access to Manhattan (a 30-min bus ride away) rather than for being in New Jersey.

Numerous *Amtrak* **trains** pass through Newark, Princeton and Trenton, en route between Philadelphia, New York and Washington DC, and *Greyhound* covers most of the state. *New Jersey Transit* (☎201/460-8444 or ☎1-800/772-2222) also offers a good train and bus service, extending to Philadelphia and New York as well as out to the coast. New Jersey's south coast is connected to Delaware by the Cape May–Lewes **ferry** (in Cape May, ☎609/886-7218; in Lewes, ☎302/645-6313).

Inland New Jersey

Travelling west on the interstates from the shore or from New York City, visitors see the New Jersey of popular imagination: heavily industrialized, a cultural and visual desert. **Newark**, the state's largest city, is perhaps the nation's drabbest, redeemed only by its efficient airport and views over the Hudson to the Statue of Liberty (which is, incidentally, in New Jersey waters). Northwest of Newark, on I-287, **Morristown**, where Washington spent two harsh winters, is now a national historic park. **Trenton**, the state capital, sits on the Delaware River at the border with Pennsylvania, something of a national joke for its motto, "Trenton makes, the world takes". Nearby **Princeton**, an Ivy League town that makes a pretty stop-off, is one place worth visiting.

The **area code** for Newark and northern New Jersey is ☎201; for Princeton and the coast it's ☎609.

Paterson

Though in some ways it's the sort of New Jersey place most people do their best to avoid, **PATERSON** is perhaps the state's most significant city. Though it last made the news in the 1970s when Bob Dylan campaigned against the trumped-up murder conviction of local boxer **Ruben "Hurricane" Carter**, its historic importance dates back to Revolutionary times, when Alexander Hamilton established the young nation's largest manufacturing complex here in 1791, taking advantage of the immense water-power of the 70ft **Great Falls** of the Passaic River. For 150 years Paterson was at the forefront of American **industry**, its mills responsible for the first Colt revolvers as well as silk fabrics, its millworkers on the front lines of the American Labor movement.

While most of the old looms have been silent since the 1950s, the millraces and buildings survive intact awaiting creative re-use. A new and expanding **museum** (Tues–Fri 10am–4pm, Sat & Sun 12.30–4.30pm; $1) is housed inside the renovated Rogers Locomotive factory at Market and Spruce, but the best first stop is the **Great Falls Visitor Center**, a block away at 65 McBride Ave (Mon–Fri 9am–4pm; ☎279-9587), for a wealth of maps and background information. Don't miss the **waterfalls** themselves, across the street; after a good rain they roar like a mini-Niagara.

Like many old mill towns, Paterson now suffers from serious decay, poverty and unemployment, so it's not really a place to linger. Still, it's easy to reach on a day trip: regular **buses** run from New York's Port Authority building (see p.60); if you're driving, take the Grand Street exit off the I-80 freeway. Once here, there are a couple of good **bars** (such as the *Question Mark* on Van Houten and Cianci, where journalist and labor activist John Reed used to drink) and **cafés** in the historic district where you can get a feel for Paterson's proudly blue-collar character.

Princeton

Staid and self-satisfied **PRINCETON**, on US-206 eleven miles north of Trenton, is home to the Ivy League **Princeton University** – the nation's fourth oldest, which broke away from the overly religious Yale in 1756. It began its days inauspiciously as Stony Brook, and then in 1724 as Princes Town, a coach stop between New York and Philadelphia. In January 1777, a week after Washington's triumph against the British at Trenton, the **Battle of Princeton** occurred southwest of town. This victory, a turning point in the Revolutionary effort, bolstered the morale of Washington's troops before their long winter encampment at Morristown to the north. After the war, in 1783, the **Continental Congress**, fearful of potential attack from incensed unpaid veterans in Philadelphia, met here for four months; the leafy, well-kept town was then left in peace to follow its academic pursuits. Graduates of the university include actor James Stewart, jazz-age writer F Scott Fitzgerald, and presidents Wilson and Madison. Today, there is little to do in this sleepy place other than tour the university and see the historic sites.

Arrival, Information and Getting Around

A shuttle bus, the *Princeton Airporter*, makes the run from Newark (1hr 30min) and JFK (2hr 40min) airports to town (daily 7am–10pm; ☎587-6600). The in-town train terminal, on campus at University Place, a block north of Alexander Road, is connected by *New Jersey Transit* "dinky" **trains** (☎201/378-6300) and *SEPTA* shuttles (☎215/574-7800) to Princeton Junction, three miles south, where both *Amtrak* and *New Jersey Transit* stop on their New York–Philadelphia runs. *Suburban Transit* **buses** (☎201/249-1100) from New York stop every thirty minutes at Nassau St.

Information, including maps and lists of events, is available from Stanhope Hall at the university (Mon–Fri 8.30am–4.30pm; ☎258-3600) or the **CVB**, 20 Nassau St (☎683-1760). The Historical Society, 158 Nassau St (☎921-6748), leads **walking tours** through town (Sun 2pm; $3), and provides **maps** so you can do it yourself.

The Town and the University

Mercer Street, the long road that sweeps southwest past the university campus to Nassau Street, is lined with elegant Colonial houses, graced with shutters, columns and wrought-iron fences. The **Princeton Battlefield State Park**, a mile out, includes the Thomas Clarke House, 500 Mercer St, a Quaker farmhouse that served as a hospital during the battle (Wed–Fri 9am–5pm, Sat 10am–noon, Sun 1–5pm). In a simple house at 112 Mercer St, back towards town, **Albert Einstein** lived while teaching at the Institute of Advanced Study.

Princeton University's tranquil and shaded campus is a beautiful place for a stroll. Just inside the main gates on Nassau Street, **Nassau Hall** (Mon–Fri 2–5pm, Sat 9am–5pm, Sun 1–5pm; free) was, when constructed in 1756, the largest stone building in the nation; its 26-inch-thick walls (now patterned with plaques and patches of ivy placed by graduating classes) withstood American and British fire during the Revolution. It was also the seat of government during Princeton's brief spell as national capital. The 1925 **chapel**, based on Kings College Cambridge, has stained glass windows showing scenes from works by Dante, Shakespeare and Milton as well as the Bible, and the Prospect Gardens, a flowerbed in the shape of the university emblem, are a blaze of orange in summer. In the middle of the campus, fronted by the Picasso sculpture *Head of a Woman*, the **University Art Museum**, not included on the standard tours, is well worth a look for its collection from the Renaissance to the present, including Modigliani, Van Gogh and Warhol, and Chinese and pre-Columbian art (Tues–Sat 10am–5pm, Sun 1–5pm; tours Sat 2pm, museum talks Fri 12.30pm & Sun 3pm; free).

While Princeton has found itself acting as a sanctuary and gathering place for exiled members of China's democracy movement since the **Tiananmen Square** massacre of 1989, a substantial number of those who visit are disarmingly conservative prospective students and their proud parents, soaking up the tales of old-boy pranks and superstitions (for example, that no student should pass through the main gates for fear of being tarnished by the ugly outside world) that prop up the Ivy League tradition. The student-led **tours** may be complacent, but they are free; they leave from the rear of the yellow **Maclean House** at 73 Nassau St (Mon–Sat 10am, 11am, 1.30pm, & 3.30pm; Sun 1.30pm & 3.30pm).

Accommodation, Eating and Drinking

The only **hotel** in the center of Princeton is the pompous, ersatz-Colonial *Nassau Inn*, on Palmer Square (☎921-7500; ⑦). Budget **motels** can be found along US-1 and in the suburb of Lawrenceville a few miles south of town, such as the functional *Sleep-e-Hollow*, 3000 US-1 (☎896-0900; ②), and the *McIntosh Inn* (☎896-3700; ③), by the Quaker Bridge Mall on US-1.

For cheap diner-type **food** try along Witherspoon Street; for a more upmarket feast, the popular *Annex*, 128 Nassau St, serves quality Italian food in a candlelit setting from $7. Vegetarians should try the *Tempting Tiger*, 14 Witherspoon St (☎924-0644), which serves healthy salads, soups and sandwiches, accompanied by classical music, from around $4 (open until 8.30pm, 5.30pm on Sat). **Nightlife** is limited, especially out of term-time, but the *Tap Room* bar downstairs at the *Nassau Inn* is usually full of ancient revellers drinking, reminiscing and enjoying live jazz.

New Jersey Shore

New Jersey's Atlantic coast, a 130-mile stretch of almost uninterrupted **resorts** – some rowdy, many pitifully run-down and faded, a few undeveloped and peaceful – has long been reliant on farming and tourism. No profitable ports were established, nor did shortlived attempts at whaling come to anything. In the late 1980s the whole coastline suffered severe and well-publicized pollution from ocean dumping, but today the beaches, if occasionally somewhat crowded, are now safe and clean, sandy, broad and lined by characteristic wooden **boardwalks**, some of which, in an attempt to maintain their condition, charge admission during the summer. The casinos of the tackily surreal **Atlantic City** are the most brazenly obvious attractions, with the restorative **Spring Lake** and historic Victorian **Cape May** offering quieter charms.

Spring Lake and Asbury Park

SPRING LAKE, about twenty miles down the Jersey coast, is one of the smallest, most uncommercial communities on the shore, a gentle respite on the road south to Atlantic City. Tourism in this elegant Victorian resort evolved slowly, without the booms, crises, resurgences and depressions of other seaside towns – partly due to the strict zoning laws prohibiting new building; and stressed-out city dwellers come here to get away from it all. You can walk the totally undeveloped two-mile **boardwalk** and watch the crashing ocean from battered gazebos, swim and bask on the white beaches (in summer, compulsory beach tags cost $2 per day, but most guest houses provide them free) or sit in the shade by the town's namesake, **Spring Lake** itself. Wooden footbridges, swans and geese, and the grand St Catherine's Catholic Church on the banks of the lake give it the feel of a country village. For the moment, what little activity there is centers on the upmarket shops of Third Avenue.

Bruce Springsteen fans can use the town as a base for visiting nearby **Asbury Park**, a decaying old seaside town where The Boss lived for many years and played his first gigs. Almost nothing remains of the carousels and seaside arcades that Springsteen wrote about on early albums such as his debut *Greetings from Asbury Park*; the sole survivor is Madame Marie's fortune-telling salon, which still stands amid the rubble and half-completed condominium developments that line the boardwalk.

Practicalities

Spring Lake is accessible by US-34 from the New Jersey Turnpike, and served by *New Jersey Transit* from New York. The *Spring Lake Hotel and Guest House Association* (☎449-1332) can help find lodging, especially on summer weekends. There are no cheap **motels**, and **B&Bs** can be expensive. One of the nicest is the easy-going *Sea Crest by the Sea*, 19 Tuttle Ave (☎449-9031; ⑤), an 1885 inn with rooms furnished individually on quirky themes, and an excellent all-you-can-eat home-cooked breakfast. *Ashling Cottage*, 106 Sussex Ave (April–Dec only; ☎449-3553; ④), overlooks the lake.

Most of Spring Lake's **restaurants** are in the elegant Victorian hotels along the seafront, and can be pricey. The **North Pavilion** on the boardwalk sells cheap breakfasts and snacks, but there are no fast-food stands along the walk itself. *Jeffrey's*, 1321 Third Ave (☎449-1661), is a no-nonsense café serving breakfast from $2, lunch from $4. *The Beach House*, 901 Ocean Ave (☎449-9646), is more upmarket, with screened-in verandah seating and healthy lunches from $5, dinner from $16. For a blowout, the *Sandpiper*, 7 Atlantic Ave (☎449-6060), serves superb fresh fish and seafood in elegant candlelit surroundings. Dinner costs around $20; bring your own bottle.

Atlantic City

> *What they wanted was Monte Carlo. They didn't want Las Vegas.*
> *What they got was Las Vegas. We always knew that they would get Las Vegas.*
> Stuart Mendelson, Philadelphia Journal, 1978.

ATLANTIC CITY, on Absecon Island just off the midpoint of the Jersey shoreline, has been a tourist mecca since 1854, when Philadelphia speculators created it as a rail terminal resort. In 1909, at the peak of the seaside town's popularity, Baedeker wrote "there is something colossal about its vulgarity" – a quality which it sustains today, even while beset by bankruptcy and decay. The real-life model for the board game **Monopoly**, it has an impressive popular cultural history, boasting the nation's first **Boardwalk** (1870), the first color **postcards** (1893), the world's first **Big Wheel** (1869) and the first **Miss America Beauty Pageant** (cunningly devised to extend the tourist season in 1921, and still held here yearly).

During Prohibition and the Depression, Atlantic City was a center for rum-running, packed with speakeasies and illegal gambling dens. Thereafter, in the face of increasing competition from Florida, it slipped into apparently terminal decline, until desperate city officials decided in 1976 to open up the decrepit resort to legal **gambling**.

The monster **casinos** that replaced the grand old hotels dominate not just the Boardwalk and the skyline, but the whole culture of the city. Their tackiness puts the lie to the would-be glamorous image; pace Stuart Mendelson, Atlantic City didn't even quite "get" Las Vegas. The place is not so much limousines and roulette as hamburgers and slot machines. As eighty percent of Atlantic City's millions of visitors are day-trippers, there's definitely more glitz than glamor, and the neglected areas inland from the casinos betray the fact that only a very few property developers have benefited from the influx of cash.

Arrival, Information and Getting Around

Travelling to Atlantic City by bus can be a real money-spinner; casino-sponsored **buses** from New York, Philadelphia and other points along the coast give away vouchers exchangeable for cash and free meals to a value well above the fare. It's hoped that you will spend all this money and more in the casinos, but you can easily cash it and leave. The bus terminal (☎347-5413) at Arctic and Arkansas avenues is served by *Greyhound* (☎345-6617) and *New Jersey Transit* (☎1-800/582-5946).

Amtrak has express **trains** from New York, Philadelphia, Washington and Baltimore, and *New Jersey Transit* ($6; ☎1-800/772-3606) **trains** run between Atlantic City and Philadelphia, from 1 Atlantic City Expressway (☎344-9013). Atlantic City International Airport is thirteen miles from downtown in Pleasantville (☎645-8882); the smaller Bader Field Airport (☎345-6402), in the center of town, has connections to Boston, Baltimore, Philadelphia and Pittsburgh.

For maps and **information**, head for the **CVB**, 2310 Pacific Ave (Mon–Fri 9am–5pm; ☎348-7100), or the **visitor center** next door (Mon–Fri 9am–4.30pm; ☎348-7044).

City Transportation

Atlantic City is easy to walk around, although it is unwise to stray farther from the five-mile Boardwalk along the ocean than the parallel Pacific, Atlantic and Arctic avenues. Ventnor and Margate to the south on Absecon Island are served by **buses** along Atlantic Avenue. *Jitneys* (☎344-8642) offers 24-hour minibus service the length of Pacific Avenue, the #1 route travelling as far as Ventnor ($1).

Various **bike rental** stands along the Boardwalk charge about $3 per hour, although cycling is only permitted from 6am until 10am in the summer.

The Town

The hopeful hordes in Atlantic City head straight for the casinos, with an ample over-spill flooding the Boardwalk and beach. Beyond the Boardwalk there is little to see, although a quick walk around the eerily quiet slums of the South Inlet district makes a chilling contrast to the manic jollity a mere block away. This is not an area in which to linger for any length of time, or indeed at all at night – the **danger** is very real.

Atlantic City's wooden **Boardwalk** was originally built as a temporary walkway, raised above the beach so that holiday-makers could take a seaside stroll without tread-

THE CASINOS OF ATLANTIC CITY

Each of Atlantic City's dozen **casinos**, which also act as luxury hotels, conference centers and concert halls, has a slightly different personality, despite the apparent uniformity of vast, richly ornamented halls, slot machines, relentless flashing lights and incessant noise, chandeliers, mirrors, and a disorienting absence of clocks or windows. Apart from a quick flutter, the real pleasure here is in people-watching; from the frisky pensioners cashing in their chips to the shady-looking compulsive types lurking at the roulette wheel. All casinos are **open** 24 hours a day, though things get pretty quiet in the wee hours. Casino **restaurants** keep their own hours, and costumed waitresses serve drinks at the tables and will supply newcomers with rule books. Although officially jeans and T-shirts are frowned upon, in practice most of the punters are extremely **casual**, even after 6pm; during the day many people seem to have just wandered in off the sands. One rule that is never waived is the **age requirement**; you must be 21 to gamble and will be asked to show **ID**.

As time goes on, these overblown amusement arcades have become more and more outrageous in order to compete with each other. By far the most ostentatious is the new kid on the block, Donald Trump's Disneyesque **Taj Mahal**. Occupying nearly twenty acres and over forty storeys high, with glittery minarets and onion domes, this gigantic piece of Far Eastern kitsch stands opposite the arcade-packed Steel Pier at the north end of the Boardwalk. It is one of the largest gambling casinos on earth, precariously tottering on the edge of bankruptcy. At the other end of the scale, the **Claridge**, Indiana Ave and the Boardwalk, dubs itself "the friendly casino" and is smaller, darker and more downmarket than the others. **Sands**, next door at South Indiana Ave, is a noisy and popular venue on a pink flamingo theme. Both these properties are slightly off the Boardwalk, accessible by a glass-covered slow-moving sidewalk with accompanying taped music from the various stars who have played Atlantic City. **Caesars**, Arkansas Ave and the Boardwalk, has an uninspired Roman theme, with statues of Greek gods, marble columns and laurel wreaths at every turn.

ing sand into the grand hotels. Alongside the brash 99¢ shops and exotically named palm-readers, a few beautiful Victorian buildings that survived the wrecker's ball invoke past elegance, despite being dwarfed by the casinos and housing fast-food joints. Early in the morning when the breezes from the ocean are at their most pleasant, the Boardwalk is peaceful, peopled only by keen cyclists and a few lost souls down on their luck.

The **Central Pier** offers all the fun of the fair, with rides, games and old-fashioned "guess your weight" challenges. A few blocks south, another pier has been remodelled into an ocean-liner-shaped shopping center. The small and faded **Arts Center and Historic Museum**, at the quiet northern end of the Boardwalk, on the Garden Pier, has a free collection of seaside memorabilia, postcards, photos and a special exhibit on Miss America, as well as travelling art shows. A block off the Boardwalk, where Pacific Avenue meets Rhode Island Avenue, and in the heart of some of the city's worst deprivation, the **Absecon Lighthouse** was active until 1933, but is now a small free marine museum, with separate entrance to the 167ft tower (June–Oct Thurs–Tues 10am–5pm, Nov–May Fri–Mon 10am–5pm; 50¢).

Atlantic City's **beach** is free, family filled and surprisingly clean considering its proximity to the Boardwalk. Beaches at neighboring **Ventnor**, a jitney-ride away, are quieter, but charge users $3.50 per week. For the same fee, New Jersey's beautiful people pose on the beaches of **Margate**, three miles south of Atlantic City; all watched over by Lucy, the Margate Elephant, 9200 Atlantic Ave. A 65ft wood and tin Victorian oddity, Lucy was built as a seaside attraction in 1881 and used variously as a tavern and a hotel. Today her huge belly is filled with a **museum** of Atlantic City memorabilia, and photos and artefacts from her own history (July–Aug daily 10am–8.30pm, April–June and Sept–Oct Sat–Sun 10am–4.30pm; $1.50).

Accommodation

Atlantic City's high **accommodation** rates get even higher at weekends and in summer, though if you book ahead and business is slow many will offer discounted **package deals**, with $200-a-night suites going for under half price. Otherwise room prices at the casinos are, not surprisingly, astronomical, but **motels** line Pacific and Atlantic avenues behind the Boardwalk, and things are cheaper in quiet Ocean City, a family resort on the mainland to the south.

The Cassino Hotel, 28 S Georgia Ave (☎344-0747). Small rooms in family-run hotel, open May–Oct. ③.

The Dunes Motel, 2819 Pacific Ave (☎344-5271). Reasonable rooms near the Boardwalk. ③.

The Irish Pub, 164 St James Place (☎344-9063). Rooms above one of the best bars in town. ③.

Shamrock Hotel, 133 St James Place (☎348-9832). Budget rooms; weekly rates from $180. ②.

Showboat Casino Hotel, On the Boardwalk at Delaware Ave (☎343-4000). The most pleasant of the huge casino hotels, with luxury ocean-view rooms. ⑤.

Eating

One side-effect of Atlantic City's rabid commercialization is an abundance of **fast food**. The Boardwalk is lined with pizza, burger and sandwich joints, and the casino cafés too dole out economical meals. Diners on Atlantic and Pacific avenues serve soul food and cheap breakfasts.

Hunan Chinese Restaurant, 2323 Atlantic Ave (☎348-5946). Reasonably priced Chinese food two blocks from the Boardwalk. Combination plates from $6.

Los Amigos, 1926 Atlantic Ave (☎344-2293). Mexican restaurant and bar, with good tortillas and enchilada meals from $7. Open until 6am.

Tony's Little Italy, S Carolina Ave and the Boardwalk. One of the better cheap and cheerful Boardwalk joints, with pizza and breakfast from $2.

White House Sub Shop, Mississippi and Arctic avenues (☎345-8599). This bright and super-efficient sandwich bar is where Bill Cosby gets his subs when in town. Prices range from $3 for half a French loaf crammed with omelette, to $7 for a full steak sandwich.

Entertainment and Nightlife

Atlantic City sells itself as the fun night-time city; but the **nightlife** centers on the casinos and Boardwalk amusements. Once you get bored with slot machines there is little else to do. Big-name entertainers perform regularly at the casinos, with tickets in the $20 range. Both the *Claridge* (☎340-3700) and the *Trop World Casino* (☎340-4000) have **comedy clubs** with shows from $10. For cheaper informal fun, good neighborhood bars include the friendly, dark-panelled *Irish Pub*, 164 St James Place (☎345-9613), which serves cheap food and often has live Irish music, and *McGuire's Pittsburgh Café*, 142 S Tennessee Ave (☎345-9607).

Cape May

CAPE MAY was founded in 1620 by the Dutch Captain Mey, on the small hook at the very southern tip of the Jersey coast, jutting out into the Atlantic and washed by the Delaware Bay on the west. After being briefly settled by New England whalers in the late 1600s, it turned in the eighteenth century to more profitable farming and, soon after, to tourism. In 1745 the first advertisement for Cape May's restorative air and fine accommodations appeared in the Philadelphia press, heralding a period of great prosperity, when Southern plantation owners, desiring cool sea breezes without having to venture into Yankee land, flocked to the fashionable boarding houses of this genteel "resort of Presidents".

The Victorian era was Cape May's finest; nearly all its gingerbread architecture dates from a mass rebuilding after a severe fire in 1878. However, the increase in car travel after World War I meant that vacationers could go further, more quickly and cheaply, and the little town found itself something of an anachronism, while the gaudier charms of Atlantic City became the brightest stars on the Jersey coast. During the 1950s, Cape May began to dust off its most valuable commodity: its history. Today the whole town is a National Historic Landmark, with over six hundred **Victorian buildings**, tree-lined streets and beautifully kept **gardens**, and a lucrative B&B industry. Avoid the few inevitable twee olde shoppes and high prices, and concentrate instead on the appealing combination of historical authenticity and good **beaches**.

Arrival and Information

New Jersey Transit (☎884-6139) runs an express **bus** from Philadelphia and the south Jersey coast, and services from New York and Atlantic City. **Flights** from New York, Philadelphia and Atlantic City touch down at the Cape May County airport (☎886-1500), five miles north on US-47, and **ferries** connect the town to Lewes, Delaware (15 per day in the summer, 4 or 5 off-season; $5 per person, $20 per car; schedules on ☎886-2718 or ☎1-800/64-FERRY). The ferry **dock** is in west Cape May, at the end of US-9.

Maps and **information** are available from the friendly *Mid-Atlantic Center for the Arts*, 1048 Washington St, the non-profit organization that masterminded Cape May's preservation move (Mon–Fri 9am–5pm; ☎884-5404). It also organizes guided **walking tours** of the town's central mansions and ninety-minute historical trolley tours of the area, and issues details of self-guided cycling tours. The *Welcome Center* at 405 Lafayette St can help with finding **accommodation** (April–Oct Mon–Sat 9am–4pm, Sun 1–3pm; ☎884-9562); other sources of information include a small booth on the southern end of Washington Street in the paved mall, and the tiny Chamber of Commerce, in the bus depot, 609 Lafayette St (Mon–Fri 9am–5pm; ☎884-5508).

Though Cape May itself is best enjoyed on foot, to venture out a bit further **bikes** can be rented from the *Village Bike Shop*, Washington and Ocean (daily 6.30am–7pm; $10 per day; ☎884-8500). The *Cape May Whale Watch and Research Center*, 1286 Wilson Drive, offers three trips around Cape May Point daily, dolphin-watching breakfast and sunset cruises and a four-hour **whale-watching voyage**. Boats leave Cape May harbor at the north end of Lafayette Street (April–Nov daily; ☎898-0055).

The Town

Cape May's brightly colored houses were built by nouveaux riche Victorians with a healthy disrespect for subtlety. Cluttered with cupolas, gazebos, balconies, and "widow's walks", the houses follow no architectural rules except excess. They were known as "patternbook homes", with designs and features chosen from catalogues and thrown together in accordance with the owner's taste. The Victorian obsession with the Orient is everywhere; Moorish arches and onion domes sit comfortably next to gingerbread and Queen Anne-style turrets.

The only old home open as a museum, the eighteen-room **Emlen Physick House**, 1048 Washington St, was built by the popular Philadelphia architect Frank Furness. It has been restored to its 1879 glory, with whimsical "upside down" chimneys, a mock Tudor half-timbered facade, and much original furniture (Mon–Thurs, Sat & Sun 10.30am–3pm; $5). Various B&Bs and hotels, given enough notice, also conduct informal tours of their premises; the *Mainstay Inn*, 635 Columbia Ave, was an elaborate Italianate 1872 gambling club (guided tour and tea daily 4pm; $5; ☎884-8690), and the *Abbey*, Columbia Ave and Gurney St, is a Gothic mansion with a 60ft tower and blood-red etched windows (tours Thurs–Sun; $3; ☎884-4506).

West of town, where the Delaware Bay and the ocean meet, the 1859 **Cape May Lighthouse**, visible from 25 miles at sea, offers great views from a gallery below the lantern (199 steps up) and a small exhibit on its history at ground level (Sat–Sun 10am–4pm; $3.50). A mile north of town on US-9, **Historic Cold Spring Village**, 735

Seashore Rd, depicts a typical nineteenth-century South Jersey farming community. Restored buildings from the region house a jail, school, an inn and shops, and there are various craft shows and special events (June–Oct 10am–4pm; $2).

Cape May's excellent **beaches** literally sparkle with small quartz pebbles. Beach tags ($2 per day) must be worn from 10am until 6pm in the summer, and are available from B&Bs, official vendors, or at **City Hall**, 643 Washington St (☎884-9525).

Accommodation

Most of Cape May's pastel Victorian homes seem to be (pricey) **B&Bs** or **guest houses**, but the resort is so popular that choice plummets on summer weekends. Standard **hotels** front the ocean on Beach Drive, and you can **camp** at *Seashore Campsites*, 720 Seashore Rd (reservations recommended July–Aug; ☎884-4010).

Abigail Adams Bed and Breakfast, 12 Jackson St (☎884-1371). High-quality lodging, April–Nov only, half a block from the sea. Rates include home-cooked breakfast and afternoon tea. ④.

Inn at Cape May, Beach Drive and Ocean Ave (☎884-3500). Once a fashionable Victorian shore-front hotel. Rooms in the main building (May–Sept) cost more than those in the small adjoining motel wing (April–Nov). ③.

The Montreal Inn, Beach Drive and Madison Ave (☎884-7011). Modern motel with standard rooms; cheaper off-season. ④.

Summer Cottage Inn, 613 Columbia Ave (☎884-4948). 1867 inn, verandahs and cupola. ④.

Queen Victoria, 102 Ocean St (☎884-8702). Over twenty rooms in four buildings including a cottage and a carriage house. Rates cover use of the library and flower gardens, as well as breakfast (in bed if desired) and afternoon tea. ④–⑤.

Eating

Cape May lacks the usual Boardwalk snack bars, but it has plenty of cheap lunch places. Dinner, however, is far more expensive. If you're staying at a B&B, you can always fill up there with homemade goodies, and make do with bar snacks at night.

Café Gazebo, 414 Washington St mall (☎884-4832). Cool, dark café with indoor gazebo and wrought-iron benches. Gourmet coffees, specialty ice creams and light lunches from $5.

The Lemon Tree, Washington St mall (☎884-2704). Cheap cheerful deli. Breakfasts, sandwiches, soups and salads. Nothing over $6.

Louie's Pizza, 7 Gurney St (☎884-0305). Fresh pizza opposite the beach from $8, or $2 per slice.

Mad Batter, 19 Jackson St (☎884-5970). Worth splashing out on, with international meals (baked clams in a tomato pesto sauce), served by candlelight in the garden, from $16. Lunch from $8.

Nightlife and Entertainment

Cape May is a friendly and laid-back place to be after dark; the day-trippers have gone home and the bars and music venues are enjoyed by locals and tourists alike. If you're after something a bit more lively, head a few miles north to the raucous nightclubs of **Wildwood**.

Carney's, 401 Beach Ave (☎884-4424). Spacious and relaxed Irish bar, with raucous live music.

The Shire, 315 Washington St mall (☎884-4700). Hip setting for excellent live blues and jazz, Latin, reggae and world music. Outside seating and reasonably priced food. A real gem.

Ugly Mug, Washington St mall and Decatur St (☎884-3459). Local favorite, with friendly bar, and chowder, sandwiches and seafood from $3.

CHAPTER THREE

NEW ENGLAND

The six New England states of **MASSACHUSETTS, RHODE ISLAND, CONNECTICUT, NEW HAMPSHIRE, VERMONT** and **MAINE** like to view themselves as the repository of all that is intrinsically American. In this version of history, the tangled streets of old Boston, the farms of Connecticut and the village greens of Vermont are the cradle of the nation. Certainly, nostalgia is at the root of the region's tourist trade; while the real business of making a living goes on in cities for the most part well off the tourist trail, innumerable small towns have been dolled up to recapture a past that is at best wishful, and at times purely fictional. Picturesque they may be, with white-spired churches beside immaculate rolling greens, but they're not always authentic: there's little to distinguish a clapboard house built last year from another, two hundred years old, which has just had its annual fresh coat of white paint.

The genteel seaside towns of modern Cape Cod and Rhode Island are a far cry from the first European settlements in New England. While the Pilgrims congregated in neat and pristine communities, later arrivals, with so much land to choose from, felt no need to reconstruct the compact little villages they had left behind in Europe. Instead, they spread themselves across existing Native American fields, or straggled their farmhouses in endless strips along the newly built highways (thus establishing a more genuinely American style of development). As the European foothold on the continent became more certain, the coastline came increasingly to be viewed as prime real estate, to be lined with grand patrician homes – from the Vanderbilt mansions of Newport to the presidential compounds of the Bush and Kennedy families.

Inland, the Ivy League colleges – Harvard, Yale, Brown, Dartmouth *et al* – still embody New England's strong sense of its own superiority – though in fact the region's traditional role as home to the WASP elite is due more to the vagaries of history and ideology than to any economic realities. Its thin soil and harsh climate made it difficult for the first pioneers to sustain an agricultural way of life, while the industrial prosperity of the nineteenth and early twentieth centuries is now a painfully distant memory.

New England is an **expensive** place to visit, especially in late September and October when visitors flock to see the magnificent **fall foliage**. Its tourist facilities are aimed at weekenders from the big cities as much as outsiders; places like **Cape Cod** make convenient short breaks for locals, but they're *not* the bucolic retreats you might expect. **Connecticut** and **Rhode Island** in particular clearly form part of the great East Coast megalopolis which stretches from Washington to Boston – you rarely escape the feeling that you're travelling through some vast suburb of New York. **Boston** itself, however, is a vibrant and stimulating city, while further up the coast the towns finally thin out and

---

ACCOMMODATION PRICE CODES

All accommodation prices in this book have been coded using the symbols below. Note that prices are for the least expensive double rooms in each establishment. For a full explanation see p.35 in *Basics*.

①	up to $30	④	$60–80	⑦	$130–180
②	$30–45	⑤	$80–100	⑧	$180+
③	$45–60	⑥	$100–130		

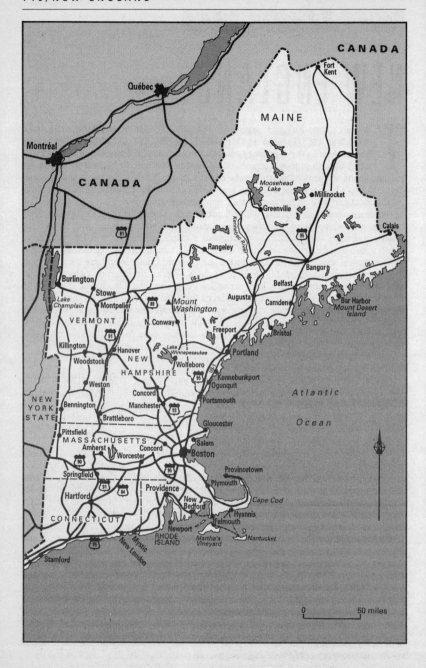

the scenery gets interesting (as does the **seafood**). Inland, too, the lakes and mountains of **Maine** and **New Hampshire** offer rural wildernesses to rival any in the nation.

History

The **Native Americans** who first peopled the northeast shoreline lived by farming and fishing along the coast in summer, and retreating with their animals to the relative warmth of the inland valleys in winter. Though the Algonquin did not always live in harmony with each other, they did manage to repel the first European invaders, earning themselves five hundred years' grace, some time around 1000 AD, by forcing the Viking Leif Ericsson to abandon the settlement of **Vinland the Good** – which may have been anywhere between Newfoundland and Massachusetts.

Within five years of Columbus' first voyage, John Cabot nosed by in 1497, in search of the Northwest Passage. Over the next century, European fishermen began to return each year, but it was not until the early 1600s that the French and English attempted to found permanent colonies, in what is now Maine. The name "New England" was given in 1614 by John Smith, who particularly appreciated the plentiful lobsters.

This was not promising land: as a character in Robert Lowell's *Endecott and the Cross* put it, "I'm not a birdwatcher or an Indian. . . . I don't see the point of this outpost of England." Without precious metals to be mined, or the potential to grow lucrative crops, the first major impetus for emigration was **religion**. Refugees from intolerance – notably the Puritans, beginning with the **Pilgrims** in 1620 – made the arduous voyage to find the freedom to build their own communities. The Pilgrims only survived at first thanks to the Indians; they were aided by a certain Squanto, who had been kidnapped, sold as a slave in Spain and returned home via England. In return, the Pilgrims forced the Indians from their terraces they had farmed for generations, dismissing as inappropriate their solution to the problems of survival in such terrain: "Their land is spacious and void, and there are few and do but run over the grass. . . . They are not industrious, neither have art, science, skill or faculty to use either the land or the commodities of it."

The possibility of a serious Indian threat was removed by victory in **King Philip's War** of 1675–76, when a leader of the Narragansett persuaded feuding groups to bury their differences in one last despairing throw. By then, white colonization was beyond the stage where it could be controlled by a few high-minded zealots. The **Salem witch trials** of 1692 provided a salutary lesson of the potential dangers of fanaticism, and as immigration became less English-based, with influxes of Huguenots after 1680 and Irish in 1708, Puritan domination decreased and a definite class structure began to emerge.

While the strand of history which began with the Pilgrims is just one among many – even forgetting the Indians, the Spanish were in Santa Fe before the Pilgrims ever left England – it is true to say that the metropolis of **Boston** deserves to be celebrated as the place where the great project of American **independence** first captured the popular imagination. The leading port of colonial America was always the likeliest focus of resentment against the latest impositions of the British government, and was ready to take up the challenge thrown down by British Prime Minister Townshend in 1766: "I dare tax America." So many of the seminal moments of the **Revolutionary War** took place here: the Boston Massacre of 1770, the Boston Tea Party of 1773, Paul Revere's ride and the first shots at Lexington and Concord in 1775.

Nationhood secured, however, New England's prosperity was ironically hit hard by the loss of trade with England, and Boston was slowly eclipsed by Philadelphia, New York, and the new capital, Washington. The **Triangular Trade** in slaves, sugar and rum provided one substitute source of income, the brief heyday of **whaling** another, and New England was also briefly at the forefront of the **Industrial Revolution**, when water-powered mills created a booming textile industry. The attempt to farm the north, however, foundered: careless techniques served to exhaust the land, and as the vast spaces of the west opened to settlement many of the inland towns fell silent.

MASSACHUSETTS

To the first colonists of the **Massachusetts Bay Company**, their arrival near the site of modern Salem in 1630 marked a crucial moment in history. **Puritans** who had decided to leave England before it was engulfed by the clearly imminent chaos of civil war, they saw their purpose, in the words of Governor John Winthrop, as the establishment of a Utopian "**City upon a hill**". Their new colony of **MASSACHUSETTS** was to be a beacon to the rest of humanity, an exemplar of sober government along sound spiritual principles. Not all those who followed, however, shared the same motivation; the story is often told of the preacher who told his congregation that they had come to New England to build a new kingdom of God, only to be challenged by a vociferous element who said that they personally had come to fish.

In their own terms, the Puritans were not successful: as waves of immigration carried all kinds of dissenters and free-thinkers from Europe, society in New England inevitably became secular. However, their **influence** remained. A clarity of thought and forcefulness of purpose can be traced from the foundation of Harvard College in 1636, through the intellectual impetus behind the Revolution and the crusade against slavery, to the nineteenth-century achievements of **writers** such as Melville, Poe, Hawthorne and Thoreau.

Other traditions too have helped shape the state – poor migrants from **Ireland** and **Italy**, freed and escaped **slaves** from the southern states, **Portuguese** seamen – even if they have not always been welcome. The anti-immigrant "Know-Nothings" of the 1850s acquired considerable public support; in 1927, the Italian anarchists **Sacco and Vanzetti** came up against conservative old Massachusetts, and were framed and executed on murder charges. As recently as the 1970s, Boston experienced racial conflicts to compare with any in the nation. There is, however, a cosmopolitan side to Massachusetts – witness the extraordinary blend of nationalities involved in the trans-global **whaling** industry of nineteenth-century Nantucket – and a strong liberal undercurrent. The high-tech promise of former Governor Michael Dukakis' "Massachusetts Miracle" may not quite have delivered lasting prosperity, but optimism and resilience still shine through.

Spending a few days in **Boston** is strongly recommended; the city is Massachusetts at its best. It's a place that feels no need to rest on its laurels – the history is there and visible, but there's a great deal of modern life and energy besides. Several further historic towns are within easy reach – **Salem** to the north, **Concord** and **Lexington** just inland, and **Plymouth** to the south. **Provincetown**, a three-hour ferry ride across the bay at the tip of Cape Cod, is a lot of fun to visit, and the rest of the Cape offers historic towns, lovely beaches – and huge crowds. **Inland Massachusetts** is much quieter; its settlements are naturally concentrated where the land gets fertile, such as along the Connecticut River valley and in the Berkshires in the west, and high real estate prices tend to ensure a rich population and a placid atmosphere.

Getting Around Massachusetts

With the single proviso that all roads in Massachusetts seem to lead to Boston, this is an easy state to tour on **public transportation**. Planes, trains and buses all radiate out from the one great city; the connections to **Cape Cod** in particular (see p.164) are absolutely legion. The *Amtrak* line which connects Boston with New York, Philadelphia and Washington is the best **train** service in the nation, and the east–west line via Worcester and Springfield gives access to Montréal, Toronto and Chicago. With the exception of the local commuter lines, trains do not, however, continue north of Boston: the only service along the coast is the summer-only service to Hyannis on Cape Cod. **Buses** from Boston are also plentiful, but the only major north–south route inland is that which runs up the Connecticut River valley.

Boston

Although the metropolitan area of **BOSTON** has long since expanded to fill the shore-line of **Massachusetts Bay**, and stretches for miles inland as well, the seventeenth-century port at its heart is still discernible. Forget the neat grids of modern urban America; the twisting streets clustered around **Boston Common** are a reminder of how the nation started out, and the city is enjoyably human in scale.

Boston was until 1755 the biggest city in America; as the one most directly affected by the latest whims of the British Crown, it was the natural focus for the opposition which culminated in the **Revolutionary War**. Numerous evocative sites from that era are preserved along the **Freedom Trail** through downtown. Since then, however, Boston has in effect turned its back on the sea. As the third busiest port in the British empire (after London and Bristol), it stood on a narrow peninsula. What is now Washington Street provided the only access by land, and when the British set off to Lexington in 1775 they embarked in ships from the Common itself. During the nine-teenth century, the Charles River marshlands were filled in to create the posh Back Bay residential area. Central Boston is now slightly but significantly set back from the water, separated by the psychological barrier of the hideous John Fitzgerald Expressway which carries I-93 across downtown.

There is a certain truth in the charge levelled by other Americans that Boston likes to live in the past; echoes of the "Brahmins" of a century ago can be heard in the upper-class drawl of the posher districts. But this is by no means just a city of WASPs; the Irish who began to arrive in quantity after the Great Famine produced their first mayor as early as 1885, and the president of the whole country within a hundred years. The liberal tradition which spawned the Kennedys remains alive, fed in part by the pres-ence in the city of more than one hundred universities and colleges.

The slump of the Depression seemed to linger in Boston for years – even in the 1950s, the population was actually dwindling – but these days the place definitely has a rejuvenated feel to it. **Quincy Market** has served as a blueprint for urban development worldwide, and with its busy street life, imaginative museums and galleries, fine red-brick architecture and palpable history, Boston is the one destination in New England there's no excuse for missing.

> The **area code** for Boston is ☎617.

Arrival and Information

Boston may not be the "hub of the universe", as Oliver Wendell Holmes liked to think, but it is at any rate the center of New England's transportation networks. Direct flights from Europe mean that for many travellers it provides their first taste of America, while efficient rail and bus services from New York, Montréal and further afield make this an obvious starting point, wherever you're heading in New England.

Air

Logan Airport (☎1-800/235-6426 or 561-1800), constantly busy with both international and domestic services, is a mere three miles from downtown Boston. It stands on an arti-ficial peninsula jutting into Boston Harbor, created by levelling three islands and destroying Revolution Wharf. As driving within the city is not to be recommended (see overleaf), it makes little sense to rent a car at the airport. A **taxi** into town costs between $10 and $15; the trip should take twenty minutes, but all traffic has to pass through the Sumner or Callahan tunnels, which can get very congested. Between 5.30am and 1am, free **buses** run every few minutes from all terminals to the airport **subway** station on the *MBTA Blue* line (see below), from where it's an easy ten-minute ride to the city center. Just as quick, and a whole lot more fun, is the **water shuttle** which connects the terminal buses with Rowes Wharf across the Harbor (Mon–Fri every 15min, 6am–8pm, Sat & Sun every 30min, noon–8pm; adults $8, kids $4; ☎1-800-23-LOGAN).

Several **bus** companies offer direct links between Logan Airport and northern New England. *Vermont Transit* (☎1-800/451-3292) covers New Hampshire's White Mountains and continues to Vermont and Montréal, while *Concord Trailways* (☎1-800/639-3317) runs to New Hampshire and up the Maine coast.

Trains

Amtrak trains along the Northeast Corridor from Providence, Washington DC and New York, and from Chicago and Canada via Springfield, as well as the summer-only Cape Cod specials, arrive in downtown Boston near the waterfront at **South Station** (☎482-3715), Summer St and Atlantic Ave. The station is currently being expanded to coordinate all Boston's buses and trains. Some *Amtrak* services also make an extra stop at **Back Bay Station** (☎348-0601), 145 Dartmouth St, on the *Orange* subway line near Copley Square. **North Station** is used only by *MBTA* commuter trains.

Buses

Boston's long-distance *Greyhound* buses (☎292-4702 or 1-800/231-2222) stop at South Station, Summer Street and Atlantic Avenue, as do *Bonanza Bus Lines* (☎720-4110), which connects the city with Woods Hole, Newport and Providence; the *Plymouth and Brockton Bus Co* (☎508/746-0378), serving Hyannis; *Peter Pan Bus Lines,* (☎426-7838) to New York and western Massachusetts; and *Concord Trailways* (☎1-800/639-3317). Some long-distance buses also operate out of Logan Airport (see above).

Information

The most convenient place to get advice and maps is the **Visitor Information Center** (daily 8.30am–5pm; ☎267-6466) at Park Street subway on the Tremont Street side of Boston Common. There's also an information booth in **Quincy Market**, and another at the **John Hancock Tower**, at Copley Square in the Back Bay area (Mon–Sat 9am–11pm, Sun noon–11pm). For **disabled information**, contact the Center for Individuals with Disabilities (☎727-5540; ☎1-800/462-8015 in Massachusetts only).

The city's main **post office** is at McCormack Station, Post Office Square, Boston MA 02109 (Mon–Fri 8am–5pm; ☎654-5686).

Getting Around

Much of the pleasure of visiting Boston comes from being in a city that was built long before cars were invented. Walking around it can be a joy; conversely, driving is an absolute nightmare. The freeways won't take you where you want to be, the one-way traffic systems can have you circling for hours without getting any nearer your destination; and if you ever do arrive there's nowhere to park. There's really no point renting a car in Boston until the day you leave.

The *Massachusetts Bay Transportation Authority* (*MBTA*, universally known as the "**T**") is responsible for Boston's **subway** system and **trolley buses**. The subway, which opened in 1897, is the oldest in the US; its first station, Park Street, remains its center (any train marked "inbound" is headed here), and is the place to pick up all schedules and information. Four lines – *Red, Green, Blue* and *Orange* – operate daily from 5am until 1am, although certain routes begin to shut down earlier. Away from downtown, the trains emerge from tunnels to run along the city's major arteries, though not all their overground stops are shown on the widely available *Rapid Transit* maps. Trains are fast and safe; only the *Orange* line might be said to be unsafe after dark.

The standard fare is 85¢, paid with tokens inserted into turnstiles, but on some incoming overground routes you have to pay extra, up to $1.75. You can buy eleven tokens for the price of ten, and a **tourist pass** covers all subway and local bus journeys at a cost of around $9 for 3 days, or $18 for a week. (All *MBTA* **information** is on ☎722-3200 Mon–Fri 7am–6pm; ☎722-5000 nights and weekends; ☎1-800/392-6100.)

The normal fare on *MBTA*'s **local buses** is 60¢, but longer distances, such as out to Salem or Marblehead, cost up to $2.50. Red double-decker *Shopper's Shuttle* buses loop regularly between Back Bay, Downtown Crossing and Faneuil, from 10am until 6pm; adults 50¢, kids 25¢. *MBTA* also run **commuter rail lines**, extending as far as Salem, Ipswich, and Concord; these are based at the venerable **North Station** (☎227-5070) on Causeway Street, under the Boston Garden.

Bicycles can be rented from the *Community Bike Shop* at 490 Tremont St (☎542-8623) and *Ferris Wheels*, 64 South St, Jamaica Plain (☎522-7082), among others.

City Tours

It's easy enough to get to know Boston by following the Freedom Trail on foot (see below). If you prefer to be guided, narrated trips run throughout the day aboard the *Beantown Trolley* (☎236-2148), and *Boston By Foot* (77 N Washington St; ☎367-2345) conduct ninety-minute walking tours for $5. Also useful are the coach excursions further afield with *Brush Hill Tours* (☎236-2148 or 1-800/647-4776).

The City

Boston has grown up around **Boston Common**, which was set aside as common land in 1634. As well as being the obvious first stop on a tour of the city, it is also a pleasant place to return to rest your legs at the odd moment throughout the day. You might even choose to take a short ride in one of the two-ton **swan boats** which paddle across the main pond of the lovely **Boston Public Garden**, across Charles Street.

The visitor center – the start of the **Freedom Trail** – is near the tapering north end of the Common. As you stand here, facing up Tremont Street with the **State House** away to your left, the main **shopping** district, **Quincy Market**, and the **waterfront** are slightly ahead but down to the right. The modern concrete wasteland of **Government Center** is straight up Tremont Street, with beyond the **North End** – first Irish, then Jewish, and now very definitely Italian. A short way behind you on the left rises **Beacon Hill**, every bit as elegant as when Henry James called Mount Vernon Street "the most prestigious address in America" (and far removed from its eighteenth-century nickname of "Mount Whoredom"). Heading away from the center down Tremont Street brings you to **Chinatown** and the **Theater District**, while grand boulevards such as Commonwealth Avenue lead west from the Public Garden into the **Back Bay**.

The Freedom Trail

Much the best way to orientate yourself to downtown Boston – and to appreciate the city's role in American history – is to walk some or all of the **Freedom Trail**. You can pick up or leave this easy self-guided route anywhere – for most of the way a line of red bricks is embedded in the pavement, elsewhere there's a painted red line – but technically it begins on Boston Common at the **Visitor Information Center**.

From here, head for the golden dome of the **State House**, which was completed in 1798 to a design by Charles Bulfinch. It remains the seat of Massachusetts' government; its most famous feature, the wooden Sacred Cod symbolizing the wealth Boston accrued from its fisheries, hangs in front of the Speaker, and faces in different directions according to which party is in office (free tours Mon–Fri 10am–4pm).

Henry James described **Park Street Church** as the "most interesting mass of brick and mortar in America"; this was where the orator William Lloyd Garrison launched

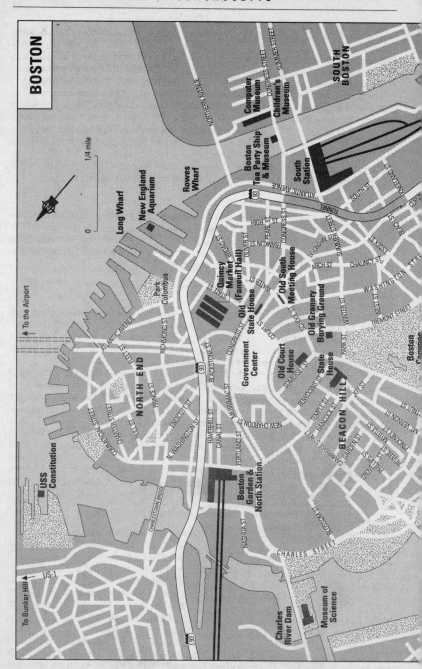

BOSTON

To Bunker Hill
US-1

To the Airport

0   1/4 mile

USS Constitution

CHARLESTOWN BRIDGE

NORTH END

COMMERCIAL STREET
CHARTER STREET
HULL ST
PRINCE ST
ENDICOTT ST
N. WASHINGTON ST
SNOW HILL ST

ATLANTIC AVENUE
RICHMOND ST

Park Columbus

Long Wharf

New England Aquarium

Rowes Wharf

NORTHERN AVENUE

Boston Tea Party Ship & Museum

Computer Museum

Children's Museum

SOUTH BOSTON

CONGRESS STREET
SUMMER STREET

93

ATLANTIC AVENUE
TUNNEL

South Station

SOUTH ST

HIGH ST
PEARL ST
FRANKLIN ST
CONGRESS ST
OLIVER ST
BATTERYMARCH ST
BROAD ST
DEVONSHIRE STREET
SUMMER STREET
KILBY ST
PURCHASE ST

Quincy Market
Old (Faneuil Hall)
State House

Old South Meeting House

ARCH ST
CHAUNCY ST
WASHINGTON ST

STATE ST
WATER ST
SCHOOL ST
WINTER ST

Old Granary Burying Ground

WEST ST
TREMONT STREET

CONGRESS ST
BLACKSTONE ST

Government Center

Old Court House

State House

PARK ST

Boston

BOWDOIN ST
SOMERSET ST
TEMPLE ST
HANCOCK ST
JOY ST

BEACON HILL

CAMBRIDGE STREET
NEW CHARDON ST
MERRIMAC ST

HAVERHILL ST
CANAL ST
PORTLAND ST

Boston Garden & North Station

NASHUA ST

REVERE ST
MYRTLE ST
PINCKNEY ST
MT. VERNON ST
PHILLIPS ST
GARDEN ST
GROVE ST
W. CEDAR ST
CHESTNUT ST

BLOSSOM ST

CHARLES STREET

Charles River Dam

Museum of Science

93

TRUST ST

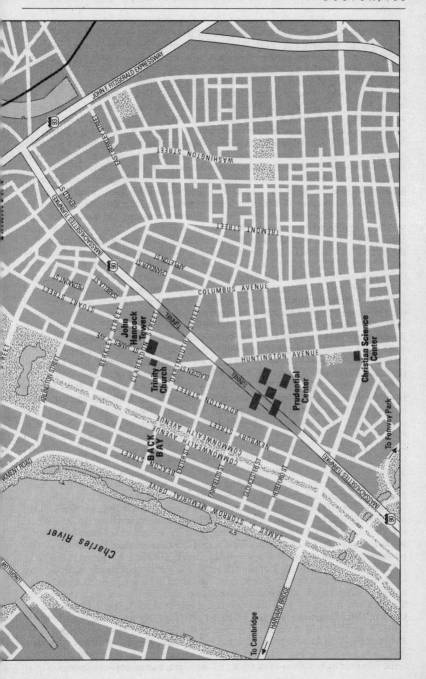

his campaign to free the slaves on July 4 1829 (July & Aug Tues–Sat 9.30am–3.30pm, otherwise by appointment; free). The 1600 graves of the **Old Granary Burying Ground** just around the corner (daily 8am–5pm; free) include those of Paul Revere, Samuel Adams and John Hancock, as well as the original Mother Goose, while **King's Chapel Burying Ground** (Tues–Sun 10am–4pm; free) contains Boston's earliest colonists and the first governor, John Winthrop. A statue of Benjamin Franklin marks the site of Boston's **First Public School**, attended by Franklin and Samuel Adams. Guests at the nearby **Omni Parker House Hotel** (not officially on the Trail) have included Charles Dickens and John Kennedy; employees, Malcolm X, Red Foxx and Ho Chi Minh. The **Old Corner Bookstore** at School and Washington was a literary salon frequented by Longfellow, Thoreau and Hawthorne; under the auspices of the *Boston Globe*, it's now the atmospheric *Globe Corner Bookstore*, specializing in travel.

Next come the Trail's two most striking and significant buildings. At the **Old South Meeting House**, Samuel Adams addressed the patriots about to carry out the Boston Tea Party on December 16 1773 (April–Oct daily 9.30am–5pm; Nov–March Mon–Fri 10am–4pm, Sat & Sun 10am–5pm; $2.50). This was no raucous and unruly mob: they were solemn men, well aware of the likely impact of their actions. The elegant **Old State House**, built in 1712 and still proud although dwarfed by surrounding skyscrapers, was the seat of Colonial government. From its balcony the Declaration of Independence was read on July 18 1776; exactly two hundred years later Queen Elizabeth II appeared on that same balcony. Inside is a museum of Boston history (daily 9.30am–5pm; $2). Outside, a ring of cobblestones marks the site of the **Boston Massacre** on March 5 1770, when British soldiers fired on a crowd which was pelting them with stone-filled snowballs, and killed five, including the black Crispus Attucks.

Modern visitors gravitate to **Quincy Market** and **Faneuil Hall** (it rhymes with *Daniel*; daily 9am–9pm; free) for the lively shops, restaurants and takeaways which made this a pioneer example of successful urban renewal (by the developer who went on to transform London's Covent Garden). Faneuil Hall was, however, once known as the "Cradle of Liberty", a meeting place for Revolutionaries and, later, abolitionists.

Passing under the six-lane JFK Expressway and into the North End, **Paul Revere House** is Boston's last surviving seventeenth-century house. Built after the Great Fire of 1676, and home to Paul Revere – patriot, silversmith, Freemason, and father of sixteen children – from 1770 until 1800 (mid-April to Oct daily 9.30am–5.15pm; Nov to mid-April daily 9.30am–4.15pm; closed Mon Jan–March; $2). Revere's famous **ride** of April 18 1775, to warn Lexington of imminent British attack, was spurred by two signal lanterns ("one if by land, two if by sea") hung from the steeple of **Old North Church** at 193 Salem St (daily, 9am–5pm; free). A little further up, from **Copp's Hill Burial Ground** (daily 8am–5pm; free) you can see across the harbor to Charlestown; as indeed could the British who planted their artillery here for the Battle of Bunker Hill.

In theory, the Freedom Trail now crosses the Charlestown bridge, but that's a long walk over. Its final two sites are better reached by the frequent **ferries** from Long Wharf to Charlestown Navy Yard (every 15–30min, Mon–Fri 6.30am–8pm, every half-hour at weekends 10am–6pm; $1 each way). First is the **USS Constitution**, also known as "Old Ironsides", the oldest commissioned warship afloat in the world. Launched in Boston in 1797, it was prominent in the War of 1812. Every July 4 it is ceremonially turned around – sailed out into the bay and its cannon fired – mainly in order to equalize the weathering on its two sides. Unless it's closed because of ongoing rehabilitation work, free tours of the ship are conducted in period costume (daily 9.30am–3.50pm). Up above, the **Bunker Hill Monument** is in fact on Breed's Hill; but this was the actual site of the battle on June 17 1775, which, although won by the British, did much to convince them that they could not hope to triumph in the end. A spiral staircase of almost three hundred steps leads to the top; nearby, a **museum** offers a multimedia presentation of the battle (summer daily 9.30am–5pm, winter 9.30am–4pm; monument free, museum $3) .

THE BLACK HERITAGE TRAIL

Massachusetts was the first state to declare slavery illegal, in 1783 – partly as a result of black participation in the Revolutionary War – and a large community of free blacks and escaped slaves swiftly grew up in the North End, and on Beacon Hill. Ironically, very few blacks now live on Beacon Hill, but the **Black Heritage Trail** through the area celebrates important sites in local black history (the various visitor centers provide maps).

Pick up the Trail either at 46 Joy St, where the **Abiel Smith School** contains a **Museum of Afro-American History** (Tues–Fri 10am–4pm), illustrating the national civil rights campaign as well as local history, or at the **African Meeting House** at 8 Smith Court (off Joy St), for displays and talks from well-informed rangers. Built in 1806 as the first African-American church in the United States, this became known as "Black Faneuil Hall" during the abolitionist campaign; Frederick Douglass issued his call here for all blacks to take up arms in the Civil War. Among those who responded were the volunteers of the **Massachusetts 54th Regiment**, commemorated by a monument at the edge of Boston Common, opposite the State House, which depicts their farewell march down Beacon Street. Robert Lowell won a Pulitzer Prize for his poem, *For the Union Dead*, about this monument; and the regiment's tragic end at Fort Wagner was depicted in the movie *Glory*. The Trail then winds around Beacon Hill, passing schools, other institutions, and residences ranging from the small cream clapboard houses of Smith Court to the imposing **Lewis and Harriet Hayden House** at 66 Phillips St, once a stop on the famous "Underground Railroad", sheltering runaway slaves from pursuing bounty-hunters.

The Waterfront

It comes as a disappointment to realize that you can't walk along Boston's **waterfront** for any distance: most of the wharfs are closed to visitors, and you can see little of the harbor from the roads and footpaths which provide access to them. If you head straight for the sea from Quincy Market, however, **Columbus Park**, next to the ugly *Marriott Hotel*, makes a nice place to sit. Originally, Faneuil Hall stood at the head of **Long Wharf**, which stuck two thousand feet out into the harbor, and was the site of the final British evacuation on March 17 1776. Then a thousand feet of water was filled in, and the **Custom House Tower** was erected to mark the end of the wharf. That remained Boston's tallest building until as recently as 1962; it too now finds itself inland, as a further thousand feet of new land has been added.

Boston Harbor Cruises ($9; ☎227-4321) from Long Wharf are not all that exciting. The port is nothing like as busy as when fishing boats lined the quays three or four deep on all sides. Instead you pass vast rows of freshly imported Japanese cars on the quayside, and get a close-up view of the airport. You can get off one cruise in Charlestown to see the *USS Constitution*, and catch the next one back for no extra charge.

Close by on Central Wharf, the **New England Aquarium** (July–Sept Mon, Tues & Thurs 9am–6pm, Wed & Fri 9am–8pm, Sat & Sun 9am–7pm; Oct–June Mon–Thurs 9am–5pm, Fri 9am–8pm, Sat & Sun 9am–6pm; adults $7.50, kids $4) has an outdoor pool of basking harbor seals. Inside, the colossal Giant Ocean Tank, a four-storey glass cylinder, contains sharks, giant turtles and tropical marine life (with an unsettling emphasis on how "delicious" certain specimens are). Scuba divers hand-feed the fish five times a day, and dolphin shows are held in a floating amphitheater alongside.

If you follow the shoreline past **Rowe's Wharf** (the base for the water shuttles to the airport), a short distance before South Station the **Congress Street Bridge** leads off to the left across the Fort Point Channel. The **Boston Tea Party Ship and Museum** (daily 9am–6pm; adults $6, kids $3) is moored to the bridge itself. This is not the original *Beaver*, one of the three ships stormed by patriots in 1773, but a replica, *Beaver II*, sailed here from Denmark in 1973. Neither is it the original mooring, which was on the now-demolished Griffin's Wharf; instead it's the site of the house where the conspirators prepared their assault. The ship is small and not desperately interesting, for adults at any rate. Displays include a relief model of Boston as it then was – virtually an island – and costumed attendants serve China tea of the same type that was thrown in the sea, provoking the British to close the port and place Boston under martial law. From time to time throughout the day there are re-enactments of the Tea Party itself.

On the far side of the bridge, a forty-foot **milk bottle**, which serves as an ice cream store and sandwich bar, marks **Museum Wharf**. Here the two most enjoyable museums in the city share the same modern building (though each has a separate entrance). The **Children's Museum** (Tues–Thurs, Sat & Sun 10am–5pm, Fri 10am–9pm, closed Mon except during school holidays; adults $5, kids $4) is an absolute kids' paradise – all its galleries invite maximum participation. The central shaft is taken up with a climbing maze-cum-sculpture, stretching three storeys, that no one over fourteen could possibly get into. One end holds a reconstructed Thirties house, looking as though the family has just nipped out – downstairs in "Grandfather's Cellar" the woodworking tools are laid out for anyone to use. At the other, a genuine Japanese dwelling offers impromptu art classes. In a soundproof booth upstairs demented kids jam on synthesized guitars; nearby a psychedelic disco raves all day.

The world's first **Computer Museum** is right alongside (same hours; $7 – you have to pay again). Reached by a glass-sided elevator, the collection opens with four history-making computers: the first, *Univac*, is seen predicting the result of the 1952 presidential election. You progress to hands-on exhibits on artificial intelligence, graphic design, and of course games. The highlight is the chance to explore a giant "**Walk-through Computer**", dissected mouse and all. You need to be computer-literate already, or at least confident, to get the most of it, and it's more fun when the place is empty, so come during the week or out of holidays.

Children might also want to visit the **Museum of Science**, in the Science Park on the Charles River Dam at the northern end of the waterfront, not far from North Station (daily 9am–5pm except Fri 9am–9pm, closed Mon except during holidays; adults $6.50, kids $4, free Wed 1–5pm). The Sun Room here takes advantage of the beautiful setting to catch light for its solar panels, while in the egg hatchery at least one new chicken always seems to be pecking its way out of the shell, to the bewilderment of its older siblings. An *OMNIMAX* cinema takes up the full height of one end of the building, and the Hayden Planetarium as ever pays its way with Pink Floyd laser shows.

Back Bay and Beyond

As each portion of the tidal flats of the Charles River was filled in, from 1857 onwards, more of the spacious boulevards and grand houses of **Back Bay** were built. Thus a walk through the area from east to west provides an object lesson in Victorian architecture. Much the most distinguished of its buildings is the Romanesque **Trinity Church** on Clarendon Street, supported on four thousand wooden pilings which have to be kept permanently moist. The church these days can always be seen reflected in the gleaming windows of the adjacent **John Hancock Tower**, whose rooftop observatory provides a glorious overall view of Boston (Mon–Sat 9am–11pm, Sun noon–11pm; $3). Construction defects caused Hancock Tower to shed three thousand panes of glass during its first year; the cost of insuring Trinity Church against damage was so prohibitive that it was cheaper to buy it outright. **Copley Square** nearby is an upmarket shopping mall with several good snack-bars and restaurants.

The **Christian Science Center** at Huntington and Massachusetts Ave is the "Mother Church" of the Church of Christ Scientist, and the home of the *Christian Science Monitor* newspaper; Nelson Mandela made a point of paying a personal visit here in 1990 to thank the paper for its support. The **Mapparium** (Mon–Fri 8am–4pm, Sat 10am–3.45pm, Sun 11.15am–3.45pm; free) is an impressive, if not utterly logical, glass globe of the world, which you can walk inside on a footbridge. Part of the interest is that it was built in 1932, and thus shows national boundaries as they were then.

Further south, beyond the boundaries of Back Bay and a long enough walk to warrant taking the *Green* subway line instead (get on a car marked "E"), is the **Museum of Fine Arts** at 465 Huntington Ave (Tues & Thurs–Sun 10am–5pm, Wed 10am–10pm; West Wing only is also open Thurs & Fri 5–10pm; adults $7, kids $3.50). From its magnificent collections of Asian and ancient Egyptian art onwards, this holds sufficient marvels to detain you all day. High points include Edward Hopper's tranquil, hopeful, *Room In Brooklyn* (American Modern); Andrew Wyeth's *Corner of the Woods* (William Coolidge); Degas' *The Little Dancer*, Gauguin's *Where do we come from, What are we, Where are we going?* (Impressionists), and Millet's *The Sower* (English and French). Don't miss the **American Decorative Arts** either: a gloriously nostalgic jamboree of coffee urns, speak-your-weight machines and reconstructed living rooms.

A smaller-scale and rather more idiosyncratic collection of fine arts can be found at the **Isabella Stewart Gardner Museum**, down the road at 280 The Fenway (Tues noon–6.30pm, Wed–Sun noon–5pm; $6, kids $3). This reconstructed Italian Renaissance villa, complete with indoor fountain, is crammed with the eclectic harvest of a lifetime spent in pursuit of the sublime – a breathtaking hotchpotch of anything from modern American to fifteenth-century Italian. Some of the most interesting works are "unlisted", such as the tapestry of a lion, a sea lion and an elephant above the door of the Italian room, or the sculpted pigeon on the nearby windowsill. Gardner insisted on the place being a pen-free zone; if you're tempted to make any notes, use a pencil.

Cambridge

The excursion across the Charles River to **Cambridge** merits at least half a day, starting with a fifteen-minute ride on the *Red* "T" line from Park Street to **Harvard Square**. This is not so much a square as a number of interlocking streets, filled with shopping malls and bookstores, at the point where Massachusetts Ave runs into JFK and Brattle streets. This is an exceptionally lively area, filled with students from nearby Harvard University and MIT; its café terraces, such as *Au Bon Pain*, make for enjoyable people-watching. The **Cambridge Discovery Booth** (June to mid-Oct Mon–Sat 9am–6pm, otherwise Mon–Sat 9am–5pm, Sun all year 1–5pm, ☎497-1630) here organizes walking tours in summer, and sells local maps and guides including the *Unofficial Guide to Life at Harvard*, produced by the students responsible for the *Let's Go* travel series.

Feel free to wander into **Harvard Yard** and around the core of the university, founded in 1636; its enormous Widener Library (named for a victim of the *Titanic*) boasts a Gutenberg Bible and a First Folio of Shakespeare. Five minutes' walk west along Brattle Street is the imposing yellow-fronted mansion known as **Longfellow House** (daily 10.30am–4.30pm; $2), after the author of *Hiawatha* who lived here until 1882; a century earlier it was briefly the headquarters of General George Washington. Dexter Pratt, immortalized in Longfellow's *Under the spreading chestnut tree, the village blacksmith stands*, lived at 56 Brattle Street, now a popular bakery and café.

Many of Cambridge's wonderful array of **bookstores**, such as *Barillari* (1 Mifflin Place) and *Words Worth* (30 Brattle St) stay open until midnight, and a wide range of cheap clothing stores and shops cater for student interests. Things in general get a bit funkier east down Massachusetts Ave towards MIT. *Cheapo Records* at no 645, by Central Square (Mon–Wed & Sat 10am–6pm, Thurs & Fri 10am–9pm), has a phenomenal selection of old **records** on two floors.

Lexington and Concord

On the night of April 18 1775, **Paul Revere** rode down what is now Massachusetts Avenue from Boston, racing through Cambridge and Arlington on his way to warn the American patriots gathered at **Lexington** of an impending British attack. Close behind him was a force of over four hundred British soldiers, intent on seizing the supplies which they knew the "rebels" had hoarded at **Concord**.

Although much of Revere's route has been turned into major freeways, and you are barely out of the Boston suburbs before you arrive in Lexington, the various scenes of the first military confrontation of the Revolutionary War – "the shot heard round the world" – remain much as they were then. The triangular **Town Common** at Lexington was where the British encountered the opposition. Captain John Parker ordered his 77 American **"Minutemen"** to "stand your ground. Don't fire unless fired upon, but if they mean to have a war let it begin here." No one knows who fired the first shot – it may have come from one of the venerable houses around the green – but the Minuteman Statue commemorates the eight Americans who died. Guides in period costume lead tours of the **Buckman Tavern**, where the Minutemen waited for the British to arrive; the **Hancock-Clarke House** a quarter of a mile north, where Samuel Adams and John Hancock were awakened by Paul Revere, is now a **museum**. All three sites are open Mon–Sat 10am–5pm, Sun 1–5pm, and admission is $5.

There were no British casualties in Lexington, but by the time they marched on Concord the next morning the surrounding countryside was up in arms. In running battles in the town itself, and along the still-evocative **Battle Road** leading back towards Boston, 73 British soldiers and 49 colonials were killed over the next two days. The relevant sites now form the **Minuteman National Historic Park**, with visitor centers at the scenic North Bridge (174 Liberty St) in Concord and Battle Road in Lexington. Paul Revere's ride is re-enacted annually on the state holiday of Patriot's Day, the third Monday in April, along with the Battle of Lexington (and the Boston Marathon).

Walden Pond south of Concord was where Henry David Thoreau conducted the experiment in solitude and self-sufficiency described in his 1854 book *Walden*. "I did not feel crowded or confined in the least", he wrote of life in his simple log cabin; the site where it stood is now marked with stones, and at dawn you can still watch the pond "throwing off its nightly clothing of mist". This pretty and popular state park was saved from development by a band of Hollywood types led by ex-Eagle Don Henley. Thoreau is interred, along with Ralph Waldo Emerson, Nathaniel Hawthorne and Louisa May Alcott, atop a hill in **Sleepy Hollow Cemetery**, just east of the center of Concord.

As well as guided **bus tours** from Boston (see p.151), **buses** run to Lexington from Alewife Station, and **trains** to Concord from North Station ($3.60 each way).

Accommodation

Good-quality budget **accommodation** is hard to find in Boston. The price of a hostel here would get you an upmarket motel elsewhere, while any hotel accommodation in walking distance of downtown for under $100 has to be considered a bargain.

Though many Boston homes offer **bed and breakfast** accommodation, very few downtown options advertise themselves directly, preferring to deal through **agencies**. Some of the nicest places are available through *B&B Agency of Boston* (47 Commercial Wharf, Boston 02110; ☎720-3540 or 1-800/248-9262; Freephone UK ☎0800/895128); *Host Homes of Boston* (PO Box 117, Waban Branch, Boston MA 02168; ☎244-1308) and *Boston B&B* (1643 Beacon St, Suite 23, Boston 02168; ☎332-4199) can also provide rooms, from around $70. Boston's **room tax** of 9.7 percent is added to all bills.

Hostels

Boston International AYH Hostel, 12 Hemenway St, Boston (☎536-9455). A little way out in the Fenway (Hynes Convention subway). Dorms $12 for members, $15 non-members. 10am–5pm lockout, midnight curfew. In summer book ahead, or check in at 8am, to be sure of a place. ①.

Cambridge YMCA, 820 Massachusetts Ave (☎661-9622) and **Cambridge YWCA**, 7 Temple St, (☎491-6050). Newly renovated single rooms in single-sex hostels, both near Central subway in Cambridge, for $30 members, $39 non-members. Book in advance. ②.

Charlestown YMCA, 150 Second Ave, Charleston Navy Yard (☎241-8400). Very new rooms, popular with military personnel. Rates include use of the excellent gym. ③.

Greater Boston YMCA, 316 Huntington Ave, Boston (☎536-7800). Best budget rooms in the Back Bay. Mixed-sex accommodation, rates include breakfast. ②.

YWCA, 40 Berkeley St, Boston (☎482-8850). Women-only singles and doubles in convenient South End location, near Arbourway Northeastern station. Non-members pay extra, weekly rates. ②.

Hotels, Motels and B&Bs

Boston Park Plaza, 64 Arlington St (☎426-2000 or 1-800/225-2008). Spacious, high-ceilinged rooms in Bill Clinton's favorite grand old Boston hotel. ⑥.

A Cambridge House, 2218 Massachusetts Ave at Porter Square, Cambridge (☎491-6300 or 1-800/232-9989). Classy restored B&B, 15 minutes' walk from Harvard Square. ④.

Lenox Hotel, 710 Boylston St (☎536-5300 or 1-800/225-7676). Lovingly maintained, medium-sized hotel in the heart of the Back Bay. ⑥.

Longwood Inn, 123 Longwood Ave, Brookline (☎566-8615). Large Victorian house, plain rooms. ③.

Susse Chalet Motor Lodge and **Susse Chalet Inn**, 800 and 900 Morrissey Blvd, Dorchester (☎287-9100 or 287-9200). Six miles southeast of downtown, just off the Southeast Expressway. High-quality double rooms, free parking. ④.

The Tremont House, 275 Tremont St, Boston (☎426-1400). Well-restored Art Deco hotel, in the Theater District two blocks from the Common. ⑤.

Eating

There is far more to eating in Boston than its image as "Beantown" might suggest. Above all, there's the **seafood**, especially lobsters, *scrod* (a generic term for young white-fleshed fish), clams (served as *steamers*, dipped in butter, or as creamy chowder) and oysters (some of the world's best come fresh daily from Wellfleet and other Cape Cod spots). You could base a day's tour of the different neighborhoods around the foods on offer: breakfast in the cafés of **Beacon Hill** or **Cambridge**; lunch in the food plazas of **Quincy Market** or **The Garage** on JFK Street in Cambridge, or dim sum in **Chinatown**; for dinner, a budget **Indian** in Cambridge, an **Italian** around Hanover Street in the North End, or expensive seafood overlooking the Harbor.

The central aisle of **Quincy Market** is superb for all kinds of takeaways, including fresh clams and lobster, ethnic dishes, fruit cocktails and cookies (all over the city, you'll find marvellous chocolate and ice cream). Groups can buy from different vendors and eat together in the central seating area, and restaurants and brasseries are on all sides.

Chinatown, where restaurants stay open until 2 or 3am, is best for **late-night** eating.

Boston

Addis Red Sea, 544 Tremont St (☎426-8727). Authentic Ethiopian food, which you scoop up using chunks of doughy flatbread. Spicy and cheap.

The Blue Diner, 150 Kneeland St (☎338-4639). Classic restored diner with lively jukebox, slowly inching its way upmarket but with excellent traditional and unpretentious American food.

Buteco II, 57 W Dedham St, South End (☎247-9249). Wide range of tasty Brazilian dishes served until 11pm, including *feijouada* stew at weekends, and Brazilian drinks. Moderately priced.

Daily Catch, 323 Hanover St (☎523-8567) and 261 Northern Ave (☎338-3093). Italian-style seafood, with a wonderful way with squid. Expect to pay up to $20.

Durgin-Park, 340 N Market St, Faneuil Hall (☎227-2038). Crowded, hurried and priding itself on surly service, but a Boston institution for its chunky prime ribs and seafood specialties – not to mention the baked beans. Shared tables, no reservations. Anything from $7 upwards.

Golden Palace, 14–20 Tyler St (☎423-4565). Chinese restaurant open until 11.30pm, with cheap and excellent dim sum daily until 3pm. $7 and upwards.

HooDoo Barbeque, 835 Beacon St (☎267-7427). Substantial barbecues, where *Green* "T" line C emerges at Audubon Circle. Good jukebox and a lively atmosphere, but the prices are not low.

Legal Sea Foods at the *Park Plaza Hotel*, 50 Park Plaza (☎426-4444). Fast-growing chain deservedly renowned for top-quality seafood. Excellent oysters.

Rebecca's, 21 Charles St (☎742-9747). High-quality Continental cuisine on Beacon Hill, open until midnight except 10pm Sun. $15 and upwards. Also good for breakfast.

Ristorante Lucia, 415 Hanover St, North End (☎367-2353). Wonderful Italian with seafood specialties and an intimate atmosphere. $10 and upwards.

Sakura-bana, 57 Broad St (☎542-4311). Smart, highly aesthetic but relaxed and far from exorbitant Japanese restaurant and sushi bar.

Thai House Restaurant, 1033 Commonwealth Ave (☎787-4242). Excellent Thai restaurant; steamed seafood and great duck from $15.

Cambridge

Bombay Club, 57 JFK St, Galeria Mall, Harvard Square (☎661-8100). One of the very best of Cambridge's many Indian restaurants. with good-value lunch buffet.

Boston Sail Loft, 1 Memorial Drive, Kendall Square (☎225-2222). Fine array of cheap seafood.

The Cajun Yankee, 1193 Cambridge St, Inman Square (☎576-1971). Gumbo, crawfish, and other Cajun specialties, with a short menu that changes daily. Reserve. $10–18.

El Rancho, 1126 Cambridge St, Inman Square (☎868-2309). Tues–Sat until 9pm. Very cheap Salvadorean restaurant; tasty Latin American food, fruit drinks but no alcohol. $4–10.

Jake & Earl's Dixie BBQ, 1273 Cambridge St, Inman Square (☎491-RIBS). Excellent, inexpensive ribs, chicken and sandwiches.

Nightlife and Entertainment

Mainstream Boston's pride and joy, the **Boston Symphony Orchestra**, is based at the Symphony Hall, 301 Huntington Ave (☎266-1492) – which Stravinsky called the best auditorium in the world – with a winter season followed by the **Boston Pops** concerts in May, June and the 4th of July. The city's **theater** scene divides into the safe productions of the Theater District (often Broadway cast-offs) and more experimental companies in Cambridge. The **Bostix** kiosk (☎723-5181) at Faneuil Hall sells tickets for all major events – as well as tours, "T" passes, and so on – with some half-price day-of-sale tickets.

Seattle bands may have attracted the music business hype so far this decade, but arguably Boston has made a more innovative and substantial contribution to **rock music**. The emergence in the late Eighties of the Pixies, Buffalo Tom and the seminal Dinosaur Jr has been followed by a fresh batch of more photogenic bands like Belly, the Lemonheads, the Juliana Hatfield Three and Drop Nineteens, who look set to make Boston and Cambridge the face of grunge rock for the rest of the century.

Note that the city's **bars** are unusually officious in demanding ID. Though not permitted to offer cut-price happy hours, some provide free early-evening snacks instead.

Bars, Cafés and Clubs

The Black Rose, 160 State St (☎742-2286). Large Irish pub right beside Faneuil Hall, with traditional music every night and Guinness galore.

Bull and Finch Pub, 84 Beacon St, Beacon Hill (☎227-9605). Its status as the original setting of TV's *Cheers* gives this place an unpleasant streak of smugness, but at least it's central and lively.

Catch A Rising Star, 30 JFK St, Cambridge (☎661-9887). The hottest of Boston's comedy clubs; at least one show every night. Admission $6 and upwards.

Chaps, 27 Huntington Ave (☎266-7778). The biggest, glitziest gay club in town.

Commonwealth Brewery Company, 138 Portland St (☎523-8383). Brew pub right by Boston Garden near North Station, serving good pub food and their own real ale.

Diamond Jim's Piano Bar, 710 Boylston St (☎536-5300). Just off the lobby of the *Lenox Hotel*, this lively late-night haunt beats the socks off karaoke – audience members take turns belting out tunes, and you can join in the energetic sing-alongs for the price of a drink.

Front, 343 Western Ave, Cambridge (☎492-7772). Live music every night, reggae at weekends.

Grendel's Den, 89 Winthrop St, Harvard Square (☎491-1160). The liveliest of Cambridge's many student-oriented bars.

Indigo, 823 Main St, Cambridge (☎497-7200). Gay women's club, Wed–Sat only. Cover $7 and up.
Other Side Cosmic Café, 407 Newbury St (☎536-9477). Popular, and trendy, café with great salads, sandwiches, beer, wine, coffee and tea. Open late, across from *Tower Records* and Mass Turnpike.
Paradise, 969 Commonwealth Ave (☎254-2052). Enjoyable rock venue for name touring bands.
Passim, 47 Palmer St, Harvard Square (☎492-7679). Long-standing "coffee-house" folk/blues venue.
Plough & Stars, 912 Massachusetts Ave, Cambridge (☎492-9653). Time-worn Irish pub with music most nights. Cover free–$6.
The Rat, 528 Commonwealth Ave (☎267-4156). Known to novices as the *Rathskeller*, and packed most nights with sweaty, drunken grunge-heads. Live bands, cover varies.

Sport

The legendary Red Sox play **baseball** at Fenway Park (Kenmore or Fenway subway on the *Green* "T" line). The whole stadium, squeezed in 1912 into the odd-shaped plot that was all its builders could buy, is painted green, including the 37ft, 6-inch wall in the left field known as the "Green Monster". (Schedules ☎267-8661; tickets, $6–16, ☎267-1700.) **Basketball**'s Celtics (☎523-6050) and **hockey**'s Bruins both play at the Boston Garden, 150 Causeway near North Station (box office ☎227-3200).

The **Boston Marathon**, first run in 1897, is now held on Patriot's Day, the third week in April, and finishes on Boylston Street near Trinity Church (details ☎338-5709).

The North Shore

As you head northwards out of Boston, you pass through a succession of rich little ports which have been all but swallowed up by the suburbs. **Lynn** has some nice bathing beaches, and claims to have given the world the game of *Monopoly* and the brown paper bag; a more obvious day trip from Boston is the half-hour ride out to witch-hunting **Salem**. Nearby **Marblehead**, on the other hand, gave us the **US Navy**: George Washington's first five vessels were built there. If you have the time, both the atmospheric old fishing ports of **Gloucester** and **Rockport** further out on **Cape Ann** have strong literary and artistic identities: T S Eliot used to come here for his family vacations, and the *Dry Salvages* of the third of his *Four Quartets* are a group of offshore rocks. They're also the best places on the East Coast for **whale-watching** trips; *Cape Ann Whale Watch* (☎283-5110 or 1-800/877-5110) offer four-hour trips for $20.

Salem and Marblehead

Ironically, **SALEM** is remembered less as the site where the colony of Massachusetts was first established, with the most elevated of intentions, than as the place where just sixty years later Puritan self-righteousness reached its apogee in the horrific **witch trials** of 1692. While the town itself was to prosper as a port – as evidenced by its fine old buildings – the witch scare did much to discredit the idea that the New World conducted its affairs on a different moral plane than the Old. Twenty Salem women were put to death as witches, thanks to a group of impressionable teenage girls who reported as truth a garbled mixture of fireside tales told by a West Indian slave, Tituba, and half-digested scare stories published by Cotton Mather, a pillar of the Puritan community.

That this unpleasant history is now the basis of a child-oriented tourist industry – all black hats and broomsticks – makes Salem an unsettling place. The **Salem Witch Museum** in Washington Square (July & Aug daily 10am–7pm, otherwise 10am–5pm; $4) draws parallels with modern racism and political persecution, but is at heart a rather tacky show of illuminated dioramas and prerecorded commentary. Innumerable other witch-related attractions in town are best ignored. Salem's later seafaring years are remembered in the **Peabody Museum** in East India Square (Mon–Wed & Fri–Sat

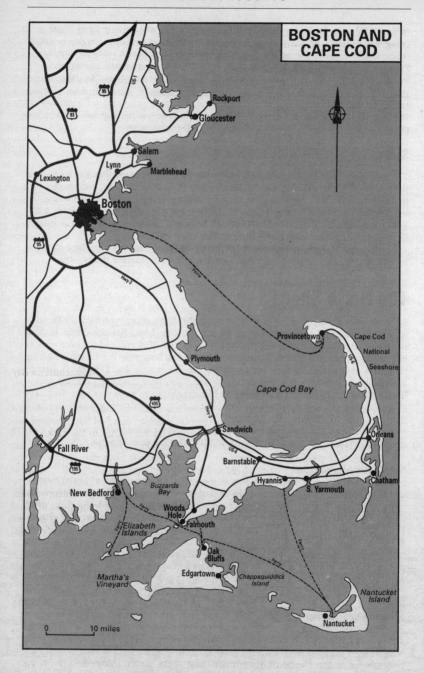

BOSTON AND CAPE COD

10am–5pm, Thurs 10am–9pm, Sun noon–5pm; $6), which since 1799 has assembled a remarkable collection of objects brought home by voyaging New Englanders. As well as extensive Japanese and Asian displays, it has one of only three existing breadfruit-wood idols of the Hawaiian god Ku, and details about the town's ships themselves.

Little of Salem's original waterfront remains, though the long **Derby Wharf** is still standing, together with the imposing **Custom House** at its head, where Nathaniel Hawthorne once worked. The **House of Seven Gables** at 54 Turner St, the star of his eponymous novel, is a rambling old mansion beside the sea (summer daily 9.30am–5.30pm; otherwise 10am–4.30pm, $6). Hour-long guided tours of the complex also take in the author's birthplace, moved here from its original site in Union Street.

Regular *MBTA* **buses** run to Salem from Haymarket Square in Boston, as well as hourly **trains** (every two hours at weekends) from North Station. If you want to **stay**, the best-value rooms are at *Hotel Lafayette*, 116 Lafayette St (☎745-5503; ③).

When Salem's witch-related attractions grow tiresome, head five miles south and east along the bay to **MARBLEHEAD**, a lovely waterfront village whose historic homes date back as far as the mid-1700s. Free walking tour **maps** are available from the information booth in the center (☎631-2868), while 250-year-old **Fort Sewall**, jutting into the harbor, gives pretty views. *Ten Mugford Street*, 10 Mugford St (☎639-0343; ④), has comfortable B&B **rooms**; *Tien's*, 12 School St (☎639-1334), serves excellent Vietnamese **meals**.

The South Shore

It can take a while to get clear of Boston heading south – especially at summer weekends, when the traffic down to Cape Cod can be horrendous. Two historic towns, one north and one south of the Cape, are worth exploring – **Plymouth** and **New Bedford**.

Plymouth

"America's Hometown", little **PLYMOUTH**, on the south shore of Massachusetts Bay 35 miles south of Boston, is given over to commemorating, in various degrees of taste and tack, the landing here of the 102 **Pilgrims** in December 1620.

A solemn pseudo-Greek temple by the sea encloses the nondescript **Plymouth Rock** where the Pilgrims are said to have touched land; as they had already spent two months on Cape Cod, and there are no contemporary references to the rock, it is of symbolic importance only. Two worthier memorials make no claim to authenticity, but meticulously reproduce the experience of the Pilgrims. Both the replica of the **Mayflower** in town, and **Plimoth Plantation** three miles south, are staffed by costumed "interpreters", each of whom acts out the part of a specific Pilgrim, Indian, or sailor. The charade visitors are obliged to perform – pretending to have stepped back into the seventeenth century – can be a little tiresome, but ultimately the sheer depth of detail in both endeavors makes them fascinating. At the Plantation, everything you see in the Pilgrim Village of 1627, and the Wampanoag Indian Settlement, has been created using traditional techniques (both April–Nov, daily 9am–5pm; *Mayflower* in July & Aug 9am–7pm; Plantation and *Mayflower* $18.50, *Mayflower* alone $6; ☎746-1622).

Plymouth's **visitor center** is in the park on North Park Ave (☎746-4779). **Motels** include the *Blue Anchor*, 7 Lincoln St (☎746-9551; ④), and the *Cold Spring*, 188 Court St (☎746-2222; ④). The *Lobster Hut* (☎746-2270) is a good **seafood** place on the front.

New Bedford

The famous old whaling port of **NEW BEDFORD**, 45 miles due south of Boston, is still home to one of the nation's most prosperous fishing fleets. New development, and a waterfront highway, has obscured some of its past, but on County Street the fine old houses still stand of which Melville commented:

> *New Bedford is a queer place. Had it not been for us whalemen, that tract of land would this day perhaps have been in as howling condition as the coast of Labrador . . . all these brave houses and flowery gardens came up from the Atlantic, Pacific and Indian oceans. One and all, they were harpooned and dragged hither from the bottom of the sea.*

The roster of the whaling ship *Acushnet*, in the **New Bedford Whaling Museum** at 18 Johnny Cake Hill (Mon–Sat 9am–5pm, Sun 11am–5pm; $3.50), shows Melville as one of the crew. Other evocative displays include a half-size replica of a whaling vessel. Immediately opposite stands the **Seamen's Bethel**; it really *does* have the ship-shaped pulpit described in *Moby Dick*, but this one was rebuilt after a later fire.

Much the most atmospheric place to **stay** in town is the *Durant Sail Loft Inn*, in the port at 1 Merrill Wharf (☎999-2700; ④), just across busy MacArthur Drive. At the same address, the *Pena Branca* (☎999-4495) is a superb and cheap Portuguese-owned **fish restaurant**. The **visitor center** is two blocks uphill at 47 N Second St (☎991-6200); **ferries** to Martha's Vineyard are detailed on p.169.

Cape Cod and the Islands

> *Here a man may stand, and put all America behind him.*
>
> Henry David Thoreau

The trouble with standing on **Cape Cod** these days is that "all America" tends to be a lot closer behind you than you might prefer. Its main tourist haunts are packed in summer, its roads circled by a grim procession of crawling vehicles, vaguely searching for some "unspoiled" bit of beach or "undiscovered" old town. Unless you have your own, preferably very secluded, place to stay, on weekends especially it's barely worth turning up between June and August and putting yourself through the hassle of trying to find what little accommodation may be available, invariably at premium prices.

Thinking of the Cape, as everyone does, as an arm, these strictures apply most forcefully to its **upper** section, the thirty-mile eastward stretch closest to mainland Massachusetts. Much the worst of the beachfront development lies along the southern shore, and **Hwy-28**, running from Falmouth via Hyannis to Chatham, gets especially clogged. Only once you get beyond the "elbow" and head north past the spectacular dunes of **Cape Cod National Seashore** do you get a feeling for why the Cape still has a reputation as a seaside wilderness. **Provincetown**, right at the end, is the one town on the Cape that can be unreservedly recommended.

Sadly, the islands of **Martha's Vineyard** and **Nantucket**, off the Cape to the south, are now also dependent on summer tourism for their livelihood. However, a trip out to Nantucket in particular does still evoke haunting memories of its proud seafaring days.

Cape Cod was named by Bartholomew Gosnold in 1602, on account of the prodigious quantities of cod caught by his crew off Provincetown. Less than twenty years later the Pilgrims landed nearby; in the few months before moving on to Plymouth they began the process, continued by generations of Europeans, of stripping the interior of the Cape bare of its original covering of thick woods.

Getting to the Cape

It was the Pilgrims who first suggested the construction of a canal between Cape Cod Bay and Buzzards Bay, so coastal shipping could avoid the dangers of the open ocean; when finally completed at the start of this century, it left the peninsula as an island. Now all traffic to the Cape bottlenecks at one or other of the two enormous bridges across the canal; you may regret trying to **drive** there on a summer Friday (or back on a Sunday). Each has an **information office** for the Cape (daily 9am–7pm) on its mainland side.

The **area code** for all eastern Massachusetts outside Boston is ☎508.

One way to dodge the traffic is to **fly**. *Business Express* (☎1-800/345-3400) serves Hyannis and Nantucket from Boston and New York; *Continental Express* (☎1-800/525-0280) leaves several times daily from Boston and New Bedford to Hyannis, Provincetown and the islands. In summer, weekend *Amtrak* **trains** usually run to Hyannis from both New York and Boston – check in advance, as these depend on a state subsidy that may not always be forthcoming. *Bonanza* **buses** run regularly from New York (☎564-8484), and the *Plymouth and Brockton Bus Co* (☎1-800/328-9997) runs to Hyannis and Provincetown from Rhode Island, Boston and New York daily (for other Boston services see p.150). **Ferries** take three hours to cross from Boston to Provincetown (see p.166); for boats to the various islands see p.169.

You can also **cycle** from Boston on the 135-mile Boston–Cape Cod Bikeway, which extends all the way up to Provincetown.

The Upper Cape

The **Upper Cape**, just across the bridges, was the first part of the peninsula to attract tourists in any numbers – and it shows. To see the various communities of the south coast as "pretty little villages" – the image they hope to project – you'd have to be wearing exceptionally rose-tinted spectacles, or blinkers. In theory, each is coyly arranged around a prim central green; but you have to fight your way through thickets of malls, motels and fast-food joints (at last count there were seventeen *Dunkin' Donuts* stands between Buzzards Bay and Hyannis) to reach their artificial hearts.

It only makes sense to stay in one of these places if you're catching a **ferry** to the islands (see p.169). Thus one obvious base is **FALMOUTH**, where central motels include the *Falmouth Marina Trade Winds* on Robbins Rd (☎548-4300; ③); the luxurious clapboard *Village Green Inn*, 40 West Main St (☎548-5621; ⑤), is in Cape terms a bargain. The *Sippewissett Campground* a couple of miles out at 836 Palmer Ave (☎548-2542) offers a free shuttle service to the ferries and beaches. Restaurants abound, but the best food is to be found in the assorted moderately priced seafood places along the waterfront at **WOODS HOLE**, four miles southwest; the *Fishmonger's Café* at 56 Water St (☎548-9148) is recommended. An exhibition near Little Harbor focuses on the sensational rediscovery of the *Titanic* in 1986 by the well-respected **Woods Hole Oceanographic Institute**, not itself open to the public.

The largest port on the Cape, and its main commercial hub, **HYANNIS**, clings a little desperately to the glamour it earned when the **Kennedy compound** at Hyannisport placed it at the center of world affairs. The Kennedys are still here, though their property can only be glimpsed, from a considerable distance, from the sea. Coincidentally enough, the town itself has become a rather anonymous playground for the over-privileged young. As well as its many motels, Hyannis has some reasonable **B&Bs**, such as the *Snow's Creek Inn*, 361 Ocean St near the harbor (☎778-4758; ③), and *Sea Gate House*, 94 Seagate Lane (☎778-5783; ③). At the *HyLand (AYH)* **youth hostel**, 465 Falmouth Rd (☎775-2970; ①), dorm beds cost $10 ($14 for non-members), and you have to check in between 5pm and 10.30pm.

Sightseeing trips on the **Cape Cod Railroad** (☎771-3788) run from Center Street in Hyannis along a meandering route to Sandwich, Buzzards Bay and Falmouth.

The Mid-Cape

The middle stretch of Cape Cod holds some of its prettiest, most unspoiled places. Time-worn old fishing communities like Wellfleet and Chatham, along with dozens of carefully maintained, mildly touristy hamlets along the many winding roads, are what most people hope to find when they come to the Cape. Cutting across the middle, the **Cape Cod Rail Trail** follows a paved-over railway track from Dennis to Eastham, through cranberry bogs and forests. It makes a good **cycling** trip; bikes can be rented in all the main towns.

CAPE COD NATIONAL SEASHORE

After the bustle of Cape Cod's towns, the **Cape Cod National Seashore** really does come as the proverbial "breath of fresh air". These protected lands, spared by President Kennedy from the rampant development further south, take up virtually the entire Atlantic side of the Cape, from Chatham north to Provincetown. Most of the way you can park by the road and strike off across the dunes to windswept beaches – though in places parking is limited to local residents. A programme of grass-planting helps to hold the whole place together; three feet of the lower Cape is washed away each year, and much of it is carried here by the sea to extend the endless beaches.

It was on these shifting sands, not then as denuded as today, that the **Pilgrims** made their first home. They obtained their water from Pilgrim Spring near Truro; at Corn Hill Beach they uncovered the freshly buried cache of Indian corn that kept them alive. After a couple of months, which they survived with the help of the Wampanoag Indians, they moved on to Plymouth (where the reconstructed Indian village at Plimoth Plantation, p.163, is based on one found at Eastham).

Displays and movies at the main **Salt Pond visitor center**, on US-6 just north of Eastham (daily 9am–4.30pm; ☎255-3421), trace the geology and history of the Cape. A road and a hiking/cycling trail head east to the sands of **Coast Guard Beach** and **Nauset Light Beach**, both of which offer excellent swimming. Another fine beach is the **Head of the Meadow**, halfway between Truro and P-Town on the northeast shore.

One desirable destination is the whitewashed old fishing community of **CHATHAM**, tucked on a protected harbor between Nantucket Sound and the open Atlantic Ocean. Hang out at the **Fish Pier** on Shore Road and wait for the fleet to come in, or head a mile south to **Chatham Light**, one of many built to protect mariners from the treacherous shoals. Tour **maps** are available from the booth at 553 Main St (☎945-5199), and the *Impudent Oyster*, just off Main at 15 Chatham Bars Ave (☎945-3545), serves excellent seafood. One of the nicest **places to stay** on the whole East Coast is the *Whalewalk Inn*, at 220 Bridge Rd in the town of Eastham (☎225-0617; ④), where rates for the lovely B&B rooms include free use of bicycles to ride the many nearby trails.

Provincetown

The compact fishing village of **PROVINCETOWN** ("P-Town") is right on the knuckle of Cape Cod's clenched fist. Silvery clapboard houses, with glorious unruly gardens, line its tiny winding streets. Provincetown is far from secluded: its population of five thousand rises tenfold in summer. Self-professed **bohemians** and **artists** have always flocked here for the dazzling light and vast beaches, and in 1914 Eugene O'Neill established the *Provincetown Playhouse* in a small hut. It has also become renowned, since the beatnik Fifties, as a **gay** and **lesbian** center. Commercialism, though rampant, is countercultural; gay, environmentalist and feminist gift shops join arty (not craftsy) galleries, restaurants and bars on the aptly named **Commercial Street.**

Provincetown retains a firm grip on its past. Strict zoning ensures that there are few new buildings in town, and there is barely a sign of ugly development. Albeit crowded and raucous from July onwards, P-Town remains a place where history, natural beauty, and, above all, difference, are respected and celebrated.

Arrival, Information and Getting Around

Provincetown lies 120 miles from Boston by land, but less than fifty by sea, nestled in the second largest natural harbor in the world (after Le Havre in France). By far the nicest way to arrive is on the **ferry**. *Bay State Cruises* leave 20 Long Wharf, Boston, at 9.30am, arriving at MacMillan Wharf three hours later, and return at 3.30pm (daily from mid-June to mid-Sept, weekends only in early June and late Sept; $15 one-way, $25 round trip; ☎723-7800 in Boston). The tiny **information center** in the Chamber of Commerce, at the end of the wharf at 307 Commercial St, sells ferry tickets (summer daily 9am–5pm, off-season Mon–Sat 10am–4pm; ☎487-3424).

It couldn't be easier to **walk** around tiny P-town, but many visitors prefer to **cycle** the narrow streets and hills. The ever-packed *Arnold's*, 329 Commercial St, rents mountain bikes and ten-speeds for $7 to $15 per day (daily 8.30am–5.30pm; ☎487-0844). For those without transport, **tours** to the more isolated dunes and moors include the *Provincetown Trolley Inc* from the town hall on Commercial St (daily 10am–7pm; $6; ☎487-9483); *Art's Dune Tours* are based at Commercial and Standish (April–Oct 10am–sunset; $7; ☎487-1950). **Whale-watching** cruises leave from MacMillan Wharf during May and September. All cost about $18–20 and sell tickets in the harbor.

The Town and the Beaches

Visitors who head straight for the beaches miss out on Provincetown's tiny core, centered on the three narrow miles of **Commercial Street. MacMillan Wharf**, always busy with charters, yachts and fishing boats (which unload their catch each afternoon), splits the town in half. Not far away in the quieter **East End**, the **Heritage Museum**, 356 Commercial St (summer daily 10am–10pm; otherwise 10am–5pm; $2), stands in an 1860 Methodist church. This well-loved collection of Provincetown memorabilia includes a 68-inch striped bass, a Portuguese altar, a model fishing schooner, and a reconstruction of the beach hut of Harry Kemp, beach-bum poet and crony of Eugene O'Neill. It also provides leaflets detailing walking tours. Further out, the delightful **Provincetown Art Association**, 460 Commercial St (summer daily noon–4pm & 7–10pm; Nov–March Fri–Sun noon–5pm; $2), displays paintings by local artists.

The 250ft granite tower of the **Pilgrim Monument and Museum** on Town Hill, in the pretty **West End** of P-Town, has an observation deck (only accessible by stairs and ramps) which looks out over the whole of the Cape (summer daily 9am–7pm; off-season 9am–5pm; $3.50). At the bottom of the hill on Bradford Street, there's a bas-relief monument to the Pilgrims' **Mayflower Compact**. Further from the wharf, the weathered clapboard houses have colored blinds, white picket fences, and wildflowers spilling out of every possible crevice. The 1746 **Seth Nickerson House**, 72 Commercial St, is the oldest house in town, built by a ship's carpenter. Tours lead through cabin-like rooms with slanting doors and crazed floorboards (June–Oct daily 10am–5pm; $2). A modest bronze plaque on a boulder at the western end of Commercial Street commemorates the Pilgrims' actual landing-place.

A little way beyond the town's narrow strip of sand, undeveloped **beaches** are marked only by dunes and a few shabby beach huts. You can swim in the clear water from the uneven rocks of the two-mile breakwater, where the seabed crunches with soft-shell clams, or head onwards through scented wild roses and beach plums to find blissful isolation. West of town, **Herring Cove Beach**, easily reached by bike or through the dunes, is more crowded but never unbearably so. In the wild **Province Lands**, at the Cape's northern tip, vast sweeping moors and bushy dunes are buffeted by a deadly sea, site of three thousand known shipwrecks. The **visitor center** (summer daily 9am–6pm; off-season 9am–4.30pm; ☎487-1256), in the middle of the dunes on Race Point Rd, has an observation deck from which you might spot a whale.

Accommodation

As well as the few motels on the outskirts, every second picturesque cottage in town seems to be a guest house. Prices are reasonable until mid-June, and off-season you can find real bargains. The *Provincetown Reservation Service* (☎487-2400 or 1-800/648-0364) and the gay-oriented *Intown Reservations* (☎487-1883 or 1-800/67P-TOWN) can usually rustle up lodging at busy times. The welcoming *Dunes' Edge Campground*, on Hwy-6 just east of the central stop lights (☎487-9815), charges $20 for its wooded sites.

Elephant Walk Inn, 156 Bradford St (☎487-2543). Central, spacious rooms, with free parking. ④.

Gull Walk Inn, 300A Commercial St (☎487-9027). All-women guest house in a quiet lane off the town center, with sun deck and sea views. ④.

Hurst House, 384 Commercial St (☎487-0990). Quiet, clean rooms in artistic house. Large doubles with shared bathroom. ③.

Joshua Paine's Guest House, 15 Tremont St (☎487-1551). Four rooms on quiet street. ③.

Eating

Food in Provincetown can be expensive: the snack bars around MacMillan Wharf are generally extortionate, and the – undeniably good – nouvelle cuisine in the trendy gay restaurants can hit $10 for a salad and a coffee. Portuguese bakeries, relics of early settlement, and bland family restaurants abound on Commercial Street.

Café Blase, 328 Commercial St (☎487-9465). Touristy pastel cafe, one of the few places with outdoor seating for people-watching. Pricey for dinner, but delicious $6 fresh fruit and waffle breakfasts.

Café Heaven, 199 Commercial St (☎487-9639). Light and airy upmarket-looking café serving all-day breakfasts, cappuccino and creative salads from $5. Closed 3–6pm, then reopens until 9pm.

Fat Jack's, 335 Commercial St (☎487-4822). Cheap no-nonsense breakfasts and daily specials.

Post Office Cafe, 303 Commercial St (☎487-6400). Small gay-run restaurant serving healthy lunches and dinners for $5–10. Gay/feminist cabaret nightly.

Nightlife and Entertainment

Each weekend, boatloads of revellers seek out P-Town's notoriously wild nightlife. From house music raves to drag cabarets, from torch singing to r'n'b, the variety is huge.

The Atlantic House, 6 Masonic Place, behind Commercial (☎487-3821). The "A-House" – a dark drinking hole of Tennessee Williams and Eugene O'Neill – is now a trendy gay music club and bar.

Colonial Tap Room, Commercial St. Ancient, dimly lit fishermen's bar. Crooked wooden floors and heavy graffiti-carved benches. Clientele includes gruff sea salts and exuberant revellers.

Crown and Anchor, 247 Commercial St (☎487-1430). Noisy pub with nightly drag cabaret.

Governor Bradford, 312 Commercial St (☎487-9618). Popular bar with live jazz, reggae and r'n'b.

Martha's Vineyard

The island of **MARTHA'S VINEYARD**, just seven miles south of Cape Cod and twenty-four miles long by ten wide, may or may not have been named for Bartholomew Gosnold's daughter Martha (some ancient maps call it *Martin's* Vineyard). The "Vineyard" part, however, was for its "incredible store of vines"; considerably more fertile than bleak little Nantucket, it has never been quite so dependent on the sea to make a living. Now more than ever tourism is at the root of the island's economy. The many second-home owners who spend the summer here get a better deal than mere day-trippers, though – some of the best beaches are off-limits to non-residents.

Ferries to the island arrive at either **Oak Bluffs**, where genteel terraced houses look down on the harbor and there's a colorful century-old fairground carousel near the jetty, or at the more upmarket **Vineyard Haven**. **Edgartown**, over to the east, is the oldest settlement on the island, and has been extravagantly dolled up for visitors (you may recognize it as the location for the *Jaws* films). A little ferry shuttles back and forth from Edgartown to adjacent **Chappaquiddick Island** (the bridge which Senator Edward Kennedy made infamous is on the far side).

The three principal island communities are connected by a regular bus service and offer full facilities and shops of every kind. They're quite mellow places to pass a summer's day, but much the best idea on a visit to Martha's Vineyard is to explore the island for yourself. Bringing a car over is expensive and rather pointless, but as soon as you get off the ferry you encounter rows of **bike** rental places. The best ride is along the State Beach Park between Oak Bluffs and Edgartown, with the dunes to one side and marshy Sengekontacket Pond to the other; purpose-built cycle routes continue to the youth hostel at West Tisbury (see below).

Trips around the west side of the island ("up-island") can be disappointing, with not a peep at the ocean beyond the private estates; however, you do eventually come to the **lighthouse** at **Gay Head Cliffs**, where the multicolored clay was once the main source of paint for the island's houses. The cliffs are not vast, and they're crumbling away so fast that it's not safe to approach them too closely. From Philbin Beach below, however, you can get near enough to wallow in some lovely mud holes. Gay Head was once famous for its Wampanoag harpooneers, such as Tashtego in *Moby Dick*.

Accommodation

If accommodation is booked up, as is very likely, the main **Chamber of Commerce** office at Beach Road in Vineyard Haven (☎693-0085) may be able to help. There are **campgrounds** near Vineyard Haven (☎693-3772) and Oak Bluffs (☎693-0233).

Attleboro House, 11 Lake Ave, Oak Bluffs (☎693-4346). Old-fashioned B&B in a distinguished harbor-view terrace – no private bathrooms. ④.

Colonial Inn, North Water St, Edgartown (☎627-4711). Extremely central white clapboard inn, part of a largish mall. Some off-season bargains, but midsummer room rates are high. ⑥.

Manter Memorial Youth Hostel (AYH), Edgartown Rd, West Tisbury (☎693-2665). A very nice setting, but not that easy to get to. April–Nov, curfew 10pm, $12 members, $15 non-members. ①.

Nashua House, Kennebec Ave, Oak Bluffs (☎693-0043). Small doubles, shared baths. ③.

Wesley Hotel, 1 Lake Ave, Oak Bluffs (☎693-6611). Huge but characterful hotel near the ferries. Most rooms are upwards of $125, but a few with shared bathrooms cost less. ④.

Eating

It's not at all hard to find something to eat on Martha's Vineyard. The ports in particular have rows of places to tempt tourists catching the ferries back. Only in Edgartown and Oak Bluffs can you order alcohol with meals, but you can bring your own elsewhere.

AJ's Seafood & Steak, Main St, Vineyard Haven (☎693-4480). Good budget food in a nice setting.

Linden Tree, Main St, Vineyard Haven (☎693-4480). Very cheap cafe with seafood and pasta.

Giordano's, Circuit Ave, Oak Bluffs (☎693-0184). Crowded and cheap Italian.

Lawry's, Main St, Edgartown (☎627-8857). Very good back-to-basics fish-market-cum-restaurant.

Louis', 102 State Rd, Vineyard Haven (☎693-3255). Lively Italian place, well priced. Salad bar.

FERRIES TO MARTHA'S VINEYARD AND NANTUCKET

Unless otherwise specified, all the ferries below run several times daily in midsummer (mid-June to mid-Sept). Most have fewer services from May to mid-June, and between mid-September and October. There is at least a skeleton service to each island, though not on all routes, all year round. Single passenger fares from the Cape to Martha's Vineyard are around $6, to Nantucket $12. Bikes are $5 extra, cars around $40.

To Martha's Vineyard

From **Falmouth** to Oak Bluffs. Passenger only. *The Island Queen* (☎548-4800).

From **Woods Hole** to both Vineyard Haven and Oak Bluffs. Car ferry. *Steamship Authority* (☎540-2022; on Martha's Vineyard ☎693-0367).

From **Hyannis** to Oak Bluffs. Passenger only. *Hy-Line* (☎778-2600 in Hyannis; ☎693-0112 on Martha's Vineyard).

From **New Bedford** to Vineyard Haven. Passenger only, $10. *Cape Island Express*

Lines (☎997-1688 in New Bedford; ☎693-2088 on Martha's Vineyard).

From **Montauk**, Long Island to Oak Bluff. Passenger only, summer Thursdays only, $40. *Viking Ferry* (☎668-5709).

To Nantucket

From **Hyannis**. Cars on *Steamship Authority* (☎228-3274 on Nantucket). Also *Hy-Line* (☎228-3949 on Nantucket).

The *Steamship Authority* in summer also runs one daily connecting service between Martha's Vineyard and Nantucket.

THE WHALERS OF NANTUCKET

Scores of anonymous Captains have sailed out of Nantucket, that were as great, and greater than your Cook.. . . For in their succorless empty-handedness, they, in the heathenish sharked waters, and by the beaches of unrecorded, javelin islands, battled with virgin wonders and terrors that Cook with all his marines and muskets would not have willingly dared.

Herman Melville, *Moby Dick*

In 1659, a sober group of 27 Quaker and Presbyterian families arrived on Nantucket and set about imposing order on the haphazard business of **whaling**. Whales had always beached themselves on the treacherous sandy shoals all around – up to a dozen might be washed ashore in a major storm – and the local **Indians** had become skilled in hunting them in nearby waters. At first, the white settlers treated the island itself as their vessel, erecting tall masts from which a permanent watch was kept for passing whales. As the years went by, they stopped waiting at home, and sent large ships out into the ocean to pursue their prey. The Wampanoag played an integral part in the process: the actual kill was effected by two rowboats working in tandem, and at least five of each thirteen-man crew, usually including the crucial **harpooneer**, would be Indian. (The common occurrence when an injured whale would speed away, dragging a boat helter-skelter behind it for endless terrifying hours, was known as a "**Nantucket Sleighride**".)

The early chronicler Crèvecoeur provides an extensive account of Nantucket as it was in 1782 in his *Letters from an American Farmer*. Although perturbed by the islanders' universal habit of taking a dose of opium every morning, he held them up as a model of diligence and good self-government. Whaling was a disciplined profession, unmarred by the stereotyped debauchery of sailors elsewhere, and to feed themselves and equip their ships the islanders kept up a shrewd and extensive trade with the mainland. At that time there were already more than a hundred ships. The whalemen were not paid; instead each had a share (a *lay*) of the final proceeds of the voyage. Crèvecoeur was impressed by the Nantucketers' ambition: "Would you believe that they have already gone to the Falkland Islands and I have heard several of them talk of going to the South Sea."

They did indeed reach the Pacific – see Chapter Sixteen, Hawaii, for an account of their experiences there. The great days of Nantucket were immortalized by Herman Melville:

And thus have these naked Nantucketers, these sea hermits, issuing from their ant-hill in the sea, overrun and conquered the watery world like so many Alexanders . . . Two thirds of this terraqueous globe are the Nantucketer's. For the sea is his; he owns it, as Emperors own empires.

In fact *Moby Dick* is a valediction; by the time it was published in 1851, Nantucket's fortunes had gone into an abrupt decline. Soon after a devastating fire in 1846, reports of the Californian Gold Rush lured young men westwards; the discovery of underground oil in Pennsylvania came as the final blow. A magazine article of 1873 reported, "Let no traveler visit Nantucket with the expectation of witnessing the marks of a flourishing trade . . . of the great fleet of ships which dotted every sea, scarcely a vestige remains."

Nantucket

The thirty-mile, two-hour sea crossing to **NANTUCKET** may not be an ocean-going odyssey, but it does set the "Little Grey Lady" apart from her shore-hugging sister, Martha. Halfway here from Hyannis, neither mainland nor island is in sight, and once you've landed you can avert your eyes from the smart-money double-deck cruisers with names like *Pier Pressure* and *Loan Star* and let the place remind you that it hasn't always been a rich folk's playground. Indeed, despite the formidable prowess of its seamen (see box), survival for early settlers on the island's barren soil was always a struggle.

The tiny cobbled alleyways of **Nantucket Town** itself, once one of the largest cities in Massachusetts, were frozen in time by economic decline 150 years ago. This area of delightful old houses is very much the center of activity. From the moment you get off the ferry you are besieged by bike rental places and tour companies. **Straight Wharf** leads directly onto **Main Street** with its shops and restaurants; the **information office** – which does *not* make accommodation reservations – is nearby at 25 Federal St (☎228-0925). The main sights in town are the excellent **Whaling Museum** (daily, 9am–6pm, summer only; $3) on Broad Street at the head of Steamboat Wharf, where you should look out especially for such scrimshaw artefacts as a set of 21 whale types carved from whales' teeth, and the astonishing harpoon corkscrewed in the "flurry" or last struggle of a dying whale, and the **Peter Foulger Museum** ($2) of island history next door.

After a stroll around Nantucket Town, the usual procedure is to cycle the seven flat miles east to the village of **Siasconset** (always abbreviated to *Sconset*), where the ancient cottages stand literally encrusted with salt, and then to meander back at will across the heaths and moorland. Buses also link Nantucket Town and Siasconset.

Accommodation

But for the **youth hostel**, accommodation on Nantucket is invariably expensive; the going rate in B&Bs and guest houses starts at $75. There are no **campgrounds**.

Cliff Lodge, 9 Cliff Rd (☎228-9480). B&B with some low-priced singles. ⑥.

Hawthorn House, 2 Chestnut St (☎228-1468). Cheap, central and well-appointed guest house. ④.

Hungry Whale, 8 Derrymore Rd (☎228-0793). Good value and friendly. ⑤.

Star of the Sea Youth Hostel (AYH), Surfside (☎228-0433). Dorm beds at Surfside Beach, 2 miles south of town. $12 members, $15 non-members. April–Oct only. Opens 5pm, curfew 10.30pm. ①.

Eating

Crèvecoeur (see box) reported that on Nantucket "music, singing and dancing are holden in equal detestation". **Seafood** fortunately is not; the only trouble is that Nantucket's restaurants, good as they may be, tend to be exceptionally expensive.

Espresso Cafe, 40 Main St (☎228-6930). Cheap, healthy lunch place. Some vegetarian dishes.

Obadiah's Native Seafood, 2 India St (☎228-4430). Good value for the island.

Rose and Crown, 23 S Water St (☎228-2595). Seafood saloon with music and comedy.

Inland Massachusetts

The 150 miles of Massachusetts which stretch inland to the west of Boston have always been obliged to play second fiddle to the state capital. Just ten years after the Revolution, the farmers who struggled to make a living from this indifferent soil so resented the imposition of taxes by the prosperous merchants of the east that they rose in **Shay's Rebellion**; their pitchforks were no match for the guns of the new nation.

These days the citizens of the west are eager to promote themselves as cultural rivals to the big city, with the **Berkshires** hosting the celebrated **Tanglewood** music festival in summer. **Amherst**, the home of Emily Dickinson, is a stimulating little college community, as is its larger neighbor **Northampton**; both have all the cafés, restaurants and bookstores you could want. Another delightful college town is **Williamstown** in the far northwest corner, set at the end of the incredibly scenic Mohawk Trail.

Worcester

Forty miles west of Boston on I-90, **WORCESTER** is Massachusetts' second largest city and the only industrial city in the US beside neither sea, lake nor river. Abbie Hoffman's hometown is not a place to spend a great deal of time, but if you're nearby the remarkable **Higgins Armory Museum**, at 100 Barber Ave (Mon–Fri 9am–4pm, Sat & Sun noon–4pm; closed Mon Sept–June; $6), houses weapons and armor from all over the world in a bizarre steel and glass office-cum-museum (note the conspicuous riveting). The enthusiasm for metalworking of the founder of the Worcester Pressed Steel Company led him to tour Europe after World War I, buying vast quantities of ancient

---

OLD STURBRIDGE VILLAGE

Halfway between Worcester and Springfield on US-20, near the junction of I-90 and I-84, the restored and reconstructed **Old Sturbridge Village** (daily 9am–5pm; $15), made up of preserved buildings brought from all over the region, gives a somewhat idealized but still engaging portrait of a small New England town of the 1830s. As in other similar places, costumed interpreters act out roles – working in blacksmiths' shops, planting and harvesting vegetables, tending cows and the like – but they pull it off in an unusually convincing manner. The site itself, with mature trees, ponds and dirt footpaths, is very pretty, and with all its crafts and diversions you could easily spend half a day here.

---

armor. You might also drop in at the **American Antiquarian Society**, 185 Salisbury St (Mon–Fri 9am–5pm, tours Wed 2pm), which holds copies of two-thirds of all the material published in America before 1821, more even than the Library of Congress.

Of local **accommodation**, the *Howard Johnson* at 181 W Boylston St (☎835-4456) starts at $65; the *Yankee Budget Motor Lodge* at 561 Lincoln St (☎852-5800) is cheaper. *Legal Sea Foods*, 1 Exchange Place (☎792-1600), is a reliable fish restaurant.

Springfield

SPRINGFIELD, at the point where I-90 crosses I-91, ninety miles from Boston at the southern end of the Pioneer Valley, has an odd assortment of claims to fame, including being the home of the Springfield Rifle and the late children's author Dr Seuss. Visitors are drawn to this unwieldy and unattractive city, split by the wide Connecticut River, by the 1890s invention of Dr James Naismith – the sport of **basketball**. Naismith designed the game as a way of providing exercise for athletes at the YMCA, and its popularity spread with amazing rapidity. After a trip to the Berlin Olympics in 1936 Naismith came up with another bright idea and established the **Basketball Hall of Fame** at 1150 West Columbus Ave, next to the river just south of Memorial Bridge (July to mid-Sept daily 9am–6pm; otherwise 9am–5pm; $6). This enjoyably traces the history of the game with movies, videos and plenty of memorabilia, and also lets you test your own skills.

Springfield's *Amtrak* station is very central, on Lyman St. Plenty of **motels** start at around $40, including the *Susse Chalet* at exit 6 off I-90 (☎592-5141; ③). *Chi-Chi's Restaurante*, 955 Riverdale Rd in West Springfield (☎781-0442), is a local institution, a massive pseudo-adobe Mexican restaurant on Hwy-5 just south of the I-91 bridge.

The Berkshires

The **Berkshire Hills**, where Massachusetts borders New York, are a cross between the English Lake District and the grand seafront resort of Newport, Rhode Island. Especially in the area nearest the Massachusetts Turnpike (I-90), the green hillsides are dotted with ostentatious Victorian mansions, while the towns are chic – if not snooty – summer tourist-traps. Further north, it's easier to escape civilization and get deep into the woods. The **Mohawk Trail** in the northwest corner passes through North Adams and Williamstown, following the very scenic route the Indians used to travel between the valleys of the Connecticut and Hudson rivers.

STOCKBRIDGE, just south of I-90 fifty miles west of Springfield, started out as "Indian Town". The Reverend John Sergeant built the simple wooden **Mission House** on Main Street in 1739 in an attempt to live in close proximity with the local Indians and convert them to Christianity by sheer force of example. His success barely lasted beyond his own death; later settlers were far less keen on having the Indians around.

The **area code** for Springfield and western Massachusetts is ☎413.

That Stockbridge today looks the archetypal New England small town – above all when there's snow on the ground – is due largely to the artist **Norman Rockwell**, who lived here for 25 years until his death in 1978. Many of his *Saturday Evening Post* covers, whose sentimentality was made palatable by his sharp wit, featured the town; a collection can be seen at the brand-new $10 million **museum** on Hwy-183 (May–Oct daily 10am–5pm; otherwise Mon–Fri 11am–4pm, Sat & Sun 10am–5pm; $8). Some of the tour guides modelled for Rockwell as children and recall that for every few minutes they managed to hold still he'd slip them one more from his large pile of nickels.

Magnificent houses in the hills around include **Chesterwood**, the luxurious home and studio of Daniel Chester French, sculptor of the Lincoln Memorial (May–Oct daily 10am–5pm), half a mile south of the new Rockwell Museum, and **Naumkeag**, which belonged to Joseph Choate, US ambassador to Queen Victoria (summer daily 10am–4.15pm; winter Sat & Sun only 10am–4.15pm). Stockbridge was also the setting for Arlo Guthrie's song, and movie, *Alice's Restaurant*.

Well-heeled tourists flock to nearby **LENOX** each year for the summer season of the Boston Symphony Orchestra at **Tanglewood**. Open-air concerts are held every Friday, Saturday and Sunday in July and August; the few covered seats are expensive and hard to get, but you can sit and picnic on the lush lawns for an admission fee of around $10. Some midweek rehearsals are also open to the public (☎637-1940 for details), and there's a jazz festival on the weekend of Labor Day.

Further north on US-7, **Arrowhead** (Mon–Sat 10am–4.30pm, Sun 11am–3.30pm; $4) near Pittsfield was Herman Melville's home while he wrote *Moby Dick*; declining popularity eventually obliged him to sell up and move to New York. The **Hancock Shaker Village** five miles west of Pittsfield survived from 1790 to 1960 (May–Oct daily 9.30am–5pm; April & Nov daily 10am–3pm; $9). Their legacy includes the large dwelling place, in which almost one hundred people slept and ate; a round stone barn for their cattle; and the garage where the last Shakers kept their cars. A more important, and much less commercialized, Shaker village, **Mount Lebanon**, is another five miles west on US-20, just over the New York state border; much has been dismantled and moved to museums, but self-guided **tours** give a sense of the Shaker way of life ($2; ☎794-9500).

Practicalities

Most of the **accommodation** in the Berkshires is concentrated in Lenox and neighboring Lee; when the Tanglewood concerts are on, prices of course go through the roof. The only rooms in Lee for under $50 are in the *Super 8 Motel* at 128 Housatonic St (☎1-800/843-1991; ③); the *Underledge Inn* at 76 Cliffwood St in Lenox (☎637-0236; ④) is a welcoming B&B inn, and the *Black Swan Inn* (☎243-2700 or 1-800/876-7926; ④) in Lee has lakefront doubles. The *Red Lion Inn* is one of the grander edifices on Main St Stockbridge (☎298-5545; ⑥); rooms are expensive, but the *Lion's Den* bar and restaurant downstairs is fun. For **food**, the *Church Street Café*, 59 Church St, Lenox (☎637-2745), is good value. Good **bars** include the *Shaker Mill Tavern*, Albany Rd, West Stockbridge (☎232-8565), and *Sullivan Station*, a converted railway station in Lee (☎243-2082).

RHODE ISLAND

RHODE ISLAND is the smallest state of the Union, at a mere 48 miles long by 37 miles wide, and tends to be overlooked as a destination, even if it is home to more than twenty percent of the nation's historical landmarks. It was established by Roger Williams in 1635 as a "lively experiment" in religious freedom. He had been expelled from Puritan Salem for his radical ideas (including the notion that Indians should be paid for their land and that there should be a complete separation of church from state), and the Massachusetts Puritans liked to call the state "**Rogues Island**".

Despite its size, Rhode Island has over four hundred miles of coastline, hacked out of the Narragansett Bay; it is in fact made up of over thirty tiny islands, including Hope and Despair. The **"Ocean State"** therefore developed through sea trade, whaling and smuggling. Partly due to this commercial power, Rhode Islanders were in the front rank of Revolutionary feeling, resenting the stringent economic pressures placed on them from England. However, no Revolutionary battles were fought on Rhode Island soil, and this turned out to be the last state to ratify the Constitution, unwilling at first to abandon its new-found freedom. Between the Revolution and the Civil War, Rhode Island shifted from a maritime economy; it led the **Industrial Revolution** when Samuel Slater created the nation's first water-powered **textile mill** at Pawtucket outside Providence. Today, although still heavily industrialized, the state's principal destinations are its two original ports: well-heeled **Newport**, yachting capital of the world with good beaches and outrageously extravagant mansions, and the Colonial college town of **Providence**. **Block Island**, about thirty miles south of Newport, has a popular state beach, while the rest of Rhode Island is largely made up of sleepy small towns and fishing ports.

Getting Around Rhode Island

Rhode Island is tiny enough to make getting around ridiculously easy. I-95, the major interstate, runs through **Providence** on its way from Massachusetts to Connecticut. The more scenic US-1 follows the coast of Narragansett Bay into Connecticut. **Newport** is accessible from Hwy-138, which connects the small islands in Narragansett Bay to the mainland. **Public transport** is good; local buses connect Providence and Newport, and *Amtrak* stops regularly in Providence. **Ferries** link Block Island and Newport.

Providence

Splayed across seven hills on the Providence and Seekonk rivers, **PROVIDENCE** was Rhode Island's first settlement, founded "in commemoration of God's providence" on land given to Roger Williams by the Narragansett Indians (his insistence that Indians should be paid for their land being waived in his own case). Now New England's fourth largest city, it has been the **state capital** since 1901, and flourished as one of the most important ports of call in the notorious "triangle trade", where New England rum was exchanged for African slaves to be sold for West Indian molasses. Since Slater's invention of the water-powered textile mill, port trade and industry have been the mainstays of the economy. Today Ivy League **Brown University** and the **Rhode Island School of Design** (RISD or "Rizdee") give the place a certain cultural verve (although admittedly that doesn't stray far from the immediate environs of College Hill on the east bank of the river), and the many original Colonial homes on **Benefit Street** emphasize a historical importance almost absent from the somewhat drab downtown across the river. Ethnic diversity is provided by **Little Italy** on Federal Hill west of the river, and fairly voluble Greek and Portuguese – and especially Cape Verdean – communities.

Arrival and Getting Around

T F Green Airport is in Warwick, nine miles south of Providence. In town, there's a brand-new *Amtrak* station at 100 Gaspee St, in a domed building a short walk southwest of the capitol. *Plymouth and Brockton, Greyhound,* and *Bonanza* **bus** lines stop considerably further out at 1 Bonanza Way (exit 25 off I-95) (☎751-8800). Bus transport within the city, and to the rest of the state, is provided by *RIPTA* (Mon–Sat 8.30am–6pm; ☎781-9400), with most local and all longer-distance buses leaving from Kennedy Plaza, where schedules are available from a rarely staffed information booth (Mon–Fri 8am–4.30pm). However, sightseeing is best done on foot.

The **area code** for the entire state of Rhode Island is ☎401.

Information

The **CVB**, 30 Exchange Terrace (Mon–Fri 9am–5pm; ☎274-1636 or 1-800/233-1636), provides maps and brochures, as does the useful **Providence Preservation Society**, 24 Meeting St in the 1772 *Shakespeare's Head*, which has self-guided walking and audio-cassette tours of the city's historic areas (Mon–Fri 9am–5pm; ☎831-7440). There's another **information center** in the Roger Williams National Memorial Park, 282 N Main St (daily, summer 9am–5pm; winter 9am–4.30pm; ☎528-5385).

The City

Providence's main attractions focus around three of its seven hills. Downtown, which centers on **Kennedy Plaza**, is sited just below **Constitution Hill. City Hall**, on the western end of the Plaza, is mainly notable for a star-spangled midnight blue ceiling in the Alderman's Chamber. Though no longer used as a train terminal, the nearby 1898 Beaux Arts **Union Station** is a fine example of the historic restoration at which the city excels. Southeast of the Plaza, the 1828 **Westminster Arcade**, the oldest enclosed shopping mall in the nation, features expensive clothes shops and a food court in a small, bright, skylit hall. **Roger Williams National Memorial Park**, at N Main and Smith at the foot of Constitution Hill, includes an original well said to be used by Williams and his followers (Nov–April Mon–Fri), while at the top of the hill, the white marble **state capitol** boasts a huge unsupported dome, second only in size to Saint Peters in Rome, topped with a statue of "independent man". A handsome full-length portrait of Washington adorns the Reception Room (free tours Mon–Sat 9am–3.30pm).

Laid-back **College Hill**, across the river, is a pretty district of Colonial buildings and museums. Part of Williams' holy experiment was the establishment of the Baptist Church in 1638. The white clapboard **First Baptist Meeting House** at the foot of the hill dates from 1775, and is remarkable for its very tall steeple. This street leads into **South Main Street**, once bustling with waterfront activity, now a small stretch of pot-pourri and pottery shops. **Benefit Street**, a block up the hill, is Providence's "**mile of history**", lined with the ice-cream colored former clapboard homes of merchants and sea captains. Now beautifully restored, the street was just a dirt path leading to grave-yards until it was improved in the nineteenth century for the "benefit of the people of Providence" – hence its name. The elegant **John Brown House**, 52 Power St at Benefit St, was home to the Donald Trump of the eighteenth century, who made his wealth from trading in slaves and with China. The first house built on the hill (nicely conspicuous from the river), it retains its original furnishings and holds displays on the formidable Brown family and the city itself (Tues–Sat 11am–4pm, Sun 1–4pm; $5).

Ivy League **Brown University** sets the tone for this three-centuries-old district with its relaxed, intellectual feel; for free tours, contact the admissions office, 45 Prospect St (Mon–Fri 8am–4pm; tours 10am, 11am, 1pm, 3pm & 4pm). Another university building, the **Woods-Gerry Gallery**, 62 Prospect St, is a solid red-brick mansion set in a tree-shaded garden with heavy stone benches, exhibiting innovative student art (Mon–Fri 11am–4pm; off-season Mon–Sat 11am–4pm, Sun 2–5pm; closed August; free). At the eastern edge of College Hill, **Wickenden Street** buzzes with a creative assortment of bookshops, cafés, and antique and thrift stores.

The small but excellent collection of the **RISD Museum of Art**, 224 Benefit St, is worthy of its status as one of the best art schools in the country, and includes ancient and Oriental works, Impressionists and Post-Impressionists, American art and Rodin's statue of Balzac (mid-June to Aug Wed–Sat noon–5pm; Sept to mid-June Tues, Wed, Fri & Sat 10.30am–5pm, Thurs noon–8pm, Sun 2–5pm; $3.50, free on Sat). Across the road, the Greek Revival **Providence Athenaeum**, 251 Benefit St, is where Edgar Allan Poe unsuccessfully wooed fellow poet Sarah Whitman. Today the library holds original Audubon prints and rare books, and the piano and hand-painted chairs in the cozy reading rooms give it the feel of someone's living room (June–Sept Mon–Fri 8.30am–4.30pm; Oct–May Mon–Fri 8.30am–5.30pm, Sat 9.30am–5.30pm; free).

Federal Hill, west of downtown, is Providence's **Little Italy**, entered through a large arch at Atwells Avenue topped by a bronze pine cone. Long a powerful Mafia stronghold, this area is one of the friendliest and safest in the city – alive with cafés, delis, bakeries and bars, and a large Italianate fountain in the Piazza de Pasquale.

Pawtucket

In 1793, Samuel Slater used technology surreptitiously imported from England to shove Rhode Island into the industrial age. His landmark **Old Slater Mill** is still in operation, in suburban Pawtucket. A ten-minute drive north to exit 28 on I-95, the **Slater Mill Historical Site**, on Roosevelt Ave, also includes in its living museum of the Industrial Revolution the 1810 Wilkinson Mill and the 1758 Sylvanus Brown House (June–Sept Tues–Sat 10am–5pm, Sun 1–5pm; March–May & Sept–Dec Sat & Sun 1–5pm; $4).

Accommodation

Downtown Providence has few cheap **rooms**, although B&B is a viable option. *B&B of Rhode Island*, Box 3291, Newport (☎401/849-1928) offers accommodation on College Hill from $60. Motorists can take advantage of the cheap hotels along I-95, or north in Pawtucket, and south near the airport at Warwick.

Church House Inn, 122 Fountain St (☎751-7209). B&B above good music venue (see opposite). Special deals on extended stays. ③.

Comfort Inn, 2 George St, Pawtucket (☎723-6700). Reasonable rooms near I-95 and Slater's Mill. ④.

Holiday Inn, 21 Atwells Ave (☎831-3900). Next to the Civic Center near Little Italy. ⑤.

The Old Court, 144 Benefit St (☎751-2002). Luxury ten-room B&B in old rectory. ⑥.

State House Inn, 43 Jewett St (☎785-1235). Pleasant, central B&B rooms in restored old home. ④.

Eating

Studenty **Thayer Street** is lined with cheap lunch places, almost all of which remain open until late. **Wickenden Street** is more alternative, and more expensive. The family-run Italian restaurants on Federal Hill serve good food at reasonable prices, and the Westminster Arcade downtown is your best bet for a quick breakfast or lunch.

Cinema Café, 204 S Main St (☎272-3315). Joined to Providence's hippest artsy cinema, this simple cafe has outdoor seating and is open late for vegetarian and international dishes from $3.

Coffee Exchange, 214 Wickenden St (☎273-1198). Trendy coffee bar. A popular meeting place for arty intellectuals. On the pavement, deckchairs and barrels act as seating and tables.

Le Grecque, 24 Arcade Mall (☎351-3454). The cheapest and most interesting food in the mall. Greek specialties include marinated chick peas and rice or spinach pies.

Kabob'n'Curry, 261 Thayer St (☎273-8844). Above-average Indian meals in trendy Thayer Street.

Trattoria d'Antuono, 351 Atwells Ave (☎272-7339). Classic Italian family-style cooking. Great fish.

Nightlife and Entertainment

As Providence's **nightlife** is largely student-generated, things get quiet during the vacations, though Thayer Street is always lively. On summer evenings, a **party trolley** with balloons and noisy music rumbles through downtown. The $6 fee includes entrance to six nightclubs on its route, and a half-price drink (Fri & Sat 8.30pm–2am; ☎861-1385). The *Cable Car Cinema* at 204 S Main St, and the *Avon Rep Cinema*, at 250 Thayer St (☎421-3315), show good independent and art **films**. The *Providence Performing Arts*

Center, downtown at 220 Weybosset St, is in a grand old art-deco movie house and hosts various shows and theater (☎421-2787). The free weekly *Nice Paper* has complete entertainment listings.

Church House Inn Red Brick Tavern, 122 Fountain St (☎351-5505). Two clubs, with live jazz, blues, reggae and Cajun music, and DJ dance one-nighters.

Club Babyhead, 73 Richmond St (☎421-1698). Indie bands and assorted dance nights.

The Last Call, 15 Elbow St (☎421-7170). Live r'n'b and jam sessions.

L'Elizabeths, 285 S Main St (☎621-9113). Upmarket, relaxed bar.

Newport

Thirty miles south of Providence, **NEWPORT** stands at the southern tip of the largest island in Narragansett Bay, **Aquidneck (or Rhode) Island**. It was established as a colony by William Coddington of Providence in 1639. Due to its excellent harbor, it grew rapidly as a port for the triangle trade, a privateering center, and a hotbed of Revolutionary feeling. **Religious tolerance** led to an influx of Jews, Quakers and Baptists who formed lucrative international trade links, but this great prosperity was severely knocked back by the **British occupation** of 1776–79, when half the population fled and much of the town was burned down. Fortunately, enough buildings survived for Newport now to rival Boston for its number of original eighteenth-century homes.

In the 1850s the town became fashionable again as a resort for wealthy Southern merchants, and very soon nouveau-riche industrialists such as the Astors, Belmonts and Vanderbilts were building "**summer cottages**" – better described as palaces – along the rocky coastline. The obscene ostentation of this era, now known in Mark Twain's disparaging phrase as the **Gilded Age**, shocked Massachusetts old wealth to the core.

Depression killed off the decadence, but Newport kept going as a naval town until the 1970s. Today the town feeds off tourism; much of it caters to the tennis and yachting set, but there are as many people looking at – and envying – the wealth as enjoying it. Though sanitized by the ugly new **America's Cup Avenue**, which replaced the sea-salt rawness of the waterfront with bars and boutiques, the rough old port still rears its boozy head, with beer and r'n'b clubs as evident as cocktails and cruises.

Arrival, Information, and Getting Around

There are actually three towns on Aquidneck Island; **Portsmouth** is at the northern edge, and then comes the appropriately named **Middletown**, with **Newport**, the southernmost, just below it. The mainland is connected to the island from I-95 on US-138 by the **Jamestown Bridge** to Conanincut Island, and from there by the **Newport Bridge**.

Newport itself, spanning only ten miles, is easy to walk around. **Thames** (pronounced *Thaymz*) Street is the main road, with Bellevue Avenue, or Mansion Row, parallel to the east. Information, auto-tape tours ($12), maps and advice are available from the large **visitor center** at 23 America's Cup Ave (daily 8am–8pm, off-season 9am–5pm; ☎849-8048 or 1-800/326-6030).

The adjacent **Gateway Center** is the terminal for *Bonanza* (☎846-1820) and *RIPTA* buses; the latter run regularly to the beaches and on to Providence (75¢–$2.25; ☎847-0209 or 1-800/662-5088). Also based at the Center are free summer **shuttle buses** connecting the main sights and shopping areas (daily 10am–7pm); the hourly **Newport Trolley** which stops at sixteen tourist attractions including the mansions (June–Sept daily 10am–3pm; unlimited rides $7.50; ☎849-8005); and *Viking Tours*, whose bus excursions take in admission to one or more mansions (☎847-6921). Rented **bikes**, good for getting to the quieter beaches, cost $10 per day from *Ten Speed Spokes*, 18 Elm St, off America's Cup Ave (Mon–Sat 9.30am–5.30pm, summer Sun noon–5pm; ☎847-5609).

The Town

Newport's main attractions are obviously its **mansions**, but there is nothing to be gained by attempting to tour them all, and although it is pleasant enough to stroll around the predominantly Colonial **downtown**, the ever-growing profusion of souvenir shops is somewhat off-putting. Otherwise, if you don't fancy beautiful-people-spotting on the harbor, you'll do better following the crowds to one of the **beaches**.

The Mansions

The phrase **"conspicuous consumption"** was coined by sociologist Thorstein Veblen, who visited Newport at the turn of the century and witnessed the desperate need felt by new entrepreneurial **millionaires** to define their fragile identities by flaunting their wealth. More than just a summer resort, Newport became an arena in which families competed with increasing mania to outdo each other – though the **"season"** of wild and decadent parties lasted only a few weeks, and many of the ten-million-dollar mansions lay empty for years at a time.

It's difficult to grasp the sheer wealth involved by merely gawking at the mansions' facades, but after being herded in and rushed through more than a couple the opulence rapidly begins to pall. Choose one to see, or two at the most. The most important stand on **Bellevue Avenue**, **Ocean Drive** and **Harrison Avenue**. The Astors' **Beechwood**, 580 Bellevue Ave (mid-May–Oct daily 10am–5pm; Nov–Dec daily 10am–4pm; Feb–May Sat & Sun 10am–4pm; $7.75), is an entertaining antidote to the drier historical drills given on other tours. Costumed actors welcome visitors as house guests who have arrived for a party held by Mrs Astor, the self-proclaimed queen of American society (she devised the notion of the **Four Hundred**, an elite of individuals whose lineage had to go back at least three generations). Anecdotes, bitchy asides and a constant stream of activity – as well as strawberry tea in the servants' kitchen – make it all great fun.

Also on Bellevue Avenue, the **Marble House** is the most over-the-top example of Gilded Age excess, with a golden ballroom and a Chinese teahouse on the grounds; it and **Rosecliff**, with its colorful rose garden and heart-shaped staircase, were both used as sets during the filming of *The Great Gatsby*. **Kingscote**, on Bellevue Ave, is a quirky Arts and Crafts cottage with a lovely interior, while the biggest and best of the lot, Cornelius Vanderbilt's **The Breakers**, on Ochre Point Avenue, is a sumptuous Italian Renaissance palace, overlooking the ocean. All except Beechwood are run by the **Newport Preservation Society**, 118 Mill St, whose combination tickets slightly help to beat the hefty individual admission prices of at least $6 (April–Sept daily 10am–5pm, otherwise schedules vary; any two houses $11, three $16, four $19; ☎847-1000).

One way to see the Bellevue Avenue mansions on the cheap is to peer in the back gardens from the **Cliff Walk**, which begins on Memorial Avenue where it meets First Beach. This three-and-a-half mile oceanside path alternates from jasmine and wild roses to unappealing concrete underpasses through perilous rocks. For those with a car, Ocean Drive continues from Bellevue Avenue where the Cliff Walk ends, following the coast eastwards and passing **Hammersmith Farm**, John and Jackie Kennedy's 28-room shingled summer home, originally owned by Jackie's mother (April–Oct daily 10am–7pm, March & Nov Sat & Sun 10am–5pm; $6.50).

Downtown

Newport's Colonial political and business center, **Washington Square**, lies just south of the Gateway Center, beginning where Thames Street meets the Brick Market. The 1762 market, off **Long Wharf** (the most important of Newport's Colonial wharves), has been reconstructed to include fairly ordinary galleries and pricey gift shops. The **Old Colony House**, one of Rhode Island's few pre-Revolutionary brick buildings and seat of government from 1739 to 1900, stands on the other side of the square (July–Sept Mon–Fri

9.30am–noon & 1–4pm, Sat & Sun 9.30am–noon; free). To the north, the **Easton's Point** district, between Washington Street on the water and Spring Street to the east, is lined with the eighteenth-century homes of ship captains; only the 1748 **Hunter House**, 54 Washington St, is open to the public (May–Oct daily 10am–5pm; $6).

The oldest religious building in town is the shabby 1699 **Quaker House**, Marlborough and Farewell, restored to its nineteenth-century appearance and completely free of adornment (mid-June to Aug Mon–Sat 10am–5pm; otherwise tours by appointment; $2). In 1790, Newport's Jewish community wrote to George Washington expressing their hopes for his new government. His enthusiastic reply advocating religious liberty is exhibited at the Georgian **Touro Synagogue**, 85 Touro St, built in 1763 and the oldest in the nation (June–Sept Mon–Fri 10am–5pm, Sun 10am–6pm; Oct–May Sun 2–4pm; free). Just next door, the tiny **Newport Historical Society and Museum**, 82 Touro St (Tues–Fri 9.30am–4.30pm, Sat 9.30am–noon), has changing exhibits on Newport's past and organizes **walking tours** through Colonial Newport on Friday and Saturday in summer at 10am ($5). Washington himself worshipped at the 1726 **Trinity Church** on Queen Anne Park, a Colonial structure based on the Old North Church in Boston and the designs of Sir Christopher Wren (June–Sept Mon–Sat 10am–4pm; Oct–May Sat & Sun 1–4pm; free). A few blocks south, the Catholic **St Marys Church**, Spring St and Memorial Blvd, is the oldest Catholic Church in Rhode Island, where Jackie Bouvier married John Kennedy (Mon–Fri 7–11am; free).

Bellevue Avenue, the street lined with most of Newport's famous mansions, also has two museums of note. The **Newport Art Museum**, at no 76, is housed in the 1864 mock-medieval Griswold House and exhibits New England art from the last two centuries (Tues–Sat 10am–5pm, Sun 1–5pm; $2.50). At no 194, the grand **Newport Casino** was an early country club which held the first national tennis championship in 1881. It is now the **International Tennis Hall of Fame**, and still keeps its grass courts open to the public. The museum includes exhibits on tennis fashion and trophies (May–Sept daily 10am–5pm; Oct–April 11am–4pm; $4).

Beaches

The indubitable attraction of Newport's shoreline, with its many coves and gently sloping beaches, is slightly marred by the fact that many are strictly private. **Gooseberry Beach**, on the southern edge of the island, is surrounded by grand houses and charges $1 admission. The town beach, **First** (or Newport, or Easton's) **Beach**, is at the east end of Memorial Boulevard. **Second** and **Third** beaches are further along the same route towards Middletown. The visitor center provides a guide to them all.

Accommodation

There are plenty of reasonably priced **guest houses** in Newport, but it's a good idea to book ahead, especially on summer weekends (when prices rocket). The visitor center (see p.177) has free phone links to inns and motels in all price ranges. By far the most prevalent form of accommodation is **B&B**. *Bed and Breakfast of Rhode Island* (☎849-1298) can find rooms from around $65, and *Anna's Victorian Connection*, 5 Fowler Ave (☎849-2489), offers a 24-hour reservation service with rooms from $35.

Commodore Perry Inn, 348 Thames St (☎846-4256 or 1-800/343-2863). Clean and comfortable rooms in prime position. ③.

Marion's House, 378 Spring St (☎848-0115). 1861 house, room rates rise at weekends. ③.

The Melville House, 39 Clarke St (☎847-0460). Colonial B&B two blocks from the harbor. ⑤.

Pembroke House, 21 Bedlow Ave (☎849-8786). Pleasant B&B. ④.

The William Fludder House, 30 Bellevue Ave (☎849-4220). 1875 home near the mansions. ④.

The Willows, 8–10 Willow St (☎846-5486). If you liked Beechwood, you'll feel right at home with the daily "living history lessons" which come with your breakfast in bed. ④.

Eating

Many of Newport's restaurants are smug and overpriced, with the result that visitors on a budget have to make do with snacks. However, there are some gems, even along touristy Thames Street, and the seafood here is well worth the blow-out if you have the extra cash.

Wave Cafe, 22 Washington Square (☎846-6060). Hip, upbeat café serving aspiring artists and poets rather than the yacht club. Crepes from $4, lunch specials with an international flavor from $5.50, flavored coffees and teas. Occasional poetry readings and exhibitions.

Muriel's, 58 Spring St (☎849-7780). French specialties, plus chowder and pasta from $10.

Salas, 345 Thames St (☎846-8772). Buzzing, friendly Italian family restaurant serving home-cooked feasts including stuffed quahog (clams) at very low prices.

Live Music

Newport is historically famed for its duo of music festivals: the **Ben & Jerry's Folk Festival** in August, followed by the **Newport Jazz Festival**. Both are held in Fort Adams State Park (☎847-3700). A lesser-known **Classical Music Festival** takes place in the mansions during July (☎846-1133).

Otherwise, there is plenty of shamelessly unrefined **nightlife**; noisy bars abound near the waterfront, and among the **live music venues** in town, two of the best are the *Blue Pelican*, 40 W Broadway (☎847-5675), which has jazz, blues, folk, Irish, reggae and world music nightly, and *Thax*, 212 Thames St (☎849-1112), which puts on r'n'b and jazz above an upmarket restaurant.

CONNECTICUT

CONNECTICUT was named *Quinnehtukqut* by the Native Americans for the "great tidal river" which splits it in two before spilling out into the Long Island Sound and washing the old whaling ports of the coast. This small and densely populated state is a sort of conservative, high-rent suburb of New York City, enabling commuters to earn Big Apple salaries while avoiding New York state and city taxes. Its first white settlers arrived in the 1630s: refugees from Massachusetts seeking liberty, good farmland and trading opportunities (not necessarily in that order). Connecticut soon became a center for "**Yankee ingenuity**", prospering through the invention and marketing (often by the notorious and not always honorable Yankee peddlers) of many a useful little household object. Although hit very badly by English raids in the Revolutionary War, its role in providing the war effort with crucial supplies made it known as "the **provisions state**". After the war, the original charter of Connecticut's first colonists was used as a model for the American Constitution and gave rise to another nickname: "the **Constitution state**". It continued to prosper during the eighteenth and nineteenth centuries, with steady industrialization and lucrative whaling along the southeastern coast. Today, much of the old industry, especially in the north, has withered away, leaving areas of green countryside, untroubled by noisy interstates, many verdant forests and the idyllic rural villages that typify New England's PR image – but also unemployment, poverty, and a degree of displacement. **New Haven** in particular, home to Yale University, faces distinctly un-New England problems like drug wars, homelessness and violent crime.

The linchpins of Connecticut's economy – insurance companies, medical research and military bases – hardly make for pleasing aesthetics, as demonstrated by the interminably dull capital city, **Hartford**, and even the historic and otherwise attractive coastline is marred by some unlovely stretches of sprawling grey concrete.

> The **area code** for the entire state of Connecticut is ☎203.

Getting Around Connecticut

Except for a few isolated areas in the north, Connecticut is well provided with major **roads**; the state also has some of the fastest drivers on the East Coast, and traffic hurtles along at well over 75mph. I-95 is the main interstate, running from New York to Rhode Island along the shore of the Long Island Sound. I-91 travels north from I-95 at New Haven, weaving its way along the Connecticut River to Vermont. However, in Connecticut, as with the other New England states, it's a shame to miss out on the quiet countryside scenery along the side roads. Although it's easy to get lost on poorly sign-posted backroads, distances are so small that this is unlikely to be a major problem.

All the major east coast air carriers **fly** to Bradley International Airport near Hartford, and *Greyhound* **buses** run to most of the main towns. *Connecticut Transit* buses (☎525-9181) serve the inland area around Hartford. *Amtrak* and *Metro North* (☎1-800/223-6052) **trains** call regularly at New Haven, Hartford, Mystic and New London, and make numerous commuter stops.

Southeastern Connecticut

The much-visited **southeastern coast** of Connecticut spans fifteen miles from Stonington in the east to Niantic in the west, bisected by the Thames (pronounced *Thaymz*) River. Each of the handful of tiny, picturesque Colonial communities and old whaling villages along the Long Island Sound is a mere stone's throw from the next. No longer are they the iniquitous and rumbustuous ports that so inspired Melville, but they're still keen to preserve a sense of their history. The restored nineteenth-century **Mystic Seaport** justifies at least a day's visit; nearby are the less lovely US Naval submarine base at **Groton** and the pretty fishing harbor of **Stonington Borough**.

Mystic

The old whaling port and shipbuilding center of **MYSTIC**, the purists will tell you, does not in fact exist; it is an area governed partly by Groton and partly by Stonington. Nonetheless, it does have a small, well-kept, and somewhat touristy **downtown**, lined with typically New England-quaint clapboard galleries and antique shops. The old bridge across the bustling **Mystic River** which divides it down the middle still opens hourly, and self-guided walking tours take in the many old houses built by well-off sea captains. The **Olde Mistick Village**, at the intersection of I-95 and US-27, is a pleasant enough outdoor mall with over sixty upmarket shops in Colonial-style buildings. For a scenic walk or bike ride away from tourists, the four-mile river road is protected from cars and development and passes by Downes Marsh, a sanctuary for osprey.

What brings the tourists to Mystic is the impeccably reconstructed seventeen-acre waterfront village of **Mystic Seaport**, at the mouth of the river, where more than sixty weathered buildings house old-style workshops, stores and a printing press. Its **Stillman Museum** exhibits exquisitely carved scrimshaw and a vast amount of products made from whales' wax-like spermaceti, as well as film of a bloody whale capture. Demonstrations of shanty-singing, fish-splitting and sail-setting, among other sea-salty pastimes, vie with storytelling and theater, while in the **shipyard** you can watch the building, restoration and maintenance of wooden ships. The pièce-de-resistance is the restored *Charles W Morgan*, a three-masted wooden Yankee **whaling ship** built in 1841. The last of its kind, the *Morgan* is an elegy to an age of exploration and arrogant expansion remembered now with a mixture of nostalgia and shame. Done up ready to embark on a two-year voyage, the ship is filled with whaling memorabilia; below deck, accessible by perilously narrow stairs, the blubber room is crowded with huge iron try-pots to melt down the stinking blubber (daily 9am–8pm in summer, otherwise 9am–5pm; $14, late-afternoon arrivals are granted free entrance on the next day; ☎572-0711).

Over six thousand weird and wonderful sea creatures glug about the **Marinelife Aquarium**, at exit 90 off I-95. The hourly *Marine Theater* is more educational than the usual performing seal show, with porpoises and a beluga whale, and there are various gooey-eyed baby seals and cute penguins to coo at (July & Aug daily 9am–7pm, last admission 5.30pm; Sept–June daily until 6pm, last admission 4.30pm; $8.50).

Practicalities

Mystic has **information offices** in the Olde Mistick Village shopping mall (Mon–Fri 9.30am–5.30pm, Sat 9.30am–6pm, Sun 10am–5pm; ☎536-1641), and in the train station, from where a special bus runs straight to the Seaport. Though the town itself is manage-able on foot, it also has a tourist trolley service which stops at the major hotels.

Accommodation in town is at a premium in July and August. B&Bs include the small *Comfort Inn*, handy for the Seaport at 132 Greenmanville Ave (☎572-8531; ③), and the rural Colonial farmhouse *Applewood Farms Inn*, five minutes north of town at 528 Colonel Ledyard Highway, Ledyard (☎536-2022; ④), whose owners will collect you from the train station if given notice. The *Seaport* **campground** is on US-184 in Old Mystic, three miles from the Seaport (☎536-4044).

Much the best-known **restaurant** is *Mystic Pizza*, at 56 W Main St (☎536-3700), a small family-run pizza place which continues to serve huge, cheap and fresh "pies", unruffled by its movie-star status. Ten minutes' drive south in the small fishing port of **Noank**, the casual summer-only *Abbott's Lobster in the Rough*, 117 Pearl St (☎536-7719), serves superb fresh steamed lobster and seafood at outdoor picnic tables. A giant New England dinner for four costs $25, a lobster plate around $18; bring your own alcohol.

Stonington Borough

STONINGTON BOROUGH, five miles east of Mystic, is an overwhelmingly pretty old fishing village, originally Portuguese but now very New England, characterized by desirable whitewashed cottages (which were once factory houses), white picket fences and colorful flower gardens. Its main street, **Water Street**, is chock-a-block with antique shops and upmarket thrift stores, crowded with well-heeled bargain hunters at the weekend. The **Old Lighthouse Museum**, at no 7, dates from 1823 and is full of local memorabilia, maps and drawings; fresh flowers everywhere add a nice touch. You can climb the stone steps and iron staircase to the top for views over the water and Connecticut's neighboring states (May–Oct Tues–Sun 11am–4.30pm; $2). The water-side itself is a great place to pass a few sunny hours, peaceful and quiet with a few bob-bing fishing boats and clean water for swimming.

If you want to **stay**, the *Farnan House*, 10 McGrath Court (☎535-0634; ④), is a simple Colonial B&B. Authentic New England clam chowder, and full meals, can be had at *Noah's*, 115 Water St (☎535-3925), an old Portuguese **restaurant** with a friendly, pine-table-trendy atmosphere and delicious home-baked cakes.

Groton

Seven miles west of Mystic Seaport, **GROTON** is a suitably unpleasant name for the home town of the hideous **US Naval Submarine Base**, headquarters for the North Atlantic fleet. The **USS Nautilus**, America's first nuclear-powered submarine, was built in Groton. In 1958, four years after it was launched, it became the first vessel to sail under the polar icecap. It's now moored on the Thames, and self-guided tours allow access to its terrifyingly claustrophobic corridors, one-person-wide in many places. The sub looks pretty much as it did in the Fifties, complete with pin-ups of Marilyn Monroe. The **Submarine Force Museum** next door has exhibits on the history of submersibles from the minuscule *American Turtle*, built in 1775, to the frighteningly powerful *Trident* (April–Oct Wed–Mon 9am–5pm; Nov–March 9am–3.30pm; free; ☎449-3558).

New London

NEW LONDON, opposite Groton on the west side of the Thames, is the closest thing the region has to a city, although it spreads over only six square miles. Originally settled in 1646, it was a wealthy whaling port in the nineteenth century and is today home to the **US Coast Guard Academy**, Mohegan Ave off I-95 (May–Oct daily 9am–5pm), where visitors can wander around a museum of coastguard history and visit the tall ship *USS Eagle* when it's in port. A self-guided walking tour of downtown passes along the prosperous Huntington Street, where four adjacent Greek Revival mansions are known as **Whale Oil Row**. For swimming and sunbathing, the **Ocean Beach Park**, Ocean Ave, has a sand beach and huge saltwater pool, as well as a wooden boardwalk (summer daily 9am–10pm; $1).

New London was the birthplace of boozy playwright **Eugene O'Neill**. His childhood home, the **Monte Cristo Cottage**, 325 Pequot Ave, is open for tours, complete with juicy details of his trauma-ridden early life – though they may already be familiar to you from his *Long Day's Journey Into Night* (Mon–Fri 1–4pm; $3). The writer's influence is felt further at the *O'Neill Memorial Theater Center*, 305 Great Neck Rd in nearby **Waterford**, an acclaimed testing ground for playwrights and actors, at which audiences can take potluck and watch new, often experimental shows in rehearsal (performances every other night in July; ☎443-5378).

Practicalities

Groton–New London Airport (☎445-8549) has a limited service to the rest of New England (and several car rental outlets); you can also arrive in New London by **ferry** from Orient Point on Long Island (*Cross Sound Ferry*, ☎443-5281). *Greyhound* (☎447-3841) and *Bonanza* both serve the town, which is the center of *SEAT*'s far from comprehensive local **buses** (☎886-2631).

The **Southeastern Connecticut Chamber of Commerce** is at 1 Whale Oil Row (☎443-8332 or 1-800/222-6783). New London is generally a less expensive place to stay than Mystic, with reasonably priced **motels** along I-95, including the *Holiday Inn*, I-95 and Frontage Rd (☎442-0631; ④). Regional **B&B**s can be booked via *Seacoast Landings B&B Registry*, 133 Neptune Drive, Groton, CT 06340 (☎442-1940).

Central Connecticut

Though **central Connecticut** is dominated by **Hartford**, the state's largest city is possibly one of the nation's dullest destinations. There's not a great deal of point in straying away from the coast, where **New Haven** is a whole lot more interesting.

Hartford

The unattractive modern capital of Connecticut, **HARTFORD** on the Connecticut River, is also the insurance center of the United States. Its central gold-domed **state capitol**, sitting on a hill in Bushnell Park, houses a small museum of Connecticut history; free tours are available during the week from 9.15am until 2.15pm. Marginally more thrilling is the antique merry-go-round in the park, which gives jangling rides for a mere 25¢. The

State Museum across the road holds Colt rifles and revolvers and the desk at which Abraham Lincoln signed the paper that emancipated all slaves during the Civil War.

The small **Hartford Atheneum** at 600 Main St, the nation's oldest public art museum, is filled with American fine and decorative arts (Tues–Sun 11am–5pm; $3, free Thurs). Nearby on Main Street, the wide-ranging **Avery Art Memorial** holds works by Picasso, Goya, Rembrandt and Cezanne.

About a mile west of downtown Hartford on Hwy-4, a hilltop community known as Nook Farm was home in the 1880s to next-door neighbors **Mark Twain** and **Harriet Beecher Stowe**, when Twain was writing *Huckleberry Finn*. Today their Victorian homes, at 351 Farmington Ave, furnished much as they were then, are open for tours (daily in summer, closed Mon in winter; $6.50 for one, $10 for both). Twain lived here from 1874 until 1891, writing many of his classic works, and he spent a fair portion of his publishing royalties building and redecorating this outrageously ornate home, with its unusual black and orange brickwork and luxurious Tiffany-filled interior.

Practicalities

Hartford, which lies at the junction of I-91 (north–south) and I-84 (east–west), is easily accessible by car. *Greyhound* (☎547-1500) and *Bonanza* **buses**, and *Amtrak* **trains**, all pull into the terminal at Union Place. If you have to stay the night, there are cheap **motels** along I-91, such as *Susse Chalet* at exit 27 (☎525-9306 or 1-800/258-1980; ③); hotels in Hartford itself cater mainly to business visitors and are correspondingly pricey. A popular **restaurant** downtown is *Brown, Thompson & Co* (☎525-1600), 924 Main St, where dinner costs around $6 and there's live comedy at the weekend (for a $10 admission charge). For further information, try Hartford's **CVB**, in the center of downtown on Civic Center Plaza (Mon–Fri 9am–4.30pm; ☎728-6789).

New Haven

NEW HAVEN, founded in 1638 by a group of wealthy Puritans from London on a large natural harbor at the mouth of the Quinnipiac River, developed a solid economy based on shipping and, later, industry. In 1716 it became the seat of **Yale University**, now the third oldest college in the States, but it was manufacturing that really brought the city into its own, late in the nineteenth century. New Haven churned out Winchester rifles, musical instruments, tools, carriages and corsets, and **Eli Whitney**, inventor of the revolutionary cotton gin, discovered in his workshop here a method of mass production that did away with expensive skilled labor. Today, however, there is little manufacturing activity left in New Haven, as it faces a damaging and profound depression.

It's an uneasy place, half tension-ridden urban wasteland and half Ivy League idyll. Town-versus-gown conflicts are so marked as to give the city a crackling energy, and New Haven is certainly less WASPish and smug than many other Ivy League towns. Drug pushing, gang wars and homelessness notwithstanding, blacks and whites – and Italians, Irish and Asians – coexist, ambivalently, in New Haven in a way unseen in the rest of New England. Even the students themselves seem a different, slightly less self-satisfied, breed from those at Princeton, say, or Harvard. The city's ethnic diversity, and the undeniable vitality provided by the much-maligned Yalies, make it a stimulating place to spend some time.

Arrival, Information and Getting Around

New Haven lies where the interstates I-91 and I-95 fork apart, and is on the main **train** line between Washington and Boston; services also run to Canada and New York. The *Amtrak* terminal is in the colossal and newly renovated **Union Station**, on Union Avenue six blocks southeast of the Yale campus downtown. To or from New York, the *Metro-North Commuter Railroad* (☎497-2089) is a better deal than *Amtrak*. *Greyhound* and *Peter Pan* (to Boston) **buses** arrive at 45 George St (☎772-2470). Upon arrival, it's advisable to catch a cab to your hotel, as the bus and train terminals are in potentially dodgy areas. One reputable firm is *Metro Taxi* (☎777-7777).

Public transportation to areas outside downtown is provided by *Connecticut Transit* (☎624-0151), 470 James St, but service is poor after 6pm. An **information booth** two blocks east of the Green at 200 Orange St has schedules (Mon–Fri 9am–5pm). There is a **visitor center** at 195 Church St, on the Green (☎787-8822).

The City

A succession of remarkably ugly buildings put up during the 1950s rather blighted New Haven, but its **downtown**, centering on the **Green**, remains both attractive and walkable, thanks in part to some sensitive restoration. This area, laid out in 1638, was the site of the city's original settlement; around the Green are three churches, a grand library and a number of stately government buildings. The park itself is now home to a handful of harmless itinerants, and borders the student-filled College and Chapel Street district. The surrounding five blocks are a genuinely lively place in which to hang out, filled with bookshops, cafés, clubs and hip clothes shops; the **Neon Garage**, an art exhibit in a real parking lot on Crown Street, is especially notable. It's quite safe to wander around, even at night, especially during term-time.

New Haven's prime attraction, **Yale University**, stands proudly right in the center of things. You can wander at will, though free hour-long student-led **tours** set off daily from the Information Office at 344 College St opposite the Green (Mon–Fri 10am–4pm; tours Mon–Fri 10.30am–2pm, Sat & Sun 1.30pm). Tours entail quite a bit of trooping to and fro, starting with the beautiful old spires and ivy-strewn cobbled courtyards of the old campus (mostly built in the Thirties, but painstakingly distressed to look suitably ancient) and ending up at the remarkable **Beinecke Rare Books Library**, 121 Wall St, where venerable manuscripts and hand-printed books can be seen with the aid of natural light seeping through the translucent marble walls (Mon–Fri 8.30am–5pm, Sat 10am–5pm, closed Sat in Aug; free). Other buildings of interest include the modernist, Louis Kahn-designed **Center for British Art**, 1080 Chapel St, where British paintings range from Elizabethan portraits to contemporary works by Peter Blake and Francis Bacon (Tues–Sat 10am–5pm, Sun 2–5pm; free). The impressive **Yale University Art Gallery**, just across the road at 1111 Chapel St, and the nation's oldest university art collection, holds American decorative arts, regional design and furniture, and African and pre-Columbian works. Among major European paintings is Van Gogh's famous *Night Café*, said by the artist to be "one of the ugliest pictures I have done" (Tues–Sat 10am–5pm, Sun 2–5pm; closed Aug; free). A quirky **Collection of Musical Instruments** is at 15 Hillhouse Ave (Tues–Thurs 1–4pm), and the **Peabody Museum of Natural History**, 170 Whitney Ave, is a solid nineteenth-century collection of fossils, skeletons, and gems (Mon–Sat 10am–5pm, Sun noon–5pm; $3.50, free Mon–Fri 3–5pm).

New Haven's close-knit **Italian District** has been based since 1900 among the well-kept brownstones and colorful window boxes of **Wooster Street**, just beyond Crown Street southeast of the Green. This was where the city's original Italian immigrants settled when they came to work on the railroad. There's little to see here except the incredibly popular restaurants, but it's well worth stopping by when there's a festival on.

Accommodation

New Haven has surprisingly few **hotels** for a city of its size; not even expensive ones for visiting Yalie parents. **B&B** from around $45 can be arranged in advance through *Nutmeg Bed and Breakfast*, 222 Girard Ave, Hartford, CT 06105 (☎236-6698). The downtown hotels, although slightly overpriced, are worth it for their convenient location and safety. Because of the shortage of rooms, be sure to book ahead if you're going to be visiting during graduation.

Colony Inn, 1157 Chapel St (☎776-1234). Luxury hotel in the center of things. ⑥.

Holiday Inn, 30 Whalley Ave (☎777-6221). Generic rooms in good central location. ⑤.

Hotel Duncan, 1151 Chapel St (☎787-1273). Comfortable rooms in old-fashioned hotel, a few steps away from Yale. ③.

Eating

You can't leave New Haven without trying the local **pizza** (known by the cognoscenti as tomato pies). The *New York Times* discovered New Haven's pizzas a few years ago, and since then there have been queues down the street at all the family restaurants in Wooster Square. There are also plenty of reasonably priced and innovative restaurants around the Green, on College and Chapel streets.

Atticus Bookstore Cafe, 1082 Chapel St, in the Yale Center for British Art (☎776-4040). Salads, soups, sandwiches, brioches and good coffee, in a relaxed bookshop open until midnight.

Bruxelles Brasserie, 220 College St (☎782-1551). Fashionable restaurant near the theaters with excellent cordon bleu food and smart crowd. Entrees, which include Louisiana stuffed trout and chicken with lemon yoghurt, start at $13.

Claire's Corner Copia, 1000 Chapel St (☎562-3888). Stodgy 1970s-style vegetarian food at moderate prices. A rather dilettante attitude to the microwave.

Daily Caffe, 316 Elm St (☎766-5063). Relaxed and arty café, open until 1am, catering to the cappuccino and Sunday papers set. Sandwiches and cakes from $2.

Louis' Lunch, 263 Crown St (☎562-5507). Small and dark ancient burger house that claims to have invented the hamburger. Highly popular, but closed, oddly enough, at the weekend.

Pepe's Pizzeria, 157 Wooster St (☎865-5762). Most popular of the Wooster Street eateries; plain, functional and friendly, with huge "combination pies" starting at $5. The secret is apparently in the coal-fired ovens and the Italian tomatoes.

Spanky's, 238 Crown St (☎562-3530). This brand new "Fifties" diner may look awful, but it can offer great music on the individual jukeboxes, juicy burgers from $5, and no-nonsense blue-plate specials like meatloaf from $8.

Willoughby's, 1006 Chapel St (☎789-8400). Self-consciously trendy gourmet coffee bar frequented by hip intellectuals and fashionable townies. Superb coffee from $1.75, sticky cakes for slightly more.

Yankee Doodle, 258 Elm St (☎865-1074). Yalies' favorite cheap caff, with original Fifties fittings and shop sign.

Nightlife and Entertainment

New Haven has an undeniably rich **cultural scene**, and is especially strong on **theater**. The *Yale Rep Company*, 1120 Chapel St (☎432-1234), which boasts amongst its eminent past members Jodie Foster and Meryl Streep, turns out consistently good shows during the school year. The *Long Wharf Theater* (☎787-4282), 222 Sargent Drive just off I-95, has a nationwide reputation for quality performances, as does the refurbished *Schubert Performing Arts Center*, 247 College St (☎562-5666).

Additionally, there are several good **bars** and **clubs**, concentrated on Chapel and College streets. The free biweekly paper *Hip*, available from the clothes shops along Chapel Street, has details of all the happening happenings in and around New Haven, while the *New Haven Advocate*, a free news and arts weekly paper, has more comprehensive listings.

Anchor Bar, 272 College St (☎865-1512). Authentic Fifties bar, one of the best spots in town. Snug plastic booths, dim orange lighting, frosted windows and a formidable matronly hostess.

Bopper's, 239 Crown St (☎562-1469). Pseudo-Fifties club with various one-nighters.

Club Heat, 216 Crown St (☎782-1238). Wild club which really wishes it were in New York, and does its best to pretend that it is.

Foundry Café, 104 Audubon St (☎776-5144). Laid-back bar with live music and a small, pretty garden.

Toad's, 300 York St (☎777-7431). Big live-music venue, where the likes of Dylan and the Stones "pop in" occasionally to play impromptu gigs.

NEW HAMPSHIRE

Long after sailors, fishermen and agricultural colonists had domesticated the entire coastline of New England, the harsh glacier-scarred interior of **NEW HAMPSHIRE**, with its dense forests and forbidding mountains, remained the exclusive preserve of the Algonquin Indians. Only the few miles of seashore held sizeable seventeenth-century communities of European settlers, such as Strawbery Banke at **Portsmouth**.

Even when the Indians were finally driven back, following the defeat of their French allies in Canada, the settlers could make little agricultural impact on the rocky terrain of this "granite state". Towns such as Nashua, Manchester and Concord grew up in the fertile Merrimack Valley, but not until the Industrial Revolution made possible the development of water-powered **textile** mills did the economy take off. For a while, ruthless **timber** companies looked set to strip all northern New Hampshire bare – very few of the trees you see now are original growth – but they were brought under control when it was appreciated that the pristine landscape of the **White Mountains** might turn out to be the state's greatest asset. Large-scale **tourism** began towards the end of last century; at one stage fifty trains daily brought travellers up to Mount Washington.

Ever since becoming the first American state to declare independence, in January 1776, New Hampshire has been proud to go its own idiosyncratic way. The absence of a sales tax, or even a personal income tax, is seen as a fulfilment of the state motto, "Live Free or Die". Alternative sources of revenue include state-owned **liquor stores** – set up after the failure of Prohibition, and enthusiastically promoted: they even have them in freeway rest areas. The state has long gained inordinate political clout as the venue of the first **primary election** of each presidential campaign, with its villages well used to playing host to would-be world leaders.

One less ideological aspect of New Hampshire's individualism is the emphasis on a healthy outdoor lifestyle. Hiking, climbing, cycling, and **skiing** are enjoyed both by energetic locals and by the many visitors who drive up from Boston and New York. The major destinations are **Lake Winnipesaukee**, and **Conway**, **Lincoln** and **Franconia** in the mountains further north. Some have grown rather too large and commercial for their own good, but if you steer clear of the paying "attractions", the lakes, islands and snow-capped peaks themselves remain spectacular. To see the bucolic rural scenery more usually associated with New England, take a detour off the main roads up the Merrimack Valley – to **Canterbury Shaker Village** near Concord, for example.

Getting Around New Hampshire

Manchester has a small airport, but travellers coming to New Hampshire from far afield usually do so via Boston's Logan Airport. *Concord Trailways* (☎1-800/258-3722; ☎1-800/852-3317 in NH) runs **buses** from there to Manchester, Concord, Conway and Franconia. *Vermont Transit* (☎1-800/451-3292) runs from Boston to Conway and Franconia, and at weekends (Fri, Sat & Sun) also connects Conway with Burlington and Montréal. The closest *Amtrak* service is to White River Junction in Vermont, across the state line from Hanover. A surprising number of **cyclists** set out to tour the mountains.

The Coast

Of all the US states with ocean access, New Hampshire has the shortest coastline – just eighteen miles. Driving north from Boston along either I-95 or the quieter US-1, you enter New Hampshire after roughly forty miles, to be confronted almost immediately by

The **area code** for the entire state of New Hampshire is ☎603.

the nuclear power plant at **Seabrook Station**, which finally opened in 1990 after years of determined opposition, not least from the irate state of Massachusetts close by.

Hampton Beach, a little further on, is a traditional family seaside resort (its free information line has the optimistic number ☎1-800/GET-A-TAN). The usual assortment of motels and fast-food places line the approaches to the crowded beaches, but this close to Boston summer **accommodation** rates are high. The *Pine Haven* at 183 Lafayette Rd (☎964-8187; ④), on US-1 four miles north of town, is one of the less expensive options. Large local **campgrounds** include *Tuxbury Pond* in South Hampton (☎394-7660).

Portsmouth

New Hampshire's oldest community, **PORTSMOUTH**, might look like a major city on the map, but once you're there it has much more of the feel of a country town. Its position at the mouth of the Piscataqua River has always made it an important port – it was the state capital until 1808 – but it has barely grown, and the spire of **North Church** in the central **Market Square** remains the highest building you'll see in town.

Of a striking selection of grand timber mansions, the 1758 gambrel-roofed, cream-and-white clapboard **John Paul Jones House** at 43 Middle St, on the corner of State St, is the most distinctive (May–Sept only, Mon–Sat 10am–4pm; $4). However, with so many old houses to see you can contentedly walk at random, and a visit to **Strawbery Banke** provides a better overview of local history. Antiquarian book dealers, such as the *Book Guild* at 58 State St, and curio shops like *Garakuta* in Bow Street, add to the pleasures of a stroll. In **Prescott Park** along the waterfront, the **Sheafe Warehouse Museum** has a fascinating free collection of mostly nautical ephemera.

Portsmouth's fortunes have long rested with its **Naval Shipyard**, visible across the bay (in Kittery, Maine; see p.203). Founded in 1800 by John Paul Jones as the US government's first shipyard, it has remained active ever since – it launched 31 submarines in 1944 alone, and built the first Polaris in 1962. During World War I, **Humphrey Bogart**, as a junior naval rating, received injuries while attempting to prevent the escape of a prisoner which left him with his trademark permanent sneer and a slight lisp.

Strawbery Banke

Hancock and Marcy streets. May–Oct daily 10am–5pm. $10 adults, $4 kids, $25 families.

The lack of any great pressure on space has made it possible to preserve ten acres of Portsmouth's original site as **STRAWBERY BANKE**. This area began life as home to wealthy shipbuilders, and was successively the lair of privateers and a red-light district before turning into respectable – and, in the Fifties, ultimately decaying – suburbia. It was then decided to re-create its former appearance, mainly by clearing away the newer buildings (only two of the houses on display had to be moved here). One or two people still live here, tucked away on the upper floors, but the whole complex serves as a living museum, which you can explore either on a guided tour or at your own whim; in either case, several of the houses have well-informed attendants.

Each building is shown in its most interesting former incarnation, whether that be 1695 or 1955; in the **Drisco House**, the first you come to, each individual *room* dates from a different era. The 1766 **Pitt Tavern** holds most historic significance, having acted as a meeting place during the Revolution for patriots and loyalists (it still functions as a masonic lodge, one of the four oldest in the US – which explains why you can't go upstairs). Tiny glasses remind you that its clientele drank gin rather than beer.

Although you may have to struggle to keep ahead of school groups, Strawbery Banke continues to undertake serious academic research. Traditional **crafts** are studied and practised; in the **Dinsmore Shop**, an infinitely patient cooper manufactures barrels with the tools and methods of 1800. The *Mills Zoldak* **pottery** shop, open year-round, produces attractive low-priced ceramics; you can visit without paying admission.

Practicalities

C&J Trailways **buses** halt at 5 Congress St, on Market Square, en route between Boston and Portland. You can pick up information from the **visitor center** at 500 Market St (Mon–Fri 9.30am–5pm; ☎436-1118), and the outside tables of the *Café Brioche* in Market Square make an obvious point from which to get your bearings.

Accommodation in the town center is restricted to B&Bs such as the peaceful, rambling seven-room *Inn at Strawbery Banke*, 314 Court St (☎436-7242; ④), and the more formal *Martin Hill Inn*, 404 Islington St (☎436-2287; ④). Of the **restaurants**, the *Stockpot*, overlooking the river at 53 Bow St (☎431-1851), specializes in paella and stir-fries, while the *Szechuan Taste* at 54 Daniels St (☎431-2226) serves good Thai and Chinese food. The lively *Washington Street Eatery* is part of Strawbery Banke, but you can sample their excellent sandwiches without entering the museum.

Hotels and motels along US-1 include the *Comfort Inn at Yoken's* (☎433-3338; ④), with pool. The adjacent *Yoken's* (☎436-8224) is a popular and inexpensive ribs restaurant, housed in New England's largest **gift shop**, a veritable goldmine of trivia.

Odiorne Point State Park

The one brief patch of semi-wilderness along the New Hampshire coast was, ironically, where the first white settlers landed in 1623. Some of the scattered ruins in marshy **Odiorne Point State Park** date from those early days; others, far more modern, were World War II defences. The two park entrances are on Hwy-1A near **Rye**, four miles southeast of Portsmouth, and a summer-only visitor center is open daily from 10am until 4pm. The offshore **Isles of Shoals**, a supposed haunt of Blackbeard the pirate, can be seen close-up on boat trips from Portsmouth Harbor (☎431-5500).

The Merrimack Valley

The financial and political heartland of New Hampshire is the **Merrimack Valley**, which first by water and now by road has always been the main thoroughfare north to the White Mountains and Québec. None is of any great interest to tourists, though all are pleasant enough, and equipped with relatively inexpensive motels.

The southernmost town on the river, **Nashua**, was named by *Money* magazine in 1987 as the "number one place to live in America". Plenty of its citizens still choose to work in Boston, though Massachusetts no longer allows employees to escape state taxes by living across the border in New Hampshire. **Manchester**, like its namesake in England, was a major nineteenth-century cotton producer. Although its massive Amoskeag Mills closed in the Thirties, it remains the largest city in the state, and is now notable mainly for the glassware, furniture and paintings in the **Currier Gallery of Art** at 192 Orange St (Tues–Sun 10am–5pm; free). The focal point of **Concord** is the gold dome of the State House, the seat of New Hampshire's state legislature; despite its small size it has 424 members, making it the fourth largest such body in the world (after the parliaments of the United States, Britain and India). Local schoolteacher Christa McAuliffe, a victim of the *Challenger* tragedy, is commemorated by a planetarium.

Fifteen miles north of Concord on Hwy-106, **Canterbury Shaker Village** (May–Oct Mon–Sat 10am–5pm; $8) was the sixth Shaker community (see pp.173, 391 and 396) Ann Lee founded in the 1780s, and grew to 300-strong by 1860. Ninety-minute tours show visitors Shaker crafts and techniques – such as box-making – and the attached *Creamery* restaurant serves Shaker food. South of Concord, outside Derry on Hwy-28, the **Robert Frost Farm** (summer daily 10am–6pm, weekends only rest of year; $2.50) has been evocatively restored to its condition when New England's poet laureate lived here from 1900 to 1911. Displays in the barn discuss his work, and a half-mile "poetry nature trail" leads past the sites that inspired many of his best-known poems.

The Lakes Region

Of the literally hundreds of lakes created by the snow-melt flowing south from the White Mountains, much the biggest is **Lake Winnipesaukee**, which forms the center of the vacation-oriented Lakes Region. Long segments of its 300-mile shoreline, especially in the east, consist of thick forests sweeping down to waters which are only disturbed by pleasure craft and dotted with little islands. The most sophisticated of the towns is **Wolfeboro**; the most fun to visit has to be **Weirs Beach**.

Ideally, you would bring your own small boat and get thoroughly lost in the maze of small channels and islets. Failing that, the **cruise ship** *Mount Washington* does daily three-hour tours in summer of the more open stretches, leaving Weirs Beach at 9am and 12.15pm, and Wolfeboro at 11am. The tours cost $12, and also call at either Center Harbor (Mon, Wed & Fri) or Alton Bay (Tues, Thurs, Sat & Sun). It's certainly a pretty ride, though it can seem a little long in the heat of the day and you might prefer to take an evening dinner cruise (July & Aug Tues–Sat). A smaller mail-boat does more local round-trips from Weirs Beach for $7.50. For all queries, ring ☎366-BOAT.

Wolfeboro

Because Governor Wentworth of New Hampshire built his summer home nearby in 1768, tiny **WOLFEBORO** claims to be "the oldest summer resort in America". Sandwiched between lakes Winnipesaukee and Wentworth, it has little to show for that history, but it's a relaxing place to spend a few hours, along the short but bustling main street, next to the quay where the *Mount Washington* comes in.

The 1812 *Wolfeboro Inn* (☎1-800/451-2389 or 569-3016; ⑤) stands in a dignified waterfront position at 44 N Main St, just a few yards from the town proper; also beside the lake, four miles north in Alton Bay, is the *Bay Side* motel (☎875-5005; ④). *Wolfeboro Campground* is on Haines Hill Rd (☎569-9881). Two branches of *Bailey's* (☎569-3662), one on the quayside and one on Main St, serve basic good-value **food**; *West Lake Asian Cuisine* (☎569-6700) in the Wolfeboro Center on Hwy-109 is an excellent, reasonably priced, **Chinese** restaurant.

The eastern shore of Lake Winnipesaukee is considerably less developed than the area around Weirs Beach, and makes for much better walking. One fascinating stop-off, a few miles north of Wolfeboro on Hwy-109, is the **Libby Museum** (summer only, Tues–Sun 10am–4pm), where the obsession of turn-of-the-century dentist Henry Forest Libby with evolution is illustrated by various ineptly stuffed animals (one can only hope that he was a better dentist than he was a taxidermist) and the skeletons of bears, orangutans, and humans. There's also a mastodon's tooth, a "Niddy Noddy" spinning device, and a fingernail supposedly pulled out by its Chinese owner to demonstrate his new Christian faith. The front steps command a superb view over the lake itself.

Weirs Beach and Laconia

The short boardwalk at **WEIRS BEACH**, the very essence of seaside tackiness even if it is fifty miles inland, is the social center in summer of the Lakes Region. Its little wooden jetty throngs with holiday-makers, the amusement arcades jingle with cash, and there's even a neat little crescent of sandy beach, suitable for family swimming. The better of its two competing **water parks** is *Surf Coaster* (summer daily 10am–8pm; $15 adults, $12 kids) on Hwy-11B just south of town, offering dramatic rides and a powerful wave machine.

Nearby **LACONIA** controls the purse-strings for Weirs Beach. **Belknap Mill** here claims to be "the oldest unaltered brick textile mill building in the United States". You might think the fact that it is now an arts center would count as some sort of alteration, but the mill machinery is still in working order in amongst the gallery space, which is the venue for evening concerts and lecture programmes.

On Father's Day weekend (the third in June), at least twenty thousand **bikers** cruise up for a gigantic motorcycle race and rally in **Loudon**. Even at quieter times, room rates are high; choices include the beachfront *Birch Knoll Motel* (April–Oct; ☎366-4958; ④), and the restaurant and B&B *Hickory Stick Farm* (☎524-3333; ④) on Bean Hill Rd, in the woods four miles south. The nearest **campground** is the *Gunstock* (☎293-4341), near Gilford six miles south (a ski resort in winter).

Meredith

MEREDITH, four miles north of Weirs Beach, is the last of Lake Winnipesaukee's resorts. In the new waterfront mall, the *Millworks Restaurant* (☎279-4116) is a nice place to eat, while the *Inn at Mill Falls* (☎279-7006; ⑤) is exceptionally comfortable.

The **Winnipesaukee Railroad** (☎279-3196) operates two-hour ($7) and one-hour ($3) scenic trips along the lakeshore between Meredith and Weirs Beach, on weekends from Memorial Day and then daily from mid-June to mid-October, including special fall foliage excursions (and even a Santa Claus special).

The only thing to admire at **Annalee's Doll Museum** (daily 9am–5pm in summer, slightly shorter hours in winter), just outside Meredith, is its effrontery in calling itself a museum. In fact it's a hard-sell toy shop, specializing in painted-felt dolls of quite stunning ugliness. Those items onto which they've managed to stitch the heads back to front are offered at a 25 percent reduction.

Northwards to the Mountains

Hwy-25 northeast from Meredith leads to Conway in the White Mountains; US-3 northwest, on the other hand, keeps you in the Lakes Region a little longer, and leads past **Squam Lake**, where the movie *On Golden Pond* was filmed. Educational tours of the **Science Center of New Hampshire** at **Holderness** (July & Aug daily 9.30am–4.30pm, May, June, Sept & Oct Mon–Fri 9.30am–4.30 pm, Sat & Sun 1–4pm; $1) lead through a largely natural landscape, in which animals such as deer, bobcat, bears and foxes are kept (mostly short-term) in enclosures.

Five miles on from Holderness at **Plymouth**, you can either rejoin I-93 as it heads into the mountains, or continue another five miles west to the **Polar Caves** (mid-May to Oct daily 9am–5pm; $8). Frankly, that would not be a good idea; whatever else the Polar Caves may be, they are not caves. They are no more than a cascade of clammy granite boulders tumbled against a hillside, between which visitors are for no discernible reason expected to find pleasure in squeezing themselves – while paying handsomely for the privilege. A large gift shop sells supremely irrelevant "souvenirs".

The White Mountains

Thanks to their accessibility from both Montréal to the north and Boston to the south, the **White Mountains** have become a year-round tourist destination, popular with summer hikers and winter skiers alike. Commercialized they may be, in built-up strips along the main highways, but the great granite massifs retain much of their majesty and power. **Mount Washington** can claim the severest weather in the world, and conditions are harsh enough for the timberline to be at four thousand feet, as compared to the norm in the Rockies of ten thousand.

Just a few high passes – here called "**notches**", only discovered with infinite pains by the early pioneers – pierce the range, and the roads through these gaps, such as the **Kancamagus Highway** between Lincoln and Conway, make for an enjoyable driving tour. However, you won't really have made the most of the White Mountains unless you also set off, on foot or on skis, across the long expanses of thick evergreen forest which separate them, with snowcapped peaks poking out in all directions.

HIKING, CYCLING AND SKIING IN THE WHITE MOUNTAINS

Hiking in the mountains is coordinated by the **Appalachian Mountain Club** (AMC), whose chain of information centers, hostels and huts along the Appalachian Trail, traversing the region from northeast to southwest, is detailed on p.194; ring ☎466-2727 for further information, and pick up a copy of the *AMC White Mountain Guide* ($16) before you attempt any serious expedition.

Downhill and cross-country **skiers** can choose from several resorts, such as *Loon Mountain* (☎1-800/227-4191 or ☎745-8111), *Ski Bretton Woods* (☎1-800/258-0330 or ☎278-5000) and *Mt Washington Valley Ski Touring* (☎356-9920 or ☎1-800/282-5220). General information on the skiing centers along I-93 is available from *Ski 93* (PO Box 517, Lincoln, NH 03251; ☎745-8101); those further east are covered by the very helpful Mount Washington Valley Chamber of Commerce (PO Box 2300, North Conway, NH 03860; ☎356-3171). Once you're in the area, North Conway is the best place for equipment rentals and other supplies.

Bikes can be rented from the *Loon Mountain Bike Center* on the Kancamagus Highway in Lincoln (☎745-8111) or *Joe Jones* on Main St in North Conway (☎356-9411).

Franconia Notch and the Old Man of the Mountains

I-93, speeding up towards Canada, and the more leisurely US-3 merge briefly about ten miles beyond **Lincoln**, to pass through **Franconia Notch State Park**. From a roadside pullout, you can look back and upwards to the **Old Man of the Mountains**. This natural rock formation, resembling an old man's profile, will no doubt already be familiar from powerfully magnified photographs – and New Hampshire's licence plates. Seen from a thousand feet below, it's absolutely tiny. It all has to be held together with wires, and one particular family has the annual responsibility of climbing up to plug the cracks made by the winter's ice.

Franconia Notch itself is a slender valley crammed between two great walls of stone. From the park **visitor center** (May–Oct daily 9am–4.30pm), you can for $6 walk along a two-mile boardwalk-cum-nature-trail to the **Flume**, to look down on the Pemigawasset River as it rages through a narrow rock-filled gorge, or take an $8 **cable-car** ride up the sheer granite face of **Cannon Mountain** (all year; ☎823-5563).

One mile south of **FRANCONIA** further on, the **Frost Place** on Ridge Rd (July & Aug daily except Tues 1–5pm; May, June, Sept & Oct Sat & Sun 1–5pm; $3) is a former home of poet Robert Frost, memorable largely for an inspiring panorama of mountains which can look almost undisturbed by human interference. If you're interested in his poetry, his farm outside Concord (see p.189) makes a better destination.

Bretton Woods

The ease with which US-302 now crosses the middle of the mountains belies the effort that went into cutting a road through **Crawford Notch**, halfway between Franconia and Conway. Just north, the magnificent **Mount Washington Hotel** (☎278-1000 or 1-800/258-0330; ⑦) stands in splendid isolation in the wide mountain valley of **BRETTON WOODS**. Its glistening white facade, capped by red cupolas and framed by the western slopes of Mount Washington rising behind, has barely changed since it opened in 1902. In its heyday, a stream of horse-drawn carriages brought families (and their servants) up from the train station, deliberately located at a distance in order to increase the sense of grandeur. Displays in the grand lobby commemorate the Bretton Woods Conference of 1944, which laid the groundwork for the post-war financial structure of the capitalist world, setting the gold standard at $35 an ounce – it's now $350 – and creating the International Monetary Fund and the World Bank.

Recent restoration has ensured that the hotel remains marvellously evocative, with its quarter-mile terrace and white wicker furniture. It's not the one featured in the movie *The Shining* (see p.872), but it has something of the same feel; even if you're not staying, you're welcome to pad down its endless corridors, or stop in for a drink. There are weekend golfing and tennis packages, and skiing in winter.

Mount Washington

The 6288ft **Mount Washington** was named for George Washington before he became President, but over the years other mountains in this "Presidential Range" have taken the names of Madison, Jefferson, and even Eisenhower. (Mount Nancy was called that long before the Reagans; and Mount Deception just happens to be close by.)

You can see all the way to the Atlantic – and right into Canada – from the top of Mount Washington on a clear day, but the real interest in making the ascent lies in the extraordinary severity of the weather up there. The wind exceeds hurricane strength on over one hundred days of each year, and in 1934 it reached the highest speed ever recorded anywhere in the world – 231mph. On the very summit, you'll see the remarkable spectacle of buildings actually held down with great chains; many have over the years been blown away, including the old observatory, said to be the strongest wooden building ever constructed. There's now a viewing platform, with a weatherproof museum and café just below. A roll call of the 103 victims to die on the mountain includes two who attempted to slide down the Cog Railway on "improvised boards".

On the way to the top, you pass through four separate climatic zones, with century-old fir and ash trees so stunted as to be below waist-height, before coming out finally amid Arctic tundra. The drive up the **Mount Washington Auto Road** (mid-May to Oct only, 7.30am–6pm in peak season) is not quite as hair-raising as you may be led to expect, though the hairpin bends and lack of guard-rails certainly keep you alert. There is, however, a $12 **toll** for private cars (plus $5 for each additional adult and $3 for kids). Specially adapted minibuses, still known as "stages" in honor of the twelve-person horse-drawn carriages which first used the road, give **narrated tours** ($16 adults, $10 kids). Driving takes thirty or forty minutes under sane conditions, though rally-drivers have done it in under ten. The record for the annual **running** race each June – heading *up* the mountain, naturally – now stands at an incredible 59min 12sec.

Last but far from least, you can also ride to the top on the coal-fired steam train of the **Mount Washington Cog Railway**, which climbs the exposed western flank of the mountain, ascending gradients of up to 38 percent on a track which was completed in 1869. It's truly a unique experience, inching up the steep wooden trestles while avoiding descending showers of coal smut. The three-hour round trip costs $35 for adults, $18 for kids over eight, and trains leave hourly (May–Nov 8am–4pm; ☎846-5404 or 1-800/922-8825) from a station six miles northeast of Bretton Woods.

North Conway

A few miles south of Mount Washington, heading past **Glen**, US-302 and Hwy-16 as they approach **NORTH CONWAY** become a veritable turmoil of shopping malls, fast-food places and theme parks such as Heritage USA and Storyland. The strip between North Conway and **Conway** proper offers all sorts of "factory outlets" (including a branch of Maine's *L L Bean's* – see p.206) for discount shopping. The towns are not terribly interesting, but there are plenty of secluded lodging options in the foothills to either side, and bars and restaurants in the malls (detailed below).

Kancamagus Highway

The **Kancamagus Highway** (Hwy-112) connecting Conway and Lincoln is the least busy road through the mountains, and makes for a very pleasant drive. Several campgrounds are situated in the woods to either side, and various walking trails are sign-posted. The half-mile hike to **Sabbaday Falls**, off to the south roughly halfway along, leads up a narrow rocky cleft in the forest to a succession of idyllic waterfalls.

White Mountains Accommodation and Eating

So many youthful hikers and skiers come to the White Mountains that for once there is a great deal of **low-budget accommodation**. However, there's quite a chasm between the hostels, costing under $20, and the inns and B&Bs which tend to start at over $60. **Campers** can pitch their tents anywhere in the White Mountains National Forest below the treeline and away from the roads, so long as they show consideration for the environment; there are also more than twenty official campgrounds (information ☎528-8727, reservations ☎1-800/283-2267). Low-priced **eating places** line the main highways.

Hostels and Mountain Huts

Apart from the hostels at Crawford Notch and Pinkham Notch, accessible to motorists, the ten Appalachian Mountain Club huts along the Appalachian Trail can be reached only on foot. In summer, they provide meals and bedding for up to one hundred people per night. Prices in all of them range from $13 to $40, according to the amount of privacy (and food) you desire. It's extremely advisable to book ahead, on ☎466-2727.

Berkshire Manor, 133 Main St, Gorham (☎466-9418). Hostel-style accommodation – shared kitchens and so on – but private rooms. ②.

Bowman's Base Camp AYH Hostel, Randolph (☎466-5130). Very basic summer-only hostel, roughly ten miles by road north of Pinkham Notch. $12 AYH members, $13 others. ①.

Crawford Notch Depot, US-302, Carroll (☎846-7773). AMC hostel; two dorms and three cabins in the heart of the mountains. See above for rates. Daily information in summer 8.30am–4.30pm. ①.

Pinkham Notch Camp, Hwy-16 (☎466-2727). AMC hostel – see above for rates – near the base of the Mount Washington Auto Road. Daily information in summer 7am–10pm. ①.

Motels, Hotels and B&Bs

The Bungay Jar, Hwy-116, Franconia (☎823-7775). B&B in superb natural setting. ④.

Eagle Mountain House, 2 Carter Notch Rd, Jackson (☎1-800/777-1700 or 383-9111). Highly atmospheric inn, recently re-built, far above the bustle of North Conway. ⑤.

The Forest – A Country Inn, Hwy-16A, Intervale (☎356-9772). Very welcoming B&B between North Conway and Jackson. ④.

New England Inn, Hwy-16A, Intervale (☎356-5541 or 1-800/826-3466). Very comfortable traditional white clapboard inn, near North Conway, with raging fireplace in winter. ④.

Raynor's Motor Lodge, south of Franconia on Hwy-18 (☎1-800/634-8187 or 823-9586). Old-style budget hotel rooms, plus a dearer fully modernized motel next door. Bicycles for rent. ③.

Saco River Motor Lodge, US-302, Center Conway (☎447-3720). Standard motel rooms. ③.

Stonybrook Motor Lodge, one mile south of Franconia on Hwy-18 (☎1-800/722-3552 or 823-8192). Another motel near the interstate. ③.

Sunny Side Inn, Seavey St, North Conway (☎356-6239). Pleasant B&B. ③.

Restaurants and Bars

The Cinnamon Tree, Pleasant St Plaza, Conway (☎447-5019). Appetizing breakfasts and snacks.

Houlighans, Kearsarge St, North Conway. Lively bar and restaurant, just off the main strip.

Red Parka Pub, US-302, Glen (☎383-4344). Evening-only barbecue restaurant with bar until 1am, live rock music at weekends.

Truants Taverne, Main St, North Woodstock (☎745-2239). Homely, very reasonable, restaurant.

West to Vermont

Much of the western side of New Hampshire, as you approach the Connecticut River which forms the entire border with Vermont, amounts to a less developed – and therefore less touristed – version of the Lakes Region. For a tranquil day or two the area around **Lake Sunapee** can be very appealing. All the local inns – such as the

Mountain Lake Inn (☎938-2136; ⑤) on Hwy-14, just south of Bradford on tiny Lake Massasecum – share a toll-free booking number (☎1-800/662-6005).

Hanover

HANOVER, near Lebanon just across from Vermont, is home to the venerable and elegant **Dartmouth College**, founded in this remote spot in the eighteenth century "for the instruction of the Youth of Indian tribes . . . and others". The main attraction here is the small **Hood Museum of Art** on the college green (Sun & Tues–Fri 11am–5pm, Sat 11am–8pm; free), which contains works by Picasso and Monet alongside genuine Assyrian bas-reliefs. In the adjacent cultural complex, the Dartmouth Film Society screens international art and classic movies ($5) year-round.

Hanover is enjoyable to wander around, with lively places to eat and drink such as *Molly's Balloon*, 43 S Main St (☎643-2570), and the panelled cellar of *Peter Christian's Tavern* at 39 S Main St (☎643-2345). Its best accommodation is in the *Hanover Inn* (☎643-4300; ⑤), overlooking Dartmouth Green from the corner of Main and Wheelock.

One unforgettable place to stay nearby is *Moose Mountain Lodge* (☎643-3529; ⑥), a steep climb up in the hills above **Etna**, looking over Vermont. All year it feels marvellously remote from the world below, but it really comes into its own for **cross-country skiing** in winter. The friendly owners expect their guests to share their enthusiasm for the country life, and charge $60 per day per person, with a good evening meal.

VERMONT

VERMONT comes closer than any New England state to fulfilling the quintessential image of small-town America, with its white churches and red barns, covered bridges and clapboard houses, snowy woods and maple syrup. No city manages a population of fifty thousand – only **Burlington** has over twenty thousand – and the chief tourist attraction is *Ben and Jerry's* ice cream factory. Though rural, the landscape is not all that agricultural, and much is still covered by mountainous forests (the state's name supposedly comes from the French *verd mont*, or green mountain). The people who choose to live here hold a lot in common; hippies and die-hard conservatives, working together to preserve their environment and lamenting the advent of yet more ski resorts.

This was the last area of New England to be settled, early in the eighteenth century. As French explorers worked their way down from Canada, American colonists began to spread north; but even as that rivalry died down, a further antipathy developed between settlers from New Hampshire and those from New York. The wealthy New York merchants who built fine homes along the Connecticut River valley thought of themselves as the "River Gods", but the hardy settlers of the lakes and mountains to the west had little time for their patrician ways. Their leader was the now-legendary **Ethan Allen**, who formed his **Green Mountain Boys** in 1770, proclaiming that "the gods of the hills are not the gods of the valley". When the Revolutionary War superseded such conflicts, this all-but-autonomous force captured Fort Ticonderoga from the British and helped to win the decisive Battle of Bennington. For fourteen years from 1777, Vermont was an independent republic, with the first constitution in the world explicitly to forbid slavery and grant universal (male) suffrage, but once its boundaries with New York were finally agreed, it joined the Union in 1791. Curiously, the two seminal figures of the **Mormon** religion were both born in Vermont shortly thereafter – Joseph Smith in 1805, and his lieutenant and successor Brigham Young in 1801.

With the occasional exception, such as the extraordinary assortment of Americana at the **Shelburne Museum** near Burlington, there are few specific goals for tourists.

The **area code** for the entire state of Vermont is ☎802.

Visitors come in great numbers during two well-defined seasons: to see the **fall foliage** in the first two weeks of October, and to **ski** in the depths of winter, when the resorts of **Killington**, and **Stowe** further north (home of the *Sound of Music*'s Von Trapp family), spring into life. For the rest of the year, you might just as well explore any of the state's minor roads which take your fancy, confident that some picturesque village will be around the next corner. There are far too many to list; we've had to leave out such prime examples as **Peru**, **Grafton** and **Middlebury**. Further information can be picked up from the official Welcome Center on each interstate as it enters Vermont.

Getting Around Vermont

Vermont Transit Lines (☎864-6811 or 1-800/451-3292) **buses** connect Montréal with Boston and New York, passing through Burlington, Montpelier, Rutland, White River Junction and Brattleboro. Other services link Stowe with Burlington, cross the north from Newport to Portland, Maine, and traverse the Green Mountains. *Amtrak* **trains** between Washington DC and Montréal stop at Brattleboro, White River Junction, Montpelier and Burlington – at inconvenient hours. The main **airport** is in Burlington.

Lake Champlain Ferries (☎864-9804) carries cars to New York at three points, including Burlington, and a six-minute ferry links Larrabee's Point with Ticonderoga further south. *Vermont Mountain Bike Tours* (PO Box 541, Pittsfield, VT 05762; ☎746-8580) and *Vermont Bicycle Touring* (PO Box 711, Bristol, VT 05433; ☎453-4811) organize **cycling tours**.

Southern Vermont

Of the two low-key towns at either end of Vermont's southern corridor – a mere forty miles from east to west and linked by Hwy-9 – **Brattleboro** has the atmosphere of a college town, but not the college, while **Bennington** has the college but not the atmosphere. The birthplace of Mormon prophet Brigham Young is marked by a monument at **Whitingham**, halfway between the two.

Brattleboro

If **BRATTLEBORO**, in the southeast corner of the state, is your first taste of Vermont, it may come as a surprise. Not the Fifties throwback you might expect, its style owes more to the Sixties, with numerous little stores catering to the youthful and vaguely "alternative" population which has moved into the surrounding hills over the last two decades. The town's one unlikely claim to fame is that this was where **Rudyard Kipling** wrote his two *Jungle Books*.

Trains follow the river into town and stop behind the Old Railroad Station, which as the **Brattleboro Museum** (May–Oct Tues–Sun noon–6pm; $2) now displays locally made Estey organs and works of art. Buses, on the other hand, merely pick up and set down next to exit 3 off the interstate, a couple of miles north. Much the best place to **stay** is in one of the lovely river-view rooms at the Art Deco *Latchis Hotel* at 50 Main St (☎254-6300; ③). Guests receive a free pass to the **movie theater** next door; there's also a good café and the on-site *Windham Brewery* (☎254-4747). The nearby *Common Ground Community Restaurant* at 25 Elliot St (☎257-0855) is a long-established **whole-food restaurant**, serving vegetarian specialties in a very pleasant glassed-in conservatory; across the street *Himmelman's Bakery* has very good pastries and espresso.

Bennington

Little has happened in **BENNINGTON** in the past two hundred years to match the excitement of the days when Ethan Allen's Green Mountain Boys were based here, known as the "Bennington Mob". A 306ft hilltop obelisk (April–Oct daily 9am–5pm; $1) commemorates the **Battle of Bennington** in August 1777, in which they were a crucial factor in defeating the British under General Burgoyne (though the battle itself was probably fought just across the border in New York).

About a mile north of the sleepy intersection at the town center, three **covered bridges** cross the Walloomsac River. Walkers set out from the southern end of the Long Trail (see below) roughly five miles east. Students from the exclusive arts-oriented Bennington College crowd into the *Blue Benn* **diner** at 102 Hunt St (☎442-8977). The *Fife'n'Drum* **motel** (☎442-4074; ③) is one of many south of town on US-7.

The Green Mountains

The **Green Mountains** which form the backbone of Vermont are not as harsh as New Hampshire's White Mountains, though the forests for which they are named are invariably buried in snow for most of the winter, and the higher roads are liable to be blocked for long periods. Here and there, denuded patches mark where trees have been shaved away to create ski-runs, but for the most part the usually peaceful **Hwy-100** running up from the south offers unspoiled mountain views to either side.

In summer, hikers take up the challenge of the **Long Trail** along the central ridge, 264 miles from north to south. This predates the Appalachian Trail, which now joins its southern portion, and was constructed by the **Green Mountain Club** (PO Box 650, Rte 100, Waterbury Center, VT 05677; ☎244-7037). Their *Guidebook to the Long Trail* ($9.95) is invaluable.

Hwy-100 Scenic Drive: Weston

One of the prettiest villages along Hwy-100 is **WESTON**, spreading beside a little river and centering on a perfect green, where a somber stone slab commemorates the seventeen local soldiers who were killed on the same day during the Civil War, at Alexandria in Virginia. Nearby, the **Farrar-Mansur House** (July & Aug Wed–Sun 1.30–4.30pm; May, June, Sept & Oct Wed–Fri 1.30–4.30pm; $2) is an early tavern which has been restored to show the lives of early settlers, while the **Weston Playhouse** is a typical little Vermont theater, putting on light summer performances (Tues–Sun; ☎824-5288).

Stores selling antiques, toys and fudge are scattered up and down the main street. The spell is slightly broken when you realize just how vast the **Vermont Country Store** south of the green really is, artfully concealed behind its modest facade. The original *Weston Village Store* opposite is more authentic, if not as comprehensive in its range of vaguely rural and domestic articles. Finished and unfinished wooden items at the **Weston Bowl Mill** on the north side of town include beautifully turned bowls.

Weston's nicest **accommodation** has to be the lovely four-room *1830 Inn on the Green* (☎824-6789; ④); among alternatives are the *Colonial House* motel (☎824-6286; ④), less than two miles south on Hwy-100, and the *Hillside* B&B (☎875-3844; ④) in Andover three miles northeast. A magnificent soda fountain dominates the 1887 mahogany bar of the lunch-only *Bryant House* **restaurant** (closed Sun; ☎824-6287), two doors down from the *Vermont Country Store* and run by the same management; the menu includes such country goodies as "johnny cakes" of cornbread with molasses.

Killington

The ski resort of **KILLINGTON**, in the center of the Green Mountains halfway between Woodstock to the east and Rutland to the west, has grown out of nothing since 1957. Despite a permanent population of perhaps fifty, it's estimated that in season there are enough beds within twenty miles to accommodate over ten thousand people each night. The two main slopes are **Killington Peak** itself (for skiing information, ring ☎422-3333) and **Pico Peak** (☎775-4345).

In winter, the Killington Access Road up from US-4 is jammed with bars and restaurants; most close in summer, though you can still take the **cable-car** (☎422-3333) up to the observation deck and cafeteria on the bleak summit. Hiking routes which meet here include the Long and Appalachian Trails. The *Cortina Inn* (☎1-800/451-6108 or 773-3331; ④) is one of several luxury **motels** on US-4 to offer reduced summer rates.

Woodstock

Since the 1790s, **WOODSTOCK**, a few miles west from the Connecticut River up US-4, has been one of Vermont's more refined centers. Hence the distinguished houses around its oval green, now largely taken over by antiques stores and tearooms. It should most certainly not be confused with Woodstock, NY, of festival fame; the closest it came to radical action in the Sixties was to build a new covered bridge.

Both of Woodstock's two main paying attractions are geared towards seeing animals close up. Part of **Billings Farm and Museum** (May–Oct daily 10am–5pm; $6) is maintained as it was on the death of its former owner in 1890, while the rest is run as a modern dairy farm; the **Vermont Raptor Center** on Church Hill Rd (summer daily 10am–4pm; winter Mon–Sat 10am–4pm; $5) treats injured birds of prey.

An information booth on the Green in summer (☎457-3555) can help with **accommodation**, such as the *Village Inn of Woodstock*, 41 Pleasant St (☎457-1255; ④), or the homely *Applebutter Inn* (☎457-4158; ④), just east on US-4 in Taftsville. You don't have to be a guest at the riverside *Lincoln Inn* (☎457-3312; ⑤), three miles west, to eat in its very reasonable dining room (Wed–Sun only); in Woodstock itself, the *Rumble Seat Rathskeller* (☎457-3609) is a bar and restaurant with an outside patio.

Quechee

In recent years, the grand houses on the hills around **QUECHEE**, eight miles west of Woodstock, have been joined by a proliferation of new condos and second homes. It's all reasonably well landscaped, but a shame nonetheless, and adds nothing to the environs of **Quechee State Park**, which was fortunately created in time to spare the splendors of the **Quechee Gorge**. A delicate bridge spans the 165ft chasm of the Ottauquechee River, and hiking trails lead down through the fir trees, where you'll find one of Vermont's many state-run **campgrounds** (☎295-2990).

A waterfall on the river turns the turbines of **Simon Pearce Glass** (daily 9am–9pm; ☎295-1470), on Main Street in Quechee itself. Housed in a former woollen mill, this is an unusual combination of glass-blowing center and restaurant, where you can watch bowls and pots being made and then eat off them. Adventurous meals start at $12.

White River Junction

Probably the most exciting thing ever to happen in **WHITE RIVER JUNCTION** was the first use of laughing gas as an anaesthetic, in 1844. But it's an invaluable transport hub; weary *Amtrak* passengers stumble off trains at unearthly hours, straight onto N Main Street, and buses run east into New Hampshire – **Hanover** (see p.195) is just across the river – and west through Vermont.

A good old-fashioned railroad hotel still survives in the town center, with good old-fashioned prices – the *Hotel Coolidge* at 17 S Main St (☎295-3118; ②), where the *Cashie's* restaurant is a bargain too. Call in at the *Catamount Brewery* down the road at 28 S Main St (☎296-2248) to try their fresh-brewed ale.

Montpelier and Barre

Another fifty miles north up I-89, **MONTPELIER** is the smallest state capital in the nation, with less than ten thousand inhabitants. The golden dome of the **capitol** is appealing in its leafy gardens, but there's nothing very much to see. Copious information on accommodation possibilities, here and throughout the state, is available from the Vermont Travel Division at 134 State St (Mon–Fri 7.45am–4.30pm, Sat 9am–3pm, Sun 11am–3pm; ☎828-3236 or 1-800/VER-MONT); budget rooms can be had at the *Vermonter Hotel* (☎479-9014; ②), southeast on US-302.

Students from the local New England Culinary Institute run both the *Elm Street Café* at 38 Elm St (☎223-3188) and the more upmarket *Tubbs Restaurant*, 24 Elm St (☎229-9202), serving excellent and inexpensive – if experimental – dishes from all over the world. The *Horn of the Moon Café*, 8 Langdon St (☎223-2895), is a wholefood bakery, while *Julio's*, 44 Main St (☎229-9348) serves delicious Mexican specialties.

The immigrant stoneworkers of the adjacent town of **BARRE** (pronounced *BA-rie*) were at the turn of this century famed for their militancy. Their most enduring memorials are the gravestones they carved themselves, in **Mount Hope Cemetery** on Hwy-14, though the Scots among them did also erect downtown a rather incongruous statue of Robert Burns. Southeast of town, you can watch workers cut huge blocks out of the earth at the world's biggest granite quarry, the **Rock of Ages** (summer daily 8.30am–5pm; free). *Arnholm's* at 891 N Main St (☎476-5921; ②) is a summer-only motel.

Waterbury

Guidebooks never paid much attention to **WATERBURY** before 1978; even then, the opening of a homemade ice cream stand on the forecourt of a gas station excited little interest. However, **Ben & Jerry's Ice Cream Factory**, one mile north of I-89 in Waterbury Center, on the way up to Stowe, has grown so huge, so fast, that it is now the number-one tourist destination in Vermont. Half-hour tours (Mon–Sat 9am–4pm; $1, kids free) feature an audio-visual presentation, a chance to look down on the workforce from an observation platform, and a free scoop of the deliciously rich ice cream that made it all possible. You're then let loose in a massive gift shop.

Waterbury is the closest *Amtrak* stop to Stowe – the station is just south of the interstate – and *Vermont Transit* buses also pass through.

Stowe

There is still a beautiful nineteenth-century village at the heart of **STOWE**, with a white-spired meeting house and a green to stroll around, though a century's experience of catering to large crowds of skiers means that it has become rather swamped by malls full of fast-food outlets and equipment stores, and sprawling complexes of condos and resort facilities. Nonetheless, the setting remains spectacular, at the foot of Vermont's highest mountain, the 4393ft **Mount Mansfield**.

Hwy-108 – **Mountain Road** – leads close to the mountain through the dramatic **Smugglers' Notch**, which is closed by snow through the winter. Weather permitting, you can get to the very top either by driving up the **Toll Road** which starts seven miles up (May to mid-Oct daily 9.30am–5pm; $8 per car), or by taking the **Gondola** (June–Oct 9am–5pm; $10; ☎253-7311) up to Cliff House, and hiking for another half-hour from there. Vermont's **State Ski Dorm** is on Mountain Rd just past the foot of the Toll Road (☎253-4010; ①). In summer, when it doubles up as an AYH **youth hostel**, dorm beds are just $12; in winter the $40 charge includes dinner and breakfast.

What really made Stowe's name as a **cross-country ski** resort was its connection with the **von Trapp family**, of *Sound of Music* fame. After fleeing Austria during the war, they established the *Trapp Family Lodge* on Luce Hill Rd (☎253-8511; ⑧). The original lodge, where Maria von Trapp held her singing camps, has burned down, and she herself died in 1987, but a new and equally luxurious building has taken its place; its *Austrian Tea Room* serves incredibly heavy Germanic cakes and pastries.

Plentiful **accommodation**, mostly on Mountain Road, includes the *Stoweflake Inn* (☎1-800/782-9009 or 253-7355; ④); the *Golden Kitz* (☎253-4217; ②), where rates double in winter; the small *Charbonneau Guest House* (☎253-7701; ②); and the central 1833 *Green Mountain Inn* (☎1-800/445-6629 or 253-7301; ⑤). The *Gold Brook* **campground** is two miles south on Hwy-100 (☎253-7683). The sunken lounge of *Hapeltons* (☎253-4653) on Hwy-100 is a nice place for a snack and a drink, and very snug in winter.

For **skiing information**, contact Mount Mansfield (☎253-7311) or Smuggler's Notch (☎1-800/451-8752 or 664-8851). **Bikes** can be rented from the *Mountain Bike Shop* on Mountain Rd (☎253-7919); an excellent biking trail climbs the mountain.

Lake Champlain

The 150-mile long **LAKE CHAMPLAIN**, which forms the boundary between the states of New York and Vermont, and just nudges its way into Canada in the north, never exceeds twelve miles in width. Across the water from the flatlands of the Champlain Valley, the impassive Adirondacks are always visible, looming up in the west. The first non-native to see the lake, Samuel de Champlain in 1609, who named it in his own honor, was also the first to claim that it held a sinuous Loch-Ness-style monster. "Champ" is now familiar as an informal symbol of the region.

The life and soul of the valley is the French-influenced city of **Burlington**, whose long-standing trade connections with Montréal have filled it with elegant nineteenth-century architecture. Within just a few miles of the center, US-2 leads north onto the supremely rural **Champlain Isles**, covered in meadows and orchards.

Lake Champlain Ferries (☎864-9804) cross the lake from Vermont to New York from **Burlington** (to Port Kent; hourly; $12); **Charlotte** (to Essex; hourly; $7); and **Grand Isle** (to Plattsburgh; year-round, every 20min; $7). All these rates are for a car and a driver; additional passengers, cyclists and walk-ons pay $2–3.

Burlington

Lakeside **BURLINGTON**, Vermont's largest "city", is one of the most purely enjoyable towns in New England, a relaxed and open-minded fusion of Montréal, eighty miles away to the north, and Boston, over two hundred miles southeast. In fact, from its earliest days Burlington looked as much to Canada as to the south. Shipping connections with the St Lawrence River were far easier than the land routes across the mountains, and the harbor became a major supply center. The city's founders included Ethan Allen and family – far from being some impoverished Robin Hood figure, Ethan was a wealthy landowner, and his brother Ira set up the University of Vermont.

Burlington today is the definitive youthful, outward-looking university town. From the bandstands to the brew pubs, this is simply a nice place to be. It's one of the few American cities to offer something approaching a café society, with a downtown, especially around the Church Street Marketplace, you can stroll around on foot, and plenty of open-air terraces. Politically too it's unusual; Bernard Saunders, the former socialist mayor of Burlington, was in 1990 elected to the House of Representatives from Vermont – the first political independent to go to Congress in forty years.

Arrival and Information

Vermont Transit **buses** stop in downtown Burlington at the corner of St Paul and Main, beside City Hall Park, but the *Amtrak* station is an inconvenient five miles north, in the small community of Essex Junction (connecting buses every half-hour; $1). The airport is two miles out along US-2, in the same general direction. Practical **information** is available from the **visitor center** at 209 Battery St (July–Sept Mon–Fri 8.30am–5pm, Sat & Sun 10am–2pm; Oct–June Mon–Fri 8.30am–5pm; ☎863-3489).

Lake Champlain Ferries (see above) leave from the jetty at the end of King Street; sightseeing cruises on the *Spirit of Ethan Allen* (☎862-9685; $8) set out from nearby Perkins Pier at the end of Maple Street. *Ski Rack*, 85 Main St (☎658-3313), rents **bikes**.

The City

Your natural inclination on setting out to explore Burlington might be to head for the **waterfront**. In fact, that's surprisingly undeveloped, though Battery Park at its northern end makes a good place to watch the sun go down over the Adirondacks – especially when there's a band playing, as there often is at weekends.

A better target is the pedestrianized **Church Street Marketplace**, a few blocks back, which holds Burlington's finest old buildings and all its modern cafés and boutiques. The free **Robert Hull Fleming Museum** on Colchester Ave (Tues–Fri 9am–4pm, Sun 1–5pm) has an interesting collection of art and artefacts from all over the world, including pre-Columbian pieces, while back at Essex Junction, the stimulating **Discovery Museum** near the river at 51 Park St (July & Aug Tues–Sat 10am–4.30pm, Sun 1–4.30pm; otherwise Tues–Fri & Sun 1–4.30pm, Sat 10am–4.30pm; $2.50) aims to excite children's interests in science and nature.

The Shelburne Museum

Hwy-7 in Shelburne, three miles south of Burlington. Mid-May to mid-Oct daily 9am–5pm. ☎985-3344. Adults $15, kids $5. Tickets are valid for two successive days.

It takes a whole day, if not more, fully to appreciate the remarkable fifty-acre collection of unalloyed **Americana** gathered at the **Shelburne Museum**. Created in 1947 by heiress Electra Webb, it centers on her parents' French Impressionist paintings, including works by Degas and Monet, displayed in a meticulous reconstruction of their New York apartment. However, Electra's own interests ranged far wider, and she put together what is probably the nation's finest celebration of its inventive past.

More than thirty buildings, some original and some newly constructed, focus on aspects of everyday life over the past two centuries; most are staffed by well-informed attendants. The village includes a General Store, complete with painted **"cigar store Indians"**, an apothecary, an early print shop, a doctor's, a dentist's and a blacksmith's. There's a **Shaker barn**, a schoolhouse, a meeting house, a covered bridge, a railroad station, and even an enormous **steam paddle-wheeler** from Lake Champlain, the *SS Ticonderoga*, with its own rock-surrounded lighthouse.

Accommodation

Burlington has no shortage of moderate accommodation, and for **camping** the lakeside *Northbeach Campsites* (☎862-0942) is less than two miles north on Institute Road.

Econo-Lodge, 1076 Williston Rd (☎863-1125). On US-2 just east of I-89, with clean basic rooms. ③.

Ho-Hum Motel, 1660 Williston Rd, 3 miles east of downtown on US-2 (☎863-4551), and 1200 Shelburne Rd, 3 miles south on US-7 (☎658-1314). Simple, reasonably priced motels. Both ③.

Mrs Farrell's Home Hostel (AYH), 27 Arlington Court (☎865-3730). A few dorm beds. $10 members, $12 others. 3 miles out from the center. ①.

Queen City Inn & Motel, 428 Shelburne Rd, South Burlington (☎864-4220). Basic motel rooms, or slightly pricier alternatives in the inn itself. ③.

YWCA, 278 Main St (☎862-7520). Women-only budget accommodation. Dorms $8, doubles $18. ①.

Eating, Drinking and Entertainment

The presence of ten thousand students during term-time ensures Burlington offers any number of inexpensive and good restaurants, as well as some pretty raucous nightspots.

Bourbon Street Grill, 213 College St (☎865-2800). Crowded and dimly lit. Cajun specials from $8.

Daily Planet, Center St behind Church Street Marketplace (☎862-9647). Innovative menu combining Asian and Mediterranenan cooking with old-fashioned American comfort food.

Five Spice Café, 175 Church St (☎864-4045). Excellent Asian food. Dim sum and vegetarian.

Oasis Diner, 189 Bank St (☎864-5308). Friendly, authentic chrome and leatherette steel-tube diner.

Vermont Pub and Brewery, 144 College St (☎865-0500). Roomy and convivial brew pub. Free little tasters of their various beers – *Dogbite Bitter* is the best – plus a good menu and live music.

MAINE

As big as the other five New England states combined, **MAINE** has barely the population of Rhode Island. In principle, therefore, there's plenty of room for its massive summer influx of visitors; in practice, the majority of these make for the southern stretches of the extravagantly corrugated **coast**. You only really begin to appreciate the size and space of the state further north, or **inland**, where vast tracts of mountainous forests are dotted with lakes, and barely pierced by roads – ideal territory for hiking and canoeing (and spotting the occasional moose).

Although Maine is in many ways inhospitable – the **Algonquin** called it "Land of the Frozen Ground" – it has been in contact with Europe ever since the **Vikings**, around 1000 AD. For the navigator Verrazzano, in 1524, the "crudity and evil manners" of the Indians made this the "Land of Bad People", but before long European fishermen were setting up camps each summer to dry their catch. Francis Bacon in turn said the English were "worse than the very Savages, impudently lying with their Women, teaching their men to drink drunke, and . . . to fall together by the eares".

North America's first agricultural **colonies** were in Maine: de Champlain's **French** Protestants near Mount Desert Island in 1604, and an **English** group which survived one winter at the mouth of the Kennebec three years later. In the face of the unwillingness of subsequent English settlers to let them farm in peace, the local Indians formed a long-term alliance with the French, and until as late as 1700 regularly drove out streams of impoverished English refugees. By 1764, however, the official census could claim that even Maine's black population was more numerous than its Native Americans.

At first considered part of Massachusetts, Maine only became a separate entity in 1820, when the Missouri Compromise made Maine a Free and Missouri a Slave state. In the nineteenth century, its people had a reputation for conservativism and resistance to immigration, manifested in anti-Irish riots. Today, the **economy** remains heavily based on the sea, although many of those who fish also farm, and long expeditions are rare. Recently they have been selling their catch direct to Russian factory ships anchored just offshore. Lobster fishing in particular has defied gloomy predictions and has boomed again, as evidenced by the many thriving **lobster pounds**.

In winter, most of Maine is under ice; summer is short and usually heralded in early June by an infestation of tiny black flies. **Fall colors** begin to spread from the north in late September – when, unlike elsewhere in New England, off-season prices apply – but temperatures drop sharply, becoming quite frosty by mid-October.

Getting Around Maine

The vast majority of visitors to Maine **drive**. Much the most enjoyable route to follow is US-1, running within a few miles of the coast all the way to Canada, with innumerable side turnings to hidden seaside villages. If you're in a hurry, I-95, initially the (tolled) Maine Turnpike, offers speedy access to Portland and beyond. In the **interior**, the roads are quiet and the views spectacular; many belong to the lumber companies, who keep careful track of who you are and where you're going (and charge you for the privilege). At any time of year bad weather can render these roads suddenly impassable; be sure to check before setting off.

Public transport, on the other hand, falls a long way short of meeting travellers' needs. The six-times-daily *Greyhound* service from Boston to Portland, three of which continue to Bangor, at least links the main towns of the southern coast, as does *Concord Trailways* (☎1-800/639-3317), but that's about all. Except in high summer, you can't get a bus any nearer to Acadia National Park or Bar Harbor than Bangor, and nothing at all runs north. Sadly, in a state which once built its industry and tourism on its railroads, there is no longer any *Amtrak* service. A Canadian train runs across the middle of the state to reach New Brunswick, but doesn't connect anywhere useful within Maine itself.

The **area code** for the entire state of Maine is ☎207.

The Maine Coast

Considering that the state has a coastline of three thousand miles, finding access to the sea in Maine can be a frustrating business. The oceanfront is monopolized by an endless succession of private homes and vacation residences – most famously that of former president Bush at Kennebunkport. In fact, only two percent of the shore is publicly owned – and not all of that is beach. Rather than long walks on coastal footpaths, travellers can expect attractive if rather commercial harbor villages, linked by roads which are mostly set well back from the water and packed with diners, motels, and factory outlets.

Europeans tend to find the landscape pretty, but not strikingly different to the Atlantic coast back home, and occasionally a bit too well manicured. The liveliest destinations are **Portland** and **Bar Harbor** (at the edge of **Acadia National Park**); there's a wide choice of smaller seaside towns, such as **Belfast** and **Wiscasset**, if you're looking for a more peaceful base. **Beaches** are more common (and the sea is warmer) further south, for example at **Ogunquit**.

The best way to see the coast itself must be by **boat**; ferries and excursions operate from even the smallest harbors, with major routes including the ferries to **Canada** from Portland and Bar Harbor, and the shorter trips to **Monhegan** and **Vinalhaven** Islands from Boothbay Harbor and Rockland respectively.

South of Portland

I-95 crosses from Portsmouth, New Hampshire (see p.188) into an area of Maine so dense with little communities that Mark Twain alleged one couldn't "throw a brick without danger of disabling a postmaster". Three miles over the border, an **information center** at **Kittery** provides copious details for the whole state (daily summer 8am–9pm; winter 9am–5pm; ☎439-1319).

If you want to avoid the tolls on the interstate and follow US-1 instead, you'll soon find yourself in **YORK**, which was in 1639 the first English city to be chartered in North America. Its seventeenth-century **Old Gaol** now serves as a museum, commemorating its own past and also that of the local Native Americans.

Ogunquit

The three-mile spit of sand which shields **OGUNQUIT** from the open ocean is Maine's finest **beach**, but the town remains small enough to be a pleasant resort. The summer season at the *Ogunquit Playhouse* (☎646-5511) usually attracts a few big-name performers. Among dozens of **motels** is the summer-only *Holiday House* (☎646-5020; ③). The Marginal Way, a not very rural clifftop path, leads from central Ogunquit to **Perkins Cove** a mile south, where well-priced **seafront restaurants** include *Barnacle Billy's* (☎646-5575).

Kennebunkport

KENNEBUNKPORT was perfectly happy as a self-contained and exclusive residential district, before its worldwide exposure as the home of **George Bush**'s "summer White House". If anything, locals seem to feel that George lowered the tone of the place by becoming president. There were complaints at having to bear the extra cost of policing (the far smaller and poorer Plains, Georgia, home of Jimmy Carter, paid up with pride), and talk of a "lower class" of gawking visitor clogging the streets and driving the old money away. However, Kennebunkport is not actually all that different from anywhere else along the coast – which is presumably what's bothering the locals. The best place to hang out (and eat seafood) is *Alisson's* at 5 Dock Square (☎967-4841), where dinner is served until 10pm, and the bar stays open until 1am. There's no great point paying in-town hotel rates when there are so many motels along the highways.

Five miles south of Portland is the **Cape Elizabeth lighthouse**, commissioned by George Washington in 1791 and familiar from postcards and posters. The *Lobster Shack* (☎799-1677) just below the light (and above the horn) is great for fresh seafood.

Portland

The largest city in Maine, **PORTLAND** was founded in 1632 in a superb position on the Casco Bay Peninsula, and quickly prospered, building ships and exporting the great inland pines for use as masts. A long line of wooden **wharves** stretched along the seafront, with the merchants' houses on the hillside above. From the earliest days it was a cosmopolitan city, with a large free black population who traditionally worked as longshoremen; there was great bitterness when Irish immigrants began to displace them in the 1830s. When the **railroads** came, the Canada Trunk Line had its terminus right on Portland's quayside, bringing the produce of Canada and the Great Plains one hundred miles closer to Europe than it would be at any other major US port. Some of the wharves are now taken up by new condo developments, though **Custom House Wharf** remains much as it must have looked when Anthony Trollope passed through in 1861 and said "I doubt whether I ever saw a town with more evident signs of prosperity." Most of the town he saw was destroyed by an accidental **fire** in 1866 (Indians in 1675, and the British in 1775, had previously burned Portland deliberately).

Grand Trunk Station was torn down in 1966, and downtown Portland appeared to be in terminal decline until a group of committed residents undertook the energetic redevelopment of the area now known as **Old Port Exchange**. Their success has revitalized the city, keeping it at the heart of Maine life – but you shouldn't expect a hive of energy. Portland is simply a pleasant, sophisticated, and in places very attractive town, not a major urban center.

Arrival and Information

Both I-95 and US-1 skirt the promontory of Portland, within a very few miles of the city center; **Portland International Jetport** (☎779-7301) is next to I-95, and connected with downtown by regular city buses. Congress Street is the main central thoroughfare, while Fore Street runs along the harbor just to the south. *Greyhound*'s coastal services (around six daily to Boston, three northwards to Bangor and, in summer, Bar Harbor) arrive at 950 Congress St (☎772-6587), at the eastern edge of downtown. The **CVB** is near the Art Museum at 142 Free St (Mon–Fri 9am–5pm; ☎772-2811).

Downtown Portland, though served by buses and trolleys, is compact enough to stroll around, and *Portland Bicycle Exchange*, 396 Fore St (☎772-4137), rents **bicycles**.

Between mid-May and October, the Prince of Fundy Company's *Scotia Prince* **ferry** leaves Portland for **Yarmouth** in Nova Scotia at 9pm each evening, returning the next day. The standard high-season fare is $93 car, $68 adult, $34 children, extra for a cabin, though there are various discount and excursion fares (details on ☎775-5616, ☎1-800/482-0955 in Maine, ☎1-800/341-7540 elsewhere).

The City

Thanks to the various fires, not all that much of old Portland survives, though various grand mansions can be seen along Congress and Danforth streets. The **Wadsworth-Longfellow House** at 485 Congress St was Portland's first brick house when built in 1785 by Peleg Wadsworth, but owes its fame primarily to Peleg's grandson, the poet Henry Longfellow, who spent his boyhood here. Tours start every hour on the hour and last around 45 minutes (June to mid-Sept Tues–Sat 10am–4pm; $3).

The **Portland Museum of Art** at 7 Congress Square is a much more modern affair, built in 1988 by the I M Pei partnership (Tues, Weds, Fri & Sat 10am–5pm, Thurs 10am–9pm, Sun noon–5pm; $3.50, free Thurs 5–9pm). All parts of the museum give superb views over the bay, including some through porthole windows; indeed on occasions the collection seems subordinate to the design, which does not allow much room for extensive displays. Normally the lower storeys are occupied by temporary exhibitions – though there's a lovely open-air garden café as well – while the works upstairs include a lively and flirtatious set of 1880s Winslow Homer engravings, some Andrew Wyeths, and an array of early nineteenth-century European ceramics commemorating heroes of the American Revolution.

For relaxed wandering, the restored **Old Port Exchange** near the quayside is quite entertaining, with all sorts of antiquarian shops, specialist book and music stores (particularly on Exchange Street), and other esoterica. Several companies operate **boat trips** from the nearby wharves, including the *Tango,* a 56ft ketch that sails around the harbor and bay from the ferry pier off Commercial St (daily in summer, 2hr trips for $20; ☎766-2751), and **whale-watching** on the *Odyssey* from Long Wharf (weekends late May to early Oct, daily in high summer; ☎642-3270). *Casco Bay Lines* offers a twice-daily mailboat all year, and additional cruises in summer, to six of the innumerable **Calendar Islands** in Casco Bay, from its terminal at Commercial and Franklin ($8 adult, $4 child; ☎774-7871). **Long, Peaks** and **Cliff islands** all have accommodation or camping.

If you follow Portland's waterfront to the end of the peninsula, the **Eastern Promenade**, which became almost exclusively residential after the last fire, is remarkably peaceful so close to downtown. A big beach lies below the headland, while at the top of Munjoy Hill above is the eight-sided shingled 1807 **Portland Observatory** (June Fri–Sun 1–5pm, July–Labor Day Wed–Sun noon–5pm; $2).

Accommodation

Finding a room in Portland is no great problem, though you can expect to pay more to stay in town than in the **budget motels** around exit 8 off I-95. The closest (summer-only) **campground** is *Wassamki Springs* (☎839-4276) off Hwy-114 towards Westbrook.

Embassy Suites, 1050 Westbrook St (☎775-2200 or 1-800/EMB-ASSY). Spacious suites for the price of a hotel room. Overlooking Portland's tiny Jetport; rates include full breakfast and afternoon cocktails. ⑨.

Hotel Everett, 51A Oak St (☎773-7882). Two blocks from the Wadsworth-Longfellow House. ⑥.

Sonesta, 157 High St (☎775-5411). Luxury central accommodation. ⑥.

Susse Chalet, 340 Park Ave (☎871-0611). Good-value doubles on the western edge of the peninsula near the Maine Medical Center. ④.

YMCA, 70 Forest Ave (☎874-1105). Men-only hostel accommodation north of Congress St near Deering Oaks Park. $20 per night, $81 per week, cash only and unfortunately often full. ①.

YWCA, 87 Spring St (☎874-1130). Very near the Museum of Art, women-only, charging $25 single, or $20 per bed in a double room. ①.

Eating

Not only is Portland rich in affordable **restaurants**, but most of its entertainment venues and bars, listed under a separate heading overleaf, serve food as well.

Amigos, 9 Dana St (☎772-0772). Good Mexican dinners for around $10, in a distinctive large clapboard property very near the port.

Baker's Table, 434 Fore St (☎775-0303). Open-air wooden-table lunch café, which becomes a formal tablecloth restaurant in the evening. The clams steamed in Bass Ale are recommended.

Boone's, 6 Custom House Wharf (☎774-5725). Traditional waterfront restaurant in old wharf buildings, overlooking the fishing docks. Good lobster and broiled seafood in general.

Fresh Market, 58 Market St (☎773-7146). All kinds of fresh pasta and noodles, including ginger and squid's ink, at reasonable prices.

Hu-Shang, 29 Exchange St (☎773-0300) and 7–13 Brown St (☎774-0800). Deservedly popular Chinese restaurants. A good lunch at either can easily cost under $8.

Raffles Café Bookstore, 555 Congress St (☎761-3930). Wholefood café and bookstore; lunch daily, dinner Thurs–Sat only.

Raphael's, 36 Market St (☎773-4500). Good but slightly pricey northern Italian food, in the same premises as *Little Willie's Lounge*, a no-cover comedy and jazz bar.

Nightlife and Entertainment

Portland's formal entertainment possibilities range from the tiny and adventurous *Mad Horse Theatre Company* at 955 Forest Ave (☎797-3338) up to the large productions at the Portland Performing Arts Center, 25A Forest Ave (☎774-0465). The free *Casco Bay Weekly* has listings of all local events; Maine's biggest gigs each summer take place roughly ten miles south of Portland at **Old Orchard Beach**.

Café No, 20 Danforth St (☎772-8114). Part wholefood café and part secondhand bookstore, which puts on live jazz and folk at weekends, in a building mostly taken up by artists' studios. Closed Mon.

Gritty McDuff's, 396 Fore St (☎772-2739). Portland's first brew pub, making Portland Head Pale Ale and Black Fly Stout. Food, folk music, long wooden benches, and a friendly (if a little self-consciously British) atmosphere, which gets rowdy on a Saturday night.

Raoul's Roadside Attraction, 865 Forest Ave (☎773-6886). Music venue – r'n'b, punk, reggae, etc – which is also a restaurant with vegetarian specials, one mile from downtown.

Three Dollar Dewey's, 135 Fore St. Raucous beer hall, with a wide selection of draught beers.

Zootz, 31 Forest Ave (☎773-8187). "Progressive" dance club hosting world-beat discos and concerts.

North Along the Coast from Portland

The coastal towns immediately north of Portland are no less commercialized than those to the south; **Freeport**, for example, is one long shopping mall, albeit a good one. However, soon after **Brunswick** I-95 veers away inland towards Augusta (see p.213), and US-1 is left to run on alone parallel to the ocean. Things become much less frenetic, and prices a whole lot lower; even on the main road you find pleasant communities like **Bath** and **Belfast**, while the many headlands can be even more peaceful. There's really no need to race the full 160 miles to Acadia National Park in one go.

Freeport

The current prosperity of **FREEPORT**, fifteen miles north of Portland, rests on the invention by Leon L Bean, in 1912, of a particularly ugly rubber-soled fishing boot. That original boot is still selling, and **L L Bean's** has grown into an enormous clothing store on Main Street which literally never closes. In theory, that's so pre-dawn hunting expeditions can stock up; all the relevant equipment is available for rent or sale, and the store runs regular workshops to teach backcountry lore. However, with the outdoor look in vogue, *L L Bean's* is now more of a fashion emporium. Freeport has expanded to welcome its 2.5 million annual customers a year with a mile-long strip of top-name **factory outlets** along US-1, most of which do give genuine reductions against usual shop prices (though coastal North Hampton, New Hampshire, offers much the same selection without Maine's hefty sales tax).

Freeport is not an ideal place to stay – everything falls quiet once the shoppers have gone home – but the *Harraseeket Inn* at 162 Main St (☎1-800/342-6423 or 865-9377; ⑥) is a wonderful clapboard B&B inn.

For a complete change of pace, head a mile south of Freeport to the sea, where the *Harraseeket Lunch & Lobster Co* (☎865-4888), extending on its wooden jetty into the peaceful bay, makes a great outdoor lunch spot. The very green promontory visible just across the water is **Wolfe's Neck Woods State Park**. In summer, for $1, you can follow hiking and nature trails along the unspoiled fringes of the headland.

Brunswick

Only a few miles further on from Freeport is **BRUNSWICK**, home since 1802 of the private Bowdoin College. Free tours of the college itself take in the intriguing **Peary-Macmillan Arctic Museum** (Tues–Fri 10am–4pm, Sat 10am–5pm, Sun 2–5pm). After decades of controversy, experts are now generally agreed that former student Admiral Robert Peary really was the first man to reach the North Pole in 1909; whatever the truth, his assembled equipment and notebooks have a powerful fascination.

It was while her husband Calvin was teaching here in the early 1850s that Harriet Beecher Stowe wrote *Uncle Tom's Cabin*, a book whose portrait of slavery had such an impact that Lincoln is said to have greeted her with the words "so this is the little lady that made this big war". The rambling old **Harriet Beecher Stowe House** at 63 Federal St (☎725-5543; ④) is now a B&B; guests stay in modern motel rooms around the back, but can use the lounge of the original house. Alternatives include the *Maineline Motel*, 133 Pleasant St (☎725-8761; ④). The *Great Impasta* at 42 Maine St (☎729-5858) serves excellent Italian food at reasonable prices.

The ideal moment to visit Brunswick is on Labor Day Weekend, when the town hosts a **Bluegrass Festival** (☎725-6009) a little way on at Thomas Point Beach, reached by following Hwy-24 from Cook's Corner. On the same road, **Orrs Island** has a well-equipped oceanfront **campground** (☎833-5595).

Bath

The small town of **BATH** has an exceptionally long history of **shipbuilding**; the first vessel to be constructed and launched here was the *Virginia* in 1607, by Sir George Popham's short-lived colony. **Bath Iron Works**, founded in 1833, attracted job-seeking Irishmen in such numbers as to provoke a mob of anti-immigrant "Know-Nothings" to burn down the local Catholic church in July 1854. The works continue to produce ships – during World War II, more destroyers were built here than in all Japan – and only admit visitors for special occasions such as ceremonial launchings. However, at the **Maine Maritime Museum**, next to the Iron Works two miles south of the town center, you can tour a functioning shipyard where apprentices learn to build wooden schooners using traditional techniques (May–Oct daily 10am–5pm; $6 adults, $3 kids).

As you head up the coast, **accommodation** starts to be better value. *Glad II* at 60 Pearl St (☎442-1191; ③) is a small (and non-smoking) B&B very near the museum; west on Bath Rd, the *New Meadows Inn* (☎443-3921; ③) serves good basic meals, and has bargain four-person cottages. The *Bakke B&B*, on Foster Point Rd in West Bath (☎442-7185; ④), is tiny and very friendly, with just one suite of two bedrooms.

The *Soup to Nuts Café* at 191 Water St (☎442-7234) is a good-value vegetarian lunch place, while the *Harbor Lights Café*, 166 Front St (☎443-9883), is a Mexican restaurant putting on live music at weekends. *Montsweag Restaurant* (☎443-6563), on US-1 in **Woolwich** just to the east, is a very inexpensive and lively seafood place, open for both lunch and dinner. Be warned that everything in Bath closes very early in the evenings.

Wiscasset and Boothbay Harbor

WISCASSET, ten miles on from Bath, is dominated by the bridge which carries US-1 over the Sheepscot River. In the shallow waters of its narrow and picturesque bay lie two forlorn **shipwrecks**, the *Luther Little* and the *Hesper*, all that remains of the last four-masted schooners in the world. As good a view of them as any is to be had from the seafood restaurant *Le Garage*, on Water St (☎882-5409). One can only hope that the large nuclear power plant south of town on Hwy-144 proves more robust.

Accommodation possibilities in the area include the down-to-earth summer-only *Whitfield Motel*, three miles south on US-1 (☎882-7137; ②), or the private lakeside **campground** *Downeast Family Camping* (☎882-5431), at Gardiner Pond, four miles north on Hwy-27, with its cathedral stand of Norway pines.

For no obvious reason, **BOOTHBAY HARBOR** at the southern tip of Hwy-27 is one of Maine's most crowded resorts. Don't plan to stay, but if you do happen to pass by, the *Lobstermen's Coop* at 99 Atlantic Ave (☎633-4900) dishes up ultra-fresh lobsters at minimal prices. *Moody's Diner* (☎236-3391) in **Waldoboro**, back on the main road east, is a long-standing haunt of police and truckers, open 24 hours and oozing nostalgia.

Rockland and Vinalhaven

ROCKLAND, where US-1 reaches Penobscot Bay roughly halfway between Portland and Bar Harbor, is the world's largest distributor of **lobsters**, and holds the Maine Lobster Festival over the first weekend of August (for more info ☎596-0376). One of the best of its traditional lobster pounds is *Miller's* (☎594-7406), on the shore of Wheeler's Bay in an isolated cove at Spruce Head on Hwy-73, which is open from 10am until 7pm in season, for succulent lobsters and steamers. South of Rockland, the pretty **St George Peninsula**, in particular the village of Tenants Harbor, inspired writer Sarah Orne Jewett's classic Maine novel *Country of the Pointed Firs*.

Between two and four **ferries** run daily throughout the year from Rockland to the island of **Vinalhaven**, which has one or two inns (but no campgrounds), a few shops, a museum and an impressive lighthouse; slightly fewer serve neighboring **North Haven**. The boats do carry cars, though the chance to hike is what attracts many visitors. The *Maine State Ferry Service* at 517A Main St (☎596-2202) has full schedules; they also operate several daily services from **Lincolnville**, where there's also a small but pleasant beach, across to **Islesboro** and the **campground** (☎289-3824) on tiny Warren Island.

Camden and Rockport

The adjacent communities of **CAMDEN** and **ROCKPORT** split into two separate towns in 1891, over a dispute as to who should pay for a new bridge over the Goose River between them. Rockport was at that time a major lime-producer, but a fire at the kilns in 1907 not only put an end to that business but also destroyed the ice-houses which were the town's other main source of income. Now it's a quiet working port, among the prettiest on the Maine coast, home to numerous lobster boats, pleasure cruisers and little else; clearly, overcute Camden has won the competition for tourists.

Camden's specialty is organizing sailing expeditions of up to six days in the large schooners known as **windjammers**. Vessels include the *Stephen Taber* (70 Elm St; ☎236-3520 or 1-800/999-7352) and the *Roseway* (PO Box 696X; ☎236-4449). Among busy **eating and drinking** spots in Camden are *Cappy's Chowder House* at 1 Main St (☎236-2254) and *Gilbert's Publick House* on Sharps Wharf (☎236-4320), which has pool tables. The *Maine Stay*, 22 High St (☎236-9636; ④), is an 1813 white clapboard inn.

Belfast

Homely **BELFAST** feels like the most lived-in and liveable of the towns along the Maine coast. Here the shipbuilding boom is long since over, but the inhabitants have had the waterfront declared an historic district, sparing it from over-commercialization and condo development. Belfast's whitewashed Greek Revival houses, dating from the 1830s, have served as backdrops to movies from *Peyton Place* to *Man Without a Face*. As you stroll around, look out for the old-fashioned *Greyhound* and *Western Union* office (complete with jukebox), and the *Cranberry Tiger* **ice cream store** (☎338-3531) at 60 Main St. If love for your product is anything to go by, the claims of Woody, its owner, to make the best ice cream in the world are entirely credible.

The **information office** (☎338-2896) at the foot of Main Street by the bay is next to the old **railroad station** used by the *Belfast and Moosehead Lake Railroad* (☎338-2330). Hour-long excursions in reconditioned Pullman cars run from here up the lush banks of the Passagassawakeag River, along track laid in 1870 to connect logging operations with the sea – though whatever impression you might get from their advertisements, the trains are pulled by diesel not steam. En route to the villages of Brooks and Burnham Junction, you pass through thick forests, at their most colorful in the fall.

Also right beside the rail terminal, *Weathervane's* seafood **restaurant** (☎338-1774) has tables on the wooden jetty outside; across the bay, *Young's Lobster Pound* (☎338-1160) has $10 fresh-boiled lobster dinners and sunset views. *Rollie's Café* back up the hill at 37 Main St (☎338-9872) is a rough-and-ready beer bar open until 1am every day of the year. For **accommodation**, try the *Hiram Alden Inn*, 19 Church St (☎338-2151; ③), a beautiful 1840 Greek Revival house run as a B&B by the genial Jim Lovejoy, the *Horatio Johnson House*, 36 Church St (☎338-5153; ③), or the three-room in *Kingsbury House*, 35 Northport Ave (☎338-2419; ③), which serves macrobiotic breakfasts.

While you're in the area, it's worth tuning into the mildly offbeat local **radio station** *WERU*, broadcasting on 89.9FM from the snooty resort of **Blue Hill** – which also holds the lively *Left Bank*, offering Thai food and good music.

Mount Desert Island

Considering that five million visitors come to **Mount Desert Island** each year, that it contains most of New England's only National Park, and that it boasts not only a genuine fjord but also the highest headland on the entire Atlantic coast north of Rio de Janeiro, it is quite an astonishingly small place, measuring just sixteen miles by thirteen. It is of course simply one among innumerable rugged granite islands along the Maine coast; the reason to come here is that it is the most accessible, linked to the mainland by bridge since 1836, and has the best facilities. The social center, **Bar Harbor**, has accommodation and restaurants to suit all pockets, there are lower-key communities all over the island, and **Acadia National Park** can offer less sedate travellers camping, cycling, canoeing, kayaking, and birdwatching.

The island was named *Monts Deserts* (bare mountains) by Samuel de Champlain in 1604 and fought over by the French and English for the rest of the century. Although all existing settlements date from long after the final defeat of the French, the name remains, still pronounced in French (more like *dessert*, actually).

Getting There

If you're **driving**, Mount Desert is easy enough to get to, along Hwy-3 off US-1, though in high summer roads on the island itself get congested (and the horse-drawn tours don't help). **Public transport**, however, is minimal. *Greyhound* buses (☎667-8596) run to Bar Harbor from Bangor for perhaps a couple of months in summer, starting in mid-June, though even that can't be guaranteed. *St Croix Bus Co* (☎454-7526) connects Ellsworth and Bar Harbor, as does *Downeast Transportation* (Mon, Wed & Fri only; ☎667-5796), which also runs buses across the island from Bar Harbor to Southwest Harbor (Thurs) and Northeast Harbor (Tues).

Nearby Trenton Airport (☎667-7432) has a limited service on *Continental Airlines* and *Bar Harbor Airlines* (☎1-800/327-8376), while the *Bluenose* **ferry** takes six hours to link Bar Harbor with Yarmouth, Nova Scotia (cars $70, adults $38, kids $18; late June to late Sept, daily from Bar Harbor at 8am; otherwise Mon, Wed, & Fri only, 8.30am. For reservations, contact *Marine Atlantic Reservations Bureau*, PO Box 250, North Sydney, NS B2A 3M3, Canada; ☎288-3395 or 1-800/341-7981; in Canada ☎902/794-5700).

The Town of Bar Harbor

BAR HARBOR began life as an exclusive resort, summer home to the Vanderbilts and the Astors; the great fire of October 1947 which destroyed their opulent "cottages" ended all that. It's now firmly geared towards tourists, though it's by no means downmarket. There's not all that much to do in town, even in high summer. However, the ambience is sufficient for it to take a while to realize that once you've strolled around the village green, and walked past the headland of the *Bar Harbor Inn* for views of the ocean and Frenchman Bay, you've seen most of what Bar Harbor has to offer.

In high season up to 21 different **sea trips** set off each day, for purposes ranging from deep sea fishing to cocktail cruises. Among the most popular are the *Acadian* **whale-watcher** expeditions, departing from the *Golden Anchor Inn* (July & Aug 8am & 1.30pm; Sept & Oct 11.30am only; ☎288-9794), and the two-hour cruises on the **three-masted schooner** *Natalie Todd* from the *Bar Harbor Inn* (daily 10am, 2pm & 6pm; $17.50; summer ☎288-4585, winter ☎546-2927).

One of the town sights in its heyday was the "Indian village", a summer encampment where Native Americans came to sell to tourists; it was cleared away in the 1930s to make room for a new ball park. Now the only signs of the island's first inhabitants are the artefacts at the **Robert Abbe Museum**, found at Fernald Point near Southwest Harbor, and attributed to a nomadic people who made birch-bark canoes. What became of them is encapsulated by a classic understatement on a map contrasting the tribal areas of 1600 with the modern reservations: "the native population did not view territorial boundaries as we do today." The museum is a couple of miles south of Bar Harbor – not a particularly pleasant walk – at Sieur de Monts Spring, just off the Park Loop Road (daily, July & Aug 9am–5pm, mid-May to June, Sept & Oct 10am–4pm; $1.50).

Bar Harbor's main **tourist information** office is at the ferry terminal (☎288-3393); in summer there's another on Kennebec Street beside the village green.

Acadia National Park

Not all of **Acadia National Park** is on Mount Desert Island – there are sections on the Isle au Haut to the west, reached by ferry from Stonington, and on the Schoodic peninsula to the east – but there's all you could want here in terms of mountains and lakes for secluded rambling, and **wildlife** such as seals, beavers, puffins and bald eagles. The two main geographical features are the narrow fjord of **Somes Sound** which almost splits the island in two, and **Mount Cadillac**, only 1530ft high but offering tremendous ocean views. The summit, the first place in the United States to see the sun rise each morning, can be reached either by a moderately strenuous climb – more than you'd want to do before breakfast – or by a very leisurely drive, winding up a low-gradient road.

Much the most enjoyable way to explore is to ride a rented **bicycle** around the fifty miles of gravel-surfaced "**carriage roads**", built by John D Rockefeller as a protest against the 1917 vote which allowed "infernal combustion engines" onto the island. Two Bar Harbor companies rent mountain bikes between 8am and 6pm, at around $9 half-day, $16 all day: *Bar Harbor Bicycle Shop*, at 141 Cottage St on the edge of town (☎288-3886), and *Acadia Bike & Canoe Co*, across from the post office at 48 Cottage St (☎288-9605). *Southwest Cycle* does the same in Main St, Southwest Harbor (☎244-5856). All provide excellent maps. Carry water, as there are very few refreshment stops inside the park. **Canoes**, **kayaks** and **bikes** are for rent, mid-May to mid-October, from *National Park Outdoor Activities Center,* 137 Cottage St in Bar Harbor (☎288-0342), which also offers guided sea kayaking trips and downhill bike rides from the top of Mount Cadillac.

The park is open all year, with a summer-only **visitor center** at the entrance to the Loop Road north of Bar Harbor (daily mid-June to Aug 8am–8pm, May to mid-June & Sept–Nov 8am–6pm; ☎288-3338), and the headquarters at Eagle Lake (daily 8am–4.30pm). There are two official **campgrounds**: *Blackwoods*, five miles south of Bar Harbor off rte 3, and *Seawall*, on rte 102A, four miles south of Southwest Harbor. Both are in woods, near the ocean, and have full facilities in summer; only *Blackwoods* is open in winter, with minimal facilities. Space can be reserved in midsummer from Acadia National Park, PO Box 117, Bar Harbor, ME 04609 (☎288-3338).

The one and only sizeable beach, five miles south of Bar Harbor, is a stunner: called simply **Sand Beach**, it's a gorgeous strand bounded by twin headlands, with restrooms, a parking lot and a few short hiking trails. The water, unfortunately, is usually arctic.

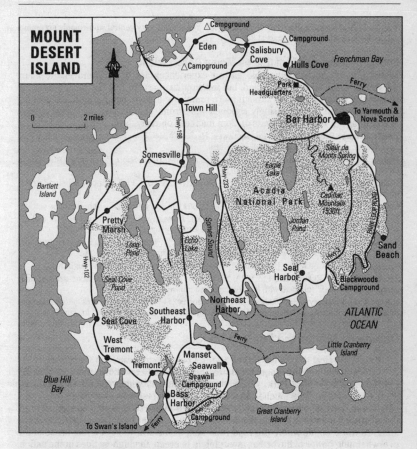

Accommodation on Mount Desert Island

Hwy-3 into and out of Bar Harbor (which is Main Street on the way south) is lined with budget **motels**, which do little to improve the look of the place but satisfy an enormous demand for accommodation. Rates increase drastically in July and August, and anywhere offering sea views will cost a whole lot more. The quieter places elsewhere on the island tend to be booked up early.

Bar Harbor Inn, Newport Drive, Bar Harbor (☎288-3351 or 1-800/248-3351). The nicest place to stay bar none, with spacious rooms looking out over the bay from the heart of town. ⑥.

Bass Cottage in the Field, Main St, Bar Harbor (☎288-3705). Ten-room old-fashioned white clapboard inn, very near the center. ③.

Maine Street Motel, 315 Main St, Bar Harbor (☎288-3188). April to mid-Nov only. Has its own restaurant next door. ④.

McKay Cottages, 243 Main St, Bar Harbor (☎288-3581). B&B in two nice old houses. ③.

Moorings Motor Sail, Shore Rd, Manset (☎244-5523). Lovely 200-year-old inn, two miles east of Southwest Harbor, May–Oct. Private beach, boats for rent next door. ③.

Mt Desert Island Youth Hostel, Kennebec St, Bar Harbor (☎288-5587). Mid-June to Aug only, beds in large dormitories for $8 AYH members, $11 non-members. Reservations essential. ①.

Penury Hall, Main St, Southwest Harbor (☎244-7102). Small B&B. ②.

YWCA, 23 Mt Desert St, Bar Harbor (☎288-5008). Year-round, very central women-only accommodation. Beds in shared rooms start at $18. ①.

Eating, Drinking and Nightlife on Mount Desert Island

Mount Desert's most memorable **eating** experiences are to be found in the many **lobster pounds** all over the island, but for nightlife as such, Bar Harbor is where the people are. Cottage Street is a much more promising area to look for food and evening atmosphere than the surprisingly subdued waterfront. The Art Deco *Criterion* cinema at 35 Cottage St (☎288-3441) puts on 2pm matinees on rainy days.

Beal's Lobster Pier, Clark Point Rd, Southwest Harbor (☎244-7178). Fresh seafood for under $10, on a rickety wooden pier crammed full of lobsters.

Bulger's Dockside Restaurant, across from Manset Town Dock, Shore Rd, Manset (☎244-5221). Ocean views from every table, seafood from $7.

Fisherman's Landing, West Street Pier, Bar Harbor (☎288-4632). Pick-your-own lobster dinners, on the dock below town. Closes at 8.30pm.

Galyn's, 17 Main St, Bar Harbor (☎288-9706). Delicious fish and prime rib in unpretentious setting.

Lompoc Café, 34 Rodick St, Bar Harbor (☎288-9392). A healthy Middle Eastern menu for $10–15, with local Thunder Hole Ale on draught and live music every night. Open 3pm–midnight.

The Opera House, 27 Cottage St, Bar Harbor (☎288-3509). Upmarket restaurant serving dinner only at around $20 per head, with framed portraits and recordings of opera legends.

Thirsty Whale, 44 Cottage St, Bar Harbor (☎288-9335). Bar Harbor's busiest late-night bar.

Triangle Seafood Restaurant, Rte 102A, Bar Harbor (☎244-9608). Excellent-value seafood daily 11am–9pm; "try it all" full meal with lobster, crab and mussels for $9.95.

Village Green Bakery Café, 150 Main St, Bar Harbor (☎244-9450). Great pastries, plus a full range of lunches and dinners, including the requisite boiled lobsters. Low prices, good for families.

Downeast Maine: the Coast to Canada

Looking at a typical map of the United States, you'd never dream that Canada stretches for five hundred miles beyond Maine to the east. In fact few travellers venture far beyond Acadia National Park, which is one reason why what's known as **Downeast Maine** remains so little touched by change. Another reason is that this is bleak and windswept country, where high cliffs are battered by harsh seas. In summer, though, the weather is no worse than in the rest of Maine, and the coastal drive can be exhilarating. At those points where the road runs next to the sea, you get a real sense of the overwhelming power of the ocean, sweeping in to create the highest tides in the nation.

A short way northeast of Acadia, a loop road leads from US-1 to the rocky outcrop of **Schoodic Point**, which offers good birdwatching, great views, and a splendid sense of solitude. Tourism is not big business in these parts, but each village has one or two B&Bs and low-priced restaurants. The fishing harbor at **JONESPORT** on Hwy-187, which deserves a detour, holds *Tootsies Bed and Breakfast* (☎497-5414; ③). A glorious high-arched iron bridge leads to the nature reserve of **Beal's Island**. **MACHIAS** back on US-1 is even more picturesque, with a little waterfall right in the middle, and was the unlikely scene of the first naval battle of the Revolutionary War, in 1775. The townsfolk commandeered the British schooner *Margaretta* and proceeded to terrorize all passing British shipping. That attack was planned in the still-standing gambrel-roofed **Burnham Tavern**. Meals are good value at *Helen's Restaurant*, 32 Main St (☎255-6506), while the *Clark Perry House*, 59 Court St (☎255-8458; ③), provides B&B accommodation.

Continuing east, and abandoning US-1 for Hwy-189, you come to the prominently striped **lighthouse** at **West Quoddy Head**, the easternmost point of the US, where an international bridge crosses to Campobello Island in Canada. The nearby settlement of **Bailey's Mistake** is named for a sea captain who beached his lumber vessel in thick fog in 1830, and chose to settle here with his crew, building homes with their erstwhile cargo, rather than face the wrath of the ship's owners back in Boston.

The border between the United States and Canada weaves through the center of **Passamaquoddy Bay**; the towns to either side get on so well that they refused to fight in the US–UK war of 1812, and promote themselves jointly to tourists as the **Quoddy Loop** (information on ☎454-2597). It's perfectly feasible to take a "two-nation vacation", but each passage through customs and immigration between **CALAIS** (pronounced *callous*) in the States and **St Stephen** in Canada does take a little while – and watch out for confusion stemming from the fact that they're in different time zones. No trace now remains of Samuel de Champlain's 1604 attempt to found a colony on the diminutive St Croix Island, which you can see from an overlook on the main road. The *St Croix Bus Line* (☎454-7526) runs a once-daily van from Calais to Ellsworth and Bar Harbor.

Inland Maine

The vast expanses of the **Maine interior**, stretching up into the cold far north, consist mostly of evergreen forests of pine, spruce and fir, interspersed by the white birches and maples responsible for the spectacular fall colors. Only in the remote north is at all much of it genuine wilderness, however; elsewhere, what you see is more likely to be either abandoned farming land, over-exploited by the pioneers, or woodlands cultivated by the timber companies.

Distances are large. Once you get away from the two largest cities nearer the sea – **Augusta**, the capital, and **Bangor** – it's roughly two hundred miles by road to the northern border at **Fort Kent**, while to drive between the two most likely inland bases, **Greenville** and **Rangeley** (where exiled psychologist Wilhelm Reich lived and is buried), takes three hours or more. Driving (there's no public transportation) through this mountainous scenery can be a great pleasure, but you do need to know where you're going. There are few places to stay, and many roads are tolled access routes belonging to the lumber companies: gravel-surfaced, vulnerable to bad weather, and in any case often not heading anywhere in particular.

This landscape has evolved in a very unusual way. Many waterfront communities grew up without roads to serve them, in the days when the timber harvest was floated downriver to the sea; other more recent settlements have only ever been accessible by seaplane. Now that mighty trucks carry the tree-trunks instead, roads are finally being pushed through, amid complaints that they are ruining the whole feel of the place.

If you have the time, this is great territory in which to **hike** – the **Appalachian Trail** starts its 2000-mile course down to Georgia at the top of Mount Katahdin – or **raft** on the **Allagash Wilderness Waterway**. Especially around **Baxter State Park**, the forests are home to deer, beaver, a few bears, some recently introduced caribou . . . and **moose**. These endearingly gawky creatures (they look like badly drawn horses, and are virtually blind), tend to be seen at early morning or dusk; in spring they come to lick the winter's salt off the roads, while in summer you may spot them feeding in shallow water.

Augusta

The capital of Maine since 1832, **AUGUSTA** is much quieter and less visited now than it was a hundred years ago. The lumber industry here really took off after the technique of making paper from wood was rediscovered in 1844, and Augusta also had a lucrative sideline – each winter hundreds of thousands of tons of **ice**, cut from the Kennebec River, were shipped out, as far south as the Caribbean, in a trade now all but forgotten by history. There are informative displays on Maine's landscape and industrial past at the lively **Maine State Museum**, a short way south of the capitol on State St (Mon–Fri 9am–5pm, Sat 10am–4pm, Sun 1–4pm).

If you plan to stay in Augusta, as usual the best-value **accommodation** is the *Susse Chalet Motor Lodge* (☎622-3776; ③), on Whitten Rd at the Maine Turnpike's Augusta-

Winthrop exit. For **food**, the lobster rolls at *Burnsie's Homestyle Sandwiches* (☎622-6425) on State St next to the capitol are favorites with the politicians, while *Hazel Green's* at 349 Water St (☎622-9903) is an atmospheric but pricey riverside restaurant.

Bangor

In its prime, **BANGOR**, 120 miles northeast of Portland, was the undisputed "Lumber Capital of the World". Every winter its raucous population of "River Tigers" went upstream to brand the felled logs, which they then maneuvered down the Penobscot as the thaw came in April, reaching Bangor in time to carouse the summer away in the grog shops of Peppermint Row. (Bangor too exported ice to the West Indies – and got rum in return.) Those days were coming to an end when in October 1882 Oscar Wilde addressed a large crowd at the new Opera House and spoke diplomatically of "such advancement . . . in so small a city".

Bangor today is not a place to spend much time, although its plentiful motels and the big new Bangor Mall on Hogan Rd north of town make it a good last stop before the interior. Its twin claims to fame are that it's the unlikely home of Stephen King, the horror fiction writer, and that it possesses what, at 31 feet, may well be the largest statue of **Paul Bunyan** in the world, excepting perhaps one or two in Minnesota (see p.000) – though it looks more like a brightly painted model airplane kit than a statue.

From mid-May until the end of July there's **harness racing** at the *Bangor Raceway* (☎947-3313), just behind the statue; admission is $1 but the potential to lose money is unlimited. The same venue hosts the **Bangor State Fair**, in the last week of July and the first in August. The *Opera House*, 131 Main St (☎947-0200), was destroyed by fire in 1914, but has now been restored and puts on film, opera, dance and theater, while a few miles north of Bangor, the *Maine Center for the Arts* (☎581-1755), at the University of Maine in **Orono**, runs a series of big-name concerts each summer. Orono is named after the eighteenth-century Chief Joseph Orono; a small island nearby is now a rather sad reservation running summer Bingo sessions.

Practicalities

Bangor is the last sizeable town along I-95, before it finally veers away from the coast and heads up the Penobscot towards Canada. It's also the end of the line for *Greyhound*, the thrice-daily service from Boston and Portland terminating at 158 Main St.

Accommodation possibilities include the *Red Carpet Inn*, opposite Paul Bunyan at 480 Main St (☎942-5282; ③), and the *Quality Inn-Phenix*, right downtown at 20 Westmarket Square (☎947-3850; ③). The *Holiday Inn* at 500 Main St (☎947-8651; ④) houses Bangor's liveliest dance venue, the *Bounty Taverne*. The best breakfasts in Bangor are at the *Bagel Shop*, 1 Main St (947-1654), the state's only kosher deli; other, equally incongruous options include a handful of Indian and Pakistani places, and the massive Mexican *Pepino's* at 105 Main St (☎947-1233).

Baxter State Park and the Far North

Driving through northern Maine can feel as though you're trespassing on the private fiefdoms of the logging companies; only Baxter State Park is public land. However, you're pretty much free to hike, camp and explore anywhere you like, so long as you let people know what you're doing (only a sensible precaution, after all). The scenery is pretty much the same everywhere, although of course to get the best of it – to experience what Thoreau described in his *Maine Woods* – you need to leave your car at some point and set off into the back woods.

Five miles north of Brownsville Junction on Hwy-11, an inconspicuous left turn leads to the **Katahdin Iron Works** at Silver Lake (daily in summer, 9am–5pm), built in

1843. It's remarkable quite how little remains of what one hundred years ago was a thriving industrial community; one solitary brick oven and the tower of the blast furnace, stark and forlorn at the end of a few miles of gravel track. In good summer weather it's possible to continue along the track across the hills to Greenville.

Further north, **Millinocket** is a genuine company town, built on a wilderness site by the Great Northern Paper Company in 1899–1900 as the "magic city of the North". Public curiosity was so great that three hundred people came on a special train from Bangor to see what was happening. Since then it has produced massive quantities of newsprint, but in 1990 the company was taken over by the Georgia Pacific Corporation, and although the townspeople made a killing from cashing in their stock, their homes are almost unsaleable, and their jobs may well not last.

Next to **Millinocket Lake**, ten miles northwest, the splendidly ramshackle old *Big Moose Inn* (Box 98, Millinocket, ME 04462; ☎723-8391; ②) and adjacent campground makes a great place to stay, with some four-person cabins. *Unicorn Expeditions* (☎725-2255) uses the inn as a base for day **rafting** and **kayaking** expeditions, and there are **dog-sled races** in February and March, as well as seaplane tours.

By now you're approaching the southern end of **Baxter State Park** itself, with on a clear day the 5268ft peak of **Mount Katahdin** visible from afar. The park was the single-handed creation of former Maine Governor Percival P Baxter, who having failed to persuade the state to buy Katahdin and the land around it, bought it himself between the 1930s and 1960s and deeded it bit by bit to the state on condition that it remain "forever wild".

Northwards to Canada

The northernmost tip of Maine is taken up by Aroostook County, which covers an area larger than several individual states. Although its main activity is the large-scale cultivation of potatoes, it is also the location of the **Allagash Wilderness Waterway**; this is where most of the **whitewater rafting** companies mentioned in this section actually carry out their expeditions.

Britain and the United States all but went to war over Aroostook in 1839; at **Fort Kent**, the northern terminus of US-1 (which runs all the way from Key West, Florida), the main sight is the solid cedar **Fort Kent Blockhouse** built to defend American integrity, and looking like a throwback to early pioneer days. *Doris' Café* (☎834-6262) at Fort Kent Mills on Hwy-11 towards Eagle Lake can provide big breakfasts.

Greenville

GREENVILLE, at the southern end of Moosehead Lake, is another nineteenth-century lumber town which now makes its living primarily from tourism. It's not exceptionally pretty and it's certainly not very large, but it is well positioned for explorations throughout the Maine woods. In town, the main attraction is the restored **steamboat** *Katahdin*, which tours the lake and also serves as the (non-profit) Moosehead Marine Museum (cruises at 10am & 2pm, daily July–Sept, Sat & Sun only in May & June; ☎695-2716).

The **Chamber of Commerce** on Main St near the T-junction at the lake (summer daily, winter Mon–Fri only; ☎695-2702) has details of **accommodation** such as the *Gray Swan Motor Lodge* (☎695-4470; ④), overlooking the lake from deep in the woods on the hill above town, and the *Greenville Inn* on Norris St (☎695-2206; ③). Among local **rafting** companies charging $55–90 for a day in the water are *Eastern River Expeditions*, PO Box 1173, Moosehead Lake, Greenville, ME 04441 (☎695-2411; outside Maine ☎1-800/634-RAFT); *Wilderness Expeditions*, The Birches, PO Box 41, N Rockwood, ME 04478 (☎534-2242); and *Allagash Canoe Trips*, Box 713G, Greenville, ME 04441 (☎695-3668). Greenville is also the largest **seaplane** base in New England; contact *Currier's Flying Service* (☎695-2778).

Rangeley

RANGELEY is only just in Maine, a short way east of New Hampshire and even less distance south of the border with Québec. Furthermore, as the cheap café-bar *Doc Grant's* (☎864-3449) on Main St makes a great show of telling you, it's equidistant (at 3107.5 miles) from the North Pole and the Equator. That doesn't mean it's on the main road to anywhere, although if you're avoiding the coast altogether you can get here direct from the northern side of the White Mountains (see p.193). It has always been a resort, served in 1900 by two train lines and several steamships, with the main attraction then being the fishing in the spectacularly named Mooselookmeguntic Lake.

This small and very homely place, nestling amid a complex system of lakes and waterways, serves as base for summer explorations, and in winter as the nearest town (and airport) to the **ski** area at **Saddleback Mountain**. Rangeley Lakes **Chamber of Commerce** at PO Box 317 (☎864-5571) has details of various activities, including snowmobiling, and dawn moose-watching **canoeing** expeditions (☎864-5136). One really fun thing to do is to take a **seaplane** trip with the *Mountain Air Service* (☎864-5307). A fifteen-minute tour, flying low over endless forests and tiny lakes, costs $30 for two; you can also arrange on the spot on the waterfront to go on the regular two-hour fire-watching tours, for $25 each person. Among other outlets, **bicycles** and **canoes** can be rented from the *Rangeley Region Sport Shop* on Main St (☎864-5615).

Rangeley also has one unlikely and not exactly orthodox tourist attraction. About halfway along the north side of Rangeley Lake, a mile up a side track off rte 16, the remote **Wilhelm Reich Museum** at **Orgonon** (PO Box 687, Rangeley, ME 04970; July & Aug Tues–Sun 1–5pm, Sept Sun only 1–5pm; $3; ☎864-3443), is where Wilhelm Reich eventually made his American home after fleeing Germany in 1933. Although he was an associate of Freud in Vienna, and wrote the acclaimed *Mass Psychology of Fascism*, Reich is best remembered for developing the orgone energy accumulator. He claimed it could create rain and dissipate nuclear radiation; sceptical authorities focused on the not very specific way in which it was said to collect and harness human sexual energy. In a tragic end to his career, Reich was imprisoned after a wayward student broke an injunction forbidding the transportation of his accumulators across state lines, and he died in the federal penitentiary in Lewisberg, PA in November 1957. He is buried here, amid the neat lawns and darting hummingbirds, and his house remains a center for the study of his work.

Accommodation in the Rangeley Area

The *Rangeley Inn* on Main St (☎864-3341; ④) stands between Rangeley Lake and the smaller bird sanctuary Haley Pond, so you can stay right in town and have a room that backs onto a scene of utter tranquillity; there's also a gorgeous old wooden dining room. Otherwise, the Chamber of Commerce can provide lists of "remote campsites" around the lake – which really are remote, several of them inaccessible by road.

Twenty miles north of Rangeley, the peaceful *Grants Camps* beside Kennebago Lake (mid-May–Sept, PO Box 786, Rangeley, ME 04970; ☎864-3608) arranges fishing, canoeing and windsurfing, with accommodation in comfortable cabins, with all meals, costing around $70 per person per day, and lower weekly rates. A more accessible campground is *Cathedral Pines* (☎246-3491) just north of **Stratton** on Eustis Rd. At its entrance stands a memorial to Benedict Arnold's expedition to Québec in 1775, which passed this way, and to Colonel Timothy Bigelow who climbed the mountain in a "vain endeavor to see the city of Québec".

To the east, the great white *Herbert Inn* in **Kingfield** (PO Box 67, Kingfield, ME 04947; ☎265-2000; ③) is something special, a classic country hotel with good meals for under $15; the *Sherbert* next door is a luxurious candy store and bakery.

CHAPTER FOUR

THE GREAT LAKES

S wept by tumultuous storms and traversed by fleets of oceangoing tankers, the interconnected **Great Lakes** form the largest body of fresh water in the world; Lake Superior alone is over three hundred miles from east to west. Left untouched, the shores of these inland seas can rival any coastline: Superior and the northern reaches of Lake Michigan offer stunning rocky peninsulas, craggy cliffs, tree-covered islands, mammoth dunes and deserted beaches. For endless stretches along Lake Erie, and the bottom lips of lakes Michigan and Huron, however, sluggish waters lap against grimy cities and the unused wharves of decaying ports.

To varying degrees, all the states that line the American side of the lakes – **OHIO, MICHIGAN, INDIANA, ILLINOIS, WISCONSIN** and **MINNESOTA** – share this mixture of natural beauty and industrial blight. Cities such as Chicago and Detroit, with all their good and bad points – and **Chicago** in particular, with its magnificent architecture, museums, music and restaurants, is an unmissable destination – should not be seen as characterizing the entire region. Within the first hundred miles or so of the lakeshores, especially in Wisconsin and Minnesota, tens of thousands of smaller lakes and tumbling streams are scattered through a spectacular rural wilderness; beyond that, you are soon in the heart of the corn belt, where you can drive for hours and encounter nothing more than a succession of crossroads communities, grain silos and giant barns. Garrison Keillor's wry stories about the fictional backwater town of Lake Wobegon (where "all the women are strong and all the men are beautiful"), set in Minnesota, carry more than a ring of truth.

The first foreigner to reach the Great Lakes, the French explorer Champlain in 1603, found the region inhabited mostly by Huron, Iroquois and Algonquin. France soon established a network of military forts, Jesuit missions and fur-trading posts – which entailed treating the Indians as allies rather than subjects. Territorial disputes with their colonial rivals, however, culminated in the **French and Indian War** with Britain from 1754 to 1761. The victorious British felt under no constraints to deal equitably with the Indians, and things grew worse with large-scale American settlement after independence. The **Black Hawk War** of 1832 put a bloody end to traditional life.

Settlers from the east were followed to Wisconsin and Minnesota by waves of **Scandinavians** and **Germans**, while the lower halves of Illinois and Indiana attracted **southerners**, who attempted to maintain slavery and resisted Union conscription

---

ACCOMMODATION PRICE CODES

All accommodation prices in this book have been coded using the symbols below. Note that prices are for the least expensive double rooms in each establishment. For a full explanation see p.35 in *Basics*.

① up to $30	④ $60–80	⑦ $130–180
② $30–45	⑤ $80–100	⑧ $180+
③ $45–60	⑥ $100–130	

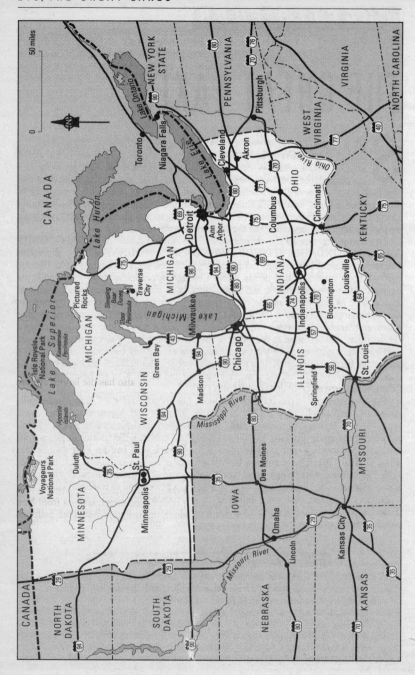

during the Civil War. These areas often still have more in common with neighboring Kentucky and Tennessee than with the industrial cities of their own states.

The impetus given to **industry** by the Civil War was encouraged by abundant supplies of ores and fuel, and efficient transport connections by water and rail. As lakeshore cities like Chicago, Detroit and Cleveland grew, their populations were swollen by hundreds of thousands of poor **blacks** brought in from the Deep South as cheap labor, particularly to work in munitions during the two world wars. But a complete lack of planning, inadequate housing provision and mass lay-offs at times of low demand bred conditions which led to the riots of the late Sixties and current inner-city deprivation. Depression in the Seventies ravaged the economy – especially the **automobile** industry on which so much else depended – and brought the unwanted title of "**Rust Belt**". Since then, urban centers have battled back with varying degrees of success.

During the summer, breezes coming off the Great Lakes keep the **temperature** down to a comfortable average of 70°F. Even in spring and autumn it can often slip below freezing in the northern reaches of the region, where winter readings of -50° are not uncommon and the lakes are frozen solid.

All the major towns of the region are easily reached by public transport. **Amtrak**'s national hub is in Chicago and routes spread across the entire region; **Greyhound** operates reasonably frequent services to nearly all urban centers. The best way to appreciate the sculpted shorelines of the lakes themselves, however, is to travel the lonely minor roads by **car**, while **cycling** in the northwest, alongside Superior and the northern parts of Lake Michigan, can be hugely enjoyable.

OHIO

OHIO, the furthest east of the Great Lakes states, clings to the southern edge of shallow Lake Erie. This is known as one of the nation's most industrialized regions, but industry is largely concentrated in the east, near the Ohio River, and to the south the landscape becomes less populated and more forested. Ohio also has the largest **Amish** population in the world, who farm in the northeast and are much less of a tourist attraction than the highly publicized Pennsylvania Dutch (see p.125).

Enigmatic traces of Ohio's earliest inhabitants can be seen at the **Great Serpent Mound**, a grassy state park sixty miles east of Cincinnati, where a cleared hilltop high above a river was reshaped to represent a giant serpent swallowing an egg, possibly by the Adena Indians around 800 BC. When the French claimed the area in 1699, it was inhabited by the **Iroquois** – Ohio means "something great" in their language. In the eighteenth century, its prime position between Lake Erie and the Ohio River made it the subject of fierce contention between the French and British; once the British acquired control of most of the French land east of the Mississippi, settlers from New England began to establish communities both along the Iroquois War Trail paths on the shores of the lake and along the Ohio River.

During the Civil War, Ohio was in the forefront of the struggle, producing two great Union generals, Ulysses Grant and William Sherman, and sending more than twice its quota of volunteers to fight for the north. Its progress thereafter has followed the classic "Rust Belt" pattern: rapid industrialization, aided by its natural resources and crucial location, which has since the Seventies foundered alarmingly.

Although the state is dominated by its triumvirate of "C"s – the cities of **Cleveland**, **Columbus** and **Cincinnati** – its most visited destinations are the **Lake Erie Islands**, which have benefited from the recent cleanup of the polluted lake and now attract thousands of mainlanders in pursuit of outdoor recreation. Cincinnati and Cleveland, the latter hit especially hard by the recession, have both undergone major face-lifts and are surprisingly attractive.

Getting Around Ohio

Amtrak **trains** between New York or Washington and Chicago stop either at Cincinnati or at Cleveland and Toledo; Toledo is also connected with Detroit, Toronto, and, via Sandusky, with Buffalo. Ohio is well served by *Greyhound* **buses**, and there are major **airports** at Cleveland and Cincinnati.

Cleveland

Nowadays few refer to the great industrial port of **CLEVELAND** – for so long the butt of jokes after the heavily polluted Cuyahoga River caught fire in the early Seventies – as the "Mistake on the Lake". Although the path back from acute recession (another Seventies legacy) is by no means complete, it's hard not to be impressed by the remarkable resurgence of Ohio's largest city. The Cleveland of the Nineties boasts a sensitive and fond restoration of the Lake Erie/Cuyahoga River waterfront, a superb constellation of museums, glittering city center malls and a new downtown superstadium. Add to that the recent arrival of several major corporate headquarters and classy hotels, and there's an unmistakeable buzz about the place.

Founded in 1796, Cleveland profited greatly, thirty years later, from the opening of the **Ohio Canal** between the Ohio River and Lake Erie. During the city's heyday, which began with the Civil War and lasted until the 1920s, its vast iron and coal supplies made it one of the most important **steel** and **shipbuilding centers** in the world. **John D Rockefeller** made his billions here, as did the many others whose now-decrepit old mansions line "Millionaires Row". That has become a no-go area, along with many other bleak and faceless danger spots; despite the investment of billions of dollars during the past decade, the scars of deprivation and neglect are still often all too visible.

City leaders have high hopes that the I M Pei-designed **Rock and Roll Hall of Fame**, due to open in 1995, will signal the emergence of their town as a major destination (an inconceivable thought a few years ago). Cleveland won the hotly contested bidding to host this national music shrine, thanks largely to Alan Freed, the local disc jockey who popularized the phrase "rock and roll" back in 1952.

Arrival, Getting Around and Information

Cleveland's busy **Hopkins International Airport** (☎265-6030) is twelve miles out in the western suburb of Brookpark. The twenty-minute **cab** ride to town costs around $20, though the *Regional Transit Authority* (*RTA*; ☎621-9500) train is only $1.50. *Greyhound* arrives in a dodgy area at 1465 Chester Ave (☎781-1400), and the *Amtrak* station (☎696-5115) is on the lakefront at 200 Cleveland Memorial Shoreway.

Cleveland is concentrated in different pockets, and as the potentially dangerous areas are scattered pretty wide (it is not safe, for example, to stray into the streets around the three-block-deep *Cleveland Clinic*, very close to the much-frequented University Circle), you're safest in a **car**. *RTA* runs an efficient **bus** service ($1) and a small *Rapid* train line ($1.50), until about 12.30am. **City tours** are provided by *Trolley Tours of Cleveland*, W Ninth St at St Clair Ave (reservations required, ☎771-4484).

Maps and **information** can be had from the Cleveland **CVB**, 3100 Tower City Center (☎621-4110), in the center of Public Square, and there's an information booth in the nearby Terminal Tower.

The City

All the main streets in Cleveland lead to the stately nineteenth-century Beaux Arts **Public Square**, at the very center of downtown. **Ontario Street**, which runs north–south through the Square, divides the city into east and west. Cleveland's most interesting areas are at two opposite ends of the spectrum: the industrial romance of the **Flats** in the northwest, and the cultural institutions of **University Circle**, east of the river.

Downtown Cleveland has recently been regaining energy; among its glamorous new shopping malls are the **Tower City Center** in the Terminal Tower, which also has an **observation deck** on the 42nd floor (Sat & Sun only) and the **Avenue**, a skylit hall of gleaming white and black marble. The **Playhouse Square Center** (☎771-4444), twelve blocks away at 1501 Euclid Avenue, is an impressive complex of three renovated old theaters. Take a look at the gorgeous lobby of the small *Ohio Theatre*, with its starlit-sky ceiling.

Just west of Public Square is the **waterfront**, where one of the nation's busiest waterways shares space with excellent bars, clubs and restaurants strung out along a boardwalk. Right by the Cuyahoga River, the Flats, long known for its excellent nightlife, relishes its industrial setting; magnificent grimy old buildings, warehouses and slag heaps appear powerful and romantic rather than depressing, a proud testimony to Cleveland's manufacturing history.

The surrounding **Historic Warehouse District**, a stretch of nineteenth-century commercial buildings between W Third and W Tenth streets given over to shops and cafés, is still being restored. To the west of the river, **Ohio City** is one of Cleveland's hipper neighborhoods, with junk stores, Victorian clapboard houses and a busy farmers' market on W 25th Street selling all manner of ethnic foods (Mon & Wed 7am–4pm, Fri & Sat 7am–7pm).

Cleveland Lakefront State Park, two miles west of downtown, is a pleasant – and clean – place to have a swim or a picnic. To see the city from the water, try the two-hour *Goodtime Cruise* (☎861-5110; $9.50) from the dock at East Ninth Street Pier.

Five miles east of downtown, the **University Circle** is a cluster of over seventy cultural institutions. The eclectic and well-contextualized **Museum of Art**, fronted by a lagoon at 11150 East Blvd, ranges from fifteenth-century Dutch tapestries to African art (Tues, Thurs & Fri 10am–5.45pm, Wed 10am–9.45pm, Sat 9am–4.45pm, Sun 1–5.45pm; free). Also notable is the **Museum of Natural History**, Wade Oval, with its exhibits on dinosaurs and Native American culture (Mon–Sat 10am–5pm, Sun 1–5.30pm; Wed 10am–10pm in summer; $4, free Tues & Thurs 3–5pm). Dotted along East and Martin Luther King boulevards, 24 small landscaped cultural gardens are dedicated to and tended by Cleveland's diverse ethnic groups, including Croatians, Estonians and Finns. **Murray Hill**, Cleveland's Little Italy, is adjacent to University Circle: an attractive area of brick streets, small delis and galleries.

Five miles out of downtown via I-71 South, the **Cleveland Zoo**, 3900 Brookside Drive (daily; summer 9am–7pm, otherwise 9am–5pm; $7), features a spectacular rainforest building stuffed with seven thousand plants and 118 species of animals including orangutans, American crocodiles and Madagascan hissing cockroaches.

Accommodation

Travellers without cars in Cleveland are limited to the somewhat expensive downtown hotels, to a small cluster of places next to the train station at W 150th St out by the airport, or a long bus ride into town. **B&B** can be arranged through *Private Lodgings*, Box 18590, Cleveland 44118 (☎321-3213).

Budgetel Inn, 4222 W 150th St (☎251-8500). Standard motel rooms; easy downtown access via train. ③.

Glidden House, 1901 Ford Drive (☎231-8900). Bed and continental breakfast in a Gothic mansion very close to downtown. ⑥.

Holiday Inn – Airport, 4181 W 150th St (☎252-7200). Relaxing hotel with good pool. ④.

The **area code** for Cleveland is ☎216.

Holiday Inn – Lakeside, 1111 Lakeside Ave (☎241-5100). By no means the best property in this chain but just about the cheapest weekday rooms downtown. Like most city center hotels it offers weekend specials. ⑥.

Lakewood Manor Motel, 12019 Lake Ave (☎226-4800). In the western suburb of Lakewood about four miles from downtown, though accessible by bus #55CX. Plain but adequate rooms. ②.

Red Roof Inn, 6020 Quarry Lane, Independence (☎477-0030). Eleven miles out from downtown, but served by public transit. ②.

Eating

The **farmers' market** in Ohio City is one of the best places for cheap and unusual picnic food, but Cleveland is also sprouting some excellent (if pricey) fine-dining restaurants downtown. The Italian places on Murray Hill are good value and popular.

Burgess Grand Café, 1406 W Sixth St (☎574-2232). Glamorous, stylish downtown café in old warehouse. Superb food, reasonably priced. Fruit and waffle breakfasts from $6. Dinner begins at $16.

Isabella's, 2025 Abington Ave (☎229-1177). Popular Italian restaurant in University Circle/Murray Hill with lunch from $5, dinner from $10, and live jazz.

New York Spaghetti House, 2173 E Ninth St (☎696-6624). Cheap, family-owned Italian restaurant.

Watermark Restaurant, 1250 Old River Rd (☎241-1600). Excellent and extensive seafood menu in a classy Flats location. Great views from the deck.

Whole Grain, 55 Public Square (☎861-0999). Cheap and healthy weekday breakfast and lunch.

Nightlife and Entertainment

For drinking, live music and dancing, several districts are worth checking out. The crowded and lively bars in the **Flats** – such as *Shooters*, 1148 Main Ave (☎861-6900) – have great views over the river, while *Peabody's* at 1059 Old River Rd (☎241-2451) is one of the best venues in a city famed for its live rock scene. In **Ohio City**, the huge mahogany bar in the *Great Lakes Brewing Co*, 2516 Market St (☎771-4404), still bears bullet holes left over from a Twenties shoot-out involving Elliot Ness.

As for more refined entertainments, the *Cleveland Opera* (☎575-0900) and *Ballet* (☎621-2260) perform in **Playhouse Square** (☎771-4444), which also hosts drama, and the *Cleveland Orchestra* (☎231-1111) is based in University Circle at Severance Hall, 11001 Euclid Ave. Current events listings can be found in the *Cleveland Magazine* and *Northern Ohio Live* available at newsstands.

The Lake Erie Islands

The **LAKE ERIE ISLANDS – Kelleys Island**, and the three **Bass Islands** further north – were early stepping stones for the **Iroquois** on the route to what is now Ontario. French attempts to claim the islands in the 1640s met with considerable hostility, and they were left more or less in peace until 1813, when in the **Battle of Lake Erie**, fought off South Bass Island, the Americans established their control over the Great Lakes by destroying the entire English fleet (for the first time in history).

The islands first tasted prosperity in the 1860s, when a boom in wine production meant that nearly every available acre was planted with grapes. Tourism arrived almost simultaneously, with steamboats bringing wealthy visitors to spend their summers in the grand hotels. However, the economy was hit hard by Prohibition and the emergence of the California wineries, as well as the advent of car travel. In the Seventies, Lake Erie's appalling pollution was the final straw for many inhabitants, who undertook a huge cleanup, both literally, of the lake, and figuratively, of the islands' image. Their plan has worked; today the islands are heavily touristed, especially in summer, with fishing and swimming the two main attractions. Those mainland towns, like **Sandusky**, that act as jump-off points for the islands, are destinations in themselves.

The Mainland

The large coal-shipping port of **SANDUSKY**, fifty miles west of Cleveland on US-2, is probably the most visited of the lakeshore towns, thanks to **Cedar Point Amusement Park**, five miles southeast of town (May–Sept daily 9am–10pm; $25, $14 after 5pm). The largest ride park in the nation, now nearly a century old, it claims to have the tallest and fastest **roller coaster** in the US, and also has a mile-long beach.

Sandusky, in its pleasant farmland setting, is a nice enough town, but there's not much to it apart from its pretty downtown square and the fast-food spots lining US-2. **VERMILION**, further east, just beyond the suburbs of Cleveland, is also known as Harbor Town for its attractive lakeside area, which has thrived since 1837. Today it is a quaint old hamlet lined with clapboard houses, cedar trees and tidy gardens. Olde-style galleries and shops hug the small downtown, a stone's throw from the boat rides, seafood restaurants and fishing boats on the dockside.

Practicalities

Two *Amtrak* **trains** pass through Sandusky daily to and from Boston; the station, at N Depot and Hayes avenues, is in a dodgy area, and unstaffed. *Greyhound* **buses** call way out at 6513 Milan Rd (☎625-6907), with a shuttle to Cedar Point and downtown ($5). Sandusky's **visitor center** is at 231 W Washington Row (daily in summer, 8am–6pm; ☎625-2984 or 1-800/255-ERIE); Vermilion's, 5495 Liberty Ave (☎216/967-4477).

Motels along Cleveland Road in **Sandusky** include the *Mecca*, 2227 Cleveland Rd (☎626-1284; ③), and the *Greentree* (☎626-6761; ③), along with its Fifties café and bowling alley, near the entrance to Cedar Point. **Camping** is available at the *Bayshore Campsite*, 2311 Cleveland Rd (☎625-7906). In **Vermilion**, rooms usually run a bit cheaper; try the *Motel Plaza*, 4645 Liberty Avenue (☎216/967-3191; ②). In **Lakeside**, a quiet Methodist retreat across Sandusky Bay, the *Lakeside Hotel* (☎798-4461; ②) offers clean simple rooms at great prices. For a good meal and live music in fun surroundings, head for *Margaritaville* in Sandusky at the junction of routes 6 and 2.

Kelleys Island

KELLEYS ISLAND is about nine miles north of Sandusky, in the western basin of Lake Erie. Seven miles across at its widest, it's the largest American island on the lake, but it's also one of the most peaceful and picturesque, home to just a hundred or so permanent residents. The whole island, green, dozy and with few buildings less than a century old, is a National Historic District. Its seventy-plus archeological sites include **Inscription Rock**, a limestone slab carved with four-hundred-year-old pictographs, east of the dock on the southern shore. The **Glacial Grooves State Memorial**, on the west shore, is a four-hundred-foot trough of solid limestone, scoured with deep ridges by the glacier that carved the Great Lakes.

Settled in the 1830s, Kelleys was at first a working island, its economy based on lumber, then wine, and later limestone quarrying. All but the latter have collapsed, though a steady tourist industry also developed and today hundreds of Clevelanders come here at weekends, to swim (from the sandy public beach on the north shore), and cycle and hike through some dramatic disused quarries, which now sprout cedars.

Practicalities

Kelleys Island's **visitor center** (☎746-2360) is on the dockside. Getting around is easy; cars are heavily discouraged, and most people, when not strolling, use bikes ($8 per

The **area code** for Sandusky and the Lake Erie Islands is ☎419.

Ferries to Kelleys Island are operated by *Neuman Boats* from Sandusky (☎626-5557) and Marblehead (☎798-5800) every hour from dawn until dusk, more frequently at weekends and during peak times (April–Nov; $8.50 return, bikes $2.50). *Kelleys Island Ferry Boat Lines* (☎798-9763) offers a year-round service from Marblehead and takes bikes free.

Ferries to South Bass Island are operated by *Put-in-Bay* (☎285-3491) from Port Clinton, ten miles away on the mainland, at regular intervals during the day; and by *Miller Boats* (☎285-2421) from Catawba Point at the end of US-53 N to Lime Kiln Dock on the southern tip of the island (March–Sept daily, hourly 7am–7.30pm; $4.50 one way).

The Jet Express takes a mere fifteen minutes to reach South Bass Island from Port Clinton. It runs until 11.30pm in the summer (April–Nov; $9 one-way; ☎1-800/2451-JET). Look out for their discount days.

Cruises operated by *Goodtime* (☎625-9692) from Sandusky's Jackson Street Pier depart daily at 9.30am and call at both Kelleys Island and South Bass Island, for a round-trip fare of $21. The *Sandusky Boat Lines* ship plies a similar route and leaves from the dock at Columbus Ave in Sandusky (☎627-0198; $23).

Flights to both Kelleys Island and South Bass Island leave daily from Sandusky. Contact *Griffing Airlines* (☎626-5161).

day) or golf carts ($45), available from *First Place Rentals*, at the top of the ferry dock (☎746-2314). A tram ($1) runs downtown from the dock, giving a short narrated tour of the island on its way. There are a few B&Bs and inns, but the island caters more for long-term stays with cottages and apartments; the *Crafts Motel & Cottages* (☎746-2281; ③) is a good all-round bet. You can camp for $12 at the first-come, first-served state Park on the north bay near the beach. The jovial *Village Pump* (☎746-2281) serves good homestyle food, beer and a smooth Brandy Alexander until 2am.

South Bass Island

SOUTH BASS ISLAND is the largest and southernmost of the Bass Island chain, three miles from the mainland northwest of Kelleys Island, and named for the excellent bass fishing in the surrounding waters. Also referred to as Put-in-Bay (the name of its one and only village), this is the most visited of the American Lake Erie Islands, with its permanent population of 450 swelling to ten times that in summer.

Just a year after its first white settlers turned up and planted their wheat, British troops invaded the island as part of the 1812 war for control of the lakes. The Battle of Lake Erie, which took place on its southeastern edge, is commemorated by the Perry's Victory and International Peace Memorial in a 25-acre park where the island dramatically nips in at the waist. You can see the ten miles to the battle site from an observation deck near the top of the 352ft stone Doric column (May–Oct daily 10am–7pm; $1).

After the war, with the lake safe from Canadian invasion, South Bass Island grew both as a port, transporting cedar to the mainland for the construction of steamboats, and as a tourist destination: in the 1890s its *Victory Hotel* was one of the largest hotels in the world. Today it's pretty much a family resort, where outdoor-lovers come to fish, camp, hike, parasail, or swim at the stone beach in the state park on the west of the island. Wine was also big business, though only one of its 26 vineyards survived Prohibition (by producing grape juice). The Heineman Winery on Catawba Avenue, the east–west road on the main body of the island, and adjacent Crystal Cave (a giant spangly geode of lilac celestite crystals) give combination tours which include a free glass of wine or grape juice (daily May–Sept 11am–5pm; $3.50).

Practicalities

Put-in-Bay's **visitor center** (☎285-2832) is in Harbor Square, downtown, just next to the northern dock. To get around, as on Kelleys Island, most people either rent **golf carts** from *Baycarts Rental* on Harbor Square ($10–20 per hour; ☎285-5785), or **bikes**, from *Island Bike Rental* at both docks (☎285-2016). A **shuttle bus** runs between the northern dock, the winery and the state park ($1), and a narrated **tram tour** sets off from the dock every thirty minutes. The local taxi will take you anywhere on the island for $2.50 per person, or $1.50 if you're staying here (7am–3am; ☎285-6161).

Hotel rooms, which range between $50 and $95, are heavily booked at the weekends and during the summer, and B&Bs often require a two-night minimum stay at the weekend. There's **camping** for $12 in the state park (get there by 9am) and at the *Foxes Campground* (☎285-5001) on the southern shore.

Put-in-Bay's wild **nightlife** pulls in revellers not only from the other islands but from the mainland. *Tippers Seafood and Steakhouse* serves fantastic seafood dinners from $14, while *Frosty's* does good pizza and beer. Numerous **live music** venues include the *Beer Barrel Saloon* – said to have the longest uninterrupted bar in the world – and the *Roundhouse*, 234 Lorain Ave (☎285-4595).

Cincinnati

CINCINNATI, just across the Ohio River from Kentucky and roughly three hundred miles from both Detroit and Chicago, is a dynamic **industrial** metropolis with a definite European flavor. Its tidy center, rich in architecture and culture, lies within a few minutes' easy walk of the arty **Mount Adams** district and the attractive **riverfront**.

The city was founded in 1788 where an Indian trading route crossed the river and was named in honor of a group of Revolutionary War admirers of the Roman general Cincinnatus who, after saving his city in 458 BC, returned to his small farm and refused to accept any reward or glory. Cincinnati quickly became an important supply point for pioneers heading west on flatboats and rafts, and its population rocketed with the establishment of a major steamboat **riverport** in 1811. Tens of thousands of **German** immigrants poured in during the 1830s.

Loyalties were split by the **Civil War**. At first merchants were perturbed by the loss of important markets; then they began to pick up lucrative government contracts, and the city decided its future lay with the Union. In the prosperous post-war decade, Cincinnati acquired Fountain Square, the prodigious Music and Exhibition Hall, a zoo, art museum, public library and the country's first professional baseball team. **Sport** remains a great source of pride; you can't be in the city for long without becoming familiar with the orange and black colors of the Bengals football team and the epic saga of the Reds' victory in the 1990 World Series.

Another Cincinnati success story is the **Rookwood Pottery**, started by Maria Storer in Mount Adams in 1880. Its distinctive tiles adorn countless downtown Art Deco landmarks, as well as the Union and Dixie Terminals.

Charles Dickens, Winston Churchill and Longfellow have all admired Cincinnati; Mark Twain, on the other hand, said that he hoped to be in Cincinnati when the world ended, as it's always twenty years behind everywhere else.

Arrival and Information

Greater Cincinnati International Airport (☎283-3151) is twelve miles south of downtown, in Covington, KY. Taxis to the city center cost $20, and *Jet'Port Express* (☎283-3702) shuttle vans half that. The **Greyhound** station is just off Broadway on the eastern fringe of the center at 1005 Gilbert Ave (☎352-6000). *Amtrak* **trains** (☎579-8506) arrive almost two miles out at 1901 River Rd, on the daytime citywide **bus** network.

Cincinnáti's main **visitor center** is at 300 W Sixth St (Mon–Fri 8.45am–5pm; ☎621-2142); there are also information booths in Fountain Square and Union Terminal.

Downtown

Downtown Cincinnati rolls back from the Ohio River to fill the flat Basin area, ringed by a disarray of rugged hills. During the city's emergent industrial years, the filth, disease, crime and general commotion of the so-called Sausage and Rat rows led the middle classes to abandon downtown en masse, an early instance of what became a common phenomenon. Nowadays, however, it has been taken over by a continental-style abundance of attractive stores, street vendors, restaurants, cafés, open spaces and gardens. Over, among and even right through the hotel plazas, office lobbies and retail areas, the **Skywalk** network of air-conditioned passages and flyovers spans sixteen city blocks. No one building or sector stands out, but the area's charm, atmosphere and cleanliness, together with the friendliness of the people, simply make it a very enjoyable place to wander round and explore.

At the geographic center of downtown, the **Genius of the Waters** in **Fountain Square** sprays a cascade of hundreds of jets to symbolize the city's trading links. Once the site of a noisy, fetid market, the square is now surrounded by a tree-dotted plaza, all but enclosed by soaring facades of glass and steel, and provides an extremely popular lunch spot and venue for daytime concerts. Looming above at Fifth and Vine streets, the 48-storey Art Deco **Carew Tower** has a viewing gallery on its top floor giving a wonderful panorama of the tight bends of the Ohio and the surrounding hillsides (Mon–Fri 9am–5pm; $1).

Just east of Fountain Square are the Art Deco headquarters of **Procter and Gamble**, manufacturers of *Ariel*, *Tide*, *Fairy Liquid* and *Old Spice*. The company was formed in 1837 by candlemaker William Procter and soapmaker James Gamble, to exploit the copious supply of animal fat from the slaughterhouses of **"Porkopolis"**. A less than open style of management has spawned tales of dubious religious and political links; the corporate logo even had to be changed to counter accusations that it was a satanic symbol. By sponsoring radio's "Puddle Family" in 1932, the company was responsible for creating the world's first **soap opera**.

The nearby **Contemporary Arts Center**, in the Mercantile Center at 115 E Fifth Street, was briefly closed by police in 1990, and its director charged with obscenity, in shocked response to a show of the homoerotic photography of Robert Mapplethorpe. Undaunted, it continues to put on multimedia modern art exhibitions (Mon–Sat 10am–6pm; $2, free on Mon). By contrast, the **Taft Museum**, just east of downtown in an immaculate 1820 Federal-style mansion at 316 Pike Street, contains a priceless collection of works by Rembrandt, Goya, Turner and Gainsborough, plus some staggering Ming porcelain and French enamels (Mon–Sat 10am–5pm, Sun noon–5pm; $2). The statue of a weary Abraham Lincoln in **Lytle Park**, in front of the museum, was criticized as unpatriotic when unveiled in 1917; it's now seen as a great example of sculptural realism.

Mount Adams and Eden Park

Just over a mile from downtown, the land rises suddenly and the streets – narrow courses with tight corners and abrupt dead ends – start to conform to the contours of **Mount Adams**. Century-old townhouses coexist with avant-garde galleries, stylish boutiques, trendy gift shops and international restaurants. During the late nineteenth century, the elegant dining rooms of Mount Adams entertained the rich and famous who wanted to escape the squalor and noise of the Basin. Today its lively bars appeal to

The **area code** for Cincinnati is ☎513; for Covington across the river it's ☎606.

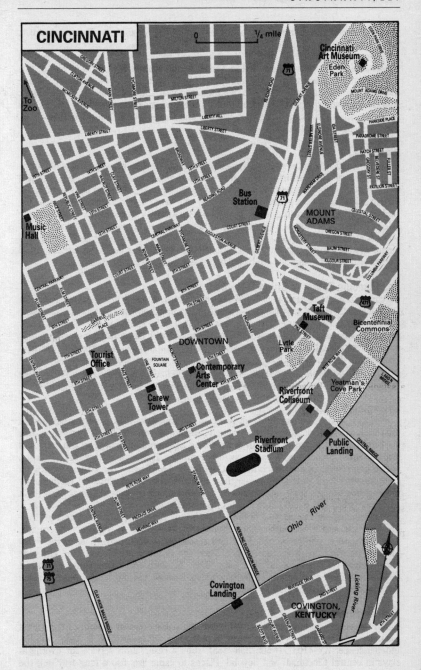

yuppies, students, hedonists and iconoclasts from all over the city. From downtown, take a taxi (around $3) or #49 bus.

Adjacent to this tightly packed neighborhood recline the rolling lawns, verdant copses and scenic overlooks of **Eden Park**. A loop road at the northern end of this former vineyard leads to the **Cincinnati Art Museum** on Art Museum Drive. Its one hundred labyrinthine galleries span five thousand years, taking in an excellent Islamic collection as well as a solid selection of European and American paintings by the likes of Matisse, Monet, Picasso, Edward Hopper and Grant Wood (Tues–Sat 10am–5pm, Sun 11am–5pm; $5, free on Sat).

Riverside

The Cincinnati side of the Ohio River seems at first to be dominated by the pallid, uninspiring **Riverfront Stadium**, home of football's Bengals and baseball's Reds. But just to the east, despite its proximity to parking lots, concrete edifices and busy interstates, the riverside takes on a greater serenity. The mile-long riverside walk begins near the stadium at **Public Landing** at the bottom of Broadway. The cobbled wharf here, the original site of the city, is a great place to take a look at immaculately painted showboats and other river craft. The *Star of Cincinnati* operates daily sightseeing and dinner **cruises** from adjacent Star Landing (☎723-0100). Further west, **Bicentennial Commons** was a two-hundredth birthday present from the city to itself in 1988.

The Museum Center at Union Terminal

Cincinnati's latest attraction is its **Museum Center**, housed in the magnificent Art Deco Union Terminal northwest of downtown, approached via a stately and imposing driveway off Ezzard Charles Drive. The last train left the station in 1972, but its newly restored lobby itself is absolutely stunning, complete with extraordinary mosaic murals and a Rookwood-tiled ice-cream parlor. Highlights of the **Museum of Natural History** are dioramas of Ice Age Cincinnati and The Cavern, which houses a living bat colony; the **Historical Society** holds a succession of well-presented short-term exhibitions (Mon–Sat & hols 9am–5pm; Sun 11am–6pm; museums $5 each or $8 combined).

Covington, Kentucky

Covington, directly across the Ohio River on the Kentucky side, is very much part of the Cincinnati hinterland. It can be reached from downtown Cincinnati by walking over the bright-blue 355-yard 1867 **John A Roebling Suspension Bridge**, at the bottom of Walnut Street, which served as a prototype for the Brooklyn Bridge. Once across, you're confronted by the much-hyped **Covington Landing** – "the largest waterfront complex on inland waters" – a collection of cafés, shops and clubs on permanently moored boats that's little more than an upmarket mall on water. The *BB* riverboat company (☎606/261-8500) offers cruises from the Landing.

Ten minutes' walk southwest of the bridge brings you to the attractive, narrow, tree-lined streets and nineteenth-century houses of **MainStrasse Village**, a Germanic neighborhood of antique shops, bars and restaurants which plays host to the lively **Maifest** on the third weekend of each May, and is the centerpiece of the city-wide **Oktoberfest** on the weekend after Labor Day. At Sixth and Philadelphia streets, 21 mechanical figures accompanied by glockenspiel music toll the hour on the German Gothic **Carroll Chimes Bell Tower**.

Accommodation

Budget travellers may have problems finding affordable downtown rooms; things don't get much cheaper until as far out as the airport. *Ohio Valley B&B*, 6876 Taylor Mill Rd, Independence, KY 41051 (☎606/356-7865), runs a reservation service for overnight stays in central Cincinnati and beyond. Places to camp are also a long way out; the nearest is the *Florence Overnite RV Park* (☎606/371-8352), 10485 Dixie Hwy (US-25), fifteen miles south in Florence, Kentucky.

Budget Inn, 3356 Central Parkway (☎559-1600). The least expensive place in uptown Cincinnati, though doubles range greatly in price. Just over three miles from downtown. ③–④.

Cincinnati Home Hostel (AYH), 2200 Maplewood Ave (☎651-2329). Dorm beds in large converted house for only $6. Two miles from downtown. ①.

Holiday Inn Downtown, 800 W Eighth St (☎241-8660). Downtown's lowest-priced rooms. ④.

Motel 6, I-75 Exit 180, Florence, KY (☎606/283-0909). Budget rates, almost twenty miles south. ①.

Quality Hotel Riverview, 666 Fifth St, Covington, KY (☎606/491-1200). Strange-looking tower hotel, with comfortable rooms, very near the interstates just south of downtown. The expensive revolving *Riverview* restaurant offers amazing views of the river (see below).

Eating

Cincinnati has some excellent gourmet and continental restaurants, but it's best known for fast-food **Cincinnati chili** chains such as *Skyline Chili*, open from breakfast to midnight at over forty sites, including Vine & Seventh streets downtown. The new **Tower Place** mall at Carew Tower at Fifth and Vine streets has a good and wide-ranging food court on its lowest level.

Celestial Restaurant, 1071 Celestial St, Mt Adams (☎241-4455). Popular French restaurant. Dinner can be very expensive, though there are good early-evening $9.95 specials, Mon–Thurs.

Dee Felice, 529 Main St, Covington, KY (☎606/261-2365). Small and atmospheric restaurant/jazz venue, specializing in Cajun cuisine, with lots of fresh seafood dishes.

La Normandie Grill, 118 E Sixth St (☎721-2761). Solid, mid-range downtown choice, well known for great steaks, chops and seafood.

Longworth's, 1108 St Gregory St, Mt Adams (☎579-0900). Good-quality meals at attractive prices in a delightful garden setting. Food served all day until midnight, and the music goes on until 2.30am.

Mike Fink, at the foot of Greenup St, Covington, KY (☎606/261-4212). Quality seafood restaurant in a fine old riverboat. Great night views of the Cincinnati skyline. Most main courses around $12.

Pigall's Café, 127 W Fourth St (☎651-2233). Newly remodelled downtown café with inventive modern cooking.

Riverview Revolving Restaurant, in the *Quality Hotel*, 666 Fifth St, Covington, KY (☎606/491-5300). Brilliant views of the river, with a full revolution each hour. The unusual cordon bleu menu, including alligator ravioli, is very expensive, but the excellent Sunday brunch is good value.

Rookwood Pottery, 1077 Celestial St, Mt Adams (☎721-5456). Snacks and burgers right inside the former kilns of Cincinnati's celebrated pottery.

Nightlife

The bars, restaurants and cafés of Mount Adams offer a great choice of music, food and atmosphere, especially good on warm summer nights when the narrow streets are full of revellers. What's on listings for the whole city are in the free *Everybody's News*.

Arnold's, 201 E Eighth St (☎421-6234). Fun and funky downtown spot. A favorite with jazz fans, though it also puts on folk and acoustic acts. Good restaurant upstairs.

Blind Lemon, 936 Hatch St, Mt Adams (☎241-3885). Extremely popular cocktail bar in a dark, cavernous setting. Acoustic music most nights.

The Pavilion, 949 Pavilion St, Mt Adams (☎721-7272). Bar with great view of the city and the Ohio River from its terraced outdoor deck.

Classical Music, Opera, Theater

Music Hall, at 1241 Elm St (☎621-1919), an 1870s conglomeration of spires, arched windows and cornices, is said to have near-perfect acoustics. Home to Cincinnati's *Opera* and *Symphony Orchestra*, it also hosts the May Festival of choral music. The *Cincinnati Playhouse in the Park* (☎421-3888), in Eden Park, puts on drama, musicals and comedies with daily performances throughout the year (except Mon).

MICHIGAN

Mention **MICHIGAN** and most people think of cars, heavy industry and inner-city Detroit. Midwesterners prefer to focus on its magnificent scenery: the beaches, dunes and cliffs along the 3200-mile shoreline of its two vividly contrasting **peninsulas** – bordering four of the five Great Lakes – rival many an oceanfront state.

The mitten-shaped **Lower Peninsula** is dominated from its southeastern corner by the industrial giant of **Detroit**, surrounded by satellite cities almost exclusively devoted to the automotive industry. In the west, the scenic 350-mile Lake Michigan shore drive passes through likeable little ports before reaching the stunning **Sleeping Bear Dunes** and resort towns such as **Traverse City** in the peninsula's balmy northwest corner. The desolate, dramatic and thinly populated **Upper Peninsula**, reaching out from Wisconsin like a claw to separate lakes Superior and Michigan, is a far cry indeed from the cosmopolitan south.

In the mid-seventeenth century, **French explorers** forged a successful trading relationship with the Chippewa, Ontario and other tribes. The **British**, who acquired control after 1763, were far more brutal: Governor Henry Hamilton was known as the "Hair Buyer of Detroit" for his advocacy of taking scalps rather than prisoners. Ever since, Michigan's economy has developed in waves, the eighteenth-century fur, timber and copper booms culminating in the state establishing itself at the forefront of the nation's manufacturing capacity, thanks to its abundant raw materials, good transport links, and the genius of innovators such as **Henry Ford**. Today, car production remains the major source of income – though just as the automobile created many of eastern Michigan's cities in the Twenties, it destroyed them during the slumps of the Seventies and Eighties – but tourism has become a four-season money-spinner.

Getting Around Michigan

It's easy to be caught out by Michigan's sheer **size**; Detroit is over 700 miles from Ironwood on the Wisconsin border (a **ferry** between Ludington and Manitowoc, Wisconsin helps to cut driving time – see p.239). *Greyhound* **buses** run regularly throughout the south, but journeys elsewhere are less frequent, and those few buses that serve the remote Upper Peninsula travel through at night. *Amtrak* **trains** between New York and Chicago stop at Detroit, Dearborn and Ann Arbor; trains into Canada leave from Windsor, just over the river from Detroit. Michigan's principal **airport** is just outside Detroit. **Cycling** is both feasible and rewarding, particularly around Traverse City; the League of Michigan Bicyclists (☎616/452-BIKE) can help with routes.

Detroit

DETROIT, the birthplace of the mass production car industry and the Motown sound, is a city with an image problem. It boasts a billion-dollar downtown development, two ultra-modern motor-manufacturing plants, some excellent museums and one of the nation's biggest art galleries. But media attention dwells instead on its huge tracts of urban wasteland, and the gun-blasted neighborhoods where the only signs of commerce are heavily fortified loan shops and food stores. Despite the fact that cities like Atlanta, Newark and Washington DC regularly post much worse crime statistics, the press still seems intent on painting Detroit as the American Beirut.

Such views incur the wrath of Coleman Young, the city's mayor for twenty years up to 1993, who claims that the press magnifies his city's problems for the simple reason that blacks run Detroit and account for 75 percent of its population. That assertion certainly carries weight, but Detroit – which has lost nearly half its citizens, almost a million people, in less than forty years – has by any standards suffered.

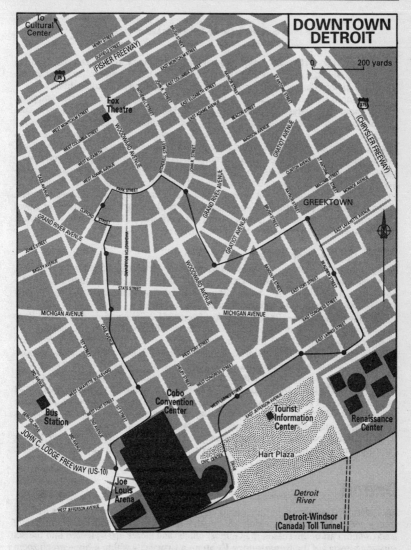

DOWNTOWN DETROIT

To Cultural Center

0   200 yards

HENRY STREET

CUSTER ROAD

(FISHER FREEWAY)

Fox Theatre

EAST MONTCALM STREET

EAST COLUMBIA STREET

EAST ELIZABETH AVENUE

EAST ADAMS AVENUE

BEACON STREET

MADISON AVENUE

(CHRYSLER FREEWAY)

WEST MONTCALM STREET

WEST COLUMBIA STREET

WEST ELIZABETH

WEST ADAMS AVENUE

WOODWARD AVENUE

WITHERELL STREET

JOHN R STREET

GRAND RIVER AVENUE

GRATIOT AVENUE

CLINTON AVENUE

MACOMB STREET

MONROE AVENUE

CASS AVENUE

PARK STREET

CLIFFORD STREET

GREEKTOWN

GRAND RIVER AVENUE

JAMES STREET

BAGLEY AVENUE

STATE STREET

WASHINGTON BOULEVARD

WOODWARD AVENUE

RANDOLPH STREET

EAST LAFAYETTE AVENUE

MICHIGAN AVENUE

MICHIGAN AVENUE

EAST FORT STREET

EAST CONGRESS STREET

CASS AVENUE

FIRST STREET

EAST FORT STREET

SHELBY STREET

WEST CONGRESS STREET

EAST LARNED STREET

EAST JEFFERSON AVENUE

WEST LARNED STREET

Cobo Convention Center

Tourist Information Center

Renaissance Center

Bus Station

SECOND AVENUE

WEST LAFAYETTE BOULEVARD

WEST FORT STREET

THIRD AVENUE

JOHN C. LODGE FREEWAY (US-10)

FIRST STREET

Hart Plaza

CIVIC CENTER DRIVE

Joe Louis Arena

Detroit River

WEST JEFFERSON AVENUE

Detroit-Windsor (Canada) Toll Tunnel

Founded in 1701 by Antoine de Mothe **Cadillac**, as a trading post for the French to do business with the Chippewa, Detroit was no more than a medium-sized port two hundred years later. Then **Ford**, **Olds**, the **Chevrolets** and the **Dodge** brothers began to build their automobile empires. Thanks to the introduction of the mass assembly line, Detroit sped into full gear in the Twenties, expanding into the countryside and booming like a mining town – fast, compulsive and indifferent to the needs of its population. The auto barons sponsored the construction of segregated neighborhoods and unceremoniously dispensed with workers during times of low demand. Such policies created huge ghettos, and the city came to the boil in July 1967 in the bloodiest **riot** in the USA for fifty

The **area code** for Detroit, Ann Arbor and Flint is ☎313.

years. More than forty people died and over 1300 buildings were destroyed. Nothing was solved, and little even improved; the inner city was left to fend for itself, and the all-important motor industry was rocked by the oil crises and Japanese competition.

No visitor to Detroit could fail to be disturbed by the divisions between rich and poor. The fact that other industrial towns have been hit equally hard by the recession is little consolation, and General Motors' seemingly endless announcements of lay-offs do not exactly bode well for the future. However, while heavily scarred and bruised, Detroit is not the apocalyptic mess some would have it. New businesses are appearing downtown, and suburban residents have started to return to its festivals, theaters, clubs and restaurants; but it makes more sense to think of Detroit as a region rather than a European-style city, and so long as you plan your time and don't mind driving, it holds an awful lot to see and do. **Downtown** is not so much the heart of the giant as just another segment, along with the huge **Cultural Center**, attractive pockets such as freewheeling **Royal Oak**, posh **Birmingham** and the Ford-town of **Dearborn**, and even nearby towns such as **Windsor, Ontario** and Ann Arbor, a short drive west.

Arrival, City Transport and Information

Most **flights** still come into **Detroit Metropolitan Airport** in Romulus (☎942-3550), thirty minutes' drive from downtown and a hefty $30-plus taxi ride, though *CTC* (☎946-1000) runs a shuttle for $12. Some airlines use the expanding **Detroit City Airport** (☎267-6400), five miles out and less than half the cab fare.

The main *Greyhound* – 1000 W Lafayette Ave (☎961-2535) – and *Amtrak* – 2601 Rose St – terminals are not in areas where it's safe to walk around at night. *Amtrak* also stops ten miles out at 16121 Michigan Ave, Dearborn, near the Henry Ford Museum and several mid-range motels. The high-tech *People Mover* elevated railway loops around thirteen downtown stations, all adorned with interesting art (Mon–Thurs 7am–11pm, Fri & Sat 7am–midnight, Sun noon–8pm; 50¢). Otherwise, public transit is inadequate. Heavily fortified *DOT* buses (☎933-1300) run a patchy inner-city service for $1 per ride, while the slightly better *SMART* buses (☎962-5515) serve suburbia. Transport in the Motor City is geared firmly toward the car; driving in Detroit is not too much of a challenge for outsiders, but you do need to know where you're heading.

At the time of writing, Detroit's **visitor center** was closed, pending a move to new premises; for city information, call ☎1-800/DET-ROIT. The main **post office** (Mon–Fri 8.30am–5pm, Sat 8am–noon; zip code 48200) is at 1401 W Fort St, at Eighth St.

Downtown

Futuristic glass-box office blocks and a tastefully revamped park overlook the deodor-ant-green **Detroit River**, but for the most part downtown can seem a rather sad and empty place. Even in the middle of the day its streets are remarkably quiet and uncrowded. Part of the reason is that most offices and stores are squeezed into the six gleaming towers of the **Renaissance Center** – a virtual city within a city – which zoom up 73 storeys from the riverbank (and offer a great view of the metropolis from an observation deck; daily, $3). This giant business, convention and retail center, known locally as the RenCen, was one of many complexes developed by **Detroit Renaissance** (a joint public/private sector project) to rejuvenate downtown in the aftermath of the 1967 riots. Seen by some as the savior of the city, the consortium is viewed less favorably by those whose small businesses and homes were compulsorily purchased to make way for its multimillion-dollar projects. Outside another massive chunk of steel and concrete, the Rubik-Cube-style **Cobo Convention Center**, stands a powerful-looking bronze statue of home-grown boxer **Joe Louis**. The Brown Bomber's wins, especially

THE MOTOWN SOUND

Mo.town (*mo'toun'*) adj [< a trademark for phonograph records, etc. <Mo(tor) Town, nickname for Detroit, Mich] designating or of style of rhythm and blues characterized by a strong, even beat.
Webster's New World Dictionary of the American Language

The legend that is Tamla Motown started in 1959 when Ford worker and part-time songwriter **Berry Gordy Jr** borrowed $800 to set up a studio. From his first hit onwards – the prophetic *Money (That's What I Want)* – he set out to create a crossover style, targeting his records at white and black consumers alike.

Early Motown hits were pure **formula**. Gordy softened the bluenotes of most contemporary black music, in favor of a more danceable, poppy beat, with **gospel**-influenced singing and clapping. Prime examples of the early approach featured all-female groups like the **Marvelettes** (*Needle in a Haystack*), the **Supremes** (*Baby Love*) and **Martha Reeves and the Vandellas** (*Nowhere to Run*), as well as the all-male **Miracles** (*Tracks Of My Tears*) featuring the sophisticated love lyrics of lead singer **Smokey Robinson**. Gordy's "Quality Control Department" scrutinized every beat, playing all recordings through speakers modelled on cheap transistor radios before the final mix.

The Motown organization was an intense, close-knit community: **Marvin Gaye** married Gordy's sister, "Little" **Stevie Wonder** was the child of the family. It did, however, move with the times, utilizing such innovations as the wah-wah pedal and synthesizer. By the late Sixties its output had acquired a harder sound, crowned by the acid soul productions of Norman Whitfield with the versatile **Temptations**. In 1968 the organization outgrew its premises on Grand Avenue; four years later it abandoned Detroit altogether for LA, to be closer to Hollywood. Befitting the MOR tastes of the Seventies, the top sellers now were the high-society soul of **Diana Ross** and the ballads of the **Commodores**. White artists began to appear on the label: Tom Jones is said to have turned down a contract, though R Dean Taylor (*Indiana Wants Me*) and the less successful Kiki Dee accepted.

The Seventies saw many top artists, dissatisfied with Gordy's constant intervention, leave the label. The crack songwriting team of Holland-Dozier-Holland, responsible for most of the **Four Tops**' hits, stayed in Detroit to produce the seminal **Chairmen of the Board** (*Gimme Just A Little More Time*), along with Aretha Franklin and Jackie Wilson.

over Italian fascist Primo Carnera for the World Heavyweight Championship in 1935, were greeted by a carnival atmosphere in the black neighborhood of Paradise Valley.

Rare green space comes among the fountains and sculptures of **Hart Plaza**, which rolls down to the river in the shade of the RenCen. It hosts free lunchtime concerts, as well as a succession of lively ethnic festivals on summer weekends. The US leg of the annual **Montreux–Detroit Jazz Festival** takes place here in early September.

Three miles further east (take *DOT* bus #25 and transfer to #4 at MacArthur Bridge), **Belle Isle** public park is a quiet inner-city island retreat with twenty miles of walkways, sports facilities, and free attractions including an aquarium, a Great Lakes Museum and elaborate gardens. It's also home to the annual **Detroit Grand Prix** for Indy cars.

The Cultural Center

Three miles northwest of downtown, next to Wayne State University, the top-class museums of the **Detroit Cultural Center** all lie within easy walking distance of each other. It's easy to spend half a day in the center, but due to stringent budgetary restrictions, you should phone for current opening times.

One hundred galleries in the colossal **Detroit Institute of Art**, 5200 Woodward Ave, trace a history of civilization, most notably Chinese, Persian, Egyptian, Greek, Roman, Italian, Dutch and American (Wed–Sun 11am–4pm; mandatory donation). No less than 93 Rembrandts, 77 Matisses and 67 Picassos are on display, as are masterpieces such as a Van Gogh self-portrait and Joos Van Cleeve's *Adoration of the Magi;* but Diego Rivera's enormous 1932 mural *Detroit Industry* steals the show. At present one wing is open in the morning and the other in the afternoon, so time your visit carefully.

The main display in the well laid-out **Museum of African-American History**, 301 Frederick Douglass St, looks at Michigan's role in the Underground Railway, smuggling slaves from the south to Canada (Wed–Sat 9.30am–5pm, Sun 1–5pm; donation). While recognizing the achievements of the city's African-Americans, the museum doesn't ignore the social and employment problems faced by young people in Detroit today. Also in the Cultural Center, the **Detroit Historical Museum**, 5401 Woodward Ave, interprets the city's past through the Streets of Old Detroit display (Wed–Fri 9.30am–4pm, Sat & Sun 10am–5pm; donation).

The Motown Museum

2648 W Grand Blvd. Tues–Sat 10am–5pm, Sun 2–5pm. $4.

Unlike cities such as Memphis, Nashville and New Orleans, Detroit is devoid of the bars, clubs and homes of its musical heroes. The golden age of Motown was very much confined to a time and a place, and, disappointingly, only at the **Motown Museum** can Tamla fans now pay homage to the world's most celebrated record label. The museum is housed in the small white and blue clapboard house that served as Motown's recording studio from 1959 to 1972. On the ground floor, Studio A remains just as it was left: battered instruments stand piled up against the nicotine-stained acoustic wall-tiles, and a well-scuffed Steinway piano all but fills the room. Upstairs, record sleeves, gold and platinum discs, sheet music and photos are diplayed almost at random on the walls and tables. Michael Jackson gets a small room to himself as a thank you for his $125,000 donation. The absence of sophisticated display is more than made up for by the enthusiastic and knowledgeable staff, who will quite happily give one person the full tour.

The **American Black Artist Museum** across the street covers all artistic disciplines and has exhibits on black historical figures (tours by arrangement; ☎872-0332).

Henry Ford Museum and Greenfield Village

20900 Oakwood Blvd, Dearborn. 10 miles from downtown, on *SMART* bus routes #200 and #250. Daily 9am–5pm; the interiors of Greenfield Village buildings are closed Jan to mid-March. $12.50 for each attraction or $22 for a two-day combination ticket. ☎271-1620.

The enormous **Henry Ford Museum** pays fulsome tribute to its founder as a brilliant industrialist and do-gooder. The former is certainly true. The hero of the "second industrial revolution" and inventor of the assembly line didn't succeed by being a philanthropist. His Service Department of 3500 private policemen prompted the *New York Times* in 1928 to call him "an industrialist fascist – the Mussolini of Detroit". To Ford, unions were "the worst things that ever struck the earth", though he was forced to let the UAW into his factories in 1943 after only 34 out of 78,000 workers voted against joining a union. Ford also bowed to the economic necessity of employing blacks, though he banned them from the model communities he built for his white workers. Instead, the company constructed a separate town, which he sardonically named Inkster.

Besides the massive "**Automobile in American Life**" exhibit, the twelve-acre museum amounts to a giant curiosity shop, holding several planes and trains, rows and rows of domestic inventions, and cabinets full of schoolchild collectables like dime novels, comics and baseball cards. Real oddities include the chair Lincoln was sitting in and the car Kennedy was riding in when each was shot, and even a test tube holding Edison's last breath. One pertinent item not on view, however, is the Iron Cross which Hitler presented to Ford (a notorious anti-Semite) in 1938.

Ford uprooted the houses of famous Americans from all over the country to relocate them in **Greenfield Village**. Among the 240 buildings, you'll find Ford's own birthplace, the Wright Brothers' cycle shop, Edison's laboratory, and Firestone's farm. Costumed staff demonstrate everything from weaving to puncture repairing.

Windsor, Ontario

The riverside cafés of the easy-going Canadian city of **WINDSOR**, due south of Detroit across the river, offer surprisingly pleasant views of their larger neighbor's skyline. Like Detroit, Windsor's main industry is auto-manufacturing, but it's much smaller and more relaxed, and makes a good place simply to hang out. The most interesting attraction in the town is booze-oriented: the **Hiram Walker plant**, where *Canadian Club* is distilled, stands just a short stroll from downtown at Riverside and Walker (free tours and samplings, Tues & Thurs at 2pm, check times on ☎254-5171).

Windsor Charter **buses** (☎519/444-4111) connect downtown Detroit and downtown Windsor for $1.50 each way. Be sure to bring the proper identification for customs and immigration officials. To drive, take the tunnel and pay the $2 toll. The **visitor center** (☎519/973-1338) is across from the bus station at 80 Chatham St.

Accommodation

Downtown Detroit caters well for expense-account travellers – its top-range hotels are as safe as any city's – but if your budget's restricted it's harder to find lodging that's both safe and cheap. A twelve percent tax comes slapped onto room bills; if exchange rates are favorable it may be worth considering staying in Windsor, Ontario.

The Atheneum, 1000 Brush Ave (☎962-2323 or ☎1-800/772-2323). Swish, new, all-suite hotel in Greektown. Some units fetch over $300 a night; others are around a third of that price. ⑥.

Country Grandma's AYH Home Hostel, 22330 Bell Rd, New Boston, MI (☎753-4901). On the outskirts of Dearborn. $9 members; $12 non-members. ①.

Fairfield Inn, 31119 Flynn Drive (☎728-2322). The best of the budget motels near the airport. ③.

Fairfield Inn – Auburn Hills, 1294 Opdyke Rd (373-2228). Clean new motel on the north edge of the metro area, close to Pontiac Silverdome. ②.

Hyatt Regency Dearborn, Fairlane Town Center, Dearborn (☎593-1234 or ☎1-800/233-1234). Candy-brown colossus with every imaginable amenity. Not cheap, but lots of specials. ⑦.

Park Avenue House, 2305 Park Ave (☎961-8310). $12 dorms (*AYH* only) in theater district. ①.

Ramada Inn – Downtown, 400 Bagley Ave (☎962-2300). Relatively inexpensive for downtown. ⑤.

Royal Windsor Hotel, 675 Goyeau St, Windsor, Ontario (☎519/253-4411). Best-value mid-priced lodgings in Windsor, still close to downtown Detroit. The nearby *Ramada* is also reasonable. ③.

Sagamore Motor Lodge, 3220 N Woodward Ave (☎549-1600). Have a look at the room first; if it's all right, then you've got a bargain, close to trendy Royal Oak. ②.

Shorecrest Motor Inn, 1316 E Jefferson Ave (☎568-3000 or ☎1-800/992-9616). Clean good-value rooms, despite exterior. Friendly family-run place in lively Rivertown, just off downtown. ④.

Teahouse of the Golden Dragon Hostel, 8585 Harding Ave, Centerline, MI (☎756-2676). Friendly home hostel in a safe district some ten miles from downtown. $6 dorms. ①.

Travelodge Dearborn, 23730 Michigan Ave (☎565-7250). Handy for *Amtrak* and Dearborn. ③.

Eating

Detroit's **ethnic** restaurants dish up the best (and some of the least expensive) food in the city. **Greektown**, just one block of Monroe Avenue between Beaubien and St Antoine streets, is crammed with authentic Greek places, and also contains *Trappers Alley*, a small mall brimming with good stalls and shops. Less commercial, but offering just as high a standard, are the bakeries, bars and cantinas of **Mexican Town**, five minutes from downtown. Suburban **Royal Oak**, ten miles north, has a wide range of vaguely alternative wholefood places, along with its bars, record and bookstores.

Elwood Grill, 2100 Woodward Ave (☎961-7485). Wonderful Art Deco building near to the Fox Theater. Gourmet burgers, sandwiches and entrees from $8 to $15.

El Zocala, 3400 Bagley Ave at 23rd St, Mexican Town (☎841-3700). It's touch and go as to whether this Mexican restaurant, revered for its margaritas and botanas (chips smothered in refried beans), or *Xochimilco's*, a couple of doors away, is the best Mex in Michigan. Try both. Most entrees $5–7.

Fishbone's Rhythm Kitchen Café, 400 Monroe St, Greektown (☎965-4600). Noisy, fun, and often packed-out Cajun joint.

La-Shish, 12918 Michigan Ave, Dearborn (☎584-4477). Brilliant juice bar, good Lebanese dishes.

New Parthenon, 579 Monroe Ave, Greektown (☎961-5111). Expensive-looking, with its pillars and Hellenic murals, but very reasonable prices for great salads, seafood and vegetarian cooking.

Old Fish Market, 156 Chatham St West, Windsor, Ontario (☎253-7417). Good and very reasonably priced seafood.

Original Pancake House, 1360 S Woodward Ave, Birmingham (☎642-5775). Uninspired decor, but superb crepes, waffles, omelettes and pancakes. Huge variety and a top choice for breakfast.

Rattlesnake Club, 300 River Place, Rivertown (☎567-4400). Owned by creative Detroit masterchef, Jimmy Schmidt, with a setting to match the exquisite food. Dinner will set you back $15–25 per entree; lunch costs less.

Old Woodward Bar & Grill, 555 Woodward Ave, Birmingham (☎642-9400). A possible first in Michigan – a smoke-free sports bar. Good food too.

Woodbridge Tavern, 289 St Aubin St, Rivertown (☎259-0578). Excellent burgers and sandwiches, with Twenties decor and a great outdoor terrace. Also live rock music Thurs–Sun.

Nightlife

There's lots to do late at night in Detroit – the city where the techno-house beat originated and is still going strong – though if you're unfamiliar with the layout it's best to travel by taxi. In the past few years young whites from the suburbs have started to come back downtown for nights out, particularly to the bars and clubs of the **Theater District**. The area centers around the glorious **Fox Theater**, 2111 Woodward Ave (☎567-6000), a huge old movie palace that's the city's top concert and drama venue. **Rivertown**, a mile from the RenCen, is renowned for its chic bistros and funky jazz and blues bars, tucked in among rambling warehouses. Canadian **Windsor** also has some good nightlife, with an age limit of 19 as opposed to Michigan's 21.

For details of events in Detroit, Ann Arbor and Windsor, pick up the free weekly *Metro Times*, and listen to the Midwest's best up-to-the-minute rock station, *89X FM*.

California's, 911 Walker Rd, Windsor, Ontario (☎519-258-1152). Inexpensive indie-band gigs (*89X* has free giveaways) in a cool bar. When the music palls, there's beach volleyball in summer.

Franklin Street Brewing Co, 1560 Franklin St, Rivertown (☎568-0390). Industrial interior and micro-brewed ales.

Industry, 15 S Saginaw St, Pontiac (☎334-1999). Girders, galvanized tables and post-industrial props blend with the Moorish moldings of the old *Eagle Theatre*, but you'll probably be too busy dancing to the best house, industrial and alternative sounds to notice. Well worth the trip out.

Metropolitan Musicafe, 326 W Fourth St, Royal Oak (☎542-1990). A bit like a *Hard Rock Café*, but with live music and without the corporate nonsense and horrible T-shirts.

Rhinoceros, 265 Riopelle St, Rivertown (☎259-2208). Poppy jazz hangout. A tight squeeze but fun.

Saint Andrew's Hall, 431 E Congress St (☎961-MELT). Cramped cavernous downtown club promoting unknown bands and top new acts. Only holds 800, so get a ticket in time, and keep the stub for free admission to the *Shelter* dance club afterwards.

Soup Kitchen Saloon, 1585 Franklin St, Rivertown (☎259-2643). Detroit's premier venue for gutsy low-down blues. A great old bar but the capacity of just 130 makes it sweaty, smoky and squashed.

Sport

Detroit teams may not pick up the major prizes too often, but it's one of the few cities with franchises competing at the highest level in all four major team sports. Baseball's Tigers (☎963-9944), featuring big-hitting Cecil Fielder, play at the venerable Tiger Stadium, near downtown at Michigan and Trumbell, though they plan on having a new home by 1995. The Redwings hockey outfit entertain at the Joe Louis Arena (☎567-6000), though both basketball's Pistons (☎377-8600) and the footballing Lions (☎335-4151) are based 25 miles north in the Pontiac/Auburn Hills district.

The Lions play in the **Pontiac Silverdome**, the venue in 1993 of the first ever indoor international soccer match, and of four World Cup games in 1994. Its great views and top-class organization have put Detroit on the map as a major sporting city.

Out from Detroit: Ann Arbor and Flint

Two interesting but very different cities are both within an hour or so of Detroit. While the highlight of the Motown hinterland is undoubtably studenty **Ann Arbor**, economically ravaged **Flint**, the home of General Motors, possesses enough interest to take care of a day.

Ann Arbor

Although its population just tops 100,000, **ANN ARBOR**, 45 minutes' drive west of Detroit along I-94, offers a greater choice of restaurants, live music venues and cultural activities than most conurbations ten times its size. The **University of Michigan** has shaped the economy and character of the town ever since it was moved here from Detroit in 1837, providing the city with a very conspicuous radical edge.

Much the best thing to do in Ann Arbor is to stroll round downtown and the campus which meet at S State and Liberty. Downtown's twelve blocks of brightly painted shops and sidewalk cafés offer all you would expect from a college town, with over forty book-shops and more than a dozen record stores. Don't miss *Border's Books*, 303 S State St (☎668-7652), nor *Schoolkid's Records*, 523 E Liberty St (☎994-8031).

Though the huge U of M campus doesn't look particularly appealing, it does emanate a sense of excitement. Worth a look are the **Ruthven Exhibit Museum**, 1109 Geddes Ave, packed with huge dinosaur skeletons, rare Indian artefacts and a planetar-ium (Tues–Sat 9am–5pm, Sun 1–5pm), and the small but eclectic **Museum of Art**, 525 S State St (Tues–Sat 10am–4pm, Sun 1–5pm).

Practicalities

Frequent *Greyhound* services to both Detroit ($11) and Chicago stop at 116 W Huron St (☎662-5511); *Amtrak* is on the north edge of downtown at 325 Depot St. The **visitor center** is at 211 E Huron St (☎995-7281).

Although most Ann Arbor **motels** target their rates at conventioneers and academ-ics, there's a *HoJo Motel* about a mile from campus on Stadium Blvd (☎971-8000; ③). Both *Super 8* (☎1-800/800-8000; ④) and the *Fairfield Inn* (☎995-5200; ④) are at the junction of I-94 and State Street. The modern downtown *YMCA*, 350 S Fifth Ave (☎663-0536; ①), open to both sexes, has single rooms with shared baths for around $30. The University of Michigan (☎763-5750) also rents rooms at its Residence Hall (②) in the suburbs, and at the downtown *Cambridge House*, 541 Thompson St (④). The nearest campground is ten miles east, at the KOA, 6680 Bunton Rd, Ypsilanti.

Restaurants worth trying include the good-value Indian *Raja Rani*, 400 S Division St (☎995-1545), and the wholefood *Seva*, 314 E Liberty Ave (☎662-1111). *Jerusalem Garden*, 307 S Fifth St (☎995-5060), serves the best falafel in town, while *Zingerman's*, 422 Detroit St (☎663-DELI), is an excellent if expensive deli.

Ann Arbor's **live music** scene has enjoyed a nationwide reputation ever since the Stooges, MC5 and Bob Seger made their names here; and, unlike many college towns, the whole place doesn't go to sleep during the summer. For news of gigs, grab a copy of *Current*, a free monthly, or tune into the eclectic student/community (ie ex-student) station *WCBN* 88.3FM. Likely venues include the jazzy *Bird of Paradise*, 207 S Ashley Ave (☎662-8310), and the often-crowded *Del Rio*, 122 W Washington Ave (☎761-2530), which serves good Mexican food and hosts free Sunday jazz sessions. The *Blind Pig*, 208 S First St (☎996-8555), *Rick's American Café*, 611 Church St (☎996-2747) and the *Students' Union*, 530 S State St (☎763-2236), all put on regular rock, blues and indie gigs. If all you want is a cool beer try the *Full Moon*, 201 S Main St (☎665-8484); it has over one hundred to choose from.

Flint

Despite being the birthplace and cradle of General Motors, little attention was paid to **FLINT** before Michael Moore's sassy documentary *Roger and Me* hit the big screen in 1989. As one would expect with any town reeling from the recent loss of 30,000 jobs, Flint, two hours north of downtown Detroit, sports a few bruises, but it still holds enough auto-industry bequeathments – along with attractive cobbled downtown streets and a youthful air supplied by a university campus – to make a visit worthwhile.

Thanks to a sizeable wagon-making industry, Flint was already calling itself "Vehicle City", by 1903. Then Billy Durant, a local wagonmaker and entrepreneur, bought David Buick's fledgling motor company and started to produce "horseless carriages". Within a few years, he had also acquired Oldsmobile, Cadillac, Pontiac and AC Spark Plugs, and formed a conglomerate he named General Motors (GM). In 1910 Durant lost control of GM and became chairman of tiny Chevrolet Motors, which sensationally bought control of the General Motors stable just five years later. Durant was again forced out of GM in 1920 and set his sights a mite lower by purchasing a bowling alley and drive-in restaurant in Flint; he died, supposedly penniless, in 1947. The alley and café may have long since disappeared but Flint still has **Buick City**, a gigantic futuristic manufacturing plant on the site of Durant and Buick's original workshop at 902 E Hamilton Ave (free tours; reserve on ☎236-4494). In contrast, the great white elephant of **Autoworld**, the $100 million auto industry theme park which the town felt would make it a top travel destination, has long since closed and stands like a sad giant on the edge of downtown.

A less glamorous view of Flint's industrial heritage is presented by the small but excellent **Labor Museum of Michigan**, 711 N Saginaw St (Tues–Fri 10am–5pm, Sat & Sun noon–5pm; $2). It pays particular attention to the **Great Flint Sitdown Strike** of 1936, when workers downed tools and occupied the Fisher and Chevy plants for 44 days, despite attempts by the National Guard to force them out, before GM became the first major company to recognize the Union of Automobile Workers.

Practicalities

The **visitor center**, 400 S Saginaw St (☎313/232-8900 or ☎1-800/288-8040), gives out discount lodging coupons. Pick of the motels is the beautiful *Holiday Inn* at US-23 and Hill Rd (☎232-5300; ⑤), though the central *Hampton Inn* has a decent restaurant at 1150 Robert Longway Blvd (☎238-7744; ③). The *Econolodge* at I-69 exit 139 (☎744-0200; ②) has a pool and jacuzzi. Inexpensive downtown burgers can be had at *Torch Bar*, 522 Buckham Alley; the *White Horse Tavern*, 621 W Coutt St (☎234-3811), has decent pizza.

The Rest of the Lower Peninsula

Though **St Joseph** is just the first of many small ports on the 350-mile trip north along Lake Michigan's eastern shore, the northwestern reaches of the peninsula are what attract sportspeople and tourists from all over the Midwest. Within striking distance of **Traverse City** are the beautiful **Sleeping Bear Dunes** and the charming towns of **Charlevoix** and **Petoskey**. At the northern tip, messy **Mackinaw City** is the departure point for the state's major tour-bus attraction, old-world **Mackinac Island**.

Southwestern Michigan

Under thirty miles north of Indiana, **ST JOSEPH** marks the start of "Harbor Country" – a string of small towns offering good swimming, boating and fishing opportunities. St Joseph's neat downtown perches on a high bluff, from which steep steps lead down to sandy Silver Beach, where each of the two parallel piers has its own lighthouse. When not swimming, pass the time watching the yachts go by while eating great **food** at *Clementine's Too*, 1235 Broad St. **Places to stay** include the classy lakeside *Boulevard Suite Hotel*, 521 Lake Blvd (☎983-6600; ⑤), and the good-value *Best Western Golden Link*, two miles from downtown at 2723 Niles Ave (☎983-6321; ②), though there's a unique option in the bizarre shape of the Frank Lloyd Wright-inspired *Snow Flake Motel*, 3822 Red Arrow Hwy, off I-94 exit 23 (☎429-3261; ②). For general information on the area, call into the **visitor center** just off I-94 exit 29 (☎925-6301).

Fifty miles north, **HOLLAND** was settled in 1847 by Dutch religious dissidents. Today's residents lose no opportunity to let visitors know of their roots: tens of thousands of tulips brighten the town in early summer, while the Netherlands museum, a Dutch village, a clog factory and the inevitable windmill all attract tourist dollars.

A further twenty miles up the shoreline, **GRAND HAVEN** boasts one of the largest and best sandy beaches on the Great Lakes, seen on a leisurely stroll along the one-and-a-half-mile boardwalk (for the most part a concrete path). At the top of Dewey Hill stands a huge electronically controlled musical fountain. The *Fountain Inn*, 1010 S Beacon Blvd (☎846-1800; ③), provides reasonable accommodation.

Grand Haven is just under one hundred miles south of **LUDINGTON**, from where the **Lake Michigan Car Ferry** departs for Manitowoc, Wisconsin (☎845-5555 or ☎1-800/841-4243; $30 per adult, $40 per car).

The Leelanu Peninsula

The southwestern edge of the heavily wooded **Leelanu Peninsula**, beyond the small port of **Frankfort**, 61 miles north of Ludington, is taken up by the **Sleeping Bear Dunes National Lakeshore**, a constantly re-sculpted area of towering dunes and precipitous four hundred-foot drops. They were named by the Chippewa, who saw the mist-shrouded North and South Manitou islands as the graves of two drowned bear-cubs, and the massive mainland dune, covered with dark trees, as their grieving mother. Fierce winds off Lake Michigan cause the dunes to edge inland, burying trees that reappear years later stripped of foliage, while the continual attack of high water undercuts the massive sand banks, occasionally sending massive chunks into the lake. Stunning overlooks can be had along the hilly nine-mile loop of the **Pierce Stocking Scenic Drive**, off Hwy-109; you can also clamber up the strenuous but enjoyable **Dune Climb**, four miles further north on Hwy-109 (best done barefoot, as shoes soon fill with sand; take sunscreen and water). The **visitor center** (☎326-5134), at the junction of highways 22 and 109, provides details on trails, campgrounds, and beaches.

The best of the villages to base yourself at is **LELAND**, fifteen miles north. Its harbor, crammed with expensive launches, also shelters a quaint collection of well-weathered sheds, known as **Fishtown**, where the day's catch used to be hauled in for gutting and smoking; most are now touristy knick-knack shops. *The Cove* at 111 River St (☎256-9834) serves up tasty Great Lakes fish and is run by the same people as the weirside burger restaurant, *Rick's Place*, downstairs. **Ferries** from Leland (☎256-9061; $18 round-trip) go to the uninhabited North and South Manitou islands. **NORTHPORT**, on the tip of the peninsula, is another relaxing little fishing village.

Traverse City

Smooth beaches and striking bay views help make lively **TRAVERSE CITY**, 242 miles northwest of Detroit, the favorite in-state resort for Michiganers. A town of just 17,000 year-round residents, it was saved from the stagnation that overtook many north

The area code for southwestern Michigan and the Traverse City area is ☎616.

Michigan communities when their lumber mills closed down, as the stripped fields proved to be ideal for fruit-growing. Today, the area's claim to be "**Cherry Capital of the World**" is no idle boast: thousands of acres of cherry orchards envelop the town, their wispy, pink blossom bringing a delicate beauty each May. The annual **Cherry Festival** is held during the first full week in July. As well as parades, fireworks and concerts, there's a chance to sample every imaginable cherry product; Coca-Cola chose the event to launch its cherry flavor a few years ago.

The neat **downtown** rests along the bottom of the west arm of **Grand Traverse Bay**, below the Old Mission Peninsula. This slender seventeen-mile strip of land, which divides the bay into two inlets, makes for a pleasant short driving tour; narrow roads slice through miles of cherry orchards and vineyards, with tremendous simultaneous views of the bay on either side. Five sandy public beaches and a small harbor can be found around the town itself. Various companies offer boat, windsurfer, jet ski and mountain bike rental (the surrounding countryside is excellent for cycling).

Practicalities

Greyhound stops near downtown at 3233 Cass Rd (☎946-5180). The **visitor center**, at 415 Munson Ave (☎947-1120), can help with finding **accommodation**, though there's a dearth of budget lodging. Both the attractive little *Bay Shore Motel*, 833 E Front St (☎946-4798; ⑤), near downtown with a private beach, and the well-maintained *Days Inn*, 420 Munson Ave (☎941-0208; ⑤), have nice rooms, as does the recently renovated *Sierra Motel*, 230 Munson Ave (☎946-7720; ④). In summer, you can get a tidy room at North Michigan Community College East Hall, 1701 E Front St (☎922-1406; ②). There's **camping** at Traverse City State Park, just outside town at 1132 US-31N (☎947-7193).

Traverse City brochures might tout its exclusive country clubs, but more affordable **places to eat** are easy to find. *Mode's Bum Steer*, 125 E State St (☎947-9832), is the town's premier rib joint; *Don's Drive-In*, 2030 US-31N (☎938-1860), is a garish pink diner with magnificent burgers and shakes, a couple of miles south of downtown. The *U & I Lounge*, 214 E Front St (☎946-8932), has to be the best bar around; besides the drink it serves up gyros, burgers and salads. *Union Street Station*, 117 South Union St (☎941-1930), has **live music** of all sorts most nights. *Larry's Place* at the *Bay Winds*, 1265 US-31N (☎929-1044), is a hectic beach bar. It's popular with students and great fun – even if there is a limit to the number of Jimmy Buffet songs you can stomach in one night.

North of Traverse City

Scenic Hwy-31 skims along Lake Michigan and through **Charlevoix** and other pretty lakeside towns on its way north from Traverse City. The northern tip of the peninsula is sullied by **Mackinaw City**, a giant parking lot for the tour buses that bring excursionists to much-hyped **Mackinac Island** – roadside hoardings advertise its attractions for a good fifty miles before you arrive.

Charlevoix, Petoskey and Harbor Springs

CHARLEVOIX boasts a positively idyllic setting, fronting onto three separate lakes: Michigan, Charlevoix and the beautiful, bowl-shaped Round Lake. Petunia-lined **Bridge Street**, the two-block downtown, looks over a picturesque, almost landlocked **harbor** on Round Lake, hemmed in on other sides by terraced ridges. Various companies offer boat trips – call in at the **visitor center**, 408 Bridge St (☎547-2101), for details – and there are two sandy beaches on the Michigan shoreline.

Lakeside hotels can charge up to $500, though *Nanny's*, 219 Ferry Ave (☎547-2960; ③), usually has some inexpensive rooms, and beds at the home hostel at 541 N Mercer St (☎547-2937; ①) cost only $8 a night. *Parkside Dining*, 404 Bridge St (☎547-9111), is a reasonably priced family-style diner with a good view of the harbor.

In the bigger and busier **PETOSKEY**, 16 miles north along US-31, high above the stony-blue waters of Lake Michigan, grand old Victorian houses encircle the nicely restored Gaslight District downtown. Budget lodging is available year-round in the clean dorms at *North Central Michigan College*, 1505 Howard St (☎347-3973; ①), for just $10. For a good deli sandwich, try *Symon's General Store*, 401 E Lake St (☎347-2438). Another 12 miles on along Hwy-119, **HARBOR SPRINGS** is a favorite haunt of the midwestern elite. Its charming main street and small shaded beach with adjacent park are certainly captivating, but the sheer ostentation puts many off this "Cornbelt Riviera" resort. The comfy *Harbor Springs Cottage Inn*, at Bay and Zoll streets (☎526-5431; ④), has the only reasonably affordable rooms.

Mackinac Island

Viewed from an approaching boat, the tree-blanketed rocky limestone outcrop of **MACKINAC ISLAND** (pronounced *Mackinaw*), suddenly thrusting out from the swirling waters, is an unforgettable sight. As you near the harbor, large Victorian houses come into view, dappling the hillsides with white and pastel shades. The most conspicuous is the imposing facade of the $250-a-night *Grand Hotel*, where even to enter the foyer costs $5. On disembarking, your attention is grabbed by rows of horses and buggies (all motor vehicles are supposedly banned from the island, though some motorized horse trailers are tucked away out back) and the omnipresent smell of fresh manure. Also ubiquitous on the island is **fudge**, a Mackinac "delicacy" which tourists purchase by the boxload from Victorian-style shops.

Mackinac's crowded main street and the contrived nostalgia can get irritating, but the island is still worth visiting, not least for the ferry ride over and the chance to cycle along the hilly backroads. Underneath the tourist trimmings is a rich history. French priests established a mission to the Huron Indians here during the winter of 1670–71, and the French army built a fort in 1715 but lost control of the island to the British within fifty years. Since independence, Mackinac has been a base for John Jacob Astor's American Fur Company, a fishing port, and a jail for Confederate officers during the Civil War. The government acknowledged its beauty by designating it as the country's second National Park, two years after Yellowstone in 1875, though management was handed over to the state of Michigan twenty years later. To get a feel for the history, hike or cycle up to the whitewashed stone **Fort Mackinac**, a US Army outpost until 1890. Its ramparts afford a great view of the village and lake below, though admission is a steep $6.

From **MACKINAW CITY**, a parasitic colony of motels, fudge and T-shirt emporia, forty miles north of Petoskey, *Shepler's* operates a smooth, reliable ferry service to the island ($13 return, $5 for bikes; ☎616/436-5023). Though the average room costs in excess of $130 per night – the least costly hotel is *Murray's* (☎847-3361; ④) – unpretentious B&Bs such as the *Bogan Lane Inn* (☎847-3439; ③) and the secluded *Small Point* (☎847-3758; ③) are more affordable. The **information kiosk** on Main Street (☎847-3783) provides full details of accommodation, horse rides and bike rental.

The Upper Peninsula

From the map, it would seem logical for Michigan's **Upper Peninsula**, separated from the rest of the state by the **Mackinac Straits**, to be part of Wisconsin. However, when Michigan entered the Union in 1837 (eleven years before Wisconsin), its legislators, keen to tap its huge mineral wealth, incorporated it into their new state.

The **area code** for Mackinac Island and the Upper Peninsula is ☎906.

Before then the UP, as it's commonly known, figured prominently in French plans to create an empire in North America. Missionaries such as Father Jacques Marquette made peace with the Indians and established settlements like the port of Sault Ste Marie in 1688. The French hoped to press further south, but before they could get much past Detroit, the British inflicted a severe military defeat in 1763.

Vast, lonesome and wild, the Upper Peninsula has lots of stunning landmarks, exemplified by the **Pictured Rocks National Lakeshore**, but few towns of interest. Most of the eastern section is marked by low-lying, sometimes swampy land in between softly undulating limestone hills. The northwest corner is the most desolate, especially the rough and broken **Keewanaw Peninsula**, and **Isle Royale National Park** fifty miles offshore. Until 1957 you could only get to the UP from lower Michigan by ferry. Today, the five-mile **Mackinaw Bridge** ($1.50 toll) stretches elegantly across the bottleneck Straits of Mackinac, with lakes Superior and Huron to either side. At night its glistening multicolored lights sparkle in the dark northern sky and are reflected in the black waters of the straits.

Sault Ste Marie

Perched at the northeast corner of the UP, 340 miles from Detroit, **SAULT STE MARIE** (known locally as *The Soo*) lies across St Mary's Rapids from the Canadian town bearing the same name. It's one of the oldest settlements in the US, not that you'd guess that from its bedraggled Fifties-looking downtown and the industrial sprawl of the waterfront. The Soo owes most of its trade and industry to the St Mary's Locks, the only water connection between Superior and the other Great Lakes, built in 1855 and later expanded to take oceangoing vessels. Four giant reservoirs raise upbound boats 21 feet to the level of Lake Superior. To see this impressive operation, which accounts for more tonnage than the Suez and Panama canals combined, take one of the Soo Locks Boat Tours ($12; ☎632-3311) from Dock #1 or Dock #2 on East Portage Ave, or watch for free from the visitor center (daily 7am–11pm).

Despite efforts to increase its tourist trade, the Soo is not a place where you'd want to spend much time, though the *Crestview Thrifty Inn*, 1200 Ashmun St (☎635-5213; ③), has clean, comfortable rooms.

Paradise

Native Americans who lived in the area around **PARADISE**, sixty miles west and north of the Soo, called it Tahquamenon (Marsh of the Blueberries). If you get here on a good summer day, the current name of this elongated lakeside village, cut out of thick dark green forests and surrounded by small, reed-cluttered ultramarine lakes, doesn't seem too far amiss. Life is slow and easy here, but the choppy waters of Superior deny absolute calm to the beach. In winter temperatures drop to -40°F and snowmobiles are the usual mode of transport. Ten miles west on Hwy-123, a popular spot for hiking, boating and camping is the **Tahquamenon Falls State Park** (daily; $3 per car), where waters, colored a translucent brown by tannic acid, spill over two sets of cataracts.

Whitefish Road winds nine miles north of town to where the shingly **Whitefish Point** nudges into the harsh waters of Lake Superior. Raging northwesterly winds building up over two hundred miles of open lake have contributed to over five hundred shipwrecks along the eighty-mile stretch of lakeshore to Munising, a story told by the **Great Lakes Shipwreck Historical Museum**, gloomily lit with doom-laden background music. It's not all ancient history; the cargo ship *Edmund Fitzgerald* foundered in 96mph gusts on November 10 1975, with the loss of its 29 crew (June to mid-Oct daily 10am–6pm; $3).

Paradise has basic but clean **accommodation** at the *Vagabond Motel* (☎492-3477; ②); *Curley's Motel* (☎492-3445; ③), at the road junction, is a definite step up with a nice beach, sports facilities and the *Yukon Bar*, full of stuffed trophies, across the road. Six-person cabins cost well under $100. You can pitch a tent at the *Superior Campground* (☎492-3249), one mile south of town near the *Birch Hill Café*, popular for its whitefish.

Pictured Rocks National Lakeshore

The 42 miles between the attractive fishing villages of **Grand Marais** and **Munising** form the **Pictured Rocks National Lakeshore**, a splendid array of multicolored cliffs, rolling dunes and secluded sandy beaches. Rain, wind, ice and sun have carved and gouged arches, columns and caves into the face of the lakeshore, all stained different hues. An unpaved road and hiking trails run beside the water, but the best way to see the cliffs is by **boat**. Three-hour narrated cruises leave from the left of the City Pier in Munising (July & Aug 5 trips daily; June, Sept & early Oct, 2 trips daily; $10; ☎387-2379). *Scotty's Motel*, 415 Cedar St in Munising (☎387-2449; ②), is a comfortable enough place to stay.

The Keewanaw Peninsula

The hundred or so miles beyond Munising become progressively more rough-hewn, culminating in the **Keewanaw Peninsula**, jutting like a dorsal fin eighty miles out into Lake Superior. Encircled by a dramatic shoreline and potted with crags and precipices, it's a great place for a short driving tour, with roads winding through forests, past old copper workings and up and down steep hills.

Halfway up the peninsula in the small college town of **Houghton**, the *Gateway Motel* on US-41 near the ferry dock (☎482-3511; ③) is good value. The *Suomi Home Bakery and Restaurant* (☎482-3220), under the covered street downtown, serves cheap pasties and Finnish food. At the northern tip of Keewanaw, best reached along Hwy-26 (The Brockway Mountain Drive) from Eagle River, handsome little **Copper Harbor** was once so rich in minerals that early miners could pick up chunks of pure copper from the lakeshore. Today you can go on an underground tour at the **Delaware Mine** (☎289-4688), ten miles west on Hwy-41. Budget accommodation is available at the *Norland Motel* (☎289-4815; ②), two miles east on US-41 next to Wilkins State Park.

Isle Royale National Park

Much closer to Canada than the US, the 45-mile sliver of **ISLE ROYALE NATIONAL PARK**, fifty miles out in Lake Superior, is in a double sense as far as you can get in Michigan from Detroit: all cars are banned and, instead of freeways, 166 miles of hiking trails lead past windswept trees and swampy lakes where moose graze. The park is usually open from mid-May to the end of September. Besides other outdoor types the only traces of human life you're likely to see are ancient mineworks – thought to be two millenia old – shacks left behind by commercial fishermen in the Forties, a few lighthouses and some park buildings. Trekking, canoeing, fishing and scuba-diving among shipwrecks are the principal leisure activities. Camping is free, but visit the park headquarters at 87 N Ripley St (☎482-0984) in Houghton before you leave the mainland, for advice on water purity, mosquitoes, and temperatures that can drop well below freezing even in summer. You can also stay at a self-catering cottage or lodge room at the *Rock Harbor Lodge*, PO Box 405, Houghton, MI 49931 (☎337-4993, Oct–April ☎502/773-2191; ⑤), where they rent motor boats and canoes for $20 a day and offer cruises for $10.

Ferries leave from Copper Harbor ($35 one-way; ☎289-4437), Houghton ($45 one-way; ☎482-0984) and Grand Portage, Minnesota ($42 one-way; 715-392-5551). If there are enough in your party, it may be just as economical to charter a **plane** from *Isle Royale Seaplane Service* (☎482-8850) in Houghton.

INDIANA

Thanks to an early nineteenth-century influx of northward migrants, **INDIANA** still displays vestiges of the easy-going South. Among these early settlers was the family of Abraham Lincoln, who set up home near the present village of Santa Claus in 1816, and stayed for fourteen years before moving to Illinois. Unlike the abolitionist Lincolns, many brought slaves to this new territory; Indiana allowed a system of "voluntary servitude" to operate right up to 1843. At the outbreak of the Civil War, thousands of ex-southerners rioted against the draft, in part expressing a concern that Indiana was every bit as subservient to the northeast as the Deep South. However, since the 1870s, industrialization has integrated Indiana into the regional economy.

Despite some beautiful dunes and beaches, the most lasting memories provided by Indiana's fifty-mile **lakeshore** (by far the shortest of the Great Lake states) are the grimy steel mills and poverty-stricken neighborhoods of towns like **Gary** and **East Chicago**. Elsewhere the state holds little to interest travellers. The central plains are characterized by small agricultural settlements, except for the sprawling capital, **Indianapolis**, which, despite a population close to a million, lacks the dynamism of nearby cities of similar size such as Louisville and Cincinnati. Hilly southern Indiana, at its most appealing in fall, is a welcome contrast to the central cornbelt.

Dozens of explanations have been offered as to why Indianans are called "Hoosiers"; the most believable is that its use spread from the days of the Ohio Falls Canal construction in the 1820s, when a contractor, Samuel Hoosier, gave employment preference to those living on the Indiana side of the Ohio River.

Getting Around Indiana

Nine different interstates – seven of them slicing through Indianapolis – provide boring but fast ways of traversing Indiana. *Greyhound* runs frequent services, particularly on I-65 between Chicago and Louisville and I-70 between the east and St Louis. **Indianapolis, Michigan City** and **South Bend** are the major stops on the three different *Amtrak* routes which cut through the state. Flights from most midwestern and eastern cities come in at **Indianapolis International Airport**.

Northern Indiana

Lying just off I-80/90, halfway along the northern fringe of Indiana, **SOUTH BEND** briefly rivalled Detroit as the country's leading car manufacturer during the early Twenties, when the now-defunct Studebaker marque was going strong. These days it's better known for the **University of Notre Dame**, the most famous Roman Catholic college in the US and home of the widely supported Fighting Irish **football** team. Free tours of the campus (☎219/239-5110) take in the gold-domed Administration Building and sights such as a replica of the grotto at Lourdes. The *Hickory Inn*, 50520 US-33N (☎219/272-7555; ②), is a budget motel three miles from the university.

Forty miles west, smaller **MICHIGAN CITY** marks the start of the twenty-mile **Indiana Dunes National Lakeshore**, intended to prevent further encroachment on the state's shoreline. There's not much to the "city" itself but it is the handiest place to stay near the lake; the *Knights Inn*, 201 W Keiffer Rd (☎219/874-9500; ②), presents the best value. Just to the west of town, the impressive **Mount Baldy** is, in fact, a giant sand dune. Good swimming beaches, and hiking trails through woods and marshes, can be found at **Indiana Dunes State Park**, twelve miles further along.

From here it's another fifteen miles west to the industrial mess of **GARY**, the largest US city founded this century and mildly famous as the birthplace of Michael Jackson. Until the US Steel Corporation built a giant foundry here in 1906, this was uninhabited bogland. These days it's basically a depressed suburb of Chicago.

Indianapolis

INDIANAPOLIS began life in 1821 when a tract of barely inhabited marshes was designated state capital. Its location in the middle of Indiana's rich farmland bore terrific commercial advantages, but the absence of a navigable river prohibited the transportation of bulky materials such as coal and iron to sustain heavy industry. Though home to over sixty car manufacturers by 1910, the city never seriously threatened Detroit's supremacy. Nevertheless, it has become one of the biggest cities in the world not to be accessible by water, attracting food, paper and pharmaceutical industries, including the giant Eli Lilly Corporation.

Today the city is trying to shake off such nicknames as *Naptown, India-no-place* and *Brickhouse in the Cornfield* in favor of its chosen designation as the country's unofficial amateur sports capital – amateur events like the Pan-American Games and national Olympic trials being worth big money these days. In recent years, it has acquired several world-class sports stadiums, along with new hotels, two museums and a zoo, and its old downtown landmarks have become shopping and dining complexes. No longer is it (quite) true that nothing happens here except for the glamorous **Indianapolis 500 car race** each May – "the most televised annual event in the world".

Arrival and Information

The fast-growing **Indianapolis International Airport** is seven miles west of downtown, on the #9 bus route ($1.25). A **taxi** into the center costs around $24, the *Shuttle Express* **van** service $14 (☎247-7301). *Greyhound* (☎635-4501) arrives at 127 N Capital Ave, just off Monument Circle, while *Amtrak*, 350 S Illinois St, is next to the fairly central Union Station complex. The **visitor center** is at 201 S Capitol St (Mon–Fri 10am–5.30pm, Sat 10am–4pm; ☎237-5206 or 1-800/323-INDY), beside the Hoosier Dome.

Downtown

Though spacious and unhurried, downtown Indianapolis lacks a nerve center, and never quite gels into a coherent entity. Streets radiate from **Monument Circle**, once the focal point of downtown but now filled with venerable but dull buildings. The challenge of climbing 32 flights of steep stairs up the 284ft **Soldiers and Sailors Monument** (there are often lines for the tiny elevator) is rewarded by an unspectacular view of the sprawling city (daily 10am–7pm; free).

The shops, cafés and lively bars of the tastefully renovated Romanesque red-brick and pink granite **Union Station** complex at Capitol and Louisiana, southwest of Monument Circle, inject some much-needed energy into downtown, while the serene tree-shaded **Lockerbie Square Historic District**, on the eastern fringe at New York and East streets, provides a small enclave of picturesque charm. Small wood-frame cottages, once home to nineteenth-century artisans, line the cobblestone streets, many of them painted in bright pinks, blues and yellows, with ornately carved porches.

Indianapolis seems a strange setting for the **Eiteljorg Museum of American Indian and Western Art** (Tues–Fri 10am–5pm, Sun noon–5pm; $2), set in a stone, wood and adobe building among the rolling greenery of White River State Park on the western edge of downtown, at 500 W Washington St. Harrison Eiteljorg, an industrialist who went West in the Forties to speculate in minerals, fell so much in love with the art of the region that he decided to bring as much of it back with him as possible. A Southwestern gallery features the work of artists from Taos and New Mexico, and the American Western gallery ranges from Frederic Remington to Andy Warhol. Artefacts from all over North America are on display in the Native American gallery.

The **area code** for Indianapolis is ☎317.

Out from Downtown

Although the bodies of former President Benjamin Harrison and Hoosier poet James Whitcomb Riley lie in the enormous **Crown Hill Cemetery**, at 38th St and Michigan Rd, the most visited grave belongs to Thirties bankrobber **John Dillinger**, supposedly buried at Section 44 Lot 94 (though some researchers allege another man was killed in his place). Designated public enemy number one, he was renowned as a daring, sharp-dressed gunman who in a brief one-year career completed thirteen bank raids, killing four policemen, three FBI agents, one sheriff and an undetermined number of innocent bystanders. Something of a folk hero, he escaped from jail twice inside a few months, but was eventually ambushed by the FBI outside a Chicago theater in 1934 (see p.259).

Opposite the cemetery at 1200 W 38th St, over 150 lush wooded acres accommodate the capacious **Indianapolis Museum of Art**. The main building, surrounded by a lake, botanical garden, sculpture courtyard and concert terrace, is fronted by the original of Robert Indiana's *LOVE* pop-art sculpture. Inside, in the tasteful galleries, the exceptional displays include neo-impressionist works, Chinese art, the Eiteljorg Collection of African Art and the largest collection of Turner paintings outside Britain (Tues, Wed, Fri & Sat 10am–5pm, Thurs 10am–8.30pm, Sun noon–5pm; free).

The Indianapolis 500

Seven miles north of downtown, the **Indianapolis Speedway** race track only stages one race per year, but that does happen to be the legendary **Indianapolis 500**. Held on the Sunday before Memorial Day, it's preceded by a month of practice to whittle the hopeful entrants down to a final field of 33 drivers, one of whom will scoop the million-dollar first prize. The two-and-a-half-mile rectangular circuit was originally built as a test track for the city's motor manufacturers, but the first 500-mile race held in 1911 – won in a time of 6hr 42min, at an average speed of 74.6mph – was a huge success, vindicating the organizers' belief that the distance was the optimum length for spectators' enjoyment. The winner's speed is likely to touch 225mph.

The big race crowns one of the nation's largest festivals, watched by 450,000 with up to 100,000 locked outside, hoping to savor at least some of the fume-laden air. At first, the city's conservative hierarchy saw it as an infringement on the traditional observance of Memorial Day weekend. However, it brings so much money into the city, with thousands of "Indy Racing" fanatics staying for the full month, that it is now exploited to the full with civic events such as the crowning of the Speedway Queen, a Mayor's Ball and street parade. Seats for the race usually sell out well in advance, but you may gain admittance to the infield, where the atmosphere makes up for the poor view, on the day.

Adjoining the track, the impressive display of race car history at the **Indianapolis Motor Speedway Hall of Fame Museum**, 4790 W 16th St, provides a good background to the hysteria (daily 9am–5pm; $1). For an extra dollar, a rickety old bus saunters around the super-smooth asphalt track, ringed by huge banked grandstands.

Accommodation

Indianapolis has plenty of places to **stay**, but few budget downtown options. The huge convention trade means there are usually a lot of empty rooms at weekends.

Fall Creek YMCA, 860 W Tenth St (☎634-2478). Single rooms for both men and women, $25. ①.

Holiday Inn Union Station, 123 W Louisiana St (☎631-2221). One of downtown's least expensive places, handy for bars and restaurants. Regular rooms and suites in converted railway carriages. ⑤.

Motel 6, 2851 N Shadeland Ave (☎546-5864). Ten minutes' drive from downtown, just north of I-70. Functional motel with a pool. ①.

North Meridian Inn, 1530 N Meridian St (☎634-6100). Medium-range motel with pool and lounge, sixteen blocks north of downtown. ④.

Renaissance Tower Historic Inn, 230 E Ninth St (☎631-2328). Just off central downtown. Rooms come complete with four-poster bed, toaster, coffeemaker and popcorn popper. ③.

Eating

Union Station, at Capitol and Louisiana streets, houses fast-food interpretations of many ethnic cuisines as well as a number of mid-price cafés and lively bars. At lunchtime, **City Market**, 222 E Market St, is a maze of lunch counters and tables where you can feast cheaply on all sorts of international food amidst a cacophonous din.

Bazbeaux, 334 Massachusetts Ave, downtown (☎636-7662), and 832 E Wheatfield Blvd, Broad Ripple Village (☎255-5711). The best pizzas in town, with a great range of toppings.

El Matador, 921 Broad Ripple Ave, Broad Ripple Village (☎251-9722). Unassuming Mexican diner.

Mugwumps, 608 Massachusetts Ave (☎635-7115). Halfway between a pub and café. International menu featuring vegetarian dishes for under $10. Gourmet coffees and teas. Live jazz Thurs–Sun.

Original Pancake House, 121 W Louisiana St (☎266-0304). Scrumptious German oven-baked pancakes made this one of *Gourmet* magazine's top ten breakfast restaurants in the USA.

St Elmo Steak House, 127 S Illinois St (☎635-0636). One of the top steak restaurants in the meat-mad Midwest. Wonderful food, if rather pompous and expensive. Expect to pay $25–30 for a meal.

Nightlife

Downtown, the area around **Union Station** buzzes in the evening as crowds go in and out of the numerous lively bars and discos. In summer, head north to chic **Broad Ripple Village** (#17 bus) at College Ave and 62nd St, packed with bars, cafés, galleries and shops. See the *NUVO* or *New Times* free papers for full details of gigs and events.

The 1927 Spanish baroque *Indiana Repertory Theatre*, 140 W Washington St (Thurs–Sun; ☎635-5252), puts on dramatic productions between October and May; the Indianapolis Symphony Orchestra has weekly concerts at the equally elaborate 1916 *Circle Theatre*, 45 Monument Circle (☎639-4300).

Broad Ripple Brew Pub, 840 E 65th St (☎253-2739). Atmospheric new brew pub, six miles north.

Chatterbox, 435 Massachusetts Ave (☎636-0584). Lively local bar, with nightly jazz except Sun.

Madame Walker Urban Life Center and Theatre, 617 Indiana Ave (☎236-2099). Black cultural and heritage center. *Jazz on the Avenue* every Fri plus regular dance events, plays and concerts.

Slippery Noodle, 372 S Meridian St (☎631-6968). Indiana's oldest bar, established in 1850. Next to Union Station. Cheap beer Mon and Tues, live blues Wed–Sat.

The Works, 4120 Keystone Ave (☎547-9210). Gay men's social club and resource center with dancing until dawn every night. Other services include private rooms, sauna and gym.

Out from Indianapolis: Bloomington

BLOOMINGTON, by far the liveliest small city in Indiana, lies 45 miles southwest of Indianapolis on Hwy-39. It owes its vibrancy to the 33,000-student Indiana University, east of downtown – best known former pupil, J Danforth Quayle – where the I M Pei-designed **University Art Museum** on E Seventh St (☎812/855-4826) holds a fine international collection of paintings and sculptures. The Indiana Hoosiers, the best-loved team in a basketball-mad state, play to a sell-out crowd every home game.

Practicalities

Greyhound, 535 N Walnut St (☎812/332-1522), runs a reliable service to Indianapolis. Bloomington's **visitor center** can be found at 2855 N Walnut St (☎812/334-8900 or 1-800/678-9828).

Inexpensive places to **stay** include the *Downtown Motel*, 509 N College Ave (☎812/336-6881; ②), and *Motel 6*, further out at 1265 Franklin Rd (☎812/332-0337; ②). The *Indiana Memorial Union* on Seventh and Park (☎812/856-6381), a good source of campus information, also offers a range of cheap places to **eat**. Student bars and cafés are strung out along Kirkwood Avenue; more formal restaurants include *Grisanti's*, 850 Auto Mall Rd (behind College Mall), which serves good-value pasta dishes, especially lasagnes, and the *Snow Lion*, 113 S Grant St, where the Tibetan entrees cost around $10.

ILLINOIS

Nearly everything in **ILLINOIS** revolves around **Chicago**, the largest and most exciting of all the Great Lakes cities. Set at the state's northeastern corner, on the shores of **Lake Michigan**, Chicago has a skyline to rival New York City plus a gamut of top-rated museums, restaurants and cafes, and innumerable bars and nightclubs paying homage to the city's strong jazz and blues heritage. Seventy-five percent of the state's twelve million population live within commuting distance of Chicago's energetic center, which controls the bulk of the state economy – Illinois is the third largest agricultural producer in the US. The sole exception to the endless flat prairies elsewhere is far to the south, where the forested **Shawnee Hills** rise between the Mississippi and Ohio rivers.

The contrast between the quiet rural hinterlands and the buzzing urban center could hardly be greater. That said, Illinois does hold a few places to look out for, though, besides a couple of mildly exciting college towns, most are of historic rather than current interest. First explored and settled by the French, in 1763 the area that's now Illinois was sold to the English, for whom it was the western extent of their vast Virginia colony. Granted statehood in 1818, Illinois remained a distant frontier until the mid-1830s when, after a series of uprisings, the native **Sauk** and **Black Hawk** were subjugated and settlers began to arrive in sizeable numbers. Among these were the first followers of Joseph Smith, founder of the Mormon Church, who established a large colony along the Mississippi at Nauvoo. The **Mormons** met with suspicion and persecution, and, after Smith was murdered by a lynch mob in 1844, fled west to Utah.

Other early immigrants included the young **Abraham Lincoln**, who practised law from 1837 onwards in **Springfield**, the state capital and home of a wide range of Lincolniana, including his restored home, his law offices and various other period buildings and artefacts, as well as his monumental tomb. Indeed, Illinois' self-proclaimed nickname – repeated on its car licence plates – is "Land of Lincoln", and many other central Illinois towns try to claim important roles in the making of the sixteenth US president, including one named Lincoln.

Getting Around Illinois

Since Chicago is the site of **O'Hare Airport**, the world's busiest, with more take-offs and landings each year than any other (though both Atlanta and Heathrow handle more passengers), as well as the hub of the national *Amtrak* **train** network, you're likely at least to pass through it. If you plan to spend time in the rest of Illinois, *Amtrak*, numerous commuter railroads, and, to a lesser extent, *Greyhound* make getting around on public transport feasible, and **cycling** is generally easy on these endless flat plains.

If you're **driving**, half a dozen interstates fan out across the country from Chicago; the famous Chicago-to-LA Route 66 has been defunct since the 1960s, though I-55 southwest to St Louis, followed by I-44 and I-40, follow its general route.

Chicago

CHICAGO is in many ways the last great American city. Though long eclipsed by Los Angeles as America's second-largest center after New York, Chicago really does have it all, with less of the hassle and infrastructural problems of its coastal rivals. Founded in the early 1800s, Chicago grew up with the country, serving as the main connection between the established East Coast cities and the wide open Wild West frontier. This position on the sharp edge between civilization and wilderness made Chicago into a crucible of innovation, and many aspects of modern life, from skyscrapers to suburbia, had their start, and their finest expression, here on the shores of Lake Michigan.

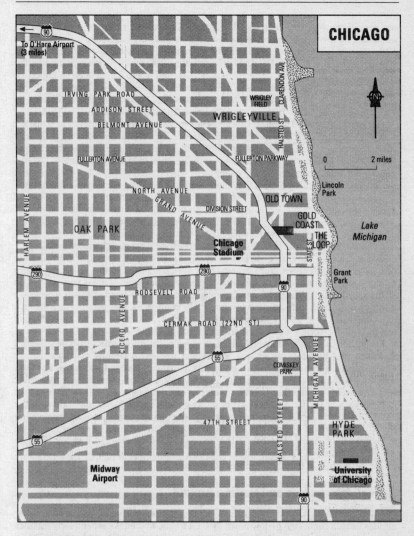

Despite burning to the ground in 1871, Chicago boomed thereafter, doubling in population every decade and reaching two million around 1900, swollen by **Irish** and **eastern European** immigrants (Chicago still ranks as the second largest Polish city in the world, after Warsaw). In the early years of this century, it cemented a reputation as a place of apparently limitless opportunity, with jobs aplenty for those willing to work. The attraction was strongest among Deep South **blacks** suffering from economic deprivation and racist terror: from 1900 to 1920 African-Americans poured in, with over 75,000 arriving during the war years of 1916–18 alone. Long hours, poor pay and squalid work-

The **area code** for Chicago is ☎312.

ing conditions were the catalysts which made Chicago the cradle of American trade unionism. By the turn of the century most workers were organized under the American Federation of Labor, and the 1894 Pullman strike saw black and white workers unite for one of the first times in the US. As hostilities intensified, the city's workers became the driving force behind the left-wing "Wobblies". Chicago has also long been an important center for black organization – both the Reverend Jesse Jackson's **Operation PUSH** (People United to Save Humanity) and the more militant **Nation of Islam**, founded by Elijah Mohammed in the 1940s, have their national headquarters on the South Side.

During the Roaring Twenties, Chicago's self-image as a no-holds-barred free market was pushed to the limit by a new breed of entrepreneur: criminal syndicates, ruthlessly run by the brazen likes of **gangsters** John Dillinger and Al Capone, took advantage of Prohibition to sell bootleg booze. Shoot-outs in the street between sharp-suited, Tommy-gun wielding mobsters were not as common as legend would have it, but the backroom dealing and iron-handed control they pioneered was later perfected by politicians such as former mayor **Richard Daley** – father of the present incumbent – who ran Chicago single-handedly from the 1950s until his death in 1976. His brutal handling of student anti-war demonstrators at the **1968 Democratic convention** remains notorious. These days, the tourist authorities play down the mobster era; few traces of the hoodlum years exist, and those that do owe more to Hollywood than contemporary Chicago.

Today, Chicago's towering **skyline** – the city has perhaps the world's best collection of **modern architecture**, from Frank Lloyd Wright houses to the 110-storey **Sears Tower** – still dominates the pancake-flat prairies for hundreds of miles around, and its status as cultural, and financial, heart of middle America is beyond question. **The Loop** downtown holds the offices of many major US companies, and some of the nation's most important **commodity markets**, which together handle the buying and selling of one-third of the world's agricultural and industrial products.

For visitors, Chicago offers a wide range of excellent **museums** (especially the **Art Institute of Chicago**), restaurants, sports and high-brow cultural activities, but its strongest suit is **live music**, with a phenomenal array of **jazz** and **blues** clubs packed into the backrooms of its amiable bars and cafés. And almost everything is noticeably less expensive than in other US cities – **eating out**, for example, costs much less than in New York or California, but is every bit as good. Though locals might deny it, the city has a surprisingly low-key and generally welcoming population – Chicagoans on the whole are proud of their city and usually keen to point out its best features. Two great ways to get a real feel for the city are to head out to ivy-covered **Wrigley Field** on a sunny summer afternoon to catch baseball's Cubs in action, or take a cruise boat under the bridges of the Chicago River at sunset.

Arrival, Information and Getting Around

Chicago's **O'Hare Airport**, the national HQ for *United*, *American* and several other airlines, is well connected to downtown by *CTA* trains, which take around forty minutes and cost just $1.50 (see overleaf). **Taxis** into town cost around $30, and can take 30–50 minutes. Another option is *Continental Air Transport*'s **van** service between the terminals and downtown hotels ($15; ☎454-7799); the highway is often clogged, so allow at least an hour for the trip. They also connect the city with **Midway Airport**, smaller than O'Hare and used mostly by domestic flights but not much easier to reach; from here the vans take around half an hour to downtown and cost $10.50.

Chicago is the base of the nationwide **Amtrak rail** system, and almost every cross-country route passes through Union Station (☎558-1075) at Canal and Adams, which has left-luggage lockers (for passengers only; $1) and is open 24 hours. **Greyhound** (☎781-2900) and a number of regional bus companies pull in to a large 24-hour station at Harrison and Jefferson, three blocks southwest; this too has left-luggage lockers.

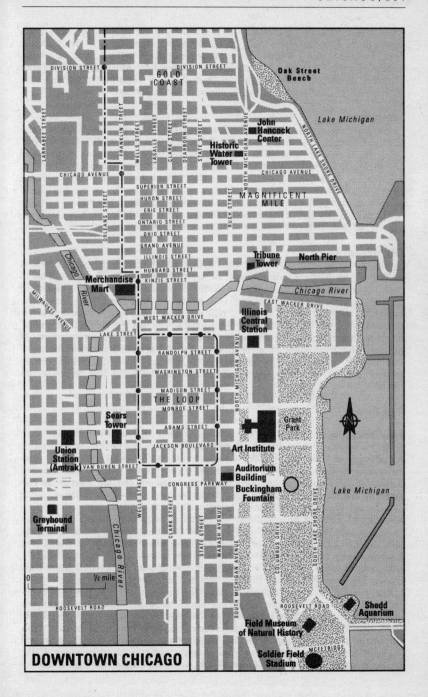

DIVISION STREET
DIVISION STREET

GOLD
COAST

Oak Street
Beach

Lake Michigan

John
Hancock
Center

Historic
Water
Tower

CHICAGO AVENUE
CHICAGO AVENUE

MAGNIFICENT
MILE

SUPERIOR STREET
HURON STREET
ERIE STREET
ONTARIO STREET
OHIO STREET
GRAND AVENUE
ILLINOIS STREET
HUBBARD STREET
KINZIE STREET

Tribune
Tower

North Pier

Merchandise
Mart

Chicago River

EAST WACKER DRIVE

WEST WACKER DRIVE

Illinois
Central
Station

LAKE STREET

RANDOLPH STREET
WASHINGTON STREET
MADISON STREET

THE LOOP

MONROE STREET

Grant
Park

Sears
Tower

ADAMS STREET

JACKSON BOULEVARD

Art Institute

Union
Station
(Amtrak)

VAN BUREN STREET

Auditorium
Building
Buckingham
Fountain

CONGRESS PARKWAY

Lake Michigan

Greyhound
Terminal

0   ½ mile

ROOSEVELT ROAD

ROOSEVELT ROAD

Shedd
Aquarium

Field Museum
of Natural History

Soldier Field
Stadium

DIVISION STREET

LARRABEE STREET
ORLEANS STREET
FRANKLIN STREET
WELLS STREET
LASALLE STREET
CLARK STREET
DEARBORN STREET
STATE STREET
RUSH STREET
NORTH MICHIGAN AVENUE
NORTH LAKE SHORE DRIVE

Milwaukee Avenue

Chicago River

WELLS STREET
CLARK STREET
STATE STREET
WABASH AVENUE
NORTH MICHIGAN AVENUE

COLUMBUS DRIVE
SOUTH LAKE SHORE DRIVE
SOUTH MICHIGAN AVENUE

MCFETRIDGE

DOWNTOWN CHICAGO

Arriving in Chicago **by road** can be memorable, racing past the gleaming glass towers of the Loop; however, traffic on the downtown expressways is pretty horrendous. **Parking** is also a problem. Perhaps the best place to leave a car is the garage under Grant Park (around $7 for 24 hours), between Lake Michigan and the Loop; entrances are along S Michigan Ave. An alternative is to utilize *CTA*'s Park and Ride scheme; call for details of suburban parking locations ($1 per day).

Information

Pick up information and maps from the **Chicago Tourism Council**, in the lobby of the Chicago Cultural Center, 78 E Washington St (daily 9.30am–5pm; ☎280-5740 or ☎1-800/ 487-2446); there's also a kiosk at 163 E Pearson St, across Michigan Ave from the Historic Water Tower on the Magnificent Mile. The Chicago Architectural Foundation's **Archicenter**, in the Monadnock Building at 330 S Dearborn St (☎922-3431), has local guidebooks and walking-tour maps, and runs good guided tours on foot, bus and bike; it also provides the guides for the excellent **Chicago by Boat** tours (see p.254).

Chicago has the world's largest **post office**, at 433 W Van Buren St (Mon–Fri 7am– 5.30pm, Sat 8am–5.30pm; ☎765-3200). The general delivery zip code is 60607.

City Transportation

Getting around Chicago is simple and quick, thanks to the **trains** and **buses** operated 24 hours a day by the Chicago Transit Authority (*CTA*; ☎836-7000). Elevated trains circle the Loop before heading out to the North Side and suburbs, and link up with other subway routes criss-crossing the city. A complete network of buses fills out the system. For $1.25 you get two hours' unlimited riding – be sure to get a 25¢ transfer ticket, if required, when you board – and there's a special all-day fare of $1.75 on Sundays and holidays. Various sightseeing companies run one-hour narrated **open-top-bus tours** of the city center for $8, starting from the Historic Water Tower, 806 N Michigan Ave.

Chicago is compact enough that **taxis** rarely cost more than $8. Cabs are readily available in the Loop (during the day at least) and on the North Side; otherwise you can book one on ☎829-4222.

The City

Lake Michigan, which provides Chicago with some of its most attractive open space (twenty miles of lakeshore lie within the city limits), serves as a clear point of reference for getting your bearings – the lake is always to the east of the urban grid. **Michigan Avenue** is the city's main thoroughfare, running between the lakeside museums and parklands, the densely packed skyscrapers of downtown and the diverse low-rise neighborhoods that spread to the north, south and west. The **Chicago River**, which cuts through the heart of downtown Chicago out of Lake Michigan, separates the business district from the shopping and entertainment areas of the North Side, which range from the upscale **Near North** and **Gold Coast** neighborhoods, to the artists' lofts and galleries of **River North**, and the more blue-collar areas of **Old Town**, **Lincoln Park**, and **Wrigleyville** – Chicago's hottest spots for nights out on a budget.

In contrast to the wealth and prosperity of the North Side, the deprived **South Side** is more like New York's South Bronx, a huge and in places desperately poor expanse with a justifiably dangerous reputation. But while large areas are definitely unsafe after dark, and dodgy even at midday, a few corners of the South Side are well worth visiting, especially the spacious **University of Chicago** campus and neighboring **Hyde Park**, site of the massive **Museum of Science and Industry** – one of the most popular museums in the US. Apart from **Oak Park** to the west, which holds the childhood home of **Ernest Hemingway** and over a dozen well-maintained examples of the influential architecture of **Frank Lloyd Wright**, suburban Chicago has little to offer.

Downtown Chicago: The Loop

It may not have anything like the sheer mass of Manhattan, or the dense warrens of the City of London, but **downtown Chicago** puts on what is perhaps the finest display of **modern architecture** in the world, from the prototype skyscrapers of the 1890s to Mies van der Rohe's modernist masterpieces and the tallest building in the world, the quarter-mile-high **Sears Tower**. Just about all these edifices are workplaces of one kind or another; the whole place is bustling in the day and virtually empty later on.

The compact heart of Chicago is known as **the Loop**, because it's circled by the elevated tracks of the *CTA* "El" trains; for a first impression of downtown, you can't beat riding a train into any of the dozen stations, and starting your explorations by seeing the energy, drive and unmasked greed exposed in the trading pits of its various **commodity marketplaces**. Half the world's wheat and corn (and pork belly futures) are bought and sold amid the cacophonic roar of the **Chicago Board of Trade**, housed in a gorgeous Art Deco tower, appropriately topped by a thirty-foot stainless steel statue of Ceres, Roman goddess of grain. From the entrance at 141 W Jackson St, at the south end of La Salle Street, take the lift to the fifth-floor visitors' gallery (Mon–Fri 9am–2pm; free), where displays trace the evolution of the various frantic shouts and signals by which trade is actually carried out. A similarly energetic ballet goes on from the early hours on Chicago's stock options exchange, the largest in the US. At the **Chicago Mercantile Exchange**, three blocks away at 30 S Wacker Drive (Mon–Fri 7.30am–3.30pm; free), precious metals, currencies and commodities are bought and sold to the tune of some $50 billion a day. The **best time to visit** any of the exchanges is just before the close of trade when the pressure is at its peak and tempers are most frayed.

A couple of other buildings in the immediate vicinity are worth nosing around. Half a block from the Board of Trade, **The Rookery**, 209 S La Salle St, built in 1886 by Burnham and Root, is one of the city's most celebrated and photographed edifices. Its forbidding Moorish Gothic exterior gives way to a wonderfully airy lobby, decked out in cool Italian marble and gold leaf in 1905 during a major remodelling by Frank Lloyd Wright; its spiral cantilever staircase rising from the second floor has to be seen to be appreciated. A couple of doors toward the Board of Trade, call in at the **Continental Illinois Bank** lobby, with its 28 Ionic marble columns and intricate murals.

Looking up at the proud facade of the **Reliance Building**, 32 N State St, you'd be forgiven for thinking it dated from the Art Deco 1930s, but it was in fact completed way back in 1895 by Daniel Burnham, who did much to shape the face of Chicago; his **Fisher Building**, with its tongue-in-cheek, aquatic-inspired ornamental terracotta, stands across from the Archicenter at 343 S Dearborn St. A block further south, the 1890 **Manhattan Building** was the world's first tall all-steel-frame building, and is generally acknowledged as the progenitor of the modern curtain-walled skyscraper; now converted into luxury flats, it preserves some noteworthy exterior ornament.

Besides office buildings, the Loop also holds some of Chicago's grandest turn-of-the-century **department stores**. On the best-looking of these, the 1889 **Carson Pirie Scott** store at 1 S State St, a magnificent ironwork facade blends botanic and geometric forms in an intuitive version of Art Moderne; its architect, Louis Sullivan, was also responsible for the gorgeous spherical bronze clocks suspended from the building's corners. Two blocks north, at State and Washington, the comparatively bland exterior of **Marshall Field's** oldest and grandest branch masks one of the world's great stores, with seven floors of merchandise corralling a multistorey escalator-filled atrium.

The Loop is usually said to end at the El tracks, but the blocks beyond this core, to either side of the Chicago River, hold plenty more of interest. Broad, double-decked **Wacker Drive**, parallel to the water, was designed as a sophisticated promenade, lined by benches and obelisk-shaped lanterns, by Daniel Burnham in 1909. It was never completed, but, despite the almost constant intrusion of construction works, it makes for a nice extended walk. The river itself had its direction reversed, around the turn of the century, in an engineering project more extensive than the digging of the Panama Canal. As a result, rather than letting its sewage and industrial waste flow east into Lake Michigan, Chicago now sends it all south into the Corn Belt.

The best way to enjoy the riverfront is on a **boat tour** from beneath the Michigan Avenue bridge, giving magnificent views of downtown and a good insight into the city's history ($8–15; daily 10am–9pm). However, half an hour's walk, especially at lunchtime when the office workers are out in force, will do the trick. Burnham's promenade runs along both sides of the river, crossing back and forth over the twenty-odd drawbridges that open and close to let barges and an occasional sailboat pass. The **State Street bridge** is a superb vantage point. On the south bank, at 35 E Wacker Drive, the elegant Beaux Arts **Jewelers Building** was built in 1926 and is capped on the seventeenth floor by a domed rotunda that once housed Al Capone's favorite speakeasy. Across the river stands what's commonly considered the masterpiece of Ludwig Mies van der Rohe – the 1971 **IBM Building** at 330 N Wabash Ave. The gentle play of light and shadow across the detailed bronze and smoked glass facade was a model for countless other less considered copies worldwide. The building is so huge that it acts as a funnel for winter winds off Lake Michigan, and heavy ropes sometimes have to be tied across the broad plaza at its base to protect people from getting blown away.

Perhaps Chicago's most successful and acclaimed building of recent years stands four blocks west at **333 W Wacker Drive**. Towering over a broad bend in the river, and bowed to follow its curve, the green glass facade reflects the almost fluorescent green of the river (recently upgraded from "toxic" to merely "polluted"); on the lower floors, a more classically detailed stone base actively addresses its stalwart elder neighbors. Further on, a newly resurrected stretch of the riverfront walk follows the western bank of the river, with open-air cafés and gardens to tempt office workers to extend their lunch breaks. Further south, and back on the Loop side of the river at S Wacker Drive and Adams, is the 1450ft tall **Sears Tower**, so huge that it has over one hundred different lifts. Two of them ascend, in little over a minute, all the way from the ground level shopping mall to the 103rd-floor **Skydeck Observatory** (9am–11pm; $6.50), from where you can pick out the city's landmarks. Look out for the distinctive triangular **Metropolitan Detention Center**, where prisoners exercise on the grassy roof, beneath wire netting to ensure they don't get whisked away by helicopter.

South Michigan Avenue and the Art Institute of Chicago

Many of Chicago's major cultural attractions are gathered on the eastern edge of the Loop, along Michigan Avenue between the city's commercial core and the shores of Lake Michigan. On the lake side of South Michigan Avenue, at the east end of Adams Street, the **Art Institute of Chicago** (Mon & Wed–Fri 10.30am–4.30pm, Tues 10.30am–8pm, Sat 10am–5pm, Sun noon–5pm; $6 suggested donation, free last half-hour each day and all day Tues) has an excellent collection of Impressionist and Post-Impressionist paintings, Asian art (particularly Japanese prints), photography and architectural drawings. The neoclassical facade of the main entrance does its best to look dignified, but the numerous added-on wings can make it hard to find your way around inside.

Most visitors head straight upstairs to the Impressionist paintings, which include a wall full of Monet's *Haystacks* captured in various lights, next to Seurat's immediately familiar pointillist *Sunday Afternoon*; a handful of Post-Impressionist masterpieces by Van Gogh, Gauguin and Matisse are arrayed nearby. Beyond here, a tortured, tuxe-doed self-portrait by **Max Beckmann** – his last Berlin painting before fleeing the Nazis – welcomes you into a crowded gallery of early twentieth-century American and European works, in which moody portraits by Balthus and Picasso, and Surrealist landscapes by Max Ernst and Yves Tanguy, hang side by side with Edward Hopper's lonely *Nighthawks* and Georgia O'Keeffe's doom-laden *Black Cross, New Mexico*.

CHICAGO FOR FREE

It's very easy to go through a lot of cash visiting Chicago – not that things are inordinately expensive, but there's just so much to see and do. On arrival, be sure to get hold of the free weekly *Reader*, an excellent source of no-cost one-off events, and the CVB's *Chicago Official Visitors Guide*.

Free **lunchtime concerts** take place most days of the week in the Cultural Center (see p.255), and during summer at the bandstand in Grant Park, the Daley Plaza at Washington and Clark, and at the first National Bank Plaza on Madison and Clark. These outdoor locations make great picnic venues, as do the Lincoln Park beaches (see p.258).

Chicago's **festivals** range from nationally known extravaganzas to small neighborhood and ethnic events (details from the *Events Hotline*; ☎744-3370 or ☎1-800-ITS-CHGO). The first mega-event of the year falls on **March 17** when, in a fit of over-exuberance, city officials dye the river green for the St Patrick's Day Parade. **June** sees blues, gospel, and the classical **Ravinia** festivals as well as a large Lesbian and Gay Pride Parade and many neighborhood celebrations. **July** brings the Independence Day fireworks, the **Taste of Chicago** gastric extravaganza and the spectacular **Air and Water Show**. The hot and funky **Jazz Festival** takes place in September over **Labor Day** weekend.

Some Chicago **museums** don't charge at all, including the **Museum of Broadcast Communications** (p.255); all except the Oceanarium have one free day per week.

Mon	Chicago Historical Society (p.259).
Tues	Art Institute of Chicago (p.254) and the Museum of Contemporary Art, 237 E Ontario St (10am–5pm; usually $4).
Wed	The Glessner and Clarke houses (p.261) charge $1; not free, but a significant saving on the usual $10.
Thurs	Field Museum of Natural History (p.256), Museum of Science and Industry (p.262) and the Shedd Aquarium (p.256; the Oceanarium entrance is $5 instead of the usual $8).

Elsewhere in the museum, keep an eye out for the pitchfork-holding farmer of Grant Woods' oft-reproduced *American Gothic* – a picture he painted as a student at the Art Institute school, and sold to the museum for $300 in 1930 – and for the delightful seventh-century Indonesian sculpted stone monkeys, in the Southeast Asian collections displayed around the McKinlock Court Garden, which in summer serves as an attractive **open-air café**. Also here, in the far east end of the complex, is the immaculately reconstructed Art Moderne trading room of the Chicago Stock Exchange, designed by Louis Sullivan in 1893 and moved here in the 1970s.

A few blocks north, the **Chicago Cultural Center** takes up most of the splendid old Public Library building at 78 E Washington St, and holds a range of free activities. As well as the city's main **visitor center**, it features various galleries (including some great photos of Chicago's most famous landmarks), major touring exhibits, and free lunchtime and evening recitals, readings and concerts (☎346-3278 for details). The highlight is the **Museum of Broadcast Communications**, where you can while away a few hours watching old adverts, newsreels and sporting moments (Mon–Thurs 10am–7pm, Fri 10am–6pm, Sat 10am–5pm, Sun noon–5pm; free).

Around the turn of the century this lakefront strip around the Art Institute on South Michigan Avenue was the city's prime entertainment district. Many of that era's grand structures preserve a sense of its unabashed artistic aspirations. The world-renowned **Chicago Symphony Orchestra**, now run by Daniel Barenboim after many successful years under the baton of Sir Georg Solti, still performs to sell-out crowds at the (Daniel Burnham-designed) **Orchestra Hall** at 220 S Michigan Ave. Down the street, the **Fine Arts Building**, at no 410, once held the offices of *Wizard of Oz* author L Frank Baum and the drafting studio of the young Frank Lloyd Wright.

Further along stand two of Chicago's most famous old **hotels**, including the recently renovated *Hilton* – the world's largest hotel when it opened in 1927 – and the more affordable and atmospheric *Blackstone*. South of here, the neighborhood income levels drop off sharply, and, apart from the Prairie Avenue Historic District described on p.261, there's little of interest before the Hyde Park district three miles south – though r'n'b fans may like to know that the southwest corner of Michigan Avenue and 21st Street held the studios and offices of **Chess Records**, immortalized in the early Rolling Stones song *2120 S Michigan Avenue*.

Grant Park

East of the Art Institute towards Lake Michigan, **Grant Park** provides a welcome but not entirely complete break from the downtown urban grid – wide strips of high-speed road and railway slice through it, so casual rambling can be frustrating. The northern half of the park, especially around the immense **Buckingham Fountain**, is its least degraded part, and the whole two hundred-acre swath is liberally sprinkled with sculptures and monuments, from a moping Columbus to a proud Plains Indian on horseback. Throughout the summer, jazz, blues and classical concerts are held in the Petrillo Music Shell, just behind the Art Institute. The **Taste of Chicago** at the end of June attracts over a million people to a week-long feeding frenzy.

The railway tracks of the Illinois Central make it annoyingly difficult to walk the mile or so from the southern end of the Loop to the southern half of Grant Park, where all the major attractions are gathered; the best route is to walk through the northern half of the park and head south along the lakeshore promenade.

The extensive and engaging **Field Museum of Natural History**, 1200 S Lake Shore Drive at Roosevelt Rd (daily 9am–5pm; $5, free Thurs), is ten minutes' walk south of the Art Institute, in a huge, marble-clad, Daniel Burnham-designed Greek temple. "Natural history" here includes anything non-white and non-European; the collection ranges from Egyptian tombs – the entire burial chamber of the son of a Fifth Dynasty Pharaoh was brought here in 1908 – to a simulated South Pacific Island, complete with mock lava flows. Folklorists in an earthen lodge in the Native American section tell myths and legends – intended for young kids but not overly sentimental or simple-minded. As you might expect, acres of embalmed and stuffed specimens highlight the flora and fauna of North America, starring a 75ft skeleton of an Aptosaurus dug up on the Great Plains.

Just across busy Lake Shore Drive, on the shores of Lake Michigan, the **Shedd Aquarium** (daily 9am–6pm; $4, free Thurs) proclaims itself, in true Chicago style, the largest indoor aquarium in the world. The uninspired 1930s structure itself is rather old-fashioned, but the lighthearted and often tongue-in-cheek displays – some use *Far Side* cartoons, while others describe a Joycean *Portrait of an Otter* – are at once informative and entertaining. The central exhibit, a 90,000-gallon re-creation of a coral reef complete with sharks (who get fed at 11am and 2pm daily), turtles and thousands of tropical fish, is surrounded by over a hundred lesser tanks. Highlights include the sluggish and comical South American freckled sideneck turtles, housed across from a four-foot, 250lb alligator snapping turtle, who trundles to the surface to breathe every half-hour.

The recently added **Oceanarium** (same hours; $8, $5 Thurs – includes Aquarium admission) provides an enormous contrast, with its modern lake-view home for marine mammals such as Pacific dolphins and beluga whales. Designed to replicate a rocky Alaskan coastline, it's a carefully disguised amphitheater for such demonstrations of the animals' "natural behavior" as jumping out of the water and fetching plastic rings. Performances are four times daily and you need a ticket; at other times you can watch from underwater galleries as the animals cruise around the tank, and listen to the clicks, beeps and whistles they use to communicate with each other. As well as a cramped tank of unhappy-looking penguins, there's an interactive exhibit on sea otters and a detailed look at the repercussions of the devastating *Exxon Valdez* oil spill.

In summer, *Shoreline Marine Sightseeing* ($6; ☎222-9328) runs hour-long **cruises** along the lakeshore from a jetty just north of the Aquarium. The predictable **Adler Planetarium** nearby (9.30am–4.30pm; free, $4 for Sky Show) is the smallest, oldest and least interesting of the Grant Park museums, but it does give one of the best views of the towering Chicago skyline; the small Meigs Field airport is just to the south, so don't be surprised if low-flying planes seem about to crash into the lake.

The Near North

Chicago's **Near North**, where you're likely to spend much of your time, has few big-name attractions, but it's great for simply wandering around, chancing upon odd **shops**, neighborhood bars and historic sites, in a generally low-rise tangle containing some of the city's most characteristic corners.

When the Michigan Avenue bridge was built over the Chicago River in 1920, the warehouse district along its north bank quickly changed into one of the city's most upmarket quarters, now known as the **Magnificent Mile** and famed for its fashionable shops and department stores. Throughout the Roaring Twenties one glitzy tower after another was thrown up along Michigan Avenue, starting in the north with the opulent **Drake Hotel** off Lincoln Park, and in the south with the white terracotta, wedding-cake colossus of the **Wrigley Building**, just over the river at 400 N Michigan Ave. Built by the Chicago-based chewing-gum magnates, the latter was eclipsed almost immediately by the "Mag Mile's" most famous structure, the **Tribune Tower**. Still housing the editorial offices of Chicago's morning newspaper, as well as, on the ground floor, the studios of its main AM radio station, *WGN* (you can peer in from the street and watch the DJs in action), the tower was completed in 1925, its flying buttresses and Gothic detailing turning its back on the then-prevalent Modern style. Look closely at its lower floors and you'll see pieces of historic buildings – like the Parthenon and the Great Pyramid – purloined from around the world by Tribune staffers and embedded here.

While the Tribune Tower anchors its southern end, the Mag Mile's northern reaches are dominated by the quarter-mile-high, cross-braced steel **John Hancock Center** at 875 N Michigan Ave. Though it's 125 feet shorter than the Empire State Building, and has since been pushed out of the top three by New York's World Trade Center and Chicago's own Sears Tower, the 360° panorama you get on a clear day from its 94th-floor **Skydeck Observatory** (daily 9am–midnight; $4) is unforgettable.

Back at ground level, you're right at the heart of Chicago's prime **shopping district**, where *Bloomingdale's*, *Neiman-Marcus* and *Tiffany & Co* rub shoulders with *Benetton* and *Nike Town*. Some front straight onto Michigan Avenue, but many of the shops are enclosed within multistorey, fabulously decorated shopping malls, all of which stay open daily from 9am until midnight, so you can window-shop after the stores have closed. In the newest and most outlandish of these emporia, **Chicago Place** at 700 N Michigan Ave, an eight-storey shopping mall is topped by a barrel-vaulted glass conservatory where you can sample fast foods from dozens of admittedly anodyne stands. Two blocks north, at the **900 N Michigan Avenue** mall, *Gucci* and *Aquascutum* fill the lower floors of the deluxe *Four Seasons Hotel*; this flashy complex is also home to the lavish *Henri Bendel*, Chicago's most exclusive department store.

Across from Water Tower Place, at the very center of this consumer paradise, stands the **Historic Water Tower** – a building you'll feel is either beautiful or grotesque. An exuberant but naive example of frontier Gothic, the stone castle, topped by a hundred-foot tower, was built in 1869 and is one of the very few structures to have survived the Chicago Fire of 1871. Across the street, the equally historic **Pumping Station** holds a **visitor center** along with the multimedia extravaganza **Here's Chicago** (hourly 10am–4pm; $5), a 45-minute guided tour through Chicago past and present.

Away from the Magnificent Mile, the area along the river, between Michigan Avenue and the lake, is being redeveloped in a major way, with giant hotel and office block complexes already under construction. The one part so far completed, **City Point**, is quite shamelessly and successfully modelled upon New York's Rockefeller Center; Daniel Burnham's riverfront promenade is also being incorporated into the plans, and, near where the river flows out of Lake Michigan, a large fountain, each hour on the hour, spurts a powerful stream of water arching across to the south bank. A block from the fountain, at 455 E Illinois St, **North Pier**, one of the few surviving riverfront warehouses, was recently restored into a carnival-like collection of restaurants and gift shops, complete with an indoor crazy-golf course that features models of Chicago's many skyscrapers. It's nowhere near as tacky as it might sound, and is certainly worth the walk. Further east along E Illinois at **Navy Pier** – venue for weekend festivals in summer and embarkation point for several boat trips – several attractions are currently being developed, including the relocated Chicago Childrens' Museum.

The more heavily industrial area west of Michigan Avenue is also experiencing a revival of sorts, though on a smaller scale and with a different character. Re-christened **River North**, the many old brick warehouses and factory premises here have been converted to house avant-garde art galleries, restaurants and nightclubs. Huron and Superior streets, around their intersection with Wells Street, hold the most concentrated collection; if you're interested in doing any degree of serious gallery-hopping, pick up a copy of the free *Chicago Gallery News*.

The Gold Coast and Old Town

As its name suggests, the **Gold Coast** is one of Chicago's wealthiest and most desirable neighborhoods, stretching north from the Magnificent Mile along the lakeshore. This residential district is primarily notable for holding Chicago's most central (and style-conscious) beach, the broad strand of **Oak Street Beach**, reached via a walkway under Lake Shore Drive, across from the *Drake Hotel*. After dark, the summertime crowds are apt to be found in the myriad bars of Rush and Division streets. The more northerly reaches of the Gold Coast, approaching Lincoln Park, are also its most exclusive, nowhere more so than the stretch of Astor Street running south from the park. **Old Town**, west of LaSalle Street to either side of North Avenue, has a much more lived-in look than does the dandified Gold Coast. Originally a German immigrant community based around the 1888 **St Michaels Church** – whose carrillon is to Old Towners' what Bow Bells are to Cockneys – today the neighborhood boasts a broad ethnic and cultural mix. While its many century-old row houses and workers' cottages are now prime real estate, as recently as thirty years ago its then-shabby housing stock and derelict factories attracted a variety of creative types. **Wells Street**, the main drag, emerged in the late 1960s as a mini-Haight Ashbury, and while almost all signs of that era have vanished (or, as in the case of the folk club *Earl of Old Town*, moved uptown), at least one survivor, the *Second City* comedy club (see p.266), is still going strong. The rest of the neighborhood is packed with some of the city's best bars, galleries and barbecue joints, and makes for a diverting afternoon's wander.

The westernmost quarter of this area, stretching from Chicago Avenue north to Division Street (locale of Studs Terkel's eponymous social documentary), is a district tourists would do well to avoid: the immense 1960s **Cabrini Green** public housing project has since eroded into one of the city's most poverty-stricken corners (recently demonized in the movie *Candyman*).

Lincoln Park and Wrigleyville

In summer, Chicago's largest green space, **Lincoln Park**, gives a much-needed respite from the gridded pavements of the rest of the city. Unlike Grant Park to the south, Lincoln Park is packed with leafy nooks and crannies, monuments and sculptures, and has a couple of friendly, family-oriented **beaches**, at the eastern ends of North Avenue and Fullerton Avenue. Near the small **zoo** (daily 9am–5pm; free), at the heart of the park, you can rent paddleboats or bikes. If the weather's bad, head for the **conservatory** (free), or visit the **Chicago Historical Society museum** (Mon–Sat 9.30am–4.30pm, Sun noon–5pm; $3.50, free Mon), at the south end of the park off Clark Street, and bone up on Chicago's captivating past; it also has a nice skylit café.

The Lincoln Park neighborhood, inland from the lake between North Avenue and Diversey Parkway, centers on **Lincoln Avenue** and **Clark Street**, which run diagonally from near the Historical Society; **Halsted Street**, with its blues bars and nightclubs, runs north–south through its heart. Any of these main roads merits an extended stroll, popping in to the many book and record stores, while smaller side streets show off why Lincoln Park is such a popular place to live. Look out for the **Biograph Theatre**, 2433 N Lincoln Ave, where **John Dillinger** was ambushed and killed by the FBI in 1934, thanks to a tip-off from his companion, the legendary Lady in Red; and **Oz Park**, at Lincoln and Webster avenues, which was the namesake, if not the inspiration, for Chicago author L Frank Baum's stories, set somewhere over the rainbow.

Chicago spreads north from Lincoln Park for block after low-rise block of houses and shops, many of which date from the late 1800s, when thousands of German immigrants settled in what was then the separate enclave of Lake View. It's now dubbed **Wrigleyville**, in honor of **Wrigley Field**, the ivy-covered 75-year-old stadium of baseball's much-loved Cubs. Along with Boston's Fenway Park (see p.161), this remains the best place to get a real feel for the game – the club is so traditional it fought the installation of floodlights right up to 1988. Even if you know nothing about the rules, there are few more pleasant and relaxing ways to spend an afternoon than drinking beer, eating hot dogs, watching the Cubs come close to winning a ball game (they haven't won anything important since World War II) and joining in the ritual seventh-inning singing of *Take Me Out To The Ballgame*, led by gravel-voiced announcer Harry Caray.

The West Side

Chicago's West Side, west of the Chicago River, was where the **Great Fire of 1871** started, supposedly when Mrs O'Leary's cow kicked over a lantern. The flames spread quickly east to engulf the entire central city, which was built of wood and fed the fire for three full days. Appropriately enough, the O'Leary cottage is now the site of the Chicago Fire Department training academy. The West Side also saw 1886's **Haymarket Riots**, when striking workers assembled at the old city market at Desplaines and Randolph streets; after a peaceful demonstration, as police began to break up the crowd, a bomb exploded, killing an officer. Another six policemen and four of the workers died in the resulting panic; four labor leaders were later found guilty of murder and hanged, despite the fact that none of them had been present at the event.

Though the West Side has little to see compared to the rest of the city, it does provide a good look at its day-to-day realities, having served as the port of entry for Chicago's myriad ethnic groups, now congregated in its distinct neighborhoods. **Milwaukee Avenue**, which stretches under the El tracks diagonally from the Loop out towards O'Hare Airport, has long been home to a sizeable eastern European community, mainly Poles – over a million altogether, including some 60,000 who came to Chicago during the martial law era of the 1980s. For an introduction, stop by the **Polish Museum of America** (daily noon–5pm; free) at 984 N Milwaukee Ave, or the **Ukrainian National Museum** (Mon–Fri 11am–4pm, Sun noon–4pm; $1), half a mile west at 2453 W Chicago Ave. **Greektown**, the few blocks of Halsted Street north of the I-290 freeway, and **Little Italy**, along Taylor Street west of Halsted, are both just a short walk from the University of Illinois subway station, on the *CTA Congress* line. On a Sunday morning, the liveliest spot on the West Side is **Maxwell Street market**, four blocks southeast of Little Italy, where blues bands busk on street corners and kielbasas replace bagels among the stallholders.

Ten miles west of the Loop, the affluent and attractive turn-of-the-century suburb of **Oak Park** has been preserved as a national historic district, thanks in part to its early influence on two very different but very American figures, **Ernest Hemingway** and **Frank Lloyd Wright**. Oak Park is easily accessible by public transport: take the Lake–Dan Ryan *CTA* El train west to the Harlem Avenue stop. The **visitor center** a block north of the station at 158 N Forest Ave (daily 9am–5pm; ☎848-1500) has an excellent walking tour map ($1) as well as guidebooks and free brochures.

Hemingway was born and grew up in Oak Park, editing his high school newspaper and living a normal middle-class life; neither his birthplace (at 339 N Oak Park Ave) nor his boyhood home (600 N Kenilworth Ave) is open to visitors, though an engaging collection of memorabilia can be seen at the **Oak Park Historical Society** (Fri 10am–2pm, Sat & Sun 1–4pm; $3) at 217 Home Ave, a block south of the station.

In 1889, a decade before Hemingway's birth, an ambitious young architect named Frank Lloyd Wright arrived in Oak Park, which he used for the next 25 as a testing ground for his innovative design theories. Most of the twenty-five buildings he put up here are in keeping with conventional Victorian design, and few are open to the public; fortunately, however, his most interesting and groundbreaking edifices are maintained as monuments. His ideal of an "organic architecture", in which all aspects of the design derive from a single unifying concept – quite at odds with the fussy "gingerbread" popular at the time – is exemplified by **Unity Temple** at 875 Lake St. Though the simplicity of this angular reinforced-concrete structure was largely dictated by economics, its unembellished surfaces contribute to a masterful manipulation of space, especially in the skylit interior, where the subtle interplay of overlapping planes and volumes creates a dynamic spatial flow. Though little noticed in the US, Unity Temple was very influential in Europe as a precursor of Modern architecture.

Frank Lloyd Wright built his small brown-shingled **home and studio**, nearby at 951 Chicago Ave, on the corner of Forest Avenue, at the age of 22 in 1889, and remodelled it repeatedly thereafter. It shows all his hallmarks: large fireplaces to symbolize the heart of the home and family; free-flowing, open-plan rooms; and the visual linking of interior and exterior spaces. The furniture of the kitchen and dining rooms is Wright's own design; he added a two-storey studio in 1898, with a mezzanine drafting area suspended by chains from the roof beams. In 1909 Wright abandoned Oak Park and his family for new pastures; he was eventually to design such landmarks as New York's Guggenheim Museum. You can see the house itself on a 45-minute guided tour (Mon–Fri 11am, 1pm & 3pm, Sat & Sun 11am–4pm; $6); lengthier walking tours, costing $10, take in the dozen other Wright-designed houses within a two-block radius.

The South Side

The **South Side** of Chicago has always had a rough deal, cursed with the presence of bad-neighbor heavy industries like the sprawling **Chicago Stockyards**, the slaughterhouses and meatpackers which Upton Sinclair exposed in his 1906 novel *The Jungle*, and whose stink covered most of the South Side up through the 1950s. The overriding impression is one of misery and downtrodden poverty, with block after block of deprived and dangerous neighborhoods. That said, there are exceptions: not just the **Prairie Avenue** and **Hyde Park** districts described below, but also the buzzing **Chinatown** around Wentworth Ave and 22nd St; the artsy, predominantly Mexican **Pilsen** district, a few blocks north and west; and the predominantly Irish, blue-collar **Bridgeport**, around Halsted and 37th – Mayor Daley's old fiefdom, the home of New Comiskey Park and baseball's White Sox (see p.267). To reach the South Side, double-decker *Illinois Central* commuter trains run beside the lake to Prairie Ave (a block from the 18th St station) and Hyde Park (near the 59th St station); *CTA* bus #1 follows Michigan Ave to the same places, while bus #8 bus runs every fifteen minutes, 24 hours a day, south through Pilsen to Bridgeport.

Two blocks east of Michigan Avenue, a mile from the Loop and only a quarter of a mile from the lake, **Prairie Avenue** started life as an exclusive suburb. Though just ten minutes' walk south from Grant Park and the Field Museum, it's best reached by cab, bus or train; the route is confusing and the streets are just not safe. As the one part of Chicago to remain unscathed in the Great Fire of 1871, this area had a brief moment of glory as the city's finest address. However, by the turn of the century the railroads had cut it off from Lake Michigan, and the expansion of the stockyards had encouraged the wealthy to flee back to their traditional North Side haunts.

One of the few structures to have survived the intervening years is the Romanesque 1886 **Glessner House**, Chicago's only surviving H H Richardson-designed house, standing sentry on the southwest corner of Prairie Ave and 18th St. Behind the forbidding stone facade, the house opens onto a garden court, its interior filled with Arts and Crafts furniture and swathed in William Morris fabrics and wall coverings. The place is maintained by the Chicago Architecture Foundation, who give guided tours on the hour (Wed & Fri 1–3pm, Sat & Sun 1–4pm; $6). A combination ticket costing $10 (Wed $1), gets you inside Chicago's oldest building, the **Clarke House** (Wed & Fri noon–2pm, Sat & Sun noon–3pm; $6) a block away at 1855 S Indiana Ave, a plain white 1836 Greek Revival pioneer home that spent many years as a community center before being prissied up as a minor museum of interior decor. Much more interesting, and proof of the wealth once concentrated here, is the lavish gothic **Presbyterian Church**, a block away at 1936 S Michigan Ave, with its Burne-Jones and Tiffany stained-glass windows.

An island of middle-class prosperity surrounded by urban poverty, **Hyde Park** is the most attractive and sophisticated South Side Chicago neighborhood. It's also one of the more racially integrated areas of the city, and among its more erudite: the **University of Chicago**, endowed by Rockefeller in 1892 and now among the top institutions in the US, has encouraged a college-town atmosphere, with bookshops and numerous cafés around its compact campus, especially along E 57th St. On the campus itself, two buildings are well worth searching out: the massive Gothic pile of the **Rockefeller Memorial Chapel**, at 59th St and Woodlawn Ave, and the Prairie-style **Robie House**, designed by Frank Lloyd Wright, two blocks north at 5757 S Woodlawn Ave. Campus tours start from the Ida Noyes Hall, 1212 E 59th St (Mon–Sat 10am).

Woodlawn Avenue runs north from the University of Chicago campus, passing one of the South Side's most popular taverns, *Jimmy's Woodlawn Tap* at 55th Street, before turning a whole lot grander. Besides its enormous mansions, Woodlawn Avenue illustrates the social and racial mix for which Hyde Park is renowned: within two blocks of each other are the Midwest's largest Jewish temple, the ornate **Isaiah Israel** at 1100 E Hyde Park Blvd, and the home of **Minister Louis Farrakhan**, leader of the Nation of Islam, which was started here on the South Side in the 1940s by the late Elijah Muhammad. In between, at 4944 S Woodlawn Ave, stands the huge brick manor where boxer Muhammad Ali lived for many years.

Just west of the university, on the edge of lush Washington Park, the **Du Sable Museum of African-American History** takes a look at the experience of Americans of African descent, from slavery to the present day (Mon–Fri 9am–5pm, Sat & Sun noon–5pm; $2.50). Named for Jean Du Sable, the Haitian-born Francophone who was Chicago's first permanent settler, it focuses on the works of WPA-sponsored artists of the 1930s and on the Black Power-era of the 1960s.

Washington Park wraps around the south of the University of Chicago campus, to join the long green strip of the **Midway** – one of the few reminders that a hundred years ago this was the site of the Chicago **World's Columbian Exposition**. Attracting some thirty million spectators in the summer of 1893 (45 percent of the USA's population at the time), the Midway was then filled with full-size model villages from around the globe, including an Irish market town and a mock-up of Cairo complete with belly dancers; these days it's used mainly by joggers and students tossing Frisbees. The cavernous **Museum of Science and Industry** at the east end of the park (Mon–Fri 9.30am–4pm, Sat & Sun 9.30am–5.30pm; $5) was, until it started charging admission in 1991, Chicago's single most popular tourist destination (and ranked second in the US); it now disputes that status with the Shedd Aquarium. Besides interactive computer displays, the best of which explores the inner workings of the brain, exhibits include a captured German U-boat, a trip down a replica coal mine, and a simulated space-shuttle journey; it's fun for kids, but adults may not feel like staying very long. The complex also hosts a giant *Omnimax* movie dome; admission is $3.50 extra.

Promontory Point juts into Lake Michigan just east of the museum, giving great views of the Chicago skyline, including a close-up look at Mies van der Rohe's first high-rise, the Promontory Apartments at 5530 S Lake Shore Drive.

Accommodation

Most central **accommodation** is oriented toward business and convention trade rather than tourism, but there are still plenty of moderately priced rooms. A good selection of clean if unexciting pre-war hotels in and around the Loop offer reasonable rates, especially at weekends, and motorists can pick from scores of motels along the interstates (parking downtown can add $15 a night to your stay). Even top-class downtown hotels are, comparatively, not that expensive. Under the *Chicago's Got It* programme, hotels in all price ranges offer discounts of fifteen to forty percent on Thursday to Sunday nights, when the business types have gone home, so you can often get a room in a really plush place for around $100. While they're not as prominent as elsewhere, **bed and breakfast** rooms are available through *Chicago B&B*, PO Box 14088 (☎951-0085), from $60 per night. Fifteen percent room tax is added everywhere to all bills.

Arlington House International Hostel, 616 W Arlington Place (☎929-5380 or ☎1-800/538-0074). Easy-going hostel open 24 hours, close to Wrigley Field and loads of good bars. Male, female and coed dorms. AAIH, IYHF & AYH members pay $14; $3 more for others. ③.

Avenue Motel, 1154 S Michigan Ave (☎427-8200 or ☎1-800/621-4196). Well placed for Soldier Field and Shedd Aquarium, almost 2 miles south of the river. Nothing fancy, but free parking. ③.

Best Western Grant Park Hotel, 1100 S Michigan Ave (☎922-2900 or ☎1-800/528-1234). Large central hotel with outdoor pool – handy for Grant Park and lakeside attractions. Good value. ④.

The Bismarck Hotel, 171 W Randolph St (☎236-0123 or ☎1-800/643-1500). Safe and clean if somewhat faded Loop hotel. ⑤.

Blackstone Hotel, 636 S Michigan Ave (☎427-4300 or ☎1-800/622-6330). Resurgent, once elegant turn-of-the-century hotel (featured in *The Untouchables*), overlooking the lake near Grant Park. ⑥.

Chicago International AYH Hostel, 6318 N Winthrop Ave (☎262-1011). Clean rooms in a safe if somewhat distant Northside neighborhood, easily accessible on the subway – take the A or B train north to Loyola Station, then walk two blocks south. Dorm beds $13 for members. ③.

Comfort Inn of Chicago, 601 W Diversey Parkway (☎348-2810 or ☎1-800/228-5150). Recently renovated medium-sized motel, with free parking and continental breakfast, near Lincoln Park. ④.

The Drake Hotel, 140 E Walton Place (☎787-2200). Chicago's society hotel, modernized without sacrificing its sedate charms. Off the Magnificent Mile; you can always just pop in for a drink. ⑧.

Executive Plaza Hotel, 71 E Wacker Drive (☎346-7100 or ☎1-800/621-4005). Magnificent setting by the Michigan Avenue bridge; an extra $10 gets a riverview. Big weekend discounts. ⑦.

Ho Jo Inn, 720 N LaSalle St (☎664-8100 or ☎1-800/446-4656). Standard *HoJo* rooms in a good near North location. ④.

International House, 1414 E 59th St (☎753-2270). Plain, pleasant rooms in summer on University of Chicago campus; not a nice part of town. AYH members $16, others $25. Reservations essential. ③.

Lenox House Suites, 616 N Rush St (☎337-1000 or ☎1/800-445-3669). Great all-suite hotel just a few blocks north of the river. ⑤.

Ohio House Motel, 600 N LaSalle St (☎943-6000). Similar to the neighboring *HoJo*. ④.

YMCA/YWCA, 33 W Chicago Ave (☎944-6211). Very plain, safe, and very central private rooms, not far from Evanston/Ravenswood. Weekly rates from $75. ②.

Eating

Chicago, famous across America for **deep dish pizzas** and barbecued **ribs**, is one of the most satisfying US cities for good, inexpensive food. Besides its all-American steak-and-potato places, a legacy of Chicago's days as the nation's meatpacker, all sorts of ethnic restaurants – Italian, Chinese, South American and eastern European – energize a dynamic and changeable eating scene. Gold Coast and Lincoln Park are the best areas. Steer clear, though, of the numerous "theme" restaurants, such as replica Fifties diners and places run by retired sports stars – where the food is usually secondary to the surroundings.

Many of the establishments listed under "Bars" and "Cafés" in the "Drinking" section also serve snacks and light meals. Dozens of cafés and fast-food joints in the Loop offer great breakfast and lunch specials.

Budget Eating: Breakfasts, Burgers and Sandwiches

Little Al's Italian Beef Barbeque, 1079 W Taylor St (☎226-4017). Fight your way to the counter for hearty sandwiches and a groaning pile of fresh french fries – all for under $4. Open until 1am.

Billy Goat Tavern, 430 N Michigan Ave (☎222-1525). Well-worn, fluorescent formica haunt of shift-working Chicago *Tribune* journalists. Cheap breakfasts, burgers and beers 7am–3am daily.

Ceres Cafe, 141 W Jackson Blvd (☎427-3443). Lively Art Deco coffeeshop, on the ground floor of the Board of Trade building, packed with TV screens quoting the latest pork belly futures prices.

Lou Mitchell's, 563 W Jackson Blvd (☎939-3111). Excellent coffee, fresh-squeezed fruit juices and delicious fresh pastries, plus carbo-loading breakfasts. Just west of the Loop.

Morrie's Old-Fashioned Deli, 345 S Dearborn St (☎922-2932). Successful imitation of a Jewish New York deli, with pickles and matzo-ball soups along with delicious pastrami sandwiches.

Oak Tree, in the 900 N Michigan Ave mall (☎751-1988). Bustling, all-American diner extremely popular for omelettes, waffles and endless cups of coffee.

West Egg Cafe, 620 N Fairbanks St (☎280-8366). Very popular – especially for Sunday brunch – artsy cafe, with sidewalk dining two blocks east of the Magnificent Mile.

American

Army and Lou's, 420 E 75th St (☎483-6550). Excellent-value, top-quality soul food in friendly South Side setting – smoked ham hocks, shrimp gumbos, mouthwatering fried chicken, and a superb range of desserts.

Eli's the Place for Steaks, 215 E Chicago Ave (☎642-1393). A favorite of old-time Chicagoans, including Frank Sinatra, who come for the thick steaks and 1940s ambience.

Shaw's Crab House, 21 E Hubbard St (☎527-2722). The swanky main room offers the freshest available fish and seafood; the less expensive oyster bar also serves up great clam and crab treats.

Twin Anchors, 1655 N Sedgewick St (☎266-1616). Zesty, melt-in-the-mouth barbecued ribs, great onion rings in friendly Old Town landmark. Unless you arrive at 5pm, you'll have to wait at the bar.

Asian

Hatsuhana, 160 E Ontario St (☎280-8287). Sit at the blond wood bar and watch the chefs prepare sea-fresh sushi or sashimi. Expensive, but not outrageous for the prime Magnificent Mile location.

Klay Oven, 414 N Orleans St (☎527-3999). East Indian restaurant offering freshly prepared meals including some unusual offerings at mid-range prices.

Mekong, 4953 Broadway (☎271-0206). Hugely popular, and unfortunately very small, Vietnamese eatery in the North. Excellent barbecue and seafood at very moderate prices. Expect to join a line.

Shilla, 5930 N Lincoln Ave (☎275-5930). Enormous, and very authentic, Korean menu with large portions. Absolutely beautiful food.

Thai Classic, 3332 N Clark St (☎404-2000). Inexpensive, low-key Wrigleyville Thai place with very good seafood specialties.

Three Happiness, 2130 S Wentworth Ave (☎791-1228). Chicago's best dim sum, in a cacophonous Chinatown haunt.

Eastern European

Galan's, 2212 W Chicago Ave (☎292-1000). Groaning plates of Ukrainian food at low prices. Set meals with potato dumplings, sausages, beef, pork or chicken paprika, plus wine, for around $15.

Irene's, 6873 N Milwaukee Ave (☎647-8147). SuperbPolish food in old-world atmosphere, out from downtown, near O'Hare Airport. Pirogis, kielbasas and plum soup, plus daily specials for under $10.

Mareva's, 1200 N Milwaukee Ave (☎227-4000). An unexpected family-run Polish restaurant in the as-yet ungentrified Near West Side. Multi-course Slavic meals with pirogis and borscht for $20–25.

French, Italian and Pizza

Ambria, 2300 N Lincoln Park West (☎472-5959). Classy but not stuffy Art Nouveau ambience, and exquisite nouvelle cuisine – tender slices of duck liver in calvados just for starters.

Avanzare, 161 E Huron Ave (☎337-8056). Spacious Near North restaurant serving top-quality northern Italian dishes for less than you'd think. Main dishes are $12–15, and the desserts are excellent.

Bacino's, 2204 N Lincoln Ave (☎472-7400). Just off Oz Park, this popular pizza place has great calzones, plus good beers and wines. There's a downtown branch at 75 E Wacker Drive.

Cafe Spiaggia, 980 N Michigan Ave (☎280-2764). Casual but top-rate Italian cafe, in the posey One Magnificent Mile building. Ultra-fresh salads, and great pizzas and pasta dishes.

California Pizza Kitchen, 414 N Orleans St (☎222-9030). Pricey but popular designer pizza chain. Barbecued chicken and Peking duck toppings served in a stagey black-tiled setting.

Edwardo's Natural Pizza Restaurant, 1212 N Dearborn St (☎337-4490). Exceptional pizza even by Chicago standards. Also at 2120 N Halsted St (☎871-3400) and 521 S Dearborn St (☎939-3366).

Gino's East, 160 E Superior St (☎943-1124). Rough-and-ready, dark wood and vinyl booth pizza parlor serving up some of the best (and cheapest) pies in the city.

Pizzeria Uno, 29 E Ohio St (☎321-1000). The place that put Chicago deep dish pizza on the map.

Middle Eastern and African

Helmand, 3201 N Halsted St (☎935-2447). An unusual Lincoln Park treat: Chicago's only Afghani food, with dishes like baked lamb with split peas, onions and a dash of coriander.

Mama Desta's Red Sea, 3216 N Clark St (☎935-7561). Hearty bread and stew finger-food in small Ethiopian restaurant. Inexpensive.

Moulibet, 3521 N Clark St (☎929-9383). Low-key but top-quality storefront Ethiopian restaurant, near Wrigley Field. Garlicky meat stews, delicately spiced vegetables, tangy *injera* flatbreads.

Spanish, Mexican and South American

Cafe Ba-ba-reeba!, 2024 N Halsted St (☎935-5000). Pricey but fun tapas bar and restaurant. Great garlic shrimp and plentiful paella, cooked in an open kitchen and washed down with Spanish wine.

Frontera Grill, 445 N Clark St (☎661-1434). Excellent, $10-a-plate Mexican-flavored restaurant using ingredients – Hawaiian seafood or smoked venison – you'd rarely find south of the border. The *Topolamba* next door offers delicious gourmet Mexican dishes but can be quite pricey.

Marco's Paradise, 3358 N Sheffield St (☎281-4848). Heaped portions of Mexican food, just down the street from Wrigley Field and jam-packed after a game. Fill up for around $5.

Mestizo, 311 W Superior St (☎787-4160). Fairly posey Mexican place, in the River North gallery district, worth a look at least for its ersatz Mayan decor; live salsa music most nights.

Rio's Casa Iberia, 4611 N Kedzie Ave (☎588-7800). Why fly to Rio de Janeiro when you can taste the best of Brazil (and Portugal and Spain) at the end of the Ravenswood *CTA* line? Not cheap at around $25 for a full meal, but great, especially the shellfish dishes.

Drinking

If not quite as wild as in the bootlegging days of speakeasies and Prohibition, Chicago remains a consummate boozer's town. From chic piano bars to spit-on-the-sawdust-floor saloons, the city has somewhere for everybody. As well as the standouts listed below, there are hundreds of equally comfortable haunts all over town, as often as not within stumbling distance of each other, and all are open to 3 or 4am, some until 5am. One thing Chicago has more of than anywhere else on earth is **"sports bars"**, where banks of TV screens broadcast Cubs, Sox, Bears, Bulls and Redwings games – great places for beer drinking and male bonding, but not for thoughtful conversation. **Division Street**, in the two blocks west of State Street, is unreconstructed breeder-bar territory, with a handful of more subtle joints tucked away on side streets off the main drag.

Cafés

Albert's Café, 52 W Elm St (☎751-0666). Tiny café, tucked away off Division Street and Michigan Avenue, with great cakes and coffees.

Café Voltaire, 3231 N Clark St (☎528-3136). Comfy couches and a nice garden attract a varied daytime crowd; live music and performances pack the downstairs cabaret at night. Good veggie food.

Caffe Trevi, 2275 N Lincoln Ave (☎871-4310). Cozy neighborhood café that makes an eye-opening antidote to Lincoln Avenue's wall-to-wall saloons, nightclubs and pool halls.

No Exit Café, 6970 N Glenwood Ave (☎743-3355). As you might guess from the name, this nearly suburban North Side café strives to preserve late 1950s Bohemianism intact for future generations.

Scenes Coffeehouse, 3168 N Clark St (☎525-1007). Clubby café just a block from N Halsted Street's alternative theaters and nightclubs, sharing space with the city's best drama bookshop.

Third Coast Coffeehouse, 1260 N Dearborn St (☎649-0730). The place to people-watch at 5am after a night in clubland. Trendy café open 24hr Tues–Sun; also at 888 N Wabash Ave (☎664-7225).

Bars and Pubs

John Barleycorn Memorial Pub, 658 W Belden St (☎348-8899). Highbrow hang-out near Lincoln Park. Lots of room, and a good range of British and Irish beers.

The Berghoff, 17 W Adams St (☎427-3170). Classic and stylish Chicago saloon – sharp-suited gentlemen behind the brass-railed bar have been pouring drinks for almost a century.

Coq d'Or, in the *Drake Hotel*, 140 E Walton Place (☎787-2200). Plush, warmly lit hideaway off the Magnificent Mile, perfect for an intimate evening cocktail or two.

Goose Island Brewing Co, 1800 N Clynborn Ave (☎915-0071). Beer brewed on the premises, and a pleasant atmosphere in West Lincoln Park.

Old Town Ale House, 219 W North Ave (☎944-7020). Bass IPA on draught and the jazziest juke-box in town. Unpretentious well-worn haunt attracting a friendly, varied crowd. Nightly until 4am.

O'Rourke's Pub, 1625 N Halsted St (☎335-1806). Spacious and comfortable Irish bar with a good jukebox and portraits of notable Irishmen on the walls. Well-kept draught Guinness.

Tap Root Pub, 636 W Willow St (☎642-5235). Ripe with Old Chicago legend – Al Capone kept his bootleg whisky next door, for example. A great place to soak up some history over a beer or two.

Zebra Lounge, 1220 N State St (☎642-5140). Ironic and erudite contrast to nearby Division Street's meatmarkets. Everything in this basement bar is covered in black-and-white stripes, and the late-night singalongs have to be seen and heard to be believed.

Sports Bars

Harry Caray's, 33 W Kinzie (☎465-9269). Chicago's biggest and best sports bar, in old River North brick warehouse. The huge bar is packed with beer drinkers until the early hours, and has floor to ceiling Cubs memorabilia – Harry Caray is a radio announcer. Very good Mediterranean food.

Michael Jordan's, 500 N LaSalle St (☎644-3865). Just one TV screen, but it's the biggest in town. Laid-back atmosphere, and Michael makes the odd appearance in the pricey restaurant upstairs.

Slugger's World Class Sports Bar, 3540 N Clark St (☎248-0055). Probably the only bar in the world with its own indoor batting cage, this raucous beer bar fairly rattles and hums during Cubs, Bears and Bulls games. During happy hour beers cost just 50¢.

Nightlife and Entertainment

From its earliest frontier days, Chicago has had some of the best **nightlife** in the US. Sweet Home Chicago, birthplace of Muddy Waters' **urban blues** as well as r'n'b's *Chess Records*, is still going strong, inspiring the energetic dancebeat of 1980s **house**

music and the hardcore bands on the *Waxtrax* label, as well as the groundbreaking **jazz** of the Art Ensemble of Chicago. **Nightclubs** aplenty are all over town, especially along Halsted Street, Lincoln Avenue and Clark Street on the North Side; the best **gay clubs** congregate in the Lincoln Park area.

More highbrow pursuits are also well provided for: the **Chicago Symphony** plays in winter at the Orchestra Hall, 220 S Michigan Ave (☎435-6666), and in summer at the Ravinia Festival, held in the northern suburbs. **Theater** is also of a high standard – among others, David Mamet and John Malkovich had their first break here. **Comedy** is particularly vibrant, with the improvisational troupe at *Second City*, 1616 N Wells St (☎337-3992), especially renowned. **Festivals** are detailed in the box on p.255.

In addition to our listings, get a rundown of what's on when you're here (and articles on local issues) from the free *Chicago Reader* (out every Thursday); the colorful *New City* is less comprehensive but still worth a look. Local **radio** stations are also good sources of information; one of the best is *WHPK* (88.5FM), which plays great jazz, blues and r'n'b without commercial interruption. The Friday editions of the daily *Tribune* and the *Sun-Times* also carry arts and music listings.

Rock Clubs

Avalon Niteclub, 959 W Belmont Ave (☎472-3020).The latest bands, plus dance floors. $5 or less.

Cubby Bear Lounge, 1059 W Addison St (☎327-1662). A sports bar during the day – right next to Wrigley Field – after dark this place transforms itself into one of the city's better live venues, popular with ageing dinosaurs more than new bands, but still fun.

Lincoln Tap Room, 3010 N Lincoln Ave (☎868-0060). Three or four indy/punk bands most nights.

Lounge Ax, 2438 N Lincoln Ave (☎525-6620). Small and always crowded old barroom that's emerged as one of Chicago's most happening new clubs.

Metro, 3730 N Clark St (☎549-3604). Multilevel dance club, converted from an old cinema. Regular concerts, often young English bands trying to break in Stateside, and DJ mixes. The best dancing is in the downstairs *Smart Bar*. The whole complex is open late – until 5am Fri and Sat.

Blues Clubs

B.L.U.E.S., 2519 N Halsted St (☎528-1012). Small and sweaty club, pulling in some of the best blues singers and players on the planet. Cover $5–15. Its more dance-oriented sister club, *B.L.U.E.S. etc*, 1124 W Belmont Ave (☎549-9436), is considerably larger and has a broader range of music.

Buddy Guy's Legends, 754 S Wabash Ave (☎427-0333). South Loop club, part-owned by veteran Chicago performer, and attracting major blues artists. Great acoustics and atmosphere.

Kingston Mines, 2548 N Halsted St (☎477-4646). Big names play the main room, local bands a smaller side room, and a huge dancefloor grooves until 4am every night; cover $4–9.

New Checkerboard Lounge, 423 E 43rd St/Muddy Waters Drive (☎624-3240). Chicago's oldest blues club, in a slightly dodgy South Side neighborhood near the *CTA* 43rd Street station.

Rosa's Blues Lounge, 3420 W Armitage Ave (☎342-0452). One of Chicago's most welcoming blues bars, with great bands and an even better sound. Well worth the $6 taxi ride from downtown.

Wise Fool's Pub, 2270 N Lincoln Ave (☎929-1510). Friendly, no-frills beer bar, two blocks from Lincoln Park. Portraits of Chicago's blues musicians cover the walls, and a blues band most nights.

Folk and World Music Clubs

At the Tracks, 325 N Jefferson St (☎332-1124). Artsy, post-industrial space, across the railroad tracks from the Loop skyline, with an unpretentious range of folksy, usually acoustic live music.

Clearwater Saloon, 3937 N Lincoln Ave (☎549-5599). Cozy, publike haunt with good, free (or very inexpensive) live folk and country most nights.

Earl's Pub, 2470 N Lincoln Ave (☎929-0660). This rough-at-the-edges Sixties holdout has good beers and live acoustic music most nights.

Wild Hare and Singing Armadillo Frog Sanctuary, 3350 N Clark St (☎327-0800). Fun if fairly anodyne reggae dance club that attracts an interesting mix of local rastas and Lincoln Park yuppies; *Exodus II*, up the street at 3477 N Clark St (☎348-3998), is closer to the real thing.

Jazz Clubs

Andy's, 11 E Hubbard St (☎642-6805). Slick, central and packed with office workers for low-priced lunch-hour and early-evening performances. A second wave appears for the nightly live shows.

The Bulls, 1916 N Lincoln Park West (☎337-3000). Chicago's best late-night hang-out, with live local groups three times nightly – last shows kick off at 1am.

Green Mill, 4802 N Broadway (☎878-5552). Atmospheric, 1930s Art Deco tavern with big band swing and other traditional jazz.

Joe Segal's Jazz Showcase, in the *Blackstone Hotel* at 636 S Michigan Ave (☎427-4300). Premier contemporary jazz in top-class setting. Dress to impress, and expect to pay $20 for a big-name star.

Dance Clubs

Cairo, 720 N Wells St (☎266-6620). Very fashionable, high-style River North hang-out for civilized decadence, divided into posey jazz bar (upstairs) and cavernous rock club (downstairs).

Club 950, 950 W Wrightwood Ave (☎929-8955). Alternative European dance; cheap drinks and no cover Mon–Thurs.

Medusa's, 3257 Sheffield Ave (☎935-3635). Housed in an old school, this offbeat and enthusiastic young people's club – there's no alcohol, and just about everyone's under 18 – is an energized counterpoint to Chicago's more studiously jaded haunts.

Neo, 2350 N Clark St (☎528-2622). Longstanding alternative club. Largest and lively dance floors; good mix in both the music and the crowd. Cover $3–5; open until 4am every night but Mon.

Shelter, 564 W Fulton St (☎648-5500). Chicago's hottest and most expensive nightspot, with assorted bars and dance floors inside and lines snaking around the block; cover around $10.

Sports

Staunchly blue-collar Chicago must be among the best US cities for watching **sports**. Though the city's two baseball teams haven't won anything big for years, Chicagoans follow their fortunes with masochistic glee. The perennially mediocre Chicago Cubs baseball team plays all summer at historic Wrigley Field on the North Side, described on p.259 (☎404-2827); the usually better Chicago White Sox are based at the ultramodern New Comiskey Park, on the South Side (☎924-1000).

In recent years the city's most successful outfit has been the Chicago Bulls basketball team, until recently lead by superstar Michael Jordan; they play in winter and spring at Chicago Stadium, 1800 W Madison St (☎943-5800), as do hockey's Chicago Blackhawks (☎733-5300). The post-Ditka Chicago Bears football team (☎663-5408) can be seen at the 66,814-capacity lakeside Soldier Field, 425 E McFetridge Drive at the bottom end of Grant Park – host of the opening ceremony and first game of soccer's 1994 World Cup.

Central Illinois

Interstates 55 and 57 slice south through the **Corn Belt** of central Illinois from Chicago. Few places warrant much attention (particularly with St Louis directly across the Mississippi in the southwest), though the state capital, **Springfield**, interestingly commemorates its former citizen, **Abraham Lincoln**. Otherwise, the college towns of **Bloomington-Normal** and **Champaign-Urbana** are the only rational urban stops.

Springfield

The Illinois state capital, **SPRINGFIELD**, spreads out from a neat, leafy, downtown grid, 165 miles south of Chicago. Abraham Lincoln honed his legal and political skills here, and tourists flock to his old homes, haunts and final resting place. What they find is neither tacky nor pompous, portraying not only the life of the sixteenth president of the USA, but also the uncertainty and turmoil of a nation on the brink of civil war.

Thirty miles northwest of Springfield on Hwy-97, **Lincoln's New Salem State Historical Site** marks where the future president first came to live in this area in 1831. In this backwoods clearing he clerked in a store, volunteered for the Black Hawk War, served as postmaster and failed in business before taking up legal studies. Today the authentically re-created village features unelaborate homes, workshops, a store and a tavern. The **visitor center** hosts a worthwhile exhibit on pioneer lifestyles (daily; April–Oct 9am–5pm; Nov–March 8am–4pm). Once established as a member of the Illinois House of Representatives, Lincoln left to pursue his career in Springfield in 1837.

Pick up tickets at the **Lincoln Home Visitor Center**, Eighth and Jackson in Springfield itself, for a narrated tour of the only house Lincoln ever owned, which he shared with his wife Mary from 1844 to 1861. Though tours are free (daily 8.30am–4.30pm; extended hours in summer) you can expect to wait: various displays and a brief film at the visitor center are good ways of passing time.

In the restored Greek Revival **Old State Capitol**, three blocks away at Sixth and Adams, Lincoln attended at least 240 Supreme Court hearings, and proclaimed in 1858 that "A house divided against itself cannot stand. I believe that this government cannot endure, permanently, half-slavery, half-freedom." Objects, busts and papers relating to Lincoln and the Democrat Stephen Douglas, whom he beat in the 1860 presidential election, can be found throughout the building (daily 9am–5pm; free). At the tastefully renovated **Lincoln Depot** on Tenth and Monroe (daily 10am–4pm; free), the newly elected president said goodbye to Springfield in February 1861 and boarded a train for his inauguration in Washington DC (a slide show illustrates the twelve-day journey). The next time he returned was in his funeral train. **Lincoln's Tomb** stands in Oak Ridge Cemetery on the north side of town. The vault, adorned with busts and statuettes, is open to the public (daily 9am–5pm).

Also in Springfield, the **Illinois State Museum**, on Spring and Edwards, is crammed with natural history, native American and contemporary art exhibits along with the interactive "At home in the Heartland" display tracing Illinois family life from 1700 to 1970 (Mon–Sat 8.30am–5pm, Sun noon–5pm; free). The **Dana-Thomas House**, 301 East Lawrence Ave, completed in 1904, survives as the best-preserved and most completely furnished example of **Frank Lloyd Wright's** early Prairie house, with over four hundred pieces of glasswork and original art light fixtures. A free tour of the house is an absolute must, though unfortunately lack of funding has cut opening hours: phone ☎782-6776 for current times.

Practicalities

Amtrak **trains** from Chicago and St Louis roll in at Third and Washington downtown, at manageable times; *Greyhound* drops off east of town at 2351 S Dirksen Parkway. The **CVB**, 109 N Seventh St (☎789-2360 or ☎1-800/545-7300), has brochures and maps.

The best selection of budget **accommodation**, including a *Motel 6* with pool (☎789-1063; ②), lies off I-55 at the Hwy-29 exit, though downtown accommodation is reasonably priced – even the swanky politicians' hotels offer affordable deals at the weekend. Central options include the *Best Western Lincoln Plaza*, 101 E Adams St (☎523-5661 or ☎1-800/528-1234; ③), with a decent café and bar, right next to the capitol and *Amtrak*. Get the feel of nineteenth-century Springfield at *Corinne's B&B Inn*, 1001 S Sixth St (☎527-1400; ④), and enjoy fresh pastries and quiches in the morning.

Springfield's cafés seem to have exclusive rights to a phenomenon known as the **Horseshoe** – ostensibly a sandwich, but fried, covered in melted cheese, and totally delicious. *Norb Andy's*, a great little jazz and blues bar at 518 E Capitol Ave (☎523-7777), musters up the best Horseshoes around. At the other end of the health spectrum, the *New Leaf Café*, 501 W Washington Ave (daytime only; ☎523-4300), serves up great California-style and veggie meals. Just north of New Salem on Hwy-97, the menu at *George Warburton's Café* (☎632-7878) holds homemade soups, breads and burgers.

WISCONSIN

As many cows as humans call **WISCONSIN** home. About four million of each eat to their hearts' content in this rich, rolling farmland, which has a higher proportion of over-weight people than any other state. However, America's self-proclaimed "Dairyland" is more than just one giant pasture. Beyond the massive red barns and silvery silos lie endless pine forests, some 15,000 sky-blue lakes, postcard-pretty valleys and dramatic bluffs. The state, whose Ojibway name means "gathering of the waters", is bordered by Lake Michigan to the east, Lake Superior in the north and, westward, the Mississippi and St Croix rivers; only the southern, Illinois, demarcation is dry.

The **history** of Wisconsin exemplifies the standard formula for westward expansion. Seventeenth-century French and British explorers began by trading with the Native Americans and soon ousted them from their land. The European settlers who followed – predominantly Germans, Scandinavians and Poles – tended to be liberal and progressive; such major national social programmes as labor laws for women and children, assistance for the elderly and the disabled, and unemployment compensation were rooted here. On the down side, Joseph McCarthy, the infamous 1950s witch-hunter, was born in Grand Chute, current headquarters of the right-wing John Birch Society.

Wisconsin today is best known for its liquids. The **milk** from all those cattle yields cheeses of all kinds, while the **beer**, as the song says, is what made **Milwaukee** famous. Sparkling **Madison** apart, Wisconsin's other cities – LaCrosse, Green Bay, Oshkosh – can veer toward the dull side, but they're also clean, safe and amiable, while its smaller towns can be distinctive and charming.

Getting Around Wisconsin

You'll be hard put to explore Wisconsin's remote north, or key locales like Door County peninsula, without a vehicle. Public transport is better in the south. Milwaukee and, to a lesser extent, Madison are hubs for *Greyhound* and *Amtrak*. Six **trains** daily connect Milwaukee and Chicago, a 90-minute journey, while one crosses the state in the south en route for Seattle, via Columbus (near Madison), Wisconsin Dells and LaCrosse.

Milwaukee

Bustling **MILWAUKEE**, the "Deutsch Athens" of southeastern Wisconsin, is a combination of the down-home and the sophisticated, known for its lakeside **festivals** and huge **breweries**. Visually it's a mix of elegant Teutonic architecture, rambling Victorian warehouses, and tasteful waterfront developments. Its prime position on the shores of Lake Michigan, at the confluence of three rivers, made it a meeting place for Native tribes long before white settlers moved in, while the opulent mansions lining the lake commemorate the industrialists who helped make this Wisconsin's economic and manufacturing capital. By 1850, less than two decades old and with a population of twenty thousand, Milwaukee already had a dozen breweries and 225 saloons. The contemporary estimate of 6000 bars – one per hundred residents – is not necessarily apocryphal.

Arrival, City Transport and Information

Milwaukee is well served by air, rail and coach. Its **airport**, eight miles south of down-town at 5300 S Howell Ave, is connected with the city center by bus #80 ($1), and by a limousine service ($7.50 single). *Amtrak* is at 433 W St Paul Ave, while *Greyhound* and *Wisconsin Coach*, serving outlying Wisconsin, operate out of the same terminal at 606

The **area code** for Milwaukee and eastern Wisconsin is ☎414.

N Seventh St (☎272-8900), as does *Badger Bus* (☎276-7490), which runs a daily express service to Madison ($14 return). Take care in or near the stations – or, for that matter, downtown as a whole – at night. **Getting around** Milwaukee is easy and inexpensive via the county's extensive **transit system** (24-hour info ☎344-6711; flat fare $1).

Milwaukee's **CVB**, 510 W Kilbourn Ave (Mon–Fri 8am–6pm; ☎273-3950 or ☎1-800/231-0903), has details on such **festivals** as the eleven-day Summerfest (late June–July 4), Great Circus Parade (mid-July) and the Wisconsin State Fair (early Aug). The main **post office** is at 345 W St Paul Ave (Mon–Fri 7.30am–6pm; ☎287-2530; zip code 53201).

The City

Downtown Milwaukee, split north to south by the **Milwaukee River**, is only a mile long and a few blocks wide. Handsome old buildings and gleaming, modern steel and glass structures are comfortably corralled together on three sides by spaghetti-like strands of freeway. **Lake Michigan** forms the fourth boundary, with its parkland, marina and the **Summerfest** grounds. The **Milwaukee Art Museum**, 750 N Lincoln Memorial Drive (Tues, Wed, Fri & Sat 10am–5pm, Thurs noon–9pm, Sun noon–5pm; $4), contains works by European masters and twentieth-century Americans. One wing – with stunning views of the lake – is devoted to a dazzlingly comprehensive collection of Post-Impressionist paintings. At the **Milwaukee Public Museum**, also downtown at 800 W Wells St (daily 9am–5pm; $5), the intertwined histories and mysteries of the earth, nature and humankind are presented with vibrant imagination, through dioramas such as The Streets of Old Milwaukee and a battle of the dinosaurs.

The blue-domed, neo-Byzantine **Annunciation Greek Orthodox Church**, standing like a mushroom crossed with a spaceship at 9400 W Congress St (9am–2.30pm; call first on ☎461-9400; $2; bus #57), was one of the last major works by native Wisconsin architect Frank Lloyd Wright. Completed in 1961, its interior is a jaw-dropping blend of the streamlined and the ornate. The 37-room **Pabst Mansion**, 2000 W Wisconsin Ave (mid-March to Dec Mon–Sat 10am–3.30pm, Sun noon–3.30pm; otherwise weekends only; $5) was built in 1893 as the castle of a local beer baron. Both the **Pabst Brewery**, at 915 W Juneau Ave (Mon–Fri 10am–3pm, June–Aug also Sat 9–11am, bus #71), and the **Miller Brewing Company** at 4251 W State St (Mon–Sat 10am–3.30pm, bus #71), offer free behind-the-scenes tours, culminating in generous samples for over-21s. The more primitive micro-brewery **Sprecher**, 730 W Oregon St (Sat 1, 2 & 3pm, $2), serves samples straight out of the barrel. *Schlitz*, the "beer that made Milwaukee famous", was bought out by *Stroh's* in the late Eighties and is now produced in Detroit.

You can also take one-hour tours of the engine plant responsible for Milwaukee's other legendary brand name, **Harley-Davidson**, out in a rough area of town on W Capital Drive at Hwy-45. It's really for Harley devotees; bikes aren't assembled here and if you don't know your shovelheads from your knuckleheads you might feel out of place (tour times vary; ☎ 535-3693). For those more interested in Harley chic, there's ample opportunity to purchase all kinds of merchandise throughout Milwaukee.

Accommodation

Lodgings in Milwaukee run the gamut from low-budget to upmarket chains. *B&B of Milwaukee Inc*, 1916 W Donges Bay Rd in nearby Mequon (☎242-9680), is a free reservation service for close on thirty B&Bs in or near the city.

Marie's, 346 E Wilson St (☎483-1512). B&B in self-contained suburb-that's-not-a suburb Bay View. Excellent morning feeds. ④.

Park East Hotel, 916 E State St (☎276-8800). Clean, very comfortable rooms in a nice part of downtown. Good value compared to the bigger hotels. ⑤.

Red Barn Hostel, 6750 W Loomis Rd (☎529-3299). 13 miles southwest, via Hwy-894 or buses #10 and #35 (best avoided at night). Hiking and biking trails. May–Oct only; $9 *AYH* members only. ①.

Robert Stevens Inn, 1457 N Franklin Place (☎224-1059). Towered Victorian restoration. All eight rooms have private baths; outdoor pool, grand piano, sitting room with fireplace. ⑤.

The Wisconsin, 720 N Third St (☎271-4900). Older downtown hotel half a block from the glassy, classy and sprawling Grand Avenue Mall, with free parking and a lounge. ③.

Eating
The Germans who first settled in Milwaukee determined its eating style – heavy on brat-wurst, rye bread and beer. Subsequent immigrants threw the collective kitchen wide open, making for a culinary cornucopia. With Lake Michigan lapping the city's feet, freshwater fish can hardly be overlooked, especially on a Friday night when fish boils (see p.273) break out all over the place. Wherever you go, portions tend to be big.

Jack Pandl's Whitefish Bay Inn, 1319 E Henry Clay St (☎964-3800). Suburban landmark famous for broiled whitefish ($9), colossal oven-baked pancakes ($8), and stein collection.

John Ernst's, 600 E Ogden Ave (☎273-1878). With the similarly pricey *Mader's* and *Karl Ratzsch's*, one of the top German institutions. Assiduous service, excellent Wiener schnitzel and lots of seafood.

The King & I, 823 N Second St (☎276-4181). Good medium-priced Thai food, downtown.

Knickerbocker Cafe, 1007 N Cass St (☎272-4661). Gorgeous little Deco-style daytime café in a venerable downtown apartment-hotel. Meals $3–6.

The Old Town, 522 W Lincoln Ave (☎672-0206). Tasty Serbian food on the Pole-dominated south side. Try a *burek*, a meat or spinach-filled pie the size of a Frisbee ($11). Live music Thurs–Sun.

Water Street Brewery, 110 N Water St (☎272-1195). Milwaukee's smallest brewery, serving good ales, ribs and salmon.

Nightlife
The concept of neighborhoods is vital to Milwaukee's nightlife. **Brady Street** in the near northeast, a counterculture haven in the 1960s, is now filled with Italian restau-rants and bars. **Walker's Point**, on the edge of downtown, has all sorts of gay and straight watering holes, while the **Polish** locals can be found further south. Downtown gets busy at the weekend, especially on Water Street between Juneau and State.

High culture in downtown Milwaukee revolves around the **Performing Arts Center** (*PAC*), 929 N Water St (☎273-7206 or ☎1-800/472-4458), and the plush, historic *Pabst Theater*, 414 E Wells St (☎278-3665). Nearby, the *Milwaukee Repertory Theater*, 108 E Wells St (☎224-9490), has a reputation for risk-taking productions.

John Hawk's Pub, 100 E Wisconsin Ave (☎272-3199). Riverside Brit-style establishment down-town. Food all day, jazz on Sat.

Louie's American-Chinese Tavern, 120 W National Ave (☎347-0524). Weird but popular bar where kimonos, a rickshaw and teahouse upstage a patio-cum-volleyball court.

Tamarack, 322 W State St (☎225-2552). Old saloon, specializing in weekend R&B – ribs and blues.

Up and Under Pub, 1216 Brady St (☎276-2677). Milwaukee's top blues bar.

Eastern Shores

North of Milwaukee, **eastern Wisconsin** is a melange of the industrial and the mari-time, with a nod to agriculture, shaped by its proximity to **Lake Michigan** and the smaller **Lake Winnebago**. Of its towns, **Appleton** was the birthplace of escapologist Harry Houdini, **Green Bay** is home to the legendary Packers, and **Oshkosh** is a household word for its overalls and baby clothes, but it's all best seen as a prelude to the most romanticized part of the state, **Door County**.

Green Bay

Few cities can be as closely associated with a sports team as **GREEN BAY** is with the footballing Packers: 108 miles north of Milwaukee, it's the smallest city in the US to have a professional sports franchise and the only one to own it. The **Green Bay Packer Hall of Fame**, 855 Lombardi Ave (daily; June–Aug 9am–5pm, otherwise

10am–5pm; $6), celebrates the dynastic years of the Sixties when the Pack won Superbowls I and II, as well as such stars of today as Reggie *Minister of Defence* White, Brett Favre and Sterling Sharpe. Stuffed with hands-on displays, movie theaters and memorabilia, the museum offers more than enough to satisfy any football fan. Packer fanatics can also tour adjacent **Lambeau Field** (summer, daily 10.30am–4.30pm; $5).

Also in this busy but not particularly attractive port, pride of place at the **National Railroad Museum**, 2285 S Broadway (May to mid-Oct, daily 9am–5pm; $4, including train ride) goes to the 1.1 million-ton 1941 Union Pacific *Big Boy* locomotive, one of a many such trains which served Green Bay's still-enormous freight depot. West on Hwy-172, opposite the airport, stands Wisconsin's biggest casino – **Oneida Tribal Bingo** (☎497-8118 or 1-800/238-4262). Tribal history, and the way in which profits from blackjack, video poker and bingo have improved education, social and health facilities, are examined at the **Oneida Nation Museum**, seven miles west of Hwy-41 as it runs south from downtown (Mon–Fri 9am–5pm, Sat & Sun 10am–2pm; $2).

The city's **visitor center** (☎494-9507 or ☎1-800/236-EXPO) sits in the shadow of the football stadium, off Lombardi Ave, near the *Bay Motel*, 1301 S Military Ave (☎494-3441; ②). *Los Banditos*, 1258 Main St (☎432-9462), serves well-priced Mexican **food**.

Door County

From **Sturgeon Bay**, 140 miles north of Milwaukee, **DOOR COUNTY** sticks for 42 miles into Lake Michigan like a gradually tapering candle. With thirteen lighthouses and a dozen fishing villages, its coastline smacks more of New England than the Midwest. The name derives from "Porte des Morts" or **"Door of the Dead"**, the French name for the treacherous eight-mile strait which severs Washington Island at its tip. Despite drawing a million-plus warm-weather tourists, the peninsula (actually an island split off from Wisconsin by a canal) is not an extended theme park. Prices can get a little steep, but you get what you pay for – a small sliver of America devoid, for the most part, of crude billboards, sloppy diners, bland chain motels and tacky amusements. Activities include browsing around galleries and attending arts festivals, as well as hiking, fishing and boating. Renting a **bicycle** (Fish Creek's *Nor-Door Cyclery* has the best models; ☎868-2275; $22 a day) gives the chance to follow an excellent **cycle trail**.

Pick up road and trail maps at the **visitor center** at 1015 Green Bay Rd in Sturgeon Bay (☎743-7873 or 1-800/52-RELAX), where you can also phone local lodgings for free.

Exploring Door County

Door County begins at its only sizeable town, **Sturgeon Bay** – a pleasant enough ship-building community, if not exactly abundant in small-town splendor. Ten miles north on Hwy-57 is the rolling **Whitefish Dunes State Park**, with its wispy sand dunes and popular mile-long beach (daily; $6 per car). A short trail leads to the spectacular rocky **Cave Point County Park** (free), studded with wind- and wave-sculpted caves. In general **beaches** are better this side of the peninsula; **Jacksonport**'s (free) Lakeside Park ranks as the best of the lot. You can also swim in several placid inland lakes.

Over on the western side, biking and hiking trails traverse the thickly forested hills of **Peninsula State Park** (situated between tiny **Fish Creek** and elegant Mennonite **Ephraim**, with its resplendent white-clapboard architecture). An observation tower and lighthouse stand on the park's extensive shoreline, while just outside it on Hwy-42 is the anachronistic *Skyway Drive-In* movie theater (☎854-9938).

Washington Island, off the peninsula's northern tip, offers a different cultural perspective. During Prohibition, the Icelandic community here convinced authorities that (40 percent alcohol) bitters were an ancient cure for rheumatism. Cases of the stuff were shipped in, and the habit stuck; go into *Nelson's Bar* in **Detroit Harbor** and you're likely to find old-timers shifting bitters by the half-pint. Motel rooms are available on Washington, but there's no such luxury on the primitive 950-acre **Rock Island** across the "Door of the Dead". Once the private estate of a millionaire, it's dotted with stark, stone buildings; no cars are allowed, so see them by foot or bike.

The islands are served by the *Washington Island Ferry* from Northport at the tip of the peninsula (daily; $7 return; cars $15, bikes $2; ☎847-2546 or 1-800/223-2094) and the *Rock Island Ferry* out of Detroit Harbor (daily, June–Sept; ☎847-2252).

Accommodation

Door County has a full range of **accommodation**, including some overpriced resorts. Prices given are for shoulder seasons (the best time to come); expect to pay up to 25 percent extra at the grander hotels in July and August, and a small weekend premium. **Camping** is idyllic; state park sites cost $10 (plus $6 daily admission, annual $28), while among recommended private campgrounds are *Patch of Pines* (☎868-3332), County Road F off Hwy-42, near Fish Creek (May–Oct, $15).

Chal-A-Motel, 3910 Hwy-42/57, Sturgeon Bay (☎743-6788). Offbeat, clean, budget motel with a huge collection of dolls, toys and old autos. ②.

Century Farm Motel, 10068 Hwy-57 (☎854-4069). Basic cottages (sleeping to six people), set in farmland halfway between Sister Bay and Ephraim. Probably the lowest prices on the peninsula. ②.

Hillside Hotel, 9980 Hwy-42 (☎854-2417 or ☎1-800/423-7023). Beautifully restored country inn on Ephraim harbor. All rooms share baths. Gourmet meals (residents only) on selected nights. ⑤.

Liberty Park Lodge and Shore Cottages, Hwy-42N, Sister Bay (☎854-2025). Spotless complex with a lakeside porch and sandy beach. Great value. ③.

Waterbury Inn, Hwy-42, Ephraim (☎854-2821). Relatively new luxury property. Lacks the olde worlde charm of places like the *Hillside*, but its nice suites come with fully equipped kitchens. ④.

White Gull Inn, 4225 Main St, Fish Creek (☎868-3517). Elegant old inn next to delightful Sunset Park. Good restaurant (breakfast not included in price), and fishboil every night in summer. ④.

Eating

One reward of a midsummer visit to Door County is the chance to sample the cherry in all its guises. Another traditional treat is the **fishboil**, a delicious outdoor ritual involving whitefish steaks, potatoes and onions cooked in a cauldron over a wood fire. Rounded off with coleslaw and cherry pie, it's widely available for around $10.

Al Johnson's Swedish Restaurant, Hwy-42 (☎854-2626). Pancakes, meatballs and other fine Scandinavian dishes; and there are goats tethered atop the sod roof.

Bayside Tavern, Main St, Fish Creek (☎868-3441). Convivial pub serving a celebrated chili, burgers and a mean Friday night perch-fry.

Dal Santo's, 341 N Third St, Sturgeon Bay (☎743-6100). Pizza, pasta, and bar snacks in an old railway depot with a good micro brewery. Their cherry ale is surprisingly palatable and refreshing.

Little Sister Resort, 360 Little Sister Rd, Sister Bay (☎854-4013). The county's best-fun fish fry: all-you-can-eat and free beer for $14 with a great lakeshore view.

Wilson's, Hwy-42, Ephraim (☎854-2041). Burgers, sandwiches and (along with the *Door County Ice Cream Co* in Sister Bay) the top ice cream on the peninsula.

Upstate Wisconsin

Sparsely settled **northern Wisconsin** has no large cities (and few small ones), and no interstates; it's a lake-studded wilderness, covered by enormous tracts of forest. You can canoe its rivers, fish for record-breakers, or ski or snowmobile cross-country trails without having to fight for space. **Bayfield** and the **Apostle Islands** in the northwest are the obvious destinations, but **Hayward**, 76 miles southeast of Superior, is home to the amaz-

The **area code** for upstate Wisconsin is ☎715.

ing **National Fresh Water Fishing Hall of Fame** (mid-April to Nov, 10am–5pm), where you're invited to "Walk through the biggest fish in the world!" – a four-storey 500-ton fiberglass monster.

The Apostle Islands

All but one of the 22 **Apostle Islands**, scattered off **Bayfield Peninsula** eighty miles east of Duluth, MN (see p.282), are designated as National Lakeshore – a prized preserve of outdoors enthusiasts seeking to recharge depleted spiritual batteries.

The jumping-off point for the islands, **BAYFIELD**, once a lumbering and fishing village, is now a pleasant soft-sell tourist trap. Its sumptuous *Old Rittenhouse Inn*, 301 Rittenhouse Ave (☎779-5111; ⑤), offers gourmet meals and swanky **rooms**; *Frostman's*, 24 N Third St (☎779-3239; ②), has clean, simple doubles. Lodges and cottages are scattered through the thirty gorgeous lakeside acres of *Rocky Run Resort* (☎373-2551; ⑤), outside **Washburn** eleven miles south. On Fridays it's worth journeying 21 miles west to **Cornucopia**, for a special Scandinavian fishboil ($10) at the *Village Inn Restaurant* (☎742-3941). Bayfield's **visitor center** is at 42 Broad St (☎779-3335 or 1-800/447-4094). Campers heading for the islands require free permits from the **visitor center** at 410 Washington Ave (daily May–Oct; ☎779-3397). *Apostle Island Cruise Service* boats (☎779-3925; $20) twist their way past all of the islands, and will set down and pick up campers.

Madeline Island

By the fifteenth century, **Madeline Island** was known to the Ojibway as *Mon-a waun-a-kauning* – home of the golden-breasted woodpecker. Frenchman Michel Cadotte founded a fur trading post there for the British in 1793, and subsequently married Equaysayway, daughter of a tribal leader, who took the name the island bears today. Madeline is now the only commercially developed Apostle, but it all remains pretty low-key. Cadotte is buried in an overgrown cemetery in its sole town, **La Pointe**.

La Pointe is accessible in summer via the 15-min ride on the *Madeline Island Ferry Line* from Bayfield (every 30min; passengers $3, bikes $1.50, cars $7; ☎747-2051). Its 165 year-round residents maintain an interesting little historical **museum** (May–Oct daily 10am–5pm; $3) while assorted sandy beaches, wide bays, scenic points and forests can be explored along 45 miles of sometimes rough road. **Bicycles** are for rent near the dock for $18 per day, **mopeds** from *Motion to Go* (☎747-6585) at around $45.

A **visitor center** on Main Street (☎747-2801) can offer advice on places to stay; the *Madeline Island Motel* (☎747-3000; ③) and *La Pointe Lodgings* (☎747-5205; ③), both near the ferry dock, are probably the best value. **Camping** sites, on top of a bluff and close to caves at **Big Bay State Park** (☎779-3346), cost $15 including park admission; reservations required. A wooden footbridge across the lagoon leads to Big Bay Town Park ($10, no reservations); the campgrounds share a splendid mile-long beach. **Eating** options are limited to the pricey but tasty *Clubhouse* (Wed–Sun only; ☎747-2612), and the low-cost *Grandpa Tony's* (☎747-3911). There are also a couple of bars.

Southern Wisconsin

Assorted highways and back roads lace up **southern Wisconsin**, passing over rolling hills and deep dales. The main conurbation of Wisconsin's most populated region, still mainly farmland, is the immensely likeable lakeside college town of **Madison**, which doubles as the state capital. **Wisconsin Dells** may have a picturesque setting, but it's just a bit too overladen with tacky attractions to make it a worthwhile stop. Stretches of the **Mississippi River**, undulating down the western border, are designated as **The Great River Road**, a scenic highway that runs from near Canada to the Gulf of Mexico.

Madison

The history books say that **MADISON**, just over an hour west of Milwaukee, was little more than a wooded, mosquito-infested swamp when it was selected to be the political nucleus of Wisconsin Territory in 1836. Today this stimulating, youthful metropolis is one of the most beautifully set cities in the US, with a handful of diverting museums.

Downtown is neatly laid out on an isthmus between lakes Mendota and Monona, with the sumptuous white granite **State Capitol** sitting benignly on a hill at its center, surrounded by shady trees, lawns and park benches. Capitol Square itself is the site of a fun farmers market (May–Oct, Sat 6am–2pm); browse late for bargains. **Madison Civic and Art Center**, close by at 211 State St (☎266-6550), offers various free performances, musicals, concerts and an interesting regional **art gallery**.

If the capitol is the city's governmental heart, the **University of Wisconsin** (average enrolment 46,000) is its spirited, liberal-thinking head, now mellowed since its protest heyday in the late Sixties. The campus "living room", **Memorial Union**, 800 Langdon St (☎262-1583), holds a budget cafeteria and pub, the *Rathskeller*, with tables strewn beneath huge vaulted ceilings and live music most nights. Out back, the spacious **UW Terrace** offers beautiful sunset views over Lake Mendota. Capitol and campus are arterially connected by **State Street**, eight tree-lined, pedestrianized blocks of restaurants, cafés, bars, and funky stores.

Practicalities

Greyhound, 931 E Main St (☎257-9511), has regular runs to Milwaukee, Green Bay and beyond. *Badger Coaches*, 601 W Washington Ave, makes two trips daily to Milwaukee ($14 return; ☎255-1511). *Alco Buses* departs from Memorial Union to Chicago's O'Hare Airport (12 daily; $18; ☎257-5593). The **visitor center** is at 615 E Washington Ave (Mon–Fri 8am–5pm; ☎25-LAKES or ☎1-800/373-MDSN).

Accommodation can be had all over the city, though the budget chains lie east, off I-90/94. *Collins House*, 704 E Gorham St (☎255-4230; ④), is a beautiful B&B a few blocks from the capitol, while the *Madison Concourse Hotel*, 1 Dayton St (☎257-6000 or ☎1-800/356-8293; ④), is even closer. The *Towers*, 502 N Frances St (☎257-0701; ②), occasionally offers bargain central rooms. State Street is a veritable smorgasbord of **food** and **drink**, from the tiny *Nepalese Himal Chuli* (no 318; ☎251-9225) to *Ella's Deli* (no 425; ☎257-8611), with its kosher food and rich ice creams. *Ovens of Brittany* (no 305; ☎257-7000), offers a great setting for breakfast (try the Brittany buns) and fine seafood in the evening. The *Essen Haus*, 514 E Wilson St (☎255-4674), is a raucous *biergarten* with a phenomenal selection of beers. *Crandall's*, in the old rail depot at 640 W Washington Ave (☎255-6070), does a tasty all-you-can-eat fish fry every Wednesday and Friday.

Besides the (often free) **entertainment** on campus, the converted railroad hotel at 636 W Washington St incorporates a live music bar, a mixed dance club (*Club de Wash* ☎256-3302), and a heavy-duty gay leather bar. The soulful neighborhood *Crystal Corner*, 1302 Williamson St (☎256-2953), puts on blues acts; *O'Cayz Corral*, 504 E Wilson St (☎256-1348), ranges through heavy metal, folk and acoustic. Full **listings** are carried by the free weekly *Isthmus*.

Baraboo

Between 1884 and 1912, the **Ringling Brothers' Circus** kept winter quarters in **BARABOO**, thirty miles northwest of Madison (see also Sarasota, p.475). The **Circus World Museum**, 426 Water St, successfully recaptures the pre-TV glory days of big-top history, via an enormous collection of memorabilia and daily performances including an old-time circus show that is both tawdry (elephants with bows on their tails doing leg

The **area code** for southern Wisconsin is ☎608.

kicks to *New York, New York*) and irresistible (daily, late July & Aug 9am–10pm; May, June, and the first halves of July & Sept 9am–6pm; $10). Every summer, in the second week of July, 75 meticulously restored circus wagons set out on a two-day rail journey through small-town Wisconsin and Illinois, culminating in a horse-drawn parade through downtown Milwaukee – an unbeatable extravaganza of Americana.

Baraboo itself is calmer, quieter and more affordable than nearby Wisconsin Dells. The colonial *Barrister's House*, 226 Ninth Ave (☎356-3344; ④), is a B&B on a high bluff. More basic rooms are on offer at the *Spinning Wheel*, 809 Eighth St (☎356-3977; ②); the friendly all-night store opposite serves as the local *Greyhound* stop. *Kristina's Family Café*, 113 Third St (☎356-3430), serves low-cost meals. Baraboo's **visitor center** is at 124 Second St (Mon–Fri 10am–4pm; ☎356-8333).

Spring Green

During his seventy-year career, Wisconsin-born architect and social philosopher **Frank Lloyd Wright** designed such structures as New York's spiralling Guggenheim Museum and Tokyo's earthquake-proof *Imperial Hotel*. Three miles south of **SPRING GREEN**, itself forty miles west of Madison on Hwy-14, tours of the grounds of Wright's former home, **Taliesin**, cost $20; double that amount gets you a look around the house itself. In town, the streamlined geometry and functional grandeur of his **Hillside Home School**, opened in 1932, exemplify Wright's break away from the boxy, fustian Victorian style (May–Oct daily, tours on the hour 9am–4pm; $9; see also p.000 and p.000). His actual studio is magnificent; there's also a jewel-like theater space. Other Wright-influenced buildings in Spring Green are the bank, pharmacy and the lounge of a mid-priced restaurant called the *Post House* (☎588-2595). All tours leave from the **Frank Lloyd Wright Visitor Center** (☎588-7948), designed by Wright in 1953 as a restaurant; it now features displays, a café and a bookstore.

From 1944 onwards, Alex Jordan built the **House on the Rock**, six miles beyond Taliesin on Hwy-23, on and out of a natural sixty-foot, chimney-like rock – for no discernible reason. He certainly never lived in it, nor did he intend it to become Wisconsin's number one tourist attraction (April–Oct daily 8am–dusk; $13). Only the first section of this multilevelled series of furnished nooks and chambers bears any resemblance to a house of any kind. With its low ceilings, indirect lighting, indoor pools, waterfalls and trees and pervasive shag carpeting, the style is a sort of Frank Lloyd Wright meets *The Flintstones*. The rest of the House is a logic-free labyrinth, containing Jordan's astounding collection of collections (antiques, nickelodeons, miniature circuses, dolls and doll's houses, maritime memorabilia, armor and firearms, ad infinitum), with little to indicate what is genuine or imitation, and no clue as to what it all means. The net effect is overwhelming and disorienting, alternately great fun and ghastly. Highlights include the **Infinity Room**, composed of three thousand small glass panels tapering to a point and cantilevered several hundred feet above the Wyoming Valley. A complex of other attractions have been added to the fifty-acre grounds, including the utterly dazzling **World's Largest Carousel** (with 269 fabulous figures and some 20,000 lights), a circus building, a giant doll's house and an olde-style shopping street.

Practicalities

Spring Green is a pretty **place to stay**, but prices can get high in summer. *Round Barn Lodge*, Hwy-14 (☎588-2568; ④), has a pool, sauna and family dining in a former dairy farm. The secluded *Wildwood Lodge* (☎588-2514; ②), between Taliesin and the House on Hwy-3, about two miles off Hwy-23, is run-down and hard to find. Locals and thespians hang out at *The Shed* (☎588-9049), an easy-going diner and bar on Lexington Street downtown. The *American Players Theatre* (☎588-7401) performs Shakespeare and other classics in a wooded amphitheater each evening from mid-June through September.

MINNESOTA

Though **MINNESOTA** is about a thousand miles from either coast, it's virtually a seaboard state, thanks to **Lake Superior**, connected to the Atlantic via the St Lawrence Seaway. The glaciers that, millions of years ago, flattened all but its southeast corner gouged out more than 15,000 **lakes**, and major **rivers** run along the eastern and western borders. Ninety-five percent of the population lives within ten minutes of a body of water, and the very name Minnesota is a Sioux word meaning "land of sky-tinted water".

French explorers in the sixteenth century encountered prairies to the south and, in the north, dense forests whose abundant waterways were an ideal breeding ground for beavers and muskrats. **Fur trading, fishing** and **lumbering** flourished, and the Ojibway and Sioux were eased out by waves of French, British and American immigrants. Admitted to the Union in 1858, the new state of Minnesota was at first settled by Germans and Scandinavians, who farmed in the west and south. Other ethnic groups followed, many drawn by the massive **iron ore** deposits of north-central Minnesota, which are expected to hold out for another two hundred years.

Minnesota still thrives on its natural resources and on a progressive social outlook typified by such Democratic heavyweights as Hubert Humphrey, Walter Mondale and Eugene McCarthy. More than half of its hardy inhabitants, who endure some of the fiercest winters in the nation, live in the southeast, around the so-called Twin Cities of **Minneapolis** and **St Paul**, attractive and basically friendly rivals who together rank as the Midwest's great civic double act for their combined cultural, recreational and business opportunities. Smaller cities include the northern shipping port of **Duluth**, the gateway to **Scenic Hwy-61** lakeshore drive, and **Rochester**, near pretty river towns like Red Wing and Winona. The tranquil waters of **Voyageurs National Park** lie halfway along the state's boundary with Canada.

Getting Around Minnesota

Minneapolis/St Paul **airport**, home base for *Northwest Airlines*, handles routes to Europe as well as domestic flights. *Amtrak* **trains** cross the state once a day east and west from Chicago and Seattle, with stops in Winona, Red Wing, St Paul (with a connecting bus to Duluth), Staples and Detroit Lakes. *Greyhound*, founded upstate in Hibbing although no longer based there, is the largest of the several **bus** companies plying Minnesota's roads. Six buses per day make the nine-hour journey to Chicago from the Twin Cities; Duluth, St Louis and Kansas City are also served several times daily from the state's major metropolis.

Minneapolis and St Paul

Commonly known as the **Twin Cities**, **MINNEAPOLIS** (a hybrid Sioux/Greek word meaning "water city") and **ST PAUL** are competitive yet complementary. Fraternally rather than identically twinned, they may be even better places to live than they are to visit, thanks to their good looks, cleanliness, cultural activity, social awareness and relatively low crime rates. About thirty of *Fortune Magazine*'s 500 top-ranking corporations are based here; many extend substantial financial support to local arts, community projects and sports. Life for a majority of Twin Citians seems so vibrantly wholesome that the most significant threat would appear to be their own creeping complacency.

St Paul has been called "the last city of the east", making Minneapolis across the curving Mississippi "the first city of the west". Only a twenty-minute expressway ride

The **area code** for Minneapolis/St Paul is ☎612.

separates their respective downtowns, but each has its own character, style and strengths. **St Paul**, the state capital – originally called Pig's Eye, for a scurrilous French-Canadian fur trader who sold whisky at a Mississippi river-landing in the 1840s – is the staid, slightly older sibling, careful to preserve its buildings and traditions. The residents are mainly German, Irish and Catholic. The compact but stately downtown is built, like Rome, on seven hills; the **Capitol** and the **Cathedral** occupy one each, august monuments that keep the city mindful of its responsibilities.

Minneapolis, founded on money generated by the Mississippi's hundreds of flour and saw mills, is livelier, artier and more modern, with skyscraping, up-to-date architecture and an upbeat and even brash attitude that never quite jeopardizes its essential affability. The mostly Slavonic, Nordic and Lutheran residents are spread over wider ground than in St Paul, with dozens of lakes and parks to underscore the city's appeal. Home-grown superstar **Prince** has cast a global spotlight on the local music scene.

Arrival, Information and Getting Around

Twin Cities International Airport lies about ten miles south of either city in suburban Bloomington. Limousine service (☎726-6400) between the airport and major hotels is around $10, although some lodgings lay on transport. **Taxis** to Minneapolis will set you back close to $25, to St Paul $15. Bus #7 goes to Minneapolis; transfer to #9 for St Paul (6am–midnight: $1.60). *Amtrak* is midway between the cities at 730 Transfer Rd, off University Ave. The *Greyhound* terminals, each in a convenient downtown location, are at 29 Ninth St in Minneapolis (☎371-3311), and, less used, Seventh and St Peter streets in St Paul (☎222-0509). *Metropolitan Transit Commission* **buses** (☎827-7733) make both cities relatively easy to explore without a car; money-saving multiple-ride tickets can be bought from 560 Sixth Ave in Minneapolis.

In Minneapolis, the **visitor center** is at 1219 Marquette Ave (☎348-4313 or ☎1-800/445-7412); in St Paul it's at 101 Norwest Center, 55 E Fifth St (☎297-6985 or ☎1-800/627-6101). The main Minneapolis **post office** is on First and Marquette (zip code 55401); St Paul's at 180 E Kellogg Blvd (zip code 55101).

Exploring Minneapolis

Laid out on a simple grid, **downtown Minneapolis** is bounded by the Mississippi River on the north side and by lovely Loring Park to the south. The riverfront, dubbed the **"Mississippi Mile"**, continues to be developed as a place for strolling, dining and entertainment. Each city has its own landing site for narrated **paddleboat** cruises (☎227-1100; $8.50, seasonal). The vast Third Avenue bridge makes an ideal vantage point for viewing **St Anthony Falls**, a controlled torrent in a wide stretch of the river. The missionary Father Hennepin discovered the Falls in 1680; the first permanent settlement of present-day Minneapolis began nearby in the early nineteenth century.

Downtown's major stores line up along the pedestrianized **Nicollet Mall**. **Hennepin Avenue**, the other main drag, is a block west. The **IDS Center**, on the Mall, is the tallest building in either city; its indoor glass atrium, the Crystal Court, is essentially modern Minneapolis' town square. Citizens escape weather extremes via a "skyway" system of elevated, climate-controlled glass walkways, connecting over forty buildings. Culturally, Minneapolis would be poorer without the **Walker Art Center**, Vineland Place (Tues–Sat 10am–8pm, Sun 11am–5pm; $3, free Thurs), on the edge of downtown, a multipurpose contemporary arts space which balances its permanent collection of sculpture and paintings (such as German expressionist Franz Marc's *Blue Horses*) with exciting temporary exhibitions. The seven-acre outdoor **Sculpture Garden** is a work of genius, its most popular piece the whimsical gigantic *Spoonbridge and Cherry* (not exactly a bridge, more like a fountain) by Claes Oldenburg and Coosje van Bruggen. One mile from downtown, at 2400 Third Ave (bus #9), the huge **Minneapolis Institute of Arts** hosts a huge and thoroughly comprehensive collection of art from 2000BC to the present (Tues, Wed, Fri & Sat 10am–5pm, Thurs 10am–9pm, Sun noon–5pm; free).

Arctic winters apart, hordes of Minneapolitans flock to the shores of the "big three", lakes **Calhoun** and **Harriet** and **Lake of the Isles**, all in residential areas within two miles south of downtown. Each July the **Minneapolis Aquatennial** celebrates the life-style fostered by the lakes with two huge downtown parades and water-based events such as milk-carton boat races. **Minnehaha Falls**, south of downtown on bus #7, was featured in Longfellow's 1855 poem *Song of Hiawatha* without his ever having laid eyes on it. The adjacent park is a favorite haunt for hikes and picnics.

Exploring St Paul

St Paul, reached along I-94 (and served by buses #16A, #21A or express route #94B), has more wealthy old homes and civic monuments than Minneapolis. Call in at the jazzy Art Deco lobby of the **City Hall and Courthouse**, Fourth and Wabasha, to see Swedish sculptor Carl Milles' revolving 36ft *Indian God of Peace*, carved in the 1930s from white Mexican onyx. The castle-like **Landmark Center**, a couple of blocks away at Fifth and Market, overlooks **Rice Park**, probably the prettiest little square in either city. Here, too, downtown buildings are linked via "skyways"; but evenings and weekends in St Paul can get very quiet. The beautifully restored **Cafesjian's Carousel** ($1 per ride) is tucked inside **Town Square Park**, a lush, multilevel indoor garden in a shopping complex. An immense steel iguana is the doorkeeper at the exciting hands-on **Science Museum of Minnesota**, 30 E Tenth St (April–Sept Mon–Sat 9.30am–9pm, Sun 11am–9pm, otherwise closed Mon; $6), which also has a domed **Omnitheater**.

A well-preserved five-mile Victorian boulevard, **Summit Avenue**, leads away from downtown. **F Scott Fitzgerald**, born nearby, finished his first success, *This Side of Paradise*, in 1918 while living in a modest row house at no 599; he disparaged the avenue as a "museum of American architectural failures". Look for the coffin atop no 465, once the home of an undertaker. Pioneer politico **Alexander Ramsey**'s house (April–Dec Tues–Fri 10am–4pm, Sat & Sun 1–4.30pm; $3.50), nearby at 265 S Exchange St in the fashionable Irvine Park district, remains a showcase of Victorian high style.

Costumed staff do a fine job of interpreting Minnesota's early nineteenth-century past at **Fort Snelling** (May–Oct daily 10am–5pm; Nov–April Mon–Fri 9am–4.30pm; $4), near the airport off highways 5 and 55. Built between 1819 and 1825 on a strategic bluff at the confluence of the Mississippi and Minnesota rivers, this was Minnesota's first permanent structure – a successful attempt by the US government to establish an official presence in the wilderness that had recently been won from Great Britain.

Annual celebrations in St Paul include a beanfeast called **Taste of Minnesota** (tons of food, live entertainment, rides and fireworks) on July 4, the nation's largest State Fair (end of Aug to early Sept), and the **Winter Carnival** (late Jan to early Feb), a frosty gala designed to make the most of the seasonal freeze via ice and snow sculpt-ing, hot air ballooning, team sports, parades and more.

The Mall of America

Equidistant from Minneapolis and St Paul, 20min south on I-494 at 24th Ave, Bloomington, MN.

Shopping addicts make the pilgrimage to the **Mall of America** from all over the Midwest – and far beyond, including parties from Japan and the regular "Shop 'Til You Drop" packages run by British operator *Major Travel* (£300; ☎071/485-7017). This mind-boggling 4.2 million square feet, four-storey monument to consumerism incorporates over four hundred stores, with a seven-acre theme park (the pay-per-ride **Snoopy Camp**) bang in the center. The futuristic superstructure contains twice as much steel as the Eiffel Tower, and there's enough room to play a week's NFL games side by side. The hands-on demonstrations at **Oshman's Supersport** – of fishing, shooting, golf, basketball etc – are the highlight of a tour, while the *Everything For A $* store is worth rooting through.

Accommodation

You're likely to pay more for lodgings downtown than in the suburbs, where dozens of cheap **motels** line I-494 near the airport, though some of the pricier central hotels offer reduced rates and special package deals on weekends.

Minneapolis

Brasie House, 2321 Colfax Ave S (☎377-5946). Attractive guest house in lively neighborhood near downtown. Three rooms with shared bath, continental breakfast. ④.

Christopher Inn, 201 Mill St, Excelsior (☎474-6816). Year-round suburban B&B on Lake Minnetonka. Good discounts off-season and midweek. ⑤.

Evelo's B&B, 2301 Bryant Ave S (☎374-9656). Three comfortable rooms in well-preserved Victorian home near bus lines, lakes and downtown. Non-smokers preferred. ③.

Fair Oaks, 2335 Third Ave S (☎871-2000). Friendly, unpretentious motor hotel near downtown, across from the Art Institute. ③.

Minneapolis Hilton and Towers, 1001 Marquette Ave (☎376-1000). The newest and classiest downtown lodgings, featuring a great gym and pool. Weekend rates under $100 a night. ⑥.

St Paul

Caecilian Hall (AYH), 2004 Randolph Ave (☎690-6604). *AYH*-only bunks ($13) and rooms. ①.

Chatsworth B&B, 984 Ashland Ave (☎227-4288). Beautiful turn-of-the-century home now run as a welcoming B&B. ③.

Como Villa, 1371 W Nebraska Ave (☎647-0471). Gay-owned Victorian B&B by Como Park. ③.

Miller B&B, 887 James Ave (☎227-1292). 1920s duplex with shared bath. ②.

Sunwood Inn, 1010 Bandana Blvd W (☎647-1637). Unique lodgings in former railroad car repair shop now attached to Bandana Square mall. Indoor pool and sauna. ④.

Eating

Preconceptions of Midwestern blandness are swiftly put to rest by an almost bewildering array of **restaurants** in Minneapolis – head for the downtown **warehouse district** or the university's **Dinkytown** – and St Paul – try **Galtier Plaza** or the **St Paul Center** downtown. Of local chains, *Lotus* serves budget Vietnamese meals, while *Key's* offers great breakfasts and fresh lunches. Be sure to sample **wild rice**, a Minnesota specialty.

Minneapolis

Broder's Cucina Italiana, 2308 W 50th St (☎925-3113). Terrific deli for eat-in or takeaway.

Cafe Brenda, 300 First Ave N (☎342-9230). Excellent, moderately priced nouvelle vegetarian cuisine in arty downtown warehouse district.

Chez Bananas, 129 N Fourth St (☎340-0032). Spicy, Caribbean-influenced food, and toys on tables.

Emily's Lebanese Deli, 614 University Ave NE (☎379-4069). Warm, low-cost local place.

Korea House, 414½ Cedar Ave S (☎339-9385). Family-owned, authentic, inexpensive.

Odaa, 408 Cedar Ave S (☎338-4959). Fine all-you-can-eat Ethiopian finger food for $10 and less.

Sawatdee, 607 Washington Ave S (☎338-6451). Flavorsome Thai food, always well prepared; entrees $8–15; also have a location in St Paul.

St Paul

Caravan Serai, 2175 Ford Parkway (☎690-1935). Afghani food, tentlike space, pillow seats.
The Deco, 305 St Peter St (☎228-0520). Scandinavian-style buffets atop riverside art museum.
Italian Pie Shoppe, 777 Grand Ave (☎221-0093). Superb deep-dish pizzas at bargain prices.
Mickey's Diner, 36 W Seventh St (☎222-5633). Landmark 24-hr diner in 1930s dining car.
St Paul Grill, 350 Market St (☎292-9292). Trad but inventive dishes in classic downtown hotel.
WA Frost, Selby and Western Ave (☎224-5715). Former pharmacy and F Scott Fitzgerald hang-out converted into plush restaurant with garden patio.

Nightlife and Entertainment

The Greater Twin Cities have been dubbed a "cultural Eden on the prairie", where 2.2 million people support ninety **theater** companies, ten **dance** troupes, twenty **classical music** ensembles and over a hundred art galleries. Sir Tyrone Guthrie began the theatrical boom back in 1963, enrolling large-scale local assistance to establish the classical repertory company (☎377-2224 or ☎1-800/848-4912) named after him. The cities now have more theaters per capita than anywhere in the US apart from New York City.

Unusually, **nightlife** in Minneapolis (and, to a lesser extent, St Paul) hasn't been siphoned off by suburbia, with one hundred thousand students to ensure a vibrant club scene. Before the Seattle music explosion, Minneapolis natives Bob Mould and Paul Westerberg pioneered the grunge sound with their seminal bands **Hüsker Dü** and **The Replacements**. The city still churns out great guitar bands such as Soul Asylum, while **Prince Rogers Nelson** continues to meddle around in his multimedia **Paisley Park** studio in suburban Chanhassen. For complete entertainment information and listings, check out the ubiquitous free weeklies *Twin Cities Reader* and *City Pages*. *Equal Time* and *Gaze* provide a similar service from a gay and lesbian perspective.

Minneapolis and St Paul Theaters

Chanhassen Dinner Theater, 521 W 78th St, Minneapolis (☎934-1525). Mainstream musicals, popular comedies and drama on three stages. Adequate meals. Thirty minutes from downtown.
Dudley Riggs' Brave New Workshop, 2605 Hennepin Ave S, Minneapolis (☎332-6620). The grandparent of local satirical comedy troupes.
Great North American History Theater, 30 E Tenth St, St Paul (☎292-3423). Original plays dealing with events and personalities from Minnesota's past.
Jungle Theater, 709 W Lake St, Minneapolis (☎822-7063). Hole-in-the-wall theater/cabaret.
Park Square, St Peter St and Kellogg Blvd, St Paul (☎291-7005). Classic plays well served.
Penumbra, 270 N Kent St, St Paul (☎224-4601). Professional African-American company.
Red Eye Collaboration, 15 W 14th St, Minneapolis (☎870-0309). Challenging experimental theater.
Theater de la Jeune Lune, First St and First Ave, Minneapolis (☎333-6200). Unique ensemble of Parisians and Minneapolitans offers dynamic, highly physical productions from a commedia base.

Minneapolis Clubs and Pubs

Fine Line, 318 First Ave (☎338-8100). Sleek, small and musically eclectic downtown club.
First Avenue and 7th St Entry, 701 First Ave (☎338-8388 or ☎332-1775). Landmark rock venue where Prince's *Purple Rain* was shot still packs 'em in with top bands and dance music.
Gay 90s, 408 Hennepin Ave S (☎333-7755). Sprawling gay club that's a downtown institution with two dancefloors, piano lounge, men's and women's bars, dining and weekend drag shows.
Glam Slam, 110 N Fifth St (☎338-3383). State-of-the-art dance club, with live acts. Dress flash.
Loon Café, 500 First Ave N (☎332-8342). Noisy, likeable sports bar with great grub (try the chilis).
Loring Bohemian Bar and Café, 1624 Harmon Place (☎338-6258 or ☎332-1617). Beautiful people with attitude drink, dine or drift upstairs to the dance/theater Playhouse.
Nye's Polonaise Room, 112 E Hennepin Ave (☎379-2021). Plenty of old-time atmosphere with both piano and polka bars, plus Polish-American restaurant.

St Paul Clubs and Pubs

The Dakota Bar and Grill, 1021 Bandana Blvd (☎642-1442). Gourmet Midwestern food and great local and national jazz in converted shopping mall locale.

Gallivan's, 354 Wabasha St (☎227-6688). Downtown white-collar pub with neighborhood feel.

O'Gara's Bar and Grill, 164 N Snelling Ave (☎644-3333). Mixed clientele drawn by grub, grog and live bands in the adjoining *Garage*.

Rumors, 490 N Robert St (☎646-2288). Downtown gay/lesbian club; exudes camaraderie.

Town House, 1415 University Ave (☎646-7087). Gay country & western bar where they'll gladly teach you the two-step.

Northern Minnesota

Minnesota's substantial northern half, overrun with forested lakes, remains much as it was when Europeans first traded with the Indians. The northwest – **the Arrowhead**, poking into Lake Superior – holds the greatest charm: most visitors choose secluded outdoor vacations centered around fishing, canoeing and snowmobiling, but there's infinite potential for driving tours in a wilderness comparable to the Alaskan interior.

The Arrowhead is anchored by busy **Duluth**, from where **Scenic Hwy-61** skirts the cliff tops over Lake Superior, passing waterfalls, state parks and neat little towns on the way north to the Canadian border. Sleepy little **Grand Marais** is poised at the edge of the wild **Boundary Waters Canoe Area Wilderness (BWCAW)** and the **Gunflint Trail**. Inland, the **Iron Range** makes a scenic route north to the idyllic **Voyageurs National Park**. Everywhere you'll find **campgrounds** and "Ma and Pa" lakeside **resorts**, havens of homely simplicity dedicated to soothing urban-ravaged souls.

Duluth

DULUTH, at the western extremity of Lake Superior 150 miles north of Minneapolis/ St Paul, forms a long crescent at the base of the Arrowhead. Named for a seventeenth-century French officer, Daniel Greysolon, Sieur du Lhut, it cascades down from the granite bluffs surrounding **Skyline Drive** (an exhilarating thirty-mile route) to a busy **harbor**, shared with inferior Superior, Wisconsin. Together these "twin ports" constitute the largest inland port in the US. Originally the main cargo was fur; now it ships grain, lumber and ore to the Atlantic via the St Lawrence Seaway.

In the 1980s, Duluth had a face-lift and began to encourage tourism. The main drawback is that it's **cold**. The seaway is frozen through the winter, and even spring and autumn evenings can be chilly. Temperatures are always significantly cooler near the lake – as fate would have it, the location of nearly all the attractions and activities.

A short walk down Lake Avenue from the **CVB office**, 100 Lake Place Drive (☎722-4011 or ☎1-800/438-5884), leads to the free **Marine Museum** in Canal Park, a vantage point to watch big boats from around the world pass under the delightfully archaic Aerial Lift Bridge (mid-June to mid-Sept, daily 10am–9pm; otherwise times vary). Originating at Canal Park, Duluth's **Lakewalk** is the free way to take in the view, though in summer you can also take two-hour **harbor cruises** (☎722-6218; $8).

Rail excursions along the Superior shoreline to pretty Two Harbors (☎722-1273; $13 for 6hr) run from **The Depot** complex at 506 W Michigan St. This also houses the Lake Superior Museum of Transportation, plus assorted smaller archives (daily 10am–5pm; $5), and is home to performing art companies at night. Duluth's Spirit Mountain **ski area** (☎1-800/642-6377) boasts the best downhill runs in the Midwest.

The **area code** for Duluth is ☎218.

Practicalities

From 2212 W Superior St, *Greyhound* **buses** connect with the upper Midwest (☎722-5591), and *Triangle Transportation* hooks up with North Dakota. **Accommodation** rates and availability fluctuate in summer; Victorian-styled B&Bs include the *A Charles Weiss Inn*, 1615 E Superior St (☎724-7016; ④), while among choice **motels** are the *Best Western Edgewater*, 2400 London Rd (☎728-3601; ④), with a good pool, and the central *Park Inn*, 250 Canal Park Drive (☎727-8821 or 1-800/777-8560; ④). Indian Point **campground**, at 75th and Grand, west off Hwy-23 (☎624-5637), has summer bayside sites.

The Italian-American **food** at *Grandma's Saloon And Deli*, 522 S Lake Ave (☎727-4192) in view of the bridge, is not for dieters. *Grandma's Sports Garden* (☎722-4722), just across a parking lot at no 425, is similarly convivial, dishing up tasty food when not functioning as either dancefloor or basketball court. Classiest of all is the revolving *Top of the Harbor* (☎727-8981), atop the *Radisson Hotel*, 505 W Superior St.

North from Duluth: Highway 61

Memorialized on vinyl by Minnesota native Bob Dylan, stunning **Scenic Hwy-61** follows Lake Superior for 150 miles from Duluth to the border, its precipitous cliffs interspersed with pretty little ports and picture-postcard picnic sites.

At **Gooseberry River State Park**, forty miles out from Duluth, the river splashes over volcanic rock through waterfalls and cascades to its outlet in Lake Superior. Like the four other state parks along Hwy-61, it provides access to the rugged two-hundred-mile **Superior Hiking Trail** (☎834-4436), divided into easily manageable segments for day-trekkers. To **camp** at any of the state parks, reserve on ☎1-800/765-CAMP.

Just beyond **Cascade River State Park**, the road dips into the somnolent little port of **GRAND MARAIS**, where a walk around the photogenic Circular Harbor will soon cure car-stiff legs. The **visitor center** on Broadway (☎237-2524 or 1-800/622-4014) has lists of outfitters for those going into the BWCAW. Inexpensive room options include the ultra-clean *Sandgren Motel*, by the lights on Hwy-61 (☎387-2975; ②), and the characterful *Harbor Inn* (☎387-2095 or ☎1-800/245-5806; ②). A backpacker haunt with a difference is the *AYH Hostel* (☎388-2241; ①) on an island in Seagull Lake; bunks cost $12 and they'll pick you up from town for a a couple of dollars. For herrings and import beer, or just a well-priced snack, head for *Sven & Ole's Pizza*, 9 W Wisconsin St (☎387-1713).

Ferries from **GRAND PORTAGE**, 45 miles nearer the Canadian border and site of an Indian-operated casino, run in summer to the desolate **Isle Royale National Park** (see p.243), 22 miles out among the sweeping waves of Lake Superior.

The BWCAW and the Gunflint Trail

The huge **Boundary Waters Canoe Area Wilderness**, west of Grand Marais, is also accessible from Tofte and **ELY**, home of the intriguing **International Wolf Center** (May–Oct; daily, 9am–6pm; free). The BWCAW is a canoe, backpack and fishing enthusiast's paradise, where overland trails or "portages" link over a thousand lakes; in winter you can ski cross-country and dogsled. The unpaved sixty-mile **Gunflint Trail** from Grand Marais cuts the BWCAW in two; otherwise there are no roads in this outback, let alone electricity, telephones or trash cans. Most lakes remain motor-free. Stringent rules limit entry to the BWCAW; in summer you need a permit (☎720-5440). If you don't want to rough it, several rustic lodges lie strung out along the Gunflint.

The Iron Range

In the inhospitable **Iron Range**, a few miles west of Ely, a number of fabulously rich mines continue to function over a century after their inception. If you're interested in surveying old workings, it's possible to descend 2300 feet at the **Soudan Underground Mine State Park**, on Hwy-1.

Seventy miles south on Hwy-169 in **CHISHOLM**, the **Ironworld USA** cultural theme park turns ecological disaster into tourist spectacle, inviting you on a trolley ride to see "the scenic wonder of an open pit mine". Further opportunities to view such wonders (this time for free) occur during the half-hour drive to **HIBBING** – a plain little community, of interest mainly as the birthplace of Robert Zimmerman in 1941. His adult persona of **Bob Dylan** debars the local **museum** in City Hall from showing any exhibits on his career.

Hibbing was also the home of America's biggest bus company; the **Greyhound Bus Origin Center**, 23rd St and 5th Ave, with the help of model buses and old adverts looks back to its roots transporting local miners to and from the pits (summer; Mon–Sat 9am–5pm; $1). The **Hull-Rust Mahoning Mine**, once the world's largest open pit-iron ore mine, now functions as a city park.

Voyageurs National Park

Made up of border lakes between Minnesota and Canada, **VOYAGEURS NATIONAL PARK** is like no other in the National Park system. To see it properly, or indeed to grasp its immense beauty at all, you need to leave your car behind and venture into the wild by boat. Once out on the lakes, you're in a great, silent world where kingfishers, osprey and eagles swoop down for their share of the abundant walleye, moose and bear stalk the banks, and sunrises and sunsets conjure up a photographer's dream.

The park's name comes from the intrepid eighteenth-century French-Canadian trappers, who took almost a year to get their pelts back to Montréal in primitive birchbark canoes, paddling for 16 hours per day and fighting off attacks from Native Americans – and each other. Their "customary waterway" became so established that the treaty of 1783 ending the American Revolution specified it as the international border.

You can't do Voyageurs justice on a day trip, though daily cruises do at least allow a peek at the lakelands (mid-May to late Sept; ☎286-5470; $10–30). If you're here for a few days, rent a **boat** (reckon on $25 a day) and camp out. It's easy to get lost in this mesmerizing maze of islands and rocky outcrops, and unseen sandbanks lurk beneath the surface – if you're at all unsure, hire a guide from one of the resorts for the first day (around $150 per 8hr day). During **freeze-up** – usually from November until April – the park takes on a whole new aura, as a prime destination for skiers and snowmobilers (rentals start from $110 per day).

INTERNATIONAL FALLS, the only sizeable nearby community, might sound attractive, but it's a messy array of motels, duty-free shops, fast-food joints and lumber yards; the falls, never more than glorified rapids anyway, were dammed in 1906.

Practicalities

Most travellers access Voyageurs from Hwy-53, which runs northwest from Duluth. The first entrance to the park comes after one hundred miles, at Orr for **Crane Lake** on the eastern extreme; 39 and 42 miles further along, highways 129 and 122 lead respectively to the **visitor centers** at **Ash River** (June–Aug; times vary; ☎374-3221) and **Kabetogama Lake** (May–Sept, Mon–Fri 9am–5pm; ☎875-2111). The main visitor center is at **Rainy Lake** (daily, summer 9am–5pm; otherwise times vary; ☎286-5258), at the westernmost entrance 36 miles further on via International Falls.

Once inside the park, you have to take a few precautions: check (natural) mercury levels in fish before eating them, don't pick wild rice (only Native Americans can do this), be wary of Lyme's Disease (a tick-induced gastric illness), boil drinking water and watch out for bears. Discuss such matters, along with customs procedures in case you venture into Canadian waters, with a ranger before venturing out.

The definitive way to experience the park is to **camp** on one of its many scattered islands, most plentiful around Crane Lake (if you don't have your own boat, cruise operators can drop you off and pick you up at a later date). There are also first-come, first-served campgrounds on the mainland at Ash River and Woodenfrog, near Kabetogama. However, most visitors shack up in one of over sixty **resorts**. Basically family-run cottages, these usually cater for weekly stays, with all meals, though you can rent rooms nightly. Most popular are those around Kabetogama, such as *Watson's Harmony Beach* (☎875-2811; ③), a great place for picking up tips on the park, *Arrowhead Lodge* (☎875-2141; ③), well known for its restaurant, and the basic, cheap and cheerful *Driftwood Lodge* (☎875-3841; ①). You can book through the Kabetogama Lake Association (☎1-800/524-9085), while resort associations for Crane Lake (☎993-2346), Ash River (☎1-800/950-2061) and Rainy Lake/International Falls (☎283-9400) can fix you up with lodgings, including houseboats (usually $1200 and up per week). The quasi-luxury *Kettle Falls Hotel* (☎374-3631 or ☎1-800/322-0886; ④), set way, way out in the park, is accessible only by boat or a ferry from Ash River.

Southern Minnesota

Southern Minnesota is split between high plains, timbered ravines and slow-flowing Mississippi tributaries in the east, and the drier, flatter prairie and chequerboard farm-land of the west. In the scenic **southeast**, spared a filing down by the last glacial advance, attractive small towns sit along the Mississippi, or on bluffs above it, in the ninety-mile **Hiawatha Valley**. Mississippi shipping helped sustain easy-going communities like **Winona, Red Wing, Lake City** (where waterskiing was invented circa 1922) and **Wabasha**, all of which share well-preserved old homes and hotels.

The agricultural and college center of **Northfield**, on I-35 a mere thirty miles south of the Twin Cities, annually commemorates the Jesse James gang's foiled attempt to rob the town bank in September 1876. **Harmony**, almost in Iowa and near Minnesota's largest **Amish colony, Lanesboro**, with a storybook setting on the hillsides of the Root River, and **Mantorville** have all kept at least one foot in the nineteenth century. Further west, **New Prague** and **New Ulm** were prime targets for the beleaguered Sioux during a six-week war with the US government in 1862.

Rochester

The metropolis of **ROCHESTER**, about eighty miles southeast of Minneapolis/St Paul, was settled in the 1850s by migrants from Rochester, New York, as a humble crossroads campground for wagon trains. After a tornado devastated the town in 1883, Dr William Worral Mayo established the huge **Mayo Clinic**, 200 First St SW (☎284-2653). Free **tours** of its skyways and subways serve as ninety-minute pedestrianized adverts for "the first and largest private group medical practice in the world" (Mon–Fri 10am & 2pm).

Rochester is crawling with **accommodation**, such as the central *Kahler Hotel*, 20 SW Second Ave (☎282-2581; ③), the *Civic Inn*, 31 NW 13th St (☎289-3343; ②), and *Heritage House*, 103 SW Third Ave (☎282-2248; ③). The *Broadstreet Café and Bar*, 300 NW First Ave (☎289-1280), a bistro in a renovated warehouse, serves excellent meals; there's live music in the cozy *Redwood Room* downstairs..

Jefferson Union Bus Depot, 405 SW First Ave (☎289-4037), is the hub for bus services. Limousines (☎288-4490) make around six runs daily to the Twin Cities' airport, and the **visitor center** is at 150 S Broadway (☎288-4331 or 1-800/426-6025).

The **area code** for southern Minnesota is ☎507.

Pipestone

PIPESTONE, eight miles east of the South Dakota border, is named for a soft red rock within the local quartzite, which was used for centuries by Great Plains Indians to make ceremonial calumets, or peace pipes. The quarry site, a kind of neutral, inter-tribal United Nations, is now the **Pipestone National Monument** (daily; $1). A self-guided trail winds from the visitor center through stands of trees, past rock formations and exposed quarry pits, and over a creek, complete with picturesque falls.

Pipestone's small historic district includes a sleepy county museum and a building with several amusing sandstone gargoyles; pick up a walking tour brochure from the **visitor center** (☎825-3316), near the junction of highways 75 and 23. You can sleep and eat at the grand old *Calumet Inn*, 104 W Main St (☎825-5871 or ☎1-800/535-7610; ④), though *Kings Kourt Motel* (☎825-3314 or ☎1-800/252-1937; ③) is less expensive. Each July the town puts on a nine-day **Indian pageant** in an outdoor amphitheater.

From a distance the red rocks at **Blue Mounds State Park**, sloping into a long cliff a few miles north of the junction of I-90 and US-75 at Luverne, create a great hump that appeared blue at sunset to approaching pioneers. Twice a year, at the equinoxes, the sun lines up with a curious 1250ft row of rocks, aligned on an east–west axis. There are seasonal **campgrounds** (☎1-800/765-CAMP) and a permanent small herd of buffalo.

CHAPTER FIVE

THE CAPITAL REGION

The city of **WASHINGTON DC**, and the four states of **VIRGINIA, WEST VIRGINIA, MARYLAND** and **DELAWARE**, constitute a cross-section of the nation. Since the days of the first American colonies, US history has been shaped here, from agitation towards independence to the battles of the Revolutionary and Civil wars. Now, the contrasts and incongruities of contemporary America are shown in high relief; the corridors of power in Washington are literally a stone's throw away from dire inner-city poverty, while nearby dozens of time-worn farming and fishing towns seem straight out of some Norman Rockwell idyll.

Early in the seventeenth century, the first British settlements began to take root along the rich estuary of the **Chesapeake Bay**; the colonists hoped for gold, but found their fortunes growing tobacco. **Virginia**, the first of all, was the largest and most populous; it originally included most of what are now Kentucky, Tennessee and Ohio, and as late as the 1790s had double the residents of any other state. What often goes unsaid, however, is that fully half the people living here were **slaves**, brought from Africa to do the back-breaking work of harvesting the tobacco. Despite its central position on the East Coast, the whole region lies below the Mason-Dixon Line – the symbolic border between North and South, drawn up in 1763 as the boundary between slave and free states – and until the Civil War, one of the country's busiest slave-markets was just two blocks from the White House.

Besides generating the bulk of colonial **wealth**, the region also produced many of early America's great leaders, from firebrand politicians like **Patrick Henry** ("Give me Liberty or Give me Death") to patrician intellectuals such as **Thomas Jefferson**. Another Virginian, **George Washington**, led the Continental Army against the British in the Revolutionary War and served as the first US president, while **James Madison** was the primary author of the Constitution.

For all its colonial importance, by the mid-nineteenth century the region had lost power and status to the burgeoning industrial and mercantile centers of Philadelphia and New York. Tensions between North and South finally erupted into the **Civil War**, of which traces are still visible everywhere. The hundred miles between the capital of the Union – Washington DC – and that of the Confederacy – Richmond, Virginia – were a constant and bloody battleground for four long years. This sense of a nation divided against itself is especially acute at the grand manor of **Robert E Lee**, the Confederacy's military leader: high on a hill overlooking the heart of Washington DC, its grounds are now filled with the war dead of the Arlington National Cemetery.

ACCOMMODATION PRICE CODES

All accommodation prices in this book have been coded using the symbols below.
Note that prices are for the least expensive double rooms in each establishment.
For a full explanation see p.35 in *Basics*.

①	up to $30	④	$60–80	⑦	$130–180
②	$30–45	⑤	$80–100	⑧	$180+
③	$45–60	⑥	$100–130		

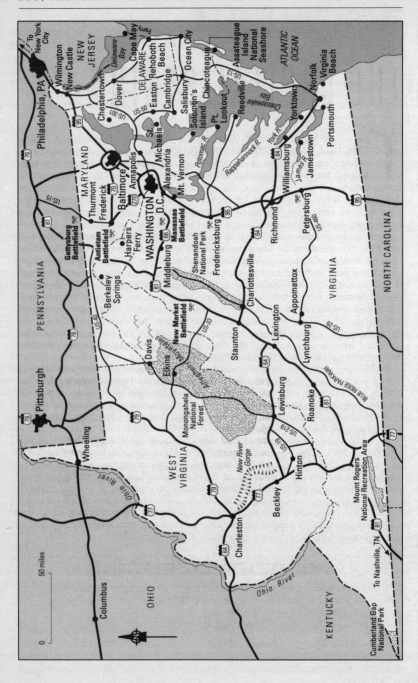

Washington DC itself, with its magnificent national showcases, is an essential stop on any tour of the region. Virginia, to the south, holds literally hundreds of historic sites, from the homes of early politicians to the colonial capital of Williamsburg, as well as the narrow forested heights of Shenandoah National Park, along the crest of the Blue Ridge Mountains. Much greater expanses of wilderness, crashing whitewater rivers, and innumerable backwoods villages await you in less-visited West Virginia.

Most tourists come to Maryland for the maritime traditions of Chesapeake Bay – though many of its quaint old villages have been gentrified by weekend pleasure-boaters. Baltimore is characterful and enjoyably unpretentious (and has a phenomenal concentration of bars), while Annapolis, the pleasant state capital, is linked by bridge and ferry to the eastern shore, where Assateague Island remains an Atlantic paradise. New Castle, across the border in Delaware, is a perfectly preserved colonial-era town; nearby are some of the East Coast's best and least crowded beaches.

WASHINGTON DC

That the marshy swamp where WASHINGTON DC now stands was chosen as the site of the capital of the newly independent United States of America says a lot about then-prevalent attitudes towards government. Washington, District of Columbia – also known as "DC" and "The District" – can be unbearably hot and humid in summer, and bitterly cold in winter. Such an unpleasant climate, it was hoped, would discourage elected leaders from making government a full-time job. This disdain for politics is still apparent: DC is run as a virtual colony of Congress, where residents have just one, non-voting representative and could not vote in presidential elections until the 1970s.

Another factor in the decision to establish the national capital here was that DC is midway between the northern cities of Boston, New York, and Philadelphia – the latter, the previous capital, was thought too exciting for a seat of government – and the rural south. It was also accessible from the sea, via the Potomac River – a bit too easily so, as demonstrated by the burning and ransacking of the city by the British during the War of 1812. Best of all, the land was cheap – the state of Maryland ceded sovereignty to the federal government, which only had to pay for the individual sites it chose for its buildings. Though the baroque plan of the city was laid out in 1800 – by a Frenchman, Pierre L'Enfant, and the black Benjamin Banneker – few buildings were put up, apart from the actual houses of government, until near the end of the century. Charles Dickens, visiting in 1842, found "spacious avenues that begin in nothing and lead nowhere".

After the Civil War, thousands of southern blacks arrived in search of a sanctuary from racist oppression; to some extent, they found one. Racial segregation was banned in public places, and Howard University, the only US institution of higher learning that enrolled black people, was set up in 1867. By the 1870s African-Americans made up over a third of the 150,000 population, but economic resources were soon stretched to breaking point. As poverty and squalor worsened, official segregation was re-introduced in 1920, banning blacks from government buildings – including, in an ironic twist, the Lincoln Memorial – and the jobs they had come to find. The situation has improved little since: DC currently has the country's highest murder rate, and appalling levels of unemployment, illiteracy and drug abuse – its longtime mayor, Marion Barry, spent the early 1990s in prison after being videotaped smoking crack cocaine after a massive, federally sponsored sting operation which many saw as racially motivated.

Arrival, Information and Getting Around

Washington DC has three major airports, two on the outskirts and one right in the city center. Dulles International Airport, thirty miles west in the depths of northern Virginia, and Baltimore-Washington International (BWI), halfway between DC and

Baltimore, get the majority of the international traffic; **National Airport**, along the Potomac River just west of the Mall, is mostly used by domestic flights. **Shuttle vans** from Dulles (*Washington Flyer*, ☎703/685-1400) or BWI (*Airport Connection*, ☎301/261-1091) to downtown Washington cost around $16 one-way, $26 round-trip. National is a whole lot more convenient, being on the DC Metro subway system.

By **train**, you arrive amid the gleaming malls of bustling **Union Station**, just two blocks north of the US Capitol; *Greyhound* **buses** stop at a modern station at 1005 First St NE (☎1-800/231-2222) in a fairly dodgy part of town, ten blocks from downtown – take a cab (around $4), especially at night. **Driving** into DC is a sure way to experience some of the worst traffic on the East Coast – the main I-95 freeway circuits Washington on what's known as the **Beltway**, jammed eighteen hours a day.

The helpful **visitor center**, 1445 Pennsylvania Ave NW (Mon–Sat 9am–5pm; ☎789-7000), has free handy guides to all the museums and attractions. **Disabled visitors** can get *Access Washington: A Guide for the Physically Disabled*, by calling ☎547-8081.

The main **post office** is across from Union Station on Massachusetts Ave and Capitol St NE (Mon–Fri 8am–8pm, Sat 8am–2pm; ☎682-9595; zip code 20002).

City Transit
Getting around DC is a cinch. Most places downtown, including all the Mall museums, the major monuments and the White House, are easily walkable from one another, and an excellent **public transportation** system – including an extensive modern subway and a network of buses – reaches outlying sites and neighborhoods. **Buses** cost $1, the **Metro subway** $1 to $2 (route information can be had at 12th and F streets NW; ☎637-7000). **Taxis** are also a good option, and not that expensive.

City Tours
During the day, narrated open-air **Tourmobiles** ($8.50, $4 under-12s) do a circuit of the major museums and sites; you can get on and off at any of a dozen different locations, and buy tickets from kiosks on the Mall or on the tram itself.

If you want to **cycle** or **cruise** along the Potomac River or the historic C&O Canal both *Thompson's Boat Center*, Rock Creek Parkway at Virginia Ave NW (☎333-4861), near the Watergate complex, and *Fletcher's Boat House*, 4940 Canal Rd NW (☎244-0461), rent out touring bikes, rowboats and canoes. In addition, mule-drawn **canal boats**, with costumed National Park Service guides, follow the old C&O Canal from behind 30th and M streets in Georgetown on a 90min narrated cruise ($5; ☎472-4376).

The City
Because the city was built from scratch, Washington's regular **town plan** is easy to grasp. Centered on Capitol Hill and its governmental monoliths, the District is divided into four **quadrants** – northeast, northwest, southeast, southwest. Dozens of broad **avenues**, all named for states, run diagonally across a standard grid of **streets**, meeting up at monumental traffic circles like Du Pont Circle. North–south streets are numbered, east–west ones are lettered (there's no J Street, an intentional slight to early Supreme Court justice John Jay, and I Street is often written Eye Street). Be very sure to note the relevant two-letter code in any **address** (NW, NE, SW, SE) which shows its quadrant; 1600 Pennsylvania Ave NW is a *long* way from 1600 Pennsylvania Ave SE.

Until you get your bearings, it's wise to stick to the established tourist trail; almost all the most famous sights are in the comparatively affluent northwest quarter. To the

The **area code** for Washington DC is ☎202.

west of the Capitol, the broad, green **Mall** holds monuments to presidents **Washington**, **Jefferson** and **Lincoln**, as well as the **White House**, official home of the current incumbent. Also here are the bulk of the city's many marvellous museums, including the national collections of the **Smithsonian Institution**.

However, there is more to Washington than an endless succession of museums and monuments, and it's well worth searching out its many attractive **neighborhoods**. Despite its violent reputation, most of the city is in surprisingly good shape, with row after row of nineteenth-century brick-fronted houses set along leafy boulevards. The oldest area, **Georgetown**, where popular bars and restaurants now line M Street and Wisconsin Avenue above the **Potomac River**, actually precedes the establishment of the District; it's a longish walk from the *Foggy Bottom* Metro. Other neighborhoods to check out are **Du Pont Circle** at the intersection of Massachusetts, Connecticut and New Hampshire avenues, which pulls a dynamic mix of yuppies, guppies and buppies; and the lower-rent, Latin American immigrant community of **Adams Morgan**, a short walk from Du Pont Circle up 18th Street at Columbia Road.

Capitol Hill

Though there's more than one hill in Washington DC, when people talk about what's going on on 'The Hill" they mean **Capitol Hill** – a shallow knoll topped by the giant white dome of the US Capitol building. Rising at the very center of the city, when Washington DC was first laid out Capitol Hill was intended to be both the symbolic and real seat of the federal government. Home of both the legislature – **Congress** – and the judiciary – the **Supreme Court** – this is still the place where the law of the land is made and refined; it also holds the newly refurbished **Library of Congress**.

US Capitol

Between Constitution and Independence avenues at the end of E Capitol St; closest Metro *Capitol South*. Daily 9am–8pm.

Visible from all over the city, and housing the nation's law-makers and tax-takers, the **Senate** and the **House of Representatives**, the **US Capitol** is one of the few places in the District where you can get a sense of the immense power wielded by the nation's elected officials – and watch them at work. The grand halls and public spaces are packed with monuments and statues of ex-politicians, while the current crop of legislators can be seen arguing over the finer points of law and policy in committee rooms and the ornate main chambers. When the lantern above the dome is lit, Congress is in session.

Begun in 1793 – George Washington, in Masonic garb, laid the cornerstone – the Capitol was repeatedly expanded over the ensuing years, and is now a confusing hybrid, hard to find your way around (the almost-constant construction and restoration work doesn't help). The **free tours** (every 15min until 3.45pm) are basically just a walk around the building; US citizens who want to see inside the legislative chambers have to arrange "VIP tours" through their representatives; foreigners, however, can simply show their passports at the visitors gallery entrances. Nine presidents, most recently JFK, have lain in state before burial in the impressive **Rotunda**, which, capped by a 180ft-tall dome, links the two halves of the Capitol – the Senate is in the north wing, the House in the south.

Library of Congress

10 First St SE; closest Metro *Capitol South*. Mon–Fri 8.30am– 9.30pm, Sat & Sun 8.30am–6pm.

In the **Library of Congress**, the largest in the world, over 95 million books and manuscripts, and countless thousands of microfilm rolls and computer discs, are arrayed on 600 miles of shelves. Set up in 1800, the entire library was burned by the British in 1814; to replace the loss, Thomas Jefferson sold the country his six-thousand-volume personal

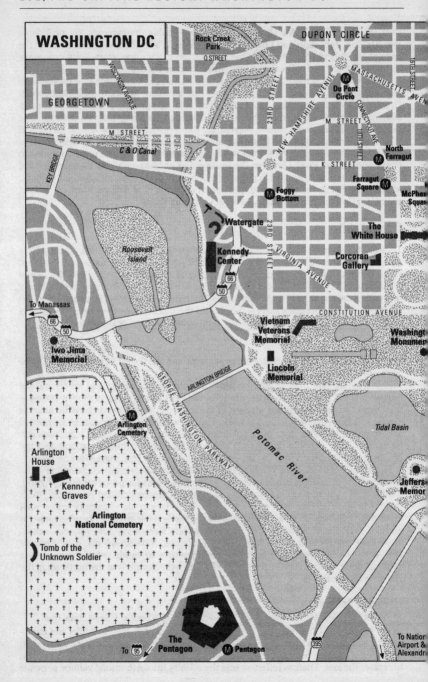

WASHINGTON DC

Rock Creek Park

DUPONT CIRCLE

Q STREET

GEORGETOWN

WISCONSIN AVENUE

23RD STREET

MASSACHUSETTS AVEN

18TH STREET

Du Pont Circle

NEW HAMPSHIRE AVENUE

CONNECTICUT AVE

M STREET

M STREET

C & O Canal

K STREET

North Farragut

Farragut Square

McPher Squar

KEY BRIDGE

Foggy Bottom

Watergate

23RD STREET

VIRGINIA AVENUE

The White House

Roosevelt Island

Kennedy Center

Corcoran Gallery

66

50

To Manassas

66

50

CONSTITUTION AVENUE

Vietnam Veterans Memorial

Washingt Monume

Iwo Jima Memorial

GEORGE WASHINGTON PARKWAY

ARLINGTON BRIDGE

Lincoln Memorial

Arlington Cemetery

Tidal Basin

Arlington House

Potomac River

Kennedy Graves

Arlington National Cemetery

Jeffers Memor

Tomb of the Unknown Soldier

To 95

The Pentagon

Pentagon

395

To Nation Airport & Alexandri

collection. In 1870, when the Library of Congress was declared the **national copyright library**, the need was felt to build a suitable home; the result, the exuberantly eclectic **Thomas Jefferson Building**, opened in 1897 across from the Capitol. The multitiered, domed octagon of the **Reading Room**, and the hundreds of mosaics, murals and sculptures, are all well worth a look. Various old books – including a Gutenberg Bible and a first folio of Shakespeare – are on display in the adjacent **James Madison Building**.

Supreme Court

First St and Maryland Ave NE; closest Metro *Union Station*. Mon–Fri 9am–4.30pm.

The **Supreme Court**, across from the US Capitol, is the final arbiter of what is and isn't legal in the country. The interior spaces of this pseudo-Greek temple, especially the courtroom itself – where guides give lectures when the court is not in session – make it worth climbing the steps and going inside. Each day, the cases to be heard are listed in the *Washington Post* newspaper (or phone ☎479-3499). Sessions begin at 10am, and last one hour per case; arrive early to be assured of getting one of the 150 seats.

The Mall

One of the main features of L'Enfant's grand plan for Washington was the provision of a large central parkland, a Grand Avenue lined by the mansions of the political elite. Today the mile-long **Mall** stretches west from the Capitol to the Potomac River. It wasn't always such a carefully manicured park, however: when the Capitol was first built, it looked out across a muddy, bug-infested swamp, and by the 1870s, the south side was lined by meat-markets and warehouses and criss-crossed by railroad tracks. A stark reminder of L'Enfant's unfulfilled dream, for over twenty years the Washington Monument was left unfinished, an ugly butt of stone cut off halfway.

DC's most popular green space, used for summer softball games and Fourth of July Beach Boys concerts, the Mall is lined by numerous museums, the White House, the understated but powerful Vietnam Memorial and the trio of presidential monuments.

Washington Monument

In the center of the Mall at 14th St; closest Metro *Smithsonian*. Daily; summer 8am–midnight, otherwise 9am–5pm.

The Mall's tallest and most prominent feature, the **Washington Monument** is an unadorned marble obelisk built in memory of George Washington, the first US president. At 555 feet it's the tallest all-masonry structure in the world. Volunteers started work on it in 1848, but various internal arguments, and later the Civil War, so disrupted construction that it wasn't completed until 1884. When the US Government took over the project in 1876, they used marble from a slightly different source; the transition line at the 150ft level where work resumed is readily apparent.

You may have to wait at the base for an hour or more to ride the elevator up. You can't walk up (not that you'd want to), but twice a day (10am & 3pm) guided walks back down point out 200-odd stones donated by various states and national organizations.

The White House

1600 Pennsylvania Ave NW; closest Metro *McPherson Square*. Continuous tours Tues–Sat, 10am–noon; ticket kiosk on the south side opens at 8am.

For nearly two hundred years, the **White House** has been the residence and office of the President of the United States. Standing at the edge of the Mall, due north from the Washington Monument, this grand, neoclassical edifice was completed in 1800 by Irish immigrant James Hoban, who modelled it on the Georgian manors of Dublin. Each of its presidential occupants has made his mark: Thomas Jefferson added the first toilets, just before the British burned it down during the War of 1812. It was quickly rebuilt and expanded, often in such a hurry that the whole building was on the verge of collapse. Harry Truman had to move out for four years from 1948 while the structure was stabilized; all the rooms were dismantled and a modern steel frame inserted. Truman also added the balcony to the familiar south side portico.

Though many visitors are surprised by how small and homey it is (Buckingham Palace it's not), security at the White House is every bit as tight as you'd imagine, and visits are limited to a brief **tour** of the ground floor reception rooms, all filled with portraits of ex-presidents. In summer, the gardens are sometimes opened for afternoon tours, and during the Christmas holidays there are special evening tours of the festively decorated interior (phone ☎456-7041 for details).

Lincoln Memorial

23rd St between Constitution and Independence avenues; closest Metro *Foggy Bottom*.

Standing at the far west end of the Mall, the **Lincoln Memorial** is modelled upon a Doric temple, enclosed by a colonnade and fronted by a long reflecting pool. During the Civil Rights march on Washington in 1963, Dr Martin Luther King Jr delivered his epic "I Have a Dream" speech, not from the steps of the White House or the US Capitol, but here. Ironically, when this monument to the Great Emancipator was dedicated in 1922, the crowds were segregated by color – even black leader Booker T Washington, who gave an address, was forced to watch from a roped-off area to the side.

The Lincoln Memorial is a fitting tribute to the man who held the country together during the Civil War and thereby put an end to slavery in the US. A craggy likeness of Abraham Lincoln sits firmly grasping the arms of his throne-like chair, deep in thought.

Vietnam Memorial

Constitution Ave at 21st St; closest Metro *Foggy Bottom*. Daily 8am–midnight.

Cutting sharply into the green lawn of the Mall, the small and simple **Vietnam Veterans Memorial** serves as a somber and powerful reminder of the nearly 60,000 US soldiers who died in Vietnam. The pathway that slopes down from the grass forms a gash in the earth, its increasing depth symbolizing the increasing involvement of US forces in the war. Alongside, a black marble wall is carved with the names of every soldier who died, in chronological order from 1959 to 1975.

The memorial was designed by Maya Lin, a 21-year-old architecture student. When it was first erected in 1982, there was some outcry by veterans groups about its anti-war connotations. By way of appeasement, in 1984 a more traditional statue of three heroic soldiers was placed nearby, under a floodlit American flag.

Jefferson Memorial

West of 14th St near Ohio Drive; closest Metro *Smithsonian*. Daily 8am–midnight.

The most recently constructed of the major Mall monuments – it wasn't finished until 1943 – the **Jefferson Memorial** is the best looking but hardest to reach of the three presidential memorials. Modelled on his country home, Monticello (see p.319), it consists of a shallow dome hovering over a bronze statue of Thomas Jefferson, the author of the Declaration of Independence and the third US president. The interior walls, encircled by an Ionic colonnade, are carved with Jefferson's words, and an inscription around the frieze reads "I have sworn upon the altar of God eternal hostility against every form of tyranny over the mind of man."

The **Tidal Basin**, which fills most of the space between the Lincoln and Jefferson memorials, was created in order to prevent the western end of the Mall, including the spots where the two memorials sit, from being inundated by Potomac floods. The reflections off it are especially pretty in spring (usually late April) when the rows of Japanese cherry trees come out in full bloom.

The Smithsonian Institution

The cream of Washington DC's remarkable panoply of historical artefacts and fine art works comes under the general auspices of the **Smithsonian Institution**, which holds the US national collections of everything under the sun. Endowed by an Englishman – James Smithson, bastard son of the first Duke of Northumberland, who never even visited the US – the Smithsonian was established in 1846 "for the increase and diffusion of Knowledge". This broad brief is reflected in its impressive range of research centers and museums, nine of which line up along the Mall, while four are located just north.

The original home of the Smithsonian, the 1849 Norman-style fortress known as **The Castle**, stands on the Mall halfway between the Capitol and the Washington Monument. It was at first devoted to scientific research, but as the Smithsonian became more of a museum, the sheer accumulation of stuff necessitated the construction of the various other buildings along the Mall. The old Castle is now the Smithsonian headquarters and main **visitor center;** pick up the latest details on all the galleries at the hi-tech information desk. The ornate tomb of James Smithson is in an alcove just off the Mall entrance, and a lovely flower-filled garden (daily 7am–9pm) fronts the Castle on the south side. To get a feel for the days when this was known as "the nation's attic", take a look in the adjacent **Arts and Industries Building** at the hundreds of objects – including a steam locomotive and Samuel Morse's original telegraph – sent here for safekeeping after the 1876 Centennial Exhibition in Philadelphia.

Admission to all the galleries is **free**. For details on current exhibitions and events dial ☎357-2700; there's a 24-hour recorded announcement on ☎357-2020.

National Air and Space Museum

South side of the Mall between Fourth and Seventh streets SW; closest Metro *L'Enfant Plaza*. Daily summer 10am–7.30pm, otherwise 10am–5.30pm.

The **National Air and Space Museum** is by far DC's most popular attraction, drawing nearly ten million people every year. Most of them may seem to be here on the day you come, but the hangar-like building can accommodate everyone without feeling crowded, and you can always see the hundreds of **historic aircraft** close up. Hanging from the rafters in the main entrance gallery, the **Milestones in Flight** include the handmade plane in which the **Wright Brothers** made the first powered flight in 1903; **Charles Lindbergh's** *Spirit of St Louis*, in which he made the first solo transatlantic crossing; and the sleek black **X-15**, the world's fastest plane. Pick up a cassette tour ($2.50) of the rest of the museum, or just wander around past Pershing and SS-20 ballistic missiles, various interactive computer exhibits, a mock-up of the Skylab space station – and a touchable piece of **moon rock** , brought back by the Apollo astronauts.

The museum also shows a rotating programme of super-large-screen **IMAX** movies (☎357-1686 for times). All have some connection with flying; the most spectacular, *The Dream is Alive*, was shot from an orbiting space shuttle.

National Museum of Natural History

North side of the Mall between Ninth and 12th streets NW; closest Metro *Smithsonian*. Daily 10am–5.30pm.

The imposing three-storey entrance rotunda of the **National Museum of Natural History** feels like the busiest and most boisterous crossroads in all of DC, with troops of screeching school kids chasing each other non-stop around the African elephant. Hundreds of other stuffed animals, tracing evolution from fossilized four-billion-year-old plankton to dinosaurs' eggs and beyond, are on display in the rest of this huge museum – pick up floor plans and guides at the information desk at the elephant's feet. However, little seems to have changed since the 1950s. The museum's old-fashioned, Eurocentric ideology is evidenced by its treatment of pre-Columbian cultures: Inca and Mayan artefacts, and an extensive array of items from Pueblo and other native Southwest desert cultures, are displayed alongside bison, bighorn sheep and other once-wild things.

Upstairs are hundreds of creepy-crawly critters – lizards, snakes, tarantulas and the like – as well as an **Insect Zoo**, filled with hundreds of bugs, which, should you so desire, you can play with. There's also a truly exceptional array of gemstones, including the legendary 45-carat **Hope Diamond**, which once belonged to Marie Antoinette.

National Museum of American History

North side of the Mall between 12th and 14th streets NW; closest Metro *Smithsonian*. Daily, summer 9.30am–7pm, otherwise 9.30am–5.30pm.

If you like kitsch, you won't want to miss the bizarre melange of cultural artefacts at the **National Museum of American History**. George Washington's wooden teeth, Muhammad Ali's boxing gloves, and the ruby slippers Judy Garland wore in the *Wizard of Oz* are set among didactic displays tracing the country's development. It's not so much a center for the scholarly study of history as a sanctuary for vanishing Americana, incorporating Model T Fords, old post offices, and even a restored, turn-of-the-century ice cream parlor, which still serves up banana splits.

As you enter from the Mall, a hilariously over-the-top patriotic sound-and-light display showcases the battered flag that inspired the US national anthem – the **Star-Spangled Banner** itself. Every hour on the half-hour the curtain is raised to expose the 30-by-45ft red-white-and-blue emblem, which survived the British bombing of Baltimore harbor during the War of 1812. On the upper floor, one gallery looks at the farm-based rural and agricultural society of the early US; across the hall, another examines the mass movement of African-Americans from southern farms to the war-time industries of northern cities. The top floor holds the oddest objects, from political memorabilia (much of it over a century old) to stamp and coin collections, old TV sets, and typewriters.

Hirshhorn Museum

South side of the Mall between Seventh and Ninth streets SW; closest Metro *L'Enfant Plaza*. Daily 10am–5.30pm.

Next to the Air and Space Museum, and housed in the most clearly modern building on the Mall – a windowless cylinder balanced on fifteen-foot stilts above a concrete plaza, it looks like a spaceship poised for takeoff – the **Hirshhorn Museum** holds the Smithsonian's extensive collection of late nineteenth- and twentieth-century art. From the main entrance on Independence Ave, escalators climb to the upper floor galleries, where major works by Picasso, de Kooning, Mondrian, Pollock, Matisse and many more are on display. The gallery downstairs hosts travelling exhibitions, and highly rated films are shown in the evenings (☎357-1300 for details).

A stimulating collection of modern **sculpture** is displayed in an open-air garden across Jefferson Drive on the Mall side of the museum. Alongside assorted Moores, Rodins, Smiths and Malliols are two expressive abstract figures by Marino Marini, and a stalwart *Yucatan Woman* by Mexican sculptor Francisco Zuniga. The landscaped garden, sunk below ground level to spare Congress members from having to look at modern art, is also a nice place for a picnic lunch.

National Museum of African Art

South side of the Mall at 950 Independence Ave SW; closest Metro *Smithsonian*. Daily 10am–5.30pm.

Filling the eastern half of the Mall's newest and most attractive building, the **National Museum of African Art** holds over six thousand sculptures and artefacts, both spiritual and functional, from the numerous tribal cultures of sub-Saharan Africa. The permanent collection ranges from Nigerian carved-ivory cult figures to Zairean mother-and-child fertility fetishes and puppet heads from eastern Mali. Around half the space is devoted to changing exhibitions on specific regions, and the gift shop sells woven and dyed fabrics and clothes as well as books and postcards.

Sackler Gallery

South side of the Mall at 1050 Independence Ave SW; closest Metro *Smithsonian*. Daily 10am–5.30pm.

The angular and pyramidal counterpart of the curved and domed African Art museum – built together in 1987, the two are linked by an aseptic rooftop flower garden – the **Sackler Gallery** contains artworks and devotional objects from Asia and the Middle East. You'll find delicate translucent jade dragons and three-thousand-year-old bronzes from China; stone deities from India and Tibet; and lushly illustrated early Islamic texts from Iran, gorgeously colored in gilt, silver and crushed stone pigments.

Freer Gallery

South side of the Mall, Jefferson Drive at 12th St SW; closest Metro *Smithsonian*.

From the day it opened in 1923, the **Freer Gallery** has been one of the more unusual Smithsonian museums. Put together and paid for by railroad millionaire Charles Freer, it revolves around over one thousand prints, drawings and paintings by London-based American artist **James McNeil Whistler** – the largest collection of his works anywhere – but also includes Chinese jades and bronzes, Byzantine illuminated manuscripts, Buddhist wall sculptures and pieces of Persian metalwork, all collected by Freer under Whistler's tutelage. Among other works are pieces by Whistler's contemporaries Winslow Homer, Albert Pinkham Ryder and John Singer Sargent.

Besides his portraits and landscapes, Whistler himself is represented by an entire room – the **Peacock Room**. Its original owner commissioned Whistler to execute a painting for the mantlepiece; the artist later covered the walls and furnishings with blue and gold painted peacock feathers. His patron hated it, so Freer bought it and shipped it over from London (he also kept live peacocks in the museum's central courtyard).

National Museum of American Art

G St between Seventh and Ninth streets; closest Metro *Gallery Place*. Open daily 10am to 5.30pm.

Separated from the main Mall galleries, the **National Museum of American Art** may not get the traffic of the other museums, but it's perhaps the most worthwhile of all. As well as mounting the most thought-provoking shows – one exhibition examining the distortion and deceit underlying early images of the American frontier earned it national notoriety – its galleries are also pleasant places to be in their own right.

When it opened in 1829, the museum was known as the National Gallery of Art – Andrew Mellon later usurped that name. Since 1968, it has shared the Greek Revival-style **Old Patent Office** with the National Portrait Gallery (see below). Works range from Revolutionary portraits and genre scenes to WPA-style social realism and contemporary works by Helen Frankenthaler, Willem de Kooning, Robert Rauschenberg and Clyfford Still. The more modern pieces are displayed on the top floor in the vaulted and colonnaded **Lincoln Gallery**, which in 1865 hosted President Lincoln's post-Civil War Inaugural Ball and is still one of DC's most celebrated interior spaces.

National Portrait Gallery

F St between Seventh and Ninth streets NW; closest Metro *Gallery Place*. Daily 10am–5.30pm.

The **National Portrait Gallery**, sharing its premises with the Museum of American Art, holds pretty much what you'd expect: paintings, sculptures and photographs of famous and not-so-famous people. Highlights include Gilbert Stuart's half-finished portrait of George Washington, a Degas portrait of Mary Cassatt, a collection of Matthew Brady's Civil War photographs and a wall full of *Time* magazine covers.

Renwick Gallery

Pennsylvania Ave at 17th St NW; closest Metro *Farragut West*. Daily 10am–5.30pm.

Housed in the red-brick 1870s French Empire-style building that was the original home of the Corcoran Gallery (see p.300), the **Renwick Gallery** devotes itself to American decorative arts and crafts. The building itself is a noteworthy piece of architecture – from the inscription above the entrance, which simply reads "Dedicated to Art", it's packed with ornate stone and woodwork. A few of the rooms, notably the **Grand Salon**, are decorated as they would have been during the Victorian era; others hold travelling exhibitions of contemporary crafts, and the fairly small permanent collection is made up of mostly modern jewellery and furniture.

Other Museums and Attractions

While one could quite easily spend a good week wandering around the Smithsonian, the national collections are by no means the only worthwhile museums in DC – or, for that matter, along the Mall. The large **National Gallery**, at the foot of the US Capitol, is the best art museum in the city, and one of the top ten in the world. Besides further top-quality art galleries, you can tour various **federal buildings** – to watch the FBI track down criminals, or count brand-new dollar bills as they roll off the presses – and venture out to see Nixon's famous pandas at the **National Zoo**, or honor the nation's dead, including the Kennedy brothers, at **Arlington National Cemetery**.

National Gallery of Art

North side of the Mall between Third and Seventh streets NW; closest Metro *Archives*. Mon–Sat 11am–5pm; Sun 11am–6pm. ☎737-4215.

Though the visually stunning **National Gallery of Art**, the nearest of the Mall museums to the Capitol, is not in fact a government institution, it fully deserves its name. It owes its prominence to the efforts of industrialist **Andrew Mellon**, who bought the building and donated most of the paintings (many were purchased from the cash-poor post-revolutionary government of the USSR, where they had previously hung in the Hermitage). His family have continued as benefactors, raising countless millions to build the new **East Building** in 1978; Walter Annenberg, whose *Reader's Digest* helped to fund Ronald Reagan's rise to political stardom, was also a major patron.

The original neoclassical gallery, designed by John Russell Pope in 1941, is now called the **West Building** and holds the bulk of the permanent collection. From its domed central rotunda, where you can pick up a floor plan and gallery guide, a vaulted corridor runs the length of the building, making it easy to keep your bearings. Galleries to the west on the main floor display major works by Renaissance masters, arranged by nationality: half a dozen Rembrandts fill the **Dutch** gallery, Van Eyck and Rubens dominate the **Flemish**, and El Greco and Velazquez face off in the **Spanish**. Downstairs, smaller galleries have a broader range, including drawings and watercolors by van Gogh, Cezanne and others, collected by Armand Hammer. The other half of the West Building holds an exceptional collection of nineteenth-century **French** paintings – Gauguin, Renoir, van Gogh, Manet, Monet *et al*. At either end of the building, the skylit, fountain-filled **Garden Courts** make an ideal place to rest weary feet.

The triangular **East Building** houses twentieth-century paintings as well as changing exhibitions. As in the Guggenheim in New York, the attention-grabbing spatial choreography of the architecture ends up overpowering the works of art. You emerge from under the oppressively low entrance into a central atrium, from where an escalator, literally carved out of a forty-foot granite wall, climbs to the main galleries – which, squeezed into the corners, seem like an afterthought. The underground concourse which links the two buildings contains a good bookstore, an espresso bar and a large cafeteria – topped by pyramidal skylights and bordered by a glassed-in waterfall.

Corcoran Gallery of Art

17th St between E St and New York Ave NW; closest Metro *Farragut North* or *Farragut West*. Tues, Wed & Fri–Sun 10am–4.30pm, Thurs 10am–9pm.

Just down the street from the White House, the **Corcoran Gallery** is one of the oldest and most respected art museums in the US; or it was, until it bowed to Jesse Helms and cancelled a retrospective of Robert Mapplethorpe's photography. Especially strong in American art – from frontier artists like Remington and Bierstadt, to portraiture by Mary Cassat and Thomas Eakins and modern works by Warhol and Rothko – it also includes a sampling of Dutch masters, medieval tapestries and French Impressionists.

Phillips Collection

1600 21st St at Q St NW; closest Metro *Du Pont Circle*. Tues–Sat 10am–5pm, Sun 2–7pm. Suggested donation $6.50.

The **Phillips Collection**, one of the country's most extensive assemblies of modern paintings, starts off with a variety of proto-modern painters such as El Greco and Turner, before hurrying via French Impressionism to the real heart of the show – hundreds of works by Picasso, Matisse, Kandinsky, van Gogh, Rothko, O'Keeffe, Klee and many others. The building adds to the experience: part is displayed in the Phillips ornate 1890s mansion, the rest in a 1960s modern purpose-built gallery space, all of it recently renovated. A popular series of free concerts takes place on Sunday evenings at 5pm in the ornate music room.

National Museum of Women in the Arts

1250 New York Ave NW; closest Metro *Metro Center*. Mon–Sat 10am–5pm, Sun noon–5pm. ☎783-5000. Admission $4.

Housed in a converted Masonic Temple, the **National Museum of Women in the Arts** has, since it opened in 1987, been the country's only museum dedicated to women artists. Though it includes hundreds of works by painters no one has ever heard of, that is of course partly the point – its curators were inspired by the fact that, as recently as twenty years ago, not one female artist was mentioned in the main American art history textbook. It also includes sculptures by Barbara Hepworth and Camille Claudel (Rodin's mistress and assistant) and paintings by Helen Frankenthaler, Georgia O'Keeffe, Mary Cassatt and Elaine de Kooning – and has one of DC's better museum cafés, the *Mezzanine Café*.

National Archives

North side of the Mall at Seventh St and Constitution Ave NW; closest Metro *Archives*. Daily, summer 10am–9pm, otherwise 10am–5.30pm. ☎501-5000.

On display inside the impressive neoclassical Greek Temple of the **National Archives** are the three short texts upon which the United States is founded: the **Declaration of Independence**, the **Constitution**, and the **Bill of Rights**. These three original sheets of parchment (the three further pages of the Constitution are not on display), drafted respectively in 1776, 1787 and 1789, are now held in helium-filled glass cases, which drop underground in case of fire or threat. You can look at them as long as you like, but if there's a crowd (there usually isn't) you have to shuffle on past.

As well as a copy of the **Magna Carta**, dating from 1297, the archives hold exhibitions and serve as the official repository of all US national records – census data, treaties (including the surrender of Japan in World War II), passport applications, as well as genealogical records – most of which are held in storage.

If you want to search out the so-called **Watergate Tapes**, which led to the downfall of President Richard Nixon, a shuttle bus will take you to where they're held (☎703/756-6498 for details).

The FBI

On Pennsylvania Ave between Ninth and Tenth streets NW, just north of the Mall; closest Metro *Federal Triangle*. Hour-long tours, Mon–Fri 8.45am–4pm. ☎324-3447.

A fortress-like modern building on Pennsylvania Avenue holds the headquarters of the FBI – the **Federal Bureau of Investigation**, the nation's elite law-enforcement organization. Set up in 1908, the FBI came into its own chasing bootleggers and bank robbers like Al Capone and Machine Gun Kelly during the Thirties. Hordes of visitors queue outside, sometimes for well over an hour, to join tours through displays of the famous gangsters and dangerous Communists and subversives from whom the FBI shields the American people (they kept extensive files on Dr Martin Luther King, Jr). Ideology aside (the FBI has only just begun to emerge from the shadow of its longtime führer, J Edgar Hoover), the tour tells all about fingerprinting, ballistics testing and other crime-fighting techniques. What really brings the crowds in, however, is the culminating display of sharpshooting and firepower: agents blast away at cut-out targets with a battery of small arms and automatic weapons.

Holocaust Memorial Museum

100 Raoul Wallenburg Place SW, off 14th St at Independence Ave. Closest Metro *Smithsonian*. Daily 10am–5.30pm. ☎488-0400.

Nothing in DC is more disturbingly unforgettable than the large and generously laid-out new **Holocaust Memorial Museum**. Commemorating the persecution and murder of six million Jews by the Nazis, it places Hitler in historical perspective while personalizing the tragic suffering of the individual victims.

Besides case after case of newspapers and newsreels documenting Nazi activities from the early Thirties through the Final Solution, chillingly evocative reconstructions and in many cases actual relics of Warsaw Ghetto streets, railroad cattle-cars and concentration camp barracks fill the top floors. The sheer numbers of people killed are evoked throughout, first by a whole room filled with shoes stolen from deportees, later by a crisp glass wall etched with the names of the hundreds of eastern European Jewish communities wiped off the map forever.

When it opened in mid-1993, huge crowds overwhelmed the museum's interactive computer systems, and the flow of people had to be controlled. At the time of writing, tickets for specific entry times were being made available free of charge at 9am on the day, and in advance through *Ticketmaster* (☎423-7328; $3 service charge).

The Bureau of Printing and Engraving

One block south of the Mall at 14th and C streets SW; closest Metro *Smithsonian*. Mon–Fri, 9am–2pm. Closed for the entire week around Christmas.

In most ways, a tour of the **Bureau of Printing and Engraving** is like visiting any other printing plant. The difference is that the presses here crank out millions of dollars in currency every day, nearly $100 billion a year. It's a surprisingly low-tech operation: the bills come off in huge sheets, which are sliced up into single bills by ordinary paper cutters, checked for defects and loaded into large wheelbarrows. The Bureau also produces all US postage stamps. A short film explains the basics of intaglio printing, and you can watch it all happen from a glassed-in upstairs gallery.

The National Zoo

3000 Connecticut Ave; closest Metro *Woodley Park/Zoo*. Daily, summer 8am–8pm, otherwise 8am–6pm.

At the **National Zoo**, just a short walk from the Metro, lush trails lead past credible and comparatively humane simulations of the natural environments of over three thousand creatures. Its star attraction is the **panda**, Hsing Hsing, one of a pair given to the US by the People's Republic of China during Richard Nixon's 1972 visit. His mate, Ling Ling, died in 1992, and you can usually see him only at feeding times (11am & 3pm). The zoo also has the expected menagerie of monkeys and chimps, birds and bees, and lions and tigers (including rare white tigers).

Arlington National Cemetery

Across the Potomac River in Arlington, VA; closest Metro *Arlington Cemetery*. Daily, summer 8am–7pm, otherwise 8am–5pm.

A poignant contrast to the grand monuments of the capital is provided by the endless sea of identical white headstones on the hillsides of **Arlington National Cemetery**. The country's most honored final resting place was first used during the Civil War, when the grand mansion at the top of the hill, and all the surrounding land, belonged to Confederate leader **Robert E Lee**. Nearly 200,000 US war dead lie here, and the **Tomb of the Unknown Soldier** remembers thousands more whose bodies were never recovered or identified. An eternal flame marks the grave of **President John F Kennedy**, near his brother Robert; among other well-known names is Pierre L'Enfant, whose gravesite offers a superb view over the Mall and the District he designed.

Unless you have strong legs and lots of time the best way to see the vast cemetery is by *Tourmobile* (see p.290), which leaves from the visitor center at the entrance. You can also walk here from the Lincoln Memorial across the Arlington Bridge.

The Pentagon

Across the Potomac along I-395. Closest Metro *Pentagon*. Mon–Fri 9.30am–3.30pm. ☎703/695-1776.

The symbol of the US military establishment is one of the largest chunks of architecture in the world: though it's only five storeys tall, the total floor area of over 6.5 million square feet is three times that of the Empire State Building. Each of the five sides is over 900 feet long, and the combined length of all the internal corridors totals up at over 17 miles; these and other useless factoids are about all you get from visiting the behemoth building, apart from the opportunity to see at first hand the people responsible for spending billions of tax dollars on those proverbial $50,000 toilet seats.

Ninety-minute **guided tours** leave every half-hour from the small waiting area inside the entrance.

Accommodation

Most DC **hotels** cater to business travellers and political lobbyists, and during the week are quite expensive. At weekends, however, many cut their rates by up to fifty percent – for a list of properties contact the **Promote DC** office (☎724-4091 or 1-800/422-8644) and ask for their *Washington Weekends*. *Washington DC Accommodations* (☎289-2220 or 1-800/554-2220) provide a general hotel reservation and travel planning service.

Similarly, a number of **B&B** agencies offer comfy doubles from around $65: try *B&B Ltd* (☎328-3510), the B&B *League* (☎363-7767) or *Capitol Reservations* (☎452-1270 or 1-800/847-4832). There's no good **camping** anywhere near DC, but besides the **youth hostel**, both the Catholic University (☎635-5277) and Georgetown University (☎687-3999) offer budget **rooms** in summer; these must be arranged well in advance.

One thing to keep in mind: DC in summer is hot and humid, and **air-conditioning** is essential for getting a good night's rest.

Allen Lee Hotel, 2224 F St NW (☎331-1224 or 1-800/462-0186). Slightly faded but clean downtown hotel, two blocks from *Foggy Bottom* Metro. ③.

Connecticut-Woodley Guest House, 2647 Woodley Rd NW (☎667-0218). Pleasant small guest house opposite the *Sheraton Washington* and near the zoo. ③.

Hotel Harrington, 1100 E St NW (☎628-8140 or 1-800/424-8532). Large, refurbished older hotel, halfway between the Capitol and the White House. ④.

Hay-Adams Hotel, 1 LaFayette Square NW (☎638-2260 or 1-800/332-3442). Beautiful and very expensive hotel overlooking the White House. Stop in for a drink if you can't afford the rates. ⑧.

International Guest House, 1441 Kennedy St NW (☎726-5808). Small, homey boarding house, offering rooms for $25 a night, with weekly rates. ①.

Kalorama Guest House, 1854 Mintwood Place NW (☎667-6369). Cozy, nicely furnished rooms spread around six houses in the lively Adams Morgan neighborhood. ③.

Marifex Hotel, 1523 22nd St NW (☎293-1885). Basic accommodation, with shared baths, near Du Pont Circle. ③.

Tabard Inn Hotel, 1739 N St NW (☎785-1277). Very pleasant small hotel, two blocks from *Du Pont Circle* Metro. Rates, for doubles with shared bath, include breakfast. ⑤.

Washington International AYH Hostel, 1009 11th St NW (☎737-2333). Huge (250 beds), clean and very central, three blocks north of Metro Center. AYH/IYHA members only, $14 a night. ①.

Eating

Just as the faces in government change with every election, so too do **restaurants** come and go more quickly in Washington than just about anywhere else in the US. Within this constant flux a few longstanding favorites endure; and certain neighborhoods – Connecticut Avenue around **Du Pont Circle**, 18th Street and Columbia Road in **Adams Morgan**, and M Street in **Georgetown** – always seem to hold a good range of dining options.

It's often said, not entirely in jest, that the best restaurants tend to come from the "trouble spots" of the world – Vietnam in the 1970s, Afghanistan and Ethiopia in the 1980s, and most recently Central America. The cafés in the main **museums** are good for downtown lunch breaks.

Downtown

AV Ristorante, 607 New York Ave NW (☎737-0550). Huge, ever-popular downtown trattoria, serving up great pizzas and daily Italian specials for under $10.

Bacchus, 1827 Jefferson Place NW (☎785-0734). Somewhat pricey but very good downtown Lebanese restaurant, with excellent hummus and tangy kebabs.

Old Ebbitt Grill, 675 15th St NW (☎347-4800). Very plush, old-style downtown tavern, with an immaculate mahogany bar, gilt mirrors and stylish clientele.

Head's, 400 First St SE (☎546-4545). Trendy Capitol Hill barbeque place featuring great ribs on a full menu of down-home dishes.

Patent Pending, Museum of American Art, Eighth and G St (☎357-2700). Located just off the sunny central courtyard in the ornate old Patent Building, with good pastries and sandwiches.

Vie de France Café, 1615 M St NW (☎659-0992). One of a chain of low-priced, lunchtime cafés featuring fresh-baked croissants.

Du Pont Circle

Afterwords Café, 1517 Connecticut Ave NW (☎387-1462). Located in the back of *Kramerbooks*, DC's best bookstore, and serving up the District's best cappuccino.

Café Tomate, 1701 Connecticut Ave NW (☎667-5505). Light, airy and very popular Du Pont Circle restaurant, with a range of freshly prepared pasta, grilled fish and meat dishes.

City Lights, 1731 Connecticut Ave NW (☎265-6688). Above average, bargain Chinese restaurant.

Food for Thought, 1738 Connecticut Ave NW (☎797-1095). Arty vegetarian café with live music.

Pizzeria Paradiso, 2029 P St NW (☎223-1245). Arguably DC's best pizzeria – certainly the most fun.

Straits of Malaya, 1836 18th St NW (☎483-1483). Unique Southeast Asian cuisine; great seafood.

Adams Morgan

Calvert Café, 1967 Calvert St NW (☎232-5431). Ancient-looking Adams Morgan café. Excellent Middle Eastern food at bargain prices. Just across Duke Ellington Bridge from *Zoo Station* Metro.

Cities, 2424 18th St NW (☎328-7194). Trendy bistro-style café. Good pizzas plus an ever-changing menu of international foods on an outdoor terrace overlooking the Adams Morgan streetlife parade.

Mixtec, 1792 Columbia Rd NW (☎332-1011). Great-tasting, low-priced Mexican food – great tacos and tortillas, plus a hangover-soothing *menudo*.

Red Sea, 2463 18th St NW (☎483-5000). Inexpensive and plentiful portions of spicy Ethiopian food.

Saigonnais, 2307 18th St NW (☎232-5300). Well-presented Vietnamese food in cozy townhouse.

Georgetown

Au Pied du Cochon, 1335 Wisconsin Ave NW (☎333-5440). Casual, comfortable, late-opening bistro.

Dancing Crab, 4611 Wisconsin Ave NW (☎244-1882). Unpretentious seafood café, specializing in Chesapeake Bay softshell crabs – all you can eat for around $15.

Madurai, 3318 M St NW (☎333-0997). DC's most popular vegetarian restaurant, serving good curries and an excellent, meat-free *kofta*.

Mr Smith's, 3104 M St NW (☎333-3104). Casual and somewhat chaotic burger bar.

Patisserie Café Didier, 3206 Grace St NW (☎342-9083). Outrageously good (and quite expensive) cakes, pastries, teas and coffees. Just off Wisconsin Ave across from the C&O Canal.

The Tombs, 1226 36th St NW (☎337-6668). Burgers and beers in a cozy, publike room.

Nightlife and Entertainment

With five different theater spaces, the **Kennedy Center** (☎467-4600), next to the Watergate complex along the Potomac River, hosts most of the capital's high-brow cultural events, as well as nightly screenings organized by the American Film Institute. *The Arena Stage*, Sixth St and Maine Ave SW (☎488-3300), puts on contemporary plays and performance pieces, as does the *Church Street Theater*, 1742 Church St NW (☎298-9000). *Woolly Mammoth*, 1401 Church St NW (☎393-3939), and *Source Theatre Company*, 1815 14th St (☎462-1073), are also worth seeking out. For half-price day-of-show theater **tickets**, call ☎TIC-KETS.

DC's **bar** and **nightlife** scene is less developed than in more settled cities. Peak times for drinking tend to be the rush hours, and comparatively few people who work in the District during the week venture back into town at the weekend. However, things are slowly improving, and in the well-worn haunts of collegiate **Georgetown** and **Du Pont Circle** you should be able to pass a pleasant evening or two.

Tickets to watch the Washington Redskins **football** team are very expensive, and usually every game sells out. They play at the RFK Stadium (☎547-9077) – also the venue of some matches in the 1994 soccer World Cup. See the free weekly *CityPaper* for up-to-date **listings** of music, theater and other events in the area – as well as good alternative features and reporting. The *Washington Blade* focuses on **gay** and **lesbian** life.

The Bayou, Wisconsin Ave and K St (☎333-2897). Georgetown's leading headbanger hang-out, right on the riverfront.

The Dubliner, 520 N Capitol St NW (☎737-3773). Bare-bones Irish bar, with Harp and Guinness on draught and no end of boisterous conversation.

15 Min, 1030 15th St NW (☎408-1855). Live bands, indie rock, poetry readings and dance music.

The Fireplace, 2161 P St (☎293-1293). Friendly, gay-oriented Du Pont Circle bar with pool tables, huge jukebox and seven-hour Happy Hour. A staging ground for the cruisey P Street Beach scene.

Hung Jury, 1819 H St NW (☎785-8181). Popular women's bar, tucked away off an alley.

J Paul's, 3218 M St NW (☎333-3450). Huge and always lively Georgetown pub.

Kelly's Irish Times, 14 F St NW (☎543-5433). Half a block west of Union Station, this crowded but comfortable pub has a good range of beers and above-average bar food.

Kilimanjaro, 1724 California St NW (☎328-3838). Restaurant and nightclub; reggae and world beat.

Mr Eagan's, 1343 Connecticut Ave NW (☎861-9609). Halfway between a honky-tonk and an Irish pub, with the cheapest drinks near Du Pont Circle.

VIRGINIA

Travelling through **VIRGINIA**, the oldest, largest and wealthiest of the American colonies and the single most powerful influence on the early United States, is a non-stop history lesson. Pretty and largely rural it may be, but the past predominates; wherever you go you're pointed toward this or that painstakingly restored two-hundred-year-old building, where something or other happened some long time ago. The more you know about it all, the more rewarding Virginia is to visit, but it can get a bit ridiculous after a while, counting the historical plaques that mark every spot where George Washington slept, Thomas Jefferson thought, or Robert E Lee tied his horse to a tree.

Virginia's recorded history began at **Jamestown**, just off the Chesapeake Bay, with the establishment in 1607 of the first successful British colony in North America. Though the first colonists hoped to find gold, it was **tobacco** that made their fortunes. The native strain – used for hundreds of years by Virginia's aboriginal population, of whom almost no trace remains – was too strongly flavored for European tastes, but when a smoother, more palatable variety was introduced in 1615 by John Rolfe – coincidentally the same man whose shipwreck on Bermuda inspired Shakespeare's *The Tempest* – tobacco quickly become the colony's major cash crop. Before long vast plantations, owned by a very few aristocratic families, sprang up along the many broad rivers that flow into the Chesapeake Bay. To grow and harvest tobacco required an immense amount of land – so the Indians had to go – and intensive labor – so the plantation owners brought in **slaves** from Africa. By the end of the seventeenth century, enslaved African-Americans accounted for nearly half of the colony's 75,000 people; a hundred years later, they numbered over 300,000.

Virginians had an enormous impact on the foundation of the nascent United States: George Mason, Thomas Jefferson, and James Madison wrote the Declaration of Independence and the Constitution, and four of the first five US presidents were from Virginia. However, by the mid-1800s the state was in decline, its once fertile fields depleted by overuse and its predominantly rural, agrarian economy increasingly eclipsed by the urban and industrialized North.

As the confrontation between North and South over slavery and related economic and political issues grew more divisive, Virginia was caught in the middle, both geographically and ideologically. Though this slaveholding state initially voted against secession from the Union, it joined the Confederacy when the **Civil War** broke out, providing its military leader, Robert E Lee, and its capital, Richmond. Four long years later Virginia was ravaged, its towns and cities wrecked, its farmlands ruined, and most of its youth dead. It has never regained its early prosperity, nor its prominence in national affairs.

Richmond itself was largely destroyed in the war; today it's a small city, with some good museums, which makes the best starting point for seeing Virginia. The bulk of the **colonial** sites are concentrated just to the east, in the **Historic Triangle**. Here the remains of **Jamestown**, the original colony, **Williamsburg**, the restored colonial capital, and **Yorktown**, site of the final battle of the Revolutionary War, lie within half an hour's drive of each other.

Another historic center, Thomas Jefferson's **Charlottesville**, sits at the foot of the gorgeous **Blue Ridge Mountains**, an hour west of Richmond. An attractive small college town in its own right, it's also within easy reach of the natural splendors of **Shenandoah National Park** and the small towns of the western valleys. **Northern Virginia**, often visited as a day out from Washington DC, holds a number of restored homes, and several preserved Civil War **battlefields**.

The **area code** for northern Virginia is ☎703.

Getting Around Virginia

Virginia is not difficult to explore. Two north–south *Amtrak* routes from Washington DC cross the state, one through Charlottesville towards Atlanta and the other through Fredericksburg and Richmond on the way to Florida; in addition, daily connections run east from Richmond to the Historic Triangle, and west from Charlottesville towards Chicago. *Greyhound* reaches dozens of smaller towns. Drivers heading south can take the stunning Blue Ridge Parkway along the Appalachians. If you've got the time, there's ample opportunity for **cycling**, whether on quiet country roads or up in the mountains, and **hiking** or **walking** tours are also worth thinking about.

Northern Virginia

Northern Virginia, almost all of which lies within commuting distance of Washington DC, holds some extremely exclusive suburbs – McLean and the rest of Fairfax County, for example, house an inordinate number of US senators. The anglophile heartland of Virginia's landed gentry – often called "Hunt Country" for its love of horses and fancy-dress blood sports – it holds well-preserved eighteenth- and nineteenth-century stately homes, cottages, churches, barns and taverns tucked away along the quiet backroads. It's all very popular with tourists, nowhere more so than **Mount Vernon**, the longtime home of George Washington. During the Civil War, **Fredericksburg** to the south witnessed the battles of Chancellorsville, Spotsylvania and the Wilderness, while **Manassas** to the west was the site of the bloody battles of Bull Run.

Mount Vernon – George Washington's Home

Set on a shallow bluff overlooking the broad Potomac River, **Mount Vernon** (daily, summer 9am–5pm, otherwise 9am–4pm; $5) is among the most attractive historic houses in the US. The country estate of **George Washington** has been maintained virtually intact since his death in 1799, with its eight-thousand acres of landscaped and planted grounds. Besides illuminating the life and times of the leader of the revolutionary armies, and the first US president, Mount Vernon also allows an eye-opening look into the aristocratic way of life of the colonial gentlemen who founded the USA.

A small museum gives an overview of Mount Vernon's history; in the house itself, the furnishings and decoration reflect Washington's preference for plain living, but few items – a reading chair with a built-in fan, and a key to the destroyed Bastille, presented by Thomas Paine on behalf of Lafayette – give much of a sense of his character. The four-posted bed upon which he died stands in an upstairs bedroom; he and his wife Martha are buried in a simple tomb on the south side of the house.

Gunston Hall – George Mason's Home

The plain brick 1755 **Gunston Hall**, home of Washington's contemporary **George Mason**, stands just around a bend in the river, ten minutes' drive south along Hwy-1 at the east end of Hwy-242 (daily 9.30am–5pm; $5). It was Mason's revolutionary idea "that all men are by nature equally free and independent and have certain inherent rights", which Jefferson incorporated into the Declaration of Independence. Mason was later one of the main framers of the US Constitution, which he then refused to support because it neither included a Bill of Rights nor abolished slavery. Unlike Washington and Jefferson, Mason eschewed public power, preferring to stay here with his family – which is understandable once you've seen the place, one of the most impressive pieces of architecture in Virginia. Most of it was designed and constructed by William Buckland; the masterful interiors, particularly in the stately drawing room, feature some beautiful carved ornament. The house fronts onto a large formal garden, and the extensive grounds are in turn surrounded by two riverfront state parks and wildlife refuges.

Manassas Battlefield National Park

Manassas Battlefield National Park spreads on grassy green hills at the western fringes of the Washington DC suburban belt, just off the I-66 freeway. Though the modern world is just outside its boundaries – after a lengthy court battle, developers were prevented in 1991 from building a tract of battle-view homes on its fringes – you don't have to know the details of what happened here to feel the numinous power of these brooding hillsides.

Soon after the first shots were fired at Fort Sumter, the first major land battle of the Civil War, known as the **Battle of Bull Run**, was fought here on the morning on July 21 1861. Expecting an easy victory, some 25,000 Union troops attacked a Confederate detachment that controlled a vital railroad link to the Shenandoah Valley. The rebels proved powerful opponents, their strength in battle earning their commander, General Thomas Jackson, the famous nickname "Stonewall". Displays in the small **visitor center** at the entrance (daily, summer 8.30am–6pm, winter 8.30am–5pm; park admission $1) describe how the battle took shape, and detail the other battles fought here over the course of the war.

Fredericksburg

Only a mile off the I-95 freeway, and easy to reach on *Amtrak* or *Greyhound*, **FREDERICKSBURG** retains a good deal of its historic feel. In colonial days, this was an important inland port, loading tobacco and other plantation products onto boats that sailed down the Rappahonock River. Dozens of eighteenth- and nineteenth-century buildings along the waterfront now hold antique stores and secondhand booksellers.

Two blocks away, in the 1816 town hall, the **Fredericksburg Area Museum**, 905 Princess Anne St (March–Nov Mon–Sat 9am–5pm, Sun 1–5pm; Dec–Feb closes 4pm; $3), has a broad range of displays tracing local history from Native American settlements to the present day. The **Rising Sun Tavern**, by the river at 1304 Caroline St, was built as a home in the mid-1700s by George Washington's brother Charles. As an inn, it became a key meeting place for patriots and a hotbed of sedition. It is now a small "living history" museum (March–Nov daily 9am–5pm; Dec–Feb daily 10am–4pm; $3), in which costumed "wenches" guide visitors around a collection of pub-games and ancient pewterware. They don't, however, serve food or drink anymore, except for the glass of spiced herbal punch you get on the tour.

Fredericksburg's important strategic location made it vital during the **Civil War**, and the land around the town was heavily fought over. Over 100,000 men lost their lives in the major battles of Fredericksburg, Chancellorsville, Spotsylvania, and countless other bloody skirmishes. The **Fredericksburg and Spotsylvania National Battlefield Park**, 1013 Lafayette Blvd south of town (visitor center daily, summer 8.30am–6.30pm, otherwise 8.30am–5pm; admission free), has informative exhibits and rents three-hour audio tours ($3 for tape and player) of the various battlefield sites.

Practicalities

Fredericksburg's **visitor center** at 706 Caroline St (☎373-1776 or 1-800/678-4748) has maps of walking tours. The town gets a lot of weekend-escape trade, and so has several good places to **eat** and **drink**. The closest contemporary equivalent to the bawdy *Rising Sun* is probably the *Irish Brigade*, 1005 Princess Anne St (☎371-9413), a lively sandwich and burger bar (open until 2am) with draught Harp and Guinness, and nightly folk and r'n'b. The cozy pub at the eighteenth-century *Kenmore Inn*, 1200 Princess Anne St, serves old-fashioned steaks and fish, and there's occasional live jazz. It also has B&B rooms furnished with antiques (☎371-7622; ④). Fredericksburg abounds in olde worlde **B&Bs** like the *Richard Johnson Inn*, 711 Caroline St (☎899-7606; ④); good motels include the *Fredericksburg Colonial Inn*, 1707 Princess Anne St (☎371-5666; ③).

Richmond and the Tidewater

At the very heart of Virginia, **Richmond** and the **Chesapeake Bay tidewater** are, in many ways, where the US was born. Not only does this fairly compact area hold some of the most important surviving colonial-era sites, it is also where the strength of the nation was tested by the traumatic Civil War. The greatest interest is to be found in the compact **Historic Triangle**, east of Richmond, and along the **Atlantic coast** beyond.

Richmond and Around

Founded in 1737 at the furthest navigable point on the James River, **RICHMOND** remained a small outpost until just before the end of the colonial era, when independence-minded Virginians, realizing that their capital at Williamsburg was open to British attack, shifted it fifty miles further inland. The move to Richmond failed to offer much protection – the city was raided many times and twice put to the torch, once by troops under the command of Benedict Arnold.

For the next 75 years Richmond flourished, its population reaching 100,000 by the time of the Civil War. Although, just a month before, Virginia had strongly opposed secession from the Union, voting two-to-one against, when war broke out Richmond was named the **capital of the Confederacy**. The massive **Tredegar Iron Works** – now being restored as a riverfront museum – became the main engine of the Confederate war machine. For four years the city was the focus of Southern defences and Union attacks, but despite an almost constant state of siege – General McClellan came within six miles of the capital as early as 1862, and General Grant steamrollered remorselessly towards it through the last months of the war – it held on until the very end. It was less than a week after the fall of Richmond, on April 3 1865, that General Lee surrendered to General Grant at Appomattox, a hundred miles to the west.

After the war, Richmond was devastated. Much of its downtown was burned, allegedly by fleeing Confederates who wanted to keep its stores of weapons, and its warehouses full of tobacco, out of the victors' hands. Rebuilding, however, was quick, and the city's economy has remained among the strongest in the South. **Tobacco** is still a major industry – machine-rolled cigarettes were invented here in the 1870s, and Marlboro-makers **Phillip Morris** run a huge manufacturing plant just south of downtown. In the mornings you can smell the sweet earthy aroma of the drying leaves. Richmond is also a leading **banking** center, and has all the modern office towers of a major American city, as well as an extensive inventory of architecturally significant older buildings.

Arrival, Information and Getting Around

Two hours' drive from Washington DC via I-95, which cuts through the east side of downtown, Richmond is also served by *Amtrak*, pulling in to 7519 Staples Mill Rd, five miles northwest of downtown, and *Greyhound* (☎353-8903), who stop just off I-64 at 2910 N Blvd, also a good way from the center. The large **airport** ten miles east of downtown is served by major carriers.

There's a large **visitor center** (daily, June–Aug 9am–7pm, otherwise 9am–5pm; ☎358-5511) near *Greyhound* at 1710 Robin Hood Rd off I-95, and a smaller but more central office at 300 E Main St (☎782-2777 or 1-800/365-7272).

Most of Richmond is compact and easily walkable, but to get to outlying places (like the stations or the Fine Art Museum) you might want to take a *GRTC* **bus** (75¢–$1.20; ☎358-GRTC). They also operate three free downtown trolleys, including one that runs to the main nightlife districts (Shockoe Slip and Shockoe Bottom) until midnight on

The **area code** for Richmond and the Tidewater is ☎804.

weekdays. **City tours** run by the *Historic Richmond Foundation*, 2407 E Grace St (☎780-0107), include some on foot (April–Oct Mon–Sat 10am–noon; $5; reserve a day in advance).

Downtown Richmond

Richmond's **downtown** centers on a few blocks rising up from the James River to either side of Broad Street. Modern office towers front onto a riverside park, while up the shallow hill in the **Court End** district, dozens of well-preserved antebellum homes provide a suitable background to some important museums and historic sites.

The **Virginia State Capitol** (daily 9am–5pm; free), which has been in use since 1788 as the seat of the state – and, during the Civil War, Confederate – government, is the focal point, visible from all over Richmond and offering a sweeping view from its columned portico. Thomas Jefferson had a hand in the design, based on his favorite building, the Roman ruin of Maison Carré in Nimes, France. The domed central rotunda, not visible from outside, holds a life-sized marble statue of George Washington, the only one modelled from life, and busts of Jefferson and the seven other Virginia-born US presidents line the walls. Likenesses of famous Virginians, including a solemn bronze Robert E Lee, fill the adjacent **Old House Chamber**, the largest room in the Capitol and the place where Aaron Burr was tried and acquitted of treason in 1807.

Just two blocks north of the Capitol on 12th St, the **Museum of the Confederacy**, 1201 E Clay St (Mon–Sat 10am–5pm, Sun noon–5pm; $4), gives an even-handed history of the Civil War, starting with a brief description of the 1850s abolitionist and states rights movements but concentrating on the various battles, from Fort Sumter to Appomattox, and on the personalities of the Confederate leaders. Next door, the so-called **White House of the Confederacy** (same hours; $7), a neoclassical mansion where Jefferson Davis lived as Confederate president, has recently been restored to its 1860s appearance. Tours of the house itself are reverential and rather dull; far more interesting is the exhibition on Davis' staff, telling how some of his slaves were supposedly "bribed" into escaping north, and a small collection of domestic memorabilia with captions hurriedly written by Davis' wife.

Two blocks to the west, the 1812 **Wickham House** now forms part of the excellent **Valentine Museum** at 1015 E Clay St (Mon–Sat 10am–5pm, Sun noon–5pm; $4, or $7 combined with Confederacy Museum). This neoclassical monolith houses a small local history museum, focusing on the experience of working-class and black Americans, as well as an extensive array of furniture and pre-Civil War clothing – whalebone corsets and other *Gone with the Wind* period costumes.

A little further west, beyond the Convention Center on Sixth St, is a neighborhood of early nineteenth-century houses, many fronted by ornate wrought-iron balconies similar to those in New Orleans' French Quarter. Known as **Jackson Ward**, and filling a dozen blocks around First and Clay streets, this has been the center of Richmond's African-American community since well before the Civil War, when Richmond had the largest free black population in the US. As well as covering local history, the **Maggie L Walker House**, 110 E Leigh St (Tues–Sun 9am–5pm; free), traces the working life of the physically disabled black Richmond woman who, during the 1920s, founded and ran the first non-white-male-owned bank in the US, now the Consolidated Bank and Trust. Plans are afoot to open a black heritage museum (details on ☎780-9093).

Shockoe Bottom, the Poe Museum and Church Hill

A short walk southeast from the Court End district, a very different neighborhood allows a glimpse at another side of the Richmond story. Split down the middle by the raised I-95 freeway, the increasingly gentrified (and regularly flooded) riverfront warehouse district of **Shockoe Bottom** still holds a few palpable reminders of Richmond's industrial past in its cobbled stone streets, among the restaurants and nightclubs.

From **Shockoe Slip**, a prettified old wharf area rebuilt in the 1890s after being destroyed in the Civil War, Cary St runs east along the waterfront lined by a wall of brick warehouses known as **Tobacco Row**.

Nearby, in Richmond's oldest building, an appropriately gloomy 250-year-old stone house at 1914 E Main St serves as the **Edgar Allan Poe Museum** (Tues–Sat 10am–4pm, Sun–Mon 1.30–4pm; $5). Poe spent much of his life in Richmond and considered it his hometown; after his mother died in 1811 when Edgar was three years old, he was raised by foster parents before leaving for the University of Virginia at age eighteen, and later returned to write the *Narrative of Arthur Gordon Pym* while working on the Richmond-based magazine *Southern Literary Messenger*.

Church Hill, a few blocks northeast, is one of Richmond's oldest surviving residential districts, its decorative eighteenth-century houses, adorned with cast-iron porches and rambling magnolia-filled front gardens, looking out over the James River. Capping the hill at the heart of the neighborhood, **St John's Church** (Mon–Sat 10am–3.30pm, Sun 1–3.30pm; $2 donation), 2401 E Broad St, which dates back to 1741, is best known as the place where, during a March 1775 debate on whether the Virginia colony should raise a militia against the British, **Patrick Henry** made the impassioned plea: "Is life so dear, or peace so sweet, to be purchased at the price of chains of slavery? I know not what course others may take, but as for me, give me liberty or give me death." His speech is re-enacted by an actor every Sunday at 2pm, after the religious services.

The Virginia Museum of Fine Arts and the Science Museum

The newest and most opulent of Richmond's neighborhoods, called the **Fan District** because its tree-lined avenues fan out at oblique angles, spreads west from the downtown area, beyond Belvedere Street (US-1). Lined by garish turn-of-the-century mansions, the Fan District's broadest street, **Monument Avenue**, was laid out in 1889 as a symbol of the city's post-Reconstruction recovery, and is marked every few hundred yards by large-scale memorial statues honoring Civil War figures Jeb Stuart, Robert E Lee, Jefferson Davis and Stonewall Jackson.

South of Monument Avenue, at 2800 Grove Ave, stands the **Virginia Museum of Fine Arts** (Tues–Sat 11am–5pm, Sun 1–5pm; $2 donation). Paul Mellon donated an extensive collection of Impressionist and Post-Impressionist paintings, displayed alongside American paintings ranging from George Catlin's romantic images of Plains Indians to the Pop Art creations of Roy Lichtenstein and Claes Oldenburg in the vast new West Wing. Other galleries contain such diverse items as Frank Lloyd Wright furniture, Lalique jewellery, and Hindu and Buddhist sculpture from the Himalayas, but perhaps the most popular part of the museum is a world-class array of over three hundred jewel-encrusted **Fabergé eggs**, crafted in the 1890s for the Russian tsars.

Accommodation

Finding well-priced **accommodation** in Richmond isn't difficult, with no shortage of anonymous downtown hotels catering to the business and government trade. You can get a feel for the old city by staying the night in a **B&B** in one of the historic quarters.

The Berkeley Hotel, 1200 E Cary St (☎780-1300). Elegant small hotel on historic Shockoe Slip. ④.

Caitlin-Abbott House, 2304 E Broad St (☎780-3746). Small B&B on Church Hill, across from St John's Church. ④.

Holiday Inn Midtown, 3200 W Broad St (☎359-4061). Good location, near the Fan District and Fine Arts Museum. ③.

Jefferson, Franklin and Adams (☎788-8000 or 1-800/424-8014). Beautifully maintained spacious grand hotel, with fabulous marble-columned lobby. ⑥.

Linden Row Inn, 100 E Franklin St (☎783-7000 or 1-800/348-7424). Historic red-brick Georgian terrace houses converted into comfortable modern hotel. ④.

Massad House Hotel, 11 N Fourth St (☎648-2893). Cheerful old hotel in Court End district. ②.

Eating

Richmond has a good choice of eating options at either end of the price spectrum, with barbecue a specialty.

Bill's Barbecue, 3100 N Blvd (☎355-9745). Great breakfasts and huge portions of barbecued chicken and ribs, plus delicious fresh pies. Seven other locations around Richmond.

Peking Restaurant, 1302 E Cary St (☎649-8888). Very good, inexpensive (especially at lunchtime) Chinese place in Shockoe Slip. Szechuan and Mandarin specialties. Also a branch at 5710 Grove Ave in the West End.

Scarlett, 1500 E Main St (☎643-0445). Splendid New American cuisine in restored Main St train station in Shockoe Bottom. Surprisingly romantic views across the tracks.

Strawberry Street Café, 421 N Strawberry St (☎353-6860). Casual and comfortable Fan District neighborhood café – mainly quiches, pastas and salads.

Third Street Diner, Third and Main St (☎788-4750). Relaxed 24hr all-American diner; splendid breakfasts, and Greek specialties. Stylish student crowd, especially at night when it's also a bar.

The Tobacco Company, 12th and E Cary St (☎782-9431). Cheerful New American food in stunningly restored three-storey tobacco warehouse, with antique elevator. Cocktail bar with nightly live entertainment in the leafy first-floor atrium.

Traveller's Restaurant, 707 E Franklin St (☎644-1040). Upmarket steak and seafood in home once lived in by Robert E Lee.

Drinking and Nightlife

Richmond's main drinking and nightlife spots are concentrated around the riverside Shockoe Slip and Shockoe Bottom areas just east of downtown, where you'll find the likes of the *Bird in Hand*, 1718 E Main St (☎788-1101), which has live music on Wednesday evening, and DJs from Friday to Saturday; the singles-scene *Shockoe Slip Café*, 1218 E Cary St (☎343-1757); or *The Flood Zone*, 18th & Main St (☎644-0935), one of Richmond's hippest live music venues. In the Fan District, try the *Paradise Café*, 2229 W Main St (☎358-6759), or the *Stonewall*, 1520 W Main St (☎359-6324).

Between October and June, *TheaterVirginia* (☎367-0840), at 2800 Grove Ave in the Museum of Fine Arts, is Richmond's best bet for live **theater**. For music and events check the listings in the free weekly paper *Night Moves* newspaper.

The Historic Triangle: Jamestown, Williamsburg, and Yorktown

The **Historic Triangle**, on the thin peninsula that stretches east of Richmond between the James and York rivers, holds by far the richest concentration of colonial-era sites in the US. **Jamestown**, founded in 1607, was Virginia's first settlement; **Williamsburg** is an animated if theatrical resurrection of the colonial capital; and it was at **Yorktown** that American independence from the English crown was finally secured. All three sites are within an hour by car, bus or train from the capital.

The I-64 freeway is the quickest way to cover the fifty miles from Richmond to Williamsburg, but once you're in the area the best way to get around is along the lushly landscaped **Colonial Parkway**, which winds west to Jamestown and east to Yorktown, twenty miles end-to-end. Most of the area's numerous tourist facilities – this is the most-visited destination in the state – are to be found around Williamsburg. We've listed a few suggestions under "Historic Triangle Practicalities" on p.315.

Jamestown National Historic Site

The first successful English colony in the New World, **JAMESTOWN** was established as a commercial venture, sponsored by King James I but paid for and owned by the **Virginia Company**. On April 26 1607 the colonists, thirty adventure-minded aristocrats and seventy-five indentured servants, arrived at the mouth of the Chesapeake Bay after four months at sea, and within two weeks established a fortified settlement upon a low-lying island forty miles up the James River.

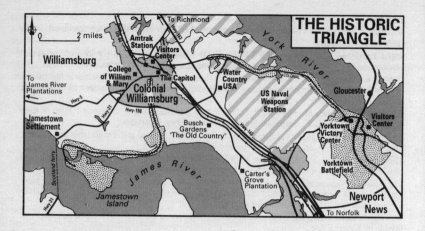

Despite the fact that Jamestown was intended to be self-supporting, not one of the party had any experience of farming or fishing – their leader, **John Smith**, wrote in 1608 that "though there be Fish in the Sea, and Foules in the ayre, and Beasts in the woods, their bounds are so large, they are so wilde, and we so weake and ignorant, we cannot much trouble them". The Virginia Company continued to send new recruits, but the loss of life was extreme: of more than seven thousand settlers who came to Jamestown in its first decade, six thousand perished within a year of arriving.

What saved Jamestown, besides the provisions brought by new settlers, was **tobacco**: by 1619 the colony was shipping some twenty tons a year back to England. As it expanded, the colony began to encroach upon the **Powhatan** Indians, who until then had been fairly peaceable. In 1622 and again in 1644 provocations caused the Powhatan to attack the Jamestown colonists, killing some five hundred settlers each time. The most serious damage to Jamestown, however, was caused by the colonists themselves, when they burned the fort to the ground in 1675 to protest the lack of protection offered them by the crown. Rather than rebuild the tiny island outpost, by the end of the 1600s they had shifted the capital and most of the commercial activity inland to Williamsburg, and Jamestown slowly disappeared.

The one bit of seventeenth-century Jamestown to survive, protected within the **Jamestown National Historic Site**, is the fifty-foot tower of the first brick church, built in 1639 – the rest was destroyed by fire in 1698. Around it are sundry unearthed foundations, as well as numerous memorial shrines and monuments.

From the **visitor center** (daily, summer 9am–6.30pm, otherwise 9am–5pm; $5 per car), where artists' drawings and audio-visual exhibits endeavor to conjure up the past, a footpath leads down to the river, where the remains of the original fortress, now underwater, are vaguely visible.

Jamestown Settlement

Next to the authentic site of Jamestown, the state of Virginia has created **Jamestown Settlement** (daily 9am–5pm; $7.50, $10 with Yorktown Victory Center, see p.315), a complex of museums and full-size replicas that elucidate the details of what went on here. A short film dramatizes Jamestown's early days, and displays explore Europe's needs for colonies, documenting the economic and social conditions, in England especially, which led to the founding of Jamestown. An informative section deals with the Powhatan, an Algonquin-speaking tribe who controlled most of tidewater Virginia.

Behind the museum, two groups of reconstructed buildings are inhabited by interpretive guides, dressed in period costumes. In the **Powhatan Village**, women wearing buckskins practice weaving and pottery, while in the larger and more convincing replica of **James Fort**, some fifteen thatched, wattle-and-daub buildings – all built using period tools – act as blacksmith shops, a storehouse, and a church. Full-sized replicas of the three **ships** that carried the first settlers here – the *Godspeed* (which retraced the route from England in 1985), the *Susan Constant* and the *Discovery* – are moored below on the James River.

Williamsburg

After mosquito-plagued Jamestown burned down, in 1699 the colonial capital was moved inland to a small village known as the Middle Plantation, soon re-christened **WILLIAMSBURG** in honor of King William III. To reflect the increasing wealth of the colony, a grand city, centering upon a mile-long, hundred-foot-wide avenue, was laid out. Suitable buildings were constructed, beginning with the **capitol** in 1704 and culminating in the opulent **Governor's Palace** in 1720. By the mid-1700s tobacco-rich Virginia was the most prosperous of the American colonies, and Williamsburg was its largest city, though with some two thousand residents not on the scale of Philadelphia, New York or Boston. Williamsburg remained the seat of colonial government, and emerged as one of the leading centers of **revolutionary thought**: at the College of William and Mary, George Wythe, Thomas Jefferson, James Monroe and George Mason argued the finer points of law and democracy, while in the capitol, and in the many raucous taverns surrounding it, firebrand politicians like Patrick Henry held forth on the iniquities of colonialism and organized the first resistance to British rule. When the Revolutionary War broke out, the government moved to the more secure Richmond, and Williamsburg slowly faded from view, all but unrecognized for its place in American history.

Fortunately, many of the colonial structures survived intact until the 1920s, when oil baron **John D Rockefeller** answered the pleas of a local priest, W A R Goodwin, to support Williamsburg's restoration. (Goodwin, who considered that cars were going to ruin American towns, and that the men who were making millions out of the car industry might feel guilty about this, had initially approached Henry Ford, who sent him packing.) Over the ensuing years, Rockefeller, with Goodwin acting as his agent, spent some $90 million buying and restoring the surviving fragments to their original condition, in many cases rebuilding replicas from scratch. In 1934 **Colonial Williamsburg** opened as the first theme park in the US to use American history for amusement, with costumed guides as interpreters. While you have to buy a (very expensive) ticket to look inside most of the buildings – see overleaf – the entire historic area, which includes many fine gardens, is open all the time, and you can wander freely down the cobbled streets and across the lush green commons. Cars are banned, and Williamsburg as a whole is a remarkably pleasant – if very crowded – place.

From the Wren Building on the William and Mary campus, built in 1716 at the west end of Williamsburg and now separated from the historic area by a mock-colonial shopping center, **Duke of Gloucester Street** runs east through the historic area to the rebuilt capitol. The first of its eighteenth-century buildings, a hundred yards along, is the Episcopalian **Bruton Parish Church** where Goodwin preached (Mon–Sat 9am–5pm, Sun noon–5pm; donations). It was built in 1715, when all white Virginians were required by law to attend services at least once a month. Behind it, the broad **Palace Green** spreads north to the rebuilt Governor's Palace (see overleaf). West of the church, the **courthouse** – built in 1770 and still in use when Rockefeller bought it – and the octagonal **Powder Magazine** face each other in the midst of the Market Square. Further along, **Chowning's Tavern**, a reconstruction of an alehouse that stood here in 1766, is one of four functioning pubs in the district. Thomas Jefferson rented a room in the (no longer used) **Market Square Tavern** across the street as a law student.

Various other buildings along Duke of Gloucester Street house blacksmiths' shops, printers or milliners, open only to Colonial Williamsburg ticket-holders. At the east end of the street, fife-and-drum corps and members of the militia assemble in front of the reconstructed capitol (see below) before the evening's march through town.

Colonial Williamsburg

Crowds flock to **COLONIAL WILLIAMSBURG** in high summer, and tickets are expensive, but a visit really is worth including in your itinerary. The meticulously restored buildings and the various interpretive activities and crafts workshops – ranging over thirty colonial trades, from apothecary to wig-making – are both entertaining and true to life. As Rockefeller's tidy influence has waned (his idea of restoration was that everything should be made to look new), Williamsburg has tried to come to grips with the less savory realities of colonial life. Thus people who used to be referred to as servants are now acknowledged to have been slaves – fully half of Williamsburg's population was African-American, and their lives and conditions are well covered. On another level, houses and outbuildings, formerly repainted every year, are now left to age naturally, and once-manicured lawns are now allowed to get (slightly at least) overgrown.

The real architectural highlight is the **capitol**, at the east end of Duke of Gloucester St. The current building, a 1945 reconstruction of the 1705 original, has an open-air ground-floor **arcade** which links two keyhole-shaped wings. The east wing housed the elected, legislative body of the colonial government, the **House of Burgesses**, while the other held the chambers of the **General Court** – where alleged felons, including thirteen of Blackbeard's pirates, were tried. The eleven justices of the General Court, all of whom were appointed by the King, served as a second legislative body, much as the US House and Senate work today; if the two became deadlocked, they'd meet jointly in a conference chamber bridging the two wings.

A number of fully stocked and fairly tacky gift shops along **Duke of Gloucester Street** have been done up as olde worlde apothecaries and silversmiths. The **Raleigh Tavern** was where the independence-minded colonial government re-convened after being dissolved by the loyalist governors in 1769 and again in 1774; the original tavern burned in 1859. Considering that most Virginians of the time, even well-to-do landowners, lived in one- or two-room log cabins, the imposing two-storey **Governor's Palace** at the north end of the Palace Green, with its grand ballroom and opulent furnishings, must have served as a telling declaration of the power vested inside.

The smaller of the two conventional museums in Williamsburg, the recently expanded **Abby Aldrich Rockefeller Folk Art Center** on the south side of town, has an intriguing collection of household implements, children's toys, and general bric-a-

---

TICKETS FOR COLONIAL WILLIAMSBURG

To set foot inside any of the more than two hundred assorted buildings that have been restored or rebuilt as part of Colonial Williamsburg, you need first to buy a ticket, either from the main **visitor center** (daily 8.30am–8pm; ☎220-7643 or 1-800/447-8679) off the Colonial Parkway, or from a smaller office at the west end of Duke of Gloucester St.

The **Basic Ticket** ($24), valid for one day only, gets you into everything except the Folk Art Center, Archeology Museum, Carter's Grove Plantation (which costs $10 on its own), Governor's Palace ($14) and the Wallace Decorative Arts Gallery ($8.50); the three-day **Royal Governor's Pass** ($26.50) covers everything except the Archeology Museum and Carter's Grove, and the **Patriot's Pass** ($29) gives you unlimited access to everything in Williamsburg for an entire year. All three include an introductory guided tour. Additional charges are made for the various special entertainment and educational events offered by Colonial Williamsburg, such as staged trials in the courthouse, evening dances, and candlelight walking tours.

brac as well as fascinating paintings and sculptures by so-called primitive or natural artists. The other, the **DeWitt Wallace Decorative Arts Museum** ($7.50), features fine furniture, as well as porcelain and portraits. Its modern galleries are underground; the entrance is through the reconstructed facade of the **Public Hospital**, two blocks south of Bruton Parish Church. The first asylum in North America, the hospital now has reconstructions of the wire cages in which many early inmates were kept, and exhibits tracing the evolution of the treatment of mental illness in the US.

Yorktown Battlefield

YORKTOWN, along the York River on the north side of the peninsula, is not much of a town, but gave its name to the decisive final battle of the **Revolutionary War**. The smallest and least visited of the Historic Triangle sites, Yorktown was little more than farmland when, on October 18 1781, overwhelmed and besieged British (and German) troops under the command of Cornwallis surrendered to the joint American and French forces commanded by George Washington. At the heart of the battlefield, a **visitor center** (daily 9am–5pm; free) has informative interpretive displays, racks of military artefacts, and a short audio-visual presentation on the war. The **Siege Line Overlook** on the roof gives good views of strategic points; maps and a cassette-taped tour are available if you want to explore in greater detail.

The **Moore House**, where the British surrender was agreed, survived later Civil War battles (and eventual use as a barn) before John D Rockefeller had it restored; it stands along the York River, a mile east of the visitor center.

Yorktown Victory Center

Though Yorktown survived the battle more or less unscathed – the fighting took place on open fields to the east, and in the waters of the Chesapeake Bay – much of the town was destroyed by fire in 1814, and very little of substance survives from the colonial days. Many of the surviving homes are privately owned, and not open to visitors. To make up for this, as at Jamestown the state of Virginia has constructed a mini-theme park – this time a re-created Continental Army encampment – as part of the **Yorktown Victory Center** (daily 9am–5pm; $7, $10 with Jamestown Settlement), west of the battlefield on US-17. It's not as extensive or convincing as the one at Jamestown, but the museum is if anything even better, focusing on the tobacco wealth of now-vanished York River towns and discussing both sides, British and American, of events leading up to the Revolution. A final gallery deals with the course and impact of the war itself.

Historic Triangle Practicalities

Of the three main sites, only Williamsburg is easily reached without a car. *Amtrak* **trains** and *Greyhound* **buses** (☎229-1460) stop at the **Transportation Center**, on Boundary St two blocks from the Governor's Palace. An airport shuttle from Norfolk Airport travels to Williamsburg for $14 (☎587-6958). Once there, the Colonial Parkway makes an excellent cycling route to Jamestown or Yorktown, but there's no other transportation available; rent a **bike** from *Bikesmith* of Williamsburg (☎229-9858).

Considering the wealth of historic structures, it's surprising how few characterful hotels or B&Bs there are. However, good-value packages, with meals, two nights' lodging, and admission are available through Colonial Williamsburg, from around $150 per person – some provide accommodation in restored eighteenth-century homes within the historic area. Otherwise **places to stay** around the Historic Triangle are generally anodyne and rarely cheap; if you get stuck, the *Williamsburg Hotel/Motel Association* (☎220-3330 or 1-800/446-9244) will try to find you a bed at no extra charge. There are plenty of motels around Williamsburg – the *Bassett Motel*, 800 York St (☎229-5175; ③), is just a few blocks from the capitol – as well as a number of "Guest Homes", where you get your own room in someone's house. One of the best of these is *Mrs Carter's*,

903 Lafayette St (☎229-1117; ②), a short walk to the historic area. For a change of pace, the *Duke of York Motel*, 508 E Water St in Yorktown (☎898-3232; ②), has bargain beachfront doubles along the York River.

Various olde worlde **restaurants** and taverns along Duke of Gloucester Street feature basic pub food as well as strolling entertainment, and can be fun if you're in the mood. If not, head west of the historic area to the **Merchants Square** shopping mall, to the excellent *Trellis Café* (☎229-8610), which serves international food in an upmarket setting. Dozens of diners and fast-food places line Richmond Road (US-60) west of Williamsburg.

The Atlantic Coast

One of the busiest of the East Coast ports, **Norfolk** sits midway along the east coast at the point where the Chesapeake Bay empties into the Atlantic Ocean. Virginia's sole heavily industrial center is not a particularly pretty place, but it does have a rich maritime and naval heritage, as well as the Chrysler Museum, one of the nation's best art galleries.

Fifteen miles east of Norfolk, along the open Atlantic Ocean, low-key **Virginia Beach** draws summer sun-seekers to the state's only real resort, surrounded by broad beaches and tidal marshlands. The rest of Virginia's Atlantic coast is on its isolated and sparsely populated eastern shore, packed full of bizarre place names – Nassawadox, Assawoman and Accomac, as well as Modest Town and Temperanceville. Its one really remarkable destination is **Chincoteague**, an island refuge straddling the Maryland border that's part of the Assateague National Seashore (see p.341).

Norfolk

A strategic location at the broad mouth of the Chesapeake Bay, and an extensive deep-water harbor, made colonial **NORFOLK** the main American port for trade with England and the West Indies – in the mid-eighteenth century it was the largest city in Virginia. After being burned by the British in 1775, and suffering naval bombardments during the Civil War, Norfolk never regained much character, and despite recent efforts to redevelop its waterfront the modern city is little more than a supply depot for the vast naval shipyards. Along with Hampton and Newport News on the north side of the James River, Norfolk is home to the largest naval base outside the USSR, and carriers, cruisers and all manner of grey steel behemoths steam past incessantly. Hour-long tours take in top-secret centers and top-brass naval officers' homes.

Five minutes from the naval base, an extraordinary array of oriental antiquities is displayed in the intimate and accessible Tudor-style former home of the Sloane family, on the Lafayette River at 7637 N Shore Rd (Mon–Sat 10am–5pm, Sun 1–5pm; $4, guided tours only). Now known as the **Hermitage Museum**, it ranges through medieval tapestries and Art Nouveau to Roman glass, Persian rugs and incredibly rare ancient Chinese ceremonial vessels.

A small **ferry** (11am–11pm; 80¢) shuttles from Town Point Park at the heart of the downtown waterfront across the harbor to the historic **Portsmouth** neighborhood, where brick-paved streets are lined by eighteenth- and nineteenth-century houses. The **Chrysler Museum**, Olney Rd and Mowlbray Arch (Tues–Sat 10am–4pm, Sun 1–5pm; $3 suggested donation), half a mile north of the downtown waterfront, holds the collection of car magnate Walter Chrysler, Jr, who was on drinking terms with Picasso. It includes a little bit of everything, from ancient Greek statuary to French Impressionist paintings to Franz Klein abstractions and Mayan funerary objects, as well as a world-class collection of Tiffany and Lalique glassware.

Two blocks from the harbor, amid the parking lots and vacant lots of downtown, the **Douglas MacArthur Memorial** on Bank St (Mon–Sat 10am–5pm, Sun 11am–5pm; free) houses the mortal remains and personal papers of the flamboyant US general. The leader of the Allied forces in the Pacific during World War II, who as head of the occupying forces wrote the constitution of Japan, MacArthur was relieved of his command during the Korean War, apparently because of his alarming desire to bomb China. Objects in the Memorial include his trademark corncob pipe and dark glasses, along with some entertaining grainy old newsreel.

The rest of downtown isn't up to much; head for Colley Ave and 21st St, lined with upmarket and innovative clothes stores, bookstores and restaurants.

Practicalities

An *Airport Shuttle* ($11.50; ☎857-1231) connects **Patrick Henry International Airport**, twelve miles north of the city, with downtown. *Amtrak* bus connections from Newport News stop at the *Howard Johnson Waterside*, 700 Monticello Ave, and *Greyhound* (☎627-5641) halts opposite at no 701. Norfolk's **visitor center** is at 236 E Plume St (daily 9am–5pm; ☎441-1852 or 1-800/368-3097).

Along with the highway motels, **accommodation** options include the modern *YMCA*, 312 W Bute St (☎622-6328; ①), with clean doubles and free use of the gym (men and women) across from the Chrysler Museum, while the quaint *Glen Coe*, 222 North St in Portsmouth (☎397-8128; ④), has **B&B** rooms. **Eat** Cajun-style seafood at the *Mason Dixon Grill*, 210 York St downtown (☎623-3872), or enjoy fresh pasta and crabcakes while sitting outside the cheerful café *Elliot's*, 1421 Colley Ave (☎625-0259). *Piranha's*, a bit of a drive north at 8180 Shore Drive (☎588-0100), is a funky venue serving Caribbean and Indian-inspired seafood cooked by celebrity chef Monroe Duncan. In summer, Waterside Park hosts the weekly *Thank God It's Friday*, a large outdoor party with live music, inexpensive beer and heaps of atmosphere. Downtown, the ornate Art Nouveau *Wells Theater* (☎627-1234) puts on plays and small concerts.

Virginia Beach

Not as huge and frenzied as Ocean Beach in Maryland, nor as wild and open as the Outer Banks of North Carolina, both in character and geography **VIRGINIA BEACH** is about halfway in between the two. The state's only summer resort has all the usual beachfront hotels and motels, as well as a boardwalk strip of bars, restaurants and nightclubs, but it also has some long stretches of golden sands, especially in **False Cape State Park**, which stretches from Virginia Beach to the North Carolina border. Closer to town, you can walk or fish – but not swim or sunbathe – on the four miles of beautifully isolated beach at the **Back Bay State Park** wildlife refuge.

During the day at least, there's not a lot to do apart from lie in the sun and play in the waves: Virginia Beach is one of the main East Coast surfing centers, hosting the summer-long *Billabong* competitions. You can rent surf, skim and boogie boards from *Wave Riding Vehicles*, 19th and Cypress (☎422-8823). Away from the sands, most of the action is along Atlantic Avenue, the beachfront main drag.

The eccentric **ARE Visitor Center**, at 67th St and Atlantic Ave (Mon–Sat 9am–8pm, Sun 11am–8pm), focuses on Edgar Cayce (1877–1945), a pioneer in ESP and hypnotism known as "the sleeping prophet" for his alleged ability, while in a trance, to diagnose and heal the ailments of individuals anywhere in the world. Visitors can use an enormous parapsychological library, or join "testings" of group ESP (June–Aug daily at 1pm).

High-tech interactive exhibits at the lovely **Virginia Marine Museum**, 717 General Booth Blvd (summer Mon–Sat 9am–9pm, Sun 9am–5pm, otherwise Mon–Sun 9am–5pm; $4.50), illustrate all things aquatic, from submarines to sea-birds. The museum organizes regular **dolphin-watching** expeditions in summer (Mon–Fri 9am; $12).

Practicalities

Greyhound drops off at 1017 Laskin Rd (☎422-2998), off 31st St, while the *Amtrak* bus connection from Newport News arrives at the *Radisson Hotel*, 1900 Pavilion Ave. The **visitor center** is located at the east end of I-44, half a mile west of the beach on 21st St (☎425-7111 or 1-800/446-8038).

Virginia Beach has one great boon for **budget travellers** – just a block from the beach, there are dorm rooms and bargain B&B doubles at *Angie's Guest Cottage B&B AYH Hostel*, 302 24th St (☎428-4690; ①/③). More upmarket, with attractive themed rooms overlooking the ocean, is the *Clarion Hotel*, 501 Atlantic Ave (☎422-3186 or 1-800/345-3186; ③–⑥).

The town also offers a good, laid-back nightlife and some great **restaurants**. Hostellers congregate most nights at the *Jewish Mother*, 3108 Pacific Ave (☎422-5430), a daytime deli and late-night beer bar with free live music; *Chicho's*, 2112 Atlantic Ave (☎422-6011), is an Italian eating and drinking spot for exuberant twentysomethings, open until 2am. The *Lynnhaven Restaurant*, at the top of the Lynnhaven Fishing Pier at the mouth of the Chesapeake Bay (☎481-0003), dishes out splendid soups, oysters, and dinners, while the *Big Tomato*, by the ocean at Second and Atlantic (☎437-0155), has a creative menu (shrimp with peanuts and peach marmalade) and a cool bar. Check *Port Folio*, the listings newspaper, for details of live music events.

Charlottesville and the Shenandoah Valley

The densely forested four-thousand-foot peaks of the Blue Ridge Mountains form a definite barrier between the history-rich worlds of tidewater Virginia to the east and the rougher river-and-valley country to the west. In between the two, at the geographical center of the state, the friendly, manageably small college town of **Charlottesville** holds two great monuments to the mind of **Thomas Jefferson**. To the west, the northern **Blue Ridge Mountains**, crowned by the dense forests of **Shenandoah National Park**, run south to Tennessee, culminating in 5729ft Mount Rogers. On the far side of the mountains, the lush Shenandoah Valley was a vital battleground during the Civil War; since then little seems to have changed.

The main highway, I-81 through the Shenandoah Valley, is joined in the north by I-66 from Washington DC and in the middle by I-64 from Richmond through Charlottesville. Numerous scenic routes are slower but more worthwhile, such as **Skyline Drive** and the **Blue Ridge Parkway**, which weave along the four-hundred–mile mountain crest. You'll definitely need a car to get the most out of it, though cycling is a good option along the many back roads, and, for hikers, the **Appalachian Trail** runs right down the middle. There are plenty of roadside motels so you needn't be too concerned about advance planning – it's a great place for aimless exploration.

Charlottesville

If you only have a couple of days to see Virginia, **CHARLOTTESVILLE**, seventy miles west of Richmond, should be near the top of your itinerary. Abounding in history, and holding some of the finest examples of early American architecture, it is at once small enough to feel comfortable in and large enough to have good restaurants and nightspots. Its compact, low-rise center is criss-crossed by magnolia-shaded streets, and makes a fine place to amble around, particularly the six pedestrianized blocks of **Main Street**, site of the nightly town promenade. However pleasant the town, the compelling attraction is the legacy of **Thomas Jefferson**, whose home and final resting place, **Monticello**, stands atop a hill just east of town, overlooking the beautifully landscaped neoclassical campus of the University of Virginia.

The University of Virginia

Though he wrote the Declaration of Independence and served as the third US president, Thomas Jefferson took more pride in having established the **University of Virginia** than in any of his other achievements, and if you're able to visit you may well share his view. In 1976 the University of Virginia was officially designated the greatest piece of architecture in the US, but the university also reveals the ideology of its patron, who besides designing every building down to the most minute detail also planned the curriculum and selected the faculty. Uniquely for universities of the time, which functioned primarily as seminaries, it was not rooted in religious training – Jefferson having been one of the prime proponents of the separation of church from the affairs of state – but emphasized instead a broadly based liberal arts education.

The highlight and architectural focus is the red-brick and white-domed **Rotunda**, modelled on the Pantheon and completed in 1821 to house the university library and classrooms. A basement gallery tells the story of the university, while upstairs three elliptical classrooms are linked by a voluptuous central hall. A staircase winds up to the **Dome Room**, where, in place of the planetarium Jefferson wanted to install, Corinthian columns rise to an ocular skylight. From the Rotunda, where 45-minute guided tours (daily 10am–4pm; free) of the campus begin, twin colonnades stretch along either side of a lushly landscaped quadrangle, linking together a string of single-storey student apartments and taller pavilions, in which professors live and hold tutorials. While the overall feel is harmonious, each individual block is unique, the differing facades and rooflines designed to show off the various orders and styles of neoclassical architecture.

Parallel to the quadrangle buildings, two further rows of dormitory buildings, the East and West Ranges, front on to serpentine walled gardens. **Edgar Allan Poe** stayed in one of these rooms while studying at the University of Virginia in 1826, but was forced to drop out after his stepfather cut off his allowance, apparently because Edgar had lost all his money gambling. His room – Number 13, of course, in the West Range – is now restored to how it would have looked when Poe was here, and is virtually the only campus interior, apart from the Rotunda, which you can visit.

Monticello – Thomas Jefferson's Home

One of America's most familiar buildings – it graces the back of the nickel coin – **Monticello**, three miles southeast of Charlottesville on Hwy-53, was the home of **Thomas Jefferson** for most of his life. A visit provides a distinctive insight into the mind and personality of the most intriguing of America's Founding Fathers. Surrounded by acres of beautifully landscaped hilltop grounds with fine views out over the Virginia countryside, Monticello is a handsome house, whose symmetrical brick facade, centered upon a white Doric portico, belies the quirky irregularities of the interior – furnished as it was when Jefferson lived, and died, here.

To see Monticello you have to join one of the **guided tours** (daily March–Oct 8am–5pm, otherwise 9am–4.30pm; $7) which leave continuously from the parking lot at the bottom of the hill. There's often a queue, especially on weekends, so try to get there as early as possible in the morning. From the outside, Monticello looks like an elegant, Palladian-style country home, but as soon as you enter the domed entrance hall, with its funhouse mirror – which reflects an upside-down image – and displays of fossilized bones and elk antlers (from Lewis and Clark's epic 1804 journey across North America, which Jefferson sponsored as president), you begin to get a sense that Jefferson was a somewhat more bizarre character than the sober statesman portrayed by most histories. His love of gadgets marked him as something of an eccentric: the weather vane over the front porch is connected to a dial, so he could see which way the wind was blow-

The **area code** for Charlottesville is ☎804; for the Shenandoah Valley, it's ☎703.

ing without having to step outside, and the house is filled with odd little contraptions such as the elaborate dual-pen device Jefferson used to make automatic copies of all his letters. Jefferson's **private chambers** are also on the tour: he slept in a tiny alcove linking his dressing room and his study, and would get up on the right side of the bed if he wanted to make some late-night notes, on the left if he wanted to get dressed.

The upstairs rooms, where Jefferson's daughter lived, are not open to the public, but in the grounds around the house you begin to see how Monticello, a 5000-acre plantation, really functioned. Extensive flower and vegetable gardens spread to the south and west, and a dank passage runs under the house from the kitchen and beer cellar (Jefferson was a keen home-brewer) to the remains of Mulberry Row, Monticello's **slave quarters** – Jefferson, who called slavery an "abominable crime", owned almost two hundred of his fellow human beings. At the south end of Mulberry Row, a grove of ancient hardwood trees surrounds Jefferson's grave, marked by a simple stone obelisk; a footpath beyond winds back down to the bottom of the hill.

Charlottesville Practicalities

Amtrak trains from DC stop in Charlottesville at 810 W Main St, and *Greyhound* pulls in a few blocks away at 310 W Main St (☎295-5131). Once you arrive, you can get around on foot or, better, by renting a **bike** for $10 from *Blue Wheel*, 19 Elliewood Ave (☎977-1870). The well-signed **visitor center** (☎977-1783) is just south of I-64.

For its size, Charlottesville has quite a broad range of **accommodation**. The usual motels line Emmet Street (US-29) at the west end of town, the least expensive being the *Econo Lodge*, 400 Emmet St (☎296-2104; ③) and the nicest the *Sheraton* (☎973-2121; ⑤) a mile north. Good-value **B&B** is available in private homes through *Guesthouses* (☎979-7264) and at the *200 South Street Inn*, 200 South St (☎979-0200; ③).

The best **eating** and **drinking** is to be had near the university and in the downtown mall. Tucked away behind the pizza and burger places like *The Virginian*, 1521 W Main St (☎293-2606), across from the campus, *Martha's Café*, 11 Elliewood Ave (☎971-7530), serves up spinach lasagnes, crab cakes and Bass Ale on draught on a leafy front patio. Downtown, *Millers*, 109 W Main St (☎971-8511), specializes in grilled meats and fish dishes and has live jazz most nights, and the *C&O Restaurant*, 515 E Water St (☎971-7044), housed in an old railroad station, has bistro-style food in the humming bar and more upscale French nouvelle cuisine in the upstairs dining room. Virginia's best selection of wines and beers, plus a range of light meals, is on tap at the *Court Square Tavern*, 500 Court Square (☎296-6111), two blocks north of the mall.

As a college town, Charlottesville isn't short of **nightlife**, whether at cafés like the *Roasted Bean*, 110 N Fourth St (☎977-JAVA), or in its two main nightclubs, *Zippers*, 1202 W Main St (☎295-7060), and *Trax*, 127 S 11th St (☎295-8729).

Shenandoah National Park

SHENANDOAH NATIONAL PARK, which contains seemingly endless acres of dark forests, rocky deep ravines and precipitous, surging waterfalls, has one of the most unusual histories of any US National Park. Far from being untouched for the past three hundred years, this "natural" landscape was created when hundreds of small family farms and homesteads were bought up by the state and federal governments during the Depression, and the land was left to revert to its natural state.

One of the most scenic byways in the US, **Skyline Drive** is a thin ribbon of pavement curving along the crest of the Blue Ridge Mountains. It starts just off I-66 near the town of **Front Royal**, 75 miles west of DC, and winds south through the park giving great views over the Piedmont to the east and lovely Shenandoah Valley to the west.

The views are especially fine, and the crowds especially large, in the fall, but any time of year you can get the best of the park's open spaces by following one of the many **hiking trails** that split off from the ridge. One favorite leaves from the parking area of *Big Meadows Lodge* in the southern half of the park and winds along to tumbling **Dark Hollow Falls**; another, leaving Skyline Drive at milemarker 45, climbs up a fairly treacherous incline to the top of **Old Rag Mountain** for 360° views out over the whole of Virginia and the Allegheny Mountains in the west. More ambitious hikers, or those who want to spend the night out in the backcountry, head for the **Appalachian Trail**; details on any of these hikes, or the required free overnight camping permit, can be picked up at either of the **visitor centers** (☎999-2266), located along Skyline Drive four miles beyond the north entrance and at milemarker 50, in the middle of the park.

Two rustic **lodges**, both near the middle of the park, offer food and beds. The north-ernmost and oldest, *Skyland Lodge*, opened in 1894, has cabins (②) and modern hotel rooms (⑤), as well as a large restaurant with panoramic views; *Big Meadows Lodge*, ten miles south, has similar facilities, and is just next to the larger visitor center. For full details of rates, contact *ARA Services* (☎743-5108 or 1-800/999-4714).

The Shenandoah Valley

The small and characterful towns of the **Shenandoah Valley**, down below Skyline Drive, are as rich in human history as any in Virginia. Many were left in ruins after the war, but have since been restored to their proud antebellum state, and numerous memorials, monuments and cemeteries line the back roads, surrounded by spacious horse farms and apple orchards.

Given its strategic importance and fertility, the Shenandoah Valley was inevitably one of the most fought-over battlegrounds in the Civil War, changing hands over seventy times at a cost of some 100,000 dead and maimed. The whole bloody story is told in evocative detail in the small but outstanding **museum** (daily 9am–5pm; $4) at the **New Market Battlefield**, just off I-81, thirty miles south of the I-66 junction. This was the scene of the legendary 1864 confrontation that involved a company of fourteen-year-old cadet-soldiers from the Virginia Military Institute.

Besides its Civil War history, the northern Shenandoah Valley also holds half a dozen of Virginia's many underground **limestone caverns**. All are privately owned and cost $4 to $10 to enter. You'll no doubt see billboards advertising each one as the best: the largest is **Luray Caverns**, twelve miles east of New Market. Further south, off Hwy-250 northwest of the town of Staunton, the **Museum of Frontier American Culture** (daily 9am–5pm; $4) brings to light how the various immigrants who settled here melded their traditions to develop a joint American culture. Most of the exhibits have to do with farming techniques and other somewhat mundane activities, but it's all engagingly presented and well worth a look.

Lexington

Though it's one of the region's smaller towns, **LEXINGTON**, in the heart of the Shenandoah Valley, definitely has the most to offer to visitors. From horse-drawn carriages parading along its quiet, brick-paved streets, to the fine rolling countryside all around – all of which may be familiar from the movie *Sommersby* – Lexington makes a great place to sit back and relax or, if you prefer, delve deep into Civil War and other military arcana at its small museums and memorials.

The most engaging of these, the **Lee Chapel** (Mon–Sat 9am–5pm, Sun 2–5pm; free), is on the attractive colonnaded campus of Washington and Lee University, a short walk north of the town center. A commodious and somber building, the chapel is named in honor of Confederate General Robert E Lee, who taught here after the Civil War. Behind the pulpit is a marble statue of Lee in repose, surrounded by an array of authentic battle flags; along with many members of his family, Lee is interred down-stairs in the chapel crypt, and his trusted horse Traveller is buried just outside.

On the comparatively bland but formidable campus of the **Virginia Military Institute**, just east of the Lee Chapel, the Military Museum (Mon–Sat 9am–5pm, Sun 2–5pm; free) tells the story of the state-supported, male-only military academy which was founded in 1836 and has the dubious claim to fame of being the only university in US history to have sent its entire student body into battle. If possible, time your visit to coincide with the 4pm Friday full-dress parade – a bit like the changing of the guard, American-style – held on the field in front of the museum.

At the opposite end of the parade ground, the **George C Marshall Museum** (daily, March–Oct 9am–5pm, otherwise 9am–4pm; free) documents the life of World War II US General and later Secretary of State George Marshall, whose plan for the reconstruction of post-war Europe earned him the Nobel Peace Prize in 1953.

The **Stonewall Jackson House**, 8 E Washington St (Mon–Sat 9am–6pm, Sun 1–5pm; $3), is where the noted Confederate general and Virginia Military Institute philosophy professor lived for fifteen years before his death at the battle of Chancellorsville. His spartan brick townhouse is furnished as it was in the years before the war, and Stonewall himself is buried, along with hundreds of his fellow soldiers, in the Stonewall Jackson Memorial Cemetery off S Main St.

Even if you're not thrilled by war stories, Lexington still makes a good stop, with its dozens of fine old homes; pick up a walking tour map from the **visitor center**, 102 E Washington St (daily 9am–5pm; ☎463-3777). The *Virginia House*, 722 S Main St (☎463-3643), hard to find on the south side of town, serves up some fine down-home **southern cooking**; if your taste tends toward tofu, you may prefer *Sprouts Natural Deli*, 110 W Washington St (☎463-1163), across from the Washington and Lee campus. A block away stands Lexington's one remarkably cheap **place to stay**, Ms Ruth Rees' $5-a-night *Tourist Home*, 216 W Washington St (☎463-3075; ①); in addition to the usual motels along the highways, the comfy German-speaking *Asherowe B&B*, 314 S Jefferson St (☎463-4219; ③), stands in the Golden Triangle six blocks west of the visitor center.

The Blue Ridge Parkway

Once out of Shenandoah National Park, Skyline Drive becomes the **Blue Ridge Parkway**, which winds southwestwards along the crest of the Appalachians at an average elevation of 3000 feet – a beautiful drive, though **I-81**, sweeping along the flank of the mountains, is a more efficient way of getting from A to B. Ultimately the Parkway leads through North Carolina and on to the Great Smokies, a route covered in detail on p.362. Within Virginia, **Roanoke** is the nicest of the nearby towns, though in summer the *Rocky Knob Cabins*, at milepost 174 on the Parkway itself, offers a memorable night's stay in the idyllic Meadows of Dan (☎593-3503; ③).

Roanoke

Sandwiched between I-81 and the Parkway, **ROANOKE** is the largest community in western Virginia, and the largest town along the Parkway. With its leisurely old-fashioned streets, however, it makes a very pleasant stop-off, focusing around its still functioning Farmers Market (Mon–Sat), and the modern Center In The Square mall.

A **visitor center** at 114 Market St (daily 9am–5pm; ☎345-8622 or 1-800/635-5535) can provide full details and walking tour maps. The *Mary Bladon House* at 381 Washington Ave (☎344-5361; ⑤), a few blocks southwest, is a welcoming **B&B**, while the least expensive of the interstate motels is the *Friendship Inn*, 526 Orange Ave NE, at exit 4E off I-581 (☎981-9341 or 1-800/424-4777; ③). The *Eden Way Place*, 307 Market St (☎344-3336), is a vegetarian café and wholefood store in the market area; *Carlos*, opposite at 312 Market St (☎345-7661), serves superb "international cuisine", predominantly Brazilian. The *Iroquois Club*, 324 Salem Ave (☎982-8879), is a lively music venue.

WEST VIRGINIA

The people of **WEST VIRGINIA** are only half joking when they call it the Ireland of the US. Generally poor and almost entirely rural – with the lowest per capita income, and the lowest crime rate, of any state – it shares a similar history of exploitation by outside powers, with **timber** and **coal-mining** companies taking advantage of the rich natural resources while giving little in return. But, quite apart from the almost Third World deprivation which endures in some areas (and which, along with John Denver songs and the barefoot hillbillies supposed to inhabit its backwoods reaches, still colors most outsiders' preconceptions), West Virginia is also, in places at least, incredibly beautiful, holding the longest whitewater rivers and most extensive wilderness areas in the eastern US. The extreme topography which has historically isolated its inhabitants now makes this a popular destination for hikers and outdoors enthusiasts, and the moonshiners of old have been replaced by ski instructors and mountain bike guides.

After it hived itself off from Confederate Virginia in the middle of the Civil War – a separation which the other Virginia has yet to recognize officially – it took many years for West Virginia to develop a political and economic identity of its own. Around the turn of the century, when railroads from the East Coast first reached into the mountainous interior, timber companies clear-cut stand after stand of forest, setting up a succession of mill towns, each dismantled in its turn when they moved on somewhere new – **Cass**, now preserved within the Allegheny National Forest, is one of the few that was left intact. Later on, coal-mining conglomerates, especially in the south, perfected the "company town" approach, wherein workers were paid a little bit less each month than the amount they owed for their company-provided food and lodging. Coal companies still exert immense power in West Virginia, but the real key to the state's future prosperity is tourism, which in places now accounts for over half their income.

The most popular destination, the restored 1850s town of **Harpers Ferry**, is barely in West Virginia at all, standing just over the broad rivers which form its Maryland and Virginia borders. To the west, the **Allegheny Mountains** stretch for over 150 miles; more than a million acres of hardwood forest rival New England for brilliant fall color. West Virginia's oldest and most attractive town, **Lewisburg**, sits just off I-64 at the mountains' southern foot, while the capital, **Charleston**, lies in the comparatively flat Ohio River valley of the west.

Getting Around West Virginia

With its many mountains and rivers making straight, flat roads virtually non-existent, getting around West Virginia is as much a part of its attraction as is any specific destination – a bike and a stout pair of legs, or a motorcycle, would be ideal, but a car is pretty necessary if you really want to see the state. *Greyhound* is basically useless, and *Amtrak*, apart from serving Harpers Ferry from Washington DC, has only one, albeit spectacular, route, running through the New River Gorge to the capital, Charleston.

Harpers Ferry and Around

HARPERS FERRY, a ruggedly sited eighteenth-century town now restored as a national historic park, gives many visitors their first and only look at West Virginia. Clinging to steep hillsides above the confluence of the Potomac and Shenandoah rivers, many of its forty-odd brick and stone buildings date from the days when George Washington set up the country's first **national munitions factory** here to arm the young Republic. During the mid-1800s Harpers Ferry was a thriving industrial complex,

The **area code** for the entire state of West Virginia is ☎304.

home to some five thousand workers and linked with the capital by the B&O Railroad and the Chesapeake & Ohio Canal, but after suffering the ravages of the Civil War and a series of torrential floods it was all but abandoned, the empty shells of its homes and factories slowly becoming overgrown by the dense forest which covers the surrounding hills. Almost all of Harpers Ferry has since been reconstructed as an outdoor museum, with a stunning combination of historical importance and natural beauty.

However pretty Harpers Ferry is – and in the fall, when the leaves blaze with color, it's hard to imagine a more picture-perfect setting – it's best known for its unique place in US history. The 1859 raid on its huge US arsenal by anti-slavery revolutionary (and borderline psychotic) **John Brown**, which rocked the already fragmenting nation, was the clearest foreshadowing of the Civil War which broke out just sixteen months later. In the hope of fomenting a widespread slave revolt, Brown and 21 other abolitionist radicals, including two of his sons and five black men, seized the munitions factory and its large store of weapons on the night of October 16. They held out for two days before US troops, under the command of Robert E Lee, stormed the buildings, killing many of the raiders and capturing Brown, who was taken to nearby Charles Town, tried, convicted of treason, and hanged.

Devastated during the Civil War – the arsenal buildings were burned in 1861 to keep the weapons out of Confederate hands, and in 1862 Stonewall Jackson captured the town and 12,500 Union soldiers – Harpers Ferry never really got back on its feet. Enough of the original buildings and cobbled streets survive to give a good sense of how things used to be, and the restoration project has so far managed to re-create the townscape without making it feel too much like a theme park.

Seeing Harpers Ferry

Almost everyone who comes to Harpers Ferry drives. Parking is virtually banned in the old town area; shuttle buses run from the large **visitor center** on US-340 (daily, June–Aug 8.30am–6pm, otherwise 8.30am–5pm) – where you pay the $2 per person, $5 per car entry fee – to the old town, dropping off outside the balconied old **Stagecoach Inn**, at the end of gas-lit Shenandoah Street in the heart of the restored area; inside there's an information desk with maps and a small bookshop. Across the street, displays in the **Master Armorer's House** will tell you everything about gun-making; adjacent buildings include a restored blacksmith's shop, a general store and a tavern, often peopled with costumed guides who act out and describe events from the town's history.

John Brown's **fort** – actually the armory's engine room where he and his raiders were captured – originally stood directly across from the tavern, and has been rebuilt a block away, near the point where the rivers meet. Other structures along **High Street** house exhibits on the Civil War and local black history, and between them a set of stone steps climbs up through the residential area to the **Harper House**, built in 1782 and preserved as a typical worker's rooming house of the period.

A footpath continues uphill past overgrown churchyards hemmed in by dry-stone walls to **Jefferson Rock**, a huge grey boulder giving a great view over the two rivers – Thomas Jefferson said that the outlook was worth a voyage across the Atlantic. If you're in the mood for a longer hike, two trails lead onwards into the surrounding forest: the **Appalachian Trail** continues from Jefferson Rock across the Shenandoah River into the **Blue Ridge Mountains** of Virginia, while the **Maryland Heights Trail** makes a four-mile round trip around the headlands across the Potomac River.

Around Harpers Ferry

Among small towns worth seeing nearby is **Charles Town**, four miles south of Harpers Ferry on US-340, where John Brown was tried and hanged; the **Jefferson County Museum** at Washington and Samuel (Mon–Sat 10am–4pm; free) tells the story of his trial, conviction, and execution, and remembers his last words: "I, John Brown, am now quite certain that the crimes of this guilty land will never be purged away but with blood." The cozy village of **Shepherdstown**, along the Potomac ten miles to the north, is prettier and better for wandering, its quaint ancient shops and cafés looking across the river to Maryland's bloody **Antietam Battlefield** (see p.336).

Further afield, and of more salubrious interest, is the old spa town of **Berkeley Springs**, now preserved intact as a state historic park, thirty miles west of Harpers Ferry on Hwy-9, seven miles south of I-70. The nearest early America ever came to having resorts like Bath in England, Berkeley Springs was a favorite summer retreat of the colonial elite – George Washington and Lord Fairfax were among the regulars who came here to "take the waters" – and assorted massage and steam bath treatments are still available in its many health farms. In summer, you can soak yourself in the old **Roman Baths**, in active use since 1815 and now run by the state. The town's **central square** is leafy and green, with footpaths fanning out in all directions, one climbing the hill up to **Berkeley Castle**, a fortress-like mid-Victorian folly above the town that originally held a large ballroom and is now used mostly for weddings.

Harpers Ferry Practicalities

As it's a popular day out from Washington DC (a daily train from DC arrives at 5.20pm, en route to Chicago), Harpers Ferry is well prepared for tourists. Olde worlde **cafés** line High Street up from the historic area – both the *Mountain House Café* (☎535-2339) and the *Garden of Food* (☎535-2202) are good and relatively inexpensive.

If you want to **spend the night**, dozens of amiable B&Bs are sprinkled around the region, like the *Highlawn Inn*, 304 Market St (☎258-5700; ④), or the *Manor Inn*, 415 Fairfax St (☎258-1552; ④), both in Berkeley Springs. In Harpers Ferry itself, the century-old *Hilltop House Hotel and Restaurant* on Ridge St (☎535-2132 or 1-800/338-8319; ③) may be showing its age, but still has reasonable prices and the best views. Budget beds can be had at the *Comfort Inn* (☎221-2227 or 1-800/228-5150; ③) on US-340, and there's lots of **camping** along the Potomac River in the C&O Canal Historic Park. The **park visitor center** has further details, as does the Jefferson County tourist bureau (☎535-2627 or 1-800/848-TOUR) across US-340.

The Allegheny Mountains

Considering that it's the most extensive wilderness area on the East Coast, within a few hours' drive of a dozen big cities, surprisingly few people have heard about, much less bother to visit, the backcountry reaches of the **Allegheny Mountains**, West Virginia's segment of the Appalachian chain. The entire 140-mile crest is protected as part of the **Monongahela National Forest**, within which numerous state parks highlight the most spectacular sights. There are no cities and few towns, public transport is non-existent and not much goes on after dark – to give an idea of how rural it is, whole counties do without a single traffic light – but if you like to backpack, ski, cycle, climb, canoe or just wander around the great outdoors, the Alleghenies are well worth a look. For maps and more detailed information, contact the state tourist office (see p.21) or the Monongahela National Forest, 200 Sycamore St, Elkins, WV 26253 (Mon–Fri 8am–4.45pm; ☎636-1800).

Blackwater Falls, the Canaan Valley and Seneca Rocks

Some of the most beautiful stretches of the Monongahela National Forest are in the northern corner of the state, where the thundering torrents of the **Blackwater Falls** pour over a sixty-foot limestone cliff before crashing down through a steeply walled canyon. South from here spreads the dense maple, oak, walnut and birch forest of broad **Canaan Valley**, while to the east rise the barren sub-arctic highlands of the **Dolly Sods Wilderness**, the whole area criss-crossed by hiking, cycling and skiing trails.

Rising up at the far end of the Canaan Valley, the state's highest point, the 4861ft **Spruce Knob**, stands out over the headwaters of the Potomac River. Even more impressive views can be had from the top of **Seneca Rocks**, eight miles to the northwest, whose 1000ft limestone cliffs are commonly considered to present the most challenging rock-climb on the East Coast. A good trail leads around the back of the North Peak if you want to take the easy way up, and the helpful **visitor center** at the junction of US-33 and Hwy-28 (daily 9am–5.30pm in summer, Sat & Sun only in winter; ☎257-4488) has details of outdoor recreation opportunities in the entire region.

The old logging town of **Davis** (population 868), just east of US-219 at the north end of the Canaan Valley, makes an obvious base, with a couple of **places to stay** – the *Bright Morning Inn* (☎259-5119; ③) on Williams Ave doubles as the town café, and the *Davis Inn* (☎259-5142; ②) has basic motel rooms. Among local **outdoor guides and outfitters**, the *Blackwater Outdoor Center* (☎259-5117) runs rafting, caving and rock-climbing trips; *Blackwater Bikes* (☎259-5286) rents out mountain bikes and offers off-road tours; and *Timberline Resort* (☎866-4801) has the state's largest downhill ski area. For more information, contact the **visitor center** (☎259-5315 or 1-800/782-2775).

Elkins and the Augusta Festival

One of the few ways visitors can experience the vibrant folkways of the West Virginia mountains is by taking part in the summer-long **Augusta Festival**, an annual celebration of arts, crafts and Appalachian culture. Held throughout July and August, just west of the Canaan Valley in **ELKINS**, the biggest town in northern West Virginia, the festival offers public workshops in such diverse down-home pursuits as banjo-playing, blacksmithing, quiltmaking and folk dancing, and after dark performers get together for a nightly hoe-down, featuring storytellers, bluegrass bands and general good times.

Find out more from the **Augusta Heritage Center**, part of Davis and Elkins College, 100 Sycamore St, Elkins, WV 26241 (☎636-1903), or stop into the *Starr Café and Bookshop*, 224 Davis Ave (☎636-7273) in the center of town. Among the most central of several B&Bs is the *Wayside Inn*, 318 Buffalo St (☎636-1618; ④).

Pocahontas County

The southern half of the Monongahela National Forest is contained within hilly **Pocahontas County**, known as "the birthplace of rivers" because it holds the headwaters of the Greenbrier, Cheat, Gauley and other great West Virginia rivers. Like most of the Alleghenies, it's a mountainous, fairly inaccessible region – two roads, US-219 and Hwy-92, wind north-to-south, with a handful of narrow tracks twisting between them – offering outstanding outdoor recreation as well as endless scenic vistas.

Besides gorgeous scenery, Pocahontas County is also home to the **Cass Scenic Railroad**, a restored, steam-powered logging railroad built in 1902. Running on narrow-gauge tracks, the chugging *Shay* locomotive carries visitors up to the top of 4842ft Bald Knob on a converted logging train, starting at the old lumber-mill village of **CASS**, five miles west of Hwy-28 near the town of **Greenbank** (Tues–Sun at 11am, 1pm and 3pm, summer only; $10; ☎456-4300). Cass has been preserved in its entirety as an historic park, where you can wander around the old loggers' cabins and company store, or stay the night in the cozy *Shay Inn B&B* (☎456-4652; ③).

An energetic five-mile walk downhill from Cass leads along the tracks to the start of the cycle-friendly **Greenbrier River Trail**, which follows the river and the railroad grade for 75 miles, coming out near Lewisburg (see below). You can also rent a **mountain bike** from *Elk River Touring Center* (☎572-3771), fifteen miles north of **Marlinton**, the county seat, off US-219 in the hamlet of **Slatyfork**, and set off into the mountains. They run a shuttle service to the trailheads and organize backcountry cycling trips and ski tours in winter, and their year-round **hotel** (③) has a hot tub and good-value restaurant. Pocahontas County **tourist bureau** (☎799-4636 or 1-800/336-7009) provides maps.

The other main attraction in this part of the Alleghenies is the birthplace of **Pearl S Buck**, author of *The Good Earth* and one of only two American women – the other being Toni Morrison – to win the Nobel Prize for Literature. Her home at **Hillsboro**, on US-219 halfway between Marlinton and Lewisburg, is packed with memorabilia.

Lewisburg and the Greenbrier Resort

Located just off I-64 on the southern edge of the Monongahela National Forest wilderness, **LEWISBURG** is the archetypal West Virginia town, its few square blocks of old buildings surrounded by rich pastureland, with good roads allowing quick access to the wilder mountain reaches. Originally a frontier outpost during the Indian Wars of the 1770s, Lewisburg was greatly prized during the Civil War for its location at the head of the Greenbrier Valley, but nowadays its attractions are those of a classic American small town, where everyone seems to know everyone else and where the houses and shops have remained in the same hands for generations.

Washington Street, the four-block business district, is lined on both sides by brick-fronted early nineteenth-century houses, and makes for pleasant wandering; no 106 has been a two-chair barber shop for over a hundred years. A block away, in a small park at 200 N Jefferson St, stands the oldest surviving structure in Lewisburg, a rough-hewn limestone shed built in 1770 to protect the still-flowing freshwater spring.

The **visitor center**, 105 Church St (☎645-1000), hands out walking tour maps of the town and can suggest driving tours around Greenbrier Valley. They also can put you in touch with various cozy **hotels**, such as the *General Lewis Inn*, 301 E Washington St (☎645-2600; ④), and suggest places to **eat**, like the innovative and inexpensive *Blue Moon Café* at 110 S Jefferson St (☎645-4548).

Just east of Lewisburg, outside the faded spa of **White Sulphur Springs**, two dozen US presidents have escaped the pressures of politics in *The Greenbrier* (☎536-1110 or 1-800/624-6070; ⑧). The grandest and plushest hotel in West Virginia, it's five-star all the way, from the pillared entrance hall to the 6500 acres of lush grounds and golf courses. Stop in for a drink or a fine meal (or just to gape) if you can't afford the room rates.

The New River Gorge

One of West Virginia's most spectacular river canyons, the **New River Gorge**, lies just thirty miles west of Lewisburg along I-64. Now protected as a national park, and stretching for over fifty miles, the thousand-foot cleft was carved through the limestone West Virginia mountains by the New River – despite its name, one of the oldest rivers in North America. Apart from one daily train (see below), there's no easy access to most of the gorge – to see it, you have to get out on the water, with the help of any of over fifty professional rafting companies – but visitor centers located near the most impressive spots give details of recreation opportunities. Just off US-19 in **Fayetteville**, the **Canyon Rim Visitor Center** sits alongside the New River Gorge Bridge, a single-span steel arch that rises nine hundred feet above the river; the smaller **Grandview Visitor Center** is located at an elbow bend in the river, five miles north of I-64 near Beckley.

Fortunately for car-less travellers, *Amtrak* trains from Washington DC pass right through the gorge on one of the most stunning railway journeys in the East. Though the ride itself is memorable enough, for a close-up look you can get off at the southern end of the gorge at the turn-of-the-century railroad town of **HINTON**. The train's only stop, it's a fascinating, if somewhat dilapidated remnant of the glory days of railroads. This almost perfectly preserved purpose-built company town – the National Park Service intends someday to restore it as a living museum – is beautifully sited, its brick-paved streets angling up from the water and lined by dozens of grand civic buildings as well as row after row of slowly decaying workers' houses. A walking tour map of Hinton is available from the Chamber of Commerce, 206 Temple St (☎466-5420).

Although the town has definitely seen better days, Hinton still makes a workable base for visitors to the gorge, with a pair of budget **motels**, the *Coast-to-Coast* (☎466-2040; ③) and the *Sandman* (☎466-1700; ③), and a couple of riverfront taverns on Hwy-20 just south of town. Local **river-rafting** firms include *New River Tours* (☎466-2288 or 1-800/292-0880) and *Cantrell Canoes* (☎466-0595).

Charleston

After leaving the gorge, the New River flows west into the Ohio and eventually the Mississippi, but not before passing through **CHARLESTON**, West Virginia's state capital and largest city. Charleston isn't a place many people set out to visit, mainly because there's not very much to see or do: the riverfront **state capitol**, designed by Lincoln Memorial architect Cass Gilbert and completed in 1932, is pleasant enough, with a small monument to black activist Booker T Washington on the grounds, but nothing really grabs you. The **West Virginia Cultural Center** (Mon–Fri 9am–8pm, Sat & Sun 1–5pm; free), next to the capitol, showcases traditional West Virginia culture, especially during the annual **Vandalia Festival**, Appalachia's largest celebration of folk arts and crafts, held on Memorial Day weekend and highlighted by lively bluegrass music and tall-tale-telling contests.

There are 300 very central **rooms** at the *Elk River Town Center Inn*, 2 Kanawha Blvd E (☎343-4521 or 1-800/765-6566; ③), and motels abound on the interstates. *General Seafood*, 213 Broad St (Tues–Sat only; ☎343-5671), is a restaurant conveniently attached to a fish market.

MARYLAND

Founded as the sole Catholic colony in strongly Protestant America, and isolated as the northernmost slave state, **MARYLAND** has always been unusual. Within its small but irregular area, it ranges from its bustling urban center, **Baltimore**, to Appalachian hill country and the sleepy fishing villages of the **Chesapeake Bay**. Once one of the world's most productive fishing areas, the Chesapeake has recently been brought back from the brink of complete annihilation due to pollution and overfishing – its abundant oyster stocks are a thing of the past, but **soft-shell blue crabs** are more plentiful than ever – and now supports a diverse, decentralized economy, buoyed by the hundreds of weekend sailors who cruise from one to another of its colonial-era towns.

Maryland's heritage isn't quite as impressive as Virginia's, and it has nowhere near as many historic sites. Its main claim to fame occurred during the War of 1812 – a last-ditch effort by British military to wrest back the colonies, in which they burned much of Washington DC. One of the main British aims in this attack, which actually took place in 1814, was to destroy the shipyards at Baltimore. The British forces failed, having been held off by a small fort at the harbor's mouth; the fort's resistance inspired an onlooker, Francis Scott Key, to write the words to the **Star-Spangled Banner**.

Maryland's largest city is the busy port of **Baltimore**, a quirky and engaging metropolis that has a couple of good museums and an extensive and enjoyable urban waterfront. **Western Maryland** stretches over a hundred miles to the Appalachian foothills, its rolling farmlands noteworthy chiefly for the Civil War battlefield at **Antietam**. Just twenty miles south of Baltimore, along the Chesapeake Bay, picturesque **Annapolis** has served as Maryland's capital since 1694. Some of the state's most worthwhile destinations, from the pretty fishing and yachting town of **St Michaels** to the untouched wilderness of **Assateague Island**, are across the Chesapeake Bay on the eastern

The **area code** for Baltimore is ☎410.

shore, connected to the rest of the state by the US-50 bridge but otherwise still a world apart – except for the sprawling resort of **Ocean City**.

Getting Around Maryland

While it's not all that easy to do, the best way to get around Maryland is by **boat**, sailing around the gorgeous Chesapeake Bay. If you lack either the money or the good luck, you can hop aboard the *Chesapeake Flyer* **catamaran** (☎639-7241) which cruises the bay from Baltimore to Annapolis and eastern shore towns of St Michaels and Rock Hall. **Cycling** is also a good option, especially on the eastern shore, where the roads are wide shouldered and little travelled, winding through cornfields from one colonial-era hamlet to another – the state tourist office (see p.20) puts out an excellent free map of the safest and most scenic routes.

Baltimore is on the main *Amtrak* line between New York, Philadelphia and Washington DC, and linked by regular buses with Annapolis.

Baltimore

I would never want to live anywhere but Baltimore. You can look far and wide, but you'll never discover a stranger city with such extreme style. It's as if every eccentric in the South decided to move north, ran out of gas in Baltimore, and decided to stay.

John Waters, *Shock Value*

BALTIMORE is among the more enjoyable stops on the East Coast. It may not have a Statue of Liberty, or even a Liberty Bell, but its closely knit neighborhoods and historic quarters provide an engaging backdrop to many diverse attractions – like the **National Aquarium**, showpiece of the resurrected Inner Harbor **waterfront** – and top-rated **museums**, which cover everything from fine arts to black history to urban archeology. That Baltimore has been home to such diverse figures as writers Edgar Allan Poe and Anne Tyler and civil rights activists Frederick Douglass and Thurgood Marshall goes some way in explaining its sometimes bizarrely varied character, but it's still hard to pin down exactly what makes it such an engaging city to visit, and to live in.

Arrival, Information and Getting Around

The spacious modern **Baltimore–Washington International Airport** (BWI), ten miles south of the city center and 25 miles northeast of DC, is one of the busier East Coast hubs. *Airport Shuttle* **vans** ($5) into Baltimore leave the terminal every twenty minutes, taking half an hour to reach downtown. **Taxis** cost around $20. *Amtrak* **trains** stop every hour or so at the restored **Pennsylvania Station**, half a mile north of downtown at 1525 N Charles St (☎539-2112), while *MARC* commuter trains (☎859-7400 or 1-800/325-RAIL) from DC stop at BWI airport before continuing to the Camden Yards station south of downtown. *Greyhound* pulls in on the west side at 210 W Fayette St.

Pick up free maps and the seasonal *Quick City* visitors guide at the **Baltimore Area Convention and Visitors Association**, 1 E Pratt St (☎837-4636 or 1-800/282-6632), across from the Inner Harbor, or its booths at the airport and train station.

City Transit

Because the city is so compact – everything of interest is within a mile of the center – you could get around quite happily on foot. If the weather's bad, or you get worn out, motorized **trolleys** (Mon–Sat 11am–7pm; 25¢) cruise the city on two circuits, one up and down Charles Street from Penn Station to the Inner Harbor, and another east from downtown to Fell's Point. A **water taxi** ($3.25 for an all-day pass) nips between the Inner Harbor and Fell's Point. The city-operated *MTA* bus, subway and light-rail

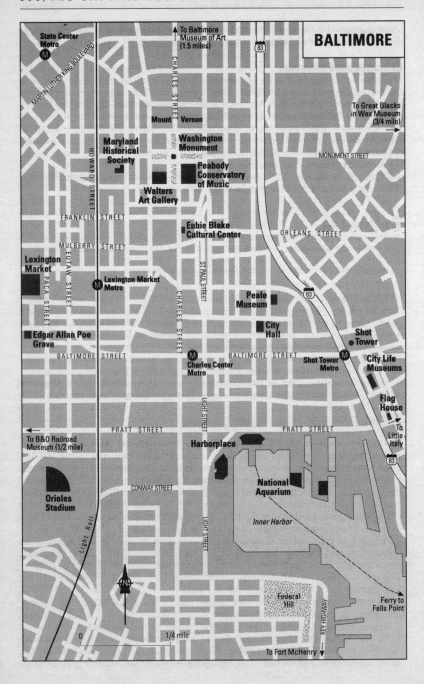

BALTIMORE

State Center Metro

To Baltimore Museum of Art (1.5 miles)

MARTIN LUTHER KING BOULEVARD

CHARLES STREET

Mount Vernon

To Great Blacks in Wax Museum (3/4 mile)

MONUMENT STREET

HOWARD STREET

Maryland Historical Society

Washington Monument

Peabody Conservatory of Music

Walters Art Gallery

ORLEANS STREET

FRANKLIN STREET

EUTAW STREET

MULBERRY STREET

Eubie Blake Cultural Center

PACA STREET

Lexington Market

St PAUL STREET

Lexington Market Metro

Peale Museum

CHARLES STREET

City Hall

Shot Tower

Edgar Allan Poe Grave

BALTIMORE STREET

BALTIMORE STREET

Shot Tower Metro

City Life Museums

Charles Center Metro

Flag House

To B&O Railroad Museum (1/2 mile)

PRATT STREET

LIGHT STREET

PRATT STREET

To Little Italy

Harborplace

CONWAY STREET

National Aquarium

Light Rail

Orioles Stadium

LIGHT STREET

Inner Harbor

Federal Hill

KEY HIGHWAY

Ferry to Fells Point

N

0 1/4 mile

To Fort McHenry

system is more useful for commuters than for visitors, but runs 24 hours and costs $1. **Taxis** include *Yellow Cab* (☎685-1212) and *Diamond Cab* (☎947-3333).

Downtown Baltimore

When the whole of **downtown Baltimore** burned to the ground in 1904, everything from the waterfront to Mount Vernon was destroyed, except for the domed 1867 **City Hall**, three blocks east of Charles Street, the main business strip. Though Baltimore quickly rebuilt, the downtown area never recovered much character, and it's not a place to spend much time. However, a few very different sorts of places give alternative looks at what makes Baltimore tick.

Downtown Baltimore's most worthwhile stop, a block north of City Hall, is usually surrounded by a fleet of armored cars (the *Brinks-Mat* garage is next door). The **Peale Museum** (Tues–Sat 10am–5pm, Sun noon–5pm; $2), at 225 Holiday St, is living proof that Baltimore's taste for the bizarre goes back well beyond John Waters. Housed in the first purpose-built museum building in the US, it traces the history of museum-making, from eighteenth-century European "cabinets of curiosities" – shrunken heads from the South Pacific, and a wax model of Daniel Lambert, who died in 1809 weighing 53 stone – through to the more didactic displays of anthropological tidbits installed by founder Charles Willson Peale in 1814. His original museum didn't survive long, and the building was later used as an early Baltimore City Hall as well as the country's first public school for black children.

A block south of City Hall, along Baltimore Street, stand the decaying remains of what was known as the **Baltimore Block,** the East Coast's largest red light district. Looming at the end of the strip, the 215ft red-brick **Shot Tower** (daily 10am–4pm; free), looking like a misplaced lighthouse, was built in 1828 as part of a munitions factory that pumped out some six thousand tons of lead shot every year: tiny drops of molten lead became nearly perfect spheres as they plummeted from the top of the tower, to drop into a deep pool of water that caused them to solidify.

West of Charles Street is Baltimore's somewhat down-at-heel central **shopping** district. Though many of the premises are boarded up and abandoned, there are a few holdouts, including the oldest and loudest of the city's covered markets, **Lexington Market**, at the center of which *Faidley's* is the best (and cheapest) place to sample oysters, clams, crabs and other Chesapeake Bay produce.

Three blocks up, at 600 N Paca St, the **Mother Seton House** (Sat–Sun 1–4pm; free) is a small, late eighteenth-century brick house where **Elizabeth Seton**, the first American woman to achieve sainthood, founded the Daughters of Charity Catholic order. Just south of the market, **Westminster Church** was built in 1852 on top of the main Baltimore cemetery, and many ornate tombs now stand in dark catacombs underneath. Among the prominent citizens buried here is **Edgar Allan Poe**, who lived in Baltimore for three years in the 1830s, marrying his 13-year-old cousin and beginning a career in journalism before moving on to Richmond, Virginia (see the Index for further references). In 1849, while passing through Baltimore, Poe – who had an obsessive fear of being buried alive – was found incoherent in a polling place and died soon afterwards. In 1875 his remains were moved from a pauper's grave and entombed within the stone memorial that stands along Green Street on the north side of the church.

Much more fun than either of these is the narrow brick rowhouse where baseball great **Babe Ruth** was born in 1895, at 216 Emory St (daily 10am–5pm; $3). Filled to bursting point with photographs, film clips and baseball memorabilia, it not only traces the life and achievements of the much-loved home-run hitter, but also serves as an enjoyable introduction to the game and its personalities. Appropriately enough, the beautiful new **Orioles Stadium** is just two blocks west, on the site of the old railroad terminus at Camden Yards (for tickets, phone *Ticketmaster* ☎423-7328).

The Inner Harbor and the National Aquarium

Sooner or later, if you're in Baltimore you're bound to be drawn down to the **Inner Harbor**, a success story of urban regeneration that leaves other cities green with post-industrial envy. Instead of the rotting wharves and derelict warehouses that stood here through the 1970s, the sparkling steel-and-glass **Harborplace** shopping mall, crammed with the likes of *Benetton* and *Laura Ashley* as well as cafés and restaurants, is now the city's pride and joy, swarming day and night with tourists and locals. Unlike Covent Garden, or Faneuil Hall in Boston, nothing here dates from before the rebuilding, but it's still quite an enjoyable place, the waterfront promenade enlivened by busking guitar players and the occasional fire-eating juggler.

To lend an air of authenticity, remnants from the city's proud maritime past have been assembled in the Inner Harbor, including the graceful **USS Constellation** (daily 10am–6pm; $2), an eighteenth-century, Baltimore-built frigate that was the US Navy's first ship. Another collection of ships – a Coast Guard cutter that survived Pearl Harbor, a Chesapeake Bay lightship, and a World War II submarine – make up the less-than-riveting **Baltimore Maritime Museum** (daily 9.30am–5pm; $3) on the next pier.

The National Aquarium

Far and away the biggest tourist attraction in Baltimore – on national holidays it rivals Walt Disney World as the most popular destination in the US – the **National Aquarium** (Mon–Thurs 9am–5pm, Fri–Sun 9am–8pm; $11) is certainly well worth seeing, so long as you avoid the weekend throngs. The main exhibition building, a rather grey, 1970s concrete space with a confusing jumble of escalators and ramps, rises in levels from a tankful of bat rays past a simulated South Pacific reef up to the rooftop rainforest garden. From here, another ramp winds down past the **Open Ocean Exhibit**, which features a number of slow-moving sharks.

While the displays in the main building are generally educational if not all that innovative or thought provoking, the separate **Marine Mammal Pavilion**, at the end of an adjacent pier, is a lot more entertaining: this is where the aquarium's trained **dolphins** and beluga **whales** are put through their paces. Half-hour shows are given every ninety minutes, with the best views to be had from either side, where transparent acrylic panels allow you to watch the animals above and below the water as they run the gamut of tail-walking, breaching, and spitting water into the audience.

Incidentally, despite the "national" in its name, this is a privately run, profit-making institution – a clever Maryland politician had a special decree passed in Congress so that it could be called the National Aquarium.

Mount Vernon

Baltimore's most elegant quarter is just north of downtown on the shallow rise known as **Mount Vernon**, where a couple of good museums sit among rows of eighteenth-century brick townhouses. It takes its name from the country home of George Washington, whose likeness tops the 165ft marble column of the central **Washington Monument**, in a small leafy park next to the aspirational spire of the sham-Gothic Mount Vernon Methodist Church at Charles Street and Monument Place. You can climb the monument for a great view over the city.

At its foot, the solemn stone facade of the Peabody Conservatory of Music hides one of the city's best interior spaces: the beautiful, skylit atrium of the **Peabody Library** (Mon–Fri 9am–3pm; free). Five tiers of intricate wrought-iron balconies rise above ground-floor displays of sixteenth-century books, including a wonderful illustrated 1555 edition of Boccaccio's *Decamarone* and a 1493 printing of the *Nuremburg Chronicles*. Two blocks west, the **Maryland Historical Society museum** (Tues–Sat 10am–5pm,

Sun 1–5pm; $2.50) has a fairly tame collection of portraits of Maryland society and docu-ments tracing local history, though its antique-filled chambers give a strong sense of the maritime wealth created here through nineteenth-century trade. A small room off the lobby holds some nifty models of Chesapeake Bay boats, and upstairs the "War of 1812 Gallery" displays the original manuscript of the lyrics to the *Star-Spangled Banner*.

Walters Art Gallery

Baltimore's best museum, the **Walters Art Gallery** (Tues–Sun 11am–5pm; $3, free Wed), on Charles Street a block south of the Washington Monument, provides a comprehensive survey of art from ancient statuary to French Impressionist painting. Its core is a large sculpture court, modelled upon an Italian Renaissance palazzo, beyond which modern galleries show off Greek and Roman antiquities, medieval illuminated manuscripts, Islamic ceramics and some very fine Byzantine silver. The top floor has the oddest organization, with pre-Columbian stone carvings displayed in a narrow corri-dor, at the end of a grand hall filled with late nineteenth-century paintings, including Manet's beer-drinking *At the Café*.

Almost everything on show was bought by William Walters, one of the first US collec-tors of **Chinese** and **Southeast Asian** art. The restored **Hackerman House** holds some especially fine pieces, including a roomful of Chinese jade figurines, a Ming dynasty handscroll, some lovely Japanese prints and a pair of polychrome and gilt temple doors, carved to look like peacock feathers. A seventh-century lacquered wood statue of a svelte Buddha is perhaps the oldest such image in the world.

The City Life Museums, Little Italy and Fells Point

A quarter of a mile east of downtown and the Inner Harbor, across the busy Falls Expressway, four small museums at 800 E Lombard St, known as the **Baltimore City Life Museums**, delve into some less frequently charted corners of history (Tues–Sat 10am–4pm, Sun noon–4pm; $4, free Sat morning). The luxurious 1820s **Carroll Mansion**, home of Charles Carroll, a signatory of the Declaration of Independence, contrasts with the **1840 House**, a reconstructed working-class cottage in which costumed guides demonstrate the domestic life of the time. The **Courtyard Exhibition Center** looks at the revitalization of Baltimore's waterfront, and archeologists at the **Center for Urban Archeology** talk about the various digs going on in the area. The nearby but separate **Flag House** and **1812 Museum** (Mon–Sat 10am–4pm; $2) was where Mary Pickersgill in 1813 sewed the 30-by-45ft US flag which inspired Francis Scott Key to write the *Star-Spangled Banner*. The actual banner is now in the Museum of American History in Washington DC, but the house is full of patriotic tributes.

The densely tangled streets of **Little Italy**, still a strongly Italian neighborhood, spread to the south and east. Besides dozens of usually very good restaurants and cafés, the area holds plenty of Baltimore's trademark stone-fronted rowhouses, almost all with highly polished marble steps. As a sort of traditional local substitute for air-conditioning, in the heat of summer people move their furniture outdoors, thereby turning each entire street into an extended living room.

Beyond Little Italy, separated from the renovated Inner Harbor by acres of derelict wharves and warehouses, stands Baltimore's oldest and liveliest quarter, **Fells Point**. Projecting into the main harbor, its deepwater frontage made it the heart of the city's extensive shipbuilding industry; the shipyards are long gone, but many old bars and pubs have hung on to form one of the best nightlife districts in the country. Specific places of interest are hard to pinpoint, though the **Pink Flamingoes** junk shop owned and run by Edith Massey, inspiration for many of John Waters' stranger films, was at 728 S Broadway, a block from the water; it's now a novelty shop specializing in Divine memorabilia.

Around Baltimore

The **B&O Railroad Museum**, housed in an 1830 passenger station at 901 W Pratt St, half a mile west of the Inner Harbor (Wed–Sun 10am–4pm; $4), commemorates the first large-scale railroad in the US, founded in 1827. It holds dozens of ornate carriages, including some wacky parasol-covered early models, and row upon row of locomotives, from steam engines to sleek 1940s diesels.

Perhaps Baltimore's most unusual museum is about a mile northeast of the center, in an old fire station off Broadway at 1601 E North Ave. The **Great Blacks in Wax Museum** (Tues–Sat 9am–6pm, Sun noon–6pm; $5) uses wax models to illustrate black history, from Egyptian pharaohs and early Muslims through to Martin Luther King, Jr, Marcus Garvey and Malcolm X. The models are posed in prop-filled dioramas – Rosa Parks being dragged off a Montgomery bus, for example, stands across from a pair of Jim Crow-era drinking fountains, a spotless enamel one labelled Whites Only and a rusty spigot for Colored People. Upstairs, figures in the Maryland Room include Baltimore-born ragtime piano player and composer Eubie Blake, and blues diva Billie Holiday, who was born and raised on Dallas Street just around the corner.

Further out on the north side, at the top of Charles Street two miles from downtown (bus #3), are the pseudo-classical modern galleries of the **Baltimore Museum of Art** (Tues, Wed & Fri 10am–4pm, Thurs 10am–9pm, Sat & Sun 11am–6pm; $2, free Thurs). As well as Italian and Dutch great works by Botticelli, Raphael, Rembrandt and Van Dyke, there is an overview of contemporary art spotlighting Gilbert and George's *Hellish* self-portrait. The standout is the Cone Collection of works by Delacroix, Degas, Cezanne and Picasso, with over a hundred drawings and paintings by Henri Matisse.

Accommodation

Apart from an attractive and central **youth hostel**, and the usual interstate **motels**, Baltimore has few budget places to stay. However, there are **B&Bs** – the *Maryland Reservation Center* (☎269-7550 or 1-800/654-9303) lists rooms in private homes from $50 per night – and inns cluster around the historic waterfront area of Fell's Point.

Admiral Fell Inn, 888 S Broadway (☎522-7377). Nicely restored historic hotel in the heart of Fell's Point, with breakfast and free parking. ⑥.

Baltimore International AYH Youth Hostel, 17 W Mulberry St (☎576-8880). $10 dorm beds in historic downtown brick rowhouse. There's an 11pm curfew, and you have to be out by 9am. ①.

Celie's Waterfront B&B, 1714 Thames St (☎522-2323). Small Fell's Point inn, on the waterfront. ⑥.

Comfort Inn, 24 W Franklin St (☎727-2000 or 1-800/228-5150). Recently modernized Mount Vernon hotel. ④.

Radisson Lord Baltimore Hotel, 20–30 W Baltimore St (☎539-8400). Plush downtown hotel, two blocks from the Inner Harbor. ⑤.

Eating

Baltimore, long known as **Crab City**, has dozens of reasonably priced, fresh **seafood** places, as well as the usual range of diners and over a dozen good restaurants side by side in Little Italy, just east of the Inner Harbor. Restaurants tend to be unpretentious and family orientated, and prices lower than elsewhere.

Bertha's, 734 S Broadway (☎327-5795). Casual but stylish seafood restaurant, tucked away behind a tiny Fell's Point bar.

Da Mimmo, 217 S High St (☎727-6876). Intimate, romantic Little Italy café, with live piano music and wide-ranging menu. Main dishes $9–15.

Faidley's, in Lexington Market (☎685-6169). Always crowded fresh oyster, clam and crab cake stand in boisterous downtown market. Fresh-shucked oysters (6 for $6), and $1.50 beers.

Louie's Bookstore Café, 518 N Charles St (☎962-1224). Busy Mount Vernon bar which also does a range of good $6–10 meals. Open late, with regular live music.

Luigi Petti, 1002 Eastern Ave (☎685-0055). Newish Little Italy trattoria, with sunny terrace.

Obrycki's, 1727 E Pratt St (☎732-6399). Baltimore's best and longest established fish restaurant, with delicious fresh crabs. Closed in winter.

John Steven Ltd, 1800 Thames St (☎276-9497). Fresh seafood, including good sushi – $5 for 6 pieces – in homey Fell's Point pub.

Women's Industrial Exchange Restaurant, 333 N Charles St (☎685-4388). Excellent-value 1940s café with full breakfasts for under $2, huge plates of chicken gumbo for $4, and great crab cakes.

Drinking and Nightlife

Baltimore's waterfront **Fell's Point** neighborhood may well have the densest assembly of drinking places in the US. One bar after another lines up along Broadway and the many smaller side streets; almost all feature some sort of entertainment, usually live bands, and on summer nights the pavements are packed solid with revellers. The city's high-brow culture is concentrated northwest of the center, along Mount Royal Ave, home of both the **Meyerhoff Symphony Hall** (☎783-8000) and the **Lyric Opera House** (☎685-5086).

For a full rundown of what's on and where, pick up a copy of the free *City Paper*, available at book and record stores all over town.

Buddy's Jazz Pub, 313 N Charles St (☎332-4200). Evening jazz, for the price of a drink or two.

Cat's Eye Pub, 1730 Thames St (☎276-9085). Cozy bar with a good range of beers.

Max's, 735 S Broadway (☎675-6297). Small but usually lively haunt pulling in some big names.

Mount Royal Tavern, 1204 W Mount Royal Ave (☎669-6686). Welcoming bar, popular with art students as well as night-capping musicians.

Old Oak Tavern, 641 Montford Ave (☎675-2565). Friendly gay and lesbian bar, a few blocks east of Fell's Point, with oak panelling and pool tables.

Wharf Rat Bar, 801 S Ann St (☎276-9034). Another well-stocked and convivial bar.

Western Maryland

Stretched between West Virginia and the razor-straight Pennsylvania border, western Maryland ranges for some two hundred miles east to west, but is in places well under five miles across. In general, the further west you go, the more mountainous and back-woodsy the feel – with a strong affinity to Maryland's Appalachian neighbors.

Though the countryside is very pretty, specific points of interest are few. Apart from the Civil War battlefield at **Antietam**, west of the only sizeable town, **Frederick**, the best reason to come is to cycle or hike the footpath of the restored old **Chesapeake and Ohio Canal**, which winds along the Maryland side of the Potomac River from Washington DC for over 180 miles to **Cumberland** in the western mountains.

Frederick and Around

One of the first towns settled in northwestern Maryland, **FREDERICK**, at the junction of I-70 and I-270 an hour west of Baltimore, was laid out in 1745 by German farmers lured from Pennsylvania by the promise of cheap fertile land. It grew to become a main stopover on the route west to the Ohio Valley, and the bulk of today's tidy town survives from the early 1800s. A **visitor center** (☎663-8703) at 19 E Church St has walking tour maps of the town, pointing out such places as the **Schifferstadt House** (Tues–Sat

The **area code** for all Maryland outside Baltimore is ☎301.

10am–4pm, Sun 1–4pm; $2), just off US-15, a stonewalled farmhouse built in 1753 and largely unaltered since. According to a romantic poem popular with turn-of-the-century schoolchildren, 95-year-old Barbara Fritchie defiantly waved the US flag while Confederate soldiers marched past from the tiny **Barbara Fritchie House**, along Carroll Creek on the west side of town. When Winston Churchill passed through, he stopped at the house and recited the poem from memory.

Camp David, the mountain retreat used by US presidents since FDR, which was where Jimmy Carter brought Menachem Begin and Anwar Sadat together in 1978 to sign the historic Camp David accords between Israel and Egypt, is hidden away in the mountains north of Frederick. Nearby **Cunningham Falls State Park** and the **Catoctin Mountain Park** both hold endless hardwood forests – great for fall color – in the midst of numerous preserved remnants of early homesteaders. Pick up details on hiking and camping in the two parks at the main **visitor center** (daily 9am–5pm; ☎663-9388), off Hwy-77 two miles west of US-15.

Besides being a nice detour off the highway, Frederick is a good base for exploring places such as **Antietam** (see below) and **Harpers Ferry** in West Virginia (see p.323). There are **motels** along both I-70 and US-15, and in town the *Tyler Spite House*, 112 W Church St (☎831-4455; ④), is a pleasant **B&B** in an elegant 1814 mansion. For a bite to **eat**, try the soups and steaks at the *Brown Pelican*, 5 E Church St, or the burgers and steamed crabs at *Cactus Flats*, off US-15 three miles north of town.

Antietam National Battlefield

The site of the bloodiest single battle in the Civil War, **Antietam National Battlefield** spreads over unaltered farmlands outside the whitewashed and balconied village of **Sharpsburg**. Here, fifteen miles west of Frederick, on the morning of September 17 1862, in an effort to consolidate rebel gains after their victory at Manassas, 40,000 troops faced a Union army twice that number. Hours later, some 25,000 from both sides lay dead or dying. The fiercest fighting, and the worst bloodshed, occurred in cornfields to the north; Union General Joseph Hooker recorded: "In the time that I am writing, every stalk of corn in the northern and greater part of the field was cut as closely as could have been done with a knife, and the slain lay in rows precisely as they had stood in their ranks a few moments before."

The battle continued throughout the day without a clear result. It may not have been decisive, but the Confederate lack of success lost them the support of their erstwhile ally Great Britain, while the Union performance encouraged Lincoln to issue the Emancipation Proclamation. Pick up a brochure and driving tour map of the park at the **visitor center**, a mile north of Sharpsburg off Hwy-65 (daily 9am–5pm; ☎432-5124). Numerous plaques and memorials have been constructed around the fields, but otherwise the site, with its various farm buildings and country churches, is unchanged, and the entire park serves as a mute but evocative memorial to the conflict.

Cumberland and the C&O Canal

The only large town in the far west of Maryland, **CUMBERLAND** started life as a coal-mining center in the late 1700s. Often confused with Daniel Boone's Cumberland Gap in southwest Virginia, this Cumberland was also an important trans-Appalachian crossing, but its main place in history is as the terminus of the ill-fated C&O (Chesapeake and Ohio) Canal, an impressive engineering feat begun in 1813 but not completed until 1850, by which time the railroads had already made it obsolete.

The **Western Maryland Station Center** (Wed–Sat 10am–5pm, Sun & Tues 1–4pm; ☎722-8226), beside the canal, can provide information on hiking, cycling, canoeing and camping; in summer, the historic trains of the **Western Maryland Scenic Railroad** set off on two-hour rides through the surrounding mountains ($9.50; ☎689-6668).

Annapolis and Southern Maryland

While Baltimore has grown into the state's largest and busiest city, **Annapolis**, Maryland's colonial and current capital, has remained more or less unchanged. Before the US broke free from English rule, this was considered to be one of the most genteel and attractive colonial centers, and though its time-worn streets are now always crowded, Annapolis is still among the more engaging small US cities. Its once-vital Chesapeake Bay **waterfront** now has little of the feel of colonial maritime life, but the real attractions of Annapolis, among its wanderable narrow streets, include fine homes, the Beaux Arts campus of the US Naval Academy, and the beautiful state capitol.

If you like the look of Annapolis, and want to get a better feel for the Chesapeake Bay region away from the crowds, head south to places like **St Mary's City** – the first capital of Maryland, completely reconstructed in the 1960s – or **Solomons Island**, one of many small Chesapeake Bay towns that seem unaltered for decades.

Annapolis

At the center of **ANNAPOLIS**, overlooking the town's baroque web of streets, the **Maryland State House** (daily 9am–5pm; free) was completed in 1779 and soon after served as an early capitol of the United States. The **Old Senate Chamber**, to the right of the grand entrance hall, is where the Treaty of Paris was ratified in 1784, officially ending the Revolutionary War; a statue of George Washington stands on the spot where he resigned his commission as head of the Continental Army, and displays document the role Annapolis played in the life of the young Republic. Free guided tours are given on the hour, or you can wander around on your own, perhaps stopping in to listen to the proceedings of Maryland's current crop of legislators, who hold court from January to April in the more modern wing to the north of the old building. Also on the grounds of the State House is the cottage-sized **Old Treasury Building**, built in 1735 to hold colonial Maryland's currency reserves.

Grand late eighteenth-century brick homes line the streets of Annapolis, but for substance and grace none surpasses the **Hammond-Harwood House** (Tues–Sat 10am–5pm, Sun 2–5pm; $3), two blocks west of the State House at 19 Maryland Ave off King George St. The warm red-brick Palladian villa, which consists of two symmetrical wings connected by a central hall, was built in 1774 to the designs of William Buckland, and is most notable for its beautifully carved decorative woodwork, especially evident in the intricate front doorway. Despite its architectural harmony, the house has had an unfortunate history, the original owner becoming so obsessed with its construction that his fiancée left him, breaking his heart and causing his untimely death at age 38; the architect Buckland also died in mysterious circumstances before the house was completed.

Another historic Annapolis mansion, the 1765 **Paca House**, 186 Prince George St (Tues–Sat 10am–4pm, Sun noon–4pm; $4), was a downmarket rooming house until the 1960s; it was restored to its period appearance in time for the 1976 Bicentennial, and boasts a splendid formal garden (a parking lot twenty years ago), which you can peer into from King George Street. Besides such elite manors, dozens of pastel eighteenth-century clapboard cottages and commercial structures fill the narrow streets that run down to the waterfront. Of those that have escaped the gentrifiers, the **Tobacco Prise House**, 4 Pinkney St (Sat & Sun 10am–4pm; $2), is a colonial tobacco warehouse that now sets out to explain the handling and storage of the valuable leaves. Further along, the **Shiplap House**, 18 Pinkney St (daily 11am–4pm; free), was built in 1715 as a tavern; now it's a small museum of Annapolis history, with an herb garden behind containing assorted medicinal plants grown in colonial times.

The Waterfront and US Naval Academy

Although few colonial sites survive along the modern **Chesapeake Bay waterfront** to give a sense of the port's former maritime strength, the rebuilt 1850s dockside city market, the **Victualling Warehouse**, at 77 Main St facing the Market Space (daily 11am–4pm; $2), is an early nineteenth-century replacement of a colonial warehouse used by the revolutionary army.

The rest of the waterfront is pleasant enough for an afternoon's wandering, especially on summer weekends when the harbor and bay are full of clanging halyards and billowing sails. In among the boat supply shops and harborside bars, the grey stone walls of the **US Naval Academy** (Mon–Sat 9.30am–5pm; free) seem designed to exacerbate the sensory deprivation endured by the over four thousand crew-cut young men and a handful of women (all of whom line up in formation outside **King Hall**, the dining commons, every day at noon) who spend four strictly disciplined years here before embarking on careers as naval officers. A small museum holds models of various British and US warships and other naval memorabilia. Guided tours of the Academy ($2) leave hourly from the visitor center in Ricketts Hall, near the main gate at the end of Randall Street, a block east of the City Dock.

Practicalities

Compared to the rest of Maryland, Annapolis is easy to reach, on *Greyhound*, *MTA* buses and, someday soon, on light rail from Baltimore. By road it's about half an hour from Washington (via US-50) or Baltimore (via Hwy-1), though parking can be difficult. A trolley bus (25¢) loops around the small and very walkable central area. Various organizations offer **walking tours**, the best being those given by *Historic Annapolis* (☎267-8149); if you'd rather see it on your own, the **visitor center** (☎268-8687) at the end of the City Dock has free maps as well as tons of practical information.

Finding a **place to stay** is not usually a problem, though prices are fairly steep. There's a free accommodation bureau (☎1-800/848-4748), or you can choose from among **B&Bs** like the central and characterful *Scot-Laur Inn*, 165 Main St (☎268-5665; ④); the pricier *Prince George Inn*, 232 Prince George St (☎263-6418; ⑤); or the small and gay-friendly *Casa Bahia*, 262 King George St (☎268-3106; ④). Dozens of motels are to be found along US-50 on the west side of town.

Restaurants and **bars** are both plentiful and good: the no-frills *Chick and Ruth's Delly*, 165 Main St (☎269-6737), does big breakfasts and has a booth on permanent reserve for Maryland's governor; the ritzier *Harry Browne's*, 66 State Circle (☎263-4332), is popular with politicos and expense-account lobbyists. You can tuck into fish and chips while people-watching from the sunny porch of the waterfront *Middleton Tavern*, 2 Market Space (☎263-3323), one of the city's oldest buildings. The *King of France Tavern* in the historic *Maryland Inn*, 16 Church Circle (☎263-2641), puts on live jazz, while *Marmaduke's*, 301 Severn Ave (☎269-5420), is a waterfront bar popular with the yachting brigades, who turn out to watch videos of themselves racing around the bay.

Southern Maryland

The little-visited back roads (there are no big roads) of **southern Maryland** in many ways resemble the agricultural Deep South. All along both main roads, US-301 from Baltimore and Hwy-2 from Annapolis, lush fields of corn and tobacco, dotted with ageing wooden barns, fill the arable lands in scattered parcels, and narrow, tree-lined country lanes open suddenly onto rivers or the broad Chesapeake Bay.

Solomons Island

Towns in southern Maryland are few and far between, but a couple are worth searching out. The old shipbuilding community of **Solomons Island**, sixty miles south of

Annapolis via Hwy-2, is not actually an island but a narrow two-mile peninsula between the Patuxent River and Back Creek Bay. The entire waterfront is dotted with homely **B&Bs** like the *Back Creek Inn* (☎326-2022; ④) and fresh seafood **restaurants** – the *Lighthouse Inn* on the bay side, and *Solomon's Pier* across the road both have sunny outdoor decks – but the best reason to stop is the **Calvert Marine Museum** (daily 10am–5pm; $3), on Hwy-2 at the north end of town. This focuses specifically on the Patuxent River, and on the unique estuarine ecosystem of the Chesapeake Bay tidal areas. Its two protected marshland wildlife areas, one saltwater and one freshwater, can be explored on raised walkways. Inside the main building, exhibits follow the development of local boat-building and commercial fishing, and dozens of historic boats are on show. In summer, an old oyster buy-boat, the *William B Tennison*, leaves from the museum dock on hour-long **cruises** (daily at 2pm; $4) around the bay.

St Mary's City and Point Lookout State Park

It's not really historic, nor even much of a city, but the reconstructed village of **ST MARY'S CITY** is well worth a look, if only for its lovely position. Set on a broad Potomac cove near the southern tip of the Maryland peninsula, twenty miles south of Solomons Island, St Mary's City is a small-scale but credible reconstruction of Maryland's first colonial capital, established here in 1634 before being moved to Annapolis sixty years later. The entire complex, including a working tobacco plantation and a replica of the tiny ship on which the first colonists arrived from England, is run as a sort of theme park, complete with costumed tour guides (daily 10am–5pm; $4). Its main feature is a rebuilding of the long-vanished **State House**, where in 1689 Protestant rebels seized control of what had been a Catholic-run colony, but it's all a bit too manicured to provide much sense of history. Nearby, and much more fun, the *Farthing's Ordinary* is a mock **tavern** selling hearty soups and sandwiches for around $6.

South from St Mary's City, the very tip of the southern Maryland peninsula was used during the Civil War as a **prisoner-of-war camp** for rebel forces captured at the battle of Gettysburg. In just over a year, from March 1864 to June 1865, over four thousand died due to the appalling conditions, including some seven hundred Union guards. Most of the Confederate soldiers were buried in a mass grave, now marked by a granite obelisk; the actual camp (the ramparts have been reconstructed and there's a small and somewhat gruesome museum) was a mile south. The point where the Potomac flows into the Chesapeake is a good place to watch the sun rise or set.

The Eastern Shore

Maryland's compelling and addictive **eastern shore**, the broad peninsula that protects the Chesapeake from the open Atlantic, holds miles of back roads perfectly suited to aimless exploration and sudden discovery, such as coming across the odd wooden farmhouse or tobacco barn standing forlornly in the middle of a field, or an old sailboat tied up to an apparently decrepit dock that springs to life when the fishing craft return. The US-50 bridge, built across the Chesapeake Bay in the early 1960s, may have made the eastern shore more accessible, but it hasn't affected its air of somnolence. Quiet country lanes head away from US-50 as it races down to the beach resort of **Ocean City**, to two-hundred-year-old waterfront towns like **Chestertown**, **St Michaels** and **Oxford**.

Chestertown and Rock Hall

A stopping place for travellers since colonial days, when it was a prime Chesapeake port, **CHESTERTOWN** is the northernmost center on the eastern shore. Stretching west along High Street from the Chester River, it's surprisingly intact, with its fine old riverfront homes, a courthouse square lined with ornate wooden cottages, and a generally langorous feel that makes it a popular weekend escape from Baltimore or DC. Many of the old houses, like the *Widow's Walk Inn*, 402 High St (☎778-6455; ⑤), have been converted into **B&Bs**, while others now house top-rated **restaurants** like the *Feast of Reason*, 203 High St (☎778-3828), and the swanky dining room of the *Imperial Hotel* (☎778-5000) across the street. The **visitor center**, 118 N Cross St (☎778-0416), has details of walking and cycling tours.

To the west of town, fifteen miles of country lanes lead down to the wharves and dockside restaurants of **Rock Hall**, an old fishing port where you can watch the day's catch being unloaded while munching on crab legs at the bare-bones *Waterman's Crabhouse* (☎778-1803) on the main pier. The *Chesapeake Flyer* catamaran service lands here (see p.329), and bikes are available for rent from the marina office.

St Michaels

A contender for prettiest harbor on the Chesapeake Bay, tiny **ST MICHAELS**, twelve miles west of US-50 on Hwy-33, is also one of its oldest ports. Founded during the mid-1600s, it grew into one of colonial America's prime shipbuilding centers; its fast sloops and shallow-draught "bugeyes" evaded British blockades during the Revolutionary War. St Michaels languished as Baltimore bloomed, but since the early 1960s it has been rediscovered, its old buildings now gentrified into art galleries, boutiques and cozy **B&Bs** like the *Hambleton Inn*, 202 Cherry St (☎745-3350; ⑤), and its wharves and docks filled with weekend sailors and fronted by restaurant-cum-bars like the *Town Dock* (☎745-5577) or *Longfellow's* (☎745-2624), both at the end of Mulberry Street.

Some corners of St Michaels survive intact, especially the old town green, **St Mary's Square**, a block off the main Talbot Street on Mulberry Street. To get a clear sense of the human and natural history of Chesapeake Bay, head north along the docks to the extensive modern **Chesapeake Bay Maritime Museum** (daily 9am–6pm; $5). It focuses on the restored **Hooper Strait Lighthouse**, at the foot of which float a few Chesapeake Bay sailboats – designed to make the most of the bay's shallow waters. Nearby, some two hundred other boats include a Native American dugout canoe, while in the museum workshop skilled artisans and legions of volunteers restore and maintain historic boats using painstaking traditional techniques.

Tilghman Island

If you want to see the real, workaday Chesapeake, **Tilghman Island**, west from St Michaels across the Knapps Narrows drawbridge, is home to most of the Chesapeake's working skipjack fleet. Partly in response to the continued depletion of oyster stocks, the government has made it illegal to harvest oysters except from small, graceful and hopelessly outmoded sailing boats called **skipjacks**, of which around thirty are still in use. Most are moored at **Dogwood Harbor**, on the east side of the island; during the fall and winter harvest, they unload at the *Harrison Oyster Packing Company*, at the foot of the bridge. You can buy oysters fresh off the boat, or sample them and other local delicacies at two very good restaurants on either side of the bridge: the *Bay Hundred* (☎886-2622) and the more upscale *Bridge Restaurant* (☎886-2500).

Oxford

Just west of US-50, or seven miles south of St Michaels via country lanes and the **Tred-Avon Ferry** – which first crossed in 1683 and has been in continuous service since 1836 – the leafy waterfront hamlet of **OXFORD** seems to have slumbered peacefully since colonial days. Along with Annapolis, this was one of two ports of entry for all colonial Maryland, a role remembered by the reconstructed one-room **Customs House** next to the ferry landing on the north side of town. After Independence, Oxford was all but forgotten; its full-time population is under a thousand, and there's hardly any tourist trade. Wandering the quiet streets, however, or along the lengthy riverfront promenade, can be quite relaxing and enjoyable. The *Town Creek* (☎226-5131) is a friendly inexpensive **seafood restaurant** with a large deck right on the main harbor, at the end of Tilghman St; the ancient *Robert Morris Inn*, on Morris St at The Strand (☎226-5111; ⑤), named for the Oxford man who personally financed the Continental army during the Revolutionary War, serves James Michener's favorite crab cakes. In the larger but less interesting US-50 town of **Easton**, the ancient *Bishop's House B&B*, 214 Goldsborough St (☎820-7290; ⑤), provides a comfortable alternative to the highway motels.

Ocean City

With over ten miles of broad Atlantic beach, a boisterous boardwalk amusement park and around half a million visitors every weekend, **OCEAN CITY** is Maryland's number one summer resort. No matter how you get here, down the coast from Delaware or across the rural eastern shore along US-50, its tower-block hotels and overcrowding will come as a shock. If you're after a quiet weekend by the sea, avoid it like the plague.

Ocean City might be good for a day out, or even a long weekend, but it's hard to imagine anyone wanting to stay very long. It is, at least, easy to reach; *Carolina Trailways* **buses** from DC end up at the southern end of town at Second St and Hwy-1 (☎289-9307). Places to **stay** are plentiful except on summer weekends, and off-season rates are at least half prime-time ones, but pleasant accommodation is rare indeed. For a **motel** near the bus station and boardwalk, try the *Oceanic* (☎289-6494 or 1-800/638-2106; ③) at the south end of Baltimore St. Alternatives range from the faded seaside grandeur of the *Commander Hotel* on the boardwalk at 14th St (☎289-6166 or 1-800/543-6986; ④), to the gleaming marble and glass of the *Cocoanut Mallory*, 60th St and The Bay (☎524-5500 or 1-800/767-6060; ⑦). If you get stuck, the **Chamber of Commerce**, on Hwy-1 at 40th St (☎289-8181 or 1-800/62-OCEAN), can usually help out.

Apart from the boardwalk fast-food joints, and the national franchises along Hwy-1 (there are three all-night *McDonalds*, for example), Ocean City has few good **eating** options. The *Angler Restaurant*, on the bay at Talbot St (☎289-7424), has fresh seafood and an all-you-can-eat salad bar; it also has nice beers, wild tropical cocktails and nightly live bands. Other **nightspots** include the *Big Kahuna Surf Club*, 18th and Hwy-1 (☎289-6331), and the all-ages *Nite Lite*, Boardwalk and Worcester (☎289-6313).

If you find yourself here in the peak of summer and want to escape the crowds, head just down the coast to **Assateague National Seashore** – a twenty-mile stretch of entirely undeveloped beach and marshland. There's a visitor center at the end of Hwy-611, five miles south of Ocean City, and **camping** right on the beach at Assateague State Park (☎641-2120). The best **lodging** is to be found near the southern half of Assateague Island, across the Virginia border in the tiny hamlet of **Chincoteague**, at either the *Main Street House B&B*, 704 N Main St (☎1-804/336-6030; ③), or the *Anchor Inn*, 534 S Main St (☎1-804/336-6313; ③).

DELAWARE

Though **DELAWARE** has its beauty spots – including some of the mid-Atlantic's best beaches – its tourist boards and PR people have their work cut out. About the only images potential visitors have of the state are negative: Delaware is known for the massive chemical plants of the **Du Pont Corporation** and **Dover Air Force Base**, as well as for tolerating shady **business** practices – half of America's largest companies have their official bases in the tiny state, thanks to the permissive tax, banking and incorporation laws (there's no sales tax either).

None of the above is likely to make you want to visit, so instead Delaware's promoters emphasize its **past** – for example, as the first ex-colony to ratify the Constitution, it claims the title of **America's First State**. Dutch whalers established a settlement at

The **area code** for the entire state of Delaware is ☎302.

the mouth of the Delaware Bay in 1631, and soon after the Swedes built a larger colony at present-day **Wilmington**. The two groups fought among themselves until the British took over in 1664. Delaware was part of neighboring Pennsylvania – Philadelphia is only ten miles north of the present, arching state border – until hiving itself off in 1776.

Much of Delaware's fortunes (and misfortunes) since then can be traced directly to the Du Pont family, who, fleeing the wrath of revolutionary France, set up a gunpowder mill that became, and has remained, the main supplier of conventional explosives to the US government. After World War I, the Du Ponts went public and made millions in the stock market frenzies of the Roaring Twenties, since when the company has diversified, its labs inventing such modern essentials as nylon and cellophane.

The Du Ponts built huge mansions for themselves in the **Brandywine Valley** north of Wilmington, near the perfectly preserved old colonial capital, **New Castle** on the Delaware Bay, just five miles south of I-95. Further south, **Dover**, the capital, may not detain you long, but beyond it the small and amiable resorts of **Lewes** and **Rehoboth Beach** mark the northern extent of over twenty miles of unspoiled Atlantic beaches.

Getting Around Delaware

Apart from **Wilmington**, which is on the main East Coast **train** and **bus** lines, Delaware is hard to get around without a car. *Greyhound* services are limited to a summer-only route from DC to **Rehoboth**, and local transport is non-existent.

I-95 and the New Jersey Turnpike converge at Wilmington, from where US-13 runs south through the state. More often called the **Du Pont Highway**, it was paid for and constructed by the industrialists so that they could ride in comfort between their Wilmington mansions and Dover. A direct car **ferry** connects Cape May, the southern tip of New Jersey, and Lewes, at the mouth of the Delaware Bay (see p.345).

Wilmington and Around

WILMINGTON may not be the most compelling place in America, but this much-maligned, medium-sized city can make for a refreshing break from the tourist trail: not only does it boast the excellent **Delaware Art Museum** and some pretty waterside parks, but the surrounding **Brandywine Valley** holds the manor homes and gardens (and factories) of the First State's First Family, the Du Ponts, all open to the public and providing an inside look at America's de facto aristocracy.

If you arrive in Wilmington by **train**, on the *Amtrak* line between New York and Washington, you'll pull in to the quirky 1907 terracotta station on the somewhat dodgy south side of the city. From here, the two main streets, Market and King, run north for about a mile to the Brandywine River, their partly pedestrianized lengths holding a standard array of stores and other small businesses, as well as a handful of restored eighteenth-century rowhouses clustered around the **Old Town Hall**, 512 Market St. The faceless grey monoliths that tower over the cityscape house the headquarters of hundreds of national companies.

A short walk north of the **downtown** commercial district, at the top end of Market Street, **Brandywine Park** comes as a welcome relief from the concrete pavements, its grassy knolls lining both banks of the Brandywine River. In the residential districts to the north are some of the city's oldest and poshest houses, many dating from the Revolutionary War, when Wilmington's flour mills fed the American forces. The nearby **Delaware Art Museum** (Tues 10am–9pm, Wed–Sat 10am–5pm, Sun noon–5pm; free), 2301 Kentmere Parkway, has a good range of works by American painters like

Thomas Eakins, Winslow Homer and Edward Hopper, as well as a comprehensive collection of English Pre-Raphaelite painting and drawing.

Most of Wilmington's surprising number of important colonial sites are hidden away amid the decrepit and heavily industrialized **waterfront** to the east of downtown. A poorly signed "historic Wilmington" loop stops first at the foot of Seventh Street, where a small monument marks the site of Delaware's first European colony, **Fort Christina**, set up by Swedish settlers in 1638. Nearby, at 606 Church St, the **Old Swede's Church** is one of the oldest houses of worship in the US, built in 1698 and still retaining its impressive black walnut pulpit.

The **tourist office** at 1300 Market St (☎652-4088) downtown has walking and driving tour maps and practical information, but unless you want to **eat** at the excellent *Waterworks Café*, 16th and French St in Brandywine Park (☎652-6022), or blow $150 on a night at the splendidly ornate *Hotel Du Pont* (☎594-3100 or 1-800/441-9019; ⑦), which fills an entire block of Market Street, there's no great reason to linger.

The Du Pont Mansions

Various generations of the Du Pont family built opulent homes in the rural Brandywine Valley northwest of Wilmington. To learn how their fortune was made, stop first at the **Hagley Museum** (daily 9.30am–5pm, Jan–March weekends only; $8), off Hwy-141 just north of Wilmington. Pierre Du Pont, the patriarch, was minister of finance to Louis XVI, but the museum begins with the foundation in 1802 of a small water-powered **gunpowder mill** along the banks of the Brandywine River. Mirroring the development of nineteenth-century American industry, the complex grew over the next hundred years to include ever-larger steam-powered and eventually electrically powered factories – almost all of which are still in working order.

The enormous pink **Nemours Mansion**, just a mile up the road, gives an idea of the wealth and power the family garnered (tours every two hours, Tues–Sat 9am–3pm, Sun 11am–3pm; $7). It was thrown up by Alfred Du Pont in 1910, modelled upon the family's ancestral home in France and surrounded by a 300-acre, Versailles-style formal garden. Two miles northwest, off Hwy-52, the one-time Du Pont family estate of **Winterthur** (Tues–Sat 9.30am–5pm, Sun noon–5pm; $9, gardens only $4) has evolved into the country's finest museum of early American **decorative arts**. Since 1927, when Henry Du Pont took over the twelve-room cottage to house himself and his antique furniture, Winterthur has grown into a vast private museum, each of its two hundred rooms showcasing a particular decorative style. Ranging from the simplicity of a Shaker cottage to a beautiful three-storey elliptical staircase taken from a North Carolina plantation home, the various pieces of furniture, textiles, silverwork and paintings – all made in America between 1640 and 1840 – are a rich catalogue of the diversity of American applied arts.

New Castle

Delaware's magnificently preserved first capital, **NEW CASTLE**, fronts the broad Delaware River, just six miles south of Wilmington via Hwy-141. Founded in the 1650s by the Dutch intent on expanding from their colony at New Amsterdam, and taken over by the British in 1664, New Castle was the main stopping point between Baltimore and Philadelphia. Though largely bypassed when railroads and highways replaced the riverboats, it has somehow managed to survive intact, its quiet cobbled streets and immaculate eighteenth-century brick houses shaded by ancient hardwood trees.

The heart of New Castle is the tree-filled **Town Green** that spreads east from the shops of Delaware Street. Laid out in 1655 by Peter Stuyvesant, it is dominated by the stalwart tower of the **Immanuel Episcopal Church**, built in 1703 and bordered by tidy rows of two-hundred-year-old gravestones. Its pristine white interior, however, is more recent, reconstructed after a disastrous 1980s fire. On the west edge of the green, the **Old Court House** was built in 1732 and served as the first state capitol. Its dainty cupola was the centerpoint from which surveyors determined the state's curved northern border, drawn up when Delaware seceded from Pennsylvania in 1776.

Fine colonial houses fill the few blocks around the Town Green. The largest, and the only one regularly open to the public, is the **George Read II House** (Tues–Sun 10am–4pm, Jan & Feb Sat & Sun only; $4), two blocks south along the river at 42 The Strand. Built between 1797 and 1804, and restored in the 1970s, the sumptuously detailed house has marble fireplaces, brightly painted walls, elaborately carved woodwork and some of the finest plasterwork ornament of the Federal period. The spacious gardens behind were laid out in 1847 to the picturesque designs of Andrew Jackson Downing. The large houses across the street, backing on to the Delaware River, also date from the early nineteenth century, and many are now run as B&Bs.

Practicalities

Many visitors are content to see New Castle, just off the interstate, as a day out from Washington DC or Philadelphia, but there's enough to merit a longer trip. For further information, or to pick up the self-guided walking tour map, call in at the **visitor center** at 220 Delaware St (☎322-9802). Comfortable **B&Bs** line the Delaware riverfront, varying from the homey, hospitable *River House*, 21 The Strand (☎328-2323; ③), to the more luxurious *Jefferson House*, 5 The Strand (☎323-0999; ⑤). There's good beer and pub-grub at the popular *Green Frog Tavern*, 114 Delaware St, while more refined tastes will enjoy the historic *David Finney Inn*, 216 Delaware St (☎322-6367), just off the Town Green.

Dover

DOVER, the capital of Delaware, is pretty much a non-event as far as tourism goes. Located in the mostly agricultural center of the state, just west of US-13 , it's basically a very small town, its low-rise business district hemmed in by blocks of suburban detached houses. South of **Lockerman Street**, the main route through town, a few, strangely somnolent governmental buildings center upon the 1792 **Old State House**, its old legislative chambers now restored as a museum (Tues–Sat 10am–4.30pm; free) and furnished with early American antiques. To the west, around the oval **Town Green**, lawyers and insurance brokers have taken over historic buildings such as the *Golden Fleece Tavern*, where Delaware's early legislators agreed to ratify the Constitution.

A short walk west of the green, the small **Delaware State Museum** (Tues–Sat 10am–4.30pm; free) is worth a look not for its fairly tedious displays of anthropological detritus – Native American shell necklaces, wooden water pipes from early Wilmington and the like – but because a small building across the graveyard holds the **Johnson Memorial**. This large and enjoyable collection of **phonographs**, dedicated to the memory of Dover-born engineer Eldridge Reeves Johnson, who helped to invent the *Victrola*, is laid out like a 1920s music store. Dozens of "talking machines", from early wind-ups to prototype jukeboxes, play period recordings, and comical photographs document early, pre-electric recording techniques – entire orchestras crowd together around huge megaphones. Pride of place goes to a painting of a dog, *Nipper*, listening to a *Victrola*, an image made familiar as "His Master's Voice". In 1929 Johnson sold the rights to his machine, and to his trademark dog, to RCA for $29 million.

Every Tuesday and Friday for over fifty years, **Spence's Bazaar**, two blocks south on Queen St at New Burton Rd, has hosted a free-for-all **flea market**. All of Dover turns out, including dozens of local **Amish**, who ride here in their ancient horse-drawn buggies to sell home-grown fruits and vegetables. Though it's not as well known as the Amish community of Lancaster County (see p.126), the area around Dover has nearly as large an Amish population, concentrated in the farmlands to the west of town; happily for them, their presence has yet to become a tourist attraction.

Practicalities

Most of Dover's **restaurants** and **hotels** are concentrated on Lockerman Street and State Street in the town center, just north of the Town Green. State Street in particular holds the *Dinner Bell Inn* at no 121 (☎678-1234) and the more pub-like *W T Smithers* (☎674-8875) across the street. US-13 highway also has some **budget accommodation**, such as the *Comfort Inn* (☎674-3300; ③) two blocks south of Lockerman Street. A **visitor center** (☎736-4266) next to the Old State House has the usual tourist information.

The Delaware Coast

The thirty-mile-long **Delaware coast** is one of the little-known jewels of the East Coast. Its one built-up resort, **Rehoboth Beach**, is a traditional seaside town, packed solid in summer, and the fishing community of **Lewes** is attractive and historic, but what really sets the area apart is the ease with which you can find long stretches of sand to yourself. For every developed stretch, about ten times more has been preserved as open space, most extensively at **Delaware Seashore State Park**, which stretches south from Rehoboth to the Maryland border.

Lewes

Whether you come down Hwy-1, or cruise across on the ferry from Cape May, New Jersey, **LEWES** makes a good introduction to the Delaware coast. Its natural harbor at the mouth of the Delaware Bay has attracted seafarers ever since a Dutch whaling company set up a small colony here in 1631. Lewes' current role as a summer resort hasn't obscured its substantial history, outlined in the mock-Dutch **Zwaanendael Museum** (Tues–Sat 10am–4.30pm, Sun 1.30–4.30pm; free), in the heart of town on Savannah Road at Kings Highway. The **tourist office** (☎645-8073) next door, housed inside a gambrel-roofed 1730s farmhouse, has walking tour maps of the rest of the town, pointing out the handful of eighteenth-century houses and outbuildings collected from around the area to form the **Lewes Historical Complex** on Front Street three blocks north. Along the canal, keep an eye out also for the **Overfalls Lightship**, which lit the entrance to Delaware Bay until 1961, and the array of cannons, one said to be from an old pirate ship, that are lined up along the top of **Memorial Park**.

Though Lewes can justly boast of being "the First Town in the First State", most people come here for the **beach** rather than history. There's an extensive strand along the usually calm Delaware Bay at the foot of the town, while **Cape Henlopen State Park**, a three-thousand-acre open space where the bay meets the open ocean just a mile east of the town center, is even better, and has the biggest sand dunes north of Cape Hatteras. Except on peak summer weekends, Lewes is quiet enough to mean you should have no trouble finding a room in **motels** like *Vesuvio's* (☎645-2224; ③) or *The Captain's Quarters* (☎645-7924; ③), both on Savannah Road near the water. Most of the **restaurants**, not surprisingly, feature seafood, the local favorite being *The Angler's* (☎645-9931), along the Lewes–Rehoboth Canal. You can **walk** almost everywhere in the compact center, or rent a **bike** from *Lewes Cycle Sport*, 514 Savannah Rd (☎645-4544). For a nice day out, or a possible next leg of your journey, take the **ferry** ($5 per person, $20 per car; ☎645-6313 or 1-800/64F-ERRY) across the Delaware Bay to the pleasant Victorian beach resort of **Cape May**, New Jersey (see p.142). It leaves every couple of hours from a terminal very near the town center, and takes seventy minutes.

Rehoboth Beach

A non-stop parade of motels and shopping malls along the six miles of Hwy-1 links Lewes with **REHOBOTH BEACH**, Delaware's largest and liveliest beach resort. Crowded all summer, but nearly empty the rest of the year, Rehoboth – which started life as a Methodist revival camp, and attracts so many escapees from DC that it's known as the Nation's Summer Capital – is more family orientated than other beach towns, lacking the nightlife of Ocean City but making up for it with miles of clean and uncrowded **sands**.

Rehoboth has less of a history than Lewes, though its wooden **boardwalk** is one of the last on the East Coast. It stretches along the Atlantic to either side of Rehoboth Avenue – always "The Avenue" – which acts as the main drag, its four short blocks clogged with souvenir shoppers browsing though the usual array of T-shirts and seaside tat. Most of the **restaurants** and **nightspots** are concentrated here, with *Thrashers French Fries* stands mixed in with the mock-Caribbean beach shack decor of the *Back Porch Café*, 59 Rehoboth Ave (☎227-3674), and boardwalk burger bars like *Obie's-by-the-Sea*, three blocks north; after dark, the action shifts to the Anglophile environs of the *Country Squire*, 19 Rehoboth Ave, which has the largest beer selection for miles.

Apart from the peak times of July and August, you shouldn't have much trouble finding a bed in one of Rehoboth's many **motels**: the *Sandcastle*, 61 Rehoboth Ave (☎227-0400 or 1-800/372-2112; ③), or the *Admiral*, a block south at 2 Baltimore Ave (☎227-2103 or 1-800/428-2424; ③), are right off the boardwalk, or if you want to avoid the crowds try *Adams Oceanfront*, a mile south of the center at 4 Read Ave in **Dewey Beach** (☎227-3030; ③). Room rates at all of the above can rise as high as $100 on summer weekends. For more information, contact the **Chamber of Commerce**, 501 Rehoboth Ave (☎227-2233 or 1-800/441-1329).

South of Rehoboth, **Delaware Seashore State Park** stretches for miles along a thin sandy peninsula, split by Hwy-1 and bound on the east by the Atlantic and on the west by various freshwater marshlands. There's little here apart from beachfront parking areas until you approach the Maryland border, where the concrete tower blocks of Bethany Beach do little to prepare you for the Costa del Sol-like concentrations of hotels and condos in **Ocean City**, ten miles further along (see p.341).

CHAPTER SIX

THE SOUTH

A s Mark Twain put it in 1882, "In the South, the [Civil] war is what AD is elsewhere; they date everything from it." Five generations later, the legacies of
years of slavery and the "War Between the States" are still evident throughout
the southern heartland states of **NORTH CAROLINA, SOUTH CAROLINA,
GEORGIA, KENTUCKY, TENNESSEE, ALABAMA, MISSISSIPPI** and
ARKANSAS. The war is the focus point for countless museums and shrines, and the
Confederate "Stars and Bars" flag remains conspicuous everywhere.

It's not, however, an area that's entirely stuck in its ways. Quite how far the "New
South" differs from the old is a matter for debate; but the last few decades have unquestionably seen the influx of high-tech industries, the emergence of liberal white politicians such as Jimmy Carter, and the growth of such dynamic urban centers as the go-
ahead black city of **Atlanta**, the birthplace of Dr Martin Luther King Jr and the venue
for the 1996 Olympics. It took suffering and bloodshed to effect the changes of the
Fifties and Sixties, but relations between black and white have improved – and are
essentially better than in many large cities elsewhere in the country.

The South has never been one uniform, homogeneous unit; even during the Civil War
there were substantial pockets of pro-Union support, particularly in the mountains.
Today the culture and make-up of the overwhelmingly black Mississippi Delta or South
Carolina are markedly different from the white hill farms in Kentucky and Tennessee,
where prohibition is still enforced. Likewise, the sun belt industries of North Carolina
and northern Alabama are far removed from the rural backwaters of southern Georgia.

However, the region still exhibits distinct social traits – particularly fundamentalist
religious views and authoritarian values – that set it apart from the rest of the country.
Life in the countryside is conducted at a slow, laid-back pace, with a code of rather
quaint manners that contrasts starkly with the impersonal edge of the bigger cities.
The much-vaunted **southern hospitality** really does exist, even if it remains tempered
by the continuing presence of rednecks.

The most exciting aspect of the southern heritage is undoubtedly its **music**.
Hundreds of thousands of fans make pilgrimages each year to the country and blues
meccas of **Nashville** and **Memphis**, the homelands of Elvis Presley, Hank Williams,
Robert Johnson, Dolly Parton and Otis Redding, and the backwoods barn dances in
Appalachia or the blues jook-joints of the Mississippi Delta and South Carolina. The
southern experience is also reflected in a rich regional **literature**, its communities and
people well documented by the likes of William Faulkner, Carson McCullers, Alice
Walker, Eudora Welty and the one-book-wonders Margaret Mitchell and Harper Lee.

ACCOMMODATION PRICE CODES

All accommodation prices in this book have been coded using the symbols below.
Note that prices are for the least expensive double rooms in each establishment.
For a full explanation see p.35 in *Basics*.

① up to $30	④ $60–80	⑦ $130–180
② $30–45	⑤ $80–100	⑧ $180+
③ $45–60	⑥ $100–130	

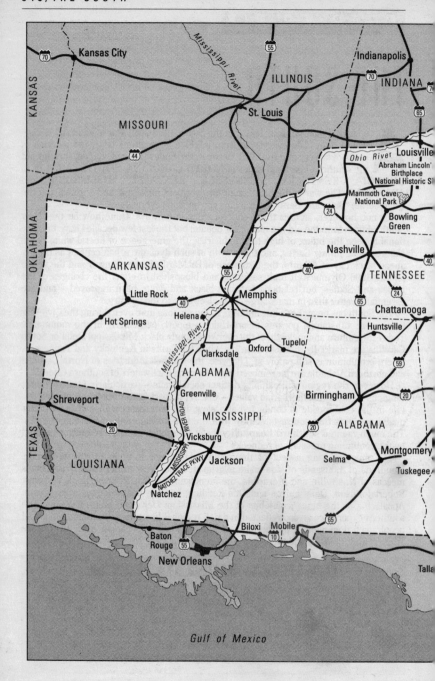

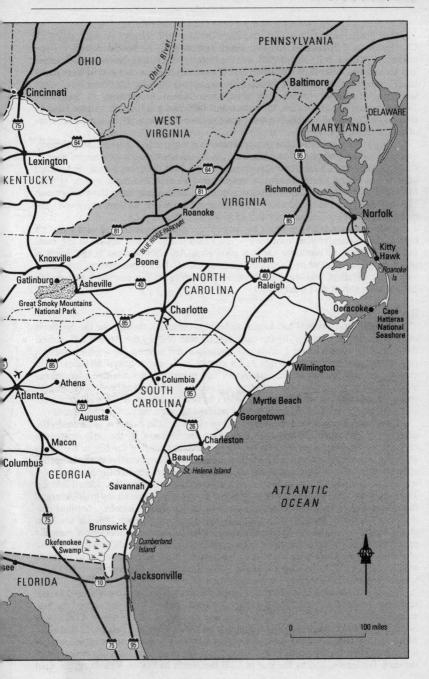

Other major destinations for travellers include the elegant coastal cities of **Charleston** and **Savannah**, frenzied beach resorts such as **Myrtle Beach**, college towns like **Athens** and **Chapel Hill**, and the historic Mississippi riverports of **Natchez** and **Vicksburg**. Away from the urban areas, much southern scenery consists of undulating, sun-scorched hillsides broken by occasional forests, but there are some surprises. Highlights include the misty Appalachian **mountains** of Kentucky, Tennessee and North Carolina, the subtropical **beaches** and tranquil **barrier islands** along both the Atlantic and Gulf coasts, and the river road through the tiny settlements of the flat Mississippi Delta.

During July and August, the **temperature** is mostly a very humid 90°F; virtually every motel, bar, restaurant and museum is air-conditioned, but you might want to schedule your visit a little either side of these months. On the coast, where the beaches offer a less expensive alternative to neighboring Florida, the main season is from Memorial Day to Labor Day, and outside of these dates many attractions are closed. The fall colors in the mountains (just as beautiful and a lot less expensive and congested than New England) are at their headiest during October.

Public transportation through the large rural expanses is poor. In any case, it's best to take things at your own pace – you'll find things to see and do in the most unlikely places – so renting a car is a good idea. **Accommodation** in the South is generally good value, while its varied **cuisine** includes highly calorific but irresistible soul food, excellent seafood, and the ubiquitous grits (maize porridge) and catfish (which has a sort of mild trout flavor).

History

The **Spanish** and **French** had begun to build settlements throughout the South as early as the 1520s. However, by the early seventeenth century the **British** had pushed them back to what are now Florida and Louisiana, and steered the region towards a role as supplier of **raw materials** to its **cotton** mills and **tobacco** factories. Both climate and soil favored staple agriculture, and massive labor-intensive **plantations** started to spring up. No self-respecting European would cross the Atlantic to pick cotton on a plantation, so the big landowners turned to **slavery** as the most profitable source of labor, importing Africans in their millions through the port of Charleston.

As the South became increasingly set in its ways, with little incentive to diversify, the northern states surged ahead in both agriculture and industry. By the early nineteenth century the southern economy was clearly subservient to that of the North: the South grew the crops, but northern factories monopolized the more lucrative **manufacturing** of finished goods. Southern politicians and plantation owners accused the North of political and economic aggression, and felt that unless slavery continued to spread into the Territories and even the free states, they would progressively lose all say in the future of the nation. The election as president in late 1860 of **Abraham Lincoln**, a hardline pro-northern candidate, brought the crisis to a head, and in February 1861 six southern states broke away to form the Confederate States of America. **Secession** radically upped the stakes in the controversy. Most northerners had been indifferent to the issue of slavery – even Lincoln, as late as mid-1861, said "I have no purpose . . . to interfere with slavery in the States where it exists" – but the potential destruction of the Union was seen as a far more serious – and treacherous – threat.

During the resultant **Civil War**, the South was outgunned and outsoldiered by the vast resources of the North. The Confederates fired the first shots and scored the first victory in April 1861 when the Union garrison at Fort Sumter (outside Charleston, South Carolina) surrendered. The Union was on the military defensive until mid-1862, when its navy blockaded the coast of Georgia and the Carolinas and occupied several key ports. Then Union forces in the west, under generals Grant and Sherman, swept through Tennessee, and by the end of 1863 the North had taken Vicksburg, the final

Confederate-held port on the Mississippi, as well as the strategic mountain-locked town of Chattanooga on the Tennessee–Georgia border. Grant proceeded north to Virginia while Sherman captured the transport nexus of Atlanta and began a bloody and ruthless march to the coast, burning everything in his way. With 228,000 men dead (a quarter of the South's adult white male population), defeat was total, and General Robert E Lee surrendered on April 9 1865 at Appomattox in Virginia.

The war was followed by a period of **Reconstruction**, when the South was occupied by Union troops. The political administrations imposed and run by northern Republicans ("carpetbaggers" or "scalawags") were characterized by corruption, but what galled southerners most was that blacks were also involved in government. When this probationary era came to an end in the mid-1870s, southern states returned to Democratic Party control; black politicians were intimidated out of office, in particular by the **Ku Klux Klan**, which was started in 1865 by ex-Confederate officers. "**Jim Crow**" segregation laws were imposed, and poll taxes, literacy tests and property qualifications disenfranchised virtually all blacks (and many poor whites).

The war left the South in chaos. One quarter of the white male population of military age was dead, and two thirds of Southern wealth had been destroyed. From controlling thirty percent of the nation's assets in 1860, the South was down to twelve percent in 1870, while the spur the war gave to industrialization meant that the North was booming. With the abolition of slavery, the plantations were no longer viable. Instead the southern economy turned to **sharecropping**, a crude barter system under which landowners provided their tenants with land, housing and even food and implements, the cost of which was later deducted (along with a high rate of interest) from the sale of crops. Most farms were too small to be economical, and sharecropping encouraged production of cash crops rather than food. As a result, the freed slaves benefited little from the abolition of the "peculiar institution": thousands were forced into debt, and and there were mass migrations to cities like Memphis and Atlanta, and to the North.

After the uncertainties of Reconstruction, industrial growth accelerated (the impetus coming ironically from northern investors who took advantage of the cheap land and labor), but by the time of the 1929 stock market crash the South still lagged well behind the North. During the **Depression**, the suffering of the region was exacerbated by the fact that its people were so poor to begin with. Roosevelt's New Deal programme, particularly the establishment of the TVA (see p.397) and road-building works, helped to alleviate immediate hardships and lay down an infrastructure to aid economic recovery, and the war effort during the early Forties stimulated industrial growth. Since the Sixties, foreign companies, particularly Japanese, have opened thousands of new factories in the South, attracted by the anti-union "Right to Work" statutes upheld by most states. What was the "Cotton Belt" now likes to go under the high-tech label of the "Sun Belt", but an overall lack of agricultural and industrial diversification still means that huge parts of the South remain overwhelmingly and disturbingly poor.

The political and legal advances of the New Deal started a more liberal trend in federal law-making. A groundbreaking 1954 Supreme Court ruling outlawed segregation in schools, but individual southern states were at best very slow to effect the required changes. The **civil rights movement**, which began when blacks campaigned for desegregation in education, soon expanded to encompass demonstrations and protests against racial barriers in other areas of life, such as the Montgomery bus boycott and the Greensboro lunch counter sit-in. Before civil rights legislation was finally imposed in the late Sixties, southern whites, led by fire-eating politicians, put up a bloody resistance to change, and left behind a catalogue of murder, attacks and harassment – particularly in Mississippi and Alabama. Modern travellers can follow in the footsteps of **Dr Martin Luther King Jr** throughout the South, from his birthhome in Atlanta, through his church in Montgomery, to the site of his assassination in Memphis, commemorated (somewhat inappropriately) by the National Civil Rights Museum.

The civil rights years left a marked effect on **party politics** in the South. Since the Civil War the region had voted almost en bloc for the **Democrats**, but as that party has become more identified with liberal reforms, greater government intervention and, especially, racial integration, there has been a marked shift towards the Republican Party, especially in presidential elections. Right-wing politicians have been forced to search for a party political home; Strom Thurmond of South Carolina and the equally vitriolic George Wallace campaigned for the US presidency under the banners of small segregationist parties, while the leading demagogue in the South today, Senator Jesse Helms of North Carolina, is a Republican. Nevertheless, many unreconstructed back-woodsmen still fight for white supremacy under the umbrella of the Democratic Party.

The dispossession of the **Native Americans** is often the forgotten chapter of south-ern history. Colonial powers at best tolerated the Indians, for the most part peaceful, agrarian tribes, and used them as allies in their imperialist wars with each other. However, after the Revolution, pressure from plantation owners and small farmers led to the forced removal in the 1830s of the "five civilized tribes" – the Cherokee, Creek, Choctaw, Chickasaw and Seminole – to malarial Oklahoma. Today only a few thousand Native Americans live in the South.

NORTH CAROLINA

NORTH CAROLINA, though the most industrialized of the southern states, remains relatively rural and poor, with just six million people spread over an area larger than England. It suffered heavily during the **Civil War**, and **Reconstruction** brought mixed fortunes: although the Democrats regained control in 1870, they ran a liberal administra-tion and were effective in stamping out the Ku Klux Klan. Since then there have been parallel traditions of radical black, and white racist, activity. **Greensboro**, for example, where **Jesse Jackson** served his political apprenticeship, was the site of the 1960 lunch-counter sit-in by black students, and also of the Greensboro Massacre of 1979 when Klansmen killed five people at a Communist Workers Party demonstration.

Geographically, North Carolina breaks down into three distinct areas: running from east to west, the coast, the Piedmont and the mountains. For visitors, the **coast** is much the most promising, with good beaches, beautiful landscapes and a fascinating history. The inner coast consists largely of the less developed **Albemarle Peninsula**, with colo-nial Edenton nearby. The **Piedmont** is dominated by manufacturing cities, and by the academic institutions of the Research Triangle: **Raleigh**, the state capital, **Durham**, home of prestigious Duke University, and villagey, trendy **Chapel Hill**. **Charlotte** bills itself as the next boom city of the South, but for the moment it's a boring mix of down-town skyscrapers and suburban malls. In the **mountains**, one of the most stunning stretches of Appalachia, the only towns of any size, Boone and Asheville, are linked by the spectacular **Blue Ridge Parkway**, while **Great Smoky Mountains National Park** overlaps the border with Tennessee.

Getting Around North Carolina

North Carolina's major **airports** are at Raleigh-Durham, a hub for *American Airlines*, and Charlotte, an arrival point for transatlantic flights on *British Airways*. A tiny airport at Manteo in the Outer Banks (☎1-800/927-3296) serves Norfolk, VA, four times daily, and has charter flights to Cape Hatteras and Ocracoke Island. Charlotte, Raleigh-Durham and Greensboro are served by *Amtrak* **trains**, but unfortunately there is no coastal route. Plenty of buses run within the Piedmont; schedules are much less frequent in the mountains and along the coast, both of which are best explored by car. The state has a good network of **cycling** routes along quiet country roads; for informa-tion contact the Dept of Transportation, 1 S Wilmington St, Raleigh (☎733-2804).

The North Carolina Coast

The North Carolina **coast**, which ranges through salt marshes, beaches, barrier islands and estuaries, holds most of the state's more interesting **historic sites**. The continent's earliest English colonists vanished inexplicably from **Roanoke Island** in 1590; just over three centuries later, the Wright brothers achieved the first powered flight at **Kitty Hawk**. The **Outer Banks**, the long reef of barrier islands which stretch down from Virginia, are in parts tacky and elsewhere beautifully unspoiled.

Edenton and the Albemarle

The huge and generally relaxed **Albemarle Peninsula** remains largely unexploited. Local towns try to make much of their **colonial history** – this was the first part of North Carolina to have permanent European settlements, around the end of the seventeenth century – but often there's not a lot left to see, except for restored eighteenth-century buildings that get a bit similar after a while.

Edenton

EDENTON, set along a beautiful Albemarle-Sound **waterfront** roughly forty miles back from the ocean and the same distance south of the Virginia border, was established as North Carolina's first state capital in 1722. A major center of unrest in the American Revolution, it remained a prosperous port until the early nineteenth century, when it began to fade. Today Edenton feels frozen some time around 1961.

As you stroll around the town – possibly aided by the self-guided walking tour issued by the **Barker House visitor center** (Mon–Sat 10am–4.30pm, Sun 2–5pm; ☎482-3663) – you'll come across an exceptional number of colonial and pre-Civil War **houses**, and the magnificent wooden **Cupola House**. St Paul's Parish Church and the Georgian Chowan County Courthouse overlooking the waterfront are fine mid-seventeenth-century structures. The **main street** is also interesting in an offbeat way: Victorian facades, old-fashioned drugstores selling home-mixed sodas, and Fifties chrome signs.

A narrated slide show at the visitor center covers colonial history well, but is less explicit about slavery. There's no mention of the remarkable **Harriet Jacobs**, a runaway slave who hid for seven years in her grandmother's attic. She finally escaped to the North through such ruses as disguising herself as a male sailor, and was eventually reunited in Boston with the two children she had had by a white man in Edenton. She wrote this amazing story as *Incidents in the Life of a Slave Girl*, which became one of the most famous published slave narratives of the nineteenth century. None of the buildings mentioned in the book is still standing, although you can get an idea of where places were from the map in the Harvard UP edition (1987).

Edenton is not a bad base for explorations of the coast. Among luxurious **B&Bs** is the *Trestle House Inn* on Soundside Rd (☎482-2282; ④), while budget **motels** include the *Coach House Inn*, 919 N Broad St (☎482-2107; ③), and the *Colonial Motel* (☎482-8010; ④) on Broad St/US-17 north, which puts on a good inexpensive **buffet** of Southern food.

Exploring the Albemarle

Albemarle **plantation** life can be sampled at **Hope**, the home of David Stone, a state governor and US senator of the revolutionary and Federal period. It's off Hwy-308, a few miles west of **Windsor**, about 25 miles southwest of Edenton (March to late Dec Mon–Sat 10am–4pm, Sun 2–5pm; $5). The house, built in 1803, is classic Southern myth: white, with a double balcony at the front, and filled with hand-carved wooden

The **area code** for the North Carolina coast is ☎910.

furniture. Admission includes entrance to the 1763 **King-Bazemore House**, a simple planter's home which holds demonstrations of colonial cooking in its working kitchen.

A clearer picture of slave life is given by **Somerset Place State Historic Site**, a plantation 25 miles southeast of Edenton at Cresswell on US-64 (summer Mon–Sat 9am–5pm, Sun 1–5pm; winter Tues–Sat 10am–5pm, Sun 1–4pm; free). This is how the lowland plantations must have looked, with fields dissolving into marshland beyond huge oaks. The wooden shacks of the slaves' quarters have gone, although you can see the foundations of the tiny shed-sized slave "hospital". The director of the site is descended from slaves who worked here.

There's a **campground** at the neighboring **Pettigrew State Park** on Phelps Lake (☎797-4475; $9), an area of mighty trees ranged around a shallow rainwater-fed lake, ideal for fishing. Even if you don't stay, take time to go down to the tiny museum at the water's edge, where the interesting display on local Native Americans includes a couple of 4000-year-old dugout canoes raised from the lake.

The southern shore of the Albemarle holds less to see, although it's pretty and unspoiled. The Memorial Museum in the city hall at **Belhaven**, 25 miles east of Washington (daily 1–5pm; free), houses an engaging collection of anything and everything, from dressed fleas (as silly as it sounds) to old tools and militaria.

The surrounding marshy countryside and tree-lined roads make for a pleasant drive, and **Lake Mattamuskeet Wildlife Refuge**, off Hwy-94 on the causeway across the lake or off US-264 near New Holland, is an amazing sight in winter, when thousands of swans migrate here from Canada. It's also a sanctuary for endangered osprey.

The Outer Banks

The **OUTER BANKS** are a series of long sand bars, sprinkled with sea oats, that stretch around 180 miles from the Virginia border to Cape Lookout, near Beaufort; a great place to wander along at your own speed, although unfortunately there's no public transportation apart from the ferries between islands and to the mainland.

The main road from the north, US-158, crosses from the mainland on a low bridge to the southern half of **Bodie Island**, where you're greeted by a roadside **visitor center** (☎261-4644). South along US-158 and the parallel shoreline Beach Road, the seaside towns of Kitty Hawk, Kill Devil Hills and Nag's Head are strung out without a break, and the fine warm-water **beaches** are lined with motels and fast-food places mixed in with the huge holiday "cottages". Note that when Outer Bank hotels describe themselves as "waterfront", it simply means they are on the coastal side of the road, not that they necessarily have ocean views.

Kitty Hawk and Roanoke Island

The **Wright Brothers National Memorial** (daily, summer 9am–7pm, winter 9am–5pm), a large granite fin atop a hill just off the main road at **KITTY HAWK**, commemorates the plucky Orville Wright's **first powered flight**, on December 17 1903. A lumpen boulder near the visitor center marks the spot where his first aircraft hit the ground, and successive numbered markers show the distance of each of his subsequent flights. A museum records the brothers' various experiments; after several years of trials with kites and gliders, visiting the Outer Banks for a few weeks at a time and living in makeshift shacks on the beach, they finally shook hands before launching their powered plane on a cold December morning. As one of the local lifeboatmen acting as ground crew remarked, "We couldn't help notice how they held on to each other's hand, sort o' like folks parting who weren't sure they'd ever see one another again." Wilbur asked the men "not to look too sad, but to . . . laugh and holler and clap . . . and try to cheer Orville up when he started." The phlegmatic Orville recorded the historic moment of take-off in his diary: "The machine lifted from the truck. . . . I found control of the front rudder quite difficult ... the machine would rise suddenly to about 10 ft and then as suddenly, on turning the rudder, dart for the ground ... time about 12 seconds."

ROANOKE ISLAND, between Bodie Island and the mainland via US-64/264 and another bridge, was the **first English settlement** in North America, founded by **Sir Walter Raleigh** in 1585. The colonists survived initial difficulties with weather, disease and Indians, and were joined by one hundred more settlers brought over by John White in 1587. When White returned three years later, however, all trace of the colony had disappeared, except for the one mysterious word "Croatoan" carved on a tree. Theories as to the fate of the "Lost Colony" have varied, although it was and is generally assumed that the settlers were massacred by hostile Indians – a key piece of early anti-Indian mythology. A rather fanciful but happier version has it that settlers and Indians banded together and marched inland, forming what is now the small and very racially mixed Lumbee tribe in southwest North Carolina.

Nothing authentic survives of Roanoke, but **Fort Raleigh**, three miles north of **Manteo** off US-64, is a conjectural and very tiny reconstruction of the colonists' earthwork fort, set in a wooded glade with a canopy of Spanish moss (daily 9am–5pm; free). Its museum explains local Indian interaction with colonists, and an outdoor amphitheater on the ocean hosts performances of *The Lost Colony*, an undeniably impressive drama (June–Aug, Mon–Sat 8.30pm; $10; ☎473-3414). In Manteo, *Elizabeth II* is a reconstruction of the **ship** used by Raleigh for his second voyage to the New World, in 1585. An excellent film in the visitor center illuminates life on board (April–Oct, daily 10am–6pm; Nov–March, Tues–Sun 10am–4pm; $3).

Good motels line the beaches north of Oregon Inlet. The *Comfort Inn*, MP 8 at Kill Devil Hills (☎480-2600; summer ⑤, winter ②), is one of the nicest, with an oceanfront pool and views of the Wright Memorial; the *First Colony Inn* is a plush B&B at 6720 S Virginia Dare Trail, Nags Head (☎441-2343; summer ⑥, winter ③). On Beach Road in Kill Devil Hills, the *Mex-Econo* (☎441-8226) – a Mexican restaurant with surf-punk decor, spray-painted toilets and good, cheapish food – doubles as a night-time music venue where punk and guitar rock bands play almost every night. Less frenetic is *Kelly's Restaurant*, 2316 S Croatan Hwy (☎441-4116), which serves delicious fresh seafood in a room filled with nautical memorabilia.

Cape Hatteras National Seashore

CAPE HATTERAS NATIONAL SEASHORE stretches south onto **Hatteras** and **Ocracoke** islands, with wonderful unspoiled beaches on its seaward side. Most tourists just drive straight through on Hwy-12, and even in high season you can pull off the road and walk across the dunes to deserted beaches. The salt marshes on the western side are also beautiful, and at the northern end of Hatteras Island the **Pea Island National Wildlife Refuge** has trails and observation platforms from which you can see a wide variety of birdlife. Over 600 ships have been wrecked along this treacherous stretch of coast since the sixteenth century. At the south end of Hatteras Island, near the early nineteenth-century black-and-white-striped **Cape Hatteras Lighthouse** (where you can climb the 208 feet to the top), a visitor center (daily 9am–5pm; free; ☎473-2111) holds displays on the island's maritime history. At Frisco, the **Native American Museum** is a loving collection of Indian arts and crafts, including a drum from a Hopi kiva (July–Aug daily 10am–8pm; Sept–June Fri–Sun 10am–8pm; free).

Various **motels**, food shops and adequate **restaurants** are scattered through the fly-blown settlements along Hwy-12. The *Cape Hatteras Motel* in Buxton (☎987-2345; ③) is a big hit with windsurfers; next door to a windsurfing store, it has a relaxed friendly atmosphere and a fish-cleaning station. **Camping** is best, however, at one of the summer-only, first-come, first-served, National Park Service campgrounds near Salvo, Buxton and Frisco. Ocracoke and Bodie Island ranger stations at the entrances to the seashore keep daily lists of what's available (or call ☎473-2111).

Ocracoke Island

OCRACOKE ISLAND (pronounced *oke-ruhcoke*) is forty minutes by ferry from Hatteras, and every bit as beautiful. The village of **Ocracoke**, at its southern tip, despite the crowds of tourists, somehow seems to have hung on to its village atmosphere, especially on the back lanes. There's nothing in particular to see, except perhaps for the harbor and squat brown lighthouse (you can't go in), and the tiny British World War II naval cemetery. You can see all this on a **trolley tour** from the *Trolley Stop* restaurant (on Hwy-12 as you come into the village; ☎928-1111; $3.50), although it's nicer just to walk or cycle – there are several **bike rental** places.

Hotels and B&Bs in Ocracoke village get full in summer, and are fairly expensive; as elsewhere on the Outer Banks, rates drop in September. The small *Sand Dollar Motel*, 123 Sand Dollar Lane (☎928-5571; ③), is reasonable, or you could sleep in one of the unusual "crows-nest" rooms in the *Island Inn and Dining Room* on Hwy-12 (☎928-4351; ③), whose restaurant is renowned for its crab cakes (☎928-7521; reserve). Other, less expensive, food options include the *Back Porch*, on the main street (☎928-6401). The fairly isolated Park Service **campground**, a few miles north, tends to be the first of the Outer Banks sites to fill up (you can reserve through *Ticketron*); commercial campgrounds in the village include *Beachcomber's* (☎928-4031).

Cape Lookout National Seashore

The mainland between Cedar Island and Beaufort is a rural backwater, sparsely settled and hardly touched by tourists. It's reasonably attractive to wander around, but towns such as **Davis** and **Smyrna** don't have any accommodation, and the most likely reason to pass through is to get to the all-but-deserted **CAPE LOOKOUT NATIONAL SEASHORE**, a narrow ribbon of sand stretching south of Ocracoke Island along two undeveloped Outer Banks, with no roads or habitation (park headquarters 3601 Bridges St, Morehead City ☎728-2250). Its few visitors share a total of around 55 miles of beach along both islands, with the marshes on the landward side supporting rich and unusual plant and bird life adapted to the harsh, salty conditions.

At the northern tip of the **north island**, across from Ocracoke, stand the pretty, strangely eerie ruins of the abandoned village of **Portsmouth**, whose last two residents left in 1971. The main ferry for the island, from **Atlantic** (Morris Marina, 3 per day each way; $12 return; ☎225-4261), lands fifteen miles south of Portsmouth, which you can only reach on foot. Two boatmen also carry groups of travellers to or from Ocracoke (Rudy Austin at ☎928-4361, or Dave McLawhorn at ☎928-5921; $15 per person). **Cabins** on the island, operated by the ferry company, cost around $10 per person; otherwise there's only primitive **camping**, with neither drinking water nor food available.

The **south island** is served in summer by two private ferries each way per day from Davis ($12 return; call Mr Alger Willis at ☎729-2791). Here, too, the ferry company manages some wood **cabins** (the smallest sleeps four people; all work out to $10 per

---

OCRACOKE FERRIES

In summer, **ferries** between Ocracoke and Hatteras leave both islands on the hour and half-hour all day, slightly less frequently before 7am and after 6.30pm. Winter sailings are on the hour all day until 6pm, then every two hours until midnight. The crossing takes forty minutes, although you may have to wait to get on in a car as there's limited space and it's loaded on a first-come, first-served basis.

Ferries from Ocracoke also head south down the coast to **Cedar Island** (2hr 15min; 8 daily each way in summer, 4 in winter; $1), and to **Swan Quarter**, on the Albemarle (2 per day all year; 2hr 30min; $1). Both require motorists to reserve in summer; at short notice you should get the day you want, if not the time. Call the port from which you want to leave: Ocracoke ☎928-3841; Cedar Island ☎225-3551; Swan Quarter ☎926-1111.

head if full). Camping is as primitive as on the north island, but the ferry will buy food for you on the mainland and bring it across, and water supply and showers are supposedly being laid on near the ferry landing. Another ferry runs to the southern tip of the south island from low-key Harker's Island, south of Smyrna, to within two miles of Cape Lookout itself and its lighthouse (*Carteret Boat Tours*, ☎728-3866; $12 return).

Shackleford Island, which does not form part of the National Seashore, is rather more varied, with high sand dunes roamed by wild horses and dwarf forests of trees hanging on in the harsh environment. Several places in Beaufort offer trips out – *Beaufort Tours* charges around $10 per person for a three- to four-hour trip (☎728-7827). They also do trips out to Carrot Island, in front of Beaufort harbor, for $5.

Beaufort

BEAUFORT, about 150 miles southeast of Raleigh just beyond the end of US-70, is probably the nicest of North Carolina's seaside towns: a relaxing place to hang out and drink cold beer, or just sit around on the waterfront. The **Maritime Museum** has good displays on local ecology and shipping history (Mon–Fri 9am–5pm, Sat 10am–5pm, Sun 2–5pm; free). In the restored area on Block Turner Street, off the waterfront, you'll find handsome **old houses**, an apothecary's shop, and the city jail. The main house serves as the town **visitor center** (Mon–Sat 9.30am–4.30pm; ☎728-5225).

B&Bs along Ann Street – named for Queen Ann, and still boasting an elm tree sent by her personally – include the forty-room *Beaufort Inn* (no 101; ☎728-2600; ③/⑤) and the friendly and intimate Victorian *Captains' Quarters* (no 315; ☎728-7711; ③/⑤), which has a wraparound verandah. Rates increase considerably in summer. **Morehead City**, a couple of miles down the coast, and the Bogue Bank resorts offer plenty of motels.

The Beaches

South of Beaufort, the beaches along the twenty-mile offshore **Bogue Bank** are always pretty crowded, especially at **Atlantic Beach** at the east end and marginally less so at **Emerald Isle**, to the west. On **Bear Island** to the south, though – reached by a summer-only ferry ($2) with a strict limit on the number of daily passengers – the stunning **Hammocks Beach State Park** has high sand dunes, a wooded shore and perfect beaches. The entrance is two miles west of **Swansboro**; register at the small park center if you want to **camp** ($4; ☎326-4881). No camping is permitted on the few days around each full moon when **loggerhead sea turtles** come ashore to lay their eggs.

On the far side of the Camp Lejeune US Marine base, **Topsail Island**, yet another sand bar of resorts, is considerably less built up than Bogue Bank, presumably because its beaches aren't quite as good. **Surf City** and **Topsail** are both slightly run-down family resorts, with shabby motels and campgrounds. Public beach access points are signposted from the main road, but in practice you can get down at lots of other places.

South on the mainland the resorts get bigger and more crowded, but are still fairly manageable. At the tip of the peninsula near Kure, **Fort Fisher State Historic Site** commands a spectacular rocky site overlooking both the sea and the mouth of the Cape Fear River. A small museum focuses on its days as a Confederate stronghold (summer Mon–Sat 9am–5pm, Sun 1–5pm; winter Tues–Sat 10am–4pm, Sun 1–4pm).

Wilmington

Though it's the largest town on North Carolina's coast, **WILMINGTON**, set back along the Cape Fear River fifty miles short of the southern border, has a welcoming down-home feel. During the Civil War, it was briefly the Confederacy's most important harbor, exporting cotton all over the world. "**Blockade-runners**" would attempt to outrun the

Union navy, racing into the safety of Fort Fisher's guns; "Rebel Rose" Greenhow, glamorous Confederate spy, drowned here during a run in 1864. Dozens of blacks were murdered in Wilmington by white mobs in the **Race Riot** of 1898 – a backlash to the election of a "Fusionist" (Republican-Populist-black) governor two years earlier.

Despite its traumatic past, Wilmington today is attractive and friendly, with a historic district, starting on the south side of Market Street and stretching east along Third Street, that feels genuinely lived-in. At 814 Market St, the free **Cape Fear Museum** (Tues–Sat 9am–5pm, Sun 2–5pm) gives a lively account of local history. The extravagant houses, ornate City Hall, and lovely old *Italian Theatre* demonstrate Wilmington's former wealth, while the cobbled streets of the **waterfront**, dotted with laid-back cafés and restaurants, are nice, if a bit too picturesque for their own good. Chandler's Wharf, an upmarket shopping mall in a restored warehouse, is typical of the area's revitalization, while the Old City market sells crafts and food in a more authentic atmosphere (Thurs–Sun). The town is also famed as the base of the *CarolCo* film company (it's on 23rd St, but there's little to see), until recently owned by Dino de Laurentis and responsible for such productions as *Blue Velvet* and *Teenage Mutant Ninja Turtles*.

Practicalities

Wilmington's **visitor center** is at 24 West Third St (☎341-4030). The **bus** station is at 201 Harnett St, a mile north of downtown off Third St (☎762-6625). When the movie stars come to town, they stay at the *Graystone Inn* on Dock and Third, with its comfortable library and shady patio (☎763-2000; ⑥); another nice alternative is to head a dozen miles east to the sea island of Wrightsville Beach, where among the string of weather-worn condos the *Holiday Inn*, 1706 N Lumino Ave (☎256-2231; ⑤), has comfortable rooms. Budget **motels** line US-17. The nearest **campground** is *Camelot Campground*, seven miles north on US-17 (☎686-7705; $13 per tent).

The town has a fairly thriving nightlife – even a small gay scene. *Crooks by the River*, 138 S Front St (☎762-8898), is an artsy hang-out serving fabulous Cajun and Southern **food**. Students and seasalts gather on the waterfront patio of the *Ice House Bar*, 115 S Water St (☎762-8898), to hear live jazz and blues, while the nearby *Barbary Coast*, 116 Front St, is a hole-in-the-wall bar much favored by Mickey Rourke.

The North Carolina Piedmont

North Carolina's **Piedmont** is a fairly industrialized area of textile and tobacco towns, mostly in decline. However, even close to the towns it can still be very rural, little changed since the 1950s. The main area of interest is the **Research Triangle** trio of neighboring college towns – **Raleigh**, the capital; relaxed **Durham**, with its strong black community; and countercultural **Chapel Hill**. **Charlotte**'s international airport provides a point of arrival for many European visitors.

Raleigh

RALEIGH, North Carolina's capital, stands on I-40 at the very heart of the state, focusing around the central, pedestrianized Capitol Square. The **Capitol** itself is worth a look if only to see the copy of Canova's bizarre statue of George Washington in Roman garb (Mon–Fri 8am–5pm, Sat 9am–5pm, Sun 1–5pm; free). Almost next door, the new **North Carolina Museum of History**, 109 E Jones St (Tues–Sat 9am–5pm, Sun 1–6pm; free) is impressively far-reaching, a chronological trot through the state's history from the viewpoint of its people, with particularly strong sections on women.

The **area code** for Raleigh and the Research Triangle is ☎919.

At lunchtime a trolley (10¢) shuttles between downtown and the four-block **city market** ranged around Martin Street and Moore Square, which holds a number of good shops and restaurants; you can watch local artists and sculptors at work in *Artspace*, 201 E Davie St (Tues–Fri 9am–5pm; Sat 10am–5pm). A little way out to the north, the impressive **North Carolina Museum of Art**, 2110 Blue Ridge Blvd (Tues–Thurs & Sat 9am–5pm, Fri 10am–9pm, Sun noon–5pm; tours daily 1.30pm; free) has an eclectic display of works from Africa and the USA. It also boasts a particularly good restaurant open for lunch from Tuesday to Sunday, tea and cakes Friday to Sunday, and dinner on Friday (☎833-3548). **Andrew Jackson** was born in a tiny hut just north of where the Capitol now stands; his birthplace has since been moved to Mordecai Historic Park, 1 Mimosa St (March to mid-Dec, Tues–Fri 10am–3pm, Sat 1.30–3.30pm; free). Here you can also see the **Mordecai House**, built by a wealthy plantation owner and continuously inhabited by the same family for the next two centuries. Inside, a delightfully ragbag display records the lives of all who lived there, including the slaves.

Practicalities

Raleigh/Durham **airport** (☎840-2123) is off I-40, fifteen minutes northwest of town. The taxi ride costs around $15, various circuitous shuttle services about $8. One daily *Amtrak* train passes on its way to New York, another on the way to Florida, drawing in at 320 W Cabarrus St. The *Greyhound* station is in a seedy part of downtown at 321 W Jones St (☎828-2567). There's a tourist office at 800 S Salisbury St (Mon–Fri 8.30am–5pm; ☎833-4636). The **visitor center** at 301 N Blount St (Mon–Fri 8am–5pm, Sat 9am–5pm, Sun 1–5pm; ☎733-3456) coordinates local walking and driving tours.

If you want to **stay**, avoid the anonymous downtown hotels and head out to Hillsborough Street near the university, where the *Velvet Cloak Inn* at no 1505 offers stylish, arty decor, free coffee and an indoor pool (☎828-0333; ⑤). At the *Quality Suites Hotel*, close to downtown at 4400 Capital Blvd, the breakfast and evening buffet are included in the price of the spacious rooms (☎876-2211 or 1-800/228-5151; ③).

Big Ed's, in the city market at 220 Wolfe St (☎836-9909), makes Southern **home-cooking** into a fine art. The breakfasts, in particular, are amazing: plates piled high with eggs, link sausage, crispy pork medallions and fluffy biscuits soaked in molasses, served in a chatty room strewn with memorabilia from the family farm. More upmarket, but just as popular, the huge *42nd St Oyster Bar*, downtown at West and Jones (☎831-2811), is always buzzing with journalists, politicians and students enjoying splendid fresh fish and seafood. Hillsborough Street, lined with bars, clubs and cafés, is the epicenter of Raleigh's excellent **nightlife**. Try *Cup a Joe* (no 3100; ☎828-9665), a bohemian coffee bar with live folk music on Friday and Saturday, or, for alternative music, the *Five O Café*, above the *Studio* arts cinema (no 2526; ☎821-4419).

Durham and Chapel Hill

Unlike the other two Research Triangle towns, Durham, twenty miles northwest of Raleigh, emphasizes its vibrant **black heritage**. The **Hayti Heritage Center**, 804 Old Fayetteville St (☎ 683-1709), hosts theater, talks and exhibitions on all aspects of the African-American experience; the center is named after the Hayti district, a black community which thrived from the 1920s until the 1960s, until Hwy-137 decimated the area. Based in a number of surprisingly small old plantation homes, seven miles north of town in rural Treburne Park, the **Stagville Center** is not a museum as such, but hosts various workshops and living history demonstrations, illustrating plantation life from the early 1800s to Reconstruction through the work of the local black craftworkers.

Durham found itself at the center of the nation's tobacco industry after farmer Washington Duke came home from the Civil War with the idea of producing cigarettes – by 1890 he and his three sons had formed the **America Tobacco Company**, one of the nation's most powerful businesses. You can trace Washington Duke's rise from humble farmer at the **Duke Homestead Historical Site**, 2828 Duke Homestead Rd about a half-mile north of I-85 (April–Oct Mon–Sat 9am–5pm, Sun 1–5pm; Nov–March Tues–Fri 9am–5pm, Sat 10am–1pm, Sun 2–5pm; free). In addition to Duke's home, there are frequent living history demonstrations, the original curing barn piled high with fragrant sheaves of the golden tobacco leaf, and a fascinating museum on the social history of tobacco farming, which explores subjects from tobacco auctions to cigarette marketing in an even-handed and lively manner.

Duke University

In 1924 the Duke family's $40 million endowment to the previously small-scale Trinity College enabled it to expand into a world-respected medical research facility, swiftly changing its name to **Duke University**. Today it is well worth stopping by the campus; on the original, east side the **Museum of Art** (Tues–Fri 9am–5pm, Sat 11am–2pm, Sun 2–5pm; free) has good African, pre-Columbian, medieval and Asian collections. The splendid Gothic west campus centers on the soaring cathedral-style chapel (daily 8.30am–5pm), which boasts one of the most powerful *Flentrop* organs in the world. Still on campus, the terraces and bowers of the beautifully landscaped Sarah P Duke Gardens are a blaze of fragrance and color surrounded by pine forest.

Chapel Hill

The village atmosphere of **Chapel Hill**, on the southwest outskirts of Durham, has been given a hip edge in recent years with the rise to national prominence of local grunge bands such as Superchunk. About fifty percent of the 40,000 population are students, and its position as a bastion of white liberalism in a poor rural state gives the town a slightly complacent air; that said, it's a pleasant enough place to hang out for a while, joining the hordes of students in the laid-back bars and restaurants along **Franklin Street**, fringing the north side of campus.

The **University of North Carolina**, dating from 1795, was the nation's first state university and holds some fine eighteenth-century buildings. The earliest is **Old East**, its original brick painted a fashionable tan in the 1840s. Evidence of the university's wealth can be seen at the splendid **Morehead Planetarium**, E Franklin St (free; star shows $3; ☎549-6863), boasting a star-gazing theater with a 68ft dome. Free guided tours of campus leave from the west entrance of the Planetarium (☎962-0045).

On Hwy-12 from Durham, **Patterson's Mill Country Store**, at the end of a rutted country lane, looks straight out of *The Waltons*, selling everything from old signs and used books to crafts, candy, soap and spices. A back room is stuffed with intriguing vials and potions; upstairs there's a bewildering panoply of tobacco memorabilia.

Practicalities

Greyhound buses draw into Durham at 820 Morgan St (☎687-4800), and to downtown Chapel Hill at 311 W Franklin St (☎942-3356). Pick up maps and local bus information from the **Greater Durham Chamber of Commerce**, 2011 N Roxboro St (☎682-2133), whose foyer is open until midnight, or Chapel Hill's **welcome center** at 113 W Franklin St (Tues–Sat 10am–4pm; ☎929-9700).

Chapel Hill is much the nicer place to **stay**, though its few hotels are often booked up; one of the most popular is the 1920s *Carolina Inn* at 211 Pittsboro St on campus, a block from downtown (☎933-2001; ③). The elegant *Siena Hotel*, 1505 E Franklin St (☎929-4000 or 1-800/223-7379; ⑤), has a good Italian restaurant.

Durham's **Brightleaf Square**, an upbeat, upmarket shopping area of restored tobacco warehouses, is a good bet for **restaurants**; try *Anotherthyme*, 109 N Gregson St, serving creative Californian-style food with no red meat. In Chapel Hill, *Crooks Corner* on Franklin St (☎929-7643) serves cordon bleu Southern cooking such as shrimp and grits or fried chicken and greens in smart surroundings. *He's Not Here*, 112 W Franklin St (☎942-7939), one of Chapel Hill's most relaxed hang-outs, has regular live bands.

Durham has historically been at the center of the North Carolina Piedmont **blues** scene, with musicians such as Reverend Gary Davis playing for tips in the 1920s at the tobacco markets in town. It hosts the Bull Durham Blues Festival in late September.

Charlotte

More than anywhere else in the region, **CHARLOTTE**, at the junction of I-77 and I-85 near the South Carolina border, can genuinely claim to have made it, a banking and transportation center that has become the largest city in the state. It has been "boosted", in much the same way as Atlanta, by ambitious business and city leaders. They like to project the image of a sophisticated, fast-lane cultural metropolis, but in fact it's somewhat soulless – it could be anywhere. Served by direct *British Airways* flights from London, however, it does make a less abrasive point of arrival in the country than the larger cities of the north.

Downtown Charlotte, known as "uptown", is an unlovely mass of skyscrapers and concrete. The medium-sized **Mint Museum of Art**, three miles east at 2730 Randolph Rd on bus #15 (Tues 10am–10pm, Wed–Sat 10am–5pm, Sun 1–6pm; $4), has a good array of Indian, pre-Columbian and African art plus historical items. The **Spirit Square Arts Center**, 345 N College St (☎1-800/922-6431; galleries Tues–Sat noon–6pm), has more art, and stages performances by the city's theater company and symphony orchestra. **Discovery Place**, 301 N Tryon St, is a kids-oriented science museum with an indoor rainforest and an Omnimax theater hosting the nation's largest planetarium (June–Aug Mon–Wed 9am–6pm, Thurs 9am–8pm, Fri & Sat 9am–9pm, Sun 1–8pm, Sept–May Mon–Fri 9am–5pm, Sat 9am–6pm, Sun 1–6pm; $5).

Paramount's **Carowinds Theme Park** (variable hours; daily early June to mid-Aug, Sat & Sun only Sept, Oct, March & April; ☎588-2600 or 1-800/888-4FUN; $22.95), ten miles south of Charlotte on I-77, is a vast conglomeration of enjoyable Americana. As well as roller coasters and other rides, Carolinan theme areas include "Blue Ridge Junction", while movie fans will relish the chance to meet sundry *Star Trek* characters and to ride the *Days of Thunder* simulator, roaring at 200mph in a stock car.

Practicalities

Charlotte's **airport** (☎359-4000), seven miles west of town on Old Dowd Rd or I-85, is served by **buses** during rush hours; **taxis** cost about $11. *Amtrak* is at 1914 Tryon St, and *Greyhound/Trailways* at 601 W Trade St (☎527-9393). The **visitor center** is at 122 E Stonewall St (Mon–Fri 8.30am–5pm, Sat 10am–4pm, Sun 1–4pm; ☎371-8700).

Most of Charlotte's identical **hotels** are aimed at the conference trade, with the less expensive ones concentrated away from the center, on I-85 and I-77. Downtown's best value can be found at the *City Center Inn*, 601 N Tryon St (☎333-4733; ②), while the tiny *Elizabeth B&B* offers two pretty rooms in an old neighborhood nearby, at 2145 E Fifth St (☎358-1368; ③/④). Of the city's many restaurants, you can enjoy cordon bleu delicacies in the *Lamplighter*, downtown at 1065 E Morehead St (☎372-5343) – reservations and jacket advised. The highly popular *Catherine's on Providence*, 829 Providence Rd (☎372-8199; closed Sun, lunch only Mon–Wed), is just as good, serving a constantly changing menu in a cosy candlelit setting. There's also a fairly active **music** scene; good live jazz can be heard at *The Jazz Cellar at Jonathan's*, 330 N Tryon St (☎332-3663), set in an expensive downtown restaurant, and country music just south of the city at *Lil' Gilleys*, 2740 Carowinds Blvd (☎548-1324). For full listings, get hold of the *Charlotte Observer*.

> The **area code** for Charlotte and the mountains is ☎704.

The North Carolina Mountains

The best way to see the **mountains** of North Carolina is from the pristine **Blue Ridge Parkway**, which runs across the northwest from Virginia (see p.322) to the Great Smoky Mountains National Park. It's a delight to drive; the vast panoramic expanses of forested hillside, with barely a settlement in sight, may astonish travellers fresh from the crowded centers of the east coast. This predominantly poor region is a traditional bastion of **bluegrass** music, as played by Doc Watson and Earl Scruggs.

The Blue Ridge Parkway

The peak tourist season for the **Blue Ridge Parkway** is October, when the leaves of the deciduous trees which cover the landscape turn from bright yellow and gold through browns to vivid red. All year round, however, this magnificent, twisting mountain road – largely built in the 1930s by Roosevelt's Civilian Conservation Corps volunteers – is a worthwhile vacation destination in itself, peppered with state-run campgrounds, short hiking trails, and dramatic overlooks. When planning your itinerary, take note that though the Parkway is closed to commercial vehicles, and only particularly crowded near one or two hyped beauty spots, the constant curves make it difficult to average anything approaching the 45mph speed limit.

Not far from the Virginia border, the summer-only *Bluffs Lodge* stands at 3750 feet in a stunning clearing, just east of the Parkway at milepost 241 (☎919/372-4499; ④), with a coffee shop and gas station on the Parkway itself.

Boone

BOONE is the most obvious northern base for exploring the mountains; the town itself holds little of interest, though as home to Appalachian State University it does have a life of its own. Corny family entertainments dot US-321 – the three-mile steam-driven *Tweetsie Railroad* is all that's left of a line across the mountains to Johnson City, TN (summer daily 9am–6pm; $13) – while pretty back roads hold offbeat settlements such as **Valle Crucis** on US-194, where the 1883 *Mast General Store* is still thriving.

Greyhound/Trailways, Boone's only long-distance transportation connection, use the station on Winkler's Creek Rd at the heart of the local *AppalCART* bus network. Bargain central **accommodation** can be had at the *Boone Trail Motel*, 820 E King St (☎264-8839; ①); alternatives south of downtown near the **visitor center** (☎264-2225) on Blowing Rock Rd (US-321) include the *Cabana Motel* (☎264-2483; ②). A mile east, the *Lovill House Inn* at 404 Old Bristol Rd (☎264-4204 or 1-800/849-9466; ④) is a pleasant little B&B. Students flock to the *Tumbleweed Grille* across from the ASU baseball field downtown (☎264-7111), which serves reasonable, filling and cheap Mexican food; nearby, the *Red Onion Café* (☎264-5470) is more sophisticated but still good value. Live music venues – especially at weekends – include *Shadracks* on Blowing Rock Rd (☎264-1737) and the *Depot St Music Hall*, 110 S Depot St (☎262-5483).

South Along the Parkway

Eight miles south of Boone, **BLOWING ROCK** is a pleasant if touristy resort just south of the Parkway, though the "Blowing Rock" itself (daily 8am–7pm; $4) – named for the legend that items such as lovelorn Indians falling from it will be blown back up by the wind – is nothing like as impressive as photos suggest. At the nearby **Parkway Craft Center** (☎295-7938), you can see traditional folk crafts being made. The **visitor center** (☎295-7851) is on the main street, together with **motels** such as the *Boxwood* (☎295-9984; ②). Just north of town, the *AYH*-affiliated **hostel** at the **Blowing Rock Assembly Grounds** (☎295-7813; $11) is a favorite haunt of Christian groups; the least expensive local **campground** is at **Julian Price Park** on the Parkway (☎963-5911; $9). At

MOUNTAIN ACTIVITIES

Organized **outdoor pursuits** available along the Blue Ridge Parkway include excellent **whitewater rafting** and **canoeing**, most of it on the Nolichucky River near the Tennessee border south of Johnson City, TN, but also on the Watauga River and Wilson Creek. Companies running trips include *Wahoo* (☎1-800/444-7238), based near Boone, and *High Mountain Expeditions* (☎295-4200) in Blowing Rock. Expect to pay around $20 for half a day, $40 for a full day (safety equipment included).

Winter sees **skiing** at a number of slopes and resorts, particularly around **Banner Elk**, 12 miles southwest of Boone. Resort accommodation is expensive, lift passes less so ($18–27 for each weekday). *Appalachian Ski Mountain* (☎1-800/322-2373) is near Blowing Rock, and *Ski Beech* (☎1-800/222-2293) is at Beech Mountain; you can pick up full lists at visitor centers. A few places also offer **cross-country skiing**, at $50 for a day tour.

Woodland's, on Hwy-12, the pork barbecue is excellent; it's also a good spot to drink beer, as is the back porch of *Holley's* (☎295-7661).

Holley's has a fine view of the privately owned **Grandfather Mountain** (5964ft), fifteen miles further south and entered near milepost 304 (daily, summer 8am–7pm, winter 8am–5pm; $9). Prices may be high, but the prospect from the top, and the "mile-high swinging bridge" between the peaks, is superb. Bears and other animals are held in habitat settings, and hang-gliders launch from the top. During the **Highland Games** and "Gathering of the Clans" in the second week in July, distantly Scottish Americans dress up in kilts and pretend to have just come in off the bonnie braes.

Of various short and easy **trails** off the Parkway hereabouts, the one leading half a mile or so up to **Rough Ridge**, near milepost 301, is especially enjoyable. Rough Ridge is one of several access points to the 11.5-mile **Tanawha Trail**, which runs along the ridge above the Parkway from Linn Cove to Julian Price Park, looking out over the lush dense forests to the east. If you plan a longer backpacking trip, equip yourself with a large-scale Forest Service map, widely available in camping stores; though the actual walking is not that difficult, it's not hard to lose yourself in the woods.

Another good hike heads through the **Linville Gorge Wilderness**, near milepost 316 a couple of miles outside Linville Falls village. The high and spectacular **Linville Falls** themselves are at one end of the wilderness; trails descend into the gorge at intervals from the dirt road which climbs from the falls parking lot. Breathtaking views from either side of the gorge look down 2000 feet to the **Linville River** below, which has perfect, long, deep swimming pools. Be warned that ascents are steep, and some of the fainter paths are near-jungle. You can also climb **Hawksbill** or **Table Rock** mountains from the nearest unsurfaced Forest Road, which leaves Hwy-181 south of the village of Jonas Ridge (signposted "Gingercake Acres", with a small low sign to Table Rock).

The unremarkable but amiable villages of **Linville** and **Linville Falls** have the usual **motels** and restaurants; Linville Falls also holds a **campground** (☎765-2681), and *Spears Restaurant* (☎765-2658) is worth a detour for its hickory-smoked pork barbecue.

The views from the Parkway in the **Mount Mitchell State Park** area, south towards Asheville, are tremendous. Sadly, however, this is largely because the trees around the summit of Mount Mitchell – the highest point in the eastern US, at 6684 feet – have been ravaged by acid rain from coal-burning industries in the Chattanooga Basin to the west, and the large barren patches leave the horizon clear.

Twenty miles southeast of the Parkway on US-64/74, the natural rock tower of **Chimney Rock** sticks out from the almost-sheer side of Hickory Nut gorge (8.30am–6pm; $7). After taking the elevator to the top, you can clamber over smaller nearby formations and walk on steps or protected walkways along the impressive cliffs. Many of the climactic moments of the movie *Last of the Mohicans* were filmed here; you may recognize the mighty waterfall which drops 400ft from the western end of the gorge.

Asheville

Encircled by a ring of interstates, and skirted to the east and south by the Parkway, modest **ASHEVILLE**, roughly 100 miles southwest of Boone, retains an appealing downtown core. Two miles south on Biltmore Ave, the **Biltmore Estate** is the largest private mansion in the US (daily 9am–5pm; $21.95). Built in the late nineteenth century by George Vanderbilt and loosely modelled on a Loire château, it's a wildly extravagant piece of nouveau riche folly; visits are expensive but entertaining, from the Victorian chic of the indoor palm court and banquet hall to the stately landscaped gardens.

Asheville's *Greyhound/Trailways* terminal (☎253-5353) is inconveniently located at 2 Tunnel Rd, two miles out of downtown on bus #13 or #14A. Central **motels** include the *Interstate*, 37 Hiawassee St (☎254-0945; ③), and the *American Court*, 85 Merrimon Ave (☎253-4427; ③); the *Beaufort House*, 61 N Liberty St (☎254-8334; ⑤), is a very grand **B&B** in spacious grounds north of downtown. The nearest **campground** is *Bear Creek RV Park*, 81 S Bear Creek Rd, off I-40 to the west (☎253-0798). The *Windmill* on E Tunnel Rd (☎253-5285) serves a surprisingly successful melange of Italian, east European and Indian dishes. *Stone Soup*, 50 Broadway St (☎255-7687), is a cooperative soup and sandwich place, closed in the evenings; in fact nightlife is pretty quiet, although *Bill Stanley's Barbeque and Bluegrass*, 20 S Spruce St (☎253-4871), is a good barbecue joint where you can hear live bluegrass and see "clogging" (clog-dancing).

Pick up information on the numerous local summer music and craft festivals at the downtown **visitor center**, 151 Haywood St (☎258-6111 or 1-800/453-2961). August's **Mountain Dance and Folk Festival** features bluegrass and traditional dancing, while the hugely enjoyable **Black Mountain Folk Festival**, held in mid-May, fourteen miles east on I-40 (1 bus a day), showcases Appalachian and world folk music, usually attracting major European and African musicians. At *McDibb's Traditional Music Café*, 119 Cherry St in Black Mountain (☎669-2456), you can hear folk and blues year-round.

Great Smoky Mountains National Park

West of Asheville, **GREAT SMOKY MOUNTAINS NATIONAL PARK** is the most visited National Park in the US. It straddles the border with Tennessee, and is covered in more detail – with a map – in our Tennessee section on p.415. In summer and fall, the North Carolina approaches to the park are every bit as clogged with traffic as those in Tennessee, and all accommodation can be booked up weeks in advance.

The largest of the possible bases is **CHEROKEE**, where a few Cherokee managed to hang on when the tribe was "removed" along the Trail of Tears to Oklahoma in 1838 (see p.552). Now known as the "Eastern Band of the Cherokee Nation", they have a small reservation on the edge of the park, which derives its main income from tourism. As a result, Cherokee itself is a mass of fast-food restaurants, cornily named motels and tacky gift shops, where the sentimentalized presentation of Indians as noble savages all but equates them with the bears of the park as just another novelty for tourists.

Away from the kitsch and cliché, however, the **Museum of the Cherokee Indian** at the north end of town (mid-June to Aug Mon–Sat 9am–8pm, Sun 9am–5pm; otherwise daily 9am–5pm; $3.50) has good archeological displays and sections on Cherokee arts and history – including Sequoyah's invention of a syllabary in 1821, to preserve the oral Cherokee culture in writing. *Qualla Arts and Crafts*, across the street, is a Cherokee-run cooperative selling traditional crafts, principally basketwork. Nearby, the **Oconaluftee Indian Village** (mid-May to Oct daily 9am–5.30pm; $8) is a reconstruction of a mid-eighteenth-century Cherokee village. Amid the log cabins, you can see demonstrations of weaving and basketmaking, as well as crafts and skills that have long since died out, such as dugout canoe construction and blowpipe hunting.

Cherokee is not much of a place to stay, without a single passable place to eat, and is unbelievably dead between about October and March. Of over fifty motels (lists from

the visitor center, ☎1-800/438-1601), the central *Thunderbird* (☎497-2212; ③) is a typical, perfectly adequate, budget option. As a reservation town, Cherokee is entirely dry.

The **Oconaluftee visitor center**, the headquarters of the North Carolina side of the
park, is a short way out of Cherokee along US-441 (summer 8am–7pm; spring and fall
8am–6pm; winter 8am–5pm; admission to the park is free; ☎497-9146). Besides good
displays on Appalachian farming life, there's a re-creation of a **pioneer village**.

Southwestern North Carolina

The area west of Asheville, and south of the national park, holds a number of dramatic
waterfalls. **Looking Glass Falls**, about twelve miles south of the Parkway on US-276,
is in a particularly beautiful section of the **Pisgah National Forest**. The falls drop 85
feet, with a great (albeit very cold) swimming hole at the bottom. **Connestee Falls**, a
few miles south on US-276 towards Brevard, is a double waterfall, even higher.
Unbridled optimists can pay to pan for **gemstones**, such as rubies, at outwashes of the
numerous gem mines near the 250ft **Cullasaja Falls**, further west on US-64.

The far west corner is famous for its superb **whitewater**, with canoeing and rafting on
the **Nantahala River**. Masses of guided raft expeditions charge around $25 for a three-
hour trip; one company, *Nantahala Outdoor Center* (☎488-6900 or 1-800/232-7238), also
runs a **youth hostel** (☎488-2175; ①). *Nantahala Rafts* (☎1-800/245-7700) is based a
couple of miles south by the river.

West of the Nantahala, off US-129 almost in Tennessee, **Joyce Kilmer National
Forest** is worth a final detour, as one of the last remaining stands of unlogged virgin
forest in the southeast. Some hardwood trees have grown to a huge size.

SOUTH CAROLINA

The relatively small state of **SOUTH CAROLINA** remains, with Mississippi, one of the
poorest and most rural pockets of the US. Politics in the first state to secede from the
Union in 1860 have traditionally been conservative. Reconstruction was mired in terrible Klan violence, while turn-of-the-century demagogues openly espoused lynching and
enforced "Jim Crow" laws with frightening zeal. It contains two of the country's most
right-wing minor universities – football-fixated Clemson, and Christian Bob Jones
University in Greenville, a training ground for the fundamentalist right.

South Carolina's fascinating subtropical coastline of **sea islands**, great beaches,
marshes and lush palmetto groves preserves traces of a virtually independent black
culture (featuring the unique patois *gullah*), from the days when slaves escaped the
mainland plantations. Beyond the grand old peninsular port of **Charleston**, arguably the
most elegant city in the US with its rainbow-colored old buildings and magnificent tree-
lined avenues, restored plantations stretch as far north as **Georgetown**, en route
towards the poseur's paradise of **Myrtle Beach**. Inland, the rolling Piedmont and flat
coastal plain hold little to see.

Getting Around South Carolina

Charleston has South Carolina's biggest **airport**, with flights to and from major towns
on the east coast. Three *Amtrak* routes cut through the state, stopping at Greenville
and Clemson in the west, Columbia and other towns in the center and Charleston on
the coast. **Buses** run along I-85 between Charlotte, North Carolina and Atlanta, and a
less regular service operates along the coast, stopping at Myrtle Beach and Charleston.

The **area code** for the entire state of South Carolina is ☎803.

Myrtle Beach and the North Coast

MYRTLE BEACH is a brazen splurge of seaside fun, an unmitigated stretch of commercial development twenty miles down the coast from the North Carolina border at the center of the sixty-mile "Grand Strand". Predominantly a family resort, it's packed fit to burst during mid-term vacations with leering, jeering students in fluorescent beach wear – if you've seen the movie *Shag* you'll know what to expect. Fans of crazy golf, water parks, funfairs and bungee jumping will be in heaven; appropriately enough, this was the birthplace of *Wheel of Fortune* star Vanna White. The **beach** itself isn't bad, with the widest stretch at North Myrtle Beach, a chain of small communities, of which Ocean Drive is the center and Atlantic Beach is exclusively used by African-Americans.

South of Myrtle Beach lie **Murells Inlet**, a fishing port with lots of good fish restaurants, and **Pawleys Island**, a secluded resort, once favored by plantation owners and today retaining a far slower pace than its neighbors. Between the two on Hwy-17, the beautifully landscaped **Brookgreen Gardens** hold a gathering of American figurative sculpture on the grounds of what was once a rice and indigo plantation, used as the setting for many of Julia Peterkin's novels of *gullah* life. There's also a wildlife area with alligator and deer (daily 9.30am–4.45pm; $5).

Practicalities

Hwy-17 (Kings Highway) is Myrtle Beach's main traffic thoroughfare, while the parallel Ocean Blvd is lined with hotels and motels. *Greyhound* **buses** from Charleston and Wilmington come in at Ninth Ave N (closed 2.30–7pm daily, and after 2.30pm on Saturday; ☎448-2471). Minimal transportation in the beach areas is provided by *Coastal Rapid Public Transit* buses (75¢ one-way; ☎248-7277).

The **visitor center** at 1301 N King's Highway (☎672-7444) can provide events listings and details of accommodation – though there's no great reason to choose any one of the countless **motels** over the rest. The *Swamp Fox*, 2311 Ocean Blvd (☎1-800/228-1894; ③–⑧), is one of the nicest places to stay, with turquoise pools, its own boardwalk, and sea views from the more expensive tower rooms. If you want burgers, standard diner meals or any one of a zillion varieties of ethnic fast food, you'll have no problem finding somewhere. Well-prepared **seafood** can be had at the classier *Sea Captain's House* at 3002 N Ocean Blvd (☎448-8082), or at a number of similar establishments in Murrells Inlet, further south. You can sit on the terrace above the ocean and watch the volleyball players at *Downwind Trading Co*, on Ocean Blvd and 28th Ave S (☎626-8000), which serves fishy pasta to an accompaniment of live music.

With nine campgrounds and two state parks, Myrtle Beach calls itself the "Camping Capital of the World"; most of the commercial **campgrounds** are concentrated along King's Highway (US-17 Business), where just south of town you'll find the vast (and pretty hellish) campground at **Myrtle Beach State Park** (☎238-5325).

As for **nightlife**, if you can't find anywhere to shag, the *Purple Gator* on Magnolia Plaza (☎449-3660) hosts good reggae and r'n'b bands. Kitschier, and more expensive,

---

SHAGGING IN MYRTLE BEACH

South Carolina's obsession with **shagging** began in the 1940s at Ocean Drive's beach pavilion, North Myrtle Beach, where r'n'b-style beach music, not accepted by the white establishment, was played to a predominantly black crowd. In the 1960s the Chairmen of the Board and the Trammps carried on the tradition, and it is still a matter of pride among many South Carolinans to know the moves of their state dance. If you want to learn to shag, or just like to watch, head for *The Pad* and *Fat Harold's* on Ocean Blvd, opposite the old pavilion in Ocean Drive, where the old pros – who attend shagging conventions here in spring and fall – strut their stuff.

are the glut of country variety shows that have recently sprung up; at the *Myrtle Beach Opry*, 19th Ave N and Hwy-17 (☎448-6779 or 1-800/446-4110; $14), powerful singers belt out extraordinarily corny rock and roll, country and bluegrass with a couple of hymns for good measure. Other live gigs and bars are listed in the fortnightly *Hot Times*.

South to Charleston: the Plantations

The waterfront of **GEORGETOWN**, the first town beyond Myrtle Beach to be anything more than a beach town, makes a refreshing and dignified contrast, while the main street has a late-Fifties feel. Ask at the **visitor center**, 600 Front St (☎1-800/777-7705), for a self-guided walking tour sheet to the fine antebellum and eighteenth-century houses in the 32-block historic district. The **Rice Museum**, under the clock tower on Front St, tells how the cultivation of rice flourished on the coast during the slavery period (April–Sept Mon–Fri 9.30am–4.30pm, Sat 10am–4.30pm, Sun 2–4.30pm; Oct–March Mon–Fri 9.30am–1pm, Sat 10am–1pm). If you want to **stay**, *530 Prince St B&B* (☎527-1114; ③) is a hospitable, if eccentrically furnished, inn in the heart of downtown.

Just north out of Georgetown on US-17, the first right turning after the bridge leads to the **Belle W Baruch Plantation** (daily 10am–5.30pm, tours Thurs only; $3). Though now fairly overgrown, the plantation is practically unique in that its original "**slave street**" is still standing, complete with wooden shacks and church. It serves as a powerful reminder of the brutal basis of antebellum southern prosperity and gentility.

Hopsewee Plantation, the grand mansion home of Thomas Lynch, a signatory of the Declaration of Independence, is set in Spanish moss-draped grounds, twelve miles south on US-17 (March–Oct Tues–Fri 10am–5pm; $5). Clouds of large and ferocious mosquitoes drift up from the adjacent river, so think twice before going in summer. The mosquito-free and less manicured **Hampton Plantation State Park**, further south, eight miles off US-17 on Hwy-857, is probably closer to the look of a typical plantation. The grounds (Thurs–Mon 9am–6pm) are pretty, but the house (Sat 10am–3pm & Sun noon–3pm; $1) is most impressive, a huge eighteenth-century neoclassical monolith, its white exterior restored but the inside still bare, with no interpretive displays as yet.

The plantation is isolated in the heart of the dense **Francis Marion National Forest**, badly damaged by Hurricane Hugo in September 1989. It's a heavily black area, particularly known for its sweetgrass basket-weaving. This craft originated with the slaves in West Africa, using tight bundles of grasses to make intricate baskets and pots. In view of the enormously time-consuming work and the cost of materials, the baskets you see being made at roadside stalls here cost upwards of $20.

Further south, beyond the forest a few miles north of Charleston, is the much-publicized **Boone Hall Plantation** (April–Sept Mon–Sat 8.30am–6.30pm, Sun 1–5pm; Oct–March Mon–Fri 9am–5pm, Sun 1–4pm; $6). A visit is a sanitized and annoying experience: the plantation may date from the late seventeenth century but the house is a

---

KUDZU

The western Carolinas are badly afflicted by **kudzu**, a leafy climbing vine introduced from Japan in 1876 for decoration and shade. Its use was encouraged by the federal government from the 1930s to stop soil erosion. Unbelievably, it can grow as much as a foot a day in hot weather, and eventually kills trees by cutting off the sunlight. So far, it has covered about two million acres of forest. In places it's amazing, totally carpeting whole stands of trees and telegraph poles and wires. South Carolina folk poet James Dickey's poem *Kudzu* portrays it as a mysterious, evil invader from the east:

> *In Georgia, the legend says*
> *that you must close your windows*
> *at night to keep it out of the house*
> *the glass is tinged with green, even so . . .*

twentieth-century reconstruction, with tours conducted by hapless young women in Southern belle costumes, who rather overplay the connections with *Gone with the Wind*. The grounds are more interesting, with a long tree-lined drive and another rare slave street, this time of small mid-eighteenth-century brick cabins that housed privileged slaves – domestic servants and skilled artisans.

Charleston

CHARLESTON, one of the most elegant cities in the US, spreads way beyond its original confines on the tip of a peninsula at the confluence of the Ashley and Cooper rivers, roughly one hundred miles south of Myrtle Beach and north of Savannah. It's a compelling place to visit, its historic district lined with tall, narrow houses of multicolored stucco, adorned with wooden shutters and ironwork balconies wrought by slaves from Barbados. The Caribbean feel is augmented by palm trees, a tropical climate and easy going atmosphere, and the town also evokes New Orleans or Savannah with its pretty hidden gardens and leafy patios.

Founded in 1670 by a group of English aristocrats as a specifically money-making venture, Charles Towne swiftly boomed as a **port** serving the rice and cotton plantations. It became the region's dominant town, a commercial and cultural center which right from the start had a mixed population, with immigrants including French, Germans, Jews, Italians and Irish as well as the English majority. One third of all the nation's **slaves** came through Charleston, sold at the market on the riverfront and bringing with them their ironworking and building skills. The town had a sizeable **free black** community, too, and its then unusually urban density allowed an anonymity and racial openness which, although still dominated by slavery, went a lot further than the rest of the South. Nevertheless there was still slave unrest, culminating in the abortive Veysey slave revolt of 1823, after which the city built the Citadel armory and later the military university to control future uprisings.

The **Civil War** started on Charleston's very doorstep, at Fort Sumter in the harbor. Fire swept through the city, destroying large chunks, in 1861; more damage was inflicted when it was taken by Union troops in February 1865. The decline of the plantation economy and slump in cotton prices led to an economic crash after the war, made worse by a catastrophic earthquake in 1886. As the upcountry industrialized, capital steadily deserted the city, and it only really recovered when World War II restored its importance as a port and naval base. Since then, a steady programme of preservation and restoration – not helped by the devastation of Hurricane Hugo in 1989 – has made **tourism** Charleston's main focus. Despite the crowds, however, it has kept its atmosphere, while retaining all the energy and life of a real, working town. The *gullah* traditions of the Sea Islands are a tangible presence here too; "basket ladies" weave their sweetgrass baskets all around the market and near the post office, and many people – black and white – possess distinctive *gullah* accents.

Arrival, Getting Around and Information

Charleston International Airport is about ten miles north of downtown, off I-26; a $13 taxi ride with *Yellow Cabs* (☎577-6565). Both *Amtrak* – 4565 Gaynor Ave, eight miles north of downtown – and *Greyhound* – stranded at 3610 Dorchester Rd, out near I-26, by the closure of its downtown depot (☎722-7721) – are in inconvenient and potentially dangerous locations. Each is a $7 taxi ride from downtown. **Public transportation** isn't bad, however. *SCE&G* buses (☎722-2226) cover most areas, including *Amtrak* and *Greyhound*, for 75¢, and the *Downtown Area Shuttle* (*DASH*; ☎724-7368) runs through the historic district south of Cannon Street (every 15min, Mon–Fri 8am–5pm only; 25¢).

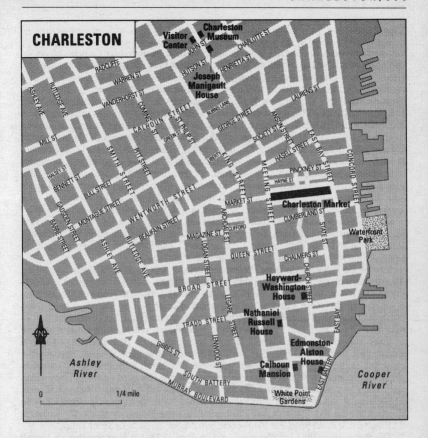

Guided Tours

Charleston is ideal for **walking tours**. *Charleston Strolls* leave from the *Omni Hotel*, 130 Market St (spring and fall only, daily 9.30am & 1.30pm; $12); the *Civil War Walking Tour* sets out from *Mills House Hotel*, 115 Meeting St (March–Dec, Wed–Sun 9am; $12); and in fall, the *Preservation Society*, 147 King St (☎722-4630), organizes candlelit tours, visiting private old homes, and offering free champagne on Saturdays (Sept–Oct only, Thurs–Sat 9pm). Although much of Charleston's beauty is owed to the black slaves who built it, the town has no formal museum of black history. However, *Al Miller*'s **black history tours** include material on the Veysey uprising, the Civil War, and the lives of the freed slaves (☎762-0051; $15).

Horse and carriage tours leaving from the market (as do less worthwhile trolley tours) include *Palmetto Carriages* (☎723-8145), which provide a lively, leisurely overview of town.You can rent **bikes** from *The Bicycle Shoppe*, 283 Meeting St (☎722-8168).

Information

Charleston's huge and well-equipped **visitor center**, 375 Meeting St (daily, summer 8.30am–5.30pm, otherwise 8.30am–5pm; ☎853-8000), gives out lots of discount coupons, leaflets and maps, and shows a film about the town ($1). The **post office** is at 11 Broad St, on the corner with Meeting St (Mon–Fri 8am–5pm, Sat 8am–noon; zip code 29401).

The City

Charleston's **historic district** is fairly self-contained, bounded by Calhoun Street on the north and East Bay Street by the river. It's best taken in by strolling at your own pace – though that pace can get pretty slow at midday in high summer, when the heat is intense. Attractive spots to pause in the shade include the swinging benches at **Waterfront Park**, a beautifully landscaped piazza with boardwalks leading out over the river, and **White Point Gardens**, by the Battery on the tip of the peninsula, where the flowers and lawns have good views across the water and a breeze even in summer.

Opposite the excellent visitor center, the **Charleston Museum**, 360 Meeting St (Mon–Sat 9am–5pm, Sun 1–5pm; $5), is the nation's oldest, dating from 1773 (although the original building no longer stands). It's something of a ragbag of city memorabilia, with video presentations on subjects from rice growing to the Huguenots. One intriguing room holds exhibits from its early collections, where pickled snakes shared space with Egyptian mummies and casts from the British Museum. The "head of a New Zealand chief" and "fine electrical machine", however, were destroyed in a fire of 1778.

Charleston's **market area** runs from Meeting Street to East Bay Street, centering on a long enclosed hall but spilling out onto the surrounding streets. Undeniably touristy, packed with hard-headed "basket ladies", this is one of the liveliest spots in town, selling junk, spices, tacky T-shirts, jewellery and rugs.

Most of the city's fine **houses** are private, and can only be admired from the outside. You're not necessarily missing all that much; the appeal of those that you can get into doesn't take long to pall. The late nineteenth-century **Calhoun Mansion**, 16 Meeting St, is among the more extreme, with its ornate plaster and woodwork, hand-painted porcelain ballroom chandeliers and similar extravagances (Wed–Sat 10am–4pm, Sun 1–4pm; $10). The Charleston Museum offers a $9 combination ticket with a visit to any one of three houses: the **Aiken-Rhett House**, 48 Elizabeth St, headquarters of General Beauregard during the Civil War; the 1803 **Joseph Manigault House**, opposite the museum; or the **Heyward-Washington House**, 87 Church St, built by a rice baron. In the heart of Catfish Row, this was the setting for Dubose Heyward's novel of black waterfront life, *Porgy*. Admission to each is $5. The neoclassical **Nathaniel-Russell House**, 51 Meeting St, is noted for its daring flying staircase, which soars unsupported for three floors, while the stately antebellum **Edmonston-Alston House** overlooks the harbor at 21 E Battery St (both Mon–Sat 10am–5pm, Sun 2–5pm; $5 each, or $8 for both).

The first shots of the Civil War were fired on April 12 1861 at **Fort Sumter**, on a small island some way out from Charleston, where the rivers meet the Atlantic. When South Carolina announced its secession, the federal government had to decide whether to re-provision its forts in the south. The commander of Fort Sumter, Major Robert Anderson, requested supplies in early 1861; when a relief expedition was sent, Confederate General Pierre Beauregard demanded the fort's surrender. In one of the ironies that so characterized the war, Beauregard, who personally coordinated the bombardment, had been the star pupil of Major Anderson's artillery classes at West Point. After a relentless barrage, the garrison gave in the next day, becoming the first prisoners of the war. The fort was re-taken by Union troops on Good Friday 1865, the very day of Lincoln's assassination, and today holds a good **museum**. *Gray Line*, among others, operates **tour boats** from the City Marina, off Lockwood Blvd (daily, spring and summer at 10am, 12.30pm & 3pm, otherwise 2pm only; ☎722-1112; $8.50 for boat and fort).

Accommodation

Though Charleston is an expensive city, and **accommodation** options are limited if your budget's tight, it's really worth trying to stay within walking distance of downtown. As well as hotels, a lot of grand historic district houses serve as **B&Bs**, with prices starting at around $65. Agencies include *Historic Charleston B&B*, 43 Legare St

(☎722-6606). Further out, the usual **budget motels** cluster around US-17 in West Ashley and Mount Pleasant, and along I-26 in North Charleston.

Bed No Breakfast, 16 Halsey St (☎723-4450). Very small downtown guest house. Large rooms but shared baths. Coffee and tea, but, as the name says, no breakfast. ③.

Cannonboro Inn B&B, 184 Ashley Ave (☎723-8572). Fine columned house with attractive patios and gardens. Very comfortable B&B rooms, and complimentary bicycles. ④.

Days Inn Historic District, 155 Meeting St (☎722-8411). Standard rooms; one of the least expensive downtown options. ③.

Eliot House Inn, 78 Queen St (☎723-1855 or 1-800/729-1855). Highly luxurious B&B in old Charleston building. Free wine and afternoon tea in pretty courtyard. ⑤.

Maison Dupré, 317 E Bay St (☎723-8691). Beautiful inn in crumbling 1804 European-style building. An idyllic garden holds fountains and a wishing well. Complimentary high teas. ④.

Rutledge Guest House, 114 Rutledge Ave (☎722-7551). Friendly inn spread through three houses on the west side of the historic district. Small student rooms are available at a discount. ③/⑤.

Eating

Eating in Charleston can be overpriced; the **historic district** is characterized by undistinguished seafood places. Cappuccino bars and cafés line Market and King streets.

Aaron's Deli, 213 Meeting St (☎723-6000). An excellent New York-style Jewish deli with great sandwiches, open until late and with acoustic folk some nights.

Bookstore Café, King and Houston (☎720-8843). Quiet café, lined, as the name suggests, with books and papers. Open until 7.30pm Mon–Fri, 2pm Sat & Sun.

Gaulart and Maliclet, 98 Broad St (☎577-9797). Wonderful French bistro, seating only nine people. Fondue dinners and croissant breakfasts. Lunch only on Mon, closed Sun.

Magnolias, 185 E Bay St (☎577-7771). Splendid nouvelle Southern cuisine – shrimp with grits, etc – in stylish monochrome setting with a circular bar.

Moultrie Tavern, 18 Vendue Range (☎723-1862). Rebel-yelling food (bean soup, okra stew), eaten off metal plates in a dark tavern full of Civil War memorabilia. Next to Waterfront Park.

Pinckney's, 18 Pinckney St (☎577-0961). Well-prepared and inexpensive seafood.

Poogan's Porch, 72 Queen St (☎577-2337). Local food in old Charleston house; crabcakes and catfish, or a five-course supper for $24.

Primerose House, 322 E Bay St (☎723-2954). Elegant food (grilled scallops, sesame chicken) in relaxed atmosphere – stone tiled floors, open brick walls, ill-matched tableware.

Roberts, in *Planter's Inn Hotel*, Market and Meeting (☎577-7645). Probably the swankiest place in town; a seven-course set dinner, served while Robert sings opera, costs $70 (including tip and wine). Reserve ahead. Mon–Fri 8pm, Sat & Sun 6pm & 8pm.

Nightlife and Entertainment

Charleston has a dynamic **nightlife**, with a wide choice of **music**, **clubs** and **bars**, especially around the market. Ask at the visitor center about its many festivals, or pick up the free monthly *Omnibus*. The **Spoleto Festival**, concentrating mainly on classical music, is held from late May until early June. October's **Moja Arts Festival** celebrates African/Caribbean theater, dance and film, with all events free or low-priced.

Blue Coyote, 61 State St (☎577-2583). Rowdy, touristy bar with live music and dance.

Cumberlands, 26 Cumberland St (☎577-9469). A nice bar and deli which puts on blues and folk.

Deja Vu, 525 E Bay St (☎722-5994). Mixed gay bar.

East Bay Trading Co, 161 E Bay St (☎723-4363). Typical noisy bar and restaurant with live music.

Henry's, 54 N Market St (☎723-4363). Flash bar, with live jazz at weekends. Also serves seafood.

Louis Charleston Grill, at the *Omni Hotel*, 130 Market St (☎577-4522). Good jazz in rather synthetic surroundings.

Myskyns, 5 Faber St (☎577-5595). Lively and unpretentious place near the market. Big blues, reggae and African artists, as well as more local rock.

Out from Charleston

The **river road**, Hwy-61, leads **north** from Charleston along the Ashley River, past a series of magnificent plantations. Many can be visited, although in best southern tradition, house tours tend to dwell on the furniture and dining habits of the slave masters rather than any more pertinent sense of social history. **Drayton Hall**, closest to Charleston at 3380 Ashley River Rd, is a particularly fine Georgian mansion, looking much as it did in the mid-seventeenth century with its handcarved wood and plasterwork (daily, March–Oct 10am–4pm, Nov–Feb 10am–3pm; $6). The nearby **Magnolia Plantation and Gardens**, ten miles from Charleston, has stunning ornamental gardens, particularly in spring when the azaleas are blooming (daily; grounds 8am–5pm, $8, rising to $9 March–May; house tours 9.30am–4.30pm, $4, $5 March–May). Canoe rides lead through the **Audubon Swamp Garden** here, a preserved swamp, complete with alligators and lush flowers. Across the Ashley River, between US-17 and I-126 west of Ashley River Bridge, **Charlestowne Landing** is a 663-acre state park (daily summer 9am–6pm; winter 9am–5pm; $5), with a restored waterfront and a replica of a seventeenth-century merchant ship, as well as hiking and biking trails and kayak rentals.

South of Charleston, **beaches** such as **Isle of Palms** and **Sullivan's Island** are heavily used by Charlestonians at weekends. The further you get from town, the more likely you are to find a stretch to yourself. The Mount Pleasant bus from Calhoun Street runs to both Isle of Palms and Sullivan's Island. If you want to stay, there are plenty of motels and eating places, and the odd decent bar, such as the *Windjammer*, 1000 Ocean Blvd, Isle of Palms (☎886-8596), open until 2am and with live rock at weekends; *Bert's Bar*, 2209 Middle St, Sullivan's Island (☎883-9318), is similar.

The Sea Islands

South of Charleston towards Savannah, the coastline dissolves into small marshy islands. **Edisto Island**, south of US-17 on Hwy-174, is typical: huge live oaks festooned with great drapes of Spanish moss line the roads, there are bright green marshes with rich bird life, and wide beaches on the seaward side. If you want to stay, there are no budget motels, but the **campground** at **Edisto Beach State Park** (☎869-2156) is near a great beach lined with palmetto trees and other semi-tropical plants.

BEAUFORT (pronounced *Byoofort*), the biggest town, has a few old houses but a slightly weird atmosphere, thanks to racial tensions and the baleful proximity of Parris Island US Marine Base, notorious for the brutality of its training regime, as mythologized in Kubrick's Vietnam film *Full Metal Jacket*. The **visitor center** at 1006 Bay St (☎524-3163) has details of tours around the small historic district and discount coupons for the motels out on US-21. In town, the *Best Western Sea Island Inn*, 1015 Bay St (☎524-4121 or 1-800/528-1234; ④), has nice rooms with an old-fashioned feel. The 1765 *Anchorage House*, 1103 Bay St (☎524-9392; reserve, closed Sun), is a romantic candlelit restaurant serving reasonably priced continental and local dishes. The *Greyhound* **bus** station is two miles north of town on US-21 (☎524-4646).

St Helena Island

Across the bridge to the southeast of Beaufort, **ST HELENA ISLAND** is among the least spoiled of the eastern sea islands. The **landscape** is gorgeous: amazing Spanish moss and enormous, wide views out across bright marshes, and small shrimp and oyster fishing communities. Occasionally you see what looks like a fleet of ships in the middle of a field, only to realize that in fact the boats are anchored in a small salt creek, hidden by bright green marsh reeds.

This is an area of strong **black communities**, descended from slaves, who were given parcels of land when they were freed by the Union army in February 1865 and who speak a dialect known as *gullah*, an Afro-English patois with many West African words. The **Gullah Institute** at the Penn Center, part of a National Historic District, off US-21, contains the **school** started for freed slaves by Charlotte Forten, a black Massachusetts teacher. Forten remarked that "I have never seen children so eager to learn . . . the majority learn with wonderful rapidity. Many of the grown people are desirous of learning to read. It is wonderful how a people who have been so long crushed to the earth . . . can have so great a desire for knowledge, and such a capability for attaining it." The school was an important retreat for civil rights leaders in the 1960s, used by Dr Martin Luther King Jr's SCLC and others. The white building set back from the road is a **museum** containing fascinating turn-of-the-century pictures of black fishermen and farmers, plus old tools and shrimp nets, and rattlesnake skins (Mon–Fri 9am–5pm; $1). Nearby, off US-21, the ruined black **Church of Ease** nestles among thick Spanish moss, with seashell-adorned interior walls.

St Helena's main **beach**, at **Hunting Island State Park** on the east shore, can get crowded, but it's simply idyllic: soft white sand, wide and gently shelving, lined with palmettos, palm trees and sea oats, and with incredibly warm water. Pelicans come in to feed, particularly in the early morning, and the shrimp fleet sails past soon after. Apart from a large **campground** (☎838-2011), there are few places to stay. Occasional road-side restaurants sell excellent fresh **seafood**. The "shrimp burger" at the *Shrimp Shack* (☎838-2962), to the east near Hunting Island, has to be seen to be believed.

The last sea island on the way south to Savannah, the resort and retirement complex of **Hilton Head Island**, is really just a huge, complacent golf course.

GEORGIA

Compared to the rest of **GEORGIA**, the largest of the southern states, the bright lights of its capital **Atlanta** are a wild aberration. Apart from some beaches and towns on the highly indented coastline, this overwhelmingly rural state is composed of slow, easy-going settlements where the best, and sometimes the only, way to enjoy your time is to sip iced tea and have a chat on the porch.

Settlement in Georgia, the thirteenth British colony (named after King George II), started at **Savannah** in 1733, intended as a haven of Christian principles for poor Britons, with both alcohol and slavery banned. However, under pressure from planters, **slavery** was introduced in 1752, and by the time of the **Civil War** almost half the population were black slaves. Little fighting took place on Georgian soil until Sherman's troops marched in from Tennessee, burned Atlanta to the ground and laid waste to all property on the way to the coast. The economy successfully re-established itself after the war; Atlanta rose from the ashes to become the communications center of the South, and attracted substantial investment in the latter years of the nineteenth century.

Today, bustling **Atlanta**, the venue for the 1996 Olympics, stands as the unofficial capital of the South. The city where **Dr Martin Luther King Jr** was born, preached and is buried bears little relation to *Gone with the Wind* stereotypes, and its forward-looking energy is held up as a role model for other cities with large black populations – though it does still suffer high levels of urban poverty and violent crime.

Atlanta's main rival as a tourist destination is the **Georgia coast**, stretching south from beautiful old **Savannah** via the **Sea Islands** to the semi-tropical **Okefenokee Swamp**, inland near Florida. To the **northeast**, the Appalachian foothills are particularly fetching in fall, while **Athens** has a reputation for producing offbeat rock groups such as **REM** and the **B-52s**. Further **south**, the agricultural heartlands are rich in musical history, but only **Macon** and ancient **Ocmulgee** provide reasons to stop.

Getting Around Georgia

Georgia's main points of interest are easily accessible, but local transportation is poor. *Amtrak* **trains** from Washington DC to New Orleans and Florida call at Atlanta and Savannah respectively. **Bus** services in most areas are patchy and infrequent, though Atlanta has regular connections to the major cities, and several daily buses along the coast call at Savannah. Atlanta has the world's largest passenger **airport**, and Savannah has a reasonable service – but air fares between the two are extraordinarily high.

Atlanta

ATLANTA is a relatively young city: only incorporated in 1847, it was little more than a minor transportation center until the Civil War, when its accessibility made it a good site for the huge Confederacy munitions industry – and consequently a major target for the Union army. In 1864 Sherman's army **burned** the city, an act immortalized in *Gone with the Wind*. Recovery after the war took just a few years: Atlanta was the archetype of the aggressive, urban, industrial "New South", furiously championed by **"boosters"** – newspaper owners, bankers, politicians and city leaders. Industrial giants who based themselves here included **Coca-Cola**, source of a string of philanthropic gifts to the city – most recently the Woodruff Arts Center. Heavy **black** immigration to Atlanta increased its already considerable black population and led to the establishment of a thriving community centered around Auburn Avenue.

The characters – politicians and newspaper people – have changed little, and the "booster" tradition has continued to the present, peaking spectacularly when Atlanta won the right to host the 1996 **Olympics**. The bid to convince the world of the city's prosperity and sophistication was led by city leaders such as ex-mayor **Andrew Young** (the first southern black congressman since Reconstruction, who became Carter's ambassador to the UN), and flamboyant *Cable News Network* owner **Ted Turner**.

Today's Atlanta is at first glance a typical huge American city: a population of 2.5 million, with the usual traffic congestion, racially segregated neighborhoods cut off from each other by roaring freeways, bright lights, and enclave mentality. That said, the city is undeniably progressive, with little interest in lamenting a lost southern past, and an economy that seems unscathed by the recession. There's a highly visible, vocal black community, with one of the largest black middle classes in the country. In 1974 Atlanta voted in the nation's first black mayor, Maynard Jackson – who returned to office in the 1980s. Add to that Atlanta's vociferous gay community, hip local neighborhoods and cosmopolitan blend of cultures, and you have a city with a dynamism and verve that's a far cry from its much-mythologized Deep South roots.

Arrival, Getting Around and Information

The colossal **Hartsfield International Airport** (☎530-6600) is a few miles south of downtown Atlanta, just inside I-285 ("the perimeter"). Road **shuttle** services such as the *Atlanta Airport Shuttle* (☎524-3400) run into the city for around $12, and it is also the southern terminus of one of the two **subway** lines, half an hour's ride from downtown. The *Amtrak* station is at 1688 Peachtree St, just north of downtown. It's too far to walk in: take bus #23 to the Arts Center subway, N5 on the northern line. *Greyhound* **buses** arrive downtown at 81 International Blvd (☎522-6300).

The subway and the wide network of **buses** are run by the *Metropolitan Area Rapid Transit Authority* (*MARTA*), and are clean, reliable, and pretty safe, operating until

The **area code** for Atlanta is ☎404.

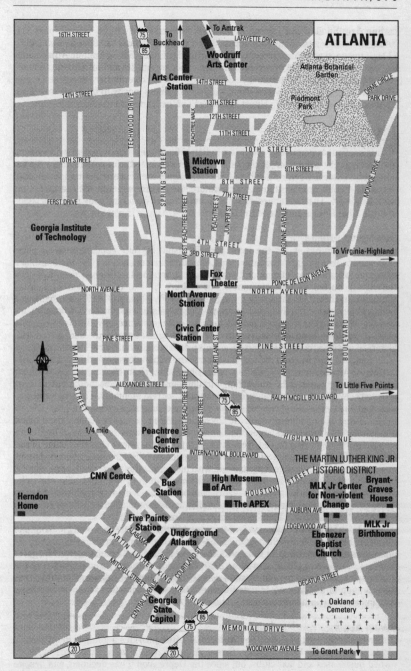

ATLANTA

16TH STREET

To Buckhead

To Amtrak

LAFAYETTE DRIVE

Woodruff Arts Center

Arts Center Station

14TH STREET

Atlanta Botanical Garden

Piedmont Park

ORME CIRCLE

PARK DRIVE

14TH STREET

13TH STREET

12TH STREET

11TH STREET

10TH STREET

TECHWOOD DRIVE

PEACHTREE WALK

10TH STREET

Midtown Station

9TH STREET

8TH STREET

7TH STREET

SPRING STREET

MONROE DRIVE

FERST DRIVE

WEST PEACHTREE STREET

PEACHTREE ST

JUNIPER ST

Georgia Institute of Technology

4TH STREET

3RD STREET

ARGONNE AVENUE

To Virginia-Highland

Fox Theater

PONCE DE LEON AVENUE

NORTH AVENUE

North Avenue Station

NORTH AVENUE

Civic Center Station

PIEDMONT AVENUE

PINE STREET

JACKSON STREET

BOULEVARD

PINE STREET

MARIETTA STREET

COURTLAND ST

ARGONNE AVENUE

ALEXANDER STREET

WEST PEACHTREE STREET

To Little Five Points

RALPH MCGILL BOULEVARD

0   1/4 mile

Peachtree Center Station

WEST PEACHTREE STREET

PEACHTREE STREET

HIGHLAND AVENUE

INTERNATIONAL BOULEVARD

THE MARTIN LUTHER KING JR HISTORIC DISTRICT

CNN Center

Bus Station

High Museum of Art

HOUSTON

STREET

MLK Jr Center for Non-violent Change

Bryant-Graves House

Herndon Home

The APEX

AUBURN AVE

MLK Jr Birthhome

Five Points Station

EDGEWOOD AVE

ALABAMA

MARTIN LUTHER KING JR AVE

Underground Atlanta

Ebenezer Baptist Church

MITCHELL STREET

COURTLAND ST

DECATUR STREET

CENTRAL AVENUE

Georgia State Capitol

Oakland Cemetery

MEMORIAL DRIVE

WOODWARD AVENUE

To Grant Park

midnight on Sunday and 1am on other days. Each trip costs $1.25 (weekly pass $11, Friday to Sunday pass $7, weekend pass $5). If you need a taxi, call *Checker Cab* (☎351-1111). One good way to explore the neighborhoods of Atlanta is on a summertime **walking tour** with the *Atlanta Preservation Center* – 156 Seventh St (☎876-2040; $5).

The CVB's **visitor center** at suite 2000 in the Harris Tower of the Peachtree Center, 233 Peachtree St (Mon–Fri 9am–5pm; ☎659-4270), caters mostly to business travellers; a subsidiary one stands at 65 Upper Alabama St in the Underground Atlanta complex.

The City

Atlanta's layout is confusing, following Indian trails rather than a logical grid system, and nearly every second street seems to be called Peachtree; take care to note whether it is Avenue, Road, Boulevard and so forth. The sights are scattered, but relatively easy to reach on public transportation. Furthermore, the **downtown** area, the Martin Luther King Jr Historic District ranged along **Auburn Avenue** and the trendy neighborhoods of **Little Five Points** and **Virginia-Highland** are all easy to explore on foot.

Downtown Atlanta

Downtown Atlanta is for the most part the usual big city concentration of glitzy skyscrapers. Its highlight, **Underground Atlanta**, which opened in 1989, is a four-block subterranean shopping, dining and entertainment area on the original site of the city (effectively buried in the late nineteenth century by the construction of railroad viaducts). In the 1970s the district, ranged around Five Points *MARTA* station, was a crime-ridden waste, but, thanks to Andrew Young's dream of a revitalized downtown, it's now one of the liveliest – albeit heavily touristy – pockets of the city. The underground maze of cobbled gaslit streets, restored to their original appearance and dotted with historical markers, is reached by steps from a piazza buzzing with street performers.

Dominating the western side of the piazza, the super-glossy **World of Coca-Cola** pavilion (Mon–Sat 10am–9.30pm, Sun noon–6pm; $2.50), with its "special look at those unforgettable commercials" and array of photographs, posters and merchandise, does little to relieve the air of unreality, especially in its surreal grand finale where space-age soda fountains jerk out a variety of sickly colas for gleeful guzzling visitors.

Northwest of the Underground, the **CNN Center** daily achieves a global penetration undreamt of by Coca-Cola's founders. The *Cable News Network* is just one of five television networks belonging to Ted Turner, whose multimedia power stretches from ownership of the Braves baseball team to movie production and distribution. Aptly, among the thousands of MGM classics now stamped with his logo is *Gone with the Wind* – witness the plethora of Tara, Scarlett and Rhett knick-knacks in the gift shop. Unlike the Coke pavilion, this is a working facility – adrenalin-fuelled guided tours rush past frazzled producers and toothy anchorpersons beaming across the planet, and there's no free soda at the end (Mon–Fri 10am–5pm; Sat & Sun 10am–4pm; $6).

The **Atlanta Public Library**, in Margaret Mitchell Square at Carnegie Way and Forsythe St (Mon & Fri 9am–6pm, Tues–Thurs 9am–8pm, Sat 10am–6pm, Sun 2–6pm), has a room devoted to *Gone with the Wind* author and Atlanta native **Margaret Mitchell**. The novel (1936) and film (1939) helped perpetuate popular images of the genteel plantation South – not least, of course, the burning of Atlanta. The tiny downtown branch of the **Atlanta History Center** (Mon–Sat 10am–6pm; free) is also here, with information on historical tours of the city.

Sweet Auburn

A mere half-mile east of downtown, **Auburn Avenue** provides a glimpse into Atlanta's black history. In its 1920s heyday "Sweet Auburn" was a prosperous area of black-owned businesses and jazz clubs, but since the Depression it has declined, and despite

THE BURNING OF ATLANTA AND THE MARCH TO THE SEA

In summer 1864, following the comprehensive Confederate defeats of Spotsylvania and the Wilderness in May, Union **General William Tecumseh Sherman** invaded north Georgia. Outflanking the much smaller Confederate forces, he laid siege to Atlanta; the city eventually surrendered at the start of September.

Sherman announced that the entire population of the city must leave forthwith, and that he would burn such of their property as he deemed necessary. The Confederate commander, General Hood, powerless to resist, expostulated: "Sir, permit me to say that the unprecedented measure you propose transcends, in studied and ingenious cruelty, all acts ever before brought to my attention in the dark history of war. In the name of God and humanity, I protest." Sherman responded: "In the name of common sense, I ask you not to appeal to a just God in such a sacrilegious manner . . . Talk thus to the marines, but not to me."

On November 16, Sherman put a torch to the city, and set out on his notorious **"March to the Sea"**. As he later exulted, "Behind us lay Atlanta, smoldering in ruins, the black smoke rising high in the air, and hanging like a pall over the ruined city."

Sherman's March is seen as an early example of total war; some accuse him of inventing the methods later followed in the Nazi *Blitzkrieg*. His explicit intention was to "make Georgia howl", via the systematic destruction of agricultural and industrial resources and terrorization of civilians. One Georgia woman noted in her diary that "there was hardly a fence left standing all the way from Sparta to Gordon. The fields were trampled down and the road was lined with carcasses of horses, hogs and cattles that the invaders, unable either to consume or carry away with them, had wantonly shot down, to starve out the people . . . the dwellings that were standing all showed signs of pillage, and on every plantation we saw . . . charred remains."

It was the final body blow to the southern war effort; though the Confederate armies struggled on for a few more months after Sherman took Savannah, their fate was sealed.

admirable efforts it has yet to succeed in reincarnating itself as a living monument to black culture and heritage.

However, several blocks have been designated as the **Martin Luther King Jr National Historic Site** (daily 9am–5pm), in honor of the reverend who won the Nobel Peace Prize at a time when he was being actively persecuted by agents of the US government. King's **birthplace**, a small, neat Queen Anne-style shotgun house restored to its 1920s appearance, stands at 501 Auburn Ave. Lively and anecdotal tours (every 30min; free) begin from the park service information station in the **Bryant-Graves House** opposite, where you can also see a slide show on the area. West along Auburn at no 449, the **Martin Luther King Center for Nonviolent Change** is privately run by King's widow (daily, summer 9am–8pm, winter 9am–5.30pm; free). Chiefly an educational and research facility, the center also features a small exhibition with King's travelling suitcase, a hand-written sermon and, rather sensationally, the key to the room in Memphis' *Lorraine Motel* where he was assassinated. A time line of his life develops a fuller history of the civil rights movement. King's body was brought here from Memphis in the early 1970s, and his **memorial**, a simple slab inscribed with the words "Free at last, free at last, thank God Almighty I'm free at last" stands in a shallow pool in the courtyard outside.

Next door, visitors are welcome to attend services at the **Ebenezer Baptist Church** (☎688-7263), where he was pastor; moves are afoot to convert this into a visitor center and build a new church across the street. Auburn remained the base for King's breathtakingly courageous campaigning during the Sixties, and his Southern Christian Leadership Conference (**SCLC**) still has its headquarters in the old Masonic building on the corner of Auburn and Hilliard. Beyond here, at 184 Auburn, the recently reopened *Royal Peacock Club* was famed from the 1930s to the 1950s for performances by Cab

Calloway, Louis Armstrong and Aretha Franklin, while the *Atlanta Life Insurance Co Building* at no 148, from 1920 to 1980 the headquarters of the nation's largest black-owned business, now holds a small selection of African-American art in the lobby.

The privately run African-American Panoramic Experience (**APEX**) at 135 Auburn (Tues & Thurs–Sat 10am–5pm, Wed 10am–6pm; Feb, June & Aug also Sun 1–5pm; $2) has an interesting collection on black history, including a reconstruction of a 1920s black-owned drugstore and an African art gallery.

Little Five Points to Emory University

Northeast of Auburn Avenue, around Euclid and Moreland, the youthful **Little Five Points** district is center of Atlanta's alternative community, a tangle of thrift stores, secondhand record stores, funky restaurants, bars and clubs. By way of contrast, just a few blocks north at 1 Copenhill Ave, on the hill where Sherman is said to have watched Atlanta burn, the ponderously reverential **Carter Presidential Center** houses a small museum on the years the former Georgia state governor spent as president, together with his collected papers and fascinating film footage (Mon–Sat 9am–4.45pm, Sun noon–4.45pm; $2.50). Northeast of here, beyond the trendy **Virginia-Highland** district, treks to Emory University campus are rewarded by the stylish, brand-new **Carlos Museum of Art and Archeology**, 571 S Kilgo St (Mon–Thurs & Sat 10am–5pm, Fri & Sun noon–5pm; $2 suggested donation). The pre-Columbian collection is particularly fine; among the extraordinary Andean ceramics note one entitled *Human as a Peanut*.

Midtown and Buckhead

Midtown stretches from Ponce de Leon Avenue to 26th Street. The wildly flamboyant Art Deco **Fox Theater** at 660 Peachtree St at Ponce de Leon (☎881-1977), with its strong Moorish theme, should not be missed. Unless you buy a ticket for one of its fairly mainstream theatrical shows, the only way to see it is on an organized tour.

A few blocks north, the huge **Woodruff Arts Center**, 1280 Peachtree St, includes the main branch of the **High Museum of Art** (Tues–Thurs & Sat 10am–5pm, Fri 10am–9pm, Sun noon–5pm; $5, free after 1pm Thurs). This stylish gallery presents excellent contemporary and non-western exhibitions – particularly strong in African art – in a beautifully laid out futuristic white glass and steel building. The temporary photographic shows, in particular, are usually excellent.

Even further north, at 3101 Andrew Drive in the affluent white suburb of **Buckhead**, the museum of the **Atlanta Historical Society** (Mon–Sat 9am–5.30pm, Sun noon–5.30pm; $6, free after 1pm Thurs), has exemplary exhibits on civil rights and the Civil War. The *Atlanta Resurgens* room features short vox-pop videos of relentless Atlantans talking positively on subjects such as "What is Atlanta's Image?", and provides good coverage of the *Cotton States and International Exposition* of 1895, the emergence of black politics, women's history, Coca Cola and *Gone with the Wind*. Every half-hour there are tours of two houses in the extensive grounds: the **Swan House**, a rather ponderous 1920s mock-classical mansion, and the **Tullie Smith Farm**, an antebellum farmhouse and garden. For a further taste of the Tara-style Old South, tour the **Governors Mansion,** 391 W Paces Ferry Rd (Tues–Thurs 10–11.30am; free).

The West End

The **West End**, Atlanta's oldest quarter, is a slightly shabby but resurgent district south-west of downtown. Historically this has been a black residential area; African-American and Haitian art is displayed at the **Hammonds House**, 503 Peeples St (Tues–Fri 10am–6pm, Sat & Sun 1–5pm; $1), and you can tour the Beaux Arts **Herndon Home**, 587 University Place, designed and lived in by Alonzo Herndon, the freed slave who founded the Atlanta Life Insurance Company. The mansion's grand interior contains the

Herndon family's original furnishings, among them fine Venetian glass (Tues–Sat 10am–4pm; free).

The fascinating **Wren's Nest**, home of *Br'er Rabbit* author Joel Chandler Harris, at 1050 R D Abernathy Blvd, shatters preconceptions about the Uncle Remus stories propagated by the racist images of Disney's *Song of the South*. Harris, a friend of Mark Twain, was a respected journalist whose column for the *Atlanta Constitution* retold the slave stories he heard while training as a printer on a plantation newspaper; recently the dialect has been reappraised as authentically African and the stories as valuable upholders of a black folk tradition. Regular storytelling sessions take place in the peaceful, untamed garden (Tues–Sat 10am–5pm, Sun 1–5pm; $3).

Grant Park

Directly south of downtown, **Grant Park** is home to the **Cyclorama**, a huge circular painting (50ft by 900ft) depicting the Battle of Atlanta, executed by a group of German and Polish artists in 1885–86. Cycloramas used to travel around the country as entertainment in the days before movies. You sit inside the circle of the painting and the whole auditorium slowly rotates twice. During the second rotation, a guide gives interesting details on the painting; look out for the hole in the wagon, originally used as a fire escape. In the accompanying museum, treating the war from the point of view of the average soldier, banks of distressing statistics are interspersed with photos and memorabilia (June–Sept 9.30am–5.30pm; Oct–May 9.30am–4.30pm; $3.50).

Adjacent **Atlanta Zoo** features such "natural habitats" as an African rainforest (summer Mon–Fri 10am–5pm, Sat & Sun 10am–6pm; winter daily 10am–5pm; $7). At weekends, a special "zoo shuttle" runs from Five Points *MARTA* station to the park.

Accommodation

Hotels in downtown Atlanta, one of the biggest convention cities in the US, feel no great need to offer special deals to individual travellers. Motorists will find the usual chains along the interstates around the perimeter, but that's a long way out. The *B&B Atlanta* agency, 1801 Piedmont Ave NE (☎875-0525; ②–⑦), will reserve **B&B** rooms.

Young foreign travellers who call in person at the CVB in the Peachtree Center can take advantage of the "International Youth Program", which coordinates reasonably priced rooms in major hotels.

Atlanta Downtown Travelodge, 311 Courtland St NE (☎659-4545). Standard rooms on the east side of downtown. ③.

Atlanta Dream Hostel, 222 East Howard Ave (☎370-0380). Friendly, hip dorm accommodation in old art gallery with beer garden, in attractive Decatur district. The owners will despatch an outrageous leopard-skin limousine to collect parties of three or more from the *Amtrak* station, if you call in advance. *MARTA* Decatur station. ①.

Atlanta International AYH, 223 Ponce de Leon Ave (☎875-9449). Dorms, with 3-day maximum stay. Part of a beautifully converted former bordello B&B. *MARTA* North Ave station. ①/⑤.

Barclay Hotel, 89 Luckie St NW (☎524-7991). Relatively inexpensive downtown hotel with rooftop pool, behind the Peachtree Center. ④.

Comfort Inn Downtown, 101 International Blvd (☎524-5555). Friendly, central chain hotel. ④.

Paschal's Motor Hotel, 830 Martin Luther King Jr Drive SW (☎577-3150). Clean smart atmospheric Fifties motel in the West End, historically important as a meeting place for King and other civil rights activists, and still attracting a predominantly black clientele. ②.

Radisson Hotel, 165 Courtland St (659-6500). Mid-range downtown hotel with wonderful indoor pool surrounded by foliage. ⑤.

Westin Peachtree Plaza, 210 Peachtree St (659-1400). Landmark luxury cylindrical tower hotel, America's tallest, right downtown. Splendid rooftop revolving restaurant, with wonderful views. ⑦.

Woodruff B&B, 223 Ponce de Leon Ave (☎875-9449). See under *AYH* above.

Eating

Atlanta has scores of good **restaurants**. Southern **soul food** is best around Auburn Ave, while downtown options are more upmarket and cosmopolitan. **Vegetarians** will find plenty of choice in Little Five Points and Virginia-Highland. For a good take-out lunch try the **Dekalb Farmers Market**, out towards Stone Mountain, with stalls selling goat stew, tofu stir-fry and glazed duck; other goodies include fresh farm-fattened catfish and pretty blue crabs, and aromatic coffees from around the world.

Addis, 453 Moreland Ave (☎523-4748). Excellent, well-priced Ethiopian food in Virginia-Highland.

The Atomic Café, 1655 McLendon Ave (☎377-6068). Artists' and beatniks' vegetarian coffeehouse, just east of Little Five Points. Particularly good for breakfast.

Auburn Ave Rib Shack, 302 Auburn Ave (☎523-8315). Good cheap ribs and soul food, very near the King Center.

Beautiful Restaurant, 397 Auburn Ave (☎233-0080). Famous down-home cooking, next to the Ebenezer Baptist Church.

Capo's, 992 Virginia Ave (☎876-5655). Casual, romantic neighborhood café. Specialties include creamy crabcakes and vegetable lasagne.

Caribbean Sunset, 60 Upper Alabama St, Kenny's Alley (☎659-4589). Good Jamaican food in the Atlanta Underground. Cocktails and live reggae too.

Danté's Down the Hatch, 86 Alabama St (☎577-1800). Popular fondue restaurant on a nautical theme in the Underground, with live jazz nightly.

Delectables, 1 Margaret Mitchell Square (☎681-2909). Atlanta's public library makes an unlikely location for one of the city's best lunch restaurants, serving salad, soups and home-baked cakes.

Eat Your Vegetables, 438 Moreland Ave (☎523-2671). Trendy health-food restaurant in Little Five Points.

Lombardi's, 94 Upper Pryor St (☎522-6568). Stylish, upbeat modern Italian food in Underground.

Majestic Diner, 1031 Ponce de Leon Ave (☎875-0276). Funky Virginia-Highland 1920s diner in *Majestic Mall*, crowded even at 5am for authentic white country cooking.

Mary Mac's Tearoom, 224 Ponce de Leon Ave (☎876-6604). Hospitable soul food cafeteria near the youth hostel.

Paschal's, 830 Martin Luther King Jr Drive SW (☎577-3150). Friendly, lively Fifties dining room in motel (see p.379); specialties include chicken hash and milkshakes.

RJs Uptown Kitchen and Winebar, 870 N Highland Ave (☎875-7775). Innovative and eclectic ethnic, vegetarian and New American cuisine in Virginia-Highland. Great wine list and microbeers.

Rocky's Brick Oven Pizza, 1770 Peachtree St (☎876-1111). Without doubt Atlanta's best pizza, served to a seriously groovy crowd.

Silver Grill, 900 Monroe Drive (☎876-8145). True Southern breakfasts with grits.

Touch of India, 962 Peachtree St (☎876-7777). Some of the best Indian food in town, at good prices in a nice midtown setting.

The Varsity, 61 North Ave (☎881-1706). Vast and usually very full midtown drive-in restaurant: a true Fifties throwback where you can eat for well under $10.

Nightlife and Drinking

Atlanta is a place where you can have a very good time; budget to blow some money hopping between its bars and clubs. The **Atlanta Underground** complex comes into its own at night; otherwise the main concentrations are in **Virginia-Highland**, **Little Five Points** and the more upmarket **Midtown**, the center of Atlanta's thriving **gay and lesbian** scene. Look out for *ETC*, the gay listings paper. Up-to-the-minute listings for all venues can be found in the free weekly *Creative Loafing*.

The A Train, Kenny's Alley, Atlanta Underground (☎221-0522). Stylish jazz club, with gospel on Sunday.

Atkins Park, 794 N Highland Ave (☎876-7249). Lively Virginia-Highland bar. Original 1920s decor.

Backstreet, 845 Peachtree St NE (☎873-1986). Hardcore gay disco.

Blind Willie's, 828 N Highland Ave (☎873-2583). The best blues venue in town, with appearances by major artists, this Virginia-Highland hang-out is also a lively bar.

Blues Harbor, 155 Kenny's Alley, Atlanta Underground (☎524-3001). Good Chicago blues bar. Rib and lobster dinners served 6–10pm.

Cotton Club Revue, 1021 Peachtree St (☎874-2523). Midtown's major venue for live rock music.

Euclid Avenue Yacht Club, 1136 Euclid Ave (☎688-2582). Classic neighborhood bar in Little Five Points. Fine pork barbecue and Brunswick stew.

Limerick Junction, 824 N Highland Ave (☎874-7147). Partially gay Irish bar in Virginia-Highland; lively, with live folk and (often dreadfully kitschy) Irish music.

Manuel's Tavern, 602 N Highland Ave (☎525-3447). Relaxed studenty neighborhood bar near the Carter Center. Wooden benches, ceiling fans and portraits of Jack Kennedy and Eisenhower.

Masquerade, 695 North Ave (☎577-8178). Groovy grunge/punk hang-out midtown: a series of three clubs – *Heaven* (live bands), *Hell* (dance music) and *Purgatory* (coffee bar).

The Point, 420 Moreland Ave (☎577-6468). Hip club in Little Five Points with studenty crowd and live bands. Cover around $5.

The Stein Club, 929 Peachtree St NE (☎876-3707). Huge, friendly, smoky downtown dive; an Atlanta institution since the 1960s.

Taco Mac, 1006 N Highland Ave (☎873-6529). Fun, studenty Virginia-Highland bar, with huge selection of beers from around the world and excellent Tex-Mex food.

Stone Mountain

Just half an hour's drive east of Atlanta, **Stone Mountain State Park** (daily 6am–midnight; $5 per vehicle) centers around a huge dome of granite, with a five-mile circumference. You can climb it in around 45 minutes, or take a cable car ($2.50), and there are various train rides, and so on, but most visitors come to see the massive 90x190ft relief of Confederates Jefferson Davis, Robert E Lee and Stonewall Jackson. Work on the colossal sculpture was started in 1924 by Gutzon Borglum, who went on to carve Mount Rushmore in South Dakota (see p.592), but was not completed until 1970. Concessions and gift shops down below supply endless souvenir kitsch, and there's a nightly laser son et lumière in the summer (9.30pm; free with entrance to park).

North from Atlanta: the Mountains

Atlanta is a short drive from some spectacular Appalachian mountain scenery, at its best in October when the fall leaves turn gold and red. **DAHLONEGA**, fifty miles northeast on US-19, makes a good general base for the area. It was the site of the first gold rush in the US, in 1828, although the Cherokees had panned for gold long before then. Over $6 million of gold coin was minted here before the Civil War; the mining industry more or less died out later in the nineteenth century. An interesting **Gold Museum** is housed in the handsome county courthouse on the main square (Mon–Sat 9am–5pm, Sun 2–5pm; $1.50). You can also pan for gold at various small mines in the area, although you're hardly likely to make your fortune. The town hosts one of Appalachia's biggest annual **bluegrass** festivals, in the third week of June.

Dahlonega's **visitor center** is across from the courthouse (☎864-3711). The *Smith House* at 202 S Chestatee St (☎864-3566; ③) has comfortable double rooms, and serves excellent food. Alternatively, you can **camp** at **Amicalola Falls State Park**, twenty miles west (☎265-2885; also cabins ③). The falls are impressive and easily accessible, and one of the many trails goes 7.5 miles north to **Springer Mountain**, the southernmost point of the superb 2000-mile **Appalachian Trail**.

The **area code** for northern Georgia, including Athens, is ☎706.

A drive through the mountains on the secondary roads takes you through endless hairpins and narrow passes; Hwy-348 ascends a particularly impressive pass at the White County line, crossed at the top by the Appalachian Trail. The towns and villages are disappointing, though, too often unremarkable or kitsch. **HELEN**, about 35 miles northeast of Dahlonega, has been turned into a pseudo-Bavarian "theme village", full of fake half-timbered houses and gift shoppes. The *Helendorf Inn* on Main St (☎878-2271; ③) overlooks the Chattahoochee River.

This area is particularly famous for its **waterfalls**: most are fairly inaccessible, and you'll need a vehicle and some patience finding your way on dirt forest roads, but they're worth the effort. Among the best are **High Shoals Falls** and **Duke's Creek Falls**, both off Hwy-75 between Helen and Hiawassee. Visitor centers in Clayton and elsewhere supply directions on how to get to them, as well as details of **whitewater rafting** expeditions on the Chattooga River in the far northeastern corner of the state. Half-day trips for beginners cost around $40, or a little more at weekends, and there are harder routes and overnight trips if you have canoeing experience. Companies include *Wildwater Ltd* (☎1-800/451-9972) and *Nantahala Outdoor Center* (☎1-800/232-7238).

Athens

The small and very likeable city of **ATHENS**, almost seventy miles northeast of Atlanta, is home to the 30,000 students of the University of Georgia, and has a liberal feel – and city government – unusual for the South. The compact downtown area north of the campus is alive with book and record stores, clubs, bars, restaurants, and cafés; Broad Street in particular is lined with sidewalk tables. It may be short on formal attractions – antebellum homes, a double-barrelled Civil War cannon on the grounds of city hall that never worked, and the Tree That Owns Itself – but it has achieved world fame in recent years as the home of such innovative rock groups as REM and the B52s, both of whom are still based here.

Pilgrims drawn by the REM connection will want to head straight for the original home of the *Automatic for the People* slogan – *Weaver D's* soul-food café, well within walking distance east of downtown at 1016 E Broad St (☎353-7797). Unaffected by its new sideline in memorabilia, it continues to serve its delicious southern fried chicken and vegetables on molded polystyrene plates. The group started out playing at the *40 Watt Club*, originally housed at 171 College Ave but now resurrected in its third and by far its largest premises at 285 W Washington St (☎549-7871), and half-owned by Barrie Buck, wife of drummer Peter Buck. These days the *40 Watt* doesn't put on as many local bands as its half-dozen nearby rival music clubs – such as the lively *Sugar Bowl* sports bar, 312 E Washington St (☎613-0021), where regular performers include Five-Eight and Nathan Sheppard – but it remains determinedly eclectic. Big-name bands tend to appear at the *Georgia Theatre*, 215 N Lumpkin St (☎353-3405), a converted movie theater which still shows films on quiet nights.

Practicalities

Greyhound, based at 220 W Broad St (☎549-2255), has a regular service to Atlanta, while the *Athens Transit System* operates buses around town, 75¢ flat fare. The **visitor center** is in a small antebellum home a couple of blocks north of campus at 280 E Dougherty St (Mon–Sat 9am–5pm, Sun 2–5pm; ☎404/353-1820).

Lodging choices include the good-value business-oriented *Courtyard by Marriott*, 166 Finley St (☎369-7000; ③), the *Downtowner Motor Inn* near the campus at 1198 S Milledge Ave (☎549-2626; ②), and B&B on a working horse farm at the *Hutchens-Hardeman House*, 5335 Lexington Rd (☎353-1855; ②). For top-quality food, your best bet is *Harry Bissett's New Orleans Café & Oyster Bar*, a simulated French Quarter restaurant at 279 E Broad St (☎353-7065), though the Mexican *Compadres*, 320 E Clayton St (☎546-

0190), is less expensive and puts on live bands. The *Athens Coffee House*, 301 E Clayton St (☎208-9711), serves excellent coffees and desserts (though not breakfasts).

Athens' two trendiest bars are *The Globe*, 199 N Lumpkin St (☎353-4721) – settle down in an old rocking chair or leather sofa and select from a huge array of beers – and the *Mellow Mushroom*, 259 E Broad St (☎613-0892).

Central Georgia

The broad expanse of **central Georgia**, south of Atlanta, is famous more for its people than for places to see. **Otis Redding**, **James Brown**, **Little Richard** and the **Allman Brothers** were all born or grew up in the area, while peanut farmer-cum-president **Jimmy Carter** came from little Plains, roughly 120 miles due south of the capital.

Few of its small towns hold very much of interest, though vegetable fanatics may enjoy **Juliette**, twenty miles north of Macon, where the original *Whistle Stop Café* is still frying the green tomatoes celebrated in the 1991 movie, and **Vidalia** further east, the self-proclaimed "Sweet Onion Capital of the World". The largest communities are the dull army center of **Columbus** and the textile town of **Macon**.

Macon

MACON, eighty miles southeast of Atlanta on I-75 where I-16 branches off to Florida, makes an attractive stop en route to Savannah, above all when its 170,000 **cherry trees** erupt with frothy blossom (celebrated by a festival in the third week of March).

As the highest navigable point on the Ocmulgee River, Macon was a major cotton port, and its spacious streets still hold over four hundred two-storey white-columned buildings. Among historic homes open to visitors, the opulent Italian Rennaissance Revival **Hay House** at 934 Georgia Ave (Mon–Sat 10am–5pm, Sun 1–5pm) is quite extraordinary – a vast mansion, topped by a cupola reached by a 28ft spiral staircase, where the job of restoration is endless.

Macon was home to Little Richard, Otis Redding (the plain Otis Redding Memorial Bridge is just east of downtown) and the **Allman Brothers**; Duane Allman and Berry Oakley, killed here in motorcycle smashes in 1971 and 1972 respectively, are buried in **Rose Hill Cemetery** on Riverside Drive, the inspiration of various of the band's songs.

Ocmulgee National Monument
Between 900 and 1100 AD, people of the Mississippian culture migrated from the Mississippi Valley to a spot a couple of miles east of modern downtown Macon, and levelled the site overlooking the Ocmulgee River that is now **Ocmulgee National Monument** (daily 9am–5pm; free). Their settlement of thatched huts has vanished, but two grassy mounds, each thought to have been topped by a temple, still rise prominently from the plateau. Near the informative visitor center, which holds artefacts from excavations in the area, you can enter the underground chamber of a ceremonial **earthlodge**. Modern wooden supports now hold up the roof, replacing the original timbers whose fiery destruction baked the clay floor, thereby preserving a ring of individually molded seats, and an extraordinary bird-shaped altar or dais.

Practicalities
The imposing **Terminal Station** at the foot of Cherry St houses Macon's **visitor center** (no 200; ☎743-3401 or 1-800/768-3401), and is scheduled to become the Georgia

The **area code** for Macon, Savannah and the Georgia coast is ☎912.

Music Hall of Fame; it's the base for Marty Willett's entertaining customized **city tours**, for which he dresses as local poet Sidney Lanier (Mon–Sat 10am & 2pm; $8).

Amtrak no longer serves Macon, but *Greyhound* provides good connections from 65 Spring St (☎743-5411). Though downtown **accommodation** is restricted to the plush B&B *1842 Inn*, 353 College St (☎741-1842; ⑤), and a giant *Radisson*, motels such as *Motel 6*, 4991 Harrison Rd (☎474-2870; ②), surround the I-475/US-80 interchange. The atmospheric wood-panelled *Len Berg's Restaurant*, in Old Post Office Alley off Walnut St (☎742-9255), serves down-home Southern food at bargain prices; *Beall's 1860*, 315 College St (☎745-3663), is much grander – the portico may be familiar from the cover of the Allman Brothers' first album.

Savannah

SAVANNAH, seventeen miles from the sea on the border with South Carolina, is the natural starting point for explorations of the short **Georgia coast**. Its appealing **Historic District**, ranged around Spanish-moss swathed squares, formed the core of the original city, while the cobbled waterfront on the **Savannah River**, key to the postwar economy, is towered over by old cotton warehouses.

Savannah was founded in 1733 by James Oglethorpe as the first settlement of the new British colony of Georgia; Oglethorpe himself was anti-slavery, but with the arrival of North Carolinan settlers, plantation agriculture, based on slave labor, thrived. The town became a major export center, at the end of important railroad lines by which **cotton** was funnelled from far away in the South. Sherman arrived here in December 1864 at the end of his March to the Sea; he offered the town to Abraham Lincoln as a Christmas gift, but at Lincoln's urgings left it intact and set to work apportioning land to freed slaves. This was the first recognition of the need for "reconstruction", but such concrete economic provision for slaves was rarely to occur again.

The plantations floundered after the Civil War; cotton prices slumped, and Savannah went into decline. There was little industry beyond the port, and as that fell into disuse and decay so too did Savannah's graceful town houses and tree-lined boulevards. It was not until the 1950s that local citizens started to organize what has been, on the whole, the successful restoration of their town – recently, and tentatively, extended to the predominantly black **Victorian District**.

Arrival, Getting Around and Information

Savannah's **airport**, served by several major airlines, is five miles west of the city. A taxi downtown costs around $15. The **bus station** (☎232-2135) is just north of downtown at 610 E Oglethorpe Ave, while the **railway station** is about three miles out, at 2611 Seaboard Coastline Drive. It isn't served by buses; a taxi in costs about $7.

The historic district is best explored on foot, but if you want to get further out, *Chatham Area Transit* (*CAT*) operates a reasonable **bus** network (☎233-5767). Route maps are available from the **visitor center**, 301 Martin Luther King Jr Blvd (Mon–Fri 8.30am–5pm, Sat & Sun 9am–5pm; ☎944-0456), which also has discount accommodation coupons and details of walking tours. Trolley and minibus tours leave from here. Romantic moonlit **horse and carriage** tours depart from outside the *Hyatt Regency* (☎236-6756; $9.50). *Gray Line Tours*, 215 W Boundary St (☎236-9604), also runs further afield. **Bicycles** can be rented from the *City Market Bicycle Shoppe*, 211 W Julian St (☎233-9401), which will deliver to hotels in the historic district.

The Town

Savannah's **Historic District** is flanked by the river, Martin Luther King Jr Blvd in the west, and to the east, Broad Street, the old commercial main street, now a depressing

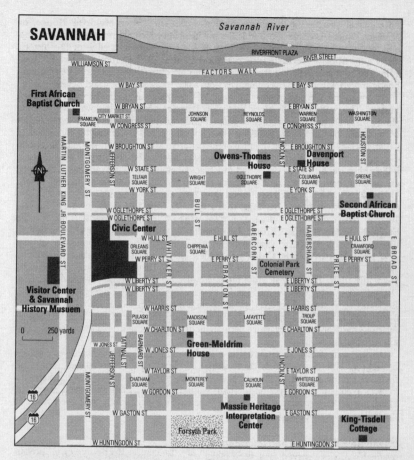

SAVANNAH

Savannah River

WILLIAMSON ST

RIVERFRONT PLAZA
RIVER STREET
FACTORS WALK

W BAY ST · E BAY ST

First African
Baptist Church

W BRYAN ST · E BRYAN ST

FRANKLIN CITY MARKET ST
SQUARE · JOHNSON SQUARE · REYNOLDS SQUARE · WARREN SQUARE · WASHINGTON SQUARE

W CONGRESS ST · E CONGRESS ST

W BROUGHTON ST · E BROUGHTON ST

W STATE ST

Owens-Thomas House

Davenport House

E STATE ST

TELFAIR SQUARE · WRIGHT SQUARE · OGLETHORPE SQUARE · COLUMBIA SQUARE · GREENE SQUARE

W YORK ST · E YORK ST

W OGLETHORPE ST · E OGLETHORPE ST

Second African
Baptist Church

Civic Center

W HULL ST · E HULL ST · E HULL ST

ORLEANS SQUARE · CHIPPEWA SQUARE · Colonial Park Cemetery · CRAWFORD SQUARE

W PERRY ST · E PERRY ST · E PERRY ST

W LIBERTY ST · E LIBERTY ST
W LIBERTY ST · E LIBERTY ST

Visitor Center
& Savannah
History Museum

W HARRIS ST · E HARRIS ST

0   250 yards

PULASKI SQUARE · MADISON SQUARE · LAFAYETTE SQUARE · TROUP SQUARE

W CHARLTON ST · E CHARLTON ST

W JONES ST
W JONES ST

Green-Meldrim
House

E JONES ST

W TAYLOR ST · E TAYLOR ST

CHATHAM SQUARE · MONTEREY SQUARE · CALHOUN SQUARE · WHITEFIELD SQUARE

W GORDON ST · E GORDON ST

16

16

W GASTON ST

Massie Heritage
Interpretation
Center

E GASTON ST

King-Tisdell
Cottage

Forsyth Park

W HUNTINGDON ST · E HUNTINGDON ST

MARTIN LUTHER KING JR BOULEVARD · MONTGOMERY ST · JEFFERSON ST · WHITAKER ST · BULL ST · DRAYTON ST · ABERCORN ST · HABERSHAM ST · PRICE ST · E BROAD ST · HOUSTON ST · LINCOLN ST · TATTNALL ST · BARNARD ST · JEFFERSON ST · MONTGOMERY ST

series of boarded-up shops and offices. You can get an overview at the **Savannah History Museum**, in the restored Railroad Station at 303 Martin Luther King Jr Blvd, behind the visitor center (daily 8.30am–5pm; $3), where an informative jaunt through Native American culture, colonial development, the river and the Civil War is let down slightly by a slide show that is less a history lesson than a hard-sell promotion for Savannah's considerable charms.

The best way to get a feel for the place is simply to wander the "tabby" streets – made from a kind of primitive concrete mashed up with oyster shells – lined with shuttered federal, Regency and antebellum houses adorned with intricate iron balconies. The shady residential **squares**, ablaze with dogwood, azaleas and magnolias, offer peaceful respite from the blistering summer heat.

Most visitors to Savannah take in one or two of its old **mansions**, such as the classic British Regency **Owens-Thomas House**, 124 Abercorn St (Feb–Dec Tues–Sat 10am–5pm, Sun & Mon 2–5pm; $5), or the red-brick Georgian **Davenport House**, 324 E State St (Mon–Wed & Fri–Sat 10am–4pm, Sun 1.30–4pm; $4). The latter, the first restoration project of the *Historic Savannah Foundation*, is sparsely furnished but boasts a wonderful elliptical staircase and delicate plaster work. The **Green-Meldrim House**, on Madison Square, is a splendid Gothic Revival mansion which Sherman used as his head-quarters (Tues & Thurs–Sat 10am–4pm; $3). At the southern edge of the historic district, the **Massie Heritage Interpretation Center**, 207 E Gordon St (Mon–Fri 9am–4pm; $1.50 donation), illuminates Savannah's architecture with displays on its neighbor-hoods and growth, and traces influences from as far away as London and Beijing.

Savannah was the port of entry for many of Georgia's slaves, and has a strong **black history**. The predominantly black **Victorian District**, southeast of downtown, is being slowly restored, and has a couple of good, if underfunded, museums. The nerve center of the restoration process is the **King-Tisdell Cottage**, 514 E Huntingdon St, owned by a middle-class black family at the turn of the century (Mon–Fri noon–4.30pm, Sat & Sun 1–4pm; $1.50). In addition to a fine collection of *gullah* baskets and African woodcarving, it illustrates the history of slaves and free blacks before the Civil War, and of the freed slaves after, commemorating Savannah's role as the site of Sherman's famous **"Field Order #15"**, which granted each freed slave forty acres and a mule. The museum also operates excellent **black heritage tours** (leaving from the visitor center, Mon–Sat 10am & 1pm; call a day in advance on ☎234-8000; $10). The two-hour tour takes in the **Second African Baptist Church**, 123 Houston St, where Field Order #15 was signed; the poor black **Yamacraw** neighborhood, now sadly run-down and depressed; and the 1777 **First African Baptist Church**, the oldest black church in North America, built by slaves. This latter, at 23 Montgomery St in the Historic District, can also be visited inde-pendently (daily 10am–2pm). Note the decorative carvings on the pews and diamond-shaped holes on the floor, ventilation for slaves escaping on the Underground Railroad. Back in the Victorian District, the airy **Beach Institute**, 502 E Harris St (Mon–Fri noon–5pm, Sat & Sun 1–4pm), Georgia's first school for freed slaves, today houses an African-American art gallery with a permanent display of extraordinary woodcarvings by folk artist Ulysses Davis.

On the **waterfront**, River Street is a lively commercial area cobbled with ballast brought by eighteenth-century cargo ships. Tall brick cotton warehouses, said to be haunted by the ghosts of the slave stevedores, are connected by iron bridges to Factors Walk and Bay Street on the bluff behind; benches along the paved Riverfront Plaza, site of a lively festival on the first Saturday of every month, give good views of the still considerable port activity.

Accommodation

By far the nicest places to stay in Savannah are the central **B&Bs** in elegant private houses, but if you're on a tight budget the usual insalubrious **hotels** congregate on and around Boundary St near the *Greyhound* station, and chain **motels** are further out on Ogeechee Rd (US-17). The *Last Minute Rooms* service can arrange fifty percent discounts on one-night stays if you call on the day (☎238-1389).

The nearest **campground** is six miles southeast, at **Skidaway Island State Park** (☎598-0393); a barrier, or "sea" island with an interesting combination of salt and fresh-water habitats.

Bed and Breakfast Inn, 117 W Gordon St (☎238-0518). Great-value B&B in 1853 town house over-looking shady square – reservations essential. German-speaking owners. ②.

Days Inn, 201 W Bay St (☎236-4440). The most affordable hotel in the Historic District, if lacking the character of the B&Bs. ④.

Gastonian Inn, 220 E Gaston Rd (☎232-2869). Splendidly romantic B&B, beloved of honeymoon couples. Two-night minimum stay. ⑤.

Mulberry Inn, 601 E Bay St (☎238-1200). Friendly *Holiday Inn*-owned hotel with B&B feel (free iced tea and cookies in the lounge). Rooftop jacuzzi, courtyard, and luxurious riverview rooms. ④.

Olde Harbour Inn, 508 E Factors Walk (☎234-4100 or 1-800/553-6533). Very luxurious B&B-style hotel in old waterfront warehouse. Fabulous full breakfasts, and wine and cheese receptions. ⑤.

Eating

Savannah has a great number of **restaurants**, with many – usually pricey – seafood places on the riverfront. The City Market, a couple of blocks south of W Factors Walk, has a couple of stylish pasta and New American restaurants.

Bistro Savannah, 309 W Congress St (☎233-6266). Delicious Cajun and far-Eastern dishes near the City Market, with a menu worthy of far more expensive restaurants.

City Market Café, 224 W St Julian St (☎236-7133). Upmarket pasta, salads and seafood for around $7. Cool brick-walled interior and pleasant outdoor seating.

Dockside Seafood, 201 W River St (☎236-9253). Traditional seafood and "low country bakes" in the riverside's oldest building, an eighteenth-century ships' chandlery.

Mrs Wilkes' Boarding House, 107 W Jones St (☎232-5997). Savannah's most famous eating place, a real Southern experience run by the redoubtable Mrs Wilkes. Everyone sits around a large table, helping themselves to delicious mounds of fried chicken, sweet potatoes, spinach, beans, spaghetti. As much as you can eat for $8. There's no sign outside; just join the line.

The Shrimp Factory, 313 E River St (☎236-4229). Good and unusual shrimp dishes on the waterfront, moderate to expensive.

Wall's BBQ, between Price and Houston in the alley between York and Oglethorpe (Wed–Sat only). Tiny and spartan, with good soul food. It's difficult to spend more than $5.

Bars, Clubs and Music

Savannah's nightlife is more laid-back than Atlanta's – if unusually strict about demanding ID. Everything is fairly close together, ranged between the City Market and the river. There's an annual **jazz festival** in late September or October. For information on this or other jazz events/venues, contact the *Coastal Jazz Association* at ☎232-2222.

The Bottom Line, 206 W Julian St (☎232-0812). Be-bop, traditional and big-band jazz in the City Market, with moderate cover charge.

Congress St Station, 121 W Congress St (☎233-2259). Attracts a younger and more studenty crowd, with progressive rock and college bands.

The Crossroads, 219 W Julian St (☎234-5438). Live blues Tues–Sat.

Crystal Beer Parlor, 301 W Jones St (☎232-1153). A convivial padded-booth bar, with moderately priced Southern food.

Hard Hearted Hannah's, *DeSoto Hilton Hotel*, 15 E Liberty St (☎232-9000). Old-fashioned night out in cosy book-lined bar; cool jazz and informal atmosphere, Mon–Sat. Watch out for veteran piano-player Emma Kelly, who knows 6000 songs by heart. Happy Hour and free *hors d'oeuvres* 5–7pm.

Malone's, 27 Barnard St (☎234-3059). Club with disco and live jazz and rock, and a younger crowd; extremely lively, crowded, and a lot of fun.

Out from Savannah

Tybee Island, 18 miles east of the city on US-80, is served by three daily *C&H* buses (☎232-7099) from the Civic Center in Savannah. Here you'll find Savannah's best – and not too overdeveloped – **beach**, as well as a 154ft lighthouse, at 30 Meddin Drive, which dates from 1736 and houses a small museum at the base. Abundant **accommodation** options include the new *Ocean Plaza Inn*, 15th St (☎786-7664; ③). *Spanky's Beachside* at 404 Butler Ave (☎786-5520) has live rock and "beach music" at weekends.

Ten miles out on 7601 Skidaway Rd on bus #16, **Wormsloe State Historic Site** (Tues–Sat 9am–5pm, Sun 2–5.30pm; $1.50) is the site of an eighteenth-century defensive plantation. The atmospheric tabby ruins of the fortified house of British settler Noble Jones are now overgrown with palms and lush forest, while the museum offers a film portraying the early settlement of Savannah, archeological finds, and demonstrations of the skills and crafts of the first settlers. **Fort Pulaski National Monument**, off US-80 E, is the most interesting of several local forts (daily summer 8.30am–6.30pm; winter 8.30am–5.15pm; $1). An impressive Confederate stronghold, it was nevertheless taken by Union troops, the first masonry fortress to be pierced by rifled cannon fire.

Brunswick and the Southern Coast

BRUNSWICK, the one sizeable settlement south of Savannah, makes an obvious base for exploring the offshore **Sea Islands**. It's not in itself very exciting, although the shrimp docks are quite interesting when the catch is brought in. The **visitor center** (daily 9am–5pm; ☎264-5337) has lists of budget **motels** and central **B&Bs** such as the *Rose Manor Guest House*, 1108 Richmond St (☎267-6369; ③). Dorm beds cost just $7 at the welcoming *Hostel in the Forest*, nine miles west of town on US-84 (☎264-9738; ①); it even boasts a couple of treehouses.

The **Hofwyl-Broadfield Plantation**, ten miles north of Brunswick on US-17, gives a vivid idea of life under slavery (Tues–Sat 9am–5pm; $1.50). A good exhibit covers the rice cultivation that made the planters so wealthy, and you can see the surprisingly modest plantation house where their descendants lived until the 1970s. Occasional **gospel** concerts are held here on summer Saturdays, with soul food on sale.

The Sea Islands

Several of the **SEA ISLANDS**, off the coast north of **Darien**, were divided after the Civil War between freed slaves. They remained poor, agricultural communities, however, and little now remains from those years for an outsider to see.

The **southern islands** are the most developed, all with swanky resort pretensions. This is largely due to **Jekyll Island**, bought in 1887 for use as an exclusive club by a group of millionaires whose absurdly opulent "village" is still standing (daily summer 10am–4pm; winter 9.30am–2pm; $2). Jekyll is the one island to hold much **accommodation**, most of it expensive; the *Clarion-Buccaneer Beach Resort*, 85 Beachview Drive (☎635-2261; ③), has the lowest rates. There's a **campground** a little further north (☎635-3021; $10), near the nesting sites of loggerhead turtles.

Most of the bigger **St Simon's Island** is still a pleasant landscape of marshes and live oaks covered with Spanish moss. At the (free) Sea Island Festival here in late August, you can hear traditional music and see folk crafts being made (☎638-9014). **Fort Frederica National Monument**, seven miles north of the causeway (daily summer 8am–8pm; winter 8am–5pm; $1.50), was built in 1736 by General Oglethorpe as the largest British fort in North America; now it's an atmospheric ruin.

To the south, **Cumberland Island** is a stunning wildlife refuge of marshes, beaches and semitropical forest, with the odd deserted planter's mansion, and wild horses. You can get there by ferry from the village of St Mary's to the south near the Florida border (out at 9am and 11.45am, returning at 10.15am and 4.45pm, taking 45min; $7.50).

Okefenokee Swamp

The dense semitropical **OKEFENOKEE SWAMP** stretches over thirty miles down to Florida from a point roughly thirty miles southwest of Brunswick. Tucked away among its astonishing profusion of luxuriant plants and trees are something like 20,000 alligators, over thirty species of snakes, and bears and pumas. You can only get in at the **Okefenokee Swamp Park**, a private charity-owned concession at the northeast end, on Hwy-177, off US-23/1, not served by public transportation (summer 9am–6.30pm; otherwise 9am–5.30pm; $8). The fee includes a half-hour boat trip through the swamp, a serpentarium, a good interpretive center on wildlife, an observation tower, reconstructed pioneer buildings – and a lot of disconcertingly large alligators.

Unlovely **WAYCROSS**, ten miles north, holds bargain **motels** such as the *Pinecrest* (☎283-3580; ①). The **Okefenokee Heritage Center** (Mon–Sat 10am–5pm, Sun 2–4pm; $4) has slightly erratic displays on the history of the swamp.

KENTUCKY

Two hundred years after it was wrested from the Indians, **KENTUCKY** still hasn't quite made up its mind as to whether it belongs in the North or the South. Both the rival presidents in the Civil War, Abraham Lincoln and Jefferson Davis, were born here, and divisions were acute between slave-owning farmers and the merchants who depended on trade with the nearby cities of the industrial north. Officially neutral, seventy thousand Kentuckians joined the Union army and forty thousand the Confederates. After the war Kentucky sided with the South in its hostility to Reconstruction, and since then it has remained solidly Democrat.

Kentucky's rugged beauty is at its most appealing in the mountainous **east** and the small historic towns of the **Bluegrass Downs**, with visits enlivened by the varied attractions of bourbon whiskey, thoroughbred horses and bluegrass music. **Louisville**, home of the **Kentucky Derby**, is a busy manufacturing and arts center; the more reserved **Lexington**, eighty miles east, is a major horse-breeding marketplace.

Getting Around Kentucky

Kentucky's limited **public transport** can be a real headache. There's a full *Greyhound* service along the interstates south of Louisville and Lexington (and both have surprisingly good city transport), but a lot of ground is left uncovered. *Amtrak* doesn't operate here at all. **Cycling** is a pleasant and manageable option; if you're **driving**, be sure to keep small change for the tolls on the state highways. Lexington has its own small airport, but it's also within easy reach of the airport for Cincinnati, Ohio, which is in Covington, Kentucky (see p.225). Louisville is served by the larger Standiford Field.

Lexington, Bluegrass and East Kentucky

The fertile **Bluegrass Downs**, just eighty miles across, form the base of America's thoroughbred racing industry, with **Lexington** quietly prospering at its heart. The name comes from the unique steel-blue sheen of the buds in the meadows, only visible in early morning during April and May. Kentucky's first white pioneers, who trekked in the 1770s through the 150 miles of wilderness now called the **Daniel Boone National Forest**, were amazed to find this "Eden" deserted while the Indians lived in much less attractive terrain. Anthropologists have now discovered that the area's twelfth-century inhabitants were plagued by fatal bone diseases, due to mineral deficiencies in the soil.

Around modern Lexington are some of the oldest towns west of the Alleghenies. However, alongside the fine scenery of the **Natural Bridge** and **Cumberland Gap** districts, eastern Kentucky also suffers from acute rural poverty.

Lexington

The productivity of the bluegrass fields has kept **LEXINGTON**'s economy ticking over since 1775, though its lack of a navigable river always made its traders vulnerable to competition from Louisville. Eighty miles east of Louisville and ninety south of Cincinnati, it still retains large numbers of fine antebellum houses. However, its current affluence dates from after World War I, when smoking caught on internationally and Lexington emerged as the world's largest burley **tobacco** market. Despite a population now exceeding 200,000, the city maintains an almost rustic atmosphere, with its most conspicuous activity the **horse** trade.

> The **area code** for Lexington and eastern Kentucky is ☎606.

Arrival and Information

Lexington's **airport** is six miles west of town on US-60W, near Keeneland racetrack (handy for the jets of the horse-breeders). *Greyhound* (☎255-4261) drops off about a mile from downtown at 477 New Circle Rd – take bus #6. *Lex-Tran* (☎252-4636) operates a good service to the University and suburbs, including a downtown trolley, but you need a car to reach the horse-related attractions. The **visitor center** is in the civic center at 430 W Vine St (Mon–Fri 8.30am–5pm, Sat 10am–5pm; ☎848-1224).

Downtown Lexington

The plush hotels, glass office blocks, skywalks and shopping malls of Lexington's city center, set in a dip on the Bluegrass Downs, crowd in on fountain-filled **Triangle Park**. Despite its age, the city lacks buildings of historical interest; the early merchants threw up mostly functional structures, preferring to get on with making money. The red-brick ivy-covered buildings of small 1780 **Transylvania University** are behind the Courthouse at N Broadway and Third Street (the name means "across the woods", an appropriate description of Kentucky at the time). At the other side of downtown, the **Art Museum** on the sprawling University of Kentucky campus displays contemporary American art and Indian artefacts (during semester only, Tues–Sun noon–5pm; free).

Lexington's Horses

Along **Paris** and **Ironworks Pikes**, northeast of Lexington, in an idyllic Kentuckian landscape, sleek thoroughbred horses cavort in bluegrass meadows. Some farms are still staked out by miles of immaculate white-plank fences, though most now use the cheaper but much less attractive black creosote to protect the wood. You can watch the horses' early-morning workouts at **Keeneland racecourse** to the west (April–Oct daily dawn–9.30am; free), after a super-cheap breakfast at the adjacent *Keeneland Kitchen*. Tasteful dark-green grandstands emphasize the crisp white rails around the one-mile oval track, and the absence of a public address system makes for a unique race-day atmosphere; thousands of puzzled voices, trying to work out which horse is which, break into loud cheers as they hurtle into the final furlong (racing for 3 weeks in April, Tues–Sun 1pm, and 3 weeks in Oct, Wed–Sun 1pm; $2–5).

Tours of horse farms used to be very popular, but owners have become reluctant to let the public get too close to the shy creatures. One exception is **Spendthrift Farm**, seven miles out at 884 Ironworks Pike (via I-75 Exit 120), which commands stud fees of up to $20,000 for its thirty stallions. From February to June, visitors come specifically to watch the horses "at stud" in a special viewing gallery. Tours are free but you should tip the groom (Mon–Sat, summer 10am–2pm, otherwise 10am–noon; ☎255-2003).

The enjoyable **Kentucky Horse Park** is a little further along at 4089 Ironworks Pike (mid-March to Oct daily 9am–5pm; otherwise Wed–Sun only; $8.95). Its museum traces the use of horses throughout history, from Roman chariot races through cavalry regiments, commercial haulage and modern sports. The 1032-acre park also features live specimens of over thirty different breeds, and a working farm.

Accommodation

Lexington has very little accommodation to offer downtown, but budget **motels** can be found around the exits from I-75. If you're stuck, *Dial-A-Ccommodations* (☎233-7299) help to find rooms. The best **campground** (☎233-4303) is at the Horse Park.

Kimball House Motel, 267 S Limestone St (☎252-9565). Much the most central option. Ten-room downtown boarding house with antique-furnished rooms. ③.

La Quinta, 1919 Stanton Way (☎231-7551). Handily placed at the I-75/I-64 intersection. ③.

University of Kentucky (☎257-3721). A few rooms available during the academic year, and plenty during the summer. ①.

YMCA, 239 E High St (☎255-9622). Dingy downtown men-only location, often fully booked. ①.

Eating and Drinking

Lexington's large student population means it has several lively youth-oriented **eating places**, besides the steakhouses catering for the horse crowd and conventioneers. Fast-food cafés, open until early evening, fill the third floor of central **Festival Market** at Main Street and Broadway; the streets around the back hold a few lively bars which flourish despite the Baptist-inspired 1am curfew on bars and clubs.

Alfalfa, 557 S Limestone St (☎253-0014). Hippyish café, near the University of Kentucky. A wide range of international, mostly vegetarian dishes. Lunch specials $3–5, evening meals under $10.

The Bar, 224 E Main St (☎255-1551). Popular, late-opening downtown gay disco.

De Sha's, 101 N Broadway (☎259-3771). *The* downtown place to be seen eating. Seafood and steak dishes in nice surroundings, if a bit pricey. Reservations required.

High on Rose Cantina, 301 E High St (☎233-2243). All-purpose diner serving good-value Tex-Mex food and beer, to a backdrop of loud music, until 1am.

Ramsey's Diner, 496 E High St (☎259-2708). Very popular and atmospheric. Tasty sandwiches, burgers and meals for $4–8. After 10.30pm cheap snacks are available from the bar, open until 1am.

The Virtual Gallery, 117 S Upper Street (☎231-1529). New (alcohol-free) venue for alternative bands and art shows.

Bluegrass Country

Apart from the horse farms directly to the north of Lexington, most places of interest lie to the south, such as the fine old towns of **Danville** and **Harrodsburg**, and the restored **Shaker Village**. After approximately forty miles the meadows give way to the striking **Knobs** – random lumpy outcrops, shrouded in trees and wispy low-hanging clouds, that are the eroded remnants of the Pennyrile Plateau.

Harrodsburg

Old Fort Harrod State Park at **HARRODSBURG**, 25 miles west of Lexington on US-68, reconstructs the first permanent English settlement west of the Alleghenies, founded in 1774 by Captain James Harrod. At the *Fort Harrod Motel*, opposite the park at 115 S College St (☎734-4189; ②), owner Marti Williamson sells and plays vintage Kentucky **musical instruments**.

Shaker Village at Pleasant Hill

The Utopian settlement of **PLEASANT HILL**, hidden among the bluegrass hillocks near Harrodsburg, was established by Shaker missionaries from New England around 1805. Within twenty years, five hundred villagers were producing seeds, tools and cloth, for sale as far away as New Orleans. During the Civil War, Union and Confederate troops alike were billeted upon the pacifist Shakers. Numbers thereafter declined until the last member died in 1923, but a non-profit organization has since 1961 returned the village to its nineteenth-century appearance.

The Shaker values of absolute celibacy, hygiene, simplicity and communal ownership have left their mark on the 27 grey and pastel-colored dwellings, which women and men entered via different doors. There are demonstrations of broom-making, weaving, quilting and other traditional crafts, and also summer excursions on the sternwheeler *Dixie Belle* (village daily summer 9am–5pm; winter hours vary; $8.50, or $11.50 with *Dixie Belle*). The *Trustees Office Inn* houses a superb **restaurant** specializing in boiled ham, lemon pie and other Kentucky favorites, and also has rooms, which should be reserved well in advance (☎734-5111; ④).

Berea

Thirty miles south of Lexington, just off I-75 in the foothills where Bluegrass meets Appalachia, the unique **BEREA COLLEGE** gives its 1500 students free tuition in return for work in any of 120 crafts ranging from needlework to wrought ironwork. Founded in 1855 by abolitionists as a vocational college for the young people of East Kentucky – both white and black – it was forcefully shut down four years later by mobs opposed to the board's support for John Brown's raid at Harper's Ferry (see p.324).

The **Appalachian Museum** on Jackson St relates the story of the region (Mon–Sat 9am–6pm, Sun 1–6pm; closed Jan). Free campus tours leave from *Boone Hall Tavern*, a student-run hotel and restaurant (☎986-9358) at Main and Prospect streets, taking in the student art gallery and the sales room (Mon & Wed–Sat).

The college's reputation has attracted many private art and craft galleries to little Berea. **Motels** clustered around the exit of I-75 include the *Red Carpet Inn* (☎986-8426; ②); the *Wanpen* nearby at 710 Chestnut St (☎986-4020; ④) serves good Asian food.

Daniel Boone National Forest

Almost the entire eastern length of Kentucky is taken up by the steep slopes, narrow valleys and sandstone cliffs of the unspoiled **DANIEL BOONE NATIONAL FOREST**. Few Americans can have been mythologized as much as **Daniel Boone**, said to have been one of Kentucky's earliest fur-trapping pioneers, in 1767. Perhaps the most famous legend tells of the time he was captured by Shawnee Indians and initiated as *Sheltowee*, or Big Turtle. Learning of plans to attack pioneer communities, Big Turtle escaped just in time to warn the citizens of his own settlement at **Boonesborough**, southeast of Lexington. But all did not end happily ever after. Boone failed to legalize his land claims, and lost practically all of the land in Kentucky he had claimed for himself and his sponsors. The resultant animosity forced the ageing frontiersman to press further west to Missouri in 1798, where he died in 1820 aged 86.

Natural Bridge and Around

The geological extravaganza of the **Red River Gorge**, sixty miles east of Lexington via the Mountain Parkway, is best seen by taking a thirty-mile loop drive from the **Natural Bridge Resort Park** on Hwy-77 near the village of Slade. Natural Bridge itself is a large sandstone arch surrounded by steep hollows and exposed clifflines; for the best panoramic view, continue to the solid span of **Sky Bridge**, which stretches along the top of a thin ridge. As well as hiking trails, canoeing, fishing, rock-climbing and camping, there's cottage **accommodation** in secluded *Hemlock Lodge* (☎663-2214; ④).

For all its natural beauty, the **Snakey Hollow** area shows stark rural deprivation. Some tourists come here to see whether Hollywood images of backwardness, incest and violence square up in real life, but it's surely best to leave such communities undisturbed.

Towards the Southeast

In 1940, "Colonel" Harlan Sanders opened a small diner at the back of a filling station in tiny **CORBIN**, ninety miles south of Lexington on I-75. His **Kentucky Fried Chicken** empire has since spread to over 58 countries. The original 100-seat restaurant, near the junction of US-25E and US-25W, has been restored with 1940s decor and memorabilia (daily 7am–11pm; ☎528-2163). The bespectacled Sanders (1890–1980) was not a soldier, but a member of the Honorable Order of Kentucky Colonels.

STEARNS, fifty miles southwest of Corbin on Hwy-92, is a classic former mining-company town, one of many such in the Appalachians, in which the company owned every building – shops, church, sheriff's office and all. As one Thirties writer put it, "with their unpaved streets and unpainted buildings (they) come into view like blighted spots on the land, with all the inconveniences and few if any of the comforts of modern towns of equal size." The **Stearns Museum** at 1 Henderson St (mid-April to Oct Wed–Sun 10am–5pm) takes a sanitized look at this history. The highlight for visitors is the eleven-mile trip on the **Big South Fork Scenic Railway** (mid-April to early Nov daily 11am & 3pm; ☎1-800/462-5664), which traverses deep woodlands and descends a rugged 600ft gorge to **Blue Heron**, another former mining community.

On the tristate border of Kentucky, Tennessee and Virginia, the **Cumberland Gap National Historic Park** is one of the most visited parts of Boone Forest. A natural passageway used by migrating deer and bison, it served as a gateway to the west for Boone and other pioneers. **Pinnacle Overlook**, a 1000ft lookout over the three states, is near the visitor center (☎248-2817) on US-25E in **Middlesboro**.

Just outside the forest boundaries on the Virginia border, there are plenty of coal-fields and lumber forests, but few people. The high death toll in underground mines and the ecological disasters of strip-mining have drawn national attention, particularly during the violent struggles of the Thirties in places such as **Harlan County**, where striking miners were killed and evicted from their homes by armed company men.

Louisville, Central and Western Kentucky

In heavily rural Kentucky, the manufacturing giant of **Louisville** stands out, with its lively cultural and racial mix. Only occasionally does it bother with the laid-back southern image other parts of the state are so keen to promote. In the **southern** hinterland, numerous small towns retain their tree-shaded squares and nineteenth-century town houses – and their strict Baptist beliefs – and the endless caverns of **Mammoth Cave National Park** attract spelunkers and hikers in their thousands. The west, where the Ohio River meets the Mississippi, is flat, heavily forested and generally less attractive.

Louisville

LOUISVILLE, just south of Indiana across the Ohio River, is firmly embedded in the American national consciousness for its multimillion-dollar **Kentucky Derby**. Each year, the horse race attracts over 500,000 fans to this cosmopolitan and well-diversified industrial city, which still bears the traces of the early French settlers who came upriver from New Orleans. A third of the USA's bourbon is made here, and it's also home to the giant Philip Morris company – manufacturers of *Marlboro* cigarettes – which until recently was the target of an acrimonious national boycott, spearheaded by Louisville's gay community, for its backing of far-right politicians like Jesse Helms.

Louisville's history revolves around a perennial rivalry with Cincinnati, a mere one hundred miles upstream. For example, despite being pro-Union during the Civil War, it promoted itself thereafter – erecting Confederate statues and so on – as the place for southern business to invest, as opposed to midwestern Yankee cities like Cincinnati.

As well as a lively arts scene and lots of citywide festivals, Louisville boasts an unrivalled network of public parks, many designed by Frederick Law Olmstead. One native son who took advantage of the recreation facilities was three-times world heavyweight boxing champion **Muhammad Ali**, who used to do his early-morning roadwork in the scenic environs of Chickasaw Park.

Arrival and Information

All major US airlines fly into **Standiford Field Airport** (☎367-4636), five miles south of downtown on I-65; take bus #2 or pay a $13 cab fare. *Greyhound* terminates at fairly central 720 W Muhammad Ali Blvd (☎585-3331). An excellent **bus** service (60¢) makes getting around easy. Some routes operate as late as 2am, and downtown **trolleys** run

The **area code** for Louisville, central and western Kentucky is ☎502.

from 7.30am to 6pm. The useful **visitor center**, at 400 S First St (Mon–Fri 8.30am–5pm, Sat & Sun 8.30am–4pm; ☎582-3732; ☎1-800/633-3384 in KY; ☎1-800/626-5646 outside KY), is the boarding point for city tours.

Central Louisville

Downtown Louisville rolls gently down towards Main Street, then abruptly lunges down to the river. **Riverfront Plaza**, between Fifth and Sixth streets, is a prime observation point for the natural **Falls of the Ohio** and the bizarre **Louisville Falls Fountain**, which every fifteen minutes sprays water from an offshore barge 375 feet into the air to form a colored fleur-de-lys, and otherwise looks like a sewage unit discharging into the river. The *Belle of Louisville*, a 1914 steam **stern-wheeler**, leaves nearby for daily cruises during summer (Tues–Sun at 2pm, also Tues & Thurs at 7pm; $7; ☎625-2355).

The most impressive modern structure along Main Street, where skyscrapers blend in with early nineteenth-century warehouses, is the extravagantly marbled **Humana Building** at no 500, the headquarters of a giant hospital group and complete with 2000-year-old Roman statues. Free tours take place on Saturday morning from 10am to 1.30pm, the 25th-floor terrace providing a great view of the Ohio (☎580-3606).

The sizeable **J B Speed Art Museum** at 2035 S Third St, in the University of Louisville campus, displays extensive collections of art and sculpture from medieval to modern times, featuring works by Picasso, Rembrandt, Rubens, Monet and Henry Moore (Tues–Sat 10am–4pm, Sun 1–5pm; $2, free on Sat).

Louisville's Horses: the Kentucky Derby

The **Kentucky Derby** is one of the world's premier horse races; it's also, as gonzo journalist Hunter S Thompson put it, "decadent and depraved". Derby Day itself is the first Saturday in May, at the end of the two-week **Kentucky Derby Festival**. Since 1875, the leading lights of southern society have gathered for an annual orgy of betting, haute cuisine and mint juleps in the plush grandstand, while tens of thousands of the beer-guzzling proletariat cram into the infield. Apart from the $20 infield tickets available on the day – offering virtually no chance of a decent view – all seats are sold out months in advance. The actual race, traditionally preceded by a mass drunken rendition of *My Old Kentucky Home*, is run over a distance of one and a quarter miles, lasts barely two minutes, and offers close to a million dollars in prize money. Only during the Superbowl do television commercials cost more.

Thoroughbreds also race at **Churchill Downs**, three miles south of downtown at 700 Central Ave, in April, May, June, October and November ($1.50; ☎636-4400), and there's harness racing at **Louisville Downs**, 4520 Poplar Level Rd ($2; ☎964-6415), most of the year.

The excellent hands-on **Kentucky Derby Museum**, next to Churchill Downs at 704 Central Ave (#4 bus), will appeal to horse-racing ignoramuses and enthusiasts alike. Admission includes a tour of the racetrack, and a magnificent audio-visual display captures the Derby Day atmosphere on a 360° screen (daily 9am–5pm; $3).

Accommodation

Most of the year, Louisville's **accommodation** is plentiful and reasonably priced, though of course it's incredibly booked up for the Derby Festival. *Kentucky Homes*, 1431 St James Court (☎635-7241), is a **B&B** reservation service. You can **camp** just over the river in Indiana at the central *KOA*, 900 Marriot Drive, Clarksville ($15; ☎812/282-4474), or occasionally at the university (☎588-6691) during festivities.

Days Inn Downtown, 101 E Jefferson St (☎585-2200). Indoor and outdoor pools. ③.

Emily Boone Home Hostel (AYH), 1027 E Franklin St (☎585-3430). Just east of the center among the shotgun houses of Butchertown. $7 plus chores. Reservations essential. ①.

Galt House, 140 Fourth St (☎589-5200). Huge, faded, riverside hotel with lots of character. ④.

Motel 6, 3304 Bardstown Rd (☎456-2861). Seven miles from downtown, near #17 bus route. ①.
Travelodge of Louisville – Downtown, 401 S Second St (☎583-2841). Rates include breakfast. ②.

Eating
Louisville's **restaurants** cater for all tastes, though downtown prices are fairly high.

Baja Bay, 1801 Bardstown Rd (☎459-6398). The best Tex-Mex in town. Try the white chili, a delicious blend of white beans, chicken, onions, cheese and sour cream. Entrees $8–12.

Dietrich's, 2862 Frankfort Ave (☎897-6076). Atmospheric converted picture house in the Crescent Hill district. Inventive seafood and meat choices cooked on a wood-burning grill. Entrees $7–20.

Lilly's, 1147 Bardstown Rd (☎451-0447). Avant-garde decor and a regularly changing menu, strong on veal and seafood. Most main courses cost around $10–12.

Old Spaghetti Factory, 235 W Market St (☎581-1070). Downtown's best value, with main dishes all under $9. Antiques and curiosities give this big-chain restaurant an individual feel.

Nightlife and Entertainment
The **Kentucky Center for the Arts** (☎584-7777 or ☎1-800/283-7777), prominent downtown between Fifth and Sixth avenues and fronted by several outlandish sculptures, is Louisville's main venue for high culture. As for **drinking** and **live music**, the two-mile strip around Bardstown Road and Baxter Avenue (bus #17) is punctuated by fun bars and restaurants; the best **gay** clubs are on the eastern edge of downtown.

Anthony's by the Bridge, 131 W Main St (☎584-7720). Sixty-nine different beers, acoustic/blues music, comedy on Friday and Saturday, and decent pasta dishes for around $8.

Butchertown Pub, 1335 Storey Ave (☎583-2242). Ever-popular live music pub in the Butchertown district near downtown. Cover under $3. Take #15 bus.

Connections, 130 S Floyd St (☎585-5742). The pick of Louisville's gay scene. At weekends this giant club, complete with terrace garden, holds over 2000, playing house and hi-energy.

Phoenix Hill Tavern, 644 Baxter Ave (☎589-4957). Premier live-music venue. Cover $2–3.

Out from Louisville
South from Louisville to Tennessee, **central Kentucky** offers great scope for a one- or two-day driving tour. There's small-town charm in **Bardstown** and Abraham Lincoln's birthplace of **Hodgenville**, while the top natural attraction is the amazing **Mammoth Cave National Park**, the largest underground cave system in the world.

Kentucky's **western** stretches don't compare with the rugged east for scenic beauty; all the significant lakes were created by damming its rivers and much of the land is scarred by strip mines, oilfields and commercial forests. There's little of real interest here except for the **Land Between the Lakes** recreation area, squeezed between Kentucky and Barkley lakes, overlapping the Tennessee border.

Fort Knox
Legendary **FORT KNOX** straddles 100,000 acres either side of US-31W, thirty miles southwest of Louisville. The bomb-proof **Bullion Depository**, surrounded by security fences, machine-gun turrets, patrol guards and huge floodlights, stores nine million pounds of the federal gold reserve behind doors weighing twenty tons apiece. No visits are allowed, and you can only stop by the roadside for a maximum of five minutes.

Bardstown and Bourbon Distilleries
Forty miles south of Louisville on US-31E, attractive **BARDSTOWN** is the place to get acquainted with Kentucky **bourbon whiskey**, created in earliest pioneer days, so the story goes, when Elijah Craig, a Baptist minister, added corn to the usual rye and barley. Named for Bourbon County near Lexington, Kentucky's whiskey soon gained a national reputation, thanks to crisp limestone water and the skills of small-scale distil-

lers. Under federal law, corn must make up at least 51 percent of all solid ingredients, and the drink must mature for two years in new oak barrels with charred interiors.

Get into the spirit at Bardstown's free **Oscar Getz Museum of Whiskey History**, 114 N Fifth St (May–Oct Mon–Sat 9am–5pm, Sun 1–5pm; otherwise times vary). Fourteen miles west at **CLERMONT**, you can tour **Jim Beam's** famous plant (Mon–Sat 9am–4.30pm, Sun 1–4pm; free). **Maker's Mark Distillery**, a small family-run operation twenty miles south of Bardstown near **LORETTO**, is an out-of-the-way collection of beautifully restored black, red and grey plankhouses, in which whiskey is still made manually (Mon–Sat 10.30am–3.30pm; closed Sat in Jan & Feb; free). However, don't expect a sample at either distillery; like most of rural Kentucky, the area is **dry**.

Abraham Lincoln Birthplace

On February 12 1809, **Abraham Lincoln**, the sixteenth president of the USA, was born in a one-room log cabin in the frontier wilds, son of a wandering farmer and, if some accounts are to be believed, an illiterate and illegitimate mother. The original dirt-floored hut, three miles south of **HODGENVILLE** on US-31E, is now enclosed in a granite and marble Memorial Building with 56 steps, one for each year of Lincoln's life. The family moved in 1811 to **Knob Creek**, seven miles east of town, where Lincoln's earliest memory was of slaves being forcefully driven along the road. Little Hodgenville, which the Lincolns left in 1816 for Indiana, doesn't overplay the presidential connection, and its homely cafés make it a good place to stop.

Mammoth Cave National Park

The three hundred miles of labyrinthine passages and domed caverns of **MAMMOTH CAVE NATIONAL PARK** lie halfway between Louisville and Bowling Green, ten miles off I-65. Its amazing geological formations, carved by acidic water trickling through limestone, include a bewildering display of stalagmites and stalagtites, a huge cascade of flowstone known as **Frozen Niagara**, and **Echo River**, 365 feet below ground, populated by a unique species of colorless and sightless fish. Among traces of human occupation are Native American artefacts, a former saltpeter mine, and the remains of an experimental tuberculosis hospital built in 1843 in the belief that the cool atmosphere of the cave would help clear patients' lungs. Access is by guided tour ($3.50–25): tickets from the **visitor center** (☎758-2251) or *Mistix*. Book ahead, especially in summer. The temperature in the caves is a constant 54°F, so take a sweater or jacket.

The park's attractions are by no means all subterranean. The scenic **Green River** cuts through densely forested hillsides and jagged limestone cliffs; you can follow hiking trails, rent canoes, or for a more leisurely trip take the *Miss Green River II* **cruise boat** ($4). **Camping** is free in the backcountry; the *Mammoth Cave Hotel* (☎758-2225) has cottages (②) and motel rooms (④).

The privately owned caves all around, many of which ruin the sights with garish light shows, and the "attractions" in nearby Cave City and Park City, are best ignored.

Bowling Green and Around

BOWLING GREEN's main claim to fame is as the only place where you can buy a drink between Louisville and Nashville, just sixty miles further southwest. It's a lively enough place, though, and offers a treat for **sports car** enthusiasts. One-hour tours of the **General Motors Corvette Plant**, on Louisville Rd, off I-65, take a step-by-step look at the manufacture of one of the great symbols of the American Dream (Mon–Fri at 9am & 1pm; free; ☎745-8419; reservations advisable).

There's another former **Shaker settlement**, with crafts displays, ten miles west of Bowling Green on US-68, in **SOUTH UNION** (April–Nov Mon–Sat 9am–5pm, Sun 1–5pm; ☎542-4167). The 1869 *Shaker Tavern*, a mile or two away on Hwy-73, serves traditional Kentucky recipes such as chess pie (reservations ☎542-6801).

TENNESSEE

TENNESSEE, one of the most visited states in the US, divides into three distinct regions. A shallow rectangle, only one hundred miles from north to south, it stretches 450 miles from the Mississippi to the Appalachians. The marshy **western** third of the state occupies a low plateau edging down towards the Mississippi. Only in the far southwest corner do the bluffs rise high enough to permit a sizeable riverside settlement – the exhilarating port of **Memphis**. Tennessee's largest city is a magnet for music fans, as the birthplace of urban blues and long-time home of **Elvis**. The fine plantation homes and tidy old towns of **Middle Tennessee's** rolling farmland reflect the comfortable lifestyle of its pioneers; if this is the heart of the Bible Belt, then **Nashville**, the state capital and **country music's** mecca, is its buckle. The mountainous **east** shares its top attraction with North Carolina – the peaks, streams and meadows of **Great Smoky Mountains National Park**.

Tennessee's first white settlers, most of them British Protestants, appeared from across the mountains in the 1770s, to settle in the hills and hollows of the Appalachians. Initially relations with the **Cherokee** were good. However, demand for land increased, and confrontations throughout the state culminated in 1838 with the forced removal of the Indians on the "Trail of Tears". One of the main congressional opponents of this process was **Davy Crockett**, familiar from legend as the heavy-drinking hunter in a coonskin cap. When **Civil War** came, the plantation owners of the west maneuvered Tennessee into the Confederacy, against the wishes of the non-slaveholding smallhold farmers in the east. The last state to secede became the primary battlefield in the west, the site of 424 battles and skirmishes.

Despite economic development to rival any in the country, soil erosion and farm mechanization led to a mass migration to the cities in the years before World War I. The fundamentalist beliefs of these transplanted hill-dwellers (whose folk and fiddle music served to spark Nashville's country scene) influenced a **prohibition** movement which kept all Tennessee bone-dry until 1939, and still sees a majority of counties forbidding the sale of alcohol. The New Deal of the Thirties brought significant changes. In particular, the **Tennessee Valley Authority**, created in 1933, harnessed the flood-prone Tennessee River, providing much-needed jobs and cheap power, and ignited the transition from an agricultural to an industrial economy.

Getting Around Tennessee

For such a popular tourist destination, Tennessee has disappointing **transportation** connections. *Amtrak* only calls at Memphis, and while *Greyhound* provides a reasonable service to major towns and cities, travelling by bus through the small towns in the east is very difficult. The **airports** at Memphis and Nashville have extensive connections throughout the USA, though fares between the two are high. If you cherish a fantasy of travelling **by boat** along the Mississippi, unfortunately only luxury craft make the trip these days, at prohibitive prices (see p.400).

Memphis

The cotton-trading capital of the Delta, **MEMPHIS**, perched above the Mississippi two hundred miles east of Nashville and three hundred south of St Louis, is one of the great romantic destinations of the South. Pilgrims come from all over the world to celebrate the city which virtually invented blues, soul and rock'n'roll. The home of *Sun Records* and *Stax* doesn't hype its heritage to the same extent as Nashville or New Orleans; instead a visit to Memphis, with its frequent festivals and vigorous nightlife, feels like an invitation to share in a genuine and enduring local culture.

Culturally and geographically, Memphis has more in common with the deltalands of Mississippi and Arkansas than with the rest of Tennessee. Founded in 1819 and named for Egypt's ancient Nile capital, its fortunes rose and fell with **cotton**. The Confederate defeat which ended the slave trade briefly plunged it into economic chaos, and severe yellow fever epidemics didn't help, but thanks to its potential for river and rail transportation Memphis soon bounced back. The nation's second-largest inland port became a major stopping-off point for **black migrants** escaping the poverty of the Delta, and many stayed, significantly shaping the city's identity and culture.

In the last few years, the tourist influx has given Memphis an appealing new self-confidence, characterized by its most dramatic sight – the extraordinary 321ft glossy stainless-steel **Pyramid** which now dominates the riverfront skyline. **Beale Street** is booming once more, perhaps a little ersatz but always entertaining, while **Elvis Presley**'s Graceland – a refreshing change from the usual "gracious Southern home" – provides an intimate and exuberant glimpse of the city's most famous son.

Arrival, Getting Around and Information

Memphis International Airport is ten miles south of downtown – a long and complicated bus trip, but just fifteen minutes by the *Yellow Cabs* **limo/van** service (☎577-7700; $7) or **taxi** ($15–18). *Greyhound* **buses** stop at 203 Union Ave at Fourth St downtown (☎523-7676), while the *Amtrak* station at 545 S Main St is in a particularly seedy and unsafe area on the southern edge of downtown.

A new downtown **trolley service** runs along the Main Street Mall from the Pyramid to Beale Street and the Civil Rights Museum (50¢ flat fare, 25¢ 11am–1.30pm); slow and infrequent *Memphis Area Transit Authority* **buses** cover nearly all the rest of the city (☎274-MATA). The two main east–west roads in town, **Poplar** and **Union** avenues, get very congested; **motorists** will often find it quicker to take a more circuitous route via the I-240 loop. Of several companies offering **city tours**, the most unusual are the garish amphibious *Delta Ducks*, 185 Union Ave (☎527-6823).

Information
Memphis' **visitor center**, 340 Beale St (summer Mon–Sat 9am–6pm, Sun noon–6pm; otherwise Mon–Fri 9am–5pm, Sat 9am–6pm, Sun noon–5pm; ☎543-5333 or 1-800/447-8278), provides invaluable advice on accommodation and getting around.

The **post office** is at 555 Third St at Calhoun (Mon–Fri 8.30am–5.30pm, Sat 10am–2pm; ☎521-2140; zip code 38101).

The City

Downtown Memphis has in the last few years started to come back to life, at the cost of losing some of its old cotton-era buildings. However, the central streets parallel to the river remain short of hotels, restaurants, and stores, and **Beale Street** on its southern fringes makes a much livelier area to stroll around, with Sun Studio nearby and the Civil Rights museum just south. The huge **Mud Island** on the river itself merits half a day, while **Graceland**, nine miles out, should on no account be missed.

The Riverfront
The northern boundary of downtown is marked by the surreal 32-storey **Pyramid**, two-thirds the size of the Great Pyramid. Completed in 1991, it was intended as a symbolic link with the Nile Delta; plans to make it an Egyptian theme park have yet to materialize,

The **area code** for Memphis and western Tennessee is ☎901.

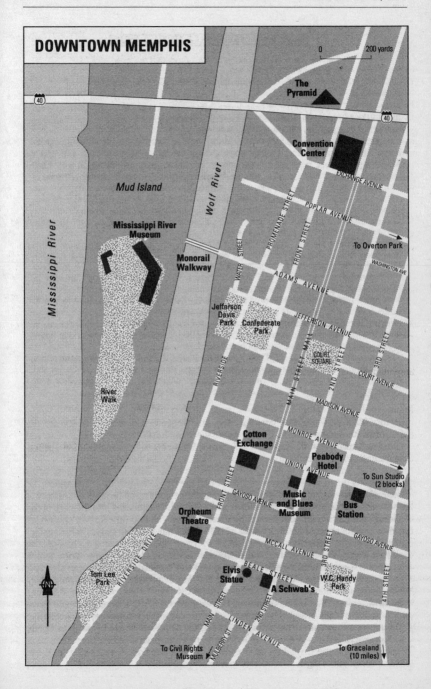

DOWNTOWN MEMPHIS

0   200 yards

The Pyramid

Convention Center

EXCHANGE AVENUE

Mud Island

Wolf River

POPLAR AVENUE

PROMENADE STREET

FRONT STREET

Mississippi River Museum

To Overton Park

WASHINGTON AVE

WATER STREET

Monorail Walkway

ADAMS AVENUE

Mississippi River

Jefferson Davis Park

Confederate Park

JEFFERSON AVENUE

RIVERSIDE

COURT SQUARE

2ND STREET

3RD STREET

COURT AVENUE

River Walk

MAIN STREET MALL

MADISON AVENUE

Cotton Exchange

MONROE AVENUE

Peabody Hotel

UNION AVENUE

To Sun Studio (2 blocks)

FRONT STREET

GAYOSO AVENUE

Music and Blues Museum

Bus Station

Orpheum Theatre

GAYOSO AVENUE

MCCALL AVENUE

3RD STREET

4TH STREET

RIVERSIDE DRIVE

Tom Lee Park

Elvis Statue

BEALE STREET

W.C. Handy Park

A Schwab's

MAIN STREET

2ND STREET

LINDEN AVENUE

MULBERRY ST

To Civil Rights Museum

To Graceland (10 miles)

THE MISSISSIPPI RIVER

I do not know much about gods; but I think that the river
Is a strong brown god – sullen, untamed and intractable.
St Louis-born T S Eliot, *The Four Quartets*

North America's principal waterway, the **Mississippi River**, starts just ninety miles south of the Canadian border at Lake Itasca, Minnesota, and winds its way 2348 miles to the Gulf of Mexico, taking in over one hundred tributaries on the way and draining all or part of 31 US states and two Canadian provinces.

One of the busiest commercial rivers in the world, it's also one of the most unconventional. Only by a quirk of history does it bear the name Mississippi; if the upper Mississippi had not been discovered and charted first, geographers might well have designated the 1403-mile longer Missouri-Mississippi fork as the main stream. Instead of widening towards its mouth, like most rivers, the Mississippi grows narrower and deeper. Its "**Delta**", over three hundred miles upstream from its mouth, is not a delta at all but an alluvial flood plain. On the other hand, its estuary deposits, which extend the land six miles out to sea every century, are comparatively paltry; Gulf currents disperse the sediment before it has time to settle.

The Mississippi is also, in the words of Mark Twain, who spent four years as a river boat pilot, "the **crookedest** river in the world". As it weaves and curls its way extravagantly along its channel it continually cuts through narrow necks of land to create oxbow lakes, meander scars, cut-offs and marshy backwaters. A bar could operate one day in Arkansas and then find itself in dry Tennessee the next, thanks to an overnight cut-off.

A more serious manifestation of the Mississippi's power is its propensity to **flood**. Although the river builds its own natural levees, artificial embankments help further to safeguard crops and homes; the entire area from Cape Girardeau, Missouri, to the sea is now virtually walled in. You can even drive along the top of the larger ones, and at times of low water some serve as makeshift beaches.

It's no longer feasible to sail Twain's route for yourself, though **riverboat excursions** operate in most sizeable river towns. Longer cruises, on the luxurious *Delta Queen* and *Mississippi Queen* paddlewheelers, are expensive; contact the *Delta Queen Steamboat Company*, 30 Robin Street Wharf, New Orleans, LA 70130 (☎1-800/543-1949).

but its 22,500-seat theater puts on Memphis' biggest concerts. Every year, the **Memphis Cook Convention Center** just to the south hosts a different major historical exhibition (April–Sept; ☎1-800/755-8777). **Main Street** south from here is now a pedestrianized mall (served by trolleys; see p.398), though it holds little retail activity.

Monorail trains and a walkway cross from Riverside Drive at Adams St to **Mud Island** (considered such an eyesore in 1917 that the city voted to blow it up), where the **Mississippi River Museum** is an enjoyable and ingenious romp through the history of the river. A full-size reconstructed steam packet somehow squeezes into the core of the building, a Disasters Theater exerts a morbid fascination, and little-known characters such as keelboatman Mike Fink – who in 1830 styled himself "half-horse, half-alligator" – are held up for inspection; there's also an overview of Memphis music. Outside, the half-mile **River Walk** is a scale model of the river itself, complete with town grids, which ends in the "Gulf of Mexico" at a swimming pool and artificial beach. You can also visit the original **Memphis Belle** nearby, a World War II bomber. (Grounds only, daily 10am–5pm, last admission 3pm, $2; museum $4 extra, last admission 3.30pm.) **Paddlewheelers** offer ninety-minute sightseeing trips at $7.50, leaving Riverside Drive at Monroe Ave (daily March–Dec; always 2.30pm, many others in season; ☎527-5694).

In between Riverside Drive and Front Street, the small tree-shaded **Jefferson Davis** and Confederate parks are popular lunchtime meeting places. When the Union took Memphis during the Civil War, thousands of dismayed residents watched from these sites as seven out of eight Confederate gunboats were sunk.

The imposing buildings of **Cotton Row**, halfway along Front St, might have seen busier days, but this is still the largest spot cotton market in the country. The Cotton Exchange Building at 84 S Front St contains a small historical exhibit on the cotton trade, but visitors are not allowed into the trading area.

At the south end of downtown, **Tom Lee Park**, the venue for major outdoor events such as "Memphis in May", commemorates a black boatman who rescued 32 people from a sinking boat in 1925 – despite the fact that he couldn't swim.

Beale Street

Beale Street began life as one of Memphis' most exclusive enclaves; its elite residents were driven out by the yellow fever epidemics, to be replaced by a diverse mix of blacks, whites, Greeks, Jews, Chinese and Italians. But it was Beale's **black culture** that gave the street its fame. This was where black roustabouts, deckhands and travellers passing through Memphis immediately headed for; rural blacks came for the bustling Saturday market; and, in times of strict segregation, Beale acted as the center for black businesses, financiers and professionals.

As the black main street of the mid-South, Beale in its Twenties heyday was jammed with vaudeville theaters, concert halls, bars and jook-joints (mostly white-owned). Along with the frivolity came a reputation for heavy gambling, voodoo, murder and prostitution. One appalled evangelist proclaimed that "if whiskey ran ankle deep in Memphis . . . you could not get drunker quicker than you can on Beale Street now."

Although Beale still drew huge crowds in the Forties, the drift to the suburbs and, ironically, the success of the **civil rights** years in opening the rest of Memphis to black businesses almost killed it off. The **bulldozers** of the late Sixties spared only the *Orpheum Theatre* and a few commercial buildings between Second and Fourth streets.

Beale Street has now been restored as an **Historic District**, its shops, clubs and cafés bedecked with Twenties-style facades and signs. Tourist money has led to extensive development, but with the exception of a few out-and-out souvenir shops most of the new businesses remain carefully in tune with the past, and for blues fans in particular its music venues – which include places owned by B B King and Jerry Lee Lewis; see p.405 – are irresistible.

A nine-foot bronze **statue of Elvis Presley** marks Beale's western end, at the junction with Main Street. Fans traditionally drop their business cards into his guitar. A few yards down at no 152, the excellent **Center for Southern Folklore** (Mon–Sat 9am–5.30pm, Sun 1–5.30pm) is not what you might expect. Without a Confederate flag or picture of Dolly Parton in sight, this oral-history project celebrates the music, food, storytelling and crafts of the people of the mid-South, with great archive film. There's a very good gift shop, and the staff are happy to advise on gig venues and places to see; they also organize tours of the Delta.

A **Schwabs Dry Goods Store**, no 163, looks much as it must have done when it opened in 1876, with an incredible array of such voodoo paraphernalia, familiar from the blues, as *Mojo Hands* and *High John the Conqueror*, as well as 99¢ neckties and Sunday School badges. Next door, the free **Memphis Police Museum**, open around the clock, holds an assortment of old photos, newspapers, and crime-fighting accoutrements. To the east, tree-shaded **Handy Park** echoes day and night to jamming blues musicians. The **Blues Foundation**, annual promoters of the National Blues Music Awards, is based at no 352, the tiny former home of **W C Handy**, who was in 1910 the first man to publish blues tunes (often blues in name only; see p.427). His *Memphis Blues* – originally *Mr Crump* – was the theme song for the 1909 mayoral election of Edward H Crump, whose crooked political machine ran the city from then until the early Fifties.

Separate buildings, one below the *New Daisy Theatre* at 330 Beale St and a newly-restored one a couple of blocks north at 97 S Second St, opposite the *Peabody Hotel* and its famous ducks (see "Accommodation", p.404), house the two halves of the **Memphis**

Music and Blues Museum. Both use photos, records, old instruments and film and TV footage to recall the musicians of Memphis, with the Beale St section focusing on the pre-Elvis years, and the Second St branch covering Sun, Stax and beyond. (Sun–Thurs 11am–6pm; Fri & Sat 11am–9pm; $5 each.)

Sun Studio

706 Union Ave. Daily; June–Aug tours 9.30am–6.30pm, store 9am–9pm; Sept–May tours 10.30am–5.30pm, store 9am–7pm. Tours $5.

Sun Studio, ten minutes' walk east of Beale, was where Elvis, Johnny Cash and others cut their first records (see box). Twenty-minute "tours" (sic) of its single room, complete with stand-up bass, drumkit and photos but measuring just eighteen feet by thirty feet, feature tapes of legendary recording sessions. Though Sun Records moved

---

THE SOUND OF MEMPHIS

Since the start of this century, Memphis has been a meeting place for black musicians from the Mississippi Delta and beyond. During the Twenties, its downtown pubs, clubs and street corners were alive with the sound of the blues. **Jug bands**, in which singers were given a bass accompaniment by blowing across the neck of a jug, were a specialty. Several songs by **Gus Cannon's Jug Stompers** – such as *Walk Right In* – became hits for white artists during the folk revival of the Sixties. Guitarist **Memphis Minnie**, **Bukka White** and **Memphis Slim** appeared at nightspots like *Mitchell's Hotel* and *Pee Wee's Saloon*, all long since defunct. After World War II, young musicians and radio DJs experimented by blending the traditional blues sound with jazz, adding electrical amplification to create **rhythm'n'blues**. Pioneers included **Bobby Bland** and **B B King**.

White promoter Sam Phillips started **Sun Records** in 1953, employing Ike Turner as a scout to comb the Beale Street clubs for new talent. Among those whom Turner helped introduce to vinyl were his own girlfriend Annie Mae Bullock (later **Tina Turner**), **Howlin' Wolf**, and **Little Junior Parker**, whose *Mystery Train* was Sun's first great recording. Phillips' conviction that "If I could find a white man who had the Negro sound and the Negro feel, I could make a billion dollars" achieved fruition in 1954, during a coffee break, when he overheard a young white man who had hired the studio to record a disc for his mother – **Elvis Presley**. Phillips dropped his black artists right away, signing other white **rockabilly** singers like **Carl Perkins** and **Jerry Lee Lewis** to make classics such as *Blue Suede Shoes* and *Great Balls of Fire*. Elvis – who in the immortal words of Carl Perkins had the advantage that he "didn't look like *Mr Ed*, like a lot of the rest of us" – was soon sold on to RCA (for just $35,000), and didn't record in Memphis again until 1969, when with songs like *Suspicious Minds* he produced the best material of his later career.

In the Sixties and early Seventies, Memphis' **Stax Records** provided a rootsy alternative to the poppier sounds of Motown. This hard-edged **southern soul** was created by a multiracial mix of musicians, Steve Cropper's fluid guitar complementing the blaring Memphis Horns. The label's first real success was *Green Onions* by studio band **Booker T and the MGs**; further hits followed from **Otis Redding** (*These Arms of Mine*), **Wilson Pickett** (*Midnight Hour*), **Sam and Dave** (*Soul Man*) and **Isaac Hayes** (*Shaft*). The label eventually foundered in acrimony; the last straw for many of its veteran soulmen was the signing of the British child star Lena Zavaroni for a six-figure sum.

Memphis has been renowned for its **gospel** music since the Thirties, when Rev Herbert Brewster wrote Mahalia Jackson's *Move On Up a Little Higher*. Following a religious revelation, the consummate soul stylist **Al Green**, who achieved chart success for **Hi Records** with *Let's Stay Together* and *Tired of Being Alone*, is now minister at the Full Gospel Tabernacle, at 787 Hale Rd in the leafy suburb of Whitehaven. Visitors are welcome at the 11am Sunday services, complete with four-piece rhythm section; continue a mile south of Graceland, then turn west (phone ahead to check he's in town; ☎396-9192). Uplifting gospel sounds can also be heard at the Mississippi Boulevard Christian Church, 205 E Raines Rd (☎345-1312), every Sunday at 8am and 11am.

out in 1959, the studio was restored in 1987, and has since been used by artists such as U2. For $49.95, you can walk in off the street – just as Elvis did – and make your own record, to a pre-recorded backing track. One room of the building still functions as an atmospheric café – see "Eating", below – and there's a gift store upstairs.

The National Civil Rights Museum

450 Mulberry St. Mon & Wed–Sat 10am–5pm, June–Aug Sun 1–6pm, Sept–May Sun 1–5pm. $5; free Mon 3–5pm.

The **National Civil Rights Museum**, a few blocks south of Beale Street, has been built around the remains of the *Lorraine Motel*, where **Dr Martin Luther King Jr** was assassinated by James Earl Ray on April 4 1968. In increasingly hard-line speeches, Dr King had explicitly linked black poverty with military spending in Vietnam. He was killed by a single bullet the evening before he was due to lead a march in Memphis in support of a strike by black sanitation workers.

The struggle for civil rights is traced from A Philip Randolph of the Brotherhood of Sleeping Car Porters, who originally called for a march on Washington in 1941, through to the Nation of Islam and the Black Panthers. Great resources have been devoted to an impressive exposition of the movement's history, though the tone veers between the over-detailed and the banal – sitting on the front seat of a reconstructed Montgomery bus triggers a recorded message instructing you to move to the back. Tours climax with Dr King's room, preserved behind a glass screen, and the balcony where he was shot; unquestionably an emotive sight, but arguably also tasteless, if not downright exploitative. Protestors continue to charge that Memphis' role in Dr King's death should be a source of shame rather than a tourist attraction, and that his memory would have been better served if the site had been used as a facility for the poor.

Graceland

3765 Elvis Presley Blvd (☎332-3322 or ☎1-800/238-2000). Nine miles from downtown, on bus route #13 from Third & Union. Ticket office open daily Memorial Day to Labor Day 7.30am–6pm; high season June–Aug 7.30am–7pm; otherwise 8.30am–5pm. Tours continue until last visitor leaves. Combined ticket to all attractions $16 – allow 3 hours; 90-min house tours only, $8. Reservations are recommended, especially during Aug (Graceland, PO Box 16508, Memphis TN 38186-0508).

In itself, Elvis Presley's **Graceland** was a surprisingly modest home for the world's most successful entertainer. It's certainly not the "mansion" you may have been led to expect, and while Elvis was clearly a man who indulged his tastes to the full, there's none of the pomposity, the acquisition of incongruous eighteenth-century European antiques, that characterizes so many other showpiece Southern residences. Visits, run under the auspices of his widow Priscilla, are affectionate celebrations of the man; never exactly tongue in cheek, but not cloyingly reverential either.

Elvis was just 22 when he paid $100,000 for Graceland in 1957. It was then considered one of the most desirable properties in Memphis, though now the neighborhood is distinctly less exclusive, its main thoroughfare – **Elvis Presley Boulevard** – lined with motels, fast-food joints, and souvenir shops. Tours start opposite the house in **Graceland Plaza**; visitors are ferried across the road in mini-buses, which depart every few minutes and sweep through the musical gate in the "**Wall of Love**", scrawled with tens of thousands of messages from fans.

It's not easy to get an accurate sense of the house's size and layout, as the rooms where Elvis' housekeeper still lives, along with the entire upstairs, are out of bounds to visitors. The interior is a frozen tribute to the taste of the Seventies – one caption explains "wild-looking stuff like this was a sort of fad at the time". Choice moments include the **Jungle Den** with its carpeted ceiling, and the navy and lemon mirrors in the **TV Room**, fitted with three screens so Elvis could watch three football games at once. In the separate **Trophy Building**, you parade past Elvis' platinum, gold and silver records, his stage costumes, outfits from some of his 31 films, and his extensive gun collection. Elvis (Jan 8 1935–Aug 16 1977), his mother Gladys, his father Vernon, and his grand-mother are buried beside the swimming pool in the **Meditation Garden** outside; his body was moved here two months after his death, when the security problems inherent in keeping it in the local cemetery became obvious.

The Plaza itself holds several enjoyable related attractions, from the wittily edited free film *Walk A Mile In My Shoes*, through the **Elvis Presley Automobile Museum** with its reconstructed drive-in movie theater and Harley Davidson golf cart, to Elvis' fully customized **airplane**, the *Lisa Marie*.

Midtown and East Memphis

The mile-long, heavily wooded expanse of **Overton Park**, three miles from downtown (#50 bus) on Poplar Avenue, holds the wide-ranging **Memphis Brooks Museum of Art** (Tues–Sat 10am–5pm, Sun 11.30am–5pm; $2, free Fri), and the **Memphis Zoo and Aquarium** (daily, April–Sept 9am–5pm, Oct–March 9am–4.30pm; $3.50, free Mon 3.30–5pm). **Overton Square**, the city's top suburban entertainment, dining and shop-ping district, is within walking distance. Just past East Parkway, the **Memphis Pink Palace Museum and Planetarium** at 3050 Central Avenue (Tues–Sat 9.30am–4pm, Sun 1–5pm; $3, free Thurs 5–8.30pm) centers on the pink marble mansion of Clarence Saunders, who founded America's first chain of self-service **supermarkets**, *Piggly-Wiggly*, in 1916. As well as a walk-through model of the first store, complete with origi-nal packets and prices, an audio-visual programme explores Memphis history.

Accommodation

Downtown Memphis has a few reasonably cheap **places to stay**, though if you're unlucky, and don't have a car, you may be stuck with a long bus journey out to the suburbs. The **visitor center** (see p.398) offers good advice, and is particularly helpful at busy times such as the anniversary of Elvis' death in mid-August.

B&B in Memphis (PO Box 41621, TN 38174; ☎726-5920) runs a reservation service, with rooms costing $56 and upwards. The closest **campground** is the *Elvis Presley Blvd RV Park*, 3971 Elvis Presley Blvd (☎332-3633), three blocks south of Graceland.

Days Inn–Downtown, 164 Union Ave (☎527-4100). Prime downtown location, good prices. ②.

Holiday Inn Crowne Plaza, 250 N Main St (☎527-7300). Flagship luxury hotel, opposite Convention Center with views of the river and Pyramid. ⑥.

India House II, 78 N Main St (☎529-9282). Very central hostel. $10 dorms, no curfew or lockout. ①.

Lowenstein-Long House/Castle Hostelry, 1084 Poplar Ave (☎527-7174). Victorian mansion a mile from downtown via bus #50, run as B&B and hostel. Dorm beds $10 (*AYH*), $13 others. ①/④.

Peabody Hotel, 149 Union Ave (529-4000 or 1-800/PEABODY). Landmark hotel, near Beale St. Don't miss the legendary ducks, which waddle from the elevator at 11am prompt, to the strains of the *King Cotton March*, spend the day in the lobby fountain, and return to their penthouse at 6pm. ⑦.

River Place Inn, 100 N Front St (☎526-0583). Riverside rooms overlooking Mud Island. ③.

Wilson World Graceland, 3677 Elvis Presley Blvd (☎332-1000 or 1-800/945-7667). Right across from Graceland, every room has fridge and microwave. Part of four-property local budget chain. ②.

Eating

Memphians are fond of their food, claiming to be the **pork barbecue** capital of the world with over one hundred specialist restaurants. There is also a good selection of reasonably priced soul-food cafés. **Downtown** has a good choice (including some pass-able cafés on Beale Street); for a bit of variety, try **Overton Square** in midtown.

Automatic Slim's Tango Café, 83 S Second St (525-7948). Trendy southwestern-themed restau-rant/nightspot, complete with tumbleweed, opposite the *Peabody*. Excellent if pricey nouvelle food.

Blues City Café, 138 Beale St (☎526-3637). City branch of Mississippi soul-food specialist *Doe's Eat Place* (see p.428). Tasty tamales, catfish and stew, popular with musicians from nearby clubs.

Little Tea Shop, 69 Monroe Ave (☎525-6000). Unusual downtown soul-food café, serving a health-conscious version of what is traditionally a very fatty type of food. Lunches cost around $5.

La Montagne, 3550 Park Ave (☎458-1060). Wholesome vegetarian and Indian specialties.

The North End, 346 N Main St (☎525-1315). Like the linked *Jake's Place* at no 356, a friendly bar-cum-restaurant opposite the Pyramid, specializing in wild-rice dishes, stir-fries and a killer hot fudge pie. Open until 3am daily, happy hour 4–7pm. Live blues 10pm–2am Wed–Sun; $2 cover Fri only.

Paulette's, 2110 Madison Ave, Overton Square (☎726-5128). An exciting fusion of American, French and Hungarian cuisine.

Public Eye, 17 S Cooper St, Overton Square (☎726-4040), and 111 Court Ave, downtown (☎527-5757). Superb pork ribs and very cheap lunch specials.

The Rendezvous, General Washburn Alley, 52 S Second St (☎523-2746). The most famous and highly regarded of Memphis' many pork barbecue joints. Huge helpings and a nice atmosphere.

Sun Studio Café, 710 Union Ave (☎521-9820). Tangy barbecues and fine desserts, at the self-same tables Elvis used. Hugely atmospheric, with definitive jukebox of Sun singles. Daily 10am–7pm.

Nightlife and Entertainment

Though **live music** is at its best in Memphis during the city's many **festivals**, such as the month-long **Memphis in May** (which also features the Barbecue Cookout Competition) and October's **Blues Memphis Week**, the blues and soul clubs of Beale Street have plenty to offer fans all year round. There's another concentration of night-spots at **Overton Square**, while the beautifully restored *Orpheum Theatre*, Main and Beale (☎525-3000), puts on Broadway shows, opera, ballet and classic films.

The best sources for **listings** are the free weekly *Memphis Flyer*, Friday's *Memphis Commercial Appeal*, and the community **radio** station WEVL (FM90, daily 6am–2am).

Barbara's, 1474 Madison Ave. Friendly country-oriented bar near Overton Square. Mainly aimed at gay women, with weekend dancing. Happy hour Mon–Fri 5–7pm.

B B King's Blues Club, 143 Beale St (☎527-5464). Beale's most popular club. Outside there's a spectacular neon guitar; inside it's spacious and atmospheric, fried chicken and beer is delivered to your table, and there's blues seven nights a week. The proprietor plays on average 8 times per year.

Green's, 2090 E Person Ave (☎274-9800). Unpretentious neighborhood venue. Live blues until 2.30am every Fri and Sat, with reliable house bands the Fieldstones and the Bluesbusters. $3 cover.

Huey's, 1927 Madison Ave (☎726-4372). Popular Overton Square venue with live jazz on Sunday afternoon, followed by an out-of-town blues band in the evening.

Jerry Lee Lewis' Spot, 326 Beale St (☎523-2727). More of a countrified rockabilly bar than a hard blues club. Menu features Jerry Lee Lewis' fried baloney; weddings performed on request.

Joyce Cobb's, 205 Beale St (☎526-0484). Sophisticated supper-club jazz; Joyce herself usually sings.

Kudzu's, 603 Monroe Ave (☎525-4924). Great downtown bar. Live weekend blues, plus pool table.

Rum Boogie Café, 182 Beale St (☎528-0150). Usually one of Beale's most crowded venues, with resident blues bands every night 9pm–1.30ªm, plus Cajun cooking and ribs. $4 cover.

Shiloh National Military Park

Approximately 110 miles east of Memphis and twelve south of Savannah, via US-64 and Hwy-22, **SHILOH NATIONAL MILITARY PARK** commemorates one of the most crucial battles of the Civil War. After victories at Fort Henry and Fort Donelson, General Grant's confident Union forces were all but defeated by a surprise early-morning Confederate attack on April 6 1862. A stubborn rump of resistance held on until around 5pm, and the Confederates elected to finish the task off the next morning rather than launching a twilight assault. However, Grant's decimated regiments were bolstered by the overnight arrival of new troops, and instead it was their dawn initiative which forced the tired and demoralized Confederates to retreat.

Shiloh was the first encounter on a scale that became common as the war continued, putting an abrupt end to the romantic innocence of many a raw volunteer soldier. Over 20,000 men from the two sides were killed or wounded. Even the Union's war-toughened General Sherman spoke of "piles of dead soldiers' mangled bodies . . . without heads and legs . . . the scenes on this field would have cured anyone of war."

The **visitor center** displays artefacts recovered from the battlefield and shows an informative twenty-minute film. A self-guided ten-mile driving tour takes in the **National Cemetery**, whose moss-covered walls contain thousands of unidentified graves (daily summer 8am–6pm; otherwise 8am–5pm; free; ☎689-5275).

Reelfoot Lake

Surrounded by a thick growth of oak and cottonwood trees, woven together by wild grape vines, the eighteen-mile **REELFOOT LAKE** in the northeastern corner of Tennessee has its own strange beauty. It was created by the New Madrid earthquakes between December 1811 and March 1812. The ground sank, huge trees snapped in half and the Mississippi was even forced to flow northwards for two days, filling the depression in a series of gigantic waves.

Between December and March, the Reelfoot Lake State Park organizes trips to catch a glimpse of the national bird, the migratory **bald eagle**. The park's **visitor center** (☎253-7756) is five miles east of **Tiptonville** on Hwy-21 on the lake's south shore. The *Blue Bank Motel* (☎253-6878; ②), in between the two, has comfortable rooms, and there are **campgrounds** in the park. The nearby *Boyette's Dining Room* (☎253-7307) is good for reasonably priced ham, chicken and catfish.

Nashville

Set amid the gentle hills and fertile farmlands of central Tennessee, **NASHVILLE** attracts six million people each year – a mixture of devoted fans and the just plain curious – to immerse themselves in **country music**. They come to enjoy themselves, and the city makes sure that they do, offering not just the relatively mainstream **Opryland**, **Country Music Hall of Fame** and **Grand Ole Opry**, but all the wonders of "Tacksville". To make the most of Nashville, you need to abandon any idea of detachment, and get out there among the nightspots and gift emporia, joining the quest for souvenir T-shirts, stetsons, rattlesnake belts and photos of your favorite star.

However, there is a real city beneath the rhinestone glitter. Nashville has been the leading settlement in middle Tennessee since **Fort Nashborough** was established in 1779. State capital since 1843, it is now the **financial** and **insurance** center of the mid-south as well as a fast-growing **manufacturing** base. Giant *Nissan* and *Saturn* motor plants have been attracted to its immediate hinterland, and rapid growth since World War II has transformed a once-compact city into a sprawling conurbation stretching out in all directions along the undulating roads, here known as **pikes**.

For all its blue-collar "Nash-Vegas" image, Nashville has maintained a strong reputation for **learning** since planter times, and is home to sixteen higher education establishments, including Vanderbilt University and the renowned black colleges of Fisk University and Meharry Medical School. The city likes to see itself as the "Athens of the South" – and, endearingly, has built a replica of the Parthenon to bolster its claim.

The other conspicuous element in Nashville's make-up is **religion**. There are over seven hundred churches, more per capita than anywhere else in the country. But what really earns it the tag of "Protestant Vatican" is the proliferation of colleges for training preachers and missionaries, church administrative offices and Bible-publishing plants.

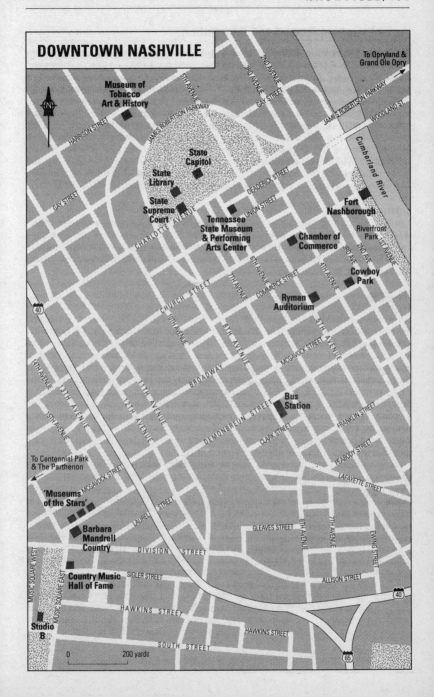

DOWNTOWN NASHVILLE

To Opryland &
Grand Ole Opry

Museum of
Tobacco
Art & History

State
Capitol

State
Library

State
Supreme
Court

Tennessee
State Museum
& Performing
Arts Center

Fort
Nashborough

Riverfront
Park

Chamber of
Commerce

Cowboy
Park

Ryman
Auditorium

Church Street

Broadway

Bus
Station

To Centennial Park
& The Parthenon

'Museums
of the Stars'

Barbara
Mandrell
Country

Country Music
Hall of Fame

Studio
B

0   200 yards

Arrival, Getting Around and Information

Nashville International Airport is eight miles southeast of downtown. Buses into town (weekdays 6.15am–10.30pm; weekend times vary) take around thirty minutes and cost 85¢. Taxis are quicker but will set you back up to $20. *Greyhound* buses arrive in a seedy part of downtown at 200 Eighth Ave S (☎256-6141); there's no *Amtrak* service.

Nashville is so spread out that a **car** is all but essential. However, the one-way system can be maddening, and the roads change name without warning. *Metropolitan Transit Authority* (☎242-4433) **buses** run until midnight to most parts of the county, from the transit mall on Deaderick St, and **trolleys** cover the entire downtown area plus Music Row for a fare of 75¢. *Grand Ole Opry Tours* (☎889-9490), *Gray Line* (☎883-5555) and *Stardust* (☎244-2335) all offer **bus tours**. Expect to pay $20 for a three-hour trip, not including admission to attractions. Architecturally oriented **walking tours** of downtown Nashville are organized in summer by *Historic Nashville* (Sat 9am; $5; ☎244-7835).

Information

On foot, it's a bit of an effort to get to the main **Tourist Information Center** (☎259-4747), across the bridge on Interstate Drive at Exit 85, off I-65. However, the **Chamber of Commerce Office** at 161 Fourth Ave N (☎259-4700) has a well-stocked rack of maps and leaflets. The **post office** is downtown at 921 Broadway (Mon–Fri 8am–6pm, Sat 8am–noon; ☎251-5321; zip code 37202).

The City

Downtown Nashville looks much like any other regional business center, dominated by office blocks and parking lots. It's perfectly possible to spend a busy day here without coming into contact with country music. A good starting point – though it borders on a rough part of town – is **Riverfront Park** at First and Broadway, a thin stretch of grass and terracing dipping down to the Cumberland River. A replica of the wooden **Fort Nashborough** stands on a promontory above the river as a monument to the city's founders of 1779 (Tues–Sat 9am–4pm; donation). Overlooking all proceedings from First Avenue, a row of craggy Victorian brick warehouses runs right through to Second Avenue where their cast-iron frontages house restaurants, bars and shops. During the religious revival of the Thirties, these streets were packed every Sunday for "free for all preachings", when zealous fundamentalists would proclaim their own brand of theology from atop any convenient box, cart or wall.

A few blocks away, the worthy **Tennessee State Museum** at 505 Deaderick St (Mon–Sat 10am–5pm, Sun 1–5pm; free) is strongest on the Civil War, highlighting the hardships of the ill-clad, ill-fed soldiers, of whom 23,000 out of 77,000 died at Shiloh alone. Other displays focus on frontier life and on black Tennesseans, looking at slavery, Reconstruction, the founding of the Ku Klux Klan and the civil rights movement.

Marking downtown's northern boundary at Sixth and Charlotte, the resplendent **Tennessee State Capitol**, modelled on an Ionic temple, looks out across the city from its hilltop perch. Earlier this century, this area was yet another "Hell's Half Acre", notorious for its drinking holes, gambling clubs, sex shows and dope dens; it's considerably tamer now, housing hotels and a huge state museum/performing arts complex.

Ten minutes' walk north, the **Museum of Tobacco Art and History** at 800 Harrison St (Tues–Sat 10am–4pm; free) takes an excellent look at "the truly American commodity". An international collection of advertisements spans a century, alongside elaborate snuff boxes, meerschaum pipes, spittoons, and displays on the use of tobacco ever since Columbus found Native Americans smoking, chewing and snorting it in 1492.

The **area code** for Nashville, and central and eastern Tennessee, is ☎615.

At the 1897 Tennessee Centennial Exposition, Nashville's "Athens of the South" exhibit featured a full-size wood-and-plaster replica of the **Parthenon**, which proved so popular with Nashville residents that the present permanent structure, in the middle of **Centennial Park** southwest of downtown at West End and 25th avenues, was built in 1931. This impressive edifice – familiar to movie-goers from the finale of Robert Altman's not-always-flattering *Nashville* – is now home to Nashville's premier **art museum** (Tues–Sat 9am–4.30pm, Sun 1–5pm; $2.50). The lower level contains American paintings; the upper hall is dominated by a 42ft replica of Phidias' statue of Athena holding Nike (the goddess of victory).

Just across West End Avenue, weatherbeaten Gothic structures sit alongside more modern utilitarian buildings on the campus of prestigious **Vanderbilt University**. This bastion of conservatism was one of the very few colleges to witness student demonstrations in *support* of US involvement in Vietnam.

Of the many buildings erected by Nashville's antebellum elite, none was more elaborate than **Belmont Mansion**, a mile southeast of the Parthenon at 1900 Belmont Blvd (June–Aug Mon–Sat 10am–4pm; otherwise Tues–Sat 10am–4pm; $4). This 36-room 1850 Italianate villa looks out across ornamented gardens that once contained a bear house and a lake stocked with alligators.

Country Music Nashville

The status of Nashville as country music's capital city dates back to the Twenties and the arrival of thousands of migrants fleeing rural poverty. The music they brought with them, rooted in the folksongs of Tennessee's first Irish and British settlers, soon mutated in the urban environment into something new, incorporating elements of Tin Pan Alley musicals, religious hymns and songs from ex-slaves.

As radios and record players became widely available for the first time, the **recording industry** began to take off, and Nashville became the obvious geographical base for the musicians of the mid-south. Radio station WSM had championed the country sound since 1925, and its live weekly Grand Ole Opry concerts (see box) spearheaded the city's burgeoning **live music** scene.

The first big commercial boom came in the decade of prosperity after World War II. Nashville proliferated with recording studios, publishing companies and artists' agencies. The big labels recognized that a large slice of the (white) record-buying public wanted something a bit safer than rockabilly. The easy-listening **Nashville Sound** they came up with, pioneered by Patsy Cline and Jim Reeves and perpetuated by the likes of Barbara Mandrell and Kenny Rogers, remains the clean-cut face of country, although country music has always had its seamier side, and the concentration of stars and music-biz executives has turned Nashville into something of a downmarket Hollywood.

Though Nashville's country scene is both conspicuous and accessible, submerging yourself in it takes time and quite a lot of money; prices are set at what the industry knows enthusiastic fans will pay. In addition to the daytime attractions mentioned below, country music venues are listed in the "Nightlife" section on p.412.

Downtown at 116 Fifth Ave, enjoyable short tours of the **Ryman Auditorium**, the former home of the Grand Ole Opry, lead through the wooden church pews of the auditorium proper and the dressing rooms, culminating in a chance to sing on the well-worn stage (daily 8.30am–4.30pm; $2.50). Around the corner, among the Broadway honky-tonks, **Hatch Show Print**, no 316, still prints and sells evocative posters from the early days of country and rock'n'roll, using the original blocks. Almost next door, **Cowboy Park** provides a surreal photo opportunity, as home to seven brightly painted "urban cowboy" sculptures, made from recycled household cans and boxes. Performers of all kinds pick out their stage costumes from the flamboyant leather and sequinned garments sold in **Dangerous Threads**, at the foot of Second Ave (no 105) nearby.

THE GRAND OLE OPRY

Nashville's radio station WSM ("We Shield Millions", the slogan of its insurance-company sponsor) first broadcast on October 5 1925. Two years later, at the start of his *Barn Dance* show, compere George D Hay announced "for the past hour we have been listening to music taken largely from Grand Opera, but from now on we will present *The Grand Ole Opry*". This piece of slang became the name of America's longest-running radio show, still going out to millions every Friday and Saturday evening on WSM-AM (650m); the original "hillbilly" jam session has become country music's elite showcase.

Swiftly outgrowing the WSM studios, the show moved in 1943 to a former tabernacle – the **Ryman Auditorium**. There it acquired a make-or-break reputation; up-and-coming singers could only claim to have made it if they had gone down well at the Opry. Among thousands of hopefuls who tried to get on the show was Elvis Presley, advised by an Opry official in 1954 to stick to truck-driving. The first appearance of **Hank Williams**, in 1949, commanded an unequalled six encores. Within four years, the Opry audience was singing his evangelical *I Saw the Light* on the news of his drink- and drug-induced death.

In the Seventies the show moved on again, this time to a new purpose-built 4424-seater theater in the **Opryland** theme park – one of many Opry spin-offs, including hotels, TV stations and a record label. Among more than sixty stars currently on the Opry roster are old-timers like Roy Acuff and Minnie Pearl, perennial superstars like Loretta Lynn, and current country chart-toppers such as Reba McEntire, Randy Travis and Ricky Skaggs.

Throughout the year, two performances on Saturday night and one on Friday night feature up to twenty acts. During the summer, an extra Friday-night show and matinees on Tuesday, Thursday, Saturday and Sunday offer fewer artists. **Tickets** are not too hard to get, especially if you book in advance. Evening shows cost $13–15; matinees are $11–13. Contact the ticket office at 2808 Opryland Drive, Nashville TN 37214 (☎889-3060).

Blue route trolleys along Broadway run just over a mile southwest of downtown to the excellent, but often crowded, **Country Music Hall of Fame**, at 4 Music Square East (daily, June–Aug 8am–8pm; Sept–May 9am–5pm; $7.50). This is packed with costumes, guitars and personal possessions of the stars, including Elvis' gold-laden Cadillac, with forty coats of paint containing crushed diamonds and oriental fish scales. Film and TV clips help to clarify the arcane distinctions between C'n'W, rockabilly, honky-tonk and western swing. Admission also includes a tour of RCA's historic **Studio B**, preserved as it was when the label moved to more modern premises in 1971. The likes of Willie Nelson, Dolly Parton and Jim Reeves recorded here, as did the Monkees and the Everly Brothers, and Elvis laid down over 200 tracks. You can follow in their footsteps by trying out all sorts of instruments, including the indispensable dobro (steel guitar).

The surrounding area, **Music Row**, is the heart of Nashville's recording industry. A minute's walk from the Hall of Fame brings you to a strip of garish souvenir shops on Demonbreun Street, and several tacky private museums honoring stars such as Waylon Jennings, Elvis Presley and Hank Williams Jr. These places charge you to see personal mementos and rubbish that the stars don't want to keep in their homes; it costs $7, for example, to visit **Barbara Mandrell Country** at 1510 Division St.

A similar assortment of "museums" and gift shops, **Music Village**, can be found in the small town of **Hendersonville**, eighteen miles north of Nashville. This is near Old Hickory Lake, where nouveau riche country stars have built their own luxury shore-side enclave, abandoning uncomfortable attempts to live in select Nashville suburbs such as Belle Meade. Tour buses bring thousands of fans to see the homes and possessions of stars such as Johnny Cash, Willie Nelson and Conway Twitty.

Opryland

Nine miles northeast of downtown on Briley Parkway, just off the I-40E loop. Daily Memorial Day to Labor Day; weekends only late March–May & Sept–early Nov. Usual summer hours 9am–9pm, otherwise considerable variation – call ☎889-6700. $22.95 one-day, $34.95 two days admission includes rides but not paddlesteamer trips ($12.95 extra) or Opry Theater tickets (see box).

There's nothing all that "country" about **Opryland**. It's basically a standard **theme park** where the staff happen to wear gingham instead of cartoon costumes. The 21 **rides** included in the price are not exceptional, though the roller coaster *Chaos* is worth trying, and there's a plethora of shooting galleries, shops and fast-food stalls – even a studio to make your own country tape – to keep you spending. Twelve stages offer music fans very professional but utterly sanitized family shows of mainstream jazz, gospel, rock'n'roll and, of course, watered-down country music.

To the north of the park, on McGavock Pike in **Music Valley**, a colony of parasitic attractions – a wax museum, a "cars of the stars" place, and so on – has sprung up around the opulent *Opryland Hotel*.

Accommodation

Well-priced **rooms** are not too hard to find in Nashville, with budget **motels** gathering a couple of miles north of downtown, off the I-65 Trinity Lane/Brick Church Pike exit. **B&B** agencies include *B&B Hospitality Tennessee,* PO Box 110227, TN 37222 (☎331-5244), and *B&B of Middle Tennessee,* PO Box 40804, TN 37204 (☎297-0883). The least costly (and nearest to Opryland) of the **campgrounds**, ten miles northeast in Music Valley, is *Fiddlers Inn Campground,* 2404 Music Valley Drive (☎885-1440).

Cabot Lodge, 1111 Airport Center at Donelson Pike North (☎883-1366). Spacious rooms 11 miles east of downtown, off I-40, convenient for the airport and Opryland. ③.

Days Inn Downtown/Convention Center, 711 Union St (☎242-4311). Excellent central downtown location, and good weekend rates. ③.

Econolodge Near Opryland, 2460 Music Valley Drive (☎889-0090). Just about the least expensive motel you'll find in this elite area. ②.

Hampton Inn, 1919 West End Ave (☎329-1144). Clean, comfortable lodgings in the pleasant Vanderbilt University area, one mile west of downtown and six blocks from Music Row. ④.

Opryland Hotel, McGavock Pike (☎889-1000). Unbelievably vast and expensive shopping mall of a place, with 2000 rooms (costing up to $2000) set out around its glass-roofed courtyards. ⑦.

Travelodge Downtown, 800 James Robertson Pkwy (☎244-2630). Situated at the north end of downtown, behind the state capitol. ③.

Tudor Inn Downtown, 750 James Robertson Pkwy (☎244-8970). Works out slightly cheaper than the neighboring *Travelodge*. ②.

Eating

Nashville is all but taken over by fast-food and family-eating chains, but downtown has a few interesting places. Otherwise you might have to rely on the large **food mall** on the top floor of Church Street Mall, between Seventh and Eighth avenues.

Bristol Bar & Grille, 113 Church St Mall (☎255-7007). The most formal option in this downtown mall, offering very good value salads, stir-fries and southwestern specialties.

Ichiban, 109 Second Ave (☎254-7185). Japanese restaurant and sushi bar, near *Dangerous Threads*.

Laurell's Second Ave Oyster Bar, 123 Second Ave (☎244-1230). Excellent selection of fresh seafood dishes; the menu often includes exotic crustaceans.

Old Spaghetti Factory, 160 Second Ave (☎254-9010). With its turn-of-the-century decor, this pasta chain is one of downtown's best-value places. Main dishes around $7, but be prepared to queue.

Rotier's, 2413 Elliston Place (☎327-9892). A basic, good-value, no-frills diner near Vanderbilt, strong on tasty southern-style dishes, including a great choice of filling vegetable plates.

Satsuma Tea Room, 417 Union St (☎256-5211). A downtown tradition popular with office workers and tourists. Tasty homemade breads and desserts with lunches under $5. Mon–Fri 10.45am–2pm.

Windows on the Cumberland, 112 Second Ave (☎244-7944). Reasonably priced daytime vegetarian café serving sandwiches, baked potatoes, beans'n'rice and salads.

Nightlife

Of all Nashville's country music venues, the main ones to **avoid** are the ersatz over-crowded clubs along the much-hyped and sleazy downtown **Printers' Alley**. The **honky-tonks** on Broadway, between Second and Fourth, are more genuine and down-to-earth, though best avoided if you're on your own. Dine-and-dance places like the *Stock Yard* offer good-quality mainstream country music (and more crowds); up-and-coming progressive country bands play smaller venues like the *Bluebird Café*. Every June, the **Fan Fair** is a week-long series of concerts and opportunities to meet the stars (contact 2804 Opryland Drive, Nashville TN 37214; ☎889-7502).

For **listings** of upcoming gigs and events, see the free weekly *Nashville Scene*, Thursday's *Nashville Banner*, or Friday's and Saturday's *Tennessean*. If you're looking for music other than country, **Second Avenue** is a popular downtown hang-out for both locals and tourists, offering everything from bluegrass to funk and punk, and various haunts of interest can be found around Vanderbilt's campus.

Nashville's prime venue for theater, dance and classical music is the **Tennessee Performing Arts Center** at 505 Deaderick St (☎741-7975). Its **symphony orchestra** also puts on weekend concerts in **Centennial Park**, at West End and 25th avenues by Vanderbilt University, between June and August.

Bluebird Cafe, 4104 Hillsboro Rd (☎383-1461). Small intimate café, six miles west of downtown, which has become *the* place to see the latest honky-tonk and new country artists. Early evening entertainment is free, but a cover of around $6 is charged after 9.30pm.

Ernest Tubb's Record Store Midnight Jamboree, 2414 Music Valley Drive (☎889-2474). A live radio show, recorded every Saturday from midnight to 1am in a wooden hut next to the shop. Ernest Tubb, pioneer of the gutsy, bluesy honky-tonk style, has passed the show on to his son, Justin. Genuinely promising newcomers as well as major Opry stars. Free.

Exit/In, 2208 Elliston Place (☎321-4400). Very popular venue near Vanderbilt putting on all sorts of rock and guitar bands, plus the occasional big name. Cover $3–6.

Grand Ole Opry, 2808 Opryland Drive (☎889-3060). See box.

Mere Bulles, 152 Second Ave (☎256-1946). Loud, lively jazz-funk café-bar. Usually no cover.

Nashville Palace, 2400 Opryland Drive (☎885-1540). Opposite *Opryland Hotel*. Resident country bands, and Opry acts on summer Mondays. A good insight into mainstream Nashville. Cover $3–5.

Station Inn, 402 12th Ave S (☎255-3307). Very popular bluegrass and acoustic venue, a mile south of downtown. Slightly above-average cover of $4–8, but free jam sessions every Sunday night.

Stock Yard/Bull Pen, 901 Second Ave (☎255-6464). Spacious dine-and-dance spot serving huge steaks. Frequented by the stars, and owned by Buddy Killen, president of *Tree International*, country music's largest publishers. As good a place as any to submerge yourself in the rhinestone scene.

Tootsie's Orchard Lounge, 422 Broadway (☎726-3739). Venerable downtown honky-tonk. Connects at the back with the Ryman Auditorium, so Opry stars could drink here between sets.

Windows on the Cumberland, 112 Second Ave (☎244-7944). Live acoustic, singer-songwriter and world music Thurs–Sat, plus good Sunday-afternoon jazz sessions.

World's End, 1713 Church St (☎329-3480). The city's friendliest gay club, for men and women.

South from Nashville

As you head southeast from Nashville, large nineteenth-century plantation homes line US-31 between suburban Brentwood and the historic town of **FRANKLIN**, eighteen miles out. One of the bloodiest battles of the Civil War occurred here on November 30 1864, when 8500 men fell in less than an hour. Despite forcing the Union troops back to Nashville, huge losses meant that the southerners could not follow up their victory. Among several strategic buildings open for visits is **Carnton Mansion** (☎794-0903), about a mile southeast of the town on Hwy-431, a former Confederate hospital where bloodstains are still visible on the floor. The town's entire fifteen-block center, now full of antique and specialty shops, is listed in the National Register of Historic Places.

Jack Daniel's at Lynchburg

The change-resistant village of **LYNCHBURG**, seventy miles southeast of Nashville, is home to **Jack Daniel's Distillery** (daily 8am–4pm; free). Founded in 1866, this is the oldest registered distillery in the country (hence the famous *No 1* appellation). Entertaining seventy-minute tours lead you through every step of the sour-mash whiskey-making process – but you can't actually sample the stuff, as you're in a dry county.

Lynchburg itself is a pretty hamlet, laid out around a red-brick courthouse, with a number of old-fashioned stores. One enjoyable throwback is *Miss Mary Bobo's Boarding House*, which serves southern dinners at a single 1pm sitting (Mon–Sat; reservations essential; ☎759-7394).

Eastern Tennessee

Until the creation of the TVA, the opening of Great Smoky Mountains National Park and the building of the interstate highways, life had continued in the remote hills and valleys of eastern Tennessee in much the same way as it had ever since the arrival of the first pioneers. Now visitors flock here for its endless expanses of natural beauty; and as a result, especially in the fall, the Smokies can get clogged with traffic. Most communities are small, and either over-touristed or just bland. The two main cities, modern **Knoxville** and picturesque **Chattanooga**, have much in common, including healthy post-World War II industrial growth, thanks to cheap TVA power.

Knoxville

Surrounded by the backwoods wilderness of the Great Smoky, the Cumberland and the Blue Ridge mountains, **KNOXVILLE**, the original capital of Tennessee, is a growing conurbation of 180,000. Modern skyscrapers, older brick buildings and a riverfront at the bottom of steep bluffs combine to give **downtown** an attractive edge, but specific places of interest are thin on the ground. On the northern fringe, the **Old City**, centered on Central and Jackson, is a rejuvenated area of shops, galleries, restaurants and nightspots in Victorian warehouses along narrow cobbled streets and railway arches.

On the western edge of downtown, the **World's Fair Park** is dominated by the futuristic **Sunsphere**, a huge glass ball mounted on a round concrete tower. The **Knoxville Museum of Art**, in the park at 410 Tenth St, features a small permanent collection of paintings and a cleverly designed sculpture garden focused on a 200-year-old elm tree. Follow Cumberland Avenue up a few blocks and you come to the large, leafy campus of the University of Tennessee. Lined with bars and diners, frequently bedecked in the orange colors of the Volunteers football team, the campus has two theaters and the free **Frank H McClung Museum** at Circle Park, which features displays on the city's archeology, art and history.

Practicalities

Greyhound buses stop in the Old City on North Central St (☎522-5141); *K-Trans* city buses run a free trolley to the campus. The **visitor center** is at 810 Clinch Ave (☎523-7263). The comfortable *Best Western Campus Inn*, 1706 W Cumberland Ave (☎521-5000; ③), is fairly central, and there's a *Motel 6* at 10115 Watkins Blvd (☎675-5700; ②). Rooms are at a premium when the Tennessee Volunteers are playing at home.

Knoxville's favorite **restaurant**, the rib specialists *Calhoun's*, overlooks the river downtown at 400 Neyland Drive (☎544-0349), and, in the Old City, the *131 Deli and Sidewalk Café* (☎523-4131) sells really tasty sandwiches. *Planet Earth* (☎522-2737) on West Jackson Street is a popular **bar** with live guitar bands most evenings. On campus, Cumberland Avenue offers a range of cheap eating options and lively drinking holes.

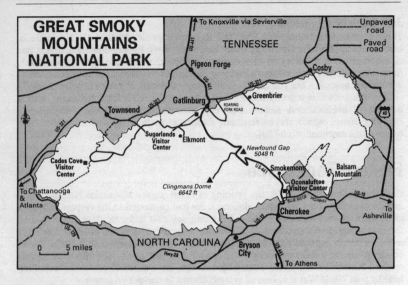

Towards the Great Smoky Mountains

The usual way to approach the Smokies from the west is on US-441 via the small market center of **SEVIERVILLE**, which evokes days gone by with its wooden-floored general stores and small cafés serving mountains of southern food to hungry farmers. A statue of **Dolly Parton** stands on the lawn outside the courthouse. Sevierville merges almost seamlessly into the six-mile strip of motels, fast-food places, clothing factory outlets, themed family attractions and souvenir shops at the dry town of **PIGEON FORGE**, while five miles further along US-441, a heavy layer of kitsch all but submerges the genuine Germanic heritage of the more upmarket "wet" tourist town of **GATLINBURG**. The long, narrow main street is packed to the point of claustrophobia with gimmicky souvenir shops, wax museums, and stalls selling sickly sweet taffy.

DOLLYWOOD

Born in 1946, one of twelve children, **Dolly Parton** lived in several modest homes around Pigeon Forge, the most isolated of them two miles from the nearest neighbor and over four miles from the mailbox. As a child she sang every week on local radio, before leaving for Nashville on the day she finished at Sevier County High School. Her first success, duetting with Porter Wagoner, came to an acrimonious end in the early Seventies, but she scored a major country hit in 1976 with *Jolene*. She then crossed over to a poppier sound, and into Hollywood films like *9 to 5* and *The Best Little Whorehouse in Texas*. Her songs have been acclaimed for their readiness to address issues like rural poverty, and refusal to tag along with the Nashville stereotype of subservient females.

Dollywood, Dolly Parton's "homespun fun" **theme park**, blends ersatz mountain heritage with the glamor of its celebrity shareholder. One section showcases Appalachian **crafts**, making everything from lye soap to horse-drawn carriages; a museum looks at Dolly herself in entertaining detail; and music shows are constantly on the go. The rides, however, are unspectacular, and cumulatively the whole place can get insufferably twee.

Dollywood is at 700 Dollywood Lane at the north end of Pigeon Forge (May–Oct & Xmas, as a rule 9am–9pm but considerable variations; $20.99; ☎1-800/DOLLYWOOD). Local **radio station** WDLY, on 105.5, is another Dolly Parton enterprise.

Practicalities

Both Gatlinburg (☎1-800/568-4748) and Pigeon Forge (☎1-800/251-9100) maintain toll-free **information** lines, and visitor centers on the main drag. **Accommodation** prices in the foothill towns fluctuate seasonally, from $20 up to $80. Motels in **Sevierville** are the best value; try the *Mize Motel* (☎453-4684; ②), one mile south at 804 Parkway. **Pigeon Forge** has literally dozens, such as the *Parkview*, 2806 Parkway (mid-March–Dec; ☎453-5051 or 1-800/239-9116; ②), and the comfortable, friendly *Shular Inn*, 2708 Parkway (☎453-2700 or 1-800/451-2376; ③). If you prefer neon lights to wilderness trails, you can camp at the *Smokies Campground*, 705 S Parkway (☎453-4129).

   Gatlinburg tends to be the most expensive, but *Bales*, 118 Bishop Lane (☎436-4773 or 1-800/458-8249; ③), and *Conner*, 840 River Rd (☎436-5147; ③), are competitively priced. It is, however, the best choice for **food**. *Linebergers*, 903 Parkway (☎436-9284), at traffic light #8, is strong on seafood and vegetable dishes. A good **breakfast** place in Pigeon Forge is the *Smoky Mountain Pancake House* at 301 N Parkway (☎453-1827).

Great Smoky Mountains National Park

The northern boundary of the **GREAT SMOKY MOUNTAINS NATIONAL PARK**, which stretches for seventy miles along the Tennessee–North Carolina border (see also p.364), is just two miles south of Gatlinburg on US-441. Don't expect immediate tranquillity, however: the roads, particularly in the fall, can be lined almost bumper-to-bumper with cars. The Smokies, within a day's drive of the major urban centers of the East Coast and the Great Lakes – and of two thirds of the entire US population – attract over nine million visitors per year, more than twice as many as any other National Park. These heavily contorted peaks are named for the **bluish haze** which hangs over them, made up of moisture and hydrocarbons released by the lush vegetation (a mature tree emits up to 900 gallons on a summer day). Since the Sixties, **air pollution** has been adding sulphates to the filmy smoke, and has cut back visibility by thirty percent. More than 120 tree species and over 1400 flowering plants clothe the mountains and meadows in color from early spring to late autumn. Sixteen peaks rise above 6000 feet, their steep elevation accounting for dramatic changes in climate.

   The most popular **times to visit** are between late March and mid-May, to see the delicate spring flowers, and during the second half of October when the hills are shrouded in a magnificent canopy of glaring reds, subtle yellows and faded browns. During June and July, rhododendrons blaze fiercely in the sometimes stifling summer heat.

   Just inside the park on US-441, the main artery running through to North Carolina, **Sugarlands visitor center** (daily, summer 8am–7pm; fall and spring 8am–6pm; winter 8am–5pm) is a useful source of leaflets covering hiking trails, driving tours, forests and wildlife. From here a ten-mile drive rises to Newfound Gap on the state line, where a seven-mile spur road winds its way up to **Clingman's Dome**, at 6643 feet the highest point in the park and in all Tennessee. A surreal concrete spiral walkway on top affords a panoramic, though hazy, view of the mountains, rather spoiled by the fact that virtually all the mature balsam firs in the area have been killed off by insect infestation.

   The scenic **Little River Road** branches off back at Sugarlands towards **Cade's Cove**, where another visitor center (with the same hours) is situated halfway round an eleven-mile driving loop, in summer and autumn always jam-packed with cars. Along the route, deserted barns, homesteads, mills and churches stand as a reminder of the farmers who carved out a living from this wilderness, before having to move out when National Park status was conferred in 1934. Quieter **Hwy-321**, on the other side of Sugarlands, branches off onto a gravel road towards the beautiful Greenbrier area.

   If you really want to get away from it all, escape onto the nine hundred miles of **hiking** trails. On the Appalachian Trail, you can now only camp in designated areas, caged-in behind iron bars to keep out the bears.

Practicalities

Hikers intending to stay out overnight require **backcountry permits**, available from visitor centers. The park also has ten developed **campgrounds**, of which the three most popular – *Cades Cove, Elkmont* and *Smokemont* – are always fully booked. Reserve in advance if you want a space in summer or fall. For details of the North Carolina side of the park, see p.364.

On Saturday, from dawn until 10am, the Cades Cove loop is reserved for **cyclists**. Bikes can be rented at the *Cades Cove Campground* (☎436-5615).

Chattanooga

Few cities are so identified with a song as **CHATTANOOGA**, in the southeast corner of Tennessee. Visitors expecting Tex Beneke and Glenn Miller's *Chattanooga Choo-Choo*, however, will be let down to find that there is no longer even an *Amtrak* service, although the town continues to celebrate its railroad history, and has plenty more to offer besides – not least its beautiful location on a deep bend in the Tennessee River, walled in by forested plateaux on three sides. This setting led John Ross, of Scottish and Cherokee ancestry, to found a trading post on the spot in 1815, and its strategic importance made it a great prize during the Civil War; victories here in 1863 were the springboard for Sherman's march through Georgia (see p.377).

The centerpiece of Chattanooga's twenty miles of reclaimed riverfront is **Ross's Landing** (the town's original name), a park at the bottom of Broad Street. Here the splendid five-storey **Tennessee Aquarium** (summer Mon–Thurs 10am–6pm, Fri–Sun 10am–8pm; winter daily 10am–6pm; $8.75) traces the aquatic life of the Mississippi from its Tennessee tributaries to the Gulf of Mexico. Cruises on the *Southern Belle* riverboat (☎266-4488), from the bottom of nearby Chestnut Street, include the daunting experience of bobbing around in the bottom of a huge lock on Chickamauga Lake.

A few blocks from the river, the **Chattanooga Regional History Museum** at 400 Chestnut St (Tue–Fri 10am–4.30pm, Sat & Sun noon–4.30pm; $2) takes a people-centered look at the area's rich history, with displays on its steel, soft-drink bottling and power industries, and on the Cherokee. A short walk further along are the grand old turn-of-the-century buildings of the lively business district, centered on Market and Broad streets. None is more eye-catching than the recently restored *Tivoli Theatre* at 709 Broad Street, whose flashing lights stand out like a beacon at night.

Two miles in from the river, in a rather depressed area, is the **Choo-Choo complex**, where the 1909 Beaux Arts style **Southern Railroad Terminal**, at 1400 Market St (☎266-5000), is now a *Holiday Inn*, the *Chattanooga Choo-Choo Hotel*. The impressive high-domed waiting room serves as the lobby, leading through to the former platform area where restored carriages act as hotel suites. Gift shops and cafés share space with a steam engine similar to the original Choo-Choo (the name given by the local paper to the first passenger train to come in from Cincinnati in 1880 – the first to link the south to the north). You're free to roam around; admission to the world's largest model railway display, on site, is $1.75. A free shuttle runs between the *Choo-Choo* and the Aquarium.

Chattanooga does, however, offer stunning six-mile rides on the real **steam trains** of the **Tennessee Valley Railroad**, crossing the river, running through deep tunnels, and turning round on a giant turntable. The two main stations, restored to their 1930s look, are at 2200 N Chamberlain Ave in east Chattanooga, and 4119 Cromwell Rd (I-75 exit 4 to Hwy-153), though some weekend routes pick up at the Choo-Choo (June–Sept Mon–Sat hourly 10am–5pm, Sun 12.30–5pm; other times call ☎894-8028).

Practicalities

A taxi downtown from Chattanooga's **airport** (☎855-2200), three miles east, costs around $12. *Greyhound* connections with Nashville, Knoxville and Atlanta come in on

THE CHEROKEE NATION AND THE TRAIL OF TEARS

During the eighteenth and early nineteenth centuries, the **Cherokee** were the most powerful Indian tribe in the tristate region of Tennessee, Georgia and North Carolina. They forged close links with white pioneers, adopting white methods in schooling and agriculture, intermarrying – and owning African slaves. The only Native Americans to develop their own written language, they had a regular newspaper, *The Cherokee Phoenix*. They even supplied soldiers for Andrew Jackson's US forces against the Creek Indians and the British in 1814, hoping to buy influence with the federal government.

Thirteen years later, against a background of aggressive territorial claims by settlers, they produced a written constitution modelled on that of the USA, stating their intention to continue to be a self-governing nation. John Ross, founder of Ross's Landing, and at most one-eighth Cherokee, was elected as the first Principal Chief in 1828 in an effort to appease and negotiate with national and state governments over their lands. However, as white demand for land increased, their former ally **Jackson**, now US president, was pressurized by the Georgians into "offering" the Cherokee western lands in exchange for those east of the Mississippi. Although the tribal leadership refused, a minority faction accepted, giving the government the get-out clause they wanted. The Cherokee were ordered to leave within two years, and 14,000 of them were forcefully removed to Oklahoma in 1838 along the horrific **Trail of Tears**: 4000 died of disease or exposure on the way. In the meantime, their land was sold by lottery and Ross's Landing was renamed Chattanooga. One thousand Cherokee managed to avoid removal by escaping into the mountains, and their descendants now occupy a small reservation in North Carolina.

The **Red Clay State Historic Park**, twenty miles east of Chattanooga off Hwy-317, recounts the old Cherokee way of life, with replica houses, tools and household implements. Its balsamic Sacred Council Spring was a meeting place for Cherokee elders.

Broad St downtown. The **visitor center**, 1001 Market St (Mon–Fri 9am–5.30pm, Sat 9.30am–1pm; ☎756-8687), provides the usual range of help, along with a useful guide for travellers with disabilities. Good-value **places to stay** downtown include the *Best Western* at 901 Carter St (☎266-7331; ③); far more atmospheric, if you can get a room on the train, is the *Choo-Choo* (☎266-5000; ⑤). There's **camping** at *Raccoon Mountain Campground*, Rte 4, Cummings Hwy (☎821-9403).

For a **breakfast** special, treat yourself to the buffet in the elegant black walnut-panelled dining rooms of the *Radisson Read House* at 827 Broad St (☎266-4121). You can get deliciously messy hoagies at the *Downtown Sub Station*, 347 Broad St (☎266-8999), and more substantially, *The Station House* in the Choo-Choo complex serves good steaks, chicken and southern food with excellent live country music from the servers. At night, *Michelangelo's Blues Club* (☎265-3327) in downtown Miller Plaza hosts live blues, jazz and rock.

Lookout Mountain

The name Chattanooga comes from a Creek word, meaning "rock rising to a point"; six miles from downtown is the rock itself, the 2215ft **Lookout Mountain**. From 3917 St Elmo Ave, on the #14 bus route, the world's steepest **incline railway** grinds its tentative way up to the top through a narrow gash in the lush forest, tackling nerve-racking gradients of up to 72.7 percent (summer daily 8.30am–9pm; winter 9am–6pm; 3–4 trips per hour; $6). Once there, a walk of a few hundred yards past exclusive homes takes you to **Point Park**, and the only statue in the country to show Union and Confederate soldiers shaking hands. This is part of the Chickamauga and Chattanooga National Military Park, covering several sites around the city and in nearby Chickamauga, Georgia. A short, steep, walking trail descends several tiers of steps to an overlook affording a not-to-be-missed view of the city and the meandering Tennessee River.

ALABAMA

Just 250 miles from north to south, **ALABAMA** ranges from the fast-flowing rivers, waterfalls and lakes of the **Appalachian** foothills to the subtropical bayous and white beaches of the **Gulf Coast**. Most of its industry is concentrated in the **north**, around rejuvenated **Birmingham**, and **Huntsville**, first home of the nation's space programme. The sun-scorched farmlands of middle Alabama envelop sober **Montgomery**, the state capital. Away from the French-influenced coastal strip around attractive **Mobile**, fundamentalist Protestant attitudes have traditionally backed a succession of right-wing demagogues, such as **George Wallace**, the four-times state governor who received ten million votes in the 1968 presidential election.

Times have moved on since the epic **civil rights** struggles in Montgomery, Birmingham, and **Selma**. Monuments and civic literature celebrate the achievements of the campaigners, and even Wallace renounced his racist views, courting – and winning – black votes in his successful campaign for governor in 1982. Even so, Alabaman blacks – a quarter of the population – still conspicuously lack political and commercial power.

Getting Around Alabama

Considering its rural nature, **public transport** is relatively good in Alabama. A daily *Amtrak* service between Birmingham and Mobile calls at Montgomery and several small towns, while the New York–Atlanta–New Orleans train stops at Anniston, Birmingham and Tuscaloosa. *Greyhound* serves the major towns and cities. Mobile, Montgomery, Huntsville and Birmingham all have small airports.

Northern Alabama

Northern Alabama, on the trailing edges of the Appalachians, is brightened up by the mountain lakes, rivers and canyons of the Tennessee River Valley. The area's first white settlers were small farmers who had little in common with the big plantation owners further south, and made various localized attempts to disassociate from the Confederacy during the Civil War. Just after the war, substantial mineral finds led to an industrial boom which peaked in the early Thirties.

Huntsville

Many southern cities aspire to blend the old with the new, but few achieve it so dramatically as **HUNTSVILLE**, just over a hundred miles south of Nashville just inside the Alabama border. Its sleepy center still recalls the days when it was dominated by cotton merchants and railroad owners. The **Huntsville Depot Transportation Museum**, 320 Church St (Tues–Sun 10am–5pm; $2.50), has an absorbing account of the city's railroad and commercial history. An excellent **trolley service** tours the town (50¢ for an all-day ticket), taking in historic **Twickenham** – the community's original name in 1808, before anti-British sentiment in the run-up to the 1812 War dictated that it should be renamed for its first settler, a Virginian named John Hunt.

Time was when Huntsville was content to be the "Watercress Capital of the World"; the great leap forward came after World War II, when the Army consolidated its **rocket and missile** research efforts in the city. Spearheading the project were **Dr Wernher von Braun** and 118 other German scientists, who came to Huntsville after a token period of rehabilitation. Von Braun's contribution of the V-2 ballistic missile to the Nazi

The **area code** for the entire state of Alabama is ☎205.

war effort is ignored by the city, which prefers to laud his later space-age achievements, such as **Explorer I**, the nation's first satellite, and the mighty **Saturn V**.

The giant **Space and Rocket Center**, five miles west of downtown on Hwy-20, off I-65 (daily summer 8am–7pm; otherwise 9am–6pm; $10.95), contains a mind-boggling array of technological exhibits, hands-on displays, and weightlessness simulators, as well as a giant Omnimax cinema. Outdoors, in the surreal Rocket and Space Shuttle parks, redundant rockets protrude skywards in the blazing Alabama sunshine; the 120-yard, four-storey Saturn V rocket is laid on its side to emphasize its immensity.

Practicalities

Huntsville's **visitor center** is at 700 Monroe St (Mon–Sat 9am–5pm; ☎533-5723). Chain **motels** on the outskirts include the *Econolodge*, 1304 N Memorial Hwy (☎539-9671; ③); the *Hilton*, 401 Williams Ave (☎533-1400; ④), is more central. Of the **restaurants**, *Bubba's*, at 105 Washington St (☎534-3133), serves burgers and ribs all day.

Birmingham

The rapid transformation of farmland into the city of **BIRMINGHAM** began in 1870, when two railroad routes met in the Jones Valley, a hundred miles south of Huntsville. What attracted speculators was not the land but what lay under it – a mixture of iron ore, limestone and coal, perfect for the manufacture of iron and steel. The expansion of heavy industry was finally brought to an abrupt halt by the Depression. Today iron and steel account for only a few thousand jobs, but new service and medical industries have helped transform this once smog-filled metropolis into a prosperous and pleasant city.

Being known as the "Pittsburgh of the South" might seem like faint praise; however, Birmingham also earned the label of the "Johannesburg of America" for the brutality and intolerance of its police force. An intense civil rights campaign in 1963 was the turning point, setting Birmingham on the road to smoother race relations.

Arrival and Information

Birmingham Airport is just three miles from downtown, but it's not served by buses; *Yellow Cabs* are on ☎252-1131. *Amtrak* pulls in at 1819 Morris Ave, downtown, and the *Greyhound* station is at 19th Street (☎252-7171), between Fourth and Fifth avenues – a rough area at night. Public transport is poor and most of the attractions are well strung out, so you need a car to see the city properly. **Visitor centers** are located at the airport (daily 8.30am–8pm; ☎254-1640), and at 1201 University Blvd (Mon–Sat 8.30am–5pm, Sun 1–5pm; ☎254-1654) on the university campus.

The City

Downtown Birmingham extends north from the railroad tracks at Morris Avenue to Tenth Avenue North, bounded to east and west by 25th and 15th streets. The landscaped greenery of **20th Street**, overlooked by a collection of early skyscrapers, is not enough to save these one-hundred-plus blocks from anonymity, with shopping now firmly anchored in the malls and suburbs.

The concrete colossus of the Birmingham-Jefferson Civic Center, at 22nd St and Tenth Ave N, contains the **Alabama Sports Hall of Fame**, a tribute to sporting greats such as 1936 Olympic hero **Jesse Owens**, Le Roy "Satchel" Paige, the first black baseball player to appear in the World Series, and boxer Joe Louis. There's even a space for George Wallace, on the rather flimsy excuse that he was state amateur boxing champion (Mon–Sat 9am–5pm, Sun 1–5pm; $2). Weave your way past the monotonous white-walled legal buildings to the nearby **Museum of Art**, 2000 Eighth Ave North, which is strong on Oriental art, American landscapes and Wedgwood pottery (Tues, Wed, Fri & Sat 10am–5pm, Thurs 10am–9pm, Sun 1–5pm; free).

A few blocks from the edge of downtown, at First Ave N and 32nd St, stand the massive sheds and tall chimney stacks of **Sloss Furnaces**, which produced pig iron to feed the city's mills and foundries from 1882 until 1971. Self-guided tours through the boilers, stoves and casting areas vividly portray the harsh working conditions endured by the ex-slaves, prisoners and unskilled immigrants. Imagining the searing heat, cramped space, the heavy loads and the putrid gaseous emissions, it's easy to appreciate why one former Sloss worker claimed "if mules had to do this work they would have banned it" (Tues–Sat 10am–4pm, Sun noon–4pm; free).

Atop **Red Mountain**, four miles south of downtown, a 55ft iron statue of Vulcan, Roman god of the forge, is the largest cast-iron statue ever made. The chubby rust-colored figure, perched high up on its 124ft pedestal, looks rather insignificant from ground level, but it's worth winding your way up the steep, verdant mountain road to relax in the peaceful grounds, or ride to the top of the tower for a superb panoramic view of the Jones Valley (daily 8am–10.30pm; $1).

Accommodation

Many of Birmingham's wide range of places to stay offer advantageous weekend rates. The nearest place to **camp** is the *Birmingham South KOA* (☎664-8832), eight miles south in Pelham, off I-65S.

Campus Inn, 800 11th St S (☎933-1900). Just south of downtown. ②.

Courtyard by Marriott, 500 Shades Creek Parkway (☎879-0400). Good-value accommodation geared for business travellers, with excellent deals at weekends. ③.

Economy Inn, 2224 Fifth Ave N (☎324-6107). The best value in downtown. ①.

Motel Birmingham, 7905 Crestwood Blvd (☎956-4440 or ☎1-800/338-9275). Pleasant rooms, though a little far out, past the airport on I-20 Montevello Exit. ③.

Eating and Drinking

The best bet in Birmingham is to ignore downtown in favor of **Five Points South**, at the foot of Red Mountain, two miles below downtown. Its narrow streets and alleys, packed with bars and restaurants, throng with revellers every weekend.

The Back Alley, Cobb Lane at 20th St S & 13th Ave (☎933-6211). Attractive restaurant famed for its desserts, on a cobbled lane in Five Points South. Main courses are mostly under $10.

Bogue's, 3028 Clairmont Ave (☎254-9780). Fantastic soul-food cafe near Five Points South offering superb value. Open during the week until 2pm and for morning brunch only at the weekend.

CIVIL RIGHTS IN BIRMINGHAM

In the first half of 1963, civil rights leaders chose Birmingham as the target of "Project C" (for confrontation), aiming to force businesses to integrate lunch counters and employ more blacks. Despite threats from Police Chief **"Bull"** Connor that there would be "blood running down the streets of Birmingham", pickets, sit-ins and marches sparked mass arrests. Over 2000 protestors flooded the jails; one was Dr Martin Luther King Jr, who wrote his *Letter from a Birmingham Jail* after being branded as an extremist by local white clergymen. Connor's use of high-pressure hoses, cattleprods and dogs against demonstrators acted as a potent catalyst of support. Pictures of snarling Alsatians sinking their teeth into the flesh of schoolkids were transmitted throughout the world, and led to an agreement between civil rights leaders and businesses in June 1963. Success in Birmingham sparked demonstrations in 186 other cities, which culminated in the 1964 Civil Rights Act prohibiting racial segregation.

The headquarters for the campaign, the **16th Street Baptist Church**, between Sixth and Seventh avenues, was the site of a sickening Klan bombing on September 15 1963, which killed four young black girls attending a Bible class. Open daily, the church contains a small shrine dedicated to the murdered girls. A bronze statue of Dr King stands across the road in Kelly Ingram Park, site of many huge rallies during the Sixties.

Cosmo's Pizza, 2012 Magnolia Ave (☎930-9971). A lively standard-priced pizza parlor popular with students and situated in the Art Deco Pickwick Plaza in Five Points South.

Manhattan, 2000 Second Ave (☎251-1832). Popular diner open for breakfast and lunch, offering good-value gyros, falafel, burgers, salads and soup.

West of Birmingham

Just west of Birmingham city limits, I-20/59 passes **BESSEMER**, a likeable small town named in 1887 after Sir Henry Bessemer, the English engineer who perfected the steel-making process. The **Hall of History Museum** in the 1916 Southern railroad depot, 1905 Alabama Ave, displays Native American artefacts alongside exhibits from the industrial pioneer years (Tues–Sat 10am–4pm; free).

TUSCALOOSA, home of the lively main campus of the University of Alabama, but little else of interest, lies 32 miles southwest of Bessemer. If you're hungry, combine eating with a view of the Black Warrior River at *Henson's Cypress Inn*, 501 Rice Mine Rd N (☎345-6963), which specializes in keenly priced seafood dishes and steaks.

Sixteen miles south on US-69, the **Mound State Monument** preserves twenty earthen mounds, carpeted in lush grass, with the largest supporting a rebuilt Native American temple. An estimated three thousand people lived here on the banks of the Black Warrior during the twelfth century; the on-site museum exhibits items found in burial grounds including jewellery, ceremonial vessels and a few skeletons.

South Central Alabama

Southern Alabama – memorably depicted in Harper Lee's child's-eye view of racial conflict, *To Kill a Mockingbird* – still consists mostly of small, sleepy, God-fearing rural communities. Only state capital **Montgomery**, with a population of just over 200,000, achieves metropolitan status. It lies in the heart of the **Black Belt**, originally named for the rich loamy soil, but these days more usually taken to refer to the region's ethnic make-up. Cotton was the major earner here until 1915, when a boll weevil infestation ended its dominance. Now it has been supplanted (officially) by soybeans, corn and peanuts – though surveys suggest that the leading cash crop is, in fact, marijuana.

Montgomery

MONTGOMERY's Black Belt position, 90 miles south of Birmingham and 160 west of Atlanta, made it a natural political center for the plantation elite, leading to its adoption as state capital in 1846 and temporary capital of the Confederacy fifteen years later. Despite its administrative importance, Montgomery is strangely quiet, largely because many businesses have relocated to the suburbs. Most neighborhoods are either exclusively white or totally black; integration sadly does not appear to be on the social agenda in the city that saw the first successful mass civil rights activity in 1955–56.

Arrival and Information

Dannelly Field Airport (☎281-5040) is fifteen miles from downtown on US-80. *Amtrak* stops at a bizarre group of converted grain silos at Commerce and Coosa by Riverfront Park, rather than the more traditional Union Station nearby, while the *Greyhound* station is even more conveniently located at 210 S Court St (☎264-4518).

The **visitor center** at 401 Madison Ave (☎262-0013) is set in a grand mansion house moved here from Tuskegee. Tours start here of **Old Alabama Town**, an area of restored houses and museums immediately behind (Mon–Sat 9.30am–3.30pm, Sun 1–3.30pm; $5). All places of interest downtown are easily walkable, though there is a handy trolley route.

CIVIL RIGHTS IN MONTGOMERY

During the Fifties, Montgomery's **bus system** – as was the norm in the South – was a miniature model of segregated society. The regulation ordering blacks to give up seats to whites came under repeated attack from black organizations, culminating in the call by the Women's Political Council for a mass boycott after **Rosa Parks** was arrested on December 1 1955 for refusing to give up her seat. Black workers were asked to walk to work, while black-owned taxis carried those who lived further away for the same 10¢ fare as buses. The protest attracted over ninety percent support, and the Montgomery Improvement Association (MIA), set up to coordinate activities, elected the 27-year-old **Dr Martin Luther King Jr** as its chief spokesperson. Meanwhile, the laid-off white bus drivers were employed as temporary police officials. Despite personal hardships, bombings and jailings, the boycott continued for eleven months, until the US Supreme Court declared segregation on public transport to be illegal in November 1956.

King remained pastor at the small brick **Dexter Avenue King Memorial Baptist Church**, surprisingly central at 454 Dexter Ave (Mon–Fri 9am–noon & 1–4pm, Sat 10am–2pm), until his move to Atlanta in 1960. A mural along a basement wall chronicles his life, while the upstairs sanctuary, much as it was during his ministry, contains his former pulpit. One block away at the corner of Washington and Hull, in front of the Southern Poverty Law Center (which specializes in helping victims of racial attacks), the deeply moving **Civil Rights Memorial** (designed by Maya Lin) consists of a black granite table that records the names of forty martyrs murdered by white supremacists and police. Cool water pumps slowly and evenly across it, and the wall behind is engraved with the quotation used so often by Dr King, "(we will not be satisfied) until justice rolls down like waters and righteousness like a mighty stream".

The City

Although 1993 saw Alabama's state flag finally replace the Confederate flag over the white-domed Greek Revival **State Capitol** at the top of Dexter Avenue, downtown Montgomery still bear reminders of its white supremacist past. A bronze star marks the spot where Jefferson Davis was sworn in as president of the Confederacy on February 18 1861 – an occasion on which his vice-president proudly proclaimed that this government was "the first in the history of the world, based upon this great physical and moral truth . . . that the Negro is not equal to the white man". Other "attractions" in this vein include the **Alabama Department of Archives and History**, next door, notable only for the lavish use of marble in its interior (Mon–Fri 8am–5pm, Sat 9am–5pm; free) and the **First White House of the Confederacy**, 644 Washington Ave, the temporary home of Jefferson Davis, now crammed with sentimental Confederate oddments (Mon–Fri 8am–4.30pm, Sat & Sun 9am–4.30pm; free).

On a different note, Montgomery was jammed with mourners in 1954 for the funeral of 29-year-old country star **Hank Williams**, who died of a heart attack on his way to a concert on the night of New Year's Eve 1953. An Alabama native from Butler County, Williams was as famous for his drink- and drug-related lifestyle as he was for writing honky-tonk classics like *Your Cheating Heart* and *I'm So Lonesome I Could Cry*. His hit single at the time of his death was *I'll Never Get Out of This World Alive*. The **Hank Williams Memorial**, a large white marble headstone complete with song lyrics and an image of the singer, dominates the Oakwood Cemetery Annex, 1304 Upper Wetumpka Rd, near downtown; Hank's statue stands at Lister Hill Plaza on N Perry St.

Reminiscent of the grounds of a large English stately home, the stunningly landscaped **Blount Cultural Park** gives some substance to the city's claim of being a regional center for the arts. Situated off Woodmere Blvd, ten miles southeast of the city, it's home to the Alabama Shakespeare Festival (☎1-800/841-4273 or ☎271-5353), which also performs contemporary works in the sumptuous Renaissance-style *Carolyn Blount Theatre* (Ms Blount's husband provided the entire funds for the park). The equally slick **Montgomery Museum of Fine Arts** (Tues, Wed, Fri & Sat 10am–5pm, Thurs 10am–9pm, Sun noon–5pm; free) spans more than 200 years of American art.

Accommodation

There are several good-value places to stay in and around downtown Montgomery, with the usual motel names all sitting alongside the highways.

Capitol Inn, 205 N Goldthwaite St (☎265-0541). Well-kept establishment on a small hill, a fifteen-minute walk from downtown. ②.

Red Bluff Cottage, 551 Clay St (☎264-0056). Friendly B&B, with good food, near the *Capitol*. ③.

Riverfront Inn, 200 Coosa St (☎834-4300). Well placed for *Amtrak* and downtown. ③.

Town Plaza Motel, 743 Madison Ave (☎269-1561). Conveniently located, but very basic. ①.

Whitley Hotel, 231 Montgomery St (☎262-6461). Twenties decor, comfortable rooms. ③.

Eating and Drinking

Downtown Montgomery is dotted with cheap cafés selling burgers or soul food; a few minutes' drive southeast, suburban **Cloverdale** offers a good selection of eating places covering every price range. Especially in the center, things get pretty quiet at night.

Corsino's, 911 S Court St (☎263-9752). Small, family-run pizza parlor, open until 9.30pm.

Farmers' Market Cafe, 315 N McDonough St (☎262-9163). Just off downtown, next to the busy marketplace; the best place for southern-style breakfast in Montgomery. Mon–Fri, 5am–2pm.

Kat & Harri's Nice Place, 1061 Woodley Rd, Cloverdale (☎834-2500). The pick of the suburban nightspots, though only really lively on Fri or Sat.

Montgomery Marina, 617 Shady St (☎259-5490). Unpretentious café and bar, pleasantly located about a mile from downtown on the banks of the Alabama River.

Vintage Year, 405 Cloverdale Rd, Cloverdale (☎264-8463). Reservations are necessary at one of Alabama's most highly rated restaurants. The haute cuisine will set you back at least $30.

Young House, 231 N Hull St (☎262-0409). Southern cooking in an 1850 house, next to the visitor center and Old Alabama Town. Lunch only.

Selma

The neat market town of **SELMA**, fifty miles west of Montgomery, became in the early Sixties the focal point of a national voting rights campaign. Demonstrations, meetings and attempts to register were repeatedly met by police violence, before the murder of a black protestor by a state trooper prompted the decision to organize the historic **march from Selma to Montgomery**. On "Bloody Sunday", March 7 1965, six hundred marchers set off across the steep incline of the imposing, narrow, **Edmund Pettus Bridge**. As they went over the apex of the bridge, a line of state troopers fired tear gas without warning, lashing out at the panic-stricken demonstrators with nightsticks and cattle-prods. This violent confrontation, broadcast all over the world, is credited with having directly influenced the passage of the **Voting Rights Act** the following year. Outside the 1965 campaign headquarters at the **Brown Chapel AME Church**, 410 Martin Luther King St, a bust of Dr King is part of a monument to the struggle. Plans are currently under way to designate the entire route of the march as a National Historic Trail.

Lined with independently owned stores and cafés, **Broad Street** is the town's busy main thoroughfare, running into the wide riverfront **Water Avenue**, which still feels set in the Forties with its frontier-style shopfronts, seed warehouses and garages. Just a few blocks away stand the beautiful homes of the town's Historic District.

Selma's history stretches back well before the Sixties; its huge arsenal and ship-building plant were prime targets for Union troops who looted and burned most buildings in March 1865. One of the few remaining plantation homes is **Sturdivant Hall**, 713 Mabry St (Tues–Sun 9am–4pm; $4), an attractively furnished house with an accessible cupola tower and lovely grounds.

Practicalities

Unfortunately, downtown Selma is devoid of places to **stay**; there are some small independent motels on the outskirts, and the *Holiday Inn* is three miles west on US-80 (☎872-0461; ②). The pick of the **soul food restaurants** is the *Downtowner*, 1114 Selma Ave (☎875-5933), open for breakfast and lunch; *Major Grumbles*, 1 Grumbles Alley (☎872-2006), is a slightly upmarket riverside pub with hot sandwiches (try the almondine flounder) and a disturbing "Indian giant" skeleton draped in a Confederate flag. The **visitor center** at 2207 Broad St (☎875-7485), north of town at the junction with Hwy-22, provides tour brochures for the Historic District and black heritage sites.

Tuskegee

TUSKEGEE, forty miles east of Montgomery, off I-85 on US-29, has played a seminal role in black history as the home of **Tuskegee University**, one of the earliest black colleges, founded in 1881 by ex-slave **Booker T Washington**. He believed that blacks should work for advances in education and employment instead of campaigning for social equality with whites, and that voting rights were worth sacrificing for a share in economic growth. To that end, the college concentrated more on crafts than academia.

Washington was seen, by the white press at least, as the most influential black figure in the country around the turn of the century, although his accommodationist approach aroused bitter opposition from black radicals like **W E B Du Bois**. In the years before his death in 1915, however, the virtual disenfranchisement of southern blacks and rising unemployment drew Washington closer to agreement with his detractors.

Today the privately run 3500-student university is short of funds and very shabby; many of the original buildings built by students are still in use, and all roads and pathways, except for those used by Ronald Reagan during a presidential visit, are full of potholes and weeds. On campus, the **George Washington Carver Museum** catalogues the work of the Tuskegee agricultural scientist who promoted self-help programmes for black farmers but is best known as the inventor of more than three hundred byproducts from the peanut and sweet potato (daily 9am–5pm; free).

The **visitor center** (☎727-6390) is inside the museum, and *Dorothy Hall* (☎727-8753; ②) on campus provides an inexpensive place to **stay** – though with nothing to see in the rest of the town, it's unlikely that you'll want to spend long in Tuskegee.

Alabama's Gulf Coast

Alabama's narrow share of the **Gulf coastline** is blessed with an abundance of fine white sand beaches, laundered by clear blue waters. The coast veers sharply inwards to accommodate the port city of **Mobile**, featuring hundreds of antebellum buildings in a tree-shaded center. Away from the water's edge, agriculture, dominated by pecan, peach and watermelon growing, flourishes on the gently sloping coastal plain.

Mobile

The busy port and paper manufacturing city of **MOBILE** (pronounced *Mo-beel*) traces its origins back to a French community founded in 1702. These early white settlers brought with them **Mardi Gras**, celebrated in Mobile continuously since 1704 – several years before New Orleans. Virtually every street is transformed in early spring by the delicate colors of azaleas, camellias and dogwoods: a beautiful complement to the many early eighteenth-century Spanish and Colonial-style buildings.

Despite this combination of bricks and bulbs, the city is unlikely to hold your attention for more than a day. Mobile survived the torches of the Union army during the

Civil War, and possesses enough antebellum buildings to designate four sizeable areas as historic districts. The obvious place to start exploring is reconstructed **Fort Conde**, whose ramparts provide a good view of the city, and of the World War II battleship **USS Alabama** permanently moored nearby. Fanning out from the fort, the Church Street Historic District holds 59, mostly pre-Civil War, buildings, as well as two free museums (both Tues–Sat 10am–5pm, Sun 1–5pm; free). The **History Museum**, 355 Government St, displays glittering Mardi Gras costumes and lavish horse-drawn carriages, while steam fire engines, resplendent in original livery, shining brass bells and trumpets, are the stars of the **Phoenix Fire Museum**, 203 S Clairborne St.

Downtown Mobile's lack of action outside of Mardi Gras is made up for by an amazing display of greenery, particularly down its main thoroughfare, **Government Street**, which is shaded by a canopy of adjoining oaks, and central Bienville Square, a popular picnic spot with free lunchtime concerts every Wednesday during summer.

Practicalities

Downtown Mobile is somewhat under the shadow of I-10, as it sweeps to meet I-65 a few miles west. *Amtrak*, 11 Government Street, and *Greyhound*, 201 Government St (☎432-9793), are both very central. Mobile's resourceful **visitor center**, located in Fort Conde, 150 S Royal St (daily 8am–5pm; ☎434-7304), can provide valuable **accommodation** discount vouchers. The cheapest downtown place is the *Oak Tree Inn*, 255 Church St (☎433-6923; ②), while the huge rooms at the *Malaga Inn*, 359 Church St (☎438-4701; ③), an 1862 twin town house, are great value, and there's a good but expensive seafood restaurant. Mobile's finest hotel, *Stouffer Riverview Plaza*, 64 Water St (☎438-4000; ⑤), has a great view of the port and reductions at weekends.

The *Back Porch*, 200 S Royal St (☎432-5875), is a friendly lunchtime **café** serving cheap subs and a renowned red beans'n'rice, while *Wintzels' Oyster House*, 605 Dauphin St (☎433-1004), serves good-value seafood platters in a determinedly eccentric atmosphere. At night, downtown Mobile is largely deserted; *G T Henry's Bar*, 462 Dauphin St (☎432-0300), is a popular pub with a pool room, loud music by independent-label bands, and a wide selection of beers.

Around the Bay Area

Twenty miles south of Mobile, off I-10, the 65 acres of landscaped color that make up **Bellingrath Gardens** include a quarter of a million azaleas. Fifteen miles further south on Hwy-193 are the quiet beaches and undisturbed pine forest of sunny **Dauphin Island**, which has a campground (☎861-2742) on its western tip.

The *Mobile Bay Ferry* links Dauphin with the larger **Pleasure Island**, five miles away (adults $1; cars $9; ☎968-7511). The real gem here, and indeed on the entire Alabama Gulf Coast, lies twenty miles west, in the shape of **GULF SHORES**, a stunning **beach** where ultramarine waters sweep gently over blinding snow-white sands, just beyond the junction of Hwy-59 and Hwy-182. Although it never gets overcrowded, the beach is particularly busy on a Sunday, when young people from all over LA – Lower Alabama in this case – choose the resort in preference to the more expensive Florida Panhandle. A smattering of lively cafés specialize in freshly caught **shrimp**; the lurid *Pink Pony Pub* (☎948-6371) is the most popular place for refreshment and music.

Tourism is Gulf Shores' only trade; if you get bored with the beach and the bars, there's not a lot else to do. **Accommodation** is pricey and often booked up during summer weekends, though the *Port of Call Motel*, one mile west on Beach Blvd (☎948-7739; ②), is reasonable. Otherwise expect to pay in excess of $70 for a double, though you can **camp** three miles further east at the Gulf State Park Resort (☎948-6353). The Gulf Coast **CVB** (☎968-8832) on Hwy-59, near Gulf Shores, provides a full range of information.

MISSISSIPPI

When cotton was king – and slavery was as yet unchallenged – **MISSISSIPPI** was the nation's fifth wealthiest state. Ever since the Civil War, it has been the poorest, its dependence on cotton now a handicap which makes it victim to the vagaries of the commodities market. Widespread poverty endured alongside pockets of enormous riches, and white Mississippi was notorious for violent resistance to black political participation. Not until the early Seventies did the church bombings and murders come to an end; no one could claim that racial tension does not exist, but matters have improved since the days of *Mississippi Burning*. The economy too has begun to pick up, though the profits brought in by the legalization of riverboat gambling may not prove durable.

The major city in this largely flat state is the capital, **Jackson**. However, historic river towns like **Vicksburg** and **Natchez** provide good reasons to stay off the interstates, and **blues** fans will need no encouragement to go exploring sleepy **Delta** settlements such as Alligator or Yazoo City.

Getting Around Mississippi
Although *Greyhound* serves most of Mississippi, including the Delta, only along the coastal stretch are services at all frequent. Jackson has the only **airport** of any size, and *Amtrak* trains from New Orleans head north to Memphis, and along the coast to Florida. Trips on the Mississippi itself are run on expensive luxury cruisers (see p.400).

The Delta

> *That Delta. Five thousand square miles, without any hill save the bumps of dirt the Indians made to stand on when the river over-flowed.*
>
> William Faulkner, *Sanctuary*

"That Delta" is not in fact a delta at all; technically it's an alluvial flood plain, a couple of hundred miles short of the mouth of the Mississippi. The name is owed to its resemblance to the fertile Delta of the Nile (which also began at a city named **Memphis**); the extravagant meanderings of the river on its way down to **Vicksburg** deposit sufficient rich topsoil to make this one of the world's finest cotton-producing regions.

The Delta is a land of scorching sun, parched earth, flooding creeks and thickets of bone-dry evergreens, best seen at dawn or dusk when the glassy-smooth Mississippi waters reflect the sun and the foliage along the banks. Just to contain the sheer volume of water is a never-ending battle, with giant levees struggling to protect the farmland. The main thoroughfare south is the legendary **Highway 61**; but exploring is best on the backroads, characterized by roadside shacks, tiny churches and the sound of the blues.

Clarksdale

CLARKSDALE, the first major town south of Memphis, may lack beauty, but it has every right to call itself the home of the blues. The quite phenomenal list of former residents in the **Delta Blues Museum**, housed in the public library at 114 Delta Ave (Mon–Fri 10am–5pm, Sat 10am–2pm), stretches through Muddy Waters, John Lee Hooker, Howlin' Wolf and Robert Johnson up to Ike Turner and Sam Cooke. They're celebrated by photos, instruments, personal possessions, videos and recordings, with the centerpiece being the "Muddywood" guitar created by Z Z Top out of wood from Waters' old cabin. Blues fans can also drop in at WROX radio, 127 Third St, where Early

The **area code** for the entire state of Mississippi is ☎601.

THE DELTA BLUES

As recently as 1900, much of the **Mississippi Delta** remained an impenetrable wilderness of cypress and gum trees, roamed by panthers and bears and plagued with mosquitoes. Bit by bit land had been cleared for cotton plantations, but, though the soil was fertile, white laborers could not be enticed to work in this god-forsaken backcountry. Since emancipation, the economy had come to depend on black **sharecroppers**, who would work a portion of the land on a white-owned plantation in return for a share (often pitifully small) of the eventual crop. As a rule, this lifestyle ensured long periods of poverty and debt interspersed with occasional windfalls; but in the Delta the returns tended to be greater than elsewhere, and blacks moved here from all over Mississippi.

In 1903, W C Handy, often credited as "the Father of the Blues" but at that time the leader of a vaudeville orchestra, found himself waiting for a train in Tutwiler, fifteen miles southeast of Clarksdale. At some point in the night, a ragged black man carrying a guitar sat down next to him and began to play what Handy called "the weirdest music I had ever heard". Using a pocketknife pressed against the guitar strings to accentuate his mournful vocal style, the man sang that he was "Goin' where the Southern cross the Dog".

This was the **Delta blues**, characterized by the interplay between words and music, with the guitar aiming to parallel and complement the singing rather than simply provide a backing. A local, place-specific music – the "Southern" and the "Dog" were railroads which crossed a short way south at Moorhead – it did not of course simply appear from nowhere. It combined traditional African instrumental and vocal techniques with the "field hollers" chanted by slaves and the reels and jigs then at the basis of popular entertainment.

Two men epitomize the Delta blues. One was **Charley Patton**, born west of Jackson in April 1891. The classic itinerant bluesman, Patton moved from plantation to plantation and wife to wife, playing Saturday-night dances with a repertoire that extended from rollicking dance pieces to documentary songs such as *High Water Everywhere*, which chronicled the bursting of the Mississippi levees in April 1927. The more enigmatic **Robert Johnson** was rumored to have sold his soul to the Devil in return for a few brief years of writing songs such as *Love in Vain* and *Stop Breakin' Down*. His *Crossroads Blues* spoke of being stranded at night in the chilling emptiness of the Delta; themes carried to metaphysical extremes in *Hellhound on My Trail* and *Me and the Devil Blues* – "you may bury my body down by the highway side / So my old evil spirit can catch a Greyhound bus and ride".

Both Patton and Johnson died in the 1930s. However, within a few years the Delta blues had been carried north to **Chicago** by men such as Muddy Waters and Howlin' Wolf. Their electrified urban blues was the most immediate ancestor of rock 'n' roll.

In addition to the towns mentioned in the text – especially Clarksdale and Helena – blues enthusiasts may want to search out the following rural sites.

Stovall Plantation. 7 miles northwest of Clarksdale on Stovall Road. Where tractor-driver Muddy Waters was first recorded; his cabin is still (just) standing.

Sonny Boy Williamson's Grave. Whitfield Church, outside Tutwiler, 13 miles southeast of Clarksdale.

Parchman Farm. Junction US-49W/Hwy-32. Mississippi State penitentiary, immortalized by former prisoner Bukka White.

Dockery Plantation. Hwy-8, between Cleveland and Ruleville. One of Patton's few long-term bases, also home to Howlin' Wolf and Roebuck "Pops" Staples.

Charley Patton's Grave. New Jerusalem Church, Holly Ridge, off US-82 6 miles west of Indianola.

Robert Johnson's Grave. Payne Chapel at Quito, off Hwy-7, roughly 6 miles southwest of Greenwood, where he was poisoned.

Getting to See Blues Events

Managing to hear live blues music in the Delta is rarely straightforward. Half the time nobody seems to know who is playing where, let alone when, and many of the "jook joints" themselves – which tend to be dark and rudimentary places, making few concessions to decor or comfort – don't have phones. On the whole, most "jookin" gets done at weekends; we list likely venues for each town. With public transport – even taxis – all but nonexistent, a car is essential.

Wright has broadcast his show since 1947 (Mon–Fri 6–10pm), and the *Barbershop*, 317 Issaquena Ave, where recording artist Wade Walton performs for visitors when he's not cutting hair. The **Stackhouse/Delta Record Mart**, 232 Sunflower Ave (☎627-2209), is stuffed with obscure records, books and Delta crafts, and the staff, who also run the *Rooster Blues* record label and a mail-order service, are very useful for gig information.

Practicalities

Clarksdale's strangest **accommodation** option has to be the *Riverside Hotel*, 615 Sunflower Ave (☎624-9163; ①), which until 1944 was a hospital, famous as the site of **Bessie Smith**'s death in 1937 after a car crash. Now it's a basic rooming house; you can find better facilities along US-61, which in town is State Street, at the *Comfort Inn* (no 710 S; ☎627-9292; ③); the *Southern Inn* (no 1904 N; ☎624-5558; ①); and the *Beacon Inn* (no 1910 N; ☎624-4391; ②). Central **restaurants** include the Lebanese *Rest Haven*, 419 S State St (☎624-9106), and soul-food specialists *Fair's*, 227 Fourth St (☎627-2747).

The most famous of Clarksdale's **jook-joints**, *Smitty's Red Top Lounge*, 377 Yazoo Ave (☎627-4421), has live blues most weekends. *Margaret's Blue Diamond Lounge*, 381 W Tallahatchie Ave (☎627-4060), usually puts on something on a Saturday night; on Sunday afternoon, try *Red's South End Disco*, 395–397 Sunflower St (☎627-3166).

Central Delta Towns

GREENVILLE, seventy miles south of Clarksdale, is the largest town on the Delta. Still an important riverport, it hosts the **Mississippi Delta Blues Festival** every September. Tree-lined avenues lead from the characterless outskirts into the business district, beyond which pallid warehouses stand in the shadow of a huge levee. Several of the flimsy shacks along **Nelson Street**, a run-down street in a potentially dangerous part of town, transform at night into blues joints which welcome visitors; *Perry's Flowing Fountain*, at no 816 (☎335-9836), is currently the most reliable. The top places to **eat** – arguably the best in the entire Delta for down-home cooking – are the original lunch-only *Doe's*, on the safer end of Nelson at no 502 (☎334-3315), and *Doe's Too*, 1525C Hwy-1 S (☎332-2171), recently opened on the main through highway.

Fifteen miles east on US-82, **INDIANOLA** is the home of the largest catfish processing company in the world, *Delta*. **B B King**, who was born here, plays an open-air home-town show once a year under the auspices of *Club Ebony*, 404 Hannah St (☎887-9915). The *Keyhole Inn* on Church St is an archetypal jook joint.

For a look at the Delta's social and economic history, call in on **GREENWOOD**, a sleepy town of 20,000 people, forty miles east on US-82, and still the country's second largest cotton exchange after Memphis. The nineteenth-century offices of downtown's Cotton Row overlook the shady Yazoo River, and graceful mansions line pretty Grand Boulevard. The **Cottonlandia Museum** (Tues–Sat 9am–5pm, Sun 1–5pm), two miles west of the town center on US-49E, focuses on the history of the Delta agriculture and its workers. Greenwood has recently begun to play on its Robert Johnson connection (he died here) by putting on the **Mississippi Crossroads Blues Festival** every May.

Northern Mississippi

Cutting its way south through Mississippi, I-55 acts as an approximate boundary between the Delta and the luscious green forests of the northeast. Of the small northern market towns, the most appealing are **Holly Springs**, whose oak-lined streets emanate from a neat courthouse square, and the old-style shopping center of **Columbus**. The only two places of major interest in the region are genteel **Oxford** and tidy blue-collar **Tupelo**, birthplace of **Elvis Presley** and **John Lee Hooker**.

Oxford

Twelve thousand residents and eleven thousand students enable **OXFORD**, an enclave of wealth in a predominantly poor region, to blend small-town charm with a busy night-life. Its central square and leafy streets have a vaguely European air about them – the town called itself after the English city as part of its campaign to persuade the **University of Mississippi** – known as Ole Miss – to locate its main campus here.

It's difficult now to believe that the leafy campus was in September 1962 the site of the most bitter display of racial hatred ever seen in Mississippi. After eighteen months of legal and political wrangling, the federal court ruled that James Meredith should be allowed to enrol as the first black student at Ole Miss. The news that Meredith had been sneaked into college by federal troops sparked a riot that left three dead and 160 injured. Despite constant threats, Meredith graduated the following year, wearing a "NEVER" badge (the segregationist slogan of Governor Ross Barnett) upside down. The **Blues Archive** (Mon–Fri 8.30am–5pm; ☎232-7753 in advance) on campus holds thousands of recordings and B B King's personal memorabilia, while the **Center for the Study of Southern Culture** looks at southern folkways (Mon–Fri 8.15am–4.45pm; free).

From Ole Miss, a ten-minute walk through lush Bailey Woods leads to secluded **Rowan Oak**, the former home of novelist **William Faulkner**, preserved as it was on the day he died in July 1962 (Mon–Fri 10am–noon & 2–4pm, Sat 10am–noon, Sun 2–4pm; free). The fictional Deep South town of Jefferson, where the Nobel Prize winner set his major works, was based heavily on Oxford and its environs.

Practicalities

Oxford's **visitor center** (☎232-2149) is in the town square. **Accommodation** options include *Ole Miss Motel*, 1517 University Ave (☎234-2424; ②), and the *University Inn*, 2201 W Jackson Ave (☎234-7013; ③). Prices go up during graduation, the Faulkner Literary Festival each August, and on weekends of football games. You can **eat** good-value Mexican meals at *Cafe Ole*, 1612 University Ave, or soul food at the *Beacon* one mile north on Hwy-7 (☎234-5041). **Nightlife** focuses on **Harrison Avenue** and the adjacent streets; clubs putting on live blues and other music include the *Gin Bar*, in an old cotton warehouse at S 14th St and Harrison (☎234-0024), and the dilapidated *Hoka* at 304 S 14th St (☎234-3057), which houses a cheap café and a small movie theater.

Tupelo

On January 8 1935, **Elvis Presley** and his twin brother Jesse were born in **TUPELO**, an industrial town in northeastern Mississippi. Jesse died at birth, while Elvis grew up to be a truck driver. Their parents, Gladys and Vernon Presley, who lived in poor-white East Tupelo, found it hard to make ends meet. Such was the financial strain of rearing the young Elvis that his sharecropper father was reduced to forgery in a desperate attempt to raise cash, and was jailed for three years. The two-room home was repossessed, and the family eventually moved to Memphis in 1948.

Tupelo **CVB**, 712 E President St (☎841-6521 or 1-800/553-0611), has details of a four-mile driving tour which takes in Elvis' first school and the shop where he bought his first guitar. The town doesn't go in for overkill, however, and has little of the tackiness you might expect. The actual **Elvis Presley Birthplace**, 306 Elvis Presley Drive, more of an emotive shrine than a glitzy tourist stop, now stands in Elvis Presley Park, near a meditation chapel built with donations from fans (May–Sept Mon–Sat 9am–5.30pm, Sun 1–5pm; Oct–April Mon–Sat 9am–5pm, Sun 1–5pm; $1).

The *Comfort Inn*, 1190 N Gloster St (☎842-5100; ③), is a central place to **stay**, with good Italian food at the nearby *Vanelli's*, 1302 N Gloster St (☎844-4410).

South Central Mississippi

South of the Delta, the rich woodlands and meadows of central Mississippi are heralded by steep loess bluffs, holding engaging historic towns such as **Vicksburg** and **Natchez**. Driving is a real pleasure, especially along the unspoiled Natchez Trace Parkway – devoid of trucks, buildings and neon signs – which runs through Jackson.

Jackson

JACKSON, halfway between Memphis and New Orleans at two hundred miles from either, has been Mississippi's state capital since 1821. Only in this century, however, has it become the largest conurbation in the state. It's now a pleasant and hospitable community which is flourishing as a center for health and technological industries.

The **Old Capitol**, now the **State Historical Museum**, charts Mississippi's unenviable history, with excellent displays on civil rights and slavery, especially the chilling notices for slave auctions (Mon–Fri 8am–5pm, Sat 9.30am–4.30pm, Sun 12.30–4.30pm; free). The "new" **Mississippi State Capitol**, 400 High St, built in 1903 as a Beaux Arts Classical showpiece, is much more ornate. In true rebel fashion, the gilt eagle on the roof looks away from Washington. A block west, the **Smith-Robertson Museum and Cultural Center**, 528 Bloom St, tells the story of black Mississippians since the French first imported slaves in 1719, through the fortunes of Farish Street, Jackson's oldest black neighborhood (Mon–Fri 9am–5pm, Sat 9am–noon, Sun 2–5pm; $1).

Practicalities

Greyhound **buses** from Atlanta, Dallas and Memphis arrive at 201 S Jefferson St (☎353-6342); **Amtrak** is at 300 W Capitol Ave. Jackson's regional **airport** is ten minutes east on I-20 – a $15 taxi ride or $10 by van (☎957-6868). *JATRAN* runs a reasonable in-town bus service until 7pm. The **visitor center** is at 1150 Lakeland Drive (summer Mon–Sat 8.30am–4.30pm, Sun 1.30–4.30pm; otherwise Mon–Fri 8.30am–4.30pm; ☎960-1800).

There are central **rooms** at the *Sun'n'Sand Motel*, 410 N Lamar Blvd beside the capitol (☎354-2501; ②), and the *Wilson Inn*, 310 Greymont St (☎1-800/333-9475; ②). Further out, the *Holiday Inn North*, 5075 I-55 North (☎366-9411; ③), has a nice pool.

Downtown Jackson more or less closes down at 6pm, though one notable exception is *Hal & Mel's Restaurant & Oyster Bar*, at 200 S Commerce St by the Mississippi State Fairgrounds (☎948-0888), which specializes in New Orleans cuisine and puts on live bands at the weekend. Details of local **blues** events are printed in the *Clarion Ledger*, or broadcast on WMPR, 90.1FM. Out in the suburbs, *Poet's*, 1855 Lakeland Drive (☎982-9711), does great things with redfish for $10 and has live music.

Vicksburg

The historic port of **VICKSBURG** straddles a high bluff on a bend in the Mississippi, 44 miles west of Jackson. During the Civil War, its domination of the river halted Union shipping, and led Abraham Lincoln to call Vicksburg the "key to the Confederacy". It was a crucial target for General Ulysses S Grant, who eventually landed to the south in the spring of 1863, circled inland, and attacked from the east. After a 47-day siege, the outnumbered Confederates surrendered on the Fourth of July – a holiday Vicksburg declined to celebrate for the next hundred years – and Lincoln was able to rejoice "the Father of Waters again goes unvexed to the sea". **Vicksburg National Military Park** (daily 8am–5pm; $3 per car), entered on US-80 (Clay St) just northeast, preserves the main battlefield. A sixteen mile loop drive through the rippling green hillsides traces every contour of the Union and Confederate trenches, punctuated by statues, refurbished cannons, and over 1600 state-by-state monuments. Also on show are the substantial remains of the iron-clad **USS Cairo**, sunk by a mine in the Yazoo River, along with artefacts found when it was salvaged a century later, and the **Vicksburg National Cemetery**, in which 13,000 of the 17,000 Union graves are simply marked "Unknown".

Vicksburg today is a bare but attractive city of precipitous streets, steep terraces and wooded ravines, its Victorian riverfront as yet unaffected by the impact of at least two floating **casinos**. As well as nineteenth-century homes, it offers the fascinating **Old Court House Museum**, on Cherry St (Mon–Sat 8.30am–4.30pm, Sun 1.30–4.30pm; $2), focusing largely on the siege; the victorious Grant, who returned as president, addressed thousands of ex-slaves from its balcony. At 1107 Washington St, an enjoyable display of old **Coca-Cola** merchandising marks the spot where the drink was first bottled (Mon–Sat 9am–5pm, Sun 1.30–4.30pm; $1.75). Three daily **hydro-jet tours** explore the Mississippi and Yazoo rivers (which have changed their course since the siege), departing from the bottom of Clay Street (March to mid-Nov; ☎638-5443; $25).

Practicalities

Vicksburg's **visitor center** is opposite the Military Park (☎636-9421 or 1-800/636-9421). Among **motels** nearby are the clean *Hillcrest*, 4503 Hwy-80 E (☎638-1491; ①), and the comfortable *Park Inn International*, 4137 I-20 Frontage Rd (☎638-5811; ③). Central **B&Bs** in historic homes include the extremely hospitable *Annabelle's*, 501 Speed St (☎634-8564 or 1-800/634-8564; ⑤), and *Cherry Street Cottage*, 2212 Cherry St (☎636-7086; ④). **Camp** at the *Battlefield Kampground*, 4407 I-20 Frontage Rd (☎636-9946).

Eat at the "round tables" all-you-can-eat *Walnut Hills*, 1214 Adams St (☎638-4910), for its superb southern fried chicken; on the other hand, the upmarket *Delta Point River Restaurant*, 4144 Washington St (☎636-5317), has a stupendous river view.

Natchez

Sixty miles south of Vicksburg, the river town of **NATCHEZ** still maintains an antebellum atmosphere, abounding in Greek revival mansions with meticulously maintained gardens. Fourteen homes stay open all year round, including the elaborate octagonal **Longwood**, 140 Lower Woodville Rd (daily 9am–5pm; $6), with its huge dome, snow-white arches and columns, and the palatial **Stanton Hall**, 401 High St (daily 9am–5pm; $5). In March and October each year, most of the rest can be seen on the **Natchez Pilgrimage** – tours, led by women wearing massive hoopskirts, which start from 100 State St ($20 per half-day tour; ☎446-6631 or 1-800/647-6742).

By the mid-sixteenth century, the sophisticated sun-worshipping local **Natchez Indians** had built a flourishing commercial empire, which they later defended in bitter running battles with the French. Ceremonial mounds, reconstructed dwellings, and a small museum can be seen at their **Grand Village**, 400 Jefferson Davis Blvd (free).

Down below the town proper, raucous **Natchez Under-the-Hill** was once known as the "Sodom of the Mississippi"; most of the old streets have eroded away, and the area is now choked by traffic for the *Lady Luck* riverboat **casino** (24-hrs; ☎1-800/722-LUCK).

Practicalities

Natchez **CVB** is at 311 Liberty Rd (☎446-6345 or 1-800/547-6724). Budget **rooms** can be had at the *Days Inn*, 109 US-61 S (☎445-8291; ②), and *Natchez Inn*, 218 John R Junkin Drive (☎442-0221; ②), but Natchez is a place to splash out on a historic **B&B**. The very friendly *Highpoint*, 215 Linton Ave (☎442-6963 or 1-800/283-4099; ⑤), is one of the best value places; others, such as the resplendent purple *Glen Auburn*, 300 S Commerce St (☎442-4099; ⑦), stretch into extraordinary realms of opulence. The *Cock of the Walk*, 200 N Broadway (☎446-8920), serves irresistibly tasty catfish, though the *Main Street Steamery*, 326 Main St (☎445-0608), may make a welcome change from fried food.

Bicycles can be rented from the *Natchez Bicycling Center*, 334 Main St (☎446-7794).

Mississippi's Gulf Coast

Mississippi's hundred-mile strip of **coast** is utterly unlike the rest of the state, cultu-rally as well as physically – a strong Mediterranean (Catholic) heritage is conspicuous amid the subtropical beauty. Some of the towns are scarred by hurricanes, but the **beaches** are often superb. Along the **Gulf Islands National Seashore**, four beautiful barrier islands boast brilliant white sand and crystal-blue waters, while the 26-mile arti-ficial **Harrison County Beach** runs parallel with the busy coast road between **Biloxi**, the major resort, and laid-back **Pass Christian**, with its fine display of live oaks.

Biloxi

Plastic, neon-lit **BILOXI** (*"Bi-lux-i"*), sprawling alongside a busy four-lane highway, cannot claim to be the prettiest resort in the world. But it's less expensive than Florida, it's not far from New Orleans, and it has sufficient diversity to satisfy beach poseurs, senior citizens and families alike. Biloxi was attracting wealthy visitors by the mid-nineteenth century, but it has never depended exclusively on tourism; seafood canner-ies line the bayou at the rear of the city, along with a massive USAF base.

The center of Biloxi is the **Loop**, where I-110 curves out over the ocean before join-ing US-90 (Beach Blvd), five minutes from shabby **Main Street**. The seafront has in the last couple of years become home to several permanently moored **casinos**, the most central being the *Biloxi Belle* (☎1-800/BILOXI-7), just east of the Loop.

Old Biloxi, at the far end of Lameuse Blvd, consists of narrow streets of stuccoed buildings, in a tree-shaded tranquillity that seems miles from the hustle of US-90. Across the highway, shrimp and oyster fleets unload their catch at the **Small Crafts Harbor**. You can rent boats to visit windblown **Deer Island**, half a mile offshore, or just to go fishing (70-min shrimping tours cost $8; ☎374-5718). A mile west, a glut of tacky shops selling T-shirts, seashells, trinkets and other ephemera marks the approach to the most popular stretch of **Harrison County Beach**, in front of the *Biloxi Hilton*.

Five miles from Main Street, the compact white raised cottage of **Beauvoir**, set in beautiful wooded grounds, was the final home of Confederate President Jefferson Davis. After two years' imprisonment at the end of the war, Davis lived here until his death in 1889. Beauvoir is now run as a shrine by the Sons of Confederate Veterans, with memor-abilia such as the 1978 joint resolution of Congress which finally restored Davis' US citi-zenship. A museum provides insights into the lives of ordinary Civil War soldiers, the amputation kit being one of the most gory reminders. ($4; daily 9am–5pm.)

West Ship Island
Hailed by *USA Today* as one of the top ten beaches in the country, the barrier island of **West Ship** was only created in 1969, when the 200mph winds and thirty-foot tide of Hurricane Camille ripped Ship Island in half. It's basically a giant sandbank, dotted with inland ponds (home to a family of alligators), marshlands, sand dunes and warm tidal pools. Everywhere you come across delicate wispy sea oats; even touching them incurs a heavy fine, as their elaborate root structure is all that holds the island together.

The small, idyllic **beach** boasts fine white sand, free showers and a reasonable café, though umbrella and deckchair rental is expensive. D-shaped Fort Massachusetts alongside was built in 1859 and captured by the Union Navy early in the Civil War. Free tours give a wonderful panoramic view from its grass-topped roof.

West Ship is the only barrier island with regular **ferries**; boats from *David M's* on the Loop near the *Isle of Capri* cost $12, take seventy minutes, and leave at 9am and noon each day during summer, arriving back at 4.45 and 7.45pm (☎432-2197). Ferries from Gulfport Yacht Harbor, at the intersection of US-90 and US-49 (☎864-1014), oper-ate the same schedules during the summer, plus daily trips during spring and autumn.

Practicalities

Biloxi's **visitor center** is at 710 Beach Blvd at Main St (☎435-6248). *Greyhound* **buses** from New Orleans and Mobile come in at 322 Main St (☎436-4336), very near the *Amtrak* station on the new New Orleans–Miami line. *Coast Area Transit* (☎896-8080) runs an hourly trolley service along the coast to the unspectacular business center of Gulfport, and serene Pass Christian. All-day passes on the *Beachcomber* line cost $2.

Room rates vary considerably according to season and ocean view, but the most convenient area to stay is the **Loop**. Options along Beach Blvd include the *Buena Vista Beach Club*, (no 911; ☎432-5511; ④); the nearby *Sun Tan Motel*, (no 780; ☎432-8641; ③); and further west near the *Hilton*, a good *Travelodge* (no 2030; ☎388-5531; ③) and the *Captain's Inn*, (no 1950; ☎388-3131; ②). The central new *Biloxi Backpackers*, just back from the *Biloxi Belle* at 128 Fayard St (☎435-2666; ①), offers $14 dorm beds, or you can **camp** at *Biloxi Beach Campground*, 1816 Beach Blvd (☎432-2755).

Baricev's, in the Loop at 633 Beach Blvd (☎435-3626), serves delicious flounder. Two miles east, there's more excellent fish at the unglamorous *Fisherman's Wharf*, 315 Beach Blvd (☎436-4513), and the *Ole Biloxi Schooner*, a few blocks back from the sea at 159 Howard Ave (☎348-8071). The Loop is liveliest at **night**, with popular haunts including *Gorenflo's*, just before the Ocean Springs Bridge, which puts on live r'n'b. *Le Bistro*, 222 Pat Harrison Ave (☎388-9366), is Biloxi's only **gay** club, playing great dance music.

ARKANSAS

Historically, **ARKANSAS** belongs very much to the American South. It sided firmly with the Confederacy in the Civil War, and its capital, Little Rock, was the scene in 1957 of one of the most notorious flashpoints of the struggle for civil rights. Geographically, however, it marks the beginning of the Great Plains. Unlike the other southern states, on the far side of the Mississippi River, Arkansas remained very sparsely populated until almost a century ago. Westward expansion was blocked by the existence of the Indian Territory in what's now Oklahoma, and not until the railroads opened up the forested interior during the 1880s did settlers stray in any numbers from their small riverside villages. Only once the Depression and mechanization had forced thousands of farmers to leave their fields did Arkansas begin to develop any significant industrial base.

In 1992, local boy Bill Clinton's accession to the presidency jolted Arkansas into national prominence. Four towns lay claim to him: Hope, his birthplace; Hot Springs, his "home town"; Fayetteville, where he and Hillary married; and, of course, Little Rock, the state capital. Of the four, only sleepy **Little Rock** and nearby spa resort **Hot Springs** are worth a trip, whatever the tourist brochures may say.

Though Arkansas encompasses the **Mississippi Delta** in the east, oil-rich timberlands in the south, and the sweeping **Ouachita** (*Wash-i-taw*) **Mountains** in the west, the cragged and charismatic **Ozark Mountains** in the north are its most scenic asset, and the main attraction for tourists are the uncrowded parks and unspoiled rivers.

"Arkansas" is a distorted version of the name of a small Indian tribe; the state legislature declared once and for all in 1881 that the correct pronunciation is *Arkansaw*.

Getting Around Arkansas

It's extremely difficult to venture beyond Little Rock and Hot Springs using public transportation. *Greyhound* runs intermittent services, while *Amtrak* cuts diagonally east–west through the state, calling at Little Rock, which also holds the only sizeable **airport**. To see the Ozarks you'll need a car.

The **area code** for the entire state of Arkansas is ☎501.

Eastern Arkansas

What's surprising about the eastern Arkansas deltalands is that they are far from totally flat: **Crowley's Ridge**, a narrow arc of wind-blown loess hills, breaks up the uniform smoothness, stretching 150 miles from southern Missouri to the atmospheric river-town of **Helena**. Despite scenic rivers and sleepy bayous, the pine-clad woodlands of the Gulf Coastal Plain in southern Arkansas are of little real interest.

Helena

The small Mississippi port of **HELENA**, roughly sixty miles south of Memphis, was once the shipping point for Arkansas' cotton crop, when Mark Twain described it as "occupying one of the prettiest situations on the river". A small historic district bordered by Holly, College and Perry streets reflects that brief period of prosperity before the arrival of the railroad left most of the river towns obsolete; today Helena's central core is little more than the slightly run-down Cherry Street on the levee.

That said, there are two good reasons to visit Helena. Musicians among its large black population have ensured that the town is an important stop for **Delta blues** enthusiasts – no great distance from Clarksdale, Mississippi (see p.426), it hosts one of the country's leading blues festivals every October. Radio station KFFA (1360m) still broadcasts the long-running *King Biscuit Time Show* (Mon–Fri 12.15–12.45pm) from the foyer of the **Delta Cultural Center** in the old train station at 95 Missouri St at the end of Cherry St: visitors are welcome. Helena was for many years the home of harmonica great **Sonny Boy Williamson**, and featured in intimate detail in many of his (usually extemporized) recordings. He used to advertise *Sonny Boy's Biscuit Meal* on the radio show, and it continues to maintain the illusion that he is present in the studio.

The Cultural Center itself is excellent, covering, among other things, the first settlers of this soggy frontier, contemporary racism, and, of course, the region's music heritage (Mon–Sat 10am–5pm, Sun 1–5pm; free). You can buy – and hear – a great assortment of blues records at *Bubba Sullivan's Blues Corner*, nearby in the small mall at 105 Cherry St: Bubba himself is a wealth of friendly information on local music events and gigs. Opposite here, the newly restored Marketplace sells a mixture of *King Biscuit* T-shirts, twee crafts and fresh produce (Fri 10am–6pm, Sat 7am–6pm).

Practicalities

Of the few places to stay the *Edwardian Inn*, 317 Briscoe St (☎338-9155; ③), on the main highway into town north of the Mississippi Bridge, is an opulent B&B with large wood-panelled rooms, slightly marred by views from the front over a chemical plant on the river. Two blocks from the Cultural Center, the friendly *Downtown Inn*, Hwy-49b and Walnut St (☎338-9125; ①), has adequate motel rooms at rock-bottom prices, though the stretch of Walnut Street north of here is best avoided. For food, *Casqui's Restaurant* opposite the Cultural Center serves a juicy "blues burger".

Central and West Arkansas

Quiet **Little Rock** stands right in the middle of the state, just fifty miles west of the rejuvenated spa town of Hot Springs, which marks the eastern gateway to the remote **Ouachita Mountains**. The rippling farmland of the **Arkansas River Valley** is sandwiched in by the Ouachita crests on the south side and the craggy ridges of the Ozarks to the north. Mining and logging communities dot the east–west-running roads, and former frontier towns like **Fort Smith** and **Van Buren** retain their Old West flavor. Fayetteville and Hope are both in west Arkansas; there's nothing to see in either.

Little Rock

The geographical, political and financial center of Arkansas, **LITTLE ROCK** is at the meeting point of its two major regions, the northwestern hills and the eastern Delta. Little Rock today has a relaxed and open feel to it – a far cry from the dramatic events of 1957 (see below) – but for a capital city, it has little to see and do beyond taking a "Clinton tour" or strolling the old streets around MacArthur Park. The **Museum of Science and History** in the park is geared largely towards kids (Mon–Sat 9.30am–4.30pm, Sun 1–4.30pm; $1, free Mon), while the adjacent **Arkansas Art Center** features work by local and international artists (Mon–Sat 10am–5pm, Sun noon–5pm; free).

The cream-colored **Old State House Museum**, 300 W Markham St, surrounded by smooth lawns and shaded by evergreens, backs onto the Arkansas River (for the convenience of early politicians). Inside, displays cover all periods of Arkansas history, but the most impressive rooms are the two senate chambers, restored to their original grandeur and uncluttered by any exhibits (Mon–Sat 9am–5pm, Sun 1–5pm; free). This was where Clinton announced his bid for the presidency on October 3 1991, and made his acceptance speech thirteen months later; a "Clinton room" is planned.

Behind the museum, **Riverfront Park**, a thin strip of greenery and fountains, runs for several blocks; a commemorative sign marks the "little rock" for which the city is named, which is just as well or you could easily miss it. The *Spirit* **paddlewheeler** sets out on one-hour cruises from just across the river (Tues–Sat 2pm; $5; ☎376-4150).

Practicalities

Greyhound (☎372-1861) arrives at 118 E Washington Ave in North Little Rock. *Amtrak* (☎372-6841) enjoys a more central location at Markham and Victory. **Taxis** don't pick up on the street, so call *Black and White* (☎374-0333); downtown to *Greyhound* costs

---

CONFRONTATION AT LITTLE ROCK

In 1957, Little Rock unexpectedly became the battleground in the first major conflict between state and federal government over **race relations**. At the time, the city was generally viewed as progressive by southern standards. All parks, libraries and buses were integrated, a relatively high thirty percent of blacks were on the electoral register and there were black police officers. However, when the Little Rock School Board announced its decision to phase in **desegregation** gradually – the Supreme Court having declared segregation of schools to be unconstitutional – James Johnson, a candidate for state governor, started a campaign opposed to interracial education. Johnson's rhetoric began to win him support, and the incumbent governor, **Orval Faubus**, who had previously shown no interest in the issue, jumped on the bandwagon himself.

The first nine black students were due to enter Central High School that September. The day before school opened, Faubus reversed his decision to let blacks enrol "in the interest of safety", only to be overruled by the federal court. He ordered state troopers to keep out the black students anyway; soldiers with bayonets forced Elizabeth Eckford, one of the nine, away from the school entrance into a seething crowd, from which she had to jump on a bus to escape. As legal battles raged during the day, at night blacks were subject to violent attacks by white gangs. Three weeks later, President Eisenhower somewhat reluctantly brought in the 101st Airborne Division, and amidst violent demonstrations the nine were at last able to enter Central High. Throughout the year, they experienced immense intimidation; when one retaliated, she was expelled. The graduation of James Green, the oldest, at the end of the year, seemed to put an end to the affair but Faubus, up for re-election, renewed his political posturing by closing down all public schools in the city for the 1958–59 academic year – and thereby increased his majority.

The school itself is an enormous brown crescent-shaped structure, more like a fortress, at 1500 S Park Avenue, about a mile from the capitol on bus route #9.

around $7. At the **visitor center**, in the Convention Center at Markham and Main (Mon–Fri 9–11.30am & 12.30–3.30pm; ☎376-4781), you can pick up details of a self-guided walking tour of Bill Clinton's Little Rock that takes in such sights as Chelsea's high school and the polling booth where Bill cast his vote for the presidency.

Finding a **room** downtown should be no problem. The *Diamond Inn*, 322 E Capital St (☎376-3661; ②), is rather basic, but has a pool, while the *Quapaw Inn*, 1868 S Gaines St (☎376-6873; ④), is a very nice B&B. Little Rock's finest **eating** is at the *Café St Moritz*, 225 E Markham St (☎372-0411), where the Swiss chef conjures up great continental seafood and superb desserts. The riverside *Cajun's Wharf*, 2400 Cantrell Rd (☎375-5351), downtown, serves well-priced Cajun seafood and doubles as a live music venue; complimentary vans will take you back to your hotel. *Juanita's Cantina*, 1300 S Main St (☎372-1228), an atmospheric and imaginative Mexican place, also hosts live bands.

Hot Springs

Fifty miles southwest of Little Rock, the spa town of **HOT SPRINGS** nestles in the heavily forested Zig Zag Mountains on the eastern flank of the Ouachitas. Its thermal waters have attracted visitors since Native Americans used the area as a neutral zone to settle disputes. Early settlers fashioned a crude resort out of the wilderness, and after the railroads arrived in 1875 it became a European-style spa. During the Twenties and Thirties, the mayor reputedly ran a gambling syndicate worth $30 million per annum, and punters included Al Capone and Bugs Malone. However, Hot Springs' popularity waned when new cures for arthritis appeared during the Fifties, and all but one of the bathhouses closed down. Today, Hot Springs encourages visitors to come to the President's "home town", where he lived between 1953 and 1964 – the **visitor center** at Central and Court provides a glossy leaflet marking his favorite haunts.

Downtown Hot Springs is crammed into a looping wooded valley, barely wide enough to accommodate Central Avenue. Eight magnificent buildings here, behind a lush display of magnolia trees, elms and hedgerows, make up Bathhouse Row. Between 1915 and 1962, the grandest of them all was the **Fordyce Bathhouse**, at Central and Reserve, which reopened in 1989 as the **visitor center** for **Hot Springs National Park** – the only National Park to fall within city limits. Its interior is a strange mixture of the elegant and the obsolete; the heavy use of marble, mosaic-tile floors and the stained-glass ceiling of the Sun Room lend it a decadent feel (daily 9am–5pm; free; ☎623-3383).

It's still possible to sample the old-time style and luxury of Hot Springs by taking a **bath**. The only establishment on Bathhouse Row still open for business is the *Buckstaff*, where a thermal mineral bath costs $11.50 (Mon–Fri 7–11.45am & 1.30–3pm, Sat 7–11.45am; ☎623-2308). Full bathing facilities are also available at several hotels. To taste the water, which lacks the strong sulphuric taste often associated with thermal springs, fill up a container at the drinking fountain at Central and Reserve.

To the rear of the *Fordyce*, two small **springs** have been left open for viewing. The **Grand Promenade** from here is a half-mile red and yellow brick walkway overlooking downtown. Trails of various lengths and severity lead up the steep slopes of **Hot Springs Mountain**. A short drive or testing two-and-a-half-mile hike through dense woods of oak, hickory and short-leafed pine takes you to the summit where the observation decks of **Mountain Tower** offer superb views of the town, the Ouachitas and surrounding lakes (daily summer 9am–9pm; other months vary; $3).

Practicalities

Greyhound (☎623-6390) operates infrequent **buses** from the capital and from Dallas, six hours away. Most places of interest are within walking distance of central accommodation, and local buses provide a reasonable hourly service to most parts of the city. **Bikes** can be rented from *Bikes Etc*, 312A Whittington Ave (☎623-BIKE).

Luxury **accommodation** is surprisingly inexpensive. Dominating the town center, the elegant twin-towered *Arlington Resort/Spa* at Central and Fountain is where Capone stayed when in town – and where President Clinton attended his Junior and Senior proms (☎623-7771; ③; bathing $12.50). The *Park Avenue Motel*, 415 Park Ave (☎623-4623; ②), is one of several neighboring budget motels. Rates rise by up to fifty percent during high season (February–April). The nearest place to **camp** is *Gulpha Gorge Campground* in the National Park, two miles out on Hwy-70B, off Hwy-70 E.

Hidden among the usual family **restaurants** is the morning-only *Pancake Shop*, 216 Central Ave (☎624-9465), whose stuffed pancakes make a filling start to the day. The excellent *Cafe New Orleans,* two doors down at no 210 (☎624-3200), serves everything from Cajun breakfasts to bargain seafood dinners. If you want to see where young Bill hung out eating chili cheeseburgers, head to *Bailey's Dairy Treat*, 510 Park Ave.

Western Arkansas

West of Hot Springs, US-270 cuts through the Ouachita Mountains, unique to the continent in that they run east–west rather than north–south. On its way to Oklahoma, the road passes over uneven crests separated by wide valleys speckled with tiny communities, so isolated that, in the Thirties, hill-dwellers supposedly spoke a form of Elizabethan English. Separating the Ouachitas from the northerly Ozarks, the **Arkansas River Valley**, a natural east–west path for bison, was used for centuries by Native Americans and white hunters before steamboats arrived in the 1820s.

Fort Smith

Now an industrial city of 70,000 people, **FORT SMITH**, on the Oklahoma border, maintains a pronounced western feel. Until Charles Isaac Parker – the "Hanging Judge" – took over in 1875, this was a rowdy pioneer town, uncomfortably close to Indian Territory, a sanctuary for robbers and bandits. Parker sent out 200 marshals to round up the fugitives; in 21 years he sentenced 160 to death and saw 79 go to the gallows. **Fort Smith National Historic Site** on Rogers Ave features remains of the original fort, Parker's courtroom, the dingy basement jail and a set of gallows (daily 9am–5pm; $2). **Old Main Street** in **Van Buren**, on the opposite bank of the Arkansas River, is a stretch of over seventy restored buildings that has been used in numerous westerns.

Lodgings in Fort Smith include the central *Days Inn*, 301 N 11th St (☎783-0271; ③), and *Regal 8*, 1021 Garrison Ave (☎785-2611; ②). For tasty home-cooked Italian food, try *Taliano's*, 201 N 14th St (☎785-2292), where meals cost between $5 and $10.

The Ozark Mountains

Although the highest peak fails to top 2000 feet, the **Ozark Mountains**, which extend beyond northern Arkansas into southern Missouri, are characterized by severe steep ridges and jagged spurs. Hair-raising roads weave their way over the precipitous hills, past rugged lakeshores and pristine rivers. When ambitious speculators poured into Arkansas in the 1830s, those who missed the best land etched out remote hill farms that represented no gain on what they had left behind in Kentucky or Tennessee. They remained utterly isolated until the last few decades; the Ozarks have now become the fastest-growing rural section of the US, a major tourist and retirement destination. Much-needed cash has flooded in, bringing with it the cafés and souvenir shops that have converted centers such as Harrison into identikit American towns.

The word *Ozark* is everywhere, used to entice tourists into music shows or gift emporia which owe more to Nashville or Taiwan than to these mountains. With all the hype, it's getting increasingly difficult to tell the genuine article from imitations, which is a good reason for visiting the state park at **Mountain View**, a serious attempt to preserve traditional Ozark skills and music. The most visited town in the region, **Eureka Springs**, just inside the Missouri border, is a pretty mountainside Victorian spa town, though not one where you should expect to find out much about Ozark life.

Mountain View

Roughly sixty miles due north of Little Rock, the state-run **Ozark Folk Center**, two miles north of the town of **MOUNTAIN VIEW** on Hwy-14, is a living history museum that attempts to show how life used to be in these remote hillsides, not reached by paved roads until the Fifties. Homestead skills are displayed in reconstructed log cabins, and folk musicians and storytellers perform throughout the park. Every night of the week live Ozark music concerts are held at 7.30pm (mid-April to early Nov daily; craft displays $4.75, concerts $5.25; ☎269-3851).

There are **rooms** at the *Lodge* (☎269-3871; ③) in the Center's grounds, and the pretty *Inn at Mountain View*, 812 Washington St (☎269-4200; ③–⑤), serves a seven-course country breakfast. Good **restaurants** include the Folk Center's down-home café and the *Catfish House* off Hwy-14 on Senior Drive, which has nightly hoe-downs (Sun–Wed 11am–8pm, Thurs–Sat 11am–9pm). For Saturday night entertainment, even in winter, it's hard to beat the friendly jam sessions in Mountain View's town square.

The **Buffalo River** – a prime destination for whitewater canoeing – flows across the state north of Mountain View. *Bennetts Canoe Rental* (☎449-6431) provides canoes and equipment and runs a shuttle bus to the river, which is at its most spectacular around **Pruitt Landing**, thirteen miles south of unremarkable **Harrison**.

Eureka Springs

Picturebook **EUREKA SPRINGS**, set on steep mountain slopes in Arkansas' north-eastern corner, began life a century ago as a health center. As that role declined, its striking location turned it into a regular tourist destination, given a kitsch edge by its specializing in weddings and honeymoons. It's an enjoyable place to stroll around, filled with tasteful Victorian buildings, and you can ride on the **Eureka Springs and North Arkansas Railway** through wooded Ozark valleys. Rolling stock includes a magnificent "cabbage-head" woodburning locomotive, and trips depart on the hour from the depot at 299 N Main Street (mid-April to Oct daily 10am–4pm; ☎253-9623).

Three miles east of town, an incredible religious complex includes the seven-storey **Christ of the Ozarks** – a surreal statue of Jesus with a sixty-foot arm span – a **Bible Museum** ($2) and a **Sacred Arts Center** ($2). Elna M Smith, whose Foundation runs the whole show, was so worried that the holy sites of the Middle East would be destroyed by war that she decided to build replicas in the Ozarks, safe from Arab attack. Minibuses whisk visitors through the **New Holy Land** theme park, past scaled-down versions of the Sea of Galilee, the River Jordan, Golgotha (Mon–Sat 9am–5pm, Sun 1–5pm). At 8.30pm, Christ's last week on earth is re-enacted in the **Great Passion Play** in a 4400-seater amphitheater (May–Oct Tues, Wed & Fri–Sun; $8–11; ☎1-800/882-PLAY).

Practicalities

Accommodation rates vary seasonally, but you can usually find inexpensive lodging just over a mile from downtown on US-62E; try *Razorback Lodge* (☎253-9182; ②). More central is *Best Western Eureka Inn* (☎253-9551; ④), at the junction of US-62 and S Main. The local **visitor center** is nearby at 81 Kingshighway (☎1-800/6EUREKA).

The *Eureka Egg Roll Emporium* at Basin Park on Spring St (☎252-8029) does cheap lunch specials, while *Joe's Mexican Restaurant*, 179 N Main St (☎253-9617), serves red snapper and seafood dishes. Just off the well-worn tourist paths, *Chelsea Corner*, 10 Mountain St, off Spring St (☎253-6723), has live music most evenings.

CHAPTER SEVEN

FLORIDA

Brochure images of tanning flesh and Mickey Mouse give an inaccurate and incomplete picture of **FLORIDA**. Although the aptly nicknamed "sunshine state" is indeed devoted to the tourist trade, it's also among the least-understood parts of the US. Away from its over-exposed resorts lie forests and rivers, deserted strands filled with wildlife, modern cities, and primeval swamps.

In many respects Florida is still evolving. A thousand people a day move to the state, now the fourth most populous in the nation. Changing demographics are eroding the traditional Deep South conservatism: the new Floridians tend to be a younger, more energetic breed, while Spanish-speaking enclaves provide close ties to Latin America and the Caribbean – links as influential in creating wealth as the recent arrival of the movie industry in central Florida, fresh from Hollywood.

The essential stop is cosmopolitan, half-Hispanic **Miami**, from where a simple journey south brings you to the **Florida Keys**, a hundred-mile string of islands known for sports fishing, coral-reef diving, and the town of **Key West**, legendary for its sunsets and anything-goes attitude. North from Miami, much of the **east coast** is disappointingly urbanized, albeit with miles of unbroken beaches flowing alongside. The residential stranglehold is finally escaped further north, where communities such as **Daytona Beach** have become subservient to the local sands.

In **central Florida** the terrain turns green, though the sole upset to the largely rural idyll could hardly be bigger: **Walt Disney World**, where tourism is practised on the scale of the infinite. If you prefer your attractions natural, skip north to the forests of the **Panhandle**, Florida's link with the Deep South, or to the towns and beaches of the **west coast**, which should be savored while progressing steadily south to the **Everglades**, an alligator-filled swath of sawgrass plain.

It makes little difference **when** you visit; warm sunshine and blue skies are a fact of life. Florida does, however, split into **two climatic zones**: subtropical in the south and warm temperate in the north. Anywhere south of Orlando has very mild winters (November to April), with warm temperatures and low humidity. This is the peak tourist season, when prices are at their highest. The southern summer (May to October), on the other hand, sees extremely high humidity – the rewards for braving the mugginess are lower prices and fewer tourists. Winter is the off-peak period north of Orlando; while snow has been known to fall in the Panhandle, daytime temperatures are generally comfortably warm. The northern Florida summer is when the crowds arrive, and when the days – and the nights – get hot and sticky.

ACCOMMODATION PRICE CODES

All accommodation prices in this book have been coded using the symbols below. Note that prices are for the least expensive double rooms in each establishment. For a full explanation see p.35 in *Basics*.

①	up to $30	④	$60–80	⑦	$130–180
②	$30–45	⑤	$80–100	⑧	$180+
③	$45–60	⑥	$100–130		

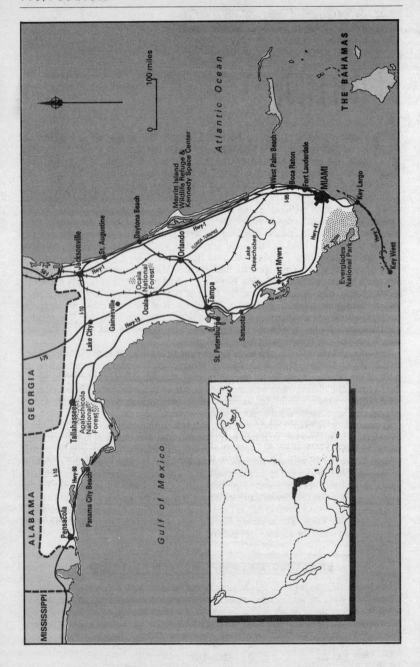

Finally, Florida has a growing reputation for **crimes** against (and even murders of) tourists. While the authorities attempt to reduce such attacks, the fact remains inescapable that planeloads of visitors who have left their cares – and sometimes their common sense – at home make an inviting target for the opportunistic criminal. The odds are astronomically against becoming a victim, but it pays to be wary at all times.

History

The **first European sighting** of Florida, just six years after Christopher Columbus located the "New World", is believed to have been made by John and Sebastian Cabot in 1498, when they spotted what is now Cape Florida, on Key Biscayne in Miami. At the time, the area's 100,000 inhabitants formed several distinct **tribes**: the Timucua across northern Florida, the Calusa around the southwest and Lake Okeechobee, the Apalachee in the Panhandle and the Tequesta along the southeast coast.

In 1513, a **Spaniard**, Juan Ponce de León, sighted land during *Pascua Florida*, the Festival of the Flowers, and named what he saw *La Florida* – or "Land of Flowers". Eight years later he returned with a mandate from the Spanish king to conquer and colonize the territory, the first of several Spanish incursions prompted by rumors of gold hidden in the north of the region. When it became clear that Florida did not harbor stunning riches, interest waned; but the arrival of French Huguenots in 1562 forced the Spanish into a more determined effort at settlement. Three years later, **Pedro Menéndez de Avilés** founded St Augustine – the longest continuous site of European habitation on the continent. In 1586 St Augustine was razed by a British naval bombardment led by Francis Drake. The ensuing bloody confrontation for control of North America was eventually settled when the British captured the crucial Spanish possession of Havana, and Spain willingly parted with Florida to get it back. By this time, aboriginal Floridians had been largely wiped out by disease, and Florida's Indian population was becoming composed of disparate tribes arriving from the west, collectively known as the **Seminoles**, who were generally left undisturbed in the inland areas.

Following American independence, when Florida was returned to Spain, the US began to think in terms of controlling the state. In 1814 a US general, Andrew Jackson, marched south, killing hundreds of Indians and triggering the **First Seminole War** – on the pretext of subduing the Seminoles but with the actual intention of taking the region. Spain formally **ceded Florida to the US** in 1819, with Jackson sworn in as Florida's first American governor and Tallahassee selected as the new administrative center. Eleven years later, the **Act of Indian Removal** decreed that all Native Americans in the eastern US should be transferred to reservations in the Midwest. Most Seminoles were determined to stay and the **Second Seminole War** broke out, with the Indians steadily driven south, away from the fertile lands of central Florida and into the Everglades, where they eventually agreed to remain.

Florida **became a state** on March 3 1845, coinciding with the prosperity brought by the railroads. As a member of the Confederacy during the **Civil War**, its primary contribution was the provision of food – a foretaste of its post-war economic role when finally re-admitted to the Union. As northern speculators began to invest in Florida, the country's newspapers extolled the curative virtues of its climate. These early efforts to promote Florida as a **tourist destination** brought in the wintering rich: Henry Flagler opened luxury resorts on the northeast coast and extended his Florida East Coast Railroad south, giving birth to communities such as Palm Beach. Henry Plant connected *his* railroad to Tampa, turning it into a thriving port city. Florida's climate enabled citrus fruits to be grown during the winter and sold to the cooler north, and the state became a major beef producer. After World War I, everyone in America wanted a piece of Florida, and chartered trains brought in thousands of eager buyers. But most deals were on paper only, and in 1926 the banks began to default. The **Wall Street Crash** then made paupers of the millionaires whose investments had helped shaped the state.

What saved Florida was **World War II**. Thousands of troops arrived to guard the coastline, empty tourist hotels provided ready-made barracks, and – most importantly – the soldiers got a taste of Florida that would entice many of them to return. In the mid-Sixties, the state government bent over backwards to help the Disney Corporation turn a sizeable slice of central Florida into **Walt Disney World**, the biggest theme park ever known. Its enormous commercial success helped solidify Florida's place in the international tourist market: directly or indirectly, one in five of the state's twelve million inhabitants now earns a living from the tourist trade.

Behind the optimistic facade, however, lie many **problems**. There's a broadening gap between the relative liberalism of the big cities and the arch-conservatism of the Bible Belt rural area: while Miami promotes its multicultural make-up, the Ku Klux Klan holds picnics in the Panhandle. Gun laws remain notoriously lax, and the multi-million-dollar **drugs trade** shows few signs of abating – at least a quarter of the cocaine entering the US is said to arrive via Florida. **Racial issues** continue to be vexed, too, with tension on several fronts: between Anglo-Americans and nouveau riche Cubans, blacks and whites, blacks and Hispanics, police and the inner-city poor. However, increased protection of the state's **natural resources** has been a more positive feature of the last decade and impressive amounts of land are under state control – overall, wildlife is less threatened now than at any time since white settlers first arrived.

Getting Around Florida

Florida is surprisingly compact, and with a **car** you'll have few problems: crossing between the east and west coasts takes only a couple of hours, and even the longest possible trip – between the western extremity of the Panhandle and Miami – can be done in a day. **Public transit**, on the other hand, requires adroit forward planning. *Greyhound* **buses** link all the major towns and cities, with both Miami and Orlando being well served, but sadly, many rural areas and some of the most enjoyable sections of the coast are off-limits.

Florida's **railroads** were built to service the boom towns of the Twenties, and consequently some present-day rural nooks have rail links as good as the modern cities. *Amtrak*'s new cross-country route runs west from **Jacksonville** via New Orleans all the way to LA, while connections with Washington DC and New York remain good. Passengers with cars only can use the daily **Auto Train** from Lorton, Virginia (just south of Washington DC) to Sanford, north of Orlando. However, on no route are there more than two services a day, and in some areas, *Amtrak* buses have replaced the trains. The southeast coast boasts a new elevated **Tri-Rail** system, ferrying rush-hour commuters between Miami and West Palm Beach.

Although **cycling** is seldom a good way to get around the cities, miles of cycle paths follow the coast, and long-distance bike trails cross the state's interior. Forget **hitching**: always dangerous (especially for women), it's illegal in Miami (where, if you did hitch, you'd be lucky to live to regret it) and on the outskirts of many other cities.

MIAMI AND MIAMI BEACH

Far and away the most exciting city in Florida, **Miami** is a stunning and often intoxicatingly beautiful place. Awash with sunlight-intensified natural colors, there are moments – when the downtown skyline glows in the warm night and the beachside palm trees sway in the evening breeze – when a better-looking city is hard to imagine. Even so, people, not climate or landscape, are what make Miami unique. Half of the two-million population is Hispanic, the vast majority Cubans. Spanish is the predominant language almost everywhere, and news from Havana, Caracas or Bogota frequently gets more attention than the latest word from Washington.

The city is no melting pot, however. Since the black ghettos first erupted in the Sixties, violent expressions of rage – most recently among Haitians and Puerto Ricans – have been a regular feature of Miami life. In 1980 it had the highest murder rate in the country, but in the last ten years it has smartened itself up considerably. One factor in that revival, strangely, has been *Miami Vice*, a TV cop show less about crime than designer clothes and fabulous subtropical scenery. The newly restored Art Deco district of **Miami Beach** – a long strip of land separating mainland Miami from the ocean – became a regular backdrop on the fashion pages of glossy magazines.

Just a century ago Miami was a swampy outpost of mosquito-tormented settlers. The arrival of the railroad in 1896 gave Miami its first fixed land-link with the rest of the continent, and literally cleared the way for the Twenties property boom. In the Fifties, Miami Beach became a celebrity-filled resort area, just as thousands of Cubans fleeing the regime of Fidel Castro began arriving in mainland Miami. The Sixties and Seventies brought decline, though with the strengthening of Latin American economic links and the upsurge in tourism, the city is now enjoying a burst of affluence. As Hispanic immigration into the US re-shapes the demography of the nation, today's Miami could well be a foretaste of tomorrow's US.

Arriving, Information and Getting Around

Miami International Airport is six miles west of the city; local bus #7 runs downtown (cab fare $15), and #42 to Miami Beach (cab fare $20). The 24-hour *Airporter*, *SuperShuttle* and *Red Top* minivans deliver you to any address in Miami for $8–15. **Greyhound's** Miami West station is a short cab ride from the airport, while the other major *Greyhound* terminal is downtown at 700 Biscayne Blvd (☎372-7222). The **train** station, 8303 NW 37th Ave, is seven miles northwest. An adjacent *Metrorail* stop provides access to downtown Miami and beyond; bus #L stops here on its way to Central Miami Beach. The **Tri-Rail** links with the *Metrorail* at 1149 E 21st St, also seven miles northwest of downtown.

For free maps and information, there's an information stand in **downtown Miami**, outside Bayside Marketplace (daily 11.30am–8pm; ☎1-800/283-2707); at **Miami Beach**, the Miami Beach Chamber of Commerce, 1920 Meridian Ave (Mon–Fri 9am–5pm, Sat 10am–4pm; ☎672-1270), is a good stop. The **post office** in downtown Miami is at 500 NW Second Ave (Mon–Fri 8.30am–5pm, Sat 8.30am–12.30pm; zip code 33101).

City Transit

Though **driving** is the most practical way to get around Miami, **bus** routes do cover the entire city – there are usually two services an hour between 6am and 7pm on weekdays, fewer at weekends; on busy routes, such as Miami–Miami Beach, buses run until 10pm or 11pm. The flat-rate single-journey bus fare is $1.25; transfers are free.

The **area code** for Miami and Miami Beach is ☎305.

Metrorail trains (5.30am–midnight) run along a single line between the northern suburbs and South Miami; useful stops are Government Center (for downtown), Coconut Grove, and Douglas Road or University (for Coral Gables). Single-journey fares are $1.25. Downtown Miami is also ringed by the **Metromover** (flat fare, 25¢), a daytime monorail loop that doesn't cover much ground but gives a bird's-eye view.

Information and free **route maps and timetables** can be had at the *Transit Service Center* inside the Metro Dade Center in downtown Miami (daily 7am–6pm; ☎638-6700). At weekends, **Breeze minibuses** run between South Beach and downtown Miami, with the aim of reducing traffic – and drunken driving – as revellers head to and from South Beach (every 15min, Fri & Sat 7pm–4am, Sun noon–4pm; $1.25).

Taxis, Cycling and Tours

Taxis are abundant; from downtown to Coconut Grove or Miami Beach costs about $8. Try *Central Taxicab* (☎532-5555) or *Metro Taxi* (☎888-8888). Otherwise, get the free leaflet, *Miami on Two Wheels,* from the CVB and **rent a bike** from one of the many outlets, such as the *Miami Beach Cycle Center*, 923 W 39th St (☎531-4161).

For an informed stroll, take one of **Dr Paul George's Walking Tours** ($13; ☎375-1625), or try the shorter **Art Deco walking tour** of South Miami Beach, which begins each Saturday at 10.30am from the *Leslie Hotel*, 1244 Ocean Drive ($6; ☎672-2014). The ninety-minute **Old Town Trolley Tour** leaves from the Bayside Marketplace every thirty minutes (daily 10am–4pm; $7).

The City

Many of **MIAMI**'s districts are officially cities in their own right, and each has a background and character very much its own. The obvious starting point is **downtown Miami**, the small, bustling nerve center of the city, overlooked by futuristic office buildings. Beyond downtown, Miami spreads out in a broad arc to the west and south. **Little Havana** is still one of the most intriguing areas, rich with Latin American looks and sounds, and immediately south the spacious boulevards of **Coral Gables** are as impressive now as they were in the Twenties, when the district set new standards in town planning. South of downtown, trendy **Coconut Grove** holds a plethora of neat streetside cafés. Make time, too, for **Key Biscayne**: a smart, secluded island community with some beautiful beaches, five miles off the mainland but easily reached by causeway. In varying degrees, all twelve miles of **MIAMI BEACH** are worth seeing – it's excellent for sunbathing and swimming throughout – but only **South Beach** will hold your attention for long. Here, rows of tastefully restyled Thirties Art Deco buildings have become the chic gathering places for the city's fashionable faces.

Downtown Miami

Don't try to relax in **DOWNTOWN MIAMI**: humanity storms down its short streets, rippling the gaudy awnings of cut-price electronics, clothes and jewellery stores, easing up only to gulp down a spicy snack and a mango juice from a roadside fast-food stand. Since the early Sixties, the predominantly Spanish-speaking businesses of downtown's square mile have reaped the benefits of any boost in South or Central American economies. Only some solid US public architecture and whistle-blowing traffic cops remind you that you're still in Florida and not on the main drag of a Latin American capital.

Nowhere offers a better first taste of downtown Miami than **Flagler Street**, very much the loudest, brightest, busiest strip. Four forbidding Doric columns mark the entrance to the **Dade County Courthouse**, at 73 W Flagler St. Built in 1926 on the site of an earlier courthouse – one-time venue for public hangings – this was for fifty years

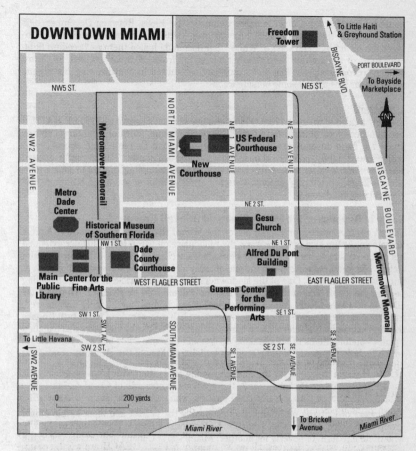

DOWNTOWN MIAMI

Freedom Tower

To Little Haiti & Greyhound Station

PORT BOULEVARD

To Bayside Marketplace

NW5 ST.

NE5 ST.

BISCAYNE BLVD

NORTH MIAMI AVENUE

NE 1 AVENUE

NE 2 AVENUE

BISCAYNE BOULEVARD

NW 2 AVENUE

Metromover Monorail

US Federal Courthouse

New Courthouse

Metro Dade Center

NE 2 ST.

Historical Museum of Southern Florida

Gesu Church

NW 1 ST.

Dade County Courthouse

NE 1 ST.

Alfred Du Pont Building

Main Public Library

Center for the Fine Arts

WEST FLAGLER STREET

Gusman Center for the Performing Arts

EAST FLAGLER STREET

Metromover Monorail

SW 1 ST.

SW 1 AV.

SOUTH MIAMI AVENUE

SE 1 ST.

To Little Havana

SW 2 ST.

SW 2 AVENUE

SE 1 AVENUE

SE 2 ST.

SE 2 AVENUE

SE 3 AVENUE

0   200 yards

Miami River

To Brickell Avenue

Miami River

Miami's tallest building, its night-time lights showing off a distinctive ziggurat peak. Little inside the courthouse is worth passing the security check for; cross SW First Avenue instead towards the **Metro-Dade Cultural Center**, an ambitious attempt by architect Philip Johnson to create a postmodern Mediterranean-style piazza. Art shows, historical collections and a library frame the courtyard, but Johnson forgot the power of the south Florida sun: rather than pausing to rest and gossip, most people scamper across the open space towards the nearest shade. Facing the plaza, the **Historical Museum of Southern Florida** (Mon–Wed, Fri & Sat 10am–5pm, Thurs 10am–9pm, Sun noon–5pm; $4) provides a comprehensive peek into the multifaceted past of south Florida. The Seminole section in particular has a strong collection of artefacts.

The Eighties saw the destruction of the decaying buildings beside **Biscayne Boulevard** (part of Hwy-1), on the western edge of downtown, to make way for the **Bayside Marketplace** (Mon–Sat 10am–10pm, Sun noon–8pm), an oversized pink shopping mall, enlivened by buskers and food stands. In case you've ever wondered, it was just to the south, on the yacht-filled marina of Bayfront Park of the Americas, that *Miami Vice*'s Sonny Crockett moored his floating home. Across Biscayne Boulevard, the **Freedom Tower**, built in 1925 and modelled on a Spanish bell tower, earned its name by housing the Cuban Refugee Center in the 1960s. Between December 1965 and June 1972, ten planes a week brought over 250,000 Cubans to Miami, allowed to leave the island by Fidel Castro. While US propaganda hailed them as "freedom fighters", most of the arrivals were simply seeking the fruits of capitalism, and, as Castro astutely recognized, any that were seriously committed to overthrowing his regime would be far less troublesome outside Cuba.

Little Haiti

Roughly a third of Miami's 170,000 **Haitians** live in what's known as **LITTLE HAITI**, a two-hundred-block area centering on NE Second Avenue, north of 42nd Street (buses #9 or #10 from downtown). Aside from hearing Haitian Creole on the streets, you'll notice the brightly colored shops, offices and restaurants. The recently opened *Caribbean Marketplace*, 5927 NE Second Ave, is an entertaining attempt to satiate tourists' curiosity – proffering a mouth-watering array of tropical fruits and Haitian delicacies, such as fried goat.

South of Downtown: the Miami River and Brickell Avenue

Fifteen minutes' walk from Flagler Street, the **Miami River** marks the southern limit of downtown. At the turn of the century, the millionaire oil baron Henry Flagler extended his railroad, which had opened up Florida's east coast, to reach Miami from Palm Beach. His *Royal Palm Hotel* (on the site of today's *Hotel Inter-Continental*) did much to put Miami on the map. One of the landowners was William Brickell, who ran a trading post on the south side of the river, an area now dominated by **Brickell Avenue** – *the* address in 1910s Miami. While the original grand homes have largely disappeared, money is still the avenue's most obvious asset: its half-mile parade of **bank buildings** is the largest grouping of international banks in the US. The rise of the banks was matched by new condominiums of breathtaking design and expense a few blocks further along, which include the most stunning modern building in Miami: **the Atlantis**, at no 2025, finished in 1983, whose focal point is a gaping square hole through its middle.

Little Havana

The impact of **Cubans** on Miami, unquestionably the largest and most visible ethnic group in the city, has been incalculable. Unlike most Hispanic immigrants to the US, who trade one form of poverty for another, Miami's first Cubans had already tasted the good life when they arrived during the late Fifties and were soon enjoying more of the same here. Some now wield considerable clout in the running of the city.

The initial home of the Miami Cubans was a few miles west of downtown in what became **LITTLE HAVANA**, whose streets, if the tourist brochures are to be believed, are filled by old men in *guayaberas* (billowing cotton shirts) playing dominoes, and exotic restaurants whose walls vibrate to the pulsating rhythms of the homeland. Naturally, the reality is quite different: Little Havana's parks, memorials, shops and food stands all reflect the Cuban experience but the streets are quieter than those of downtown Miami (except during the Little Havana Festival in early March). There isn't a great deal actually to see; the appeal of the place is almost all atmosphere.

Along the neighborhood's main strip, SW Eighth Street, or **Calle Ocho**, tiny cups of Cuban coffee are consumed from streetside counters, the odors of cigars being rolled and bread being baked waft across the pavement, and shops sell *santeria* (a Voodoo-like religion of African origin) ephemera beside six-foot-high models of Catholic saints.

Between Twelfth and Thirteenth avenues, the simple stone **Brigade 2506 Memorial** remembers those who died at the Bay of Pigs on April 17 1961, during the abortive invasion of Cuba by US-trained Cuban soldiers. Depending on who tells the story, the action was either merely ill conceived or else highlighted the lack of commitment to Cuba by the US. Veterans of the landing gather here for each anniversary, middle-aged men dressed in combat fatigues making all-night-long pledges of patriotism. A few yards away the **Maximo Lopez Domino Park** fills a corner of 14th Avenue. Entry to the open-air tables is (quite illegally) restricted to men over 55; this is one place where you *will* see old men in *guayaberas* playing dominoes.

Coral Gables

All of Miami's constituent cities are fast to assert their individuality, but none has a greater case than **CORAL GABLES**, south of Little Havana. Twelve square miles of broad boulevards, leafy side streets and Spanish and Italian architecture form a cultured setting for a cultured community. Coral Gables' creator was a local aesthete, **George Merrick**, who raided street names from a Spanish dictionary to plan the plazas, fountains and carefully aged stucco-fronted buildings. Following the first land sale in 1921, $150 million poured in, which Merrick channelled into the biggest advertising campaign ever known. However, Coral Gables took shape just as the Florida property boom ended. Merrick was wiped out, and died as Miami's postmaster in 1942. Coral Gables never lost its good looks, and remains an impressive place to explore. Merrick wanted people to know they'd arrived somewhere special, and eight grand **entrances** were planned on the main approach roads (though only four were completed).

The best way into Coral Gables is along NW 22nd Street. Once across Douglas Road, this becomes the **Miracle Mile** (in fact only half a mile long). Dominated by department stores, travel agents, and a staggering number of bridal shops, it gets more and more expensive and exclusive as you proceed west – note the arcades and balconies, and the spirals and peaks of the **Colonnade Building**, no 133–169, completed in 1926 to accommodate George Merrick's office. Further west, along Coral Way, the **Coral Gables House**, no 907 (Sun & Wed 1–4pm; $2), was Merrick's boyhood home. In 1899, when George was 12, his family arrived here from New England to run a 160-acre fruit and vegetable farm. The farm was so successful that the house quickly grew from a wooden shack into an elegant dwelling of coral rock and gabled windows (a combination that inspired the name of the future city).

Merrick's crowning achievement was the **Biltmore Hotel**, 1200 Anastasia Ave, wrapping its broad wings around the southern end of De Soto Blvd, its 26-storey tower visible across much of low-lying Miami. Everything about the *Biltmore* was over-the-top: 25ft-high fresco-coated walls, vaulted ceilings, immense fireplaces and custom-loomed rugs. In 1986, $40 million was spent on restoration, but the company involved collapsed and the great building has only recently reopened. Free **historical tours** leave from the lobby every Sunday at 1.30pm, 2.30pm and 3.30pm.

Coconut Grove

A stamping ground of down-at-heel artists and writers through the Sixties and Seventies, **COCONUT GROVE** has been turned by a business-led revitalization into a hang-out for the glitterati: art galleries, fashionable cafés and restaurants, and towering bay-view apartments mark its central section. But Coconut Grove also retains much of value from its formative years. A century ago, a strange mix of Bahamian salvagers and New England intellectuals laid the foundations of a fiercely individual community, separated from the fledgling city of Miami by a dense wedge of tropical foliage.

In 1914, farm machinery mogul James Deering blew $15 million on re-creating a sixteenth-century Italian villa within this jungle. A thousand-strong workforce completed his **Villa Viscaya**, 3251 South Miami Ave (daily 9.30am–5pm; $8), in just two years. Deering's madly eclectic art collection, and the concept that the villa should appear to have been inhabited for four hundred years, results in a thunderous clash of Baroque, Renaissance, Rococo and Neoclassical fixtures and fittings, and even the land-scaped **gardens**, with their fountains and sculptures, aren't spared the pretensions. Vulgar as it is, Villa Viscaya is one of Miami's better sights, and is rightly one of the most visited. **Guided tours** leave frequently from the entrance loggia and provide solid background, after which you're free to explore at leisure.

Blatant statements of wealth predominate as you approach central Coconut Grove. The marina on **Dinner Key** sports lines of $100,000 yachts, and the neighboring **Coconut Grove Exhibition Center** is usually consumed by top-of-the-range car and interior furnishing shows. It was at the Dinner Key Auditorium (a forerunner of the Exhibition Center) in 1969 that rock legend **Jim Morrison**, singer with the Doors, dropped his leather trousers to expose his private parts during the band's first – and last – Florida show, bringing the band more infamy than they knew what to do with.

Key Biscayne

A compact, immaculately manicured community, decorated by rows of coconut palms, **KEY BISCAYNE**, five miles off mainland Miami, is a great place to live – if you can afford it. The moneyed of Miami fill the island's upmarket homes; Richard Nixon had a presidential winter house here. The only way onto Key Biscayne is along the four-mile **Rickenbacker Causeway** ($1 toll), a continuation of SW 26th Road just south of downtown, which soars high above Biscayne Bay, giving a gasp-inducing view of the Brickell Avenue skyline. As well as by car, you can cross by bike, bus (#B), or on foot.

Crandon Park Beach, a mile along Crandon Blvd (the continuation of the main road from the causeway), is one of the finest landscaped beaches in the city. Three miles of yellow-brown beach line fringe this grassy, palm-dotted park, and give access to a sandbar enabling knee-depth wading far from shore.

Crandon Boulevard terminates at the entrance to the **Bill Baggs Cape Florida State Recreation Area**, four hundred wooded acres covering the southern extremity of Key Biscayne. An excellent swimming **beach** lines the Atlantic-facing side of the park, and a boardwalk cuts around the wind-bitten sand dunes towards the **Cape Florida lighthouse**, built in the 1820s. Only with the ranger-led **tour** (daily except Tues at 9am, 10.30am, 1pm, 2.30pm & 3.30pm; $1) can you climb through the 95ft-high structure – attacked by Seminoles in 1836 and incapacitated by Confederate soldiers to disrupt Union shipping during the Civil War – which now serves as a navigational beacon.

Miami Beach

A long slender arm of land between Biscayne Bay and the Atlantic Ocean, three miles off mainland Miami, **MIAMI BEACH** was an ailing fruit farm in the 1910s when its Quaker owner, John Collins, formed an unlikely partnership with a flashy entrepreneur called Carl Fisher. With Fisher's money, Biscayne Bay was dredged. The muck raised from its murky bed provided the landfill to transform this wildly vegetated barrier island into a carefully sculptured landscape of palm trees, hotels and tennis courts.

Occupying the southernmost three miles, the one genuinely exciting part of Miami Beach is **SOUTH BEACH**, with its pastel-colored Art Deco buildings. Hundreds of these late-Thirties gems are concentrated between 5th and 23rd streets, and best assessed along **Ocean Drive**, where a line of revamped hotels have made much of their design heritage. Swarms of photographers and film crews zoom in on what has become – thanks to the visuals of *Miami Vice* and the fashion photography of Bruce Weber – the hottest high-style backdrop in the world.

Socially, South Beach is unsurpassed. By day, ravers soak up the rays on the beach; by night, the ten blocks of Ocean Drive are the heart and soul of the biggest party in Miami, as chic terrace cafés spill across the specially widened sidewalk. Just a few blocks from Ocean Drive, the streets are much less photogenic, still bearing the scars of the poverty-stricken Seventies. Provided you stick to the main streets and exercise the usual caution, however, none of South Beach is unduly dangerous.

Accommodation

Though Miami's small size means that you can stay just about anywhere and not feel isolated, most **hotels** and **motels** are on **Miami Beach**, an ideal base for nightlife and beachlife. Typical summer rates are $40 to $75, rising to $60 to $85 in winter. **Downtown Miami** has few affordable rivals to the expense-account chain hotels; **Coral Gables** is appealing but pricey; and the stylish high-rises of **Coconut Grove** are a jet-setters' preserve. Budget alternatives are limited to the **youth hostels** in Miami Beach.

Colony Hotel, 736 Ocean Drive (☎673-0088). Beautifully refurbished Art Deco delight. ⑤–⑥.

Doubletree at Coconut Grove, 2649 S Bayshore Drive (☎1-800/528-0444). Elegant high-rise with cozy rooms and great views, just a quarter of an hour's walk from the local cafés and bars. ⑦.

Gables Inn, 730 S Dixie Hwy (☎661-7999). Basic but clean and the cheapest in the area. ③.

The Golden Sands, 6910 Collins Ave (☎1-800/932-0333). Nothing flash and mostly filled by package-touring Europeans, but likely to turn up the cheapest deals in this pricey area. ③.

Hostel International of Miami Beach, at the *Clay Hotel*, 1438 Washington Ave (☎534-2988). AYH hostel, impeccably positioned in the heart of South Beach, with beds in small dorms for $10 ($13 for non-IYHA-members), plus some private singles and doubles. ①.

Hotel Place St Michel, 162 Alcazar Ave, Coral Gables (☎444-1666). Small, romantic hideaway, with pastel decor and European antiques. Rate includes breakfast. ⑤.

Howard Johnson, 200 SE Second Ave, downtown (☎1-800/654-2000). Standard chain-hotel but the lowest-priced rooms this close to the heart of downtown Miami. ⑤.

Leslie, 1244 Ocean Drive (☎1-800/338-9076). Excellent location on beachside Art Deco strip, and striking design – bright colors and crooked mirrors. Rooms come with tape-players and TVs. ⑤–⑥.

Miami Beach International Travelers Hostel, 236 Ninth St (☎534-0268). Beds in 4-person dorms for $12 per person, in South Beach. ①.

Occidental Parc, 100 SE Fourth St (☎1-800/521-5000). A good choice, delectably positioned beside the Miami River. All rooms are suites with small kitchens. ⑥–⑦.

Park Central, 640 Ocean Drive (☎538-1611). Among the best of the Art Deco piles, retaining ceiling fans as well as regular air-conditioning. ⑥–⑦.

The Tropics, 1550 Collins Ave (☎531-0361). New Miami Beach hostel, a minute from the beach. Dorms for $12, plus some private doubles. ①/②.

Eating

Apart from seafood – every bit as good as you'd expect so close to tropical waters – **Cuban** food is what Miami does best. Countless family-run diners serve identical meals at a fraction of the prices of the fancier Cuban restaurants (mostly in Little Havana and Coral Gables) now being discovered by the critics. **Haitian** food is the current rage, closely followed by Argentinian, Jamaican, Nicaraguan and Peruvian cooking.

Aux Palmistes Chez Julie, 6820 NE Second Ave, Little Haiti (☎759-8527). Where Little Haiti dines on home-cooked fried pork, goat and fish. Closed Mon. Live music at weekends; see opposite.

Ayestaran, 706 SW 27th Ave, Little Havana (☎649-4982). Long a favorite Cuban restaurant among those in the know, especially good value for its $5 daily specials.

Bimini Grill, 620 NE 78th St, downtown (☎758-9154). Florida bayou-style food in a wooden shack on a river bank: barbecued meats and Caribbean conch fritters among the treats.

Captain Dick's Tackle Shack, 3381 Pan American Drive, Coconut Grove (☎854-5871). Filling seafood and salads, in the shadow of Miami City Hall, at rock-bottom prices.

Don't Say Sandwich to Me, 1331 Washington Ave, Miami Beach (☎532-6700). Every quick eat imaginable. Cheap Sunday brunch, too. Open 24 hours.

El Corral, 3545 Coral Way, Coral Gables (☎444-8272). Appealingly priced Nicaraguan restaurant where anything that isn't beef isn't taken seriously – carnivores' heaven.

El Inka, 1756 SW Eighth St, Little Havana (☎845-0243). The city's oldest and best Peruvian restaurant, famed for its spicy meats and seafood, and doing extraordinary things with squid.

News Café, 800 Ocean Drive, Miami Beach (☎538-6397). Fashionable sidewalk café with front-row seating for the South Beach promenade. Weekends open 24 hours.

Rita's Italian Restaurant, 7232 Biscayne Blvd, downtown (☎757-9470). Family-run Italian diner with check tablecloths, hearty portions and good prices – and an owner inclined to burst into song.

Sundays on the Bay, 5420 Biscayne Blvd, Key Biscayne (☎361-6777). The biggest and most enjoyable brunch in Miami; make a reservation to avoid queueing.

Versailles, 3555 SW Eighth St, Little Havana (☎444-0240). Chandeliers, mirrored walls, a great atmosphere, and wonderful inexpensive Cuban food.

Wolfie's, 2038 Collins Ave, Miami Beach (☎538-6626). Long-established deli drawing late-night clubbers – served generous helpings by waitresses with beehive hairdos. Open 24 hours.

Drinking, Nightlife and Entertainment

Miami folk usually **drink** in restaurants, clubs and discos, but some of the bars and pubs listed below are suited to an early-evening tipple, and others make prime vantage points to watch the city's posers come and go. Miami's **clubs** – especially those specializing in **salsa** or **merengue** (a slinky dance music from the Caribbean), and hosted by Spanish-speaking DJs – are rated as among the hippest in the world.

Miami is virtually impossible to **get around** at night without a car or taxi, but most of the action takes place at the walkable South Beach. Friday's *Miami Herald* carries full weekend entertainment **listings**; the free weekly *New Times* has reliable information on cafés and clubs. The free *TWN* (*The Weekly News*), available from the bars and clubs of Coconut Grove and South Beach, is the key source of **gay and lesbian info**.

If you want to try out the local **sports** scene, the *Florida Dolphins*, the state's only professional football team, play at the Joe Robbie Stadium, 16 miles northwest of downtown (box office Mon–Fri 10am–6pm; ☎620-2578).

Bars and Pubs

Bayside Seafood Restaurant, 3501 Rickenbacker Causeway, Key Biscayne (☎361-0808). Friendly beer-drinking crowd beside the bay.

Clevelander, 1020 Ocean Drive (☎531-3485). Miami Beach's ultimate poolside sports bar, with pool tables, sports-tuned TVs and partially-clothed athletic physiques attacking the brews.

Coco Loco's, in the *Sheraton*, 495 Brickell Ave, near downtown Miami (☎373-6000). No better place to round off a day downtown; pricey drinks, but for a dollar you help yourself to a big buffet.

Firehouse Four, 1000 S Miami Ave, downtown (☎379-1923). Filled by day with expense-account eaters, in the evening Miami's oldest fire station building makes a fine spot for a drink.

Monty's Bayshore Restaurant, 2560 S Bayshore Drive, Coconut Grove (☎858-1431). Drinkers often outnumber the diners, drawn by the gregarious mood and the views across the bay.

Rebar, 1121 Washington Ave (☎672-4788). The South Beach bar for the fashionably grungy.

Shagnasty's Saloon & Eatery, 638 S Miami Ave, near downtown Miami (☎381-8970). The hip yuppie's happy-hour hang-out, with free appetizers and many discounted drinks.

The Spot, 216 Española Way (☎532-1682). Trendy Miami Beach biker bar made famous by its former owner, actor Mickey Rourke.

Clubs and Discos

Les Bains, 753 Washington Ave (☎532-8768). Only the trendy-looking are admitted to this South Beach version of an upscale European disco. If you're too jaded to dance, try your hand at blackjack.

Bash, 655 Washington Ave (☎538-2274). Co-owned by Sean Penn and Mick Hucknall. Intimate bar and beckoning dance floor, though many revellers get no further than the garden. No cover.

Bonfire, 1060 NE 79th St, Little Haiti (☎756-0200). Smooth and danceable salsa. Wed–Sun; $2–5.

Cameo Theatre, 1445 Washington Ave (☎673-8679). Each night this Art Deco one-time movie theater sees different activity, from disco to punk to world beat. Attracts a young crowd; cover varies.

Club Tipico Dominicano, 1344 NW 36th St, Little Havana (☎634-7819). Top merengue DJ hosting the sessions Fri–Sun; $5.

Warsaw Ballroom, 1450 Collins Ave, Miami Beach (☎1-800/9-WARSAW). While not exclusively gay, this is the busiest and biggest gay disco in town; lesbian night Wed.

Live Music

In a city that still goes crazy over the studio-based latin-pop of local girl Gloria Estefan, you might not expect to find a **live music** scene at all in Miami. In fact, an impressive number of **venues** – many of them poky clubs or the back rooms of restaurants – host bands throughout the week. **Reggae** is strong; Miami has a sizeable Jamaican population, and there are regular appearances by local as well as flown-in acts.

Aux Palmistes Chez Julie, 6820 NE Second Ave, Little Haiti (☎759-8527). Great live Haitian music from 10pm to 4am on Fri & Sat. Free–$5.

Hungry Sailor, 3064½ Grand Ave, Coconut Grove (☎444-9359). Reggae bands fill the tiny corner stage of this would-be English pub almost every night. Free–$2.

Peacock Café, 2977 McFarlane Rd, Coconut Grove (☎442-8833). Back-room lounge features jazz, blues and occasional rock acts. Cover varies.

Stephen's Talkhouse, 616 Collins Ave (☎531-7557). Coffeehouse ambience that makes a comfortable setting for semi-established bands, of various musical persuasions.

Tobacco Road, 626 S Miami Ave, downtown Miami (☎374-1198). Earthy r'n'b from some of the country's finest exponents. Free–$5.

THE FLORIDA KEYS

Fiction, films and folklore have given the **Florida Keys** – a hundred-mile chain of islands that runs to within ninety miles of Cuba – an image of glamorous intrigue they don't really deserve. Instead, fishing, snorkelling and diving dominate, and are ruthlessly hawked at every opportunity. Here and there some idiosyncratic history rears its head, and terrific untainted natural areas include the **Florida Reef**, a great band of living coral just a few miles off the coast. But the various keys are really only stops on the way to fascinating **Key West**. Once the richest town in the US, and the final dot of North America before a thousand miles of ocean, it holds plenty of congenial bars in which to waste away the hours, watching the famous spectacular **sunsets**.

> The **area code** for the Florida Keys is ☎305.

Travelling through the Keys could hardly be easier. There's just one route all the way through to Key West: the **Overseas Highway (US-1)**. The road is punctuated by **mile markers (MM)** – posts on which mileage is marked, starting with MM127 just south of Miami and finishing with MM0 in Key West. The motels and restaurants strung along the highway often use the mile markers as addresses.

Key Largo

The first and largest of the keys, **Key Largo** is also the dullest, though it does boast a fine opportunity to visit the Florida Reef, at the **John Pennecamp Coral Reef State Park** at MM102.5 in North Key Largo (daily 8am–sunset; cars and drivers $3.75, passengers 50¢). This protected 78-square-mile section of living coral reef is rated by experts as one of the most beautiful in the world. If possible, take the **snorkelling tour** (9am, noon & 3pm; $24), or the **guided scuba dive** (9.30am & 1pm; $30), though less demanding is the **glass-bottomed boat tour** (9.30am, 12.30pm & 3pm; $15).

Even from the glass-bottomed boat, you're virtually certain to spot lobsters, angelfish, eels and jellyfish along the reef, and shoals of silvery minnows stalked by angry-faced barracudas. The reef itself is a delicate living thing, composed of millions of minute coral polyps extracting calcium from the sea water and growing from one to sixteen feet every thousand years. Sadly, it's far easier to spot signs of death rather than life: white patches show where a carelessly dropped anchor, or diver's hand, has scraped away the protective mucus layer and left the coral susceptible to terminal disease.

Key Largo and Tavernier

South of the park, the people of Rock Harbor recognized a good thing when they saw one and changed the name of their community to **KEY LARGO** after the success of the 1948 film in which Humphrey Bogart and Lauren Bacall grappled with Florida's best-known features – crime and hurricanes. Yet the movie's title was chosen for no other reason than it suggested somewhere exotic, and the film, though set here, was almost entirely shot in Hollywood. This being the case, the real town of Key Largo is totally boring; if you want a place to stop, keep moving ten miles on to the far more homely **TAVERNIER**. Here, the **Harry Harris Park**, off the Overseas Highway along Burton Drive, often has free live music at weekends around its picnic tables.

If you're going to explore North Key Largo and the Coral Reef State Park at length, you'll have to sleep and eat in either Key Largo town or Tavernier. The **Florida Keys Visitor Center**, 103400 Hwy-1, MM106 (Mon–Sat 9am–6pm; ☎1-800/822-1088), has more information. Most local **motels** offer diving packages: try *Ed & Ellen's Efficiencies*, 103365 Overseas Hwy (☎451-4712; ②), with a two-night minimum; the beach cottages at the *Sea Farer*, MM97.8 (☎852-5349; ③); or the *Hungry Pelican*, MM99.5 (☎451-3576; ③). There's good seafood at the *Fish House*, MM102.4 (☎451-4665).

The Middle and Lower Keys

Once over Long Key Bridge, you're into the **Middle Keys**, a sensible base for seeing the Keys without uprooting yourself too often. The largest of several islands, Key Vaca holds the nucleus of the area's major settlement, **MARATHON**. On first sight the town is as uninspiring as Key Largo, but it does at least have a couple of small **beaches**. Sombrero Beach, along Sombrero Beach Rd (off the Overseas Highway near MM50), has good swimming waters and shaded picnic tables; Key Colony Beach four miles north is prettier and quieter.

Marathon has several well-equipped **resorts**, such as *Sombrero*, 19 Sombrero Blvd (☎1-800/433-8660; ⑤–⑦), or *Banana Bay*, 4590 Overseas Hwy (☎1-800/488-6636; ⑤–⑦), as well as a good supply of cheaper **motels**. For **eating**, *Herbie's*, 6350 Overseas Hwy (☎743-6373), is justly busy on account of its inexpensive seafood, while *Porky's Too BBQ*, MM45 (☎743-6637), provides platefuls of beef and chicken.

The Lower Keys

Starkly different to their northerly neighbors, the **Lower Keys** are quiet, heavily wooded and predominantly residential. Built on a limestone rather than a coral base, these islands have a flora and fauna all their own.

The first place of consequence you'll hit after crossing Seven Mile Bridge is **Bahia Honda State Recreation Area** (daily 8am–sunset; cars $3.25, pedestrians and cyclists $1), one of the Keys' prettiest places. Its lagoon has a beckoning natural **beach** and two-tone ocean waters. The best diversion, though, is a visit to **Looe Key Marine Sanctuary**, signposted from the Overseas Highway on Ramrod Key – a five-square-mile protected reef area, in every part the equal of the John Pennecamp Coral Reef State Park. The **sanctuary office** (Mon–Fri 8am–5pm; ☎872-4039) can provide free maps, but to visit the reef you'll need the services of a dive shop; the nearest is the neighboring *Looe Key Dive Center* (☎1-800/942-5397).

In the main Lower Keys settlement, **Big Pine Key**, the **visitor center** is at MM31.9 (Mon–Fri 9am–5pm, Sat 9am–3pm; ☎872-2411). Of the **motels**, *Looe Key Reef Resort*, MM27.5 (☎872-2215; ③), is ideal for visiting the marine sanctuary. The **B&Bs** along Long Beach Drive on Big Pine Key are cozy, but book early: *Deer Run*, MM32.5 (☎872-2015; ⑤), *Barnacle*, MM32.5 (☎872-3298; ⑤), and *Casa Grande*, 33MM (☎872-2878; ④).

Key West

Much closer to Cuba than to mainland Florida, **KEY WEST** often seems pretty tenuously bound to the rest of the US. Famed for their tolerant attitudes and laid-back lifestyles, the thirty thousand islanders seem adrift in a great expanse of sea and sky, and – despite a million tourists per year – the place resonates with an individual spirit that hits you the instant you arrive. Yet as wild as it may at first appear, Key West today is far from being the dropouts' mecca of a mere decade ago. Much of the sleaziness has been brushed away through a steady process of restoration, setting the course for the advent of a sizeable holiday industry. But Key West is still resolutely non-conformist – a deliciously seductive place – and in particular, the liberal manners have stimulated a large **gay** influx. The sense of isolation from the mainland is best appreciated by adjusting to the mellow pace: amble the streets, make meals last for hours, and pause regularly for refreshment in the numerous bars.

Arriving and Getting Around

Both the **Welcome Center** on North Roosevelt Blvd (daily 9am–5pm; ☎296-4444) and the **Key West Chamber of Commerce**, Mallory Square, 402 Wall St (daily 9am–5pm; ☎294-2587), can give precise dates for Key West's annual **festivals**, the best being the *Old Island Days* (Jan–April) celebrating Key West's history, the *Conch Republic Celebration* in April, and the *Fantasy Fest* in late October, a gay-dominated version of Mardi Gras. A number of weekly **free publications** list current events, like *Island Life* and the gay-oriented *What's Happening*. The **Greyhound** station is at 615½ Duval St (☎296-9072); confusingly, its entrance is on Simonton St, a block east of Duval St itself.

It's best to explore the narrow streets of the mile-square Old Town – which contains virtually everything that you'll want to see – by **walking**. You could do it on foot in little more than a day, though dashing about isn't the way to enjoy the place. **Bikes** can be rented from *Adventure Scooter & Bicycle Rentals*, 708 and 925 Duval St, or the youth hostel (see opposite).

Around the Old Town

Anyone who saw Key West two decades ago would now barely recognize the Old Town's main promenade, **Duval Street**. Teetering just on the safe side of seedy for many years, much of the street has been transformed into a tourist strip of boutiques and beachwear shops. It's never boring, and the mile-long swath it cuts right through the Old Town makes it easy to regain bearings after forays into the side streets.

The **Wrecker's Museum**, 322 Duval St (daily 10am–4pm; $2), gives some background to the industry on which Key West's earliest good times were based: salvaging cargo from foundering vessels. Judging by the choice furniture that fills the house, Captain Watlington, the wrecker who lived here from the 1830s, did pretty well. Further up, at 516 Duval St, the **San Carlos Institute** (daily 9am–5pm; $3) has played a leading role in Cuban exile life since it opened as the San Carlos Institute in 1871. Financed by a grant from the Cuban government, the present building dates from 1924 and holds a commendable account of Key West history and Cuban life in the town. Across its grounds are spread soil from Cuba's six provinces, and there is a cornerstone taken from the tomb of Cuban independence campaigner José Martí.

As you approach the southern end of Duval Street, everything, whether house, motel, filling station or restaurant, advertises itself as "the Southernmost . . .". Accurately, the **southernmost point** in Key West, and consequently in the continental US, is at the intersection of Whitehead and South streets; a daft-looking buoy marks the spot.

In the early 1800s, thousands of dollars' worth of salvage was landed at the piers, stored in the warehouses, and flogged at the auction houses on **Mallory Square**, just west of the northern end of Duval Street. By day, the square is a plain souvenir market, with overpriced ice cream, trinkets and T-shirts, but at night there's a tourist-oriented (but fun) **sunset celebration**, when buskers and fire-eaters create a merry backdrop to the sinking of the sun. More entertaining than the square during the day is the small gathering of sea life inside the adjacent **Key West Aquarium**, 1 Whitehead St (daily summer 10am–6pm, winter 10am–7pm; $6), where porcupine fish and longspine squirrel fish leer out from behind glass. Small sharks are known to jump out of their open tanks during the **guided tours**, conducted roughly every two hours.

In **Mel Fisher's Treasure Exhibit**, 200 Greene St (daily 9.30am–5pm; $5), not far from the aquarium, an impressive emerald cross, a liftable gold bar, and countless vases and daggers are displayed alongside the obligatory cannon, pulled up from two seventeenth-century wrecks. Fisher was running a surf shop in California before he arrived in Florida armed with ancient Spanish sea charts and, in 1985, discovered the *Neustra Señora de Atocha* and *Santa Margarita*, both sunk during a hurricane in 1622, forty miles southeast of Key West. The haul was said to be worth millions of dollars.

For all the atmosphere of the streets and alleys, Key West's most popular tourist attraction is the **Hemingway House**, at 907 Whitehead St (daily 9am–5pm; $6). The compulsory half-hour **guided tours** deal, sadly, more in fantasy than fact: although Ernest Hemingway owned this large, vaguely Moorish house for thirty years, he lived in it for barely ten, and even the authenticity of the furnishings is disputed by his former secretary. Hemingway bought the house in 1931, when it was seriously run-down, and some of the writer's most acclaimed novels, such as *For Whom the Bell Tolls* and *To Have and Have Not*, were produced in the study (in an outhouse which Hemingway entered by way of a rope bridge). Divorced in 1940, Hemingway boxed up his manuscripts and moved them to a back room at the original *Sloppy Joe's* (see opposite) before heading off for a house in Cuba with his new wife, journalist Martha Gellhorn.

Accommodation

It's essential to make a **reservation** in Key West during winter; call the place directly as early as possible. The town operates a free room booking service on ☎1-800/732-2006.

Angelina Guest House, 302 Angela St (☎294-4480). Simple but well-priced regular rooms; spending a little more brings kitchenettes and suites, good value for four people sharing. ④.

Blue Parrot Inn, 916 Elizabeth St (☎1-800/231-BIRD). Dating from 1884 and offering a heated pool and continental breakfast, as well as comfortable, nicely furnished rooms. ⑥.

Eden House, 1015 Fleming St (☎1-800/533-KEYS). Relaxing hideaway, with wicker furnishings and a fish-filled pool. The cheaper rooms share a bathroom; the priciest have jacuzzis. ④–⑦.

Key West Hostel, 718 South St (☎296-5719). Youth hostel; members $14.25, others $17.50. ①.

Southern Cross, 326 Duval St (☎1-800/533-4891). Key West's oldest hotel offers no-frills rooms; get one at the rear if you want to avoid the night-time hubbub along Duval St. ⑤.

Southernmost Motel, 1319 Duval St (☎1-800/354-4455). The US's most southerly motel, decked out in tropical shades and with a poolside tiki bar. Ten minutes' walk from the heart of Key West. ⑤.

La Terraza de Marti, 1125 Duval St (☎296-6706). Tree-studded hotel complex, popular with gay visitors. Rooms face a beckoning pool. Bars, discos, a classy restaurant, and handy for the town. ⑥.

Tilton Hilton, 511 Angela St (☎294-8694). Key West's cheapest hotel but otherwise one with little to recommend it. The rooms are very basic; be sure to see yours before paying for it. ③.

Eating

In Key West, it's de rigeur to sample **conch fritter**; the stand at Duval and Fleming does the best in town for under two dollars. Also, if you've not tried it before, don't leave without tasting **Cuban food**, as there are several excellent restaurants in town.

A&B Lobster House, 700 Front St (☎294-2536). Overlooking the town's harbor, there could be no more scenic setting to indulge in fresh seafood or sample the offerings of the raw bar.

Around the World, 627 Duval St (☎296-2115). Dishes drawn from every corner of the globe; if nothing appeals tuck into the sizeable salads and enjoy the extensive selections of wines and beers.

Bo's, 429 Duval St (☎294-9272). Inexpensive over-the-counter fish'n'chips and conch fritters.

Dim-Sum, 613 Duval St (☎294-6230). Thai, Indonesian and Burmese specialties are the core of an exotic Asian menu; don't expect dinner to be less than $20.

Key West Cookie Company, 621 Duval St (☎294-3969). Freshly baked cookies to nibble in the street, inexpensive lunch specials and the best *café con leche* between Miami and Havana.

Mangoes, 700 Duval St (☎292-4606). Eat indoors or outdoors under huge umbrellas; seafood and a variety of vegetarian dishes created with a Caribbean slant.

South Beach Seafood & Raw Bar, 1405 Duval St (☎294-2727). Casual ocean-front dining at its best with the seafood selections; large portions of chicken, beef and ribs are also on offer.

Drinking and Nightlife

The anything-goes nature of Key West is exemplified by the **bars** which make up the bulk of the island's nightlife. Gregarious, rough-and-ready affairs, often open until 4am and with regular live music, the best bars are grouped around the northern end of Duval Street, no more than a few minutes' stagger from one another.

Bull & Whistle Bar, 224 Duval St (no phone). Features the best of the local musicians each night. Check the list on the door to see who's playing – or just turn up to drink.

Captain Tony's Saloon, 428 Greene St (☎294-1838). Rustic fisherman's saloon. The original *Sloppy Joe's* (see below), a noted hang-out of Ernest Hemingway. Live music of various kinds nightly.

Green Parrot Bar, 601 Whitehead St (☎294-6133). A Key West landmark since 1890, this bar draws local characters to its pool tables, dartboard and pinball machine. Live music at weekends.

Margaritaville, 500 Duval St (☎292-1435). Owned by legendary Florida balladeer Jimmy Buffett, this rowdy place keeps the alcohol and music flowing. Live bands play nightly.

Sloppy Joe's, 201 Duval St (☎294-5717). Despite the memorabilia and the crowds, this enjoyable bar – with live music nightly – is not the one Hemingway made famous; see *Captain Tony's*, above.

THE EAST COAST

Stretching from the northern fringe of Miami to the very northeastern edge of the state, the Atlantic **east coast** runs for over three hundred miles – largely the sun-soaked Florida of popular imagination, with palm-dotted beaches and warm ocean waves. That said, the first fifty-odd miles of coast are deep within the sway of Miami – back-to-back conurbations often with little to tell one from the next. **Fort Lauderdale**, at least, is certainly distinctive, though its reputation for rowdy beach parties is now well out of date. Further north, **Boca Raton**'s hallmark is the Mediterranean Revival architecture seen also in nearby **Palm Beach,** inhabited almost exclusively by multi-millionaires. North of here, though, much of the coast is still substantially free of commercial exploitation – with the single exception of the **Space Coast** centering on the **Kennedy Space Center**. Beyond the excesses of **Daytona Beach**, the plentiful evidence of Florida's early European landings is nowhere better displayed than in the comprehensively restored **St Augustine**, where Spaniards established North America's earliest foreign settlement.

By car, the scenic route along the coast is **Hwy-A1A**, which sticks to the ocean side of the **intracoastal waterway**, formed when the rivers dividing the mainland from the barrier islands were joined and deepened during World War II.

Fort Lauderdale

A thinly populated riverside trading camp at the turn of the century, seven miles of palm-shaded white sands and a low-budget Hollywood film later conspired to turn mild-mannered **FORT LAUDERDALE** into a town with a global reputation for rumbustu-ous beachlife. The 1960 teen-exploitation movie, *Where the Boys Are*, instantly made Fort Lauderdale the US's number one Spring Break venue, drawing hundreds of thou-sands of students to a frenzy of under-age drinking and lascivious excess. Not surpris-ingly, this hindered the town's chances of attracting regular tourists, and in the late Seventies the local authorities enacted strict laws to restrict boozing and wild behavior around the beach. Fort Lauderdale was left dominated by a mix of wealthy retirees and affluent yuppies, desperate to play down the beach-party tag and play up the town's settler-period history.

Anonymous bank buildings and tall glass-fronted offices make a uninspiring initial impression, but lately a multimillion-dollar effort has prettified **downtown Fort Lauderdale** with parks and promenades, linked by the pedestrian **riverwalk** along the north bank of the New River. You can follow the riverwalk to the **Historic District**, where the 1907 **King-Cromartie House** features many then-futuristic fixtures – includ-ing the first indoor bathroom in Fort Lauderdale, gleefully pointed out by the period-attired tour guides. To give perspective on the old buildings, the **Historical Society Museum**, 219 SW Second Ave (Tues–Sat 10am–4pm, Sun 1–4pm; $2), mounts tempo-rary displays and stocks historical books and pamphlets.

Like most visitors, though, you've probably come for the **beach** and its bars, and the action there is still what Fort Lauderdale does best, even if the glory days have been and gone. Leave downtown along **Las Olas Boulevard**, lined by trendy shops, art galleries and restaurants. Once across the arching intracoastal waterway bridge, about two miles on, you're within sight of the ocean and the mood changes appreciably. Where Las Olas Boulevard ends, **beachside Fort Lauderdale** begins – T-shirt, sunscreen and swimwear stores are suddenly everywhere. Along the seafront, **Ocean Boulevard** bore the brunt of Spring Break partying, but only a few beachfront bars suggest the carousing of the past. The sands, though, are by no means deserted or dull – and still get a fair number of whooping students each spring.

Practicalities

All the public transportation terminals are in or near downtown: the *Greyhound* **bus** station is at 515 NE Third St (☎305/764-6551), the **train** and *Tri-Rail* stations two miles west at 200 SW 21st Terrace (☎305/464-8251) – take buses #9, #10 or #81 to the center. While downtown, get information from the **CVB**, 200 E Las Olas Blvd (Mon–Fri 8.30am–5pm; ☎305/765-4466).

The handiest **local bus** service is #11, which runs twice every hour along Las Olas Blvd between downtown Fort Lauderdale and the beach. Or use the **Water Taxi** (☎305/565-5507), a small boat which will deliver you almost anywhere along Fort Lauderdale's many miles of waterfront; single journeys are $5, an all-day ticket $13.

Beachside **motels** line Bayshore Drive and Birch Road. Quiet places with pools, a few minutes from the beach, include *Pillars Waterfront Motel*, 111 N Birch Rd (☎305/467-9639; ②–③), and *Southern Shores*, 3017 Bayshore Drive (☎1-800/827-6232; ②–③). At the beachside **youth hostel**, *Sol Y Mar*, 2839 Vistamar St (☎305/566-1023; ①), members pay $12, others $15.

For **eating**, check out the scruffy but likeable *Ernie's BBQ Lounge*, south of downtown at 1843 S Federal Highway (☎305/523-8636) – a local legend for its glorious conch chowder (add sherry to taste). *Southport Raw Bar*, 1536 Cordova Rd (☎305/525-CLAM), is a boisterous local bar offering succulent crustaceans and well-prepared fish dishes, while *Franco & Vinny's Mexican Cantina*, 2870 E Sunrise Blvd (☎305/565-3839), serves Mexican favorites at giveaway prices near the beach. *The Floridian*, 1410 E Las Olas Blvd (☎305/463-4041), is a characterful downtown coffee shop, providing breakfast, lunch and dinner to an eclectic and interesting crowd.

Boca Raton

BOCA RATON (literally "the mouth of the rat"), twenty miles north, is populated by the executives of numerous local hi-tech companies, such as IBM. More noticeably, it has an over-abundance of Mediterranean Revival architecture, a style prevalent here since the Twenties and kept alive all over the **downtown** area by strict building codes. New structures are compelled to use arched entranceways, fake bell towers and red-tiled roofs whenever possible. Too contrived for comfort, perhaps, but it certainly stands out.

It all goes back to **Addison Mizner**, the "Aladdin of architects" (see the box overleaf), who swept in to Boca Raton on the tide of the Florida property boom, bought 1600 acres of farmland and began selling plots of a future community. Mizner envisioned gondola-filled canals, a luxury hotel, and a great cathedral, but his plan was nipped in the bud by the economic crash and he went back to Palm Beach with his tail between his legs. Bankruptcy notwithstanding, the few buildings he completed left an indelible mark. The million-dollar *Cloister Inn* grew into the present $200-a-night *Boca Raton Resort and Club*, a pink palace of marble columns, sculptured fountains, and carefully aged wood, which can be viewed on guided tours (Dec–April; $4; ☎407/395-8655).

Boca Raton's most explorable **beachside** area is **Spanish River Park** (daily 8am–sunset; cars $2, pedestrians and cyclists free), a couple of miles north of downtown. Most of these fifty acres of vivid vegetation and high-rise greenery are only penetrable on trails through shady thickets.

Practicalities

The **Chamber of Commerce**, 1800 N Dixie Hwy (Mon–Fri 9am–5pm; ☎407/395-4433), supplies the usual details. The best-value **motels** near the beaches are *Shore Edge*, 425 N Ocean Blvd (☎407/395-4491; ③), and *Ocean Lodge*, 531 N Ocean Blvd (☎407/395-7772; ③). You'll save money by sleeping inland at the *Econo Lodge*, 2899 N Federal Highway (☎1-800/624-3606; ②).

Palm Beach

A small island town of palatial homes and gardens, and streets so clean you could eat your dinner off them, **PALM BEACH** has been synonymous for nearly a century with the kind of lifestyle only limitless loot can buy. The nation's nobs began wintering here in the 1890s, after Henry Flagler brought his East Coast railroad south from St Augustine and built two luxury hotels on this then-secluded, palm-filled island. Since then, tycoons, sports aces, aristocrats, rock stars and CIA directors have flocked here, eager to become part of the Palm Beach elite and enjoy its aloofness from mainland – and mainstream – life. Joe Kennedy – father of John, Robert and Edward – bought the so-called Kennedy Compound here in 1933, the focus in 1991 of much prurient interest as the scene of the events which culminated in the acquittal of his grandson William Kennedy Smith on charges of sexual battery.

Summer in Palm Beach is very quiet – and the least costly time to stay. The winter months, from November to May, see a whirl of elegant balls, fund-raising dinners and charity galas, as well as the polo season – watching a chukka or two is the only time Palm Beach denizens show themselves in the less particular environs of West Palm Beach (on the mainland).

The main residential section of Palm Beach – **the town** – is where you should spend most of your time. Start by strolling by the designer stores and high-class art galleries on **Worth Avenue**, on the southern boundary of town. It's cruised by Rolls Royces, Mercedes and Jaguars, and filled by some of the most upmarket stores and restaurants anywhere in the US. The most appealing aspect of the street is its **architecture**: stucco walls, Romanesque facades, and passageways leading to small courtyards where miniature bridges cross non-existent canals and spiral staircases climb to the upper levels.

Along **Cocoanut Row**, the white Doric columns fronting **Whitehall** (Tues–Sat 10am–5pm, Sun noon–5pm; $5) make it the most overtly ostentatious home on the island: a $4-million wedding present from Henry Flagler to his third wife, Mary Lily Kenan. As in many of Florida's first luxury homes, the interior design was pillaged from the great buildings of Europe: among the 73 rooms are an Italian library, a French salon, a Swiss billiard room, a hallway modelled on St Peter's, and a Louis XV ballroom. All are stuffed with ornamentation, but they lack aesthetic cohesion. Informative 45-minute **free guided tours** depart continuously from the 110ft hallway, and will leave you giddy with the tales of the earliest Palm Beach excesses.

Practicalities

Even by walking you'll get the measure of Palm Beach in a day. Either drive in along Hwy-A1A from the south, or arrive on foot using one of the two bridges over Lake Worth from West Palm Beach, which is the nearest **bus** and **train** stop.

The **Chamber of Commerce**, 45 Cocoanut Way (Mon–Fri 9am–5pm; ☎407/655-3282), provides maps and information. However, you'll need plenty of money to **sleep** in Palm Beach: rates of $200 a night are not uncommon. *Palm Beach Historic Inn*, 365 S County Rd (☎407/832-4009; ③–⑤), is a B&B with the best rates in town, but you'll need to book early. Otherwise come between May and December, when *The Chesterfield*, 363 Cocoanut Row (☎1-800/CHESTR-1; ③–⑥), the *Colony*, 155 Hammon Ave (☎1-800/521-5525; ③–⑥), and *The Plaza Inn*, 215 Brazilian Ave (☎1-800/832-8666; ③–⑥), have their lowest rates. It's far cheaper to stay outside Palm Beach and visit by day.

As for **eating**, *TooJay's*, 313 Poinciana Place (☎407/659-7232), is a bakery and deli with omelettes under $6; *Green's Pharmacy*, 151 N County Rd (☎407/833-4443), has a steady supply of diner food; and *Testa's*, 221 Royal Poinciana Way (☎407/832-0992), does exquisite seafood and pasta. If money is no object – and you're dressed to kill – make for *Café L'Europe*, 150 Worth Ave (☎407/655-4020). Spend less than $50 each in this super-elegant French restaurant and you'll still be hungry.

A former miner and prize-fighter, **Addison Mizner** was an unemployed architect when he arrived in Palm Beach in 1918. Inspired by the medieval buildings he'd seen around the Mediterranean, Mizner built the **Everglades Club**, at 356 Worth Ave – the first public building in Florida in the Mediterranean Revival style. The success of the club, and the house he subsequently built for society bigwig Eva Stotesbury, won Mizner commissions all over Palm Beach as the wintering wealthy decided to swap suites at one of Henry Flagler's hotels for a "million-dollar cottage" of their own.

Brilliant and unorthodox, Mizner's loggias and U-shaped interiors made the most of Florida's pleasant winter temperatures, while his twisting staircases to nowhere became legendary. Mizner used untrained workmen to lay crooked roof tiles, sprayed condensed milk onto walls to create an impression of centuries-old grime, and fired shotgun pellets into wood to imitate worm holes. By the mid-Twenties, Mizner had created the Palm Beach Style, and he later fashioned much of Boca Raton.

The Space Coast

The so-called **SPACE COAST**, the base of the country's space industry, occupies a flat, marshy island bulging into the Atlantic. Many visitors are surprised to find that the land from which the Space Shuttle leaves earth is also a sizeable wildlife refuge.

The Kennedy Space Center

Space vehicles continue to be developed, tested, and blasted into orbit at the **Kennedy Space Center**. Confusingly, the first launches were from the US Air Force base on Cape Canaveral (renamed Cape Kennedy 1963–73), from which unmanned satellites are still sent up. After the space programme was expanded in 1964, the center of activity became Merritt Island, between Cape Canaveral and the mainland.

Arrive early at **Spaceport USA** (daily 9am–6pm or later; free), reached via Hwy-405 from Titusville or Hwy-3 off Hwy-A1A, to avoid the crowds (thinnest on weekends and during May & Sept). The **museum** holds actual mission capsules, space suits, models of satellites, the Viking craft used on Mars, and a replica space-shuttle flight deck; the firework-like rockets which launched the early space shots stand outside in the **Rocket Garden**. Next door, the **Galaxy Theater** alternates two dramatic *IMAX* movies ($4).

The **"Red" bus tour** (2hr; $7) is the only way to see the rest of the Merritt Island space complex; buy tickets for it as soon as you arrive. It first crosses the "crawlerway" – the huge tracks along which the space shuttles are wheeled to the launch pad – on the way to the 52-storey **Vehicle Assembly Building** where the shuttles are assembled and fitted with their payloads. With luck, a door may be open and you'll get a slight sense of the innards of one of the world's largest structures. The most impressive part of the tour is, perversely, also the most contrived: a simulated Apollo countdown and take-off watched from behind the blinking screens of a mocked-up control room. For the dates and times of **launches** from the Space Center, phone ☎1-800-SHUTTLE; free passes can be reserved on ☎407/452-2121 (8am–4pm). Almost as good a view can, however, be had from anywhere within a forty-mile radius of the Space Center.

Staying over: Cocoa Beach
Unquestionably the best base from which to see the Space Coast, **COCOA BEACH** is just a few miles south on a ten-mile strip of shore washed by some of the biggest surfing waves in Florida. **Motel** bargains include an *Econo Lodge*, 5500 N Atlantic Ave (☎1-800/446-6900; ②), *Motel 6*, 3701 N Atlantic Ave (☎407/783-3103; ②), and the *Wakulla Motel*, 3550 N Atlantic Ave (☎407/783-2230; ③).

Merritt Island Wildlife Refuge

NASA doesn't have Merritt Island all to itself, but shares it with the **Merritt Island National Wildlife Refuge** (daily 8am–two hours before sunset; free), which allows alligators, armadillos, racoons and bobcats – and one of Florida's greatest gatherings of bird life – to live out their primeval existence beside some of the human world's most advanced technology. Winter is the **best time to visit**, when the island's skies are alive with tens of thousands of migratory birds from the frozen north, and mosquitoes are nowhere to be found. At any other period, and especially in summer, the island's Mosquito Lagoon is worthy of its name; bring ample insect repellent.

Seven miles east of Titusville on Route 406, the six-mile **Black Point wildlife drive** gives a solid introduction to the basics of the island's ecosystem; pick up the informative free leaflet at the entrance. Be sure to do some walking within the refuge, too. Off the wildlife drive, the five-mile **Cruickshank trail** weaves around the edge of the Indian River; or drive a few miles further east along Route 402 – branching from Route 406 just south of the wildlife drive – and tackle the half-mile **Oak Hammock trail** or the two-mile **Palm Hammock trail**, both accessible from the same parking lot.

Daytona Beach

The consummate Florida beach town, with its T-shirt shops, amusement arcades, and wall-to-wall motels, **DAYTONA BEACH** owes its existence to twenty miles of light brown sand where the only pressure is to strip off and enjoy yourself. For decades, life here has revolved around two major annual invasions. Thousands of leather-clad motorcyclists still arrive for the early March **Bike Week** races at the Daytona International Speedway, but Daytona has recently – and very controversially – decided to put a stop to its March and April **Spring Break** ritual, when half a million college kids come to indulge in underage drinking and libido liberation. Just how quickly that becomes a thing of the past remains to be seen, but its demise may at least give the town a chance to reveal its truer nature, as a small, medium-paced, down-to-earth resort.

Without a doubt, the best thing about Daytona Beach *is* the seemingly limitless **beach**: 500ft wide at low tide and fading dreamily into the heat haze. Pioneering auto enthusiasts such as Louis Chevrolet, Ransom Olds and Henry Ford came to these firm sands during the early 1900s to race prototype vehicles beside the ocean. The land speed record was regularly smashed, five times by millionaire British speedster Malcolm Campbell who, in 1935, roared along at 276mph. When high speeds made racing on the sands unsafe, the **Daytona International Speedway** was built, an ungainly configuration of concrete and steel three miles west of downtown along International Speedway Blvd (bus #9). Opened in 1959, it has a capacity of 150,000 and hosts eight major race meetings each year, starting in early February with the **Rolex 24**, a 24-hour race for GT prototype sports cars. A week or so later the qualifying races start for the biggest event of the year, the **Daytona 500** stock-car race in mid-February. Tickets for this sell out well in advance, and you should book accommodation at least six months ahead (cheapest tickets $20–25 for cars, $10–15 for bikes; ☎253-7233).

Though they can't capture the excitement of a race, guided minibus **tours** (daily 9am–5pm except race days; $3), take you around the remarkable curves, whose gradients make this the fastest – 180mph is not uncommon – racetrack in the world.

Practicalities

As Ridgewood Avenue, **US-1** steams through mainland Daytona, passing the *Greyhound* station at no 138 S (☎253-6576). By car, keep to **Hwy-A1A** (known as Atlantic Ave), which enters beachside Daytona. Local buses connect the two (☎761-

7700; no night or Sunday services); the bus terminal is at the junction of Palmetto and Volusia avenues in mainland Daytona. A "trolley" runs along the beach.

From mid-May to November, scores of small **motels** on Atlantic Avenue slash their rates. Any of the following makes a good beach base: *Catalina* (no 1400; ☎255-4588; ②–③); *Daytona Shores Inn* (no 805; ☎253-1441; ①–③); and *Robin Hood* (no 1150; ☎252-8228; ②–③). The big and superbly positioned **youth hostel**, at 140 S Atlantic Ave (☎258-6937; ①), charges members $12, others $15.

Good places for **lunch** include *Julian's*, 88 S Atlantic Ave (☎677-6767), a dimly lit mock-Tahitian lounge with great food, or *Lighthouse Landing* (☎761-9271), beside the Ponce Inlet Lighthouse, for fresh fish dishes. Big eaters will relish three **buffet restaurants**: *Kay's Coach House*, 734 Main St (☎253-1944), *Shoney's*, 2558 N Atlantic Ave (☎255-9054), and *Checkers*, 219 S Atlantic Ave (☎239-0010).

The nucleus of the **beachside action** is *HoJo's Party Complex*, 600 N Atlantic Ave (☎255-4471; $3–10), with bars, discos, and live rock and reggae. Simply for a **drink**, the *Boothill Saloon*, 318 Main St (☎258-9506), and *Froggies*, 800 Main St (☎253-0330), are enjoyable, or try *The Oyster Pub*, 555 Seabreeze Blvd (☎255-6348), where there's beer, dirt-cheap oysters and a loud jukebox.

St Augustine

Few places in Florida are as immediately engaging as **ST AUGUSTINE**, which has the size and even some of the looks of a small Mediterranean town. The oldest permanent settlement in the US, with much from its early days still intact along its narrow streets, it also offers two alluring lengths of beach just across the bay.

Ponce de León touched ground here in 1513, but European settlement began when Pedro Menéndez de Avilés put ashore on St Augustine's Day in 1565. Sir Francis Drake's ships razed the town in 1586, the first of many battles with the British before Florida was eventually ceded to Britain in 1763. By then the town was a major social and administrative center, soon to be capital of East Florida. Subsequently, Tallahassee (see p.480) became capital of a unified Florida, and St Augustine's fortunes waned. Expansion largely bypassed the town – a fact inadvertently making possible the **restoration programme** that has turned this quiet community into a fine historical showcase.

Arrival and Information

The *Greyhound* station, 100 Malaga St (☎829-6401), is a fifteen-minute walk from the center. St Augustine is best seen **on foot**, though a **sightseeing train** tours the main landmarks (170 San Marco Ave; daily 8am–5pm; $7). There's no public transit; if you don't have a car, get to the beaches, two miles away, by rented **bike** (from *Buddy Larsen's*, 130 King St; ☎824-2402), or **taxi** (☎824-8161). The **visitor center**, 10 Castillo Drive (daily 8.30am–5.30pm; ☎825-1000), shows a free film on the history of the town, and can fill you in on the numerous local festivals. Harbor **cruises** ($7) leave five or six times a day from the City Yacht Pier, near the foot of King Street.

The Old Town

St Augustine's historic area – or **Old Town** – along St George Street and south of the central plaza carries the well-tended evidence of the Spanish period. It may be small, but there's a lot to see: an early start, around 9am, will give you a lead on the tourist crowds and should enable a good look at almost everything inside a day.

> The **area code** for Daytona Beach and St Augustine is ☎904.

Given the fine state of the **Castillo de San Marcos** (Mon–Sat 8.45am–4.45pm, Sun 8.45am–6pm; free; regular free talks on the fort and local history), on the northern edge of the Old Town beside the bay, it's difficult to credit that the fortress was started in the late 1600s. Its longevity is down to its design: a diamond-shaped rampart at each corner maximized firepower, and 14ft-thick walls reduced vulnerability to attack. Inside, there's not a lot beyond a small museum and echoing rooms to admire, but venturing along the 35ft-high ramparts gives an unobstructed view over the city.

The eighteenth-century **City Gate** marks the entrance to **St George Street**, once the main thoroughfare and now a tourist-trampled pedestrianized strip. A fair-sized plot at St George and Cuna is taken up by the **Spanish Quarter Living Museum** (daily 9am–4pm; $5). In its eight reconstructed homes and workshops, volunteers disguised as Spanish settlers go about their daily tasks at spinning wheels, anvils and foot-driven wood lathes. It's not at all bad, but try to visit early in the day; crocodile lines of camera-wielding tourists substantially lessen the effect.

In the sixteenth century, the Spanish king decreed that all colonial towns had to be built around a central plaza; thus St George Street runs into **Plaza de la Constitucion**, a marketplace from 1598. On the north side of the plaza, the **Basilica Cathedral of St Augustine** (free tours Mon–Sat 1–3pm, Sun 1–5pm) adds a touch of grandeur, although it's largely a Sixties remake of the late eighteenth-century original.

Tourist numbers lessen as you cross **south of the plaza** into a web of quiet, narrow streets, just as old as St George Street. At 4 Artillery Lane, the **Oldest Store Museum** (summer Mon–Sat 9am–5pm, Sun 10am–5pm; rest of the year Mon–Sat 9am–5pm, Sun noon–5pm; $3.50) does an excellent job of re-creating a general store of the 1880s, filled to the rafters with foods and drinks, medicinal potions, and oversized consumer essentials such as cigar molds and wooden washing machines.

Close by, at 20 Aviles St, the **Ximenze Fatio House** (March–Aug, Thurs–Sat & Mon 11am–4pm, Sun 1–4pm; free) was favored by travellers who predated the town's first tourist boom, drawn by the airy balconies added to the original structure, which was built in 1797 for a Spanish merchant. More substantial history is unfurled a ten-minute walk away at the **Oldest House**, 14 St Francis St (daily 9am–5pm; $5), which is indeed the oldest house in town, and was occupied from the early 1700s by the family of an artillery hand at the castle.

The Beaches

Some fine **beaches** – packed at weekends – lie just a couple of miles from the Old Town. Across the bay, **St Augustine Beach** is family terrain, but the **Anastasia State Recreation Area** (daily 8am–sunset; cars $3.25, cyclists and pedestrians $1) offers a thousand protected acres of dunes, marshes and scrub, linked by nature walks. In the other direction (take May St, off San Marco Ave), **Vilano Beach** pulls a younger crowd.

Accommodation

Most of St Augustine's visitors stay between May and October, when rates rise by $10 to $20. Many restored inns in the Old Town offer **bed and breakfast**, and there are cheap **motels** outside the center along San Marco Avenue.

American Inn, 42 San Marco Ave (☎829-2292). The least expensive motel near the Old Town. ①.

Anchorage Motor Inn, 1 Dolphin Drive (☎829-9841). Waterside location, across the bay. ②–③.

Carriage Way, 70 Cuna St (☎829-2467). One of the Old Town's best-priced B&Bs. ③–④.

Kenwood Inn, 38 Marine St (☎824-2116). Handily positioned B&B in the Old Town. ③–④.

Vilano Beach Motel, 50 Vilano Rd (☎829-2651). This laid-back motel is one of the best beach bargains, a great base for enjoying the North Beach. ②.

Youth Hostel, 32 Treasury St (☎829-6163). The town's only hostel accommodation, very near the plaza. Members $10, others $13; third night for half price. ①.

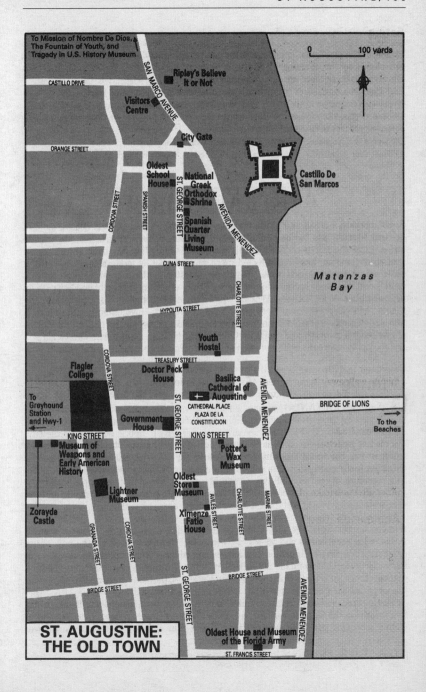

To Mission of Nombre De Dios,
The Fountain of Youth, and
Tragedy in U.S. History Museum

CASTILLO DRIVE

SAN MARCO AVENUE

Ripley's Believe
It or Not

Visitors
Centre

City Gate

ORANGE STREET

Oldest
School
House

ST. GEORGE STREET

National
Greek
Orthodox
Shrine

Spanish
Quarter
Living
Museum

CORDOVA STREET

SPANISH STREET

AVENIDA MENENDEZ

CUNA STREET

*Matanzas
Bay*

CHARLOTTE STREET

HYPOLITA STREET

Youth
Hostel

CORDOVA STREET

TREASURY STREET

Doctor Peck
House

Flagler
College

Basilica
Cathedral of
Augustine

ST. GEORGE STREET

CATHEDRAL PLACE

AVENIDA MENENDEZ

BRIDGE OF LIONS

To
Greyhound
Station
and Hwy-1

PLAZA DE LA
CONSTITUCION

Government
House

To the
Beaches

KING STREET

KING STREET

Museum of
Weapons and
Early American
History

Potter's
Wax
Museum

Oldest
Store
Museum

Lightner
Museum

Zorayda
Castle

Ximenez
Fatio
House

AVILES STREET

CHARLOTTE STREET

MARINE STREET

GRANADA STREET

CORDOVA STREET

ST. GEORGE STREET

BRIDGE STREET

BRIDGE STREET

AVENIDA MENENDEZ

ST. AUGUSTINE:
THE OLD TOWN

Oldest House and Museum
of the Florida Army

ST. FRANCIS STREET

0   100 yards

Castillo De
San Marcos

Eating

Eating in the Old Town is unusually expensive, and many of its cafés and restaurants are closed in the evening. If this is a problem, head across the bay to Anastasia Boulevard, where there are several good places.

Café Camacho, 11 Aviles St (☎824-7030). Cut-rate breakfasts and good-sized lunches.

Gypsy Cab Company, 828 Anastasia Blvd (☎824-8244). Greek and Italian food amid Art Deco style.

Scarlett O'Hara's, 70 Hypolita St (☎824-6535). Tasty soups and salads in the Old Town, and open in the evening for excellent fried crayfish suppers.

O'Steen's, 205 Anastasia Blvd (☎829-6974). Fish and shrimp feasts until 8.30pm.

El Toro Con Sombrero, 10 Anastasia Blvd (☎842-8852). Rowdy bar with Mexican food, jumping until 1am.

CENTRAL FLORIDA

Encompassing a broad and fertile expanse between the east and west coasts, most of **central Florida** was farming country when vacation-mania first struck the beachside strips. Over the last two decades, this picture of tranquillity has been shattered: no section of the state has been affected more dramatically by modern tourism, and the most visited part of Florida is also one of the ugliest. A clutter of freeway interchanges, motels and billboards arches around the small city of **Orlando**. The blame lies with its near-neighbor, **Walt Disney World**, which has sucked millions of people into the biggest and cleverest theme park complex ever created – involuntarily sparking off a tourist-dollar chase of Gold Rush magnitude on its outskirts. The rest of central Florida is markedly less brash and, north of Orlando particularly, rural towns like Ocala still typify Florida before the arrival of the highways and made-to-measure vacations.

Orlando

It's ironic that **ORLANDO**, a quiet farming town twenty years ago, now has more people passing through its environs than any other place in the state. Although reminders of the slow-paced Florida of an earlier era are easy to find in and around the city, the closest most people come is to the strings of motels along Hwy-192, fifteen miles south, or **International Drive**, five miles southwest – a brand new boulevard of hotels, shopping malls and restaurants, so short of character it could be molded from plastic. The reason is, of course, Walt Disney World, which pulls 25 million people a year to a previously featureless plot of scrubland. It's possible to pass through Orlando and not visit Walt Disney World, but there's no way you can escape its influence.

Nevertheless, despite enormous expansion over the last decade, Orlando itself remains impressively free of the commercialism that surrounds it. There is a small group of high-rise banks and offices in the compact downtown area but the bulk of the city comprises smart residential districts enhanced by recreational **parks** and several **lakes**. Historical leftovers and art collections spread through several sections will fill a diverse day – and, for anyone whose knowledge of the state begins and ends with theme parks, will give at least a brief taste of genuine Florida living.

The international **airport** is nine miles south of downtown Orlando; shuttle buses run to any hotel in the Orlando area for $10–15. Local bus #11 serves downtown Orlando (a 45-min journey; until 7.40pm Mon–Sat, 6.20pm Sun & hols). A taxi to downtown,

The **area code** for Orlando and central Florida is ☎407.

International Drive or the motels on Hwy-192 costs around $40. **Bus and train** arrivals are downtown, at the *Greyhound* terminal, 555 N Magruder Ave (☎843-7720), or the *Amtrak* station, 1400 Slight Blvd. Pick up the free *Official Visitor's Guide to Orlando* at the **visitor information center**, 8445 International Drive (daily 8am–8pm; ☎363-5871).

Getting Around: Visiting the Theme Parks

Local **buses** converge on the downtown Orlando terminal between Central and Pine streets: if you take route #8 to International Drive, you can catch a private **shuttle bus** to Walt Disney World. These connect the main accommodation areas with Walt Disney World, Sea World and Universal Studios – phone at least a day ahead to be picked up. *Rabbit Bus* (☎291-2424) charges $8 return to Walt Disney World, $5 to Sea World and Universal Studios; or try *Mears Transportation Service* (☎423-5566). If you don't rent a car, **taxis** are the only way to get around at night – try *Yellow Cab* (☎699-9999).

Accommodation

If you're going to Walt Disney World, Orlando is the obvious base. The only budget choices are two hostels in **downtown Orlando**, which is where you'll have to stay if you're dependent on public transit. Scores of plain but cheap motels line **Hwy-192** between Walt Disney World and Kissimmee. Most package tourists end up in pricey chain hotels on **International Drive**; independent travellers who show up on spec during the slow winter periods may find some bargains.

A1 Motel, 4030 W Hwy-192 (☎1-800/231-9196). Medium-sized motel. Closer to Kissimmee than Walt Disney World, it shaves a few dollars off the rates of its counterparts a few miles west. ①–②.

Casa Rosa, 4600 W Hwy-192 (☎1-800/432-0665). A generally quiet and relaxing motel with mood-enhancing Mediterranean-style architecture. ①.

Days Inn Lakeside, 7335 Sand Lake Rd (☎351-1900). Enormous branch of the nationwide chain in a winning lakeside location along International Drive, with a small beach and three pools. ③–④.

Harley Hotel, 151 E Washington St (☎352-0008). Historic, now modernized hotel by Lake Eola. ④.

Heritage Inn, 9861 International Drive (☎1-800/447-1890). Plain rooms at modest rates, plus pool and breakfast buffet. A kitsch shrine to Southern Victoriana, with live jazz some evenings. ③–④.

Maple Leaf Motel, 4647 W Hwy-192 (☎396-0300). Several people sharing a room will find the special offers here very attractive; features include cable TV, a pool and coin-op laundromat. ①.

Orlando International Youth Hostel, 227 N Eola Drive (☎843-8888). In an atmospheric residential area. Beds in small dorms for $12 (non-members $15), private singles and doubles under $30. ①.

Red Roof Inn, 9922 Hawaiian Court (☎352-1507). Unelaborate but perfectly serviceable budget-range base on International Drive, with a pool and a coin-op laundromat. ②–④.

Young Women's Community Club, 107 E Hillcrest St (☎425-2502). Women aged 16–54 who are AYH members can get a dorm bed here for $10; the facilities include a pool and small gym. ①.

Eating

The only problem with **eating** in the Orlando area is wading through the choices. Downtown and its environs hold the pick of the locals' haunts, while tourist custom around International Drive results in a glut of overpriced eating places, but spread among them are some inexpensive all-day buffets and serious gourmet restaurants.

Cricketers Arms, Mercado Mediterranean Mall, 8445 International Drive (☎254-0686). Fish and chips, pies and pasties complement a range of imported ales and lagers at this inexpensive nook.

El Bohio Café, 5756 Dahlia Drive (☎282-1723). Generous portions of Cuban food downtown.

Lilia's Philipine Delights, 3150 S Orange Avenue Drive (☎851-9087). Mouthwatering downtown selection of Filipino dishes, sadly of varying quality. If you're seriously hungry, go for the whole pig.

Medieval Times, 4510 Hwy-192 (☎1-800/229-8300). Knights swordfight and joust on horseback as you tuck into a feast inside a replica eleventh-century castle.

Ming Court, 9188 International Drive (☎351-9988). Chinese cuisine of an exceptionally high standard makes this the best dining spot on International Drive; not as costly as you might expect.

Le Peep, 250 S Orange Ave (☎849-0428). Quick bites downtown – sandwiches, soups, pancakes etc.

Walt Disney World

As significant as air-conditioning in making the state' what it is today, **WALT DISNEY WORLD** turned a wedge of Florida cow fields into one of the world's most lucrative vacation venues within ten years. The immense and astutely planned empire also pushed the state's media profile through the roof: from being a down-at-heel mixture of cheap motels, retirement homes and clapped-out alligator zoos, Florida suddenly became a showcase of modern international tourism.

Walt Disney World is very much the pacesetter among theme parks: it goes way beyond Walt Disney's original "theme park" – Disneyland, which opened in Los Angeles in 1955 (see p.775) – delivering escapism at its most technologically advanced and psychologically brilliant across an area twice the size of Manhattan. In a crime-free environment where all-American values dominate and the concept of good clean fun finds its ultimate expression, Walt Disney World often makes the real world – and its problems – seem like a distant memory.

Costs may come as a shock, especially to families (who should note that the whole place is much less geared to kids than might be expected), but the admission fee allows unlimited access to all the shows and rides in the relevant park. There's a strict embargo on bringing **food and drink** into the parks, where restaurants and snack bars are plentiful but pricey. The themed **hotels** within Walt Disney World itself can also be expensive (averaging around $200 per night), and require advance reservations.

Seeing Walt Disney World: the Main Parks

Walt Disney World's three main theme parks are quite separate entities. The **Magic Kingdom** is the Disney park everyone imagines, where Mickey Mouse mingles with the crowds – very much the park for kids. Recognizable for its giant, golfball-like geosphere, **EPCOT Center** is Disney's celebration of science and technology; boring for young kids, it's a sprawling area that involves a lot of walking. The newest and most easily assimilated of the three, **Disney-MGM Studios**, suits almost everyone; its special effects are enjoyable even if you've never seen the movies they're based on. Doing justice to all three parks will take at least four days – one day should be set aside for rest – and you shouldn't tackle more than one on any single day. If you only have one day to spare, pick the park that appeals most and stick to it.

THE WORLD OF WALT DISNEY

When brilliant illustrator and animator Walt Disney devised the world's first theme park, LA's Disneyland (see p.775), he left himself with no control over the hotels and restaurants which quickly engulfed it, preventing growth and racking off profits Disney felt were rightly his. Determined not to let that happen again, the Disney corporation secretly bought up 27,500 acres of central Florida farmland, acquiring by the late Sixties a site a hundred times bigger than Disneyland. With the promise of a jobs bonanza for Florida, the state legislature gave the corporation the rights of any major municipality: empowering it to lay roads, enact building codes, and enforce the law with its own security force.

Walt Disney World's first park, the Magic Kingdom, which opened in 1971, was a huge success. Unveiled in 1982, the far more ambitious EPCOT Center represented the first major break from cartoon-based escapism, but its rose-tinted look at the future received a mixed response. Partly due to this, and some cockeyed management decisions, the Disney empire (Disney himself died in 1966) faced bankruptcy by the mid-Eighties. Since then, clever marketing has brought the corporation back from the abyss – although EuroDisney looks an increasingly embarrassing undertaking – as it aims to increase Walt Disney World's 100,000 daily visitors and stay ahead of its rivals.

The **busiest periods** are mid-February to August, and from Christmas Day to New Year's Day. The slowest months are January, September, October and November. The **busiest day** is Tuesday, with Friday and Sunday the least crowded. If you **arrive early** at a park (say, 8am), you can easily get through the most popular rides before the mid-afternoon crush. For details of **getting there from Orlando**, see "Orlando", p.465.

Opening Times and Tickets; and Pleasure Island
Each park **opens** daily from 9am to 11pm between February and August, and otherwise from 9am to 9pm, with extended hours on holidays. **One-day tickets** cost $35 (under-tens $28; children under three free) from any park entrance, and allow **entry to one park only**, with unlimited passouts. To see more than two of the parks, use a **passport**, permitting entry to all three parks and free use of the shuttle buses. **Four-day passports** cost $125 (children $98); **five-day passports** cost $170 (children $135).

The **parking lots** (fee $4) are enormous, so make at least a mental note of where exactly you're parked to save hours of embarrassed searching later on. A complex **transportation system** uses buses and a monorail to cover Walt Disney World, linking the hotels and parking lots with the main attractions.

The Magic Kingdom
The **Magic Kingdom** firmly follows the formula established by California's Disneyland, dividing into the four sections **Adventureland**, **Tomorrowland**, **Fantasyland** and **Frontierland** (in declining order of merit). Some rides are identical to their Californian forebears; some are greatly improved. Like its older relative, the only way to deal with the place is enthusiastically, by going on every ride you can.

The ride with the cleverest special effects also has the fastest-moving queues, so hold back from joining the **Pirates of the Caribbean** – a hair-raising boat ride through a pirate attack on a Caribbean island – until the mid-afternoon crowds jam-pack everything else. **Space Mountain** offers a gut-churning trip around distant galaxies on a ferocious switchback, and **Splash Mountain** (memorably satirized by *The Simpsons*) does much the same, using water to great effect. People with weak hearts steer towards the less frenetic runaway train of **Big Thunder Mountain Railroad**. Elsewhere, the most bizarre sight comes with the **Tropical Serenade**, where The Enchanted Tiki Birds – "AudioAnimatronic" robots of birds, flowers and Tiki-god statues – sing and whistle through a programme of South Seas musical favorites.

EPCOT Center
Even before the new Magic Kingdom opened, Walt Disney was developing plans for **EPCOT Center**, or Experimental Prototype Community of Tomorrow, conceived in 1966 as a real community experimenting and working with the new ideas and materials of the technologically advancing US. The idea failed to shape up as Disney had envisioned: EPCOT didn't open its gates until 1982, when global recession and ecological concerns had put paid to utopian notions based on the infallibility of science. One drawback of this park is simply its immense size: twice as big as the Magic Kingdom and very sapping on the feet.

Inside the unmissable 180ft geosphere (unlike a semicircular geodesic *dome*, the geo*sphere* is completely round), *Future World*, a reminder of the park's original concept, details the history and possible advances to be made in agriculture, transportation, energy and communications. The best of the rides here – all corporately sponsored, so don't expect any mention of alternative power or global warming – are **Universe of Energy**, a venture into the dinosaur-era, when fossil fuels were being formed; **Wonders of Life**, a fantastic voyage through the body's immune system; and **The Living Seas**, Disney's retort to Sea World (see opposite), the world's largest artificial saltwater environment, occupied by a multitude of dolphins, sharks and sea lions.

Disney-MGM Studios

When the Disney corporation began making films and TV shows for adults – most notably *Who Killed Roger Rabbit* – they also set about devising a theme park to entertain adults as much as kids. Buying the rights to the Metro-Goldwyn-Mayer (MGM) oeuvre of films and TV shows, Disney acquired a vast repertoire of instantly familiar images to mold into shows and rides. Opening in 1990, **Disney-MGM Studios** served to mute the opening of Florida's Universal Studios (see opposite), and at the same time found an extra use for the real film studios based here – the people you'll see laboring over storyboards aren't there for show, they are genuinely making films.

If you arrive early, avoid a long wait in the sun later on by going straight on the two-hour **Backstage Tour**, visiting film production facilities and venturing around Disney's animation studios: the interest level fluctuates but you won't have had your money's worth if you miss it. The same applies to the **Indiana Jones Stunt Spectacular**, re-creating – and explaining – many of the action-packed set pieces from the Spielberg films. **Star Tours**, a flight-simulator trip piloted by *Star Wars* characters R2D2 and C-3PO, is the most physical ride in the park by a long way – passengers' seatbelts are carefully checked before lift-off. For laughs, go to **Superstar Television**, which plucks volunteers from the crowd to read the news, appear in *The Lucy Show* or team up with *The Golden Girls* – one place in Walt Disney World where the fun is spontaneous.

Walt Disney World Accommodation

If you want to be in Walt Disney World even when you're asleep, you'll be relieved to find a number of fully equipped resort-style Disney-owned **hotels** scattered around the complex (transportation by boat, bus or monorail is complimentary between them and the main theme parks). Predictably, prices are much higher – sometimes above $300 per night – than you'll pay elsewhere. Three Disney hotels, however, are specifically intended for the less affluent visitor, averaging $80–90 a night.

Though rooms may be available at short notice during quiet times, you should book as far ahead – nine months is not unreasonable – as possible. **Reservations** can be made through a single phone number: ☎407/W DISNEY.

Dixie Landing Resort. A moderately priced, Southern-themed hotel in the Disney Village area, with rooms in the "manor house" or in the "bayou cottages" set in the grounds. ④–⑤.

Port Orleans Resort. Gaze from your wrought-iron balcony across the mini New Orleans re-created in this resort's courtyard, in Disney Village. ④–⑤.

Caribbean Beach Resort. Disney's first attempt to create a "budget-priced" hotel still works rather well; the rooms at this plushly landscaped property in the EPCOT Resort are located in one of five lodges, each of which has its own pool. ④–⑤.

The Dolphin. Disney's latest and greatest hotel, topped by a giant sculpted dolphin, decorated in dizzying pastel shades and with reproduction artworks from the likes of Matisse and Warhol. ⑧.

Contemporary Resort. The Disney monorail runs right through the center of this Magic Kingdom hotel, which takes its design ideas from the futuristic fantasies of Tomorrowland. ⑨.

Fort Wilderness Resort and Campground. Hook up your RV or pitch your tent for $35–46, or rent a six-berth trailer for around $160. In the Magic Kingdom area.

Disney Nightlife: Pleasure Island

From around 9pm, each Walt Disney World park holds some kind of closing time bash, usually involving fireworks and fountains. For more solid night-time entertainment, the corporation devised **Pleasure Island**, exit 26B off I-4, a remake of an abandoned island, whose pseudo-warehouses are the setting for a mixture of vaguely enjoyable themed bars and nightclubs. The most enjoyable are the *Comedy Warehouse* and the *Adventurers Club*, loosely based on a 1930s gentlemen's club. Walking around Pleasure Island is free, as is the live open-air music, but to go inside any of the nightclubs – which are open from 7pm until 2am – you need a $13.95 **ticket** from one of the booths at the entry points, which lets you wander in and out of them all (assuming you're over 21 and have the ID to prove it).

Universal Studios and Sea World

If you've spent time at Walt Disney World and enjoyed it, you'll find it hard to resist the other two attractions in the Orlando area, which sit either side of the International Drive visitor information center on the way back towards downtown Orlando.

Universal Studios

Half a mile north of Exit 30B off I-4. Daily, winter 9am–7pm, longer in summer. $33 for ages 10 and older, $26 ages 2–9; two day passes for $53 and $42 respectively.

All the predictions suggest that Florida will be the US moving-image capital of the next century. The opening of **UNIVERSAL STUDIOS** in 1990 did nothing to dampen such speculation. Florida's Universal, like its competitor Disney-MGM, is a working studio, filling more than four hundred acres with the latest in TV and movie production technology and already turning out major features – as well as a bunch of tedious sitcoms. As a theme park, however, Universal is still struggling to justify the hype which surrounded its opening. Overall, the rides are more spectacular than those at Disney-MGM, with less emphasis on movie nostalgia – but the park has a less homely feel and only the very energetic can take it all in inside a day.

For sheer excitement, nothing in the park compares to **Back to the Future**, a bone-shaking flight-simulator time trip from 2015 to the Ice Age. Next best is **Ghostbusters**, for its finely judged mix of audience participation and inventive special effects. Moving on, neither the rickety **Earthquake – The Big One**, a ride into an 8.3 Richter-scale earthquake aboard a San Francisco subway train, nor the six-ton version of King Kong in **Kongfrontation**, which attacks your cable car amid cracks of thunder and lightning high above New York's East River, is particularly memorable – or worth a lengthy wait. Similarly, **ET's Adventure** is a rather dull ride on pretend bicycles to ET's home planet, although ET speaking your name as you leave is a pleasing touch. Elsewhere, there are attempts to demystify production techniques, the most successful being **Alfred Hitchcock: The Art of Making Movies**, exploring some of the visual tricks employed by Hitchcock, with intriguing glimpses of some of Hitch's better films.

Sea World

6227 Sea Harbor Drive. Daily, winter 9am–7pm, longer in summer. $31.95.

SEA WORLD, the cream of Florida's sizeable crop of marine parks, should not be missed; and be sure to allocate a whole day to see it all. The big event is the *Shamu* show – twenty minutes of tricks performed by a playful killer whale. With substantially less razzmatazz, plenty of smaller tanks and displays explain more than you need to know about the undersea world. Among the highlights, the **Penguin Encounter** attempts to re-create Antarctica with scores of waddling birds scampering over an iceberg; the occupants of the **Dolphin Pool** assert their advanced intellect by flapping their fins and drenching passers-by; and **Sharks!** includes a walk through a glass-sided tunnel, offering the closest eye-contact you're ever likely to have with a shark and live to tell the tale. Most impressive of all, however, at least for thrills and spills, is **Mission Bermuda Triangle**.

THE WEST COAST

In three hundred miles from the state's southern tip to the border of the Panhandle, Florida's **west coast** embraces all the extremes. Buzzing, youthful towns neighbor placid fishing hamlets; mobbed holiday strips are just minutes from desolate swamplands. Surprises are plentiful, though the coast's one constant is proximity to the Gulf of Mexico – and sunset views rivalled only by those of the Florida Keys.

The largest city, **Tampa**, won't unduly detain you, though it does have more to offer than its corporate towers initially suggest – not least its long-established Cuban community. For the mass of visitors, though, the Tampa Bay area begins and ends with the **St Petersburg beaches**, whose miles of sea, sun and sand are undiluted vacation territory. South of Tampa, a string of barrier-island beaches runs the length of the Gulf, and the mainland towns which provide access to them – such as Sarasota and Fort Myers – have enough to warrant a stop. But really, the best move is inland, to the **Everglades National Park**, explorable on simple walking trails, by canoeing, or by spending the night at backcountry campgrounds with only the alligators for company.

Tampa

A small city with an infectious, upbeat mood, **TAMPA** only takes a day to explore thoroughly; but you'll depart with a lasting impression of a city on the rise. The business hub of the west coast, Tampa has been one of the major benefactors of the recent flood of money into Florida – of which it lavishes an impressive amount on a cultural diet envied by many of its larger rivals. In spite of this, Tampa gets scant regard from most visitors, who aim straight for the Gulf coast beaches half an hour's drive west and miss out totally on its urban energy.

Tampa began as a small settlement beside a US army base built to keep an eye on the Seminoles during the 1820s. In the 1880s the railroad arrived, and the Hillsborough River on which the city stands was dredged to allow sea-going vessels to dock. Tampa became a booming port, simultaneously acquiring a major tobacco industry as thousands of Cubans moved north from Key West to the new cigar factories of neighboring Ybor City. The Depression saw off the economic surge, but the port remained one of the busiest in the country and tempered Tampa's post-war decline. While the social problems that blight any US city are evident, there seems little to stand in the way of Tampa's continued emergence as a forward-thinking and financially secure community.

Arriving, Information and Getting Around

The city's **airport** (☎870-8700) is five miles northwest of downtown: local bus #30 is the least costly connection, or use the *Central Florida Transit* minivans ($10; ☎276-2730). If you're heading for St Petersburg use the around-the-clock *Limo Inc* buses (☎572-1111); flat fare to any coastal accommodation is $25. **Taxis** (try *United*, ☎253-2424, or *Yellow*, ☎253-8871) to downtown or a Busch Blvd motel cost $12 to $15; to St Petersburg or the beaches, $35 to $45. All the major **car rental** companies have desks at the airport. *Greyhound* **buses** terminate downtown at 610 Polk St (☎229-2174); **trains** arrive at 601 Nebraska Ave (☎221-7600).

In downtown Tampa, get general information from the **visitor center** at 111 Madison St (Mon–Sat 9am–5pm; ☎1-800/44-TAMPA). The **Ybor City Chamber of Commerce** is at 1513 Eighth St in Ybor City (Mon–Fri 9am–5pm; ☎248-3712).

The **area code** for Tampa, the west coast and the Everglades is ☎813.

Although both downtown Tampa and Ybor City are easily covered on foot, to travel between them without a car you'll need to use **local buses** (☎254-HART), whose routes fan out from Marion Street in downtown Tampa. Useful numbers are #8 to Ybor City and #30 to the airport. Rush-hour commuter buses run **between Tampa and the coast** – #100 to St Petersburg and #200 to Clearwater. Alternatives are the numerous daily *Greyhound* buses or the twice-daily *Amtrak* bus.

Downtown Tampa

Upright office towers are proof of **downtown Tampa**'s prosperous present. Aside from riverside warehouses in various states of dilapidation around the northern end of the pedestrianized **Franklin Street** (once the district's main drag and still the best place to get your bearings), recalling the city's past is largely left to plaques detailing everything from the passage of sixteenth-century explorer Hernando de Soto to the site of Florida's first radio station. None of the contemporary buildings in downtown Tampa better reflects the city's striving for cultural articulacy than the **Tampa Museum of Art**, on the banks of the Hillsborough River at 601 Doyle Carlton Drive (Tues–Sat 10am–5pm, Sun 1–5pm; $3.50; free guided tours daily at noon & 1pm). The highly regarded museum specializes in classical antiquities and twentieth-century American art: selections from the permanent modern stock are cleverly blended with prime loaned specimens of recent US painting, photography and sculpture.

Further south, you'll feel like an insignificant speck at the feet of the city's tallest structures. For a better view of them – and their surrounds – make the short monorail ride (from the top of the Fort Brooke Parking Garage on Whiting Street) to **Harbor Island**, a large shopping mall on a small island dredged from the Hillsborough Bay. From here you'll see the silver minarets, cupolas and domes on the far side of the river, sprouting from the main building of the University of Tampa – formerly the **Tampa Bay Hotel**, and financed by steamship and railroad magnate Henry B Plant. To reach it, walk across the river on Kennedy Boulevard and descend the steps into Plant Park.

The structure is as bizarre a sight in today's Tampa as it was on its opening in 1891, when its five hundred rooms looked out on a community of just seven hundred souls. Plant had been buying up bankrupt railroads since the Civil War, steadily inching his way into Florida to meet his steamships unloading at Tampa's harbor, and was wealthy enough to put fantasies of creating the world's most luxurious hotel into practice without worrying about the cost. But lack of care for the fittings (the hotel was only used during winter and left to fester during the scorching summer), and Plant's death in 1899 hastened its transformation from the last word in comfort to a pile of crumbling plaster. The city authorities bought it in 1905 and halted the rot, leasing it to the fledgling Tampa University 23 years later. In a wing of the main building, the **Plant Museum** (Tues–Sat 10am–4pm, Sun noon–4pm; $3) holds what's left of the hotel's furnishings, which were largely the fruits of a half-million-dollar shopping trip across Europe and Asia by Plant and his wife.

A few strides from the museum, the former lobby makes a popular rendezvous for the university's two thousand students. You can roam around much of the building at will, but the details only fall into place on the **free guided tour**, departing from the lobby at 1.30pm on Tuesday and Thursday (Sept–May only).

Ybor City

In 1886, as soon as Henry Plant's ships ensured a regular supply of Havana tobacco into Tampa, cigar magnate Don Vincente Martinez Ybor cleared a patch of scrubland three miles northeast of present-day downtown Tampa and laid the foundations of **YBOR CITY**. Around twenty thousand migrants, mostly Cuban, settled here and created a Latin American enclave, producing the top-class hand-rolled cigars that made Tampa the "Cigar Capital of the World". However, mass-production, the popularity of cigarettes, and the Depression proved a fatal combination for skilled cigar makers: as unemployment struck, Ybor City's tight-knit blocks of cobbled streets and red-brick buildings became surrounded by drab low-rent neighborhoods.

Over the last few years, efforts to mold Ybor City into a tourist attraction have saved many older buildings from dereliction. As yet, visitors are too few to over-commercialize the place: shops still sell hand-rolled cigars, and the smell of Cuban bread and freshly brewed coffee are never far off. Take it in by strolling the ten blocks of Seventh and Eighth avenues east of 13th Street. The **Ybor City State Museum**, 1818 Ninth Ave (Tues–Sat 9am–noon & 1–5pm; $1), helps you grasp the main points of Ybor City's creation and its multiethnic make-up. The factory where the cigar-rolling took place is now converted into shops, restaurants and snack bars as **Ybor Square**, 1901 13th St (Mon–Sat 9.30am–5.30pm, Sun noon–5.30pm). Standing on the factory's steps in 1893, the Cuban poet and independence fighter José Martí called for "money, machetes and manpower" for the country's anti-Spanish struggles – expatriate cigar workers responded by contributing ten percent of their earnings.

Accommodation

Tampa is not generously supplied with low-cost **accommodation**; you'll almost certainly save money by sleeping in St Petersburg or at the beaches. There are some good deals, though, in the **motels** along Busch Blvd, six miles north.

Economy Inn, 1810 E Busch Blvd (☎1-800/527-0605). Plain, simple motel near Busch Gardens. ②.

Garden View, 2500 E Busch Blvd (☎933-3958). No-frills but dependable accommodation. ②.

Golden Key, 2523 E Busch Blvd (☎933-6760). Another standard strip motel. ②.

Hampton Inn, 4817 W Laurel St (☎878-0778). Best value near the airport. ③.

Riverside, 200 N Ashley Drive (☎1-800/AT TAMPA). Good, bright downtown hotel, where arriving on spec on a quiet day should secure lower than usual rates. ④–⑥.

Eating

Choice and quality are features of Tampa **eating**, though in downtown you'll need to be content with the basic lunchtime sandwich stops servicing office folk. Ybor City, not surprisingly, is the place to go for Cuban food.

Café Creole & Oyster Bar, 1330 Ninth Ave, Ybor City (☎247-6283). This café excels in spicy Cajun dishes – try the filling gumbo seafood soup.

Columbia, 2117 Seventh Ave, Ybor City (☎821-0983). Refined Spanish and Cuban food, served in the same place since 1905.

Eighth Avenue Bistro, 1906 Avenida de Cuba, Ybor City (☎248-8283). Trendy stop for creative sandwiches and burgers.

Gladstone's Grilled Chicken, 502 Tampa St (☎221-2988). Poultry like you've never tasted before.

New Soul Sandwich Shop, 518 N Willow Ave (☎251-3720). Southern staples, like fried chicken and collard greens, added to the standard sandwich fillings.

Silver Ring, 1831 E Seventh Ave, Ybor City (☎248-2459). The *Silver Ring* has been serving simple but authentic Cuban sandwiches for nearly fifty years.

Nightlife

Many live music venues and nightclubs have tempting **drink** reductions, although the most cost-effective way to booze is at the **happy hours** all over the city – just watch for the signs. For **nightlife listings**, read the free *Creative Loafing* and *Tampa Tonite*, or buy the Friday edition of the *Tampa Tribune*.

Comedy Works, 3447 W Kennedy Blvd (☎875-9129). Long-running comedy club; cover $3–10.

Irish Pub, 1721 E Seventh Ave, Ybor City (☎248-2099). Convivial spot for late-night drinking.

The Ritz, 1503 E Seventh Ave, Ybor City (☎247-PLAY). Tampa's only purpose-built theater. Two stages see fringe and bigger-budget mainstream productions, costing $10–15, as well as live music.

Skipper's Smokehouse, 910 Skipper Rd (☎971-0666). Dependable for live blues and reggae.

Three Birds Bookstore and Coffee Room, 1518 Seventh Ave, Ybor City (☎247-7041). A hang-out of Tampa's coffee-drinking literary crowd; poetry readings on Thursday and Saturday.

St Petersburg

Declared the healthiest place in the US in 1885, **ST PETERSBURG**, twenty miles from Tampa on the eastern edge of the Pinellas peninsula, wasted no time in attracting the recuperating and the retired, at one point putting five thousand green benches on its streets to take the weight of elderly backsides. By the early 1980s, few people under the age of fifty lived in the town, and no one was surprised when it became the setting for the 1985 movie *Cocoon*, in which a group of local geriatrics magically regain the vigor of their youth. Right now, St Petersburg itself seems to be emulating them. The average age of its residents has been almost halved, the revamped pier is a great place for open-air socializing, and – most remarkably of all – the town has acquired a major collection of works by Salvador Dali: reason enough to be in St Petersburg, if only as a day's break from the St Petersburg Beaches, nine miles west.

Few places make a less likely depository for a huge museum of works by Dali than St Petersburg, but the **Salvador Dali Museum**, 1000 S Third St (Tues–Sat 9.30am–5.30pm, Sun noon–5pm; $5), stores more than a thousand paintings from the collection of a Cleveland industrialist who struck up a friendship with the controversial artist in the Forties. **Free tours** begin whenever sufficient people gather, and trace a chronological path around the works, from early experiments with Impressionism and Cubism to the seminal Surrealist canvas *Persistence of Memory*.

Once you've dealt with Dali, the quarter-mile-long **pier**, jutting from the end of Second Ave N, is the center of gravity in town. It often features browsable arts and crafts exhibitions, and tourist literature is piled at a desk near the inverted-pyramid-like building at its head, whose five storeys are packed with restaurants, shops and fast-food counters. At the foot of the pier, the **Historical and Flight One Museum** (Mon–Sat 10am–5pm, Sun 1–5pm; $4.50) modestly recounts St Petersburg's early twentieth-century heyday as a winter resort; its free *Historic Downtown Walking Tour* brochure pinpoints some of the town's older buildings within easy reach.

Practicalities

The *Greyhound* **bus** station is at 180 Ninth St (☎898-4455); the **train** station, 3601 31st St, is two miles west of downtown. There are no trains between Tampa and St Petersburg, just an *Amtrak* bus link. The **visitor center** is at 100 Second Ave N (Mon–Fri 9am–5pm; ☎821-4715).

Sleeping in St Petersburg can be less costly than doing so at the beaches. There are two **youth hostels** (members $12, others $15): *St Petersburg International Hostel*, 215 Central Ave (☎822-4095; ①), and the *St Petersburg AYH Hostel*, 326 First Ave (☎822-4141; ①). **Motels** can be exceptionally cheap, too – under $30 during the summer, under $40 in winter. Of dozens along Fourth St, the closest to the center are *Banyan* (no 610 N; ☎822-7072; ①–②), *Landmark* (no 1930; ☎895-1629; ①–②), and *Kentucky* (no 4246; ☎526-7373; ①–②). For an excellent and inexpensive seafood meal, head for *Fourth Street Shrimp Store*, 1006 Fourth St N (☎822-0325), or the innovative *Seabar*, 4912 Fourth St (☎527-8728), where you select your meal from the display and have it cooked to your desire.

The St Petersburg Beaches

Drab suburbs stretch west from St Petersburg, covering virtually all of the Pinellas peninsula, a bulky thumb of land poking between Tampa Bay and the Gulf of Mexico. Framing the Gulf side of the peninsula, a 25-mile chain of barrier islands forms the **St Petersburg Beaches**, one of Florida's busiest coastal strips. When the resorts of Miami Beach lost their allure during the Seventies, the St Petersburg Beaches grew in popularity with domestic travellers, and more recently they've become a major destination for package-holidaying Europeans. The sands are broad and beautiful, the sea is warm, and the sunsets are fabulous – but in no way is this Florida at its best or most diverse.

All **buses** to the beaches originate in St Petersburg at the **Williams Park terminal**, at the junction of First Ave N and Third St N; an information booth there has route details.

The Southern Beaches

In twenty-odd miles of heavily touristed coast, only **PASS-A-GRILLE**, at the very southern tip of the barrier island chain, has the look and feel of a genuine community – two miles of tidy houses, cared-for lawns, small shops, and a cluster of bars and restaurants. On weekends, informed locals come to enjoy one of the area's liveliest set of sands. A mile and a half north of Pass-a-Grille, the **Don Cesar Hotel**, 3400 Gulf Blvd (free guided tours on Fri at 11.30am; ☎360-1881; ⑦), is a grandiose pink castle, filling seven beachside acres. Opened in 1928, its glamour was short-lived; during the Depression part of the hotel was used as a warehouse, and later as the spring training base of the New York Yankees baseball team. The building received a $15-million rejuvenation during the Seventies, and regained its function as a hotel – a base for anyone with upwards of $150 a night to spare (and where much of Robert Altman's movie *Health* was shot).

Keeping to Gulf Boulevard brings you into the main section of **ST PETERSBURG BEACH**, uninspiring rows of hotels, motels and eating places grouped along Gulf Boulevard. Further north, **TREASURE ISLAND** is even less varied tourist territory, culminating in the wood-walled, tin-roofed shops of **John's Pass Village**, 12901 Gulf Blvd. Immediately north, Gulf Boulevard crosses an arching drawbridge into **MADEIRA BEACH**, which is essentially more of the same – although, if you can't make it to Pass-a-Grille, the local beach justifies a weekend fling.

The Northern Beaches

Much of the northern section of Sand Key, the longest barrier island in the St Petersburg chain and one of the wealthier portions of the coast, is taken up by stylish condos and time-share apartments. It ends with the pretty **Sand Key Park**, where tall palm trees frame a scintillating strip of sand. Among the nearby high-rises which somewhat mar the view is the *Sheraton Sand Key Resort*, venue of the liaison between TV evangelist Jim Bakker and model Jessica Hahn in 1987, which led to the fall from grace of the media preacher and, for a time, greatly boosted the hotel's custom.

Sand Key Park occupies one bank of Clearwater Pass, across which a belt of sparkling white sands characterizes the holiday town of **CLEARWATER BEACH**, whose streets still retain an endearing small-town feel. There are regular bus links between Clearwater Beach and the mainland town of Clearwater – across the two-mile causeway – where you'll find connections to St Petersburg and a *Greyhound* station.

Beach Practicalities

Hotels here tend to be filled with package tourists, and are always pricier than the **motels** that line mile after mile of Gulf Boulevard – typically $40 to $55 in winter, $10 to

$15 less during the summer. Remember, too, that you'll pay $5 to $10 extra for a room on the beach side of Gulf Boulevard compared to an identical room on the inland side. Pass-a-Grille makes the best base: choose between the *Keystone Motel*, 801 Gulf Way (☎360-1313; ③); *Pass-a-Grille Beach Motel*, 709 Gulf Way (☎1-800/544-4184; ③); or the cottages of *Gamble's Island's End Resort*, 1 Pass-a-Grille (☎360-5023; ④).

It's easy to find a decent place to **eat** around the beaches. *Hurricane Seafood Restaurant*, 807 Gulf Way (☎360-9558), sports a well-priced menu of the freshest seafood; *Pep's Sea Grille*, 5895 Gulf Blvd (☎367-3550), creates inspired matings of pasta and seafood; *Debby's*, 7370 Gulf Blvd (☎367-8700), serves substantial breakfasts and lunches at insubstantial prices; *Doe-Al*, 85 Corey Circle (☎360-7976), knocks out gigantic platefuls of Southern favorites; and in Clearwater Beach, *Frenchy's Café*, 41 Baymont St (☎446-3607), cooks up grouper burgers and shrimp sandwiches.

Sarasota

Rising on a gentle hillside beside the blue waters of Sarasota Bay, **SARASOTA** is one of Florida's better-off and better-looking towns, and also one of the state's leading cultural centers. It's home to numerous writers and artists, and the base of several respected performing arts companies. Despite periodic conservative flappings, the community is far less stuffy than its wealth, and the abundance of Neoclassical statues, fountains and manicured lawns decorating it, suggest. Downtown Sarasota itself has less impact than the Ringling estate on the town's northern edge – home of the art-loving millionaire from whom modern Sarasota takes its cue – and the barrier island beaches, a couple of miles away across the bay.

Northern Sarasota: the Ringling House and Museums
Don't fail to tour the house and art collections of **John Ringling**, a multimillionaire who gave Sarasota a taste for fine arts that it's never lost. One of the owners of the fantastically successful *Ringling Brothers Circus*, which toured the US from the 1890s, Ringling acquired a fortune estimated at $200 million (see also p.275). Recognizing Sarasota's investment potential, Ringling built the first causeway to the barrier islands and made this the winter base for his circus. His greatest gift to the town, however, was a Venetian Gothic mansion and an incredible collection of European Baroque paintings, displayed in a purpose-built museum beside the house.

To get to the **Ringling house and museums** (daily 10am–5.30pm, Oct–June Thurs 10am–10pm; $8.50), three miles north of downtown Sarasota beside US-41, use **buses #2 or #10**. Begin your exploration by walking through the gardens to the former Ringling residence, **Ca' d'Zan** ("House of John", in Venetian dialect), a gorgeous piece of work serenely situated beside the bay and – unlike contemporary mansions elsewhere in Florida – a triumph of taste and proportion. On trips to Europe to scout for new circus talent, Ringling became obsessed with Baroque art and acquired more than five hundred old masters: a gathering now regarded as one of the finest collections of its kind in the US. To display the paintings, a spacious **museum** was built around a mock fifteenth-century Italian palazzo. As with Ca' d'Zan, the very concept seems absurdly pretentious but, like the house, the idea works; the architecture matches the art with great aplomb. Five enormous paintings by Rubens, commissioned in 1625, and the painter's subsequent *Portrait of Archduke Ferdinand*, are the highlights, though there's also a wealth of talent from Europe's leading schools of the mid-sixteenth to mid-eighteenth centuries.

The **area code** for the Sarasota area is ☎813.

The Sarasota Beaches

Increasingly the stamping ground of European package tourists, spilling south from the St Petersburg Beaches, the white sands of the **Sarasota beaches** are gradually losing much of their scenic appeal to towering condos. For all that, they're worth a day of anybody's time, with the two islands on which they lie, Lido Key and Siesta Key, reachable by car and buses from the mainland. There is, however, no direct link between them.

The Ringling Causeway – take buses #4 or #18 – crosses the yacht-filled Sarasota Bay from the foot of Main Street to **Lido Key** and flows into **St Armands Circle**, a glorified traffic circle ringed by upmarket shops and restaurants. Continuing south along Benjamin Franklin Drive are the island's most easily accessible beaches, ending after two miles at the more attractive **South Lido Park** (daily 8am–sunset; free), a belt of dazzlingly bright sand beyond a large grassy park.

The bulbous northerly section of **Siesta Key**, reached by Siesta Drive off US-41 about five miles south of downtown Sarasota (bus #11), holds the bulk of the tadpole-shaped island's residents, on streets which twist around a network of canals. To escape the crowds at **Siesta Key Beach**, beside Ocean Beach Blvd, continue south past Crescent Beach, and follow Midnight Pass Rd for six miles to **Turtle Beach**, a small body of sand which has the island's only campground.

Practicalities

In downtown Sarasota, *Greyhound* **buses** stop at 575 N Washington Blvd (☎955-5735), and the *Amtrak* bus from Tampa pulls up at the **local bus terminal** on Lemon Ave, between First and Second streets (where you catch the buses out to the Ringling house or the beaches). A good way to explore the town and the islands is by **renting a bike** for around $20 per day from *Sarasota Bicycle Center*, 4048 Bee Ridge Rd (☎377-4505). Call at the **visitor center**, 655 N Tamiami Trail (Mon–Fri 9.30am–5pm, Sat 9am–noon; ☎1-800/522-9799), for the customary discount coupons and leaflets.

On the mainland, **motels** run the length of US-41 between the Ringling estate and downtown Sarasota, typically charging $25 to $40. Prices are higher at the beaches, with the lowest rates on Lido Key at the *Gulf Side Motel*, 138 Garfield Drive (☎388-2590; ③), and the *Lido Apartment Motel*, 528 S Polk Drive (☎388-1004; ②).

Fort Myers

FORT MYERS, fifty miles south, may lack the élan of Sarasota, but it's nonetheless one of the up-and-coming communities of the southwest coast, having recently undergone considerable expansion. Fortunately, most of the growth has occurred on the north side of the wide Caloosahatchee River, which the town straddles, allowing the traditional center, along the waterway's south shore, to remain relatively unspoiled.

Once across the Caloosahatchee River, US-41 strikes **downtown Fort Myers**, picturesquely nestled on the river's edge, where the community first took root and now very much the commercial base. You'll need to look to the creditable exhibitions of the **Fort Myers Historical Museum**, 2300 Peck St (Mon–Sat 9am–4.30pm, Sun 1–5pm; $2.50), for thorough insights into the past, which include the exploits of Doctor Franklin Miles, the local man who developed *Alka Seltzer*.

In 1885, six years after inventing the light bulb, **Thomas Edison** collapsed from exhaustion and was instructed by his doctor to find a warm working environment or face an early death. Vacationing in Florida, the 37-year-old Edison bought fourteen acres of land on the banks of the Caloosahatchee River and cleared a section of it to spend his remaining winters (he lived to be 84) at what became the **Edison Winter Home**, 2350 McGregor Blvd (guided tours every half-hour; Mon–Sat 9am–3.30pm, Sun

12.30–3.30pm; $10), a mile west of downtown. Edison's house (which you can only glimpse through the windows) is an anticlimax, its plainness probably due to the fact that he spent most of his waking hours inside the **laboratory**, attempting to turn the latex-rich sap of *solidago Edisoni* (a strain of goldenrod weed which he developed) into rubber. When the tour reaches the engrossing **museum** the full impact of Edison's achievements becomes apparent: a design for an improved ticker-tape machine provided him with the funds for the experiments which led to the creation of the phonograph in 1877, and financed research that resulted in the incandescent light bulb. Here, too, you'll see some of the ungainly cinema projectors derived from Edison's *Kinetoscope* – which brought him a million dollars a year in royalties from 1907.

The Fort Myers Beaches

Still being discovered by the holidaying multitudes, the **Fort Myers beaches**, fifteen miles south of downtown, are appreciably different in character from the west coast's more commercialized beach strips, with a cheerful seaside mood that's worth getting acquainted with. Accommodation is plentiful on and around Estero Blvd – reached by San Carlos Blvd, off McGregor Blvd – which runs the seven-mile length of **Estero Island**. Most activity revolves around the short fishing pier and the **Lynne Hall Memorial Park**, at the island's northern end.

Estero Island becomes increasingly residential as you press south, Estero Boulevard eventually swinging over a slender causeway onto the barely developed **San Carlos Island**. A few miles ahead, at the **Carl Johnson Park** (daily 8am–5pm; $1.50), a foot-path picks a trail over a couple of mangrove-fringed islands and several mullet-filled creeks to **Lovers Key**, a spectacularly secluded beach. If you don't fancy the half-mile walk, a free trolley will transport you between the park entrance and the beach.

Practicalities

To get from downtown to the beaches, take any bus to the Edison Square mall, then use #50 to Summerlin Square, from where a trolley continues to Estero Island and Carl Johnson Park (no local public transit on Sun). The *Greyhound* station is at 2275 Cleveland Ave (☎334-1011), just south of the downtown **Chamber of Commerce**, at 1365 Hendry St (Mon–Fri 9.30am–5pm; ☎334-1133).

Accommodation costs in and around Fort Myers are low between May and mid-December, when $10 to $20 gets lopped off the standard rates. Downtown, look along First St – *Sea Chest* (no 2571; ☎332-1545; ②–③) and *Ta Ki-Ki* (no 2631; ☎334-2135; ②–③) are among the cheapest – and there are many more along Cleveland Ave. At the beaches, try Estero Blvd and be prepared to spend $70, though in midweek you might find lower rates at *Beacon* (no 1240; ☎463-5264; ③–④); *Gulf* (no 2700; ☎463-9247; ③–④); or *Laughing Gull Cottages* (no 2890; ☎463-1346; ③–④).

The Everglades

Whatever scenic excitement you might anticipate from one of the country's more cele-brated natural areas, there's nothing to herald your arrival in the **EVERGLADES**, seventy miles south of Fort Myers – one of the natural world's most remarkable ecosystems. From the monotonous course of US-41, the most dramatic sights are small pockets of trees poking above a completely flat sawgrass plain. Yet these wide open spaces resonate with life, forming part of an ever-changing ecosystem, evolved through a one-off combination of climate, vegetation and wildlife.

Appearing as flat as a table-top, the oolitic limestone on which the Everglades stand actually tilts very slightly towards the southwest. For thousands of years, water from summer storms and the overflow of nearby Lake Okeechobee has moved slowly through the Everglades towards the coast. The water replenishes the sawgrass, growing on a thin layer of soil formed by decaying vegetation, and gives birth to the algae at the foot of a complex food chain which sustains much larger creatures, most importantly **alligators**. After the floodwaters have reached the sea, drained through the bedrock or simply evaporated, the Everglades are barren except for the water accumulated in ponds – or "gator holes" – created when an alligator senses water and clears the soil covering it with its tail. Besides nourishing the alligator, the pond provides a home for other wildlife until the summer rains return. **Sawgrass** covers much of the Everglades but where natural indentations in the limestone fill with soil, fertile tree islands – or **"hammocks"** – appear, just high enough to stand above the flood waters.

Several **Native American tribes** once lived hunter-gatherer existences in the Everglades; the shell mounds they built can still be seen in sections of the park. In the nineteenth century, Seminoles, fleeing white settlers from the north, also lived peaceably in the area. By the late 1800s, a few towns had sprung up, peopled by settlers who, unlike the Indians, looked to exploit the land. As Florida's population grew, the damage caused by hunting, road building, and draining for farmland gave rise to a significant **conservation** lobby. In 1947, a section of the Everglades was declared a National Park, but unrestrained commercial use of nearby areas continues to upset the Everglades' natural cycle. The 1500 miles of canals built to divert the flow of water away from the Everglades and towards the state's expanding cities, the poisoning caused by agricultural chemicals from local farmlands, and the broader changes wrought by global warming, could yet turn Florida's greatest natural asset into a wasteland.

The Everglades National Park

Throughout this century the Everglades' boundaries have steadily been pushed back by urban development, and the **Everglades National Park** bestows federal protection to only a comparatively small section around Florida's southeastern corner. It's in the park that the vital links holding the Everglades together become apparent: the all-important cycle of wet and dry seasons; the ability of alligators to discover water; the tree islands which provide sanctuaries for animals during the floods; and the forces, such as human demands for farmland and fresh water, which threaten to tear them apart.

Everglades City and Around

Purchased and named in the Twenties by an advertising executive dreaming of a subtropical metropolis, **EVERGLADES CITY**, a few miles south off US-41 along Route 29, now has a population of just under five hundred. Most who visit are solely intent on diminishing the stocks of sports fish living around the mangrove islands – the aptly titled **Ten Thousand Islands** – arranged like jigsaw-puzzle pieces around the coastline.

For a closer look at the mangroves, which safeguard the Everglades from surge tides, take one of the park-sanctioned winter-only **boat trips** (departures half-hourly 9.30am–5pm; $9–12) from the dock on Chokoloskee, a blob of land – actually an Indian shell mound – marking the end of Route 29. The dockside **visitor center** (daily 8.30am–5pm; ☎695-3311) provides details on the cruises and the excellent ranger-led **canoe trips** (winter Sat at 10am). In Chokoloskee, you can rent an RV by the night for $45 to $60 at *Outdoor Resorts* (☎695-2881), or get a cottage in the grounds of the *Everglades Gun & Lodge Club*, 200 Riverside Drive (☎695-4211), for around $50.

The Miccosukee Indian Village and Shark Valley

Driven out of central Florida by white settlers, several hundred Seminole Indians retreated to the Everglades during the nineteenth century, and their descendants – the

Miccosukee – still live here, though the coming of US-41 brought a fundamental change in their lifestyle as they set about grabbing their share of the tourist dollars. Four miles east of Forty Mile Bend, the **Miccosukee Indian Village** (daily 9am–5pm) symbolizes their uneasy compromise. In the souvenir shop, good-quality traditional crafts and clothes stand side-by-side with blatant tack, and in the "village" (entry $5), men turn logs into canoes and women cook over open fires. It's such a contrived affair that anyone with an ounce of sensitivity can't help but feel uneasy.

A mile east of the Indian Village, **SHARK VALLEY** (daily 8.30am–6pm; cars $3, pedestrians and cyclists $1) epitomizes the Everglades' "River of Grass" tag. From here, dotted by hardwood hammocks, the sawgrass plain stretches as far as the eye can see. Aside from a few simple walking trails close to the **visitor center** (daily, winter 8.30am–5.15pm, reduced hours in summer; ☎305/221-8776), you can see Shark Valley only from a fourteen-mile loop road, ideally covered by renting a **bike** ($2.50 per hour). Alternatively, a highly informative two-hour **tram tour** (winter hourly from 9am; summer at 9am, 11am, 1pm & 3pm; $6) stops frequently to view wildlife – but won't allow you to linger in any particular place, as you'll certainly want to do.

Flamingo

The **Flamingo** section of the park – the entire southerly portion – holds virtually everything that makes the Everglades tick: spend a day or two here and you'll quickly grasp the fundamentals of its complex ecology. From the **park entrance** (always open; cars $5, pedestrians and cyclists $2), the road passes the **main visitor center** (daily 8am–5pm; ☎305/253-2241) and continues for 38 miles to the tiny coastal settlement of **FLAMINGO**, perched on Florida's southern tip, a former fishing colony now comprising a marina, hotel and campground. A century ago, the only way to get here was by boat – it was so remote it didn't even have a name until the opening of a post office made one necessary. Then "Flamingo" was chosen, due to the abundant roseate spoonbills – pink-plumed birds which the locals failed to identify correctly as they killed them for their feathers.

Flamingo now does a brisk trade servicing the needs of sports fishing fanatics. On land, the **visitor center** (daily 8am–5pm; ☎695-3101 ext 182) and the marina of the *Flamingo Lodge*, the park's only hotel, are the activity bases. From the marina, the informative **backwater cruise** (daily at noon & 3pm; $9; reservations on ☎305/253-2241) makes a two-hour foray around the mangrove-enshrouded Whitewater Bay.

Park Practicalities

US-41 skirts the northern edge of the park, providing the only land access to the Everglades City and Shark Valley park entrances, and to the Indian Village. To reach the Flamingo entrance, you'll need to touch the edge of Miami and head south. There's **no public transit** along US-41, or to any of the park entrances. **Entering the park** is free at Everglades City; at Shark Valley and Flamingo you'll pay $3 and $5 respectively per car. Tickets are valid for seven days.

The park is **open all year**, but the most favorable time to visit is **winter** (Nov–April), when the receding floodwaters cause wildlife to congregate around gator holes, ranger-led activities are frequent and the mosquitoes are bearable. In **summer** (May–Oct), afternoon storms flood the prairies, park activities are substantially reduced and the mosquitoes are a severe annoyance.

There are two well-equipped **campgrounds** at Flamingo, and many backcountry spots (free, but you need a permit, issued at the visitor centers) on the longer walking and canoe trails. Spare space at Flamingo (which fills quickly) can be checked on the board just inside the park entrance. The only **rooms** within the park are at *Flamingo Lodge* (☎695-3101 or ☎305/253-2241; ④–⑤); make reservations for November to April months in advance.

THE PANHANDLE

Rubbing hard against Alabama in the west and Georgia in the north, the long, narrow **Panhandle** has much more in common with the states of the Deep South than with the rest of Florida. City sophisticates have countless jokes lampooning the folksy life-styles of the people here, but you won't get a true picture of Florida without seeing at least some of the Panhandle. Indeed, a century ago, the Panhandle *was* Florida. At the western edge, **Pensacola** was a busy port when Miami was still a swamp. Fertile soils lured wealthy plantation owners south and helped establish **Tallahassee** as a high-society gathering place and administrative center – a role which, as the state capital, it retains. But the decline of cotton, the chopping down of too many trees, and the coming of the East Coast railroad eventually left the Panhandle high and dry. Much of the inland region still seems neglected, and the **Apalachicola National Forest** is perhaps the best place in Florida to disappear into the wilderness. The **coastal Panhandle**, on the other hand, is enjoying better times, and despite rows of hotels, much is still untainted, with miles of blindingly white sands.

Tallahassee and Around

State capital though it is, **TALLAHASSEE** is a provincial city of oak trees and soft hills that won't take more than two days to explore in full. Briefcase-clutching bureaucrats set the mood around its small grid of central streets, where you'll find plentiful reminders of Florida's formative years. When Florida was incorporated into the US, Tallahassee was made its administrative base – the local Native Americans, the Tamali tribe, being unceremoniously dispatched to make room for the trio of log cabins in which the first Florida government sat in 1823. However, Tallahassee's own recent fortunes have been hindered by the lightning-paced development of south Florida, and – oddly distanced from most of the people it now governs – the city remains a conservative place.

A fifty-million-dollar eyesore dominates the square mile of **downtown Tallahassee** – the vertical vents of the towering **New Capitol Building**, at the junction of Apalachee Parkway and Monroe St (Mon–Fri 8.30am–5pm; free). The seat of Florida law-making consequently resembles a gigantic air-conditioning machine. Florida's growing army of bureaucrats had previously been crammed into the ninety-year-old **Old Capitol Building** (Mon–Fri 9am–4.30pm, Sat 10am–4.30pm, Sun noon–4.30pm; free) that stands in the shadow of its replacement. Altogether on a more human and welcoming scale, it's hard to credit that the Old Capitol's walls once echoed with the decisions that shaped modern Florida, though proof is provided by the absorbing exhibits contained within the side rooms.

For a more rounded history – easily the fullest account of Florida's past anywhere in the state – visit the **Museum of Florida History**, 500 S Bronough St (Mon–Fri 9am–4.30pm, Sat 10am–4.30pm, Sun noon–4.30pm; free). Detailed accounts of Paleo-Indian settlements, and the significance of their burial and temple mounds – some of which have been found on the edge of Tallahassee – are valuable tools in comprehending Florida's prehistory, and the imperialist crusades of the Spanish are outlined with copious finds. There's disappointingly little on the nineteenth-century Seminole Wars – one of the bloodier skeletons in Florida's closet – though there's much on the turn-of-the-century railroads that made Florida a winter resort for wealthy northerners.

Arrival and Information

The *Greyhound* **bus** terminal is at 112 W Tennessee St (☎222-4240), within walking distance of downtown and opposite the local bus station. You can get a **free ride** into downtown Tallahassee from the bus station with the **Old Town Trolley**, which runs to

The **area code** for Tallahassee, and the rest of the Panhandle, is ☎904.

the Civic Center (near the New Capitol Building) and back at fifteen-minute intervals on weekdays (7am–6pm). Otherwise, downtown Tallahassee is best seen **on foot**.

The **Chamber of Commerce**, 100 N Duval St (Mon–Fri 8.30am–5pm; ☎681-9200), has stacks of leaflets relating to the city and the surrounding area. For material covering Tallahassee, the rest of the Panhandle and much of the rest of the state, use the **Tallahassee Area Visitor Information Center** (Mon–Fri 8am–5pm, Sat & Sun 8.30am–4.30pm; ☎1-800/628-2866) on the ground floor of the New Capitol Building.

Accommodation

Accommodation in Tallahassee is only in short supply during the sixty-day sitting of the state legislature from early April, and on fall weekends when the Seminoles football team are playing at home. **Hotels** and **motels** on N Monroe Street, about three miles from downtown Tallahassee, are considerably less expensive than those downtown.

Econo Lodge, 2681 N Monroe St (☎1-800/424-4777). Dependable motel chain with good rates. ②.

Holiday Inn, 316 W Tennessee St (☎1-800/HOLIDAY). Cheapest downtown hotel choice. ④.

Osceola Hall, 500 Chapel Drive (☎222-5010). $25-a-night rooms in summer on the Florida State University campus. ①.

Super 8, 2702 N Monroe St (☎386-8818). Regular motel facilities between I-10 and downtown. ②.

Eating

With so many politicos passing through, there's plenty of good **food** in Tallahassee; the presence of 25,000 students at its two universities keeps it affordable.

Andrew's Adams Street Café, 228 S Adams St (☎222-3446). Stylish lunch café.

Andrew's Second Act, 102 W Jefferson St (☎222-3446). Pricey evening meals in a classy restaurant.

Barnacle Bill's, 1830 N Monroe St (☎385-8734). Low-cost seafood, in a riotous atmosphere. Live Fifties music.

China Garden, 435 W Tennessee St (☎561-8849). Chinese lunch and dinner buffets for $5–6.

Mom and Dad's, 4175 Apalachee Parkway (☎877-4518). Delicious homemade Italian food.

Drinking and Entertainment

Bolstered by the students, Tallahassee has a strong nightlife, with a leaning to social **drinking** and **live rock music**. There's also a fair amount of **drama**, headed by the student productions at the *University Theater*, on the FSU campus (☎644-6500), and the *Tallahassee Little Theater*, 1861 Thomasville Rd (☎224-8474).

Andrew's Upstairs, 228 S Adams St (☎222-3446). Hosts modern jazz combos.

Calico Jack's, 2745 Capitol Circle (☎385-6653). Beer, oysters, and rock'n'roll records in a less student-dominated environment.

Halligan's, 1700 Halstead Blvd (☎668-7665). Popular for its pool tables and chilled mugs of beer.

The Moon, 1020 E Lafayette St (☎222-6666). Big-name live bands appear here.

The Warehouse, 706 W Gaines St (☎222-6188). Intimate venue, mixing rockabilly, avant-garde music and performance art.

Wakulla Springs

Fifteen miles south of Tallahassee on Hwy-61, **Wakulla Springs State Park** (daily 9am–5.30pm; cars and drivers $3.25, pedestrians and cyclists $1) holds what is believed to be one of the biggest and deepest natural springs in the world, pumping up half a million gallons of crystal-clear pure water from the bowels of the earth every day – though it would be difficult to guess that from the calm surface.

It's refreshing to **swim** in the cool liquid, but to learn more about the spring, take the fifteen-minute **glass-bottomed boat tour** ($4.50), and peer down to the swarms of fish hovering around the 180ft-deep cavern through which the water comes. Half-hour **river cruises** ($4.50) bring glimpses of some of the park's legged inhabitants: deer, turkeys, herons and egrets – and the inevitable alligators – among them. If *déjà vu* strikes, it may be because a number of movies have been shot here, including several of the early Tarzan movies and parts of *The Creature from the Black Lagoon*.

The Apalachicola National Forest

With swamps, savannahs and springs dotted liberally about its half-million acres, the **APALACHICOLA NATIONAL FOREST** is the inland Panhandle at its natural best. Several roads enable you to drive through a good-sized chunk, with many undemanding spots for a rest and a snack, but to see deeper into the forest you'll have to make an effort: exploring unhurriedly and at length, following one of the hiking trails, taking a canoe on one of the rivers, or simply spending a night under the stars at one of the basic campgrounds. Driving through the forest on Hwy-65, or around it on Hwy-319, you'll eventually pass the large and forbidding area believably called **Tate's Hell Swamp**. This is a breeding ground for the deadly water moccasin snake, and gung-ho locals sometimes venture into the swamp hoping to catch a few snakes to sell to the less reputable zoos; you're well advised to stay clear.

The main **entrances** to the forest are off Hwy-20 and Hwy-319; three minor roads, highways 267, 375 and 65, form cross-forest links between the two. **Accommodation** is limited to camping; apart from Silver Lake (nine miles east of Tallahassee; $4), all the campgrounds are free with basic facilities.

Panama City Beach

An orgy of motels, go-kart tracks, mini-golf courses and amusement parks, **PANAMA CITY BEACH** is entirely without pretensions, capitalizing as blatantly as possible on the appeal of its 27-mile beach. The whole place is as commercial as can be, but with the shops, bars and restaurants all trying to undercut one another, there are some great bargains to be found – from T-shirts and cut-price sunglasses to cheap buffet food. Throughout the lively summer (the so-called "100 Magic Days"), accommodation costs are high and advance bookings essential. In winter, prices drop and visitors are fewer; most are Canadians and – increasingly – northern Europeans, many of whom have no problems sunbathing and swimming in the cool temperatures.

Getting a tan, running yourself ragged at beach sports, and going hammer-and-tong at the nightlife are the main concerns in Panama City Beach – you'll be regarded as a very raw prawn indeed if you go around demanding history, art and culture. If you get restless, try go-karting (around $5 for ten laps), one of the amusement parks (usually $12 for a go-on-everything day ticket), a fishing trip (take your pick of the party boats on the Thomas Drive marina, around $25 a day) or scuba-diving (several explorable shipwrecks litter the area; details from any of the numerous dive shops).

Practicalities

Greyhound **buses** pick up and drop off at the *Exxon* station, 17325 W Hwy-98, fifteen minutes' walk from the nearest motels. Travelling by bus, however, you may well end up in **Panama City** (917 Harrison Ave; ☎785-7861), eight miles east of Panama City Beach; four daily *Greyhound* services link the two towns.

Places to stay are plentiful, but fill with amazing speed, especially on weekends. As a very general rule, **motels** at the eastern end of the beach are smarter and slightly pricier than those in the center, and those at the western end are quiet and family oriented. The cheapest places to **eat** are the buffet restaurants on Front Beach Rd, charging $4 to $10 for all you can manage. Or try one of the regular **lunch or dinner** restaurants, like *Hickory Key Smoked BBQ*, 4106 Thomas Ave (☎234-2717), known for its barbecued meats and formidable seafood platter, and *Shuckum's Oyster Pub & Seafood Grill*, 15618 W Hwy-98 (☎235-3214).

Really to get into the swing of things, visit one of the two beachside **nightlife** fleshpots, *Club La Vela*, 8813 Thomas Drive (☎234-3886), or *Spinnaker*, 8795 Thomas Drive (☎234-7882), each of which has dozens of bars, several discos, live bands, and a predominantly under-25 clientele.

Pensacola and Around

Tucked away as it is at the western end of the Panhandle, you might be inclined to overlook **PENSACOLA**, built on the northern bank of the broad Pensacola Bay and five miles inland from the nearest beaches, particularly as its prime features are a naval aviation school and some busy dockyards. Pensacola is, however, an historic center: occupied by the Spanish from 1559 – only the hurricane which ended their settlement prevented it becoming the oldest city in the US – it repeatedly changed hands between the Spanish, French and British before becoming the place where Florida was officially ceded by Spain to the US in 1821.

Pensacola was already a booming port by the turn of the century, when the opening of the Panama Canal was expected to boost its fortunes still further. The many new buildings which appeared in the **Palofax District**, around the southerly section of Palofax Street, in the early 1900s – with their delicate ornamentation and attention to detail – reflect the optimism of the era. Between 1870 and 1930, Pensacola's professional classes took a shine to the area just across Wright Street from Palofax called **North Hill**, commissioning elaborate homes in a plethora of fancy styles. Strewn across the fifty-block area are Neoclassical porches, Tudor Revival cottages, low-slung California bungalows, and the rounded towers of the finest Queen Anne homes – though as none is open to the public, if you want to see them you should contact the visitor center for details of special tours (see following page).

In earlier times, Native Americans, pioneer settlers and seafaring traders had gathered to swap, sell and barter on the waterfront of the **Seville District**, about half a mile east of Palofax Street. Those who did well took up permanent residence, and many of their homes remain in fine states of repair, forming – together with several museums – the **Historic Pensacola Village** (daily 10am–4pm; $5.50). One payment secures admission to all of the museums and former homes in an easily navigated four-block area.

Around Pensacola: Santa Rosa Island

On the other side of the bay from the city, the glistening beaches of **Santa Rosa Island** (the barrier island that runs sixty miles from Fort Walton) are ideal for sunbathing, and an endless row of windswept sand dunes demands investigation.

PENSACOLA BEACH in particular has everything you'd want from a Gulf coast beach: mile after mile of fine white sands, rental outlets for water-sports equipment, a busy fishing pier and a sprinkling of motels, beachside bars and snack stands. It's hard to beat for uncomplicated oceanside recreation, but while sunning yourself, don't ignore what lies a short way west. At the **GULF ISLANDS NATIONAL SEASHORE**, on Fort Pickens Rd (9am–sunset; cars $3, pedestrians and cyclists free), vibrant white sands are walled by a nine-mile-long stretch of high, rugged dunes, and the only reminder of civilization is a foliage-encircled campground.

Practicalities

At the foot of the three-mile Pensacola Bay Bridge into the city (on the city side), the **visitor center** (daily 8am–5pm; ☎1-800/343-4321) is packed with the usual worthwhile hand-outs. The **Greyhound** station is seven miles north of the city center at 505 W Burgess Rd (☎476-4800); bus #10 links it to Pensacola proper. **Local buses** serve the city but not the beach; the main terminal is at Gregory and Palofax.

Plenty of **budget chain hotels**, all $30 to $50 per night, line N Davis Blvd and Pensacola Blvd, the main approach roads from I-10. Of the central options, cheapest are the *Seville Inn*, 221 E Garden St (☎1-800/277-7275; ②), and *Days Inn*, 710 N Palofax St (☎438-4922; ②–③). Lowest priced **at the beach** are *Barbary Coast*, 24 Via De Luna (☎932-2233; ③–④), *Gulf Aire*, 21 Via De Luna (☎932-2319; ②–③), and *Tiki House*, 17 Via De Luna (☎934-4447; ①–③).

CHAPTER EIGHT

LOUISIANA

S
wathed in the romance of pirates, voodoo and Mardi Gras, **LOUISIANA** is undeniably special. Its history is barely on nodding terms with the view that America was the creation of the Pilgrim Fathers; its way of life is proudly set apart. This is the land of the rural French-speaking **Cajuns** (descended from eighteenth-century French-Canadian refugees), and the haughty **Creole** aristocrats of jazzy, sassy **New Orleans**. (The term Creole covers those born in the state to non-Anglo colonists – famed in days gone by for their glittering masked balls, family feuds and duels – as well as native-born French-speaking slaves.) **North Louisiana** – Protestant Bible Belt country, complete with cotton fields, southern belles, and fine old plantation homes – is more "Southern" than the marshy bayous, shaded by ancient cypress trees and laced by wispy trails of Spanish moss, of Catholic **south Louisiana**. Louisiana's spicy homecooked **food**, almost weekly **festivals**, and lilting French-based dialect – and above all its music (**jazz**, **r'n'b**, **cajun** and its bluesy black counterpart, **zydeco**) – draw from all these cultures.

The **French** first settled Louisiana in 1682, braving swamps and plagues to harvest the abundant cypress, but the state was sparsely inhabited before its first permanent settlement, the trading post of **Natchitoches**, was established in 1714. In 1764, Louis XV secretly handed all French territory west of the Mississippi to his **Spanish** cousin, as a

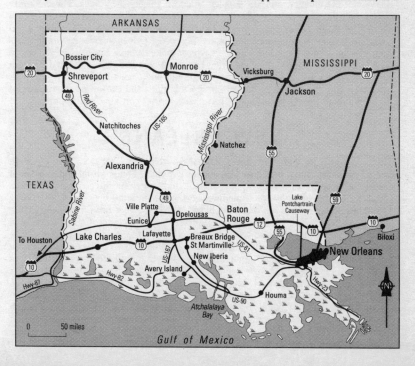

safeguard against the British, and Louisiana remained Spanish until it was ceded to Napoleon in 1801, under the proviso that it should never change hands again. Just two years later, Napoleon needed cash and struck a bargain with Jefferson, known as the **Louisiana Purchase**. This sneaky agreement handed over to the US all French lands between Canada and Mexico, from the Mississippi to the Rockies, for a total cost of $15 million. The subsequent "Americanization" of Louisiana was much resisted by the proud Creoles, and the state eventually joined the Confederacy in 1861. There were, however, important differences between Louisiana and other slave-driven Southern states. Here slavery was more in the West Indian mold than the Anglo-American. The **Black Code** of Louisiana, established by the French, upheld by the Spanish and then effectively broken by the Americans, gave slaves rights unparalleled elsewhere, including permission to marry, meet socially and take Sundays off. The black population of New Orleans in particular was renowned as exceptionally literate and cosmopolitan.

Louisiana was economically rather than physically scarred by the Civil War, with few important battles fought on its soil, and in time it recovered, benefiting from rich **agricultural** land, the mighty Mississippi River and offshore **oil**. Today **tourism** is crucial, but despite rabid commercialism, Louisiana stays unique, with an intriguing and compelling mix of upbeat, quirky, laid-back ease.

Getting Around Louisiana

Louisiana is crossed east–west by two major interstates, I-20 in the north and I-10 in the south. New Orleans is very much the hub, served by I-55 and I-59 from Mississippi. I-49 sweeps across southeast to northwest, connecting Cajun country with the north.

The main international **airport** is in New Orleans; regional airlines serve the rest of the state and surrounding areas. *Greyhound* **buses** connect all the major towns with the rest of the country, and are supplemented by smaller local lines. Three *Amtrak* **trains** daily link New Orleans with the east and west coasts, and with the north central states. The *Sunset Limited* departs New Orleans three times weekly for New Iberia and Lafayette, and onwards to Los Angeles; the *City of New Orleans* arrives in New Orleans from Chicago every afternoon; and the *Crescent* makes a daily run from New York to New Orleans. There are three connecting buses to Baton Rouge; two arrive daily from New Orleans (in the afternoon and evening), and one comes in three times a week from Lafayette. In addition to the Mississippi's bridges and causeways, **ferries** cross the river at both New Orleans and St Francisville, further north in Cajun country.

NEW ORLEANS

There's a whole lot more to **NEW ORLEANS** – the "Big Easy", the "city that care forgot" – than its tourist image as a non-stop party city. At once sordid and sublime, it careers along under an infuriating double think. In between having enormous amounts of fun, you're always liable to be pulled up short by the divisions between rich and poor (and more explicitly, between white and black). A mere stone's throw from the partying and the money-making in the **French Quarter**, for example, on Canal Street or in Lafayette Square, dispossessed New Orleanians beg on the street. Even so, the city's vitality and *joie de vivre* are real, buffeted but not beaten by the vagaries of commercialism and poverty. The melange of cultures and races that built the city still gives it its heart; not exactly "easy", but quite unlike anywhere else in the States – or in the world.

New Orleans began life in 1718 as a set of shacks on a disease-ridden marsh. Its prime location led to rapid development, and with the first mass importation of African **slaves** as early as the 1720s its unique demography began to take shape. The **French** and **Spanish** colonists were initially fierce rivals, but economic necessity soon forced them to learn to live together.

Lake Pontchartrain

LAKESHORE DRIVE

City Park

GENTILLY BLVD

LAKE PONTCHARTRAIN CAUSEWAY

CAUSEWAY BOULEVARD

New Orleans International Airport

KENNER

METAIRIE

New Orleans Museum of Art

Louis Armstrong Park

To the Chalmette Plantation

FRENCH QUARTER

ST. CLAUDE AVE.

CANAL STREET

RAMPART ST.

Louisiana Superdome

Tulane University

Loyola University

Audubon Park

Zoo

CARROLLTON AVE.

Mississippi River

NAPOLEON AVE.

ST. CHARLES AVE.

LOUISIANA AVE.

Bus Station

Train Station

GARDEN DISTRICT

Ferry

ALGIERS

MISSISSIPPI RIVER BRIDGE

TCHOUPITOULAS ST.

Ferry

WEST BANK EXPRESSWAY

NEW ORLEANS

0   2 miles

By the end of the eighteenth century, the **port** was flourishing, the haunt of smugglers, gamblers, prostitutes, pirates and escapees from the French Revolution and West Indian slave rebellions. New Orleans was thus already a diverse and many-textured city when it experienced two quick-fire changes of government, passing back into **French** control in 1801 and then being sold to **America** under the **Louisiana Purchase** two years later. This heralded the most bitter transition in the city's history, literally splitting it into two sections. The Americans who migrated here in droves were seen as crass and uncouth by the Creoles and hated by the blacks, upon whom they placed previously unknown restrictions. Unwelcome in the French Quarter, the newcomers were forced to settle in the areas now known as the **Central Business District** and the Garden District. Canal Street divided the two sectors, and even today the median strip in the middle of the main roads is called "the neutral ground".

Creoles and Americans came together briefly in 1815, defeating the British in the **Battle of New Orleans** which ended the War of 1812 and secured American supremacy in the States. The victorious general, **Andrew Jackson**, became a national hero; his army was made up of pirates (supplied by the notorious **Jean Lafitte**, previously a sworn enemy of the Americans), slaves, Creoles and Native Americans.

New Orleans' subsequent **"Golden Age"** as a finance center for the cotton-producing South, also trading in tobacco, cotton and indigo, lasted until the Civil War. The flood of immigrants included Irish, Germans, and Sicilians (by 1890, New Orleans was famed as the American seat of the **Mafia**, still a tangible presence today). However, the Union troops who occupied the city and sealed off the Mississippi until 1872 isolated it from its markets. As the North industrialized, and other southern cities grew, the fortunes of New Orleans took a downturn. Both the coming of **rail**, which diminished the importance of the river, and the abolition of **slavery** marked the end of the glory days.

Jazz exploded into the bars and the bordellos at the turn of the century, and, along with the development of **Mardi Gras** as a tourist attraction, breathed new life into the city. Even so, it was the less romantic duo of **oil** and the **petrochemical** industry that really saved the economy – until the slump of the 1950s pushed New Orleans well behind other US cities. The oil crash of the early Eighties gave it yet another battering, but battle-scarred New Orleans remains, against the odds, simply irresistible.

However, in view of recent violent incidents, visitors to New Orleans should be aware that, although the heavily touristed French Quarter is comparatively safe, to wander beyond it – even just a couple of blocks – can place your **personal safety** in jeopardy. Be careful, and at night always take a cab.

Finally, due to its swampy climate, New Orleans can be unbearably **hot**; if you can, it's well worth trying to avoid coming in **summer**, the off-season.

Arrival, Information and Getting Around

New Orleans International **Airport** (☎464-0831), twelve miles northwest on I-10, has an information booth (10am–10pm) in its baggage claim area. **Taxi** fares into town are around $21 for one or two people, $8 for each extra person (*United Cabs* are on ☎524-9606), and **minibuses** (☎469-4335) will take you to your hotel (tickets, $10, available in the baggage claim area or from the bus driver). A **public bus** from the airport goes to the downtown side of Tulane Ave (daily 6am–5.40pm; every 30min; $1.10; ☎737-9611).

Greyhound (☎525-9371) comes in next to *Amtrak* at the Union Passenger Terminal, 1001 Loyola Ave near the Superdome. This area, ten minutes from Canal St, is dangerous at night; catch a taxi.

City Transportation

Although New Orleans is easy to walk around – the French Quarter is definitely best enjoyed by a leisurely stroll – its **public transportation** is good. The *Regional Transit Authority* (Plaza Tower, 101 Dauphine St, Mon–Fri 8.30am–5pm; 24-hr information ☎569-2700) runs **buses** from Canal Street across the city well into the night (fares 80¢–$1). An *Easy Rider* shuttle bus runs from the Convention Center to the Riverwalk (Mon–Sat 6.30am–6.30pm; 50¢). The **St Charles streetcar** (a National Historic Monument) rumbles from Canal Street along St Charles Avenue in the Garden District, to Audubon Park, 24 hours a day. Settling back on the old wooden benches next to an open window is an ideal way to tour the city on the cheap ($1 each way). Seven other streetcars run along the riverfront ($1.25) and for a mere 60¢ you can also catch the **Vieux Carré minibus** through the Quarter (5am–7pm). *VisiTour* **passes**, available from major hotels, give unlimited travel on all streetcars and buses ($4 per day, $8 for three days).

Around Jackson Square on the river, **horse-drawn carriages** give narrated rides through the Quarter, but the price ($8) and the unhappy horses, decked out in funny hats, can be a turn-off. Instead, join locals on the **commuter ferry** crossing from Canal Street to suburban Algiers, for a good view of activity on Old Man River. A night ride makes a cheap alternative to "romantic" moonlit paddle boat cruises; you save about $35, but miss out on the live jazz accompaniment.

Bicycles can be rented from *Olympic Bicycle Rental*, 1506 Prytania St (☎523-1314) and the *Marquette House Youth Hostel* (see p.495).

The **area code** for New Orleans is ☎504.

CITY TOURS AND RIVER CRUISES

Both *Gray Line* (☎587-0861) and *New Orleans Tours* (☎592-0560) offer similar **bus tours** of the city (2hr; $15), the plantations (7hr 30min; $33), and New Orleans' nightlife (2hr 30min; $35). The *Friends of the Cabildo* leads **walking tours** from the Presbytere in Jackson Square (2hr; Tues–Sat 9.30am & 1.30pm, Sun 1.30pm; $7 – no reservations required).

One pleasant, if overpriced, way to while away a few hours is on a **river cruise**. The *Creole Queen* paddlewheeler and *Cajun Queen* riverboat (☎524-0814) leave from Riverwalk Mall on Canal Street; trips include excursions to Chalmette Plantation ($13), and 8pm Dixieland jazz dinner cruises ($39). *Natchez* (☎586-8777), from behind the Jackson brewery, has a 7pm jazz cruise (nightly March–Nov, Fri & Sat only Nov–March).

Information

For detailed information on the city, and excellent self-guided walking tours, drop in at the **New Orleans Welcome Center** in the French Quarter at 529 St Ann St (daily summer 10am–6pm; winter 9am–5pm; ☎566-5068). The official **post office** is at 701 Loyola Ave (Mon–Fri 8am–4.30pm, Sat 8am–1pm; ☎589-1112; zip code 70140), but an equivalent service is offered in the French Quarter by *French Quarter Postal Emporium*, 940 Royal St (Mon–Fri 9.30am–6pm, Sat 10am–3pm; ☎525-6651).

The City

One of New Orleans' many nicknames is "the **Crescent City**", for the way it nestles between a bend in the Mississippi River and the southern shore of Lake Pontchartrain. Streets curve to follow the river, making its layout somewhat confusing. Locals have their own terms for directions; remember that **upriver** from Canal Street (the widest main street in the nation) is south, **downriver** is north.

The city's spiritual center is the surprisingly small **French Quarter** (or Vieux Carré), site of the original settlement **downtown**. Also downtown, the **CBD** (Central Business District), the early "American section", spreads from Canal Street to Howard Avenue, and includes, towards the lake, the gargantuan Superdome. The **Garden District**, uptown, offers a quite different taste of New Orleans.

The French Quarter

Breathtakingly beautiful, depressingly tacky, the **French Quarter** is the heart of New Orleans. Each block, with its overhanging lacy ironwork balconies, crumbling pastel stucco walls, shutters and high-walled cobbled courtyards, smacks of history and legend. Official tours are useful for orientation, but it's most fun simply to wander – and you'll need a couple of days at least to do it justice, absorbing the jumble of sounds, people, sights and smells. Early morning, in the pearly light from the river, is a good time to explore, as sleepy locals wake themselves up with strong coffee in the neighborhood cafés, shops crank open their shutters, and all-night revellers stumble home. You can almost feel the build-up of adrenaline, and when the first trumpet moans through the air, it's as if a morning bell has sounded. New Orleans puts on its party face and the day begins.

The Quarter is laid out in a grid, with central **Jackson Square** facing the Mississippi. The architecture is predominantly Spanish colonial, with a strong Caribbean influence, and dates from the end of the eighteenth century, after most of the original French buildings had been devastated by two great fires in 1788 and 1794. Today the Quarter is home to offices, shops, galleries, restaurants, bars and apartments.

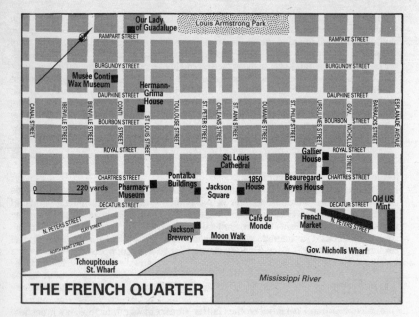

THE FRENCH QUARTER

Jackson Square

Jackson Square, as the *Place d'Armes* once used for public meetings and executions, is now a well-kept park where artists, horse-drawn carriages and buskers congregate to entertain picnicking office workers and tourists, presided over by an equestrian statue of Andrew Jackson himself. The Spanish-style **St Louis Cathedral**, in the middle of Chartres Street facing the river, is the third church on this spot, built in 1794 after the first two were destroyed by fire and hurricane. Jackson laid his sword on its grand gold and wooden altar in thanks for victory at the Battle of New Orleans. Devout worshippers stream in, illustrating New Orleans' claim to be the most Catholic city in America.

Next door, the stately **Cabildo**, with its impressive ironwork balcony, was the seat of the first Spanish government. After the Louisiana Purchase (signed on the second floor), it was used as the city hall and state supreme court, and rebuilt in 1851 to look more French. Today it is part of the State Museum. Sadly, this grand old building closed due to fire damage in 1988; when this book went to press it was due to reopen early in 1994. On the other side of the cathedral, the **Presbytere**, bought from the Church by the city in 1853, is now part of the **State Museum**, exhibiting antique portraits, musical instruments, maps, toys, and decorative art (Tues–Sun 10am–5pm; $3).

The smart red three-storey **Pontalba Buildings**, on St Peter and St Ann bordering the Square, were designed in 1850 by the eccentric Baroness Pontalba (who donned trousers to oversee the work at every stage). Planned as both business and residential units to draw activity back into the Quarter, hard hit by American success in the CBD, they are a source of much pride to the city. The restored **1850 House** at 523 St Ann St displays the ostentatious tastes of a well-to-do Creole family (Tues–Sun 10am–5pm; $3).

Decatur Street and Esplanade Avenue

For good views of the **Port**, cross Decatur Street to the **Moon Walk**, a wooden promenade where buskers serenade you as you gaze over the river. Downriver along Decatur, the **French Market**, a marketplace since the 1720s, spills over with bric-a-brac; directly behind it, the old **Farmer's Market** sells fresh produce, along with overpriced foodie souvenirs – crab boil, tabasco sauce, etc – around the clock. The weekend flea market is full of bargain oddities, as are the rummage stores opposite on Decatur, among them *Noney's* (no 1224), with unusual antiques and bulging bags of colorful Mardi Gras beads, or *Jazzrags* nearby (no 1232), a good place for quality secondhand clothes at low prices.

Continuing downriver, you'll come to the outer boundary of the Quarter, **Esplanade Avenue**, a broad oak-lined boulevard lined with grand nineteenth-century Creole mansions. The **Old US Mint**, on the 400 block, houses the **Jazz Museum**, tracing the history of the music that New Orleans calls its own, through photographs, old letters and adverts, with a lively jazz soundtrack and videos. A Mardi Gras exhibit explains the complexities of the carnival, with lots of old costumes, and the original 1906 "Streetcar named Desire" stands in the grounds (Tues–Sun 10am–5pm).

Along Chartres and Royal Streets

A left turn at the 600 block of Esplanade Avenue brings you to the **Old Ursulines Convent** at 1114 Chartres St. Built in 1750, this is the only remaining example of French colonial architecture in the States, and quite possibly the oldest building in the whole Mississippi valley. The **Beauregard-Keyes House** opposite at no 1113 (Mon–Sat 10am–3pm; $4) owes its name to Confederate General Pierre **Beauregard**, who ordered the first shot of the Civil War at Fort Sumter and rented a room here when desperately poor and unemployed in later years, and to local novelist Frances Parkinson **Keyes**. She refurbished this "raised cottage", (with the basement on the ground floor), as her winter home in the 1940s. Her novels – including *Madame Castel's Lodger*, about the "Beauregard period", which features the house – are on sale.

A block north at 1132 Royal St, the **Gallier House**, dating from 1860, is a great little museum (Mon–Sat 10am–3.45pm, Sun 12.30–3.45pm; $4), demonstrating such typical features of French Quarter residences as the outdoor cistern and cooling system, and the safe for storing tea and coffee – precious commodities of the time. The view across the French Quarter from the lacy iron balcony upstairs, where you're left in peace after the tour to linger and sup free coffee, is superb.

Behind St Louis Cathedral, the small iron-fenced garden of **St Anthony's Square** was the scene of numerous celebrated duels in the 1830s. The narrow lane alongside (favorite haunt of pavement artists) is known as **Pirate's Alley**, one of the many supposed locations of secret *rendezvous* between Jean Lafitte and Andrew Jackson to plan the Battle of New Orleans in 1815. It's highly unlikely that this is true – the road was only built in 1831 – but the story is nevertheless a New Orleans legend.

The scholarly **Historic New Orleans Collection** at 533 Royal St looks quite appropriate amongst all the antique shops and swanky art galleries. Exhibits in the dignified 1792 building, one of the few survivors of the 1794 fire, include old maps, drawings and documents relating to the Louisiana Purchase (Tues–Sat 10am–4.45pm; $2). You'll need to take a guided tour to see the best of the collection, but on the ground floor a free gallery focuses on local art and culture.

Less learned, but just as informative, is the quirky **Historical Pharmacy Museum**, in an old apothecary a block away at 514 Chartres St, illustrating medicine from the twelfth century onwards (daily 10am–5.30pm; $1). Its hand-carved rosewood cabinets are cluttered with intriguing dusty phials, ancient lotions, potions and powders. Shelves heave with *gris-gris*, jars of leeches for blood-letting (to remove irritability) and Creole "female tonics" (used to cure "all the various form of female weakness").

Exchange Alley, in the 600 block (between Chartres and Royal) of Conti Street just west of the Pharmacy Museum, was another of the city's favorite duelling spots, known in the 1830s as the "street of the fencing masters". Many of these duelling teachers also hired themselves out as assassins, who operated by provoking their prey into unwinnable duels, and consequently the street saw some pretty bloody goings-on.

MACABRE NEW ORLEANS

Voodoo

Voodoo was brought to New Orleans by African slaves, for whom Catholicism provided good cover for praying to their own gods. French and Spanish authorities tried to suppress what they saw as subversive devil-worship, but under American rule, partly due to the lifting of a ban on importing slaves from Haiti and the West Indies, voodoo flourished. As the weekly slave gatherings at **Congo Square** (now Louis Armstrong Park), with dancing, singing and weird ceremonies, turned into a tourist attraction for whites, the authentic worship of African gods shifted underground. The fascination and repulsion felt by the white community for this sexual, exotic, snake worship were fuelled by frequent reports of white women dancing naked at rituals. New Orleans' most famous voodoo priest was **Marie Laveau**, of mixed African, white, and Native American blood, who prepared spells for all walks of New Orleans life – wealthy Creoles and Americans as well as slaves. Although she died in 1881, her legend persists, with her grave(s) frequently visited (see below) and her memory revered.

The Historic Voodoo Museum at 723 Dumaine St contains various ceremonial objects, paintings, spells and *gris-gris* – pouches carried for good luck, filled with amulets, charms and herbs. (Daily 10am– dusk; $5.)

Psychic readings are widely available; they're fun, but can be pricey. Try at the tiny *Marie Laveau's House of Voodoo*, 739 Bourbon St (☎581-3751), *Voodoo Macumba*, 813 Toulouse St (☎588-1462), or *Bottom of the Cup*, 616 Conti St (☎524-1557).

The Cities of the Dead

So much of New Orleans is at, or below, sea level that early settlers who buried their dead found that the corpses would gruesomely float to the ground. Graves began to be placed, Spanish-style, in above-ground vaults, surrounded by small fences and gardens. The **cemeteries** grew to resemble cities, laid out in "streets" and taking on an eerie appearance as the tombs crumbled, tilted over and fell apart. This creepiness isn't totally imaginary, either, though armed muggers, rather than ghosts, haunt the cemeteries today. You should **never** venture here alone. Nearly all the city tours (see p.489) include a quick trip around one of the graveyards.

St Louis Cemetery No 1, 400 Basin St between Toulouse and St Louis streets, is the oldest city of the dead. This small graveyard dates from 1788, and is full of crooked mausolea jutting into narrow, twisting pathways. Its spook value is enhanced by Marie Laveau's grave, covered with red brick-dust crosses. If you turn around and knock on the slab three times, and mark a cross on her tomb with the brick provided, her spirit will grant you any favor. Mysteriously, they say, the grave is always in immaculate condition, compared to the decay that surrounds it.

St Louis No 2, N Claiborne Ave and Bienville St, is more orderly, with many well-kept graves in Greek Revival style. Marie Laveau is supposedly buried here, too, and another vault daubed with red crosses marks the spot. This one grants the wishes of any woman seeking a husband.

St Louis No 3, 3421 Esplanade Ave, is a peaceful burial ground mostly used by religious orders; all the priests of the diocese are buried here, and fragile angels balance on top of the tombs.

A Haunted House

The striking grey and black **LaLaurie Home** at 1140 Royal St is New Orleans' most famous **haunted house** (though not open to the public). It belonged to socialite Delphine LaLaurie, who although seen whipping a young slave on the roof was merely fined when the same girl "fell" from the roof to her death. Whispers about her cruelty were horribly verified when neighbors rushed in after a fire in 1834, to find slaves choked by neck braces, handcuffed and immobile, locked in a dingy attic. The next day an angry mob gathered outside the house. Delphine escaped in a carriage, and fled to France, as her home was ripped apart. Many claim to have heard the hissing of a whip and ghostly moans from the building at night; some have seen a little girl stumble across the rooftop ...

Bourbon Street

If you continue lakeside, and cross Royal Street again, Conti Street will lead you up to **Bourbon Street**, the most famous – and tackiest – pocket of the city. Lined with strip joints, neon bars and souvenir shops, with a couple of great bars (see p.499), it is in fact one of the least appealing streets of the Quarter. Half a block north at 820 St Louis St, the restored 1831 **Hermann-Grima House** illustrates the lifestyle of middle-class Creoles in the city's Golden Age (Mon–Sat 10am–3.30pm; $4; ☎525-5661). Cookery demonstrations are held in the kitchen every Thursday from October to May.

Quiet **Dauphine Street**, just north, home to a large gay community, has a peaceful atmosphere that welcomes tourists without being touristy. By following it a block west and then turning north you'll come to the **Musee Conti Wax Museum** at 917 Conti St (daily 10am–5.30pm; $5.70), which tells the story of New Orleans through lurid tableaux, including voodoo, gambling and jazz, and a waxwork house of horror, with much shrieking and wailing. **Our Lady of Guadalupe** church at 411 N Rampart St, on the corner of Conti St, is notable for its statue of "Saint Expedite", mysteriously delivered here in a crate simply stamped *expedite*. There's a jazz mass held every Saturday night, but take special care when walking around the area, especially near **Louis Armstrong Park**, one of the most dangerous areas in the city.

Outside the French Quarter

The unattractive riverside **World Trade Center** at 2 Canal St has an observation deck on the 31st floor, and a slide show about New Orleans (daily 9am–5pm; $2). The *Top of the Mart* bar on the 33rd floor offers equally fabulous views, without the entrance charge. Also on the river, the impressive **Aquarium of the Americas**, near the Canal Street wharf, holds an Amazon rainforest and a Caribbean reef. Its exotic sea creatures include killer sharks that zoom towards those who dare to cross the glass underwater tunnel (Sun–Wed 9.30am–6pm, Thurs 9.30am–9pm, Fri & Sat 9.30am–7pm; $8.75).

During the Civil War, the (then incomplete) **Customs House** at 423 Canal St (Mon–Fri 9am–4.30pm) was headquarters to Union General Butler, known scornfully as "Spoons" Butler for his kleptomaniac habit of pilfering the cutlery from his hosts. Finally completed in the 1880s, it has a huge marble hall on the second floor, in which fourteen towering columns of white Italian marble support the dazzling white and gilt ceiling.

The **St Charles streetcar** from Canal Street offers a leisurely trip to many of New Orleans' sights. **Lafayette Square** was the American version of the *Place d'Armes*, now filled with lost souls despite the city's efforts to turf them out. It may not look much today, but it has been the site of some pretty dramatic events, including acting as a military camp in an 1858 mini-Civil War between Creoles and Americans battling over city elections. A few hundred yards away, the **Confederate Museum** at 929 Camp St tells the story of the Confederacy cogently and poignantly (Mon–Sat 10am–4pm; $3).

The Garden District and Audubon Park

The grand residential **Garden District**, two miles upriver from the French Quarter, was built in the 1840s by rich Americans, who loved to display their wealth through spacious landscaped gardens, as opposed to the cramped confines of the Creole courtyards in the Quarter. Tropical bushes and magnificent oaks flourish in the fertile soil, while the ornate buildings, raised to avoid water damage, evoke the Deep South in a profusion of porches, columns and balconies. Look out for the **Brown House** at 4717 St Charles Ave, and the 1941 replica of **Tara**, the house in *Gone with the Wind*, at no 5705. You can't miss the **Wedding Cake House** at no 5809. It suits its name, an ostentatious Colonial-Greek Revival building, with balconies, cornices and lots of columns. The Welcome Center provides a self-guided walking tour, but the homes are only open to the public during the Spring Fiesta (see box on festivals, p.498).

Peaceful **Audubon Park** is full of lagoons, ancient oaks overhung with wispy Spanish moss, palms and fountains, with a swimming pool, jogging paths and bikes for the more active. New Orleanians are justifiably boastful about the spectacular **Audubon Zoo** at 6500 Magazine St behind the park, featuring as it does a white tiger, white alligators, and reconstructions of a Louisiana swamp, as well as Australian and African habitats (Mon–Fri 9.30am–5pm, Sat & Sun 9.30am–6pm; $7). You can walk through the park to the zoo, or take a shuttle bus from the park gates. The **Pitot House** is within walking distance at 1440 Moss St. This West Indies-style plantation house on the Bayou St John is the only remaining of its kind in the city, and is furnished with antiques (Wed–Sat 10am–3pm, but sometimes closed Sat; $3; ☎482-0312).

Approaching Lake Pontchartrain

The lakeside edge of the CBD would be pretty lifeless without the magnificent home of the New Orleans Saints football team, the **Superdome**. At 680ft in diameter, 27 storeys high, and covering 52 acres, this is one of the largest buildings in the world. You can't really conceive of its hugeness until you venture inside (tours 10am, noon, 2pm, & 4pm; $4; ☎587-3810). This area, though safe enough in the day, is a no-go zone at night.

Even further towards the Lake is New Orleans' 1500-acre **City Park**, site of the **Dueling Oaks**, under which Creoles and Americans met at dawn to defend their honor. The nearby **New Orleans Museum of Art**, set among the lagoons, has works by Degas, Picasso, and Dufy, Rodin sculptures, pre-Columbian pieces from Central America, and some Fabergé jewelled eggs (Tues–Sun 10am–5pm; $3).

The Chalmette Plantation

The **Chalmette Plantation**, six miles downriver from Canal Street, is the site where Jackson's ragbag army defeated the British in 1815. There isn't much to show for it, apart from bare fields and the simple Beauregard plantation home. Jean Lafitte National Historical Park rangers provide a self-guided walking tour, and give talks in the small visitor center four times daily. The plantation can be reached on a steamboat excursion or from Hwy-46, and is open from 8am until 5pm daily.

Accommodation

Room rates in New Orleans, never low, increase considerably for Mardi Gras, the Jazz Festival, and the Sugar Bowl, when reservations should be made as much as a year ahead. Even during the off-season it's a good idea to call before you arrive; this is not a city in which you'd want to be stranded overnight. Private double rooms are available in summer at **Tulane** (27 McAlister Drive; ☎865-5426; ②) and **Loyola** (6363 St Charles Ave; ☎865-3735; ③) universities, both on the St Charles streetcar line.

Bed and breakfast inns in old Creole cottages or townhouses are some of the most beautiful, and cheapest, lodgings in the city. Contact *New Orleans Accommodations and B&B Reservation Service*, PO Box 8163, New Orleans, LA 70182 (8.30am–4.30pm;

ACCOMMODATION PRICE CODES		
All accommodation prices in this book have been coded using the symbols below. Note that prices are for the least expensive double rooms in each establishment. For a full explanation see p.35 in *Basics*.		
① up to $30	④ $60–80	⑦ $130–180
② $30–45	⑤ $80–100	⑧ $180+
③ $45–60	⑥ $100–130	

☎838-0071), or *B&B Inc*, 1021 Moss St, Box 52257, New Orleans, LA 70152 (☎488-4640 or 1-800/729-4640), which can root out quaint and affordable guest houses for as little as $35. Although it is far nicer, and, in general safer, to stay in the French Quarter, options further out include some good, simple guest houses along Prytania Street, near St Charles Avenue – but do exercise caution when walking here at night. The **Welcome Center** in Jackson Square (see p.489) offers a room booking service.

French Quarter

Chateau Motor Hotel, 1001 Chartres St (☎524-9636). Simple rooms in prime position, with a pleasant outdoor café and pool. ④.

French Quarter Maisonettes, 1130 Chartres St (☎524-9918). Peaceful, popular B&B. Flagstone courtyard with fountain, tropical plants and climbing vines. Closed July, booking essential. ③.

Hotel Provincial, 1024 Chartres St (☎581-4995). Antique-filled rooms opening onto peaceful courtyard in the quiet end of the Quarter. Outdoor pool, restaurant and bar. ④.

Hotel St Pierre, 911 Burgundy St (☎524-4401). Two-storey Creole cottages. ④.

Hotel Villa Convento, 616 Ursulines St (☎522-1793). Simple guest house in Creole townhouse. ④.

905 Royal Hotel, 905 Royal St (☎523-0219). Small, established European-style guest house. ④.

Outside the Quarter

Cairo Pete's Backpacker Hostel, 4220 Canal St (☎488-0341). New hostel with lively atmosphere and clean rooms, on bus routes #41, #42 and #43. Dorm beds $10. ①.

The Frenchmen, 417 Frenchmen St (☎948-2166). B&B rooms overlooking a pretty courtyard in two 1860 townhouses, on the fringes of the French Quarter across from the Old US Mint. Also a pool. ⑤.

La Salle Hotel, 1113 Canal St (☎523-5831 or 1-800/521-9450). Near the French Quarter on the city's main thoroughfare. Cheap student rates. Large, plain, clean rooms. Seedy area at night. ②.

Longpré Guest House, 1726 Prytania St (☎581-4540). 1850s Italianate townhouse with relaxed, backpackers' atmosphere. Hostel beds and private rooms. ①/②.

Marquette House Youth Hostel, 2253 Carondelet St (☎523-3014). Antebellum house and cottages one block from streetcar in the Garden District. Clean, functional rooms, including private doubles and apartments, and no curfew. Reservations recommended, and for Mardi Gras should be paid in full well in advance. ①/②.

Prytania Inns, 1415, 2041 & 2127 Prytania St (☎566-1515).Over 50 German-owned rooms in historical houses a block from the streetcar. Gourmet breakfast $5. ⑤.

St Charles Guest House, 1748 Prytania St (☎523-6556). Bohemian guesthouse with friendly local owners. Rooms range from extremely basic Cajun cabins for backpackers to plusher doubles. Pool, terrace and small café serving free breakfast. ①–④.

YMCA, 936 St Charles Ave (☎568-9622). Next to Lee Circle, on the streetcar route. Co-ed dormitory, or double rooms with shared shower. Clean and safe. ②.

Eating

Eating out in New Orleans is delectable, a big occasion that can last the whole night. The food is a spicy and substantial mix of French, Spanish, African and Cajun; it's also delightfully cheap. The mainstay of most menus are **gumbo** – a thick soup of seafood, chicken, and vegetables (*gumbo* is the Bantu for okra, a prime ingredient) – and **jambalaya**, a paella jumbled together from the same ingredients. Many dishes are served *etouffé*, literally "smothered" in a spicy tomato sauce.

It's still just about possible to distinguish Cajun from Creole cooking, although differences have become blurred over the years. **Creole** food derives from the French and Spanish colonists and their black slaves. A lot of it, like red beans and rice (traditionally Monday lunch), shows a strong Caribbean influence. **Cajun** food is more rustic, based upon the *roux*, a tasty brown sauce, and using shallots, parsley, peppers, pork and garlic. By their very nature, Cajun meals, feasts created from scraps, can look vile, hence the prettified versions served up in many so-called "Cajun" restaurants. Moreover, much that claims to be Cajun – for example, blackened and deep fried dishes – simply isn't.

The swankiest New Orleans restaurants – *Antoine's, Arnaud's, Brennan's, Commander's Palace* and *Galatoire's* – serve Creole haute cuisine, often accompanied by live jazz in a formal setting. All but *Galatoire's* are very expensive ($30–50), and men must wear jacket and tie, but the food is exquisite. It's even more fun, though, and considerably less costly, to root out home-cooking in small local places, or, even further down the scale, to snack on *Lucky Dogs* hotdogs, as featured in John Kennedy Toole's sleaze farce *A Confederacy of Dunces*. The obscene giant hotdog carts, shoved by some of the city's most eccentric characters, are a much-loved institution, and can be seen trundling through the French Quarter at all hours.

Other specialities are **po-boys**, giant French-bread sandwiches crammed with oysters, shrimp or almost anything else, along with a lot of spicy sauces, and **muffulettas**, the Italian version, stuffed full of aromatic meats and cheese and dripping with olive dressing. Once looked down on as "trash" food, but now a favorite delicacy, **crawfish** look like baby lobster and are served in everything from omelettes to bisques.

Finally, European-influenced New Orleans is probably *the* American city for **coffee**, drunk in copious amounts, fresh, strong and aromatic.

French Quarter

Acme Oyster House, 724 Iberville St (☎522-5973). Fresh oysters shucked on marble counters. Increasingly popular with tourists for its authentic atmosphere but still a favorite with local police officers and business people. $6 for a dozen oysters on the half-shell; seafood po-boys for $5.50.

Bella Luna, 914 St Peter's St (☎529-1583). Swanky Creole restaurant with an unbelievably romantic view of the river from the terrace. Main courses, which include grilled salmon and scallop brochette and marinated baby back ribs, range from $13 to $25.

Café Pontalba, Chartres and St Peter's St (☎522-1180). Most casual of the Jackson Square restaurants, serving burgers and seafood for higher prices and with more tourists than elsewhere in town.

Central Grocery, 923 Decatur St (☎523-1620). Old Italian deli; the best muffulettas in New Orleans. Take-out only.

Galatoire's, 209 Bourbon St (☎525-2041). Splendid, top-of-the-range Creole food in grand, mirror-lined dining room. No reservations, so expect long lines, especially at lunchtime. Jacket and tie required in the evening and Sun. Closes 9pm.

Gumbo Shop, 630 St Peter St (☎525-1486). Old-fashioned but touristy, in one of the oldest buildings in the Quarter. Huge seafood gumbos and jambalayas, also sandwiches and po-boys.

Johnny's Po-boy, 511 St Louis St (☎524-8129). Family-owned restaurant serving po-boys, a fantastic gumbo (with garlic bread) and all-day breakfasts to a friendly mix of locals and visitors.

Kaldi's Coffeeshop, 941 Decatur St (☎586-8989). One of the hippest spots in town, serving fresh-brewed coffees, including Ethiopian decaf and iced Venetian *creme caffe*, to a trendy student and gay crowd in weathered wooden surroundings. Sit at the huge open window and watch the world go by, or browse through the piles of books and magazines. Local musicians frequently play for tips.

Molly's at the Market, 1107 Decatur St (☎525-5169). Dark bar and café with a neighborhood feel, frequented by politicians, media celebs, and regulars who never seem to leave. Po-boys, snacks, all-you-can-eat shrimp for $10 and full meals with free bread pudding.

Old Dog New Trick Café, 307 Exchange Alley (☎522-4569). Modern, intimate vegetarian café serving mid-range soup, pizza, pasta and burgers, with outdoor seating.

Quarter Scene, 900 Dumaine St (☎522-6533). Cheerful, laid-back restaurant in one of the Quarter's more peaceful streets. Splendid breakfast specials include omelettes smothered in shrimp, artichoke and cheese, for around $7.50. Open 24hrs except Tues (closes 11.30pm) and Wed (closes 8.30pm).

Royal Café, 706 Royal St (☎528-9086). Upmarket Cajun and Creole cuisine with European and nouvelle influences, in one of the Quarter's most beautiful buildings. Balcony tables available.

Outside the Quarter

Albertos, 611 Frenchmen St (☎949-5952). Creole cuisine with Italian flair; lots of seafood pasta dishes. A 24-hour bar, but the restaurant itself closes at 11pm. Dinner won't cost more than $12.

Chez Helene, 1530 W Robertson St (☎947-0444). Simple, good Creole soul food at reasonable prices, including fried chicken, corn bread and red beans and rice. Newer branch in the *De la Poste* hotel, 316 Chartres St, in the French Quarter.

Mother's, 401 Poydras St (☎523-9656). A real institution. Exposed brick walls, formica tables and concrete floors, and great food. Mountainous po-boys, gumbo, red beans and rice, traditional hash browns and sausage. Try shrimp *etouffée* omelette for Sunday breakfast, or turtle soup for lunch.

Pie in the Sky, 1818 Magazine St (☎522-6291). Hip café in the warehouse district serving pizza pies, focaccia sandwiches and good coffee, with frequent live jazz.

Entertainment and Nightlife

New Orleans positively reels under the energy of its ever-present **live music**. From the most lonesome busker, through the shiny uptown jazz bands, to the big-name Neville Brothers, music remains integral to the economy and the ideology of the city.

To try and decide what to do on any given night, you could be terribly organized, checking in the *Lagniappe* supplement of the *Times-Picayune* on Friday, or in the monthly listings papers *Offbeat* and *Wavelength*, and asking in French Quarter record stores. You could just as well, on the other hand, take pot-luck. Nothing compares with wandering into a local bar for a quick drink, only to be overwhelmed by the superb music coming from the unprepossessing band in the corner.

One of the most exciting features of New Orleans nightlife is that doors are always open, and with 24-hour drinking licences common, the music often doesn't get going until around midnight. Sleazy Bourbon Street strip clubs and hip uptown blues bars alike, everything can be seen – and heard – from the streets. It is also, unlike in any other American city, legal to drink alcohol in the streets; indeed, for some visitors it's almost *de rigueur*. If you hear something you like, but don't want to pay the cover charge – low or nonexistent in bars, but as much as $10 in some clubs – you can just stand outside with a "beer to go" from another bar. Ultimately, however, it's simply a false economy to skimp on entertainment in New Orleans.

Jazz

It is generally agreed that **jazz** was born in New Orleans, shaped early this century by the twin talents of **Louis Armstrong** and **Joe "King" Oliver** from a diverse heritage of African and Caribbean slave music, Civil War brass bands, plantation spirituals, black church music and work songs. It suits the city well: hard to define, improvisational, and ranging from melancholic to jubilant, upmarket to downright seedy.

In 1897, New Orleans' council, unable to control the city's prostitution, gambling and drinking, decided to restrict the bordellos and saloons to an area skirted by Iberville and Lower Basin streets, named **Storyville** after the mayor. This soon filled with newly arrived ex-plantation workers, seamen and gamblers, and from the "mood setting" tunes played in the brothels, to bawdy saloon gigs, there was plenty of opportunity for musicians to develop personal styles. Children too young to enter the bars set up makeshift "spasm bands" in the streets. Their legacy lives on in the streetwise ragamuffins on every corner, tap dancing, shoe-shining and playing trumpet.

Jazz was originally looked down upon by the white establishment as the "filthy" music of poor blacks, and Storyville was officially closed in 1917. Many jazz artists left the city, or gave up playing altogether, during the Depression (King Oliver died an impoverished janitor); but in the Fifties, the city fathers literally changed their tune, and began to promote jazz as a tourist attraction. The double-edged nature of the music – indigenous and authentic, and at the same time a commercial construction – persists. The quality ranges from **good** to **exceptional**; badly played jazz is almost nonexistent, and, thankfully, the best is not confined to the tourist traps.

MARDI GRAS

New Orleans' **Mardi Gras** (French for *Fat Tuesday*) began in the 1740s with grand balls marking the end of Carnival season, on the eve of Lent. As befits its origins in the *Carnelevamen*, the debauched "farewell to flesh", however, from early days it was known for cavorting, outrageous costumes, drinking and general bacchanalia. It has developed into a unique celebration, inextricably linked with the city's social structures. Although it is the busiest tourist season – it's practically impossible to find a room in New Orleans around the end of February – Mardi Gras is not held for commercial reasons; it's a party held by New Orleans for New Orleans, with tourists as unofficial guests.

It was the birth of the **krewe** system – with the unexpected appearance in 1857 of a stately moonlit procession calling itself the *Krewe of Comus, Merrie Monarch of Mirth* – that really gelled Mardi Gras, bringing together the populist street festivities and the elite social functions. Initiated by a group of Anglo-Americans, the idea of secret carnival clubs was taken up enthusiastically by New Orleans aristocracy. About sixty different krewes now equip colorful floats, leading processions on different – often mythical – themes. These themes, and the identity of the King and Queen (usually an older, politically powerful man and a young debutante), are completely unknown outside the krewes until the Big Day. Not all krewes are aristocratic; there are women-only krewes, "populist" ones open to anyone who can afford to join, and also three important **black** groups. The best known is **Zulu**, established in 1909 when a black man mocked Rex, King of Carnival, by dancing behind his float with a tin can on his head. They now parade in grass skirts and war paint. The eerie torch carriers of **Comus** parade at night, hooded and in flowing smocks, sparking bitter debate about whether the servile role demeans blacks, and the **Mardi Gras Indians** dance and chant in elaborate feather headdresses.

One important Mardi Gras ritual is the flinging and catching of **"throws"**. Beads, beakers and doubloons (toy coins marked with the insignia of individual krewes) are scattered amongst street revellers. Souvenirs vary in worth; the cheap and colorful strings of beads that adorn balconies everywhere are least valuable, while the coconut handed down from the float of the Zulu krewe is worth its weight in gold.

The **gay** community also has a lot of fun during Mardi Gras. Subversive gay parades and balls parody the "straight" Carnival, and the French Quarter is dominated by elaborate gay fancy-dress competitions.

The two weeks leading up to Mardi Gras are filled with processions, parties and balls, but excitement reaches fever pitch on the Tuesday itself, after a great, free, public masked ball in the Spanish Plaza the night before. Shambolic walking clubs, floatless, open the day, playing raucous jazz as they stride through the city. Zulu arrives at 9am, Rex appears before lunch, and the dramatic torchlit parade of Comus is the grand finale. By midnight, the police are clearing away die-hard revellers, and repentance can begin.

OTHER NEW ORLEANS FESTIVALS

French Quarter Festival, in early April. The Quarter is even more alive than usual, with jazz competitions, tours of private patios, free concerts, talent contests and a giant jazz brunch in Jackson Square.

Jazz and Heritage Festival, held at the end of April and start of May at the Fairgrounds Race Track. Ten outdoor stages host traditional jazz, r'n'b, gospel, African, Caribbean, Cajun, blues, ragtime, folk, bluegrass and country music, with evening performances at the *French Quarter Storyville Jazz Hall*, a marquee on the river, and the *Theater of the Performing Arts*, 801 N Rampart St (☎522-

0592). Hundreds of unofficial street bands, local arts, crafts and food. Contact PO Box 53407, New Orleans, LA 70153 (☎522-4786).

La Fête, in June/July. Food festival, with stalls all over town selling Cajun and Creole food from the simple to the outlandish.

Spring Fiesta, on the first Friday after Easter. The only time of the year when many of New Orleans' private homes are open to the public. Tours through plantation homes, French Quarter Creole cottages and patios, and Garden District mansions, many of them conducted by the owners. Public classical concerts and opera are held all around town.

Jazz funerals still occur – decorous and haunting affairs, with dirges and hymns expressing intense grief, followed by a burst of musical joy at the prospect of eternal life. Mostly occurring in the poorest neighborhoods, and not intended as tourist attractions, they are, along with brass band street parades, announced on *WWOZ* Radio (90.7 FM). A weekly **jazz mass** is celebrated at the Lady of Guadalupe church (see p.493). For the latest jazz happenings, call the **Louisiana Jazz Federation Hotline** (☎522-JAMS).

Jazz venues

The Columns Hotel, 3811 St Charles Ave (☎899-9308). Comfy uptown bar, with good modern jazz.

The Famous Door, 339 Bourbon St (☎522-7626). One of Bourbon Street's oldest authentic clubs, which never seems to close.

Gazebo Café and Bar, 1018 Decatur St (☎522-0862). Modern jazz in the center of the French Market, weekdays noon–6pm, trad jazz Sat–Sun from 11am.

New Storyville Jazz Hall, 1104 Decatur St (☎525-8199). Family place, with top-quality Dixieland bands, and occasional contemporary sets. Street musicians play on Sunday evening.

Palm Court Jazz Café, 1204 Decatur St (☎525-0200). Adjacent to the warehouse of the Jazz Foundation building. Great place for early evening trad jazz, with a good restaurant serving inexpensive shrimp, jambalaya and chicken dinners. Blues on Wed. Closed Mon & Tues.

Petroleum Lounge, 1501 St Philip St (☎523-0248). Authentic local bar, featuring New Orleans brass bands, and a brass band jukebox. Frequented by local musicians.

Preservation Hall, 726 St Peter St (☎522-2238 day, ☎523-8939 night). Not a bar or club, more like a shabby front room. No seats, drinks or air-conditioning, but long lauded as the best, if not the only, place to hear traditional jazz. Always full of smug tourists, with lines hours before the doors open at 8pm. Inside it's a zoo; old black musicians playing in an atmosphere kept deliberately derelict to titillate tourists. The $3 cover and the lengthy set (until well after midnight) are the main bonuses.

Snug Harbor, 626 Frenchmen St (☎949-0696). Excellent intimate jazz club, with a hassle-free atmosphere. Two shows a night, 9 and 11pm. Full meals and a friendly bar open long after the live music stops. Cover often around $10, but it's OK to sit and hear the music from the bar.

Other Live Music

Despite its heavy investment in traditional jazz, New Orleans is by no means just a jazz city. The **"New Orleans sound"** is characterized by the soulful r'n'b feel of the much-loved Neville Brothers, as well as the Cajun, gospel, blues, zydeco and rock, that play all over, all the time. **Blues** has always been big in this boozy, dreamy city, though influenced more by neighboring Texas than the country blues of the Mississippi delta. Piano blues lived alongside jazz in Storyville, and was continued by Tuts Washington and Professor Longhair. Look out especially for blues shouter J Monque D, who howls down the walls of many an uptown bar, and two exceptional blues singers: Irma Thomas and the powerful gospel and blues fusion of Marva Wright.

Bars and Live Music in the French Quarter

Crescent City Brewhouse, 527 Decatur St (☎522-0571). New bar with balcony opposite the *Jackson* brewery, serving traditionally brewed beers to a high-spirited crowd.

Lafitte's Blacksmith Shop, 941 Bourbon St (☎523-0066). Dim and ancient wooden bar frequented by artists and writers (how they see by candlelight remains a mystery). A front for Lafitte's plottings, unchanged since the eighteenth century, with a far better Hurricane rum cocktail than *Pat O'Brien's*.

The Mint, 504 Esplanade Ave (☎525-2000). Rumbustious gay bar, with rowdy sing-alongs, ragtime piano, and drag acts. Cover around $2.

Napoleon House, 500 Chartres St (☎524-9752). Once the home of Mayor Girod, who schemed with Jean Lafitte to rescue Napoleon from St Helena in 1821. A civilized bar, with taped classical music, fading Napoleonic memorabilia, old wooden tables on the street and delicious muffulettas.

Old Absinthe Bar, 400 Bourbon St (☎525-8108). Tiny dark bar with the original fixtures of the first New Orleans absinthe bar (nearby at 240 Bourbon St, but a lot less lively), including a marble absinthe fountain and ancient ceiling fans. Great jazz and r'n'b, noon until 3am. Small cover Fri & Sat.

Pat O'Brien's, 718 St Peter St (☎525-4823). Famous for inventing the sickly sweet Hurricane and for its riotous piano bar. Push your way to the front, request a song from the two warring piano players (who know every song ever written), and brace yourself for a raucous night. Open until 4am.

Rhythms, 227 Bourbon St (☎523-3800). Formerly the *Bourbon Street Gospel and Blues Club*, and featuring just that. Regular shows from the outstanding Marva Wright and Irma Thomas.

Bars and Live Music Outside the Quarter

Benny's Bar, 938 Valence St (☎895-9405). Authentic, seedy local blues bar, also putting on r'n'b and reggae. Music starts after midnight. No cover charge.

Café Brazil, 2100 Chartres St (☎947-9386). Self-consciously bohemian bar on the fringes of the Quarter, with eclectic live music nightly, occasional poetry readings and film shows. Good coffee bar and art gallery during the day.

Jimmy's, 8200 Willow St (☎861-8200). Very noisy student club. Only charges for big-name acts.

Lion's Den, 2655 Gravier St at Broad Ave (☎822-9591). Owned by r'n'b singer Irma Thomas, who performs regularly. Dodgy area; take a taxi and dress down.

Maple Leaf Bar, 8316 Oak St (☎866-9359). Shabby, friendly, cheap bar with superlative Cajun, zydeco and blues. Chess and darts, poetry readings on Sunday afternoon and Cajun dance lessons.

Michaul's, 701 Magazine St at Girod (☎522-5517). Predominantly a touristy Cajun restaurant, with live music and free Cajun dance lessons.

Muddy Water's, 8301 Oak St (☎866-7174). Blues, r'n'b, and good $2 meals. Many people wander all night between this and the *Maple Leaf* opposite. Cover varies.

Tipitina's, 501 Napoleon Ave (☎897-3943). Famed venue, named for a Professor Longhair song and venue for a Neville Brothers live album. An unpretentious and friendly hall hosting the smallest Cajun bands to the biggest acts. Joyful Sunday afternoon Cajun dances, $4 with free jambalaya.

The Warehouse Café, 636 Tchoupitoulas St (☎586-1282). More a warehouse than a café, with a trendy clientele and eclectic live music.

CAJUN COUNTRY

Cajun country stretches across southern Louisiana from **Houma** in the east, via **Lafayette** and Opelousas, into Texas. It's a region best enjoyed away from the larger towns, by visiting its many old-style hamlets, which despite modernization can still be found, cut off from civilization in soupy bayous, coastal marshes, and inland swamps.

Cajuns are descended from the French colonists of Acadia, part of Nova Scotia which was taken over by the British in 1713. The Catholic Acadians, who had quietly fished, hunted and farmed for more than a century, refused to renounce their faith and swear allegiance to the English king, and in 1755, the British brutally expelled them all, separating families and burning towns. About 2500 ended up in French Louisiana, where they were given land and enabled to set up small farming communities, to rebuild the culture they had left behind. Hunting, farming and trapping, they lived in relative isolation until the 1940s when major roads were built, immigrants from other states poured in to work in the oil business, and accordionist Iry Lejeune popularized **Cajun music** nationally. Since then, the history of the Cajuns has continued to be one of struggle. Towns like **Lafayette** were hard hit by the oil slump, the erosion of coastal wetlands threatens the existence of Houma and Morgan City; the silting up of the Atchafalaya Basin is having adverse effects on fishing and shrimping, and many coastal towns were severely battered when Hurricane Andrew hurtled up from the Gulf of Mexico.

The popular image of the Cajuns as partying, funloving people is borne out at their many local dances, or *fais-do-dos*. These singing, dancing celebrations, held with an unremitting frequency, are a good place to absorb the uniqueness of the culture, as well as trip a quick two-step. The French creole dialect of the older inhabitants, with its strong African and English influences, has primarily been kept alive by music (after Roosevelt's administration decreed that all American children should speak English in schools, French was practically wiped out in Louisiana). The favorite Cajun phrase, *lache pas la patate* – "don't let go of the potato" – is an encouragement not to give up that suits this enduring culture to a tee.

Although **Baton Rouge**, the capital of Louisiana, is not actually in Cajun country, heading out this way from New Orleans, via the **plantations** on the banks of the Mississippi, makes a good approach.

Northwest from New Orleans: Plantation Country

The fastest roads out from New Orleans towards the west are the major I-10 and US-61; far more pleasant, though, is to follow Hwy-18 beside the grassy levee along the Mississippi. It's not a particularly eventful drive, winding through flat fertile farmland, but you can stop off at several large and spectacular plantations along the way, from where French farmers – or rather, their slaves – once loaded cotton, sugar or indigo onto riverboats berthed virtually at their front doors.

At first, the road runs in the shadow of giant oil and chemical plants, prodigious sugar refineries, and even a nuclear power station, before emerging to pass levee-side clusters of small houses, tiny stores and pristine white churches. From **Edgard**, 25 miles along, you can cross the river to the **San Francisco House** (daily 10am–4pm; $6.50), two miles south of **Reserve** on Hwy-44. Built in the "Steamboat Gothic" style, its rails, awnings and pillars designed to re-create the ambience of a Mississippi showboat, the elaborate facade is matched by a lavish interior of Victorian furniture, decorative ceilings, marble work and cypress moldings. Back on Hwy-18, **Oak Alley**, six miles upriver from Vacherie, is a Greek Revival mansion dating from 1839 – the magnificent oaks which form a canopy over the driveway are 150 years older (daily 9am–5pm; $6.50).

The restored plantation cottages at **Tezcuco** (daily, summer 9am–5pm, winter 9am–4pm; $5.50), about an hour's drive from New Orleans on Hwy-44, are now used as delightful overnight accommodations, complete with porches, rocking chairs, and, in some cases, fireplaces and libraries (☎562-3929; ④). Rates include a bottle of wine on arrival, full Creole breakfast served in your room and a tour of the main house, an Antebellum raised cottage built in Greek Revival style.

Eighteen miles south of Baton Rouge on the west bank, **Nottoway** is the largest surviving plantation home in the South, a huge white Italianate edifice of 64 rooms, 200 windows, and 165 doors. Tours cost $8 but you can get a peep at this "white castle" from the road (daily 9am–5pm). The house is also used as an inn and restaurant.

Baton Rouge

When French explorers first came upon the site of **BATON ROUGE** in 1699, they found poles smeared in animal blood to designate the separate hunting grounds of the Houmas and Bayougoulas Indians. The area on these shallow bluffs therefore appeared on French maps as *Baton Rouge* – "red stick". Now capital of Louisiana and the country's fifth biggest port, Baton Rouge is an easy-going city for its size. It must also be one of America's greenest conurbations, its avenues canopied in oak and elm. Little happens in the central downtown section, but several parts of town are worth strolling around.

Louisiana State Capitol

Surrounded by fifty acres of showpiece gardens, the magnificent Art Deco **Louisiana State Capitol** serves as a monument to **Huey Long**, the "Kingfish". The larger-than-life state governor ordered its construction in 1931 and was assassinated in its corridors just four years later. Long was first elected governor in 1928 after a vehemently anti-big-business campaign, and swiftly concentrated power into his hands. His massive programme of public works included financing charity hospitals by heavy taxes on the big oil and gas corporations. Variously labelled a demagogue, communist and fascist, he set himself apart from other southern populists of the time by refusing to exploit the race issue. Just as his appeal – with slogans like "Every Mar. a King" – began to reach national proportions, with a bid for the presidency in the offing, he was shot by a local doctor whose exact motives remain unknown.

Other controversial figures to have worked in the building include the segregationist country singer Jimmie Davis, better remembered for writing *You Are My Sunshine* and riding his horse up the steps of the capitol than for any political skills, and David Duke, the former Grand Wizard of the Ku Klux Klan who was elected as a state representative in 1989 and was the unsuccessful Republican candidate for governor in 1991.

Tours of this stunning building, with its huge murals and sculptures, are enlivened by Louisiana's maverick political history. Guides point out stray bullets in the marble pillars of the ground-floor corridor and a pencil embedded in the ceiling of the legislative chamber by an exploding bomb. Long decreed that nothing in Baton Rouge could be taller than the 450ft capitol, so its 27th-floor observation deck is the best vantage point to look out over miles of greenery and the sluggish Mississippi (daily 8am–4pm; free).

The Riverfront

Mark Twain referred to Baton Rouge's **Old State Capitol** (in use from 1850 to 1931) as "that monstrosity on the Mississippi". A grey crenellated structure on a lumpy mound overlooking the river, penned in by an ugly wrought-iron fence, it looks like a cross between a castle and a cathedral, without the particular merits of either. Inside, a chunky iron staircase spirals up towards an elegant glass dome which casts splashes of colored light onto the central hall (Tues–Sat 9am–4.30pm; free). Plans are underway to develop a museum of Louisianan government in the building.

The **LSU Rural Life Museum**, 4560 Essen Rd at I-10, is a splendid collection of restored buildings, among them stores and cottages, re-creating pre-industrial life in a sultry garden setting (Mon–Fri 8.30am–4.30pm; $2).

One-hour harbor tours on the *Samuel Clemens* **riverboat** (summer daily 10am, noon & 2pm; winter Wed–Sun same times; $5) leave from the end of Florida Blvd, passing under the Baton Rouge Bridge. This was perhaps the most ingenious of Huey Long's constructions; his stipulation that it should have a clearance of just 65 feet ensured that big boats could go no further north, thereby boosting the port trade of Baton Rouge several times over.

Practicalities

Regular *Greyhound* **buses** to Baton Rouge come in at 1253 Florida Blvd, fifteen minutes from downtown in a dodgy area (☎343-4891). Except for route #7 to LSU, the local buses provided by *Capital City Transportation* (☎336-0821) are very infrequent.

Full **information** is available at the **visitor center** in the Capitol (daily 8am–4.30pm; ☎383-1825 or 1-800/527-6843). Downtown offers few **places to stay**; the most convenient is the comfortable *Ramada Hotel*, 1480 Nicholson Drive (☎387-1111 or 1-800/228-2828; ④). This is halfway between the center and the elegant shady campus of **Louisiana State University**, a mile south, which itself offers rooms (☎387-0297; ②). Large, very comfortable rooms at the *Best Western Chateau Louisianne Suite Hotel*, off I-10 at 710 Lobdell Ave (☎927-6700; ④), are ranged around a New Orleans-style atrium.

Downtown, you can lunch well with the politicos in the capitol's dining room for around $3, while the *Frostop Drive Inn*, 402 Government St (☎344-1179), provides a chance to wash down burgers and dogs with frozen root beer, amid Fifties decor and *Wurlitzer* sounds. At *Phil's Oyster Bar*, 5162 Government St (☎924-3045), the specialty is super-fresh oysters, and bargain Cajun and pasta dishes. *Ralph and Kacoo's*, 6110

Bluebonnet Rd (☎766-2113), serves seafood from catfish to crawfish, all heavily breaded, for around $10. It's a favorite of local boy Jimmy Swaggart, cousin of Jerry Lee Lewis and self-styled "old-fashioned, Holy Ghost-filled, shouting, weeping, soul-winning, gospel-preaching preacher". Further along Bluebonnet Rd, *Mulate's* (no 8322; ☎767-4694) offers fried, breaded Cajun food, plus live music and dancing nightly.

About 17 miles west of town, accessible from I-10 or US-190, *Joe's Restaurant* (Tues–Sun 11am–2pm & 5–9pm; ☎637-2625) on Hwy-77 in Livonia is one of the region's best, an old store set among moss-draped live oaks, serving seafood, quail, *boudin* (spicy Cajun sausage) with pepper jelly and other home-cooked Cajun treats.

Much of the city's **nightlife** revolves around the student bars on and near Highland Avenue; *Bayou*, 124 West Chimes St (☎346-1765), is a hip bar with pool tables, as seen in *sex, lies and videotape*. One neighborhood blues club that has been adopted by the student population – although the area should still be approached with extreme caution – is *Tabby's Blues Box*, 1314 North Blvd (☎387-9715), where veteran local bluesman Tabby and friends perform in spartan surroundings.

Lafayette and Around

LAFAYETTE, 130 miles northwest of New Orleans on I-10, is geographically central in Cajun country, and is the key city for its **oil** business. Originally named Vermilionville, after the orangey bayou nearby, it was renamed in the 1880s when the railroad came to town. Today Lafayette is a surprisingly quiet place, a city with a small-town feel, with absolutely no "downtown". It does offer, however, some lively Cajun history and good restaurants – and makes the best base for exploring the Cajun swamps and bayous.

Arrival, Information and Getting Around
Greyhound arrives in Lafayette at 315 Lee Ave (☎235-1541), and *Amtrak* a few blocks north at 133 E Grant Street. The **bus** system is of little use to visitors, but companies running local **tours** include *Acadiana To Go*, 619 Woodvale Ave (☎981-3918), and *Allons à Lafayette*, 127 Baudoin St (☎269-9607). If you need a taxi, try *Cajun Cabs* (☎235-7515). The Lafayette Parish **CVB** is at 16th and Evangeline Thruway (Mon–Fri 8.30am–5pm, Sat & Sun 9am–5pm; ☎232-3808 or, outside Louisiana, 1-800/346-1958).

The Town of Lafayette

In the center of Lafayette, such as it is, stands the Romanesque **St John's Cathedral**, 914 St John St, and the old **cemetery**, where the crumbling raised graves include that of Jean Mouton, the town's Cajun founder. Each of the magnificent branches of the 450-year old gnarled **St John Oak**, spreading over 200 feet opposite, weighs 70 tons. Three blocks north, the small **Lafayette Museum**, at 1122 Lafayette St (Tues–Sat 9am–5pm, Sun 3–5pm; $3), was the "Sunday home" – used as a townhouse after mass before the family returned to their plantation – of Jean's son Alexandre, Louisiana's first Democratic governor. It is filled with family memorabilia and Mardi Gras costumes.

The quirky red-brick **Old City Hall** at 217 Main St now houses *CODOFIL*, the organization dedicated to the preservation of Louisiana French; the concrete monstrosity across the road is the new City Hall. The campus of the **University of Southwestern Louisiana**, south of the center, boasts a swamp – complete with alligators, turtles, water birds and tattered Spanish moss – next to the Student Union.

The great energies Lafayette has put into tourism since the oil slump have created two excellent reconstructions of early Cajun communities. **Vermilionville**, at 1600 Surrey St across from the airport, is the easier to reach: an impressive living-history exhibition on the Bayou Vermilion, exploring the culture of Cajuns, Native Americans and Creoles (Mon–Thurs 9am–5pm, Fri–Sun 9am–9pm; $8). Plantation slave buildings sell coffee, beignets, and *boudin*, and stage cookery demonstrations. A large barn serves as a theater, with storytellers, dances, plays, and·noisy *fais-do-dos*, and the restaurant next door serves good Cajun lunches. Costumed craftspeople explain their work in Cajun French, and a simple chapel and cemetery host lectures on religious traditions, from voodoo to the *traiteurs*, Cajuns believed to have healing powers.

Ten miles or so from the visitor center, Lafayette's other folk-life museum, the **Acadian Village** at 200 Greenleaf Rd, depicts early nineteenth-century Cajun life along the bayous. Original structures – homes, stores, and a chapel – line a sluggish bayou set in gardens and woodlands, and are filled with traditional furnishings and crafts. The gift shop sells books, prints, crafts and food (daily 10am–5pm; $5).

Accommodation

Budget **rooms** are easy to find in Lafayette. Chain hotels line Evangeline Thruway just south of I-10, and US-90 and Hwy-182 towards New Iberia. **B&Bs** are welcoming and reasonably cheap, but you must book ahead (contact *Southern Comfort B&B Reservation Service*, 509 Fern St, New Orleans; ☎504/861-0082). There's **camping** at *Acadiana Park Campground*, 1201 E Alexander St (☎234-3838), northeast of town.

Bois des Chênes, 338 N Sterling St (☎233-7816). Very good B&B two miles from I-10, in the carriage house of Charles Mouton's 1821 plantation home. Rates include free bottle of wine and a remarkable breakfast. Also do good swamp tours (see p.506). Reservations required. ④–⑤.

Days Inn, 1620 N University Ave (☎237-8880). Comfortable, very big rooms northwest of town. ②.

Hotel Acadiana, 1801 W Pinhook Rd (☎233-8120). Luxury hotel near the airport and Vermilionville. Jacuzzis and outdoor pool. ③.

Mouton Manor, 310 Sidney Martin Rd (☎237-6996). Two rooms in 1806 Cajun plantation house north of town, in lovely three-acre setting, surrounded by pecan trees. ③.

T'Frere's House, 1905 Verot School Rd (☎984-9347). Hospitable, antique-filled B&B, with complimentary mint juleps. ④.

Eating In and Around Lafayette

For many Cajuns, learning to **cook** is a rite of passage as important as one's first fishing trip or *fais-do-do*. Eating is inseparable from dancing and music; evening – or afternoon, or even morning – entertainment revolves around local family-run restaurants which act as impromptu dance halls (see opposite). If you don't feel like dancing yourself, you can just watch, while downing a seafood dinner.

Cajun food is characterized by its use of anything going (they say a true Cajun cooks every part of a pig but its squeal). Basic, one-pot cooking it may be, but it's difficult to eat badly – and hard to spend over $15. Cajuns eat out all the time – Lafayette sells more restaurant food per person than any other city in America. At lunchtime, takeaway *boudin* goes down a treat, as do finger-licking specialties like rich pork cracklin' washed down with frosty beer. Some of the restaurants below are a short drive from town, but well worth the cab fare if you have no car.

Bayou Boudin and Cracklin, Bayou Teche, Hwy-94, Breaux Bridge (☎332-6158). Restored nineteenth-century Cajun country cottage selling *boudin*, hogshead cheese and crawfish balls, all prepared on the spot from traditional recipes.

Poche's Market and Restaurant, 3015A Main Hwy, Poche Bridge (☎332-2108). Out-of-the-way little Cajun fast-food place near Breaux Bridge, selling succulent crawfish *boudin*, pralines and cracklin', and home-cooked blue-plate specials.

Poor Boy's Riverside Inn, 240 Tubing Rd, Lafayette (☎837-4011). Good, reasonably priced Cajun food – alligator, catfish, crawfish – in refined atmosphere.

Prudhommes Cajun Café, 4676 N E Evangeline Thruway Service Rd, Carencro (☎896-7964). Run by the sister of New Orleans chef Paul Prudhomme. Down-to-earth country restaurant; exquisite shrimp *etouffé*, seafood-stuffed eggplant, banana bread and sweet potato muffins. Closes 2.30pm Sun.

CAJUN MUSIC

It's easy to "pass a good time" in Cajun country, with dances and *fais-do-dos* held tradition-ally on weekends. **Cajun music** is a jangling, infectious melange of accordion, violin and triangle, with traces of country, swing, jazz and blues. **Zydeco** is similar, but more blues-based, and more often played by black musicians. The nasal singing bears only a passing resemblance to the language spoken in France. Music is never performed without space for **dancing**; everyone from the smallest child to aged grandparent can join in. If you don't know how to two-step, ask someone to show you. Venues include restaurants (see oppo-site), simple dance halls, record stores and the streets themselves.

Downtown Alive!, downtown Lafayette (☎268-5566). Free street dances, including well-known Cajun and zydeco artists. Fri 5.30–8pm, April–June and Sept–Nov only.

El Sid O's Zydeco Club, 1523 N St Antoine St, Lafayette (☎237-1959). Dances Fri–Sun. Good house bands.

Four Seasons Lodge, 4855 W Congress Ave, Lafayette (☎989-2421). Live swamp-pop, coun-try and show-stopping soul from raven-haired veteran Warren Storm. Tues–Sat 9pm–2am.

Mulate's, 325 Mills Ave, Breaux Bridge (☎1-800/634-9880). Touristy but fun Cajun restau-rant. Seafood dinners under $15, big-name Cajun and zydeco music for no extra charge. Dancing nightly, and daily at noon. 15min from Lafayette on Hwy-94, a mile off I-10.

Prejean's, 3480 US-167 N, Lafayette (☎896-3247). Unfussy restaurant. A separate oyster bar serves reasonably priced fish and alligator to a lively local crowd. Dancing begins at 7pm.

Randol's, 2320 Kaliste Saloom Rd, Lafayette (☎981-7080). Locally famed dance hall serv-ing fresh seafood dinners (and specializing in soft-shell crabs). Their nightly *fais-do-dos* are occasionally televised.

Rendezvous des Cajuns, Liberty Center for Performing Arts, Second St and Park Ave, Eunice (☎457-7389). Live Cajun/zydeco radio and TV show, mostly in French, every Sat 6–8pm; also joke-tellers and recipes.

Savoy Music Center Accordion Factory, Eunice (☎457-9563). A popular Cajun record shop, producing accordions in its back room. Lively Sat-morning jam sessions, starting at about 9am and lasting until noon.

Slim's Y-Ki-Ki, Washington Rd, Opelousas (☎942-9980). Zydeco music and dancing.

Toby's Little Lodge, Opelousas (☎948-7787). Live French radio show with music and dancing.

CAJUN FESTIVALS

Cajun **festivals** (genuinely lively and enthusiastic local events, not concocted to attract tourists) are held almost daily, it seems, to celebrate anything from frogs to new harvests. They're a wonderful way to experience the food and music of the region, although for some of the larger events, it's a good idea to book a room in advance; the rest of the world is catching on to the fun, and Lafayette, especially, gets crowded.

Mardi Gras. Second only to the New Orleans bash, this pre-Lenten party begins on the Saturday before "Fat Tuesday", with street dancing. Cajun Mardi Gras differs from its city cousin; although there are private balls and parties, it is a far more pagan affair. The rural villages around Lafayette, like Eunice, Church Point and Mamou, are the scene of the *Courir du Mardi Gras* (see p.507).

Festival International de Louisiane, usually third week of April. Huge festival in Lafayette, with participants from all over the French-speaking world. Particular emphasis on indigenous music and food.

Breaux Bridge Crawfish Festival, first full weekend of May, Parc Hardy, Breaux Bridge. Crawfish-eating and peeling contests, craw-fish *etouffé* cook-offs, and crawfish races.

Festivals Acadiens, Third week of Sept in Lafayette. Cajun, zydeco and traditional French bands play all day (☎232-3737).

Southwest Louisiana Zydeco Festival, Saturday before Labor Day at the Southern Development Farm, Hwy-167, Plaisance. Zydeco performers play "black Creole" music, with regional cuisine and African-American arts and crafts (☎942-2392; $8).

Cajun Heritage and Music Festival, Second weekend of Oct. The Acadian Village is alive with music, auctions, storytelling, and Native American chanting.

Louisiana Yambilee, last week in Oct. Opelousas, yam capital of the world, goes all out to celebrate the sweet potato. Food stalls, sweet potato auctions, music, *Miss Yambilee* and *Lil' Miss Yum Yum* contests.

Touring Cajun Country

North of Lafayette, the **Cajun Prairie** has been described by folklorist Alan Lomax as the "Cajun Cultural Heartland". A patchwork of rice and soybean fields scattered with crawfish ponds, the region has a few tiny towns well worth visiting, where you'll be greeted with genuine warmth and interest from locals.

GRAND COTEAU, off I-49 ten miles north of Lafayette, is a picture-perfect little town, with whitewashed buildings – including a dazzling white chapel – and prettily winding roads. Since 1866, when a dying woman was miraculously healed by the intercession of a saint, in the **Academy of the Sacred Heart**, 1821 Academy Rd, devout Cajun Catholics have come here on pilgrimage. You can tour the old classrooms of this beautifully columned former school, and follow a long path through the ornate gardens, canopied by huge old oaks (Sun 1–4pm; $5).

The 1831 **Chretien Point Plantation**, 17 miles northwest of Lafayette on I-10, is Louisiana's oldest Greek Revival building. Its main staircase was the model for Tara in *Gone with the Wind*. Mrs Chretien, left to run the plantation after her husband's death in 1832, was very much in the Scarlett O'Hara mold. She scandalized the community by drinking, smoking, gambling and sitting with the men after dinner, and once shot an intruder, whose ghost roams the corridors. Bullet holes in the front door date from 1863, when Mrs Chretien's son showed a Masonic sign to an attacking Union general, who thereupon directed fire over the roof. Some outbuildings were destroyed, but the house and its inhabitants remained unharmed (daily 10am–5pm; $5.50).

Predominantly French-speaking **OPELOUSAS**, twenty miles north of Lafayette on I-49, was the boyhood home of Jim Bowie, Texas Revolutionary hero and inventor of the Bowie knife. The **Jim Bowie Museum**, 220 Academy St, is filled with his personal possessions (daily 8am–4pm; free; ☎948-6263). Opelousas' two other great claims to

---

SWAMP TOURS

Swamp tours are available from many landings in the **Atchafalaya Basin**. The basin is an eerie place; almost all its cypresses were harvested last century, and now just the twisted silhouettes of their stumps poke out of the sluggish waters. Cars cut right across on the enormous concrete I-10, and most of the old houseboats have been abandoned, or are used for weekend retreats. There is, however, plenty of wildlife, including sunbathing alligators and scores of fishing boats. Tours are conducted by Cajuns who see the basin as more than just a tourist attraction, and provide fascinating personal commentaries.

Angelle's Atchafalaya Tours, Whiskey River landing, Henderson. Twenty minutes from Lafayette, along I-10 and then Hwys 347 and 332, this quiet landing is run by the Angelle brothers, who also own the restaurant (and informal dance hall) on the bank. Taking a 2-hr Sunday afternoon tour and then returning to eat fresh crawfish at a *fais-do-do* is a wonderful way to spend a Cajun country day. (Daily 10am, 1pm and 3pm, extra 5pm tour in the summer; no reservations required; $8.50; ☎228-8567.)

Bois des Chênes Tours (☎233-7816). $30-per-person tours through various swamp locations, including a stopover for lunch at a backwoods hunting/fishing lodge owned by French-speaking Louisianans.

McGee's Basin Swamp Tours (☎228-2384). Tours leave McGee's Landing, on Rte 5 in

Henderson (a favorite fishing spot) at the same times as the *Angelle* tours, for similar price.

Annie Miller's Terrebonne Swamp and Marsh Tours (☎504-879-3934). 3-hr boat trips through the wildlife of the bayou. Two trips daily, March–Oct, from Miller's Landing on Big Bayou Black, in Houma (pronounced *Homer*), an oyster and shrimp fishing center on the soggy Bayou Terrebonne.

Zam's Bayou Swamp Tours, 135 Bayou Rd, Kraemer (☎504-633-7881). Not one of the furthest-reaching tours, but the main attraction is Edwin "Papa Gator" Tregle, alligator-trapper *extraordinaire*, who sells all manner of gnarled knick-knacks in the trading post. Tours at 10.30am, 1.30pm & 3.30pm daily; $12.50. The restaurant, unsurprisingly, serves assorted gator delicacies.

fame are as the birthplace of the great zydeco musician **Clifton Chenier** and – less trendily – as **yam** capital of the world.

To learn a little about the Cajun Prairie, head for friendly **EUNICE**, about 25 miles west of Opelousas. The exemplary **Prairie Cajun Cultural Center**, 250 W Park Ave (daily 8am–5pm; free), holds a far-reaching display of exhibits on local life, ranging across family, language, food, music and farming. Time your visit to enjoy one of Eunice's splendid down-home foodstops; *Johnson's Grocery,* 700 E Maple St (☎457-9314), serves fat, juicy *boudin* from 6am, and *Ruby's,* on Walnut and Second, dishes out Cajun lunches for around $3. Although there's little else to see in Eunice, it's at the hub of the region's music scene (see p.505); the regular **Liberty Center** and *Savoy Music Center Accordion Factory* bashes are supplemented by the riotous annual *Courir du Mardi Gras,* when masked horsemen in colorful capes gallop through the countryside, gathering ingredients for the community Mardi Gras gumbo from the neighbors.

From here it's a short way north to **VILLE PLATTE**, and *Floyd's Music Store,* 434 E Main St, owned by dashing Floyd Soileau, the world's chief distributor of South Louisiana music, and stocking everything from zydeco re-issues to contemporary swamp pop. If Mr Soileau isn't around, you could well find him listening to the rocking jukebox a couple of doors down at the *Pig Stand Restaurant,* 318 E Main St (☎363-2883), where giant plates of mouth-watering fried chicken, smothered sausage and barbecue come heaped with rice, gravy, black-eyed peas and potato salad.

South of Lafayette

South of Lafayette is bayou country, a marshy expanse of rivers and lakes dominated by the mighty Atchafalaya swamp. Unsurprisingly, the economy is based on fishing and shrimping, with hunting in the forests and sugar fields. Old **ST MARTINVILLE** on the Bayou Teche, just off US-90 a dozen miles south of Lafayette, was a major port of entry for exiled Acadians. The **Evangeline Oak**, on Port Street where it meets the bayou, marks where Emmeline Labiche, the inspiration for Longfellow's *Evangeline,* disembarked after her hard journey from Nova Scotia, only to hear that her lover was engaged to another. In the nineteenth century this little country town was known as "le petit Paris", filled with French Royalists fleeing the Revolution and re-creating a glittering city life of soirées and balls. It was later decimated by yellow fever, fire and hurricane, and is now just a peaceful hamlet, kept going by day-trippers from Lafayette.

The eighteenth-century St Martin de Tours **Catholic Church**, 103 Main St, contains a gold and silver sanctuary light and intricate carved font said to have been gifts from Louis XVI and Marie Antoinette. Next door, the friendly little **Petit Paris museum** exhibits fabulous local Mardi Gras costumes. Behind the church, on the left, the **Evangeline Monument** was donated by the producers of the 1929 movie *The Romance of Evangeline,* and is modelled on Dolores del Rio, its star. From here you can walk along the bayou on a wooden boardwalk. North of town on Hwy-31, the **Longfellow-Evangeline State Commemorative Area** (daily, summer 9am–7pm; winter 9am–5pm; $2 per car) on the bayou contains a **Creole Plantation House**, made with the bousillage mixture characteristic of early Louisianan buildings, and held together by wooden pegs. If St Martinville's sleepy charm wins you over you might want to **stay**; try the *Old Castillo Hotel and Restaurant,* 220 Evangeline Blvd next to the Evangeline Oak (☎394-4010; ④), a comfortable mid-nineteenth-century hotel, once favored by French aristocrats. The food here is also good, with alligator, fish and home-made bread.

AVERY ISLAND, seven miles southwest of the bayou town of **New Iberia** along a toll-road, is not an island at all; it's the tip of a massive salt dome. **Tabasco sauce** is still prepared from a family recipe in the *McIlhenny* factory, using the hot chili peppers that grow here (Mon–Fri 9–11.45am & 1–3.45pm, Sat 9am–11.45am; free). The steamy 200-acre **Jungle Gardens** are full of exotic camelias, azaleas and irises, and serve as a sanctuary for blue herons, black ibises and snowy egrets (daily 9am–6pm; $5).

MORGAN CITY, about thirty miles southwest of Franklin on the Atchafalaya River, was where the first *Tarzan* was filmed in 1917. It's shown daily at the **Information Center**, 725 Myrtle St (daily 8am–4pm; ☎384-3343), from where you can also buy tickets for daily guided walking tours of the **Swamp Gardens** opposite, which trace the settlement of the Atchafalaya Basin (daily 8am–4pm; $2).

NORTHERN LOUISIANA

North Louisiana is at the heart of the region known as the **Ark-La-Tex**, a blend of the cotton fields, Bible Belt mentality and soft drawl of the Deep South, with the ranches and oil (and passion for country music) of Texas, and hilly Arkansan forests (resplendent in the fall). **Shreveport**, its key city, has more in common with, say, Tyler, Texas, than New Orleans. Having been settled by the Scottish and Irish after the Louisiana Purchase, the area is strongly Baptist, with less of a penchant for fun than south Louisiana. At least it shares its profusion of **festivals**; Shreveport's **State Fair** is a real c'n'w hoedown, with rodeos and big-name country performers.

Natchitoches

Tiny **NATCHITOCHES** (pronounced *Nakitish*), in the sleepy cotton fields of the Cane River, is the oldest European settlement in Louisiana, having begun life as a French trading post in 1714. A Catholic oasis in a Protestant desert, it was swiftly fortified when its Spanish and Native American customers started to combine aggression with commerce.

With its lovingly restored Creole architecture, Natchitoches' exquisite **Front Street** on the river looks a lot like New Orleans' French Quarter. The lacy iron balconies, spiral staircases and cobbled courtyards are complemented by friendly old-style stores such as *Kaffies* haberdashers. The 1717 **Immaculate Conception Catholic Church**, at Second and Church, has many of its original French features, including glass chandeliers and a hand-carved font. A nearby **Starwalk** commemorates celebrities with local connections, such as John Wayne, Clementine Hunter (see opposite), and the cast of *Steel Magnolias*, which was filmed and set here in 1988, and centered on the lives of a group of strong women. **Fort St Jean Baptiste**, at Mill and Jefferson, is a five-acre reconstruction of the town's 1716 fort, with rough wooden and adobe buildings, all enclosed by a tall wooden fence (daily 9am–5pm; $2).

Kate Chopin – whose nineteenth-century novel *The Awakening*, about a married woman's desire for independence, shocked the nation – is celebrated by the **Bayou Folk Museum** in her nearby hometown of **Cloutierville** (Mon–Sat 9am–5pm, Sun 1–5pm; $2).

Practicalities

Natchitoches lies seventy miles southeast of Shreveport, on Hwy-6 off I-49. *Greyhound* (☎352-8341) comes in on the west side of town, on Caspari St near the university, but there's no public transit or taxi; to avoid being stranded the car-less should reserve accommodation in advance at a **B&B**, and arrange to be collected. One of the most welcoming is the *Fleur de Lis*, 336 Second St (☎352-6621; ④, prepaid reservations only), with its romantic verandah and huge communal breakfasts; the *Jefferson House*, by the river at 229 Jefferson St (☎352-3957; ④), is also nice.

The **visitor center**, 781 Front St (Mon–Sat 9am–5pm, Sun 10am–2pm; ☎352-8072), provides self-guided walking and driving tours, will put you in touch with tour companies, and can help find accommodation. Good places to **eat** include the chintzy *Just Friends* at 746 Front St (☎352-3836), and *Lasyone's Meat Pie Kitchen* (☎352-3353), around the corner at 622 Second St. Lasyone, the chef, happily chats to customers gobbling his special meat pies (spicy, flaky and lightly fried), red beans and sausage, fresh corn bread and rich cream pies. Come early for dinner; it closes at 7pm.

The Cane River Plantations

The rural **Cane River roads** are dotted with ramshackle houses and small farms. As you drive past the dungareed farmers sitting on porches, and the women hanging out washing, you'll come across many **plantation homes**, some overgrown and in sad disrepair, others beautifully restored and well-kept.

Melrose (daily noon–4pm; $4), sixteen miles south of Natchitoches on Hwy-119, has a romantic history. It was granted in 1794 to Marie Coincoin, a freed slave, by her owner, Claude Metoyer – the father of ten of her fourteen children. By the 1830s, the slave-operated plantation had grown to 12,000 acres, and Coincoin was able to buy freedom for two of her children and one of her grandchildren. At the turn of the century, "Miss Cammie" Henry turned the crumbling Melrose into an arts community, visited by writers such as John Steinbeck and William Faulkner. In the 1940s a black field worker, **Clementine Hunter**, started to paint vivid images of rural life, using left-over materials. She lived to be over one hundred, and her works are on show in the upper storey of the 1800 **African House**, which resembles a Congo mud hut and was used as the slave jail. A short film about Melrose is shown in the **Big House** – a typical plantation home, part brick, part wood.

Shreveport

SHREVEPORT, in Louisiana's northwest corner, was established in 1839, after Henry Miller Shreve had spent seven years clearing a 160-mile logjam which clogged the Red River. Built on land "given" by the Caddo Indians to Shreve's business partner Larkin Edwards (or so he claimed), it was a prosperous cotton, lumber and oil port until the river rebelled, silting up so seriously that it was no longer navigable.

Despite the depression caused by the oil slump, Shreveport remains the hub of the Ark-La-Tex, flying the flags of all three states. Links with Texas are especially strong; in 1873 there was even a short-lived bid to annex Shreveport and all the land west of the Red River to the Lone Star state.

This city of steakhouses, cowboy boots and Stetsons has always tapped its feet to country music, and in the 1930s and 1940s was home to radio's **Louisiana Hayride**. The show is now broadcast on the first and third Saturday of each month from the *Airline High School* in **Bossier City** across the river, also notable for its restaurants and the Louisiana Downs racetrack.

Arrival, Information and Getting Around

Shreveport Regional Airport is five miles southwest of downtown, where *Greyhound* arrives on Fannin St (☎424-4061). The city bus system, *Sportrans*, is little use for seeing the scattered attractions, running every half-hour to Bossier and the shopping malls, but few places else. The **visitor center** at 629 Spring St (Mon–Fri 8am–5pm; ☎222-9391), has an historical walking tour of the downtown area.

The City

Activity in downtown Shreveport focuses on the green riverfront. Great energies are going into revitalization, but it's not all that exciting, and for most of the year offers little more than pleasant views and walks. There are, however, some lively annual festivals, such as the two-day **Festa Italiana** in October, a celebration of Italian food and culture which includes the *La Gran Del Naso Piu Grandios*, when big noses compete on their character, shape, size and appearance. Early in October, the eight-day **Red River Revel** incorporates classical and country music, clogging and street entertainment.

The old-fashioned donut-shaped **Louisiana State Museum**, in the State Fairground, has a large collection of artefacts from **Poverty Point**, in the far northeastern corner of the state. All that remains of this ancient pre-Caddoan settlement, in use from around 1700 BC and thought to be the earliest community in the Mississippi valley, is a series of huge concentric earthern ridges (Tues–Sat 9am–4.30pm, Sun 1–5pm; free).

Southeast of downtown, on the campus of Centenary College, the small **Meadows Museum of Art** exhibits the works of Jean Despujols, commissioned in the 1930s by the French Society of Colonial Painters to travel through Indochina. He spent twenty months painting priests, chiefs and young men and women; his diaries, which are apparently a bit raunchy, are as yet unpublished. The paintings, though, make interesting ethnographic records (Tues–Fri 1–5pm, Sat & Sun 2–5pm; free).

An interesting view of nineteenth-century local life can be had at the **Pioneer Heritage Center**, on the campus of Louisiana State University at 8515 Youree Drive. Costumed guides give tours through five restored buildings and give demonstrations of making cypress shingles, bricks and lye soap (March–Dec Sun 1.30–4.30pm; $1).

The gardens of the **American Rose Center**, sixteen miles west, contain thousands of species of rose and hundreds of other flowers, and has serpentine paths shaded by towering cypress trees and dotted with statues and gazebos. Open all year, they are at their best during the blooming season, April to October (daily 10am–6pm; $3).

Accommodation

Shreveport's **accommodation** options are uninspiring but adequate. The cheapest are near the airport on Monkhouse Drive, or on I-20 around downtown, though in the eagerness to attract conventions, even upmarket hotels are reasonably priced. If you're **camping**, try *KOA Shreveport/Bossier*, I-20 exit 10 (☎687-1010).

Best Western Chateau Suite Hotel, I-20 at Spring St (☎222-7620). Luxury downtown hotel. River views, a pool, and free transportation to the airport and bus station. ⑤.

Days Inn, 4935 W Monkhouse Rd (☎636-0080). Comfortable rooms, free transportation to bus station and nearby airport. ③.

Fairfield Place B&B, 2221 Fairfield Ave (☎222-0048). Victorian inn in old part of town, gourmet breakfast included. Reservations essential. ④.

Eating

Shreveport's cuisine pilfers elements from Southern, Tex-Mex, and Louisiana cooking, resulting in delicious dishes like shrimp with guacamole and fluffy cornbread, as well as the usual gumbo and jambalaya.

The Acadiana Café, 4100 Barksdale Blvd (☎746-9461). Simple wooden Bossier City restaurant serving excellent – and inexpensive – Cajun and Creole seafood and crawfish.

The Centenary Oyster House, 1309 Centenary Blvd (☎221-7596). Gourmet burgers and raw oysters at reasonable prices. Live weekend entertainment, open Mon–Sat until 2am.

City Grille, 211 Texas St (☎221-3685). Downtown pastel-and-pine lunch place. Great, innovative, nouvelle Southwestern cuisine ranging from $5 pasta lunches to $16 dinners.

Don's Seafood, 3100 Highland Ave (☎865-4291). Cajun seafood dishes, crawfish, gumbo and red beans and rice, at remarkably low prices.

Nightlife and Entertainment

Shreveport's music scene remains vibrant: bluesy, distinctly country, and quite different from the Cajun or jazz heard in south Louisiana. The high spot is the black-oriented **Good Times Festival** in mid-June.

Ark-La-Tex Round-up, 4725 Greenwood Rd (☎861-1539). Live music every first and third Sat.

Enoch's Café, 1911 Centenary Blvd (☎222-9942). Shack-like venue, serving Cajun food and featuring regional musicians, poetry readings and lively blues jams. Open until 1am Mon–Sat.

Strand Theater, 619 Louisiana Ave (☎226-1481). Restored 1920s theater; blues, jazz, comedy and drama.

CHAPTER NINE

TEXAS

Still cherishing the memory that from 1836 to 1845 it was an independent nation in its own right, **TEXAS** stands out as distinct from the rest of the United States. While its sheer size – eight hundred miles from east to west and nearly a thousand from top to bottom – gives it a great geographical diversity, its shared history, culture and ideology bind it firmly together. Independence is key to the Texan mentality; from the overriding distrust of government – any government – to the absence of unionized labor. As the anti-litter campaign has it, "Don't mess with Texas".

Preconceived ideas about what exactly is "Texan" are soon shattered. Each of the major tourist destinations has its own distinct character. Hispanic **San Antonio**, for example, with its Mexican population and historic importance, has a laid-back feel absent from the big-city neurosis of **Houston** or **Dallas**, while trendy **Austin** revels in a lively music scene and intellectualism found nowhere else.

Regional differences are vast. The swampy, forested **east** is more like Louisiana than the pretty **Hill Country** or the agricultural plains of the **Panhandle**, and the tropical

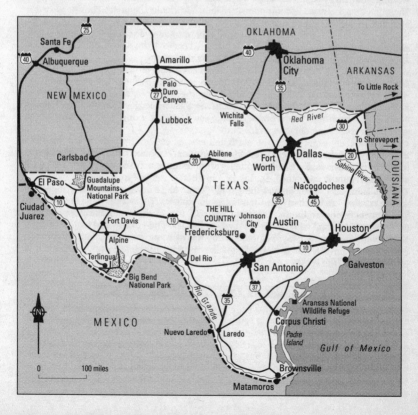

Gulf Coast has little in common with the mountainous **deserts** of the west. Changes in **climate** are equally dramatic; snow is common on the Panhandle, whereas the humidity of Houston, in particular, is only made bearable by non-stop high-power air-conditioning.

One thing shared by the whole of Texas is the constant boasting – everything has to be bigger and better than anywhere else. Such chauvinism is tempered both by a delight in self-parody and by the state's melting-pot of cultures. The much-cited Texan **friendliness** is not imaginary; to be unwelcoming would simply be unpatriotic. Texas is, after all, named for an Indian word meaning friend, *tejas*, and a visit here, especially to the Panhandle or the Hill Country, is not for those who want to be alone.

History

Early inhabitants of Texas included the Caddo in the east and nomadic Coahuiltecans further south. The **Comanche**, who arrived from the Rockies in the 1600s, soon found themselves at war when the **Spanish** ventured in, looking for gold. In the 1700s, threatened by French hopes of westward expansion from Louisiana, the Spanish began to build **missions** and forts, although these had minimal impact on the nomadic way of life. When Mexico won its independence from Spain in 1821, Texas was part of the deal. At first, the Mexicans were keen to open up their land, and offered generous incentives to settlers. Stephen Austin ("the father of Texas") established Anglo-American colonies in the Brazos and Colorado River valleys. However, the Mexican leader Santa Anna soon became alarmed by Anglo aspirations to autonomy, and his increasing restrictions led to the eight-month **Texan Revolution** of 1835–36. Legions of tourists are drawn by the romance of the Revolution to **San Antonio**, site of the legendary **Battle of the Alamo**, which though a military disaster presaged independence. Today's street names echo the conflict: Crockett, Travis, and Bowie were all heroes at the Alamo, and Houston was the general who finally led the army to victory at San Jacinto.

The short-lived **Republic of Texas**, which included territory now in Oklahoma, New Mexico, Colorado, Kansas and Wyoming, served to define the state's identity. In 1845, Texas joined the Union on the understanding that it could secede whenever it so wished. This is still written into the constitution, as is the proviso that it can, at any time, divide itself into five separate states. You'll see the **Lone Star** emblazoned on everything from advertising to architecture.

The influence, especially in the north and east, of settlers from the southern states and their attendant slave-centered cotton economy resulted in Texas joining the **Confederacy**. No major Civil War battles were fought on Texan soil, however, and it remained relatively unscathed. During Reconstruction, settlers from both the North and the South began to pour in, and the phrase "Gone to Texas" was familiarly applied to anyone fleeing the law, bad debts or unhappy love affairs. This was also the period of the great cattle drives, when the longhorns roaming free in the south and west of Texas were rounded up and taken to the railroads in Kansas. The Texan – and national – fascination with the romantic myth of the **cowboy** has its roots in this era, and still prevails; today his regalia – Stetson, boots and bandana – is virtually a state costume, especially in Fort Worth and the West.

ACCOMMODATION PRICE CODES

All accommodation prices in this book have been coded using the symbols below. Note that prices are for the least expensive double rooms in each establishment.
For a full explanation see p.35 in *Basics*.

①	up to $30	④	$60–80	⑦	$130–180
②	$30–45	⑤	$80–100	⑧	$180+
③	$45–60	⑥	$100–130		

Along with ranching and agriculture, **oil** has been crucial. After the first big gusher in 1901, at Spindletop on the Gulf Coast, the focus of the Texan economy – and culture – shifted almost overnight from agriculture towards rapid industrialization. Boom towns flew up as wildcatters chased the wells, and millions of dollars were made as ranchers, who had previously thought their land only fit for cattle, sold out at vast profit. Texas today produces one-third of all the oil in the United States, and the sight of nodding pump jacks is one of the state's most potent images.

Getting Around Texas

Texan distances are best negotiated by **car**; in fact in the larger cities like Dallas or Houston to drive is all but essential. **Greyhound** routes are concentrated between the major cities of the east and the central region, though buses also serve the Gulf Coast, the Rio Grande valley, West Texas and to a lesser extent the Panhandle. **Amtrak** has two main routes. The *Sunset Limited*, between Miami and LA, passes through Houston, San Antonio (at 3am), and El Paso three times weekly, also stopping at Alpine (for Big Bend). The *Texas Eagle* links Chicago and LA daily via all these cities and Dallas/Fort Worth and Austin. **Flying** saves time and can be very cheap; look for price wars between airlines such as *Southwest*, *Chapparal* and *Texas*. Over thirty cities have airports.

Where Texas really falls down is on **public transport** within the cities themselves; mass transit has proved impractical in a state where long distances – in Houston many people travel at least thirty miles to work – and low petrol prices make the love affair with the car almost inevitable. **Hitching** is not to be encouraged, and **cycling** only really makes sense within cities such as Austin and San Antonio.

SOUTHERN TEXAS AND THE GULF COAST

The coastline of south Texas curves from Beaumont (the site of the first major oil strike in Texas) on the much-touristed **Gulf Coast**, down past the urban monster of Houston, to the Rio Grande, the border with Mexico. Giant, cosmopolitan **Houston** dominates everything; its great wealth has led to a thriving arts scene, but ultimately it overpowers, rather than relates to, the rest of the region. Geographically and culturally, this area has two distinct faces. To the east are the seaside resorts of the prairie, rolling away from the hills and forests of east Texas. Much of the coast is feeling the strain of rapid property development and commercialization, but there are still unspoiled stretches along the **Padre Island National Seashore**. In the south, a Hispanic influence spreads north from the fertile Rio Grande valley. The border towns here have little charm except as points of entry to Mexico for cheap shopping and entertainment. A hot, swampy climate is one factor uniting south Texas. Houston, especially, is unbearable in the summer, one reason for the mass exodus to the coast.

Houston

HOUSTON is an ungainly beast of a city, crazed and confused by overdevelopment during the oil boom and then traumatized by the sudden slump of the early Eighties. It's a suffocating place, choking with traffic, and facing crime rates shooting as high as its surreal space-age downtown skyline. Yet for all this, its sheer energy, its relentless Texan pride, and above all its refusal to take itself totally seriously, give it a perverse appeal. That Howard Hughes came from Houston makes absolute sense; eccentric, domineering and sordid, the millionaire typified all that makes the city intriguing.

The **area code** for Houston is ☎713.

There is no good reason why Houston exists at all; it was founded on a muddy mire in 1837 by two brothers from New York who hoped it would become the capital of the new Republic of Texas. For all their wild claims about its potential as a port, and its (imaginary) urban attractions, the more promising site of Austin was made capital in 1839. However, by then drunken and diseased Houston had somehow established itself as a commercial center. Oil – discovered in 1901, and, like the city itself, unpredictable and heading for obsolescence – became the foundation, along with cotton and real estate, of vast private fortunes. However, the contradictions of urban life are still writ large, and abject poverty (not least among the blacks who migrated here from the rural South in the 1960s) coexists with ostentatious wealth.

Arrival, Information and Getting Around

Downtown Houston is at the intersection of interstates 10 (San Antonio–New Orleans) and 45 (Dallas–Galveston), with most of what you'll want to see encircled by Loop 610, now being widened on the west to include the huge Galleria mall. **Houston Intercontinental Airport** (☎230-3000), 25 miles north, is linked by the *Express Bus* ($9.75), which drops off at the *Hyatt Regency* in the center, the Medical Center to the south, and the Galleria. Taxis cost from $26 to $45. **Hobby Airport**, seven miles north, just west of I-45, has information centers in each terminal, and the van service (☎644-8359) into town costs $5. The downtown **tourist office** is at 3300 Main St (Mon–Fri 8.30am–5pm; ☎523-5050).

Amtrak arrives at 902 Washington Ave downtown. Have your camera ready for a splendid view of the skyline, though the station itself is small, isolated, and barely served by taxis. Try to arrive here, or at the large and modern *Greyhound* terminal (2121 Main St; ☎759-6565), during daylight.

City Transportation

There are few options for non-drivers in Houston. The *Metro Buses* are predominantly for commuters, **taxis** (most reliable firm – *Yellow Cabs*, ☎236-1111) are expensive, and the humid climate and huge distances make walking unappealing. However, in the face of crippling traffic congestion, efforts are being made to encourage mass transit. Furious debates are raging about the possible construction of an underground rail system. Maps of the city's **bus** routes can be had from the Customer Service Center, 912 Dallas Ave (Mon–Fri 10am–6pm). Local fares are 85¢, while the downtown *Texas Special* shuttles cost 25¢. Full information is on ☎739-4000.

Gray Line Tours runs daily **coach tours** for $20 (602 Sampson St; ☎223-8800).

The City

It's demoralizing and unwise to try and see too much of Houston in one go; best to concentrate on **downtown** or the **Museum District**, which can be walked around at leisure. Houston's human face is most evident in the **Montrose** area, on the way to yuppification but still home to eccentrics and bohemians.

Downtown

Since the oil crisis in the early Eighties, the frenzy of skyscraper-building has slowed down, but Houston's skyline remains an unforgettable monument to an earlier age of certainty. Observation floors on the **Texas Commerce Tower**, 600 Travis St, and the **Texaco Plaza** offer views of the endless plateau over which the city spreads.

Most people escape the heat by staying underground, in the four miles of air-conditioned **tunnels** entered from the *Hyatt Regency* or the Main Street banks. Don't bother to explore these, however; they're a confusing and unaesthetic way for visitors to get around, despite the city's pride in their shops and restaurants. One consequence of this subterranean world is a surreal, dreamlike isolation above ground, as the plate-glass towers shimmer with reflections of the modern sculptures scattered at every turn (such as the Mirós outside the Texas Commerce Tower).

Nestling below the skyscrapers, **Sam Houston Historical Park** on Bagby St contains restored structures such as a church and shop, while **Market Square** features some of the original buildings at the heart of the early city, including the 1860 Creole *La Carafe*, at 813 Congress St. Once a trading post, it is now a laid-back bar complete with shadowy corners and old wooden floors.

Even if you can't afford a performance in the **Theater District**, west of Milam St between Preston and Rusk, visit the **Wortham Theater**, 500 Texas St (☎237-1439), which houses the city's opera and ballet. The beautifully sculpted interior, perfect acoustics and secluded private bars take the breath away, as does the knowledge that the whole set-up cost $70 million – all raised in 1987, before the theater was even built.

The Museum District and the Rice University Area

Five miles southwest of downtown, the oak-lined boulevards of the quiet and leafy **Museum** and **Rice** districts are enjoyable to explore on foot. There are students everywhere, cycling, walking or just lounging on the grass, and several good bookshops.

An airy and naturally lit building at 1515 Sul Ross – designed by Renzo Piano, who contributed to the Pompidou Center in Paris – houses the **Menil Collection**. Among the superb works gathered by oil millionaires Jean and Dominique de Menil, African and Egyptian sculpture share space with Picasso, Léger and Magritte (Wed–Sun 11am–7pm; free). A little way east, the minimalist Ecumenical **Rothko Chapel**, 1409 Sul Ross (daily 10am–6pm), contains fourteen morose paintings commissioned from Mark Rothko shortly before his death. The artist considered these to be his most important works, but many people today deride the building's resemblance to a nuclear bunker. The broken obelisk in the small park outside is dedicated to Martin Luther King Jr.

At the intersection of Bissonet with Main, the **Museum of Fine Arts** features an eclectic collection from all eras, with Renaissance art especially well represented (Tues, Wed, Fri & Sat 10am–5pm, Sun noon–6pm; $3, free Thurs 5–9pm). Crane your neck upwards from the Matisses and Rodins in the pine-shaded **Cullen Sculpture Garden** outside to the downtown skyline. In a city with no zoning regulations, such architectural incongruity springs on you constantly.

Hermann Park, three miles south of downtown, is a pleasant green space, with its own Japanese meditation garden. Its excellent **Museum of Natural Science** (Mon–Fri 9am–5pm, Sat 9am–6pm, Sun noon–6pm; $2.50, free Thurs 9am–noon) includes exhibits on natural history, an IMAX theater, and a stunning gem collection. There's also a good coffee shop and a fountain shaped like Texas. The park is best avoided at night.

The Galleria and Around

The ultra-modern **Galleria** hypermall lies just west of the loop, on Westheimer. Over three hundred smart shops, movie theaters, and restaurants, plus a skating rink and a glass-floored jogging track, pay homage to Houston's love affair with modern architecture, upmarket style and Texan tack. Across the way, a waterfall-sized fountain cascades outside the black glass **Transco Tower**, looming breathtakingly high when lit at night.

Montrose

Bohemian and fun **Montrose** begins at the junction of Smith and Elgin. It's all quirky sleaze, abounding with tattoo parlors, vintage clothing stores, art galleries, and junk shops full of barbed-wire cacti and other curiosities. Unfortunately, plans are underway, spearheaded by a group of wealthy young Texans, to redevelop this as "the Old Westheimer District", erecting old-fashioned gas street lamps and other such unnecessities. The teenagers who once cruised the streets on Saturday night have been cleared away and the strip joints closed down, but this has long been the base for a very visible and strong gay community, and a high concentration of gay bars and clubs remains.

Accommodation

There's little call for budget accommodation in central Houston, where most visitors have cars; cheap hotels are concentrated near the Astrodome and outside the Loop, and motorists should try I-45, or the Katy or Southwest freeways.

You might also arrange **bed and breakfast** accommodation in advance; the human touch can be welcome in a city this potentially alienating. As well as the places listed below, try *B&B Texas Style*, 4224 W Red Bird Lane, Dallas TX 75237 (☎214/298-8586).

Grant Inn, 8200 S Main St (☎668-8000). Reliable motel near the Astrodome. ②.

The Highlander, 607 Highland Ave (☎861-7545). Luxurious B&B northwest of the city, with shady garden, porch, pool and whirlpool. ④.

Perry House Houston International Hostel, 5302 Crawford St (☎523-1009). Near Herrmann Park in a pleasant neighborhood. ①.

Sara's Bed and Breakfast, 941 Heights Blvd (☎868-1130). Less than four miles northwest of downtown, near Memorial Park. A chintzy Victorian house with a fine view of downtown Houston, serving continental breakfasts on the porch. ③.

YMCA, 1600 Louisiana Ave (☎659-8501). Clean downtown dorms, $15. ①.

Eating

There's plenty of variety in Houston's **food**; the large immigrant population has left its mark. Look out for Mexican, Vietnamese and even Indian restaurants, and the many good delis – such as the eight outlets of *Antone's Deli* – serving huge salads and sandwiches with an international flavor.

Andy's Home Café, 1115 E 11th St (☎861-9423). Good late-night Tex-Mex food, and huge breakfasts at reasonable prices.

Goode Company, 5109 Kirby Rd (☎522-2530). Fabulous barbecue, with creative menu, and c'n'w atmosphere.

India's Restaurant, 5704 Richmond Ave (☎226-0130). One of Houston's best north Indian restaurants, specializing in tandoori.

A Moveable Feast, 2202 W Alabama Ave (☎528-3585). Ideologically sound vegetarian food.

Treebeard's, 315 Travis St (☎225-2160), and 1100 Louisiana St (☎752-2601). Cheap and tasty downtown Cajun lunches, Mon–Fri 11am–2pm.

Van Loc, 3010 Milam Ave (☎528-6441). Popular Vietnamese and Chinese place, open until 3am at the weekend.

Entertainment and Nightlife

There's no shortage of things to do in Houston; just check the listings in the free *Houston Press*, or the more alternative *Public News*, and you'll find everything from feminist events to Pakistani costume shows. **Cajun** and **zydeco** has been significant in Houston since a wave of migration from rural Louisiana in the early 1960s, and there's a strong **blues** tradition, but you'll have to head outside the Loop for **country and western** music; most urban Houstonians are too hip to hoe down. **Miller Outdoor Theater** in Hermann Park, at 2020 Hermann Drive (☎520-3290), has free symphony concerts, ballet and opera on summer evenings, a Juneteenth Blues festival and a Shakespeare Festival around the end of July. The **Alley Theater** at 615 Texas Ave

(☎228-8421) offers last-minute discount seats, and *Showtix* (☎785-2787), at 11140 Westheimer Ave, has half-price theater, dance and music tickets.

On summer Thursday evenings downtown Houston hosts a giant street party with live music and drinks.

Bars and Clubs

Axiom, 2425 McKinney Ave (☎224-1240). Seriously trendy club, offering avant garde multimedia art/video/music performances.

Bon Ton Room, 4216 Washington Ave (☎864-0010). Good live R&B, between downtown and Memorial Park, plus some of the best Cajun and zydeco musicians around.

Cody's Bar, 3400 Montrose Ave (☎522-9747). Established jazz club with balcony seating. Tues–Sat.

Etta's Lounge, 5120 Scott St (☎528-2611). Old blues bar, south of downtown.

The Last Resort, 1403 Nance St (☎226-8563). East of downtown, in an arty and isolated area. Once a house of ill repute; knock twice on the closed door to get in. Good, cheap Tex-Mex food and live bands in the back garden; but you can just drink all night if you prefer.

Around Houston

Houston's double-edged status as having both historical importance and all the trappings of a twenty-first-century "space city" is neatly demonstrated by two possible excursions, both about twenty miles south of the city.

San Jacinto Battleground State Historical Park

San Jacinto Battleground, 21 miles southeast of Houston, was the site of a fifteen-minute fight, two months after the Alamo in 1836, in which the Texans all but wiped out the superbly trained Mexican army. You see little but miles of flat land from the observation deck ($2) of the tallest **monument** in the world (570ft, topped by a 35ft Lone Star), but the **Museum of History** inside is more interesting, with the stirring and emotive 35-minute movie *Texas Forever!* (daily, park 8am–7pm, museum 9am–6pm, $3.50).

NASA

NASA has been controlling space flight from the **Space Center**, 25 miles south of Houston off I-45 (on bus #246 from downtown), since the launch of Gemini 4 in 1965. As a working facility, it's not really geared to tourists; all tours are self-guided, although you are rushed through the (tiny) Mission Control Room itself with a quick-fire lecture. Behind-the-scenes tram tours of the complex start with an impressive array of hands-on exhibits at the visitor center (daily 9am–4pm; free); you get to try on space helmets, inspect moonrocks and some remarkably cranky-looking rocket replicas, join astronauts and scientists in the cafeteria, and stock up on tacky space-age presents.

The Gulf Coast

You only have to look at the number of condo developments along the **Gulf Coast** to see that this is a major tourist destination. The climate ranges from balmy at **Galveston** to subtropical at the Mexican border, but everywhere it's windy; **Corpus Christi** rivals Chicago as gustiest city in the States, and devastating hurricanes in the early 1900s all but ruined the traditional economy. The fierce tide, progressively gnawing away at the beaches, must place tourism itself in jeopardy; but for the moment, Galveston offers history, shopping and low-key relief from uptight Houston, while Corpus Christi to the south makes the best base for the beaches of Padre Island National Seashore. Rockport, a weathered resort on Hwy-35, is convenient for the Aransas National Wildlife Refuge, sheltering endangered whooping crane, armadillo and alligators.

Galveston

In 1890 **GALVESTON** was a thriving port, far larger than Houston; many newly arrived European immigrants chose to stay here in "the Queen of the Gulf". The building of Houston's Ship Canal, after the hurricanes of 1900 killed over six thousand people and washed away much of the land, left the coastal town to fade slowly away. Its recent revitalization as a historic district and beach resort has renewed spirits somewhat, but just beneath the pastel prettiness of the restored Victorian architecture and the relentless positivism of the inhabitants is a deathly stillness, as if the place is holding its breath, waiting to see if this time it can succeed without calamity or disaster.

Galveston's old Santa Fe depot at 25th St and the Strand is now a **Railroad Museum**, displaying steam trains, Pullman cars and endless artefacts relating to train travel in a skilful evocation of a lost era (daily 10am–5pm; $4). Eerie white statues stand around in the waiting room; pick up a telephone and listen to their conversations.

In town, the **Strand**, once "the Wall Street of the Southwest", has been fitted with gaslights, upmarket shops, restaurants and galleries. Old houses are everywhere, such as the ostentatious **Bishop's Palace**, 1402 Broadway (summer daily 10am–5pm; winter Wed–Mon noon–4pm; $3), with its stained glass, mosaics, and marble; the antebellum **Ashton Villa**, 2328 Broadway (summer daily 10am–5pm; winter Mon–Fri 10am–4pm, Sat & Sun 10am–5pm; $3), which shows a film about the 1900 hurricane; and the 1839 **Samuel May Williams Home**, 3601 Avenue P (summer Mon–Sat 10am–5pm, Sun noon–5pm; winter closes 4pm; $3), a New England residence moved here from Maine.

The **beaches** of Seawall Boulevard are a constant reminder of Galveston's struggle simply to exist: murky, rocky, and protected behind a ten-mile-long seawall from the ever-encroaching tides and the threat of further hurricanes. **Stewart Beach Park**, the most convenient beach for the seawall, gets very crowded; the wide **R A Apfell Park**, further east, is marginally quieter, possibly thanks to its $5 admission fee.

Practicalities

Greyhound takes about ninety minutes to cover the fifty miles from Houston, arriving at 4913 Broadway ($6 by cab from the center). There is no *Amtrak* service. **Trolleys** link the **visitor centers** at 2016 The Strand (daily 9.30am–5.30pm) and 21st St and Seawall Blvd (same hours) with all the points of interest, at $2, or $4 for a narrated tour (daily 10am–9pm; every thirty minutes).

Hotels in Galveston are pricey in summer and at weekends, but bargains can be found at other times. Rates at the *Commodore on the Beach*, 3618 Seawall Blvd (☎763-2375 or 1-800/231-9921; ④), for example, can drop considerably off-season, while the *Holiday Inn on the Beach*, at no 5002 (☎740-3581; ⑤), only charges its full rates at weekends. *Gaido's Seaside Inn* (☎762-9625; ③) is another popular choice on Seawall Blvd, with a good fish restaurant (see below). Away from the beach, *The Inn on the Strand*, 2021 The Strand (☎762-4444; ④), has nice large rooms.

Nightlife in Galveston doesn't amount to much, though the *Beach Club* (☎765-5922) in Stewart Beach Park puts on live music. Otherwise, catch up on some sleep, or put all your energies into having a good meal out. One of the best seafood **restaurants** is at *Gaido's*, mentioned above. If you can stomach the dubiously racist decor, *Yaga's Café*, 2314 The Strand (☎762-6676), serves delicious Caribbean-style seafood and chicken, and has live music at night.

Corpus Christi

The unabashed resort town of **CORPUS CHRISTI** is reached along the coast on Hwy-35 from Houston or Galveston, or on I-37 from San Antonio. Originally a rambunctious trading post, it too was hit by a fierce hurricane, in 1919, but managed to pick itself up,

The **area code** for Galveston is ☎409; for Corpus Christi it's ☎512.

shake itself down and industrialize. It's now a center for naval air training, petroleum and ranching; apart from fishing, sailing and water sports, there's not a great deal to do. If you're tiring of the outdoor life, the impressive collection of the Philip Johnson-designed **Art Museum of South Texas**, 1902 N Shoreline Blvd, includes Monet and Picasso (Tues–Fri 10am–5pm, Sat & Sun noon–5pm; $2), while the **Corpus Christi Museum**, 1900 N Chaparral St, specializes in hands-on natural history exhibits and naval aviation (Tues–Sat 10am–5pm, Sun noon–5pm; $2).

Practicalities

Greyhound arrives at 702 N Chaparral St downtown (☎884-9474). The **visitor center** (Mon–Fri 8.30am–5pm; ☎882-5603) is at 1201 N Shoreline Blvd, in the heart of all tourist activity, about a mile south of downtown. Daytime **buses** operate downtown (except Sun). A 25¢ **trolley** runs from the motels on Shoreline Blvd to the large Padre Island and Sunrise shopping malls.

Budget **motels** – inaccessible without a car – line Leopard Street in the northwest. Along Shoreline Blvd, the *Bayfront Inn* at no 601 is a good deal (☎883-7271; ③), while the *Quality Hotel Bayfront*, 601 N Water St, offers bay-view rooms (☎882-8100; ③). Of Corpus' many downtown **restaurants** *Ray's*, 920 Louisiana St (☎883-1413), serves reliable Tex-Mex specials from Monday to Saturday. *The Lighthouse* at 444 N Shoreline Blvd (☎883-3982) does good **seafood**, pricier than downtown but in a great location on the marina. For nightlife, try *Cantina Santa Fe*, 1011 Santa Fe Ave downtown, which often features live music.

South Towards Mexico

The disconnected islands of **Padre Island National Seashore** stretch just offshore for 110 miles south of Corpus Christi, almost down to the Mexican border. The frontier between **Brownsville** and **Matamoros** is not, however, very interesting; for a brief taste of Mexico, head almost due west from Corpus one hundred miles to **Laredo**. US-83 runs along the Rio Grande between Brownsville and Laredo. Away from the coast, the fertile landscape begins to dry out and citrus groves give way to the brush and mesquite of a region of huge ranches, where Mexican *vaqueros* once held sway.

Padre Island National Seashore and Brownsville

Padre Island National Seashore is not quite as unspoiled these days as its reputation might suggest, with its ranks of condos advancing steadily, but it remains a good destination for bird-watching, beachcombing and camping. Pick up details at the Park HQ, on the main route out from Corpus Christi, at 9405 S Padre Island Drive (Mon–Sat 8.30am–4.30pm; ☎937-2621). Infrequent buses run from Corpus Christi to the tip of Padre Island, and there is a taxi shuttle service into the park (☎949-8850). Note that an impassable canal divides the island, meaning that the pricier and much more touristed **South Padre Island** in the south can only be accessed from the mainland.

Brownsville, just across from South Padre Island, is a scruffy semitropical resort, populated by retired Texans on winter vacation, where you'll hear more Spanish spoken than English. To cross the border into **Matamoros**, walk across the bridge at International Blvd (a *Maxi-Taxi* costs 25¢). Wealthier than Brownsville, and considerably larger, the Mexican city is not terribly inspiring, but it has a good market, Mercado Juarez, on calles 9 and 10, and an untouristy Main Plaza at Calle 5, dominated by the cathedral. If you're intending to stay in Mexico, pick up a tourist card from the Mexican Consulate at 10th Ave and Washington St in Brownsville.

NUEVO LAREDO: A MEXICAN BORDER CROSSING

It's an easy walk across the bridge from San Agustin Plaza in Laredo (on payment of a small toll) to the typical Mexican border town of **Nuevo Laredo**; so easy that this is the most popular crossing along the entire frontier, with most trippers coming simply for evening meals and weekend shopping. There is a lively atmosphere, with all the tourist shops and restaurants concentrated near the bridge, on "the strip", Avenida Guerrero. Most take American dollars, and bargaining is acceptable at some of them.

Seven blocks down Avenida Guerrero, the Main Plaza is the social center of town. The *Cadillac Bar*, Avenida Ocampo and Calle de Belde, was the first of its **bars** and **restaurants** to encourage tourism here, serving drinks to Texans escaping Prohibition. It's a bit tacky now; better to head for *Nuevo Leon*, 508 Avenida Guerrero, for *cabrito* (barbecued goat), guacamole and cold beer, or further off the beaten track to the faded but authentic *Rincon del Viejo* at 4834 Avenida Gonzalez, which offers *cabrito*, *fajitas* and *alambres*, and occasional mariachi shows. As a whole though, Nuevo Laredo lacks real charm, and can be particularly depressing after dark; have a meal, but give the nightlife a miss.

As with all border crossings, expect to undergo full immigration procedures when you attempt to re-enter the United States.

Laredo

The dusty and poverty-stricken smuggling center of **Laredo** has seen greater days. Santa Anna marched his troops through in 1836, and in 1840, the city was the center of Zapata's Mexican separatist protest. The capitol of his short-lived Republic still stands on Zaragoza St in the historic district, now housing the small **Republic of the Rio Grande Museum** (Tues–Sun 10am–noon & 1–5pm; free). San Agustin Plaza, the site of the original Spanish settlement, has been restored with cobbled streets and Victorian buildings, as has El Mercado, on San Agustin Ave, the former hub of downtown activity.

Greyhound arrives at Matamoros and San Bernardo downtown (☎723-4324). The visitor center is at 2310 San Bernardo Ave (Mon–Fri 8am–5pm; ☎722-9895). **Hotels** include *La Quinta*, 3600 Santa Ursula Ave (☎722-0511; ④), and the more central *La Posada*, 1000 Zaragoza St (☎722-1701; ⑤), where the dining room offers a big lunch buffet and good steaks. The sometimes-rowdy *Unicorn Restaurant and Pegasus Bar*, 3810 San Bernardo Ave (☎727-4663), serves an eclectic lunch and dinner menu, and *El Meson de San Agustin*, 908 Grant St (☎722-9727), specializes in Oaxaqueñan dishes.

CENTRAL TEXAS

Central Texas stretches from the prairies of the northeast through the green and fertile Hill Country into the chalky limestone landscape of the west, and includes two of Texas' most pleasant cities: **San Antonio** and **Austin**. Austin in particular, the capital city and home to the progressive University of Texas, helps to give the region an intellectual and political feel uncharacteristic of the rest of the state.

Agriculture has been the mainstay of the economy here ever since the resistant Comanche population was finally packed off to reservations in the 1840s. The slave-driven cotton plantations of the south and east have gone, but the small communities set up by Polish, Czech, Norwegian and Swedish immigrants in the **Hill Country** maintained, even until very recently, the traditions, architecture and languages of their homelands. Great cattle drives came trampling through after the Civil War, and played a large part in the development of San Antonio.

The **area code** for Laredo, San Antonio and Austin is ☎512.

San Antonio

With neither the twenty-first-century skyline of an oil town, nor the tumbleweed-strewn landscape of the Wild West, attractive and festive **SAN ANTONIO** looks nothing like the stereotyped image of Texas – despite being pivotal in the state's history. Standing at a geographical crossroads, it encapsulates the complex social and ethnic mixes of all Texas. Although the Germans, among others, have made strong contributions to its architecture, cuisine and music, today's San Antonio is predominantly **Hispanic**; abundant Tex-Mex restaurants, the prevalent Catholicism, a Mexican university campus, and advertising billboards in Spanish all attest to a long history of "Texican" culture.

Founded in 1691 by Spanish missionaries, San Antonio became a military garrison in 1718, and was settled by the Anglos in the 1720s and 1730s under Austin's colonization programme. It is most famous for the legendary **Battle of the Alamo** in 1836, when the Mexican General Santa Anna, seeking to curb the aspirations of the Anglo-Americans, wiped out a band of Texan volunteers: thus the claim to be "birthplace of the revolution", borne out by its role during Texas' ten subsequent years of independence. After the Civil War, it became a hard-drinking, hard-fighting "sin city", at the heart of the Texas **cattle** and **oil** empires. Drastic floods in the 1920s left it riddled with slums, poverty and crime, but the sensitive WPA programme which revitalized two of its prettiest sites, **La Villita** and the **River Walk**, laid the foundations for a future as a major tourist destination. San Antonio is now the ninth largest city in the US, but it retains an unhurried, organic feeling, thanks to a winning combination of small-town warmth, respect for diversity and a self-confidence rooted in its own history.

Arrival, Information and Getting Around

San Antonio International Airport (☎821-3411) is just north of the I-410 loop which encircles most of the sights. *Star Shuttle* (☎366-3183) runs the 20-min journey downtown ($7; every 15min 6am–6.45pm, every 45min 6.45pm–midnight). Taxis cost about $12 (*Yellow Cabs*, ☎226-4242). *Amtrak* serves San Antonio at 1174 E Commerce St, while *Greyhound/Trailways* (☎270-5800) arrive at 500 N St Mary's St, supplemented by the regional *Kerrville Bus Co*, 1430 E Houston St (☎227-6592).

Pick up information on **city transit** from the **visitor center** at 317 Alamo Plaza downtown (Mon–Fri 8.30am–6pm, Sat & Sun 8.30am–5pm; ☎299-8155), or call the *VIA Metropolitan Transit Service* (☎227-2020). **Buses** are reliable; journeys within the I-410 loop cost just 40¢, but many routes stop at 5pm. Four downtown **trolley** routes serve the major attractions for a mere 10¢, from Alamo Plaza. *Gray Line*'s **bus tours** (☎227-5371) are only really of much use as a way to see the most distant missions (2hr; $16). **Walking tours of downtown** leave from outside the *Hyatt* on the 100 block of Loyola St (90-min; Wed–Fri 10am, Sat & Sun 10am & noon; $5), and 40-min **river trips** depart regularly until after dark from various points along the River Walk ($3; ☎222-1701). The *River Limo*, a large black boat, is more of a taxi service ($2.50). You can rent **bicycles** from *Bike San Antonio*, 210 Navarro St (daily 8am–7pm; ☎225-7045).

The main **post office** is next to the Alamo at 615 E Houston St (Mon–Fri 8.30am–5pm; ☎227-3399; zip code 78205).

The Alamo and the Other Missions

The Alamo is the most famous – for reasons which have nothing to do with its original purpose – of a trail of Catholic missions established by the Spanish along remote stretches of the San Antonio River early in the eighteenth century. San Antonio's most distinctive landmark, it is smack in the center of downtown, but for a real sense of early Spanish influence in Texas, it's important to make an effort to get out and see the more

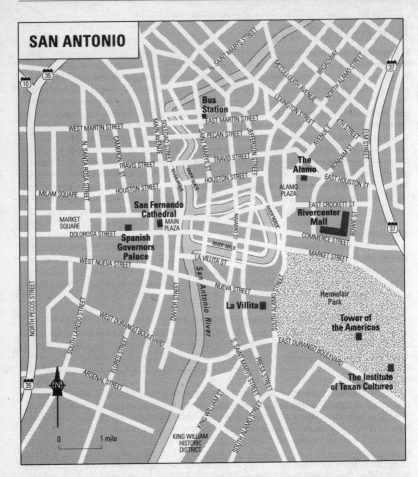

distant, less touristed missions. Each was laid out like a small fortified town, with the church as aesthetic and cultural focus. The goal was to strengthen Spanish control by "converting" the Coahuiltecans – in practice, using them as workforce and army. The missions flourished from 1745 to 1775, but couldn't survive the ravages of disease and attack from Apaches and Comanches, and fell into disuse early in the nineteenth century. To get a sense of the history of the Alamo you could head first for the nearby **Rivercenter Mall**, where the Battle is re-enacted on a six-storey, Texas-scale IMAX screen; fact and sentiment may converge, but it takes a callous viewer not to be affected by the rousing patriotism of the finale.

The Alamo

Houston, Crockett, Bonham and Alamo streets. Mon–Sat 9am–5.30pm, Sun 10am–5.30pm. Free.

All that is left of the original fort of the **Alamo** is the **chapel**, with a large arched facade of delicately carved sandstone, and the **Long Barracks**, now a **museum**. The first of the Spanish missions, established as San Antonio de Valero in 1718, it only became known as the Pueblo del Alamo in 1801, after secularization, when it was named for the Mexican hometown of a Spanish cavalry unit which used it as a base. The **Battle**, immortalized in film and song, occurred on March 6 1836, when all of the 189 men who had held out for thirteen days against the vastly superior Mexican troops were killed, a massacre dismissed by Santa Anna as "but a small affair". The rebels consisted of a few native – Hispanic – Texans, and a majority of volunteers (adventurers like Davy Crockett and Jim Bowie, and aspiring colonists from other states), dreaming of Texan autonomy and driven by the battle cry of "Victory or Death".

Though a constant stream of bus tours makes visits crowded and hectic, they're crucial to understanding the pride and stubbornness of Texas. The battle memorabilia in the **chapel** is undeniably emotive, with poignant letters sent home by soldiers preparing to die, and the **Long Barracks Museum**, hidden away southwest of the shrine's main entrance, includes two slide shows on the history of the missions and the battle.

Take time also to sit in peace in the four-acre grounds, a haven from the downtown commotion just outside the walls, dotted with lush blooms, palms and cacti, and holding an irrigation ditch filled with fat fish.

The Other Missions

The **Mission Trail** runs nine miles south along the river from Alamo St, down S St Mary's St and onto Mission Rd, and can be reached by bus #40. Each of the remaining four missions has been restored to act as an interpretive center illustrating some aspect of mission life (all daily summer 9am–6pm; winter 9am–5pm; free), while the churches themselves still serve active parishes.

Mission Concepcion, 807 Mission Rd, with its distinctive twin towers and cupola, was built between 1731 and 1751. Colorful scraps of original frescoes can still be seen, along with bullet holes from rougher days. Exhibits here concentrate on the religious function of the missions. The 1720 **Mission San Jose**, 6539 San Jose Drive, which interprets the mission as a social and defence center, is the most complete of all, with what is believed to be the only unrestored mission fort in the USA. Other notable features include the beautiful carved-stone ornamentation, especially the ornate rose window. A Mariachi Mass is held here each Sunday at noon. Of the two smaller and more isolated missions, **Mission San Juan**, 9102 Graf Rd, has displays on the mission as economic center (as well as a unique delicate bell tower), while **Mission San Francisco de la Espada**, 10040 Espada Rd, looks back on its educational role.

Around the Town

Since mission times, the **San Antonio River** has been the key to the city's fortunes. Destructive floods in the 1920s, and subsequent oil drilling, reduced its flow, leading to plans to pave the river over. Instead, a careful landscaping scheme, started in 1939 by the WPA, created the Paseo del Rio, or **River Walk**, now the aesthetic and commercial focus of San Antonio. Below street level, the walk is reached by steps from various spots along the main road and crossed by humpbacked stone bridges. Cobbled paths, lined with tropical plants and shaded by pine, cypress, oak and willow, wind for two and a half miles (21 blocks) beside the jade-green water, with much of the city's eating and entertainment concentrated along the way. You can catch a river taxi at various points (see p.521), but strolling is as much fun and cheaper, watching as the river slowly changes character between the lively Rivercenter Mall and the quieter, more parklike outskirts.

La Villita ("little town"), on the River Walk opposite Hemisfair Park, was San Antonio's original settlement, occupied in the mid- to late eighteenth century by Mexican "squatters" with no titles to the land. Only when its elevation enabled it to survive fierce floods in 1819 did this rude collection of stone and adobe buildings become suddenly respectable. It is now a National Historic District, turned over to a dubious "arts community" consisting mostly of overpriced craft shops (daily 10am–6pm). It's at its best off-season or at dusk, when the crowds dwindle and the muted colors, smells and noises evoke earlier times. In contrast, the 25-block **King William Historic District** southwest, between the river and S St Mary's St, contains the elegant late-nineteenth-century homes of German merchants. A surprise in this Mexican-feeling city, it remains a fashionable residential area.

The best of several museums in **Hemisfair Park** on S Alamo St is the **Institute of Texan Cultures**, 801 S Bowie St (Tues–Sun 9am–5pm; free). This maps the social histories of thirty diverse "Texan" cultures, with especially pertinent Afro-American and Native American sections, and an intriguing corner devoted to short-lived attempts to introduce the camel to West Texas as a beast of burden. Two of the park's other buildings house the **Mexican Cultural Institute**, filled with changing exhibits of historic and contemporary Mexican art (Tues–Fri 9am–5.30pm, Sat & Sun 11am–5pm; free). But for its observation deck (daily 8am–11pm; $2.50), the ugly 750ft **Tower of the Americas** is devoid of interest.

Across the river at 115 Main Plaza, the 1731 **San Fernando Cathedral** is the oldest cathedral in the US, though it's underplayed as a tourist attraction. Nobody really believes that the Alamo heroes are buried here, whatever might be said, but its importance to the community is paramount. Mariachi Masses are held on Sunday at 9am and 12.15pm. Two blocks west at 105 Plaza de Armas, the beautifully simple whitewashed **Spanish Governors Palace** was home to Spanish officials during the mission era. Just one storey tall, it's not really a palace, but its flagstone floors, low doorways and beamed ceilings, religious icons and ornate wooden carvings give it wonderful atmosphere, and it provides an illuminating glimpse of the lifestyles of the civil and religious authorities in this remote outpost. Don't miss the cobbled courtyard, with its mosaic floor, lush palms and cooling fountain (Mon–Sat 9am–5pm, Sun 10am–5pm; $1).

Market Square, a couple of blocks further northwest, dates from 1840. Its outdoor restaurants and bustle are still at the heart of the city's life; fruit and vegetables are on sale early in the morning, while the shops are a compelling mix of color and kitsch. **El Mercado**, an indoor complex, supposedly resembles a traditional Mexican market, selling gifts, jewellery and oddities. Amongst the tourist tack a few of the shops are great, even if the air-conditioning, piped music, and indignant refusal of the shopkeepers to engage in haggling do little to convince you of the authenticity of the venture.

About two miles south of the city, the surreal **Buckhorn Hall of Horns, Fins and Feathers** at the *Lone Star Brewery*, 600 Lone Star Blvd, is a monument to Texan excess. During San Antonio's heyday as a cowtown, cowboys, trappers and traders would bring in their cattle horns to the *Buckhorn Saloon* in exchange for a drink. Thousands are now on display, mounted as trophies, chandeliers and chairs, along with endless cases of *Lone Star* memorabilia, and a wax museum. The $4 admission includes two complimentary glasses of the "National Beer of Texas"; lovers of kitsch will find it a bargain (daily 9.30am–5pm; ☎270-9465).

It's also worth getting to the **McNay Art Museum**, 6000 N New Braunfels Ave, at US-81 Austin Highway (Tues–Sat 10am–5pm, Sun noon–5pm; free). This exquisite Moorish-styled villa was built in the Fifties to house the art collection of millionaire and folk artist Marion McNay, which includes New Mexico crafts, Gothic and medieval works as well as Post-Impressionists. Its garden is a haven of tranquillity. Buses #11 (Nacogdoches) or #14 (Thousand Oaks) serve the museum from downtown.

Accommodation

The luxury of a moonlit amble along the river back to your hotel is one of the best reasons for visiting San Antonio, so it's worth making a determined effort to stay in the center. However, downtown is monopolized by luxury hotels, and a car is virtually a prerequisite for finding budget lodgings. There are clusters of reasonably priced **motels** just north of Brackenridge Park on Austin Hwy, or, convenient for the airport, on I-35 north towards Austin.

With enough notice, *Bed and Breakfast Hosts*, 166 Rockhill (☎824-8036), can arrange rooms in a castle, a Victorian residence in the King William District, or less pricey alternatives (③–⑥; deposit often required).

Alamo Travelodge, 405 Broadway (☎222-9401). Four blocks from the Alamo. Facilities include bar, restaurant and pool. ④.

Best Western Crockett Hotel, 320 Bonham St (☎225-6500). Historic hotel with modern facilities, in excellent location just opposite the Alamo. ⑥.

Bullis House Inn International Hostel, 621 Pierce St (☎223-9426). Across from Fort Sam Houston, two miles northeast of the center (bus #11). A good place to meet people, with pool and kitchens. Call ahead to reserve in summer. ②/③.

Coliseum Inn, 365 N Pan Am Expressway (☎225-8000). Functional hotel, opposite the hostel. ③.

Elmira Motor Inn, 1126 E Elmira St (☎222-9463). Very cheap and basic downtown rooms. ②.

Holiday Inn Market Square, 318 W Durango St (☎225-3211). Good rooms near old market. ④.

Menger Hotel, 204 Alamo Plaza (☎223-4361). Texas' most famous hotel during the great cattle drives; Teddy Roosevelt recruited his "Rough Riders" here in 1898 for the Spanish-American War. ⑥.

Eating

Not surprisingly, San Antonio has good **Tex-Mex** food in all price ranges. Many visitors head straight for the Mexican restaurants on the River Walk; however, charming as it is to eat al fresco beside the river, don't be seduced to such an extent that you never venture above ground. Even downtown, there are many good, local eating places. Downstairs at the **Rivercenter Mall** is packed with assorted fast-food stalls.

A H Burritos, 516 Houston St (☎223-0608). Extremely inexpensive, friendly local restaurant two doors down from *Woolworths* in the shadow of the Alamo. Fine breakfasts of huevos rancheros, while for dinner, shrimp and steak are the most expensive items, at $6 each.

Casa Rio, 430 E Commerce St (☎225-6718). The oldest, most established place to eat on the River Walk, with excellent cheap Mexican food (a huge "deluxe dinner" costs around $6).

The Guenther House, 129 E Guenther St (☎227-1061). Delicious cookies and cakes from 75¢, in a cool green flour-mill-cum-museum in the King William District. Good breakfasts and lunches.

La Margarita, 120 Produce Row in the Market Square (☎227-7140). Touristy Mexican restaurant, with outdoor seating; a favorite pitch with the strolling mariachis.

El Mirador, 722 S St Mary's St (☎225-9444). Wonderful Mexican breakfasts and lunches for under $5. Specialties include *xocetl* (chicken broth) and *Azteca* (spicy tomato) soups. Closed Sun and Aug.

Mi Tierra, 218 Produce Row (☎225-1262). In the bustling old market building, across the alley from *La Margarita*, open 24 hours. Midnight snacks, or full meals. Bar until 2am.

Paesano's , 1715 McCullough Ave (☎226-9541). Lively Italian restaurant with a garlicky menu. The *Shrimp Paesano* is delectable – a welcome change from burritos.

Zuni Grill, 511 River Walk (☎227-0864). Creative Southwestern food in one of the most stylish River Walk restaurants. Main courses around $14.

Entertainment and Nightlife

With its abundance of picturesque settings, San Antonio is a great city for **festivals**. During August's **Texas Folklife Festival** in Hemisfair Park, ten stages reflect the state's huge diversity of music, ranging from gospel to Lebanese. May's **International Conjunto Festival**, at the *Guadalupe Cultural Arts Center* on Guadalupe St (☎271-9070), west of downtown, celebrates the German/Mexican country music of south and central Texas.

Check in the free weekly *Current* for gigs, films and events. The live jazz and flamenco in the restaurants along the **River Walk** tends to be rather sanitized, while **St**

Mary's St (just beyond the bus station towards the art museum) is the main strip for college clubs and bars. The outdoor **Arneson River Theater**, opposite La Villita, where the river separates the audience from the stage, has live music during the summer.

The Blue Bonnet Palace, 16842 I-35 N, Schertz (☎651-6702). A bit of a trek, north of the airport, but very popular, with country bands 9pm–2am on Fri and Sat. The highlight is the live bull-riding rounds at 10pm and 11.30pm – real urban cowboy stuff. Cover $5–10.

Floore Country Store, 14464 Old Bandera Rd (☎695–8827). Old country dance hall, with outdoor dancing.

The Menger Hotel, 204 Alamo Plaza (☎223-4361). Inexplicably furnished to replicate the tap-room at the House of Lords, the hotel's *Roosevelt Bar* is a good place for a cold beer next to the Alamo.

St Mary's Bar and Grill, 3000 St Mary's St (☎737-3900). $3 for R&B, Fri and Sat.

Tycoon Flats, 2926 N St Mary's St (☎737-1929). A variety of live music with no cover charge. Patio restaurant serves good veggie food for about $5. Closed Mon.

Austin

AUSTIN was only a tiny community on the verdant banks of the (Texas) Colorado River when Mirabeau B Lamar, president of the republic, suggested in 1839 that it would make a better **capital** than swampy and disease-ridden Houston. Early building had to be done under armed guard, as angry Comanche watched from the surrounding hills, but despite its perilous location, the city thrived.

These days it wears its status as capital of Texas very lightly; sightseeing rates as a low priority against simply hanging out. This laid-back and progressive city has been a haven since the Sixties for artists, musicians and writers, and an air of creativity hangs over the place. Many visitors come specifically for the **music**. Local musicians are renowned for their innovative re-workings of Texas' country, folk, and R&B heritage, often severing their rural roots to use Austin's enthusiastic environment as a springboard to national recognition. During the mid-Eighties it was the launchpad of the "New Country" sound, exemplified by Steve Earle and Lyle Lovett, and musicians hungry for fame still tumble out of buses from all over Texas to seek their fortunes in the hundreds of live venues.

Austin is one of the few cities in the state where walking, cycling, and reading on the grass are more common than driving around in big cars. It may not have completely avoided the usual problems of urban growth – until recently it was Texas' fastest-growing city, and ugly suburbs have shot up to threaten its small-town feel – but it feels beautifully safe for visitors, even women travelling alone. The presence of the vast UT campus adds to the atmosphere, even if the students' demented support of the "Longhorns" football team can get wearing.

Within the city limits the great park system offers numerous hiking and biking trails and a wonderful spring-fed swimming pool. Looking further afield, Austin makes a fine base for exploring the green **Hill Country** that rolls away to the west.

Arrival, Information and Getting Around

Austin spreads about twenty miles north–south and eighteen miles east–west, severed by I-35 (between Dallas and San Antonio) to the east. The Colorado River runs south of downtown. Flights come in conveniently close to downtown, at the **Municipal Airport** on I-35 and Airport Blvd, east of Guadalupe St and the university.

Greyhound, 916 E Koenig Lane (☎458-5267), and *Amtrak*, 250 N Lamar Blvd, are both some way out of the center. You can catch buses from the Highland Mall a few blocks east of the *Greyhound* station. **Taxis** are reliable and cheap; if you can't hail one down or find a rank, try *American Cabs*, ☎452-9999.

Walking is an easy and pleasant way of getting around, either independently or on one of the organized **walking tours** that leave from the south entrance of the Capitol (March–Nov Thurs–Sat 9am, Sun 2pm). Austin also has a good **mass transit** system. The *Capital METRO* bus runs downtown, crosstown and through the campus, for 50¢, with extra university shuttle routes – distinguishable by the longhorn emblem beside the route number – during term time (Mon–Sat 6am–midnight, Sun 6am–8pm). Schedules are available from the information kiosk at Fifth St and Congress Ave (in front of the NCNB building; Mon–Fri 8.30am–5.30pm), or you can call the *METRO* information line, ☎474-1200. The *Dillo Express*, also run by *METRO*, is a free downtown **trolley** system, running three routes every ten to forty minutes between 6.30am and 7pm on weekdays. *Rose Maries Tours* (☎441-0790) runs **tours** of the city and Hill Country excursions. **Bicycles** can be rented from *Bicycle Sport Shop*, 1603 Barton Springs Rd (Mon–Fri 10am–8pm, Sat 9am–6pm, Sun 11am–5pm; ☎477-3472).

The **visitor center** is at 300 Bouldin Ave (Mon–Fri 8.30am–5pm; ☎478-0098 or 1-800/888-8AUS), and there's a State Tourist Information Center (daily 8am–5pm) in the foyer of the state capitol. The **post office** is at 300 E Ninth St (Mon–Fri 7.30am–6pm, Sat 8am–noon; ☎929-1252; zip code 78767).

The Town

The Texas **State Capitol**, between 11th and 14th streets, is over 300 feet high, taller than the national capitol in Washington, with a pink granite dome that dominates the downtown skyline. The chandeliers, carpets and even the door hinges of this colossal building are emblazoned with lone stars and "TEXAS" motifs, a theme continued in the new underground annexe, a sleek maze of marble halls (daily 8.30am–4.30pm; public tours every 15min; free). Nearby, the antebellum **Governors Mansion**, 1010 Colorado St, contains displays on Texan history (free tours Mon–Fri every 20min 10–11.40am). **Congress Avenue**, a stretch of 1950s shops and muted office buildings which slopes south from the capitol down to the river, is worthy of a stroll; at dusk 750,000 **bats** – the world's largest urban bat colony – emerge in a large cloud from their hang-outs under the bridge. **Sixth Street**, also known as Old Pecan Street, runs west from I-35 to Congress St, and is the focus of much of the city's nightlife, as well as featuring many renovated buildings, galleries and hip shops. The elegant Romanesque *Driskill Hotel*, on the corner with Brazos St, has its own self-guided walking tour, with a glossy leaflet recounting the hotel's many links with government since 1886. Between Fifth and Sixth, just west of Lamar Blvd, the magnificent 600-year-old **Treaty Oak** is the last of the Council Oaks where treaties were signed with Native Americans. Poisoned in 1989, the tree is often surrounded by flowers, offerings and prayers.

Two interesting museums in the east of the city are the **George Washington Carver Museum** of local black history at 1165 Angelina St (Tues–Thurs 10am–6pm, Fri & Sat noon–5pm; free), which each Saturday hosts free concerts, and the **Elizabet Ney Museum** at 304 E 44th St. This latter, a German-influenced castle-like building in a leafy historic residential area, preserves the last studio, with maquettes and finished marbles, of Austin's most celebrated sculptor (Wed–Sat 10am–5pm, Sun noon–5pm; free).

Zilker Park, across the river from *Amtrak* and southwest of the center (bus #30 from 10th and Congress), is one of the best of the many fine parks in the city, a perfect retreat on sweaty Austin afternoons. One of its main attractions is the spring-fed (and deliciously cold) **Barton Springs Pool**, a turquoise rectangle shaded by pecans (April–Oct Fri–Sun, Tues & Wed 9am–10pm, Mon & Thurs noon–10pm; $2 Mon–Fri, $2.25 Sat & Sun). You can paddle in the pebbly creek below the pool free of charge, and you'll also find hiking and biking trails, a miniature railroad winding beside the river (daily 10am–dusk; $1.25), and, to the west, the wildlife garden of the **Austin Nature Center** (Mon–Fri 8am–5pm, Sat 10am–5pm; free). South of the pool on Robert E Lee Rd, the **Umlauf**

Sculpture Garden (Thurs, Sat & Sun 1–4.30pm, Fri 10am–4.30pm; $2) is a tranquil grassy enclave dotted with over 100 works in bronze, terracotta, wood and marble.

The **Laguna Gloria Art Museum**, 3809 W 35th St (Tues–Sat 10am–5pm, Sun 1–5pm; also Thurs 5–9pm, when admission is free; $2 at all other times; tours Sun 2pm), a beautiful 1916 Mediterranean villa overlooking Lake Austin in the northwest of town, was once owned by Clara Driscoll, who at 22 bought the Alamo for the Daughters of the Republic of Texas. It now features changing exhibits of twentieth-century American art, and has a replica of the rose window at the San Jose Mission in San Antonio. Don't miss **Mayfield Park** next door, a peaceful idyll complete with waterlilies and stroppy peacocks. **Mount Bonnell**, further north on the Colorado River, gives quite spectacular views over the city and surrounding countryside.

Around the University

Having its own oil well (the drilling rig *Santa Rita No 1* on San Jacinto Blvd) has made the **University of Texas** one of the world's richest universities. Its unparalleled collection of manuscripts by contemporary authors is available to scholars amid tight security in the **Harry Ransom Center**; stories abound of the sums lavished to acquire work from relative unknowns who might some day achieve fame. The Center, in the southwest corner of campus, also houses an **art gallery** (Mon–Sat 9am–5pm, Sun 1–5pm; free), with a Gutenberg Bible as well as contemporary Latin-American and American paintings. One of Austin's grimmest memories is of the day in 1966 when a gunman climbed the campus administration building, the **UT Tower** on Guadalupe St, to take potshots at passers-by; look rather than enquire, if you want to make any friends here. Student-guided tours of the campus and its museums leave the information center in the main building twice daily on weekdays and once on Saturday (term-time only).

The stretch of **Guadalupe Street** running along campus north from Martin Luther King Blvd to 24th St is known as the Drag. A focus of student activity, and lined with cafés, vintage clothes shops and bookstores – try *Europa Books* at no 2406, the best place in town for contemporary and alternative American literature – it was also subject of *Down on the Drag*, a song by Joe Ely, one of Austin's many adoptive rock'n'roll heroes.

The **LBJ Library and Museum** (daily 9am–5pm; free), on the northeast edge of campus at 2313 Red River St, traces the career of the brash and egotistical Lyndon Baines Johnson from his origins in the Hill Country to the House of Representatives, the Senate and the White House. The curious circumstances of his first senatorial election in 1948 (confirmed only after some "overlooked" votes – all written in the same hand – were found three days after his opponent had been elected) go unmentioned. John Kennedy is said to have made Johnson his vice-president to avoid his establishing a rival power base; but in the aftermath of Kennedy's assassination, Johnson's administration (1963–68) was able to push through a far more radical programme than Kennedy ever attempted. Johnson's nemesis, Vietnam, is presented here as an awful mess left by Kennedy for him to clear up, at the cost of great personal anguish. There's a replica of the Johnson Oval Office at the White House, as well as a wonderfully corny set of political campaign memorabilia from Roosevelt to Bush; some of the badges are on sale.

Accommodation

I-35 and Congress Ave are Austin's budget **hotel** strips, but **B&Bs** are better options; there are good ones in most areas of the city.

Austin International AYH Hostel, 2200 S Lakeshore Blvd (☎444-2294). Southeast of downtown (via bus #8 to Pleasant Valley and S Lakeshore) beside Town Lake. AYH $10, others $15. One double room has a water bed. ①.

Best Western Quarters at the Capitol, 300 E 11th St (☎476-7151). Comfortable rooms with pool and airport shuttle. ③.

Carrington's Bluff, 1900 David St (☎479-0638). Very good B&B, central but countrified, a block from Lamar at Martin Luther King Blvd. Shady verandah, friendly hosts, and gourmet breakfast. ③.

Driskill Hotel, 604 E Brazos St at E 6th (☎474-5911). Glamorous historic hotel in great location. ⑥.

Woodburn House, 4401 Avenue D (☎458-4335). Small B&B in the leafy Hyde Park area, within walking distance of the university. Reservation and deposit required. ③.

Eating

Radical Austin has many more vegetarian and wholefood **restaurants** than is usual in Texas; even chicken-fried steak can be found prepared healthily. Add this to the fact that sitting on your own reading a book over your meal is not seen as aberrant behavior, and you have a city in which eating out can be a real pleasure. Barton Springs Rd towards Zilker Park is known as "restaurant row", and plenty of good budget restaurants near the university cater to the students especially along Guadalupe St – look for the crowds. Alternatively, try the local restaurants along Lamar Blvd beyond the *Amtrak* station.

The Broken Spoke, 3201 S Lamar Blvd (☎442-6189). Neighborhood honky-tonk bar. No-nonsense waitresses slap down excellent chicken-fried steaks for around $5.

Catfish Station, 408 E 6th St (☎477-8875). Fresh catfish dinners in modish surroundings, with live jazz, r'n'b and reggae.

City Grill, 401 Sabine St (☎479-0817). Converted warehouse serving mesquite-grilled seafood and beef. If you like your food hot, try the Szechuan tuna, with Chinese chili and Szechuan mayonnaise.

Good Eats Café, 1530 Barton Springs Rd (☎476-8141). High-quality, reasonably priced healthy home-cooking. The restaurant also organizes early-morning walking tours in the area.

Matt's El Rancho, 2613 S Lamar Blvd (☎462-0355). Huge, rowdy Mexican restaurant with very mixed crowd. Food is authentic and cheap. Long queues, but great margaritas.

Mother's Café, 4215 Duval St (☎451-3994). Healthy international vegetarian food; delicious enchiladas, noodles and crepes. Traditional Southwestern breakfasts include unbeatable banana and walnut pancakes. Bookish clientele and chirpy waiters.

Ruby's BBQ, 512 W 29th St at Guadalupe St (☎477-1651). Reasonably priced barbecue (all natural brisket, no hormones or additives) and Cajun food, behind *Antone's Blues Club*. Open for live blues until 3.30am on Fri and Sat.

Serrano's, 1105 Red River St (☎322-9080). Lively Mexican restaurant – fajitas, veggie dishes and ceviche – in great location overlooking Symphony Square (see under Nightlife).

Threadgill's, 6416 N Lamar Blvd (☎451-5440). An Austin institution since Kenneth Threadgill was given the first licence to sell beer in the city after Prohibition. Real home-cooking at bargain prices, with free seconds of wonderful vegetables like black-eyed peas and okra. Lively atmosphere, with occasional live fiddle music, folk, or country and western bands. A must.

La Zona Rosa, 612 W 4th St (☎482–0662). Searing chili in trendy surroundings; often live music.

Nightlife

The only problem you'll have with Austin **nightlife** is being spoiled for choice. In Sixth St in particular, virtually every building houses a club or a bar, most of which have no cover charge on Thursday (remember to always carry ID). Two excellent local newspapers, the *Daily Texan*, the UT paper (Thurs), and the *Austin Chronicle* (Fri) carry listings and news of community and cultural issues.

Something is always going down on campus. Big drama and dance names appear in the **Performing Arts Center**, 23rd St and E Campus Drive (☎471-1444), and you can see **independent movies** at the *Dobie Cinema*, 2021 Guadalupe and 21st. The *Velveeta Room*, 317 E Sixth St (☎469-9116), puts on comedy on Wednesday and Thursday nights. The same people run *Esther's Pool*, 525 E Sixth St (☎320-0553; $12), home of *Esther's Follies*, Austin's hippest and funniest cabaret, which combines spoofs of local and national politicians with Texas-style singing and dancing. The *404 Club*, 404 Colorado St (☎499-0088), is a house music club with a gay and straight crowd.

Live Music

Although Austin's folk revival in the Sixties attracted sufficient attention to propel **Janis Joplin** on her way from Port Arthur, Texas, to stardom in California, the city first achieved prominence in its own right as the center of **"outlaw country"** music in the Seventies. **Willie Nelson** and **Waylon Jennings**, disillusioned with Nashville, spearheaded a movement which reworked sentimental country and western with an incisive injection of rock'n'roll. The audiences in Austin, far removed from the hard-drinking honky-tonk crowds of West Texas, provided an environment which encouraged and rewarded risk-taking and experimentation. These days the **"Austin sound"** is a melange of country, folk, blues, psychedelic and "alternative" influences, very much reliant on acoustics and guitars. Austin's laidback college-based scene was recently epitomized in Richard Linklater's offbeat, low-budget, independent movie *Slacker*.

The tradition of black Texas bluesmen such as Blind Lemon Jefferson and Blind Willie Johnson still lives on; *Antone's Blues Club* on Guadalupe is the place to hear **live blues**, while the enthusiastic and knowledgeable staff in *Antone's Record Store*, opposite, can provide advice on what to see on any given night. **Folk** music, traditional or with a punk twist, is also thriving, with an annual **folk festival** at Rod Kennedy's *Quiet Valley Ranch* in Kerrville (☎257-3600). The three-day **South by Southwest Music Festival**, held in the third week of March, features the best bands from Austin and around the world; the price of a wristband (about $30) admits you to all the shows in town.

Antone's, 2915 Guadalupe St (☎474-5314). Hot, sweaty and crowded; the best blues club in the city, with big-name national and local acts nightly.

The Back Room, 2015 East Riverside Drive (☎441-4677). Big-name bands in popular venue within walking distance of the youth hostel.

The Broken Spoke, 3201 S Lamar Blvd (☎442-6189). Neighborhood restaurant and stomping country music hall, with all the trappings but well away from the center. The barn-like dancefloor regularly attracts the best Texan acts on the circuit. Dancing begins at 9pm.

Cactus Café, Texas Union, 24th St and Guadalupe St (☎471-8228). One of Austin's favorite venues. Consistently good country, rock and folk music; regular showcase for new acts.

Carlin's, 416 E Sixth St (☎473-0905). Typical Sixth St bar in established old jazz club, with live R&B, soul, blues and jazz, 9.30pm–2am.

The Carousel Lounge, 1110 E 52nd St (☎452-6790). Cultish carnival-style piano bar, complete with carousel behind the bar. Clientele is part elderly, part hipster, smooching to blind piano man Jay Clark's romantic tunes. A long way out, near Robert Mueller Airport. Thurs–Sat until 1am; no cover.

Emo's, 603 Red River St (☎477-EMOS). Launch pad for Austin's best alternative bands, with a mixed crowd from frat-rats through punks to cowboys. Free entrance for over 21s; minors pay $5 cover.

The Hole in the Wall, 2528 Guadalupe St (☎472-5599). Fantastic, very Texan bar right next to campus, with live music from reggae to jazz.

Joe's Generic Bar, 315 E Sixth St (☎480-0171). Relaxed bar with very mixed crowd.

Liberty Lunch, 405 W Second St (☎477-0461). Established club for hippest local and national acts.

Symphony Square, Red River Rd (☎476-6064). Rough-hewn outdoor amphitheater, below street level on the river, hosting good jazz and classical concerts in summer.

Top of the Marc, 618 W Sixth St (☎472-9849). Exclusively jazz, conveniently sited above a deli.

The Hill Country

The rolling hills, lakes and valleys of the **HILL COUNTRY**, north and west of Austin and San Antonio, were inhabited mostly by Apache and Comanche until after statehood, when German and Scandinavian settlers arrived. Many of the log-cabin farming communities they established are still here, such as **New Braunfels** (famous for its sausages and pastries) and **Luckenbach**. You may still hear German spoken, and German influence is felt in local food and music; *conjunto*, for example, is a blend of Tex-Mex and accordion music.

The whole region is a popular retreat and resort area, with some wonderful hill views and lake swimming, and a lot of good places to camp. Among its numerous state parks is the **Lyndon B Johnson State and National Historical Park**, 65 miles west of Austin on US-290, preserving LBJ's birthplace (1908) and the ranch house where Lady Bird Johnson still lives (daily 8am–5pm; 1hr 30min tours leave from the visitor center). A Living History Farmstead depicts German family life in the early 1900s. Johnson's boyhood home (daily 9am–5pm; guided tours every 30min) is at **Johnson City**, fourteen miles further east; for a good lunch, stop off here at the *Hill Country Cupboard*, at the junction of US-281 and US-290.

Fredericksburg

FREDERICKSBURG, smack in the middle of the Hill Country, might at first glance look like a pastiche of a German village, overrun by Biergartens and gingerbread storefronts. In fact at core it's still pretty much the town founded by six hundred enterprising Germans in 1846. They managed to make – and, uniquely, keep – treaties with the local Comanche, and their community, based on hard work and perseverance, survived through epidemics and civil war.

During the weekend, crowds of daytrippers from San Antonio and Austin wander Main Street's galleries, craft shops and antique stores, or sit in the numerous twee tea rooms. Several original structures make up the **Pioneer Museum** at 309 W Main St, including a church and a store (summer Mon–Sat 10am–5pm, Sun 1–5pm; winter weekends only). The **Nimitz Hotel**, 340 E Main St, with its looming tower that looks like a steamboat, was once the last hotel on the military road to California. Now it's a museum honoring Fleet Admiral Nimitz, the grandson of the hotel's original owner, and commander of the Naval forces in the Pacific in World War II (daily 8am–5pm; $3). Look out also for the quirky limestone and pink granite *Bank of Fredericksburg*.

Practicalities

Like the rest of the Hill Country, Fredericksburg has no *Greyhound* or *Amtrak* service; it's reached via either US-290 from Austin or US-87 from San Antonio. The **CVB**, in the Market Square at 106 N Adams (Mon–Fri 8am–5pm, Sat 9am–noon & 1–5pm; ☎997-6523), has details of the budget **hotels** along E Main St; the *Best Western Sunday House*, 501 E Main St (☎997-4333; ④), is one of the more luxurious, with a pool. **Bed and breakfast** is big business in historic Fredericksburg; try *B&B of Fredericksburg*, 102 S Cherry St (☎997-4712; ①–⑤). There's **camping** in the Lady Bird Johnson Municipal Park, three miles southwest on Hwy-16 S, or in the Enchanted Rock State Natural Area, detailed on the following page.

Restaurants and bakeries line Main St, many of them doing cheap lunch specials. At no 218, *Dietz Bakery* is the oldest in town, a good place for tasty breads and biscuits. You can eat more substantially at *Friedhelm's Bavarian Inn* (no 905; ☎997-7024), which specializes in starchy plates of dumplings and sauerkraut (closed Mon).

Luckenbach

LUCKENBACH, about ten miles southeast of Fredericksburg, has become a cult destination since Willie Nelson and Waylon Jennings recorded the song *Let's Go to Luckenbach, Texas* ("where ain't nobody feelin' no pain") in the Seventies. Its charm is that nothing happens, apart from a bit of guitar-picking and card-playing, the occasional dance and a "ladies-only" chili cookoff on the first Saturday in October. Call the *General Store* (☎997-3224) – which, as virtually the only building in town, acts as bar, post office and dance hall – to see what may or may not be happening. To reach Luckenbach, drive east from Fredericksburg along US-290 and then south on RR 1376 and about another five miles to Luckenbach Rd; that there are no signs is all part of the fun.

Enchanted Rock State Park

Eighteen miles north of Fredericksburg, more than a thousand acres of hills and streams in the shadow of a 500ft dome of pink granite have been designated as **ENCHANTED ROCK STATE PARK**. The Comanche attributed magical powers to the rock; in fact its nocturnal creaks and groans are due to contraction after the day's heat. In 1841, Texas Ranger Jack Hays, renowned for his brutality, fought with Indians on its summit; today crowds of visitors huff and puff their way up there for the wonderful views. The park (☎915/247-3903) is open for day use 8am–10pm; there's plenty of **camping** in the tent area near the parking lot, and primitive camping spaces for backpackers along the four-mile Loop Hiking Trail, but no facilities for vehicular camping.

NORTH AND EAST TEXAS

Early immigration into north and east Texas, during the days of the Republic and following the devastation of the Civil War, was largely from the southern states. In the 1930s, the northeastern oil fields near **Tyler** (a drab town only redeemed by its beautiful rose gardens) proved to be the richest ever found in the US. The whole region is now predominantly agricultural, with logging important in the densely forested east. The grand exception is, of course, the **Metroplex** – the area which includes **Dallas** and **Fort Worth**. The main tourist attractions and cultural life of the region are concentrated here; but if you enjoy exploring small-town America, and have a car, the north and east can yield more subtle pleasures. Fans of the Wim Wenders movie will want to check out **Paris, Texas**, northeast on US-82, and four **National Forests** in the east offer unsurpassed opportunities for outdoor living: Angelina, Davy Crockett, Sabine, and Sam Houston. The forest supervisor (☎713/632-4446) in Lufkin, midway between Davy Crockett and Angelina on US-59, has details of free and private **camping** facilities.

East Texas

The tall pine forests of east Texas bear more relation to Louisiana than to the rest of the state; while undeniably Texan, the locals also identify themselves culturally and geographically with the adjacent corners of Arkansas and Louisiana – the "**Arklatex**". Thus you'll find jambalaya and gumbo in restaurants along with standard Texan dishes.

Burial sites and reconstructed dwellings of the sophisticated **Caddo** Indians, an early southeastern mound-building culture, can be seen at the **Caddoan Mounds State Historic Site**, thirty miles west of Nacogdoches on Hwy-21. Active between the ninth and fourteenth centuries, the site includes videos on Caddoan history and a self-guided walking tour (Wed–Sun 8am–5pm; $3 per car, $1 for pedestrians and cyclists).

Big Thicket National Preserve

The **BIG THICKET NATIONAL PRESERVE**, south of the Piney Woods on US-96, is a remarkable composite of natural elements from the southwestern desert, central plains and Appalachian Mountains, with swamps and bayous to boot. Once the area offered ideal refuge for outlaws, runaway slaves and gamblers; now it just hides a huge variety of plant and animal life, including deer, alligator, armadillo, possums, hogs and panthers, and over three hundred species of birds. Wild flowers, orchids and towering trees share space with cacti and yucca.

Check in at the **visitor center** (daily 9am–5pm), south of Angelina National Forest on FM 420 off US-69, just south of Wildwood, before entering the site; casual rambling isn't allowed, and hiking or canoeing is best done with the Preserve guides. There is primitive **camping** in designated areas.

Nacogdoches

NACOGDOCHES, north of Angelina National Forest on US-59, claims to be the oldest town in Texas. One of the state's first five Spanish **missions** was established here in 1716, to keep a watchful eye on the French in Louisiana, and a pyramidal **Caddo Indian Mound** in the 500 block of Mound St testifies to more ancient history. The *Sterne-Hoya House*, 211 S Lanana St, the town's oldest surviving and unreconstructed home, illustrates early pioneer life (Mon–Sat 9am–noon & 2–5pm; free).

La Hacienda, 1411 North St (☎409/564-6487), is the best place to **eat** in town, serving Mexican food in a prairie-style ranch home. If you want to **stay**, the *Haden-Edwards Inn*, 106 Lanana St, is a good B&B close to downtown (☎409/564-9999; ③). The **Chamber of Commerce** is at 1801 North St (☎409/564-7351).

Dallas

Contrary to popular belief, there's no oil in glitzy, status-conscious **DALLAS**. Since its foundation as a prairie trading post, by Tennessee lawyer John Neely Bryan and his friend Mr Dallas in 1841, successive generations of **entrepreneurs** have amassed wealth here through trade and finance, using first cattle and later oil reserves as collateral. One early group of European settlers, the Socialist Réunion co-operative of the 1850s, had to pack up and move on due to an inability to adapt to local farming methods. The city still prides itself on their legacy of arts and **high culture**.

The power of **money** in Dallas was demonstrated in the late 1950s, when its financiers threw their weight behind integration. Potentially racist restaurant owners or bus drivers were pressurized not to resist the new policies, and Dallas was spared major upheavals. Rioting, after all, would have been bad for business. The city's image was, however, catastrophically tarnished by the **assassination** of President Kennedy in 1963, and it took the building of the giant DFW Airport in the Sixties, and the twin successes of the *Dallas* TV show and the Cowboys football team in the Seventies, to restore confidence. Then boom turned to crash once more. Unemployment and the demise of the Ewings – not to mention an appalling crime rate – all took their toll, but the indomitable entrepreneurial spirit remains and, after a slump in the late 1980s, the Cowboys are back in the big time.

Competitive with Houston, and smug about its cowtown neighbor Fort Worth, Dallas boasts of its "sophistication" and its "old" wealth. For all that, the stuffiness is tempered by a typically Texan delight in self-parody, and there's still fun to be had if you know where to look – especially in the alternative **Deep Ellum** district, with its superb restaurants and nightlife.

Arrival, Information and Getting Around

Dallas is served by two major **airports**. **Dallas/Fort Worth** (DFW; ☎574-6701), as big as Manhattan and the world's second busiest airport, is exactly midway between the two cities (around 18 miles from each). Telephones in the baggage claim area link up to a variety of different **shuttle buses**, all at about $10; **taxis** cost around $20 (☎574-5878 for both). **Lovefield**, used mostly by *Southwest* airlines, lies about nine miles northwest of Dallas (for information on ground transportation call ☎670-6080).

Dallas proper is circled by inner loop 12 (or Northwest Highway) and the outer loop I-635 (which becomes LBJ Freeway). A **car** makes sense in a city this size, though the main sights of downtown's Central Business District are easy to tour on foot. Get hold of

The **area code** for Dallas is ☎214.

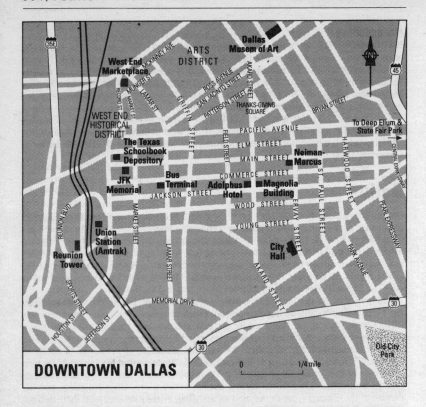

DOWNTOWN DALLAS

0   1/4 mile

the CVB's **walking** guide from the **visitor centers**, at 603 Munger Ave, in the West End Marketplace (Mon–Sat 10am–8pm, Sun noon–8pm), at the CVB, 1201 Elm St (Mon–Fri 8.30am–5pm; ☎746-6677), and in *Amtrak*'s 1916 Union Station, west of downtown at 400 S Houston St (daily 9am–5pm). *Greyhound* is at 205 S Lamar St downtown (☎655-7000).

Downtown, *Hop-a-buses* (which for no obvious reason look like frogs, kangaroos or rabbits) operate for a 25¢ fare (Mon–Fri 6.30am–6.30pm), linked to the *DART Bus Service* (☎979-1111; 75¢). The *McKinney Trolley* runs north from the downtown Museum of Art to the McKinney Ave restaurant strip (one-way 75¢, day passes $3; every 15–30min, Sun–Thurs 10am–10pm, Fri & Sat 10am–midnight). *Gray Line Tours* (☎824-2424) does all-day ($35) and half-day ($20) **city tours**, plus a $25 Saturday trip to Southfork, and *Longhorn Tours* (☎228-4571) has a four-hour trip to the Mesquite Rodeo (see p.537; $23). The *West End Cab Co* is a reliable city **taxi** company (☎902-7000).

The **post office** is at 400 N Ervay St (Mon–Fri 8am–6pm; ☎953-3045; zip code 75201).

The City

Downtown Dallas is a hymn to commerce. Many of its skyscrapers are landmarks in themselves; at night the red neon *Mobil Pegasus* on the 1921 Magnolia Building on Akard and Commerce appears to gallop over the city, while over two miles of green neon delineate the 72-storey NCNB Texas Plaza. The original **Neiman Marcus** department store, set up in 1907 by sister and brother Carrie Neiman and Herbert Marcus and famed for its glamorous Christmas catalogue, is still there on Main St, an inspiration to all keen young business people (Mon–Sat 10am–5.30pm). One small refuge is the quiet **Thanks-Giving Square** at the corner of Akard, Ervay, Bryan and Pacific (Mon–Fri 9am–5pm, Sat & Sun 1–5pm), with its meditation garden, descending walkways, fountains and modern spiralling chapel – though even here pealing bells boom out at regular intervals. South of the square on Ervay St looms the precarious upside-down pyramid of **City Hall**, possibly familiar as the police station in the film *Robocop*.

North of the West End, the **Arts District** boasts the wide-ranging **Museum of Art**, 1717 N Harwood St, with an especially impressive pre-Columbian collection (Tues & Wed 11am–4pm, Thurs & Fri 11am–9pm, Sat & Sun 11am–5pm). This is free, except for the Reves Collection of Impressionists, Post-Impressionists, and decorative arts ($3). Two blocks east, at 2301 Floral St, the magnificent **Morton H Meyerson Center**, designed by I M Pei, is the home of the symphony orchestra. The vast geometries of glass, onyx and wood inside cost $80 million, as the tour guides won't let you forget.

Tourists flock to the restored red-brick warehouses of the **West End Historical District**, the site of the original 1841 settlement on Lamar and Munger, for its eighty stores and fifty restaurants. The indoor **marketplace** has become something of an amusement arcade, with tacky gift shops, crazy golf and fast food; hidden away on the third floor, the **JFK Assassination Information Center** ($4) feels slightly out of place. Strongly in favor of the conspiracy theory, backed up by newspaper clippings, photographs and a "strange deaths" section illustrating how eighteen key witnesses were killed in the three years after the assassination, this small museum also acts as a research center selling books and videos.

The city's first park, **Old City Park**, 1717 Gano St, at I-30 and Harwood St, now serves as both recreational area and museum, charting the history of Dallas from 1840

THE ASSASSINATION OF PRESIDENT KENNEDY

It was 12.30pm on November 22 1963, as John F Kennedy greeted the crowds of Dallas from his ceremonial motorcade, when the shots rang out over Dealey Plaza which killed the president and ended the "Camelot" era.

Within hours, a gunman's nest was discovered in the nearby Texas Schoolbook Depository, and one of its employees, **Lee Harvey Oswald**, was arrested. Two days later, he in turn was shot and killed in a police station by nightclub owner **Jack Ruby**, who said he wanted to spare Kennedy's wife Jackie from having to testify at Oswald's trial. The **Warren Commission**, which investigated the assassination, concluded that Oswald had acted alone, but **conspiracy** theories have flourished ever since. Most accept that Oswald (an ex-marine who defected to Russia and returned with a Russian wife) fired the shots, but see him as the fall guy in a larger plot, variously attributed to the Mafia, anti-Castroists, Cuba, the KGB and US government agencies. Claims by witnesses to have heard shots on the famous **Grassy Knoll** on the north side of Elm St remain unsubstantiated, but visitors can usually be found sniffing around here for clues – along with self-styled guides, ready to engage them in costly conversation. Senate inquiries were finally closed down by the Justice Department in 1988, arguing that there was no "persuasive evidence" of any plot.

Dealey Plaza, a small park on Houston St's triple underpass, is one block east of the Dallas Historical Plaza on Main and Market, where an open cenotaph enclosing an eight-foot flat granite block, designed by Philip Johnson, stands as the **Kennedy Memorial**. The **Texas Schoolbook Depository** itself, at 411 Elm St, is now the Dallas County Administration Building, the top floor of which houses a **museum**, *The Sixth Floor* (Sun–Fri 10am–6pm, Sat 10am–7pm; $4). Displays build up a suspenseful narrative, with the infamous blurred 8mm images of Kennedy crumpling into Jackie's arms left until the end, at which point there's likely to be much sobbing from moved visitors, who exorcise their grief by writing in the "memory book". The "nest" has been re-created and, whatever you feel about Oswald's guilt, it is undeniably chilling to look down at the streets below and imagine the mayhem they must have seen that day.

to 1910 through more than thirty buildings relocated from towns in north Texas, among them farmhouses, a bank, a train station, a store, a church, and a schoolhouse (daily dawn–dusk; free; tours Tues–Sat 10am–3pm, Sun 1.30–3.30pm; $4).

Dallas' coolest district is **Deep Ellum**, five blocks east of downtown between the railroad tracks and I-30 at Elm and Main. Famous in the Twenties for its jazz and blues clubs (and supposedly named by Blind Lemon Jefferson), the old warehouse district now accommodates avant garde galleries, theaters, street-hip clothes stores and excellent restaurants and clubs. To the despair of its original inhabitants – note the *Yuppies go home* graffiti – prices are rocketing as the area goes mainstream. However, its sense of rebellion and nonconformity makes a great antidote to the prevalent stuffiness of Dallas.

The adjacent **State Fair Park**, a gargantuan Art Deco plaza bedecked with endless Lone Stars, was built to house the Texas Centennial Exposition in 1936; its **Cotton Bowl** stadium (☎638-BOWL) was the natural choice to host soccer's World Cup in 1994. Among its museums are the **Dallas Museum of Natural History** (daily 9am–5pm; $4), boasting reconstructions of a mammoth from the Trinity River and a 32-foot sea serpent; the hands-on **Science Place** (daily 9.30am–5.30pm; $5.50) and its planetarium ($2); the **Dallas Aquarium** (daily 10am–4.30pm; $1), built at the same time as the park; and the soon-to-be-opened **Museum of Afro-American Life and Culture**. The centerpiece, though, has to be the magnificent **Hall of State Building**, an Art Deco treasure of bronze statues, blue tiles, mosaics and murals, with rooms decorated to celebrate the different regions of Texas. For three weeks in October the Park spills over with more than three million revellers enjoying the riotous **State Fair** itself.

Southfork Ranch (daily 9am–5pm; $8), the former TV home of the Dallas soap's wheeling and dealing Ewing clan, lies about 25 miles northeast of Dallas, beyond I-635 on 3770 Hogge Rd at Plano. Having lain dormant for two years after 1991, it has recently been kitted out as a Western mini-theme park, with a **museum** in which you can see the gun that shot JR, and have your photo taken – wearing a cowboy hat – at JR's desk; a proposed exhibit on Texas ranching; plenty of Stetson-obsessed gift shops; and *Miss Ellie's Deli*. The **Ranch House** itself is surprisingly small – all the show's interior scenes were shot in California, and the exterior views used a very wide angle lens.

Accommodation

Rooms are very expensive in Dallas, though the posh downtown hotels do special **weekend** deals. Chain **motels** are concentrated a long way out, on the freeways. **Bed and breakfast** can be arranged through *B&B Texas Style*, 4224 W Red Bird Lane (☎298-8586 or 298-5433; from ③). A reservation service, on ☎1-800/428-4464, can help find rooms in any locale and price range in the Dallas/Fort Worth area. There's **camping** in the pretty *Lewisville Lake Park* on the Kingfisher Trail, a mile east of I-35 in Lewisville.

Adolphus Hotel, 1321 Commerce St (☎742-8200). Stunning historic hotel downtown, decorated with antiques. Said when it was built in 1912 to be the most beautiful building west of Venice, Italy, today it is still by far Dallas' most glamorous place to stay. ⑧.

Aristocrat Clarion Hotel, 1933 Main St (☎741-7700). Good-quality rooms, great central location. ④.

Best Western Market Center, 2023 Market Center Blvd (☎741-9000 or 1-800/275-7419). Two miles from downtown. Complimentary breakfast. ③.

Dallas Grand Hotel, 1914 Commerce St (☎747-7000). Downtown luxury hotel. ⑤.

Delux Inn, 3111 Stemmons Hwy (☎637-0060). Good, bargain rooms, but a long way northwest. ①.

Econolodge, 9356 LBJ Freeway (☎690-1220). Standard motel rooms. ②.

Holiday Inn Downtown, 1015 Elm St (☎748-9951) and **Holiday Inn Park Center**, 8102 LBJ Freeway (☎239-7111). Neither is cheap, but both do weekend specials. *Downtown* ⑤, *Park Center* ④.

The Mansion on Turtle Creek, 2821 Turtle Creek (☎559-2100 or 1-800/527-5432). Voted the best hotel in the US and ninth in the world by *Condé Nast Traveler* in 1992. ⑧.

Ramada Hotel at Convention Center, 1011 S Akard (☎421-1083). Reliable rooms, heated pool. ③.

Eating

The less expensive – and less pretentious – of Dallas' five thousand restaurants are concentrated in **Lower Greenville Ave** and trendier **Deep Ellum**, where even the excellent New American cuisine won't break the bank.

Aca y Alla, 2914 Main St (☎748-7140). Wood-grilled nouveau Mexican food in Deep Ellum hot spot.

Aw Shucks, 3601 Greenville Ave (☎821-9449). Cheap and cheerful oysters, catfish and shellfish.

Billy Blues Barbecue, 2020 N Lamar Blvd (☎871-0661). Splendid barbecue, $10.25.

Blind Lemon, 2805 Main St (☎939-0202). Casual Deep Ellum hang-out. A DJ spins Seventies funk.

The Butcher Shop Steakhouse, 808 Munger Ave (☎720-1032). Popular West End restaurant where you cook your steak, chicken or fish to taste, around an open charcoal pit. From around $7.

Deep Ellum Café, 2706 Elm St (☎741-9012). The first restaurant in the area. Very popular, serving delicious New American food for around $10. Open until midnight on Fri and Sat.

Dinger's Catfish Café, 8989 Forest Ave (☎235-3251). Mesquite-grilled whiskery aquatic vertebrates served to a hip crowd.

8.0, 2800 Routh St (☎979-0880). Sassy American and Southwestern food popular with late-night revellers enjoying the extensive jukebox.

Good Eats, 702 Ross Ave (☎744-EATS). Healthy Texan home-cooking in colorful West End café. Variable quality but plenty of fresh vegetables, and a sumptuous banana cream pie.

Mia's, 4322 Lemmon Ave (☎526-1020). Mexican family restaurant, and *Dallas Cowboys'* favorite.

Tejas Café, 2909 McKinney Ave (☎871-2050). Stylishly downbeat Tex-Mex decor, friendly waiters, great food. Happy hour and free buffet, Thurs & Fri 4–8pm. Specialties include blackened fajitas, $9.

Tolbert's, 1800 N Market St (☎969-0310). X-rated chili in touristy West End chain restaurant, plus Tex-Mex and vegetarian options, all for under $8.

Nightlife and Entertainment

The place to head for nightlife in Dallas has to be edgy off-beat **Deep Ellum**, where among the trendy clubs the innovative **Pegasus Theater**, 3916 Main St (☎821–6005), puts on avant garde and independent plays. Elsewhere nightlife is pretty formal. Mainstream attractions include the **Symphony Orchestra** at the showpiece *Morton H Meyerson Center* (☎670-3600), and the **Dallas Black Dance Theater** at 2627 Flora St (☎871-2376). In June and July, free **Shakespeare in the Park** performances are held in Fair Park (☎954-0199).

For a real Wild West night out, head to the **Mesquite Rodeo**, well out of town on I-635 at Military Parkway (April–Sept, Fri & Sat 8pm; ☎285-8777; $8). A bizarre alternative is the **Medieval Times Dinner and Tournament**, 2021 N Stemmons Freeway (☎761-1800; $28–34.50) where sorcery, falconry and jousting are presented to a crowd wearing inelegant paper hats and banqueting without the benefit of cutlery.

Full listings can be had from Thursday's *Dallas Observer*, Friday's *Dallas Morning News*, the events information line (☎746-6679), or the blues hotline (☎521-BLUE).

Arcadia, 2005 Greenville Ave (☎826-7554). Big-name bands.

Bar of Soap, 3615 Parry Ave (☎823-6617). Groovy pub-cum-laundromat on the outskirts of Deep Ellum, opposite Fair Park.

Club Clearview, 2806 Elm St (☎283-5358). Three-in-one Deep Ellum warehouse; an intimidatingly cool dance club, trippy video room with virtual reality games, and big touring acts in *The Live Room*.

Cowboys, 7331 Gaston Ave at Garland Rd, east of Greenville (☎321-0115). Large honky-tonk with big-name country acts, Tues–Sun 4pm–2am. Free dancing lessons Sun 4–7pm.

DaDa, 2720 Elm St (☎744-DADA). Famed Deep Ellum club where Edie Brickell and the New Bohemians began their days. Acoustic jam Sun 3–9pm, live bands and club nights.

Dallas Alley, 2019 Lamar St in the West End Market Place(☎720–0170). One cover charge (around $8) gets you into eight very touristy clubs and five live venues.

Exodus, 210 N Crowdus St (☎748-7871). Reggae club in Deep Ellum.

July Alley, 2809 Elm St (☎747–2809). Severely stylish Deep Ellum bar.

Fort Worth

Yes, Dallas does have something Fort Worth doesn't have – a real city thirty miles away.
Amon Carter, publisher, philanthropist, Fort Worthian

FORT WORTH, often dismissed as some kind of poor relation of Dallas, in fact has a rush and energy lacked by its stuffier neighbor thirty miles to the east. Unashamed of its origins as a lawless frontier cowtown, this is one of the most "Western" cities in Texas. In the 1870s it was the last stop on the great cattle drive to Kansas, the **Chisholm Trail**; when the railroads arrived, it became a livestock market in its own right, with its own packing houses, while remaining a haven for cowboys and outlaws. The **cattle** trade is still a major industry, after aviation and defence, but the city can also pride itself on a thriving cultural life. Unlike the more anxious Dallas, Fort Worth doesn't feel the need to brag about its many excellent **museums**. For a place so **wealthy** (the grand **Western Hills** area has proportionately more millionaires than any other US locale), it's surprisingly laid-back. It is a truly cosmopolitan city, comfortable with itself, where cowboys and roustabouts will happily down a few beers with modern jazz fans.

Arrival, Information and Getting Around

The main road between Fort Worth and Dallas, **I-30**, cuts the city east–west; loop 820 encircles it. An *Airporter* express **bus** (☎334-0092; $7) runs to and from DFW Airport, seventeen miles northeast (see p.533). The city's public transit system, **The T**, also operates **free buses** downtown, running north on Throckmorton St and south on Houston St; $3 two-day *Visitour* passes give unlimited travel on *T* services (☎871-6200). *Amtrak* runs daily to Houston and Chicago from 1501 Jones St.

There are three **visitor centers**: in the **stockyards** at 130 E Exchange Ave (daily 10am–5pm; ☎624-4741; walking tours Mon–Sat 10am, 1pm & 3pm, Sun 1pm & 3pm; $1.50), downtown in the **CVB** at 415 Throckmorton St, and in the Science Museum at 1501 Montgomery St. The downtown and stockyard areas are well patrolled and safe to walk around after dark; if you'd prefer a **taxi**, call *American Cab Co* on ☎429-8829.

The City

The chief focus of **downtown** Fort Worth is **Sundance Square**, a leafy, redbrick-paved area of shops, restaurants and bars along the 300 block of Main and Houston, ringed by glittering skyscrapers and pervaded with a genuine enthusiasm for the town's rich history. Notice the carvings of longhorn skulls everywhere, and the many *trompe l'oeil* murals – especially the Chisholm Trail mural on Fourth St between Main and Houston. **The Sid Richardson Collection of Western Art**, tucked away at 309 Main St, has a small but excellent collection of late works by Remington, including some of his best black-and-white illustrations, and early elegaic cowboyscapes by Charles Rusell (Tues–Fri 10am–5pm, Sat 11am–6pm, Sun 1–5pm; free).

Naming the square after the Sundance Kid isn't particularly appropriate; he, and such other outlaws as Bonnie and Clyde, would have spent their time a few blocks south, just north of I-30 at the city's original settlement. Even into the 1950s "**Hell's Half Acre**" was renowned for bawdy lawlessness; these days it's much less exciting, although the bubbling fountains and pools of its central **Water Gardens** offer refreshing respite.

The **Cultural District**, on the western border of downtown, is an impressive area of museums and art galleries. The finest collection is at the **Kimbell Art Museum**, 3333 Camp Bowie Blvd (Tues–Sat 10am–5pm, Sun 11am–5pm; free), where European art – Van Dyck, Hals, Rembrandt, Picasso, Goya and Gainsborough – is displayed in a splendid vaulted, naturally lit building designed by Louis Kahn. American art in the **Amon Carter Museum**, 3501 Camp Bowie Blvd (Tues–Sat 10am–5pm, Sun 1–5.30pm; free) includes great photographs of Western landscapes, while the **Modern Art Museum**, 1309 Montgomery St (Tues–Sat 10am–5pm, Sun 1–5pm; free), specializes in twentieth-century abstracts. South of here the **Museum of Science and History** (Mon–Thurs 9am–5pm, Fri–Sat 9am–8.30pm; free) includes a planetarium and an IMAX theater.

In the lively, interactive **Cattleman's Museum**, west of downtown at 1301 W Seventh St (Mon–Fri 8.30am–4.30pm; free), the changing economic face of the cattle trade is traced from the days of open range, via the great cattle drives, to modern ranching and latterday cowboys – with displays of fetishistic spurs, assorted tangles of barbed wire and some good stuff on early women pioneers.

However, museums, no matter how good, aren't necessarily what you want from a cowtown. The ten-block **Stockyards Area**, centered on Exchange Ave two miles north of downtown, is a glorious evocation of the days when Fort Worth's stockyards made this "the richest little city in the world". It's much more than a cynical creation for cowboy-hungry tourists. Look out over the wooden sidewalks and old shopfronts, listen to the bellows of the rodeo cattle, and you can almost see the dust rising and the snorting herds being driven through. Along with the restaurants and bars, the stores will have western-wear obsessives in heaven. Look out for *Fincher's* rodeo equipment store and *M L Leddy's* saddle shop; and check out the *Maverick Trading Post*, packed with hip, bright cowgirl regalia, and with a bar serving good cold beers. They encourage you to drink first and buy later; this is not a good idea. In comparison, the shops and restaurants in the **Stockyard Station Market**, a brick-floored enclave in the old hog pens, are more squeaky clean; one of the best is the stylish *Southwestern Furniture Shop*, with its own prairie dog colony. From here the magnificent *Tarantula* steam train puffs along a nostalgic route to Eighth Ave downtown (departs 1.15pm, 3.30pm, 5.45pm; 30min trip).

The stockyards no longer host live **cattle auctions**; instead, images are beamed by satellite into the huge 1902 **Livestock Exchange Building** at 131 E Exchange Ave, home of the **Stockyards Museum**. The Mission-style **Cowtown Coliseum** next door, used for rodeos and concerts, is fronted with a bust of Bill Pickett, the black rodeo star who invented the unsavory but effective practice of "bulldogging" – stunning the bull by biting its lip. Horseback **trail rides** along the old Chisholm Trail leave from *Cowtown Corrals*, 500 NE 23rd St (☎740-0852; $20 per hour; trail camps Fri & Sat 7–11pm).

Accommodation

Fort Worth is blessed with plenty of reasonably priced accommodation, even downtown. The liveliest places to stay are in the stockyards; more standard motel rooms can be found along the South freeway.

Miss Molly's Bed and Breakfast, 109 W Exchange Ave (☎626-1522). Quirkily furnished old bordello in the stockyards, if you can't resist cowboy kitsch. Friendly hosts, gourmet breakfast. ④.

Park Central Hotel, 1010 Houston St (☎336-2011). Centrally located, convenient for downtown. ②.

Ramada Inn Midtown, 1401 S University Drive (☎336-9311). West of town. ③.

Remington Hotel, 600 Commerce St (☎332-6900). Excellent location, footsteps away from Sundance Square and the bus station. ④.

Stockyards Hotel, 109 E Exchange Ave (☎625-6427). Historic stockyards hotel, reputedly a favorite haunt of Bonnie and Clyde, with Western, Mountain Man, Indian and Victorian themed rooms. *Booger Red's Saloon* boasts funky saddle barstools. ⑥.

Eating

If you love **steak**, Fort Worth is the place. Meat here is hefty, fresh, and prepared with a lot of tender loving care, especially in the stockyard area, where the many good home-cooking cafés are frequented as much by cattle ranchers as by visitors. Vegetarians will do less well; try the upmarket restaurants downtown.

Cattleman's Steak House, 2458 N Main St (☎624-3945). Dim lighting, wall-sized portraits of prize steers. A Fort Worth institution for its steaks and margaritas. Dinner is around $12.

Deep Ellum Café, 400 Main St (☎332-2232). Offshoot from one of Dallas' hippest restaurants, serving New American seafood and pasta with live jazz accompaniment.

Joe T Garcia's, 2201 N Commerce St (☎626-4356). Nationally famed Mexican restaurant in the 1930s home of its owners, serving hefty set tortilla/fajita dinners ($10–15) and frosty margaritas. Outdoor seating next to the family swimming pool.

Juanita's, 115 W Second St (☎335-1777). Downtown Mexican restaurant with an uptown feel; specialties include quail in tequila. Moderately priced lunch specials.

Owen's Family Restaurant, 1700 S University Drive (☎336-6644). Very cheap home-cooking near the cultural district.

The Star Café, 111 W Exchange Ave (☎624-8701). Famed for its gruff service, sumptuous steaks grilled in lemon butter – and low prices.

Nightlife and Entertainment

You'd be hard pushed not to find something to your taste amid Fort Worth's late-night drinking and carousing. Bar crawling is safe and fun, and there's a great mix of live music venues (though the pick-up joints in the Stockyards are best avoided). Call ☎548-7337 for a telephone **listings** guide. As well as the regular cowboy venues below, the **Chisholm Trail Round Up** (second weekend in June) and **Pioneer Days** (three days in late September) are two hugely enjoyable annual western-style celebrations in the stockyards. *Cowtown Coliseum* holds championship **rodeo** (April–Sept, Sat 8pm; $8), and special occasions throughout the year. There's a rodeo hotline on ☎336-8791.

Billy Bob's, 2520 Rodeo Plaza (☎624-7117). Mon–Sat 11am–2am, Sun noon–2am; rodeos Sat 9pm and 10pm. The largest honky-tonk in the world, down in the stockyards, with live bull-riding, pool tables, bars, restaurants and stores, and big-name concerts. Live music nightly. Tours Mon–Sat 11am, 2pm & 4pm, Sun 2pm & 4pm.

The Caravan of Dreams, 312 Houston St (☎877-3000). One of the best spots in town, a superb downtown jazz club and experimental theater with friendly, stylish crowd. A beautiful building, with great murals and a rooftop bar and greenhouse. Regularly attracts big-name acts.

Casa Manana Theater, 315 Main St (☎332-6221) and 3101 Lancaster Ave in the cultural district (same phone). Live alternative comedy and plays.

J&Js Hideaway, 3305 W Seventh St (☎877-3363). Neighborhood bar in the cultural district.

White Elephant Saloon, 106 E Exchange Ave (☎624-1887). $2 cover on Friday; Fri & Sat noon–2am, Sun–Thurs noon–midnight. Notoriously wild and authentic stockyards saloon with a cowboy hat hall of fame; prop yourself up at the long wooden bar and listen to cowboy singer Don Edwards.

Towards the Panhandle

Routes west from central Texas lead you through the state's "backyard", where farmlands and rough-cut juniper-covered hills give way to treeless sandy landscapes. Of the towns, only **Abilene** on I-20 towards Lubbock, and **Wichita Falls** on US-287 to Amarillo, near the border with Oklahoma, are even marginally interesting enough to be possible stopovers for long-distance drivers. In theory, this is rich oil-bearing land, but the cities have taken a battering since the slump.

Abilene and Sweetwater

ABILENE has a certain curiosity value as an oppressively God-fearing Bible city, though that's no great incentive to get off one of the six *Greyhound* buses which pass through each day. If you have to stay, and don't fancy the interstate motels, *Bolin's Prairie House*, downtown at 508 Mulberry St, offers B&B rooms (☎915/675-5855; ③).

Dozy **SWEETWATER**, further west on I-20, began as a general store for buffalo hunters in 1877, and is now notable for its **rattlesnake round-up** on the second weekend of March, when you can try fried snake (tough but tasty), or buy a transparent toilet seat with a rattler coiled in it. Of the motels along Georgia Street, one of the nicest is the *Ranch House Motel and Restaurant* (☎915/236-6341; ②).

Wichita Falls

The prettiest thing about **WICHITA FALLS** is its name; it's an unromantic and heavily industrial city. Reliable **motels** such as *La Quinta* (☎817/322-6971; ③) line US-287. The city's **restaurants** are in general uninspired, though *McBride Land & Cattle Co*, 501 Scott St (☎817/692-2462), does good steak and frogs' legs. The fifty-foot **waterfalls** to the north, once home to Wichita Indians, were reconstructed in 1987 after being washed away earlier this century. Fifteen miles southeast, **Lake Arrowhead** (which is dotted with large oil derricks) offers **camping** facilities along with nature trails.

THE PANHANDLE

The inhabitants of the **PANHANDLE**, the southernmost portion of the Great Plains, call it "the real Texas"; it certainly fulfils the fantasy of what Texas should look like. When Coronado's gold-seeking expedition passed this way in the sixteenth century, they drove stakes into the ground across the vast and unchanging landscape, despairing of otherwise finding their way home. Hence the name *Llano Estacado*, or staked plains, which still persists today.

Once the buffalo – and the Indians – were driven away from what was seen as perilous and uninhabitable frontier country, the Panhandle began, around the 1870s, to yield great **natural resources**. Helium – especially in Amarillo – and oil, as well as **agriculture**, have brought wealth to the region, home to some of the world's largest **ranches**.

The Panhandle may hold few actual tourist attractions, but its rural charm and quirkiness is far removed from the eastern cities. **Music** has particular significance in a region famous for songwriters such as Buddy Holly, Roy Orbison and Joe Ely; while most musicians relocate to cosmopolitan music centers like Austin, they don't forget – and are not forgotten by – their birthplace. Above all, the fiercely proud and exceptionally hospitable **people** of the Panhandle, still facing hardship and struggle in their battles with the elements, make it special, along with the starkly romantic landscape, strewn with tumbleweeds and mesquite trees – and, of course, those big, big skies.

Lubbock

LUBBOCK, the largest city in the Panhandle, has long been the center of its commerce and transportation, roughly one hundred miles northwest of Abilene and the same distance south of Amarillo. At first this was cattle-grazing land, but the discovery of copious underground water made agriculture profitable. The prosperity of the city was built on cotton; in recent years government restrictions have hit prices hard, and the days of self-sufficient farming look numbered. You may, however, still see solitary cotton fields defiantly standing on the outskirts, where stubborn farmers have refused to sell out.

With its fields, farms, lumpen bungalows and faceless block buildings, Lubbock is relentlessly ordinary-looking, its muted downtown area dotted with fading Fifties shopfronts. Which is not to say that it's dull; though Southern Baptism has left its mark and this is officially a "dry" city, Lubbock has a pervasive sense of fun which can't just be put down to the students from Texas Tech.

The **area code** for the Panhandle, including Lubbock and Amarillo, is ☎806.

BUDDY HOLLY

Lubbock's claim to world fame is as the birthplace of Charles Hardin Holley on September 7 1936. Inspired by the blues and country music of his childhood – and a seminal encounter with the young Elvis Presley, gigging in Lubbock at the *Cotton Club* – **Buddy Holly** was one of rock'n'roll's first singer-songwriters. The Holly sound, characterized by steady strumming guitar, rapid drumming, and his trademark hiccoughing vocals, was made famous by hits such as *Peggy Sue, Rave On, Not Fade Away, Oh Boy!* and *That'll Be The Day*; but Buddy himself was killed at the age of 22 by the Iowa plane crash of February 2 1959 ("the day the music died"), that also claimed the Big Bopper and Ritchie Valens.

An eight-foot bronze **Buddy Holly Statue**, on Eighth St and Ave Q, towers over a **Walk of Fame** of plaques to local performers like Roy Orbison and Waylon Jennings (the bassist for Buddy's final concert). Other sites around town include:

Buddy's birthplace. 1911 Sixth St. Now a vacant lot.

J T Hutchinson Junior High School, 3102 Canton Ave. Buddy and friend Bob Montgomery performed here in the sixth grade. Souvenirs are on sale.

Lubbock High School, 2004 19th St. Buddy and Bob, who graduated in 1955, won the school's "Westerners Round Up" with *Flower of my Heart*.

Tabernacle Baptist Church, 1911 34th St. A percentage of Buddy's royalties still go to the church which saw his baptism, wedding, and funeral.

Radio Station KRLB, 6602 Quirt Ave. Opened in 1953, this was the first full-time country music station in the States. Buddy and Jack Neal had their own show.

Fair Park Coliseum, Tenth St and Ave A. Where Buddy opened shows for Bill Haley and Elvis Presley. His "discovery" here in 1955 led to a contract with Decca.

Home of Buddy in 1957, 1305 37th St. Now a private home.

Buddy's grave, in Lubbock cemetery at end of 34th St. Take right fork inside the gate, and the grave, decorated with flowers and guitar picks, is on the left, halfway down the road.

Arrival, Information and Getting Around

Loop 289 circles Lubbock proper, with the **airport** (☎762-6411) a few minutes north. I-127 slashes through to the west, north to Amarillo and south to Tahoka. **Buses** come in downtown at 1313 13th St (☎765-6644). The **citibus** system (☎762-0111) runs commuter routes within the loop, stopping at around 6pm (Mon–Sat only). The **visitor center** is at 14th St and Ave K (Mon–Fri 8am–5pm; ☎763-4666 or 1-800/692-4035).

The Town

Downtown Lubbock, and the university, are on the northern side of town. Few buildings of interest survive, thanks to the construction boom of the 1950s and a tornado in 1970. However, you can get a stimulating overview of local history at the university's **Ranching Heritage Center**, Fourth St and Indiana Ave (Mon–Sat 10am–5pm, Sun 1–5pm; free). Over thirty original ranch buildings, from simple cowboy huts to grand overseers' houses, are set in a harsh landscape spiked with cacti and mesquite. There's an excellent museum on pioneer and cowboy history, and demonstrations on making lye soap, sourdough and quilts. The adjacent **Texas Tech Museum** (closed Mon) has further southwestern displays and a room of Buddy Holly memorabilia.

Nearby, the **Lubbock Lake Landmark State Historical Park** archeological site (daily, July–Aug 8am–8pm, Sept–June 8am–5pm; guided tours Sat 9am–noon; $1) has yielded an impressive array of artefacts spanning 1200 years, although to the untrained eye it resembles little more than a dry gravelly site buzzing with gigantic Texan insects. As indeed may **Prairie Dog Town**, in Mackenzie State Park, where six hundred cuddly little rodents are attempting to re-populate the world and gain their revenge for the attempts of government officials and irate ranchers in the 1930s to poison them into extinction. A prairie dog is a kind of fat barking hamster with a waggly tail; this cute and intelligent lot seem to be enjoying themselves immensely.

Three miles east of the loop on Hwy-1585, the *Llano Estacado* **winery** started as the hobby of two university professors. It might look incongruous, set amid scrubby pastureland and cotton fields, but its success has led Lubbock to pin great hopes on the potential of wine to revitalize and diversify its flagging economy. Visitors are given a guided tour and free tasting – many cautious Texans, brought up on beer, don't like paying for an unfamiliar drink until they've tried it. Europeans, who are looked on as connoisseurs, can expect to be questioned on their favorite vintages during the sociable and informal tasting sessions (Mon–Sat 10am–4pm, Sun noon–4pm; ☎745-2258).

Accommodation

Prices are very reasonable in this region, and rooms are plentiful, so there should be no problem finding somewhere to stay. Ave Q has a string of good, reliable chain hotels.

Days Inn, 2401 Fourth St (☎747-7111). Central motel with pool. ②.

The Lubbock Inn, 3901 19th St (☎792-5181). A pool with waterfalls, and free breakfast. ③.

La Quinta Motor Inn, 601 Ave Q (☎763-9441). Free coffee, adjacent to a 24hr restaurant, and just across from the Buddy Holly Statue. ③.

Eating

Lubbock has a surprising variety of eating places, with good barbecue and Tex-Mex and even some New American restaurants. However, many of even the most upmarket restaurants close before 10pm.

The County Line, half a mile west of I-27 in Escondido Canyon (☎763-6001). Mediterranean decor, Forties music, and the best barbecue in Lubbock, with all-you-can-eat specials for around $15.

The Depot, 19th St and Ave G (☎747-1646). In the old Santa Fe train depot. It looks a bit formal, but there are always a lot of students around. The food is very good, verging on the cordon bleu, especially their huge Sunday brunches.

Santa Fe, Fourth St and Ave Q (☎763-6114). Bulging enchiladas, gargantuan burritos and standard Tex-Mex favorites, in an unrowdy family atmosphere.

Well Body Natural Foods, 3651 34th St (☎793-1015). Health-conscious veg, chicken and fish in a no-smoking environment.

Entertainment

The best entertainment the Panhandle has to offer is at its **annual events**. Rodeos are always rip-roaring fun; Texas Tech holds one each October in Fair Park, and the **ABC Rodeo** is at Lubbock Municipal Coliseum every spring. In the same spirit, there are twirling contests, bull-riding, big-name country performers and livestock exhibits at the **Panhandle South Plains Fair** in late September and early October.

Despite its rich musical heritage there isn't a great deal of **nightlife** in Lubbock; most of the local musicians decamp to Austin. The oddly named *Lubbock Avalanche-Journal* carries listings.

Main Street Saloon, 2417 Main St (☎762-0940). Live rock and blues, jam sessions Sunday evening.

Midnight Rodeo, S Loop 289 and University Ave (☎745-2813). Tues–Sun until 2am. Huge c'n'w club; pool tables, lanky cowboys and coiffed Texan belles. Great fun, even for a woman on her own.

Jiggers Up, 4802 Ave Q (☎744-5061). Country jam sessions on Sunday evenings.

Amarillo

AMARILLO may seem cut off from the rest of Texas, up in the northern Panhandle, but it stands on one of the great American cross-country routes – I-40, once the legendary **Route 66** – roughly 300 miles east of Albuquerque and 250 miles west of Oklahoma City. *Amarillo* is the Spanish for "yellow" – the name comes from its characteristic yellow soil. An early promoter of the city was so delighted with its potential – as a site for lucrative buffalo hunting (for those who braved the Apache and Comanche threat) and as excellent ranching land – that he painted all the buildings bright yellow.

Today, sitting on ninety percent of the world's helium and hosting a world-class cattle market, Amarillo is a prosperous but surprisingly uneventful city. The small "**old town**" consists of a few tree-lined streets and staid old homes; some of the less twee antique stores along **Sixth Street** (the old Route 66, known here as "Old San Jacinto") serve equally well as museums of pioneer life. Following Sixth St ten miles west onto I-40 brings you to **Cadillac Ranch**. An extraordinary vision in the middle of nowhere, ten battered roadsters stand upended in the soil, their tail fins demonstrating the different Cadillac designs from 1949 to 1963. Some of the time they're crumbling with rust and defaced with graffiti (encouraged by the designer, eccentric helium millionaire Stanley Marsh III Marsh, on whose land the cars are planted); occasionally they're shiny blue or red after having been painted for a photo shoot.

Amarillo is also host to the world's stompingest, snortingest **livestock auction**, in the stockyards at S Manhattan and Third St, on the east side of town. There are regular tours (☎373-7464), and the auction proper is held on Tuesday morning.

If you enjoy playing cowboys, it's fun to visit one of the many grand old Panhandle **ranches** to have diversified towards tourism. Some just open for the day; others provide (usually expensive) accommodation. The ranchers who entertain you are often natural showmen and women, whose welcome is utterly genuine, though they'd rather be working the animals for real than running a theme park. Attractions at **Bootsteps Guest Ranch** (5 miles west of Amarillo on I-40, then 6 miles north to Patrick Pass; ☎1-800/692-1338), include horse-drawn hay rides, goat milking, horseshoe tossing and cow-chip throwing, with a flapjack breakfast or barbecue on arrival, for $20.

Practicalities

Amarillo has no **public transport** to speak of, but car drivers will find it easy to navigate. *Greyhound* comes in downtown at 700 S Tyler St (☎374-5371). The **CVB** is at 1000 Polk St (☎374-1497 or 1-800/654-1902).

Innumerable budget **hotels** are concentrated along I-40. For a little luxury, *Harvey Hotel*, 3100 I-40W, is good value (☎358-6161 or 1-800/922-9222; ④). Texana fans will love the tongue-in-cheek western camp of the *Inn of the Big Texan*, 7701 I-40E on exit 75 (☎372-5000 or 1-800/657-7177; ②). It's also home to the *Big Texan Steak Ranch*, which as well as serving fried rattlesnake and buffalo chili offers the 72oz steak challenge: if you can eat it all, you get it free. Other popular Amarillo restaurants include the *Iron Horse Cafe*, 401 S Grant St (☎373-1591), which serves moderately priced lunches to assorted cowboys and locals, and at the other end of the scale, the self-consciously bohemian *OHMS Gallery Café*, 619 S Tyler St (Mon–Fri 10am–4pm; ☎373-3233).

Canyon

The one "sight" in the former cattle town of **CANYON**, fifteen miles south of Amarillo on I-27, is a must. The **Panhandle-Plains Historical Museum** (June–Aug Mon–Sat 9am–6pm, Sun 1–6pm; Nov–May closes 5pm; free, donation requested) has exhibits of restored pioneer buildings, artefacts of the Plains Indians, histories of Texas ranching, natural history displays, and a collection of western art. Even the history of the oil and gas industry is made interesting. For **food**, head for the *Cowboy Café*, 15th St and Hwy-60, with giant cowboy "Tex" standing outside.

Palo Duro State Canyon Park

PALO DURO CANYON, 12 miles east of Canyon and 20 miles southeast of Amarillo, is one of Texas' best-kept secrets. Plunging 1200 feet from rim to floor, it splits the plains wide open and offers breathtaking views and colors, especially at sunset and in spring, when the whole chasm is scattered with wildflowers. Pillars of sturdy sandstone loom over the flame-colored rocks, which Coronado's explorers named "Spanish Skirts" on account of their stripy flounces.

The **park** itself is located in the most scenic part of the sixty-mile canyon ($2 per car; visitor center daily 8am–5pm; interpretive center June–Aug, Wed–Sun 11am–7pm). You can explore the depths by **train** (the *Sad Monkey Railroad* runs daily April–Sept, at weekends all year; ☎488-2222; $2.50) or on **horseback**, though backpackers and hikers may want to escape the tourist busloads by following the Prairie Dog Town fork into more remote sections of the park. To **camp**, advance reservations are recommended (☎488-2227). The *Goodnight Trading Post* opposite the Pioneer Amphitheater at the northern end of the park sells gas and snacks. The Convention and Visitors Council in Amarillo organizes a special half-day tour between April and September, which includes breakfast (and cow-chip throwing) at the **Figure 3 Ranch** on the rim of the Canyon.

You may balk at heart-warming musical spectaculars, but the outdoor *TEXAS!* has an undeniable pull in an area not exactly throbbing with nightlife, with the dramatic prairie sky as a ceiling, a 600ft cliff as a backdrop, and genuine thunder and lightning (June–Aug, Mon–Sat 8.30pm; $6–10; pre-show chuckwagon barbecue 6pm; ☎655-2181).

WEST TEXAS

WEST TEXAS is the stuff of Wild West fantasy: parched deserts, ghost towns, looming mesas, and above all the sense of utter isolation. Although the area south from the Panhandle down to Del Rio on the Rio Grande is, for convenience, also known as west Texas, the fantasy really begins west of the River Pecos; you can drive for hours without a sign of life to reach **El Paso**, Texas' shabby westernmost city. Most travellers only venture into the desolation to explore **Big Bend National Park**, nearly three hundred miles southeast of El Paso in the curve of the Rio Grande.

Minimal rainfall and harsh land were not the only hindrances to settlement. The **Apache** and **Comanche**, though accustomed in the 1820s to trading with Mexican *comancheros*, were infuriated when hapless white pioneers began to trickle in during the 1830s. With their horsemanship and ability to find scarce water supplies, the Indians posed a real threat; upon statehood, federal money helped to set up a string of cavalry forts to protect Mexican and Anglo settlers from attack. As trading posts and cattle ranges began to spring up after the Civil War, the paramilitary **Texas Rangers** were sent out on violent vigilante missions. Eventually, as in the Panhandle, a brutal programme of buffalo slaughter, supported by the US Army, starved the Indians out. Not long afterwards, **oil** hit west Texas and boomtowns appeared, with all the attendant lawlessness, gun-slinging and brawling.

Davis Mountains

The temperate climate of the verdant **Davis Mountains**, south of the junction of I-10 and I-20, make them a popular summer destination for sweltering urban Texans, while the glassy, starry nights facilitate the work of the **McDonald Observatory**, about twenty miles north of Fort Davis on Hwy-118 (tours of dome and 107-inch telescope daily 9am–5pm). Nocturnal "star parties" here provide the opportunity to look at the constellations for yourself (every Tues, Fri & Sun, 9pm). **Fort Davis State Park** offers good hiking, and fishing and swimming at the foot of the canyon in Limpia Creek. Rooms at its adobe *Indian Lodge* are clean and comfortable – and often booked up, so call in advance (☎915/426-3254; ④).

The **area code** for west Texas, including El Paso, is ☎915.

Fort Davis, a one-street town at the junction of Hwy-118 and Hwy-17, is a peaceful base for exploring the state park, en route to or from Big Bend. *The Old Texas Inn*, above a wood-fronted drugstore, has clean, colorful B&B-style rooms; breakfast is served in the café downstairs, accompanied by country tunes on the jukebox (☎915/426-3118; ③). The slightly more expensive *Limpia Hotel*, opposite (☎1-800/662-5517; ③), serves home-cooked dinners in its cozy dining room. There's pleasantly little to do in Fort Davis at night, though you can buy "membership" to the *Limpia Hotel* bar for $3.

The last town on the way to Big Bend is uninteresting **Alpine**, on Hwy-90 at the edge of the desert, about 65 miles northwest of the northernmost tip of the park. Both *Amtrak* and *Greyhound* stop here; if you need a room, try *Highland Inn* (☎837-5811; ②), just one of a series of adequate hotels on E Hwy-90. No public transportation runs on to Big Bend; drivers continuing to the park should take US-90 east, and turn onto US-385 to Marathon.

Big Bend National Park

The **Rio Grande**, flowing through 1500ft gorges, makes a ninety-degree bend south of Marathon, to form the southern border of **BIG BEND NATIONAL PARK** – thanks to its isolation, one of the least visited of the US national parks, but fully deserving of its status, and very much of a kind with the great desert parks of the Southwest.

The Apache, who forced the Chisos Indians out three hundred years ago, told that this hauntingly beautiful wilderness was used by the Great Spirit to dump all the rocks left over from the creation of the world. A breathtaking million-acre expanse of pine-forested mountains and ocotilla-dotted desert, Big Bend has been home to prospectors and smugglers, a last frontier for the true-grit pioneers at the end of the nineteenth century who took advantage of the rich cinnabar deposits for mercury mining. Today there is camping in specific areas, and some trailer parks, but much of the park remains barely charted territory, the ruins of primitive Mexican and white settlements testament to its power to defeat earlier visitors. Wild animals have fared somewhat better; coyotes, roadrunners and javelino (an odd-looking bristly black pig with a pointy snout) all roam free. Violent contrasts in topography and temperature result in dramatic juxtapositions of desert and mountain plant and animal life. Despite the dryness, tangles of pretty wild flowers and blossoming cacti, including peyote, erupt into color each April.

The most interesting route into Big Bend is from the west. You can't follow the river all the way from El Paso, but Hwy-170 – the **River Road**, reached on Hwy-67 south from Marfa, where James Dean made *Giant* – runs through spectacular desert scenery for around thirty miles west from Ojinaga, climbing stark buttes where you can peep down to the river below. Before reaching the park boundary just beyond Study Butte, you pass through the haunting communities of Lajitas and Terlingua (see opposite).

Once in the park, unless you're prepared to do some strenuous hiking there are few opportunities to see the river itself; the main road is obliged to run across the desert north of the outcrop of the Chisos Mountains. A spur road starting west of the headquarters at **Panther Junction** leads south for six miles, up into the alpine meadows of the **Chisos Basin**, ringed by dramatic (though not amazingly high) peaks. The one gap in the rocky wall here is the **Window**, looking out over the deserts and reached by a relatively simple trail. Driving twenty miles southeast of Panther Junction brings you to the riverside **Rio Grande Village** – unless you choose to detour just before, to bathe in some rather dilapidated natural **hot springs** which feed into the river. A footbridge crosses from near the village to the Mexican hamlet of Boquillas.

At three separate stages within the park boundaries the river runs through gigantic **canyons**. The westernmost, the **Santa Elena**, is the most common **rafting trip**, being accessible from a put-in at Lajitas. Although there is virtually no whitewater, it boasts the technically challenging Rock Slide, and two ethereal Mexican side canyons which can be hiked, as well as stretches where the river swirls between awesome high rock walls, striated at an angle that makes it seem you're plunging into an abyss. It's possible to drive within the park to the eastern end of the canyon, where the towering cliffs suddenly come to an end and the river meanders through marshy fields; a short hike from here shows the gorge in all its splendor.

The ease of crossing the **international frontier** adds an extra frisson to the Big Bend experience, although you can get no further into Mexico than sandbanks populated by browsing burros. This area is so remote that casual traffic across the river is regarded as insignificant; police checks for illegal immigrants take place roughly fifty miles north of Big Bend, on each of the main roads.

Park Practicalities

The park headquarters at **Panther Junction** (daily, 8am–7pm; ☎477-2251), where you pay the $5 entrance fee, holds orientation exhibits and has a daytime gas station. Camping is first-come first-served. **Rio Grande Village** has another visitor center, hot shower facilities in the grocery store, a laundromat, and a daytime gas station. When its $5 campground is full, there are also $3 primitive camping facilities, with pit toilets. Further free primitive **campgrounds** are scattered along the 36 marked hiking trails. These have no facilities, and you'll need a wilderness permit from Panther Junction, map, compass, flashlight and first-aid kit before you can venture onto the trails.

The **Chisos Basin**, which holds a visitor contact station, a store and a post office, is the site of the park's only roofed accommodation. The motel-style *Chisos Mountains Lodge* offers balcony rooms with gorgeous views; you'll often hear javelinos snuffling for food outside your door (reservations essential; ☎477-2291; ④); its adequate cafeteria restaurant closes at 7.30pm. As well as hiking in the basin, you can go **horse riding** with *Chisos Remuda Saddle Horses* (half-day $20, full-day $45; ☎477-2374).

Terlingua and Lajitas

Some of the long-abandoned mercury mining communities on the fringes of Big Bend are now stuttering back to life as alternative tourist centers. **TERLINGUA** in particular, a strangely appealing little ghost town scattered across the scrubby hills along Hwy-170, is populated by the adventurous types who work for the local rafting companies, along with assorted drifters lured by the solitary desert life. Near its fly-blown cemetery, against a backdrop of evocative ruins, the hugely atmospheric *Starlight Theater, Bar and Restaurant* (☎371-2326), with its post-modern reinterpretation of Southwestern decor, is the perfect place to enjoy a cold beer, soaking up the haunting desert view; it also serves food, and puts on evening shows in summer. Nearby, the *Desert Deli and Diner* (☎371-2305) serves sandwiches and coffee in a ramshackle hippy setting. A mile or so east along the highway, the *Kiva Bar and Restaurant* (☎371-2250), attached to the RV-oriented *Big Bend Travel Park*, is hollowed into the rock, and attracts a young crowd to its New-Age bar and evening gigs.

Allow around $85 for a full day's **rafting** along Santa Elena Canyon (see opposite). *Far Flung Adventures*, based next door to the *Starlight* in Terlingua, runs all the Big Bend routes, as well as many other southwestern rivers, and also does memorable multi-day music trips with well-known Texan musicians (☎371-2489 or 1-800/359-4138).

Lajitas, west of Terlingua, is the main put-in for rafting trips, but has largely been taken over by the somewhat ersatz *Lajitas on the Rio Grande* resort complex, with its four separate hotels (☎424-3471 or 1-800/527-0478; ④). However, it remains worth visiting if only to meet its distinguished **mayor** – Clay Henry, the beer-drinking goat, whose bottle-littered pen stands outside the adobe *Lajitas Trading Post*.

Finally, **Study Butte**, near the park at the junctions of hwys 170 and 118, holds a couple of stores and gas stations, as well as the *Big Bend Motor Inn* (☎371-2496; ④).

El Paso

Back when Texas was still Tejas, **EL PASO**, the second oldest settlement in the United States, was the main crossing on the Rio Grande. It still plays that role today, its 600,000 residents joining with another 1.2 million across the river in **CIUDAD JUAREZ**, Mexico, to form the largest binational (and bilingual) megalopolis in North America. At first sight it's not an especially pretty place – massive railyards fill up much of downtown, belching smelters of poisonous copper mills line the riverfront, and the northern reaches are blighted by the giant Fort Bliss military base, where two museums trace the military history of the city from adobe Spanish outpost to largest air defence center in the western world. Its dramatic setting, however, where the Franklin Mountains meet the Chihuahua desert, gives it a certain bold, rough pioneer edge, bearing more relation to old rather than New Mexico, with little of the pastel softness of the southwest US. Local legend has it that when Wyatt Earp arrived in sharpshooting El Paso, he thought it too wild for him, and boarded the first train to Tombstone.

Downtown El Paso holds surprisingly little to see; what character it has continues to be shaped by the **US–Mexico border**. In times past outlaws and exiles from either side of the border would take refuge across the river, and the traffic remains considerable and not entirely uncontroversial. Manual workers come north to find undocumented jobs, and US companies secretly dump their toxic waste on the south side. The border itself, the Rio Grande, has caused its share of disagreements: the river changed course quite often in the 1800s, and it was not until the 1960s, when it was run through a concrete channel, that it was made permanent. An attractive park, the **Chamizal National Memorial** (daily 8am–5pm; free) on the east side of downtown off Paisano Drive, has a small museum discussing the history of cross-border disputes, and throughout the summer hosts a variety of fiestas and cultural events. The **Cordova Bridge** heads acoss the river into Mexico, where there's a larger park and a number of museums; there are no formalities, so long as you have a multiple-entry visa for the US and don't travel more than 25 miles south of the border. A **trolley** departs hourly across the border from the visitor center, although at $10 for a round trip (unlimited stops, mostly at tacky new malls) it's no bargain.

Although El Paso is predominantly Hispanic, there is also a substantial population of **Tigua Indians**, a displaced Pueblo tribe, based in a reservation on Socorro Drive southeast of downtown. The reservation's arts and crafts center is open to the public, selling pottery and textiles and hosting occasional festivals. Adjacent to the reservation, the simple **Ysleta del Sur**, the oldest mission in the United States, marks the beginning of a **mission trail** running alongside scruffy cotton, alfalfa, chili, onion and pecan fields. Two miles east, the **Socorro mission**, moved from its original seventeenth-century site on the river, shows an unusually heavy Indian influence; the crenellation on either side of the bell tower represents a Tigua rain god. Still an active church, inside it is relatively unadorned, with hand-carved ceiling beams and lattices. Off the beaten track, six miles further along the trail, the cathedral-style **San Elizario** was the chapel for the Spanish military, with whitewashed walls, jewel-colored stained glass and a decorative tin ceiling.

Splendid views of three states and two nations can be had from the **scenic drive** along the southern rim of the Franklin Mountains; especially dazzling at night, when the lights of the city resemble a fistful of diamonds flung down into the vast flat valley.

In **Concordia cemetery**, just north of I-10 at the Hwy-54 and Gateway West interchange, a shambling collection of crumbling stones and plain wooden crosses commemorate assorted pioneers and desperados. The grave of John Wesley Hardin, much romanticized gunslinger, is marked by a crooked headstone northwest of the Chinese graveyard, a section walled-off since the Chinese built the railroads in the 1880s.

Practicalities

El Paso's **airport** is about twenty minutes' drive northeast of downtown; *Sun Metro* buses run until 7pm each night, and it's a $10 cab fare, although most downtown hotels offer free van connections. Otherwise, shuttle services run to El Paso and Alamagordo (☎1-800/872-2702), and throughout southern New Mexico (☎1-800/288-1784). *Greyhound* **buses** stop at 111 San Francisco Ave (☎544-7200) in the center of El Paso, while *Amtrak* **trains** pull in to the Daniel Burnham-designed Union Station at 700 San Francisco Ave slightly to the west.

For full information on El Paso and its Mexican neighbor, contact the downtown **visitor center** (☎544-0062 or 1-800/351-6024), at 5 Civic Center Plaza in the Convention Center complex. Of **places to stay**, the *Travelodge City Center*, 409 E Missouri Ave (☎544-3333; ③), has large, comfortable rooms and a Mexican restaurant, while the atmospheric *Gardner Hotel*, 311 E Franklin St – where John Dillinger stayed in the 1920s – has hostel accommodation and a few private rooms (☎532-3661; ①). At the other end of the scale is the luxurious *Paso del Norte Hotel*, 101 S El Paso Ave (☎534-3000; ⑥), which has a swanky Southwestern restaurant and a wonderfully romantic bar, topped with a colorful Tiffany dome and surrounded by rose and black marble.

For some of the best **Tex-Mex food** anywhere, try *Forti's Mexican Elder*, 321 Chelsea St (☎772-0066), just east of downtown, where a tableful of juicy enchiladas and rellenos costs around $10. The Tigua reservation's *Ysleta del Sur* restaurant (☎859-3916) is a popular lunch-spot, serving reasonably priced chili-charged stews and Mexican-Indian meals. Downtown the *San Francisco Grill*, opposite the *Paso del Norte* at 127-A Pioneer Plaza (☎545-1386), is one of El Paso's hippest spots, serving New American brunch, lunch and dinner in upbeat surroundings.

After dark, you might want to head across the border to **Ciudad Juarez**: the Hemingwayesque *Kentucky Club Cantina*, 629 Avenida Juarez just south of the Santa Fe Street bridge, or the more touristy *Chihuahua Charlie's*, 2525 Triunfo de la Republica near the Plaza de Toros Monumental (the main bullfight arena), are both tried and tested haunts. The latter is more comfortable for women travellers.

El Paso is also the home of *Tony Lama*, makers of top-quality **cowboy boots**, available at substantial discounts at 204 Mills St (☎532-6052).

Guadalupe Mountains National Park

Roughly one-hundred miles east of El Paso, Hwy-62/180 climbs towards Carslbad Caverns (see p.683) along the southern fringes of the **Guadalupe Mountains**, once a stronghold of the Mescalero Apaches. The National Park here is very much a hiking and camping destination, barely penetrated by road and without accommodation, food, or even gas. It's possible to hike right to the top of Guadalupe Peak, at 8749 feet the highest point in Texas, but most walkers head for the gruelling seven-mile trek through **McKittrick Canyon**, climbing from bare desert into lush mountain forests beside sheer canyon walls.

CHAPTER TEN

THE GREAT PLAINS

T he **GREAT PLAINS**, stretching west of the Mississippi through **OKLAHOMA**, **MISSOURI**, **KANSAS**, **IOWA**, **NEBRASKA**, and **SOUTH** and **NORTH DAKOTA**, are lumped together in the popular imagination as an unappealing expanse of unvarying flatness and conservative "Mid American" values, a huge national joke to be passed through as fast as possible. Once, however, this was the **West**, a vast empty canvas on which outlaws, fur-trappers, buffalo hunters and cowboys painted their dreams. In the 1870s, the wide open range of the lone prairie, which had originally been known as the **Great American Desert** but was now promoted as a bountiful Garden of Eden, inspired such fascination that General Custer was moved to call it "the fairest and richest portion of the national domain". As well as the main routes west (the Oregon and Santa Fe trails through Missouri, Kansas and Nebraska), the plains were criss-crossed by the Pony Express, cattle trails and railroads. Today the massive Gateway Arch in **St Louis** celebrates the traders, explorers and pioneers who followed their destinies further and further west.

Early maps show the "Desert" as uninterrupted by towns or roads; even today there are fewer towns, spaced further apart, on the plains than anywhere else in the nation, and the population has steadily dropped since the 1930s. One sinister note echoes through this openness and emptiness: most of the nation's **nuclear missiles** – marked by unprepossessing concrete blocks fenced into empty fields – sit patiently beneath a land already ravaged and destroyed by greed.

For the plains, today so apparently uneventful, share a trauma-scarred history. The systematic destruction by white settlers of the awesome herds of **bison** presaged the virtual eradication of the **Plains Indians**. Reservations, agencies and "assigned lands" dwindled as the natural resources of the area attracted white settlement; after 1874, when **gold** was discovered in the Black Hills, the fate of the Native Americans was practically sealed. However, thanks to warriors like **Crazy Horse** and **Sitting Bull**, the struggle for control of the plains was by no means as easy as the Hollywood Westerns imply. Today the region is troublingly ambivalent about this history: many of its museums and monuments to the Native Americans can seem as much a veiled celebration of as an apology for the destruction of their culture.

The plains are more comfortable, however, playing **cowboys**, priding in a romantic myth of the Wild West and flaunting sanitized versions of wicked old cowtowns like **Deadwood** in South Dakota, **Dodge City** (once called the "Beautiful, Bibulous Babylon of the Frontier") in Kansas, and **St Joseph**, Missouri, the birthplace of the Pony Express. **Calamity Jane**, **Wild Bill Hickok**, **Billy the Kid** and **Annie Oakley** all left

---

ACCOMMODATION PRICE CODES

All accommodation prices in this book have been coded using the symbols below. Note that prices are for the least expensive double rooms in each establishment.
  For a full explanation see p.35 in *Basics*.

①	up to $30	④	$60–80	⑦	$130–180
②	$30–45	⑤	$80–100	⑧	$180+
③	$45–60	⑥	$100–130		

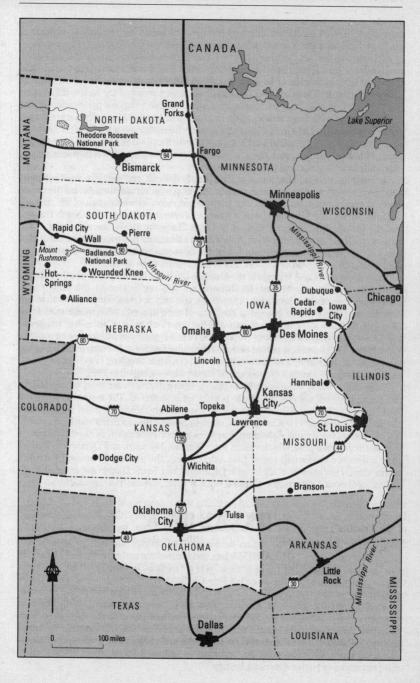

their mark here when this was the wild frontier, and today, in the sandy scrublands of northern Nebraska and North Dakota, you can still see real cowboy and cattle country.

After Reconstruction, Southern blacks came here in search of an egalitarian future, and black colonies sprang up all around the region. The dreams soon died, though, and there are few black faces to be seen nowadays. There is, however, more evidence of nineteenth-century **Russian** and **German** settlement; many of the oldest families on the plains are descendants of Mennonites who escaped religious persecution in the 1870s, bringing with them new farming methods that heralded the region's great agricultural prosperity. The Great Plains still provide the nation with much of its food and export two-thirds of the world's **wheat**, seas of which can be seen waving over the flat fields of Iowa, Nebraska and Kansas. The economy has also been dependent on **oil**, especially in Oklahoma, and **gold** in the Dakotas.

Defining the geographical limits of the plains is difficult, and the term itself is almost a misnomer – there are vast flat expanses and long uninterrupted roads, but there are also canyons, forests, and splashes of unexpected color, as well as two of the nation's mightiest rivers: the **Missouri**, which weaves its course southeast from North Dakota, and the **Mississippi**, which it joins at St Louis. Since the 1950s, the siphoning of the underground Ogallala aquifer from Nebraska to Oklahoma has transformed much that was once dusty desert into verdant fields; the consequences of overuse (ensuring the depletion of the reservoir in another fifty years) remain to be seen.

The woods, caves and springs of the **Ozarks**, the lunar landscapes of South Dakota's **Badlands**, and stately **Mount Rushmore** are the region's most touristed areas. Otherwise, there are few immediate attractions, and only St Louis stands out as an urban destination. Drama comes instead in the form of such unpredictable **weather** as freak blizzards, dust storms, lightning storms and the notorious "twister" tornados. Images of the devastating Thirties' dustbowl Depression (when topsoil was whisked as far away as Washington DC) remain as potent as the Technicolor fantasy of Dorothy and Toto being swept up from Kansas by a tornado to the land of Oz, while **flooding** is a constant threat, as seen when huge swathes of Iowa and Missouri were swamped in 1993.

A **car** is practically obligatory in the plains, where distances are long, roads straight and seemingly endless, and the sparse population is scattered. The main routes (I-94, I-90, I-80, I-70, I-40) cross east–west, making it frustratingly difficult to travel north–south. *Greyhound* **buses** travel the interstates, often bypassing the small towns which provide a real sense of the region. Subsidiary bus lines include *Jack Rabbit* in South Dakota, as well as the *Jefferson Line*, which covers Iowa, Kansas, Missouri, and Oklahoma. True to their image as a crossroads rather than a destination, the plains are crossed by *Amtrak* **trains** almost exclusively at night, with Oklahoma and South Dakota not covered at all. St Louis, Missouri, is the major **airport**, while Wichita, Kansas, is a regional hub.

OKLAHOMA

Ridiculed by the rest of the nation as boring, and forever the butt of jokes at the expense of the "Okies", **OKLAHOMA** has had a traumatic and far from dull history. In the 1830s, all this land, held to be useless, was set aside as **Indian Territory**; a convenient dumping ground for the so-called Five Civilized Tribes who blocked white settlement in the southern states. The Choctaw and Chickasaw of Mississippi, the Seminole of Florida, and the Creek of Alabama were each assigned a share, while the rest (though already inhabited by indigenous Indians) was given to the Cherokee from Carolina, Tennessee and Georgia, who followed in 1838 on the four-month trek notorious as "the Trail of Tears" (see p.417). Today the state has a large Indian population – *oklahoma* is the Choctaw word for "red man" – and even the smallest towns tend to have museums of Native American history.

Once white settlers realized that Indian Territory was, in fact, well worth farming, they decided to stay. The Indians were relocated once more, and in a manic free-for-all scramble in 1889, entire towns sprang up literally overnight. Those who jumped the gun and claimed land illegally were known as Sooners; hence Oklahoma's nickname, the **Sooner State**. White settlers didn't have an easy life, however, facing, after great oil prosperity in the Twenties, an era of unthinkable hardship in the Thirties. The desperate migration, when whole communities fled the dust bowl for California, has come to encapsulate the worst horrors of the Depression, most famously in John Steinbeck's novel (and John Ford's film) **The Grapes of Wrath**, but also in Dorothea Lange's haunting photos of itinerant families, hitching and camping on the road, and in the sad yet hopeful songs of Woody Guthrie. Since the slump of the early Eighties, the region is facing another crisis, and its major downtown areas are uncannily still.

Oklahoma is not the flat and unchanging expanse of popular imagination. Most of its places of interest, such as attractive **Tulsa**, lie in the hilly wooded northeast; only the sparse and treeless west is devoid of appeal, on the far side of the central "tornado alley" prairie grassland which holds the state's hard-hit capital, **Oklahoma City**. The lakes and parks of the south, which bears more than a passing resemblance to neighboring Arkansas (complete with mountains, foliage and bluegrass music), have made tourism Oklahoma's second industry after oil.

Getting Around Oklahoma

Car travel is the only rational way to explore Oklahoma, which has no *Amtrak* service. *Greyhound* **buses** speed along I-35 and I-40, which converge on Oklahoma City, but public transportation within the towns is minimal. Tulsa and Oklahoma City have airports. **Route 66**, which passes through both on its way from Missouri to Texas, is no longer a national highway, but if you have plenty of time (and sturdy tires; much of the road is in a bad way), makes a nostalgic alternative to the interstates. A booklet available at the Tulsa CVB details the small communities and ghost towns en route.

Eastern Oklahoma

Eastern Oklahoma includes the "Green Country" of the northeast, patterned with the foothills of the Ozarks, and woods, streams, lakes and rivers that make it a popular camping destination. Art Deco **Tulsa** is its cultural center; **Tahlequah** and **Pawhuska** are the capitals of the Cherokee and Osage nations respectively.

Tulsa

Tulsa is a good-looking city, thanks in part to the striking Art Deco architecture that dates from its Twenties heyday as an immensely wealthy oil town. Despite – or possibly because of – its pleasant atmosphere, two excellent museums, and thriving high arts scene, the city tends towards complacency. In addition, the overriding Bible Belt mentality is hard to ignore; even in the hip *Tulsa Press* a regular feature reviews local churches, whimsically named *Pew View*.

Arrival, Information and Getting Around

Tulsa International Airport (☎838-5000) lies just minutes east of downtown. Hwy-169 from Kansas City skirts its east side; I-244, which gives access from the south, is also the main route east–west across town. *Greyhound* comes in downtown to 317 S Detroit Ave

The **area code** for Tulsa and eastern Oklahoma is ☎918.

(☎584-4427). The **CVB**, 616 S Boston Ave (☎585-1201 or 1-800/558-3311), provides a self-guided walking tour of downtown – such as it is – as well as local **bus** schedules; services operate (if you're lucky) between 6am and 5pm (60¢, transfers 5¢).

The City

Downtown Tulsa's most obvious landmark is the ornate Art Deco **Union Depot**, on the First St and Boston Ave Overpass, built in the early Thirties and now housing offices. The **320 Boston Building** on Boston Ave, known in the Twenties as the "Oil Bank of America", is worth a look for its huge brass doors, stone archways, gargoyles and hand-painted ceilings. Further along the other side of the road, another distinctive Twenties skyscraper, the **Philtower**, 527 S Boston Ave, has a green and red tiled sloping roof and crouching gargoyles, a lobby richly decorated in brass and marble, and a small gallery of Tulsa history. **Lyon's Indian Store**, on the southwest corner of Seventh and Main, is an old trading post selling authentic goods made by over thirty Oklahoman tribes, including feather headdresses, bead work, rugs and jewellery. The huge and gloriously exuberant Art Deco **Boston Avenue Methodist Church**, 1301 S Boston Ave – at 255 feet high, it's practically cathedral-sized – offers good views of the city from its fourteenth storey (free tours Mon–Fri 9am–4pm, Sun at 12.15pm).

Outside downtown, to the south, the 75ft **Creek Council Oak**, 18th St and Cheyenne Ave, marks the spot where the Creek Indians ended their tortuous migration from Alabama in 1836, and founded Tulsa on the Arkansas River. The tree became a tribal meeting site, used ceremonially until 1896. The airy and stylish **Philbrook Art Center**, 2727 S Rockford Rd, in the house of oilman Waite Phillips in well-heeled Mapleridge, is a Florentine-style mansion set in Gatsbyesque acres. Though displays include Native American pottery, African sculpture, Chinese jades and Renaissance paintings, the house itself is every bit as decorative as the art, with ostentatious marble floors, indoor fountains and sweeping staircases. The gardens, with crumbling paths, pretty fountains and fantastic hill views are also worth exploring (Tues, Wed, Fri & Sat 10am–5pm, Sun 1–5pm, Thurs 5–8pm; tours Thurs, Sat & Sun; donation).

Oral Roberts University, 7777 S Lewis Ave, is a must for kitsch obsessives. University, hospital and television station all in one, the concept was inspired by visionary Oral Roberts – who back in 1987 announced that God had decided to "call him home" unless he could raise 4.5 million dollars before a certain deadline. Roberts retreated to a lonely vigil at the top of his **Prayer Tower**, a kind of B-movie space ship; he got his money (or God's; the distinction was unclear), though his credibility was dented when the tower was struck by lightning at the crucial moment. You can now see a sycophantic exhibition, complete with heavenly choir, on the great man's life (Mon–Sat 10.30am–4.30pm, Sun 1–5pm). There's an 80ft-high pair of hands in prayer on the grass outside the **City of Faith Medical Center**, where a multimedia "journey through the Bible" (the first eight books of it) runs every twenty minutes (same hours).

The **Gilcrease Museum**, 1400 Gilcrease Museum Rd, just northwest of downtown, is set in the gently rolling **Osage Hills**, with a fine vista from the back and good view of downtown from the front. Thomas Gilcrease, of Indian heritage, grew very rich after oil was found on his land. His private collection of western art includes Native American works, as well as excellent Remingtons, Russells and Morans (Mon–Sat 9am–5pm, Sun 1–5pm; free tours daily at 2pm).

To experience Tulsa's cowboy history, make for the **Ted Allen Ranch**, seven miles west along 181st St at 19600 S Memorial Drive, Bixby. This working horse ranch opens daily at 9am; activities include riding, overnight campouts, moonlit hayrides and rodeos (☎366-3010; prices vary). There's a music show and chuckwagon supper (steak, beans, baked potato and coffee) each Friday and Saturday at 7.30pm, from April to September. The band is good, with the fastest fiddle-playing and throatiest yodelling this side of Missouri, and Ted Allen's laconic humor makes it all great fun.

Accommodation

Most of Tulsa's **budget hotels** are on the interstates and along **East Skelly Drive** forking southwest from I-44. There's **camping** at the *KOA*, 193 East Ave (☎266-4227). For details of **B&Bs**, contact *Ozark Mountain Country B&B*, Box 295, Branson, MO 65726 (☎417/334-4720).

Best Western Trade Winds East, 3337 E Skelly Drive (☎743-7931). Comfortable rooms. ③.

Crosswinds, 8201 E Skelly Drive (☎665-6800). Free breakfast and popcorn. ③.

Lexington Hotel Suites, 8525 E 41st St (☎627-0030). Luxury doubles, with breakfast. ④.

YMCA, 515 S Denver Ave (☎583-6201). Men-only downtown accommodation. ①.

Eating

Tulsa's **restaurants** are diverse and scattered; good options can be found along E 15th Street and S Peoria Avenue, while downtown holds several down-home diners.

Back Bay Gourmet, 1536 E 15th St (☎584-2300). Pricey, but special. Items on the varied menu include goat cheese won ton with basil chili sauce.

Casa Bonita, 2120 S Sheridan Rd (☎587-4411). Lively Mexican-themed restaurant, serving large spicy dinners in the atmosphere of your choice, from mysterious caves to rowdy Mexican villages.

15th Street Grill, 1542 E 15th St (☎587-4411). Art Deco seafood and pasta joint. Lunch $5–8.

Metro Diner, 3001 E 11th St (☎592-2616). Fifties-style diner east of downtown, serving good home-baked pies and chicken-fried steaks, as well as great ice cream sodas.

The Orange Blossom Cafe, 3523 S Peoria Ave. Hip hang-out on the main stretch along the river. Homemade soups and chocolate cake, plus choc fudge coffee. Live jazz Fri & Sat.

Nightlife and Entertainment

There is even less to do in **downtown** Tulsa after dark than during the day; 15th and Cherry streets just south, and S Peoria Ave by the river, are much more lively. If you visit in September, try to catch the **Chili Cookoff and Bluegrass Festival**, featuring spicy chili competitions, clogging, and bluegrass gigs. Newssheets like the *Monthly Uptown News*, *Tulsa World* and *Tulsa Press* (the "teepee") carry full nightlife listings.

Club One, 3200 S Riverside Drive (☎743-1665). R'n'b during the week, All Star Blues jam Wed.

Discoveryland, 10 miles west on W 41st St (☎245-0242 or 1-800/338-6552). Outdoor performances of Rodgers and Hammerstein's *Oklahoma!* Mon–Sat, June–Aug. $12; pre-show barbecue 5.30pm, $8.

Joey's Blues Bar, 6825 S Peoria Ave (☎481-8787). Favorite blues venue.

Spotlight Theatre, 1381 Riverside Drive (☎587-5030). Art Deco building that for forty years has hosted the melodrama *The Drunkard*, accompanied by pretzels and sandwiches, every Sat.

The Sunset Grill, 3410 S Peoria Ave (☎744-5550). Hip live bands, and a free midnight buffet.

Claremore

Thirty miles northeast of Tulsa on Route 66, **CLAREMORE**, the birthplace of **Will Rogers**, populist comedian, journalist and Twenties film star, is a shrine to a man being slowly forgotten as his films are no longer seen. His career began with a vaudeville show that included lassooing a horse and its rider, while giving a witty commentary, and he was renowned for his pithy and good-natured one-liners. Incredibly, when he died in a plane crash in 1935 there was a nationwide thirty-minute silence. One of his most famous statements, "I never met a man I didn't like", is inscribed on his statue at the **Will Rogers Memorial**, on Will Rogers Boulevard on Hwy-88, which displays his possessions, such as his "gag book", together with stills and clips from his films.

Bartlesville

For forty miles north of Tulsa, the monotony of the plains is relieved only by clumps of spindly scrub oaks. Then comes quiet **BARTLESVILLE**, dominated by the extraordinary **Price Tower**, designed by Frank Lloyd Wright in 1956 – an ugly cantilevered green oddity at Sixth and Dewey, which resembles a tall tree. The **Frank Phillips Home**, 1107 S Cherokee Ave, built in 1908 by the founder of Phillips Oil, displays oil wealth at its gaudiest, with gold faucets, mirrored ceilings and marble floors. More impressive is his **Woolaroc Ranch**, thirteen miles southwest in the Blackjack Hills, now a wildlife refuge and museum of western art and history. Over 60,000 artefacts are scattered through seven huge rooms. Paintings and decorative art line the walls, from Native American works to the epic western scenes of Remington and Russell, while artefacts of various tribes, pioneers and cowboys are gathered in too great an abundance to take in. Look out for the 95-million-year-old dinosaur egg, exquisite Navajo blankets, scalps taken by Indians and Buffalo Bill's weathered saddle (Tues–Sun 10am–5pm; $4).

For **lodging**, choose between the *Travelers Motel*, 3105 Frank Phillips Blvd (☎333-1900; ②), and the luxurious *Ramada Inn*, 1410 SE Washington Blvd (☎333-8320; ④).

Tahlequah

Forty-five minutes' drive south from Tulsa on Hwy-51, **TAHLEQUAH** is the capital of the **Cherokee** nation, formed in 1839 when the Trail of Tears finally reached its end. The sophisticated Cherokee had a written constitution, published the first newspaper in Indian Territory (in both Cherokee and English) and set up the Cherokee female seminary, the first higher education school for women west of the Mississippi. It stands today on the campus of the **Northeastern State University** on Hwy-82, which has more Native American students than any other academic institution in the US.

Tahlequah itself is uncommercialized, and the **Cherokee Heritage Center**, three miles south at Tsa-La-Gi, presents Native American life to tourists with more dignity than might be expected. Historical artefacts in the museum include wooden ceremonial masks, and a display covers the Cherokee alphabet (Mon–Sat 10am–5pm, Sun 1–5pm; $3.50). A reconstructed seventeenth-century Indian village gives arts and crafts demonstrations (May–Aug Mon–Sat 10am–5pm, Sun 1–5pm; $4.50), and a "Trail of Tears" drama is put on in the summer (Mon–Sat 8pm; $9; ☎456-6007).

In the winter, the place is pretty much dead; in summer it's not a bad idea to take a **room** in the *Tahlequah Motor Lodge*, 2501 S Muskogee Ave (☎456-2350; ③), or the *Lodge of the Cherokees*, south on Hwy-62 (☎456-0511; ③). The *Restaurant of the Cherokees* (also ☎456-0511) specializes in traditional smoked dishes.

Muskogee

The Creek Indians, relocated to **MUSKOGEE** in the 1830s, established the town as the central meeting place of the Civilized Tribes; Indian leaders gathered here in 1905 to draw up a plan for a separate Native American state, which was never to be. The arrival of the railroad in the 1870s and the discovery of oil in 1903 both guaranteed that the town would be usurped by white settlers. The **Five Civilized Tribes Museum**, Honor Heights Drive, Agency Hill, tells the Native Americans' story through costumes, documents, photographs and jewellery, with a reconstructed trading post and a print room (Mon–Sat 10am–5pm, Sun 1–5pm; $3). Muskogee is an appealing place, and a good base for the crystal-clear **Lake Tenkiller**, thirty miles southeast on US-64. Surrounded by woods, cliffs and quiet beaches, the lake is perfect for fishing, boating, swimming and scuba diving, and has camping facilities, but is (unsurprisingly) heavily touristed.

Oklahoma City and Westwards

If you're heading west, your last stop in Oklahoma is likely to be the capital, **Oklahoma City**, smack in the center of the state. Beyond that, the Great Plains stretch in all their emptiness, the endless horizons broken only by small agricultural communities. The **southwest** is the most densely populated, as it is crossed by the two main routes to Texas – I-40 west to Amarillo, and I-44 south to Wichita Falls; to the north, in the **Oklahoman Panhandle**, ranches and tiny hamlets are the only signs of life.

Oklahoma City

OKLAHOMA CITY was created in a matter of hours on April 22 1889, after a single gunshot signalled the opening of the land to white settlement. What was barren prairie at dawn was by nightfall a city of ten thousand. In 1911, the capital was moved here from nearby Guthrie, and in 1928 oil was discovered. Sitting on one of the nation's largest oilfields, the city was brought up short by the slump in the Eighties. However, it is also the largest stocker and feeder cattle market in the world, and is trying to revitalize its pitifully depressed economy by developing tourism, aided by the presence of the unmissable **National Cowboy Hall of Fame**.

Arrival, Information and Getting Around

Will Rogers Memorial Airport, 6100 Terminal Drive (☎681-5311), lies southwest of the city, within about fifteen minutes of the hotels and motels. *Airport Limousine Inc* (☎685-2638) runs $9 downtown shuttles. Public transportation, far from adequate, is based at 20 W Reno Ave (☎235-7433), southeast of the Myriad Gardens and north of I-40. Buses run daily except Sunday until 7pm (75¢). You can rent **bikes** from *Miller's Bicycle Distribution*, 715 W Boyd Ave (☎321-8296).

The **visitor center** is downtown at 4 Santa Fe Plaza (Mon–Fri 8am–4.30pm; ☎278-8912), around the corner from *Greyhound* at 427 W Sheridan Ave (☎235-6425); the **post office** is at 320 SW Fifth St (Mon–Fri 8.30am–5.30pm, Sat 9am–noon; zip code 73125).

The City

Urban renewal in Oklahoma City's **downtown** is based around the renovated warehouses of **Bricktown**, on Sheridan Ave east of the Santa Fe Railroad, which is developing into a reasonable eating and nightlife center. The city's skyscrapers are low key and old fashioned, and there is no real sense of commercial activity; even in the middle of the day it can be depressingly quiet. **Myriad Gardens** on Sheridan Ave, prettily landscaped with hills, gardens and waterways, give great views across to the brick-towered downtown skyline, and on a sunny day the **Crystal Bridge** tropical botanical garden, in a glass tube in the middle of the park, abounds in garish exotic blooms.

As well as a couple of historical museums, the **Capitol Complex**, just north of downtown, includes the unprepossessing **capitol** (free tours daily 8am–3pm), which may lack the usual dome but has a working oil well in its grounds. The **Heritage Hills** area nearby, where the cattle barons, oil millionaires and bankers used to live, is now run-down and seedy in parts, with many buildings abandoned. Of the two of its mansions open to the public, the Victorian-style **Overholser Mansion**, 405 NW 15th St, is to be preferred to the **Oklahoma Heritage Center**, 201 NW 14th St, only because the latter holds the unrelentingly tedious "Oklahoma Hall of Fame" portrait gallery.

Two much quirkier attractions lie in the northeast of the city. **Enterprise Square USA**, 2501 E Memorial Rd between I-35 and Eastern Ave, is an outrageous barrage of propaganda about the glories of free enterprise – and a hallucinogenic nightmare to boot. Giant consumer products loom above your head, the George Washingtons on huge dollar bills sing the national anthem with eyes rolling and heads bobbing, and a crazed "government" computer becomes more and more manic until threatening to

---

The **area code** for Oklahoma City and western Oklahoma is ☎405.

self-destruct (moral – don't let government interference obstruct freedom of choice). Complicated computer games gauge how successful you are in different "careers"; fragile egos should beware: it's a blow to go bankrupt setting up your gardening business when the eight-year-old on the next computer is happily balancing the economy (Mon–Fri 9am–4pm, Sat 9am–5pm, Sun 1–4pm; $5).

The **National Cowboy Hall of Fame**, ten minutes' walk south at 1700 NE 63rd St, is a real treat. Sitting atop Persimmon Hill overlooking Route 66, it combines "high art" and popular art in one loving collection. In the works of Remington and Russell – rugged landscapes, stoical cowboys with horses or in comradely groups – the link between western art and western movies is very clear. The paintings look like film stills, and titles such as *Waiting for Trouble* evoke the cinema's endlessly reworked myths of the West. Large exhibitions focus on contemporary Native American work, much of it colorful, bitter and subversive. John Wayne's collection is a delight for the cowboy fetishist, and the Western Performers Hall of Fame pays homage to movie cowboys and gals in hilariously reverent oil paintings and memorabilia. The poignant *End of the Trail* sculpture, 18ft high, portrays an Indian slumped exhausted – or dead – over his horse. In the garden, dotted with horse graves, corny epigraphs send the much-loved deceased beasts to "Hoss Heaven" (daily summer 8.30am–6pm; winter 9am–5pm; $5).

Oklahoma City's **stockyards**, in the southwest on Agnew Ave and Exchange St, are the busiest in the world, and well worth a visit, though vegetarians and animal-lovers should steer clear. This is the real thing, stomping, snorting and smelly, with scrawny animals shunted in and out of tiny pens for auction. The roughnecks that spend their lives here, smoking, chatting, even sleeping, take no apparent notice of the quick-fire auctioneer, but nonetheless millions of heads of cattle per year are bought and sold, and it can make addictive entertainment. Sales begin at 8am Monday to Thursday, and fizzle out by late afternoon. Early in the week is the best time to visit.

Accommodation

Rooms are very cheap; try along the interstates, especially S I-35, for chain motels. B&Bs are a good deal, but even the downtown luxury hotels can be affordable.

Best Western Saddleback Inn, 4300 SW Third St (☎947-7000). Three blocks northeast of I-40, on the west side of town. $52–67. Pseudo-Indian decor, but luxurious touches like poolside service. ④.

Country House, 10101 Oakview Rd (☎794-4008). Two-room B&B near Lake Draper in the far southeast of the city. ② and ③.

Howard Johnson West, 400 S Meridian Ave (☎943-9841). Good rooms, breakfast included. ③.

Ramada Inn South, 6800 S I-35 (☎631-3321). Directly east of the airport, with functional rooms. ②.

The Sheraton Century Center, 1 N Broadway (☎235-2780). Downtown luxury hotel. ⑤.

Eating

Beef is, of course, good in Oklahoma City, especially around the stockyards. The warehouse restaurants of **Bricktown** are popular with the after-work and singles crowd.

Applewoods, 4301 SW Third St (☎947-8484). Famed in the city for its good steaks and all-you-can-eat apple fritters. They're greasy and rich, but fill you up.

The Cattlemen's Cafe, 1309 S Agnew Ave (☎236-0416). Cattlemen from the adjacent stockyards eat in a comfortable publike atmosphere. The restaurant, which has served beautiful steaks since 1910, was allegedly won in a crap game in 1946. Lunchtime specials.

Molly Murphy's House of Fine Repute, I-40 and Meridian Ave. Fancy-dressed staff shout at and humiliate customers, who are expected, each time *Car Wash* is played, to leap up, gather at the salad bar (a 1962 Jag) and groove on down. Even so, the food is good, and moderately priced, with fish, chicken, steaks and burgers, and you might manage to hide behind a beleaguered birthday group.

Piggy's, 303 E Sheridan Ave (☎232-3912). Good plain barbecue and beans in Bricktown, accompanied by a lively, youthful Dixieland house band.

Pump's, 5700 N Western Ave (☎840-4369). Budget Mexican food, omelettes, burgers and sandwiches in an old gas station. Regular happy hours and discounts.

Nightlife and Entertainment

Oklahoma City can be pretty dodgy at night, especially in the isolated downtown – and it's a long way from the cutting edge as regards live music or dancing. **Norman**, home to the University of Oklahoma, has campus nightlife, but it's a thirty-minute drive south. Wednesday's *Oklahoma Gazette*, along with lively articles, carries good listings.

Black Liberated Arts Center, 1901 N Ellison Ave (☎528-4666). Northwest of downtown, a variety of black theater and musical events during the winter season.

Jokers Comedy Club, 2925 W Britton Ave (☎752-5270). Comedy shows nightly.

O'Briens Piano Bar, 104 E Sheridan Ave (☎235-3434). Bricktown dive based on the famous New Orleans bar, with good boozy karaoke nights. Everyone tries very hard to have fun.

Oklahoma Opry, 404 W Commerce Ave (☎632-8322). Authentic country shows, Sat at 8pm. $6.

Guthrie

GUTHRIE, thirty miles north of downtown Oklahoma City on I-35, was the capital from statehood in 1907 until 1911. Today the 1400-acre **Guthrie Historical District** forms a remarkably complete collection of restored Victorian architecture. The **State Publishing Museum**, 301 W Harrison Ave, exhibits printing technology from the earliest newspaper printed in Oklahoma Territory, and the ornate Doric **Scottish Rite Masonic Temple**, 900 E Oklahoma Ave, the largest Masonic complex in the world, features hundreds of bright stained-glass windows. Guthrie is also home to the **Lazy E Arena**, four miles east of downtown, a huge site which hosts world champion rodeos and roping competitions, as well as big-name concerts (☎282-3004).

Guthrie has two good **B&Bs** – the *Stone Lion Inn*, 1016 W Warner Ave (☎282-0012; ④), and *Harrison House*, 124 W Harrison Ave (☎282-1000; ④), in Guthrie's first bank building. The **visitor center** is at 223 South First St (☎282-1947).

MISSOURI

The state of **MISSOURI**, where the forest meets the prairie and the Mississippi River meets the Missouri River, has just two significant cities. Dominant **St Louis** sits midway down its eastern fringe; **Kansas City** is almost directly across on the western border. The pair are linked by I-70, but there's not much in between to warrant stopping off. In contrast, the **south** features the beautiful hillsides, streams and ragged lakes of the **Ozark Mountains** as well as the booming country and western town of **Branson**, while in the **east**, small river towns such as Mark Twain's **Hannibal** and serene **Ste Genevieve** brighten the course of the Mississippi. The **northwest**, home of the Pony Express and outlaw Jesse James, still strikes up images of frontier times.

Although the first French colonists honored the claims of local Native Americans, such as the original Missouri, when the area was sold to the US in 1803 as part of the Louisiana Purchase the Indians were driven west by a great rush of settlers. In the 1840s and 1850s immigrants from Germany and Ireland flooded into the east. Outnumbering their pro-slavery predecessors, they swung the balance in favor of staying in the Union during the Civil War. However, Confederate guerrilla forces attracted considerable support among the western slave-owners. Meanwhile Missouri, and St Louis in particular, was establishing itself as an important gateway to the West.

Today, the **"Show Me State"** (so called because of the supposed scepticism of the typical Missourian) retains a conservative air, particularly in the rural areas.

Getting Around Missouri

The central corridor between Missouri's two main cities, St Louis and Kansas City, is well served by *Greyhound*; the journey takes around six hours. Chicago and Memphis are both five hours from St Louis. Infrequent *Greyhound* buses run through the southeast, to Springfield and a few Ozark towns, but you'll need a car to see the mountains and the river towns in the north. St Louis (*TWA*'s main hub) and Kansas City have major **airports**. Daily *Amtrak* **trains** between Chicago and LA call at St Louis, KC and assorted small towns; each day, two other Chicago trains terminate in St Louis, and one continues to Houston. Both KC and St Louis are on the daily route to New Orleans.

Eastern Missouri

The Mississippi defines Missouri's eastern border, absorbing major tributaries of the Missouri, Ohio, Illinois and Des Moines rivers. Innumerable towns sprang up along the river, their aspirations reflected by such classical names as Alexandria, Antioch and Athens. **Hannibal**, the boyhood home of Mark Twain, is the largest in the northeast, while Gallic **Ste Genevieve** is the prettiest in the south. All have, however, decreased in size with the growing pre-eminence of **St Louis**. Away from the river, the land rises to the **Ozark Plateau**, whose deep green valleys are cut by swift clear streams.

Hannibal

HANNIBAL might well have been just another medium-sized river settlement, had not Samuel Langhorne Clemens, who renamed himself **Mark Twain** after the cry of pilots on the Mississippi, spent his boyhood here. Although Hannibal does have other industries, downtown is little more than a Twain theme park, with attractions such as museums, donkey rides and wax displays. Businesses include the *Clemens Hotel*, *Tom'n'Huck Motel*, *Injun Joe Campground* and even the *Mark Twain Roofing Company*.

What Twain actually felt about his own town is largely unknown. He wrote surprisingly little about it in his extensive non-fiction works, though you could say he spoke with his feet when he left for good at seventeen to become a journeyman printer, riverboat pilot, journalist and writer. However, those of his books most specifically set in Hannibal – the *Adventures of Tom Sawyer* and the sequel *Adventures of Huckleberry Finn* – provide vivid accounts of growing up in this often rowdy frontier riverport.

Hannibal is shambolically picturesque. Squeezed between two steep bluffs – Tom Sawyer's **"Cardiff Hill"** to the north and **Lover's Leap** to the south – the once-busy riverside is now largely quiet except for the occasional creaking of a crane loading grain or cement. Antique, souvenir and gift stores line the north end of **Main Street**, near the short cobbled incline of **Hill Street**, among whose original buildings are Twain's father's law office, the home of the real-life Becky Thatcher (Sawyer's first love), and the **Tom Sawyer Boyhood Home** where Twain himself lived between 1844 and 1853. Adjoining the home, the Mark Twain Museum includes such memorabilia as first editions, letters, photos, original artwork and one of his trademark white suits (daily summer 8am–6pm; otherwise times vary; $4).

South of Hannibal, Hwy-79 leading to St Louis offers one of the most **scenic drives** along the Mississippi, almost continuously broken by thin, elongated, thickly wooded islands and bounded by towering limestone bluffs.

Practicalities

Motel rates in Hannibal vary wildly according to season. The very central *Best Western Hotel Clemens*, 401 N Third St (☎248-1150; ④), with a pool and breakfast, is pretty good value, while the *Econolodge*, 612 Mark Twain Ave (☎221-1490; ②), on the edge of downtown, is more basic. You can **camp** at the shaded *Mark Twain Campground* (☎221-1656), a mile south of the town on Hwy-79.

The **area code** for St Louis and eastern Missouri is ☎314.

Call in at the *Mark Twain Family Restaurant*, Third and Hill (☎221-5300), for Tom Sawyer burgers or Huck Finn shakes. The downtown bar *Kelly's Etc*, 306 N Third St (☎248-1266), serves budget meals. The **CVB** is at 320 Broadway (☎221-8300).

St Louis

Perched just below the confluence of the Mississippi and Missouri rivers, three hundred miles south of Chicago and north of Memphis, cosmopolitan **ST LOUIS** (pronounced, whatever any song might say, as *Lewis*) owes its vaguely European air to its history and developed cultural infrastructure. Any city capable of producing two of the twentieth century's greatest poets – T S Eliot and Chuck Berry – must have a whole lot going for it.

St Louis was founded in 1764 by the French fur trader **Pierre Laclede**, but the American immigration that followed its sale to the US under the Louisiana Purchase all but extinguished the refinement it had gained during French and Spanish rule. It subsequently became crucial as the major gateway for pioneers on the wagon trails westward. Transportation – first steamboats, then trains and now air haulage – has long been the basis of its considerable industrial strength. However, St Louis has not always had an easy ride. Downtown reached a nadir during the Seventies, but the past decade has seen a remarkable turnaround, with attractions on the revitalized **riverfront** including the magnificent **Gateway Arch** and the restored warehouses of **Laclede's Landing**.

Try not to leave without sampling the **suburbs**. To the west lie arty **Central West End** and studenty **University** (or "U") **City**, on either side of prodigious **Forest Park** with its museums and playing fields. The blue-collar **southside** features the markets, antique shops and jazz pubs of **Soulard** and the Italian shops and cafés of the **Hill**. Directly across the river in Illinois, **East St Louis**, once the stomping ground for jazz stars like Miles Davis and John Coltrane, has very little to offer visitors.

Arrival and Information

Lambert-St Louis International Airport is ten miles southeast of downtown – $25 by taxi or $1 by bus. Some *Greyhound* buses call at the airport, though their main terminal is downtown at 809 N Broadway (☎231-7800). *Amtrak* stops at 550 S 16th St, at Market Street downtown. The *Bi-State Transit System* (☎231-2345) operates the *Metro Link*, a new **light rail system** serving the airport and most of the significant tourist sights; rides cost $1 (free downtown 10am–3pm). *BSTS* **buses** also go to all of the city's suburbs, but services can be slow and infrequent. You can rent a **bicycle** from any of five branches of *Touring Cyclist* (☎739-4648).

The city's **visitor centers** are at 445 North Memorial Drive, near the riverfront, and at 308 Washington Ave, in the massive Cervantes Convention Center (daily 10.30am–4.30pm; ☎241-1764 or 1-800/888-FUN1). The **post office** is at 1720 Market St (Mon–Fri 7am–5pm; ☎436-5255; zip code 63166).

The Riverfront

The one-and-a-half-mile cobbled granite **wharf** along the Mississippi used to lie in the shadow of a dense tangle of warehouses and factories. When river trade decreased these became an embarrassing eyesore. Though most were ripped down, some restored structures between Eads and Martin Luther King bridges now form **Laclede's Landing Historic District**, their cast-iron facades fronting antique stores, office suites, restaurants and live music venues. Hidden among the business premises, the **National Video and Coin-op Museum**, 801 N Second St (Mon–Sat 10am–10pm, Sun noon–8pm; $3), is packed with games from the past two decades; admission includes four tokens to use on classic pinball machines and what are now obsolete arcade pieces.

On the **waterfront** itself, where roustabouts once handled cargoes of cotton and ores, assorted permanently moored vessels hold museums, theater shows, a heliport,

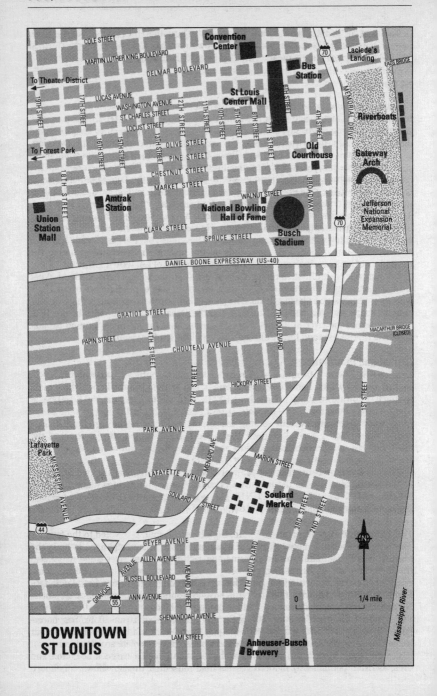

DOWNTOWN
ST LOUIS

casinos and even a floating *Burger King*. **Cruises** aboard replica paddlewheelers leave from under the Gateway Arch (April–Nov, daily 10am–5pm; $7.50; ☎621-4040).

Ten minutes' walk south, over thirty blocks of derelict buildings were ripped down to clear space for the **Jefferson National Expansion Memorial**, dedicated to the US president who negotiated the Louisiana Purchase and thereby opened up the west, and to the pioneers who journeyed along the Oregon and Santa Fe trails. Its highlight, the **Gateway Arch**, was completed in 1965, a 630ft stainless steel parabola of quite majestic symmetry; in technical terms it's a weighted catenary curve, an outline formed by a heavy cable hanging freely from two points. The arch is at its most striking when its gleaming coat catches a stray reflection – perhaps a rich red sunset or a firework display. This unusual monument has been universally adopted as the city's emblem, used in all sorts of corporate logos and insignia.

So long as you're not claustrophobic, it's fun to take the four-minute **tram ride** up the hollow curving Arch. Tiny five-seater capsules carry you to a viewing gallery, repeatedly stopping to shift position so you don't arrive at the top upside down. Unfortunately, after such an epic ride, the view is disappointing. Lengthy queues build up during summer, but you can pick up a numbered ticket earlier in the day and come back at the allotted time (daily, summer 8.30am–9.20pm, otherwise 9.30am–5.20pm; $2.50).

In a massive bunker beneath the Arch, the **visitor center** (☎425-4465) screens a riveting film about the construction of the monument, and another on the Lewis and Clark Expedition, which set off from St Louis in 1804 to explore the Missouri River and the water communications to the Pacific Ocean. It returned two years later with details of trade routes, Native American settlements and observations of animal and plant life. Exhibits in the spacious **Museum of Western Expansion** (daily summer 8am–10pm; otherwise 9am–6pm; $1) recount the story, drawing heavily on the pair's very readable journals. The **Arch Odyssey Theater**, in the same building, beams visual epics onto a four-storey screen (daily; summer 8.30am–8.30pm, otherwise 9.15am–4.45pm).

Central Downtown

One block from the Arch along St Louis' main east–west thoroughfare, Market Street, old photographs at the stately **Old Courthouse Museum** record the development of the city and the settling of the West (daily 8am–4.30pm; free). Two restored courtrooms were the site of the trial of **Dred Scott**, a black slave, who argued that having spent time with his owner in non-slave Illinois and Wisconsin, he had the right to be set free. His case was upheld in 1850, but overturned two years later. On appeal, the Supreme Court declared that Scott, born a slave in a slave state, might like any other chattel be taken anywhere his master chose to go. The decision, which meant that the US Constitution saw slaves as legitimate personal property, sent shock waves through the corridors of government and hastened the onrush of the Civil War. Scott himself, by now a nationally known figure, was voluntarily freed by his new owner, but died a year later.

The **National Bowling Hall of Fame**, Eighth and Walnut, is devoted to the favorite sport of such diverse figures as Martin Luther and Homer Simpson, tracing its history from ancient Egypt to the present (summer Mon–Sat 9am–7pm, Sun noon–7pm; otherwise daily noon–5pm; $4, free Sun). Bowling was not always the slick commercial sport it is today; excessive betting on games got it denounced by the church in fifteenth-century Germany and, three centuries later, the behavior of drunken fans led to all alleys being shut down in London.

Further along Market Street at 18th St, the focal point of the giant **Romanesque Union Station** is a 230ft clock tower. Built in 1884 and closed as a railway station in 1979, it now houses a hotel and two floors of shops, cafés and bars, with an artificial lake, where you can rent boats, at the rear. The *Hyatt Hotel*'s ornate lobby, once the station's main waiting room, is well worth visiting for a coffee or just a look.

Thomas Stearns Eliot, who as a naturalized Englishman won the 1948 Nobel Prize for Literature, was born in St Louis on September 26 1888. His family were Unitarian aristocrats who traced their ancestry back to the earliest days of settlement in New England; his grandfather, the Rev William Eliot, founded St Louis' Washington University. Eliot lived in the city until he was seventeen, and went to school at Smith Academy on Union Ave, a period which he later referred to as one of the happiest of his life. The "Prufrock" of his first major poem, *The Love Song of J Alfred Prufrock*, was a St Louis furniture dealer; "the yellow fog that rubs its back upon the window-panes" was the smog drifting across the Mississippi from the city's factories.

Once Eliot moved to Boston, to attend Harvard University, and then on to Europe, he rarely returned, and he deliberately threw off his drawling St Louis accent. The house in which he was born, at 2635 Locust St, has long since been torn down, and the only memorial to him in the city is the incongruous brass star set into the sidewalk of Delmar Boulevard as part of the St Louis Walk of Fame.

Another honoree of the Walk of Fame, **Chuck Berry**, first saw the light of day on October 18 1926 at 2520 Goode Ave – hence his most famous song, *Johnny B Goode*. Berry played his earliest gigs at the *Cosmopolitan Club* at 17th and Bond in East St Louis. Initially seen as a bizarre hybrid, a black hillbilly singing country and western, within a few months of his first recording for *Chess Records* in Chicago (*Maybellene*, in 1955) Chuck Berry's blend of razor-sharp lyrics and incisive guitar (not to mention his legendary business acumen) had made him the definitive rock'n'roll songwriter.

West of Downtown

The **Theater District**, three miles west of downtown, is staked out with ornate street lamps along Grand Avenue between Lindell and Delmar boulevards. Bright posters advertise the current shows at the **Fabulous Fox Theater**, 527 N Grand Ave, where you can have a look at its magnificent Siamese-Byzantine interior and massive Wurlitzer organ (tours at 10.30am Tues, Thurs & Sat; ☎534-1678; $3).

About a mile further west, on the edge of Forest Park, trendy shops, wine bars and turn-of-the-century mansions line the leafy thoroughfares of the **Central West End** district. A few blocks away at 4431 Lindell Blvd, the Romanesque-Byzantine **Cathedral of St Louis**, referred to by locals as the New Cathedral, houses the world's largest collection of **mosaic art** (daily May–Sept 9am–8pm; Oct–April 9am–5pm; donation).

The decision to site **Forest Park** four miles directly west of downtown (#93 bus) aroused much criticism during the 1870s, opponents claiming that its inaccessibility would make it merely a pleasure ground for the local rich. It's larger than New York's Central Park, and every bit as full of attractions; in summer, the 12,000-seat amphitheater is regularly filled for the **Muny** concert series (June–Aug; ☎361-1900). *Shuttle Bugs* – bright-red buses with black spots – scurry around its roadways.

Standing on **Art Hill** in the central west section of the park, the striking Beaux Arts **St Louis Art Museum** is the only surviving structure from the 1904 World's Fair. Its brief – to cover international art from prehistoric times onwards – may be ambitious, but none of the galleries can be considered as weak points or fillers. It houses one of the world's most extensive collections of **German Expressionism**, devoting an entire gallery to the powerful, spiralling and jagged images of Max Beckmann, and its **pre-Columbian artworks** cover every significant style, medium and culture from Mexico to Peru (Tues 1.30–8.30pm, Wed–Sun 10am–5pm; daily tours at 1.30pm; free).

In addition to the animals in its "cageless displays", the free **St Louis Zoo**, set in beautiful grounds, boasts a "Living World" exhibit in which Charles Darwin has evolved into an animatronic robot giving synopses of his theories (daily 9am–5pm).

The main strengths of the **History Museum**, on the northern fringe of the park, are the thematic collections of old pictures of St Louis documenting river life, black music in the city and Charles Lindbergh's 1927 flight in the *Spirit of St Louis* (sponsored by the city's aircraft industry) from New York to Paris (Tues–Sun 9.30am–4.45pm; free). Though the main section of the **St Louis Science Center** is across I-64, you can also enter it through the park; use one of the radar guns on the covered access bridge to check the speed of cars on the freeway below. General admission is free, but it costs a couple of dollars a time to get into the planetarium, Omnimax Theater and other major exhibits (Mon–Thurs & Sun 9.30am–5pm, Fri & Sat 9.30am–9pm).

Southside

The tens of thousands of Germans who came to St Louis in the mid-eighteenth century settled mostly in the **southside**, which has retained a noticeable Teutonic influence. They were skilled brewers; only one of the breweries they opened from the 1850s onwards still stands, but it does happen to be the largest in the world. The **Anheuser-Busch** plant, at Broadway and Pestalozzi, produces a sizeable proportion of the company's 1.1 billion-plus cases of beer each year, including *Budweiser* and *Michelob*. The buildings themselves are architecturally interesting: over one hundred intricate red-brick structures. The free eighty-minute tours are mostly company PR, but they're still good fun, and you get two glasses of the company product at the end before you're shunted into the gift shop (summer Mon–Sat 9am–4pm; otherwise Mon–Fri only).

A few blocks toward downtown, the colorful **Soulard Market**, at Broadway and Lafayette, is a great place to pick up picnic items and fresh fruit, especially on a Saturday. The terraced streets behind it hold the city's best **blues and jazz pubs**.

Red, white and green fireplugs let you know that you're in the nearby thirty-square-block **Hill** district, a small, neat **Italian** community. At its heart, **St Ambrose Church** displays a statue of Italian immigrants; all around, the aroma of freshly baked bread drifts out of the small specialty bakeries that share the area with one-room grocery stores and dozens of restaurants.

Further west at 4344 Shaw Blvd, the 79-acre **Missouri Botanical Garden** is a haven of peace and tranquillity, just a few hundred yards from busy I-44. The grounds contain everything from a magnificent Japanese Garden, surrounding a small lake and adorned with stepping stones, arched bridges and wooden teahouse, through scented, rose and English woodland gardens to the Climatron, a huge greenhouse that re-creates a tropical rainforest complete with waterfalls and cliffs (summer, daily 9am–8pm; otherwise 9am–5pm; $2, free until noon Wed & Sat).

St Charles

The beautiful little rivertown of **ST CHARLES**, 25 miles from downtown St Louis and forever threatened by flooding – in 1993 it briefly became an island in the swirling waters – is redolent with lazy charm. Three small though distinct **historic districts** are crammed with antique stores, specialty outlets and good cafés such as the Victorian tea room in the *Lindsey-Gardner House*, 803 S Main St (☎946-8154). Lewis and Clark set up strategic camp here in 1804, and are remembered in the interesting small museum.

St Charles' **CVB**, 230 S Main St (☎946-7776 or 1-800/366-2427), has details of downtown's growing range of elegant and amply porched **B&Bs**; we list the youth hostel below. The popular **KATY Trail**, which hugs "Big Muddy" for fifty miles along the route of an old railroad, is excellent for cycling (rentals available on the riverfront) or even a leisurely stroll. Gambling and show boats are anchored along the riverbanks, while the *Spirit of St Louis Riverboat* operates **cruises** from 1000 Riverside Drive (☎946-1000).

Accommodation

St Louis may be a business center – complete with huge new convention hall – but good-value **lodging** can still be found downtown, with appealing weekend rates. For **B&B**, contact the *Greater St Louis Reservation Service*, PO Box 30069, MO 63119 (☎961-2252).

Best Western Inn At The Park, 4630 Lindell Blvd (☎367-7500 or 1-800/373-7501). Good motel on northeast corner of Forest Park, right by the cafés of Central West End. ④.

Days Inn At The Arch, 333 Washington Ave (☎621-7900). Great location, at a great price. ③.

Drury Inn – Union Station, 201 S 20th St (☎231-3900 or 1-800/325-8300). Very tastefully restored accommodations. ⑤.

Huckleberry Finn Youth Hostel, 1904-6 S 12th St (☎241-0076). Dormitories and single rooms. On the edge of a dodgy area, so it's best to take #13 bus. $12 AYH, $14 non-members. ①.

Lewis & Clark Hostel, in *Noah's Ark Motel*, I-70 & S Fifth St, St Charles, MO (☎946-1000 or 1-800/332-3448). $12 bunks in very pleasant town close to St Louis. Airport and downtown pickups. ①.

Motel 6, 4576 Woodson Rd (☎427-1313). Good value, with outdoor pool. Close to the airport. ②.

Regal Riverfront Hotel, 200 S Fourth St (☎241-9500 or 1-800/325-7353). Ideal downtown setting; newly renovated and with all the facilities you would expect from a hotel of its size. ⑤.

Super Inn, 1100 N Third St (☎421-6556). The least expensive downtown option, just a few strides from Laclede's, though it's not a pleasant walk late at night. ③.

Washington University, Big Bend and Wydown blvds (☎889-5050). Rooms on campus between June and mid-August for around $18 per person. Ideal for U City shops and Forest Park. ②.

Eating

Italian food dominates St Louis cuisine, from humble salami sellers upwards. Most of the friendly Irish pubs serve beef sandwiches and stew. University City's **Delmar Boulevard** offers African, Middle Eastern, Chinese, Indian and other ethnic places. More expensive cafés are located in Laclede's Landing and the Central West End.

Duff's, 392 N Euclid Ave, Central West End (☎361-0522). Small, relaxed, and moderately priced. International menu with a heavy flavor of France. Good homemade desserts and Sunday brunch.

John D McGurk's Irish Pub, 1200 Russell Blvd at 12th St, Soulard (☎776-8309). Fresh-baked soda bread, corned beef'n'cabbage, Irish stew and imported Guinness. Live Irish music every night.

O'Connell's Pub, 4652 Shaw at Kingshighway (☎773-6600). The best burgers in the city, and the beef sandwiches aren't bad either. Near the Hill district.

Red Sea, 6511 Delmar Blvd, U City (☎863-0099). Cheap and cheerful Ethiopian restaurant; *berbere* sauce with everything. The decor is basic and the service slow, but the food's great.

Rigazzi's, 4945 Daggett Blvd, the Hill (☎772-4900). Popular trattoria, famous for "frozen fish bowls" of beer. Over thirty different pasta dishes, all at $8, plus pizzas, veal, chicken and steak entrees.

Saleem's, 6501 Delmar Blvd, U City (☎721-7947). "Where garlic is king" and St Louisians reckon you get the best ethnic food in the city. Lebanese and continental menu; reasonably inexpensive.

Sunshine Inn, 80 N Euclid Ave, Central West End (☎367-1413). Innovative vegetarian menu, plus a few chicken and seafood dishes. Great salads made even better by their unusual dressings.

Ted Drewe's Frozen Custard, 6726 Chippewa Ave (☎481-2652). A legendary slice of Americana. Try a "concrete" – an ice cream so thick that it won't budge if you turn your cup upside down.

Nightlife

Downtown St Louis' highest concentration of bars and clubs can be found in **Laclede's Landing**, presenting nightly jazz, blues, rock and reggae. Some of the outlying districts are well worth checking out in the evening; these include the Loop in **U City**, whose bars and cafés are not just popular with students, and the slightly more upmarket cafés and wine bars of **Central West End**. Unpretentious **Soulard** is the place to go for good jazz and blues. Every spring, the four-day Mid-America Jazz Festival brings the top names together for performances all over St Louis.

Don't forget also to check out the **Theater District**, centered on North Grand Boulevard in midtown, home to stage shows and the St Louis Symphony Orchestra (☎534-1700). Excellent listings can be found in the free weekly *Riverfront Times*.

Blueberry Hill, 6504 Delmar Blvd, U City (☎727-0880; band info ☎726-0066). Crammed full of memorabilia, with the downstairs dedicated to Elvis and a jukebox acclaimed by *Cashbox* as the best in the country. Live entertainment every weekend, good drinks and burgers at any time.

Cicero's Basement Bar, 6510 Delmar Blvd, U City (☎862-0009). Downstairs club putting on jazz fusion, acoustic and "alternative" music.

1860 Hard Shell Cafe & Bar, 1860 S Ninth St, Soulard (☎231-1860). One of the liveliest bars in Soulard with dancing to blues, r'n'b and soul bands. Also serves good cajun and fish dishes.

Kennedy's Second Street Co, 612 N Second St, Laclede's Landing (☎421-3655). Good, noisy bar featuring all kinds of bands.

Mississippi Nights, 914 N First St, Laclede's Landing (☎421-3853). Top venue for non-stadium bands in the city.

Other World, 1624 Delmar Blvd, downtown (☎436-2114). House, techno, hardcore, alternative sounds and live bands in popular two-floor club.

South of St Louis

The French and German heritage of tiny **STE GENEVIEVE**, sixty miles south of St Louis, is conspicuous through its architecture, cafés and festivals, though its graceful old French homes, characterized by vertical log construction, are constantly imperilled by flooding; the damage of 1993 remains apparent. The *Ste Genevieve Inn*, Main and Merchant (☎883-3562; ②), offers rooms downtown, while Amish variations on catfish, chicken and seafood are on the menu in the *Anvil Saloon*, 46 S Third St (☎883-7323).

CAPE GIRARDEAU looks down on the Mississippi from a rocky ledge 55 miles downriver. Among its antebellum and Victorian buildings, the *Port Cape Girardeau*, 19 N Water St (☎334-0954), serves tasty ribs. The *Cape Budget Inn* at I-55 exit 96 (☎334-0501; ②), with indoor and outdoor pools, is good value. The road continues south to Arkansas through reclaimed swamplands, rich in wheat, corn and melons but little else.

Kansas City

KANSAS CITY, 250 miles due west of St Louis, straddles the state line between Kansas and Missouri. Virtually all its main points of interest are on the Missouri side, where the fountains, boulevards, and Art Deco and Mediterranean-style buildings, and the slow but encouraging revitalization of downtown, are unusual and welcome features in a Midwestern city. Kansas City, Kansas, on the other hand, is a dull sprawl of suburbs that doesn't have much to attract visitors.

Kansas City was a convenient staging post for 1830s wagon trains heading west. Its consequent prosperity (and rough and tumble "sin city" image), which lasted well into the 1850s, was brought to an abrupt end by the Civil War. However, its fortunes revived in the 1870s, when the railroads brought the boom in meat packing responsible for the development of the huge stockyards, which finally closed down in 1992.

Thanks to Mayor Pendergast, an outrageous figure with whom the city still has a love-hate relationship, its many jazz clubs continued to sell alcohol during Prohibition. As in Chicago and New Orleans, speakeasies, brothels and gambling dens went hand in hand with superlative **jazz** – and, to a lesser extent, blues – spawning the careers of Count Basie, Duke Ellington and, in the Fifties, Charlie Parker. KC's resurgent jazz scene, fine restaurants, high-spending Royals and Chiefs sports teams, and theme parks help make it a popular short-break destination for the people of the western Heartland.

Arrival, Information and Getting Around

From the **airport** (☎243-5237), 25 miles northwest of downtown, a convenient forty-minute **shuttle bus** (half-hourly, 6am–11.30pm; ☎243-5000) heads to major downtown hotels ($12) and Westport ($15). The equivalent taxi ride costs around $30.

The isolated *Greyhound* terminal lies well out from downtown at 12th and Troost (☎698-0080). *Amtrak* is next to the old Union Station at 23rd and Main opposite the

The **area code** for Kansas City and around is ☎816.

Crown Center. Routes served by *Metro Buses* (☎221-0660) include extensive downtown coverage, and out to Independence. Five trolleys loop continuously between downtown, the Crown Center, Westport, and the Country Club Plaza ($4 round trip).

Visitor centers are at 1100 Main St (Mon–Fri 8.30–5pm; ☎221-5242 or 1-800/767-7000) and 20 E Fifth St in River Market (Mon–Fri 10am–4pm, Sat 8am–4pm, Sun noon–4pm; ☎842-4386). The main **post office** is close to *Amtrak* at 315 W Pershing Rd (Mon–Fri 8am–6.30pm, Sat 8am–12.30pm; ☎374-9275; zip code 64108).

The City

Kansas City is doing a good job of reinvigorating its **downtown**, putting the commercial and residential needs of its citizens first. Most sights lie further south, though wandering past the restored lofts and small businesses of the **Garment District**, between Sixth and Ninth streets, makes a nice route to **City Hall**, 414 E 12th St, a fine Art Deco building with an observation deck on its thirtieth floor (Mon–Fri 8.30am–4.15pm; free.) Also downtown is the redeveloped historic district of **River Market**, with colorful shops, cafés and a lively farmer's market at Fifth and Walnut. A good but pricey museum in the complex – **"The Treasures of the Steamboat Arabia"** – tells the story behind the recent salvaging of a sidewheeler which sank on its way to Omaha in 1856. Perfectly preserved artefacts afford unexpected and intriguing insights into frontier life (Mon–Sat 10am–6pm, Sun noon–5pm; $6).

The sprawling concrete **Crown Center**, on Grand and Pershing, owned by *Hallmark Cards*, calls itself "a city within a city", with apartments, shops, restaurants, offices, hotels, cinemas and an ice rink. Interesting displays in its splendidly awful **Hallmark Visitors Center** trace styles of greeting cards alongside political and cultural changes, demonstrating printing processes and hand decoration, but it's a strain to keep a straight face at the sentiment that cards are "messengers of the heart" which "aid humans in their love for one another" (Mon–Fri 9am–5pm, Sat 9.30am–4.30pm; free). The nearby and vacant **Union Station** is a Kansas City landmark: huge, and still riddled with the bullet holes from a Pretty Boy Floyd shoot-out. Across from the Crown Center and Union Station at 100 W 26th St, the tall skinny **Liberty Memorial** commemorates World War I, with a small museum and a life-scale trench. There's a good view from its 217ft observation deck (Wed–Sun 9.30am–4.15pm; $1).

The **18th and Vine Heritage District**, south of I-70 as it sweeps east–west, was the hub of the city's 1920s **jazz scene**. It holds little to see now, beyond depressing empty lots and a few good clubs, though plans – which include jazz and Negro Leagues Baseball museums – are underway to revitalize the area. The **Black Archives of Mid America**, 2033 Vine St, is a gallery of black arts, painting and sculpture, with extensive research facilities (Mon–Fri 9am–4.30pm; $1).

Westport, an attractive district of good restaurants, cafés and trendy shops between 39th and 45th streets, was the original jumping-off point for the Santa Fe Trail. Stop off for a drink at the city's oldest building, *Kelly's Westport Inn*, 500 Westport St, a shabby but friendly red-brick bar. Five miles south of downtown, beginning at 47th and Main, the elegant **Country Club Plaza** dates from the early Twenties. Tree-shaded and upmarket (with branches of *Gucci* and *Saks*), its tiling, mosaics, fountains and orange trees evoke the streets of Spain, and a replica Sevillan tower completes the effect.

Highlights of the extensive **Nelson Atkins Museum of Art**, 4525 Oak St, include superb Oriental exhibits, plus Van Goghs, Monets and Rembrandts, with twelve Henry Moore sculptures in a landscaped setting (Tues–Thurs 10am–4pm, Fri 10am–9pm, Sat 10am–5pm, Sun 1–5pm; $4, free on Sat). The pretty **Toy and Miniatures Museum**, 5235 Oak St, houses an offbeat collection of antique toys, games and puppets (Wed–Sat 10am–4pm, Sun 1–4pm; $3.50).

Way up in the north of town at 3218 Gladstone Blvd, the **Kansas City Museum** is worth the effort (take bus #30) if only for the ice creams from its restored 1910 drugstore. You can also see Native American artefacts and costumes, a natural history hall, and a planetarium (Tues–Sat 9.30am–4.30pm, Sun noon–4.30pm; donation).

When the midwestern humidity gets too much, head for the tropically themed water world, **Oceans of Fun**, or the adjoining **Worlds of Fun**, with its 140-plus rides, out at exit 54 of I-435 (late May–early Sept; $17 for each park).

Independence and Liberty

Bus #24 goes to the small town of **INDEPENDENCE**, twenty minutes east of the city and most famous as the former home of President Harry S Truman. The **Truman Library** on US-24 and Delaware St includes a reconstruction of his White House office, and chilling documents pertaining to the development of the atomic bomb (daily 9am–5pm; $2). The Victorian Truman Home, a mile south at 219 S Delaware St, is decorated as it was when used as the summer White House (tours 8.30am–5pm; $1).

Jesse James staged the first ever daylight bank robbery in 1866 in what's now the **Jesse James Bank Museum**, on the Old Town Square of **LIBERTY**, fifteen miles east of downtown Kansas City. Among the memorabilia and dusty relics of early banking, you can see the vault and the safe that he raided (daily 9am–5pm; $2).

Accommodation

Kansas City's budget motels lie along the interstates or out towards Independence, but reasonable central options do exist. For **B&B**, contact *Kansas City B&B*, Box 14781, Lenexa, KS 66215 (☎913/268-4214). The most central **place to camp** is at the *Trailside Camper's Inn* (☎1/800-748-7729) at I-70 exit 24, though there are more scenic sites thirteen miles from downtown in the 1500-acre woods of Wyandotte County Park, on N Hwy-5 at 91st St, which also contains a 330ft lake (☎229-0550).

Best Western Seville Plaza, 4309 Main St (☎561-9600). Very central, close to Westport. ④.

Comfort Inn, 801 Westport Rd (☎931-1000). In lively Westport with free continental breakfast. ④.

Embassy on the Park, 1215 Wyandotte Ave (☎471-1333). Recently renovated downtown hotel, in slightly isolated location. Free buffet breakfast, evening cocktails, local calls and gym. ④.

Historic Suites of America, 612 Central St (☎842-6544 or 1-800/733-0612). Large beautiful rooms with fully equipped kitchens in the heart of the Garment District. Free breakfast and cocktails. ⑤.

Travelodge Midtown, 3240 Broadway (☎531-9250). Functional motel, eight blocks from Westport and on a frequent downtown bus route. ②.

Eating

Barbecue, once the unfashionable food of the poor, is big news in Kansas City; cheap, cheerful, hickory-smoked and served with tasty sauces. Restaurants in the **Crown Center** are quite good but overpriced; many require formal dress. The **Plaza** has some great places, but again, they're expensive; relaxed Westport is a better bet.

Arthur Bryant's, 1727 Brooklyn Ave (☎231-1123). *The* place for barbecue, a mile east of downtown in a desolate area. The largest portions you will ever see of barbecue and beans; the $5 combo plate easily feeds two hefty appetites. The murky bottles in the window contain the crucial sauces. This is serious business – be sure not to dawdle in the queue, as novices are given short shrift.

Bristol Bar & Grill, 4740 Jefferson Ave (☎756-0606). Great seafood in the Plaza.

California Taquera, 2316 Summit Ave (☎474-5571). Dingy little daytime-only café with the most authentic Mex food in KC. Close to downtown, surrounded by Mexican bars, bakeries and cantinas.

Hereford House, 20th and Main St (☎842-1080). KC's top steak house, in a handy downtown spot.

Jerusalem Cafe, 431 Westport Rd (☎756-2770). Small Middle Eastern restaurant, open until about 9pm, serving superb falafel and kebabs.

Lucille's, 1604 Westport Rd (☎561-5119). Attractive Fifties diner, open 24hrs Fri & Sat. Huge portions. Top-class curly fries, burgers, omelettes and malts.

West Side Café, 723 Southwest Blvd (☎472-0010). Fun café in a former filling station serving seriously good food from around the world; Jamaican, Brazilian and Lebanese to name just three. No liquor licence; drinkers have to go next door to the similar *Boulevard Café* (☎842-6984).

Nightlife and Entertainment

Check out Kansas City's reviving **jazz** and **blues** scene, especially the authentic dives holding wonderful jam sessions into the early hours. Friday's *Kansas City Star* carries listings, as does *Pitch*, a free monthly. You can also call *The Blues Society* (☎531-7557); *The Kansas City Jazz Embassadors* (☎942-3349); or the *Jazz Hotline* (☎931-2888).

Downtown is otherwise pretty dead by mid-evening, and most people head to **Westport** for nightlife from country and western to alternative rock. In the summer, big-name bands play **free concerts** in the square at Crown Center; bring your own picnic and booze, and get there early for a good position. Showtime is 8pm Friday.

Birdland, 1600 E 19th St (☎842-8463). Seedy and authentic jazz club, in historic 18th and Vine area.

Blayneys, 415 Westport Rd (☎501-3747). Live music in the cellar, with blues every Monday.

Club Eblon, 1601 E 18th St (☎221-6612). Nicely restored jazz club in the 18th and Vine district.

The Edge, 323 W 8th St (☎221-8900). Popular warehouse dance club; good mixed gay nights.

Grand Emporium, 3832 Main St (☎531-1504). R'n'b, blues, reggae and jazz with really good Cajun and Jamaican food. Voted the best blues club in America by the National Blues Foundation.

Kiki's Bon Ton Maison, 1515 Westport Rd (☎931-9417). Louisiana-style food, plus Cajun and zydeco music on Wed & Sat.

Mutual Musicians Foundation, 1823 Highland Ave (☎421-9229). National Historic Landmark in the 18th and Vine district. Fierce jam sessions begin at 1.30am Fri & Sat, musicians competing in a frenzy for hours. It can get a bit rough, and is not recommended for women alone.

Phoenix Piano Bar and Grill, Eighth St and Central Ave (☎472-0001). Downtown piano jazz featuring Saturday afternoon sessions.

The Point, 917 W 44 St (☎531-9800). Friendly blues and jazz bar midway between Westport and the Plaza; local favorite Irma McBride sings here once a week.

Shadow, 510 Westport Rd (☎561-2222). Rock club, specializing in indie bands and proving that there's more to the KC music scene than jazz, blues and Melissa Etheridge.

St Joseph

Sixty miles north of Kansas City, **ST JOSEPH** boomed as a supply depot for the California Gold Rush, and today is still a busy manufacturing town. For a brief eighteen months, starting in 1860, it was the home of the legendary **Pony Express**, which delivered mail all the way to Sacramento, California, by continuous horseback relay. The Pony Express was a financial disaster, driven out of business by its inability to compete with the transcontinental telegraph, but riders such as Buffalo Bill Cody and Pony Bob Haslam remain immortal. The full story is told at the **Pony Express Museum**, 914 Penn St, attractively set in the company's original stables (April–Sept daily; $2.50).

It was in St Joseph, on April 3 1882, that the notorious Jesse James was shot in the back by Robert Ford, a member of his own gang. Countless books and films have portrayed Jesse James as a latterday Robin Hood; in fact, he spent most of the Civil War riding with a band of Confederate guerillas. The **Jesse James Home**, a one-storey frame cottage, is at 12th and Penn (April–Oct daily; Nov–March Tues–Sat; $3).

Other Jesse James museums are dotted about town, but St Joseph isn't much of a place to hang around. If you do want to leave the (tedious) drive to Kansas City or Omaha for another day, you'll find **motels** strung along I-29.

Southwest Missouri – Ozark Country

There's little to see south of Kansas City before the **Ozark Mountains**. Occupying most of southern Missouri and northern Arkansas (see p.437), the area remained frontier territory until the timber companies moved in at the end of the century. When they moved on, the hill-dwellers were left to eke out a living from the denuded terrain. Severe droughts forced many to leave for the cities. For those who remained, fishing resorts and tourist attractions supply some work, though the region remains poor and economically backward. None of the Ozark peaks is particularly high, but the roads through switch, dip, climb and swerve to provide stunning views of steep hillsides, thick with oak, elm, hickory and redbud and quite resplendent in the fall.

Though the region's main city is **SPRINGFIELD**, the gateway to the Ozarks 170 miles south of Kansas City, the country music town of **Branson** is more popular by far.

Branson

Nestling among beautiful Ozark lakes, the resort of **BRANSON** (year-round population 5000), 40 miles south of Springfield on US-65, is, according to the *AAA*, the second biggest auto destination in the country after Orlando. Over five million visitors a year are attracted to what's become known as the "Ozark Disneyland" by thirty-plus music venues (almost all of a country bent), a few theme parks and lots of good ol' family fun.

"**The Strip**", until recently merely Hwy-76, abounds with theaters owned and performed in by big-name stars. The spectrum ranges from Willie Nelson, Loretta Lynn and Mel Tillis, through MOR acts like the Osmond family, Japanese fiddler Shoji Tabuchi, and ancient crooner Andy Williams to banal mountain humor joints like *Baldknobbers* and *Presley's* (not *that* Presley). Lesser lights include Tony Orlando's *Yellow Ribbon Theater*, and Jim *Spiders and Snakes* Stafford's place. Tickets for a two-hour show are no bargain, at an average of $18, but there's no shortage of takers in summer for most, if not all, of the town's 40,000 seats – a figure said to exceed that of Nashville. Branson shows are firmly geared towards families; you won't find anything remotely progressive or avant-garde, not even from the often-enterprising Mr Nelson.

If you're simply intent on passing through as quickly as possible, be warned that the roads get packed, and it's not unheard of to take two hours to drive through Branson.

Practicalities

During the main season (May–Oct), it's more or less impossible to find a **place to stay** for under $50 a night; weekend rates rise higher still. *Branson Vacation Reservations* (☎1-800/221-5692) will try to sell you a package deal, but can also book you into a motel, including one of six *Best Westerns* (☎1-800/528-1234; ④). Most **places to eat** are of the fried food/family diner ilk, though it's worth searching out the fat-free menu at *McGuffey's on the Strip*, and the Greek cuisine at *Dimitri's*, downtown.

KANSAS

Today's cutesy, gingham-pinafore image of **KANSAS**, associated with *Little House on the Prairie* and *The Wizard of Oz*, is a far cry indeed from the troubled history which made it known as "bleeding Kansas". It took three hundred years after Coronado came in search of gold in 1541 before pioneers established trails across the region, and Kansas' bid for statehood in 1861 is often cited as the catalyst for the Civil War. The 1854 Kansas-Nebraska Act, which gave both territories the right to self-determination over slavery, led to fierce clashes between Free Staters and pro-slavery forces. Runaway slaves from the south were given passage through the area, aided by abolitionist John Brown, and Kansas eventually joined the Union as a free state.

After the war, the mighty cattle drives from Texas made towns like **Abilene**, **Wichita** and **Dodge City** centers of the "**Wild West**". The debauched, male image of the West, spawning such "heroes" as Wyatt Earp and Wild Bill Hickok, is, however, challenged in Kansas, which as well as being the first state to give women the vote in municipal elections, boasts the nation's first female mayor and senator, as well as aviator Amelia Earhart and the battling Prohibitionist Carry Nation.

In 1874, Russian Mennonites brought the grain that was to transform the state into the bountiful "bread basket" which now harvests most of the nation's wheat. However, only in the west do miles of golden corn sway in Kansas' infamous gusty wind. The green and hilly northeast, patterned with woods and lakes, is home to the unattractive industrial city **Topeka**, liberal college town **Lawrence**, and the dull suburbs of Kansas City (though downtown lies across the state line in Missouri). The wild and sparse northwest is pioneer country, while the once-wicked cowtown **Dodge City** is in the southwest. **Wichita**, Kansas' largest city, lies in the south central area.

Getting Around Kansas

Greyhound **buses** run to all Kansas' main cities, supplemented by erratic smaller companies; service to the west and southwest is especially poor. The most frequent routes run from Kansas City to Albuquerque via Wichita (about 5 daily; 10–12 hr) with one or two buses per day along I-70 to Denver. *Amtrak* **trains** head east–west between LA and Chicago through the center of the state calling, usually in the middle of the night, at Lawrence, Topeka, Emporia, Newton (for Wichita, but without a connecting service), Dodge City and Garden City. Wichita has the state's biggest airport.

East Kansas

Undulating **east Kansas** is laced with lakes, streams and rivers. The northeast, once crossed by the Oregon, Santa Fe and Smoky Hill trails, and now home to both **Topeka** and **Lawrence**, is more heavily visited than the southeast, where the major sight is TV's *Little House on the Prairie*, just south of Independence on SW US-75. The heritage of Kansas' four Indian tribes is still visible. Annual **powwows**, held in the major towns as well as the reservations of the northwest, have become important dates in the calendar.

Lawrence

The mellow town of **LAWRENCE** lies on the Kansas River, roughly halfway between Kansas City and Topeka, around thirty miles from either. Tree-lined streets, a welcoming historic downtown and an aura of old-hippy artsiness make it an appealing destination, with a cultural energy owed in part to the University of Kansas, and a long liberal and intellectual history. Founded by the New England Emigrant Aid Company in 1854 and a center of Free State activities, Lawrence was the site of a violent Civil War skirmish in 1863, when Missourian Confederate guerrilla Quantrill led about 300 men on the town, killing over 150, wounding hundreds more, and setting the place alight. Rebuilding was quick, however, as evidenced by the limestone and brick buildings of today's downtown, centered on Massachusetts Street, and the State University campus, which stands on a steep, tree-covered grassy bank known as Mount Oread.

Studded with cafés and eclectic shops, downtown Lawrence is a delight to walk around – and just as busy outside of termtime, when day-trippers flock in from less congenial Kansan cities. However, most of the town's formal attractions are congregated on campus. The **Museum of Natural History**, on Jayhawk Blvd along the crest of the hill, holds a chronological panorama of North American flora and fauna, as well as Custer's beloved, enormous – and now stuffed – horse, Comanche, the centerpiece of an exhibit on the Battle of Little Bighorn (Mon–Sat 8am–5pm, Sun 1–5pm; donation). Across the road, the **Museum of Anthropology**, in Romanesque Dyche Hall, presents African and Eskimo artefacts (Mon–Sat 9am–5pm, Sun 1–5pm; free). The **Spencer Art Museum**, on Mississippi St, specializes in world art, with an Oriental gallery, Old

The **area code** for Lawrence and east Kansas is ☎913.

Masters and Pre-Raphaelites. Graphic art from the Sixties includes some Warhols and exceptional photographs, from Diane Arbus' disturbing portraits to Weegee's documentary exposés of New York City life. Its gift shop does a great line in surreal and offbeat postcards (Tues–Sat 8.30am–5pm, Sun noon–5pm; free).

Indian traditions are preserved and packaged for the public each year by the exhibitions of the **Lawrence Indian Arts Show**, held throughout the city from mid-September to the end of October. One venue is the **Haskell Indian Junior College** at 23rd and Massachusetts, where the **Hiawatha Visitor Center** and the **American Indian Athletic Hall of Fame** are open year-round by appointment (☎794-8404).

Practicalities

Amtrak comes into Lawrence at 413 E Seventh St, and *Greyhound* to the tiny hut at 1401 W Sixth St (☎843-5622). The kitsch Fifties-style *Lawrence Bus Co* runs local buses. The **CVB** is downtown on Eighth and Vermont (Mon–Fri 8.30am–5pm; ☎865-4411).

Adequate but dull budget rooms can be found near the bus station at the *Virginia Inn*, 2907 W Sixth St (☎843-6611; ②), or the *Westminster Inn*, 2525 W Sixth St (☎841-8410; ②). If you have a little extra cash, head instead to the lovely all-suite *Eldridge Hotel*, at Seventh and Massachusetts (☎749-5011 or 1-800/527-090; ④); twice burned down by pro-slavery forces, it has been restored to an evocative faded elegance, and houses the stylish *American Bistro* (☎841-8349) as well as an atmospheric sports bar in the basement. You can **camp** near downtown at Riverfront Park (permits Mon–Fri 8am–5pm; ☎841-7222) or three miles out along W 23rd Street at Clinton Lake (☎843-7665).

Two healthy **places to eat** stand side by side on campus – the *Yellow Sub* (☎841-3268) and the *Glass Onion* (☎841-2310), both at 12th St and Mount Oread, serve lunch in a laid-back atmosphere with sweeping views. Downtown, the *Paradise Café*, 728 Massachusetts St (☎842-5199), does veggie burgers, soups and salads; meat-lovers can fill up with the hickory-smoked barbecue at *Buffalo Bob's Smokehouse*, nearby at no 719 (☎841-6100). Best of all are the nachos and gourmet pizzas at the exquisite *Teller's*, across the street in a beautifully restored bank building (no 746; ☎843-4111) .

Lawrence's **nightlife** is dominated by students. Popular Massachusetts St bars include the *Free State Brewing Co* (no 636; ☎843-4555) and the *Jazzhaus* (no 926; ☎749-3320), while the cavernous *Bottleneck*, 737 New Hampshire St (☎841-5483), is the place to go for live rock music. *Liberty Hall*, 642 Massachusetts St (☎749-1912), once a social and political center, housed Lawrence's first newspaper, until it was burned down by pro-slavery agitators in 1856. Today it puts on art-house films, plays and concerts.

West Through Kansas

Further west across Kansas, three towns re-create the state's Wild West heritage, although only in the westernmost, **Dodge City**, does the scrubby landscape conform to the cowboy-movie image. **Abilene**, if less famous than Dodge City, has as many outlaw and gunslinging stories, and **Wichita**, about 200 miles southwest of Kansas City, holds an excellent, authentic reconstruction of frontier days in its Cowtown Museum.

Abilene

Like all the old cattle-trail cowtowns, **ABILENE**, 115 miles west of Lawrence on I-70, claims to have been the riproaringest of the lot. By the time legendary lawman Wild Bill Hickok became its marshal in 1871, the unruly behavior was already dying down, and little today reminds you of those raucous days. Doing its best, though, is **Old Abilene**

The **area code** for west Kansas, including Wichita and Dodge City, is ☎316.

Town, at SE Sixth and Kuney, a replica of the town during its cattle boom, complete with stagecoach rides. Gunfights are held on Sunday at 2.45pm and 4pm, with cancan dancers at 2.15pm and 3pm (daily March–Sept 8am–8pm; Oct & Nov 10am–5pm; donation).

These days, Abilene prefers to stress its connections with Dwight Eisenhower. The **Eisenhower Center**, 201 SE Fourth St, includes his boyhood home, with its original furnishings, the obligatory film show and many photos and papers. The former president and his wife are buried in the meditation chapel (daily 9am–5pm).

Abilene's **visitor center** is at 201 NW Second St (☎263-2231). Most of its budget motels are off I-70 at Hwy-15. The very basic *Diamond*, closer to downtown at 1407 NW Third St (☎263-2360; ➀), offers free transportation to the bus depot.

Wichita

WICHITA, about 165 miles southwest of Lawrence on I-35, is the largest city in Kansas, severed by the Arkansas River, which forks just north of downtown into the Big and Little Arkansas rivers (incidentally, Kansans take umbrage if you pronounce it Arkansaw; pronounce it here the way it is spelled). Originally settled by the Wichita Indians, who by 1865 had been relocated to Oklahoman Indian Territory, Wichita grew up as a stop on the Chisholm Trail. Its glory days were to be short-lived, however, as farmers, angry about the damage done by stampeding cattle, erected fences which forced the drives onto different trails further west, creating new cowtowns such as Dodge City. Today three of the world's major aircraft manufacturers (*Beech, Cessna* and *Lear*) are based here, and although downtown is wilting a little, Wichita remains attractive thanks to its great museums and a rich arts scene.

Downtown Wichita is a rapidly emptying casualty of the exodus to the suburbs, enlivened mainly by the public art and sculpture that pops up unexpectedly all over the place, in tree stumps and empty lots. The exceptional **Wichita-Sedgwick County Historical Museum**, 204 S Main St, is in **Old City Hall**, a heavy stone building decorated with turrets, gargoyles and arches. The cosy interior is crammed with exhibits on everything from the Wichita Indians through decorative art to Carry Nation, whose initial zeal for singing hymns to errant drunks grew into a campaign against everything from tobacco to corsets (Tues–Fri 11am–4pm, Sat & Sun 1–5pm; $1). The stately church with vivid stained-glass windows at 601 N Water St houses the **First National Black Historical Society** of Kansas, an eclectic antidote to more mainstream views of Great Plains history, with details on Buffalo Soldiers, inventors and early black Wichitans, and some African art (Mon & Fri 10am–2pm, Sun 2–6pm; free).

Excellent museums in the **Riverside** stretch of parkland (which also holds walking and bike trails) include the **Mid-America All-Indian Center and Museum**, 650 N Seneca Drive (Tues–Sat 10am–5pm, Sun 1–5pm; $2). The 44ft *Keeper of the Plains* statue, facing east at the confluence of the Little and Big Arkansas rivers, was designed in the 1970s by a Kiowa-Comanche artist, Blackbear Bosin, and dedicated by Native Americans and city officials smoking the peace pipe. It's an eerie sight at dusk, reaching into the sky with some unknown offering. The museum itself is small, with changing exhibits of traditional and contemporary Native American art: clothing and beadwork, pottery and baskets, paintings and prints. Western artist C M Russell is the best represented of the veritable who's who of American painters assembled at the **Wichita Art Museum**, 619 Stackman Drive (Tues–Sat 10am–5pm, Sun noon–5pm; free); there's also a great café. **Old Cowtown**, 1871 Sim Park Drive, is an outside exhibit re-creating the buildings of 1870s Wichita. Looking and feeling like a movie set, the area includes – along with some docile Longhorns – the city's first one-room jail, a school room, a store, a smithy and old homes (daily 10am–5pm; until 6pm Sat & Sun in summer; $3).

To the north of the city, the surreal geodesic **Pyradomes**, 3100 N Hillside Ave, house the Garvey Center for the Improvement of Human Functioning, which aims, by using holistic medicine, to find a cure for cancer by the year 2000. It's all very worthy, but weird: road signs, for example, tell you to "de-stress to 25". Tours include a video show and individual sample "nutrient profiles" (daily at 1.30pm; $4; ☎682-3100). In the southeast of the city, the products of Wichita's plane industry are on display at the **Kansas Aviation Museum**, 3350 George Washington Blvd in the old Art Deco air terminal (Tues–Fri 10am–4pm, Sat 11.30am–4.30pm; free).

Practicalities

Domestic **flights** arrive at the Mid-Continent Airport, five miles southwest of downtown on Hwy-54 W (Kellogg Drive). *Amtrak* stops at Newton, a small Mennonite town 25 miles north, with a local bus connection to Wichita throughout the day; *Greyhound* comes in to 312 Broadway Ave, two blocks east of Main Street. *Starline* city buses (☎265-7221) are slow and unreliable. The resourceful **CVB** is in the heart of downtown on the corner of Douglas and Main (Mon–Fri 8am–5pm; ☎265-2800).

Budget **lodgings** in Wichita are plentiful, especially near the airport on W Kellogg Drive, such as the *Econolodge* (no 6245; ☎945-5261; ②). On the opposite flank of the city is a good *Fairfield Inn* at 333 S Webb Rd (☎685-3777; ②). Downtown's best value is the *Wichita Royale*, 125 N Market St (☎263-2101; ⑤), with a pool and free breakfast. *USI Campgrounds*, 2920 E 33rd St (☎838-8699), is the closest place to **camp**.

Though filled with good **places to eat**, downtown has few options for drinking or clubbing. There's great food (try the wild mushroom strudel) at the *Old Mill Tasty Shop*, 604 E Douglas Ave (☎264-6500), complete with marble soda fountain. Tasty fajitas and live music attract crowds to the southwestern *Two Feathers*, 108 E Second St (☎262-8300), while *Willie C's Café and Bar*, 650 S West St (☎942-4077), provides a good breakfast and snack menu. For the best steaks in town, head further out to *Scotch and Sirloin*, 3941 E Kellogg Blvd (☎685-8701).

Dodge City

DODGE CITY, 150 miles west of Wichita, is perhaps the most famous of all America's cowtowns. It has certainly been committed to celluloid more times than any other, in Thirties westerns like *My Darling Clementine* and *Dodge City*. However, this wildest of Wild West cities had a heyday of only a decade, from 1875 until 1886. Established in 1872 with the Santa Fe Railroad, which transported the hides of the millions of buffalo roaming the plains, by 1875 the town of traders, trappers and hunters had to find a new economic base – the buffalo had been exterminated. The era of the great cattle drives was already under way, and Dodge City became a den of iniquity where gambling, drinking and general lawlessness were the norm. Such wickedness led to gunfights galore, and the notorious Boot Hill cemetery (where the villains were buried with their boots on) was kept busy by charismatic lawmen such as Bat Masterson and Wyatt Earp.

Dodge City today is rather more staid and (outside of the two-week Dodge City Days and Rodeo each July), is content to replay its movie image in the relatively small and touristy **Historic Front Street**, where you'll find, along with the old jail, a schoolhouse and a smithy, plenty of "authentic" western entertainment: stagecoach rides, medicine shows, gunfights and melodramas, and dancing at the **Long Branch Saloon**. The **Boot Hill Museum**, 500 Wyatt Earp Blvd, is on the site of the original Boot Hill graveyard.

Other sights in town include the **Home of Stone**, 112 E Vine St, an emotive memorial to pioneer mothers, often forgotten amid the macho Wild West myth-making. The house looks pretty much as it would have in 1881, with domestic memorabilia from early plainswomen (June–Sept Mon–Sat 9am–5pm, Sun 1–5pm). **El Capitan**, at Second St and Wyatt Earp Blvd, is a massive bronze Longhorn, facing south towards an identical north-facing statue in Abilene, West Texas. Together they mark the beginning and the end of the cattle drives.

Practicalities

Greyhound **buses** from Wichita arrive twice daily at 2425 E Central Blvd (☎225-1617). *Amtrak* comes in right downtown, at Central and Front, in the historic Santa Fe Station. Call the **CVB** (☎227-2176) for advice or information, or drop in at Fourth and W Spruce. There is no public transport, but *Gunsmoke Historical Tours* run trips to historical sites and a working Longhorn ranch, from the booth on the Boot Hill parking lot.

Of inexpensive **motels** along Wyatt Earp Boulevard (not very convenient for downtown), the *Astro* (no 2200; ☎227-8146; ②) offers free rides to the train and bus stations, and the *Dodge House Inn Motel* (no 2408; ☎225-9900; ②) has a reliable restaurant. The *Western Inn Motel*, two miles east on US-50 (☎225-1381; ②), is opposite the bus station. **Camping** is an option even for the carless; the lakeside *Water Sports Campground Recreation*, 500 Cherry St (☎225-9003), lies ten blocks south of Front St (☎225-9003).

IOWA

Although at times serene, and almost always verdant, nothing about **IOWA** truly stands out: this 55,000-square-mile chunk of the Great Plains doesn't even manage to be completely flat, it just wobbles up and down a little. The state is the very essence of smalltown America, close to the geographical center of the mainland US, and coming 25th out of fifty states in size, population and level of personal income. Even the cities seem at times merely to be villages grown large.

Iowa's history, too, has been relatively uneventful. It was opened for settlement after the Black Hawk Treaty of 1832, a one-sided exercise in negotiations with the Sauk, conducted after many of them had been chased down and slaughtered in neighboring Wisconsin and Illinois. The northern European migrants who replaced them made agricultural development their prime concern, turning Iowa into the **"Foodbasket of America"** – a role it usually achieves with scrupulous efficiency, although the severe floods of 1993 saw the entire state declared a disaster area.

Getting Around Iowa

Greyhound **buses** out of Chicago call on all Iowa's major towns, with at least four services per day in each direction along I-80. St Louis is also well served by six daily buses from Des Moines and Iowa City; these towns are connected less frequently with Minneapolis/St Paul. Amtrak's east–west route misses the cities, stopping instead at assorted small communities in the south, though a bus usually makes the short trip to Des Moines from Osceola. The only sizeable **airport** is in Des Moines. Somewhat surprisingly, Iowa is a rather good place for **cycle touring**. Each year the amazingly popular cross-state bike ride – the RAGBRAI – attracts thousands of entrants, any of whom can tell you that the plains aren't always flat (tour details ☎515/284-8000).

Eastern Iowa

Eastern Iowa, in the Mississippi River hinterland, is liberally sprinkled with agribusiness towns that display the continuing influence of their central and northern European pioneers, plus **religious communities** – Amish, Mennonite and the Amana Colonies. All are easily accessible from **Iowa City**, home to a huge university and lively nightlife. Riverside towns such as northerly **Dubuque** and **Burlington**, near the Missouri state line, have been enlivened since 1991 by riverboat gambling, though so far low-stake

The **area code** for eastern Iowa is ☎319.

poker and roulette games can only be played on board Mississippi paddlewheelers, decked out in less-than-authentic Mark Twain-era trimmings.

Dubuque and Cedar Rapids

The handsome town of **DUBUQUE**, overlooked by rocky bluffs on the Mississippi around 150 miles west of Chicago, was founded as the first white settlement in Iowa by French-Canadian leadminers in 1788. In the nineteenth century it became a boisterous riverport and logging center. Buildings from this era still stand, but the companies that use them are now concerned with meatpacking and other food industries.

You can travel along the high-banked Mississippi on a **paddlewheeler** cruise with *Roberts River Rides* (May–Oct daily; $7 for 90min; ☎583-1761), or on board one of the more expensive gambling boats. Close to the harbor, **cable-cars** grind their way in summer up the at-times sheer bluff from Fourth Street to residential Fenelon Place, for a fine view across the Mississippi to Illinois and Wisconsin. The *Julien Inn*, 200 Main St (☎556-4200; ③), is a comfortable downtown **place to stay**, while the *Richards House B&B*, 1492 Locust St (☎557-1492; ⑤), veers toward olde worlde luxury.

Seventy miles southwest, **CEDAR RAPIDS**, home of *Quaker Oats*, is Iowa's industrial leader. In the late 1840s, a meatpacking boom lured thousands of Czechs here. The **Czech Village**, 16th Ave SW and First St, features the excellent bakery *Sykora's*, gift shops, traditional houses and a small museum of national costumes and pioneer artefacts. The **Museum of Art**, 410 Third Ave SE, boasts a comprehensive collection of paintings by Grant Wood, best known for his woozy, pastel depictions of Thirties farmlife (Tues, Wed, Fri & Sat 10am–4pm, Thurs 10am–7pm, Sun noon–3pm; $2.50). The *Village Inn Motor Hotel*, 100 F Ave NW (☎366-5323; ③), has reasonable rooms.

The Amana Colonies

The **AMANA COLONIES** spread from the intersection of hwys 151 and 220, midway between Cedar Rapids and Iowa City. They were founded in 1855 by the **Community of True Inspiration**, pacifist German refugees (not linked to the Amish or Mennonites) who believed that God spoke through prophets – themselves, for example – rather than ordained ministers. Members led a simple collective lifestyle: each family lived in its own home, but they all ate together and shared profits from the farms. During the Depression, communal ownership became increasingly difficult to maintain, and in 1932 stock was redistributed among all the adults. However, they did keep up their commitment to close family ties, a sense of community and religious principles. On Sunday mornings, you can still see women church members wearing the traditional black cap, shawl and apron, with men dressed in equally somber attire. Church services for visitors, held in English, take place at 10am each Sunday in Middle Amana.

The largest of the seven separate villages in this immaculately serene valley, where neat plank fences divide the rolling meadows, is **AMANA**, whose twee streets are lined with restaurants and craft shops, a brewery, winery and woollen mill – plus a small and somewhat self-congratulatory **museum**. Picturesque **HOMESTEAD** is enhanced by a walking trail around the dam on a scenic bend of the Iowa River, built centuries ago by Indians to concentrate fish into one area and thus allow them to be caught more easily.

Practicalities

Conventional addresses are not used in the Amana Colonies, but points of interest are well signposted. The **visitor center**, near the junction of hwys 151 and 220 (☎622-3828), has details of **B&Bs**. Old-style German **food** can be eaten at the *Amana Bread & Pastry Shop* (☎622-3600) in Amana village and *Hahn's Hearth Oven Bakery* in Middle Amana. South Amana's *Colony Market Place Restaurant* (☎622-3225) offers sausages galore.

Iowa City

IOWA CITY, on I-80 55 miles west of the Mississippi, is refreshingly young at heart. The restored gold-domed **Old Capitol** is a reminder of its days as state capital, before government was transferred to the more central Des Moines. Residents were placated by getting the University of Iowa instead. The arty shops and sidewalk cafés of the compact, partly pedestrianized downtown touch the east end of campus, but its red and grey buildings, closeted by tall dark trees, remain aloof from the rest of the town.

Greyhound stops at 404 E College Ave (☎337-2127), just off downtown. The **CVB** is at 325 E Washington St (☎337-6592). *Iowa House* is a comfortable central **hotel** in the Union building (☎335-3513; ③); dorms at the tidy *Wesley AYH Hostel*, 120 N Dubuque St (☎338-1179; ①), cost $12. To the west, inexpensive motels in Coralville include the clean *Capri*, 705 Second St (☎354-5100; ②). Bargain **food** is easy to find, be it fresh pasta and Cajun dishes at the trendy *Kitchen*, 9 S Dubuque St (☎337-5444), or the burgers next door at *Mickey's* (☎338-6860), a friendly, dimly lit Irish bar.

Central and Western Iowa

Pigs outnumber people in central Iowa. The only city amongst the cornfields, state capital **Des Moines**, struggles to lift the monotony, and many visitors may prefer the college town of **Ames**. The humdrum west has little to offer.

Des Moines

DES MOINES, near the center of Iowa amid tree-covered hills at the confluence of the sluggish Des Moines and Racoon rivers, owes its origins to a military fort set up in 1843. It had already grown into a trading center for farmers by the time the eighteen-year-old Frederick Hubbell arrived in 1855; within a decade he had founded the Equitable Life and Insurance Corporation to service their need for investment capital. Other companies soon realized the potential of agrarian business, and today the city is the world's third largest **insurance** center, behind London and Hartford, Connecticut. Illustrious former denizens of Des Moines include **Ronald Reagan**, who started out as a sportscaster on Radio WHO, and **John Wayne**, born and raised in nearby Winterset.

Arrival and Information

Des Moines' *Greyhound* station (☎243-5211) is just northwest of downtown at 1107 Keosauqua Way. From the very efficient transfer mall at Sixth and Walnut, *MTA* buses (☎283-8100) run practically everywhere in the city. The **visitor center** occupies Suite 222, 601 Locust St (☎286-4960 or 1-800/451-2625).

The City

The steel and glass skyline of **downtown Des Moines**, most of which shot up during the Eighties, is testimony to its ever-growing insurance trade. Towering above all is the boxy, 44-storey **801 Grand** building, headquarters of the Principal Financial Company. For such a fast-track financial center, the streets are curiously empty; pedestrians instead use the **Skywalk**: a three-mile network of air-conditioned corridors linking twenty blocks of offices, banks, parking lots, restaurants, hotels and movie theaters.

Most businesses stand on the west bank of the Des Moines River, which cuts downtown in two. In 1857, a group of speculators attempted to shift the commercial hub to the east side by bribing commissioners to site the **state capitol** at E Ninth St and Grand

---

The **area code** for central and western Iowa is ☎515.

Ave. Their hopes of huge spin-offs were dashed when the nationwide financial crash later that same year saw property prices collapse. As a result, the five-domed Italian Renaissance-style mass, on the crest of a steep hill, is now detached from the heart of the city. A short walk downhill, displays in the futuristic pink and brown **Iowa State Historical Building** at E Sixth and Locust (and topped by a strange neon figurine) cover Indian civilization, pioneer times and the development of Iowan farming (Tues–Sat 9am–4.30pm, Sun noon–4.30pm; free).

Three miles west, the impressive **Des Moines Art Center** at 4700 Grand Ave is housed in a trio of buildings designed by Eliel Saarinen, I M Pei and Richard Meier. Works by Matisse, Picasso and Renoir stand alongside twentieth-century Americans such as Wood, Hopper and O'Keeffe. The most dynamic exhibits are in the mixed-media wing, especially the giant disturbing Anselm Keifer canvas (Tues, Wed, Fri & Sat 11am–5pm, Thurs 11am–9pm, Sun noon–5pm; $2.50, free daily until 1pm & all day Thurs).

Accommodation

Downtown Des Moines caters mostly for insurance company business, but still offers some fairly inexpensive places to stay. You can **camp** in summer at the Iowa State Fairgrounds Campgrounds, E 30th St and Grand Ave (☎262-3111).

Best Western Starlite Village, 929 Third St (☎282-5251). Reasonable downtown rooms. ④.

Hotel Fort Des Moines, Tenth St and Walnut Ave (☎243-1161). Grand old historical downtown hotel; not exactly inexpensive, but frequent special offers worth enquiring about. ⑥.

Motel 6, 4817 Fleur Drive (☎287-8961). Clean rooms near the airport. ②.

YMCA, 101 Locust St (☎288-0131). Slightly faded men-only downtown rooms, $22; weekly rates. ①.

YWCA, 717 Grand Ave (☎244-8961). Clean dorm-style rooms for women in a safe part of downtown; $9 a night with discount for weekly stays. ①.

Eating, Drinking and Nightlife

That Iowans eat well is reflected in the quality – and quantity – of food on offer in Des Moines' restaurants.

French Quarter Bar & Restaurant, 100 Court Ave (☎246-9820). The New Orleans-style cuisine is pricey, as are the drinks, but the Fri–Sun jazz sessions ($2 cover) usually make a visit worthwhile.

Juke Box Saturday Night, 208 Third St (☎243-0707). Favorite weekend gathering place for young Des Moines with guitar bands at low cover charges.

Julio's, 308 Court Ave (☎244-1710). Lively, reasonably priced Tex-Mex café.

Kaplan Hat, 307 Court Ave (☎243-1414). Art Deco restaurant noted for its doorstopper sandwiches, blue plate specials and, most of all, its stuffed pork chops for $10–14.

Stella's Blue Sky Diner, 400 Locust St, in Capitol Square building (☎246-1953). Kitsch diner decked out in lurid pinks, turquoises and yellows. Burgers and fries ($4) washed down with divine chocolate, peanut butter and banana malts. Mon–Sat 8am–6pm; a must for lunch.

Out from Des Moines

Ten miles west of downtown Des Moines (I-80 exit 125), the **Living History Farms** in Urbandale trace the evolution of agriculture on the plains. Self-guided tours lead from the oval bark homes of an eighteenth-century Iowan settlement, through an 1850s homestead, to a look at the high-tech methods of today (May–Oct Mon–Sat 9am–5pm, Sun 11am–6pm; $7). If you want to continue the yokel theme, eat colossal portions of meat loaf and chops in the *Iowa Machine Shed Restaurant* (☎270-6818), or stay in the country-style *Comfort Suites Hotel* (☎276-1126; ④); both are next to the farm entrance.

Thirty miles north of Des Moines, **AMES** is the home of Iowa State University. Smaller and slightly less trendy than Iowa City, it's still a lively little community (by Iowan standards at least), and has recently earned itself a place on the stadium rock roster, attracting all manner of big-name bands. **Room** rates are reasonable out at the *Super 8*, I-35 and Hwy-30 (☎232-6510; ②), three miles from campus; the *Great Plains Sauce and Dough Co*, 129 Main St (☎232-4263), is popular for its unusual pizzas.

In sleepy, run-down **WINTERSET**, 25 miles southwest of Des Moines, the modest former home of the local pharmacist at 224 S Second St is now a museum to his son, Marion Robert Morrison, born in 1907, who grew up to become Hollywood hardman **John Wayne**. His first lead role was in 1930 but real stardom didn't come for another nine years, as the Ringo Kid in John Ford's *Stagecoach*. Three decades later, Wayne claimed his only Oscar as Rooster Cogburn, the drunken one-eyed marshal in *True Grit*. Among the photos, personal belongings and mementos is a glowing personal endorsement of the "Duke" from his buddy Ronald Reagan, who shared his political views, if not perhaps his acting abilities (daily; April–Dec 10am–5pm, Jan–March noon–5pm).

In contrast to the never-say-cry persona of Big John, as the setting for 1993's best-selling tearjerker *The Bridges of Madison County*, this area has pierced hearts across the nation. For the record, Madison County boasts six beautifully restored nineteenth-century **covered bridges**.

NEBRASKA

Hell, I thought I was dead too. Turns out I was just in Nebraska.

Gene Hackman in *Unforgiven*

Though modern transcontinental travellers tend to see **NEBRASKA** in much the same light as did the early pioneers, heading west during the Gold Rush – as just another dreary expanse of prairie to get through as fast as possible – this flat and sparsely populated state in fact encompasses quite a few places of interest. However, its most appealing cities, commercial **Omaha** and the livelier state capital, **Lincoln**, are separated by a good three hundred miles of underwhelming livestock-rearing flatlands from the western **Panhandle**, where the landscape finally erupts into giant sand hills and valleys, broken by towering rocky columns and hemmed in by sheer-faced buttes.

Western Nebraska was still embroiled in vicious and bloody battles against Native Americans long after the east had been settled; from the first serious uprising in 1854, it was 36 years before the US Army could make white control unchallengeable. Close to the South Dakota state line, **Fort Robinson**, where Crazy Horse was murdered, remains one of the West's most evocative historic sites.

Without navigable rivers, Nebraska had to rely on the **railroads** to help populate the land. During the 1870s and 1880s, rail companies, encouraged by grants that allowed them to accumulate one sixth of the state, laid down such a comprehensive network of tracks that virtually every farmer was within a day's cattle drive of the nearest halt. Thus the buffalo-hunting country of the Sioux and Pawnee was turned into high-yield farmland, which today has few rivals in terms of **beef** production.

Getting Around Nebraska

Omaha **airport** offers the best domestic links, though planes from other regional cities also fly to Lincoln. Several *Greyhound* **buses** traverse I-80 each day on the coast-to-coast marathon, stopping at all major towns. *Amtrak* **trains**, travelling through the night, follow a similar route and call at Omaha, Lincoln, Hastings, Holdredge and McCook. Driving I-80 can get tedious; if you're not in a rush, Hwy-2 is a good alternative.

Eastern Nebraska

The silt-laden **Missouri River** separates eastern Nebraska from both Iowa and Missouri on the far side. This stretch of the "Big Muddy" offers few natural ports, and **Omaha** remains the only riverfront community of any size. **Lincoln**, 58 miles southwest, is the state's capital and seat of its university.

Omaha

Although **OMAHA**, Nebraska's largest and most easterly city, is visibly a prosperous place, with a great zoo, several museums and a lively entertainment district, the atmosphere remains sedate and predominantly suburban. As a major terminus on the first transcontinental railroad, Omaha made a logical alternative to distant Chicago as a marketplace for Wyoming and Nebraska ranchers to sell their herds of cattle. By the turn of the century massive stockyards spread along the southern edge of town, and the city still handles well over one million head of livestock per year.

The broad sweeping thoroughfares of **downtown Omaha** have been all but killed off by the drift to the city's myriad malls, though you'll find good bars and cafés along the cobbled streets of the **Old Market** district, plus interesting specialist shops such as the *Antiquarian Bookstore*, 1215 Harney St (☎341-8077), packed with dusty volumes (and local bohemians). The nearby **Heartland Park of America**, at Eighth and Douglas – ideal for a picnic – holds a huge electronically controlled fountain. Behind its pink marble Art Deco exterior, the **Joslyn Art Museum**, 2200 Dodge St, contains an interesting range of Indian art and twentieth-century American paintings (Tues–Sat 10am–5pm, Sun 1–5pm; $2, free Sat before noon).

The **Great Plains Black Museum**, in the city's predominantly black north side at 2213 Lake St (Mon–Fri times vary; ☎345-2212), presents the history of African-American people on the prairies. One stimulating section focuses on blacks in the frontier army. In the main recently freed slaves, who could find no work in the Deep South after the Civil War, they were often sent as advance parties in to the most hostile and dangerous regions; it was Native American warriors who first called them **"buffalo soldiers"**, because of their tightly curled hair and the color of their skin. **Malcolm X** was born in Omaha in May 1925, though his family moved to Michigan immediately thereafter, in the face of Ku Klux Klan death threats to his father, a preacher who followed the back-to-Africa teachings of Marcus Garvey.

The **Henry Doorly Zoo**, 3701 S Tenth St (daily 9.30am–5pm; $8), rightfully considers itself as one of the best zoos in America. It started off with two buffalo borrowed from Buffalo Bill; now there's a gigantic free-flying aviary, some rare white Siberian tigers and a magnificent bear canyon, as well as the **Lied Jungle**, an indoor rainforest housing tropical wildlife from South America, Asia and Africa. An elevated walkway, with a swaying rope bridge, leads into a world populated by pygmy hippos, gibbons, leopards, crocodiles, parrots, butterflies – and the aptly named Howler monkeys.

Practicalities

Omaha's *Greyhound* station is at 1601 Jackson St (☎341-1900); *Amtrak* trains depart very late at night, and arrive long before the city wakes up, at 1003 Ninth St (☎342-1501). Both depots are well placed for downtown. Local public transport is poor.

The **CVB**, at 1819 Farnham St (☎444-4660 or ☎1-800/332-1819), offers discount vouchers for **motels**, which congregate around I-80 and 84th St. Rooms at the circular, almost cute, and certainly pretty unusual *Satellite Motel*, 6006 L St (☎733-7373; ②), come clean and at good prices, while downtown's *Excel Inn*, 221 Douglas St (☎345-9565; ②), although on a seedy block, is considered safe. The well-kept *Sleep Inn*, out by the airport at 2525 Abbott Drive (☎342-2525 or 1-800/62SLEEP; ③), makes for a quiet night.

The **Old Market** district, centered on Tenth and Howard streets, has the liveliest **restaurants** and **bars**. The *Indian Oven*, 1010 Howard St (☎342-4856), a superb Asian restaurant, features *paneer* and vegetable dishes on its extensive menu. Both *M's Pub*, 422 S 11th St (☎342-2550), serving the best bar food in town, and *The Bistro*, Twelfth

---

The **area code** for Omaha and eastern Nebraska is ☎402.

and Harney (☎346-4060), home of some great gourmet dishes, appear posh but are pleasantly informal. Whether you fancy terrific desserts or a light meal, the *Garden Café*, 1212 Harney St (☎422-1574), won't break the bank. The *Howard Street Tavern*, 1112 Howard St (☎341-0433), is a reliable rock venue with a good grunge bar upstairs.

Lincoln

Were it not for Omaha, 58 miles northeast, **LINCOLN** would be in the back of beyond; the next major point of civilization to the west is Denver, Colorado, 480 miles further along I-80. As tiny Rochester, it was selected to be **state capital** in 1867 – on the condition that it change its name to Lincoln in honor of the recently assassinated president. Such was the disappointment in the territorial seat of government, Omaha, that state officials had to smuggle documents, books and office furniture out of the city in the middle of the night to avoid armed gangs.

Lincoln now serves as an oasis of culture for a large chunk of the plains. At night, when the students emerge, its compact downtown comes into its own. O Street (the subject of Ginsberg's poem *Zero Street*), is the main drag; 13th and 14th streets are packed with good bars and places to eat.

Dwarfing the rest of **downtown**, the central tower of the 1932 **Nebraska state capitol**, 1445 K St, protrudes four hundred feet into the sky. Topped by a twenty-foot statue of a sower on a pedestal of wheat and corn, its remarkable phallic appearance – an adventurous departure from the usual architecture of state capitols – has prompted the nickname "penis of the prairies". For once there's no golden dome, and the superb iridescent murals in the foyer are a welcome alternative to old portraits, flags and emblems. From the fourteenth-floor observation deck you can survey the flatness of the surrounding farmland (Mon–Fri 8am–5pm, Sat & hols 10am–5pm, Sun 1–5pm; free).

Twelve thousand years of life on the plains are covered at the free **Museum of Nebraska History**, 15th and P, where displays focus on anthropology rather than history (Mon–Sat 9am–5pm, Sun 1.30–5pm). The Elephant Hall, a gallery of towering mammoth, mastodon and four-tusker skeletons, is the highlight of the U **of N State Museum** at 14th and U (Tues–Sat 8am–5pm, Sun 1.30–5pm; $1.50). A few blocks away, the **Sheldon Memorial Art Gallery**, 12th and R, traces the development of American art, and has a twenty-piece sculpture garden (Tues, Wed & Fri 10am–5pm, Thurs & Sat 10am–5pm & 7–9pm, Sun 2–9pm; free). The 76,000-seater **Memorial Stadium** (tickets ☎472-3111), at the northern end of campus at the end of Vine Street, is where the brutal "Big Red" Cornhuskers invariably thrash the footballing opposition.

Practicalities

Lincoln's *Greyhound* station is downtown at 940 P St (☎474-1071), while *Amtrak* passes through 201 N Seventh St at crazy early-morning hours. *Lincoln Transystem* (☎476-1234) runs good local buses. The **visitor center** is at 1221 N St (☎476-7551 or ☎1-800/423-8212). Except on football weekends, it's easy to find inexpensive **accommodation** out by the airport, off I-80 exit 399 – at the *Motel 6* (☎475-3211; ②), for example. Downtown, however, has a shortage of budget **rooms**: the *Ramada*, 141 N Ninth St (☎475-4011; ④), is good value, though the *Cornerstone* **AYH Hostel**, 640 N 16th St (☎476-0355; ①), on the edge of campus, offers basic members-only bunks for $9.

Valentino's, 13th and Q (☎475-1501), is a good Italian **restaurant**; the food and beer come well recommended at the *Crane River Brewpub and Café*, 11th and P (☎476-7766). *The Zoo*, 136 N 14th St (☎435-8754), attracts big-name jazz and blues acts who drop in en route between Chicago and Kansas City; *Duffy's Bar*, 1412 O St (☎474-3543), pulls a younger crowd and some good rock bands. Just across the street is *O'Rourke's Lounge* – a lively, well-priced hang-out. The **Historic Haymarket District**, down by *Amtrak*, also holds assorted good bars and restaurants.

Western Nebraska

After the unerringly flat journey across eastern Nebraska, the far west comes as a refreshing change. In the **Panhandle**, as it's often called, wave upon wave of rumpled sandy hills, thinly coated with prairie grass, back off towards the horizon like a sea in constant turmoil. Early pioneers wrote the area off as unproductive, and it remained barren until massive irrigation work at the start of this century enabled agricultural settlement. In the northwest the sandhills yield to classic John-Ford-style western scenery: pancake-flat valleys, criss-crossed by dry meandering river beds and corralled by crusty, contorted bluffs under the constant shadow of fast-moving clouds. Emigrants on the Oregon Trail used the bizarre outcrops which sprout along the way as "road signs" to let them know that their trek across the plains was coming to an end.

Across I-80

Interstate-80 is one of the most popular coast-to-coast routes simply because it's the shortest. Scenery is not its strongest suit, and the central swath through 450 miles of Nebraskan farmland is not always a prospect drivers cherish. If time doesn't matter, then it's best to head northwest at dreary Grand Island, 93 miles west of Lincoln, onto **Scenic Hwy-2** for a lonesome yet exhilarating drive through the Sandhills.

If you stick to I-80, decent pull-off points are few and far between. **KEARNEY**, a mildly interesting college town at exit 272, has a strip of inexpensive restaurants and studenty bars, but not really much else. Just over halfway across the state at exit 177, **NORTH PLATTE** makes a big deal about its **Buffalo Bill Ranch Historical Park** (daily 8am–8pm; $2 per car), another property of the ubiquitous William "Buffalo Bill" Cody. Today the ranch is run by the state, which places more emphasis on history than tacky folklore. Cody's mansion and various barns can be examined; activities include a nightly rodeo in summer. The *Rambler Motel*, 1420 Rodeo Rd (☎532-9290; ②), has comfortable **rooms** and an outdoor pool, while the authentic Mexican cantina *La Casita*, 1911 E Fourth St (☎534-8077), boasts an irresistible **Elvis room**.

Thirty miles west another restaurant sets out to entertain vexed drivers, in the one-horse hamlet of **PAXTON**, off exit 145. **Ole's Big Game Lounge & Grill** serves tasty fried food, with over two hundred wildlife trophies from around the world mounted on walls, cabinets and shelves. Fascinating, but not a place for the animal rights activist.

Ogallala, twenty miles along, sits just nine miles south of "Big Mac" – **Lake McConaughy** reservoir, famous for fishing, water sports and the sandy beaches along its 105 miles of shoreline. From Ogallala, it's 165 miles to Cheyenne, WY, though Sidney (exit 59) takes you into the rugged Oregon Trail country (see overleaf).

Scenic Hwy-2 and Alliance

Scenic Hwy-2 meanders and dips for over 330 miles from I-80 to South Dakota's Black Hills. It passes through the **Sandhills** – a mesmerizing landscape carpeted with short-grass prairie and softened by delicate wildflowers and shiny ponds. Apart from a few farmsteads, grain silos and tiny churches, all you're likely to see on the open road are lazing cattle, a few sluggish rivers and the occasional mile-and-a-quarter-long freight train weaving its way through the hills. It's a long, desolate yet incredibly beautiful drive through an anachronistic corner of the US, where small towns are all spick-and-span and everyone could well know each other's name; **BROKEN BOW**, 77 miles north of I-80, features one of the neatest town squares in the heartland.

The **area code** for western Nebraska is ☎308.

The road dawdles for another 200 miles through scattered villages before drifting into **ALLIANCE** – a nice enough little prairie town, which attracts over 50,000 people per year for its one big attraction. **Carhenge**, two miles north on Hwy-385, is a rough copy of Stonehenge, made with old cars rather than stone. Erected in a cornfield during a family reunion in 1987, this intriguing collection of Chevys, Cadillacs and Plymouths, painted a brooding battleship grey and tilted at unusual angles, has to be the best picnic site in America's heartland. To some it's an ingenious piece of pop art; others view it as great black humor or an appalling eyesore; and a few fundamentalist Christians suspect it to be a Satanic shrine. Certainly, the Nebraska Dept of Roads saw nothing amusing about the project. They rapidly declared it a junkyard, and ordered the City of Alliance to remove it – whereupon the city, realizing they had the only tourist attraction within a fifty-mile radius, redrew its boundaries to avoid having to enforce the order. Relentless state officials attempted to dispose of the monstrosity by ordering the construction of a slip road, parking lot and other facilities; locals rose to the challenge by forming the **Friends of Carhenge**, whose work seems to have secured the monument's future.

The helpful downtown **CVB** office (☎762-1520) provides information and sells Carhenge souvenirs. You can get clean **rooms** at *McCarroll's Motel*, 1028 E Third St (☎762-3680; ②), or the *Super 8*, 1419 W Third St (☎762-8300; ②). *Ken & Dale's*, 123 E Third St (☎762-7252), serves succulent all-day breakfasts and great pecan pancakes.

The Oregon Trail Landmarks

Two of the first landmarks encountered by travellers on the Oregon Trail (see p.000) were the lumpy **Courthouse and Jail rocks**, just beyond the likeable little town of **BRIDGEPORT**, 36 miles south of Alliance. Fourteen miles west, along Hwy-92, the much-painted and photographed **Chimney Rock** rises almost five hundred feet above the North Platte River. Although this phallic outcrop's nineteenth-century stature may have been chipped away by erosion and lightning, it remains one of the most recognizable and memorable landmarks in the West.

The twin towns of **GERING** and **SCOTTSBLUFF**, 25 miles further west, are the commercial center for the farmlands of western Nebraska. Southwest of Gering, the rugged 800ft rampart of **Scotts Bluff National Monument** (daily, summer 8am–6pm, otherwise 8am–5pm; $4 per car) stands like a Nebraskan Gibraltar. Known to the Sioux as *Me-a-pa-te* ("hill that's hard to get around"), it earned its anglicized name in 1828 after fur trader Hiram Scott was mysteriously found dead at its base. Treks to the top are rewarded with a magnificent view, and the entrance fee includes the absorbing **Oregon Trail Museum**, which relates the experiences of the early migrants. South of Gering, the spiky **Wildcat Hills** hold some delightful vistas and hiking terrain.

Well-kept **rooms** are available in the *Lamplighter Motel*, 606 E 27th St, Scottsbluff (☎632-7108 or ☎1/800-341-8000; ②); the fully licensed *Mason Jar*, 3810 N Tenth St, Gering (☎632-4177), is the best spot for family-style **food**. The towns' **visitor center** can be found at 1721 Broadway, Scottsbluff (☎632-2133).

Fort Robinson State Park

Some eighty miles north of Scottsbluff, just west of **Crawford** village, **Fort Robinson State Park**, beside 1000ft crenellated cliffs in the inhospitable White River Valley, preserves the spot where the US Army coordinated its campaign to rid the gold-rich Badlands of the native Sioux. Today, it's a cross between a dude ranch, a mini-college campus and a living history village; a cosmeticization which makes the memories of the obliteration of an entire way of native life all the more poignant.

Restored fort buildings contain period furnishings, and there are two small museums. A simple stone marks the spot where Crazy Horse was bayoneted to death;

CRAZY HORSE

The life of Oglala Sioux leader Crazy Horse is shrouded in confusion, misinterpretation and controversy. So thoroughly did the most enigmatic figure in Plains Indian history avoid contact with whites outside of battle that no photograph or even sketch of him exists; unlike other Indian chiefs, he refused to visit Washington DC or talk to reporters.

Crazy Horse earned his title as a youth, after he single-handedly charged rival Arapahoe and took two scalps. The finest moment in a brilliant military career came in June 1876 when he led a thousand warriors in inflicting a stinging defeat on the superior forces of General George Crook at the Battle of the Rosebud River. Only eight days later Crazy Horse headed the attack at the Battle of Little Bighorn, where Custer and his entire company were killed (see p.645).

After Little Bighorn, US Army efforts to round up the Indians redoubled. In May 1877, Crazy Horse surprised friend and foe alike by leading nine hundred of his people into Fort Robinson. They gave up their weapons and Crazy Horse, keen to stay in his native land (unlike Sitting Bull, who had retreated to Canada), demanded that the buffalo grounds along the Powder River should remain in Indian hands. Tensions at the army camp rose after a rumor went around the barracks that the Sioux chief had come to murder General Crook. Crazy Horse was arrested on September 5 1877; during a tussle outside the fort jail, he was bayoneted three times, dying the next morning.

Quite why this undefeated warrior should have surrendered without a fight, and whether he fell victim to a deliberate assassination, remain unclear. What is certain is that his death signalled the closing chapter of the Indian Wars. The Oglala Sioux were forcibly moved to the poor hunting country of Missouri, and settlers immediately swept in their thousands into western Nebraska, South Dakota, Wyoming and Montana.

Crazy Horse, so one story goes, was buried by his family in an unmarked grave in an out-of-the-way creek called Wounded Knee – the very place where thirteen years later three hundred Sioux men, women and children were slaughtered in the bloody finale to over half a century of barbarism (see p.589).

the tour train ($1) acknowledges it with a mere ten-second halt. Good-value **horse rides** pass some wondrously weird rock formations, and *Fort Robinson Lodge* (☎665-2660; ①) has nice **rooms** as well as bargain cottages; the *Lodge*'s restaurant serves cheap **buffalo tacos** and other beef and bison recipes.

The town of **CHADRON**, 23 miles east of Fort Robinson, is worth a visit principally for the **Museum of the Fur Trade**, three miles east on US-20 (summer only; daily, 8am–5pm; $1.50) – a valuable historical archive illustrating the grossly unfair barter system which operated between fur traders and local Indians.

SOUTH DAKOTA

The wide-open spaces of the Great Plains roll away to infinity to either side of I-90 in **SOUTH DAKOTA**. Though the land is more green and fertile east of the Missouri River, vast numbers of high-season visitors speed straight on through to the spectacular southwest, site of the **Badlands**, and the adjacent **Black Hills** – two of the most dramatic, mysterious, and legend-impacted tracts of land in the US. For the whites, they encapsulate a wagonload of American notions about heritage and the taming of the West. To Native Americans they are ancient, spiritually resonant places.

The science-fiction severity of the Badlands resists conversion into easy tourist palatability. The bigger, more user-friendly Black Hills, home of that most patriotic of icons, **Mount Rushmore**, can be more actively experienced (hiking trails, mountain lakes and streams, scenic highways) and exploited (via dozens of physical, historical and plain commercial attractions, and the mining of gold and other metals).

Time and Hollywood have mythologized the larger-than-life personalities for whom the Dakota Territory served as a stomping ground; **Custer** and **Crazy Horse** battled here for supremacy over the plains, while **"Wild Bill" Hickok** and **"Calamity Jane"** were denizens of the once-notorious Gold Rush town of Deadwood. On a more contemporary note, **Dances with Wolves**, Kevin Costner's award-winning epic shot in the state, continues to boost South Dakota's tourism image.

Sioux tribes dominated the plains from the eighteenth century, having gradually been pushed westwards from the Great Lakes by the encroaching whites. To these nomadic hunters, unlike the gun-toting Christian settlers and federal politicians, the concept of owning the earth was utterly alien. They fought hard to stay free: the Sioux are the only Indian nation to have defeated the United States in war and forced it to sign a treaty (in 1868) favorable to their race. Even so, they were compelled, in the face of a gung-ho gold rush, to relinquish the sacred Black Hills, and ultimately the choice lay between death or confinement on reservations. For decades their history and culture was outlawed; until the 1940s it was illegal to teach or even speak their language, Lakota. More Sioux live on South Dakota's six reservations now than dwelled in the whole state during pioneer days, but their prospects are often grim. Nowhere is the legacy of injustice better symbolized than at **Wounded Knee**, on the Oglala Sioux **Pine Ridge Reservation** – scene of the infamous 1890 massacre by the US Army, and also of a prolonged "civil disturbance" by the radical American Indian Movement in 1973.

Native American traditions are celebrated by music, dance and socializing at **powwows**, held in summer on the reservations; the state tourist office can supply dates and locations. Apart from powwows, South Dakota summers are taken up with historical celebrations, volksmarches (a friendly sort of community walking exercise), ethnic festivals and rodeos. The state has 170 parks and recreation areas for hikers and campers. In winter, downhill **skiing** is limited to Terry Peak and Deer Mountain outside **Lead** in the Black Hills; cross-country and snowmobiling are more prevalent.

Getting Around South Dakota

You'll be hard put to see much of South Dakota without a car. *Amtrak* routes bypass the state entirely, while *Greyhound* and *Jack Rabbit* (☎1-800/759-8687) bus lines serve points between Rapid City and Sioux Falls, sites of the two major airports. *Powder River* buses (☎1-800/442-3682) serve Black Hills towns such as Deadwood, Rapid City and Hot Springs, as well as making a two-hour trip to Cheyenne, WY.

East of the Missouri

For tourists, little in eastern or central South Dakota constitutes the essential. **Sioux Falls**, the state's biggest city, is faceless but handy. As one of the country's quietest and smallest capital cities, **Pierre** has its charms. **Mitchell** has a few curiosities, while **Yankton**, comfortably ensconced beside the Missouri across from Nebraska, is a gemlike historic town with the excellent Lewis and Clark Recreation Area on its doorstep. The town marks the start of an alternative cross-state route to I-90, trundling through nearby **Vermillion**, home to the exceptional Shrine to Music Museum, plus the Rosebud and Pine Ridge reservations. About sixty miles northwest of Sioux Falls, **De Smet**, known as "Little Town on the Prairie" thanks to the autobiographical books of Laura Ingalls Wilder (though the TV location is in Kansas; see p.572). You can tour eighteen sites she mentions for smatterings of history, pretty scenery and homely pride. **Chamberlain**, where I-90 shoots down a steep bluff and over the Missouri River, provides the most spectacular vistas in the eastern part of the state.

The **area code** for the entire state of South Dakota is ☎605.

Mitchell

MITCHELL makes a mildly diverting stop on the endless drive along I-90. The **Corn Palace** at 604 N Main St (summer daily 8.30am–10pm, winter Mon–Fri 8.30am–5pm) has been pegged as "the world's largest birdfeeder"; the first Corn Palace was built in 1892 to encourage settlement and to display products of the rich local soil. Topped with brightly painted onion-shaped domes and minarets like some kitsch Moorish transplant to the cornbelt, the exterior of this auditorium is decorated annually (at a cost of about $35,000) with large murals depicting farming and other outdoor scenes. The artists' materials consist exclusively of native corn, grains and grasses of varied but entirely natural color, all grown by local farmers. Mounted on wooden panels, their designs are sprayed with preservatives and repellents to ward off birds. Further examples of this rural folk art are found inside, along with Mitchell's **visitor center** (☎996-7311).

Other ways to while away time in Mitchell include a gallery devoted to a Yanktonai Sioux painter; a surprisingly interesting museum of dolls such as a salt-carved Shirley Temple; a pioneer museum; and a prehistoric Native American village. Both the *Best Western* (☎996-5536; ③) and *Super 8* (☎996-9678; ②) **motels** lie just off I-90 exit 332. The chef-owned *Town House*, 103 N Main St (☎996-4615), is a good place to grab a meal.

The Badlands

The White River **BADLANDS** could be considered a pocket-sized cousin of Arizona's Grand Canyon. Beyond the family resemblance what's most impressive about the "Badlandscape" is not its scale, as at the Canyon, but rather its sheer strangeness. More than 35 million years ago this area of southwest South Dakota was a saltwater sea; later it became a marsh, into which sank the remains of such prehistoric mammals as saber-toothed tigers and three-toed horses, to be covered with white volcanic ash. Drying as it evolved, the terrain became unable to support the deep-rooted shrubs or trees that might have preserved it, and over the last few million years erosion has slowly eaten away layers of sand, silt, ash, mud and gravel, to reveal rippling gradations of earth tones and pastel colors. The friable earth is carved into all manner of shapes: pinnacles, precipices, pyramids, knobs, cones, ridges, gorges or, if you're feeling poetic, lunar sandcastles and cathedrals. The Sioux dubbed these incredible contortions of nature *Mako Sica*, literally "land bad"; early French trappers echoed that with *Mauvaises Terres Traverser*, or "bad lands to travel across"; they have also aptly been described as "hell with the fires out". Despite this daunting reputation, animals such as bighorn sheep, mule deer and prairie dogs are at home here, while on average a million visitors pass through each year.

The most spectacular formations can be found within the **Badlands National Park**, particularly its northern sector, while the southern stretches are encompassed by the poverty-stricken Pine Ridge Indian Reservation. Clean-cut **Wall**, just a few miles north of the park boundaries, is the most-visited commercial center in the region.

Badlands National Park

About one tenth of the Badlands – the most amazing parts – were during the Seventies declared a **National Park** (open year-round). Its two most accessible entrances are off I-90 at exits 131 (Northeast entrance) and 109-110 (at the town of Wall), and connected by the forty-mile paved loop of Hwy-240, peppered with scenic overlooks. Visitors can backpack or climb just about anywhere; short **helicopter** rides over this spooky terrain leave from outside the northeast entrance (from $20; ☎433-5322). The Badlands' rainbow colors are most vibrant at dawn, dusk and just after rainfall.

Hiking information can be obtained from the **Ben Reifel visitor center** (summer 7am–dusk; otherwise 8am–4.30pm; ☎433-5361; $5 per vehicle), five miles from the Northeast entrance. There are two **accommodation** options nearby; *Cedar Pass Lodge*, operated by the Oglala Sioux, has comfortable doubles (mid-April to Oct; ☎433-5460; ②), while the *Badlands Budget Host Motel* (June to mid-Sept; ☎433-5335 or ☎1-800/999-6116; ②) costs a few dollars less. Another **visitor center** – White River – stands on Hwy-27 in the less-visited and less spectacular southern end of the park. A handful of seasonal **campgrounds** operate both in the park and Wall.

Wall

The town of **WALL**, eight miles north of the Badlands, may look like nothing special, yet thanks to **Wall Drug**, begun modestly in 1931 as a pharmacy and veterinary supplies shop on Main Street, it's known around the world. You'll learn about *Wall Drug*'s presence long before you reach it. Over five hundred billboards along I-90 tout its wares, and by the time you get to exit 110 (the one with the 85-foot *Wall Drug* dinosaur), you'll be compelled to pull off and see what all the fuss is about.

Behind the hype, which extends to advertising on London buses, lies a kitschy emporium which serves up to twenty thousand visitors per day. You can fill up in the 530-seat café-cum-western art gallery, or just enjoy the wall-to-wall collection of photos, memorabilia, animal trophies and mechanical displays like the Cowboy Orchestra and the Chuckwagon Quartet. The merchandise runs a gamut from quality (an excellent western bookstore, and a complete trail outfitters) to junk (anyone for a rattlesnake mold?). Most of all, there's the crackpot cornucopia atmosphere of this ultimate family store, a downmarket, down-home Disneyland wallowing in nostalgia.

There's absolutely no reason to **spend the night** in Wall, but if you're stuck try the *Best Western Plains Motel*, 712 Glenn St (☎279-2145; ③), or the slightly less expensive *Super 8* next door (☎1-800/843-1991; ③). The *Cactus Restaurant Lounge* on Main Street (☎279-2561) serves reasonable food.

Pine Ridge Indian Reservation

Pine Ridge, the second largest Indian reservation in the United States, overlaps the southern Badlands. It is also located in the nation's poorest county. Its prefab homes and beat-up trucks blend sadly and uneasily with the surrounding dry grasslands, rocky bluffs and tree-lined creeks.

The largest town, also called Pine Ridge, comprises a collection of shabby, paint-stripped structures. Just as the surrounding scrubland contrasts starkly with the former homelands of the Sioux in the lush Black Hills, these sorry communities are as far as you can get from the cozy mom-and-apple-pie atmosphere of towns like Wall. In many ways the reservation towns are an even more bitter pill to swallow than places like the nearby site of the Wounded Knee massacre: nowhere is America's disparity of wealth and opportunity so evident as in this area, which posts the highest poverty and alcohol-related death statistics on the continent.

Wounded Knee is just one of several hugely significant historic sites on the reservation, marked by peeling, hand-painted tin signs as opposed to the slick decals which commemorate soldiers, bureaucrats and politicians elsewhere in the state. **Red Cloud Indian Mission School**, a few miles west of the town of Pine Ridge on US-18, holds an Indian art show each summer featuring work by thirty different tribes. The school has a permanent display of star quilts (a Sioux tradition), paintings and a gift shop (all open Mon–Fri 9am–5pm, Sat & Sun by appointment). The **Oglala Nation Fair**, the first weekend in August, includes a powwow and rodeo. For details, contact the Oglala Sioux Tribe, Pine Ridge, SD 57770 (☎867-5771).

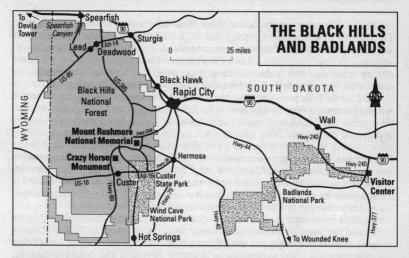

Wounded Knee

No other atrocity against Native Americans remains so potent and poignant as the massacre at **WOUNDED KNEE**. On December 29 1890, the US Army delivered a coup de grace to the vestiges of Plains Indian resistance, killing several hundred unarmed Sioux men, women and children. Most were **Ghost Dancers**, followers of a messianic cult who believed that by ritualistic, trance-inducing dancing and singing they could recover their lost land, ancestors and way of life. It was triggered by a misunderstanding during a tribal round-up. A deaf Indian, asked to surrender his rifle along with his peers, instead held it above his head, shouting that he'd paid a lot for it. An officer grabbed at the gun, it went off, and the troops started shooting.

A commemorative sign and a stone monument, surrounded by a chain-link fence, mark the victims' shabby collective gravesite, in a desolate spot off Hwy-27 toward the bottom of Pine Ridge Reservation. Somehow it has an intangible feeling of grief and anger, the mass murder here having left an indelible scar on all First Americans. Eighty-three years later, members of the radical American Indian Movement (AIM) grabbed headlines by occupying Wounded Knee in a dispute over the federal imposition of a tribal government; they were eventually dispersed by armed FBI agents and a paramilitary unit. More peaceably, since the mid-1980s the **Sitanka Wokiksuye** movement has organized an annual pilgrimage to Wounded Knee, in which an ever-growing number of Indians brave the often harsh winter weather to come by horse and travois, thereby symbolically releasing the spirits of their dead ancestors and mending the sacred hoop of the Sioux nation. It's difficult to say what influence, if any, the movement has had in Washington DC, but moves are afoot to designate the gravesite a national monument.

The Black Hills

> *Our people knew there was yellow metal in little chunks up there, but they did not bother with it, because it was not good for anything.*
>
> Black Elk, Oglala Sioux holy man

The timbered, rocky **BLACK HILLS** rise like an island from a sea of rolling hills and flat grain-growing plains, stretching for a hundred miles between the Belle Fourche River in the north and the Cheyenne to the south, and varying in width from forty to sixty miles. For many generations of Sioux, their value was and still is immeasurable. The Hills are "the heart of everything that is", a kind of spiritual safe, a place of gods and holy mountains where warriors went to speak with Wakan Tanka (the Great Spirit) and await visions. They were dubbed Paha Sapa, or Black Hills, even though they are actually mountains (the highest, Harney Peak, rises 7242 feet), and the blue spruce and Norway pine trees that cover them only appear to be black from a distance.

Thinking the Hills were worthless, the United States government drew up a **treaty** in the mid-nineteenth century that gave them and most of the land west of the Missouri River to the Indians. All such treaties were destined to be broken when the discovery of gold turned the Indians' Eden into the white explorer's Eldorado, and fortune-hunters came pouring in. The story has an incomplete postscript: in 1980, the US Supreme Court ordered the federal government to pay the Sioux $105 million in **compensation** for the illegal seizure of the Hills in 1877. After heated debate amongst Indian representatives, this settlement was rejected and a steering committee subsequently formed to campaign for the return of the Hills themselves to the tribes. The legal battle continues today, often hindered by a lack of consensus among the Native Americans.

The Hills today combine tourism with conservation. Despite the real danger of the entire area becoming an ersatz western theme park – as evidenced by its T-shirt stores, pseudohistorical wax museums, cowboy supper shows, and water slides – marketing and merchandising aren't so extensive as to rob the Hills of all their beauty or dignity.

The more thickly wooded north is noted more for urban activities, with the casino town of **Deadwood** its busiest spot. No place in the Hills is much more than ninety minutes from the four presidential heads carved into **Mount Rushmore**, but even more remarkable is **Crazy Horse Mountain**, the world's most ambitious work-in-progress. In the shade of these great monuments, the more unspoiled southern hills are home to the bison of **Custer State Park** and **Wind Cave National Park**, along with the town of **Hot Springs**.

Finally, a word about **gold**. Numerous outlets sell the area's distinctive grape-leaf design. The Hills variety has a frosted finish and comes in three shades – yellow, green and pink; the last two are alloys, made by mixing gold with silver and copper or zinc.

The North Hills

The predominantly privately owned northern Black Hills are more commercialized than their southern siblings, with **Rapid City**, the hub, surrounded by more interesting smaller towns such as **Sturgis**, **Spearfish** and **Deadwood**. The back roads, especially in the **Spearfish Canyon** area, form a network of prime driving country.

Rapid City

Though South Dakota's second largest town, **RAPID CITY**, is all but swamped with family-fun attractions, it makes a convenient base to explore the charms of the Black Hills' lesser communities. In town, the **Sioux Indian Museum**, 515 West Blvd (Tues–Sat 10am–5pm, Sun 1–5pm; free), houses rare artefacts and contemporary art; a not-for-profit craft gallery – *The Tipi Shop* – occupies the premises next door. The surrounding scenery can be put in context with a visit to the **Museum of Geology**, 501 E Joseph St (Mon–Sat 8am–6pm, Sun noon–6pm).

Rapid City offers both the best and the cheapest **lodgings** in the Black Hills. The Bavarian wood trimmings and Sioux soft furnishings of the delightful *Hotel Alex Johnson*, 523 Sixth St (☎342-1210 or ☎1-800/888-2539; ⑨), provide a great escape from dull corporate decor. *Rapid City AYH Hostel*, 815 Kansas City St (☎342-8538; ①) in the YMCA building, costs $9 for a bunk with free access to a gym and pool. Both the **food and beer** made on the premises at *Firehouse Brewing Co*, 610 Main St (☎348-1915), are worth sampling. The **visitor center** is located in the Civic Center, 444 Mount Rushmore Rd (☎343-1744 or ☎1-800/478-3223).

Sturgis

The sleepy town of **STURGIS**, thirty miles north of Rapid City, comes to life in a big way during the second week of August, when the world-famous **Sturgis Rally and Races** (PO Box 189, SD 57785; ☎347-3245) packs out virtually every motel and campground in the region with motorcycle enthusiasts. For the rest of the year, bikers have to make do with an abundance of **Harley souvenirs** in the downtown stores and the worthy **National Motorcycle Museum**, 2438 S Junction Ave (summer Mon–Fri 8am–5pm, Sat 10am–4pm; otherwise Mon–Fri 9am–5pm; $2.50). East of town, off Hwy-34, the volcanic outcrop which dominates **Bear Butte State Park** stands as a lonely sentinel, detached from the rest of the hills. This site, said to be the original location of the **Sun Dance** ceremonies, holds great religious significance for Native Americans, hundreds of whom come here on retreat each year – to avoid interfering, it's best to check with the park's **visitor center** (☎347-5240) before setting out on any of its excellent short hikes.

Of the wide range of **motels** in Sturgis, the reasonably central *Junction Inn*, 1802 S Junction Ave (☎347-5675; ③), represents the best value. The lure of **breakfast**, burgers and overpriced souvenirs is hard to resist at the garish *Roadkill Café*, 1333 Main St (☎347-5675). Sturgis **visitor center** (☎347-2556) lies just off I-90 exit 32.

Deadwood

One of the West's wildest Gold Rush towns, **DEADWOOD**, in a deep gulch high in the hills 42 miles northwest of Rapid City, has the rare accolade of being a National Historic Landmark in its entirety. Within a year of the discovery of **gold** here in 1876, six thousand gold-diggers swarmed in to stake their claims; con artists, outlaws and other dubious frontier types were not far behind. Among them were James Butler, aka **Wild Bill Hickok** – sometime spy, scout, bullwhacker, stagecoach driver, sheriff and gambler, who spent only a few weeks in Deadwood prior to his murder by a young drifter named Jack McCall – and Martha **"Calamity Jane"** Canary Burke, a coarse illiterate alcoholic, whose checkered career included stints as dishwasher, muleskinner, scout, prostitute, nurse and Wild West Show performer. She died penniless in 1903, her last wish to be buried beside Hickok high above town in **Mount Moriah Cemetery**.

Gambling was outlawed in Deadwood in 1889, the year South Dakota achieved statehood, but betting parlors and brothels flourished well into this century. Now the old ghosts of the raunchy past have been revitalized, since the passing of limited stake gambling legislation in 1989 (state residents recently voted down a proposal, sponsored by Kevin Costner who part-owns a casino in town, to raise the stake limit from $5 to $100). With a residential population of only 2000, Deadwood is now booming again, but at a cost: the economy is almost totally based on gaming and real estate prices have soared so high that no non-gambling business can afford to be on Main Street.

A visit to Deadwood is nevertheless essential, if only to see that Sin City can flourish even in a God's Country like the Black Hills. Topping the list of **places to stay** is *Adams House*, 22 Van Buren St (☎578-3877; ⑤), an antique-stuffed Victorian B&B. Main Street boasts two grand old hotels – the *Bullock* (no 633; ☎578-1745 or 1-800/336-1876; ④) and the *Franklin Hotel* (no 700; ☎578-2241 or 1-800/888-1876; ④) – though slot machines now encroach on their Victorian charm. *Saloon #10*, 657 Main St (☎578-3346), has decent food, sawdust floors and lots of memorabilia. Above the door is the chair in which Hickok was supposedly sitting when shot dead while holding two aces, a pair of eights and the nine of diamonds, forever after christened the Dead Man's Hand. The **visitor center** is at 735 Main St (☎578-1876).

Spearfish Canyon Area

Aspen, birch and white spruce spread over the towering limestone cliffs above the nine-teen-mile **Spearfish Canyon National Scenic Highway**, which starts on Hwy-14A half an hour's drive west of Deadwood, and threads past sights such as Bridal Veil and Roughlock falls. The route reveals almost as many gastronomic pleasures as it does scenic ones. Twenty minutes out of Deadwood, *Latchstring Village* (☎584-3333) treats those who have been exploring the site of the nearby winter camp in *Dances with Wolves* with excellent trout and homemade bread. Marking the southern mouth of the canyon at the junction of hwys 14A and 85, the *Cheyenne Crossing Country Store* (☎584-3510) is a must for those with a hearty appetite; popular menu items include all-day breakfasts with buffalo sausage, enormous Indian tacos and fried bread.

Marking the canyon's north end, **SPEARFISH** itself reels in the crowds for the **Black Hills Passion Play**, held thrice weekly throughout summer. Burgers and inventive specialty snacks provide the reason to drop into the restaurant at *Lown House B&B* on Fifth and Jackson (☎642-5663; ④), which also has good-value rooms (the loft sleeps six comfortably). Other recommended lodgings are the *Canyon Gateway*, right at the mouth of the canyon (☎642-3402 or ☎1-800/281-2402; ③), and for tenters, the well-shaded *City Campground* (☎642-3744; $9), off I-90 exit 12.

From Spearfish, the spectacular **Devils Tower** stands just an hour's drive away across the Wyoming state line (see p.632).

The South Hills

The **southern Black Hills** encompass lower foothills and wooded pastureland; from a purely physical standpoint, they are more attractive than the north, drawing visitors more for scenery and wildlife than kitsch or gambling. The two big mountain carvings, **Mount Rushmore** and **Crazy Horse**, mark the northern end of the region, **Custer State Park** and **Wind Cave National Park** account for much of the central zone, and the pleasant town of **Hot Springs** sits on the southern edge.

Mount Rushmore National Monument

America's two largest stone carvings are a mere seventeen miles apart, spitting distance when you consider the scale on which they're conceived. The better-known **Mount Rushmore National Monument**, 24 miles southwest of Rapid City off US-16A (☎574-2523), originally dubbed The Shrine of Democracy, is the lynchpin of the Hills' tourist circuit. Only New York City's Statue of Liberty rivals it as a globally recognized symbol of American aspirations and ideals. In 1923, state historian Duane Robinson and the sculptor Gutzon Borglum, known for carvings such as the leaders of the Confederacy in Stone Mountain, Georgia (see p.381), talked over the possibility of turning the imposing fingers of granite known as the Needles into dramatic patriotic sculpture. They discussed depictions of such heroic figures of the West as Lewis and Clark, Buffalo Bill Cody and Jim Bridger. Borglum opted for a nearby mountain named after New York attorney Charles E Rushmore, upon which he would fashion the faces and heads of four certifiably great American presidents: **George Washington, Thomas Jefferson, Abraham Lincoln** and Borglum's buddy, **Theodore Roosevelt.**

Borglum talked, dreamed and worked big. "American art ought to be monumental in keeping with American life", he opined. Sixty when the project began in 1927, he died, $200,000 in debt, just a few months prior to its final dedication fourteen years later. His son Lincoln carried on. Inclement weather and uncertain funding had meant that the actual sculpting time was about six and a half years, with a total cost of $989,000. Half a million tons of rock were removed to reach the softer, more malleable granite from which the heads were drilled and chiselled into recognizability. Ninety percent of the carving, however, was done with dynamite.

DRIVING TOURS IN THE SOUTHERN HILLS

Although the entire Black Hills region is classic auto-touring country, four roads in the southern hills stand out. It's possible to drive them all in half a day, though the number of scenic overlooks and sightings of wild animals means it usually takes longer. The first three routes lie within Custer State Park, which charges an $8 per car usage fee.

The seventeen miles of **Iron Mountain Road** (US-16A), starting two miles east of Custer State Park's Game Lodge, run up and over 5500ft Iron Mountain and finish near Mount Rushmore. This engineer's nightmare is a sightseeing motorist's delight, with three pig-tailed bridges and a trio of one-lane tunnels – cleverly designed to frame the Rushmore monument when travelling northward. You may well bump into the park's famous "begging burros" along the way: tame and disarming four-legged panhandlers who stick their snouts through the windows of passing vehicles in search of hand-outs.

The **Needles Highway** (Hwy-87, open mid–April to mid–Oct) winds for fourteen miles through pine forests and past the eponymous jagged granite spires, up to the park's higher elevations, between Sylvan and Legion lakes. A 6400ft summit faces Harney Peak, the state's highest point at 7242 feet. Look out for Needle's Eye, a gap in one of the pinnacles that measures three to four feet wide and fifty to sixty feet long.

The eighteen-mile **Wildlife Loop** wraps around the park's southern edge. Sunrise and sunset are prime times to spy such critters as elk, bighorn sheep, antelope, deer, burros and, the most plentiful, bison.

One final unmissable drive in the southern hills twists through **Wind Cave National Park**. This classic native grass prairie land is home to deer, antelope, elk, coyote, prairie dogs and a 350-head herd of buffalo, a sizeable portion of whom hang out by the scratching posts at the junction of hwys 385 and 87.

The Big Four gaze out impassively, cheek by jowl, arguably a greater engineering feat than an artistic one. Each head is about sixty feet from chin to crown. (The Statue of Liberty's head is only seventeen feet.) Lincoln, Borglum's favorite, has an eighteen-foot-long nose, the glint in each eleven-foot-wide eye is thirty inches, and his mole is sixteen inches in diameter. If he and his fellow presidents had been done full-figure to scale, they'd stand 465ft tall and be able to stride across the Potomac River in Washington DC without getting their knees wet. Rumors about expanding the monument to include other presidents (FDR, Eisenhower, JFK, Reagan) or icons such as John Wayne, Elvis Presley and even Mickey Mouse seem unlikely at best, sacrilegious at worst.

The best time to view Rushmore is dawn or dusk – fewer people, good lighting. By congressional decree, there is no admission charge. The nearest town is the tourist trap **Keystone**, which you would do well to avoid for quieter, and less costly, pastures.

Crazy Horse

In 1939, prompted by the sight of the Rushmore monument nearing completion, Sioux leader Henry Standing Bear wrote to Korczak Ziolkowski, who had just won first prize for sculpture at the New York World's Fair, proclaiming that Indians "would like the white man to know that the red man has great heroes, too". The chief invited him to take on a similar project, and less than a decade later, with just $174 to his name and pushing forty, the Boston-born orphan moved permanently to the Black Hills to undertake a vastly more ambitious scheme than Rushmore – the **Crazy Horse Mountain Memorial**, on US-16, six miles north of Custer (☎673-4681).

The subject, the revered warrior Crazy Horse (see p.585), on horseback, so appealed to Ziolkowski that he set out to make his monument the biggest statue in the world; and the work he began on Thunderhead Mountain in 1948 didn't stop with his death in 1982. His wife and most of their ten children (and doubtless their children's children) continue to realize his vision. Though the monument is still very much in the process of becoming itself, the face is taking a most recognizable form and should be completed by the end of the century; it could well be another fifty years before the icon is entirely finished. The twenty-foot scale model in the courtyard of the visitor center is thirty-four times smaller than the end result, which will be 563ft high and 641ft long. An estimated four thousand people could stand atop Crazy Horse's outstretched arm, while all four Rushmore heads could fit in his head, from which will jut a 44ft stone feather. Nor do the plans stop with the carving: Ziolkowski's descendants hope to build a North American Indian museum, university and medical training center on the land stretching between the current **visitor center** and the monument.

Ziolkowski himself raised and spent $4 million on the project. His belief in free enterprise means that Crazy Horse has received no federal or state funds, instead relying entirely on admissions and contributions. He twice turned down $10 million in federal funds, claiming the government had no right to be involved after all the treaties it had broken with the Sioux. The site, open dawn to dusk year-round, is free to Indians. Non-Indians over six pay $5 each; car-loads are let in for $12. It's a bargain. Apart from the monument, the premises contain a big barn full of Indian artefacts and crafts, several rooms devoted to Ziolkowski's life and work, a good café and an extensive gift shop. Coffee and souvenir stones are free. On the first weekend in June, the public is invited to walk to the top of the mountain and see the work close-up.

Custer State Park

The 73,000 billboard-free and sublimely scenic acres of **CUSTER STATE PARK** fill much of the southern central Black Hills, a perfect antidote to the commercial crassness of much of the rest of the region. Custer's main driving tours alone (see p.593) can take up the best part of a day, though to appreciate its beauty it's best to forsake the car and

---

THE BISON OF THE GREAT PLAINS

In the fifteenth century, the Great Plains were roamed by one hundred million shaggy, short-sighted **American bison** (popularly known as buffalo, a corruption of the French *boeuf*). Apart from eating their flesh, Native Americans used the fur and hide for clothing and shelter, the bones for weapons, utensils and toys, and the droppings for fuel. Eliminating the bison en masse was a mercilessly effective way to deplete the Indians as well. By 1900 there were fewer than a hundred bison left in the entire country.

Custer State Park was instrumental in helping to raise that meager number to today's national head count of 120,000. Its 1500 bison constitute the country's second largest publicly owned herd, beaten only by Yellowstone Park. However, over ninety percent of bison in the US are now privately owned – the meat, said to be higher in protein and lower in cholesterol than either chicken or tuna, is becoming something of a cross between a novelty and a delicacy item in restaurants (you can try it in burger form at the *Custer State Park Game Lodge*). The *Triple U Ranch*, outside Pierre, South Dakota, boasts the largest single herd, 3500 strong, though Jane Fonda and Ted Turner own around 4000, split between their ranches in Montana and New Mexico.

The Custer State Park bison are free to roam where they please until either the last Monday of September or the first Monday in October, when the park stages its annual **round-up**. From selected viewing points, the public is welcome to witness one of the Midwest's more thrilling occasions. Modern technology has invaded cowboy territory. Helicopters, jeeps and pick-up trucks, as well as riders on horseback, steer the often recalcitrant herd down a six-mile "corridor" and into a series of pens. There the calves are branded and vaccinated, and the whole herd sorted to determine which five hundred will be auctioned off on the third Saturday in November. Proceeds from the sale account for twenty percent of the park's annual revenue.

Don't let the tranquil, easy-going appearance of North America's biggest mammal lull you into a false sense of security. An average bull can stand six feet high at the hump, weigh up to a ton, outrun a horse, turn on a dime and gore a human most efficiently.

explore some of the wilderness. Pleasant hiking and biking trails criss-cross the park, and concession firms offer horseback rides, boat rental and cross-country drives in open-topped jeeps. For further information, drop into the Peter Norbruck **visitor center** (☎255-4464) on Hwy-16A. Park entrance fees run at $3 per person or $8 per vehicle; the pass lasts for five days and gets you into all other state parks.

As long as nightlife isn't high on your agenda, the park is a splendid **place to stay**. Tucked in the northwest corner on its own artificial lake, *Sylvan Lake Resort* (☎574-2561; ④) is open year-round. Its 31 comfy cabins are spread beneath the pines, while the tasteful main building holds more traditional rooms; you can eat at the *Lakota Dining Room*. Reservations at the park's other three resorts can be made on ☎1-800/658-3530. The best-known is the *State Game Lodge* (④) on Hwy-16A; President Coolidge planned to stay for a week when he arrived in 1927, but found it so much to his liking that he trailed his aides over from DC and ran the country from the lodge for the entire summer. His room is still available for rent. Custer State Park also has ten **campgrounds** (☎255-4000), costing $10 a night plus park entrance fees.

Custer

In little **CUSTER**, five miles west of the park on US-16, the *Bavarian Inn* on the main highway has classic German dining and rooms (☎673-2802; ③); the *Bunkhouse Hostel*, 120 Mt Rushmore Rd (☎673-3029; ①), charges $10 for a bunk, with free cookouts and a volleyball court. Of many garish campgrounds, *Flintstones Bedrock City* (☎673-4079 or 1-800/992-9818), with its own small theme park, manages to steal the show. The **visitor center** is at 447 Crook St (☎673-2244 or ☎1-800/992-9818); look out for the bargain daily **happy hour** (times vary) at the down-to-earth *AJ's Saloon* on the main drag.

Wind Cave National Park

Beneath wide-open rangelands, **WIND CAVE NATIONAL PARK**, ten minutes north of Hot Springs, comprises over 65 miles of mapped underground passages etched out of limestone. One of the largest caves in the US, it was discovered in 1881 when a loud whistling noise on the plains led a settler to a hole in the ground – the cave's only natural opening. The wind, caused by differences between atmospheric pressures in the cave and outside, was apparently enough to blow the discoverer's hat off. Nowadays rangers lead **tours** ($5) from the **visitor center** (daily, June–Sept 8am–7pm, Oct–May 8am–5pm; ☎745-4600) into the cave, pointing out delicate features such as frosting and boxwork along the way. If you come in summer, forget the standard walking tours and opt for the ones which allow you to crawl around and explore the caves by candlelight.

Hot Springs

The Black Hills' southern anchor, **HOT SPRINGS**, differs from other regional towns in that it hasn't tarted up its downtown to look like some movie set. It doesn't need to. Several dozen utilitarian yet handsome sandstone structures dominate its center, through which flows the sprightly Fall River.

Battles over the town's thermal pools have caused as much grief as the clamor for gold. Before white settlement, the Sioux drove out the Cheyenne, and later landowners, speculators and settlers dodged and outwitted each other for ownership of the springs. The disputes ceased in 1890 when Fred Evans incorporated numerous small springs and one mammoth hot water pool into a spa center. Today, **Evans Plunge**, on the north edge of town, is a popular family-fun center, where three great slides zoom down into the 87° waters (daily; summer 6am–10pm, otherwise times vary; $7).

The unique **Mammoth Site** on Hwy-18 By-Pass is the only in-situ display of mammoth fossils in the US. Building on a housing project in 1974 came to an abrupt halt when a tractor driver unearthed a seven-foot tusk. Paleontologists from the University of Nebraska soon declared that the workers had discovered the 26,000-year-old grave of at least forty Columbian and Woolly mammoths. Instead of removing the bones and displaying them in some distant museum, it was decided to construct a huge hangar-like building over the site. Fascinating tours explain how these ten-ton mammoths, along with camels, bears and rodents, were trapped in a steep-sided sinkhole (a pond formed by a collapsed underground cave) and were gradually covered by sediment. Complete skeletons and tiny bones like the delicate hyoid (a tongue bone) are easy to pick out in the excavation site, which is still being uncovered slowly by groups of summer volunteers. The museum holds interpretive displays, a fiberglass model, and an excellent book and gift shop (daily, mid-May to Aug 8am–8pm; otherwise times vary; $4).

Seven miles south of Hot Springs, the huge reservoir of the **Angostura Dam State Recreation Area** ($3 per person), set against contorted sandstone bluffs, is a picture-perfect spot for boating and jet skiing. Equipment can be rented from *Breakers Beach Club*, a small hut offering beer, snacks and beach volleyball, at the north entrance.

Information for visitors to Hot Springs is available from the cabin on N River St or from the CVB, 801 S Sixth St (☎745-4140 or ☎1-800/325-6991). Accommodation rates are a bit more reasonable than in the hectic northern towns. Its *Super 8 Motel*, Hwy-18 By-Pass (☎745-3888; ③), is unusual in having a bar and restaurant, both of which are recommended; alternatives include the old, faded, riverside *Braun Hotel*, 902 N River St (☎745-3187; ②), and the sumptuous *Villa Teresa B&B*, 801 Almond St (☎745-4633; ④). *Yogi's Den*, 625 N River St (☎745-5959), a lively lounge, serves up good burgers.

NORTH DAKOTA

NORTH DAKOTA has no instantly recognizable national landmarks, nor is the state's history particularly lurid or glamorous. It seems like somebody's quiet afterthought, a place to pass through. Grain silos loom on the horizon, the haystacks resemble bread-loaves. In the summer, with the sun baking in a defiantly blue sky and the wind raking strong fingers through tall fields of golden wheat and flax, North Dakota epitomizes all things rural American. Charming, picturesque – and a bit maddening.

The influx of Europeans into the Dakota Territory, spurred by the Homestead Act of 1862, precipitated a population and agricultural boom that lasted into this century. As in South Dakota, the fertile east is more thickly settled than the west, where vast cattle and sheep ranges predominate. From **Fargo**, the state's largest city, I-94 passes through the central capital of **Bismarck**, and on to the **Bad Lands** of the west, once cherished by President Theodore Roosevelt. Though the national park bearing his name is a key destination, Roosevelt would surely not be pleased about the continuing disfiguration of much of western North Dakota by strip mining operations.

Getting Around North Dakota
Amtrak runs one train per day in each direction between Fargo and Williston in the northwest, via Grand Forks. **Greyhound** is the major interstate bus operator; two buses per day make the ten-hour-trip from Minneapolis/St Paul to Bismarck via Grand Forks and Fargo, before heading west along I-94 into Montana. A number of local companies run a patchwork service to smaller towns off the main interstate route.

East of the Missouri

North Dakota has far more land east of the big winding **Missouri River**, its uneven dividing line, than west. The **Red River Valley**, the state's furthest eastern strip, has some of the nation's richest soil and two sizeable cities, easy-going **Grand Forks** and the less attractive **Fargo**.

Pelicans, geese, swans, prairie chickens and ring-necked pheasants live off the sloughs and potholes of the rolling, glaciated prairie of south-central North Dakota, while lakes and woodland dominate the north and the Canadian border. **Fort Totten Indian Reservation** at Devils Lake is midway between Grand Forks and the low-slung Turtle Mountains, which are topped by Lake Metigoshe and the **International Peace Garden** (more of a political symbol than a compelling sight).

Grand Forks

GRAND FORKS sits eighty miles north of I-94, right next to Minnesota and just 75 miles south of the Canadian border. Even before its foundation a century ago, fur traders had used the area to rest and barter during their travels between Winnipeg and Minneapolis. It's a small, friendly, outdoorsy city, with nineteen parks and several tree-lined avenues of fine homes. The compact downtown sports a handful of idiosyncratic bars and cafés that spill over the bridge into East Grand Forks, Minnesota.

The most interesting distractions can be found on the red-brick main campus of the **University of North Dakota**. The **North Dakota Museum of Art** (Mon, Wed & Fri 9am–5pm, Thurs 9am–9pm, Sat & Sun 1–5pm; reduced outside termtime) offers an eclectic assortment of contemporary art and top touring exhibits. Fascinating tours of the **Center for Aerospace Science**, one of the largest civilian pilot-training schools in the world, take in the state-of-the-art Atmospherium (☎777-2791; by appointment).

Practicalities

The **visitor center** is housed in a converted railway depot at 202 N Third St (☎746-0444 or ☎1-800/866-4566). *Greyhound* is a bit out of the way at 1325 Demers Ave (☎775-4781); *Amtrak* more so at no 5555. *Triangle Transportation* (☎218/773-2631) runs buses into Minnesota out of East Grand Forks from 1611 Central Ave NW.

Downtown's *Best Western Town House*, 710 First Ave N (☎746-5411; ④), is Grand Fork's most luxurious **motel**; for about $10 less you can stay in the kitsch splendor of the *Best Western Fabulous Westward Ho* on Hwy-2 (☎775-5341; ④), and swim in its cowboy boot-shaped pool, while nearby there's a budget *Super 8*, 1122 N 43rd St (☎775-8138; ②). *Lord Byron's*, 521 S Fifth St (☎775-0194; ④), is one of a number of comfy Victorian **B&Bs**. The most serene place to **camp** lies 22 miles west on Hwy-2 in the grounds of Turtle River State Park (reservations; ☎594-4445).

Sanders 1907, 312 Kittson Ave (☎746-8970), is a handsome hole-in-the-wall **restaurant** with an eclectic European menu. *The Windmill*, 213 S Third St (☎775-7641), serves steaks, seafood and burgers on its riverside patio, while just a few minutes' walk over the bridge in east Grand Forks is the convivial Art Deco *Whitey's Bar & Café*, 109 de Mers Ave East. The lurid *Red Pepper*, on the edge of town at 1011 University Ave (☎775-9671), dishes up low-price chili, subs and baked potatoes until 1.30am.

Devils Lake

The town of **DEVILS LAKE**, ninety miles west of Grand Forks on Hwy-2, shares its name with the state's largest natural body of water, which has four state parks and five private campgrounds on its 300 sprawling and irregular miles of shoreline. Downtown holds a smattering of nineteenth-century buildings and a few rough-and- ready bars. Most of the **places to stay**, such as the *Artclare Motel* (☎662-4001; ②), are strung along Hwy-2; more expensive resort accommodation can be found on the west side of Creel Bay, about eight miles from town, where you can also rent boats and pontoons.

The **area code** for the entire state of North Dakota is ☎701.

Fort Totten Indian Reservation, fourteen miles south and site of one of the best preserved frontier military posts (mid-May to mid-Sept daily 8am–5pm), hosts the thrilling **Fort Totten Days Powwow and Rodeo** during the last weekend of each July (daily admission $3, $5 for all three days). It's an impassioned, alcohol-free, multitribal party in which hundreds of magnificently clothed dancers of all ages compete for cash prizes.

The West

Anyone with a hankering to play cowboy could do worse than follow in the footsteps of **Theodore Roosevelt,** who declared "I never would have been President if it had not been for my experiences in North Dakota." Roosevelt initially came to the state in search of spiritual and physical renewal after the deaths (on the same day) of his mother and first wife. He dubbed what he discovered during his few years in this "grimly picturesque" area, with its clear skies, panoramic views and weird, colorful land forms, a "perfect freedom". The National Park named after him is the choicest destination in the **North Dakota Bad Lands** (distinct from South Dakota's Badlands) that dominate the state's western half.

The **Missouri River** wriggles like a giant raggedy worm out of Montana, down past the capital, **Bismarck,** and into South Dakota. En route it is transformed into Lake Sakakawea, a virtual inland sea nearly two hundred miles long that's the state's premier water playground. Scenic state hwys **1804** and **1806** follow the routes mapped out by the Lewis and Clark expedition in those respective years.

Bismarck and Mandan

The West seems to begin as soon as you cross the Missouri River from **BISMARCK,** a capital city with a small-town feel, to **Mandan.** Both were founded in 1872, Bismarck as a military camp to protect railroad crews from hostile Indians and outlaws. Its original name, Edwinton, was changed by the secretary of the Northern Pacific Railroad, both in honor of German Chancellor Otto von Bismarck and in the hope of attracting Teutonic settlers. Though the scheme failed, the name stuck. The city survived an early lawless period (present-day Fourth Street was once dubbed "Murderers' Gulch") and a major fire to become first the territorial and then the state capital.

Contemporary Bismarck is pretty much contained within the oblong between I-94 in the north and Main Street to the south. Locals are proud of their nineteen-storey limestone **Capitol,** 600 E Blvd, dating from the mid-1930s and set at the crest of a public park. The interior, a model of spatial economy and marbled Art Deco elegance, is open for free guided tours weekdays, year-round. Across the street, the superb **North Dakota Heritage Center** (Mon–Thurs 8am–5pm, Fri 8am–8pm, Sat 9am–5pm, Sun 11am–5pm; free) divides the state's past into six resonant sections, from the dinosaurs onwards. Look out for Sitting Bull's painted robe and the bison "smell box".

The major reason to venture into **MANDAN** is **Fort Lincoln State Park,** five miles south of downtown via Hwy-1806, where the centerpiece is the **Custer House** (May–Sept 9.30am–8.30pm; $3), an admirable reconstruction of the 1874 original designed by the brutally ambitious, indefatigable horseman himself. The guided tour supplies nuggets of quirky information about him (he loved to eat raw onions), his devoted wife Libbie (who wore wigs of his curly blond hair to fancy dress balls), and their household prior to his death at Little Bighorn in 1876. Nearer the river, five earthlodge reconstructions stand on the site of the once-vast On-a-Slant village, occupied by the Mandan (or River Dweller) tribe from about 1610 to the early 1800s. The Mandan were particularly helpful to the Lewis and Clark expedition and this village is said to be where the soldiers met the teenage girl **Sakajawea** who helped guide them through the Shoshone lands and onto the Pacific. The site and adjacent historical museum are somewhat run-down, but be sure to make it up to the bluff above the village, for fine views of the Missouri. If you don't have a car you can reach the park via **trolley** from Mandan's Third Street Station (☎663-9018; $5 round trip), or by the **Lewis and Clark Riverboat** from Riverboat Junction, I-94 Exit 157 (daily, summer only; ☎224-0455; $12).

Practicalities

Bismarck's *Greyhound* terminal (☎223-6576) is at 1237 W Divide St, off I-94, exit 35; its **visitor center** is at 523 N Fourth St (Mon–Fri 8am–5pm; ☎222-4308). For clean, though small, downtown doubles, try the *Fleck House*, 122 E Thayer Ave (☎255-1450; ②). Great rooms, a pool and free breakfast are on offer at the *Fairfield Inn*, 135 Ivy Ave (☎223-9293; ②), while Mandan's *Days Inn*, I-94, exit 31 (☎663-0001; ③), is also reasonable. For **camping** off the beaten track, try the excellent Cross Ranch State Park (vehicle fee $2, campsites $5–8; ☎794-3731), thirty minutes' north of Bismarck on route 112A. Overlapped by a six-thousand-acre Nature Preserve, the park features sixteen miles of trails. Alternatively you can camp at Fort Lincoln State Park (☎663-9571).

Dining and **nightlife** are plentiful in Bismarck. *Peacock Alley*, Fifth and Main (☎255-7917), in a downtown hotel that was once the headquarters of the progressive Non-Partisan League, serves Cajun, Italian and American cuisine, with lunch specials in the classy adjoining bar. *Fiesta Villa* (☎222-8075), across the street in a converted railway depot, features a patio, live music and an extensive Mexican menu. *The Drumstick*, 307 N Third St (☎223-8444; closed Sun), is a classic low-cost diner rightly proud of its home cooking and 24-hour breakfasts. In Mandan, the *Drug Store and Soda Fountain*, 316 W Main St (☎663-5900), is a good place to grab a cheap lunch and an ice cream.

Theodore Roosevelt National Park

The **THEODORE ROOSEVELT NATIONAL PARK**, a huge tract of multihued rock formations, rough grassland and lazy streams, is split into north and south units approximately seventy miles apart, the area between comprising a checkerboard of federal, state and privately owned territory. Exploring the park's 110 acres is like entering different rooms: from desert to woods to mountains. Each of the two units is at its subtlest at sunrise or sundown, the best times to observe such fauna as elk, antelope, bison and several fascinating, closely knit prairie dog communities (both open daylight hours May–Oct; vehicles $3, pedestrians $1).

Your first taste of the larger, more popular southern unit is likely to be at the breathtaking **Painted Canyon**, seven miles east of the town of **Medora** off I-94, exit 8. Here and elsewhere in the park, the land is like a sedimentary layer cake that for millions of years has been beaten by hard, infrequent rains, baked by the sun into a kaleidoscope of colors and cut through to the base by erosive streams and rivers. A mile-long nature hike begins at the end of the canyon's boardwalk.

The southern unit's main **visitor center** in Medora (June–Aug 8am–8pm; otherwise 8am–4.30pm; ☎623-4466) runs tours, nature walks and campfire programmes in high season. Out back, the simple cabin was used by the young Roosevelt while a partner in the Maltese Cross Ranch (free guided tours daily until 4.15pm). A highlight of the scenic 36-mile loop road is the sublime view from **Wind Canyon**, ten miles out of Medora. Peaceful Valley Ranch (☎623-4496), six miles from Medora and a mile from the park's Cottonwood Campground ($8 fee), arranges **horseback tours** in summer.

The northern unit, off Hwy-85 near **Watford City**, receives only a tenth as many visitors and is on the whole less spectacular, though its fifteen-mile scenic drive ends at **Oxbow Overlook**, a magnificent cul de sac. Its **visitor center** is open daily between May and September (9am–5pm), and on weekends and limited holidays the remainder of the year. Squaw Creek Campground ($8) operates on a first-come, first-served basis.

Medora

MEDORA, the southern gateway to Theodore Roosevelt National Park, languished in obscurity until the early Sixties, but has become one of North Dakota's principal attractions, an inoffensively touristy place with enough to keep you busy, and reasonably interested, for a day. The biggest noise in town is the **Medora Musical** (Mon–Fri 7.30pm, Sat & Sun 7pm; $10–12), a pseudo-western, super-Americana variety show staged beneath the stars in a vast, modern amphitheater. If a man balancing on a board balanced on a bowling ball to a cover version of the *Hawaii Five-O* theme is your idea of a great time, book on ☎623-4433.

Greyhound **buses** ply the Bismarck–Medora route twice daily, stopping at the *Dietz Motel*, 401 Broadway (☎623-4455). The Medora Foundation (☎623-4422, or ☎223-4800 in off-season) has a monopoly on **accommodation**, operating the *Rough Riders Hotel* (③), which has a reliable dining room, and the seasonal *Medora* (③) and *Badlands* (②) motels, both of which have outdoor pools. The *Medora Campground* (☎623-4435) caters for both tents and RVs.

CHAPTER ELEVEN

THE ROCKIES

E xploring the Rocky Mountain states of **COLORADO**, **WYOMING**, **MONTANA** and **IDAHO** could literally take forever. Stretching over one thousand miles from the virgin forests on the Canadian border to the desert of New Mexico, America's rugged spine encompasses an astonishing array of **landscapes** – geyser basins, lava flows, arid valleys and huge sand dunes – each in its own way as dramatic as the magnificent white-topped peaks. The geological grandeur is enhanced by **wildlife** such as bison, bears, moose and elk, and the conspicuous legacy of the miners, cowboys, outlaws and Native Americans who fought over the area's rich resources during the nineteenth century.

Apart from the **Anasazi** cliff-dwellers, who lived in southern Colorado until around 1300 AD, most **Native Americans** in this region were nomadic hunters. They inhabited the eastern extremities of the Great Plains, the richest buffalo-grazing land in the continent. Spaniards, groping through Colorado in the sixteenth century in search of gold, were the first whites to venture into the Rockies. But only after the territory was sold to the US in 1803 as part of the **Louisiana Purchase** was it thoroughly charted, starting with the **Lewis and Clark** expedition which traversed Montana and Idaho in 1805. As a result of their reports of copious quantities of game, the fabled "**mountainmen**" had soon trapped the beavers to the point of virtual extinction. They left as soon as the pelt boom was over, however, and permanent white settlement did not begin until gold was discovered at Denver in 1858. Within a decade, speculators were plundering every accessible gorge and creek in the four states in the search for valuable ores. When the construction of transcontinental rail lines and the establishment of vast cattle ranches to feed the mining camps dictated the slaughter of millions of buffalo, conflict with the Indians became inevitable. The **Sioux** and **Cheyenne**, led by brilliant strategists such as Sitting Bull and Crazy Horse, inflicted decisive victories over the US Army, most notably at Little Bighorn – "**Custer's Last Stand**". However, a massive military operation cleared the region of all warring Indians by the late 1870s.

Most of those who replaced the Indians saw the Rockies strictly in terms of profit: they came, took what they wanted and left. Most of the small communities in this isolated terrain remain exclusively dedicated to coal, oil or some other single commodity. All too often the uncertain tightrope walk between boom and bust is evident in their run-down facades.

Each of the four states has its own distinct character. **Colorado**, with fifty peaks over 14,000 feet, is the most mountainous and the most highly populated – friendly,

---

ACCOMMODATION PRICE CODES

All accommodation prices in this book have been coded using the symbols below. Note that prices are for the least expensive double rooms in each establishment. For a full explanation see p.35 in *Basics*.

①	up to $30	④	$60–80	⑦	$130–180
②	$30–45	⑤	$80–100	⑧	$180+
③	$45–60	⑥	$100–130		

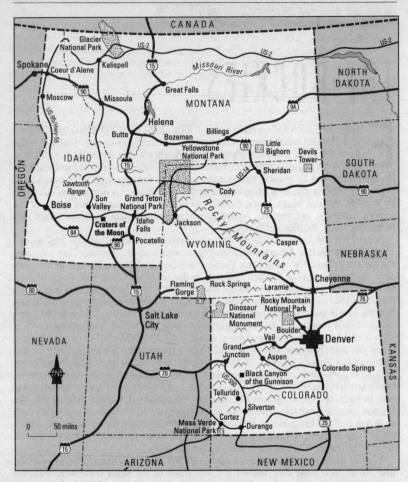

sophisticated **Denver** is the only major metropolis in the Rockies. It's also the most visited, in part because it's that much more accessible, but the numbers remain low enough not to detract from its role as a summer paradise for cyclists and whitewater enthusiasts, and home to the best ski resorts in the country. Less touched by the tourist circus is vast, brawny **Montana**, where the "Big Sky" looks down on a glorious verdant manuscript scribbled over with gushing streams, lakes and tiny communities.

Away from gurgling, spitting **Yellowstone**, adjacent **Grand Teton** park and the nearby Bighorn Mountains, vast stretches of scrubland fill **Wyoming**, the country's least populated state. Rugged, remote and desolate **Idaho** holds some of the Rocky Mountain's last unexplored wildernesses, most notably the mighty Sawtooth range.

You can usually reckon on temperatures in the high sixties Fahrenheit between early June and early September, though in the mountains you have to be prepared for wild local variations – and, of course, the higher you go the colder it gets. The altitude is high enough to warrant a period of acclimatization, while the intensity of the sun at these elevations can be uncomfortably fierce. Spring (the "mud season"), when the snow melts, is the least attractive time to visit the Rockies, and while the delicate golds of quaking aspen trees light up the mountainsides in fall, things are generally a bit cold for enjoyable hiking or sports. Most **ski** runs are open by late November and operate well into March. The coldest month is January, when temperatures of -50° F are common.

Attempting to rush around every national park and major town is a sure way to miss out on one of the Rockies' real delights – coaxing a car along the tight switchback roads that wind up and over precipitous mountain passes. At some point it's worth forsaking motorized transport, to see at least some of the area by **bike**; the Rockies contain some of the most rewarding and challenging cycling terrain on the continent.

COLORADO

COLORADO is one of the least homogenous of the United States, ranging from the flat and endless plains of the east to the colossal mountains of the west. In the north, **Native Americans** hunted and trapped in lush mountain valleys in summer, and returned to the prairies for the winter; in the south, the Anasazi of Mesa Verde grew corn on their isolated mesas and shared in the great early civilization of the southwest.

Different parts of what's now Colorado accrued to the US at different times; the east and north were acquired under the **Louisiana Purchase** in 1803, while the south was won forty years later in the war with **Mexico**. (Mexican land grants were honored by the Americans, which accounts for a still-strong Hispanic influence.) Gold-hungry Spaniards came through in the sixteenth century, and Colonel Zebulon Pike ventured into the mountains in 1806, but the Native American way of life only became seriously threatened with the discovery of **gold** west of Denver in 1858. (At that time Colorado was still part of Kansas Territory; it became a territory in its own right in 1861, and a state in 1876.) The distractions of the Civil War gave the Indians the opportunity to fight back, but they were soon overwhelmed. From then until the end of the century, Colorado boomed; the quantities of gold and silver extracted from the mountains do not really compare with the riches found in California, but they were sufficient to fuel a rip-roaring frontier lifestyle. At first, too, absentee landlords attempted to exploit massive **ranches** on the plains, but their complete disregard for conservation ensured that the droughts and storms of 1886 and 1887 swept away the topsoil.

For the modern visitor, the obvious first port of call is **Denver**, at the eastern edge of the Rockies and much the biggest city for 600 miles. Nearby to the north are the go-ahead college town of **Boulder** and the spectacular **Rocky Mountain National Park**. The majority of the resorts which have made Colorado the continent's foremost **skiing** destination snuggle into **central** Colorado: **Summit County** attracts the most visitors, **Vail** is considered best for terrain, **Aspen** boasts the glitziest après-ski scene, and **Crested Butte** is the most relaxing. To the **southwest**, untouched old mining towns can be explored along the **San Juan Skyway**, while **Mesa Verde National Park** preserves perhaps the most impressive of all the cliff cities left by the ancient Anasazi.

Getting Around Colorado

Much the biggest **airport** in Colorado is in Denver. Shuttle buses radiate from there to all the main towns and ski resorts – as do commuter-style aircraft. Denver is also a major hub for *Greyhound* **buses** to all neighboring states. *Amtrak* **trains** run straight across the middle of Colorado, timed in both directions to pass through magnificent Glenwood Canyon in hours of daylight, but little more useful in terms of getting from A to B than the hugely enjoyable *Durango & Silverton Narrow Gauge Railroad* in the southwest.

Colorado is also one of the best destinations in the world for **cyclists**, hosting numerous championships. The State Department of Highways (4201 E Arkansas Ave, Denver, CO 80222) produces excellent maps and guides to cycle routes in the state.

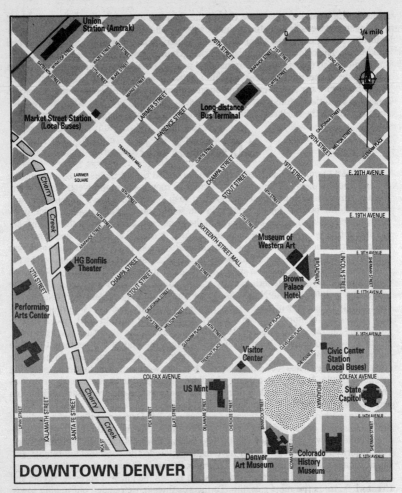

DOWNTOWN DENVER

Denver

Its skyscrapers marking the final transition between the Great Plains and the American West, **DENVER** stands at the threshold of the **Rocky Mountains**. Despite being known as the "**Mile High City**", and serving as the obvious point of arrival for travellers heading into the mountains, it is itself uniformly flat. The majestic peaks are clearly visible, but they only begin to rise roughly fifteen miles west of downtown, and Denver has, during the last century, had plenty of room to spread itself out.

Mineral wealth has always been at the heart of the city's prosperity, with all the fluctuations of fortune that entails. Though local resources have been progressively exhausted, Denver has managed to hang on to its role as the most important commercial and transportation nexus in the state. Its original "foundation" in 1858 was pure chance; this was the exact spot where small quantities of **gold** were first discovered in

Colorado. There was no significant river, let alone a road, but prospectors came streaming in, regardless of prior claims to the land – least of all those of the **Arapahoe Indians**, who had supposedly been confirmed in their ownership of the area by the Fort Laramie Treaty of 1851. Various communities had their own names for the city; with the judicious distribution of whiskey, one faction persuaded the rest to agree to "Denver" in 1859. The hope was to ingratiate themselves with the governor of the Kansas Territory, James Denver; but as it turned out, he had already resigned. The newspaperman Horace Greeley passed through in the early days, and described the place as a "log city of 150 dwellings, not three-fourths completed nor two-thirds inhabited, nor one-third fit to be".

There was actually very little gold in Denver itself; the infant town swarmed briefly with disgruntled fortune-seekers, who de-camped when news came in of the massive gold strike at Central City. Denver survived, however, prospering further with the discovery of **silver** in the mountains. All sorts of shady characters made this their home; "Soapy" Smith for example (see p.895) acquired his nickname here, selling bars of soap at extortionate prices under the pretence that some contained $100 bills. When the first railroads bypassed Denver – the death knell for so many other communities – the citizens simply banded together and built their own connecting spur.

These days, Denver is a welcoming and enjoyable city to visit. Tourism is based on getting out into the wide open spaces rather than on sightseeing in town, but somehow its isolation, a good six hundred miles from any conurbation of even vaguely similar size, gives its two-million population a refreshing friendliness; and in a city which is used to providing its own entertainment there always seems to be something going on. Denver may perhaps be less the loose-living city Kerouac wrote about in *On The Road*, and more the Eighties oil-boom metropolis familiar from *Dynasty*, but as its recent acquisition of a major-league baseball team confirms, it's still a place where things happen.

Arrival, Information and Getting Around

In March 1994, Stapleton International Airport closed down completely, and the enormous new **Denver International Airport** opened, 24 miles northeast of downtown, out on the plains beyond Stapleton. This ultra-high-tech facility, which appears to be roofed with a series of fiberglass tents and commands a broad view of the Rockies, is claimed to have the most sophisticated and efficient baggage-handling system in the world.

Direct **bus services** to other parts to Colorado, operating throughout the year, include *Charles Limousine*, to **Estes Park** (up to 6 daily; $24; ☎1-800/950-3274 or 586-5151); *Airport Express*, to **Fort Collins** ($14; ☎599-0505), and **Cheyenne** and **Laramie** in Wyoming ($26 & $31; ☎482-0505); *Resort Express*, to Silverthorne and Breckenridge in **Summit County** ($38; ☎1-800/334-7433 or 468-7600); and, logically enough, *Vans to Vail* run to **Vail** ($44; ☎1-800/222-2112 or 476-4467).

Amtrak **trains** arrive on the northwest side of downtown Denver at the old **Union Station** on Wynkoop Street, and the *Greyhound* **bus terminal** is every bit as close to the action at 1055 19th St (☎292-6111). *Discover Colorado Tours* runs **tours** of the city, as well as Rocky Mountain National Park and the surrounding area (☎277-0129).

The best place to pick up **information** about the city is the **Denver Metro CVB**, near the Capitol at 225 W Colfax Ave (summer Mon–Fri 8am–6pm, Sat 9am–5pm, Sun noon–4pm; otherwise Mon–Fri 8am–5pm, Sat 9am–1pm; ☎892-1112), though there's also an informal morning-only advice center for travellers arriving at the *Greyhound* terminal. The main downtown **post office** is at 1823 Stout St (Mon–Fri 8am–5pm; zip code 80201); a 24-hour postal service is available at the Terminal Annex, 1595 Wynkoop St (☎297-6325).

The **area code** for Denver and northern Colorado is ☎303.

City Transit

Downtown Denver is fairly easily negotiated on foot, with the occasional help of the very regular **free buses** running for a mile up and down the 16th Street pedestrian mall at its heart. *RTD* local **buses** (☎299-6000), with frequent services to Boulder and Golden, and to the airport, radiate from the underground **Market Street Station** at Market and 16th. The two main areas outside the city center that you might wish to visit are **City Park**, on the airport bus route, and **Cherry Creek** mall, which is served by buses #1, #2 and #3 (every half-hour during the day, then hourly until 11pm).

The City

Though oil money brought a hectic spate of high-rise construction in the early Eighties, creating the "17th Street canyon", **downtown Denver** remains recognizable as the gold-rush town of the 1860s. It's very easy to pick out the oldest sections on a map; though an endless regimental grid stretches for miles in all directions, at its very heart one small area of tightly packed streets stands at a sharp angle to the rest. Much of the day-to-day activity of Denver takes place along **16th Street** here, which but for its free buses is a pedestrian zone; however, the shops are not especially stimulating, and it holds nothing of any great historical interest.

For a quick appreciation of Denver's geographical position, head for the **State Capitol**. The thirteenth of the steps up to its entrance is exactly one mile above sea level; turn back and look west, and you get a commanding view – zealously protected by building regulations – of the Rockies swelling on the horizon. The Capitol is a rather predictable copy of the one in Washington DC, but the free tours (Mon–Fri 9am–3.30pm, Sat 10am–1pm) are pleasantly informal, and you can climb its dome for an even better view. The world's entire supply of red onyx was used to make its wainscoting.

Civic Center Park, right in front of the Capitol, contains two of Denver's finest museums. The **Art Museum** at 100 W 14th Ave (covered in grey glass tiles) has paintings from around the world, but it's most noteworthy for its superb examples of Native American craftwork, with marvellous pieces by the Plains Indians and the Hopi. Some of the pre-Columbian art from central America – particularly the extraordinary Olmec miniatures – is also spectacular (Tues–Sat 10am–5pm, Sun noon–5pm; $3, free Sat).

The most interesting features of the **Colorado History Museum** at 1300 Broadway are to be found in the downstairs galleries. Several dioramas, made under the auspices of the WPA in the Thirties, show historical scenes in fascinating detail, starting with the Anasazi of Mesa Verde, and following up with trappers meeting with Indians at a "fair in the wilderness" in the early 1800s, and a model of Denver in 1860. An exhaustive archive of **photographs** of the early West showcases the work of W H Jackson, who died at the age of 99 in 1942 (Mon–Sat 10am–4.30pm, Sun noon–4.30pm; $3.50).

Free tours of the **US Mint** on Cherokee Street to the east reveal millions of fresh coins gushing from the presses in a flurry of flashing metal; greedy daydreams are held in check once you notice the machine-gun turrets on the exterior, mounted at the height of the Depression (May–Aug Mon–Fri 8am–3pm; Sept–April Mon–Fri 8.30am–3pm).

It was in the **Larimer Square** district, now between 14th and 16th streets, not far from Union Station, that William Larimer put up Denver's original log cabin. That burned down in a general conflagration within a few years, whereupon a city ordinance decreed that all new construction should use brick. Restored to its late Victorian appearance, Larimer Square provides a small-scale focus for shops, bars and restaurants.

Many of the paintings at the **Museum of Western Art** at 1727 Tremont Place have more historic than artistic significance, though stimulating works by Georgia O'Keeffe hang alongside the usual pieces by Frederick Remington et al (Tues–Sat 10am–4.30pm; $3). The building itself was once Denver's leading brothel, discreetly connected by an underground passage to the grand triangular *Brown Palace Hotel* across the road.

The city's black community is most prominent in the old **Five Points** district, northwest of downtown, where the **Black American West Museum** at 3901 California St provides ample evidence of an enduring black presence. Perhaps one third of all cowboys are thought to have been black, many of them slaves freed by the Civil War who left the South and found work as cattle hands (Wed–Fri 10am–2pm, Sat 10am–5pm, Sun 2–5pm; $2.50).

Two or three miles east of downtown en route to the airport, the enormous **City Park** is home to the **Denver Museum of Natural History**, 2001 Colorado Blvd (daily 9am–5pm; $5). As with many such museums, its brief extends beyond the (very good) dinosaur exhibits and wildlife displays to include anthropological material on Native Americans, which, though fascinating, does seem rather out of place. There's also a large **zoo** nearby (daily summer 10am–6pm; winter 10am–5pm; $5).

Denver's most popular shopping center these days is the newly renovated and very glitzy **Cherry Creek Mall**, a few miles southeast of downtown. Opposite its main entrance is one of the best **bookstores** in the US, the *Tattered Cover Bookstore* at 2955 E First Ave (☎322-7727), which spreads over four extremely well-stocked floors.

Finally, twenty miles west of downtown, high above the *Coors*-brewery town of Golden, **Buffalo Bill's Grave and Museum** on Lookout Mountain is the final resting place of William Cody, famed frontiersman, buffalo-hunter, army scout and showman who died in Denver in 1915 (see also p.635). Though now surrounded by huge electricity pylons, the gravesite offers great views in both directions, over the city and out to the mountains. The adjacent museum features posters, rifles, clothing, paintings and Indian artefacts (May–Oct daily 9am–5pm; Nov–April Tues–Sun 9am–4pm; $2).

Accommodation

Denver has a good selection of central budget **accommodation**, ranging from hostels to motels and homely B&Bs, as well as various grand historic downtown hotels. Two specialist **agencies** with reasonably priced properties in Denver and throughout Colorado are *B&B Colorado*, PO Box 12206, Boulder, CO 80303 (☎1-800/373-4995) and *B&B Rocky Mountains*, PO Box 804, Colorado Springs, CO 80901 (☎719/630-3433).

Broadway Plaza Motel, 1111 Broadway (☎893-3501). Downtown motel. ②.

Brown Palace, 312 17th St (☎534-3231). A real relic of another era. Huge downtown landmark, with very classy restaurants. A former fireplace in the lobby now holds the *Beyond Denver* store. ⑥.

Denver International Youth Hostel, 630 E 16th Ave (☎832-9996). Four blocks from the capitol, dorm beds for $7. ①.

Franklin House B&B,1620 Franklin St (☎331-9106). Simple and very inexpensive rooms (one with en-suite bath) in welcoming family inn a mile east of downtown, with complimentary breakfast. ②.

Melbourne Hotel and Melbourne International Hostel, 607 22nd St (☎292-6386). An easy – if not all that safe – walk from the center. Dorms from $10, singles $20, doubles $25. No curfew. ①.

Motel 6, 12020 E 39th Ave (☎371-1980). Standard motel just off I-70 at Peoria, between downtown and the airport. ②.

Oxford Alexis Hotel, 1600 17th St (☎628-5400). Grand traditional Western hotel. ⑥.

Queen Anne Inn, 2147 Tremont Place (☎296-6666). Central and very hospitable B&B; each of the ten rooms in this nineteenth-century house is tastefully decorated to an individual theme. ④.

Eating

As well as plenty of Western-themed steak and barbecue places, Denver has a cosmopolitan selection of international restaurants, particularly Mexican. Of the several distinct districts where restaurants are concentrated, **Larimer Square** is probably the most easily accessible on foot, and has a wide enough selection to suit most tastes. Bear in mind that several of the city's **brew-pubs** serve good quality meals.

Casa Bonita, 6715 W Colfax Ave (☎232-5115). Absolutely wild Mexican place, seating 1200 diners, along way out on Colfax. Gunfights, cliff divers, abandoned mines to explore . . . the only weak link is the food itself, but it's all a lot of fun, especially if you have kids in tow, and far from expensive.

Hog Heaven, 1525 Blake St (☎572-7828).Great Southern cooking – ribs, fried chicken and collard greens – amid entertaining pig-themed decor, two blocks from Larimer. Bargain *cava* champagne.

Green's Natural Foods Café, 320 E Colfax Ave (☎831-1315). Innovative and very cheap vegetarian specialties, as well as organic meat dishes and healthy seafood.

Josephina's, 1433 Larimer Square (☎623-0166). Busy Italian restaurant with lively bar.

La Bonne Soupe, 1512 Larimer Square (☎595-9169). Bistro-style French food, well prepared.

Old Number One Firehouse Restaurant, 1326 Tremont Place (☎892-1100). Unusual lunch-only venue; quality standard meals in a building jammed with ancient fire engines.

Paramount Café, 511 16th St (☎893-2000). Pleasant downtown lunchspot. In summer, you can sit out on the patio right on the 16th Street mall, and watch the world go by.

Zenith American Grill, 1735 Arapahoe St (☎820-2800). New and very trendy black and white styled "New Western" restaurant. Expensive but memorable.

Nightlife and Entertainment

Business is booming for **brew-pubs** in downtown Denver. Following in the successful footsteps of the *Wynkoop* (see below), others have opened up around the 16th Street mall, and the city center is usually alive at night. For news of **musical** happenings, consult Friday's free *Westword*, or the "Weekend" section in the *Denver Post*. Each May, Civic Center Park in front of the Capitol sees the **Capitol Hill Peoples' Fair**, while August's **Taste of Colorado** is a heady outdoor mix of food and live music.

The remarkable **Red Rocks Amphitheater** (☎694-1234), twelve miles west of downtown Denver, has been the setting for thousands of rock and classical concerts; U2 recorded their massively successful *Under a Blood Red Sky* album here. This 9000-seater venue is squeezed between two 400-foot red sandstone rocks that seem to glow in early morning and late evening. The park is open free of charge during the day.

Denver's pride and joy, the modern **Denver Center for the Performing Arts** on 14th and Curtis, hosts nightly musical, dramatic and other performances (information ☎893-4000, tickets ☎893-4100). Facilities in the complex include three **theaters**, as well as the **Symphony Hall** (which is in the round, giving it superb acoustics).

El Chapultepec, 20th and Market St (☎295-9126). Tiny venue with live jazz every day.

Herman's Hideaway, 1578 S Broadway (☎778-9916). Mainstream but interesting rock club.

Rock Bottom Brewery, 1001 16th St (☎534-7616). Large, light and always busy central brew-pub, with a wide-ranging menu of freshly cooked food.

Ruby, 708 E 17th Ave (☎831-8990). Eclectic live music from all over the world.

Wynkoop Brewing Co, 1634 18th St (☎297-2700). Good home-brewed beers, bar food, and a lively atmosphere, opposite Union Station. Downstairs, *Jazz Works* puts on live jazz and other music.

Northern Colorado

The major attractions for visitors in the Denver area is **Rocky Mountains National Park** to the northwest. Though on the map the distances involved may not look that great, it would be a mistake to attempt to see the whole park on a day trip from Denver. Segments of the loop drive this involves can be very slow and laborious, and in a single day it's more realistic just to dip a few miles into the park's eastern fringes.

However, **Grand Lake**, near the western entrance, makes a more attractive stopover than overblown **Estes Park** on the east, and **Winter City**, on US-40 between I-40 and Grand Lake, is an affordable and enjoyable ski resort. The road west across northern Colorado passes through another ski center, **Steamboat Springs**, en route to remote **Dinosaur National Monument**, which spreads into Utah and is covered on p.744.

Boulder

BOULDER, just 27 miles northwest of Denver on US-36, is one of the liveliest college towns in the country, filled with a young population which seems to divide its time between phenomenally healthy day-time pursuits and almost equally unhealthy night-time activities. It was founded in 1858 by a prospecting party who felt that the nearby Flatiron Mountains, the first swell of the Rockies, "looked right for gold"; in fact they found little, but the community grew anyway.

While Boulder itself is not a destination which repays all that much exploration, it makes an excellent place to return to each night after a day in the mountains. Downtown centers on the pedestrian mall of **Pearl Street**, lined with all sorts of cafés and stores – including several places where you can rent mountain bikes. At the *Boulder Arts and Crafts Cooperative* at no 142 (☎443-3683), seventy artists take it in turns to sell each others' work. The most obvious short excursion is to drive or hike up nearby Flagstaff Mountain, for views over town and further into the Rockies; any road west joins up with the Peak to Peak Highway which heads through spectacular scenery to Estes Park and Rocky Mountain National Park. Extensive **cycle paths** also lead into the mountains.

The adventurous **University of Colorado** is a dependable source of entertainment and culture. Its mid-April Conference on World Affairs attracts an eclectic and surprisingly high-powered assortment of world figures to a sort of free-for-all think tank, while it plays host each summer to the Colorado Music Festival, in the Chautauqua Auditorium (☎449-1397), and the Colorado Shakespeare Festival (☎492-8181).

Practicalities

Local and long-distance **buses** come into Boulder at the Transit Center, 14th and Walnut (☎299-6000); there are regular services to Denver and its airport (half-hourly 8am–6pm, hourly 5–8am & 6–11pm). The hospitable **visitor center** is at 2440 Pearl St (Mon 9am–5pm, Tues–Fri 8.30am–5pm; ☎1-800/444-0447 or 442-1044).

Even if you're not staying at the showcase *Hotel Boulderado*, 2115 13th St (☎442-4344; ⑨), it's an atmospheric place to wander into for a drink, and to listen to the free evening jazz. The *Foot of the Mountain*, 200 Arapahoe Ave (☎442-5688; ③), is a friendly log-cabin-style **motel**, nine blocks from downtown beside Boulder Creek. In summer only, there's a welcoming **youth hostel** at 1107 12th St near the campus (☎442-9304; ①); dorm beds cost $12, and you can also get single and double rooms.

You won't have any problem finding **bars** and **restaurants** downtown, especially around the Pearl Street area. *Sushi Zanmai*, 1221 Spruce St (☎440-0733), is a friendly good-value sushi place, with karaoke and live music; the *Siamese Plate*, 1575 Folsom Ave (☎447-9718), serves superb and well-priced Thai meals. The *Walrus Café*, 1911 11th St, is a late-opening bar with cheap food.

Rocky Mountains National Park

You don't have to go to **ROCKY MOUNTAINS NATIONAL PARK** to appreciate the full splendor of the Rockies; it is simply one small section of the mighty range, measuring roughly twenty-five miles by fifteen miles. A tenth of the size of Yellowstone, it attracts the same number of visitors – around three million per year – and with the bulk of those coming in high summer, the one main road through the mountains can get incredibly congested. However, it is undeniably beautiful, straddling the Continental Divide at elevations often well in excess of ten thousand feet. A full third of the park is above the tree line, and large areas of snow never melt; the name of the **Never Summer Mountains** speaks volumes about the long, empty expanses of arctic-style tundra. Lower down, among the rich forests, are patches of lush greenery; you never know when you may stumble upon a sheltered mountain meadow flecked with colorful flowers. Parallels with the European Alps spring readily to mind – helped, of course, by the heavy-handed Swiss and Bavarian themes of the motels and restaurants in the vicinity.

This is not an area where humans have ever made their homes, though it lies on the route of old Indian trails, and the Ute would come here to hunt in summer. Early white mining ventures came to nothing, and the region was dedicated as a national park in 1915. The original proposal was for it to be much bigger, extending from Wyoming to Pikes Peak; the existing boundaries were drawn up as a compromise, after long negotiations with Colorado's powerful logging and mining interests.

Approaching the park from the **east** you barely penetrate the foothills of the Rockies before you arrive at the gateway town of **ESTES PARK**, 65 miles northwest of Denver (and 90 miles southwest of Cheyenne). At the end of the nineteenth century, Estes Park was the private hunting preserve of the Irish Earl of Dunraven; once he was squeezed out, the town took on the more democratic function it still serves, of providing visitors with food, lodging and other services. In itself, it's not an attractive place, but its presence does at least ensure that all the necessary evils of mass tourism in the area are confined into one neat valley. The park headquarters and main **visitor center** (June–Aug daily 8am–9pm, Sept–May Mon–Fri 8am–5pm; information ☎586-2371, weather ☎586-2385; admission $5) is a couple of miles north, on US-36.

To reach the **western** entrance, 85 miles from Denver, turn north off I-70 onto US-40; a small detour beyond the junction takes you to the former mining community of **GEORGETOWN**, where over 200 Victorian buildings line the immaculate streets. The **Georgetown Loop Railroad** departs from 100 Loop Drive on a tortuous six-mile trip, at one point spiralling over itself (summer daily 10am–4pm; $12; ☎569-2403).

US-40 itself negotiates **Berthoud Pass** en route to **GRAND LAKE**, a lot lower-key than Estes Park and considerably nicer. This unlikely **yachting** center, high in the mountains, consists of one main boardwalk-lined street alongside the lake itself, lined with family amusements, lodgings and restaurants. The **Kawuneeche visitor center** is one mile north of town (daily, June–Aug 7am–7pm, Sept–May 8am–5pm; ☎627-3471).

Exploring the Park

The showpiece of the park is **Trail Ridge Road**, between Estes Park and Grand Lake. This 45-mile stretch of US-34, said to be the highest highway in the world, affords a succession of tremendous views, and several short trails leave parking lots along the way. There are no services en route, and rangers advise that you allow three to four hours' driving time. The road is normally open from Memorial Day to mid-October; at other times there is no way to cross the park. As the winter progresses and the snow falls, it is blocked progressively lower down, but you can always expect to get as far as **Many Peaks Curve** from the east or the **Colorado River Trailhead** from the west.

As the road itself is so busy, the park is best appreciated by getting out of your car and **hiking**; the road itself is just too busy. Recommending any one trail above another is futile, as it depends so much on how many people are around; enquire at one of the visitor centers when you arrive. While a hike on the tundra is (literally) the high spot of any visit, the ecosystem is so delicate that, if you do so, it is essential to stay on the paths. You should also be aware of quite how delicate your own system is at this altitude: the slightest exertion can strain even the healthiest constitution.

Between June and September, the informative **Alpine Visitor Center**, halfway along Trail Ridge Road at Fall River Pass, marks the center of the park; the rangers here put on a twice-weekly educational puppet show for kids. You can also drive here in summer along the unpaved **Old Fall River Road**, the first road to be built in the park. This runs through the bed of a valley carved by glaciers into a U-shape, so it doesn't have open mountain vistas, but it's much quieter than the Trail Ridge, and there's far more chance of spotting **wildlife**. Animals roaming the park include moose, coyote, mountain lions, beavers (often seen at work in the rivers), and a total population of perhaps thirty brown bears, which with a plentiful natural food supply tend to avoid contact with humans. The central and southern tracts of this wilderness are all but impenetrable; only a well-planned hiking expedition can get you into the remoter forests and valleys.

Just inside the park, near the Estes Park entrance, a spur road, open year-round, leads south to two small and pristine alpine lakes. To ease the traffic in summer, a free and very regular **shuttle bus** from the Glacier Basin parking area runs the last few miles up to **Bear Lake** (8am–5.30pm), which is the park's single most definitive view-point, with the mountains framed to perfection beyond the cool still waters. **Sprague Lake**, lower down, has been landscaped to provide access for disabled visitors; a dead-level paved path encircles the shore, while the free **Handicamp** campground is exclusively for the use of wheelchair-bound travellers (contact the park HQ for details).

Park Practicalities

Public transit to Estes Park from Denver includes the *Estes Park Bus Company* (☎586-8108) and *Charles Limousine* service (see p.605). However, you can't see the place on foot; if you're not driving, you can either pick up a **tour** from Estes Park, which with admission (not always included in the quoted price) should cost around $20, or do the whole thing from Denver, with *Gray Line* for example (☎289-2841).

Five official **campgrounds**, at Moraine Peak, Glacier Basin, Aspenglen, Longs Peak and Timber Creek, provide the only accommodation within the park. All fill early each day; in summer, reservations are essential. Longs Peak imposes a maximum stay of three days, the rest allow one week. For **backcountry camping** you need a free permit, again valid for a maximum of seven days in summer (☎586-4459).

Estes Park abounds in lodges, motels and places to eat; the Chamber of Commerce has full details (☎1-800/443-7837). Options include the *Alpine Trail Ridge Inn*, 927B Moraine Ave (☎1-800/223-5023 or 586-4585; ③), and the "Irish B&B" *Emerald Manor*, 441 Chiquita Lane (☎586-8050; ④), offering antique-filled rooms with mountain views. Dorm beds cost $7.50 at the summer-only *AYH* **youth hostel**, five miles north of town at the *H Bar G Ranch*, 3500 H Bar G Rd (late May to mid-Sept, members only; ☎586-3688; ①). The relaxed *Friar's* at 157 W Elkhorn Ave (☎586-2806) has an extensive menu, and *Tamaki's* in Stanley Village Shopping Center (☎586-6046), serves nice sushi.

Grand Lake, too, has a **youth hostel** in summer; the gorgeous rambling *Shadowcliff*, perched on stilts high in the woods on Tunnel Road (☎627-9966; June–Sept only; ①/③), has budget dorms for $10 and conventional motel rooms. The *Western Riviera Motel & Cabins* occupies an attractive spot down by the lakeside at 419 Garfield Ave (☎627-3580; ③/④), and the venerable old *Corner Cupboard Inn*, nearby on Main St (☎627-3813), serves delicious meals. Many of the motels insist on weekly rates.

Winter Park

The former railroad center of **WINTER PARK**, 30 miles south of Grand Lake and 67 miles northwest of Denver, may not be Colorado's trendiest resort, but its wide variety of ski and bike terrain, friendly atmosphere and good-value lodgings draw over one million visitors a year. As the **only publicly owned resort** in the state, it has great facilities for kids, female and disabled skiers – and the new 200-acre **Discovery Park** charges just $18 a day for beginners. Experienced skiers relish the new mogul runs on the awesome **Mary Jane Mountain**, and the fluffy snows of the Parsenn Bowl.

In addition to skiing, you can **snowmobile** the Continental Divide on a one-hour tour with *Trailblazers* in Fraser ($35; ☎726-8452), or around a 1200-yard course at Mountain Madness ($2; ☎726-4529) just north of town, or race downhill on a tube at *Fraser Valley Tubing Hill* (☎716-5954). **Summer** visitors enjoy six hundred miles of **mountain bike** trails, as well as Saturday night **rodeos**, chairlift rides, the super-fun **Alpine Slide** and a number of contemporary music festivals.

Practicalities

Year-round service to Winter Park is provided by *Greyhound*, stopping downtown outside the **visitor center** on Vasquez Rd (☎726-4118 or 422-0666), and *Amtrak*, five miles north in Fraser. The **Rio Grande Ski Train** does round trips from Denver almost every Saturday and Sunday during ski season, leaving at 7.15am and starting back at 4.15pm (☎296-ISKI; $35 return). The best value **van** service is run by *Gart Bros* (☎398-LIFT), whose thirty percent discount on lift tickets goes a long way to paying off the $16 one-way fare. Excellent winter **shuttle buses** mean that a car is not essential.

Winter Park offers the best choice of **rooms** among Colorado resorts. As well as **condos** (bookable through *Winter Park Central Reservations*; ☎726-5587 or 1-800/453-2525; ④ and up) and **B&Bs** (☎726-5039; ④), inexpensive **motels** include the downtown *Sundowner* (☎726-8222; ③), and there are two **hostels** – the central *AYH Hostel*, PO Box, 3323, CO 80482 (☎726-5356; reserve; ①) and the less convenient *YMCA Snow Mountain Ranch*, a few miles north on Hwy-40, which has good group rates (☎887-2152; ②). On the face of it, Winter Park's six **ski lodges**, such as downtown's *Arapahoe Ski Lodge* (☎726-8222 or 1-800/338-2698; ⑦), may seem expensive, but these delightful old-style inns offer unmatched comfort, facilities and value for skiers.

Nightlife starts at the base of the ski lifts in *The Slope* (☎726-5727), before progressing downtown to the likes of *Lani's Place* (☎726-9674), good for low-cost margaritas and Mexican food, and *Deno's* (☎716-5332) with its 100-plus beers and tasty pasta. The classiest place to eat, the *Lodge at Sunspot* (☎726-5514), sits on the 10,700-foot summit.

Steamboat Springs

With its wide surrounding valleys, **STEAMBOAT SPRINGS**, 65 miles north of Vail, looks like no other Colorado mountain resort. Its roots are in ranching rather than mining, and downtown still evokes a pioneer feel – until you spot the upmarket boutiques. In this ski-mad town, rancher-types judge the quality of snowfall by the number of fence wires it covers; they're usually satisfied with a three-wire winter, which corresponds to its average snowfall of 325 inches per year.

The town's not desperately attractive **ski resort** (lift tickets $41), snuggled into Mount Werner five miles south of downtown, is complemented by such activities as **bobsled rides** at the small downtown **Howelson Hill Ski Area** ($8; ☎879-8499), sled-dog expeditions, hot air ballooning and snowmobiling. A favorite year-round activity is to let all the stress seep out at the secluded 160° **Strawberry Park Hot Springs** (daily; 10am–10pm; $5), ten miles north of town and only accessible by 4WD in winter.

Practicalities

Most winter visitors fly into Yampa Valley Airport, 22 miles out , though it's possible to drive, weather permitting, from Denver over scenic **Rabbit Ears Pass**. From town, SST buses (☎879-3717) run the five miles to the ski resort for 50¢. Slopeside **lodging**, such as the comfortable *Best Western Ptarmigan Inn* (☎879-1730; ⑦), costs a lot more than downtown options like *Alpiner Inn* (☎879-1430; winter ⑤, summer ③), or *Nite's Rest Motel* (☎879-1212; winter ④, summer ②). *Steamboat B&B*, 442 Pine St (☎879-5724; ⑤), provides comfort and a hearty start to the day. *Steamboat Central Reservations* (☎879-0740 or 1-800/922-2722), can supply information on lodging and packages.

For **food**, *Cugino's*, 825 Oak St (☎879-5805), serves inexpensive homestyle pasta and pizza; *La Montana* in the ski area (☎879-5800), offers big portions of quality Mexican food. There's a good American menu at the *Ore House*, Hwy-40 and Pine Grove Rd (☎879-1190), as well as a lively bar – *The Loft* – upstairs. If you've got money to spare, try the delicious $45 prix fixe dinner at *Hazie's*, up on the mountain, (☎879-6111 ext 465), which includes a free gondola ride. Microbrewed ales are available at *Heavenly Daze Brew Pub* and the *Steamboat Brewery and Tavern*, also serving gourmet pizza and pasta.

Central Colorado

West out of Denver, I-70 rollercoasts for 275 miles to the Utah desert, through a patchwork of granite peaks, pine forests, wide locked-in valleys and red sandstone cliffs. This splendid scenery, once the domain of trappers, miners and outlaws, is now enjoyed by legions of **cyclists**, **skiers** and **hikers**. **Aspen** and **Vail** are the best known of the twenty-plus mountain resorts, but don't overlook the wonderful old mining town of **Crested Butte**, or **Summit County** with its four top-class ski areas.

The **Colorado National Monument**, a deep multicolored canyon just outside **Grand Junction** in the far west, stands out as the finest single spectacle, while the brooding **Black Canyon of the Gunnison** is also worth a look; the best view is from the north rim outside of Hotchkiss, eighty miles south of Glenwood Springs.

Colorado Springs

Seventy miles south of Denver on I-25, **COLORADO SPRINGS** was originally developed in 1871 as a vacation spot by railroad tycoon William Jackson Palmer. He attracted so many English gentry to the town that it earned the nickname of "Little London". Despite sprawling for ten miles alongside I-25, modern Colorado Springs, a bastion of conservatism compared to liberal Denver, still retains much of Palmer's vision. Contributing factors include a high military presence, fundamentalist religious organizations, the exclusive Colorado College, and a well-to-do Anglo-American community.

Motorists whisk through the incredible **Garden of the Gods**, on the west edge of town off US-24W, without bothering to get out of their vehicles. This gnarled, twisted and warped red sandstone rockery was lifted up at the same time as the nearby mountains, but has since been eroded into finely balanced overhangs, jagged pinnacles, massive pedestals and mushroom formations. Among outstanding features are **High Point**, which has the best view, **Balanced Rock** and the **Central Garden**. The **visitor center** has details of hiking trails (daily, summer 9am–5pm; winter 10am–4pm; free).

At the **Pro Rodeo Hall of Fame**, 101 Pro Rodeo Drive, off I-25 Exit 147 (daily summer 9am–5pm; otherwise 9am–4.30pm; $5), videos and displays explain the sport's various disciplines. The **US Air Force Academy**, just north off I-25 Exit 156B, puts on a parade ground-show every weekday at 12.10pm when the 4400 cadets march to lunch. Of more interest, even to those not of a military bent, is the **NORAD** (North American Aerospace Command), buried deep inside Cheyenne Mountain behind 25-feet-thick doors, and resting on giant metal springs. Tours are conducted every Saturday morning, but tend to be booked up well in advance (☎554-3841).

Practicalities

Colorado Springs' **visitor center** is at 104 S Cascade St (☎635-1632 or 1-800/368-4748). *Greyhound* (☎635-1505) stops at 327 S Weber St downtown. Local tours with *Gray Line*, 322 N Nevada Ave (☎633-1747), cost between $30 and $45.

Accommodation is easy to find. The best value downtown is the oldish but clean *Dale Motel*, 620 W Colorado Ave (☎636-3721; ②), though the spacious *Heartstone Inn B&B*, 506 N Cascade St (☎473-4413; ⑤) doesn't overcharge. The clean and neat *Garden of the Gods Motel*, 3704 W Colorado Ave (☎475-9450; ①/③), has motel rooms, $12 dorm beds (*AYH* members only), and a $15 campground.

Characterful places to **eat** downtown include the *Red Top*, 1520 S Nevada Ave (☎623-2444), a Fifties-style diner famous for its six-inch burgers; and the excellent vegetarian *Olive Branch*, Boulder and Tejon (☎475-1199). Out in Old Colorado City, four miles

The **area code** for Colorado Springs and central Colorado is ☎719.

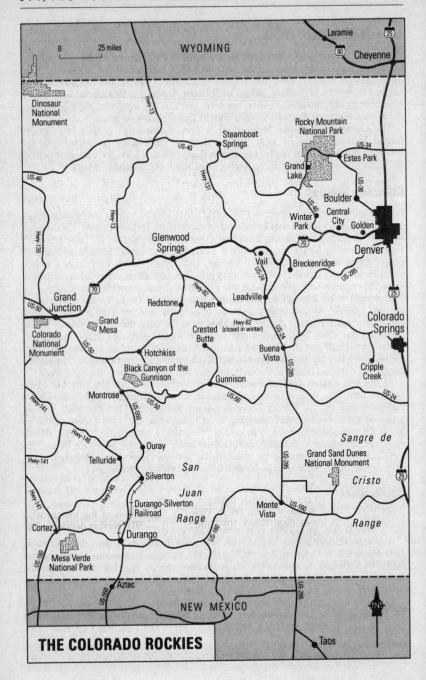

THE COLORADO ROCKIES

west, the family-owned *Henri's Mexican*, 2427 W Colorado Ave (☎634-9031), pulls in the crowds for home-style food and superb margaritas. Nearby, one of the best **bars** in the city, *Meadow Muffins*, 2432 W Colorado Ave (☎633-0583), is festooned with movie memorabilia and serves good burgers, sandwiches and salads.

Pikes Peak

Though there are thirty taller mountains in Colorado alone, **Pikes Peak**, just west of Colorado Springs, is probably the best known – largely because the view from its summit inspired Katherine Lee Bates to write the words to *America The Beautiful*. The 14,110-foot peak was first mapped by Zebulon Pike in 1806, who never climbed it himself. By the end of the century wagon trails had been built to take rich tourists like Ms Bates to the top. In 1929 it took Bill Williams, a Texan, twenty days and 170 changes of trousers to scale the mountain, pushing a peanut with his nose.

You can reach the top by a long **hike**, or by a difficult **toll road** ($5), which is not at all enjoyable for the driver. The thrilling **Pikes Peak Cog Railway** grinds its way up an average of 847 feet per mile on its ninety-minute journey to the summit; from 11,500 feet onwards it crosses a barren expanse of tundra, scarred by giant scree flows. From the bleak and windswept top, it's possible to see Denver seventy miles north, and the endless prairie to the east, while to the west mile upon mile of giant snowcapped peaks rise into the distance. The train leaves from 515 Ruxton Ave, **Manitou Springs**, six miles west of Colorado Springs (mid-June to Oct; $23, reservations advised; ☎685-5401).

The Cripple Creek Area

Fifty miles or so out from Colorado Springs, the much-chronicled gold camp of **CRIPPLE CREEK**, named for a calf that broke its leg trying to jump over a tumbling stream, nestles in a grim volcanic bowl on the west flank of Pikes Peak. In 1891, a cowhand, Bob Womack, was the first to discover gold on this poor cattle-raising land. Elated by his find, he sold his share for $500 and spent the lot on whiskey. Others were more fortunate: a total of over $500 million worth of gold was extracted. By the turn of the century 25,000 people lived in a town boasting eight newspapers, numerous banks, splendid hotels, department stores, elegant homes and even a stock exchange.

Today the main street of this isolated outpost backs onto a forbidding rocky plateau, and most of its Victorian buildings have fallen silent. Dust storms come howling through, and a herd of donkeys, descended from former pit animals, roams wild.

Scenic four-mile steam trips on the **Narrow Gauge Railway**, Fifth and Car (June to mid-Oct daily 10am–5pm; $6; ☎689-2640), trundle past abandoned mines. One mile north on Hwy-67, ex-miners take you a thousand feet underground to see gold veins in **Mollie Kathleen's Mine** (daily 9am–5pm; $7; ☎689-2466). The grand old *Imperial Hotel* (☎689-2922; ④) is a unique place to **stay**.

Six bumpy miles south, the less lavish **Victor** is where most of the miners who worked in Cripple Creek lived. *Zeke's*, 108 Third St (☎636-3091), serving delicious chili and cold beers, is the best place for a meal in either town.

Summit County

The mix of purpose-built ski resorts, old mining towns, snow-covered peaks, alpine meadows and crystal lakes that make up **Summit County**, lie alongside I-70, around seventy miles west of Denver. Before white settlement, the Utes hunted here every summer: the swanky *Keystone Ranch Golf Club* now occupies the meadow where they pitched their tepees. During the late nineteenth century the county witnessed several gold mining booms; dilapidated **ghost towns** cling to the mountainsides, but one settlement that survived is **BRECKENRIDGE**, whose streets are lined with brightly painted Victorian houses, shops and cafés. This is the liveliest of Summit County's four towns, though **FRISCO**, stretching sedately along a quiet valley, appeals to those looking for a less hectic pace. Both the other towns, **DILLON** and **SILVERTHORNE**, are dull, though the latter contains dozens of cut-price factory outlet stores. The villages at **Keystone** and **Copper Mountain** resorts are also unexciting.

Arrival and Information

By **car**, Summit County takes about two hours from Denver. Greyhound **buses** stop in Frisco and Copper Mountain; *Resort Express* runs to Silverthorne and Breckenridge from Denver Airport ($38; ☎1-800/334-7433 or 468-7600). *Summit Stage* (☎453-1241) provides free local transportation. The main **visitor center** (☎668-5800) stands by the lake at the end of Frisco's Main Street.

Outdoor Activities

Winter is still the busiest time in Summit County, with its four top-class ski areas. **Breckenridge Ski Area**, the oldest of the resorts, spans four peaks and offers ideal terrain for all skiers, as does the plush **Keystone Resort**, where the biggest night-ski operation in the US permits skiing until 10pm. The smallest resort in the county, **Araphahoe Basin**, offers great above-tree line bowl skiing. All three are owned by the same company and covered by one $38 lift ticket, making this the best value-for-money deal in the country. The slopes at the other ski area, the ingenious **Copper Mountain** ($72 for two days), are divided into three clear sections to keep beginners, intermediates and experts out of each other's way. The **Ski The Summit Pass**, allowing unlimited access to all four ski areas, costs $148 for four days, $222 for six.

In summer, fat-tire freaks and aspiring Lance Armstrongs alike will be happy with the opportunities for **cycling**, particularly the stretch between Frisco and Breckenridge; *Racer's Edge* in Breckenridge (☎453-0995) rent out the best cycles. Each resort runs chairlift or **gondola rides** to the top of the mountains, which as well as stunning views, provide access to great **hiking** and cycling trails. Breckenridge also offers toboggan rides down the dry **Alpine Slide** (summer daily 10am–5pm; $5).

Accommodation

Lodgings in Summit County cover all price ranges. Frisco has the best-priced inns and motels, with the inexpensive *Frisco Bay Inn* (☎668-5222; ③), *Sky-Vue* (☎668-3311; ③), and *Snowshoe* (☎668-3444; ③), complementing the excellent *Frisco Lodge*. There are a few downtown **B&Bs** in Breckenridge, where otherwise accommodation usually means a slopeside condo; the *Breckenridge Resort Chamber* (☎453-2913 or 1-800/221-1091; 0800/897491 in the UK), can advise on prices and package deals. Resort accommodations at both Copper Mountain (☎1-800/458-8386; 0800/89-4964 in the UK) and Keystone (☎1-800/222-0188; 0800/89-8727 in the UK) are first class, but so too are the prices; virtually nothing costs under $100 a night, unless you're lucky with a package.

Alpen Hutte Lodge, 471 Rainbow Drive, Silverthorne (☎468-6336). Clean bunkrooms in comfortable environs. Winter $25. Summer $20. ①.

Cotten House B&B, 102 S French St, Breckenridge (☎453-5509). Centrally located Victorian home with full breakfast. Winter ⑤, summer ③.

Fireside Inn, 114 N French St, Breckenridge (☎453-6456). Cosy B&B rooms, as well as a few bunk beds costing $30 per night in winter, $20 in summer. ① and ④.

Frisco Lodge, 321 Main St, Frisco (☎668-0195 or 1-800/279-6000). Great old-style accommodation. In winter, the price differentials for en-suite rooms are pretty extreme. Winter ④, summer ③.

Eating

With the exception of Keystone Resort, Summit County hasn't developed a reputation for fine dining, though there's no end of good-value places to eat.

Alpenglow Stübbe, Keystone Mountain (☎468-4161). The best dining experience in Summit County – take the free gondola ride to the top of 11,444-foot North Peak and feast on New American cuisine with a Bavarian edge in beautiful surroundings. It doesn't come cheap though, and nor does the other great place to eat in the resort: the rustic, hyper-gourmet *Keystone Ranch* (☎468-2316).

Blue Moose, 540 S Main St, Breckenridge (☎453-4859). Inventive international menu, with lots of vegetarian dishes for well under $10.

Fatty's, 106 S Ridge St, Breckenridge (☎453-9802). Great pizza and pasta at good prices.

Mi Casa, 600 Park St, Breckenridge (☎453-2071). The best Mexican food in the county. Fajitas are good value, as is the daily 4–6pm happy hour.

Drinking

Immediate apres-ski boozing is good on the slopeside bars of all four resorts. As the night goes on, Breckenridge offers the most choice, with several late-night music venues, though Frisco too has its moments.

Breckenridge Brewery & Pub, 600 S Main St, Breckenridge (☎453-1550). Good-quality micro-brew ales; bottles only $1 from 9pm until closing time every Monday.

Gold Pan, 105 N Main St, Breckenridge (☎453-5499). The only place you could get a drink in Colorado during Prohibition. Nowadays it's a lively bar and pool hall.

Moosejaw, 208 Main St, Frisco (☎668-3931). Dark wooden bar serving great burgers to 2am.

Shamus O'Toole's Roadhouse, 115 S Ridge St, Breckenridge (☎453-2004). Dingy-looking bar attracting a motley crew of bikers, bohemians and boozers. Rowdy, fun and a generous happy hour.

Leadville

Standing at an elevation of over 10,000 feet, eighty miles west of Denver, **LEADVILLE** is the highest incorporated city in the US, with a magnificent view across to broadshouldered, ice-laden mounts **Elbert** and **Massive**, Colorado's two highest peaks. As you approach from the south, your first impression is of giant slag heaps and disused mining sheds, but don't let this put you off: Leadville is rich in character and romance.

Fables abound of gunfights, miners dying of exposure and graveyards being excavated to get at the seams. **Horace Tabor**, a storekeeper who grubstaked goods to prospectors in exchange for a share in potential profits, hit lucky when two prospectors developed a silver mine that produced $20 million inside a year. Tabor collected a one-third share and left his wife to marry local waitress "Baby Doe" McCourt in the socialite wedding of 1883, attended by President Chester Arthur. By the time of his death in 1899, Tabor was financially ruined. Baby Doe took his dying injunction to "hold onto the Matchless" – his only remaining mine – literally. She died there, emaciated and frostbitten in a crude wooden shack, 36 years later. The godforsaken wooden outhouses of the **Matchless Mine** are still there, two miles out on Seventh Street ($2).

Tenth Mountain Sports, 112 E Seventh St (☎486-2202), rent equipment for **rafting** or **mountain biking** expeditions, as well as **skis**. At **SKI Cooper**, ten miles north of Leadville, lift tickets cost $18, and two-hour lessons are just $15 (☎486-3684).

Practicalities

Leadville's **visitor center** is at 809 Harrison Ave (☎486-3900). The landmark *Delaware Hotel*, 700 Harrison Ave (☎486-1239 or 1-800/748-2004; ③), offers free breakfasts; the *Leadville Country Inn*, 127 E Eighth St (☎486-2354 or 1-800/748-2354; ④), is a little more intimate. There's good Mexican food at the *Grill*, 716 Elm St (☎486-9930), and the spartan *Cantina*, one mile south on Hwy-24 (☎486-9927; traditional dancing at the weekend). For large family-style meals, try the *Golden Burro*, 710 Harrison Ave (☎486-1239).

Among Leadville's great **bars**, the *Pastime Salon*, 120 W Second St (☎486-9986), housing an 1870s Chinese bar, offers a great mountain view from its patio, and serves delicious wings and burgers, while the wood-panelled *Silver Dollar Saloon*, 315 Harrison Ave (☎486-9914), of similar vintage, is filled with Irish memorabilia.

Aspen

Coffee-table magazines might have you believe that a toll gate outside **ASPEN** only admits film stars and the super-rich. This elite **ski resort**, two hundred miles west of Denver via Leadville, is indeed home to the likes of Cher, Jack Nicholson, Goldie Hawn and John Denver, but it's a perfectly affordable place for anyone to come in summer – unless you're on an absolute shoestring budget. Visiting in winter requires more cash, though you can save money by skiing the less expensive Aspen Highlands slopes.

From inauspicious beginnings in 1879, this pristine mountain-locked town raced to become the world's top silver producer. By the time the silver market crashed fourteen years later, it had acquired tasteful residential palaces, grand hotels and an opera house. In the Thirties the population slumped below seven hundred; ironically, it was the anti-poverty WPA programme that gave the struggling community the cash to build its first crude ski lift in 1936. Entrepreneurs seized the opportunity presented by the varied terrain and plentiful snow, and the first chairlift was dedicated on Aspen Mountain in 1947. Skiing has since spread to three more mountains, and the jet set arrived in force during the Sixties. **Development** is a burning political issue; tight architectural constraints have been put on businesses (*McDonalds* are forbidden a neon sign), but the last decade has seen yet more tacky Scandinavian-style lodges and condo blocks.

Arrival and Information

In winter, **Independence Pass** on Hwy-82, which provides the quickest access to Aspen, is closed, and the detour through Glenwood Springs adds an extra seventy miles to the trip from Denver. The **airport** (☎920-5380) is four miles north of town on Hwy-82; if you fly into Denver on *Continental* or *United*, connecting flights only cost another $40 or so. In winter eight flights per day come from Denver, and three per week from Chicago, Dallas and LA; in summer, there are just two per day from Denver. *American* and *Delta* fly into Eagle Airport, eighty minutes from Aspen by car or by *Colorado Mountain Express* (☎1-800/525-6363). Once in Aspen, there's no problem **getting around**; the *Roaring Fork Transit Agency* (daily, summer 7am–midnight, winter 7am–1am) runs a free skiers' shuttle between the four mountains, charges nothing for journeys within the town, and also serves the airport ($1) and outlying areas.

Aspen's main **visitor center** is in the Wheeler Opera House, 320 E Hyman Ave (☎925-1940). An excellent source of local gossip, news, and food and drink offers, is the free *Aspen Daily News* ("If you don't want it printed, don't let it happen").

The Town and the Mountains

There's not all that much to do in Aspen itself, apart from sitting around the pedestrianized streets and watching the world go by, or browsing in the stores and galleries. The best account of Aspen's mining past is to be had at the **Aspen Historical Society**, 620 W Bleeker St (Tues–Sun 1–4pm; $3).

Three of Aspen's four mountains are run by the **Aspen Ski Co**: the mogul-packed monster of **Aspen Mountain**, looming over downtown, is for experienced skiiers only; **Buttermilk** is great for beginners, with an excellent ski school that offers a three-day guaranteed "Learn to Snowboard" programme for $99; and the wide-open runs of **Snowmass**, though mostly for intermediate skiers, feature some testing routes. Daily ski-lift tickets cost $45; savings can be made on multiple purchases. The other mountain, **Aspen Highlands**, can't boast the same high-tech lifts or as many celebrities, but is cheaper at $34 per day. **Rental** of skis, boots and poles usually costs around $18 a day – you can also rent snowshoes, to indulge in the latest Aspen fad of trekking up and down the mountains. Slightly more thrilling is **paragliding**: various companies can teach you in four days for $450. However, the town's best value has to be its fifty miles of groomed **Nordic ski trails** – the most extensive free cross-country trail network in the US.

Cycling is the main summer pursuit; *The Hub*, 315 E Hyman Ave (☎925-7970), has a wide choice of bikes, while *Timberline*, 204 S Galena St (☎925-9237), is the cheapest for fat-wheelers. Both also rent rollerblades. The **Roaring Fork River**, surging out of the Sawatch range, is excellent for kayaking and rafting, but sections can be dangerous and each summer sees a few fatalities. *Blazing Paddles* ($47 for a half-day float trip; ☎925-5651) are not the lowest-priced company, but they do have a good safety record.

If you fancy **walking** in the mountains, a **gondola** climbs from 601 Dean St to the summit of Aspen Mountain (Fri–Wed 9.30am–3pm; $12; ☎925-1220 ext 3598). Even more alluring is the landscape around the twin purple-grey peaks of the **Maroon Bells**, fifteen miles southwest, soaring above the dark blue Maroon Lake. The road is closed between 8.30am and 5pm, except for overnight campers with permits, travellers with disabilities, and *RFTA* buses which leave every half-hour from downtown ($3.50 return). Details on hiking are available from the ranger office, 806 W Hallam St (☎925-3445).

Accommodation

Aspen Central Reservations (☎1-800/262-7736 or 925-9000) run a superb service, and don't mind if you ask for the cheapest available room. They also arrange package deals combining accommodation with lift tickets. Rates vary considerably even in winter; the least expensive times to come are in the "**value seasons**" (last week in Nov, first two weeks of Dec & first two weeks of April). Between mid-December and January 4, you'll do well to find a double for under $100. Money can be saved by renting a **condo**, or **camping**; the ranger office (☎925-3445) can advise on free wilderness sites and **campgrounds** such as *Maroon Creek* or smaller places out towards Independence Pass.

Alpine Lodge, 1240 E Hwy-82 (☎925-7351). The least expensive rooms in Aspen, a short walk out of town. Choice of en-suite or shared bathrooms. Clean and friendly. Winter ④, summer ③.

Aspen Manor Lodge, 411 S Monarch St (☎925-3001). Good clean rooms, central location, and generous continental breakfast. Winter ⑤, summer ④.

Christmas Inn B&B, 232 W Main St (☎925-3822). Friendly, family-run motel, two minutes' walk from downtown. Free continental breakfast, free ski shuttle. Winter ⑤, summer ④.

Little Red Ski Haus, 118 E Cooper St (☎925-3333). Some private rooms, plus clean dorm bunks for $40 in winter, $25 in summer. Discounts for longer stays. Winter ② and ⑤, summer ① and ④.

St Moritz Lodge and Hostel, 334 W Hyman Ave (☎925-3220). Good rooms, ideal for families, and (not great) hostel accommodation. Winter ② and ⑦, summer ① and ⑤.

Swiss Chalet, 435 W Main St (☎925-8297). Good value, with kitchenettes. Winter ④, summer ③.

Eating and Drinking

Many of Aspen's eighty cafés and restaurants charge over $25 for an entree, but good budget places exist and competition is keen.

Bahn Thai, 308 S Hunter St (☎925-5518). Good lemon grass soup, saté and vegetable dishes.

Explore Booksellers and Coffeehouse, 211 E Main St (☎925-5336). Great wholefood and dessert menu at reasonable prices to an accompaniment of classical music. Open daily 10am–midnight.

Little Annie's, 517 E Hyman Ave (☎925-1098). Lively, popular and unpretentious. Potato pancakes ($4) and hearty stews ($5) for lunch. Huge trout, chicken, beef or rib dinner platters for $12.

Red Onion, Cooper St Mall (☎925-9043). Aspen's oldest bar, serving big portions of Mexican food and good burgers. A popular après-ski spot, especially for its jello shots.

Wienerstube, 633 E Hyman Ave (☎925-3357). The best breakfast in Aspen: eggs benedict, Austrian sausage, Viennese pastries among other things.

Woody Creek Tavern, Woody Creek (☎923-4585). Seven miles north along Hwy-82, right on River Road, and then first left. Cult bar where ranch hands and rock stars shoot pool, drink imported beers and eat Tex-Mex food. The regular haunt of gonzo journalist Hunter S Thompson.

Entertainment and Nightlife

Going out in Aspen, the capital of après-ski, is fun all year round and need not be expensive. Check the free papers for special offers. In summer, downtown hosts several top-notch festivals. The **Aspen Music Festival**, between late June and late August, features international performers (☎925-9042); July and early August see the **DanceAspen** festival. Mid-January's **Winterskol** includes sporting events, parades and concerts.

The Bar, 315 Dean St in the *Ritz-Carlton* (☎920-3300). Jazz every night; no dress code, no cover.

Double Diamond, 450 S Galena St (☎925-5886). Aspen's top live music venue. Usually free before 10pm with reasonable drink prices.

Jerome Bar, 330 E Main St in the *Jerome Hotel* (☎920-1000). Grand historic bar; drink and mingle with the well-heeled hotel guests.

Legends of Aspen, 325 E Main St (☎925-5860). Popular sports-type bar opposite the *Jerome*, usually offering good-value drinks specials, plus tasty chicken wings and "lips".

Shooters, 210 S Galena St (☎925-4567). Swinging country and western below the *Hard Rock Café*.

Vail

Compared to most other Colorado ski towns, **VAIL**, 122 miles west of Denver off I-70, is a new creation. Only a handful of farmers lived here before the resort, a collection of fake Tyrolean-style chalets and concrete-block condominiums, opened in 1952. During the Ford administration, it served as the western White House; Gerald Ford and his wife still live here, hosting annual celebrity golf and skiing competitions.

According to *SKI* magazine, Vail is the top **ski** destination in the US – but not for its aesthetic beauty. What lures the ultra-rich (more conspicuous than in Aspen) is the exceptional quality of snow, the sheer variety, and the huge number of lifts (expensive at $45 a day, though the ticket also lets you ski Beaver Creek, ten miles west and home of America's top-rated ski school). You can also speed down a 3000-foot **bobsleigh run** for $15 a time, or go **mountain biking**: one good option is to take the gondola from Lionshead center (mid-June to Aug 10am–4.30pm; $15) and ride down the mountain.

Practicalities

Vail spreads for eight miles along the narrow valley floor, with successive nuclei from east to west at Vail Village, Lionshead, Cascade Village and West Vail. Beaver Creek, home of the Fords, lies a further ten miles west. The entire complex is pedestrianized; there's no charge for the parking lots in summer, and *Vail Buses* run free year-round shuttles. *Vans to Vail* (☎476-4467) serve Denver airport, though Eagle County Airport, used by *American Airlines* among others, lies just 35 miles of Vail.

For information on skiing and accommodation, contact *Vail Reservations* (☎1-800/525-3875 or 845-5745; ☎0800/891673 by fax from the UK), or call into a **visitor center** at either Vail Village or Lionshead. Finding an affordable place to **stay** can be a problem. The best bets are in **West Vail**, at the *Roost Lodge* (☎476-5451; winter ⑤, summer ④), or *Days Inn* (☎476-6317; winter ⑤, summer ④). By Vail standards at least, the condos in **Avon**, just below Beaver Creek, are inexpensive. Rates in **Vail Village**, the main social center, are higher; try *Tivoli Lodge* (winter ⑥, summer ④), or the sumptuous *Mountain Haus* (winter ⑦, summer ⑥). The *Eagle River Inn*, 145 N Main St (☎1-800/344-1750 or 827-5761; winter ⑥, summer ⑤), is a B&B decked out in tasteful Santa Fe style in the hamlet of **Minturn**, seven miles south of Vail on US-24.

Eating out can also prove expensive. *Jackalope* in West Vail Mall (☎476-4314) is a lively bar and pool hall serving basic Mexican and American food. *Vendetta's*, 291 Bridge St in Vail Village (☎476-5070), offers fine Italian lunch specials and pasta dinners.

Nightlife revolves around **The Circuit** on Bridge Street, Vail Village. Most people tour between the bars and discos. The checklist of places to see and be seen includes *The Club* (live music), the *Red Lion* (British-style pub), upstairs at *Vendetta's* (the ski patrol hangout) and *Nick's*, below *Russell's Restaurant*, which plays reasonable dance music. One nice alternative is to go out to Minturn, home of excellent good-value restaurants such as the *Saloon* and the unpretentious *Minturn Country Club*.

Glenwood Springs

Busy – if not downright hectic – **GLENWOOD SPRINGS** sits at the end of impressive Glenwood Canyon, 160 miles west of Denver and within easy striking distance of Vail and Aspen. Long used by the Utes as a place of relaxation, the **hot springs** here were the target for unscrupulous speculators who broke treaties and established resort facilities in the 1880s. The sulfurous smell that hits you on the north side of the river emanates from **Glenwood Hot Springs Pool**, 410 N River St. Billed as the "world's largest outdoor mineral hot springs pool", it sports an exhilarating hydrotube water slide (daily, summer 7.30am–10pm, winter 9am–10pm; $7). The natural subterranean steam baths of the Yampah Spa Vapor Caves are adjacent (daily 9am–9pm; $7).

Some of the west's most colorful characters came here in the early days, including Dr John R **"Doc" Holliday**, a dentist better known as a gambler, gunslinger and participant in the gunfight at the OK Corral (see p.694). A chronic tuberculosis sufferer, Holliday came to the springs for a cure but died just a few months later in November 1887 at the age of 35. He is buried on a bluff overlooking the town in the picturesque Linwood Cemetery. In the paupers' section, you can find the grave of Harvey Logan, alias bankrobber Kid Curry, a member of Butch Cassidy's notorious gang.

Whitewater Rafting, I-70 exit 114 (☎945-8477), charges $35 for a float trip, $40 for a whitewater ride along a fairly placid twenty-mile stretch of the Colorado River. **Hiking** trails past streams and waterfalls criss-cross the White River National Forest surrounding the town, while the nearby family-oriented *Ski Sunlight* complex offers some of the least expensive **skiing** in the region (☎945-7491).

Practicalities

Amtrak arrives at 413 Seventh St in Glenwood Springs, at the end of a scenic route through the canyons, gorges and valleys of central Colorado. *Greyhound* (☎945-8501), travelling along the less inspiring I-70, stops close to downtown. The **visitor center** can be found at 1102 Grand Ave (☎945-6589).

The enthusiastically run *Glenwood Springs AYH Hostel*, near downtown at 1021 Grand Ave (☎945-8545 or 1-800/341-8000; ①), offers beds in a spacious dorm for $10 per night, plus a full kitchen, darkroom facilities, and a wealth of local knowledge. Reasonable motels include the *Cedar Lodge*, 2102 Grand Ave (☎945-6579; ③). The *Daily Bread Café & Bakery*, downtown at 729 Grand Ave (☎945-6253), serves up delicious fresh breads, pastries, soups and salads. A little further out, the *19th Street Diner*, 1908 Grand Ave (☎945-9133) offers budget Mexican meals, with a good bar open until 1am.

Crested Butte

The beautiful Victorian mining village of **Crested Butte**, 230 miles southwest of Denver, almost died off in the late Fifties when its coal deposits were exhausted. However, the development of 11,875-foot **Mount Crested Butte** into a world-class **ski resort** in the Sixties, and a **mountain bikers'** paradise two decades later, means that today it can claim to be the best year-round resort in Colorado. The old town is resplendent with gaily painted clapboard homes and businesses, and zoning laws ensure that condos and chalets are confined to the resort area, tucked in behind the foothills, three miles up the road. The rapid transition from near-ghost town to sporting heaven lured young people from throughout the West, to produce an addictive laid-back atmosphere.

Arrival and Information

Crested Butte is not an easy place to get to, especially in winter and spring when **roads** can be cut off by snow and avalanches. Most skiers **fly** in: ten flights per day from Denver, and at least one per week from Atlanta, Dallas and Houston, touch down at

Gunnison Airport. From here, *Alpine Express* (☎641-5074; $35 round-trip) will drive you the 28 miles to your accommodation. Once in Crested Butte there's no need for a car; **buses** ply the three-mile route between the town and resort every fifteen minutes. The **visitor center** (☎349-6438) is in the bus station at the resort.

The Town and Mountain

Pretty as it is, it doesn't take long to take in Crested Butte's tiny downtown during the day, leaving lots of time for exploring the mountain and environs.

In **skiing** circles, the Butte is best known for its extreme terrain, with lifts serving out-of-the way bowls and faces which, in other resorts, would only be accessible by helicopter. While this inspires hundreds of ski rats to make Crested Butte their winter home, the combination of good runs and an easy-going attitude helps beginners get a lot better. The big deal in recent years has been the **Ski For Free** period, usually lasting a month from Opening Day in mid-November, when lift tickets really do cost $0.00 (usually $41), there are no catches and free "never-ever" lessons for absolute beginners are thrown in. Cross-country, especially telemark, skiing attracts thousands, while snowmobiling ranks as a great way to rest your legs. For something a little different, try a horse ride through the snow with *Fantasy Ranch* (☎349-5425).

Summer in Crested Butte is becoming as popular as winter – during **Fat Tire Week** in early July, rooms get booked up well in advance. This is premier mountain bike country. You can spend days riding trails around the mountain, but for a special adventure hop over to Aspen on the rocky and jagged 21-mile **Pearl Pass** – 190 miles shorter than the road.

Accommodation

The choice in Crested Butte lies between staying up at the ski area or downtown; in the end it makes little difference as you're likely to flit between the two areas every day. *Crested Butte Vacations* (☎349-2222, or 1-800/341-5431, or 0800/894-085 from the UK) can book accommodation and advise on money-saving package deals. In any case, be sure to reserve a room in advance during winter.

Claim Jumper B&B, 704 Whiterock Ave (☎349-6471). One of the classiest B&Bs in Colorado. Six uniquely themed rooms amid a jumble of Americana. Winter ⑤, summer ④.

Crested Butte Lodge, Crested Mountain Village (☎349-4660 or 1-800/433-5684). Built in the Sixties, this is the oldest and most characterful place to stay in the resort. Winter ⑤, summer ④.

Forest Queen Motel, Second and Elk (☎349-5336). Clean and basic motel rooms. Also a few dorm beds for $20 or so, but these are usually booked up in advance. Winter ④, summer ②.

Purple Mountain B&B, 714 Gothic Ave (☎349-5888). Spacious lodge with good rooms, full breakfast and an inspirational view of Mount Crested Butte. Winter ⑤, summer ④.

Food and Drink

Crested Butte lays claim to a surprising number of gourmet restaurants which charge much less than their equivalents in the more glitzy resorts. Good, reasonably priced food is also easy to find; even next to the ski lifts, a filling lunch can be had for $5. The early apres-ski center is *Rafters*, right by the ski lifts. By early evening most visitors have found their way to downtown, for no-nonsense local bars such as *Kochevars* and *The Talk of the Town*. If you enjoy meat-market discos, then Crested Butte is not the resort for you; it's way too cool for that.

Artichoke, Crested Mtn Village (☎349-5257). Pick of the slopeside lunchspots. Big, hot sandwiches and fries go for $6, the eponymous soup for $2.

Bakery Café, Third & Elk (☎349-7280). Best breakfast in town – oven-fresh muffins, breads and pastries, plus great selection of coffees and juices.

El Dorado Balcony, 215 Elk Ave (☎349-7280). Upstairs bar, popular with locals, featuring reasonably priced drinks and some fine bands.

Powerhouse, 130 Elk Ave (☎349-5494). It's hard to say whether the Mexican food is better here or at nearby *Donita's Cantina*, but this restaurant's setting – a fondly restored 1880s generating station with a huge wooden bar – gives it the edge.

Penelope's, 120 Elk Ave (☎349-5178). Regular visitors to the Butte argue over where to find the best food in town. *Penelope's*, set in a greenhouse at the rear of a Victorian cottage, simply doesn't produce an entree that's less than excellent, and a four-course meal yields change out of $40 per person. Worthy runner-up awards go to the *Timberline*, *Le Bosquet* and *Soupçon*.

Grand Junction

GRAND JUNCTION, 246 miles west of Denver on I-70, is often neglected as a destination, even though its immediate environs abound with outdoor opportunities, and within a fifty-mile stretch you can trace the transition from fertile valley to full-blown desert. Another town which sprang into life in the 1880s with the arrival of the railroads, it now makes its living primarily through the oil and gas industries. Although initial impressions are bound to be unfavorable – an unsightly sprawl of factory units and salesyards lines the I-70 Business Loop – downtown is much better, with leafy boulevards encircling a small, tree-lined, historic and retail district.

The Colorado section of Dinosaur National Monument – see p.744 – is 90 miles north of Grand Junction along Hwy-139, but the town itself holds the **Dinosaur Valley Museum**, 362 Main St (summer daily 9.30am–5.30pm; winter Tues–Sat 10am–4.30pm; $3.50). This houses reconstructed reptiles along with giant bones excavated locally.

Grand Junction offers a wide range of **cycling** terrain, from canal paths to rigorous mountain trails. Bikes can be rented from the *Bike Peddler*, 701 First St (☎243-5602). There's great **hiking** beside the rippled, purple-grey **Book Cliffs**, paralleling the town on the north side, whose subtle changes of color throughout the day are a delight.

Practicalities

Amtrak stops at Second and Pitkin. *Greyhound* buses serve Durango, Denver and Salt Lake City from 230 S Fifth St (☎242-6012). The **visitor center**, 759 Horizon Drive (☎243-1001), provides a very helpful service. Budget **motels** on the interstate – such as the good-value Palamino, 2400 North Ave(☎242-1826; ②), with its neat little pool and fine neon sign – offer rock-bottom rates; alternatives include the downtown *Two Rivers Inn*, 141 N First St (☎245-8585; ②), and the friendly *Gate House B&B*, 2502 N First St (☎242-6105; ③). The *Hotel Melrose*, 337 Colorado Ave (☎242-9636; ①), a hostel close to *Amtrak* and *Greyhound*, charges $16 per person for a room without bath ($25 en-suite).

You can eat well for under $10 at the *River City Café & Bar*, 748 North Ave (☎245-8040), while the *Good Pasture* in the *Friendship Inn Motel*, three miles out at 733 Horizon Drive (☎245-7200; ②), looks like another boring family diner, but serves a very health-conscious and good-value menu.

Colorado National Monument

Millions of years of wind and water erosion have gouged out the brightly colored rock spires, domes, arches, pedestals and balanced rocks of the **COLORADO NATIONAL MONUMENT**, from the edge of the cliffs just four miles west of Grand Junction. This painted desert of warm reds, stunning purples, burnt oranges and browns is also home to a high arid vegetation of piñon pine, yucca, sagebrush and Utah juniper. There's an entry fee of $3 per car, good for seven days.

The best of many overlooks along the twisting, curving 23-mile **rim drive** (a 39-mile round trip from Grand Junction) is the **Book Cliff View**, or the **Parade of the Monoliths**, just off the rim road at the sign for Window Rock Trail. Short hikes include the one-hour **John Otto's Trail**, affording close-up views of several monoliths; longer trails get right down to the canyon floor. You can **camp** for $6 in the park's *Saddlehorn Campground* ($6), or pitch a tent anywhere more than a quarter of a mile off the road.

Grand Mesa

The **GRAND MESA**, thirty miles east of Grand Junction on Hwy-65, via I-70, is at 10,000 feet the world's largest flat-topped mountain, created over a period of 600 million years by erosion wearing away the softer rock which surrounded a 400-foot lava flow. Though its full extent can only really be grasped from thirty miles away, visitors who ascend the twisting Hwy-65 to the plateau are rewarded by a tranquil landscape, covered by pine and aspen groves with over 200 lakes, colored by the reflections of shoreline trees. **Lands End Road**, an 11-mile dirt track, comes out to a stunning panorama; lakes, plains, sand hills and smaller mesas separate thick forest on the left from desert on the right, with the snow-crested San Juan peaks far off in the background.

Pretty campgrounds dot the east side near Alexander Lake (details from the ranger office; ☎242-8211), as do a motel and basic cafés. At the bottom of the Mesa, five miles north of **Cedaredge**, the hospitable *Llama's B&B* on Hwy-65 (☎856-6836; ④) offers fantastic breakfast served on a sun deck, and a chance to meet some llamas.

Southwest Colorado

The high mountain passes of southwest Colorado are classic mining territory; dotted through the valleys you'll find all sorts of well-preserved late Victorian frontier towns. As the pioneers moved in, first illegally and then backed by the US government, they drove the Ute Indians away into the poorer land of the far southwest.

The San Juan Skyway

From Durango, the main town of southwest Colorado, the dramatic **SAN JUAN SKYWAY** completes a loop of over two hundred miles through the mountains, north along US-550 and then back via Hwy-145 and US-160. The stretch of road north of Durango, negotiating its way over stunning high passes, is known as the **Million Dollar Highway**, for the amount of gold in the gravel that was used in its construction.

Durango

DURANGO, named for Durango Mexico and now twinned with it, too, was founded in 1880 as a rail junction for the gold-rush community of Silverton, 45 miles further north. The **steam trains**, which still run the same spectacular route through the Animas Valley, remain the foundation of Durango's tourist economy; the **Durango & Silverton Narrow Gauge Railroad** runs up to four return trips daily between May and October, from a depot at the south end of town ($42 round-trip; reserve tickets at least two weeks in advance; 479 Main Ave; ☎247-2733). Shorter excursions, still covering the most scenic areas of the route, run from late November through to New Year's Day.

There's not very much to see in the town itself. It makes a good base for Mesa Verde (see below), but otherwise the main activity is all kinds of outdoor pursuits. Durango is a sometime host of the World Mountain Bike Championships; try the gruelling circuits for yourself on a bike rented from *Hassle Free Sports*, 2615 Main Ave (☎259-3874).

Greyhound services between Denver and Albuquerque call in at 275 E Eighth Ave (☎259-2755). Durango's **visitor center**, near the train station (☎247-0312 or 1-800/525-8855), has full lists of **accommodation**, topped by the landmark *Strater Hotel* at 699 Main Ave (☎247-4431; ☎1-800/247-4431 out of state; ④), and rounded off by the $10 dorms at the *Durango Youth Hostel*, downtown at 543 E Second Ave (☎247-9905; ③). The innumerable **motels** north of town along Main Avenue double their rates in summer; try the *Siesta* (no 3475; ☎247-0741; ①/③), or the *Silver Spur* (no 3416; ☎247-5552; ②/④). The *Scrubby Oaks*, three miles east at 1901 Florida Rd (☎247-2176; ③), is a good-value mountain-view **B&B**. There are plenty of places to **eat** and **drink**; *Carver's*

Bakery & Brewpub, 1022 Main Ave (☎259-2545), buzzes all day and well into the night, while *B W Shay's*, 948 Main Ave (☎247-4144), serves good Mexican and American food.

Silverton

Journey's end for the narrow-gauge railroad comes at **SILVERTON**, spread across a small flat valley but surrounded by high mountains. It's one of the most atmospheric of Colorado's mountain towns, with wide dirt-paved streets leading off towards the hills to either side of the one main road. Silverton's zinc and copper mining days only came to an end in 1991; the population has dropped since then, but those that remain have so far resisted suggestions that its future lies in legalizing gambling to draw in tourists. Meanwhile, the false-front stores along "Notorious Blair Street", paralleling the main drag, recall the days when Bat Masterson was the city marshal – and are the scene of a daily shoot-out at 5.30pm (even if they are now mostly T-shirt emporia).

The majority of visitors to Silverton are day-trippers, and to spend a night here is to step back a century. Bargain **accommodation** is to be had at the *Triangle Motel*, 848 Green St (☎387-5780; ②), at the south end of town, which also offers good-value two-room suites and jeep rental. The more formal *Wyman Hotel*, 1371 Greene St (☎387-5372; ③), is also more central. The *French Bakery*, 1250 Greene St (☎387-5423), serves food from sandwiches through to full meals, and has the budget and somewhat rundown *Teller House Hotel* upstairs (☎387-5423; ②). Nearby, *Romero's* at 1151 Green St (☎387-9934), is an enjoyable Mexican *cantina*.

Ouray

The equally attractive mining community of **OURAY** lies 23 miles north of Silverton, on the far side of the 11,018ft **Red Mountain Pass**, where the bare rock beneath the snow really is red, thanks to mineral deposits. The Million Dollar Highway twists and turns, passing abandoned mine workings and rusting machinery in the most unlikely and inaccessible spots; back roads into the mountains offer rich pickings, for hikers or drivers with 4WD vehicles.

Ouray itself nestles into another cosy and verdant valley, between the **Box Canyon Falls** park in the south and the commercially run **Ouray Hot Springs** in the north. At the *Box Canyon Lodge*, 45 Third Ave (☎387-5423; ③), you can bathe in natural jacuzzis; the refurbished B&B *St Elmo Hotel*, 426 Main St (☎325-4951; ④), has a good restaurant.

Telluride

TELLURIDE, 120 miles northwest of Durango on Hwy-145, is another former mining village, which in the 1880s was briefly home to the young Butch Cassidy who robbed his first bank here in 1889. These days Telluride is better known as the home of a top-class ski resort that rivals Aspen as the prime winter destination for the stars. It has, however, achieved this status without losing its character – the wide main street, a National Historic District with low-slung buildings on either side, still heads directly up towards one of the most stupendous mountain views in the Rockies. Healthy young bohemians with few visible means of support but good ski equipment seem to form the bulk of the 1200 citizens, while most of the glitzy visitors tend to hang out two miles above the town in **Mountain Village**; the two places will be connected by a free year-round gondola service from summer 1994.

Continental and *United* provide a shuttle service from DIA to **Telluride Airport**, nine miles east of town. *Telluride Transit* buses provide a free shuttle service in winter; during the warmer months you might like to rent a **bike** from *Olympic Sports*, 150 W Colorado Ave (☎728-4477). **Accommodation** is much less expensive in summer than during ski season, though prices do go up for the Bluegrass Festival in June, the Jazz Festival at the beginning of August and the Film Festival at the start of September.

Telluride Central Reservations (☎728-4431 or 1-800/525-3455) co-ordinates lodging and package deals, with free lift tickets during the first month of the season if you stay in a participating lodge. Skiing comes half-price if you stay at any one of seven neighboring towns. Of specific places, the 1895 *New Sheridan Hotel*, 231 W Colorado Ave (☎728-4351; ② to ⑥) offers some bargain rooms with shared bath, and the *Victoria Inn*, 401 W Pacific Ave (☎728-6601; ④ and ⑤) has clean doubles.

Eddie's, 300 W Colorado Ave (☎728-5335), serves good Italian food and home-brewed ales; other brew pubs in the town include the bakery-bar *Baked In Brewed In Telluride*, 127 S Fir St (☎728-4775), and the *San Juan Brewing Co* in the Historic Depot, 300 S Townsend Ave (☎728-0100).

Cortez

The town of **CORTEZ**, in the far southwest corner of Colorado, consists basically of one long stretch of highway (US-160), roughly 25 miles up from the **Four Corners Monument** which marks the meeting place of Colorado, New Mexico, Arizona and Utah. Its primary function is an overnight stop for travellers heading to or from the canyonlands of northern Arizona, very handy for visitors to Mesa Verde National Park. Nothing in town commands much attention, though the giant **Sleeping Ute Mountain** to the southwest, visible from all over, makes a dramatic backdrop, looking uncannily like a warrior god asleep with his arms folded across his chest.

The **Colorado Welcome Center** at 928 E Main St (☎565-3414 or 1-800/346-6528) has information on the entire state. Budget **motels** include *El Capri*, 2110 S Broadway (☎565/3764; ③), and the *Arrow*, 440 S Broadway (☎565-7778; ②). *Stromsted's*, 1020 S Broadway (Hwy-666; ☎565-1257) is a classy and convivial place to **eat**.

Mesa Verde

MESA VERDE NATIONAL PARK, the only national park in the US exclusively devoted to archeological remains, is set high in the plateaux of southwest Colorado, entered off US-160 halfway between Cortez and Mancos. It's an astonishing place, so far off the beaten track that its extensive **Anasazi ruins** were not fully explored until 1888.

Between the time of Christ and 1300 AD, Anasazi civilization expanded to cover much of the area now known as the **"Four Corners"**. Their earliest dwellings were simple pits in the ground, but before they vanished from history they had developed the architectural sophistication needed to build the extraordinary complexes of Mesa Verde. Most of the best preserved Anasazi relics are in the modern states of New Mexico, Arizona and Utah; see p.675 for more background information, and a list of other sites.

Mesa Verde is a densely wooded plateau, cut at its southern edge by sheer canyons which divide the land into narrow fingers. The Anasazi are thought to have been the only inhabitants the region has ever had; no one has lived here since the thirteenth century, and neither have any traces been found of a human presence before 500 AD. The people who built their first pithouses here in the sixth century were already skilled potters leading a stable agricultural life; they owned domesticated turkeys and grew corn. After several hundred years, they moved off the mesa tops and began to construct spectacular multistorey apartments and entire communities, nestling in rocky alcoves high above the canyons. Quite why they did so is not clear; the Round Towers in the Cliff Palace, for example, cannot have served as lookouts, while Spruce Tree House could hardly have been built for defence, as it's simply not defensible. Neither is it known why they eventually left; elsewhere there are signs that the Anasazi were violently displaced by marauding newcomers, but at Mesa Verde the soil may just have become too depleted for them to stay on.

Touring the Park

The road up from the park entrance twists and climbs for around fifteen miles – giving dramatic views along the way – before reaching the main **Far View visitor center** (daily 8am–5pm; ☎529-4461). Just beyond this, the road divides to the two main constellations of remains: Wetherill Mesa to the west, and Chapin Mesa further south.

Wetherill Mesa, usually accessible between late May and early October, is a tortuous twelve-mile drive. A small visitor center assigns tickets for mini-train tours of the plateau; time spent waiting can be occupied by walking down to examine nearby **Step House**. The train drops visitors off at the impressive **Long House**, for hour-long ranger-led tours, which descend sixty or so steps to reach its large central plaza, and scramble around its 150 rooms and 21 kivas. The ruins here are said to be especially authentic, having been "re-stabilized" in recent years, rather than subjected to the extensive rebuilding of the better-known sites elsewhere in the park earlier this century.

A couple of miles down the road from the visitor center towards Chapin Mesa, you pass **Far View** itself on the left. This mesa-top pueblo, abandoned in the early 1200s, depended for its water on **Mummy Lake**, an artificial reservoir ninety feet across by twelve feet deep, holding half a million gallons, which was fed by a five-mile canal.

The **museum** at the park headquarters, as you come onto **Chapin Mesa**, contains excellent displays on the Anasazi – although unfortunately many artefacts from Mesa Verde were shipped away at the turn of this century. **Spruce Tree House** here is the only ruin which can be seen in winter. In summer, a one-way driving loop takes you past the **Square Tower House**, the unfinished mesa-top **Sun Temple**, and on to the **Cliff Palace**. The largest Anasazi cliff dwelling to survive, this once housed over two hundred people; now its adobe towers, smoothly blending in with the surrounding rock, provide a haunting evocation of a lost and little-known world – when the crowds aren't too great. Ladders lead down from the main plaza into circular kivas. Inside some of the structures, fading Anasazi murals can still be discerned.

To visit **Balcony House**, further on, you may have to wait to join one of the fifty-strong groups which set out on ranger-led tours every half-hour. The tours involve scrambling up three large ladders, and crawling through a narrow tunnel – all the while teetering above a steep drop into Soda Canyon. Unless you share the fearless Anasazi attitude to heights, you might prefer to give this fascinating fortress-like edifice a miss.

Park Practicalities

Mesa Verde can get very crowded in high summer; the best times to visit are in May, September and October. The park and the museum stay open all year round, though most of the sights are inaccessible, as detailed above, and the concessions such as gas, food and lodging only operate between mid-May and mid-October.

Most visitors stay in nearby towns; the only **rooms** in the park itself are at *Far View Motor Lodge*, at the summit of Navajo Hill near the visitor center (Box 277, Mancos, CO 81328; ☎529-4421; ⑤). The ranger at the park entrance knows if rooms are available. You can **camp** at the first-come, first-served *Morefield Campground*, four miles up from the entrance (☎529-4421), and there are also several commercial campgrounds nearby.

Greyhound **buses** will theoretically drop passengers at the park entrance, but that's no help when it comes to seeing the ruins themselves; if you don't have your own transportation, you'd do best to take one of the many daily **bus tours** from Durango.

Ute Mountain Tribal Park

Mesa Verde abuts against the Ute Mountain Indian reservation, to the south. Anasazi remains spread over the large, inaccessible **Ute Mountain Tribal Park** can be explored on Ute-guided tours, which start from the *Ute Mountain Pottery*, 15 miles south of Cortez on Hwy-666 (June–Oct, daily 8am; ☎565-8548). Visitors should bring their own sturdy vehicles and all supplies, and can expect some strenuous hiking.

WYOMING

Pronghorn antelope all but outnumber people in wide-open **WYOMING**, the ninth largest but least populous state in the union, with just 460,000 residents. Above all, this is classic **cowboy country** – the inspiration behind *Shane*, *The Virginian* and countless other western novels – where the days of the open range are evoked by rodeos, country and western dancehalls and ranchwear stores. The state emblem, seen everywhere, is a hat-waving cowboy astride a bucking bronco.

Northern Wyoming is the prime tourist goal, with close to three million per year heading for the simmering geothermal landscape of **Yellowstone National Park**, and the craggy mountain vistas of the adjacent, and equally outstanding, **Grand Teton National Park**. Wedged in between Yellowstone and South Dakota to the east are the helter-skelter **Bighorn Mountains**, likeable old-West towns such as **Buffalo** and the otherworldly outcrop of **Devils Tower**.

The meagre supply of buffalo in early Wyoming caused fierce intertribal wars over hunting grounds and kept the **Native American** population down to around 10,000. However, Sioux, Cheyenne and Blackfoot combined to inflict notable defeats on the US Army before it could clear the way for pioneer settlement in the 1870s. The cattle ranchers and sheep-farming homesteaders who followed engaged in violent **range wars** over grazing rights to the wiry grasslands.

Unlikely as it may seem, this rowdy, heavily male-dominated state was the first to grant all women the vote in 1869 – a full half-century before the rest of the country, on the grounds that the enfranchisement of women would attract settlers and hasten statehood, which depended upon population. A year later Wyoming appointed the country's first women jurors, and the "Equality State" elected the first female US governor in 1924.

The absence of rivers to irrigate farmland has effectively put a lid on agricultural and population growth. Any weatherbeaten, Wrangler-clad stranger is more likely, these days, to be an oil roustabout than a genuine cowboy, fuel and mineral extraction having replaced livestock as the mainstay of the economy in the early part of this century.

Getting Around Wyoming

One daily *Amtrak* **train** crosses southern Wyoming in daylight hours in each direction. *Greyhound* **buses** operate along I-80 through the south, and to the western entrance to Yellowstone Park. The rest of the state is covered by regional bus companies; it takes considerable time and planning to get where you want to go. Jackson now has the state's largest **airport**, though flights also go to Casper and Cheyenne. **Cycling** across northern Wyoming can be great fun, though check the contours for the easiest way over the Bighorn Mountains.

South and Central Wyoming

State capital **Cheyenne** is the only town of real note in the lower two-thirds of Wyoming. Set in the heart of rich prairie – a surprise after the scrubland, mountain and desert of most of the region – it has closer economic ties with Omaha or Denver than with the rest of Wyoming. The more northerly oil city of **Casper** stressed that point in its unsuccessful bids to become the seat of government. West of Cheyenne, smaller **Laramie** possesses an agreeable frontier feel, but lacks real spark. The spectacular wilderness of the **Wind River Range**, accessible from **Pinedale** and **Lander**, accounts for most of the west central portion of the state.

The **area code** for the entire state of Wyoming is ☎307.

Cheyenne

With its ranchwear shops and honky-tonk saloons, **CHEYENNE** looks at first like an overgrown cowboy town. But a quick walk around reveals a diverse community, shaped by railroads, state politics, and even nuclear arms. When the Union Pacific Railroad reached this site in 1867, soldiers had to drive out the **"Hell on Wheels"** brigade of gamblers, moonshiners and hard-drinking gunmen who kept one jump ahead of the railroads, claiming land and then selling it for huge profit before moving on to the next proposed terminal. Union Pacific's sprawling yards and fine old terminus now mark the eastern edge of downtown, while to the west the city's long-standing military installation was expanded in 1957 to house the first US intercontinental ballistic missile base.

The **approach** into Cheyenne, dropping into a wide dip in the plains, leaves enduring memories for most travellers. With the snow-crested Rockies looming in the distance and short, sun-bleached grass encircling the town, the sky suddenly appears gargantuan, dwarfing the city's leafy suburbs and everything else below it.

Sixteenth Street is the retail and entertainment heart of Cheyenne. Five minutes' walk north up leafy Capitol Avenue near the unspectacular State Capitol, the **Wyoming State Museum**, at Central Ave and 24th St, takes a sober look at Wild West history (Mon–Fri 8.30am–5pm, Sat 9am–5pm; summer also Sun 1–5pm; free). The **Cheyenne Frontier Days Old West Museum**, five minutes' drive from downtown at Eighth and Carey, is more lighthearted, telling how the railroad came to town, with some great old engines (June–Aug Mon–Sat 8am–7pm, Sun 10am–6pm; Sept–May Mon–Fri 9am–5pm, Sat & Sun 11.30am–4.30pm; $3).

Along with the world's largest outdoor **rodeo**, the nine-day **Cheyenne Frontier Days** festival in late July celebrates **cowboy culture** with concerts by top country stars, parades, chuckwagon races, air shows and free pancake breakfasts. For the rest of the year, you'll have to make do with the **Old Cheyenne Gunfight**, at Sixteenth and Carey (summer Mon–Fri 6pm, Sat "high noon"; free), in which gunslingers act out incidents from the town's turbulent first decade, or the twice-weekly **night rodeo** held on Tuesdays and Wednesdays between mid-June and mid-September.

Practicalities

Greyhound **buses** (☎634-7744) run east and west along I-80 and south to Denver, while *Powder River* (☎635-1327) buses travel through eastern Wyoming to Montana and South Dakota. Both companies share the depot at 1503 S Capitol Ave, a two-block walk from the **visitor center**, 301 W 16th St (Mon–Fri 8am–6pm; ☎778-3133 or 1-800/426-5009), which operates a ninety-minute **trolley tour** of Cheyenne in summer for $6.

Although places to **stay** are normally inexpensive, prices double during the Frontier Days. Budget motels, such as the *Super 8* at no 1900 (☎635-8741; ②), line up along West Lincolnway (a continuation of 16th Street), but the best value can be found downtown in the large, clean rooms of the *Plains Motel*, 1600 Central Ave (☎638-3311; ②). **Campers** are advised to head for *AB Camping*, at 1503 W College Drive (☎634-7035).

Cheyenne has no shortage of diners serving cowboy-sized breakfast and lunches, such as the excellent *Driftwood Café*, 200 E 18th St (☎634-5304). *Los Amigos*, 620 Central Ave (☎638-8591), offers tasty home-style Mexican food, and the best c'n'w sounds can be heard at the spacious *Cowboy South*, 312 S Greeley Highway (☎637-3800).

Laramie

LARAMIE lies fifty miles west of Cheyenne on I-80, or slightly further via the spectacular Happy Jack Road (Hwy-210), which slices through plains studded with bizarrely shaped boulders and outcrops. At first Laramie seems typical of rural Wyoming, but behind downtown's quaint Victorian facades lurk hard-rocking record stores, vegetarian cafés, and secondhand bookstores – unusual for rodeo land, and due to the University of Wyoming, whose campus spreads east from the town center.

The centerpiece of the ambitious **Wyoming Territorial Park**, west of town at 975 Snowy Range Rd (June–Aug daily 11am–8pm; otherwise times vary; $5.95), is the old territorial **prison**. A touch over-restored, it holds informative displays on the Old West, women in Wyoming and huge mugshots of ex-convicts, among them Butch Cassidy, who was incarcerated here for eighteen months from 1896, for cattle-rustling.

In summer, scenic one-day **train trips** run across the Snowy Range of the Medicine Bow Mountains to Walden in Colorado; contact the *Greyhound* station for details.

Practicalities

Greyhound is at 1358 N Second St (☎742-0896), just north of downtown. Room rates are good at the downtown *Travel Inn*, 262 N Third St (☎745-4853; ②), and *Motel 6*, 621 Plaza Lane (☎742-2307; ①). *El Conquistador*, 110 Ivinson Ave (☎742-2377) serves adequate Mexican food; for a few dollars more, there's a healthfood and nouvelle menu at *Jeffrey's Bistro*, 123 Ivinson Ave (☎742-7046). Students, yuppies and bikers pack out the frontier-style *Buckhorn Bar*, 114 Ivinson Ave (☎745-3554); the friendly *Cowboy Saloon*, 108 S Second St (☎721-3165), is a fun place to go and hear some country music.

The Medicine Bow Mountains

Just outside Laramie, **Hwy-130** dips into the huge wind-gouged bowl of **Big Hollow**, then passes through rustic Centennial and starts the steep climb up the **Medicine Bow Mountains**. Overlooks at the top of the 10,847-ft Snowy Range Pass present picturesque alpine lakes and meadows, tight against steep mountain faces.

Forty-nine miles out from Centennial, stylish **Saratoga** is hemmed in by the Snowy and Sierra Madre ranges. The **Hobo Hot Springs** on Walnut Ave is a free outdoor pool fed by natural 114°F springs. Easily the best place to stay is the antique-furnished *Wolf Hotel*, 101 E Bridge St (☎326-5525; ②). *Wally's*, 110 E Bridge St (☎326-8472), serves up great pizzas, vegetarian food and a mean steak sandwich.

Southwest Wyoming

The long and monotonous drive across southern Wyoming on I-80 – the route also followed by *Amtrak* – holds little to delight the eye, though geologists and fossil enthusiasts will be in their element, and it may provide some travellers with their first introduction to the red-rock scenery of the west.

Rawlins, 100 miles west of Laramie, offers little more than clean rooms in the *Hi-Top Motel*, 713 W Spruce St (☎324-4561; ②), and an excellent Mexican cantina, *Rose's Lariat*, 410 E Cedar St (☎324-5261). Just west, the Continental Divide briefly splits into two separate strands in the **Great Divide Basin**. In theory, rain that falls here remains here, unable to flow towards either ocean – unfortunately virtually none does, and the brick-red hell of the **Red Desert** stretches implacably away to the horizon.

Rock Springs and Green River

ROCK SPRINGS, the largest town in southwest Wyoming, is also unquestionably the ugliest, a down-at-heel mining community that experienced its latest short-lived boom in the 1980s. However, it is a possible stop-off on both *Greyhound* and *Amtrak* for connections to Jackson and the national parks, using the *Rock Springs–Jackson Bus Line*, 913 Second St (☎362-6161). If you need to stay overnight, the *Lamplighter Motel*, beside *Greyhound* at 1004 Dewar Drive (☎362-6673; ②), has reasonable rooms, and the nearby *Kilpeppers*, at 1030 Dewar Drive (☎382-1012), serves good family-style meals.

Ramshackle **GREEN RIVER** is 14 miles west. Wedged between high buttes, and sliced through by the railroad, the interstate, and the Green River itself, it's not an easy place to find your way around. *Embers*, opposite *Amtrak* at 95 E Railroad Ave (☎875-9983) is the most popular eating spot, while the *Coachman Inn*, 470 E Flaming Gorge Way (☎875-3681; ②) is a good-value motel. **Campers** should take note that both Green River and Rock Springs lie within easy reach of **Flaming Gorge Natural Recreation Area** (covered on p.745). Roads south from each of them run through the empty hills to look down over incandescent orange rocks and a dramatic artificial lake.

Fossil Butte National Monument

Roughly 70 miles northwest of Green River – and reached by turning north from I-80 just west of the "world's largest service station" at Little America – **Fossil Butte National Monument** preserves a fossilized cross-section of the fish population of a 50-million-year-old lake. From a distance, you can clearly see the relevant pale limestone strata on the flat-topped Butte itself, but the various trails turn out to show you less than the displays at the **visitor center** (daily, June–Aug 8am–7pm, Sept–May 8am–4.30pm; free; ☎887-4455). Enquiring minds will be more stimulated by the open quarry face at Dinosaur National Monument, around 200 miles southeast (see p.744).

Twelve miles east of the monument, and isolated from the world by 50 miles of open rangeland in every direction, **Kemmerer** was the unlikely home of the first of over 1900 *J C Penney* stores. It's still there on Main Street, along with assorted fossil shops.

Casper

Dreary **CASPER**, halfway up Wyoming on I-25, may not seem an obvious place to visit, but at a good 150 miles from anywhere of similar size it makes a likely pit-stop. Originally at the spot where the Oregon Trail crossed the North Platte River – you can visit a reconstruction of the 1860s **Fort Caspar** which gave it its (misspelled) name – Casper has been since 1890 the center of Wyoming's oil region. Its population – and appearance – fluctuate between periods of high and low demand; right now, the economy is ticking along rather well, though with the exception of a couple of retail blocks along E Second Street downtown still hasn't shaken off the signs of harder times.

Practicalities

Powder River **buses**, serving Cheyenne, Billings and Rapid City, pull in at 315 N Wolcott St (☎266-1904), south of the **visitor center** at 500 N Center St (☎234-5311 or 1-800/852-1889). Of Casper's bargain **motels**, the downtown *Galley Motel*, 310 N Center St (☎234-4330; ①), is clean, and the *Showboat Motel*, 100 W F St (☎235-2711; ②), with its flashing neon lights and waterbeds, is pleasantly kitsch. You can **camp** high on nearby Casper Mountain (☎472-0452), 12 miles south. The *Cheese Barrel*, 544 S Center St (☎235-5202), serves great breakfasts and sticky cheese bread.

The Wind River Range

Roads to Grand Teton and Yellowstone national parks from southern Wyoming skirt the **Wind River Mountains**, the state's longest and highest range, with some challenging backpacking terrain. No roads cross the mountains; you can either see them from the **east**, by driving through the Wind River Indian Reservation on US-26/287, or from the less accessible **west**, by taking US-191 up from I-80 at Rock Springs.

Wind River Indian Reservation

The **Wind River Indian Reservation** occupies a large (and largely forgotten) swathe of west central Wyoming, always overshadowed by the high snow-capped peaks to the west and south. It extends roughly seventy miles from the natural spa of **Thermopolis** in the east, through arid grasslands and dessicated uranium-rich badlands, to **Dubois** in the west, with at its heart the rich fishing grounds of the cottonwood-lined Wind River itself. The reservation was created in 1863 as a permanent home for the Eastern Shoshone, but through administrative oversight and indifference soon came to accommodate the Northern Arapaho as well. Near **Fort Washakie** – named for the centenarian Chief Washakie, who held the Shoshone together throughout the period of white expansion – is the (possible) grave of **Sacajawea**, the former guide of Lewis and Clark.

The reservation's largest town, **Riverton** on US-26, 120 miles west of Casper, is still reeling from the end of the uranium boom. Lodging in **Lander**, on US-287, includes $5 dorm beds at *Ma's Boarding House* on Mortimer Lane (☎332-3123; ①), and budget rooms at the *Teton Motel*, 586 Main St (☎332-3582; ①). In nearby **Sinks Canyon State Park**, the Popo Agie River plunges underground, only to re-emerge half a mile later in a huge spring (trail information from the ranger office at 600 N US-287 in Lander).

Dubois

The former logging town of **DUBOIS** (*"dew-boys"*), squeezed into the northern tip of the Wind River valley as the mountains begin in earnest, and an oasis among the badlands, turned to tourism after its final sawmill closed in 1987. Given a head start by being just fifty miles southeast of Grand Teton National Park (via the dramatic **Togwotee Pass**), Dubois is home to the biggest herd of bighorn sheep in the lower 48 states, and celebrates that fact with its 1993-opened **National Bighorn Sheep Center**.

Motels such as the kitchenette-equipped *Branding Iron*, 401 W Ramshorn St (☎455-2893; ②), and *Trail's End*, 511 W Ramshorn St (☎455-2540; ①), make Dubois a bargain alternative to Jackson (see p.642). Its main evening activity is watching country crooners in classic Western bars such as the *Rustic Pine*, 199 E Ramshorn St (☎455-2430).

Pinedale

On the western side of the Wind River Range, tiny well-to-do **PINEDALE** on US-191 offers unrivalled access to the mountains. Once also a major logging center, it now attracts second-homeowners and backpackers. The **Museum of the Mountain Men**, 700 E Hennick St (summer only; Tues–Sat 9am–5pm, also Sun in midsummer noon–5pm), commemorates its role as a rendezvous for fur-trappers in the 1830s.

A 16-mile road winds east from Pinedale past Fremont Lake to **Elkhart Park**, from where trails lead past beautiful **Seneca Lake** and along rugged Indian Pass to the glaciers and 13,000-ft peaks (info from 210 W Pine St; ☎367-4326). *Rock Springs–Jackson Bus Line* serve Pinedale once a day. Clean basic **rooms** are available at the *Sundance Motel*, 148 E Pine St (☎367-4336; ②). Try the *Wrangler Café*, 310 E Pine St (☎367-4233), for breakfast, or the Mexican food at the *Corral Bar*, 30 W Pine St (☎367-2469).

Northwest and North Central Wyoming

Northern Wyoming has a whole lot more to offer than a handy route between the Black Hills and Yellowstone. The surreal volcanic monument of **Devils Tower**, the abrupt **Bighorn Mountains** and the desertscape of the **Bighorn Basin** are the major natural attractions in a land steeped in the history of Indian wars, outlaw activity and pioneer hardships. Small towns such as unassuming **Buffalo** and more commercialized **Cody**, developed by Buffalo Bill himself, are potential stopovers.

Devils Tower

Though Congress designated **DEVILS TOWER**, fifty miles from South Dakota in far northeastern Wyoming, to be the country's first national monument in 1906, it took Steven Spielberg's inspired use of it as the alien landing spot in *Close Encounters of the*

Third Kind to make this eerie 867-foot volcanic outcrop a true national icon. Plonked on top of a thickly forested hill, itself a full six hundred feet above the peaceful Belle Fourche River, it resembles a giant wizened tree stump; but, painted ever-changing hues by the sun and moon, it can be hauntingly beautiful. Sioux legend says the tower was formed after three young girls jumped onto a boulder to escape a vicious bear. They were rescued when the great god, seeing their plight, made the rock rise higher and higher; the bear's desperate efforts to climb up scored the sides of the column.

Four short trails loop the tower, beginning from the **visitor center** (daily summer 8am–7.45pm; otherwise 8am–4.45pm; ☎467-5501) at its base. The entrance fee per car is $3, and you can camp for $6 a night – arrive early or you'll end up paying more than twice that at one of the nearby commercial campgrounds.

Buffalo

Snuggled among the southeastern foothills of the Bighorn Mountains, quiet, attractive **BUFFALO** is unaffected by the bustle of the nearby I-90/I-25 intersection. Although **Main Street**, now lined with frontier-style stores, was an old buffalo trail, the town was named for an early resident's home of Buffalo, New York. The **Jim Gatchell Museum**, 10 Fort St, stacked full of Old West curiosities pertaining to soldiers, ranchers and Native Americans, is well worth a visit (June–Aug daily 9am–8pm; free).

Pick up information from Buffalo's **visitor center**, 55 N Main St (☎684-5544 or 1-800/684-5122). Decent **rooms** can be had at the *Mountain View Motel*, 585 Fort St (☎684-2881; ②), and the tasteless *Canyon Motel*, 997 Fort St (☎684-2957; ①). *Steve's*, 820 N Main St (☎684-5111), serves exquisite seafood and beef dishes at good prices.

Fort Phil Kearney
Fort Phil Kearney, the bloodiest of the western army forts, stood 17 miles north of Buffalo, off I-90. Only operative from 1866 to 1868, it was repeatedly stormed by Sioux, Apache and Cheyenne, and destroyed by jubilant Sioux when finally abandoned in 1868. A **museum** tells the story of the 1866 **Fetterman Massacre**, when Captain William Fetterman (who bragged that with eighty men he could whip any Indians in battle) ignored strict orders and was lured into the path of over a thousand Sioux warriors. Fetterman and his eighty soldiers were killed, the first US Army defeat ever to leave no survivors. Monuments mark this and other battlesites (mid-May to Sept, daily 8am–6pm; Oct to mid-May, Wed–Sun noon–4pm; free).

Through the Bighorn Mountains

Of the three scenic highways through the **Bighorn Mountains**, US-14A from **Burgess Junction**, fifty miles west of Victorian **Sheridan**, is the most spectacular. The massive and heavily wooded Bighorns soar abruptly from the plains to over 9000 feet; the loftiest peaks, protruding above the timberline, seem strikingly bald beside their dark-coated neighbors. The road edges its way up Medicine Mountain, on the windswept western peak of which the mysterious **Medicine Wheel** – the largest such monument to remain intact – stands protected behind a wire fence. Local Indian legends offer no clues as to the original purpose of these flat stones, arranged in a circular "wheel" with 28 spokes and a circumference of 245 feet – the pattern suggests sun-worship or early astronomy. Even if US-14A isn't closed by snow (usually Nov–May), the precipitous dirt track (past an incongruous radar dome) on which drivers can approach to within a mile of the Medicine Wheel, before hiking the rest of the way, may be impassable.

The route down the west side, with gradients of ten to twenty percent and three awesome runaway truck ramps, is said to have cost more to build per mile than any other road in America. Tight hairpin bends, passing almost vertical drops, keep the driver's eyes off the magnificent overlooks, but the best view comes near the bottom when the road belches you out into the **Bighorn Basin**. At first sight, this ultra-flat, sparsely vegetated valley, walled in by mighty mountains on three sides and ragged foothills to the north, seems like a land that time forgot.

Bighorn Canyon National Recreation Area

Before US-14A gets to Lovell, Hwy-37 turns north to the **Bighorn Canyon National Recreation Area**, an unexpected red-rock wilderness straddling the border between Wyoming and Montana. No road runs the full length of the canyon, which since being flooded by the 525-ft Yellowtail Dam (only accessible from Montana) has become primarily the preserve of watersports enthusiasts. In summer, **boat tours** (☎548-6418) leave from **Horseshoe Bend**, where the marina (☎548-7766) rents out assorted equipment, and a shadeless beach of red sand offers swimming in the bizarrest of settings. The **Devil's Canyon overlook** a few miles north affords landlubbers a rare opportunity to gauge the hideous depth of the abyss.

A **visitor center** just east of Lovell on US-14A (summer daily 8am–6pm, otherwise Sat & Sun 8am–5pm; ☎548-2251) supplies information on all activities.

Cody

CODY, 79 miles east along US-14 and the North Fork of the Shoshone River from Yellowstone, was the brainchild of investors who in 1896 persuaded "Buffalo Bill" Cody to get involved in their development company, knowing his approval would attract homesteaders and visitors alike. During summer, tourism is big business, but underneath all the Buffalo Bill-linked attractions and paraphernalia, Cody manages to retain the feel of a rural western settlement. It's certainly not a place where you would have expected avant-garde painter **Jackson Pollock** to have been born and brought up.

The wide dusty main thoroughfare, **Sheridan Avenue**, holds an array of souvenir and ranchwear shops, and is the scene of parades and rodeos during the annual **Cody Stampede**, held on the weekend of July 4. Between June and August, there's a **rodeo** every night at the open-air stadium on the road to Yellowstone (8.30pm; $6).

Buffalo Bill Historical Center

720 Sheridan Ave. June–Aug, daily 7am–10pm; May & Sept, 8am–8pm; April, Tues–Sun 8am–5pm; March & Nov, Tues–Sun 10am–3pm; closed Jan & Feb; 2-day pass $7; ☎587-4771 or 1-800/227-8483.

One of the nation's most comprehensive collections of western Americana, Cody's giant **Buffalo Bill Historical Center** comprises several distinct museums. Artefacts from William Cody's various careers, such as guns, gifts from European heads of state, billboards, clothes and dime novels help the **Buffalo Bill Museum** to chronicle the years of the Pony Express, Civil War, Indian Wars and Wild West shows.

The lives of western Native Americans are celebrated in the **Plains Indian Museum**, which at the end of each June organizes the musical and dance performances of the **Plains Indian Powwow**. The museum's permanent historical collection is given a tragic note by the display of Ghost Dance shirts. In the late 1880s, the religious revelation of the Paiute prophet Wovoka swept the western tribes. He declared that ritual purification through song and dance would hasten the day when all whites would be buried by a heaven-sent fall of soil, and their dead warriors, along with huge herds of buffalo, would return to the Plains. The US Army condemned Ghost Dances as unacceptable shows of resistance, and mobilized troops to disrupt ceremonies.

In the beautifully laid-out **Whitney Gallery of Western Art**, the contrasting styles of Frederic Remington and Charles M Russell command most attention. The propagandist Remington dwells on conflict, depicting the Indian as a savage in the path of progress, while Russell's work shows a consistent respect for Native American life.

BUFFALO BILL

The much-mythologized exploits of **William Frederick "Buffalo Bill" Cody**, born in Iowa in 1846, began at the age of just eleven, when the murder of his father forced him to take a job as an army despatch rider. An early escape from ambush brought Cody fame as the "Youngest Indian Slayer of the Plains"; four years later, he became the youngest rider on the legendary **Pony Express**. After a stint fighting for the Union, Cody found work – and a lifelong nickname – supplying buffalo meat to workers laying the transcontinental railroad. He killed over 4200 animals in just eighteen months, before rejoining the army in 1868 as its chief scout. In the next decade, when the Plains Indian Wars were at their peak, he earned a Congressional Medal of Honor and a remarkable record of never losing any troops in ambushes. Among battles in which he took part was the 1877 encounter with Sioux forces when he killed – and scalped – Chief Yellow Hand.

By the late 1870s, exaggerated accounts of Cody's adventures were appearing back east in the "dime novels" of Ned Buntline, and with the Indian Wars all but over he took to guiding Yankee and European gentry on buffalo hunts. He referred to the vacationers as "dudes", and called his camps "dude ranches". The theatrical productions he laid on for his rich guests developed into the world-famous **Wild West Show**. First staged in 1883, these spectacular outdoor carnivals usually consisted of a re-enactment of an Indian battle such as Custer's Last Stand, featuring Sioux who had been present at Little Bighorn, trick riders, buffalo, clowns, and exhibition shooting and riding by the man himself. The show spent ten of its thirty years in Europe, and made Buffalo Bill "the most famous and recognized man in the world". Dressed in the finest silks and sporting a well-groomed goatee, Cody stayed in the finest hotels and dining with heads of state; Queen Victoria was so enthusiastic in her admiration that rumors circulated of an affair between them.

In later life, a mellowing Cody played down his past activities, to the point of urging the government to respect all Indian treaties and put an end to the wanton slaughter of buffalo and game. Although the Wild West Show was reckoned to have brought in as much as one million dollars per year, his many investments failed badly, and, in January 1915, a penniless 69-year-old Buffalo Bill died at his sister's home in Denver. His grave can be found atop Lookout Mountain, outside Golden, Colorado (see p.607).

Practicalities

For information and accommodation reservations, contact Cody's **visitor center** at 836 Sheridan Ave (Mon–Sat 8am–7pm, Sun 10am–3pm; ☎587-2297). Cody is the site of the Yellowstone Regional Airport, primarily connected with Denver by *Continental*. *Powder River* at 1701 Sheridan Ave (☎587-5544) runs one-day Yellowstone tours, and **float trips** on the Shoshone are available from, among others, *Wyoming River Trips* (☎587-6661).

Cody's showpiece Western **hotel**, the *Irma* at 1192 Sheridan Ave (☎587-4221 or 1-800/745-4762; ④), was named for Buffalo Bill's daughter in 1902, and retains a superb original cherrywood bar. Among good-value motels, the friendly *Skyline Motor Inn*, high above town on the main through highway at 1919 17th St (☎587-4201 or 1-800/843-8809; ②), stands out. Sheridan Avenue is very much the place for an evening's entertainment. Having eaten at the *Irma*'s always packed ribs restaurant, call in for a drink at the authentic *Golden Eagle Bar* at no 1219, or the tamer *Proud Cut Saloon*, no 1227. *Kathryn & Co*, no 1272, is the venue for the morning espresso and breakfast.

Wapiti Valley

The drive west from Cody to Yellowstone is a superb preparation for the splendors of the park itself, skirting the artificial lake created by the Buffalo Bill Dam before running alongside the Shoshone River through the open high **Wapiti Valley**, the heart of Wyoming's "beef country", and finally climbing through the rugged mountains to Sylvan Pass. Lodges and campgrounds appear at intervals without impinging on the magnificence of the landscape. Exactly halfway along, the *Mountain View Lodge and*

Motel (☎587-2081; ③) commands an awesome prospect of the valley. Inside, the atmospheric dining room is festooned with hunting trophies and guns.

Yellowstone National Park

Millions of visitors each year come to **YELLOWSTONE NATIONAL PARK**, America's oldest national park and the largest in the lower 48 states, to glory in its magnificent mountain scenery and abundant wildlife, and above all to witness hydrothermal phenomena on a unique scale. Measuring roughly sixty miles by fifty miles, and slightly overlapping from Wyoming's northwestern corner into Idaho and Montana, the park centers on a 7500-ft-high plateau, the caldera of a vast volcanic eruption which occurred a mere 600,000 years ago. Into it are crammed more than half the world's **geysers**, in which the rain and snow that seeps through the bedrock escapes the pressure-cooker conditions under the surface in intermittent spectacular blasts, plus thousands of **fumaroles** jetting plumes of steam, **mud pots** gurgling with acid-dissolved muds and clays, and **hot springs**.

Combine the **colors** of the Grand Canyon of the Yellowstone, limpid Yellowstone Lake, the wildflower meadows and the rainbow-hued geyser pools; the **sounds** of subterranean rumblings, belching mud pools, and steam hissing from the mountainsides; and the constant **smells** of drifting sulfurous fumes, with the presence of browsing bull moose, shambling bears, heavy-bearded bison, herds of elk and everywhere scurrying **marmots**, and Yellowstone amounts to an extraordinary experience. If you allow yourself to get frustrated by the inevitable crowds and expense, you'll be missing something very special. The key to appreciating the park is to take your time, and to plan carefully; above all, try to allow for a stay of at least three days.

Arrival and Information

Two of the five main **entrances** to Yellowstone are in Wyoming, at **Cody** in the east and **Grand Teton National Park** to the south. The others are in Montana: **West Yellowstone** (west), **Gardiner** (north) and **Cooke City** (northeast). Most roads are open from May to October only (see box). Admission – $10 per car ($4 for each pedestrian or cyclist) – is good for seven days, and includes entry to Grand Teton park.

The **park headquarters** are at **Mammoth Hot Springs** near the north entrance (daily, June–Sept 8am–7pm, otherwise 9am–5pm; ☎344-7381). Tune into 1606 AM for weather information, and consult the *Yellowstone Today* freesheet for activities and current regulations. Other, summer-only, **visitor centers** are located approximately every twenty miles along the main **Loop Road**. Each issues backcountry hiking permits, and has an exhibit on a different aspect of the park – natural and human history (Mammoth Hot Springs), geothermal activity (Old Faithful and Norris), wilderness areas and the 1988 fires (Grant Village), wildlife (Fishing Bridge), and geology (Canyon). National Park Service leaflets (25¢ each) cover the important landmarks.

To get to Yellowstone by **bus**, take *Karst Stage* (☎406/586-8567) from Bozeman, via West Yellowstone or Gardiner; *Powder River Transportation* (☎1-800/442-3682), who run tours and one-way trips from Jackson, Cody or West Yellowstone; or *TW Services* (☎344-7311) from West Yellowstone, Gardiner or Billings, who also run one-day tours inside the park ($22–25). *Greyhound* run as far as West Yellowstone (☎406/646-7666).

Touring the Park

All of Yellowstone's major sights are labelled and signposted within a few hundred yards of the 142-mile **Loop Road**, a figure-of-eight circuit fed by roads from the five entrances. Although the **speed limit** is a radar-enforced 45mph, the traffic makes jour-

A BRIEF HUMAN HISTORY OF YELLOWSTONE

Although Native Americans had long hunted in what is now **Yellowstone National Park**, they were decimated by disease (and in their absence, the wildlife was thriving) by the time the first white man arrived in 1807 – **John Colter**, a veteran of the Lewis & Clark expedition (see also p.647). His account of the exploding geysers and seething cauldrons of "Colter's Hell" was widely ridiculed. However, as ever more trappers, scouts and prospectors hit upon Yellowstone, the government eventually sent out survey teams in 1870. Just two years later, Yellowstone was set aside as the first **national park**, in part to ensure that its assets were not entirely stripped by hunters, miners or lumber companies.

At first, management of the park was beset by problems; Congress devoted enthusiasm but little funding towards its protection. Irresponsible tourists stuck soap down the geysers, ruining the intricate plumbing; bandits preyed on stagecoaches carrying rich excursionists; and the Nez Percé even killed two tourists as they raced through the park (see p.659). Congress took the park out of civilian hands in 1886, and put the army in charge. By the time they handed over to the newly created National Park Service in 1917, the ascendancy of the automobile in Yellowstone had begun.

The conflict between tourism and wilderness preservation has raged ever since. The elimination of predators such as mountain lions and wolves let the elk herd grow unsupportably large; the former policy of permitting bears to feed from tourist scraps resulted in maulings, a far cry the friendly image of TV's *Jellystone* bears, Yogi and Boo Boo. Ecologists now argue that the park cannot stand alone as some pristine paradise, but must be seen as part of a much larger "Greater Yellowstone Ecosystem".

The **fires** that razed 36 percent of the park in 1988 once again focussed attention on Yellowstone's environmental policies. Despite President Reagan's dismay, park authorities insisted the burn was a natural part of the forest's ecocycle, clearing out 200-year-old trees to make way for new growth. The scarred mountainsides are now clearly recovering.

ney times hard to predict. To get the most out of a visit, even if you're short on time, choose one or two areas to explore thoroughly.

Only in the early morning is **cycling** bearable or safe; there are no mountain bike trails. Though you can expect to **walk** considerable distances along the canyon and geyser trails, it's an idea to leave backcountry hiking for the more exciting **Grand Teton National Park** – which doesn't have the mosquitoes.

The following account runs clockwise around the Loop Road, from Old Faithful to the Yellowstone Lake area, both of which lie in the southern reaches of the park.

Geyser Country: From Old Faithful to Mammoth Hot Springs

For well over a century, the dependable **Old Faithful** has been the most popular geyser in the park, erupting more frequently than any of its higher or larger rivals. As a result, a half-moon of concentric benches, backed by visitor facilities including the gigantic log-built *Old Faithful Inn*, now surround it at a respectful distance on the side away from the Firehole River. On average, it "performs" for the expectant crowds every 78 minutes, with a minimum gap of half an hour and a maximum of two hours; approximate schedules are displayed in the nearby visitor center. The first sign of activity is water splashing repeatedly over the rim. After several minutes, a column of water shoots to a height of 100 to 180 feet, spurting out a total of 11,000 gallons.

Two miles of boardwalks lead from Old Faithful to dozens of other geysers in the Upper Basin. If possible, try to arrive when **Grand Geyser** is due to explode. This colossus blows its top on average just twice a day, for twelve to twenty minutes, in a series of four powerful bursts which climb to 200 feet. At the far end of the trail, the deep blue color of the **Morning Glory Pool** is caused by algae.

Other highlights along the banks of the Firehole River, usually lined with browsing buffalo, include the fluorescent intensity of the **Grand Prismatic Spring** at Midway

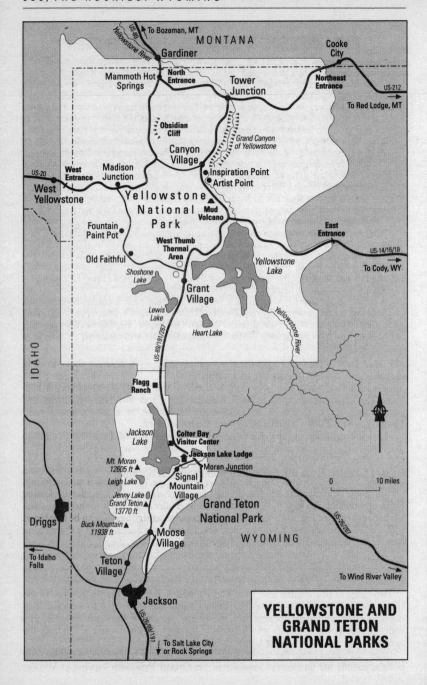

**YELLOWSTONE AND
GRAND TETON
NATIONAL PARKS**

WINTER IN YELLOWSTONE

Blanketed in four feet of snow between November and April, Yellowstone takes on a whole new appearance: a silent and bizarre world where waterfalls freeze in mid-plunge, geysers blast towering plumes of steam and water into the cold, crisp air, and buffalo, beards matted with ice, stand around in huddles. Only the road from Gardiner to Cooke City via Mammoth Hot Springs is kept open (and the Beartooth Highway is closed), and you can only stay at Mammoth Hot Springs and Old Faithful (accessible by snowmobile).

Winter vacationing in Yellowstone took off in a big way in the Sixties. *TW Services* run **snowcoach** tours of the west side of the park from Flagg Ranch at the southern entrance, West Yellowstone and Mammoth Hot Springs ($60–80). *Alpen Guides* (☎406/646-9591) run slightly cheaper excursions out of West Yellowstone. **Snowmobile** rental, generally cheapest in West Yellowstone, costs around $100 a day. Much less expensive is **cross-country skiing**; several miles of groomed trails explore the park's west side.

Geyser basin. Thirty miles north of Old Faithful, in the less crowded **Norris Geyser Basin**, two separate trails explore a pallid primeval landscape of whistling vents and fumaroles. **Steamboat**, the world's tallest geyser, forces near-boiling water over 300 feet in the air, but only functions once or twice a year, whereas the whirlpool-pattern eruptions of the **Echinus Geyser** occur every 35 to 75 minutes. The **Evening Primrose Spring** is a flower-shaped crater filled with iridescent yellow mud.

At **Mammoth Hot Springs**, at the northern tip of the Loop Road, terraces of barnacle-like deposits cascade down a vapor-shrouded mountainside. Tinted a marvellous array of greys, greens, yellows, browns, and oranges by algae, they are composed of travertine, a form of limestone which, having been dissolved and carried to the surface by boiling water, is deposited as tier upon tier of steaming stone.

Tower and Roosevelt Areas

The main landmark of Yellowstone's **Tower** and **Roosevelt** areas, east of Mammoth Hot Springs, is **Mount Washburn**, the park's highest peak, whose lookout tower can be reached by an enjoyable all-day hike or a gruelling cycle ride. A more manageable trail leads down to the spray-drenched base of **Tower Fall**. From Tower Junction, US-212 wanders away east through the meadows of serene **Lamar Valley**, where moose and buffalo graze, towards the ice-packed peaks of the **Beartooth Mountains**.

The Grand Canyon of the Yellowstone River

The Yellowstone River roars and tumbles for 24 miles between the sheer golden-hued cliffs of the 1540-foot **Grand Canyon of the Yellowstone**, its course punctuated by two narrow but striking **waterfalls**: the 109-foot **Upper Falls** and the thunderous **Lower Falls**, plummeting 308 feet. Both rims of the canyon offer superb vistas, short trails and intense scenery, but the north side is the more popular, as sightseeing can be combined with a visit to the nearby stores and snackbars. To see some bears, head for the viewing area at the intersection of the Tower and Northern Rim roads at dawn or dusk.

On the south rim, **Artists' Point** looks down 700 feet to the river, swirling between mineral-stained walls. Nearby, Uncle Tom's Trail descends deep into the canyon, to a gently vibrating, spray-covered platform right in the face of the Lower Falls. A few miles south, the river widens to meander over tranquil, marshy **Haydn Valley**. Buffalo, elk and deer congregate here, so it's an unsuitable place to go on foot.

The ominous rumblings and sulfurous stench of the **Mud Volcano** area make it the moodiest and ugliest of the park's thermal regions. A one-mile boardwalk winds through gurgling pools of sickly brown and yellow mud, past trees that have been steamed to death, to the bleak, barren shores of Sour Lake: an unnerving sight at the best of times, at dusk it makes a chemical waste dump look appealing.

Yellowstone Lake

North America's largest alpine lake, the deep and (usually) deceptively calm **Yellowstone Lake**, fills the eastern half of the Yellowstone caldera. At 7733 feet above sea level it's high enough to be frozen for half the year, but in summer it's filled with tourists out on cruises ($6.75 for one hour), rowboats ($4.50 per hour), motor launches ($19.75 per hour) and fishing expeditions. *TW Services* maintains two "villages" beside the lake – **Fishing Bridge**, long scheduled for closure to preserve grizzly populations, and its replacement, the newer and much-opposed **Grant Village**.

Accommodation in the Park

A lucrative monopoly on accommodation within the park is held by *TW Recreational Services Inc*. Reservations, strongly recommended during July and August, are essential over public holiday weekends (PO Box 165, Yellowstone Park, WY 82190-0165; ☎344-7311). Prices beyond the park boundaries are a little lower, but staying inside can be relaxing; none of the rooms has a TV, and only a few après-hike revellers stay up past midnight. Every location has a lodge building offering dining facilities (closing at 9.30pm) and sometimes a laundromat, grocery store, gift shop and gas station.

Canyon Lodge Cabins. Half a mile from the Grand Canyon of the Yellowstone. All en-suite. ③.

Grant Village. Spartan rooms on the southwest shore of Yellowstone Lake. ④.

Lake Yellowstone Hotel and Cabins. Grand Colonial-style hotel rooms, and dark and dingy en-suite cabins. The *Sun Room*, looking over the lake, makes a great place for an evening drink. ③/④.

Mammoth Hot Springs Hotel & Cabins. Right at the north end of the park. Very basic *Rough Rider* cabins, without shower or toilet, en-suite cabins, and hotel rooms. ①/②/③.

Old Faithful Inn and Lodge. Not surprisingly, a very popular location. Assorted rooms in the amazing inn – said to be the world's largest log building – plus *Rough Rider* and en-suite cabins. ①/②–⑧.

Roosevelt Lodge Cabins. The cheapest place to stay in the park, at $20 for a rustic shelter that has no bedding. *Rough Rider* and en-suite cabins. ①–③.

Accommodation in Gateway Towns

In addition to **Jackson** (see p.642) and **Cody** (p.634) in Wyoming, the small towns just outside the park's western and two northern gates offer alternative and somewhat cheaper lodging, as well as more nightlife. **West Yellowstone**, the largest, at the west entrance, is disfigured by gift stores and fast-food joints, though the surrounding national forestlands are well worth exploring. The hamlet of **Gardiner** lies next to the northwest entrance, just five miles from Mammoth Hot Springs, while the one-street villages of **Silver Gate** and more developed **Cooke City** are three and ten miles respectively from the northeast entrance on US-212.

Alpine Motel, US-212, Cooke City (☎406/838-2371). Basic but clean rooms. ②.

Alpine Motel, 120 Madison Ave, West Yellowstone (☎406/646-7544). No-frills lodgings. ②.

Blue Haven Motel, Gardiner (☎406/848-7719). Basic cabins with kitchenettes. ②.

Brandin' Iron Motel, 201 Canyon Ave, West Yellowstone (☎406/646-7664 or 1-800/231-5991). Bright new motel with hot tubs. ③.

Hillcrest Motel, US-89, Gardiner (☎406/848-9353). Slightly pokey rooms with kitchenettes. ②.

Hoosier's Motel, US-212, Cooke City (☎406/838-2241). Immaculate modern motel. ③.

Parkview Cabins, US-212, Silver Gate (☎406/838-2371). Cabins, plain or with kitchenettes. ②.

West Yellowstone Int'l Hostel and **Madison Hotel**, 139 Yellowstone Ave, West Yellowstone (☎406/646-7745). Clean, friendly old wooden hotel, with dorm beds and rooms. Summer only. ①/②.

Camping

The **National Park Service** (☎344-7381) operates eleven **campgrounds** in the park. All operate on a first-come, first-served basis, except for **Bridge Bay**, where reservations can be made through *Mistix* (☎1-800/365-2267). With a total of less than 2000 spaces, it's best to turn up very early in the morning. Fees are $6 to $10 per night.

Mammoth Hot Springs is the only campground open year round; most of the others operate between late May and September. In the northeast of the park, Slough Creek, Tower Fall and Pebble Creek are all small, very scenic and extremely popular locations. You can also camp at Madison, Norris, Indian Creek, Lewis Lake and Grant Village, which has the best shower and laundry facilities. Due to prowling bears, spaces at Canyon Village and Fishing Bridge are restricted to hard-sided vehicles.

To camp in the **backcountry** you need a wilderness permit, free from visitor centers or ranger stations. Camping is also available at commercial grounds in the gateway towns, and in neighboring National Forests such as Gallatin (☎344-7381) to the northwest and Shoshone (☎527-6241) to the east.

Eating

Snack bars and **restaurants** inside the park are expensive; even buying food at the general stores can work out pricey. The gateway towns hold few culinary delights, but do offer cheaper prices and more variety. In **West Yellowstone**, the *Running Bear Pancake House*, 538 Madison Ave, is good for breakfast, and the down-home *Thiem's Café*, 38 Canyon St, does the best lunches. The *Town Café* in Gardiner has a huge salad bar, while the stylish *Beartooth Café* in Cooke City is probably the best place for breakfast, burgers and inexpensive dinners in any of the peripheral towns.

Grand Teton National Park and Jackson Hole

The classic triangular peaks of **GRAND TETON NATIONAL PARK**, which stretches for fifty miles between Yellowstone and Jackson, are every bit as dramatic as the mountains of its congested neighbor, and a visit should be more than an afterthought on the route south. Though not especially high or extensive by Rocky Mountain standards, these sheer-faced cliffs make a magnificent spectacle, rising abruptly to tower 7000 feet above the valley floor. A string of gem-like lakes is set tight at the foot of the mountains; beyond them lies the broad, sagebrush-covered **Jackson Hole** (a "hole" was the pioneers' term for a flat, mountain-ringed valley), broken by the winding Snake River.

Shoshone Indians knew the mountains as the *Teewinot* ("many pinnacles"), but the present name, meaning big bosom, was given by lonesome French-Canadian trappers in the 1830s. After Congress set the mountains aside as a national park in 1929, it took another 21 years of legal wrangling for Grand Teton to reach its current size – local ranchers protested that the economy of Jackson Hole would be ruined if any further land was surrendered to tourism. Meanwhile, John D Rockefeller Jr bought up a large swathe of Jackson Hole and presented it to the government for free (on the condition that the *Grand Teton Lodge Company*, which he then owned, would be the exclusive operator of park concessions).

Seeing the Park

No road crosses the Tetons, but those that run along their eastern flank were designed with an eye to the mountains, affording stunning views at every turn. Two excellent side trips are the **Jenny Lake Scenic Loop**, leading to a face-to-face encounter with towering, partly hunchbacked **Grand Teton Mountain**, and the narrow track up **Signal Mountain**, which gives a fine view of the main Teton block and Jackson Hole.

Hiking trails, too, have been laid out so that no time is wasted in getting to the highlights. One easy and popular walk is along the sandy beaches of **Leigh Lake**, where the imposing 12,605-foot **Mount Moran** bursts out dramatically from the lake shores. Also very accessible are the cascading **Hidden Falls**, reachable by a two-mile walk along the south shore of Jenny Lake; it's more fun to take the shuttle boat ($3.50

return) across the lake, and walk the remaining 800 yards. For the more adventurous, the rocky nine-mile trail from Hidden Falls through U-shaped **Cascade Canyon** leads to aptly named **Lake Solitude**. Another strenuous hike, and an excellent way to reach treeline in a short distance, is the five-mile trail from **Lupine Meadows**, just south of Jenny Lake, skirting small glacial pools like Amphitheater and Surprise lakes.

On the flat roads of the Hole, **cycling** is a joy; rent a bike down in Jackson, or from *Dornan's* in Moose (☎733-3314). To admire the Tetons from **water**, take a float trip along the Snake River (see p.643) or rent a rowing boat from Colter Bay (☎543-2811) or Signal Mountain marinas (☎543-2831). In winter, all hiking trails are open to cross-country **skiiers**, and **snowmobiles** can be rented from various outlets in Jackson.

Practicalities

Shuttle buses to the park run from Jackson and Yellowstone. The **visitor centers** are just off the main road in **Moose** (daily all year, June to early Sept 8am–7pm, otherwise 8am–5pm; ☎733-2880) to the south, and at **Colter Bay** (daily, June to early Sept 8am–7pm, May 8am–5pm; ☎543-2467), halfway up, on the east shore of Jackson Lake. The **Indian Arts Museum** at Colter Bay should on no account be missed; it's a magnificent collection of Plains Indian craftwork, watched over by experts. A 24-hour recorded message (☎733-2220) and the free *Teewinot* newspaper give details of ranger-led activities. The entrance fee of $10 per car ($4 for each pedestrian or cyclist) also covers Yellowstone.

Rooms, services and activities within the park are managed by the *Grand Teton Lodge Co* (PO Box 240, Moran, WY 83013; ☎543-2811); reservations are essential in summer. Prices for the comfortable rooms in *Jackson Lake Lodge* depend on whether or not you want a mountain view (⑤/⑦); *Colter Bay Village Cabins* are more utilitarian (②, or ③ en suite), and in high summer they also have $20 "Tent Cabins" of log and canvas – potentially pretty cold at night. On the park perimeter, the basic *Atkinson's Motel* is in Moran (☎543-2442; ②), and there are motels in Jackson (see below).

All of the five summer-only park **campgrounds** work on a first-come, first-served basis. Visitor centers or entrance stations can advise on availability. Individual campgrounds tend to fill in July and August as follows: Jenny Lake (8am), Signal Mountain (10am), Colter Bay (noon), Lizard Creek (2pm) and Gros Ventre (evening). For backcountry camping, you need a permit from the Moose ranger station (☎733-2880).

The park restaurants and snack bars, especially at Colter Bay, are good but a little pricey. *Dornan's* (☎733-2415), however, just outside the southern entrance in Moose, serves all-you-can-eat pancake breakfasts for $6 and rib dinners for $12. For the ultimate in relaxation, have an early-evening drink in *Jackson Lake Lodge's Blue Heron Lounge*, where you can recline in comfortable chairs and watch the ever-changing blues, greys, purples and warm pinks of Mount Moran through huge picture windows.

Jackson

The overgrown community of **JACKSON** is tucked in at the end of Jackson Hole, ten miles from Teton park's southern gate. Hunched around a tree-shaded square, marked by an arch of elk antlers at each corner, the Old-West-style boardwalks of **downtown** front designer clothes shops, craft shops and over thirty galleries. Every summer evening, except Sundays, an amateurish shootout is staged in the town square. In winter, time is better spent visiting the **National Elk Refuge** on the north edge of town, where you can take a horse-drawn sleigh ride among a 10,000-strong herd of elk (late Dec to late March, daily 10am–4pm; $7; ☎733-9212).

In recent years, Jackson has become the center of a **ski-ing** boom, with the season running from early December to early April. Summer visitors can enjoy **chairlift** rides up 7751-ft Snow King Mountain (part of the **Snow King** resort; ☎733-5200 or 1-800/ 522-5464) from Snow King Ave, six blocks from the town square (daily 10am–6pm; $4), coming down by hiking, cycling or the thrilling **Alpine Slide** ($4 a go). Out at **Teton Village**, home of the **Jackson Hole** resort (☎733-2292), aerial **trams** swoosh their way 10,536 feet to the top of Rendezvous Mountain for a spectacular panorama of the valley and mountain ranges (June–Aug 9am–7pm; May & Sept 10am–5pm; $14; ☎733-2292).

Information, Activities and Transportation

Jackson's **visitor center** is at 532 N Cache St (☎733-3316), next to the Bridger-Teton National Forest Headquarters (☎733-2752), which provides details of hiking and back-country camping. *START* buses (☎733-3135) run to Teton Village, twelve miles north-west, while the *Grand Teton Lodge Company* (☎733-2811) and *Powder River* operate services to the parks. *Jackson–Rock Springs* vans (☎733-3135) connect with Rock Springs, 165 miles southeast, the closest *Greyhound* stop.

Jackson's **airport** is actually within the national park, eight miles north; it's linked to town by *All Star Transportation* van service ($7; ☎733-2888) or $20 taxis.

Dozens of companies in Jackson offer **float trips** on the Snake River. *Fort Jackson Float Trips*, 315 W Broadway (☎733-2583), do good-value five-hour trips for around $30 including lunch, while *Leisure Sports*, 1075 Hwy-89S (☎733-3040), offers reasonable rental rates for rafts, kayaks, tubes and bikes. Horse rides at the *OK Corral Ranch* (☎733-6556), ten minutes' drive south on Hwy-191, cost as little as $12 for two hours.

Coach tours are available from *Gray Line*, 330 N Glenwood St (☎733-4325), who whisk you through both Teton and Yellowstone parks on a brisk one-day drive for $40. *Powder River Tours*, 565 N Cache St (☎733-2136), which spends a full day in the Tetons, with a boat trip on Jenny Lake, for $36, is a better option. Guided **bike tours** in the area are run by *Teton Mountain Bike Tours* (☎733-0712) for around $10 per hour.

Accommodation

Accommodation in Jackson tends to come at above average prices, though during winter, motel rates are generally 25 percent lower. The closest **camping** is at the *Jackson Hole Campground* (☎733-2927), off West Broadway.

Antler Motel, 50 W Pearl St (☎733-2535). Very central motel, but reasonably quiet. ③.

AYH Hostel, Teton Village Ski Resort (☎733-3415). $17 for a dorm bed, in the ski area a dozen miles northwest, with private rooms for non-members. ①–②.

Bunkhouse in the Anvil Motel, 215 N Cache St (☎733-3668). $20 beds in clean but large dorm. ①.

Moose Meadows, 1225 Green Lane, Wilson (☎733-9510). Informal and very welcoming B&B set in plenty of space six miles west of town at the foot of the Teton Pass. ④.

Snow King Lodge, 470 King St (☎733-3480). The best-priced of the central motels. ③.

Woods Motel, 120 N Glenwood St (☎733-2953). Budget motel not far from the visitor center. ③.

Eating and Nightlife

The year-round tourist trade makes Jackson Wyoming's liveliest night-time commu-nity, with an ever-changing cast of **restaurants** and **nightspots**.

Anthony's, 62 S Glenwood St (☎733-3717). Good Italian food – imaginative and well-priced.

The Bunnery, 130 N Cache St (☎733-5474). Great breakfasts, stuffed omelettes and sandwiches.

Cadillac Grill, 55 N Cache St (☎733-3279). Fancy Art-Deco restaurant on the main square. Huge burgers, but also buffalo, wild boar, caribou, antelope and seafood entrees for $12 to $20.

Dynamic Health, 130 W Broadway (☎733-5418). Vegetarian menu; burgers, tofu, fruit smoothies.

Mangy Moose, Teton Village (☎733-9779). Antique-laden music venue, good for rock and reggae.

Million Dollar Cowboy Bar, 25 N Cache St (☎733-2207). Glitzy Western-themed bar, with saddles for seats and a large dancefloor.

Spirits of the West, 385 W Broadway (☎733-3854). Down-to earth-local bar.

MONTANA

MONTANA is Big Sky country. The entire state is blessed with a huge blue roof, which perfectly complements its beautiful **west**. A magnificent northernmost cap for the US Rockies, this is a region of snowcapped summits, turbulent rivers, spectacular glacial valleys, heavily wooded forests and sparkling blue lakes, at their most dramatic in **Glacier National Park**. By contrast, the **eastern** two-thirds is high prairie: sun-parched in summer and wracked by icy blizzards each winter.

Preconceptions of a desolate land populated by cowpunchers are soon shattered; each of Montana's small cities has its own proud identity. The university and sawmill community of **Missoula**, for example, possesses a high-culture feel absent from the heavily Irish, copper-mining town and union stronghold of **Butte**, while state capital **Helena** still harks back to its prosperous gold mining years.

The fur-trappers and gold miners who were the first whites to brave this inhospitable terrain soon moved on, but as white settlers invaded Indian hunting grounds, conflict was inevitable. A key plank of army strategy was to starve the Indians into submission: "For the sake of a lasting peace let them [professional hunters] kill, skin and sell until the buffalo are exterminated. Then your prairies can be covered by the speckled cow and the festive cowboy," declared General Philip Sheridan. By the late 1870s the buffalo were almost gone, and most of Montana had been cleared for settlement.

The speckled cow and festive cowboy were not in for an easy time. The horrendous winter of 1886 wiped out many herds, and the "sodbusters" who planted wheat in the wake of bankrupt ranchers often fared little better. Plagues of grasshoppers, droughts, falling wheat prices and erosion of the topsoil caused farms to fail everywhere in the Twenties, during which time Montana was the only state to record a population decline.

Wheat has since made a revival, and now, with lumbering and coal mining, forms the base of Montana's economy. Another significant money-earner is tourism, though the harsh climate restricts the season to the months between June and September.

Getting Around Montana

Considering Montana's size and sparse population, transport connections are good. *Amtrak* **trains** cross the north, stopping east and west of Glacier National Park without making it easier to see the park itself. *Greyhound* and regional **bus** companies like *Intermountain* (north from Butte and Missoula to Glacier; ☎442-5860) and *Rimrock* (east–west from Billings to Missoula; ☎1-800/255-7655) serve towns on I-90 and I-15.

The best way to get around this huge state is by car, with practically every interstate exit in western Montana leading to areas of mountain solitude, interesting landmarks or small communities. *Delta Airlines* offer the most **flights** to Montana, landing in seven towns. Western Montana is great **cycling** territory; the *Bikecentennial* organization, whose national headquarters are in Missoula (see p.650), can provide special maps.

Eastern Montana

Before ranchers and farmers settled the flat prairie of **eastern Montana**, it was prime **buffalo** territory: one early traveller waited three nights while a massive herd crossed his path. Native Americans fought hard to hold onto their land; the crushing defeats they inflicted on the US Army include the legendary victory at **Little Bighorn**.

The eastern Montana plains are intermittently broken by mountains, of which the most impressive are the icy **Beartooth Range**, crammed between the village of Red Lodge and Yellowstone. Don't expect much from the region's towns; most are lazy farm supply centers, and down-at-heel **Billings**, Montana's largest city with a population of just over 70,000, doesn't have much more to offer.

Little Bighorn Battlefield National Monument

56 miles southeast of Billings; entrance 2 miles east of I-90 on US-212. Visitor center and museum: daily summer 8am–8pm, spring & fall 8am–6pm, winter 8am–4.30pm; ☎638-2622. Battlefield: daily 8am–dusk; $3 per car, free passes available for cemetery only.

In June 1876 massive US Army detachments were sent to southeastern Montana to subjugate the Sioux and Cheyenne. A key unit in the campaign was the crack **Seventh Cavalry**; at its head was the flamboyant **Lt-Colonel George Armstrong Custer**.

Few if any US soldiers have achieved the fame or opprobrium of Custer. During an erratic career, he graduated last in his class at West Point in 1861; was the US Army's youngest-ever major general; was suspended for ordering the execution of deserters from a forced march he led through Kansas primarily to see his wife; and became notorious for allowing the murder in 1868 of almost 100 Cheyenne women and children.

On June 25 1876, Custer's was the first unit to arrive in the **Little Bighorn Valley**. Disdaining to await reinforcements, he set out to raze a teepee village along the Little Bighorn River – which turned out to be the largest-ever gathering of Plains Indians. As a party of his men pursued fleeing women and children, they were encircled by 2000 Sioux and Cheyenne warriors emerging from either side of a ravine. The soldiers dismounted to attempt to shoot their way out, but were soon overwhelmed; simultaneously, Custer's command post on a nearby hill was wiped out. Archeologists have discounted the idea of Custer's Last Stand as a heroic defiance in which Custer was the last cavalryman left standing; the battle lasted less than an hour, with the white soldiers being systematically and effortlessly picked off. The most decisive Native American victory in the West – led by Sitting Bull – was also their final great show of resistance. An incensed President Grant piled maximum resources into a military campaign that brought about the effective defeat of all Plains Indians by the end of the decade.

You can trace the course of the battle on a five-mile self-guided car tour through the grasslands, following the high ridge overlooking the valley, or on a narrated bus tour ($2). White marble tablets mark where individual soldiers fell, and a sandstone obelisk stands above their mass grave on "Last Stand Hill" (Custer himself lies in West Point Military Academy). Dioramas in the visitor center outline the battle, while the US military cemetery nearby holds the dead of all America's wars.

Hardin

Little Bighorn is the focus of the Crow Indian Reservation. Little **HARDIN**, 13 miles northwest, makes its living from tourists seeking authentic Indian artefacts and other western mementoes. Each year, on the weekend closest to the battle's anniversary of June 25, the **Little Bighorn Days** festival centers around re-enactments of the battle at a site eight miles west of the town (*not* at the original battlefield). Other activities include Indian dancing, downtown parades, dinner dances and a rodeo.

The least expensive place to **stay** is the *Western Motel* at Hwy-313 and W Third St (☎665-2296; ②). The central *Lariat Motel*, 709 N Center Ave (☎665-2683; ③) is a little more atmospheric, with the friendly snack bar *Margaret's Chat'n'Chew* next door.

Billings

By Montana standards, **BILLINGS** is a big city. Its dramatic setting, bounded on its north and east sides by the 400-foot crumpled sandstone cliffs of the **Rimrock**, certainly makes it something more than a pockmark on the prairie. The town itself, however, consists largely of run-down housing projects, and a city center whose shops have transferred out to the malls. Scarring its west side are the tracks and warehouses of the Northern Pacific Railroad, whose president, Frederick Billings, gave the city its name.

The **area code** for the entire state of Montana is ☎406.

On the Rimroad, right by Logan Airport, the free **Peter Yegen Jr Museum** (Mon–Fri 10.30am–5pm, Sun 2–5pm) is a fascinating jumble, devoted to eastern Montana pioneers. Oddities among the cabinets of weapons, fossils and domestic equipment include a stuffed two-headed calf and a display of dozens of types of barbed wire.

Billings' **bus station**, served by *Greyhound* along I-90 and I-15, and *Powder River*, north from Wyoming, is at 2501 First Ave N (☎245-5116). The *Best Western Ponderosa Inn*, next door at 2511 First Ave N (☎259-5511; ②), provides acceptable **rooms**, costing slightly more than the motel chains lined along I-90, off exit 446, such as *Motel 6* at 5400 Midland Rd (☎252-0093; ②). *Miyajima Gardens*, at 5634 Midland Rd (☎245-8240), serves *teppan yaki* meals, stir-fried at your table, and more familiar Japanese dishes. Downtown, *Casey's Golden Pheasant*, 109 N Broadway (☎256-5200), is a jazz/blues bar with good Cajun food; *Pug Mahon's*, 3011 First Ave N (☎259-4190), pulls in the crowds for Irish cooking and Guinness.

Red Lodge and the Beartooth Scenic Highway

The village of **RED LODGE**, sixty miles south of Billings at the foot of the awesome Beartooth Mountains and originally founded to dig coal for the transcontinental railroads, makes for an altogether more pleasant stop. Shops, cafés and bars line the main thoroughfare of Broadway, with a wide variety of food, including Mexican, at *Bogart's* (no 11 N; ☎446-1784), and sandwiches at the *City Bakery* (no 104 S; ☎446-2100). The *Carbon County Coal Co* (no 119 S; ☎446-3333), has live music most nights.

Few of the **motels** grouped south of town match the prices for the clean rooms, sauna and whirlpool at the central, big red *Pollard Hotel*, 2 S Broadway (☎446-2860; ②). Camping at the *KOA* (June–Sept; ☎446-2364), two miles north, costs around $15.

During winter, Red Lodge acts as a base for skiiers using Red Lodge Mountain (☎446-2610; lodging reservation service on ☎1-800/444-8977), six miles west on US-212, where ski lifts cost $23 a day (discounts Mon & Tues from early Jan).

Red Lodge faced extinction in 1924, when its largest coal mine closed, but its future was secured by the construction of the 65-mile **Beartooth Scenic Highway** to Cooke City at the northeastern entrance to Yellowstone National Park (see p.640). Other roads in the Rockies may be higher, but none gives quite such a top-of-the-world feeling as this succession of tight switchbacks, steep grades and exciting overlooks. Even in summer the springy tundra turf of the 10,940-foot **Beartooth Pass** is covered with snow that (due to algae) turns pink when crushed. All around are gem-like corries, deeply gouged granite walls, stretches of scree and huge blocks of roadside ice.

Western Montana

The **western** third of Montana sees the state at its best – from Big Timber westwards, I-90 squeezes between dramatic mountain ranges, making an exhilarating approach to Yellowstone country, replete with outdoor opportunities and bustling communities. The only mining camps to grow into substantial permanent settlements were state capital **Helena** and craggy **Butte**, which made its money from copper. Between them they conjure up more of a feel for the rambunctious times, the lust for profit and the post-bust hardships of the era than all the hyped-up ghost towns in the Rockies combined.

Bozeman

Pretty, tree-lined **BOZEMAN** lies deep in the lush Gallatin Valley, 142 miles west of Billings and a mere eighty miles north of Yellowstone. Founded by farmers in 1863, it's the only sizeable town in Montana not to owe its roots to mining, railroading or lumbering, and the absence of slag heaps, shabby warehouses or railyards makes a refreshing change. The smart-looking shops along the busy Victorian Main Street just beg to be window-shopped. South of downtown, as Montana State University peters out into a beautiful wilderness in the shadow of the mountains, the huge **Museum of the Rockies** at S Seventh Ave and Kagy Blvd (summer daily 9am–9pm; otherwise Mon–Sat 9am–5pm, Sun 12.30–5pm; $5) holds dinosaur finds, exhibits of Indian weapons and a fine selection of western landscape paintings. There's also a **planetarium**.

Bozeman is well placed for those in search of outdoor activities. The ranger office, 601 Niles Ave (☎587-6920), provides details of local walking trails, and *Chalet Sports* at Main and Willson (☎587-4595) rent out mountain bikes and ski equipment.

Practicalities

Greyhound and *Rimrock* cruise the interstates from 625 N Seventh St (☎587-3110), while *TW Services* puts on one bus per day to Yellowstone (see p.636). **Visitor centers** are at 1001 N Seventh Ave (summer-only) and 1205 E Main St (☎586-5421).

Central **motels** include the *Royal 7* (☎587-3103; ③) and the *Rainbow* (☎587-4201; ②), at 310 and 510 N Seventh Ave; the *Bozeman Inn* at 1235 N Seventh Ave (☎587-3176 or 1-800/648-7515; ③) is more luxurious, while the *Backpackers Hostel*, 405 W Olive St (☎586-4659; ①), has bunk beds for $8. There's **camping** 11 miles west at the *KOA*, 133 Lower Rainbow Rd (☎586-6492), next to the Bozeman Hot Springs bathing pools.

Homely *Colombo's*, at 1003 W College Ave (☎587-5544), dishes up affordable feasts of spaghetti and pizza. In the downtown *Baxter Hotel*, 105 W Main St (☎586-1314), the *Bacchus Pub* serves gourmet burgers and fine soups such as wild rice, bacon and cheese with mountains of bread for around $5. The *Spanish Peaks Brewery* at 120 N 19th Ave (☎585-2296) is open daily for food and home-brewed beer.

Missouri Headwaters State Park

Officially, the Missouri River begins its circuitous journey to the Mississippi, and eventually the Gulf of Mexico, at the confluence of the Jefferson, Madison and Gallatin rivers. Three miles north of I-90, halfway between Bozeman and Butte, and maintained as the **Missouri Headwaters State Park** ($3 per vehicle; camping $6), these marshy grasslands beneath a shallow bluff were identified by Lewis and Clark in July 1805. Three years later, **John Colter**, a veteran of that expedition who was the first to describe Yellowstone (see p.637), was captured here by a party of Blackfeet, who after killing his companion stripped him and made him run for his life. Colter killed the one pursuer who kept up with him, hid under a snag, and reached safety on the Bighorn River a week later. Fur trappers who followed in the wake of Lewis and Clark included Kit Carson; traces remain of the nineteenth-century town they created.

Butte

Eighty miles west of Bozeman, copper-mining **BUTTE** is bunched on a steep, almost treeless hillside. Massive black headframes of long-abandoned pits soar up among paintbare homes, stark grey business premises, and a ring of surface workings and dirty-yellow slag heaps. The disorderly landscape is so ugly, it's captivating.

Exploration of this friendly town soon reveals a community rich in ethnic and trade union culture. Among immigrants to leave their mark were the **Irish** – Butte still hosts the biggest St Patrick's Day celebrations in the Rockies, with an estimated 40,000 customers passing through the famous old *M&M Bar* every March 17 – and miners from **Cornwall**; the traditional pastie is still served in most cafés.

From its early days, Butte stood out as the "Gibraltar of Unionism" in the anti-union West. Miners used their collective strength to obtain a minimum wage and an eight-hour day, and it became impossible to get work without a union card. Such confidence bred radicalism, and Butte sent the largest delegation to the founding convention of the IWW (the "Wobblies") in 1906. The eventual consolidation of mining operations under the huge Anaconda Company led to inter-union rivalries and rioting.

From the vantage point of the town's only significant clump of greenery, reached by climbing West Park St, you can examine the ecological disaster below. A few yards on, the excellent free, volunteer-run **World Museum of Mining** is packed with memorabilia from the boom years (summer 9am–9pm, otherwise 10am–5pm; closed Dec–March). Its 37-building **Hell Roarin' Gulch** re-creates a cobbled-street mining camp, complete with saloon, bordello, church, schoolhouse and Chinese laundry. Above it all looms the blackened headframe of the Orphan Girl mineshaft.

The town's largest mine, the grotesque 2500- by 1800-yard **Berkeley Pit**, was abandoned in 1983, but today you can see the partly water-filled mess from a viewing platform on Continental Drive (summer 8am–9pm; free). At night floodlights illuminate the 90-foot **Our Lady of the Rockies** statue. Built entirely by voluntary labor, it was set in place on top of the Continental Divide, some 3500 feet above Butte, by helicopter.

Practicalities

Greyhound and *Intermountain Transit* **buses** drop off in downtown Butte. In summer, regular 90-minute **trolley tours** of town ($5) leave from the **Chamber of Commerce**, 2950 Harrison Ave (☎494-5595), out on the "Flat" by the interstate near the chain **motels**. The efficient *Best Western Butte Plaza*, 2900 Harrison Ave (☎494-3500 or 1-800/543-5814; ④), has good rooms and a large pool; downtown, the motels are a bit rougher, though the family-owned *Eddy's* at Front and Montana (☎723-4364; ①) is great value.

Gamer's Confectionery, 15 W Park St (☎782-7367), is a good spot for breakfast, pot pies and pasties, where you ring up the sale yourself and take the change in the antique cash register. Savings on decor and a huge custom allow the roomy *M & M Bar*, 9 N Main St, to serve bottled beer at $1 and the cheapest, grease-laden breakfasts in town. The recently refurbished *Silver Dollar Saloon*, 133 S Main St (☎782-7367), the most sumptuous bar in Butte, features live jazz and blues most nights.

Helena

In 1864 a party of disheartened prospectors working over the present site of **HELENA**, more or less halfway between Yellowstone and Glacier, decided to have one final dig along a likely-looking ravine – and struck lucky on what is now **Last Chance Gulch**, the town's attractive main street. More than $20 million of gold was extracted, but Helena retained an orderly appearance, set neatly at the foot of two rounded mountains with a fine view over the golden-brown **Prickly Pear Valley**. Over fifty successful prospectors remained here as millionaires, and their palatial residences still enhance the west side of town. Hollywood star Gary Cooper was born and brought up in this quintessentially Western town; actress Myrna Loy also lived here as a child, and is commemorated by a performance center.

Inside the massive neoclassical **State Capitol**, atop a small hill surrounded by lawns at Sixth and Montana, huge murals by "cowboy artist" C M Russell depict scenes from Montana history. You can see more of his work at the free **State Historical Museum**, 225 N Roberts St, as well as early photographs of pioneer life (summer Mon–Fri 8am–6pm, Sat & Sun 9am–5pm; otherwise Mon–Fri 8am–5pm, Sat 9am–5pm). The majestic red-tiled spires of the **Cathedral of St Helena** rise 230 feet at 530 N Ewing St; elaborate Bavarian stained glass, white marble altars and gold leaf decorate the interior.

Practicalities

Between them, *Intermountain* and *Rimrock* (who link with *Greyhound*), offer connections throughout Montana from Helena's bus station at 5 W 15th St (☎442-5860). East-west (Denver–Seattle) buses come through each evening; the north–south routes run morning and evening. Between mid-May and September an imitation steam train runs hour-long **tours** from the corner of Sixth Ave and Roberts St (50¢). There's a **visitor center** at 201 E Lyndale Ave (☎442-4120 or 1-800/743-5362).

The northernmost blocks of Last Chance Gulch form a low-key pedestrianized mall, decorated with mining-themed sculptures and fountains, and enlivened by bars, sidewalk coffee shops and restaurants. They also hold two exceptionally cheap **hotels**: the $12–16 doubles in the *Iron Front* (no 415; ☎443-2400; ①) are clean but come without a bath or shower; en-suite doubles cost $18 at the *Park* (no 432; ☎442-0960; ①). Nearby, *Bert and Ernies* (no 361; ☎443-5680), is a well-priced and classy **restaurant**, with saloon bar, while the *Windbag Saloon* (no 19; ☎443-9669), is a big old barn of a place that serves a reasonable pint of Guinness, and incorporates *Big Dorothy's Grill*. *Aunt Bonnie's Books* at no 419 has a wide selection of new and secondhand **books** on local themes. Visitors looking for more comfortable lodgings should head for the *Sanders B&B*, 328 N Ewing St (☎442-3309; ③), with its antique furnishings and gourmet breakfasts.

Gates of the Mountains

Sixteen miles north of Helena off I-15, you can take a two-hour **boat tour** through the **Gates of the Mountains** (daily June–Sept; $7.50; ☎458-5241). This dramatic stretch of the Missouri River, which enters a gorge between sheer 1200-ft cliffs that rise abruptly from the northern shores of a tranquil lake, was named by Meriwether Lewis (of the Lewis and Clark expedition).

Missoula

Blue-collar and academic cultures converge in **MISSOULA**, framed by the Bitterroot and Sapphire mountains, to produce one of the most vibrant and friendly small towns in the country. It's a town of contrasting faces – truck salesyards and bookstores, continental cafés and gun shops – where nearly everyone seems to be connected to either the city's huge sawmills or the 10,000-student University of Montana.

The **visitor center**, across the river from the campus, at 825 E Front St (☎543-6623 or 1-800/526-3465) can provide details on **trails** such as one leading from their office up **Mount Sentinel**, embellished by a huge concrete letter "M". The top gives a great view of the area, especially the rugged Hellgate River canyon. Other worthwhile trails traverse the **Rattlesnake Wilderness**, which, despite its name, has no serpents. The most developed of three small **ski** areas nearby is the **Snowbowl**, twelve miles northwest, which boasts a summer **chairlift** (Fri, Sat & Sun; $5; $2 for bikes; ☎549-9777).

Free tours of the Forest Service **Aerial Fire Depot and Smokejumper Center**, ten miles out of town on US-93, look at the methods used to train smokejumpers, highly skilled firefighters who parachute into forested areas to stop the spread of wildfires. A small visitor center explains their work (mid-May to mid-Sept, daily 9–11am &1–4pm).

Missoula is home to a surprising number of **authors**, among them crime writers James Lee Burke and James Crumley, and several good bookstores. *Freddy's Feed and Read*, for example, at 1221 Helen Ave (☎549-2127), is a fine deli which also sells a wide selection of fiction and unexpected titles.

Practicalities

Greyhound, *Rimrock* and *Intermountain* share the **bus depot** at 1660 W Broadway (☎549-2339). **Motels** along East Broadway, between downtown and campus, include the *Downtown Motel* (no 502; ☎549-5191; ②); the large well-equipped *Reserve Street Inn*, 4825 N Reserve St (721-0990; ④) is near the interstate west of downtown. *Goldsmith's B&B Inn*, 809 E Front St (☎721-6732; ③), beside the river across from campus, offers comfortable rooms and award-winning food. The *Birchwood AYH Hostel*, 600 S Orange St (☎728-9799; ①), charges $6 a night and has lots of space for cycles.

MISSOULA AND BIKES

Missoula has enjoyed close ties with **cycling** since 1896, when it became home to the 25th Infantry Bicycle Corps, founded to test the military potential of bikes as a means of transporting troops in mountainous regions. Its tasks included a 1900-mile ride to St Louis, where the army decided against the use of cycles and the soldiers came home by train.

Today Missoula is one of the best cities for cycling in the country, offering dozens of great road and dirt bike routes. The council even employs a bicycling co-ordinator (☎523-4626), but the best source of information and trail maps is *Bikecentennial*, 113 E Pine St (☎721-1776; see also p.29). The *Braxton Bike Shop*, 2100 South Ave W (☎549-2513), rents out good-quality cycles and can also advise on routes.

For tasty Italian **food**, join the inevitable queue at *Zimorino's Red Pies Over Montana*, 424 N Higgins St (☎728-6686); try the white pizza or any of the specialty sauces. The *New Pacific Grill*, 100 E Railroad Ave (☎542-3353), produces inventive American dishes like the jalapeno-fuelled *violence chicken* for $8.50, while cheap and filling Greek salads and kebabs are the specialties at *Zorba's*, 420 S Orange St (☎728-9259).

Bars and Entertainment

When Milo Milodragonovitch, the heavy-drinking, coke-snorting private eye in James Crumley's *Dancing Bear*, was left battered and bleeding miles from Missoula, he was consoled by the knowledge that soon he would be back in what he considered to be "the town with the best bars in a state of great bars". It's hard to argue with either claim.

The bar Milodragonovitch uses as an impromptu office is based on *Charley B's*, 428 N Higgins Ave – a dark, dingy, no-frills local. The equally rough-and-ready *Top Hat*, 134 W Front St (☎728-9865), features live rock and rockabilly bands most nights. The *Rhinocerous* (*Rhinos*), 158 Ryman Ave (☎721-6061), attracts students and yuppies, as does the *Iron Horse Brew Pub*, 100 W Railroad Ave at N Higgins Ave (☎721-8705), which brews its own *Bayem* beer in the former railroad station. Also worth checking out are the sporty *Union Club*, 208 E Main St (☎728-7980), and the *Missoula Club*, hiding behind a neon "Burgers and Beer" sign at 139 W Main St (☎728-3740).

The Flathead Valley

The sheer splendor of the remote 28-mile-long **Flathead Lake** provides a welcome diversion on the long route north towards Glacier National Park, reached by following US-93 north from I-90, nine miles west of Missoula, up to the Flathead Indian Reservation. Between Polson in the south and Somers in the north, US-93 follows the lake's western shore, while the smaller Hwy-36 runs up the east. Both offer superb views of the deep Alpine waters; US-93's curve around Elmo in the west, where conical **Wild Horse Island** rises starkly from the crystal-blue depths, is especially memorable.

Flathead Lake is a major destination for **watersports** enthusiasts, with the prime spot for launching fishing and pleasure boats being **Bigfork** in the northeast. Both *Bigfork Marina* (☎837-5556) and *Bayview Resort* (☎837-4843) rent vessels of all sizes, from canoes up to motorized launches. If you feel more comfortable on an organized cruise, summer options include the *Far West* (☎857-3203) from Somers, and the *Port Polson Princess* (☎883-2448) from *KwaTaqNuk Resort* at Polson.

General information on the Flathead Valley can be had on ☎1-800/543-3105. **Polson** has the most extensive range of facilities; *Best Western*'s *KwaTaqNuk Resort* has a pool and its own marina with boat rentals, at 303 Hwy-93 E (☎883-3636 or 1-800/882-6363; ⑤); the *Port Polson Inn*, also overlooking the lake from Hwy-93 E (☎883-5385 and 1-800/654-0682; ④), is slightly less expensive. If you're passing through, it's worth pausing at *Orchards Landing* (883-4644), a good-quality lakeside restaurant.

Kalispell

Thirty miles southwest of Glacier park, and fifteen miles north of Flathead Lake, largish **KALISPELL** corners a significant portion of the tourist trade en route to Glacier. There's not much to do here, but in high season it may be the closest place you'll get to stay to the park. Stylish **accommodation** options include the venerable *Kalispell Hotel*, First and Main (☎752-5145; ④), and various levels of luxury at the mansion-style B&B *The Whitney*, 538 Fifth Ave E (☎755-3456 or 1-800/426-3214; ③–⑤); the clean and central *Four Seasons Motel*, 350 N Main St (☎755-6123; ③), is also good value. Less expensive still are *Motel 6*, 1540 US-93S (☎752-6335; ②), and the *AYH* hostel, 2155 Whitefish Stage Rd (☎756-1908; ①), for $8 ($10 in winter). For **food**, try the breakfasts or salads with purple sauce at *Sky Jordan*, 127 N Main St (☎752-6170), or the pizzas and sandwiches in the grand old-fashioned *Moose's Saloon*, 173 N Main St (☎755-2337).

Whitefish

The resort and lumbering village of **WHITEFISH**, 17 miles north of Kalispell, makes a more pleasant stop, though accommodation is limited. Hacked out of thick forests, it lies on the south shore of beautiful Whitefish Lake in the shade of the *Big Mountain Ski Resort* (☎862-3511). The narrow roads round the lake and foothills deserve to be **cycled**; bikes can be rented from *Glacier Cyclery*, 336 Second St (☎862-6446).

The least expensive **motel** in Whitefish is the *Downtowner*, 224 Spokane Ave (☎862-3511; ③); **B&Bs** in the area include *The Castle*, 900 S Baker Ave (☎862-1257; ④), and the more rural *Crenshaw House*, three miles south of town at 5465 Hwy-93 (☎862-3496 or 1-800/453-2863; ④–⑦). For good steak and seafood dinners, go to the lively *Stumpjumpers* bar, 115 Central Ave (☎862-4979), which also has a cheaper bar menu. The *Great Northern Bar & Grill*, 27 Central Ave (862-2816) is a bar with pool tables, deli meals and live music, while Sebastian's, 214 Central Ave, does $3 lunch specials. *Bookworks* at 110 Central Ave is a good bookstore for titles of local interest, especially wildlife.

Amtrak drops off downtown on Central Avenue, while *Intermountain* **buses** (☎563-5246) call in on their way between Missoula and Glacier during summer.

Glacier National Park

Two thousand lakes and a thousand miles of rivers, threading between thick forests and glorious meadows, weave a blue and green carpet below the tightly packed peaks of **GLACIER NATIONAL PARK** – a haven for bighorn sheep, mountain goats, black bears and threatened grizzlies, wolves and mountain lions. Though the park still holds 50 small glaciers, its name comes from the fact that these immense valleys were carved by huge flows of ice, millennia ago. Crisp air, freezing waterfalls and year-round snow combine to give the impression of being very close to the Arctic Circle; in fact, the latitude here is lower than London.

Arrival and Information

Visitor centers can be found just inside the park's **western** (Apgar) entrance on the shores of beautiful McDonald Lake, twenty miles east of Whitefish and a mere 35 miles south of the Canadian border, and the main **east** gate at St Mary, seventy miles west of **Shelby** (Apgar open mid-June to early Sept daily 8am–8pm; May to mid-June and early Sept–Oct daily 8am–5pm; Nov–April Sat & Sun 8am–5pm: St Mary open Memorial Day to Labor Day only, daily 8am–9pm in mid-summer, otherwise 8am–5pm). Another visitor center stands at the top of Logan Pass on the Going-to-the-Sun road – the one through road between the two entrances, which is usually only passable between mid-June and mid-October. The park itself is open all year round, however, and it's well worth entering as far as Lake McDonald or St Mary's Lake even when the road is blocked and the visitor centers are shut. The entrance fee of $5 per vehicle is good for seven days; all park information is on ☎888-5441.

Glacier combines with the adjacent, much smaller, Waterton Lakes National Park (☎403/859-2224) in Canada to form the **Waterton-Glacier International Peace Park**, though Going-to-the-Sun road does not pass that way. Both parks operate their own fees and regulations, and to get to Waterton's separate entrance, north of St Mary, you have to pass customs and pay an extra $4 a day (or $9 for four days).

The southern border of the park is skirted by the low-lying US-2, which remains open all year and constitutes an attractive alternative drive. *Amtrak* **trains** follow the same route, stopping at West Glacier, a short walk from the west gate, and in the south at East Glacier (thirty miles south of St Mary) and Essex Park. *Intermountain* **buses** (☎563-5246) operate fairly frequent buses during summer from Missoula, Kalispell, Whitefish, and, to the east, Great Falls. Travellers arriving on public transportation are faced with the problem of how to see the actual park; a **shuttle service** makes five daily three-hour runs between West Glacier and St Mary (July–Labor Day, ☎862-2539; $14 one-way), while **sight-seeing tours** in bright red vintage "jammer" buses leave from the main lodges (☎226-5551; half-day $20, full-day $50).

Exploring the Park

Driving the fifty-mile **Going-to-the-Sun road** from west to east (which can take several hours, even when summer restrictions on vehicle size – aimed primarily at banning RVs – are in force) creates the illusion that you will be climbing forever. After a stealthy ascent of the foothills, when the road appears to be heading straight into the huge bare mountain that fills the entire windscreen, each successive hairpin confronts you with a new colossus. At the east end of ten-mile **Lake McDonald**, the road starts to climb in earnest. Snowmelt from waterfalls gushes across the road, spilling over the sheer drops on the other side. The winding route nudges over the **Continental Divide** at **Logan Pass** (6680ft) – a bewildering area where the peaks that looked so unscaleable from the valley floor are now mere hillocks of ice. Four miles on, there's an overlook at **Jackson Glacier**, one of the few glaciers visible from the roadside. Once you get down to the east gate, continue about five miles southeast on US-89 for a stunning view of the start of the Great Plains, which stretch 1600 miles east to Chicago.

Good short **trails** start from **Avalanche Creek** on the west flank of the Divide. The **Trail of the Cedars** leads through dark forest to a wall of contoured vivid red sandstone, from where a four-mile path continues gently uphill, past several waterfalls, to glacier-fed **Avalanche Lake**. Another popular trail begins at Logan Pass, following a boardwalk across beautiful wildflower meadows framed by craggy peaks en route to serene **Hidden Lake**. At **Swiftcurrent Lake**, north of the east entrance and reached by the minor Many Glacier entrance, an easy two-mile trail runs along the lakeshore, and an exciting nine-mile trail heads to **Iceberg Lake**, so called for the blocks of ice that float on its surface even in midsummer.

Cycling in Glacier, assuming you have the appropriate sprockets and calf muscles, can be tremendous fun. However, the roads are narrow and winding, and bikes are banned in July and August from sections of Going-to-the-Sun road during peak hours. Bikes can be rented at the Apgar service area, which also offers horses.

Tour boats explore all of the large lakes, charging $6 to 8 for one-hour trips, including sunset cruises on Lake McDonald and St Mary's Lake. You can also rent canoes, rowboats and outboards. The lakes, teeming with cutthroat trout, are excellent for **fishing**; regulations are outlined in a free pamphlet available from visitor centers.

Both *Glacier Raft Co* (☎888-5454 or 1-800/332-9995) and *Wild River Adventures* (☎387-0453 or 1-800/826-2724), based outside the west gate, offer half-day ($29) and full-day ($57 including lunch) **float trips** down the middle fork of the Flathead River, which runs along the park boundary.

Park Practicalities

All **accommodation** within the park is run by *Glacier Park Inc* (May–Sept, East Glacier Park, MT 59434, ☎226-5551; otherwise Station 1210, Greyhound, Phoenix, AZ 85077, ☎602/207-6000). Most rooms cost over $80, though there are less expensive options at the *Swiftcurrent Motor Inn* on the upper east side (③; basic cabins ①), the lakeside *Rising Sun Motor Inn* (④), seven miles in from the east gate at St Mary's, and the *Village Inn* (④), which fronts onto McDonald Lake with stunning views.

Information on lodging in the immediate vicinity is available from Glacier Country (☎1-800/338-5072). Just outside the western entrance, the *Apgar Village Lodge* (☎888-5484; ③) has clean rooms. An unusual B&B on the southern boundary is the *Izaak Walton Inn* at **Essex** (☎888-5700; ④), halfway between the east and west gates. *Amtrak* stops at the front door of this grand 1939 building, originally used to house railway workers charged with keeping the lines clear in winter. There are two **youth hostels**: the *North Fork AYH* in **Polebridge** (☎756-4780 or 756-5174; ①), thirty miles north of the west gate on a gravel road, and *Brownie's Grocery & AYH Hostel*, 1020 Hwy-49 (☎226-4426; ①), near *Amtrak* in the village of East Glacier Park. Popular alternative bases to the west of Glacier include **Whitefish** and **Kalispell** – see p.651.

The park's eleven **campgrounds**, all first-come first-served, fill up by late morning during July and August; ask at any visitor center for locations and availability. Most are open from late May to mid-September, though you can camp at *Apgar* or *St Mary* at any time of the year. For overnight backpacking, get a free permit from any visitor center.

Only a few places serve **food** in the park, and it tends to be pricey and bland.

IDAHO

IDAHO, sandwiched in between Washington, Oregon and Montana, was the last of the states to be penetrated by whites, and rivals Alaska in the sheer scale of its barely explored **wilderness** areas. Though much of its scenery amply deserves National Park status, its citizens have long been suspicious of encroachment by federal government and tourism alike, and only now is its potential for adventurous travel being appreciated.

With a marked absence of urban centers (the pleasant state capital **Boise**, in the south, being the only real exception), Idaho is very much a destination for the outdoors enthusiast. Natural wonders in its five-hundred-mile stretch include **Hell's Canyon**, America's deepest river gorge, the dramatic **Sawtooth National Recreation Area**, and the black, barren **Craters of the Moon**. Beyond these, **hikers** and **backpackers** have the choice of no fewer than 81 mountain ranges, interspersed with virgin forests and lava plateaus, while the mighty **Snake** and **Salmon** rivers offer endless scope for **fishing** and **whitewater rafting** (for details contact the Idaho Outifitters and Guides Association, PO Box 95, Boise ID 83701; ☎342-1348).

In 1805, **Lewis and Clark** declared central Idaho's bewildering labyrinth of razor-edge peaks and wild waterways to be the most difficult leg of their mammoth journey from St Louis to the Pacific. Only their Shoshoni guides enabled them to get through; to this day, there is no east–west road. Reports of game animals tripping over each other in their profusion attracted the usual legions of itinerant trappers, but the gold rush of the 1860s and white pressure for land hastened the violent end of traditional life: four hundred Shoshoni men, women and children were killed along the Bear River in 1863, the Nez Percé were driven out (see p.659), and by the end of the 1870s the "Indian problem" had been eradicated. The name "Idaho", incidentally, was invented by a mining lobbyist, who felt it sounded Indian; it was originally proposed for what is now Colorado.

The **area code** for the entire state of Idaho is ☎208.

The central wilderness still divides the state into two very distinct halves. The heavily forested **north**, interspersed with glacial lakes now fronted by resorts like **Sandpoint** and **Coeur d'Alene**, has always had strong trading links with Spokane in Washington; in the **south**, irrigation programmes from the 1880s onwards – partly instigated by Mormons – transformed the scrubland to either side of the Snake River into the fertile fields responsible for the state's licence-plate tag of "Famous Potatoes". Idaho's isolation, and small (1 million) population, have kept it largely out of the mainstream of recent US history; indeed, its remoteness has attracted assorted unwelcome guests – survivalists awaiting the Second Coming and/or nuclear holocaust.

Getting Around Idaho

Bus services between north and south Idaho are nonexistent, and a car is essential for extensive travel. Two *Amtrak* routes cross the state, both ultimately linking Seattle with Chicago. Sandpoint is the only stop on the northern line, though Spokane is not far across the border. Boise and other smaller towns are served on the southerly route between Portland and Salt Lake City. Boise also has an **airport**, though Spokane and Salt Lake City can be more convenient for northern and southern Idaho respectively.

Southern Idaho

To drivers on the interstates, southern Idaho appears to consist of little more than miles of vegetable fields and a few rocky or sandy desert stretches; only state capital **Boise** provides any urban interest. A trip into the interior along US-20, however, brings you to the spectacular ragged outcrops of the **Sawtooth Mountains**. During summer, the much-hyped **Sun Valley** ski resort is a good base for cyclists and canoeists, and has the only good bars and restaurants in this remote zone.

Idaho Falls

Of the two largest towns in southeast Idaho, **IDAHO FALLS** makes a better overnight stop than down-at-heel Pocatello, being approximately 100 miles from Craters of the Moon to the west and Yellowstone and Grand Teton to the northeast. The first sign you see of this likeable community, as you approach along I-15, sixty miles north of Pocatello, is its seven-tier wedding-cake Mormon temple, rising from the flat Snake River Valley. The falls for which the town was named are now entirely tamed, with a long low concrete dam running diagonally across the river very near downtown – but they form a pleasant focus for the greenbelt of parkland that lines both banks.

Much of the country en route to Yellowstone is every bit as spectacular as in the National Parks, and far less crowded; the magnificent **Mesa Falls**, for example, are a worthwhile brief detour along Hwy-47 roughly forty miles short of West Yellowstone.

Practicalities

Hotels and restaurants are congregated on the west bank of the river, near the interstate, while the old downtown area on the east side retains a fair number of shops. The new **visitor center** at 504 Lindsay Blvd (☎523-1010 and ☎1-800/634-3246), has information on the whole area, including a large relief model of the entire valley. The bizarre towering *Westbank Inn at the Falls* at 475 River Parkway (☎523-8000 or 1-800/432-1005; ②) has some of the least expensive rooms in town, while the larger *Best Western Stardust*, nearby at 700 Lindsay Blvd (☎522-2910; ③), offers very good value indeed at its *Snake River Smokehouse* (☎523-1865), where ribs are the specialty. Other good restaurant choices include the more upmarket *Sandpiper* at 750 Lindsay Blvd (☎524-3344).

Craters of the Moon National Monument

The eerie **CRATERS OF THE MOON NATIONAL MONUMENT** is around ninety miles west of Idaho Falls, less than twenty miles beyond Arco. At first sight, these 83 square miles look like a sooty-black wasteland, but closer inspection reveals a surreal cornucopia of lava cones, buttes, craters, caves and splatter cones. Here and there, sagebrush clings to the bleak soil, and trees have been battered by the fierce winds into bonsai-like contortions. All these features were formed without the aid of a volcano as such; instead, at roughly two-thousand-year intervals over the last thirteen thousand years, successive waves of lava have oozed from gaping wounds in the earth's crust. The next wave is thought to be due any time now.

The park **visitor center** is on US-20 (all year, daily 8am–6pm; ☎527-3257); entrance is $3 per car, and spaces at the *Lava Flow* **campground** are $5 (May–Oct). A seven-mile loop road, open late April to mid-November, leads to assorted cones and monoliths with trails of varying difficulty – don't stray from the trails, as the rocks are razor-sharp and can reach temperatures of 200°F. "**Caves**" formed by molten lava tubes can be explored, alone or on ranger-led tours (summer daily 9am, 11.30am, 2pm & 4pm).

Halfway between the park and Idaho Falls on US-20, the unassuming red-brick Experimental Breeder Reactor No 1 (**EBR-1**) – in lay terms, the **world's first nuclear power station** – stands just south of the 890-square-mile Idaho National Engineering Laboratory (aka nuclear waste dump). Even the first prototype nuclear submarine was built and tested here. Now decommissioned, it's a free museum.

Sun Valley

Although these days **Sun Valley** is the common label for the entire Wood River Valley area – in the center of southern Idaho, 150 miles west of Idaho Falls and east of Boise – technically it is just the name of a ski resort. This was the Thirties brainchild of Union Pacific Railroad chairman Averell Harriman, who discovering his railroad was obliged to maintain a passenger service decided an Alpine ski center would be an ideal stimulus to tourism. His scout, Austrian ski champion Count Schaffgotsch, set out to find dry powder snow on open treeless slopes, sheltered by higher mountains and not at too strenuous an elevation. Having turned down Aspen for being too high, he decided **Dollar** and **Baldy Mountains** fitted the bill, here in the relatively gentle foothills of the Sawtooths near the old sheep-ranching village of **KETCHUM**. The Sun Valley name was chosen because the snow remained even in the brightest winter sun; early brochures showed skiiers stripped to the waist. The world's first chair lift was built here in 1936, and the resort was an instant success.

Sun Valley's season runs from late November through April; as well as downhill skiing (daily lift rate $42, multi-day reductions) you can also set off cross-country. Ketchum itself is a lively little town with plenty of accommodation, and an oasis of nightlife in this otherwise thinly populated zone. Up to a point, it resembles the Colorado ski towns, though summer trade is nowhere near as busy. Among summer outdoor activities are **cycling** along thirty miles of excellent trails – including the former railroad tracks, long since paved over – and **rafting** on the rivers to the north (see below). Ernest Hemingway completed *For Whom The Bell Tolls* as a celebrity guest in the resort in 1939, and lived in Ketchum for the last two years of his life, before his suicide; his very plain grave can be found in the town cemetery.

Practicalities

Sun Valley Stages (☎1-800/821-9064) run shuttle buses from Boise and Idaho Falls, and there's a free in-town service between 7.30am and midnight. Ketchum's **visitor center**, at no 400 on the short Main Street, runs a free reservation service for **accommodation** (daily 9am–5pm; ☎726-3423 or 1-800/634-3347). The 600-room resort is expensive (☎622-4111 or 1-800/786-8259; winter ⑦, summer ⑨); more reasonable and central options in Ketchum include the comfortable *Lift Tower Lodge* (☎726-5163 or 1-800/462-8646; ③), the well-appointed *Ketchum Korral Motor Lodge* (☎726-3510 or 1-800/657-2657; ④), and the slightly more luxurious *Best Western Tyrolean Lodge* (726-5336 or 1-800/333-7912; ⑤). Room rates are lowest in spring and fall.

Louie's, Sun Valley Rd and Leadville St (☎726-7775), cooks up great pizzas, while *China Pepper*, in the new 511 Building at Fifth and Leadville (☎726-0959), has superb Asian specialties, such as Thai ginger rolls. The village also has a number of decent drinking spots. *X's Trough & Brewpub* on Main St (☎726-2267) has a copious selection of its own and other brewers' beers, as well as bar food. The *Main Street Bookcafé*, nearby at 201 N Main St (☎726-3700), is a nice hangout during the day, and the *Elephant's Perch*, 220 East Ave (☎726-3497), rents out sports equipment of all kinds.

Sawtooth National Recreation Area

North of Ketchum and Sun Valley, Hwy-75 climbs through ever-larger mountains and forests – where Clint Eastwood filmed *Pale Rider* – to top out after twenty miles at **Galena Summit**, one of the most spectacular panoramic viewpoints in all the Rockies. Spreading out far below, the meadows of the Sawtooth Valley stretch northwards, bearing minimal traces of the long-abandoned gold mining settlements. The simple road meanders beside the young **Salmon River**, whose headwaters rise somewhere in the forbidding icy peaks to the south; and the serrated ridge of the **Sawtooth Mountains** forms an impenetrable barrier along the western horizon.

Backpackers are guaranteed solitude in these high fastnesses, dotted with remote lakes – pick up details of primitive **camping** sites and hiking trails at the **Sawtooth National Recreation Area** headquarters (☎726-8291), eight miles out of Ketchum. Beside **Redfish Lake**, a prime salmon-spawning location just east of Hwy-75, sixty miles north of Sun Valley, the attractive and deliberately low-key *Redfish Lake Lodge* offers motel rooms and cabins (Memorial Day to early Oct; 774-3536; ③–⑤).

At tiny **Stanley**, a few miles north, dirt roads radiate from the junction of Hwys 75 and 21, with assorted Western-style motels and restaurants such as the *Sawtooth Hotel* (☎774-9947; ③), and *Danner's Log Cabin Motel* (☎774-3539; ②). Out of season Stanley virtually closes up; in summer its main activity is organizing **rafting trips** of all levels of difficulty and luxury (check in advance; weather conditions – such as heavy snowmelt – can make conditions too dangerous). Operators include *The River Company* (Stanley ☎774-2244; Sun Valley ☎726-8890).

Boise

Anywhere in the US, the strikingly verdant community of **BOISE** (pronounced *Boy-zee*) would come across as a bustling and likeable small city; located in arid southwestern Idaho, it's all the more appealing. The town straddles I-84, just 350 miles from Salt Lake City to the southeast and a trifling 490 miles from Seattle in the northwest.

The town grew up under the protective wing of Fort Boise, established in 1862 for the benefit of pioneers using the Oregon Trail. After adapting (or misspelling) the name originally given to the area by French trappers – *les bois*, the woods – the earliest residents boosted the town's appearance by planting hundreds more trees.

To explore Boise's compact, friendly **downtown**, start from the central **State Capitol** at Jefferson St and Capitol Blvd. This squat replica of the national Capitol exhibits gemstones such as the star garnet, found only in Indo-China and Idaho. **Old Boise Historic District**, nearby, is a once-elegant area of brick houses currently undergoing extensive restoration. The **Idaho Basque Museum and Cultural**

Center at 607 Grove St is located in a former boarding house that was for many years home to Basque immigrants fresh from northern Spain, who came to central Idaho, with its similarly rocky terrain, to employ their shepherding skills. The museum traces the Basque cultural heritage, and hosts regular traditional dance nights (Tues–Fri 10am–3pm, Sat 11am–2pm).

It's impossible not to be impressed by the contrast between the urban greenery and the humpy desert hills all around. The city is rightly proud of the **Greenbelt**, almost ten miles of paths that criss-cross the sluggish, brown **Boise River** to link nine separate parks. In Julia Davis Park, the **Idaho Historical Museum** chronicles the experience of the Chinese miners of the 1870s and 1880s, who picked over mines long since abandoned by whites. The state legislature, controlled by unreconstructed Confederates who had fled the South after the Civil War, did nothing to stamp out racial violence, and forced the Chinese to pay $4 a month, a considerable amount at the time, just to live in the Territory (Mon–Sat 9am–5pm, Sun 1–5pm; free).

The **Old Idaho Penitentiary** nestles beneath desert hills at 2445 Old Penitentiary Rd, off Warm Springs Ave (daily summer noon–5pm; otherwise noon–4pm; $3). This imposing sandstone-walled citadel feels like a desolate outpost, despite being just a mile from downtown. Constructed in 1870 to hold robbers, rustlers and other desperadoes, it remained open until 1974. Self-guided tours take you through the cramped solitary confinement unit, and the gallows room where the last hanging in Idaho was carried out in 1957. Restoration work has sensibly avoided trying to make this brutal prison look more palatable. A small museum displays confiscated weapons and mugshots of former inmates, including one Harry Orchard who blew up the state governor in 1905 and served out his sentence here, dying in 1954 aged 88.

Practicalities

Greyhound buses stop at 1212 W Bannock St (☎343-7531) and *Amtrak* pulls in at 1701 Eastover Terrace; both are on the edge of downtown. The **visitor center** is at 100 N Ninth St (☎344-7777). Downtown's best bargain for **rooms** is the landmark *Idanha Hotel*, 928 Main St (☎342-3611; ②), topped by a castellated mansard roof and black turrets. Further out, the *Capri Motel*, 2600 Fairview Ave (☎344-8617; ①), and the nicer *Seven-K Motel*, 3633 Chinden Blvd (☎343-7723; ①), are even less expensive. The *AOK Americana Kampground*, 3600 Americana Terrace (☎342-9691), is a little expensive at $16 but right in the heart of town, across the river from Ann Morrison Park.

At the **Boise Towne Square Mall** beside I-84 at Franklin and Cole, 28 different fast-food outlets share a common eating area, while *Milford's Fish House* in the Eighth Street Marketplace, 404 S Eighth St (☎342-8382), serves good fish and has a wide selection of beers. The *Piper Pub & Grill*, Eighth and Main (☎343-2444), serves reasonable burgers and bar food on its outdoor terrace, and *Cristina's*, Fifth and Main streets (☎385-0133), is a first-class bakery with great pastries and tasty lunches; try the atomic taco. *Pengilly's*, 513 Main St (☎345-6344), is the town's most atmospheric **bar**, though Boise also now has its own microbrewery, the *Table Rock* at 705 Fulton St (☎342-0944).

Northern Idaho

The wilderness peaks and pinnacles of the Sawtooth, Salmon River and Clearwater mountains make travelling through the heart of Idaho impossible. There are only two routes from south to north: up the eastern fringe from Idaho Falls, or, more enjoyably, along US-95 via Hwy-55 out of Boise. At first barren and infertile, not until just before Lewiston does the scenery unfold into superb pastoral farmland. The Nez Percé hunted buffalo, gathered berries and fished here for hundreds of years, until gold was discovered and they were forced to beat a bloody retreat.

The heavily forested far north of the Idaho Panhandle is broken by hundreds of deep glacial lakes, the largest of which have resort towns such as Coeur d'Alene and Sandpoint. While not major destinations, they can make good one- or two-day stops.

Hell's Canyon Region

From the busy but not over-commercialized little watersports' resort of **McCall**, 110 miles north of Boise, Hwy-55 climbs steadily to merge with US-95 and follow the turbulent **Little Salmon River**. Just south of the hamlet of Riggins, thirty miles on, comes the only good opportunity to see **Hell's Canyon** from Idaho. With an average depth of 5500 feet this is the deepest river gorge in the USA, though its low-relief formation, hemmed in by a series of gradually ascending false peaks, means that it lacks the impact of the steep-walled Grand Canyon. Nevertheless, it is impressive, with Oregon's Wallowa and Eagle Cap ranges rising behind it and the river glimmering far down below. Hwy-241 leads towards the overlooks; the final few miles of dirt road require a 4WD vehicle and permission from the forest ranger office (☎628-3916). The canyon is also accessible by road from Oregon (p.881) and by boat from Lewiston.

Riggins itself reclines in a steeply rising T-shaped canyon. This is prime **whitewater rafting** country, and outfitters, spread along a one-mile stretch of the one-street village, outnumber cafés and shops. The Chamber of Commerce (☎1-800/755-8894) has details. From Riggins, US-95 heads north along the Salmon River Valley for 30 miles to the rumpled terrain around **White Bird**, the start of Nez Percé Indian country.

There are few compelling reasons to visit industrial **LEWISTON**, 110 miles north of Riggins (which was Territorial capital for one brief year before Boise took over). One is to drive down the old road into town from the top of Lewiston Hill, just north – what seems like an intricate network of roads criss-crossing a series of mounds is, in fact, a single tarmac ribbon, which twists and turns for several miles down the steep hillside – although as the crow flies the distance is no more than a mile. Another is the **Lewiston Round-up**, a massive rodeo held on the second weekend of September.

For the rest of the year, the main reason to subject yourself to the nasty smells emanating from the local paper mills is for the fantastic journey down Hell's Canyon on the Salmon River. Boats sail past abandoned mine shafts and Indian caves, with mountain goats, bobcats, snakes and birds of prey adding further interest. Of the various outfitters, *Snake River Adventures*, 227 Snake River Ave (☎1-800/262-8874), offer the best value; a 180-mile round trip from 7.30am to 5pm costs $65 including lunch. Contact the **visitor center**, 2207 E Main St (☎1-800/473-3543), to check other prices.

Moscow

The thirty miles of US-95 between Lewiston and **MOSCOW** wind through the beautiful rolling hillsides of the fertile Palouse Valley – a patchwork of green lentils, bright yellow rape, soft white wheat and (100-foot-thick) black topsoil. Roadside red barns and farmhouses complete a marvellous rural picture.

With only 10,000 year-round residents and a similar number of University of Idaho students, Moscow is a friendly, culturally rich town which makes a good overnight stop. Bookstores, galleries, bars and sidewalk cafés line up along tree-shaded, part-pedestrianized **Main Street**, the only shopping thoroughfare. Theater, music and avant-garde cinema are on offer throughout the year, while summer sees a sprinkling of big-budget arts festivals.

The town's name might raise a few eyebrows, but it's pretty ordinary compared to the first settlers' choice of Hog Heaven. A proposal to rename it Paradise was seen as a trifle over-the-top; the present title comes from one early resident's home town in Pennsylvania.

THE NEZ PERCÉ INDIANS

The first whites to encounter the **Nez Percé Indians** were the weak, hungry and disease-ridden Lewis and Clark expedition in 1805. Though the Native Americans had the explorers at their mercy, they gave them food and shelter, and cared for the animals until the party was ready to carry on westward.

Relations between the Nez Percé (so called by French-Canadian trappers for their shell-pierced noses) and whites remained excellent for over half a century – until the discovery of gold, and white pressure for space, led the government to persuade some renegade Nez Percé to sign a treaty in 1863, taking away three-quarters of tribal land. As settlers started to move into the hunting grounds of the Wallowa Valley in the early 1870s, the majority of the Nez Percé, under the leadership of **Chief Joseph**, refused to recognize the agreement. In 1877, after much vacillation, the government decided to enact its terms, and gave the tribe thirty days to leave. The Indians asked for more time to round up their livestock and avoid crossing the Snake River at a dangerous time; the general in charge refused.

The ensuing tensions resulted in skirmishes which caused the deaths of a handful of settlers – the first whites ever to be attacked by Nez Percé – and a large army force began to gather to round up the Indians. Chief Joseph thereupon embarked upon the famous **Retreat of the Nez Percé**. Around 250 warriors (protecting twice as many women, children and old people) outmaneuvered army columns many times their size, launching frequent guerrilla attacks in a series of hair-breadth escapes. After four months and 1700 miles, the Nez Percé were cornered just thirty miles from the relative safety of the Canadian border. Chief Joseph (reportedly) made his much-quoted speech of surrender:

> *Hear me my chiefs! I am tired. My heart is sick and sad. From where the sun now stands I will fight no more forever.*

The Indians had been told that they would be put on a reservation in Idaho; instead, they were taken to Oklahoma, where marshy land caused a malaria epidemic. Chief Joseph died in 1904 on the Colville reservation in Washington, but decades later the Nez Percé were allowed to return to the northwest, where today some 1500 live in a reservation between Lewiston and Grangeville – a minute fraction of their original territory.

The **Nez Percé National Historic Park**, containing 24 separate sites, is spread over 12,000 square miles of north central Idaho. At the visitor centre in **Spalding**, ten miles east of Lewiston, the Museum of Nez Percé Culture is good on arts and crafts but weak on history; the heavily ravined **White Bird Battlefield**, seventy miles further south on US-95, was where the Indians inflicted 34 deaths on the US Army at no cost to themselves in the first major battle of the retreat. Further exhibits on Nez Percé history can be found in the Wallowa County Museum in Joseph, Oregon (see p.881).

Practicalities

Moscow's **visitor center** is at 411 S Main St (☎882-1800); *Greyhound* (☎882-5521) stops at the *Royal Motor Inn*, 120 W Sixth St (☎882-2581; ②). For a bit more comfort, try the *Mark IV Motor Inn*, 414 N Main St (☎882-7557; ③), which has a nice pool.

Several likeable **coffeeshops** feature live acoustic and classical music in the evening; *Café Spudnik* at 215 S Main St (☎882-9257), also does well-priced international cuisine. *Mikey's Gyros*, 527 S Main St (☎882-0780), offers cheap, simple Greek food.

Coeur d'Alene

When US Army Chief of Staff William Tecumseh Sherman set up camp in 1877 on the present site of **COEUR D'ALENE**, ninety miles north of Moscow on US-95, he found the sparkling blue lake, surrounded by wildflower borders and lush forest, so appealing that he ordered a fort to be built here. Another large structure now stands on the beautiful shoreline of long, narrow Lake Coeur d'Alene; looking not unlike an office block, the phenomenally expensive **Coeur d'Alene Resort** (*Condé Nast* called it the best resort in inland America; it boasts the world's only floating golf green) completely dominates downtown. Not surprisingly, it's a bitter local debating point.

Downtown is unremarkable, verging on the tacky with its sidewalk cafés and pricey shops. Directly east of the resort, a small public beach backs onto a balmy park area. Scenic **lake cruises** leave from the nearby City Dock (summer daily 1.30pm, 4pm & 6pm; $8.50; ☎765-4000). You can also see the lake on a twenty-minute **sea plane flight** from here, for $25 (☎664-2842).

Greyhound use the **bus station** at 1923 N Fourth St (☎664-3343), a mile north of downtown. There's a **visitor center** at Front Ave and Second St (☎1-800/232-4968). Both the *El Rancho Motel*, 1915 E Sherman Ave (☎664-8794 or 1-800/359-9791; ②), and the *Lake Drive Motel*, 316 Lake Drive (☎667-8486; ②) have central **rooms**. The unpretentious B&B *Sleeping Place of the Wheels*, two miles from downtown at 3308 Lodgepole Rd (☎765-3435; ②), is also good value (and charges just $22 for one person). The *Third Street Cantina*, 201 N Third St (☎664-0693), serves Mexican-style fish dishes; *Natural Food & Restaurant*, Third and Lakeside (☎664-0581), does vegetarian lunches. *T W Fisher's* is a friendly brew pub, at 204 N Second St (☎664-2739).

East from Coeur d'Alene on I-90

Fifty miles along the interstate towards Missoula, Montana (see p.649), the run-down streets, thrift shops and basic bars of **WALLACE** evoke images of its silver-mining days. The 75-minute **Sierra Silver Mine Tour** leaves by trolley car from 420 N Fifth St every half-hour, on a fun trip which takes you a thousand feet underground (summer daily 9am–4pm; $6). The *Silveradough Bakery* on Bank St serves large lunches for just $4. In summer 1991, the FBI seized all the slot machines and gaming tables in town in a much-publicized raid.

Sandpoint

Forty-four miles north of Coeur d'Alene in the shadows of the spiky Selkirk Mountains, **SANDPOINT**, northern Idaho's most attractive resort, is at the northwestern end of Lake Pend Oreille (pronounced *Pon-duh-ray*). Smaller and less commercialized than Coeur d'Alene, Sandpoint's lazy downtown is brightened by Cedar Street Bridge Public Market, a covered mall of stalls, shops and cafés overlooking placid Sandy Creek.

Accommodation possibilities include the *Lakeside Resort*, beside the lovely white sandy beach at 106 Bridge St (☎263-3717 or 1-800/543-8126; ③); the *K2 Motel*, 501 N Fourth St (☎263-3441; ②); and the $10 dorm beds at *Whitaker House B&B*, 410 Railroad Ave (☎263-0816; ①). *Amtrak* passes through early in the morning in both directions, while *Empire Bus Lines*, 402 Fifth Ave (263-7721), serve the rest of Idaho.

CHAPTER TWELVE

THE SOUTHWEST

The four sparsely populated Southwest desert states of **NEW MEXICO,**
ARIZONA, UTAH and **NEVADA** are extraordinary, unforgettable, and absolutely unique. They stretch from Texas to California across an elemental landscape ranging from towering monoliths of stark red sandstone to snow-capped
mountains, on a high desert plateau which repeatedly splits open to reveal deep yawning canyons. The raw power of the scenery, uninterrupted from horizon to horizon, is
overwhelming, and it is complemented by the emphatic presence of numerous Native
American cultures and the palpable legacy of America's Wild West frontier.

Among the earliest inhabitants were the mysterious **Anasazi**; the remains of their
sophisticated cliff palaces and cities are scattered throughout the region, but all appear
to have been abandoned around seven hundred years ago. However, the **Pueblo**
people of New Mexico and the **Hopi** in Arizona still follow much the same peaceful lifestyle, in more or less the same places, and are thought to be their direct descendants.

More war-like tribes, such as the **Navajo** and the **Apache**, began to migrate to the
Southwest early in the sixteenth century. They adopted local agricultural and crafts
techniques and appropriated vast tracts of territory, which they in turn soon found
themselves having to defend against bands of European immigrants. The first such, in
1540, was a party of **Spanish** explorers led by Coronado, who spent two years searching for the mythical El Dorado-style Seven Cities of Cibola. A hundred years later
Spanish friars returned to establish Catholic missions, many of which are still intact.
Although the religion took a strong hold, particularly in New Mexico, white American
traders had already come to dominate the region's economy by the time the newly
independent Republic of **Mexico** superseded Spain in 1820. Thirty years later, following war with Mexico, the **United States** took over the entire Southwest, and large
numbers of outsiders began to pass through on their way to Gold Rush California.

Thereafter, increasingly violent confrontations took place between the US government and the Native Americans. The entire Navajo Nation was rounded up and forcibly
removed to the barren plains of eastern New Mexico in 1869 (though it was eventually
allowed to return to northeastern Arizona), and the **Apache**, under warrior chiefs
Cochise and Geronimo, fought extended battles with the US cavalry. Though the nominal intention was to open up Indian lands to American settlers, few such groups ever
succeeded in extracting a living from this harsh terrain.

One exception were the **Mormons** (or Church of Christ of Latter Day Saints),
whose flight from religious persecution brought them by the late 1840s to the alkaline
basin of Utah's Great Salt Lake. Through sheer hard work, and the cooperative

---

ACCOMMODATION PRICE CODES

All accommodation prices in this book have been coded using the symbols below.
Note that prices are for the least expensive double rooms in each establishment.
For a full explanation see p.35 in *Basics*.

①	up to $30	④	$60–80	⑦	$130–180
②	$30–45	⑤	$80–100	⑧	$180+
③	$45–60	⑥	$100–130		

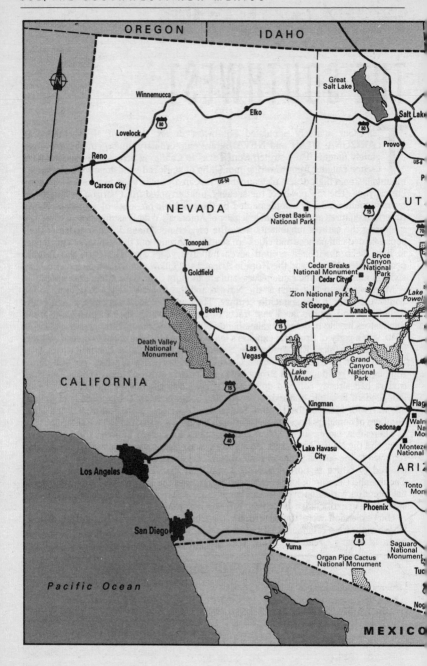

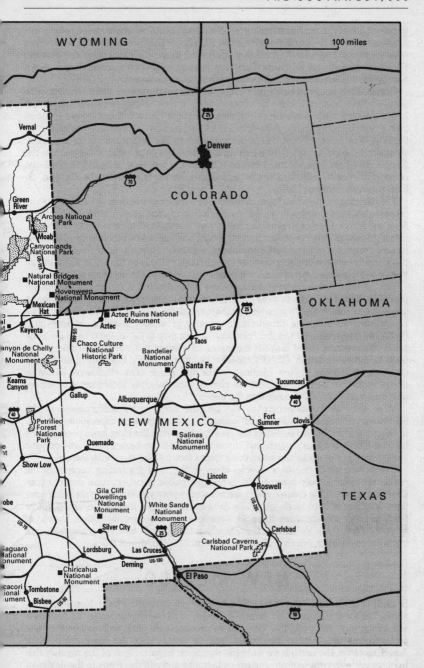

management of limited water resources, they established what amounted to an independent nation, with outlying communities all over the Southwest. Even here they met with resistance, and until the Civil War intervened, there was a real possibility that the US might declare war on them. They now amount to seventy percent of the state's population, and remain in virtual control of the Utah government.

Despite their common heritage, each of the four Southwestern states remains quite distinct. **New Mexico** bears the most obvious traces of long-term settlement, the Indian Pueblos of the north coexisting alongside major towns, laid out around spacious plazas, which clearly retain their Spanish colonial identity. In **Arizona**, the history of the Wild West is more conspicuous, in towns such as Tombstone, site of the legendary shootout at the OK Corral. Over a third of the state belongs to Indian tribes such as the Apache, Hopi and Navajo, most of whom live in the red-rock lands of the northeast corner, on remote desert mesas or amid the splendor typified by the **Canyon de Chelly** and **Monument Valley**.

The canyon country of northern Arizona – even the immense **Grand Canyon** – won't prepare you for the uninhabited but compelling landscape of **southern Utah**, where **Zion** and **Bryce Canyon** are just the best known of a string of national parks and monuments. **Moab**, poised in the east between majestic **Canyonlands** and surreal **Arches**, has become a mecca for youthful outdoors enthusiasts. **Nevada**, on the other hand, is nothing short of desolate; gamblers are lured in their millions by the bright lights of **Las Vegas**, and to a lesser extent Reno, but away from the casinos there's little to see or do.

You can count on warm sunshine anywhere in the Southwest for nine months of the year, with incredible sunsets most evenings. Summer is the peak tourist season, for no good reason – air temperatures topping 100° can make outdoor life unbearable, while in late summer awesome thunderstorms sweep in without warning, causing flash floods and forest fires. By October, perhaps the best time to come, the crowds are gone and in the mountains and canyons the leaves turn bright red and gold. Winter brings snow to higher elevations – there's excellent skiing in northern Utah and in the Sangre de Cristo mountains of New Mexico – while springtime sees wildflowers bloom in otherwise barren desert. Note that the climate varies sharply according to elevation, with mountains often 30° cooler than the plains.

More than almost anywhere in the US, the backcountry wildernesses of the Southwest are ideal for (well-planned) **camping** and backpacking expeditions. It's vital to be prepared for the harshness of the desert, where even the most basic needs can be hard to fill; always carry water, and if you venture off the beaten track let someone know where you're going and when you'll return (see p.42 for more information).

Unless you have your own vehicle, many of the most fascinating corners of the region are quite simply inaccessible. Scheduled public transport runs almost exclusively between the big cities – which are not at all where you should be spending your time. Hitching is hard work, especially in summer, but not impossible, and if you're ready to tackle the immense distances, cycling is also a worthwhile option. Dozens of specialist companies, detailed in the text which follows, can take you whitewater rafting, mountain biking, hot-air ballooning, or on backcountry desert tours.

NEW MEXICO

Settled in turn by Native Americans, Spaniards, Mexicans and Yankees, **New Mexico** is among the most ethnically and culturally diverse of all the United States. Each successive group has built upon the legacy of its predecessors; their various histories and achievements are closely intertwined, and in some ways the late-coming white Americans from the north have had little significant impact. Signs of the region's rich heritage are everywhere, from ancient pictographs and cliff dwellings to the design of the state's license plates, taken from a Zia Indian symbol for the sun – the one near-constant fact of life in this arid land.

New Mexico's indigenous peoples – especially the **Pueblo Indians**, clear inheritors of the city-building Anasazi – provide a sense of cultural continuity. Despite the **Pueblo Revolt** of 1680, which forced a temporary Spanish withdrawal into Mexico, the mission-ary endeavor here was in general less brutal than elsewhere. The proselytizing padres eventually co-opted the natives without destroying their traditional ways of life, incorpo-rating local deities and celebrations into Catholic ritual and practice. Somewhat bizarrely to outsiders, grand churches still stand at the center of many Pueblo settle-ments, often adjacent to the kivas, and almost always built in the local adobe style.

The Americans who took over from the Mexicans in 1848 saw New Mexico as a useless wasteland, and left it relatively undisturbed in their eagerness to develop California. In fact, apart from a few mining booms and range wars – such as the so-called Lincoln County War which brought **Billy the Kid** to fame – New Mexico was more or less forgotten until the US finally got around to making it a state in 1912. During World War II, it was the base of operations for the top-secret **Manhattan Project**, which built and detonated the first atomic bomb, and since then America's premier weapons research outposts have been located here. By and large people here work close to the land, mining, farming and ranching, with tourism increasingly underpinning it all.

Northern New Mexico centers on the magnificent landscapes of the Rio Grande Valley, which contains its two finest cities – the artists' colony and winter resort of **Taos**, with its nearby Pueblo, and **Santa Fe**, the adobe-fronted capital. More than a dozen Pueblo villages can be found in the mountainous area between the two, while to the west lie the evocative Anasazi ruins at **Bandelier** and **Chaco Canyon**. The broad swath of **central New Mexico**, along the I-40 transcontinental highway – the succes-sor of the old **Route 66** – pivots around the state's biggest city, **Albuquerque**, with the extraordinary mesa-top Pueblo village of **Acoma** ("Sky City"), an hour's drive to the west. In wild and wide-open **southern New Mexico**, the yawning **Carlsbad Caverns** are the main attraction, while here, as all over the state, you can still stumble upon old mining and cattle-ranching towns which have somehow hung on since the end of the Wild West.

Getting Around New Mexico

Public transport is rare in New Mexico; Santa Fe, for example, does not have a rail service. *Amtrak* **trains** do, however, pass through Albuquerque, pitstop for transconti-nental *Greyhound* **buses** and site of the only major **airport** – linked by shuttle services with the rest of the state. Texas' **El Paso** (see p.548) is a more convenient transporta-tion hub for Carlsbad. A few companies offer guided **coach tours** in the Santa Fe and Taos area, but as usual, getting around is really best done by **car**.

Northern New Mexico

The northern third of New Mexico, high in the sharp peaks of the Sangre de Cristo mountains, is the New Mexico of popular imagination, with its pastel colors, vivid desert landscape, and adobe architecture. Ranging along the headwaters of the Rio Grande, the amiable frontier town of **Taos** was immortalized by Georgia O'Keeffe and D H Lawrence, and is remarkable chiefly for the multistorey dwellings of neighboring **Taos Pueblo**. Significantly bigger, but less attractive, the state capital **Santa Fe** 75 miles southwest is the only real city in the region. Even so, with well under 100,000 residents it is hardly metropolitan in scale, and the narrow streets of its small historic

The **area code** for the entire state of New Mexico is ☎505.

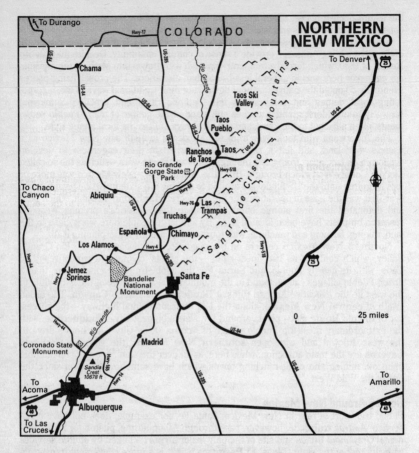

NORTHERN NEW MEXICO

center, though regularly thronged with tourists lured by the high-profile hype, retain the feel of long-gone days.

An hour's drive west from Taos or Santa Fe brings you to **Bandelier National Monument**, where ancient cliff dwellings have been carved out of the same forested volcanic plateau which also holds the eerie Los Alamos National Weapons Lab. Much further afield, but well worth an extended visit, **Chaco Canyon** holds the remains of one of the largest pre-Columbian cities in North America.

Taos

Part Spanish colonial outpost, part hangout for bohemian artists, and home to the most memorable of the Pueblo Indian villages, tiny **TAOS** has managed to retain its rough-hewn charms despite a constant stream of tourists. This attractively unpretentious town of less than five thousand people is made up of three separate communities: **Taos** itself, around the plaza; sprawling **Ranchos de Taos** five miles to the south; and the Indian community of **Taos Pueblo** two miles north. Another five miles north, the challenging slopes of **Taos Ski Valley**, at Wheeler Peak, the highest point in New Mexico, are usually open to skiers between late November and early April (lift tickets $35; information ☎776-2291; resort reservations ☎1-800/776-1111).

The landscape in which they stand is stunning, with the pine-forested Sangre de Cristo mountains rising high above dry, sunbleached foothills, undulating along the banks of the Rio Grande. Year-round the sun burns down with the magical New Mexico "light" that artists – and tourist boards – rave about: **Georgia O'Keeffe** did most of her signature desert abstractions around Taos, and spent the last fifty years of her life near Abiquiu, forty miles west. **D H Lawrence**, who lived here in the 1920s, wrote "there are all kinds of beauty in the world, but for greatness of beauty I have never experienced anything like New Mexico"; a small shrine holding his mortal remains overlooks the upper Rio Grande, twenty miles northwest of town.

Arrival, Information and Getting Around
Greyhound (☎758-1144) arrive in Taos on Hwy-68, a mile south of downtown; *Faust Transportation* (☎758-3410 or 1-800/345-3738) run shuttles from Albuquerque airport for $30. Drivers are most likely to come in past the motels along Hwy-68 to the south; keep going, and park near the plaza or at Kit Carson State Park a hundred yards north.

Basic orientation can be had from the new **visitor center** at the intersection of Hwys 68 and 64 (daily 9am–5pm; ☎758-3873 or 1-800/732-8267), or the **information booth** in Taos' leafy and low-key plaza. Walking is the best way to get around the compact town center, though in summer, the *Pride of Taos* open-air **trolley** loops around the plaza, Taos Pueblo and Ranchos de Taos, stopping at hotels and motels. Another option is to **rent a bike** from *Taos Trading Post*, 231 Paseo del Pueblo Sur (☎758-4293), two blocks south of the plaza on Hwy-68, or *Native Sons Adventures*, 813A S Hwy-68 (☎758-9342).

Taos Plaza and the Millicent Rogers Museum
The old Spanish **plaza**, still at the heart of Taos, is now ringed by jewellery shops, art galleries and restaurants; all conform to the predominant Pueblo motif of rounded brown adobe plaster. Specific sights are few – a small museum ($3) off the elderly lobby of the *La Fonda de Taos* hotel has a collection of sexy but amateurish paintings by D H Lawrence, and the tree-filled square itself is often animated by guitar-toting buskers – but the surrounding streets are perfect for an aimless stroll, and it's easy to spend half a day just mooching around. Some of the best places to eat or drink, as well as a number of top-notch art and crafts galleries, are on **Bent Street**, a block north of the plaza. *Moby Dickens* at no 124 is a fine bookshop specializing in historic and contemporary Taos. Bent Street takes its name not from any irregularities, but from the first American governor of New Mexico, Charles Bent, whose house has been preserved as a museum of frontier Taotian life (daily 10am–5pm; $1).

Just east of the plaza, across Hwy-68 at the end of Taos' sole surviving stretch of wooden boardwalk, is the dusty but evocative adobe abode where mountain man and part-time US cavalry officer **Kit Carson** (see p.972) lived for 25 years in the mid-1800s. It's now a rather flavorless museum, filled with saddles, rifles, and Wild West paraphernalia (daily 9am–5pm). Two blocks south of the plaza on Ledoux St, the much-restored 1790 house of artist and collector Ernest L Blumenshein, co-founder of the town's 1920s arts colony, displays paintings and furniture (daily 9am–5pm). A $3 admission fee covers Carson's home, the Blumenshein house and the Martinez Hacienda (see overpage).

Two miles north of Taos Pueblo on Hwy-68, the **Millicent Rogers Museum** (summer daily 9am–5pm, otherwise Wed–Sun 10am–4pm; $3) shows off a superb collection of craftworks. Objects range from pre-Columbian Zuni and Hopi pottery to contemporary black-on-black pieces by Pueblo potter Maria Martinez, and beautiful Navajo blankets. Affecting exhibits trace the development of Spanish Colonial religious art in the heathen New World; the highlight is a seventeenth-century "Death Cart", in which a skeleton holding a bow and arrow rides in the back of an ornate funeral carriage.

Taos Pueblo

Two miles north of Taos Plaza, half a mile east of Hwy-68. Usually open for tours daily 8am–5.30pm.
$5 per car, plus $5 for still photography and $10 for a video camera.

At the intact and flourishing community of **Taos Pueblo**, the Rio Pueblo de Taos flows
down the hills from the sacred Blue Lake, inaccessible to outsiders, to run between two
multistorey adobes: Hlauuma, the north house, and Hlaukwima, the south house.
These have been continuously inhabited for some eight hundred years, jointly forming
the most impressive Native American dwelling place still in use. Its 150 full-time residents have made few concessions to the modern world, living without toilets, running
water, or electricity (although many others choose to live in newer homes nearby).
Whenever sufficient visitors are waiting, short tours of the complex provide an introduction to its traditions and culture; though you do not enter the actual adobes, some
smaller buildings are open as craft shops.

For most of the year, Pueblo life continues with scant regard for the intrusion of
tourists, but feast days and dances can be spectacular. These are held regularly
throughout the summer; the biggest parties are the **Corn Dances** in June and July and
the **Feast of San Gerónimo** at the end of September, when hundreds and even thousands of outsiders flock to join the general revelry.

Ranchos de Taos

Spreading south from the central plaza area, to either side of Hwy-68, the **Ranchos de
Taos** were once the farms that fed the townspeople of Taos. Each rancho had its own
main house, or hacienda; one has been restored as a museum of colonial life. The
Martinez Hacienda (daily 9am–5pm; $3, see previous page), two miles southwest of
the plaza on Ranchitos Rd, was built in 1804 by an early mayor of Taos. Two dozen
thickly walled adobe rooms are wrapped around lushly landscaped patios and
furnished to recreate the typical family home of local Spanish gentry.

The massively buttressed adobe church of **San Francisco de Asis** turns its back to
the passing traffic four miles south of the plaza on Hwy-68. One of colonial New
Mexico's most splendid architectural achievements, with subtly rounded walls and
corners disguising its underlying structural strength, the church was one of painter
Georgia O'Keeffe's favorite subjects. Inside, there's a marvellously ornate reredos
amidst the typically overwrought clutter of devotional objects and artworks, but the
neighboring buildings – such as an old barn converted into a drive-through taco stand
and liquor store – do little to enhance its situation.

Accommodation

Taos has accommodation to meet all needs, though rates rise dramatically in ski season.
A couple of clean and pleasant **hostels** provide bare-bones bunks or simple rooms; a
handful of anodyne **motels** line Hwy-68. For a few dollars more, you can avail yourself of
atmospheric **B&B** inns or luxury hotels. *Taos Central Reservations* (☎1-800/821-2437)
will reserve lodging in advance.

Abominable Snowmansion Hostel, in the mountains near Taos Ski Valley (☎776-8298). Dorm
beds $12.50, and bargain private rooms; prices double during ski season. ①/③.

El Rincon, 114 Kit Carson Rd (☎758-4874). Peaceful adobe B&B east of the plaza. ③–⑥.

Koshari Inn, off Kit Carson Rd (☎758-7199). Inexpensive and hospitable accommodations on the
east side of town. ③.

Plum Tree Hostel, Hwy-68 (☎758-4696 or 1-800/678-7586). Riverside hostel-cum-B&B near Rio
Grande Gorge State Park, 15 miles south of Taos on main road (and *Greyhound* route). $12.50 dorm
beds, and some private rooms. ①/②.

Taos Inn, 125 Paseo del Pueblo Norte (☎758-2233 or 1-800/TAOS-INN). Central Taos landmark,
with the nicest rooms in town. Their *Doc Martins* restaurant (no relation to the English bootmakers),
serves expensive, immaculate grilled meats and other New Mexican favorites, while the *Adobe Bar*
is a congenial drinking spot, with a huge roaring fire and free live music most nights. ⑤.

THE PUEBLOS

Two distinctive but interrelated groups, the native **Pueblo Indians** and the descendants of the early Spanish colonists, have together contributed much to the unique culture of northern New Mexico. At first, the people we now call Pueblo Indians welcomed the Spanish, but they soon came to resent the imposition of Catholicism and the virtual enslavement of Pueblo laborers. In the **Pueblo Revolt** of 1680, the various tribes banded together and ousted the entire colonial regime, killing scores of priests and soldiers and sending hundreds more south to Mexico. However, after the Spanish returned in 1693 the Pueblos showed little further resistance, and have coexisted surprisingly amicably ever since, accepting aspects of Catholicism – most pueblos have a large adobe church at the core – without giving up their traditional beliefs and practices.

All the pueblos have been modernized to some extent, but all proudly retain the "Old Ways". Saints' days, major Catholic holidays such as Easter and Jan 6, and even the Fourth of July, are celebrated with a combination of native traditions and Catholic rituals, featuring elaborately costumed dances and massive communal feasts. The most impressive – and most touristed – of the pueblos is at **Taos**, but many of the less well-known ones are as worthwhile to visit, particularly if you're interested in such Pueblo arts and crafts as their fine pottery.

Seven pueblos in the area between Taos and Santa Fe area have joined with Taos Pueblo itself to promote themselves as the **Eight Northern Indian Pueblos** (☎852-4265). Visitors to each are required to **register** at a visitor center, and pay a fee, usually $3 to $5 to park plus $5 for a camera permit, but there's no extra charge for feast days or dances. Always behave respectfully when visiting – don't go "exploring" places which are off limits to visitors, such as shrines, kivas or private homes.

Nambe Pueblo (☎455-2036), thirty miles north of Santa Fe, then three miles east on Hwy-503. Among the most beautifully sited of the pueblos. Elk Dance on Oct 4, and the Fourth of July is celebrated with a staged ceremonial dance at the foot of cascading Nambe Falls.

Picuris Pueblo (☎587-2957), 25 miles south of Taos on Hwy-75 near Penasco. Tiny remote village, in the forefront of the Pueblo Revolt. Tours of ruins and an interesting small museum (daily 9am–7pm). Buffalo Dance on Feb 2.

Pojoaque Pueblo (☎455-2278), on US-84 fifteen miles north of Santa Fe. Although the old pueblo is in ruins, having been abandoned after a smallpox epidemic in 1895, the tribe runs a large museum and shop on the highway, with information and artefacts from all Tewa tribes.

San Ildefonso Pueblo (☎455-2273), 15 miles north of Santa Fe just west of US-84. The best museum, with exhibits of excellent black pottery, including pieces by Maria Martinez which fetch thousands of dollars. Main festivities include Jan 23, and the large festival of Pueblo arts and crafts, held on the third weekend in July.

San Juan Pueblo (☎852-4400), five miles north of Española off US-68 east of the Rio Grande. Large restored pueblo still standing on the site of the first Spanish capital of New Mexico. *Tewa Indian Restaurant* open Mon–Fri 9am–2.30pm. Feast days June 13 and June 24.

Santa Clara Pueblo (☎753-7326), on Hwy-30 one mile west of Española. Very fine pottery, feast day Aug 12. Eleven miles beyond the village, up in the hills at 7000 feet, the Puye Cliff Dwellings are an extensive wind-blown ruin claimed as the tribe's ancestral home. Reminiscent of Bandelier (see p.674), two tiers of hollowed-out "apartments" can be explored by scrambling up ladders against the cliff-face (daily, summer 9am–6pm, winter 9am–5pm; $4 self-guided, $5 with guide). There's camping in the Santa Clara Canyon, further on.

Tesuque Pueblo (☎983-2667), on US-64/84 nine miles north of Santa Fe. Traditional pueblo near the Santa Fe Opera, with a campground (mostly RVs) overlooked by the remarkable Camel Rock. Free admission. Corn Dances first Sat in June and Nov 12.

See also **Acoma** (p.681), **Zuni** (p.683), and the **Hopi Mesas** (p.711).

Taos Super 8 Motel, 1347 S Hwy 68 (☎758-1088). Cheapest among the franchise motels lining Hwy-68 south of town. ③.

Taos Trace, Arroyo Hondo (☎776-2538). Tasteful rural B&B rooms in friendly small house, 14 miles northwest of Taos Plaza in old Hispanic village. Shared bathrooms. ③.

Eating, Drinking and Nightlife

Taos is too small to have much nightlife, but for eating it caters to all tastes and budgets. Look out for the itinerant catering trucks which roam the streets, particularly along Hwy-68 south of the plaza, selling top-rate tacos, burritos and burgers.

Apple Tree Restaurant, 123 Bent St (☎758-1900). Good, cheap Mexican and international food.

Bent Street Deli & Cafe, 120 Bent St (☎758-5787). Just off the plaza. Airy, partly outdoor place for cheap breakfasts and lunches. A variety of Mexican food and two dozen sorts of sandwiches.

Floyd's Lounge, 819 S Hwy-68 (☎758-4142). Scruffy bar; regular live bands and no frills.

Stakeout Grill and Bar, Outlaw Hill off Hwy-68. Well-hidden, unpretentious, and very popular restaurant in a truly stunning setting. Very big – and very good-value – steak dinners. Only accessible by car; head four-plus miles south from Taos then climb east up a dirt track.

Wild and Natural Café, 812 Paseo del Pueblo (☎751-0480).Three-course vegetarian dinners for around $8. Good espresso and dessert bar. Mon–Sat 11am–9pm.

Chama

Eighty-five miles northwest of Taos on US-64 – which crosses the dramatic Rio Grande Gorge Bridge – or a hundred or so miles from Santa Fe via US-84 – beyond Abiquiu and the red rocks around Ghost Ranch – tiny **CHAMA** is the base for trips on the **Cumbres and Toltec Scenic Railroad** (☎756-2151) Daily excursions run through the High Brazos mountains on the border with Colorado; you can either take a van to Antonito, CO, and return by train ($50, dep Chama 8am), or take a round trip for the day by train to a point halfway along ($32, dep 10.30am).

Chama's venerable *Shamrock Hotel* (☎756-2416 or 1-800/982-8679; ②) is directly opposite the station; the *Gandy Dancer* is a three-bedroom B&B in an old wooden mansion nearby at 299 Maple St (☎756-2416 or 1-800/982-8679; ④).

The High Route

One satisfying tour of the Pueblo region follows what's known as "**The High Route**" between Taos and Santa Fe, taking you high into the pines and aspens of the Sangre de Christo Mountains, and passing by a number of pueblos as well as dozens of timeless devoutly Catholic villages still occupied by direct descendants of the Spaniards. Dotted with isolated, tin-roofed shacks and barns, these hills are said to be the heartland of the secretive **Penitentes**, fanatical Catholics who, during Lent, form dawn processions along the ridges, flagellating themselves with yucca whips while chanting prayers. The High Route emerges onto US-68/84 north of Santa Fe near Nambe Pueblo (see p.669).

Chimayo

The quaint mountain village of **CHIMAYO**, 25 miles north of Santa Fe at the junction of Hwy-503 and Hwy-76, is the site of New Mexico's most famous Spanish colonial church, the 1816 adobe **Sanctuario de Chimayo**, a squat, twin-towered chapel, set behind an enclosed courtyard and filled with a mind-boggling array of devotional objects. A smaller chapel, facing the Sanctuario across a gravelled parking lot, contains a small statue of *Santo Niño*, the Lost Child, to whom expectant mothers bring offerings such as tiny pairs of shoes.

Two properties belonging to the Jaramillo family, resident since 1695, make Chimayo an appealing overnight destination. The *Restaurante Rancho de Chimayo*, Hwy-503 (☎984-2100), must be the best traditional New Mexican **restaurant** around, serving superb *flautas* and a mouthwatering *sopapilla*, stuffed with meat and chilis, on a lovely sun-drenched outdoor patio. Across the road, the rambling adobe *Rancho de Chimayo* itself (PO Box 11, Chimayo, NM87522; ☎351-2222; ④), has lovely **B&B** rooms.

Higher up in the mountains, in the quiet hamlet of **Las Trampas**, another powerfully evocative adobe church, **San Jose de Garcia**, stands stern and imposing above the highway. If it's closed, ask for the caretaker in the small store opposite.

Santa Fe

During the 1980s **SANTA FE** became the most stylish destination in the US. What was once an honorable and well-meaning campaign to preserve the town's unique blend of Native American and Spanish traditions had grown into a frenzied promotion of Santa Fe chic, with upwards of a million and a half tourists every year descending upon the city of 65,000 residents. New hotels were built, old ones upgraded, and smart New York or LA boutiques and art galleries opened up outlets in Santa Fe, replacing hardware stores with international couture. But the early 1990s see a different Santa Fe; many of the shops and galleries that sprang up during the tourist boom have now gone, and Santa Feans at last have a chance to rediscover what it was people liked about their town.

There is a lot to like about Santa Fe. In 1609, ten years before the Pilgrim Fathers arrived at Plymouth Rock, **Spanish missionaries** established Santa Fe as the northernmost capital of their colonial empire. It has been the capital of New Mexico ever since, and the adobe houses and baroque churches they laid out at the foot of the mountains survive fairly intact under the surface glitz of the modern American city.

Arrival and Getting Around

For all its fame, Santa Fe is surprisingly far off the beaten path. There's no rail link, despite having the *Atcheson, Topeka and Santa Fe Railroad* named after it – *Amtrak* **trains** stop once a day in **Lamy**, fifteen miles southeast, to be met by the connecting *Lamy Shuttle* (☎982-8829) – and the airport is served only by small commuter planes. The nearest major airport is at Albuquerque, an hour's drive away. *Shuttlejack* (☎982-4311 or 1-800/452-2665) run **buses** from Albuquerque, and *Greyhound* has regular services from all over the Southwest to a terminal just south of the plaza at 858 St Michaels Drive (☎471-0008). If you **drive** in on I-25, you have to negotiate your way through a long sprawl of motels and fast-food restaurants to reach the center of town.

Almost everything to see in Santa Fe is within walking distance of the central plaza, and erratic buses serve the state museums to the southeast. Coupons obtainable at the public library on Washington St, across from the Palace of the Governors, save fifty percent on **taxis** (☎982-9990). For a guided tour of the town or its environs, contact *Afoot in Santa Fe* in the *Inn at Loretto*, 211 Old Santa Fe Trail (☎983-3701).

The **Santa Fe CVB** (Mon–Fri 9am–5pm; ☎984-6760 or 1-800/777-CITY), two blocks from the plaza at 201 W Marcy St, has the usual ad-packed information.

The Plaza

Santa Fe's old central **plaza** is still the focus of town life – especially during the annual **Indian Market** on the weekend after the third Thursday in August, when buyers and craftspeople come from all over the world, and during the Labor Day weekend for the **Fiesta de Santa Fe** – but apart from an influx of art galleries and stylish restaurants, the web of narrow streets around it has changed little in the intervening years. Although when the Yankees took over in 1848 they neglected the adobes and chose to build in wood, many of the finer houses have survived, thanks in part to a 1930s preservation campaign. Since then almost every non-adobe structure within sight of the plaza, even the downtown *Woolworth's*, has been designed or redecorated to suit the city-mandated Spanish Revival mode, with oddly canted, rounded mud-colored plaster walls supporting roof beams made of thick pine logs (called *vigas*). Santa Fe today, in fact – at least at its core – looks much more like its original Spanish self than it did a hundred years ago.

One of the main models for Santa Fe's revived architectural unity fills the entire northern side of the plaza. The **Palace of the Governors** (daily 10am–5pm; closed Mon in Jan & Feb) is a low-slung, originally sod-roofed structure constructed in 1610 as the headquarters of Spanish colonial administration. This humble-looking edifice is thus the oldest public building in the US; its name may now seem misleadingly grand, but it used to be much bigger. The arcaded adobe veranda along its front serves as a shaded market for local Indian crafts-sellers, and the well-preserved interior, organized around an open-air courtyard, houses part of the **Museum of New Mexico**, most of which is clustered together a mile to the southeast. A three-day pass to all parts of the museum costs $5, and covers the Coronado, Jemez, Fort Sumner and Lincoln state monuments elsewhere in New Mexico; each individual section costs $3.

On the plaza's northwest corner, and also part of the Museum of New Mexico, the **Museum of Fine Arts** (daily 10am–5pm) is one of the few major art museums to be started by artists, as opposed to educators or collectors, and focuses on painting and sculpture by mostly local artists. Many of the **Georgia O'Keeffe** paintings come from the artist's own collection, in her home and studio near Abiquiu, forty miles northwest.

The Churches of Santa Fe

After the plaza area, the most attractive corner of central Santa Fe is across the river, three blocks to the southwest along Guadalupe Street around the small but beautiful **Sanctuario de Guadalupe** (daily 9am–4pm; donations). Built at the end of the eighteenth century and recently restored, with a fine Baroque reredos, the shrine during Spanish and Mexican times marked the end of Camino Real highway from Mexico City. The surrounding neighborhood was later to become the main point of arrival into Santa Fe for trains on the Denver and Rio Grande railroad. Old warehouses and small factory premises nearby, like the **Sanbusco Center** on Montezuma Ave, have recently been converted to house boutiques, art galleries and restaurants.

If you follow the tiny Santa Fe River upstream, or walk two blocks east from the plaza, you approach a strange building looming at the top of San Francisco Street, looking out of place among Santa Fe's earthy adobes. **St Francis Cathedral**, the first church west of the Mississippi to be designated a cathedral, was built in 1869 by **Archbishop Lamy**. The French-educated Lamy, the title figure in Willa Cather's novel *Death Comes for the Archbishop*, had the building designed along elevated European lines.

Another nearby church, the **Chapel of Loretto**, a block away at the start of Old Santa Fe Trail, is known for its so-called Miraculous Staircase, an elegant spiral built without nails or obvious means of support. During construction, the church's designer is said to have been killed by Lamy's cousin, and for years there was no way up to the choir loft. Then an unknown carpenter arrived, built the stairs, and disappeared.

Two blocks south, across the river along the Old Santa Fe Trail, is the ancient **San Miguel Chapel**. Only a few of the massive adobe internal walls survive from the original 1610 building, most of which was destroyed in the 1680 Pueblo Revolt. The chapel is the heart of the old *Barrio de Analco* workers' district, whose many two-hundred-year-old houses now form one of Santa Fe's most appealing residential neighborhoods.

The New Mexico State Museums

East of central Santa Fe, gallery-lined **Canyon Road** – which stakes a claim to being the oldest street in the US, dating from Pueblo days – climbs a steady but shallow incline along the river bed lined by dozens of more fine adobes. A mile south along Camino del Monte Sol, on Camino Lejo two miles southeast from the plaza, is Santa Fe's other concentration of museums. The main attraction here, the third of the New Mexico Museum quartet, is the **Museum of International Folk Art** (daily 10am–5pm), which holds an astonishing range of artefacts from all corners of the globe – and sells many of them in its gift store. One huge room contains detailed and colorful dioramas depicting life in virtually any country you might care to think of, while the Hispanic Heritage Wing is an engaging reminder of just how close New Mexico's ties have always been with Mexico itself. The **Museum of Indian Arts and Culture**, fourth of the four, sets out to provide insight into the ways of life followed by New Mexico's various Native American tribes – but is not as successful as the Indian Pueblo Cultural Center in Albuquerque (see p.679). The larger, private **Wheelwright Museum of the American Indian** (Mon–Sat 10am–5pm, Sun 1–5pm; $2 donation), designed to look like a Navajo hogan, stands behind the folk art museum, and focuses primarily on Navajo sand paintings and ceremonials. Its carefully chosen Anasazi ceramics are quite exquisite.

Accommodation

Places to **stay** in Santa Fe don't come cheap, especially not during the peak summer months, when every bed in town can seem to be taken. **Cerrillos Road** (US-85), the main road into Santa Fe from I-25, holds most of the town's **motels** and its one **hostel**. Everything gets more expensive as you approach the center, though **B&Bs** make an attractive alternative to the overpriced hotels around the plaza. If you get stuck, phone the CVB's **accommodations hotline** (daily 4–10pm; ☎986-0043 or 988-4252) or commercial agency *Santa Fe Central Reservations* (☎983-8200 or 1-800/982-7669).

Budget Inn, 725 Cerrillos Rd (☎982-5952 or 1-800/288-7600). The closest in of the chain motels. ②.

El Paradero, 220 W Manhattan Ave (☎988-1177). B&B near Guadalupe St restaurant district. ④.

El Rey Inn, 1862 Cerrillos Rd (☎982-1931). Most characterful and best value of the Cerrillos Road motels, and surprisingly stylish. ③.

Grant Corner Inn, 122 Grant Ave (☎983-6678). Considerable luxury, and great breakfasts, just two blocks from the plaza. ⑤.

Hacienda Vargas, 1431 El Camino Real, Algodones (☎867-9115 or 1-800/732-2194). Relaxing rural B&B in lovely restored adobe former trading post, thirty miles southwest. ④.

Inn of the Anasazi, 113 Washington Ave (☎988-3030 or 1-800/688-8100). No expense spared and surprisingly exquisite adobe hotel just north of the Plaza, with superb restaurant. ⑦.

Preston House, 106 Faithway St (☎982-3465). Queen Anne B&B, set in peaceful garden behind the Cathedral. ③–⑥.

Santa Fe International AYH Hostel, 1412 Cerrillos Rd (☎988-1153). Under a mile from the plaza, this is the cheapest place in town, with dorm beds for $11 and private rooms for $25. ①.

Eating

Santa Fe has been one of America's culinary hot spots for at least the last decade, rivalling California Cuisine. Many of the newer restaurants will put a sizeable hole in your wallet, but you needn't break the bank to get a good meal. Some of the best places are collected along Guadalupe Street, five minutes' walk from the plaza.

The *Santa Fe School of Cooking*, in the Plaza Mercado at 116 W San Francisco St (☎983-4511) holds regular lunchtime classes in preparing Southwestern specialties, culminating in the opportunity to eat the lot (2hr 30min; $25–40).

Coyote Café, 132 W Water St (☎983-1615). Super-trendy, money's-no-object restaurant just off the plaza. Its open kitchen puts out delicious grilled meats and other trademarks of so-called "New New Mexican" cuisine; if you just want a taste, there's a cheaper rooftop bar and cafe upstairs.

Guadalupe Café, 313 Guadalupe St (☎982-9762). Central, good-value meals all day. Closed Mon.

The Palace Restaurant, 142 W Palace Ave (☎982-9893). Very good local Italian place, set around a courtyard. Closed Sun.

Tecolote Café, 1203 Cerrillos Rd (☎988-1362). Inconspicuous joint, a little way south from the center, serving magnificent breakfasts – burritos, creamy eggs benedict, etc. Closed Mon.

Tomasita's, 500 S Guadalupe St (☎983-5721). Lively, unpretentious place, cranking out platefuls of tasty Mexican food, plus margaritas by the liter, inside the old railroad station. Closed Sun.

Zia's, 326 S Guadalupe St (☎988-7008). Flashy, high-tech diner. All American meats and fish dishes.

Nightlife and Entertainment

The CVB can give details about the well-respected *Santa Fe Opera*, held during July and August in a magnificent amphitheater north of town (☎982-3855), and the various local music and arts festivals, while the *Cinematheque*, in the Center for Contemporary Art, 291 Barcelona Rd (☎982-1338), shows the most interesting films in New Mexico. Check the free weekly *Reporter* or the *Pasatiempo* section of the Friday *New Mexican* paper for up-to-date **listings**.

All the town's hotels and restaurants have their own **bars**, but straight drinking places are surprisingly few and far between. *Evangelo's*, 200 W San Francisco St, is the only good bare-bones bar near the plaza, with a pool table and a jukebox. *Mr Rs*, 2911 Cerrillos Rd (☎473-4138), puts on nonstop country music every night, and *Club West*, 213 W Alameda St (☎982-0099), has live reggae, blues and bluegrass.

Bandelier National Monument

Cut into the forested mesas of the Pajarito Plateau, 35 miles northwest of Santa Fe, the **cliff dwellings** and Anasazi ruins of **BANDELIER NATIONAL MONUMENT** ($5 per car) are spread across fifty square miles of pine woods and deep stream-cut gorges. However, all its most important features are concentrated along a paved, mile-long loop trail through **Frijoles Canyon**, off Hwy-4 at the end of a narrow switchbacking road (which often gets congested in summer). The **visitor center** at the start of the trail gives an excellent overview of the site, with displays of pottery and jewellery, models of the ruins, full-scale reconstructions of pueblo interiors and fascinating photographs of local Indian life at the turn of the century.

The ancient settlement at Bandelier – named for the amateur archeologist Adolph Bandelier, who first publicized the place in the 1880s – dates from the very end of the Anasazi period (see opposite). It is thought that some time around 1300 AD various itinerant groups of Anasazi and other tribes, seeking sanctuary from drought and invasion, gathered here to build a community which amalgamated their assorted cultures. Quite possibly, the people of Bandelier were the direct ancestors of today's Pueblo Indians.

The first stop along the trail is the remains of **Tyuonyi**, a circular, multistoreyed village of some four hundred rooms, of which only the ground floor and foundations survive. A side path leads up to dozens of **cave dwellings**, their rounded chambers scooped out of the soft volcanic rock; you can scramble up to, and even enter, some of them, to peer out across the valley. The main trail continues to the **Long House**, an 800ft series of two- and three-storey houses built side by side against the canyon wall. Though most of the upper storeys have collapsed, you can still see the morticed holes that held up the roof beams; above these are rows of carved petroglyphs, mostly figures and abstract symbols. Half a mile beyond that, along the stream up the canyon, a reconstructed kiva sits in **Ceremonial Cave**, protected by a rock overhang 150 feet above the canyon floor. To reach it you have to climb a succession of rickety ladders and steep stairs cut into the crumbly rock – not for the faint-hearted.

Much less visited than Frijoles Canyon is the **wilderness** of the rest of the monument, open to more energetic hikers. A trail south of the visitor center comes out after one and a half miles at the **Lower Falls**, at their best in late spring, and then carries on another ten minutes to the Rio Grande. Other routes lead to the **Stone Lions Shrine**, where two very eroded carved mountain lions repose in a small clearing, and the **Painted Cave**; for all these, you need a (free) permit from the visitor center. As well as backcountry sites, there's a very nice **campground** on Frijoles Mesa, just beyond the Hwy-4 turn-off, a half-hour hike up the Frey Trail from Frijoles Canyon.

Grayline run half-day **coach tours** to Bandelier from Santa Fe ($30; ☎983-9491), though you may well find that they don't allow you as much time here as you'd like.

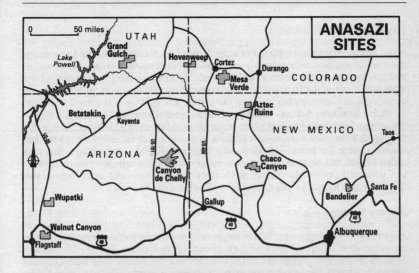

THE ANASAZI

Few visitors to the Southwest are prepared for the awesome scale and beauty of the desert cities and cliff palaces left by the ancient **Anasazi**. Signs of their civilization are to be found all over the high plateaus of what is now the **"Four Corners"** district, around the meeting point of the states of Colorado, New Mexico, Arizona and Utah.

The earliest humans reached the Southwest around 10,000 BC; the Anasazi made their first appearance as the **Basketmakers**, near the San Juan River, at about the time of Christ. Named for their woven sandals and bowls, they lived in pits in the earth, roofed with logs and mud. Over the course of a thousand years, the Anasazi adopted an increasingly settled lifestyle, becoming expert farmers and potters. Their first free-standing houses on the plains were followed by multistoreyed **pueblos**, in which hundreds of families lived in complexes of contiguous "apartments". The astonishing **cliff dwellings**, perched on precarious ledges high above remote canyons, which they began to build around 1100 AD, are an indication that things were going wrong; these were the first Anasazi settlements to show signs of defensive fortifications. A severe drought towards the end of the thirteenth century made competition for scarce resources even fiercer, as aggressors moved into the area. At this point the Anasazi disappear from history; it is thought that they moved eastwards and joined forces with other displaced groups in a coming-together which eventually produced the modern **Pueblo Indians**.

Among the most significant **Anasazi sites**, in the order they appear in this book, are:

Mesa Verde. Magnificent cliff palaces, high in the canyons of Colorado. See p.626.

Bandelier National Monument. Large riverside pueblos, and cave-like homes hollowed from volcanic rock. See p.674.

Chaco Canyon. The largest and most sophisticated freestanding pueblos far out in the desert. See p.676.

Aztec Ruins. Accessible ancient pueblo, notable for restored great kiva. See p.677.

Wupatki. Several small pueblo communities, built by assorted tribal groups. See p.702.

Walnut Canyon. Numerous canyon-wall houses above lush Walnut Creek. See p.702.

Canyon de Chelly. Superbly dramatic cliff dwellings in glowing sandstone canyon; now owned and farmed by the Navajo. See p.708.

Betatakin. Canyon-side community set in a vast rocky alcove in the Navajo National Monument. See p.713.

Grand Gulch Primitive Area. Barely explored ruins in the wilderness. See p.736.

Hovenweep. Enigmatic towers poised above a canyon. See p.737.

Los Alamos

If you approach Bandelier from the east, you'll pass **Los Alamos National Laboratory**, the main US center for the research and development of **nuclear weapons** (as well as neurobiology, computer science, and solar and geothermal energy). Virtually all the work at this, one of the foremost scientific research establishments in the world, is military-based, and consequently most of the complex is offlimits – the small and over-simplified **Bradbury Science Museum** (Tues–Fri 9am–5pm, Sat–Mon 1–5pm; free) is the only part you can visit. What's both remarkable and unnerving about the place is that the people who work here seem oblivious to the fact that not every everybody has learned to love the Bomb. The local radio station (106.7FM – great Fifties' tunes) is called *KBOM*, and museum guides glow with excitement as they describe their weapons' devastating power. Judging by the visitors' register, a sizeable percentage of visitors come here as a sort of pilgrimage from Hiroshima and Nagasaki.

Jemez Springs

The countryside to the west of Bandelier provides an unexpectedly lush counterpoint to the dry-as-dust terrain of most of New Mexico. Hwy-4 circles beyond Los Alamos through the gorgeous pinewoods and wide meadows of the **Jemez Mountains**, passing along the edge of the broad green expanse of **Valle Grande**. The geological forces which created this now-extinct volcanic caldera are responsible for numerous local **hot springs** that bubble up from underground at a sybaritically soothing 120°-plus.

Thirty miles from Bandelier, the tiny roadside hamlet of **JEMEZ SPRINGS** can offer a **hostel**-cum-B&B, the *Canyon Quarters* (☎829-3584; ①/③), and good **food** at the *Chile Bowl Cafe and Motel* (☎829-3692) and *Los Ojos Restaurant and Saloon* (☎829-3547), complete with pool tables and cheap beers till 2am. The small Jemez State Monument ($2) protects the remains of **Jemez Pueblo**, one of the last holdouts against the colonial Spanish, half a mile north of the village, but the most appealing reasons to pass this way are further north along the lovely Jemez River. Just over five miles from the village, at the foot of the aptly named **Battleship Rock**, there's a fifty-foot-long pool of steaming clear water; a couple of miles further on, on a hillside promontory between mileposts 24 and 25, **Spence's Hot Spring** has to be one of the most beautifully sited natural springs in North America. At sunset especially it's irresistible. Half a dozen waterfall-connected pools provide a range of temperatures to suit any body, from the high 90s in the lower pools to a blissful 104° at the top; local custom calls for bathing suits on weekend nights, otherwise it's clothing optional. To get there cross the river over a fallen tree and then climb up the canyon, keeping to the left for about ten minutes' walk uphill.

Chaco Canyon

Protected by the US government as the Chaco Culture National Historic Park, the hundreds of **Anasazi ruins** dotted around **CHACO CANYON** include the remains of what's generally considered to be the **largest pre-Columbian city** in North America. To archaeologists, Chaco is the greatest architectural achievement of the Anasazi people. Enough is still standing to take your breath away, although scattered over 35 square miles of scrubby high-desert plains, the buildings are not as immediately striking or photogenic as those at Mesa Verde or Canyon de Chelly, and their isolation – two hours' drive from the nearest paved road, and without food or lodging – makes them the least visited of all the major Anasazi sites.

The park **visitor center** (daily, summer 8am–6pm, otherwise 8am–5pm; ☎988-6727) is at the east end of Chaco Canyon. From there, an eight-mile paved road loops to the west around a circuit of the principal structures. The biggest and most intriguing of the lot, **Pueblo Bonito**, is a four-storied D-shaped structure, almost perfectly aligned east–west and dating from the eleventh century. Its lack of any external doors led early archeologists to see its main purpose as being defensive; they conjectured that it housed around a thousand people, though some modern theories see it as more of a trading center and storehouse. Certainly it was the central focus for an economic and political community of perhaps five thousand people, spread over the southern Colorado Plateau. Today its finely dressed stone walls and doorways only hint at its former grandeur; a trail guide (50¢) explains the history and construction techniques, leading you through basement rooms into the two central courtyards, and the **great kivas** which were its religious and social focal point.

The smaller complex of **Chetro Ketl**, quarter of a mile to the east, was built slightly after Pueblo Bonito. It shows Chaco-style masonry construction at its most sophisticated, with horizontal rows of large, squared-off stones chinked with smaller, flatter stones and set into a bed of adobe mortar with a mosaic-like precision. Another sign of the Chacoans' engineering capabilities is the extensive system of **stone-built causeways** cutting straight over and occasionally even through the mesa tops to some 75 outlying communities, including one that stretched all the way to Aztec Ruins, 45 miles north (see below). All in all over four hundred miles of arrow-straight roads, averaging thirty feet in width, have been uncovered around the Chaco backcountry, though most are barely perceptible to the naked eye; the short film *Sundagger*, shown at the visitor center, explores the astronomical and religious significance of Chaco remnants found on distant Fajada Butte. Ironically, Chaco today has become a unique place to come for **star-gazing**. As the nearest city lights are over a hundred miles away, and the park is six thousand feet above sea level, the crystal-clear night sky is usually swimming with stars.

Both the two main **routes to Chaco Canyon** entail driving at least twenty miles over rough but passable dirt roads. Roads within the park are paved; do not, however, try to drive to or from the park during or within a day after a rainstorm, as you're likely to get stuck in the mud. Marginally the better route comes in from the north or east from Hwy-44; from the south turn off I-40 onto Hwy-371 at **Thoreau** and follow it until the Hwy-57 turn-off, two miles north of the Navajo Nation town of **Crownpoint**. To pick up food and supplies, or if you want to spend the night in the area to get an early start, your best bet is the uranium mining town of **Grants**, on I-40 between Albuquerque and Gallup (see p.682). Within the park, unless you camp out in the backcountry you're limited to a fairly basic **campground** ($6), half a mile east of the visitor center.

Aztec Ruins National Monument

AZTEC RUINS NATIONAL MONUMENT preserves what was basically an outlyer Anasazi settlement, roughly halfway between the larger and more significant communities of Chaco Canyon and Mesa Verde in southern Colorado (see p.626). It is much more accessible than Chaco, lying just off US-550. The main structure (misnamed Aztec by pioneer Americans) was an E-shaped compound of some 500 rooms; unlike other sites the **great kiva** here has been rebuilt and can be entered. Always circular in shape – modelled on the ancient pit houses even when built above ground – kivas were strictly male preserves, often augmented by secret passageways so priests, and mysterious voices, could emerge from unexpected directions. Similarities between such kivas and modern Hopi practices are one reason for regarding the Hopi as descendants of the Anasazi. The nearby **visitor center** (daily 8am–6.30pm) has a good range of Anasazi artefacts, and rangers lead walking tours of the ruins throughout the day.

In the town of **AZTEC**, you can grab an early breakfast or a steak dinner at the hearty *Aztec Restaurant*, 107 Aztec Blvd (☎334-9586); rooms can be had at the *Enchantment Lodge*, 1800 W Aztec Blvd (☎334-6143; ②), or the slightly cheaper *El Aztec Motel*, 221 S Main St (☎334-6300; ②).

Albuquerque and Central New Mexico

Although to most travellers **central New Mexico** is an area to be got through as quickly as possible, it does hold isolated pockets of interest, along with its scenery. Dozens of all-American small towns hang on to the last remants of **Route 66**, the winding old "Chicago-to-LA" transcontinental highway which has by and large been bypassed by high-speed Interstate 40.

Albuquerque – far and away New Mexico's largest city, with a third of the state's population – sits dead center, at the intersection of I-40 and I-25. It's also a main stop on the *Amtrak* and *Greyhound* routes, and holds New Mexico's only major **airport**.

The area **east of Albuquerque**, stretching along the I-40 corridor towards Texas, is among the most desolate parts of the Southwest, flat and dry and nearly devoid of interest to the casual traveller. One or two towns have enough of a claim to fame to deserve a quick detour off the Interstate, mostly due to some **Wild West** hero who passed through – Kit Carson and Billy the Kid, to name two. The mountainous region to the **west of Albuquerque** has more to see – not only **Acoma Pueblo**, the mesa-top community known as "Sky City" for its incredible position on a 500ft-high desert tableland, but also the volcanic badlands of **El Malpais National Monument**.

East of Albuquerque: Tucumcari, Clovis and Fort Sumner

The long line of truck stops, diners, and motels at **TUCUMCARI**, the biggest town between Albuquerque and Amarillo, TX (see p.543), have made it a favorite I-40 pit-stop, punctuated with neon signs. During the day you can while away an hour at the mind-bogglingly bizarre Tucumcari Historical Research Institute Museum at 416 S Adams St (Tues–Sat 9am–5pm, Sun 1-5pm; $2), which boasts one of the world's greatest collections of **barbed wire**. On a more practical level, *Greyhound* stops at 118 E Center St (☎461-1350). Literally thousands of inexpensive **rooms** lie along this stretch of old Route 66; the *Buckaroo Motel*, 1315 W Tucumcari (☎461-1650; ①), is typical. *El Toro Café* makes a mean burrito at 107 S First St (461-3328).

CLOVIS, 85 miles southeast of Tucumcari on the Texas border, has twice shifted human history in its tracks. Once was at the very dawn of time; skeletons of hunters found here alongside mammoth and giant bison are the first known signs of a human presence in the Southwest. Just 12,000 years later, a bespectacled teenager, **Charles "Buddy" Holly**, nipped across from nearby Lubbock, Texas (see p.542) to record a few tunes with his band, the Crickets – *Peggy Sue*, *That'll Be the Day* and a dozen others. Norman Petty's small studios, which also gave Roy Orbison his first break, are now a museum, open irregular hours (☎763-3435). The midsized railroad and ranching community of Clovis, meanwhile, has lapsed into another 12,000-year slumber.

FORT SUMNER, sixty miles west of Clovis and 45 miles south of I-40, means different things to different people. To the Navajo, Fort Sumner was where frontiersman and US Army colonel **Kit Carson** dragged them to in 1864 after destroying their orchards and burning their villages in Arizona (see p.709). To Wild West fanatics, Fort Sumner is a pilgrimage spot because it holds the grave of legendary outlaw **Billy the Kid**, gunned down here by Pat Garrett in 1881. Both tales are told in the small **Fort Sumner Museum** (daily 9am–5pm; $2), two miles east of town on US-60, behind which a steel cage protects the tombstone of Billy the Kid from would-be memento seekers; a brass plaque nearby is all that marks the site of the vanished Army outpost.

Albuquerque

ALBUQUERQUE, right at the heart of New Mexico, is with half a million people the state's fastest-growing city, but it's not one of the more attractive. Founded beside the

Rio Grande in 1706 and named in honor of the Spanish Duke of Alburquerque, it had a pivotal position on the Old Chihuahua Trail between Santa Fe and Mexico. Sprawling, disjointed and in places intimidating, it feels more like an overgrown highway town than the economic engine it really is, and holds little to detain you longer than a day. However, the **Old Town** area retains its **Spanish plaza** intact, and the excellent **Indian Pueblo Cultural Center** is close at hand. Every October Albuquerque hosts the nation's largest **hot-air balloon** rally, attracting upwards of 100,000 people to its mass ascensions, and all year enjoyable day trips can take you up 10,500ft **Sandia Peak** for a stunning sunset view, or south to the ancient pueblos of **Salinas National Monument**.

Arrival and Information

Albuquerque's **International Airport**, two miles south of the city center, is the only major airport for hundreds of miles, linked by shuttle services such as *Shuttlejack* (☎1-800/452-2665) and *Faust's* (☎1-800/345-3738) to Santa Fe and Taos. You can reach downtown via *Sun Tran* **buses** (60¢), or *Yellow Cab* (☎247-8888) and *Checker Cab* (☎243-7777) **taxis** (about $4). *Amtrak* **trains** (one daily from east and west) arrive at a small station behind the modern *Greyhound* terminal, 300 Second St SW (☎247-3495), which has good-sized left-luggage lockers. Both terminals are in an otherwise abandoned area, five easy minutes' walk south of downtown.

A useful free listings-packed magazine, *The Art of Visiting Albuquerque*, is available from the main **tourist office** downtown at 121 Tijeras Ave NE (Mon–Fri 8am–5pm; ☎243-3696 or 1-800/284-2282), or from the Old Town booth (Mon–Sat 10am–5pm, Sun 11am–5pm) opposite the west side of the plaza.

Old Town

Once you've cruised up and down **Central Avenue**, looking at the flashing neon and 1940s architecture of this twenty-mile stretch of Route 66 (regular *Sun Tran* buses do it all day for 60¢), most of what's interesting about Albuquerque is concentrated in **Old Town**, the recently tidied-up old Spanish heart of the city. The tree-filled **main plaza** is overlooked by the twin-towered adobe facade of **San Felipe de Neri church**, and circled by horse-drawn carriages that you can hop on for a short tour ($3). It's a very pleasant place to wander or have a meal, even if there's not a whole lot to do. One of the more bizarre of the many knick-knacky shops is the *Rattlesnake Museum* west of the plaza, with live rattlers on display (and rattlesnake curios on sale); also nearby is *Gus' Trading Post*, at 2026 Central Ave SW, one of the best-value shops in the entire Southwest for buying the perfect bolo tie or other piece of Indian **jewellery**.

The one place worth spending some time, especially if you've got kids in tow, is the **New Mexico Museum of Natural History**, four blocks northeast of the plaza at 1801 Mountain Rd NW (daily 9am–5pm; $4), which has full-scale, animated models of dinosaurs, a simulated volcanic eruption and a replica of an Ice Age snow cave, as well as an engaging, handleable collection of fossils and dinosaur bones. For a more up-to-date look at the local ecology, head two miles north from Old Town along Rio Grande Blvd to the **Rio Grande Nature Center** (daily 10am–5pm; $1). Informative displays describe Albuquerque's wildlife, and two short but much appreciated nature trails along the riverside feel far removed from the city.

Indian Pueblo Cultural Center

2401 12th St NW, one block north of I-40. Daily 9am–5.30pm. $2.50. ☎843-7270.

The **Indian Pueblo Cultural Center** is a stunning museum and crafts market owned and operated as a co-operative venture by the diverse Pueblo Indians of New Mexico. The modern building is modelled on traditional Pueblo architectural forms, organized in a horseshoe shape around a central courtyard where Pueblo dances are held every Saturday and Sunday at 11am and 2pm (April–Dec only; free).

This is New Mexico's one major museum about Indians to be curated by Indians, and the displays downstairs have a clear and distinct point of view: *Our Land, Our Culture, Our Story*, as the sign at the entrance puts it. The shared Anasazi heritage which lies at the root of Pueblo culture is explained in detail, while the final few exhibits express the betrayal felt by the Native Americans when the Spanish strangers they welcomed and helped turned into conquerors and oppressors; in contrast to other museums, history here ends with the Pueblo Revolt of 1680. Modern Pueblo life is discussed in a series of video tapes, and there's an outstanding selection of covetable pottery and jewellery both on display and on sale in the various stores upstairs, with works from each of the Pueblo tribes (the Zia ceramics are a highlight). A good-quality café serves assorted Pueblo specialties (daily 7.30am–3.30pm).

Sandia Crest and the Turquoise Trail

The forested 10,500ft peaks of the **Sandia Crest** tower over Albuquerque to the east, affording particularly beautiful views from the top at and after sunset, when the city lights sparkle below. In summer it's a good 25° cooler up here than in the valley, and in winter you can go downhill or cross-country skiing (lift tickets $24 per day; ☎296-9585). If you don't want to drive the scenic but twisting twenty-mile route from Albuquerque, take the **Sandia Peak Aerial Tram** (daily summer 9am–10pm, otherwise shorter hours; $11; ☎298-8518), at 2.7 miles the world's longest single-span tramway, from the end of Tramway Rd at the northeast edge of the city.

Sandia Crest also makes a good stop on the way to or from Santa Fe. Rather than take the I-25 freeway, detour along Hwy-14, the so-called "Turquoise Trail", which passes between the Sandia and Ortiz mountains through ghostly mining camps like **Golden**, site of the Wild West's first gold discovery, **Cerrillos**, thought to have been the source of virtually all the turquoise in the ancient Southwest; and the New Agey village of **MADRID** (pronounced *MAD-rid*), where since the mid-1970s a community of arts-and-craftsy ex-hippies has resurrected the shacks and company stores of an old coal-mining town, complete with an enterable mine shaft behind the lively *Mine Shaft Tavern*.

If you do drive the I-25 route, be sure to stop off along the way at **CORONADO NATIONAL MONUMENT**, just off the freeway eighteen miles north of Albuquerque (daily, summer 9am–6pm, winter 8am–5pm; $2). Named for the Spanish explorer who wintered here in 1540 (and who, in frustration at not finding any of the vast riches he was searching for, tortured and brutally murdered a number of local Indians), the monument consists of a large **adobe pueblo** beside the Rio Grande. You can enter its restored kiva to see reproductions of its multihued murals. The originals, preserved in the visitor center, include scenes of a rabbit hunt – the animals are still abundant in the undergrowth by the river.

Salinas National Monument

About an hour south of Albuquerque's city limits, off US-60 in the southern section of the Cibola National Forest, the **SALINAS NATIONAL MONUMENT** (daily 8am–5pm; free) serves as a memorial to the Pueblo-Spanish encounter. Its three parts preserve the remnants of three separate but interrelated pre-colonial Indian **pueblos**, with their associated **missionary churches**. The largest stands on a low hill 26 miles south along Hwy-14 from the monument's visitor center in **Mountainair**; the impressive 300-room **Gran Quivira** is the only one to have been more than minimally excavated. Abandoned in 1672, partly due to Apache raids, the pueblo holds some unusual hidden kivas, tucked away deep in the complex after the Spaniards demanded the destruction of those they could see. The main feature of **Quarai**, located eight miles north of US-60 on Hwy-55, is the massive fortress-like stone church **Nuestra Senora de la Concepcion**, which stands above mounds of unexcavated ruins; **Abo**, the smallest and least interesting of the three sections, is just off US-60 nine miles west of Mountainair.

Accommodation

Central Avenue, the old Route 66 artery, holds the bulk of Albuquerque's budget accommodation; all along its twenty-mile stretch are the blinking neon signs of dozens of $25-a-night motels. There are also a few more upscale hotels downtown, and a number of national chains near the airport.

Albuquerque International Hostel, 1012 Central Ave SW (☎247-1813). Near Old Town, a mile west of downtown. Dorm beds for $10 and bargain doubles. ①.

Barcelona Court, 900 Louisiana Ave NE (☎255-5566 or 1-800/222-1122). Just off I-40, three miles east of downtown, this spacious family-orientated hotel includes full breakfasts and evening cocktails. Each room has an en-suite kitchen. Low midweek rates. ⑤.

Casas de Sueños, 310 Rio Grande Rd (☎247-4560). One of the most pleasant places to stay in all of New Mexico. Beautifully furnished, exotic (as in the extraordinary *Caracol* room coiled above the entrance) and friendly B&B very near Old Town, with themed cottages and smaller rooms. ⑤.

Comfort Inn – Airport, 2300 Yale Rd SE (☎243-2244). The best-value place to stay near the airport, with free airport shuttle. ③.

El Vado, 2500 Central Ave SW (☎243-4594). Classic Route-66-style motel near Old Town. ②.

Monterey Motel, 2402 Central Ave SW (☎243-3554). Another Old Town motel. ②.

La Posada de Albuquerque, 125 Second St (☎242-9090 or 1-800/777-5732). Historic, elegant downtown hotel; its spacious and atmospheric bar puts on occasional live jazz. ⑤.

Eating, Drinking and Nightlife

Albuquerque's **restaurants** are spread out fairly evenly over the hundred-square-mile city area, so you'll either have to take your chances in the city center area or hop in the car and drive somewhere. Most of the more reputable **bars** and **nightclubs** are inside the larger chain hotels. For **dancing**, you can two-step with throngs of urban cowboys at *Caravan East*, 7605 Central Ave NE (☎265-6993), or groove to the contemporary, almost underground sounds at *Beyond Ordinary*, 211 Gold Ave (☎764-8858). The "Pueblo Deco" *KiMo Theatre*, 419 Central Ave NW (☎243-4500), puts on live bands.

Artichoke Café, 424 Central Ave SE (☎243-0200). Good, varied menu. Closed Sun, & Mon pm.

Frontier Restaurant, 2400 Central Ave SE (☎266-0550). Basic diner food, open all day.

Garcia's Kitchen, 1736 Central Ave SW (☎842-0273) and 1113 Fourth St NW (☎297-9149). Good value diner food. The Central Ave branch, near Old Town, is worth a look for its neon sign alone.

La Hacienda, 302 San Felipe St (☎243-3131). The best bet in Old Town, with an outdoor patio overlooking the plaza and good-value Mexican cooking.

Monte Vista Fire Station, 3201 Central Ave NE (☎255-2424). Upmarket haunt, housed in restored fire station, serving up fine grilled meats and fish.

Route 66 Diner, 1405 Central Ave NE (☎247-1421). East of Old Town, near the University of New Mexico, with standard all-American meals and a usually lively, late-night clientele.

West of Albuquerque: I-40 to Arizona

Driving between Albuquerque and Arizona you could easily be so put off by the parade of billboards and hoardings offering cheap cigarettes and Indian jewellery that you'd miss out on some of central New Mexico's most interesting places, such as **Acoma Pueblo** and **El Malpais National Monument**, which lie just south of I-40.

Acoma Pueblo

Daily, summer 8am–7pm, winter 8am–4.30pm. Closed July 10–13. $6, plus $5 for photo permit.

The ancient mesa-top community of **ACOMA PUEBLO**, twelve miles off the interstate 55 miles west of Albuquerque, has been continuously inhabited for over 800 years, which makes it one of the oldest settlements in North America (rivalled by the Hopi Mesas – see p.711). Though it has become heavily dependent upon tourism – even hosting the Miss America swimsuit competition – its setting remains as dramatic as ever, and "Sky City" still has a certain aloof detachment from the modern world.

To see Acoma, you have to join one of the hour-long guided **tours** that leave regularly from the small museum/gift shop at the base of the 350ft mesa, climbing to the top by bus. The main stop is at the **San Esteban del Rey** mission, a thick-walled adobe church completed in 1640. Its earthen-floored nave is capped by a roof made of pine logs, which are said to have been carried here from the top of Mount Taylor, twenty miles away, without once touching the ground. Catholicism did eventually take root among the Pueblo people, but tales of the early mission days often speak of the Spanish priests as harsh and unfeeling taskmasters, and many came to rather sticky ends. The sheer visual impact of the building is undeniable, but in part that's due to its sheer incongruity, and it's striking that the Acomans obviously never felt inclined to follow its architectural example. Instead they went on constructing the multistorey stone and adobe houses around which the tour then proceeds. Few of these are now lived in with any regularity, as most Acomans prefer to live down below where they can get electricity and running water – and jobs. Villagers do, however, come up here during the day to sell pottery and fry-bread.

If you choose not to take the bus back down, you can instead walk by the old path, scrambling over boulders and through narrow clefts and using toeholds and notches worn away since time immemorial. Away to the east, legend has it that the forbidding **Enchanted Mesa** once held its own Pueblo community; the only access to the top was via a system of ropes strung between the mesa itself and an adjoining rock pillar. When that pillar collapsed one day while the men were away from the village, the women and children were left stranded on the top, their cries for help fading as they starved away.

El Malpais National Monument

At its western edge, Acoma Pueblo is bounded by the barren badlands of **EL MALPAIS NATIONAL MONUMENT**, whose subsurface tunnels and tubes attract potholers and geology buffs, but hardly anyone else. Most of this remote land is accessible only by four-wheel-drive vehicles, in good weather, though you can get a good look at it by driving the one paved road, Hwy-117, which passes through the **Narrows**, a glossy black formation at the base of 500ft sandstone cliffs. More ambitious visitors may want to hike the Zuni–Acoma Trail, a fifteen-mile round trip through four distinct lava flows, or explore the **Big Lava Tubes** further west.

You can get up-to-date information on El Malpais at the National Park Service office, 620 E Santa Fe Ave (☎285-5406), along old Route 66 in **GRANTS**. Something of a thriving metropolis for these parts, Grants has a couple of good cafés – try the beefy *Sirloin Stockade* at 1140 E Santa Fe Ave or the New Mexican specialties at nearby *Maria's Diner* – and half a dozen budget motels just off I-40, including *Travelodge* (☎287-2991; ③) and *Motel 6* (☎285-4607; ③). The comprehensive and enjoyable **New Mexico Museum of Mining** at 100 Iron St (Mon–Sat 10am–4pm, Sun 1–4pm; $2) focuses on the local **uranium mines**, and gives you a chance to descend into one.

Gallup

Just half an hour from the Arizona border, 65 miles west of Grants, the famous **Route 66** town of **GALLUP** is a handy I-40 pitstop, but otherwise uninteresting. A five-mile line of the old Route 66 frontage contains some of the **least expensive motels** in the US, ranging from the *Ambassador*, 1601 W Rte 66 (☎722-3843; ③), and the *Colonial*, 1007 W Coal Ave (☎863-6821; ③), to the pricier national chains. Unless you're falling asleep at the wheel, the only place really worth stopping for in Gallup is the *El Rancho Hotel*, 1000 E Rte 66 (☎863-4408 or 1-800/543-6351; ③), built in 1937 by the brother of D W Griffith as a home from home for the many Hollywood stars who needed a place to stay while filming nearby. Nowadays you can ogle their photos in the spacious Spanish Revival lobby, grab a bite in the café or spend the night in the *Ronald Reagan Room*, the *Marx Brothers Room* or the *Mae West Room*.

Gallup has evolved into a major commercial center for the Navajo Nation and other nearby Native American communities, who come together here on the second weekend in August for the **Inter-Tribal Indian Ceremonial**, the largest such gathering anywhere. Four days of dances and crafts shows have as their highlight a Saturday morning parade through the town.

Zuni Pueblo and Inscription Rock

ZUNI PUEBLO, just off Hwy-602 35 miles south of Gallup, is the sole survivor of the quasi-historical golden "Seven Cities of Cibola" sought by Coronado – not that it ever had any gold. Noted today for its immaculate mission church and elaborate masked dances, and for the intricate fetishes carved by Zuni craftspeople, it holds the Zuni Tribal Fair in late August. Half an hour east of Zuni on Hwy-53, **Inscription Rock**, officially known as El Morro National Monument, is a sandstone cliff marked on by centuries of travellers from ancient Anasazi to conquistadores and modern Kilroys. If you want to stretch your legs, climb the mile-long trail to the top to see the extensive, recently excavated Anasazi ruins of **Atsinna**, which around 1300 AD was inhabited by some 1500 people.

Southern New Mexico

Most of the travellers who come to southern New Mexico are here to visit **Carlsbad Caverns National Park**. Crassly commercialized it may be, but, like the Grand Canyon, it's too amazing a geological spectacle to miss. To the northwest of Carlsbad, the **Sacramento** and **Jicarilla** mountains – home to the large Mescalero Apache reservation as well as some rough-and-ready resorts with alpine settings to match Taos – rise out of the desert plains once roamed by Billy the Kid and other Wild West heroes. West of the mountains spread the desolate dunes of the **White Sands**, half national park, half missile and bombing range, with the rolling hills of the **Rio Grande Valley** beyond. The little-visited southwest corner – just an hour west of El Paso, Texas, the region's only city, via I-10 – is among the most attractive reaches of the Southwest, with dozens more ghost towns and some fine scenery, plus the undisturbed pre-Columbian remains of the **Gila Cliff Dwellings National Monument**.

Carlsbad Caverns National Park

Despite being a good hundred miles from the nearest sizeable town, in the remote southeastern corner of New Mexico, **Carlsbad Caverns** are among New Mexico's most visited tourist destinations. At least 250 million years of oozing dribbling water have transformed what was once a submarine limestone reef into a vast network of tortuous and eerie tunnels, punctuated by colossal lightless halls, which have literally hollowed out the insides of a mountain. However crowded the place may get (and summer holiday weekends are *very* busy), the descent through these swirling shapes of liquid rock is oddly peaceful, in fact virtually mesmerizing.

The national park consists of the two largest caves, with a separate admission fee for each one. Tickets for both are sold at the **visitor center** (daily, summer 8am–7pm, otherwise 8am–5pm; ☎785-2232), at the top of the Guadalupe Crest on a narrow twisting seven-mile road west of US-62, which has a relief model and photographs of the caverns, a restaurant and fairly tacky gift shop, a creche and even a kennel. Most of the year, you are only likely to have to wait first thing in the morning, when everyone tries to beat the rush. Guided tours are offered in winter; in summer you're on your own, though you can rent a radio (50¢) for a broadcast description of the various forms. Even when surface temperatures reach 100°, it's usually pretty cool (around 56°) down below.

To Holbrook, AZ
To Albuquerque
Salinas National Monument (Quarai)
Fort Sumner
US-60
US-285
US-60
Quemado
Salinas National Monument (Abo)
To Clovis
25
US-60
Salinas National Monument (Gran Quivira)
Socorro
San Antonio
Bosque del Apache National Wildlife Refuge
Hwy-12
Carrizozo
Trinity Site (First Atomic Explosion)
US-380
Lincoln
US-285
Gila Wilderness
Ruidoso
Roswell
ARIZONA
Gila Cliff Dwellings National Monument
JORNADA DEL MUERTO
Mescalero Apache Reservation
US-70
Rio Grande
Truth or Consequence
Hwy-78
US-180
Gila River
To Globe, AZ
Silver City
US-54
Alamogordo
US-285
To Tombstone, AZ
Lordsburg
US-70
Deming
US-180
White Sands National Monument
Carlsbad
US-180
Las Cruces
Rock Hound State Park
Mesilla
US-54
Carlsbad Caverns National Park
Whites City
Pancho Villa State Park
25
El Paso, TX
US-180
Guadalupe Mountains National Park
US-80
Hwy-11
MEXICO
0   25 miles
SOUTHERN NEW MEXICO

Carlsbad Cavern (daily, summer 8.30am–5pm, shorter hours in winter; $5, Golden Eagle pass not valid) is the biggest of the lot, and the easiest to get a look at. All its formations, however delicate, are a uniform stone grey; the rare touches of colour are provided by slight red or brown mineral-rich tinges. Early visitors were dropped down in buckets and guided through on ropes; nowadays you can walk a three-mile trail, known as the "Blue Tour", which winds steeply down from the giant gaping mouth at its entrance and passes numerous formations along the way. You miss the best of the experience if you choose to ride the modern elevator straight to the half-mile-long **Big Room** at the bottom, though the gift shop and cafeteria down there, 750 feet underground, is totally surreal; moves to close it althogether have so far been stymied by the popular affection for this strange Fifties-style installation. All visitors are obliged to ride the elevator back out.

Carlsbad Cavern is closed to the public early in the afternoon, in time for the nightly aerobatics show put on by the **millions of migratory bats** that make their homes here between spring and October, hanging upside down in the caves throughout the day. At dusk (or a bit later) black clouds of the little creatures ascend in spirals from the mouth of the caverns, right by the visitor center, and spread out over the desert for their nightly feed, returning before dawn. Park rangers are on hand to give a free and informative "Bats aren't as bad as you think" presentation, and to answer questions.

The much less visited **New Cave**, 25 miles southwest of the visitor center, can only be seen on a somewhat strenuous guided tour ($6.50, and you must have a flashlight and stout shoes; ring the visitor center for times and reservations). It's much less developed, and will appeal to anyone wanting a bit of extra adventure. One especially beautiful cave, **Lechuguilla**, is so dangerous and difficult that it's off limits to all but the most expert cavers; others have to content themselves with the marvellous pictures of its delicate crystalline formations in the visitor center.

Carlsbad Practicalities

No matter how you get to Carlsbad Caverns, you have to cross seemingly endless miles of the Llano Estacado, the deathly flat rangeland that covers southeast New Mexico and the Texas Panhandle. The route from El Paso, Texas, has the distinct advantage of passing through **Guadalupe Mountains National Park**, a beautiful though little-visited complement to Carlsbad which offers superb camping (see p.549).

There are quite a few motels on all the main roads, but the best **places to stay** are at the entrance to the park, right on US-285 in **WHITE'S CITY**. This is basically one big tourist complex (☎785-2291 or 1-800/CAVERNS) – three motels, a $10-a-night youth hostel, an RV park and a couple of restaurants – all owned and operated by the White family. *Greyhound* buses (operated by *T&NMO*) stop here three times daily; White's City run minivan trips into the park ($15 round-trip). The town of **Carlsbad** itself, 25 miles north of White's City, holds little of interest outside its many motels, such as the *Park Inn International*, 3706 National Parks Hwy (☎887-2861; ③).

Ruidoso

The Sacramento, Capitan and Jicarilla mountains, which rise at the western edge of the Llano Estacado, 85 miles northwest of Carlsbad, form a rare respite from the scrubby flatness. Spread out along winding roads that cut through dense groves of pine, fir and aspen, the main town here, **RUIDOSO**, is the fastest-growing resort in the Southwest, with dozens of motels and mountain lodges along the banks of the Ruidoso ("Noisy") River. At the Ruidoso Downs racetrack just east of town, the new **Museum of the Horse** (daily, summer 9am–5.30pm, winter 10am–5pm) celebrates all matters equine with artworks and such memorabilia as horse-drawn Russian sleighs. Ruidoso is especially popular with Texans, who flock here in summer for the refreshing cool mountain air (and to bet on the horses), and in winter to hit the 12,000ft slopes at **Ski Apache** (☎336-4565), a downhill ski area operated by the Mescalero Apache tribe (although it's not on their land; they bought it as a going concern). Après-ski activity centers on the hilltop *Inn of the Mountain Gods* (☎1-800/545-9011; ⑤), a luxury resort complex with some lively bars and restaurants.

Despite scores of inexpensive **motels**, such as *Apache Motel*, 344 Sudderth Ave (☎257-2986; ②), and *Pines Motel*, 620 Sudderth Ave (☎257-2334; ②), Ruidoso can't always handle the demand for **rooms** on summer weekends. B&Bs in the immediate vicinity include the welcoming *Sierra Mesa Lodge*, ten miles north near the ski area at Fort Stanton Rd in Alto (☎336-4515; ⑤). The best **food** is at *My Sister's Place*, 1501 Sudderth Ave, or the *Circle J Barbeque*, 1845 Sudderth Ave, and the **visitor center** is at 720 Sudderth Ave (☎257-7395 or 1-800/253-2255).

Lincoln County

One of the most enduring of New Mexico's many legendary Wild West figures was a Brooklyn-born one-time bus boy named William Bonney, better known as **Billy the Kid**. Many towns lay claim to him, but he first came to fame as an eighteen-year-old in the **Lincoln County War**, which erupted in 1878 in the frontier town of **LINCOLN** when rival groups of ranchers and merchants fought to gain control of the town and the hundreds of square miles of grazing lands that surround it. Today Lincoln, on Hwy-380 roughly halfway between Carlsbad and Albuquerque, is probably the best place to get a feel for those lawless years; the entire town, consisting of some two dozen frontier-era buildings along Main Street, has been preserved pretty much intact. There are two good museums: one inside the restored **Lincoln County Courthouse** at the west end of town tells all about Billy the Kid and his various jailbreaks and escapades, and a more modern one on the east side details local Native American cultures, with an eye-opening exhibit about a unit of black cavalrymen who were stationed at nearby Fort Stanton, fighting Apaches. Admission to the museums, along with other smaller displays in various houses and stores, costs $4. The *Wortly Hotel* (☎653-4500; ③) serves good meals throughout the day.

West of Lincoln are the scenes of yet more violence – both natural and thermonuclear. **Valley of Fires State Park**, a six-mile-wide black lava flow, bordering US-380 west of the small town of Carrizozo, forms an incredible contrast with the bleached desert of the White Sands fifty miles to the south (see below). Across the desert thirty miles to the west, at the **Trinity Site**, the first **atomic bomb** was detonated on July 16 1945, blasting the sands below Ground Zero into a thick slab of radioactive glass. Anything that was here when the bomb exploded was either destroyed or has been dug up and carted away, so there's very little to see; in any event, the whole area is on the White Sands Missile Range, and is off limits except for twice-yearly tours.

The White Sands National Monument and Alamogordo

Filling a broad valley west of Ruidoso and the Sacramento Mountains, the **White Sands** are 250 square miles of glistening, three-storey high dunes, not of sand but of finely ground gypsum eroded from the nearby peaks. Unfortunately, most of the desert valley is under the control of the US military, who use it as a missile range and training ground for pilots, and as a landing site for the **space shuttle**; only the southern half of the dunes is protected within the White Sands National Monument (often closed for an hour or two at a time while missile tests are underway). The best place to start is at the **visitor center**, just off US-70, which illuminates the uniquely evolved plants and animals that dwell here – it's not as lifeless as it first appears. An eight-mile paved road ($3) stretches into the heart of the dunes, where you can scramble and slide in the sheer white landscape. Don't forget to bring water.

ALAMOGORDO, which sits at the base of the Sacramento Mountains, sixteen miles east of the Monument along US-54, holds the nearest food and lodging options as well as a very tacky but barely memorable *International Space Hall of Fame*.

The Rio Grande Valley

From White Sands, US-70 heads southwest across the Tularosa Valley to **LAS CRUCES** – "the Crosses" – a large, modern farming community on the Rio Grande at the junction of I-10 and I-25. The town takes its name from the dozens of white crosses set up in the sands to mark the graves of early travellers killed by Apaches in 1830, but any real sense of its history is pretty well buried by motels and fast-food franchises.

North from Las Cruces towards Albuquerque, I-25 stretches for miles along the Rio Grande, passing a number of irrigation reservoirs and the elderly resort town of **TRUTH OR CONSEQUENCES**, which renamed itself after a 1950s TV show for the sake of a bit of fame. One of the few places here to tempt you off the highway is 120 miles north of Las Cruces, halfway to Albuquerque: the **Bosque del Apache Wildlife Refuge**, a great place for seeing migratory birds and the only spot where you can see the Rio Grande in its (relatively) natural state.

Mesilla

The little-changed Spanish colonial village of **MESILLA**, just south of I-10 two miles west of Las Cruces, was until the 1870s one of the Southwest's biggest towns, with upwards of eight thousand inhabitants. During the Civil War it even served briefly as the Confederate capital of New Mexico and Arizona, but it went into swift decline when the railroad bypassed it in favor of Las Cruces in 1881. A couple of good **restaurants** – the *Double Eagle* for steaks and *El Patio Cantina* for beers and Mexican food – are housed in old frontier buildings around the central plaza. Many of these adobes now house art galleries and souvenir shops, while the small **Gadsen Museum** (daily 9–11am & 1–5pm; $2), just east of Hwy-28 two blocks from the plaza, recounts the town's history and details the events leading up to the Gadsen Purchase in 1854, when the US bought thirty thousand square miles of Mexican land west of the Rio Grande. The *Meson de Mesilla* (PO Box 1212; ☎525-9212 or 1-800/732-6065; ③) is a thirteen-room B&B and restaurant five minutes' walk from the plaza.

The Southwest Corner

I-10 heads west from Las Cruces across the wide open rangeland that fills out the southwest corner of New Mexico, also known as the "**Bootheel**" for the way it steps down toward Mexico. It's so sparsely inhabited, there are roughly three square miles per person. Towns are few and far between: **DEMING**, sixty miles west of Las Cruces, has a few motels and cafés and is one of two places where *Amtrak* trains stop. Even if you're racing through on the interstate, make time for the very good **Luna Mimbres Museum** (Mon–Sat 9am–4pm, Sun 1.30–4pm) which relates the region's Native American and Wild West past, and has a great show of minerals and gemstones. If you've got more time, check out **Rock Hound State Park** ten miles southeast of town, one of the few places in the Southwest where you are encouraged to take away stones such as agates, onyx and geodes. Thirty miles south of Deming, just on the US side of the Mexican border, **Pancho Villa State Park** is a sixty-acre desert botanical garden on the site where the thousand-strong forces of the outlaw Mexican revolutionary Pancho Villa did battle in 1916 against the US cavalry, after being chased out of Mexico by his erstwhile allies. It's a nice place to camp (except in summer, when it's baking hot), and you can cross over the border to sleepy **Las Palomas** for a *cerveza* or two.

The other main town in the southwest corner, **LORDSBURG**, on I-10 twenty miles before Arizona, has a line of petrol stations, cafes and motels but little else. Just two miles south sit the remnants of **Shakespeare**, one of the best preserved and most easily accessible of the area's dozens of **ghost towns**. To see it you have to join an (unfortunately rare) guided tour (every other Sat & Sun, 10am–2pm; $2; ☎542-9034).

Silver City

Rarely visited and almost entirely wilderness, the semi-arid forested volcanic **Mogollon** and **Mimbres mountains** soar above the high desert plain of southwest New Mexico to over 10,000 feet. But for a number of copper mines, the area is protected within the **Gila National Forest**. The mountains are some of the most remote in the US, little altered since the days when they were the homelands (and strongholds) of Apache warriors Cochise and **Geronimo** – who was born here at the headwaters of the Gila River.

Halfway up the mountains, the biggest settlement, **SILVER CITY**, lies 45 miles north of I-10 at the junction of US-180 from Deming and Hwy-90 from Lordsburg. The Spanish came here in 1804, sold the Mimbreño Indians into slavery, and opened the **Santa Rita copper mine**, just east of town below the Kneeling Nun monolith; but the town was re-established in 1870 as a rough-and-tumble silver camp – Billy the Kid spent most of his childhood here. A fine selection of ornate old buildings is scattered along avenues of elms and in the surrounding hills. The excellent **museum** at 312 W Broadway (Tues–Fri 9am–4.30pm, Sat & Sun 10am–4pm; donations) tells the boom-and-bust tales while quoting from Lewis Mumford, and holds fine specimens of Casas Grandes pottery, beautiful Navajo rugs, and basketry from all the major Southwest tribes. Three blocks east, the original Main Street was washed away in a great flood and has become the cottonwood-shaded **Big Gulch Park**. Bullard Street holds atmospheric saloons and cafés like the *Silver Cafe* and the *Corner Cafe*.

Just outside town, the *Bear Mountain Guest Ranch* (☎538-2538; ⑤) is the best **place to stay** in southwest New Mexico, with very pleasant rooms in a large 1920s ranch house. Room rates include three full meals. Myra McCormick, who has run the place for 33 years, regularly guides bird-watching trips (warblers and Western Tanagers are often sighted – and heard – nearby) and can suggest or arrange a variety of multiday cycling, mountain-biking, or cross-country skiing tours of the surrounding area. If you just want a place to sleep, there are half a dozen motels along US-180.

Gila Cliff Dwellings National Monument

Beautiful, twisting Hwy-15 threads north from Silver City into the mountains, passing the picturesque old mining camp of Pinos Altos on its way to the **Gila Cliff Dwellings National Monument**. From a small visitor center at the end of the road, a mile-long trail loops along a year-round stream before climbing the side of the canyon, where you get your first view of the substantial and only slightly restored **ruins**. All six of these cliff dwellings, set back in deep caves some two hundred feet above the canyon floor, were abandoned about seven hundred years ago by their builders, the **Mogollon** people, who had lived here for just forty years. They may not be as architecturally impressive as those of Mesa Verde (see p.626), but exploring them alone – you can wander freely through the chambers, and the chances are there will be no one else around – really encourages you to imagine yourself as one of the original occupants.

The largest of the caves, near the end of the trail, holds some fifteen rooms, looking out at the cottonwoods and ponderosa pines of the canyon. The south-facing caves stay warm in winter, but are well enough shaded to keep cool in summer. Keep an eye out for the various pictograph figures above the cave entrances, before you climb down the wooden ladder and circle back down the cliff face to the car park. There's **camping** nearby along the Gila River, and excellent hiking (plus a couple of natural **hot springs**) in the adjacent Gila Wilderness Area.

ARIZONA

The tourism industry in **ARIZONA** has, literally, one colossal advantage – the **Grand Canyon** of the Colorado River. It's the single most awe-inspiring spectacle in a land of unforgettable geology, and one of the few places in the world which you absolutely *have* to see at least once in your life; but surprisingly enough the Grand Canyon is by no means the most interesting or memorable destination in the state. It's quite inhuman in scale, whereas other parts of Arizona have an abiding emotional impact precisely because of the sheer drama of human involvement in this forbidding but deeply resonant desert landscape.

Over a third of the state still belongs to the **Native Americans** who have lived here for centuries, and who outside the cities form the majority of the population. In the so-called **Indian Country** of northeastern Arizona, a sovereign state within the US, the reservation lands of the **Navajo Nation** hold the stupendous **Canyon de Chelly** and dozens of other marvellously sited **Anasazi ruins** as well as the stark rocks of **Monument Valley**. The Navajo surround the homeland of one of the most stoutly traditional and least reconstructed of all Native American tribes, the **Hopi**; even the most determinedly cynical of visitors is likely to be overwhelmed by the extent to which their ancient **mesa-top villages** remain distanced from the maelstrom of modern America. The third main tribal group are the **Apache**, in the harshly beautiful southeastern mountains, who were virtually the last of the Native Americans to give in to the overwhelming power of the white American invaders.

> The **area code** for the entire state of Arizona is ☎602.

Away from the reservations, **Wild West** towns like **Tombstone**, site of the famed gunfight at the OK Corral, give a clear sense of the Arizona's characteristically rough-and-ready, pioneer mentality; this was the last of the lower 48 states to join the Union, in 1912. The **cities**, however, are not much fun. In **Phoenix**, the capital, well over a million souls are scattered over a 500-square-mile morass of shopping malls and tract-house suburbs; **Tucson** is a bit more civil, but still wears thin after a day or so.

Getting Around Arizona

Arizona is better served by public transportation than much of the Southwest, but it can still be an effort to get around without a car. *Greyhound* **buses** stop at all the major cities and at most towns along the interstates, while *Amtrak* **trains** cross the state on two of their transcontinental routes (via Tucson and Phoenix in the south, or Flagstaff further north). *Nava-Hopi* (☎1-800/892-8687 or 774-5003) and *Amtrak* buses connect Flagstaff with the Grand Canyon, which also has a small airport, but otherwise seeing the backcountry – and especially the reservations – is all but impossible without a car. The largest airport is at Phoenix, and assorted good-value short-hop **flights** cover the larger centers. The only worthwhile **bus tours** visit the area around Flagstaff.

Tucson, Phoenix and Southern Arizona

Most of Arizona's compelling attractions are in its northern reaches, but the **southern** half of the state holds ninety percent of its people, all its significant cities and several important historic sites. Apart from a couple of Spanish missions, the bulk of what there

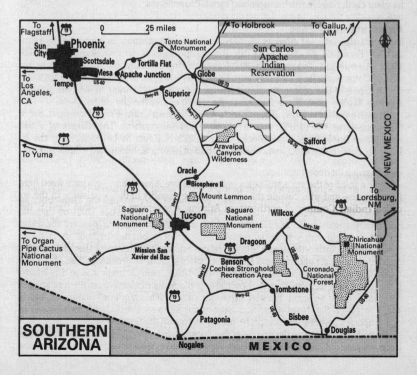

is to see is frontier Americana, especially in **Tombstone**, in the southeast corner, perhaps the best known Wild West town, where a dozen saloons serve tourists and local ranchers in relatively equal numbers. **Phoenix**, the state capital, is huge, sprawling and dull; **Tucson** makes a better base for visiting this part of the world, and for trips south of the border into Mexico. Though the open spaces of southern Arizona can be harsh and violent – most of the southwestern quarter, along the parallel I-8 and I-10 highways, is used as a bombing range – the bleakness is balanced somewhat by the many nature reserves which protect its amazing flora and fauna, such as the magical **Aravaipa Canyon Wilderness**, the remote **Organ Pipe Cactus National Monument** on the Mexican border, and **Saguaro National Monument** just outside Tucson.

Tucson

After serving as a colonial outpost under the Spanish and Mexicans, and then as territorial capital for both the US and Confederate governments, **TUCSON** (pronounced *too-sawn*) – a mere sixty miles north of Mexico on the cross-country I-10 interstate – has grown into a modern mini-metropolis of nearly a million people without entirely sacrificing its historic quarters. Now equal parts college town and retirement community, it's one of the more attractive big cities of the Southwest – which admittedly isn't saying much. Although it suffers from the same Sunbelt sprawl as Albuquerque and Phoenix, it does have a wanderable center, some enjoyable restaurants, and a pretty good nightlife, energized by the 35,000 students at the University of Arizona. It is also redeemed by having so much superb landscape within easy reach, from the forested flanks of Mount Lemmon to the rolling foothills of **Saguaro National Monument** with its giant cacti, real-life roadrunners and rare Gila monsters.

Arrival and Information

Tucson International Airport, eight miles south of downtown, is connected by regular *Sun Tran* bus #8 (60¢) or by the $11 shuttle vans of *Arizona Stagecoach* (☎889-1000). *Amtrak* and *Greyhound* (☎792-0972) both stop centrally, on Toole Ave to either side of Congress St, just off Broadway. Everywhere in town is pretty much within walking distance of the center, though if it's too hot you might want to ride the **Fourth Avenue Trolley** (25¢) out to the university, a mile east of the city center.

　　Tucson's **visitor center**, at 130 S Scott Ave downtown (Mon–Fri 8.30am–5pm, Sat & Sun 9am–4pm; ☎624-1817), has free maps and information. The *Southwest Parks Association* **bookstore**, three blocks away at 223 N Court St (☎792-0239) in the El Presidio district, stocks Arizona's best selection of historical, hiking and wildlife guides.

The Town

Tucson has two main centers: the **historic core** along the (usually bone-dry) Santa Cruz River, bisected by Congress Street, and the quarter around the **University of Arizona** campus, a mile to the east. The city was founded in the late 1700s by Catholic missionaries who came from Mexico, then a Spanish colony, to convert the Pima Indians. Nothing very substantial remains from this era, but hundreds of artefacts are now displayed inside the many historic adobe homes in and around the **El Presidio** district of cafés, art galleries and B&Bs, two blocks north of Broadway. The oldest, **La Casa Cordova** on Meyer St, dates from the 1850s, after Arizona was in US hands. Informative (and free) walking tours of the four-block district leave from the tree-shaded courtyard of the adjacent **Tucson Museum of Art**. This modern building, at 140 N Main St (Tues–Sat 10am–4pm, Sun noon–4pm; $2, free Tues), holds exhibitions of contemporary painting and sculpture, mostly to do with the Southwest.

　　Three blocks south, in the middle of the Tucson Convention Center complex, a single hundred-year-old house is the sole survivor of a once-extensive neighborhood of adobe homes torn down during the mid-1960s in the name of urban renewal. Known as the **Fremont House** (Wed–Sat 10am–4pm; free) because frontier American explorer John C Fremont lived in it for a few months in the 1870s, it belonged for many years to Leopoldo Carrillo, one of Tucson's wealthiest merchants. Though much restored, it still gives a vivid sense of the more civilized side of frontier life, from the high-quality furniture and the saguaro-rib ceilings to the fig-tree-shaded rear courtyard gardens.

Tucson's other main area of interest is around the University of Arizona, which spreads between Sixth St and Speedway Blvd a mile east of dowtown. The highlight is the **Arizona State Museum** (Mon–Sat 9am–5pm, Sun 2–5pm; free), where an exceptionally comprehensive assembly of Native American artefacts from the very earliest days traces the evolution of the various Southwest tribes. The campus also holds one of the world's finest photography archives. The **Center for Creative Photography** (Tues–Fri 10am–5pm; free) is a repository of the collected works (negatives, prints and journals) of Richard Avedon and Ansel Adams, among others. The **art museum** next door on Speedway Blvd has some morbid Spanish retablos and assorted modern pieces, in particular some fine cubist sculpture by Lipchitz and Picasso.

Old Tucson and the Desert Museum

Twelve miles west of the university on Speedway Blvd, en route to Saguaro, **Old Tucson** (daily 9am–5pm; $8.95) is an entertaining if contrived Wild West amusement center. It's built around a movie set and sound stage constructed for a 1930s Hollywood western, and later used for numerous TV shows and commercials. Nowadays you can ride a stagecoach or an old coal-fired steam train, and watch a bawdy music hall show in the saloon or a gunfight on Main Street.

Much more worthwhile, especially if you've got kids, is the **Arizona-Sonora Desert Museum** (daily, summer 7.30am–6pm, winter 8.30am–5pm; adults $6, ages 6–12 $1), two miles further west in **Tucson Mountain Park**. Museum exhibits inside the Congdon Earth Sciences Center explain the geology and ancient history of the region, and a series of dioramas are filled with tarantulas, rattlesnakes and other creepy crawlers. Outside, bighorn sheep, mountain lions, jaguars and other rarely seen denizens of the desert prowl in credible simulations of their natural habitats, while hawks and bald eagles fly about in a large aviary. One of the best and most educational zoological centers in the US, the museum is as much an animal rescue center as it is a zoo: almost all the animals you see had been injured in some way before ending up here, and would be unable to survive on their own in the desert.

Saguaro National Monument

Saguaro National Monument, part of which stretches north from the Desert Museum, gives you the chance to wander through weird forests of forty-foot, multi-limbed Saguaro (*SWAH-row*) **cacti**. It's divided into two separate sections. The smaller, more accessible (and much more popular) parcel, here on the northern slopes of Tucson Mountain, is ideal for visits of an hour or two, as you can drive through the best bits on a scenic nine-mile paved loop. The more remote section, seventeen miles east of Tucson in the **Tanque Verde** mountains north of I-10, is better if you have the time and inclination to backpack overnight: it has miles of trails, and the cacti look particularly strange by moonlight. **Visitor centers** (daily 9am–5pm) at the entrance to each of the areas make good first stops; a $3-per-car fee is collected at the eastern section only, and there's no water in either part.

Accommodation

Accommodation in Tucson ranges from affordably bohemian downtown hotels to outrageously expensive dude ranches on the outskirts. Prices, especially in the upper echelons, fluctuate considerably – when the mercury rises, rates drop – and some places are open only in the peak winter and spring months. *Premiere B&B Inns of Tucson*, PO Box 237, Tucson AZ 85719 (☎628-1800), can put you in touch with selected B&Bs.

The Arizona Inn, 2200 E Elm St (☎325-1541 or 1-800/933-1093). Arizona's most comfortable and elegant resort, this desert oasis has been a winter favorite for numerous presidents, Rockefellers and the Duke and Duchess of Windsor. It remains surprisingly unstuffy – and not all that expensive, though rates – which include a gourmet breakfast – rise in peak season (Jan–May). A lovely high-ceilinged dining room serves fresh and well-prepared food. ⑤/⑥.

Congress Hotel, 311 E Congress St (☎622-8848 or 1-800/722-8848). Very central and bohemian downtown hotel, with vintage Art Deco furnishings. The Dillinger gang were once arrested here; now it's a hostel with some simple private doubles. There's a small brakfast café and a lively bar downstairs, and at night this is one of the hottest spots in town, with loud music and dancing. ①/②.

Days Inn – Santa Rita, 88 E Broadway (☎622-4000). At the heart of downtown. Handy for the El Presidio district and Congress Street, but in itself fairly anonymous. ③.

El Presidio Inn, 297 N Main Ave (☎623-6151). Nicely furnished Spanish colonial rooms in historic downtown B&B. ④.

Triangle L Ranch, Box 900, Oracle (☎623-6732 or ☎1-800/266-2804). Double rooms in private cottages, set on the oak-shaded foothills of Mount Lemmon, 35 miles north of central Tucson. Perfect for birdwatchers or just a quiet getaway. ④.

Eating

Dining out in Tucson is characterized by some Mexican places, and a few entertaining restaurants specializing in Wild West cowboy food – huge steaks, burgers and bowls of chili. As well as downtown – where virtually everywhere stops serving by 9pm – upmarket restaurants congregate in the exclusive St Philip's Plaza, a few miles north.

Bowen and Bailey Café and Greengrocer, 135 S Sixth St (☎792-2603). Upmarket, European-style café-deli. Tasty patés and salads as well as more hearty dishes for breakfast, lunch and dinner.

Café Magritte, 254 E Congress St (☎884-8004). As you might guess, an arty café, with an eclectic – but not expensive – menu to match the offbeat clientele. Great desserts, coffees, and digestifs.

Café Terra Cotta, 4310 N Campbell Ave (☎577-8100). Inventive and fairly expensive Southwestern cooking, including pizzas fresh from a wood-burning oven.

Courtyard Caf', 186 N Meyer Ave (☎622-0351). Outdoor grill in historic El Presidio adobe courtyard, with good-value salads, burgers, beer and wine.

Daniel's Restaurant and Trattoria, 4340 N Campbell Ave (☎742-3200). Stylish black decor, North Italian specialties, and some delicious breads.

El Adobe, 40 W Broadway (☎791-7458). Long-standing local favorite for large portions of Mexican food and some of the Southwest's best margaritas.

Janos, 150 N Main St (☎884-9426). Tucson's trendiest hot spot, serving inventive cuisine in an immaculate El Presidio adobe home. Very expensive, dinner only, excellent desserts.

Ranchers Club, 5151 E Grant Rd (☎323-6262). Tucson's best (and biggest) cuts of beef – 48-oz steaks – carefully grilled over your choice of desert mesquite or subtle cherrywood flame, plus excellent soups and salads in classy but unpretentious surroundings.

Drinking and Nightlife

Nightlife in Tucson focuses on Congress Street downtown, with its gaggle of arty cafés and nightclubs, and in particular the *Hotel Congress* (see above). A handful of studenty places can be found near the university plus half a dozen country and western saloons on the outskirts. Most venues double as bars or restaurants. For a full rundown, check the listings in the free *Tucson Weekly*. The *Tucson Jazz Society* (☎743-3399) promotes gigs all over town.

Café Sweetwater, 340 E Sixth St (☎622-6464). Casual, thirty-something café and bar with regular live jazz.

Cushing Street Bar, 343 S Meyer (☎622-7984). Likely spot to catch good live music of all sorts, near the Fremont House.

The Green Dolphin, 95 N Park Ave (☎622-6099). Popular student rock venue.

Muddbugg's, 136 N Park Ave (☎882-9844). Live rock and R&B, near the university.

South to the Border: Tumacacori and Nogales, Mexico

South from Tucson, I-19 heads straight for the Mexican border, 65 miles away, passing some tangible reminders of the region's Spanish and Mexican heritage. The first of these, the pristine white **Mission San Xavier del Bac** (daily 9am–6pm; donations), lies just west of the freeway, five miles from downtown Tucson on the fringe of the vast arid plain of San Xavier Indian Reservation. Built in 1778 and definitely showing its age, the crumbling church is a curious mix of the baroque aspirations of the Catholic missionaries who designed it, and the folksy, handcrafted details of the Indians who built and have maintained it. The best time to come is on Sunday morning, when the congregation can be so big that many have to stand outside and listen through the darkened doorway.

In many ways an even more evocative memorial to the missionary effort, the massive adobe church at the heart of the **Tumacacori National Monument** was ravaged by the elements for almost a hundred years before the US government took steps to preserve it. The hulking structure, built around 1800, has been re-roofed and stabilized, but the internal walls have been left as they were found, the exposed, unplastered adobe of the more damaged parts pointing out the delicacy of the surviving, finely sculpted detailing. A very good museum is housed in the small **visitor center** at the entrance, and a self-guided tour map ($1) tells the mission story.

Nogales, Arizona and Nogales, Mexico

Twenty miles south of Tumacacori, an hour from Tucson, sits the largest and most pleasant of the Arizonan–Mexican border towns, **NOGALES**. The contrast between the sedate, ordered streets on the American sites and the jumbled white-washed houses clinging to the hillside in Mexico hits you as soon as you come in sight. Promoted as "Ambos Nogales" (both Nogales), it seems to get the same number of people going each way – Mexicans coming north to stock up at *Safeway*, and gringos heading south to buy cheap beer and maybe a rug or a hammock.

Though revolutionary bandit Pancho Villa used to hang out on the Mexican side, and iconoclastic jazz great **Charles Mingus** was born on the US side, there are no real sights; it's basically a lively, large-scale street market. Nogales is not nearly as seedy as Ciudad Juarez, and nowhere near as much a tourist rip-off as Tijuana: to get a brief taste of Mexico, it's not bad at all. Dollars are the most common currency, and border formalities are minimal, and extremely unceremonious – you simply walk through a gap in a wire fence (foreign visitors should check that their visa status entitles them to re-enter the US; if you're on or eligible for the Visa Waiver Scheme (see p.8), you're fine.

To head any further south into Mexico, you have to get a tourist visa just beyond the border crossing. From there, take a taxi (around $6) the couple of miles south to the long-distance bus station, from which regular buses head to Hermosillo, Guaymas (a good overnight stop), and Los Mochis, the start of the Copper Canyon Railroad.

Patagonia and the Sonoita Creek Bird Sanctuary

A longer but much more beautiful route between Nogales and Tucson, Hwy-82 avoids the interstate by looping northeast from Nogales through the lush **Sonoita Valley** in the craggy mountains of the Coronado National Forest. At the end of a mile-long dirt road from Fourth Street in the dusty cattle-ranching town of **PATAGONIA**, the **Sonoita Creek Bird Sanctuary** is a dense stand of oaks and cottonwoods that's home to an amazing variety and density of songbirds and raptors, including finches, warblers, hawks, kestrels, woodpeckers and cardinals. The place is amazingly green throughout the year – in fact the Sonora is known as the greenest desert on earth. Twelve miles north of Patagonia, Hwy-83 veers off to the northwest to rejoin I-10 just east of Saguaro National Monument; Hwy-82 cuts east toward Tombstone, 35 miles away.

The Southeast Corner

Amongst thousands of acres of unspoiled and magnificent wilderness, southeast Arizona contains numerous well-preserved and highly atmospheric **ghost towns**. While I-10 buzzes along from the New Mexico border, the more scenic US-80 makes a grand tour of the region. Even if you're racing through this barren country, set aside an hour at least for the excellent **Amerind Foundation Museum** (daily 10am–4pm; $2), just off the interstate 65 miles east of Tucson at exit 318, for one of the best anthropological museums in the US, broad in scope and focusing in turn on the native cultures of the Southwest, the Pacific Northwest, and Central and South America.

Tombstone and Bisbee

From the I-10 truck stop of **Benson**, 45 miles east of Tucson, US-80 cuts off south 22 miles to the most famous Wild West town of all, **TOMBSTONE**. Known as "The Town Too Tough to Die", and fabled for its daily shootouts in the streets, Tombstone is so steeped in its own mythology that it's impossible to separate the facts from the tall tales, but whether you're a history buff or just want to play outlaw for a day it's still hard to beat. Tombstone only began life as a silver-boomtown in 1877, and by the end of the 1880s it was all but deserted again. However, on the day which gave it the notoriety which has kept it alive, its population stood at over ten thousand. It was 2pm on October 26 1881 when **Doc Holliday**, along with **Wyatt Earp** and his brothers Virgil and Morgan (who all served as local sheriffs), confronted a band of suspected cattle rustlers in the legendary **Gunfight at the OK Corral**. What exactly occurred is far from certain – apart from the fact that the showdown in fact took place on Fremont Street, a block from the OK Corral – but within a few minutes three of the suspects were dead. The Earps were accused of murder but charges were eventually dropped.

Much of the town, including the OK Corral, is preserved as a national historic site. Though dependent upon tourism, its dozen or so saloons, bars and cafés are also frequented by local cowboys and ranchers, giving the town an authentic edge to counterbalance its more contrived aspects – such as the wax dummies of the Earp brothers in the *Historama*, next to the OK Corral. The best time to visit is during **Helldorado Days** in late October, when the air is cooler and the sun less harsh, but the streets are full of gun-toting strangers acting out gun battles and stagecoach robberies.

BISBEE, 25 miles south, has a similar murder-and-mayhem mythology, and it too has managed to keep going with most of its historic structures intact. Until 1974, Bisbee had one of the largest and most profitable **copper mines** in the world – over four million tons of high-grade ore were dug from its depths. A handful of spit-and-sawdust saloons and restaurants still line Brewery Gulch, the main drag, but Bisbee's centerpiece remains the grand old *Copper Queen Hotel*, 11 Howell Ave (☎432-2216; ④), with its plush bar and shady pavement café.

From Bisbee, US-80 swerves to the east along the Mexican border to **DOUGLAS** (said to be one of the major throughways for drug traffickers and the slave trade in illegal Mexican farm laborers) before circling northwards through the untouched mountain fastness of the Chiricahua and Pendregosa mountains. Apache warriors Geronimo and Cochise both availed themselves of this stark and often impassable terrain when escaping from the US cavalry, and the entire range is now kept in its natural state, within the **Coronado National Forest**. For details on hiking and exploring, contact the US Forest Service in Tucson at 300 W Congress St (☎670-6483).

Southwest Arizona

There's virtually nothing in the vast desert plain of southwest Arizona to tempt you off the twin freeways that sprint to California. The US Army stages tank battles in its Yuma

Proving Grounds between I-10 and I-8, while the Air Force drops bombs and tests Stealth technology in the more mountainous region bordering Mexico. The largest town, **YUMA**, is little more than an oversized pitstop for freight trains and cross-country truckers, with 25 motels and a dozen diners along its Fourth Avenue. **Yuma Territorial Prison**, now a state park (daily 8am–5pm; $2) beside the Colorado River, was known a century ago as the "Hell Hole of Arizona", holding over a hundred of the Wild West's most violent criminals. Its first inmates were forced to build the adobe walls which later held them; there's a small museum, and you can wander around the grounds and cell blocks at will.

North of Yuma along the Colorado River, three **wildlife refuges**, the **Kofa**, **Cibola** and **Imperial**, line the banks of the Colorado River. Established to protect herds of mule deer and bighorn sheep as well as thousands of migratory Canadian geese, the parks aren't really designed for human visitors, and are virtually inaccessible without a four-wheel-drive vehicle. It is, however, worth making the effort to reach the five-hundred-square-mile **Organ Pipe Cactus National Monument**, 55 miles south of the town of **GILA BEND**. Besides the unusual Organ Pipe, which grows in groups of tubular "pipes" from a shared root system, with a sweet fruit once prized by Native Americans, there are acres of spectacular saguaro, ironwood and other desert dwellers. Before you set off through the reserve, stop at the **visitor center** (daily 8am–5pm), which will tell you what to look out for on the two scenic loops along good dirt roads, one of 21 miles up the Ajo Mountains and the other twice as long across the Puerto Blanco plain. The copper-mining company town of **AJO**, fourteen miles north of the park, holds the nearest food and lodging options.

Phoenix

The state capital and largest city in Arizona, **PHOENIX**, can't seem to rid itself of its reputation as the most unpleasant city in the Southwest – imagine Las Vegas without gambling, or LA without a beach, and you have a good idea what it's like. Founded in 1864, it was little more than a small farming town until the 1930s when the first tourists arrived to enjoy the (then) clean air and (very) warm weather – Phoenix in summer is the **hottest** city outside the Middle East, with daytime highs rarely dipping below 100°. At first a few winter resorts and dude ranches brought in vacationers from back East, but the city really took off in the postwar, post-automobile era, and its population multiplied from 30,000 to some 600,000 between 1940 and 1975. Many of the immigrants were retirees, settling in pre-fab communities like **Sun City** on Phoenix's western edge.

Since then the Phoenix **sprawl** has engulfed the neighboring communities of Scottsdale, Mesa, and Tempe to become the tenth largest city in the US, and there's no end in sight: Motorola, IBM and other high-tech firms have set up assembly plants on the still cheap land, and, following a lengthy legal battle with their Californian and Mexican neighbors, the city has recently completed an aqueduct from the Colorado River to secure its precious water supply. A nice but far from thrilling network of canals fans out across the desert, pleasant for cycling or strolling. Otherwise there are a couple of small museums, but Phoenix's main activity seems to be killing time beside the **pool** – its posh resort hotels must have the most extravagant swimming pools in the world – or popping into the many art galleries and upscale shopping malls.

Arrival and Information

Sky Harbor International Airport, just east of downtown, is a main hub for *America West* and many other airlines, receiving flights from all over the western US. Rent a car there, or ride the free *DASH* **Shuttle vans** (Mon–Fri 6.30am–6pm; ☎253-5000), or take **bus #13** to the center. *Amtrak* **trains** come into grungy old Union Station, on the south side of downtown at Fourth Ave and Harrison St; *Greyhound* arrives at Fifth Ave and

Washington St (☎248-4040), opposite the Civic Center. Getting around without a car isn't ideal – it can take hours to cross town – but it's not impossible: *Phoenix Transit Service (PTS)* has regular **buses** for 75¢ a ride or $2.50 all day; pick up a system map and other information from the **visitor center** (☎254-6400) at Second Ave and Adams St in the Civic Center.

The city's relentless grid of streets does little to encourage casual strolling, but does make **orientation** quite straightforward: basically, numbered **avenues** (1st–115th and beyond) run north to south, intersected by east–west **streets** named for US presidents (Van Buren, for some reason, is the main one). Most of the main sights are within walking distance of the Civic Center.

Civic Center

Civic Center, long a black hole at the city center, was the subject of a major international design competition some years ago, resulting in some attractive gateways and street lights but as yet no real change. Phoenix's two most worthwhile stops are on the north side of downtown, a few blocks up Central Avenue. At 1625 N Central Ave, the **Phoenix Art Museum** (Tues & Thurs–Sat 10am–5pm, Wed 10am–9pm, Sun 1–5pm; $3, free Wed) bravely tries to trace the history of art, with a handful of forgettable paintings by middleweight Old Masters; it does better, not surprisingly, on Western art.

The **Heard Museum** at 22 E Monte Vista Rd (Mon–Sat 10am–5pm, Sun noon–5pm; $4), three blocks north and a block east of Central Avenue, provides an excellent introduction to the craftswork of Arizona's many Indian reservations. It displays top-notch Navajo rugs and Hopi kachina dolls (some 400 of which were donated by arch-conservative Arizona senator Barry Goldwater), as well as the personal collection of Grand Canyon promoter Fred Harvey. Outside, in a peaceful sculpture garden full of primitive Olmec-style figures, are dozens of cacti, including agaves, ocotillos, prickly pears, and a statuesque saguaro.

West of Civic Center the sparkling copper dome of the disused **Arizona State Capitol** stands amidst the low-level sprawl. Inside it, a small **museum** (Mon–Fri 8am–5pm; free) illuminates the state's colorful – if often violent – history. In between Civic Center and the Capitol, at 1002 W Van Buren St, the tiny **Arizona Museum** (Wed–Sun 11am–4pm; free) has enagagingly unpretentious exhibits tracing regional history from Anasazi days to statehood.

If Phoenix gets too hot to bear, the coolest place to beat the heat is on the east side of town at the *Island of the Big Surf* **water park**, at 1500 N McClintock Ave (March–Sept only, Tues–Sun 8am–6pm; ☎947-7873), where you can ride five-foot waves or careen down multistorey waterslides into a giant freshwater lagoon.

Accommodation

The nicest (and most expensive) of Phoenix's **hotels** tend to be in Scottsdale, away on its northeastern edge. A strip of **motels** lines Black Canyon Highway (I-17) on the north side of town, and there are a dozen more in the Mormon community of Mesa to the east side. The Phoenix visitor center has a toll-free **hotline** for those wishing to book a room – ☎1-800/528-0483, or ☎1-800/992-6005 within Arizona.

Budget Lodge Motel, 402 W Van Buren St (☎254-7247). Reasonably attractive rooms at attractive rates. ②.

Howard Johnson Lodge, 124 S 24th St (☎244-8221). Standard doubles near the airport. ③.

Motel 6, 1511 S Country Club Drive (☎834-0066). Budget doubles in Mesa; also at 336 W Hampton Ave (☎844-8899). ②.

San Carlos Hotel, 202 N Central Ave (253-4121 or 1-800/528-5446). Atmospheric Twenties hotel in downtown Phoenix, with tasteful good-value rooms. ④.

Valley of the Sun International Hostel, 1026 N Ninth St above Roosevelt St (☎262-9439). Dorm beds for $11, a 15-min walk from the Civic Center. Also very inexpensive bike rental. ①.

YMCA, 350 N First Ave (☎253-6181). Grungy but central single rooms for men and women, with shared bathrooms. ①.

Eating

It might seem like heaven for **fast-food** fans, but by and large eating out in Phoenix is hard work and not much fun. Everything is hidden away in malls, with no neighborhood cafés and surprisingly few coffeeshops or diners. At least there are quite a few good **Mexican** places.

Baxter's, 4515 Cactus Rd (☎953-9200). Good-value Western-themed barbecue joint.

Ed Debevic's, 2102 E Highland Ave (☎956-2760). Burgers-and-fries retro-Americana.

Julio's Barrio, 7243 E Camelback Rd (☎423-0058). Good, inexpensive Mexican food in an upbeat 1930s Scottsdale diner.

La Pasadita, 1731 E Van Buren St (☎253-7237). East of the Civic Center; hard to beat for a lunch-time burrito.

FUTURISTIC VISIONS IN THE DESERT

Despite the general lack of aesthetic sensitivity in Phoenix, it has managed to attract some of the more visionary designers of the twentieth century, most notably **Frank Lloyd Wright**, who came to the city to work on the *Biltmore Hotel* and stayed for most of the next 25 years before his death in 1959. The **Taliesin West** studio that he used in winter is at the northeastern edge of the Phoenix sprawl, on 108th St just north of Shea Blvd. It's now an architecture school and a working design studio, with regular multimedia exhibits of the man's life and work. Hourly tours, including a saccharine hagiography, are offered throughout the winter and on request in summer (daily 10am–4pm; $5; ☎860-2700).

Less well known, but in many ways more compelling, is the **Cosanti Foundation**, four miles west of Taliesin at 6433 Doubletree Rd (daily 9am–5pm; $3; ☎948-6145) in Paradise Valley. The buildings, designed by **Paolo Soleri**, an Italian-born ex-student of Wright, and constructed out of rammed earth and concrete, have a much more organic feel than Taliesin. Crafts workshops make bells and cast bronzes, and a small museum shows drawings and models of Soleri's life work: **Arcosanti**, a space-age, environmentally sensitive and in general unique project slowly but surely emerging from the desert just an hour's drive north, a mile east of I-17 at Cordes Junction.

Set on the rim of a beautiful high desert canyon, and designed to be (someday) an entirely self-sufficient community of 5000 people, Arcosanti is the clearest embodiment of **Arcology** – Soleri's ideal blend of architecture and ecology. Three-hour guided tours are given throughout the day ($5 donation; ☎632-7135), and an airy and spacious café serves healthy and tasty meals. Arcosanti hosts a very popular series of outdoor summer **concerts**, and you can **stay the night** for a very reasonable $15–25; if you like what you see, sign up for one of the month-long workshops and help out with the construction.

A more controversial enterprise looms out of the desert southeast of Phoenix, in a high-security compound off Hwy-77 near the town of **Oracle**. The giant Plexiglass bubble known as **Biosphere-2**, originally financed by Texas tycoon Ed Bass, was constructed by a cultish group of retired actors and Sixties ex-radicals as a veritable Noah's Ark. Stocked with 4000 species of plants and animals, it was designed to allow them and their investors to live happily ever after . . . on **Mars**. Despite much debate in the scientific community as to the precise merits of the exercise, a small party of experimenters emerged in September 1993 having survived being sealed into the dome for two full years. During that time, emergency oxygen was twice pumped in to avoid suffocation; they grew 88 percent of their own food, and lost 13.65 percent of their body weight.

The site has become one of Arizona's most popular tourist destinations. **Guided tours**, lasting 2hr 30min, take in a walk through greenhouses that simulate the various environments inside, a chance to peep through the wall, and even to look in on the "ocean biome" from underneath (daily, every 30min, 9am–4pm; $11.95; ☎896-2108 or ☎1-800/828-2462). There is lodging at the *Inn at the Biosphere* (☎825-6222; May–Sept ③, Oct–April ⑤).

The Orangerie, in the *Biltmore Hotel*, 24th St and Missouri Ave (☎955-6600). Extremely good but outrageously pricey restaurant in a resort hotel on the northeastern side of the city. Top-quality, stylish American food in gorgeous Art Deco surroundings; formal dress except in high summer.

Nightlife and Entertainment

Not surprisingly, **nightlife** in Phoenix tends toward cowboy dance halls and Top 40 discos in the big hotels. One of the nicest **bars** in town is in the *Biltmore* (see above), but budget travellers stuck here for longer than expected will find hundreds of places to drown their sorrows. For a rundown of **what's on** musically, pick up the free *New Times Weekly* in local record- or bookstores, or check out standbys like the *Sun Club*, 1001 E Eighth St (☎968-5802), *Char's Blues*, 4631 N Seventh Ave (☎230-0205), or the headbanging *Mason Jar*, 2303 E Indian School (☎956-6271). The *Scottsdale Center for the Arts*, 7383 Scottsdale Mall (☎994-2787), puts on a fairly upmarket series of jazz, ballet, and chamber music concerts, as well as weekend cinema classics.

East of Phoenix: The Superstition Mountains and Aravaipa Canyon

Whatever its faults, at least Phoenix lies within easy reach of the intriguingly named and haunting **Superstition Mountains** that rise to the east. The main route through the angular mountains, Hwy-88 (popularly known as the **Apache Trail**), is full of cars on a summer weekend; the road cuts off northeast from US-60 about ten miles east of downtown Phoenix. Despite the many dams along the Salt River it makes for a pleasant drive, with lots of picnic spots and campgrounds. The road turns to gravel just beyond the funky hamlet of **Tortilla Flat** (named after the Steinbeck novella), before reaching the cliff dwellings of **Tonto National Monument** (daily 8am–4pm; $3 per car), where the remains of a large pueblo built in the mid-fourteenth century by Salado Indians are preserved in the mouths of three distinct caves.

Hwy-88 rejoins US-60 at the nondescript mining town of **GLOBE**, on the western edge of the two-million-acre Apache Indian Reservation roughly sixty miles south of the spectacular **Salt River Canyon**. Globe offers the small but diverting **Gila County Historical Museum**, 1330 N Broad St (summer only, Sat & Sun 10am–5pm; free), but is most worth a look during the **Apache Days** celebration on the third weekend in October, when Native Americans of all tribes come together for a three-day street fair. The *Ember Motel*, 1105 Broad St (☎425-5736; ②), has a pool, and *La Luz del Dia* bakery and café on Broad St at Mesquite does tasty burritos made from fresh tortillas.

Aravaipa Canyon

The mountainous Apache Indian reservations stretch east of Globe almost to the New Mexico border, while Hwy-77 heads south toward Tucson through the heart of Arizona's copper-mining territory. Some of the landscape is terribly scarred, but one of the prettiest spots in the entire state, **Aravaipa Canyon**, can be reached 46 miles south of Globe and then eleven miles east on a well-maintained, mostly dirt road. A wilderness area managed jointly by the US government and the Arizona Nature Conservancy, Aravaipa, with its numerous side canyons, forms a microcosm of the desert, ranging from saguaro cactus on sun-drenched hillsides to giant cottonwood trees along a deep gorge, carved from luminous red volcanic stone by the erosive effects of **Aravaipa Creek** – one of the few year-round desert streams. It's a great place to experience the desert in its wild state, but you need to come prepared. It has no trails, no established campgrounds, and no signs; but on the other hand there are rattlesnakes, scorpions, and the hot summer sun. In order to ensure solitude, only fifty people are allowed to be in the thirty-square-mile wilderness at any one time; get a permit ($1.50 a day), and more information by contacting the Bureau of Land Management, 425 E Fourth St, Safford AZ 85546 (☎428-4040).

Central Arizona

The interstate I-40 crosses through the center of Arizona, skirting the **Navajo Reservation** which fills the northeastern corner of the state. Though the narrow strip of land to either side can be extraordinarily beautiful, with double rainbows reaching across the desert plain and fiery dawns blazing along the horizon, it holds few specific places worth stopping for until you come to the **Flagstaff** area. Itself a pleasant town, Flagstaff makes a base for several interesting excursions – to ancient **Indian sites** and the New Age mecca of **Sedona**, but above all through the forests to the **Grand Canyon**. Beyond Flagstaff to the west, there is once again little of interest.

East of Flagstaff

The widely touted **Meteor Crater** (daily 8am–5pm; $6), six miles south of the interstate on a well-marked road 38 miles east of Flagstaff, might possibly have been interesting 22,000 years ago, when a meteorite blasted a huge hole, nearly a mile across and over five hundred feet deep, into the scrubby plateau, but is only worth visiting today for those who are obsessed with astronauts. The private and unimaginative **Astronauts Hall of Fame** (daily dawn to dusk; $6) commemorates the fact that the first men on the moon were trained on its otherworldly surface (and according to sceptics faked their entire mission here). You cannot hike into the actual crater.

Two old Route 66 towns, **WINSLOW** and **HOLBROOK**, are kept alive by transcontinental truckers. Each has a strip of motels – try the *Town House Lodge* in Winslow (☎289-4611; ②) or the *Comfort Inn* in Holbrook (☎524-6131; ②) – and not much else. Winslow is a bit more interesting (*Evelyne's Tavern* is worth checking out); Holbrook, 32 miles further east, is so dull that its visitors guide consists almost entirely of TV listings.

The Petrified Forest and the Painted Desert

At **Petrified Forest National Park**, which straddles I-40 a dozen miles east of Holbrook, a fossilized prehistoric forest of gigantic trees is gradually being unearthed by erosion. The original cells of the wood have been replaced by multicolored crystals of quartz. Cross-sections, cut through with diamond saws and polished, look stunning, and can be seen in the two **visitor centers**, roughly thirty miles apart at the north and south entrances. On the ground, however, the trees are not all that exciting: segmented, crumbling and very dark. Here and there rough concrete walkways have been laid over the terrain – and often over the tree trunks themselves. The **Long Logs Walk** near the southern entrance is probably the best section; but they're still just a bunch of logs lying in the sand, even if they are stone logs.

The park's Indian **relics** include the reconstructed seven-hundred-year-old **Agate House** on Long Logs Walk, built entirely from petrified wood but somehow completely unatmospheric. Ten miles further on, one of the many petroglyph-covered rocks to be known as **Newspaper Rock** lies at the foot of a rocky incline. Close access is strictly forbidden, and in the absence of the official park telescopes you can just peer hopefully at the indistinct and undeciphered scribbles.

The northern section of the national park is renowned for its views of the **Painted Desert**, an undulating expanse of sand dunes which at different times of day take on different colors (predominantly blueish shades of grey and reddish shades of brown). It's a god-forsaken and eerie landscape, if not one that lives long in the memory.

Flagstaff

Although some of its old streets are still redolent with Wild West charm, **FLAGSTAFF**'s real significance has always been as a center for transport and trade. Its main thoroughfare, Santa Fe Avenue, was once Route 66, and before that, the pioneer trail west; while for more than a century, the Santa Fe Railroad has run right alongside.

The first white settlers arrived in 1876, lured from Boston by widely published accounts of mineral wealth and fertile land – and soon moved on, disappointed, towards Prescott. However, they stayed long enough to celebrate the centenary of American independence by flying the Stars and Stripes from a towering pine tree. This flagpole itself became a familiar landmark on the route west, and as the community grew it inevitably became known as Flagstaff. Right from the start, it was a cosmopolitan town, with a strong black and Hispanic population working in the (originally Mormon-owned) lumber mills and in the cattle industry, and Navajo and Hopi Indians heading in from their nearby reservations to trade.

Today, Flagstaff makes an ideal base for travellers, with hotels, restaurants, bars and shops aplenty within easy strolling range of the center (and the food and lodging chains a couple of miles away beside the interstate). There's not all that much of interest in the town itself, but the countryside in every direction is very much worth exploring.

Public Transportation – and Getting to the Grand Canyon

As the nearest town of any size to the Grand Canyon, seventy miles northwest (see p.715), Flagstaff remains the major junction for road and rail passengers. *Amtrak* trains still pull in at the wooden station house right in the heart of town, a minute's walk from the helpful **visitor center** at 101 W Santa Fe Ave (Mon–Sat 8am–9pm, Sun 8am–5pm; ☎1-800/842-7293 or 774-9541). Though the Santa Fe Railroad is busy with freight, the only passenger **trains** which stop here each day are the 7.15am to Albuquerque and the 9.10pm to Los Angeles. *Greyhound* (☎774-4573) and *Nava-Hopi* (☎774-5003 or 1-800/892-8687) **buses** pull up at 399 S Malpais Lane, south of the tracks a few minutes' walk away. Both serve long-distance east–west routes, and run south to Phoenix via Sedona.

Three buses run to the **Grand Canyon** each day in summer; the *Amtrak* connection, at 7.50am ($12 one-way), and *Nava-Hopi* services from the *Greyhound* station at 8.20am and 5.30pm ($25 return). Both *Nava-Hopi Tours* and the slightly more energetic *Northern Arizona Wilderness Tours* at 284 Toho Trail (☎525-1028) run (hurried) daily **excursions** in the vicinity, as well as to Navajo and Hopi country and beyond.

The least expensive **car rental**, which shared between a group should cost less than the bus, is *Budget Rent-a-Car* at 100 N Humphreys St (☎724-2763). To rent a **mountain bike**, try *Cosmic Cycles*, 113 S San Francisco St (☎779-1092).

The Museum of Northern Arizona

The exceptional **Museum of Northern Arizona** (daily 9am–5pm; $3), three miles northwest of Flagstaff on US-180 (and not on a local bus route), covers geography, flora and fauna, but places its main emphasis on documenting Indian life. It provides an excellent run-through of the **Anasazi** past and contemporary Navajo, Havasupai and Hopi culture, as well as actively encouraging the development of traditional and even new skills among Native American craftworkers. The exquisite inlaid silver jewellery now made by the Hopi stems, for example, from a museum-backed programme to find work for Hopi servicemen returning from World War II.

At all times there are marvellous pots, rugs and kachina dolls on display – and marvellous ones do exist, despite the low standards often seen elsewhere – but *the* time to come is for one of the Indian Craftsmen Exhibitions each summer. The **Zuni** show lasts for five days around Memorial Day weekend in late May; the **Hopi** one is on the weekend closest to July 4, and the nine-day **Navajo** event is at the end of July and the start of August, with every item for sale. There are also temporary shows of local (not always Indian) arts and crafts, and a well-stocked bookstore.

A **nature trail** runs through a small canyon next to the museum. On the road back towards town, the **Coconino Center for the Arts** is a gallery and concert hall specializing in works by local artists, while just behind it the co-operatively run **Art Barn** has a wide selection of crafts for sale.

Lowell Observatory

Astronomer Dr Percival Lowell established the **observatory** at the top of Mars Hill, a mile west of downtown Flagstaff, in 1894. Here he deluded himself that he'd discovered canals on Mars; but here too he performed the calculations which led to the discovery of the planet Pluto in 1930. Serious work continues, but there are daily guided tours at 1.30pm, and stargazing sessions from 8pm to 10pm every Friday which provide an opportunity (weather permitting) to look through the original telescope (☎774-2096).

Practicalities

Three very cheap and basic **hostels** right in the center of town offer dorm beds for around $11 and private rooms for under $30: *Weatherford Hotel*, 23 N Leroux St (☎774-2731; ①), *Du Beau Motel*, 19 W Phoenix Ave (☎774-6731 or 1-800/332-1944; ①), and the summer-only *Downtowner*, 19 S San Francisco St (☎774-8461; ①). The Monte Vista at 100 N San Francisco St (☎779-6971; ③) is a very pleasant little hotel with more comfortable rooms, each named for a film star. Budget **motels** abound along the interstate in the Butler Avenue area. The best **campground** is three miles south on US-89A, at *Fort Tuthill County Park* (☎774-5139).

For **food**, *Charley's Pub and Restaurant* in the *Weatherford Hotel* makes a classy if unlikely contrast with the hostel rooms upstairs, serving good cheap food accompanied by live music (cocktail piano at lunch, bands at night). The area around San Francisco Street, south of the tracks and near the university, has largely been taken over by the alternative student crowd. The *Mad Italian* (no 101; ☎779-1820) is a highly sociable **bar** with several pool tables, while *Hassib's* (no 211; ☎774-1037) does a variety of mid-Eastern and European dishes.

Around Flagstaff

The area around Flagstaff is extraordinarily rich in natural and archeological wonders, with three national monuments – **Sunset Crater**, **Wupatki**, and **Walnut Canyon** – within 25 miles. Of these, only Sunset Crater even has a campground, and none has indoor lodgings. The one alternative base to Flagstaff, Sedona (see below), is that bit further away and that bit more expensive, and there's no scheduled public transport, so if you don't have your own vehicle you'll have to take a guided tour.

Sunset Crater and Wupatki

The **San Francisco Volcanic Field** north of Flagstaff, of around four hundred volcanoes, is prominent on the western horizon from the Hopi Mesas, and its peaks are said to be the home of their powerful kachina spirits. At certain times of year the Hopi make pilgrimages on foot from the mesas to shrines hidden in the mountains.

Several hiking trails lead into the San Francisco Peaks, and a chair lift operates in summer (May–Oct daily 10am–4pm; ☎779-1951; $7) from the **Fairfield Snowbowl** almost to the summit of Mount Agassiz (12,350ft), though you can't hike any further from there. For a brief period each winter this becomes a mildly hectic ski area.

Some of the volcanoes are still active, though the most recent eruption was that of **Sunset Crater** (twelve miles from Flagstaff on US-89), around 1066 AD. In addition to the impression this made as a spectacle, it had a profound impact on local population and economy. Thick deposits of ash for miles around opened up previously infertile land to cultivation, accelerating if not triggering a land rush which threw different Indian cultures into contact and competition for the first time. The crater was named by John Wesley Powell for the many colors of its cone, which swells from a black base through reds and oranges to a yellow-tinged crest. It's too unstable for walkers to be allowed onto the rim, but a trail passes through "Ice Caves" and lava tubes around its base. The National Monument **visitor center** is nearby (open all year, at least 8am–5pm; $3 per car; ☎556-7042), opposite the *Bonito Campground* (mid-May to mid-Oct).

A dozen miles further north, the ancient ruins at **Wupatki National Monument** appear to show different tribal groups living side by side in harmony (daily, summer 8am–7pm, otherwise 8am–5pm; $3 per car; ☎774-7000). The Sinagua were joined here by many others, including the Anasazi, after the Sunset Crater explosion. When the rich new soil created by the eruption had been exhausted, around 150 years later, they all moved on once more. The specific site known as Wupatki (*tall* or *big house*) is just the largest of innumerable sites here, standing proud on its natural foundations of red sandstone. Many others remain unexcavated; there may well be further finds as significant as the oval ball court, reminiscent of the great Mexican civilizations, discovered in 1965.

Walnut Canyon National Monument

Between 1100 and 1250 AD **Walnut Canyon**, ten miles east of Flagstaff just south of I-40, was home to a thriving Sinagua community, who lived in small family groups rather than in communal pueblos. Literally hundreds of their **cliff dwellings** can still be seen nestling beneath overhangs in the sides of the canyon. They simply walled off alcoves where the softer levels of the striated rock had eroded away, and then put up partitions to make separate rooms.

A large scenic window in the **visitor center** (daily, summer 7am–6pm, otherwise 8am–5pm; ☎526-3367) gives an excellent overall view. **Walnut Creek** itself, long since diverted to provide Flagstaff's drinking water, now runs very dry, but you can still see how fertile this valley must have been when the Sinagua first arrived. Trees cling to the porous rock to shade the ancient dwellings, and the vegetation thickens down to a valley floor dense with black walnut and oak. A short trail of steep steps leads down from the visitor center and across a narrow causeway to an isthmus of rock high above a gooseneck of the creek. Along the path, you can go inside several Sinagua homes; note the T-shaped doorways, that could only be entered head first, and the ceilings blackened by the smoke of generations of fires. Lots of petroglyphs have been found in the other ruins visible to all sides of the canyon, though none remain on the trail.

Another trail follows the rim of the canyon. Its main purpose is as a less strenuous walk, leading to a picnic area and to some surface ruins (in the dissimilar pueblo style), though you could keep going to turn this into a lengthy hike. There is no accommodation, and only minimal snack food, available at the canyon.

Sedona and Red Rock Country

US-89A threads its way south from Flagstaff down **Oak Creek Canyon** to emerge after 28 miles at **Sedona**, on the threshold of the extraordinary **Red Rock Country**. Up from the valley rise giant mesas and buttes of stark red sandstone, where Zane Grey set a number of his Wild West adventures. The boom-and-bust mining town of **Jerome** looks down from a mountainside to the south, while back beside I-17 towards Phoenix are the haunting Sinagua ruins of **Tuzigoot** and **Montezuma Castle**.

Oak Creek Canyon

Claims that Oak Creek Canyon is a serious rival to the Grand Canyon are somewhat exaggerated. However, you *can* drive right through it, and with its sheer walls striped in vivid horizontal bands of color, its sparkling streams and densely wooded glens, and its facilities for camping, eating and generally playing around, anywhere else in the world this would be an unmissable attraction.

Lookout Point, its northern end, appears suddenly a dozen forested miles out of Flagstaff. The road then drops sharply to run alongside **Oak Creek** itself. The lowest level in the rocks to either side, often obscured by maples, cedars, oaks and pine, is the bright red Supai sandstone. Above that rise layers of white sandstone, buff limestone, and finally black basalt, all testifying to a geological history which has fluctuated from harsh desert to sea bottom. Temperatures are cool enough to make fishing, picnicking and hiking expeditions welcome escapes. **Slide Rock State Park** ($5) is a natural water chute, where families can swim and slide across smooth boulders set in the river bed. The absence of still water in Oak Creek means that it's almost insect-free.

The canyon floor is quite narrow, and has been heavily developed with leisure facilities, though at least careful landscaping makes most of these inconspicuous; good places to stay include the well-equipped log cabins at *Don Hoel's Cabins* (☎282-3560; ③). Only those **campgrounds** that are at river (and road) level can stay open year-round; these include *Bootlegger* and *Pine Flat* (both ☎282-4119). The most popular place to **eat** is *Garland's* (☎282-3343), which has a different small menu each night.

Sedona

SEDONA itself adds nothing to the beauty of the scenery. Architecturally, it's a real mess, with all manner of pseudo-historical buildings – such as Sacajawea Mall and the Sinagua Shopping Center – lining its narrow main road. Fifty years ago this was a small Mormon settlement, unmarked on most maps. Now it's a major artistic and spiritual community (and retirement center) which locals like to think of as "the next Santa Fe".

An intriguing blend of influences is at work in Sedona. Since Page Bryant, author and psychic, "channelled" the information in 1981 that Sedona is in fact "the heart *chakra* of the planet", and pinpointed her first **vortex** (see box below), the town has achieved its own personal growth and blossomed as a focus for **New Age** practitioners of all kinds. Even the most hard-nosed commercial operation here can seem just a front for the real business of holding earnest conversations about the state of each other's psyches. At the same time, this is the heartland of support for former Arizona senator Barry Goldwater, the most right-wing Republican presidential candidate this century,

---

VORTEX TOURS OF RED ROCK COUNTRY

What to a traditional tour guide is a big red rock called "Snoopy" or "Garfield" is to the enterprises below a "sacred energy area" or a "beacon vortex". Combining New Age mysticism with (a version of) Native American wisdom, a "vortex" is a point at which psychic energies can be channelled for personal and planetary harmony.

Huge crowds of alternative practitioners came to Sedona a few years back for the "Harmonic Convergence"; the one unsatisfied customer was the gentleman who brought his mouth-organ, under the impression that it was a harmonica convergence.

Kachina Riding Stables (☎282-7252). Horseback trips, largely geared around eating (in traditional cowboy style).

Northern Light Balloon Expeditions (☎282-2274). Balloon trips with champagne picnics.

Pink Jeep Tours (☎282-5000). You can't miss this lot in downtown Sedona. Quite exceptionally garish "4-wheelin' vehicles", crunching around in 3hr off-road tours.

Sedona Llama Treks (☎284-0233). You don't actually ride the llamas, they just carry your lunch, with "chilled wines and outrageous desserts". You can stay out all night with one if you want.

Sedona Red Rock Jeep Tours (☎1-800/848-7728 or 282-6826). 3hr Sacred Earth Tours. While bombing around the desert in a jeep, you can "learn to smudge and walk in balance", to "work with crystals and . . . tap the energy of the earth's power spots to enhance personal growth" and "focus on the need to offer love and healing to our earth, as well as each other".

Time Expeditions (☎282-2137). Up to 3hr in a jeep with an anthropologist.

so there's a strong element of "pay no taxes/take no welfare" mixed in too. The whole thing is kept ticking over by the very rich, who dominate the property market and expect to have their expensive tastes catered for.

Greyhound **buses** between Flagstaff and Phoenix stop in downtown Sedona, just before the road junction known as the "Y". Walking along the busy main street, you can hear the synchronized chirruping of the crickets in Oak Creek down below. One branch of town continues intermittently for several miles along US-89A, while a short way along Hwy-179 towards the interstate you come to the comparatively tasteful **Tlaquepaque** shopping center. If you don't have much time to spend exploring, a cruise along US-89A enables you to see most of the sights, albeit from a distance; the best parts are south along Hwy-179 within Coconino National Forest. The closest **vortex** to town is on **Airport Mesa**; turn left up Airport Road from US-89A as you head south, about a mile past the "Y". The vortex is at the junction of the second and third peaks, just after the cattle grid. Further up, beyond the precarious airport, the **Shrine of the Red Rocks** looks out across the entire valley.

Sedona is an expensive place to **stay**; you can get better deals at Cottonwood, Jerome and near Montezuma Castle. Contact the Chamber of Commerce near the "Y" (☎1-800/288-7336) for details of luxury B&Bs. What pass here for budget **motels**, all just north of the "Y", are the *Star*, 295 Jordan Rd (☎282-3641; ②), *Canyon Portal*, 210 N US-89A (☎282-7125 or 1-800/542-8484; ③) and *La Vista*, 500 N US-89A (☎282-7301; ②).

With **restaurants** of all styles and prices, you're spoilt for choice. Several of the more expensive are in Tlaquepaque; otherwise *Eat Your Heart Out* at 350 Jordan Rd (☎282-1471) is recommended as an Italian and continental café, and *Food Among the Flowers* is a very reasonable vegetarian place at 2445 W US-89A (☎282-2334). This latter, well west of the "Y", shares its premises with *The Center in Sedona for the New Age* (☎282-1949). Sedona's superb setting and New Age connections have put it on the circuit for big-name **musical** events, including the *Jazz On The Rocks* festival each September (☎282-1935).

As well as the *Greyhound* link, the *Sedona–Phoenix Shuttle* **bus** (☎282-2066) runs thrice daily; and five daily return **flights** to Phoenix are operated by *Air Sedona* (☎282-7935 or ☎1-800/535-4448). Two companies rent **bikes**: *Canyon Country Mountain Bikes* at 245 N US-89A, inside *Sedona Sports* (☎282-6985), and *Sedona Mountain Bike Rental* at 376 Apple Ave downtown (☎282-2164).

Jerome

The former mining town of **Jerome**, once the fourth largest community in Arizona, stands high above the Verde Valley on US-89A about thirty miles south of Sedona. It's conspicuous from quite a distance; an enormous letter "J" is etched deep into the hillside above it, and a large chunk of that hillside is missing altogether, having been blown apart for **opencast copper mining**. This land abounds in mineral wealth – thick veins of copper are interspersed with gold and silver, and an endless supply of limestone is still extracted for cement – but serious exploitation only started in 1876. The **United Verde** mine was partly financed by New Yorker Eugene Jerome (a cousin of Winston Churchill's mother, Jennie Jerome), who insisted that the new town bear his name. Until the current tortuous road was built, the only way up to Jerome was the precipitous railway connecting the mine with the world's largest copper smelter (the smokestacks are still there) at Clarkdale.

With its vastly disproportionate population of young males, Jerome was known as a hard-drinking and hard-living town. The young **Pancho Villa** started out in life by supplying its drinking water, using a relay of two hundred burros, and for a brief period the International Workers of the World (the "**Wobblies**") were a strong presence; several hundred miners and "outside agitators" were literally railroaded out of town in July 1917 and dumped unceremoniously in the remote deserts of southwest Arizona.

Harsh economic realities have always determined local fortunes. Plenty of copper remains in the earth; although the Depression hit hard, the mine was only closed when cheap imported copper in the early 1950s made it uneconomic to continue, and there's every possibility that as prices rise, it will reopen. To keep the mineral rights from reverting to the state, the present owners are obliged to keep on researching and prospecting; in fact they consistently do more than they have to, and have reportedly found enough gold to cover their expenses.

Even as recently as the 1970s, this was a **ghost town** in which it was possible to turn up and move into an empty house. Many who did so are still here, making a living from arts and crafts, and the town itself has made a dramatic recovery. It's a bit of a tourist trap, but is nonetheless fascinating to explore. The hillside is so steep that the stone houses (it was far too expensive to haul timber up here) tend to have two storeys at the front and four or five at the back. Under the repeated concussion of over 200 miles of tunnels being blasted into the mountainside, the whole town used to slip downhill at the rate of five inches per year, and the **Sliding Jail** on Hull Avenue came to rest 225 feet from where it was built.

Both the two old-style **hotels** on Jerome's Main Street – *Connor Hotel* (no 168; ☎634-5792; ②), and the *Miner's Roost* (no 309; ☎634-5094; ②) – have **bars**, and the latter also operates a **café**, *Betty's Ore House*. Perched above the valley two blocks below Main Street is the small antique-filled *Nancy Russell's B&B*, 3 Juarez St (☎634-3270; ④). The *English Kitchen* (☎634-2132) has been at 119 Jerome Ave since 1899. Under Chinese ownership, it was an opium den; later the Wobblies held their meetings downstairs. Now it's open for breakfast and lunch every day except Monday, and its terrace offers a commanding view of the valley. Many of the **shops** stock only tacky souvenirs, but interesting crafts showrooms on Lower Main Street include the *Knapp Gallery* and, next door, *Made in Jerome Pottery*.

Motels and every fast-food outlet imaginable can be found in **Cottonwood,** a big new retirement center on the valley floor. The *Sundial Motel*, 1034 N Main St (☎634-8031; ②) and the *View*, 818 S Main St (☎634-7581; ③), are on the one old street which survives amid the sprawl.

Tuzigoot

Between Cottonwood and Clarkdale, at **Tuzigoot National Monument,** the roofless but impressive remains of a **Sinagua pueblo** stand forlorn on the crest of a long ridge. The ground floor alone had 77 rooms, and shows signs of repeated additions; this may have been a final enclave, where the Sinagua gathered against encroaching drought before abandoning the area early in the fifteenth century. Artefacts at the **visitor center** (daily, summer 8am–7pm, otherwise 9am–5pm; $3; ☎634-5564) include turquoise mosaics and shell jewellery.

Montezuma Well and Montezuma Castle

Two further Sinagua sites constitute **Montezuma Castle National Monument**, very near I-17 forty miles south of Flagstaff and twenty miles from Sedona. **Montezuma Well** was once underground, but became a lake, 470 feet across, when the rock above it caved in. A phenomenal 1.9 million gallons per day of precious water emerges from the depths, used by farmers today as it was by the Sinagua who built their homes around it in the thirteenth century. You can still see their irrigation ditches, now with solid linings formed by calcium deposits.

Five miles south, **Montezuma Castle** is a superbly preserved **cliff dwelling** in an idyllic setting just above Beaver Creek. Filling an alcove in the hillside with a wall of pink adobe, its five storeys taper up to fit the contours of the rock. Apparently the fingerprints of the masons are still visible on the bricks, and the sycamore beams are still firmly in place, but visitors are no longer permitted to climb up. The ruins of an even larger dwelling "next door", which was burned out around 1400, can be examined more closely. This had 45 rooms, as well as little "cupboards" recessed into the walls.

The **visitor center** at the castle (summer 8am–7pm, otherwise closes earlier; $3; ☎567 3322) has informative displays on the Sinagua, including a macaw skeleton which suggests trade with the Mexican civilizations thousands of miles to the south. There is no connection with the Aztec ruler Montezuma, though the well does appear on a deer-skin map which belonged to Cortes himself, so presumably his men passed this way.

Two motels stand at nearby **Camp Verde**: *Fort Verde* (☎567-3486; ②) and *Chapparral* (☎567-3451; ②). *Cliff Castle Lodge* (☎567-6611; ⑤) on the approach road to Montezuma Castle is a luxury hotel built in what might conceivably have been Anasazi style, had the Anasazi ever felt the urge to build enormous hotels.

West of Flagstaff: I-40 to California

Everything along I-40 west of Flagstaff is dominated by being on the main route between Las Vegas and the Grand Canyon. The first town you reach, **WILLIAMS**, seems to exist solely to capture the passing tourist trade, though it livens up come winter, when the slopes of Mount Williams and the rest of the surrounding **Kaibab National Forest** offer good skiing, particularly for cross-country aficionados. Further west 45 miles, at the town of Seligman, one of the longest surviving stretches of the old Route 66 heads off on a northern loop through the **Hualapai Indian Reservation** and a dozen quickly fading towns, **Peach Springs** in particular, that look straight out of *The Grapes of Wrath*. With its old diners and dusty grand hotels, it makes a great detour on what is otherwise a very dull drive; it also provides the best access to the less visited western reaches of the Grand Canyon, around emerald **Havasu Canyon** (see p.720).

Apart from needing to fill your tank, or fill up on fast food, there's little reason to stop at **KINGMAN**, the largest town in western Arizona, from where US-93 branches north to Las Vegas and I-40 continues to Los Angeles.

Lake Havasu City

Forty miles southwest of Kingman, ten miles from the California border, a detour south brings you to one of the more bizarre sights of the American desert – the old grey stone of **London Bridge**, reaching out to an artificial island across the stagnant waters of the dammed Colorado River at **LAKE HAVASU CITY**. It has to be said that it looks a hell of a lot better here in the middle of the desert, with the Chemehuevi Mountains as a backdrop, than it ever did between South London and the City. The resort's developer, Robert P McCulloch, bought the bridge (under the impression it was Tower Bridge – or so the story goes) for 2.4 million dollars in the late 1960s, and painstakingly shipped it across the Atlantic chunk by chunk before reassembling it over a channel dug to divert water from Lake Havasu, creating an island on the other side of the bridge known as Pittsburgh Point.

One *Greyhound* **bus** daily stops outside *McDonalds*, 100 Swanson Ave, on its way to Las Vegas. **Motels** are abundant; the *Windsor Inn Motel*, 451 London Bridge Rd (☎855-4135; ②), has especially low rates, while *Pioneer Hotel of Lake Havasu*, 271 S Lake Havasu Ave (☎1-800/528-5169; ③), which costs a little more, but has its own casino. Among several good-value **restaurants** is *Shrugrue's* in the Island Fashion Mall at the end of London Bridge, which serves fresh fish, salads and pasta.

About twenty miles south of town, clearly signposted from Hwy-95, the **Colorado River Indian Reservation** (daily 8am–sundown; $3) has a collection of prehistoric giant rock figures, or *intaglios*, made by "carving" the desert floor, shedding the darker top layer of rock to reveal the lighter layers of sand beneath. The figures are so huge (up to 160 feet) that it's hard to tell what you're looking at, but gaze long enough and you can discern a four-legged animal, and a human and spiral design.

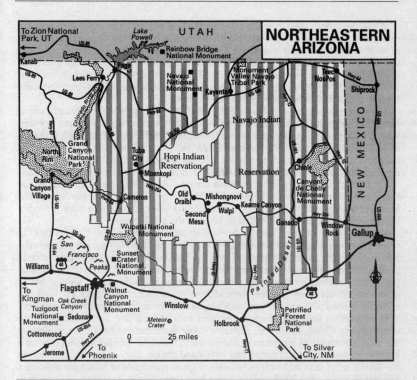

Northeastern Arizona: Indian Country

The deserts of northeastern Arizona, popularly known as **Indian Country**, hold some of the most fascinating **pre-Columbian ruins** in North America, in the most striking settings imaginable. The cliff palaces of **Canyon de Chelly**, and **Betatakin** and **Keet Seel** in the Navajo National Monument, are among the greatest architectural achievements of the **Anasazi**, made that much more special by the fact that the lands on which they stand are still lived in and worked by their heirs, the Navajo and Hopi.

The **Navajo Nation**, the largest Indian reservation in the US, fills most of the region, lapping over into western New Mexico and stretching to include the majestic sandstone pillars of Monument Valley in southernmost Utah. Historically, the migrant Navajo have been adept at absorbing other cultures, and in modern times they've embraced the American Way – driving pickup trucks and wearing baseball caps emblazoned with the names of their favorite tractor, fertilizer or football team. But to speak of them as constituting a separate and sovereign nation within the United States is not some polite fiction. You get a very real sense of travelling through a foreign country. The Navajo have their own police and legal system, and though everyone can speak English, Navajo is still the native tongue: a language so complex that it was used as a secret military code during World War II. High-tech supermarkets mark their prices in Navajo, and the reservation follows its own rules over Daylight Saving; in frontier-style towns like Tuba City the time on the clock can vary according to whether you're in an American or a Navajo district. Tune into the Navajo Nation **radio station**, KTNN 740AM, for a sense of the Navajo-American melange.

While the Navajo were here long before the Spanish, let alone white Americans, it seems that to the **Hopi** people, who have lived high on multi-fingered mesas at the heart of what is now the Navajo reservation for nearly a thousand years, they will always be interlopers. Far outnumbered by the Navajo, who began to encroach upon their territory around five hundred years ago and eventually surrounded them completely, the Hopi are renowned for their richly spiritual and antimaterialistic way of life, which they celebrate in elaborate dances and religious ceremonies.

However much others may like to muse about the spirituality and meaningful way of life of the Native Americans, the people here suffer from the same problems as everywhere in the modern world, if not worse. Unemployment is staggeringly high (upwards of 50 percent), poverty is rife (average family income is around $6000 per year), and drug and alcohol problems take a heavy toll. Things may perhaps be slowly changing for the better; education, for instance, which until the 1960s was available almost exclusively through missionary schools which forced students to adopt their faith before they could study, is improving immensely. Also, for the Navajo in particular, money has begun to flow in from the (admittedly contentious) sale of the right to mine the valuable deposits of coal and uranium that lie beneath the bleak surface.

Visiting Indian Country can be fascinating and rewarding, but it's important to respect the people and places you encounter. The Anasazi have long since vanished – Native Americans come here from all over the Southwest and beyond to take pride in their heritage – but many of the relics they left behind are on land that is still of spiritual significance to their modern counterparts. Similarly, it is offensive to photograph or otherwise intrude upon peoples' lives without permission; the reason the Hopi, for example, banned photography was largely because it was such an interfering nuisance.

On a practical note, don't expect extensive **tourist facilities**. Towns such as Tuba City, Kayenta, Chinle, the Navajo capital Window Rock, and the Hopi's Keams Canyon are mostly outposts of government bureaucracy, with little to offer visitors beyond a handful of places to eat and even fewer hotels and motels. They only come alive during the annual tribal fairs and rodeos, which are great opportunities to sample delicacies like Navajo tacos, or to buy jewellery direct from craftspeople. At other times, you may well be better off staying near I-40 to the south, in Winslow or Holbrook.

Eastern Navajo Reservation

By the time white immigrants began to arrive in force during the early nineteenth century, the Navajo – who call themselves *Dineh*, "The People" – had lived a settled lifestyle in Arizona for hundreds of years; within a generation they had lost almost everything. When the Yankees took over from the Mexicans, things just got worse, hitting bottom in 1864 when Kit Carson rounded up every Navajo he could find and forced them to move to Fort Sumner in the desolate plain of eastern New Mexico (see p.678). A few years later the Navajo were allowed to return, the US government granting them most of the vast acreage they hold today (lawsuits arising from territorial disputes with the Hopi dragged on until 1978 before eventually being decided in favor of the Hopi). Most of the 100,000 Navajo today are spread out on small holdings, working the land as shepherds and farmers, though many craftspeople also live by selling their wares from small stands set up along highways and in tourist stops.

The seat of the Navajo Tribal Council, the reservation's governing body, is on its eastern edge, along the New Mexico border. It was based for fifty years at Fort Defiance, a US cavalry outpost, until in the 1930s **WINDOW ROCK** was established as a new capital. Named for the natural stone arch on its northern side, it's not a great place to get a grasp of Navajo culture, but does at least have gas stations, shops, and a **motel**, the *Navajo Nation Inn* on Hwy-264 (☎871-4108; ③). The adjacent **Navajo Tribal Museum** (free) gives the background on tribal history and displays high-quality craftswork.

Thirty miles west of Window Rock on Hwy-264, or 35 miles north of I-40 on US-191, sits the small village of **Ganado**, named after Chief Ganado Mucho ("Won a lot"), who in 1868 signed the treaty giving the Navajo the million-acre parcel they inhabit today. A mile west of the village, which sits astride the highway crossroads, is the **Hubbell Trading Post**. When the Navajo returned from their incarceration at Fort Sumner, with their livelihood in tatters, it was mainly thanks to independent traders that they were able to survive the first few years and adapt to the whites' dominion. **John Hubbell** encouraged the Navajo to develop their crafts skills, and provided them with food and supplies in exchange for their woven blankets and other crafts. By the 1880s his trading post here had become the main interface between the Navajo and the outside world. The buildings are preserved as they were then, with most of the place still functioning much as it ever did, and in the visitor center next door Navajo artisans work amid historical photos and documents.

Canyon de Chelly

A short distance east of **Chinle**, another thirty miles north on US-191, twin sandstone walls emerge abruptly from the desert floor, climbing at a phenomenal rate to become the awesome thousand-foot cliffs of **Canyon de Chelly National Monument**. Between these sheer sides, the meandering course of the Chinle Wash can be discerned by its fringe of cottonwoods as it winds through grasslands and planted fields. Here and there a Navajo hogan stands in a grove of fruit trees, a straggle of sheep is penned in by a crude wooden fence, or ponies drink at the water's edge. And everywhere, perched above the valley on ledges in the canyon walls and dwarfed by the towering cliffs, are the long-abandoned adobe and stone dwellings of the Anasazi.

There are two main canyons, which branch apart a few miles upstream; Canyon de Chelly (a corruption of the Navajo *tségi*, and pronounced *de shay*) to the south and Canyon del Muerto to the north. Each twists and turns in all directions, scattered with vast rock monoliths, while several smaller canyons break away. The whole labyrinth threads its way upwards for thirty miles into the Chuska Mountains.

Visits are constrained by the nature of the terrain and by the fact that the monument retains great symbolic significance for the Navajo (despite the fact that they did not themselves build the cliff dwellings). There is no paved road, and you can only enter upon the canyon floor in the company of one of the many Navajo guides who daily career along the sandy river bed in four-wheel-drive jeeps and trucks.

History

The first known inhabitants of the canyon were the **Anasazi** Basketmakers, around 300 AD. During the next thousand years, before the Anasazi disappeared from history, they had advanced from living in pit houses dug into the soil to building elegant cliff dwellings, and developed fine pottery and weaving (for more on the Anasazi, see p.675). For some centuries thereafter, the Hopi came here to farm each summer, returning for the winter to the mesas to the east, but as time went by, Navajo migrants from the north and west eventually displaced the Hopi altogether. In places, Anasazi, Hopi and Navajo petroglyphs are side by side on the rock.

From 1583 onwards, the Navajo were locked with the Spanish in a bloody cycle of armed clashes and slave raids. The US Army too failed in repeated attempts to dislodge the Navajo, though no treaty could restrain the rapacious pressure for land by New Mexican settlers, as well as Utes, Paiutes, Apaches and Comanches. The end appeared to have come with the brutal roundup and deportation (the "Long Walk") of the entire Navajo people, completed by Kit Carson in 1864 when he starved the last of them down from Navajo Rock and destroyed their homes, livestock, and, worst of all, their beloved peach orchards. So barbaric was their imprisonment at Fort Sumner, however, that

Congress soon allowed them to return. To this day, 25 Navajo families still farm the Canyon de Chelly in summer, the matrilineal descendants of the women between whom it was re-apportioned in the 1870s.

The View from Above: The Rim Drives

Each of the two "rim drives" from the visitor center is highly recommended for its succession of spectacular overlooks, which provide the only unaccompanied way to see the canyon. Allow two to three hours for each of the forty-mile round trips. Thefts from cars have been a major problem, and it's wise to follow the prominent warnings.

The furthest point of the **South Rim drive** along Canyon de Chelly is the astonishing **Spider Rock**, twin eight-hundred-foot pinnacles of rock that reach to within two hundred feet of the canyon rim. At **Sliding House Overlook**, the Anasazi ruins seem to be slipping down the canyon walls towards the ploughed Navajo fields below. **White House Overlook** presents the highly photogenic White House Ruins, and is the only point from which you are permitted to hike alone into the canyon, taking perhaps 30 to 45 minutes to get down and a good hour to get back up. The trail itself is very safe, though it is frustrating at the bottom to find that you are forbidden to walk for more than a hundred yards in either direction. Be prepared to wade the wash, though there may be a rudimentary log walkway. **Junction Overlook** is at the meeting point of the two canyons; as you scramble across the bare rocks you can see Canyon de Chelly narrowing away, with a hogan immediately below.

The **North Rim Drive** runs twenty miles up Canyon del Muerto to **Massacre Cave**, where the Spanish expedition of 1805, led by Lieutenant Narbona, is thought to have killed around one hundred Navajo women, children and old men. The "cave" is just a pitifully exposed ledge, upon which the huddled group were easily picked off by the Spanish, using ricochets off the overhang above. Visible from **Mummy Cave Overlook** is the House Under The Rock, with its central tower in the Mesa Verde style – the single most striking ruin in the monument. Of the two viewpoints at **Antelope House Overlook**, one is opposite Navajo Rock, the isolated natural fortress where the Navajo were besieged for three months in 1863, climbing by means of pole ladders drawn up behind them and using a human chain to carry water to the top. At the other viewpoint you see the ruins of Antelope House far below, and across the wash the Mummy Cave, where the embalmed body of an old man was found wrapped in golden eagle feathers.

In the small town of **TSAILE**, a short way beyond the monument along the North Rim Drive, the Navajo Community College has a stimulating Indian-run museum of ancient and modern cultures (Mon–Fri 8.30am–noon & 1–4.30pm). It is possible to hike into the Canyon del Muerto from this end, although you have to hire the necessary Navajo guides back in Chinle.

Into the Canyons

Tours of the canyon floor, organized by *Thunderbird Lodge* (see below), zigzag along the washes, which vary from two or three feet deep during the spring thaw to completely dry in summer. For most of the year, the bone-shaking tours are in open-top flatbed trucks, lurching over the rutted earth, and the heat can be incredible; in winter they carry on in glass-roofed army vehicles with caterpillar tracks. To reach as far as Spider Rock, you have to take the full-day tour ($53), but the half-day trip at $33 still enables you to see a wide variety of sites and terrain.

Virtually all the ruins face south to catch the sun, with cold storage chambers deep in shady recesses. Many look more inaccessible than they were, due to rock falls and the erosion of toe- and hand-holds carved into the soft sandstone. The first stop on the tours is at the fenced-off **Antelope House Ruins** in Canyon del Muerto, made of shaped sandstone blocks around a central tower. The wall paintings here are not Anasazi, but were painted in the 1830s by the same Navajo as the "Spanish Mural" a little further along, showing a Spanish lieutenant, priest and troops advancing through the canyon. At the adjacent **Standing Cow Ruin**, a Navajo hogan is built on the foundations of an Anasazi kiva; when the Navajo first returned from Fort Sumner, in their urgent need for shelter they converted some Anasazi ruins for their own use.

The **White House Ruins** are a short distance up Canyon de Chelly. The ground-level buildings here used to be four storeys high, with ladders from the roof reaching up to those on the ledge above.

Practicalities

For the moment, Canyon de Chelly remains remarkably unspoiled. As well as being friendly and informative guides, the Navajo are excellent stewards of the monument. However, facilities are overstretched, and it's essential to book your **accommodation** well in advance. There are only two options: *Canyon de Chelly Motel* (☎674-5875; ④) in Chinle, and *Thunderbird Lodge* (☎674-5841; ⑤), very near the canyon entrance. The *Lodge* has a cheap and good cafeteria and a well-stocked gift shop, and arranges the standard sightseeing tours (if you take a tour on the day you leave, be sure to check out your room first; they charge $5 per hour extra after 11am). The adjacent (free and minimally equipped) *Cottonwood Campground* has pleasant sites among the trees. For **food**, the *Canyon de Chelly Restaurant* nearer town has virtually the same menu as the *Thunderbird* cafeteria; at both places, the Navajo taco is the best value. Chinle itself is a brief nondescript straggle on the highway, with service stations, *Taco Bell*, *Kentucky Fried Chicken*, a post office and a laundromat.

The **visitor center** (daily, May–Sept 8am–6pm, otherwise 8am–5pm; ☎674-5436) on the road from Chinle has informative displays, and provides guides for unorthodox hiking or motorized expeditions. For a group, having your own personal guided tour need not be any more expensive. Ernest Jones' *Canyon Hiking Service* (☎674-5326) offers daily **hikes** into the canyon for around $15 per person, and an overnight backpacking hike from the White House ruins, starting at 6pm on Friday, for $20. *Justin's Horse Rentals* (☎674-5678) and *Twin Trail Tours* (☎674-5985) organize **horseback** trips.

The Hopi Mesas

The **Hopi** people are virtually unique in the United States; they have lived continuously in the same place for over eight hundred years. Some invaders have come and gone in that time, others have stayed; but the villages on **First**, **Second** and **Third mesas** have endured, if not exactly undisturbed then at least unmoved.

One simple reason is that only the Hopi possess the art to support themselves in this unpromising environment. Although the mesa-tops themselves, six hundred feet from the desert floor, are all but barren, and rain is pitifully scarce, the **Black Mesa** to which they are attached is tilted at just the correct angle to deliver a tiny subterranean layer of water to the washes down below the villages. The Hopi can thus practice "dry farming", rigorously preserving enough precious liquid to grow their crops of corn, beans and squash on hand-tilled terraces. This is a way of life that has, however, been forced upon them; centuries ago, they would farm in summer as far afield as the fertile Canyon de Chelly, and return to the mesas in winter. Then the Navajo came and steadily cut them off from their grazing lands and pastures.

Each of the dozen or so settlements on the mesas centers around a **plaza**, where countless generations have built new houses on top of the old ones as they crumble into sand. Often the main entrance is via the roof, reached by a wooden ladder. A few buildings are now constructed of grey breeze-blocks, but still they blend almost imperceptibly with the ruins that trail away down the slopes. Many of the villages stand on open seams of coal – which is how the Black Mesa gets its name – and massive chunks of coal lie scattered around. Outhouses are dotted across the hillsides, and all waste was traditionally thrown over the edge of the mesa to tumble down and fertilize the terraces – a conservationist policy that works less well now that refrigerators and old bedsteads are being thrown over too.

There are now around ten thousand Hopi, about as many as there were in 1650, which constitutes a recovery from the early twentieth century when just 2500 were left. Visitors are treated with great hospitality, but the Hopi are clearly not interested in turning themselves into a tourist attraction. Accompanied tours of almost all the villages are permitted, though unless there's a dance or ceremony going on you don't see all that much apart from the houses themselves and the distant desert views.

Visiting the Hopi Mesas

The mesas are roughly fifty miles north of I-40, reached by Hwy-87 from Winslow or Hwy-77 from Holbrook. Hwy-264 runs east to west along the foot of the mesas, from the US Bureau of Indian Affairs outpost at **Keams Canyon** to the half-Hopi, half-Navajo town of **Moenkopi**.

The essential first stop, at the very heart of the mesas, is the **Hopi Cultural Center**, which serves as motel, restaurant, information center, gift shop, and museum. This is the place to find out what's going on; the friendly staff are happy to volunteer details of forthcoming dances and events. Much of the **museum** (Mon–Fri 9am–5pm, Sat & Sun

---

THE HOPI CALENDAR

Hopi spirituality, which sees human existence as a cyclical but essentially progressive passage along the road of life, has much in common with Tibetan and Hindu mysticism. Briefly, the Hopi believe that they have evolved through four distinct worlds. In each one, an initial state of innocence has given way to a time of forgetfulness and corruption, and the people have fanned out across the earth to search for the "Place of Emergence" into the next. Here in the fourth world, life is once more difficult, as each individual struggles towards a knowledge of his or her origins, only to be blocked by materialism and selfishness. Hopi mythology describes history as an endless series of migrations, within and between the successive worlds; many of the journeys described seem to correspond to actual geographical features of the Americas. The various partings and reunions that occurred in the current world before the Hopi settled into their present home account for the subdivision of the tribe into the dozen **clans**, each of which has its own clear secular and religious responsibilities.

Over and beyond the clans, the most important forces in Hopi religion are the **kachina** spirits. More akin to angels than to gods, these invisible life forces – who bring rain and crops, and ensure health and welfare, but also occasionally misbehave – are said to be present on the mesas for the first half of each year. Masked and costumed dancers take on the roles of the various kachinas in an elaborate **ritual calendar**, culminating in a sixteen-day sequence of ceremonies each July, once the corn has begun to sprout, when the kachinas return to their homes in the San Francisco Peaks, sixty miles to the west. Carved **dolls** modelled on the different kachina spirits are given to children; these are without religious significance, but have become very popular crafts objects.

Hopi **dances**, held in the central plazas of the mesa-top villages, take place throughout the year, usually at the weekend, so that those Hopi who live and work off the reservation can attend. Specific timings tend not to be announced until a few days before the ceremonies take place; for information, contact the Cultural Center at Second Mesa. Quite whether outsiders are welcomed at festivities varies from year to year; the current tendency is towards excluding tourists, thanks in part to the offence caused by the publication in 1992 of a *Marvel* comic book that characterized the kachinas as violent avengers. If you are permitted to attend a dance, be sure to maintain the appropriate distance – and don't attempt to take photographs. The legendary **Snake Dance**, in which members of the Snake clan dance with live snakes between their teeth, is held alternately in Shungopavi and Mishongnovi, and is likely to remain closed to outsiders.

9am–4pm; closed Sun in winter; $3) is devoted to describing various Hopi arts and crafts, with choice examples of pottery and silver overlay jewellery, a recent specialty. It also provides a lot of historical background – particularly to do with the long-running dispute with the Navajo – as well as brief descriptions of each of the mesa-top villages.

The most impressive of the Hopi villages, particularly if you can manage to be there at sunset, when the desert panorama seems set alight and the sacred San Francisco Peaks stand in sharp silhouette, is ancient **WALPI**. Standing all alone on a narrow mesa, connected to the other First Mesa villages by a neck of stone that drops straight down three hundred feet to either side, Walpi is the most unchanged of the Hopi villages, home to some 35 people who do without electricity or running water. To see it, take Hwy-264 to the modern town of **Polacca**, then drive a mile or so up the twisting paved road until it ends at the Ponsi Hall Community Center in the village of **Sichomovi**. From the small museum, guides will take you on half-hour tours (9am–5pm; donations), taking in the recently stabilized main plaza, where the famed Snake Dances are held. Depending on the time of year, you'll either be in a group of twenty or so, or on your own, but be sure to ask the guide to point out the steep stairway that drops down to the cornfields four hundred feet below.

The best place to **stay the night** on the Hopi Reservation is the modern motel at the Hopi Cultural Center (☎734-2401; ④); rooms are usually booked solid a week or more in advance, especially during the most popular festivities. In the cafeteria you can get good solid meals – or try **blue cornflakes** for breakfast. Fairly basic double rooms are available at the *Keams Canyon Motel* (☎738-2297; ②), along Hwy-264 at the eastern edge of the reservation; there's a popular café here too, open until 9pm only and dishing up local-style fast food (including exceptionally tough mutton). Some Hopi have established a great rapport with the Rastafarians; top-name **reggae** bands regularly come from Jamaica to play here. No alcohol is sold on the reservation.

Navajo National Monument

Made up of three separate Anasazi sites spread over the forested Shonto Plateau in the northwest quarter of the reservation, the **Navajo National Monument** protects some of the largest and most beautifully sited cliff dwellings in Arizona. From behind the good **visitor center** (daily 8am–5pm) at the end of paved Hwy-564, ten miles north of US-160, a short walkway crosses the plateau to a viewpoint where you can peer across a canyon to **Betatakin**, a 135-room masonry structure tucked away in a large natural alcove halfway up a 700-foot-high, brilliant red sandstone cliff. A powerful telescope on the overlook enables you to see the exceptionally well-preserved ruins in detail, looking as if they were abandoned just a few years ago. The ladders are new additions, but the visible roof beams are the original timber. To see Betatakin up close, you have to join one of the six-hour ranger-guided hikes (May–Sept only; daily 9am), which leave from the visitor center. Numbers are limited, and no advance bookings are taken, so get here as early as possible on the day – or stay the previous night at the very attractive free **campground** in the forest next to the visitor center.

The other two ruins within the monument are much more difficult to get a look at; in fact the small **Inscription House** ruin has been closed to visitors for many years because of its structural instability, and there are no plans to re-open it. During the summer you can still visit **Keet Seel**, one of the best-preserved Anasazi sites in the Southwest, though it's a sixteen-mile round trip from the visitor center. The largest cliff dwelling in Arizona, consisting of over 150 rooms and four kivas, Keet Seel is well worth the effort it takes to reach, especially if you can stay the night at the small **campground** near the site. Horseback trips are also available for $40 per day, though all visitors must get a permit at least a day in advance (☎672-2366), and be escorted through the site by the park ranger. (The box on p.675 gives more background on the Anasazi.)

Practicalities

Most people pass through this area on their way to somewhere else, so there aren't many places to **stay**. **TUBA CITY**, to the west of the monument, has the $10-a-night **hostel** beds at the Grey Hills Inn and Hostel , which also has budget private doubles (☎283-6271; ①), a short way east of the point where US-160 meets Hwy-264 from the Hopi Mesas, and the *Tuba City Motel* (☎283-4545; ③). It also hosts the three-day **Western Navajo Fair** each October. The coal and uranium mining town of **KAYENTA**, 22 miles northeast of the monument at the junction of US-160 and US-163, holds two more expensive options: the *Wetherill Inn* (☎697-3231; ④), and the *Holiday Inn* (☎697-3221; ④), inside which there is a distinctive and good-value **restaurant**.

The road north to Kayenta beside the Black Mesa is paralleled by the railroad which carries coal from the mines up to the **Navajo Generating Station** at **Page** (see p.739).

Monument Valley

The bizarre fiery-red sandstone towers of **Monument Valley**, silhouetted for a good thirty miles against the desert horizon as they loom over US-163 on both sides of the Arizona–Utah border, form one of the more unforgettable landmarks of the Southwest. This otherworldly skyline has been featured in countless Westerns from *Stagecoach* onwards, but even such worldwide exposure can't dilute the visual impact of the red-rock buttes and jagged pinnacles. They are quite simply an amazing sight, especially at sunset when the rock seems to glow even more brightly than the sun itself.

The biggest and most impressive of the monoliths are a pair called **The Mittens**, one East and one West, each of which has a distinct thumb splintering off from its central bulk. The taller of the two rises a thousand feet above the valley floor, with sand dunes lapping at its base. Over a dozen other spires are spread around nearby, along with some rock art panels and an assortment of minor but nicely sited Anasazi ruins.

The whole Monument Valley area is on Navajo reservation land, this portion of which is set aside as the **Monument Valley Tribal Park**. Though you can see almost everything from the highway, the best views are to be had from the small **visitor center** (daily, summer 7am–sunset, otherwise 7am–5pm; $2.50), four miles east of US-163 and surrounded by Navajo selling crafts and trinkets.

While it is possible to see Monument Valley up close by jolting around a restricted dirt road in your own vehicle, the **jeep** or **horse** tours led by Navajo guides into the backcountry are very much recommended; a two-hour jeep trip costs from around $15 per person from the various stalls, or slightly more if organized through the visitor center or *Goulding's Lodge* (see below). As well as stopping at such movie locations as the **Totem Pole** (on top of which Clint Eastwood had some perilous moments in *The Eiger Sanction*), these pause so you can watch (and ideally buy) weaving at a Navajo hogan.

Backpackers can wake up to the sight of Monument Valley, though you need to arrange for a guide to accompany you for the duration of your visit.

Practicalities

There's not much choice as far as sleeping and eating options go: right next to the visitor center there's the very exposed *Mitten View* **campground**, which costs $10, and the only nearby place to stay indoors, *Goulding's Lodge* (☎801/727-3231; ⑤), is over the Utah border, two miles west of US-163 on the road which extends from the Monument Valley visitor center. *Goulding's* has been here since 1924, when it opened as a trading post; it's now a plush resort with pricey motel rooms, a fairly good restaurant, a general store and gas station, and a small movie museum. They also offer **guided tours**. Twenty-five miles north, further into southern Utah, the San Juan River towns of **Mexican Hat** and **Bluff** (see p.737) also make good bases for visiting the area.

The Grand Canyon

Although three million people come to see the **GRAND CANYON OF THE COLORADO** every year, it remains beyond the grasp of the human imagination. No photograph, no set of statistics, can prepare you for such vastness. At more than one mile deep, it's an inconceivable abyss; at from four to eighteen miles wide it's an endless expanse of bewildering shapes and colors, glaring desert brightness and impenetrable shadow, stark promontories and soaring never-to-be-climbed sandstone pinnacles. Somehow it's so impassive, so remote – you could never call it a disappointment, but at the same time many visitors are left feeling peculiarly flat. In a sense, none of the available activities can quite live up to that first stunning sight of the chasm. The **overlooks** along the rim all offer views that shift and change unceasingly from dawn to sunset; you can **hike** down into the depths on foot or by mule, hover above in a **helicopter** or raft through the **whitewater rapids** of the river itself; you can spend a night at **Phantom Ranch** on the canyon floor, or swim in the waterfalls of the idyllic **Havasupai Reservation**; and yet that distance always remains – the Grand Canyon stands apart.

Until the 1920s, the average **visitor** would stay for two or three weeks. These days it's more like two or three hours – of which forty minutes are spent actually looking at the canyon. The vast majority come to the **South Rim** – it's much easier to get to, there are far more facilities (mainly at the Fred Harvey-owned **Grand Canyon Village**), and it's open all year round. There is another lodge and campground at the **North Rim**, which by virtue of its isolation can be a whole lot more evocative, but at one thousand feet higher this is usually closed by snow from mid-October until May. Few people visit both rims; to get from one to the other demands either a two-day hike down one side of the canyon and up the other, or a 215-mile drive by road.

Finally, there's a definite risk that on the day you come the Grand Canyon will be invisible beneath a layer of **fog**; many people blame the 250 tons of sulfurous emissions pumped out every day by the Navajo Generating Station, seventy miles upriver at Page.

Admission prices to the park, valid for seven days on either rim, are $10 per vehicle, or $4 per pedestrian or cyclist.

Getting To and From the Canyon

The most usual approach is by **road** from the south, turning off I-17 at either **Williams** or **Flagstaff**. The final twenty miles of the plain is covered by a thick ponderosa pine forest. The canyon itself is not visible from any distance – often not even from the rim road – so the restored **steam trains** which take 2hr 45min to run the 64 miles up from Williams have few scenic delights to offer. They pull in at the picturesque village station (daily; April–Sept, departing Williams 9am & 10am, and the canyon 3.30pm & 4.30pm; otherwise 10am from Williams and 4.30pm from the canyon; no service Jan & Feb; return fare $50 adults, $25 children under 12; ☎1-800/THE-TRAIN).

Nava-Hopi **buses** (☎774/5003) start from *Bright Angel Lodge*, where you can buy tickets. Each day there's a direct service to Flagstaff at 9.45am, and one via Williams at 5.45pm (fare $14). The *Amtrak* bus to Flagstaff leaves daily at 5.25pm (see p.700).

The **airport** is just outside the park at Tusayan; hourly shuttle buses run the seven miles to the village, and *Budget* and *Dollar* rent cars. *America West* (☎1-800/247-5692) fly to Flagstaff, Phoenix and Las Vegas; *Scenic Airlines* (☎1-800/634-6801) and *Air Nevada* (☎1-800/634-6377) operate scheduled flights to Las Vegas only, and scenic charters throughout the region. Planes no longer fly directly above the canyon, but the Las Vegas flights give a good view and for as little as $60 save an awful lot of time.

During high season (roughly May–Sept) free **shuttle buses** operate every fifteen minutes within the village itself, and along the West Rim Drive (which at those times is barred to motorists), stopping at the main overlooks.

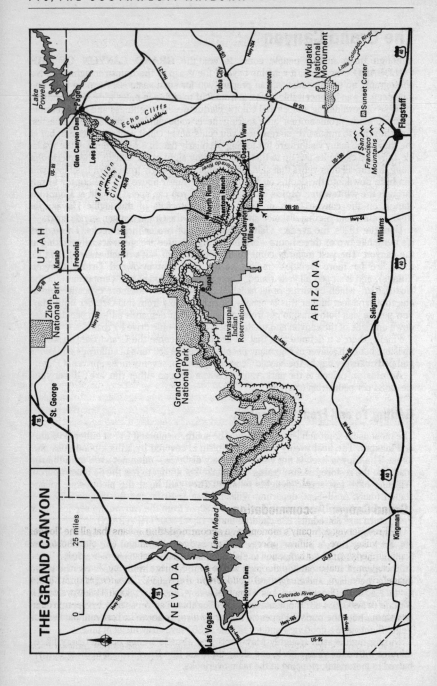

THE GRAND CANYON

GEOLOGY AND HISTORY OF THE CANYON

Layer upon layer of different rocks, readily distinguished by color, and each with its own fossil record, recedes down into the Grand Canyon and back through time, until the strata at the river bed are among the oldest exposed rocks on earth. And yet how the canyon was **formed** is a mystery. Satellite photos show that the Colorado actually runs through the heart of an enormous hill (what the Indians called the *Kaibab*, the mountain with no peak); experts cannot agree on how this could happen. Studies show that the canyon still deepens, at the slow rate of 50ft per million years. Its fantastic sandstone and limestone formations were not literally carved by the river, however; they're the result of erosion by wind and extreme cycles of heat and cold. These features were named – **Brahma Temple, Vishnu Temple**, and so on – by Clarence Dutton, a student of comparative religion who wrote the first Geological Survey report on the canyon in 1881.

It may look forbidding, but the Grand Canyon is not a dead place. All sorts of desert **wildlife** survive here – sheep and rabbits, eagles and vultures, mountain lions, and, of course, spiders, scorpions, and snakes. The **human** presence has never been on any great scale, but signs have been found of habitation as early as 2000 BC, and the **Anasazi** were certainly here later on. A party of **Spaniards** passed through in 1540 – less than twenty years after Cortes conquered the Aztecs – searching for cities of gold, and a Father Garcés spent some time with the Havasupai in 1776. **John Wesley Powell**'s expeditions along the fearsome and uncharted waters of the Colorado in 1869 and 1871–72 were what really brought the canyon to public attention. A few abortive attempts were made to mine different areas, but facilities for tourism were swiftly realized to be a far more lucrative investment. With the exception of the Indian reservations, the Grand Canyon is now run exclusively for the benefit of visitors; although even as recently as 1963 there were proposals to dam the Colorado and flood 150 miles of the Canyon, and the Glen Canyon dam has seriously affected the ecology downstream.

Grand Canyon Village

Grand Canyon Village is not a very stimulating place to spend any time. However, in the absence of significantly cheaper accommodation within fifty miles (for example, in **Tusayan** at the park entrance), there's little option but to stay here. The centerpiece is the magnificent **terrace**, in front of *Bright Angel Lodge* (usually the liveliest spot in town) and the black-beamed 1905 *El Tovar Hotel*, that gives many visitors their only look at the canyon – though the Colorado itself is too deep in the Inner Gorge to be seen from here. Further back are more lodges and gift shops, and employee housing, while about a mile east through the woods are the informative **visitor center** (8am–dusk; ☎638-7888), the **post office**, the **general store**, and the **campground**.

Grand Canyon Accommodation

The Fred Harvey company's monopoly on **accommodation** means that all the "lodges" in the village are at similar prices, with no budget alternative. (A youth hostel was condemned as unfit for habitation in 1990, and there are no plans to re-house it .) To see the canyon, it makes little difference where in the village you stay. Even in the "rim-edge" places – *El Tovar Hotel* (⑥), and *Bright Angel* (③), *Thunderbird* and *Kachina* lodges (both ⑤) – few rooms offer much of a view, and in any case it's always dark by 8pm. Further back are the *Maswik Lodge* (③; cabins can be shared between groups), *Yavapai Lodge* near the visitor center (④), and *Moqui Lodge* at the park entrance (④).

All in-park **accommodation reservations** are handled by *Grand Canyon National Park Lodges*, PO Box 699, Grand Canyon, AZ 86023 (same-day ☎638-2631, advance ☎638-2401).

Camping facilities (and a laundromat) are available at the *Mather* campground ($10; ☎638-7888) near the visitor center, at least one section of which is open year-round. If you arrive on foot, you don't need a reservation; all vehicles (there's an RV park as well) should, however, check in well in advance (you can book through MISTIX on ☎1-800/365-2267). The summer-only *Desert View* campground 26 miles east is first-come first-served, and has no hook-ups. It's also possible to camp inside the canyon itself, if you first obtain a free permit from the **Backcountry Reservations Office** at the village campground – indeed you can camp anywhere in the national forest that is more than six hundred feet from a roadway.

If all the park accommodations are full, the nearest alternative is the underwhelming service village of **TUSAYAN**, just over a mile south of the park entrance. *Seven Mile Lodge* (☎638-2291; ③), offers the least expensive rooms; *Red Feather Lodge* (☎638-2414; ⑤), is a little more comfortable. Much the most popular of the commercial campgrounds – with families, at least – is *Flintstone's Bedrock City* (☎635-2600; ⑤), 22 miles south at the junction of Hwys 64 and 180, which has its own prehistoric theme park.

Grand Canyon Eating

Thanks to the canyon's remoteness and lack of water, **food prices** tend to be well above average; if you're on a tight budget, bring your own. However, *Yavapai* and *Maswik* lodges have reasonable basic cafeterias, open until l0pm. *Bright Angel Lodge* has its own restaurant as well as the *Arizona Steakhouse*, both also open until l0pm, and both costing $15 to $30. At *El Tovar*, where the dining room looks right out over the canyon, the sumptuous menu is, however, enormously expensive. Breakfast is the most affordable; lunch and dinner can easily cost upwards of $40.

In Tusayan, *Hit the Spot Bar* (☎638-2035) is the liveliest place for a drink, and serves standard food; *We Cook Pizza* nearby (☎638-2278) is good but very pricey.

Along the South Rim

It's possible to walk along the South Rim for several miles in either direction from the village, the first few of them on railed and concreted pathways. The most obvious short excursions are to see the sun rise and set. At or near the village, the giant wall that reaches out in the west overshadows much of the evening view. If, however, you walk right out to Hopi Point at its end, looking down as you go onto the Bright Angel Trail as it winds across the Tonto Plateau, you may well see a magical **sunset**, with the Colorado – 350 feet wide at this point – visible way below.

The best place within walking distance to watch the **dawn** is Mather Point, a mile east of the visitor center. Nearby, if you can tear your eyes away from its panoramic bay windows, the **Yavapai Geologic Museum** (summer, daily 9am–7pm) has illuminating displays on how the canyon may have been formed.

Further dramatic views are available along the **East Rim Drive** – although unless you take an excursion you'll need your own vehicle to see them. **Desert View**, 23 miles out from the village, is at 7500 feet the highest point on the South Rim. Visible to the east are the vast flatlands of the **Navajo Nation**; to the northeast, **Vermillion and Echo Cliffs**, and the grey bulk of **Navajo Mountain** ninety miles away; to the west, the gigantic peaks of **Vishnu** and **Buddha Temples**. Through the plains comes the narrow gorge of the **Little Colorado**; somewhere in the depths, before it meets the Colorado itself, is the *sipapu*, the hole through which the Hopi believe that men first entered this, the Third World. The odd-looking construction on the very lip of the canyon is **Desert View Watchtower**, built by Fred Harvey in 1932 in a conglomeration of Native American styles (though a steel frame props it all up) and decorated with Hopi pictographs. It contains a gift shop, as does the general store a few yards away.

Groups of tarantulas are often seen in the evenings at Desert View, scuttling back into the warmth of the canyon for the night.

Tusayan Ruin, three miles west of Desert View (and not to be confused with modern Tusayan) is a genuine Anasazi pueblo, though not comparable in scale to the relics elsewhere in this region.

Into the Canyon

A descent into the Grand Canyon offers something more than just another view of the same thing. Instead you pass through a sequence of utterly different landscapes, each with its own distinct climate, wildlife, and topography. It's a hostile environment, and one to be treated with respect. The basic rules are, first, that whatever time you spend hiking down, you should allow twice that to get back up again, and second, carry (and drink) at least one litre of water per person.

The temperature at river level is on average 20° higher than on the South Rim, and there's far less rain. The **ecology** down here is changing fast since Glen Canyon Dam was completed 25 years ago. Previously, up to a million tons of earth and rock hurtled past Phantom Ranch each day. Now it's more like 80,000; trees are establishing themselves that would previously have been swept away, and fish are becoming extinct.

There's only space here to detail the most popular **hiking trail**, the **Bright Angel**. Many of the others, such as the **Hermit**, date from the days prior to 1928, when the obstreperous Ralph Cameron controlled access to the Bright Angel and many other rim-edge sites by means of spurious mining claims, and Fred Harvey had to find other ways to get its customers down to the Colorado. These other trails tend to be over-grown now, or partially blocked by landslides; check before setting out.

Bright Angel Trail

The **Bright Angel Trail**, followed on foot or mule by thousands of visitors each year, starts from the wooden shack in the village which was once the Kolb photographic studio. Allowing four or five hours to hike the 9.6 miles down to **Phantom Ranch**, and another eight or nine to get back up again, you should think carefully before attempting the round trip in one day. Many hikers choose instead to go as far as **Plateau**

GRAND CANYON TOURS AND ENTERTAINMENTS

Fred Harvey do at least two short daily **coach tours** along the **rim** to the west and east of the village, a **sunset trip** to Yavapai point, and **mule** rides to Phantom Ranch. They also run a five-hour **Smooth Water River Raft Excursion** through Marble Canyon ($75); whitewater rafting trips in the canyon proper (see below) are booked up literally years in advance, so this is probably your only chance of a trip along the river at short notice. Details from lodge Transportation Desks, or on ☎638-2401.

Unless otherwise specified, all these companies are in **Tusayan**, at or near the airport.

Airplane tours cost from around $55 for 30min ($30 child) up to as long as you like for as much as you've got:
Air Grand Canyon (☎1-800/AIR-GRAND or ☎638-2686); *Grand Canyon Airlines* (☎1-800/528-2413 or ☎638-2407); *Windrock Aviation* (☎1-800/24ROCKY or ☎638-9591).

Helicopter tours, from $75 for 30min:
AirStar Helicopters (☎638-2622); *Grand Canyon Helicopters* (☎638-2419); *Kenai Helicopters* (☎638-2412).

Wilderness River Adventures (Box 717, Page, AZ 86040; ☎1-800/528-6154 or ☎645-3279). 3–12-day **whitewater raft trips** through the canyon, by the operators of Fred Harvey's half-day trip detailed above.

Grand Canyon IMAX Theater (daily March–Oct 8.30am–8.30pm, Nov–Feb 10.30am–8.30pm; $7 adults, $4 kids; ☎638-2468). One of the most popular attractions, a 34-minute giant-screen film show of death-defying feats in and above the canyon.

Point on the edge of the arid Tonto Plateau, an overlook above the Inner Gorge from which it is not possible to descend any further. In summer, you can obtain water along the trail, and only need to carry one litre of water per person; in winter, when there is none, you should carry two.

The first section of the trail was laid out by miners a century ago, along an old Havasupai route. There are two short tunnels in its first mile. After another mile, the **wildlife** starts to increase (deer, rodents and the ubiquitous ravens), and there are a few **pictographs** which have been all but obscured by graffiti.

At **Indian Gardens**, almost five miles down, there's a ranger station and campground with water. Here the trails split, to Plateau Point or down to the river via the **Devil's Corkscrew**, constructed by the WPA in the 1930s. It leads through sand dunes scattered with cacti and down beside **Garden Creek** to the Colorado, which you then follow for more than a mile to get to Phantom Ranch.

Phantom Ranch

It's a real thrill to spend a night at the very bottom of the canyon, in the 1922 **Phantom Ranch**. You can only get there after an all-day hike on foot or mule, and in any case the cabins are reserved exclusively for the use of excursionists on Fred Harvey two-day mule trips ($259 per person for one night, $359 for the winter-only two-night trips). There may however be $22 dorm beds. All supplies reach Phantom Ranch the same way you do, so meals are expensive, a minimum of $10.50 for breakfast and $17 for dinner. Hikers must register with the *Bright Angel* transportation desk the day prior to their reservation, by 4pm, or on that day call ☎638-2631 ext 6576 to confirm. Do not hike down without a reservation.

The **suspension bridge** here was set in place in 1928 (hanging from twin cables carried down on the shoulders of 42 Havasupai). The delta of **Bright Angel Creek**, named by Powell to contrast with the muddy **Dirty Devil** stream a short way upriver, is several hundred feet wide here, and strewn with boulders. All the water used on the South Rim now comes by pipeline from the North Rim, and crosses the river on the 1960s Silver Bridge nearby. (Do not drink the water from any streams you pass, as it's swarming with illness-inducing bacteria.)

Havasupai

The **Havasupai Indian Reservation** really is another world. A 1930s anthropologist called it "the only spot in the United States where native culture has remained in anything like its pristine condition"; things have changed a little since then, but the sheer magic of its turquoise waterfalls and canyon scenery make this a very special place. Traditionally, the Havasupai lifestyle was to spend summer on the canyon floor and winter on the plateau above. When the reservation was created in 1882, they were only granted land at the bottom of the canyon, and not until 1975 did the concession of another 251,000 acres up above make it possible to resume their ancient pattern.

Havasu Canyon is a side canyon of the Grand Canyon, about 35 miles as the raven flies from Grand Canyon village, but almost 200 miles by road. Turn off the Interstate at Seligman or Kingman, onto AZ-66 which curves north between the two, stock up with water and petrol, and then turn on to Arrowhead Hwy-18. The road ends at **Hualapai Hilltop**, an eight-mile hike from the village of **Supai**.

Plans to build a road – or even a tramway – down into the canyon have always been rejected, in part because much of the income of the five or six hundred Havasupai comes from guiding visitors on foot, mule or horseback. Beyond Supai the trail becomes more difficult, but leads to a succession of spectacular waterfalls, including **Havasu Falls**, one of the best for swimming, and **Mooney Falls**, which was named after an unfortunate prospector who dangled here for three days in the 1890s, at the end of a snagged rope, before falling to his death.

A **campground** (☎448-2141) stretches between Havasu and Mooney Falls, and Supai itself holds *Havasupai Lodge* (☎448-2111; ③), along with a café, a general store, and the only post office in the US still to receive its mail by pack train. From time to time Supai is hit by freak floods – most recently on Labor Day 1990 – which can result in the temporary closure of the campground and hotel.

Around to the North Rim

The 215-mile route by road from Grand Canyon Village to the North Rim follows AZ-64 along the East Rim Drive to Desert View, then passes an overlook into the gorge of the Little Colorado, before joining US-89 after fifty miles at **CAMERON**. The *Cameron Trading Post* has the best selection of Native American crafts in the Grand Canyon area, and remains a trading center for the Navajo Nation (with some of its business still conducted by barter). It has a **motel** (☎679-2231; ③), and a cafeteria serving reasonable food.

Fifteen miles north of Cameron comes the junction with US-160, which heads northeast via **Tuba City** (where there's more accommodation; see p.714) towards Monument Valley and Colorado. Continuing north, after another forty miles of barren wasteland US-89 branches off to climb the mesa to the right, heading for Page and Glen Canyon Dam (see p.738).

Lee's Ferry

The direct route to the North Rim, now US-89A, crosses the Colorado at last over the single arch of Navajo Bridge, almost five hundred feet above the river. Until the bridge was completed in 1929, a ferry service operated at **LEE'S FERRY**, six miles north. This was established in 1872, at the instigation of the Mormon Church, by John D Lee, at the only spot within hundreds of miles to offer easy access to the banks of the river on both sides. The Colorado, however, could still be a raging torrent, and the crossing was carried out in both directions by casting out and struggling across while being swept downstream, in constant danger from currents and winds. Lee himself was on the run after the **Mountain Meadows Massacre** in Utah in 1857, when a wagon train of would-be settlers was slaughtered by an armed white band clumsily disguised as Indians. He remains a hero to some Mormons (a local plaque calls him "a man of good faith, sound judgment and indomitable courage"); those who have read Mark Twain's account of the massacre in *Roughing It* may disagree. He was finally apprehended and executed in 1877.

The ferry service was abandoned after a fatal accident in June 1928. A crucial piece of equipment needed to finish the bridge on the left bank was stranded on the right bank; the only way to get it across was to take it eight hundred miles by road, via Las Vegas.

Lee's Ferry is the launching point for **whitewater rafting** trips – boats setting off from here can't leave the canyon before Diamond Creek, twelve days away by muscle power – and the end of Fred Harvey's smooth water trips from Glen Canyon Dam (see p.719). It has a few relics of Lee's days, as well as a half-sunk steamboat, hauled from San Francisco in 1911 and abandoned as a failed experiment after only five trips. There's also a **campground** (☎355-2334), while back on US-89A beneath the red of the **Vermilion Cliffs** are three successive motels – *Marble Canyon Lodge* (☎355-2225; ③), *Cliff Dweller's Lodge* (☎355-2228; ③), and the slightly lower-priced *Lee's Ferry Lodge* (☎355-2223; ③) – all with restaurants.

The turning south to get to the North Rim, off US-89A onto AZ-67, comes at **JACOB LAKE**, which has an *Inn* (☎643-7232; ③) and **campground**, but not much else. From here – along a road which is closed in winter – it's 27 miles on to *Kaibab Lodge* (☎638-2389) and another fourteen to the canyon itself.

The North Rim

The **North Rim** of the Grand Canyon is nothing like as developed for visitors as the south. It's higher, and bleaker, with a succession of viewpoints that offer a radically different perspective on the chasm below. Tourist facilities, concentrated at **Bright Angel Point**, open for the season in mid-May and remain in operation until the first major snowfall of winter, which usually comes towards the end of October. Of the different grades of **accommodation** at the *Grand Canyon Lodge* (all ③), the cheapest deal is a *Pioneer Cabin*, holding four or five people. Advance reservations are essential; contact *TWA Services*, Box 400, Cedar City, Utah 84721 (☎801/586-7686). The *Lodge* has a restaurant, a general store, a post office and a gift shop, and its **information desk** (8am–6pm; ☎638-7864) co-ordinates **mule rides** along the rim or into the canyon, and **bus tours**. Just over a mile north is *North Rim Campground*, where spaces can be reserved – though it's not necessary for backpackers – through any *Ticketron* outlet, or on ☎340-9033.

UTAH

With the biggest, most beautiful and most pristine landscapes in North America, **UTAH** has something for everyone: from brilliantly colored canyons, across endless desert plains, to thickly wooded and snow-covered mountains. This unmatched range of terrain, almost all of which is unspoiled (and unpopulated) public land, makes it *the* place to come for **outdoor pursuits** – from hiking to off-track mountain biking, white-water rafting, and skiing.

Southern Utah has more **national parks** than anywhere else in the US; in fact it has been proposed that the entire area should be one vast national park. The most accessible parts – such as **Zion** and **Bryce Canyon** – are, of course, by far the most visited, but lesser-known parts like **Arches** and **Canyonlands** are every bit as dramatic. Huge tracts of this empty desert, in which beautiful pre-Columbian pictographs and Anasazi ruins lie hidden, are all but unexplored; seeing them in safety requires a good degree of advance planning and self-sufficiency.

The rest of Utah, though not as spectacular, is far from dull. In the **northeast**, the **Uinta Mountains** remain uncrossed by road and form one of the most extensive wilderness areas outside Alaska, and **Flaming Gorge** and **Dinosaur** preserve more desert splendor. In the predominantly flat and dry **northwest**, the granite mountains of the **Wasatch Front** form a towering wall over state capital **Salt Lake City** – a surprisingly attractive and enjoyable stopover – while Alta, Snowbird, and Park City offer some of the best **skiing** in North America.

Led by Brigham Young, Utah's earliest white settlers – the **Mormons** – arrived in the Salt Lake area in 1847, and set about the massive irrigation projects that made their agrarian way of life possible. At first they provoked great suspicion and hostility back east; Congress turned down their first petition for statehood in 1850, in part because of the religious significance of the proposed name – **Deseret**, a Mormon word meaning "honeybee" (the state symbol is still a beehive, to denote industry). The Republican convention of 1856 railed against slavery and polygamy in equal measure – the potential was there for a Civil War with the Mormons, had the South not intervened. Relations eased when the Mormon church realized in 1890 that it would do better to drop polygamy on its own terms before it was forced to do so. Statehood followed in 1896, and a century on, seventy percent of Utah's two million population are Mormons. The Mormon influence is especially visible in the layout of Utah's towns, where residential streets are as wide as interstates, and all are numbered block-by-block according to the same logical if ponderous system.

> The **area code** for the entire state of Utah is ☎801.

Despite Brigham Young's early opposition to the **search** for mineral wealth, Mormon businessmen became renowned as fiercely pro-mining and anti-conservation. Only since the early 1980s – once the uranium bonanza was definitely over – has tourism been appreciated as a major industry, and former mining towns such as Moab developed facilities for wide-eyed travellers smitten by the lure of the desert. Increased tourism has also led to a relaxation of Utah's notoriously arcane **drinking laws**; patrons of licensed restaurants can now purchase beer, wine and mixed drinks.

Getting Around Utah

It's nearly impossible to get anywhere in Utah without your own **car**. *Amtrak* and *Greyhound* serve Salt Lake City and a few provincial towns, but practically nowhere else. However, a couple of firms offer **coach tours** of the national parks, and if you're feeling adventurous, southern Utah also has an unbeatable range of mountain-biking, river-rafting, even hot-air ballooning opportunities: see p.735 for a list of companies.

Southern Utah: the National Parks

There's nothing quite like **southern Utah** anywhere else in the world. In this infinite elemental landscape, hardly touched by civilization, 11,000ft peaks, covered in dense stands of conifers, aspens and maples, rise above awesome sandstone canyons that have been carved like some intricate geological jigsaw puzzle into the fiery red desert by some of the mightiest stretches of America's most powerful rivers.

The southwestern national parks, **Bryce Canyon** and the overwhelming **Zion**, are the easiest to reach (just off I-15, the only interstate), and can therefore get crowded, but remain absolutely magnificent; to the east, **Capitol Reef**, **Canyonlands** and **Arches** national parks are drier, hotter and much harsher, with massive humps of bare stone standing out of the arid plateaus. Smaller national monuments and state parks are scattered everywhere: Cedar Breaks, Kodachrome Basin, Newspaper Rock and Dead Horse Point, to name an evocative few.

The very best way to experience the region is as the first explorers did: by **water**. Dozens of companies offer river-rafting trips, floating downstream, and camping out under the clear night sky to experience the sights, sounds and smells of the desert. It's a tough land, and a rough one for travellers: there are fewer roads here than anywhere else in the US, which means that almost nobody gets far into the deep backcountry, and even within the national park lands, overground access is more often than not limited to heavy-duty, high-clearance four-wheel-drive vehicles, **hikers** and, increasingly, to **mountain bikes**.

The Towns: St George and Cedar City

Southern Utah's two biggest towns, **St George** and **Cedar City**, are fifty miles apart on I-15 en route between Las Vegas and Salt Lake City. Both make reasonably pleasant and serviceable bases, if not ones that are likely to detain you for very long.

St George

ST GEORGE was the winter home of Brigham Young and other early Mormon leaders, who came to "Utah's Dixie" to bask in its comparatively mild climate. Set at the foot of a broad reddish-brown sandstone cliff, it's a pretty enough town, centering around the fine 1877 **LDS Temple** at 200 E and 500 S, the oldest still in use anywhere.

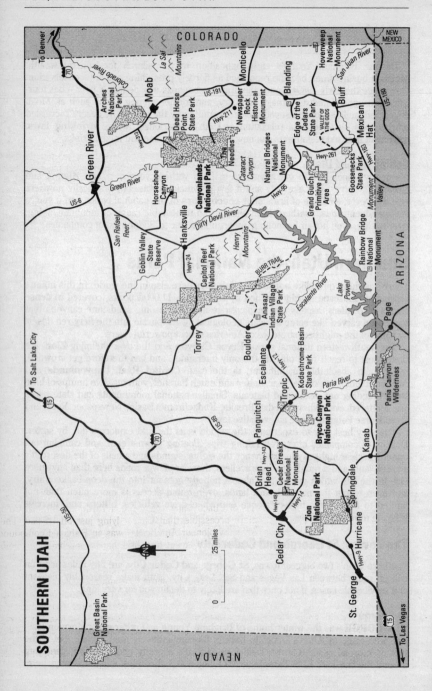

SOUTHERN UTAH

0 _____ 25 miles

The rest of the town holds quaint houses built by Mormon pioneers, including Brigham Young's much-restored **adobe house** on 200 North First West; pick up a walking tour map there or at the **visitor center** (Mon–Fri 9am–5pm; ☎628-1658) in the old **County Courthouse** at 97 E St George Blvd.

Virtually all St George's commercial life takes place along the main drag, St George Boulevard, where **motels** include the excellent-value *Red Mesa* (no 247 E; ☎673-3163; ①), complete with pool, and the *Dixie Palm* (no 185 E; ☎673-3531; ①). *Greyhound* **buses** between Las Vegas and Salt Lake City stop outside the good-value *Trafalgar Restaurant* (no 76 W; ☎673-2933); other central eating possibilities include the classier Italian dishes at *René's* (no 430 E; ☎628-9300), and the various restaurants in the popular Ancestor Square development. The Hwy-9 turn-off to Zion and Bryce is ten miles north of town; *Toraco* (☎628-8687) and *Scenic America* (☎586-9496) run guided **coach tours** through both parks from St George, the only way to get there without a car.

Cedar City

CEDAR CITY, 53 miles north of St George and approximately half its size, is not particularly more worthy of a stop. Founded as an iron-mining town in the late 1850s, it's now kept alive by the Southern Utah State College on its western fringe, and by the flood of theater-goers who come to watch the enthusiastic productions of the **Utah Shakespeare Festival**, held on the campus every summer (☎586-7880).

Main Street is handy for food and lodging. The *Sugar Loaf* (no 261 S; ☎586-6593), has Navajo tacos and standard coffeeshop meals; *Sullivan's* (no 86 S; ☎586-6761) is similar. Everything shuts at 9pm apart from *Ed and Deb's Truck Stop*, a 24-hour diner just west of I-15 on the northern fringes of town. The least expensive **beds** are on Main Street south of town; motels with pools include the *Astro Budget* (no 323 S; ☎586-6557; ②) and the *Thrifty* (no 344 S; ☎586-9416; ②). Hwy-14 heads east from the town center through the Dixie National Forest to Cedar Breaks and Bryce Canyon.

Zion National Park

To many visitors, **ZION NATIONAL PARK** is the most beautiful of southern Utah's parklands, combining dense riparian forests, cascading waterfalls and hanging gardens with magnificent canyons and sheer rock faces. It effectively consists of two sections, stretching southeast from I-15 between St George and Cedar City. The main part, the dramatic chasm of **Zion Canyon** in the southeast corner, 21 miles off the interstate via Hwy-9, holds the most impressive sights, and gets most of the tourist traffic. Further northwest, and reached by a separate entrance, are the finger canyons of the **Kolob Plateau**, where cliffs of brilliant red sandstone soar thousands of feet above maple- and aspen-lined stream valleys.

Zion Canyon

In **Zion Canyon**, mighty walls of Navajo sandstone rise nearly half a mile above the groves of box elders and cottonwoods that line the loping **Virgin River**. The awe of the early Mormon settlers who called this "Zion" is reflected in the names of the stupendous slabs of rock along the six-mile paved road from the park entrance – the Court of the Patriarchs, the Great White Throne and Angel's Landing. The road ends at the foot of the Temple of Sinawava, beyond which the gentle **Gateway to the Narrows** trail continues on another half a mile up the canyon, to the point where the river fills the entire floor (a very welcome bathing spot in drier seasons). It's a fine walk to the end of the trail and back, but at certain times of year (check with the visitor center) determined hikers can continue on, wading through the chilly river thigh- or even neck-deep for some eight miles to reach **The Narrows**, where the canyon is only twenty feet across and the walls tower some eight hundred feet straight up. It's best done as an overnight trip, camping out in one of the many enticing side canyons that splinter off the main gorge.

Less ambitious walkers might prefer to wander up to **Weeping Rock**, an easy half-hour round trip from the road to a gorgeous spring-fed garden that dangles from a rocky alcove. From the same trailhead, a mile beyond *Zion Lodge*, a more strenuous and exciting route cuts through narrow **Hidden Canyon**, whose mouth turns into a waterfall after a good rain. Directly across from the lodge a short (two-mile round-trip) and fairly flat trail winds up at the **Emerald Pools**, a series of three clearwater pools, the best (and furthest) of which has a small sandy beach at the foot of a gigantic cliff; at certain times of the year a broad waterfall sprinkles down over the trail.

The single best half-day **hike** climbs up to **Angel's Landing**, a narrow ledge of whitish sandstone protruding out some 1750 feet above the canyon floor. Starting on the same trail as for the Emerald Pools, the Angel's Landing trail switchbacks up sharply through the delightful coolness of **Refrigerator Canyon** before emerging on the canyon's west rim; near the end you have to cross a heart-stopping five-foot neck of rock with sheer drops to either side (there's a steel cable to grab hold of). Allow two hours up and an hour back down for Angel's Landing; backpackers can continue another twenty miles to the gorgeous Kolob Canyons district (see below).

The high dry plateau above and to the east of Zion Canyon is a complete contrast to the lush Virgin River gorge. The most dramatic sight is the blind **Great Arch**, best seen from the turnouts before the mile-long tunnel, beyond which the **Canyon Overlook** nature trail gives a good introduction to the flora and fauna of the park, such as the speedy lizards which race from rock to rock. The road then climbs through smooth slickrock sandstone and bizarrely eroded **hoodoos**, passing the angular Checkerboard Mesa before heading on to the North Rim of the Grand Canyon (see p.722).

Practicalities

Located just beyond the park entrance, north of Springdale on Hwy-9 (admission $5 per vehicle), the **visitor center** has maps and information on hiking trails and weather conditions, plus evening slide shows (daily, May–Sept 8am–9pm, otherwise 9am–5pm; ☎722-3256). The only **food and lodging** within Zion itself is at *Zion Lodge*, set amid rolling and well-shaded lawns near the Great White Throne (open all year; ☎586-7686; ④). Even if you can't get a room here – they're often booked up by tour groups – it's well worth stopping for lunch on the terrace of the fine old wooden dining room. The first-come, first-served *South* and *Watchman* **campgrounds** ($7) are just across from the visitor center; get there early to be sure of a space in summer.

The best alternative to the in-park lodge is *Cliffrose Lodge*, 281 Zion Park Blvd (☎772-3234; ④), among the cottonwoods along the Virgin River half a mile south of the park entrance in the small town of **SPRINGDALE**. Elsewhere along Zion Park Blvd (which doubles as Hwy-9), Springdale also holds *Flanigan's Inn* (no 428; ☎772-3244; ③), and an attractive and colorful five-room B&B, *Under The Eaves* (no 980; ☎772-3457; ③), as well as **restaurants**. *Sparky's*, in a converted church (no 868; ☎772-3901), is good for lunch or a light dinner; the *Driftwood* is reliable for breakfast (no 1515; ☎772-3262). For solid **Tex-Mex food** after a day on the trails, head to the *Bit and Spur Saloon* on the west edge of town (no 1212; ☎772-3498); it's the liveliest **bar** in this corner of Utah, with the only good margaritas for miles.

Cyclists should be warned that bikes cannot be ridden through the tunnel by which Hwy-9 leaves Zion Canyon east towards Mount Carmel; rangers can arrange lifts.

The Kolob Canyons

Although the immaculate **Kolob Canyons** are just three miles off I-15, twenty miles south of Cedar City, this section of Zion receives far fewer visitors than Zion Canyon itself. Here too the focus is on **red rock canyons**, which in the Kolob seem somehow redder, and the trees greener (and then in their turn redder, when the maples turn color in fall), than those down below.

The view from the five-mile paved road that heads up from the small but worthwhile **visitor center** (daily May–Sept 8am–5pm, otherwise 8am–4.30pm; ☎722-3256) is amazing, but hiking off along either of two main trails will give you a feeling for what makes this place so special. The first and shorter of the two starts two miles from the visitor center and follows Taylor Creek on a five-mile round trip to **Double Arch Alcove**, a spectacular natural amphitheater roofed by twin sandstone arches; there's also a small waterfall a quarter of a mile further along. The other trail starts from the north side of the parking area at Lee Pass, four miles beyond the visitor center, and follows a well-marked route past LaVerkin Falls seven miles to **Kolob Arch**, the world's longest natural rock span at over 300 feet across. There are no campgrounds in the Kolob Canyons.

Cedar Breaks National Monument

The shortest drive between Zion and Bryce, along the Virgin River and then north on US-89 across the high plain of Long Valley, is spectacular enough, but the longer route through the maple and aspen groves of the **Dixie National Forest** is even more dramatic. Halfway between Cedar City and US-89, Hwy-148 cuts sharply north through the eerie fringes of **CEDAR BREAKS NATIONAL MONUMENT**, where the soft sandstone has crumbled away from the edge of a high wooded plateau to create a fairy-land amphitheater of bizarre and brilliantly colored formations.

Cedar Breaks is in a sense just a small-scale version of Bryce Canyon to the east, but that's no reason not to come here ($3 fee per vehicle). Most of the plateau is over 10,000 feet high, so it's usually quite cold; in fact the roads through are often blocked by snow until June. **Point Supreme**, with a small summer-only visitor center (June–mid-Oct only, 8am–6pm), snack bar, and campground ($5), is a mile into the park from the south, and gives the best view.

Brian Head and Panguitch

A couple of miles north of Cedar Breaks, **Brian Head** is the highest town in Utah, and the site of southern Utah's only downhill ski resort (mid-Nov to May; $28 per day; ☎677-2035). Accommodation possibilities include the *Cosmos Motel*, 56 N Hwy-53 (☎677-3663; ②), which has its own restaurant, and the *Bristlecone Hostel*, 1035 Bristlecone Lane (☎677-3663; ①); room rates double in the ski season.

Heading east from Cedar Breaks towards Bryce Canyon, Hwy-143 passes through pine forests and across lava flows – there's a half-mile lava tube at **Mammoth Cave**, poorly signed south of Panguitch Lake in the middle of the forest. Beyond the lake the road drops down into the broad Sevier River valley at the squeaky-clean Mormon farming town of **PANGUITCH**, where you'll find eight gas stations (one, *Todd's Truck Stop*, is open 24hr), a dozen budget motels, such as the *Color Country*, 526 N Main St (☎1-800/225-6518; ②), and not much else.

Bryce Canyon National Park

The surface of the earth can hold few weirder-looking spots than **BRYCE CANYON**. Named for Mormon settler Ebenezer Bryce, who despaired of making a living in this wasteland – and memorably declared that it was "a helluva place to lose a cow" – it is not in fact a canyon at all. Along a twenty-mile shelf on the eastern edge of the thickly forested Paunsaugunt Plateau, eight thousand feet above sea level, successive strata of dazzling colored rock – yellows, reds, whites and flaming oranges – have slipped and slid and washed away to leave a menagerie of multihued and contorted **stone shapes**.

Like Cedar Breaks, the formations here have been eroded out of the muddy sandstone by a combination of freezing winters (the temperature drops below zero two hundred nights out of the year) and summer rainstorms. Some resemble elephants, giraffes, or alligators; a good dozen or so look like **Elvis**. The racks of top-heavy pinnacles known as "**hoodoos**" were formed when the harder upper layers of rock stayed firm as the lower levels were worn away beneath them. These hoodoos – **Thor's Hammer**, visible from Sunset Point, is the most alarmingly precarious – look down into technicolor ravines, all far more vivid than the Grand Canyon and much more human in scale. The whole place is at its most inspiring in winter when the figures stand out from a blanket of snow.

The single road that runs south from Hwy-12 about 25 miles east of Panguitch passes by the entrance station ($5 fee per vehicle) before arriving at the **visitor center** (daily 8am–5pm; ☎834-5322). A couple of miles south, you come to a succession of scenic overlooks, and a network of trails drops abruptly from the rim into **Bryce Amphitheater** – be prepared to walk back up the same distance that you go down. The two most popular overlooks are on either side of *Bryce Canyon Lodge* (see below): the more northerly, **Sunrise Point**, is 350 yards from the parking lot and so is slightly less crowded than **Sunset Point**, where most of the bus tours stop. A good three-mile hike switchbacks steeply from Sunset Point through the cool 200-foot canyons of **Wall Street**, where a pair of 800-year-old fir trees stretch to reach daylight. It then cuts across the surreal landscape into the basin known as the **Queen's Garden**, where the stout and remarkable likeness of Queen Victoria sits in majestic condescension – pointed out by a brass plaque – before climbing back up to the rim. A dozen trails criss-cross the amphitheater, but it's surprisingly easy to get lost, so don't stray from the marked routes.

Sunrise and Sunset points notwithstanding, the best view at both sunset and dawn (which is the best time for taking pictures) is from **Bryce Point**, at the southern end of the amphitheater. From here, you can look down not only at the Bryce Canyon formations but also take in the grand sweep of the whole region, east to the **Henry Mountains** and north to the Escalante range. Most people only get as far as Bryce Amphitheater, but the park stretches another 25 miles south, passing the intensely colored **Natural Bridge**, an 85ft rock arch spanning a steep gully, at about the halfway point. For backpackers, the **Under-the-Rim Trail** winds from Bryce Point 22.6 miles to Rainbow Point, and numerous trails connect to the road above. It's also possible to avoid the crowds in summer by entering the park from below, via a two-mile trail and three-mile dirt road from the Hwy-12 village of **Tropic** (see opposite).

Practicalities

No regular scheduled transportation serves Bryce, though *Scenic Airlines* (☎1-800/634-6801) fly here from the Grand Canyon and will arrange ground transit; otherwise you'll have to drive or join a tour from St George (see p.725).

Much the best place to **stay**, if you can manage it, is the *Bryce Canyon Lodge*, one hundred yards from the rim between Sunrise and Sunset points (May–mid-Oct only; ☎834-5361; ④), where rustic cabins cost a few dollars more than basic doubles. It also has a dining room, a grocery store, a laundromat and public showers. Standard **motels** nearby, each with its own pretty ordinary restaurant and open all year (room rates are much lower in winter), include the large *Ruby's Inn* just north of the park entrance (☎834-5341 or 1-800/528-1234; ④), the *Bryce Village Motel* (☎834-5303; ④), and the slightly more distant *Bryce Canyon Pines* (☎834-5336; ④) along Hwy-12 west of Bryce.

The two **campgrounds** within the park are near the visitor center; both *Sunset Campground*, near Sunset Point, and *North Campground* are first-come, first-served and cost $6 per night. There's a slightly more deluxe campground at *Ruby's Inn* ($11). Backpackers can choose from dozens of sites below the rim, all south of Bryce Point; pick up the required free permit at the visitor center, and take lots of water.

Bryce Canyon to Capitol Reef: Scenic Highway 12

Turning its back on the grand amphitheater of Bryce Canyon, the tiny hamlet of **TROPIC**, which strings along Hwy-12 eight miles east of the park entrance, seems almost embarrassed about the flamboyant geological phenomena ranged along the ridge above it. The practical-minded people of this Mormon farming community (pop. 380) don't especially concern themselves with tourists, but they have restored Ebenezer Bryce's log cabin, which stands next to the *Pioneer Village* motel-cum-restaurant (☎679-8546; ③). An unmarked road heads west from the cabin two miles to the park boundary, from where it's a two-mile hike up to the main formations.

At the even smaller speck of a town called **Cannonville**, nine miles south, a part-paved road turns sharply south toward **Kodachrome Basin State Park**, another collection of strangely contorted stone hunks. What makes the formations here unusual is that they weren't so much eroded as extruded by mineral-laden geysers forcing their way up through softer stone, which has resulted in rounded, svelte shapes such as the phallic oddity that towers 150 feet over the attractive **campground** ($8, including hot showers).

Beyond Cannonville Hwy-12 curves along the edge of the Table Cliff Plateau before dropping down into the remote canyons of the **Escalante River**, said to be the last river system to be discovered within the continental US and site of some of the finest backpacking routes in the Southwest. As soon as you walk even a hundred yards off the main highway, you're in a wilderness which few travellers ever see.

ESCALANTE, 33 miles east of Cannonville, is just another roadside town, with a scattering of budget motels including the *Moqui* (☎826-4210; ②) and the *Circle D* (☎826-4297; ②), which has an adequate café. The Escalante BLM **ranger station** (Mon–Fri 8am–4.30pm; ☎826-4291), a mile west of town, has up-to-date information and maps, and can suggest hiking or mountain biking trips into beautiful and relatively unvisited backcountry. From **Calf Creek**, sixteen miles east of Escalante, a well-marked trail leads just under three miles upstream to a lovely shaded dell replete with a 125ft waterfall; there's a nice campground ($4 per night) at the trailhead. More ambitious trips start from trailheads along the dusty but usually passable Hole-in-the-Rock Road, which turns south from Hwy-12 five miles east of town; from **Hurricane Wash**, 35 miles along, you can head to the sandstone bridges and arches of Coyote Gulch. The best times for hiking are late spring, when there's lots of water, and fall, when the leaves turn color.

Until the mid-1980s, when it was paved through to Capitol Reef, Hwy-12 ended at **BOULDER**, thirty miles beyond Escalante. **Anasazi State Park** (daily 9am–5pm; $1), which holds the excavated and partially reconstructed remains of a small Anasazi village, is set on a shallow knoll overlooking Boulder Creek. Beyond Boulder, Hwy-12 makes a gorgeous drive up onto the Aquarius Plateau, with marvellous vistas to the east across waves of gold and red sandstone outcrops; there's a lovely **campground** ($6) at Oak Creek fifteen miles along. Due east from Boulder all except twenty miles of the old dirt **Burr Trail** has (controversially) now been paved, to provide easy access to the Waterpocket Fold and the southern reaches of Capitol Reef National Park.

Capitol Reef National Park

CAPITOL REEF sounds like something you'd be more likely to find off the coast of Australia than in the heart of the Utah desert, but in most respects its towering ochre, white, and red **rock walls** and deep **river canyons** are of a piece with the rest of the region. The outstanding feature is a multilayered, thousand-foot-high reeflike wall of uplifted sedimentary rock, a section of which reminded an early traveller of the grand dome of the US Capitol. Stretching for over a hundred miles north to south, but only a few miles across, the seemingly impenetrable barrier of the **Waterpocket Fold** was warped upwards by the same process that lifted the Colorado Plateau, and the sharply defined sedimentary layers on display here trace over two hundred million years of geological activity. The Waterpocket Fold is sliced through in a number of places by deeply incized river canyons – some only twenty feet wide, but hundreds of feet deep – often accessible only on foot.

The one paved road through the park, Hwy-24, cuts across the northern half of the Fold, following the deep canyon of the Fremont River; motorists who stick to this road do not incur an entrance fee. Beneath the enormous and very prominent **Castle**, the **visitor center** (daily, June–Sept 8am–7pm, otherwise 8am–4.30pm; ☎425-3791) has explanatory exhibits and a campground ($6). To the west, the **Goosenecks Overlook** gazes down five hundred feet into the entrenched canyons cut by Sulphur Creek. In **Fruita** to the east, a schoolhouse and a thriving orchard are all that's left of a former Mormon community. Beyond the schoolhouse along the highway are some extraordinary **Fremont petroglyphs**, figures of Bighorn sheep and stylized spacepeople chipped into the varnished red rock a thousand years ago; a five-minute radio broadcast (AM 1540) describes their makers. Further along, 4.5 miles east of the visitor center, one of Capitol Reef's best **day hikes** heads up along the gravelly river bed through **Grand Wash** – a beautiful (and usually quite cool) canyon where, it's said, Butch Cassidy and his gang used to hide out.

Few other paved routes run through the park, so to reach the spectacular backcountry canyons you may have to put up with many miles of dusty and spine-rattling roads – renting a mountain bike is a good idea. The popular **Scenic Drive** ($3 fee per vehicle), recently paved for most of its length, heads twelve miles south from the visitor center, past the top of Grand Wash to **Capitol Gorge** and back. A more adventurous sixty-mile loop trip explores **Cathedral Valley** in the north, while a 125-mile southern route starts at the foot of the volcanic Henry Mountains, then follows the Burr Trail through Muley Twist Canyon (a good overnight stop), and continues west to the town of Boulder (see p.729). Detailed, well-illustrated maps and guides ($1) are available at the visitor center.

The nearest food and lodging to Capitol Reef is eleven miles west, in the rapidly growing small town of **TORREY**, where options include the *Chuck Wagon*, 12 W Main St (☎425-3288; ②), the *Best Western Capitol Reef Resort*, 2600 E Hwy 24 (☎425-3761; ③), and the *Capitol Reef Inn*, 360 W Main St (☎425-3271; ②), which has a small café.

Goblin Valley

Fifty fairly desolate miles east of Capitol Reef along Hwy-24, you reach the tiny crossroads of **Hanksville**. Twenty miles north on Hwy-24, a right turn takes you onto a 32-mile dirt road to a real anthropological and artistic wonder – the rock paintings of **Horseshoe Canyon**, a remote subsection of Canyonlands National Park (see p.733).

Half a mile further north on Hwy-24, a side road to the east veers off to **GOBLIN VALLEY STATE PARK**, where thousands of gnome-like figures loom out of the soft Entrada sandstone. The Carmel Canyon trail loops for over a mile through a throng of misshapen rock pillars, many of which seem to have eyes and other human features. There's a well-equipped **campground** ($8) if you want to see the place by moonlight, when it looks especially spooky.

Green River

The uneventful riverside town of **GREEN RIVER**, just east of the Hwy-24 junction, is the largest community on a two-hundred-mile stretch of I-70. One very good reason to visit is the central **John Wesley Powell River History Museum** (daily, summer 9am–9pm, otherwise 9am–5pm; $1). This recounts the epic journeys of the Canyonlands region's first true explorer, John Wesley Powell, featuring the anything-but-dry personal accounts of the men who first successfully navigated the Colorado River from near its source all the way through the Grand Canyon. An entertaining film and numerous models trace the development of river craft from Native American dugouts to turn-of-the-century steamships and today's motorized rafts, and the museum also has a wide range of information on the region. In summer **raft trips** from the museum dock float downriver to the **Crystal Geyser**, a hundred-foot cold-water gusher, and every Memorial Day hundreds of boats set out on weekend-long convoy trips that cruise down the Green River to its confluence with the Colorado, then head upriver to Moab.

Green River makes a very good base for exploring this part of Utah, with its dozen bargain-priced **motels**, including the *Robber's Roost*, 135 W Main St (☎564-3452; ①), and the *Oasis*, 118 W Main St (☎564-8272; ①), which also has a handy café.

Canyonlands National Park

Utah's largest and most magnificent national park, **CANYONLANDS** spreads over 525 very remote square miles at the confluence of the Green and Colorado rivers, displaying red rock canyons and wild rivers in all their natural glory. Each of its three very distinct sections is separated from the others by a drive of at least one hundred miles. According to writer Edward Abbey, the hard-headed local business community only agreed to the creation of the national park in 1964 upon the understanding that its different parts would be linked by a loop drive, of which the focus would be the "Confluence Overlook". In the absence of such a road, Canyonlands remains the state's least visited park, but for travellers prepared to make the effort – and especially **hikers** happy to venture down the abandoned trails left by uranium miners – it's a supremely rewarding opportunity to experience the untamed desert.

The dramatic **Island-in-the-Sky** district, Canyonlands' highest and northernmost parcel, stands on a precipitous plateau some two thousand feet above the two rivers. South of here, the sandstone spires and narrow canyons of **The Needles** are a favorite destination for outdoors enthusiasts. Each of these districts has a state park along its approach road – **Dead Horse Point** and **Newspaper Rock** respectively. The third and wildest area, where 4WD is essential for the very rough roads, is **The Maze**, a jumble of canyons, towers, buttes and mesas in which you may not see another person.

In many ways the best impressions of the Canyonlands region are to be had not from above but from the rivers below, looking up at the canyon walls and relaxing in the restful solitude of the rushing waters. However, as there's no easy way in or out, it takes at least a week to get through, starting at Green River or Moab and being brought out at Lake Powell, a hundred or so miles downstream. Much of the way the waters are smooth and unchallenging, but just beyond the confluence **Cataract Canyon** contains some of the most intense whitewater rapids in the US.

No public transportation or guided bus tours go to any part of Canyonlands, though specialist companies will take you into the backcountry and you can see the whole park from the air with *Redtail Aviation* (☎259-7421). Most operators are based in Moab (see p.735), which also holds the nearest food and lodging, and the park's headquarters (information on ☎259-7164).

Island-in-the-Sky and Dead Horse Point

Reached by a good road that climbs steadily up from US-191, 21 miles south of I-70, the **Island-in-the-Sky** district looks out over hundreds of miles of flat-topped mesas that drop in two-thousand-foot steps to the river. It's the highest, driest and most sparsely vegetated section (there's no water available anywhere on the plateau); from any of the half-dozen overlooks along the main roads you might catch a glimpse of the coyotes, foxes and Bighorn sheep which roam the rocky ledges below. The best panoramas of the lot come at the southern end of the main road, from **Grand View Point**.

Another paved road cuts north from the heart of the park to the jagged 1500ft crater of **Upheaval Dome**, thought to have been created by a meteorite. Just beyond the junction, a mile-long dirt road cuts west to the **Green River Overlook**, where you can peer down at the river as it flows through **Stillwater Canyon**. Near the overlook is the only **campground** (no water) in the district. There's a visitor center (daily 8am–4.30pm) on the road in; just past here the **Shafer Trail** drops steeply down to the White Rim, a broad sandstone step one thousand feet above the rivers. An old mining road runs along this ledge above the Colorado, then back up along the rim of the Green River canyon, making a 110-mile loop trip that's ideal for mountain bike or 4WD tourists; reservations are required for the backcountry campsites (available by post only; call ☎259-4351).

On the way in to the Island-in-the-Sky, a turn-off long before the visitor center cuts across south to the smaller but equally breathtaking **Dead Horse Point State Park**, at the very tip of a narrow mesa, which looks straight down two thousand feet to the twisting Colorado River. Cowboys used the mesa – under a hundred feet across at its thinnest point – as a natural corral, herding up wild horses then blocking them in behind a piñon pine fence which still marks the neck of the mesa. One band of horses was left here too long and died – hence the name. There's a **campground** ($8) and visitor center two miles from the point.

The Needles and Newspaper Rock

Taking its name from the thousands of colorful sandstone pillars, knobs and hoodoos that punctuate its many lush canyons and basins, the **Needles** district allows a more intimate look at the Canyonlands environment than does Island-in-the-Sky. Here you're not always gazing thousands of feet downwards or scanning the distant horizon; instead you can wander through seemingly endless acres of stone figures.

The road ends with a great collection of **mushroom-shaped hoodoos** at the **Big Spring Canyon Overlook**. A memorable and demanding 5.5-mile hike from here remains the only way to get to the Confluence Overlook, a thousand feet above the point where the Green River joins the muddy waters of the Colorado, to flow together, parallel but separate, towards fearsome Cataract Canyon. Various short walks head off the road at selected viewpoints; one of the best is **Pothole Point**, a mile before Big Spring Canyon. A longer day trip, or a good overnight hike, leaves from near the *Squaw Flat* **campground** ($6 March–Oct, when water is available; free rest of year) to the green meadow of Chesler Park, cutting through the narrow cleft of the Joint Trail. Check in at the visitor center (daily 8am–4.30pm) near the park boundary to get up-to-date information, as well as backcountry permits if you plan to camp out. The only way to **reach the river** from within the park is by taking the hot and dry trail down through Lower Red Canyon to Spanish Bottom; this is the start of the Cataract Canyon rapids, so don't try to swim across.

The 35-mile drive in to the Needles from US-191 is among the prettiest in the state, winding along Indian Creek through deep red rock canyons lined by pines and cottonwoods. **Newspaper Rock**, twelve miles in, is the best of many similarly named sites; here hundreds of tiny **petroglyphs**, many of which show deer, antelope, bear claws, and helmeted human figures, have been etched in the jet black desert varnish of a red sandstone boulder by centuries of passing hunters and travellers. There's a lovely (free) streamside **campground** just across the road.

The Maze and Horseshoe Canyon

Only about one in a hundred of the half a million visitors who come to Canyonlands every year makes it into the harsh backcountry of the remote **Maze** district. Filling up the western third of the park, on the far side of the Colorado and Green rivers, the Maze is noted for its ancient rock-art panels and for its many-fingered box canyons, accessible only by jeep or by long, dry hiking trails. If you're tempted, stop into the Hans Flat ranger station, 46 miles east of Hwy-24.

Pretty, tree-lined **Horseshoe Canyon**, reached via a long, long dirt road that loops south from Green River itself and joins Hwy-24 just south of Goblin Valley (see p.730), contains the greatest concentration of **ancient rock art** in the Southwest. Hundreds of perfectly preserved pictographs were painted onto the red sandstone walls of its "Great Gallery", some time between 500 BC and 500 AD. Most show life-sized human figures, some weirdly elongated, others draped in robes. To get to the paintings, follow the road signs to the Horseshoe Canyon trailhead, then hike a steep mile down into the canyon, and two miles upstream to the gallery.

Arches National Park

Edward Abbey, who spent a year as a ranger at **ARCHES NATIONAL PARK** in the 1950s, wrote in *Desert Solitaire* that its arid landscape was as "naked, monolithic, austere and unadorned as the sculpture of the moon". It certainly is one of the least terrestrial places on this planet. Massive fins of red and golden sandstone stand to attention out of the bare desert plain, and over 1800 natural arches of various shapes and sizes have been cut into the rock by eons of erosive weathering. Apart from the single ribbon of black tarmac that snakes through the park there's nothing even vaguely human about it. The narrow, hunching ridges are more like dinosaurs' backbones than solid rock, and under a full moon, at twilight, or watching the lightning strikes of a distant thunderstorm, you can't help but imagine that the landscape has a life of its own.

While you could race through in a couple of hours, to do Arches justice you should plan to spend a whole day at the very least. A twenty-mile road cuts uphill sharply from US-191 and the park **visitor center** (daily 8am–4.30pm), where exhibits explain the fairly simple process by which the arches are formed and point out some of the more photogenic examples. The first possible stop is the south trailhead for **Park Avenue**, an easy trail leading one mile down a scoured rock-bottomed wash. If you stay on the road, the **LaSal Mountains Viewpoint** provides a grandstand look at the distant peaks rising over 12,000 feet above the surrounding desert, as well as the huge red chunk of **Courthouse Towers** closer at hand. Beyond the Towers, the road follows the foot of the salmon-colored Entrada sandstone of the **Great Wall**.

At roughly the center of the park, **Balanced Rock** is a fifty-foot boulder atop a slender 75ft pedestal. A turning to the right (east) winds for about two miles through the Windows section, where a half-mile trail loops through a dense concentration of massive arches, some over 100 feet high and 150 feet across; a second trail, fifty yards beyond the main one, leads to **Double Arch**, a staunch pair of arches that together support another arch overhead. In the **Cove of Caves**, to the right on the way back, a dozen more arches form a semi-circular arcade at the top of a sandstone amphitheater.

Beyond Balanced Rock the main road drops downhill for two miles past Panorama Point and the turn-off to **Wolfe Ranch**, where a century-old log cabin now serves as the trailhead for the three-mile round trip to the rather bulbous **Delicate Arch**, standing at the brink of a deep canyon, with the rugged La Sal mountains in the distance. Three miles beyond the Wolfe Ranch turn-off, the deep, sharp-sided mini-canyons of the **Fiery Furnace** section form a (usually quite cool) labyrinth, through which rangers lead hikes throughout the day during spring, summer and fall.

The road continues on to the **Devil's Garden** trailhead. Eight major named arches, as well as dozens of others neither named nor marked by signs, are visible from here, while an easy one-mile walk brings you to the impressive 306-foot span of **Landscape Arch**. Some of the main arches are on short spur trails off the main route; seeing them all, and returning from Double O Arch via the longer primitive trail, requires a total hike of just over seven miles. Arches' only **campground** ($5, water available March–Nov only) is across from the trailhead, and fills daily between mid-March and October, often by early morning. All individual sites are on a first-come first-served basis; no reservations are taken. Check in at the visitor center or get a permit there for back-country camping, allowed anywhere in the park that's a mile from the road and half a mile from any trail. Rock-climbing is permitted except on named features, but it's easy to get stuck and rescues are expensive, so think before you set off.

Moab

Southeastern Utah's biggest center, **MOAB**, makes a refreshing change from the smug dullness of many other Utah towns. Founded in the late 1800s, it was hardly a speck until the 1950s, when prospector Charlie Sheen discovered uranium in the nearby hills. When the ensuing mining boom finally waned, the conservative hold of Moab's industrialists and landowners waned with it, and the town threw in its lot with tourism. A whole-hearted transformation has taken place; most of Utah's adventure travel outfits are now based here, the old uranium trails are used by mountain bikes and jeeps, and the influx of lycra-clad visitors and new residents has energized the atmosphere.

The **Moab Museum**, 118 E Center St (daily 1–9pm; donations), thoroughly and enjoyably explores local history, from the region's prehistoric inhabitants, Ute Indians and the early Spanish and Yankee explorers, up to the present day (Charlie Sheen still visits the town from time to time). Moab is also the unlikely home of the **Hollywood Stuntman's Hall of Fame** (daily 9am–9pm; $3), 111 E 100 North St, an extensive archive of odds and ends from Sean Connery's hairpiece to the hat Steve McQueen wore in *The Magnificent Seven*.

Practicalities

The **visitor center**, on the north side of town at 805 N Main St (☎259-8825 or 1-800/635-6622), has stacks of information (look out for the handy *Moab Happenings* newsletter), or you can find out about local events from the excellent *Back of Beyond Bookstore*, 83 N Main St (☎259-5154), which has all the best hiking, cycling and natural history guides, alongside *Earth First!* tracts and the complete works of Moab-based writers Edward Abbey and Zane Grey.

Despite the current construction rate of around half a dozen new motels each year, all **rooms** in town are taken on many nights between March and November, so reservations are strongly recommended. In winter room rates can drop as low as $25 per night, but little can be found for that in season. Reasonable options include the *Canyonlands*, 16 S Main St (☎259-5167; ③), and the *Apache*, 166 S 400 East St (☎259-5727; ③), where John Wayne stayed while filming *Rio Bravo* in the nearby canyons. The amiable *Lazy Lizard* (not-just-for-youth) **hostel**, south of the center (near the bowling alley) at 1213 S Hwy-191 (☎259-6057; ①), has $10 dorms, a hot tub and very laid-back atmosphere. The people who run it can pick you up at the *Amtrak* stop at Thompson, or from *Greyhound* in Crescent Junction, the nearest public transportation.

Pack Creek Ranch, a dozen miles off the highway south of town (PO Box 1270; ☎259-5505; ⑦) is a full-board B&B run by Ken Sleight, once a close associate of Edward Abbey; rates of $65–80 per person include trail rides on horseback.

For a cold **beer** and a good **meal** after a day on the trails, head for either *The Poplar Place*, First North and Main St (☎259-6018), a nice bar with fine Anasazi-themed iron-work and good pizzas, or *Eddie McStiff's* at 57 S Main St (☎259-2337), a brew pub with some interesting beers, including raspberry and blueberry, and a varied but consistently tasty menu. Genuine gourmet dining can be had at the expensive but exquisite *Center Café*, 92 E Center St (☎259-4295); at the other end of the spectrum the old-fashioned soda fountain inside the *General Store* at 38 N Main St does good sandwiches, while *Honest Ozzie's Desert Oasis*, 60 N 100 West St (☎259-8442), is an anarchic **vegetarian** café. There's also an atmospheric if over-priced option on the highway north of town, the *Grand Old Ranch House* (☎259-5753).

Natural Bridges National Monument

One of the prettiest and least-travelled highways in southern Utah, **Hwy-95**, runs for over a hundred miles southeast from Capitol Reef, through dozens of red rock canyons and across the Dirt Devil and Colorado rivers, before topping out on the sagebrush plains of San Juan County. It's a fine drive in itself, but it also gives access to the marvellous collection of sandstone spans at **NATURAL BRIDGES NATIONAL MONUMENT**, forty miles west of US-191. Three canyons come together here, and at each junction the streams which carved them have also formed sandstone bridges, the largest of which, **Sipapu Bridge**, is 268 feet across at its base and over two hundred feet high. You can see the bridge from the nine-mile paved road which loops through the monument, or walk less than a mile down into the canyon for a closer look. **Kachina Bridge**, the next along the road, is nearly as high but twice as thick, and has

---

ADVENTURE TRAVEL OUTFITS IN SOUTHEAST UTAH

Moab is the main center for companies running **adventure trips** through the backcountry and along the raging waters of southern Utah. Varying from half-day jaunts to weeklong expeditions, such trips not only get you to places you'd never otherwise reach, but also provide a sense of the region's natural splendor that can't be had from a car or on foot.

River Rafting

Among Moab's dozen licensed operators offering motorized one-day trips along the Colorado River for around $40 are *Western River Expeditions* (☎942-6669 or 1-800/453-7450), *Adrift Adventures* (☎259-8594 or 1-800/874-4483), and *Tag-a-Long Expeditions* (☎259-8946 or 1-800/453-3292). The short trips start northwest of Moab near the butte known as Fisher Towers, and arrive near town in the afternoon; many companies give passengers the chance to float quieter stretches in two-person kayaks. **Oar-powered** trips are slower but much quieter, and less expensive than motorboat trips. Longer (2–7-day) trips head through Cataract Canyon and other wild Canyonlands spots.

Mountain Biking

The Moab area is ideally suited to mountain-bike touring. The most popular half-day route, the **Slickrock Bike Trail** starts about three miles east of Moab, following a clearly marked and very challenging ten-mile loop over the sandstone knobs with views of the La Sal mountains and the Colorado River; wear a **helmet**, take lots of **water**, and keep an eye and an ear out for motorcyclists, who are also allowed on the trail. The Slickrock Trail is too dangerous for inexperienced riders, who are recommended to explore the dirt roads leading through the redrock country of Kane Creek, west of town.

Bike shops offering daily rentals and guided tours include the *Rim Cyclery*, 94 W 100 North St (☎259-5333 or 1-800/626-7335), *Kaibab Mountain Bikes*, 37 S 100 West St (☎259-7423), and *Nichols Bike Stop* (☎259-7882 or 1-800/635-1792).

Jeep Tours

Most of the thousands of miles of **jeep trails** around Moab were built years ago by miners and haven't been maintained since. The tourist office puts out a free map and guide to some of the more popular ones, and you can rent a four-wheel-drive jeep or pickup truck from *North Main Service* (☎259-5242), at 284 N Main Street.

Guided jeep tours ($50–75 per day) are offered by *Lin Ottinger's Tours* (☎259-7312), *Canyonlands Tours* (☎259-5865 or 1-800/342-5938) and *Tag-a-Long Tours* (see above).

Scenic Flights

From a small airfield twenty miles north of Moab on US-91, *Redtail Aviation* (☎259-7421), run unforgettable flights over the Canyonlands area and beyond – a perfect opportunity to appreciate the labyrinthine complexity of the Maze, to see the confluence of the two great rivers, and even to pick out inaccessible Anasazi ruins, and well worth the $60 per person rate for a one-hour reconnaissance.

Anasazi pictographs at its base. The oldest, slimmest and most fragile of the bridges is **Owachomo**, 1.5 miles up Armstrong Canyon or along the mesa-top road; it spans 180 feet but is only nine feet thick at its thinnest point. A long and fairly strenuous eight-mile trail along the canyon bottom leads past all three bridges, as well as numerous **Anasazi dwellings**.

Admission to the monument is $4 per vehicle. The **visitor center** (daily 8am–4.30pm), four miles off Hwy-95, has free trail guides and a slide show explaining how the bridges are formed, as well as a brief introduction to the Anasazi sites. **Camping** is allowed only in the small campground near the visitor center, which has the only drinkable water in the monument.

Blanding, Monticello and Grand Gulch

Due east from Natural Bridges forty miles along Hwy-95, solidly Mormon **BLANDING** offers little to the traveller apart from **Edge of the Cedars State Park**, a mile west. A small group of ruins, including a ceremonial kiva, has been restored, but surrounded as they are by suburban tract houses they're not exactly atmospheric. Inside the modern museum (daily 9am–5pm; $1) are dozens of carefully executed replicas of the Glen Canyon **Anasazi pictographs** now buried under Lake Powell.

The smaller town of **MONTICELLO**, 21 miles north of Blanding on US-191 near the turn-off for The Needles section of Canyonlands National Park (see p.731), makes a better base. Its strip of budget **motels** includes *Canyonlands Motor Inn* at 197 N Main St (☎587-2266; ②) and *Navajo Trail* at 240 N Main St (☎587-2251; ②).

Good large standard **meals** can be had at the *Juniper Tree*, 133 E Central Ave (☎587-2870), and *The Chuck Wagon* café at 296 N Main St (☎587-2803) is open all day. There's also a **movie theater** at 696 E Hwy-666 (☎587-2535), and a 24-hour *Trailside* gas-station-cum-general-store, at 251 N Main St. As the seat of San Juan County, Monticello is the best place to pick up information on the region: among the plentiful material at the **visitor center** around the side of City Hall, 117 S Main St (☎587-2231) is information on the many "undiscovered" Anasazi sites scattered through the region.

If you are interested in Anasazi culture, and want to experience it as closely as possible in its unreconstructed state, head to the **Grand Gulch Primitive Area**, which stretches for some fifty miles to the south of Natural Bridges Monument. The sharply twisting and, despite the ugly name, in places astoundingly beautiful canyon drops down to the San Juan River, and its sheer walls shelter dozens of undisturbed Anasazi cliff dwellings and hundreds of intriguing pictographs. Coyotes, mule deer, ringtailed cats and even a few mountain lions still roam the area. The Kane Gulch ranger station, five miles south of Hwy-95 along Hwy-261, marks the main trailhead; sign in here before heading off to explore, and don't disturb anything you come across. **Dark Canyon**, to the north of Natural Bridges, has yet more sites and is even less visited than Grand Gulch. (See the box on p.675 for more about the Anasazi.)

Mexican Hat, Bluff and the San Juan River

From Natural Bridges and the Grand Gulch area, Hwy-261 runs south for some 25 miles before coming to what looks like a dead end at the edge of Cedar Mesa. From here, high above the eerie sandstone towers of the **Valley of the Gods** (where much of *Thelma and Louise* was filmed) the road turns to gravel before dropping over a thousand feet in little over two twisting hairpin-turning miles down what's called the "**Moqui Dugway**". Six miles from the foot of the switchbacks, the barely marked Hwy-316 shoots across what seems like a flat valley floor to yet another overlook, this time high above the San Juan River at the extraordinary and aptly named **Goosenecks State Park**. A textbook example of what geologists call an entrenched meander, the river, a thousand feet below, snakes around in such convoluted twists and turns that it flows six miles in total for every one mile west.

Back on Hwy-261 and just south, **MEXICAN HAT**, now a sleepy river-rafting center, was once a frenzied gold-mining camp – it takes its name from a **sandstone hoodoo**, just off the road on a dirt track overlooking the river, that looks more than a little like a south-of-the-border sombrero. It's just a cluster of buildings on the banks of the river, but it's good fun and makes a good base for visiting Monument Valley, twenty miles to the south (see p.714). The best place to **stay** is the *San Juan Inn* (☎683-2220; ③), right on the river, which has its own grocery store and trading post, plus the amiable *Olde Bridge Bar and Grill*, with cold beers and Navajo tacos. Nearby is the more basic summer-only *Canyonlands Motel* (☎683-2230; ②); *Peregrine River Outfitters* (☎683-2206) run a range of river tours.

Many of the rafts that come out of the water at Mexican Hat went in at **BLUFF**, twenty miles upstream. US-163, the road between, doesn't follow the river very closely but is still a pleasant drive, and the town itself has a number of **Mormon pioneer houses** along its back streets. Good **cafés** in Bluff include the *Sunbonnet* and the *Turquoise*, both open all day, and the *Cow Canyon Café* has delicious down-home dinners – and an enticing (and reasonably priced) resort, the *Recapture Lodge* (☎672-2281; ②), which offers nightly slide shows and informal (and informative) guided tours of the surrounding landscape. The *Kokopelli Inn* on US-191 (☎672-2322 or 1-800/541-8854; ②), is a budget alternative.

Hovenweep National Monument

In a gorgeous desert setting, at the head of a narrow stream-cut canyon in the middle of nowhere, **HOVENWEEP NATIONAL MONUMENT** consists of the evocative remains of a small but self-sustaining ancient **Anasazi community**. Hovenweep is related to the bigger and better-known cities at Mesa Verde and Chaco Canyon, and if you've been to them you may be disappointed by the scale of things here; on the other hand, the integrity of the remains here afford a glimpse of Anasazi culture unavailable elsewhere. The one unique feature of Hovenweep is its series of **towers**, built of stone along the canyon rims and under the cliffs; there are also numerous kivas and pit houses and some rock art panels.

Getting out here to the Utah–Colorado border takes some doing. The best route takes Hwy-262 east from US-191, midway between Bluff and Blanding; others come in from the north, and from Cortez, Colorado (which involves several miles of driving on unpaved roads). All the routes converge at the small **visitor center**, where rangers grow corn and other foodstuffs favored by the ancients in the adjacent garden.

A half-mile loop, detailed in the **trail guide** (35¢), starts nearby at the grandly named **Hovenweep Castle**, erected some eight hundred years ago at the edge of a tree-shaded canyon. Continuing around the canyon head, the trail drops down to **Square Tower Ruin**, near the base of which a small spring was the only water source for the entire three-hundred-strong community. Opposite, the remains can be seen of the multistorey **Talus Pueblo** that used to reach up to Hovenweep Castle on the rim above; the rocky ruin has not been excavated, and it is important that you do not climb on it. The trail climbs back up to the top a hundred feet to the right, from where another trail leads through the sagebrush, cliff rose and junipers along the rim to **Tower Point**. Here another tower overlooks a fine view of two canyons, the desert plain, and the distant Ute Mountains.

Another, slightly longer but worthwhile walk from the visitor center – one mile total – heads west into **Little Ruin Canyon**, passing some (much vandalized) Anasazi granaries and a **petroglyph** panel depicting snakes and birds, directly beneath Tower Point. On the south side of the canyon, you can climb up to **Twin Towers**, then work your way back to the north rim to examine the fortress-like **Stronghold House**, which was once the top of a series of structures stepping down to the canyon floor. The last of the ruins on this trail is the exceptionally well-built **Unit-type House**, inside which the Anasazi used niches in the walls to observe the sun at summer and winter solstices.

Suggestions that Hovenweep had some special astronomical significance seem more plausible once you've spent the night in the small **campground** here; the beautifully clear **night sky** displays more stars than you ever saw in your life.

Lake Powell and Glen Canyon National Recreation Area

Sadly but surely, the mighty rivers and canyons of southern Utah come to an abrupt and ignoble end at the Arizona border, where the **Glen Canyon Dam** stops them dead in the stagnant waters of **LAKE POWELL**. Ironically, the lake is named for John Wesley Powell, the first white man to explore the canyonlands in depth, and the first of any color to run the Colorado River through the Grand Canyon. The roaring torrents with which he battled are now forever lost beneath these placid blue waters, and the blocked-up Colorado, Green, Dirty Devil, San Juan and Escalante rivers are now a playground for houseboaters and water-skiers. The construction of the dam in the early 1960s outraged **environmentalists** – Edward Abbey's *Monkey Wrench Gang* made their first big splash here, sabotaging bulldozers and simulating huge cracks in the dam at the opening ceremonies – and **anthropologists** – innumerable Anasazi pictographs are submerged hundreds of feet below the surface. It has created one of the most peculiar – and utterly unnatural – landscapes imaginable, the deep and tranquil lake a surreal contrast with the surrounding dry slickrock and sandstone buttes.

Lake Powell has 1960 miles of shoreline, which is more than the entire Pacific coast of the US, and 96 water-filled side canyons. The water level fluctuates considerably, so for much of the time the rocks to all sides are bleached for many feet above the current waterline, with a dirty-bath tidemark sullying the golden sandstone. Most of the many summer visitors bring their own boats, or rent a vessel from one of the three marinas that fringe the lake.

If you're passing through, by far the most accessible stop is **Wahweap Marina**, just off US-89 on the way between Zion and the Grand Canyon, where the *Wahweap Lodge*, owned and operated by *ARA Leisure Services* (☎602/269-9408 or 1-800/528-6154; ④), has comfortable lakeside rooms and some of the best food within a day's drive.The same company arranges **houseboat rental** from Wahweap or other Lake Powell mari-

---

RAINBOW BRIDGE

The spectacular **Rainbow Bridge National Monument**, the world's largest natural bridge, lies about fifty miles by water from Wahweap, Bullfrog, or Halls Crossing, and can also be reached on foot or horseback across (very) rough canyon country from the Navajo Reservation (hiking permits must be obtained from the Navajo Tribe).

Guided boat tours from Wahweap (daily, 7.30am & 1pm; $50) are the easiest way to see Lake Powell's many landmarks – Gunsight Butte, Castle Rock, the Navajo Generating Station – and tour guides will point out which TV commercials were filmed where. Rainbow Bridge itself lies a mile or two down a side canyon, which narrows and winds until petering out at a jetty floating in a morass of pond scum. From there a ten-minute walk leads to the astonishing giant sandstone gateway, springing up nearly 300 feet from just above the waterline, with Navajo Mountain visible through its magnificent smooth curve. Its upper section is composed of Navajo sandstone, while the base belongs to the harder Kayenta formation, not as easily cut by flowing water; despite the increase in tourism since the creation of the lake, it remains an inspiring sight, and a place of especial importance to the Navajo.

nas; boats sleep four persons (or more) and cost from $450 for three nights in winter, $700 in summer. There's **camping** on the shore of the lake at each of the marinas.

Lake Powell can also be seen from the **ferry** ($9 per car) which links Hwy-276 between Halls Crossing and Bullfrog marinas two-thirds of the way up-lake; from here the Burr Trail heads across the Waterpocket Fold to the town of Boulder (see p.729).

Self-guided tours of the **Glen Canyon Dam** start from the **visitor center** (daily 9am–4pm) and climb down to the huge 1.1 million kilowatt hydroelectric turbines. For the first eleven miles south, the Colorado River flows smoothly through Marble Canyon, lined with sandy beaches and wildflowers and home to blue heron and golden eagles. Half-day rafting trips as far as Lee's Ferry provide an easy taster; if you keep going, the rapids begin and there's no way out before the Grand Canyon.

The nearest budget accommodation to Lake Powell is across the Arizona border in **PAGE**, where you'll find gas stations, motels, and cafés as well as banks with ATMs. You can continue on from here into the Navajo and Hopi lands of northeast Arizona.

Northern Utah

Compared to the scenic splendor of the southern half of the state, northern Utah holds little to interest the tourist, although Salt Lake City, the capital, is by far the state's largest and most cosmopolitan urban center. The **northeast corner** has coal mines, old railroad towns and, along the Wyoming border, the **Uinta Mountains**, uncrossed by road and showing hardly a sign of civilization. From the **northwest**, the harshly alkaline Great Basin plain stretches uneventfully west across Nevada to California.

Salt Lake City

Disarmingly pleasant and easy-going, **SALT LAKE CITY** is well worth a stopover of a couple of days, but not perhaps a thrilling destination in itself. Its setting is, however, superb, towered over by the **Wasatch Front**, which marks the dividing line between the comparatively lush eastern and the bone-dry western halves of northern Utah, and offers great hiking or cycling in summer and fall and, in winter, some of the world's best skiing. People elsewhere in the US tend to imagine Salt Lake City as one step away from *The Stepford Wives* in terms of spontaneous public fun, and they're not far wrong. There is a fundamental lack of things to do, in the way of museums or other cultural diversions, but if you're willing to switch gears and slow down, its unhurried pace, and the lack of pretence and the positive energy of its people, can make for a surprisingly enjoyable experience.

Arrival, Getting Around and Information

Salt Lake City is very much at the center of Utah's transportation networks, with long-distance **buses** (160 W South Temple Blvd; ☎355-4684) and **trains** (400 W South Temple Blvd; ☎364-8562), arriving downtown, while the state's main **airport** is just four miles west. From there, *Super Express* shuttles (☎250-4600) provide a 24-hour door-to-door service, charging $9 for the first person to any downtown destination and $4 for each additional passenger; they also run to Park City and the ski resorts in winter. *Utah Transit Authority*'s local **bus** #50 serves the airport hourly; the skeletal *UTA* system also includes free journeys within a fairly restricted downtown area. For **motorists**, Salt Lake City is very straightforward to negotiate, with I-15 and I-80 traversing downtown and extraordinarily plentiful parking on the sweeping one-way principal boulevards.

This sprawling, mostly low-rise city incorporates a number of outlying communities like Provo, Bountiful, and Ogden, but most of what there is to see is concentrated in the walkable compact downtown area. *Gray Line* (☎521-7060) and *Scenic West Tours* (☎572-2717) both offer a wide range of guided **bus tours**, from half- and full-day jaunts around the city to multiday trips to the various national parks. To reach the best parts of the surrounding mountains, however, you'll need a car, or a cycle and strong legs; **bikes** can be rented from *Wasatch Touring*, 702 E 100 South St (☎359-9631).

Visitor centers supplying comprehensive information on the city itself can be found downtown at 180 S West Temple Blvd (daily 9am–5.30pm; ☎521-2868) or in Terminal 2 of the airport (daily 9am–10pm). For details on the rest of Utah, stop by the *Utah Travel Council* office, across from the capitol (summer Mon–Fri 8am–7pm, Sat 9am–4pm, Sun 1–4pm; otherwise Mon–Fri 8am–5pm, Sat 9am–4pm; ☎538-1030). The main **post office** is at 250 W 200 South St (Mon–Fri 8am–5.30pm, Sat 8am–1.30pm; ☎532-5902; zip code 84101).

Temple Square and Downtown Salt Lake City

The geographical – and spiritual – heart of Salt Lake City is **Temple Square**, the world headquarters of the **Mormon Church** (or Church of Christ of Latter Day Saints – LDS) and the only real public space in the whole city. Of its two **visitor centers**, north and south, the north has video introductions to Mormon belief – *Christ in America*, for example, explains how Jesus preached to the native Americans after His resurrection – while the smaller south one displays replicas of the golden plates from which Joseph Smith transcribed the Book of Mormon. LDS literature is available at both places, though they encourage you to allow missionaries to hand-deliver it to your home; dozens of smiling young Mormon missionaries are in constant attendance.

The architectural and religious focus here is the monumental **Temple** itself, completed in 1893 after forty years of intensive labor. The multispired granite edifice rises to 210 feet above the city – it's not the tallest building on the mainly flat skyline but, thanks to its crisply angular silhouette, it's just about the only interesting one. Only confirmed Mormons may enter the Temple, and even they do so only for the most sacred LDS rituals – marriage, baptisms and "sealing", the joining of a family unit for eternity. Across the plaza from the Temple stands the odd oblong shell of the **Tabernacle**, concert hall and home to the world-renowned **Mormon Tabernacle Choir**. Guests are welcome at the 9.30am Sunday broadcast, and you can also attend rehearsals on Thursday evenings at 8pm; the marvellous organ is played at 2pm on Sundays, and for the rest of the week at noon daily. All events on Temple Square are free.

A block east of Temple Square along South Temple Street, the **Beehive House** is a plain white Puritan-style house with wraparound verandahs and green shutters. Erected in 1854 by church leader **Brigham Young**, it's now a small museum of pioneer life, restored to the style of the period. Free twenty-minute tours, which you have to join to see much of the house, are given at least every half-hour.

Just over West Temple Street from Temple Square is the one place you might actually plan to spend some time. The **Family History Library** (Mon 7.30am–6pm, Tues–Fri 7.30am–10pm, Sat 7.30am–5pm; free) was set up by the LDS church so that its members could trace their ancestors and then baptize them into the Mormon faith by proxy, but it's open to all faiths. Without rival the most exhaustive genealogical library in the world, the library is housed in an attractive modern building and is surprisingly user-friendly, giving immediate access, through CD discs and banks of computers, to the birth and death records of over fifty countries dating back in many cases more than five hundred years. All you need is a person's name and place of birth, a few approximate dates and you're away; out of respect for the personal privacy of those still living, most of the information pertains to centuries prior to our own. Volunteers will help you if you need it, but leave you alone until you ask. Next door to the library, there's a free **Museum of Church History and Art** (Mon–Fri 9am–9pm, Sat & Sun 10am–7pm).

The area southwest of Temple Square is undergoing a rapid transformation, with a massive new "Salt Palace" convention center and sports arena (home of the Utah Jazz basketball team). The surrounding district of brick warehouses around the Union Pacific railway tracks is quickly filling up with designer shops and art galleries, signs that even Mormons can be yuppies. Further west, the "other side of the tracks" around the I-15 freeway, however, remains one of the city's most run-down and forgotten areas, the last resort of transient winos and Utah's growing homeless population.

Capitol Hill

Looking at the layout of Salt Lake City, you'd think that the Mormons would have located their Temple on the gentle hill above today's Temple Square. They chose not to, however, and when Utah became a state in 1896 the prominent site was adopted by the new state government. Considering the longstanding mutual distrust between the Mormon Church and the US government – in the 1870s and earlier the US Army was often on the verge of attacking the Mormons – the fact that the state government overlooks the Mormon headquarters shows how willing Mormon leaders were to accommodate US demands; they also dropped polygamy from the official church practices.

The grandly domed and imposing **Utah state capitol**, modelled as ever upon the US Capitol, is as much worth a visit as any of Salt Lake City's other buildings. Along with all the plaques and monuments you might expect to find, the corridors of power are packed full of earnest and rather diverting exhibits of great Utah moments: the basement area in particular is packed with anomalous historical what-nots, ranging from mining dioramas to the *Mormon Meteor*, the 18-cylinder, 750-horsepower car in which Ab Jenkins raced across the Bonneville Salt Flats in the 1950s (see p.743).

Now called **Capitol Hill**, the neighborhood around the capitol holds some of Salt Lake City's finest turn-of-the-century homes, with dozens of ornate Victorian houses lining Main Street and Quince Street to the northwest; walking tour maps of the district are available from the *Utah Heritage Foundation*, 355 Quince Street. Directly opposite the front of the capitol stands another architectural landmark, **Council Hall**, the old Territorial Legislature building that was dismantled and rebuilt here in the 1960s. The main chamber off the entrance has been restored to its period appearance, and the rest of the building now houses the *Utah Travel Council* (see p.740).

Accommodation

Salt Lake City has a good **hostel** and a number of cheap **motels**, most of which are walkably close to the downtown center, as well as some rather more luxurious hotels and **B&B** inns offering the usual homespun charm.

Avenues Youth Hostel, 107 F St (☎363-8137). Clean, standard rooms, five blocks east of Temple Square, with dorm beds for $13. ①.

Best Western Olympus, 161 W 600 South St (☎521-7373). Good-value mountain-view rooms downtown, convenient for *Amtrak* and interstates. ④.

Brigham Street Inn, 1135 E South Temple Blvd (☎364-4461). Luxurious, peaceful – and rather inconspicuous – B&B a few blocks east of downtown towards the mountains. ⑤.

Colonial Village Motel, 1530 S Main St (☎486-8171). Basic motel, well out from the center. ①.

Doubletree Inn, 215 W South Temple Blvd (☎531-7500). Plush modern hotel, with indoor pool, in Salt Palace complex. ④.

Motel 6, 176 W 600 South St (☎531-1252). Standard rooms, near *Amtrak*. ②.

Peery Hotel, 110 W 300 South St (☎521-4300 or ☎1-800/331-0073). Refurbished 1910 downtown landmark. ④.

Pinecrest Bed and Breakfast Inn, 6211 Emigration Canyon Rd (☎583-6663). Top-quality accommodation in six-acre pine forest, high above the city, with massive breakfasts. ⑥.

Saltair Bed and Breakfast Inn, 164 S 900 East St (☎533-8184 or 1-800/733-8184). Utah's oldest B&B, housed in landmark historic home. ③.

Shilo Inn, 206 S West Temple Blvd (☎521-9500). Clean modern rooms in downtown tower, with pool, sauna and gym. ④.

Travelodge-Temple Square, 144 West North Temple Blvd (☎533-8200). Most central and least expensive of three local *Travelodges*. ③.

Quality Inn-City Center, 154 W 600 South St (☎521-2930). Spacious, recently remodelled downtown motel, with swimming pool. ③.

Eating

Eating out in all-American Salt Lake City is not the most exciting event, but food is generally good value. A few comparatively stylish spots cater to upmarket professional types, but by and large places are unpretentious and family-orientated.

Asakusha Sushi, 321 S Main St (☎364-7142). Central Japanese dining, tasty if rather upmarket, with American and Japanese-style formal seating and a sushi bar.

Bill and Nada's Café, 479 S 600 East (☎359-6984). All-American 1940s diner, open 24hr. Great for breakfast, but worth a visit anytime for its ace jukebox, the best west of Memphis – packed with Hank Williams, Patsy Cline, blues and bebop tracks.

Café Pierpoint, 122 W Pierpoint Ave (☎364-1222). Large downtown Mexican restaurant, with top-quality *ceviche* and gourmet dishes as well as the usual standards, all competitively priced.

Lamb's Restaurant, 169 S Main St (☎364-7166). Great breakfasts, best eaten at the long shiny counter, and excellent-value set meals throughout the day in Utah's oldest restaurant.

Market Street Grill, 48 Post Office Place (☎322-4668). The nearest Salt Lake City comes to a New York City bar and grill, serving up steaks and fresh fish dishes in the main room and all sorts of drinks in the adjoining *Oyster Bar*. Full meals from $12–25.

Rio Grande, 270 S Rio Grande (☎364-3302). Spirited and stylish Mexican cantina housed in the old Denver and Rio Grande railroad station, still used by *Amtrak*, three blocks west of downtown.

Ruth's Diner, 2100 Emigration Canyon Rd (☎582-5807). Good-value indoor and patio dining, often accompanied by live music, set in and around old railroad carriages in the mountains just three miles east of town. Wide selection of fresh dishes, great salads and Utah's best breakfasts.

Santa Fe Restaurant, 2100 Emigration Canyon Rd (☎582-5888). Sophisticated upmarket sister restaurant to *Ruth's* (above). Eclectic menu of the best of Southwest cuisine as well as brilliantly presented grilled meats and fish, and an excellent $9.95 Sunday brunch.

Star of India, 171 E 200 South St (☎363-7555). Good basic curries in no-frills downtown locale.

Drinking and Nightlife

Salt Lake City doesn't roll up the pavements after the sun goes down, despite the bizarre (if slowly liberalizing) prohibitions on alcohol. Many drinking venues are technically private clubs, in which a nominal membership fee entitles the cardholder and up to five guests to two weeks' use of the facilities. To find out about the surprisingly broad range of fringe art, music and clubland happenings, pick up either the Mormon-controlled *Deseret News* or the comparatively liberal, non-LDS *Salt Lake Tribune*. If you're going to spend more than a day here, you'll have a better time if you head first to the *Cosmic Aeroplane* bookstore at 258 E 100 South St, and pick up free papers like the fortnightly *The Event* or the monthly *Catalyst*; or tune to community radio station KRCL 91FM .

The Bar and Grill, 60 E 800 South St (☎533-0340). Prime venue for alternative and local bands.

Bar X, 155 E 200 South St (☎532-9114). Lively downtown bar packed with urban cowgirls and pool sharks.

The Bay, 404 S West Temple Blvd (☎363-2623). No booze, no smoking, but lots of young bodies grooving on the three-level dance floors.

Java Jive, 2132 South Highland Drive (☎486-8066). Jazz and acoustic music in coffeehouse atmosphere.

Squatters Pub, 147 W 300 South St (☎363-2739). Casual, friendly brew-pub with a range of beers available until midnight every day.

Club Zephyr, 301 S West Temple Blvd (☎355-5646). Salt Lake's premier live venue, with semi-famous names most nights. Upmarket clientele, elegant decor, cover $5–15.

Park City

Despite Brigham Young's strictures against prospecting for precious metals – he feared a Gentile "Gold Rush" – the first mining camp at **PARK CITY**, just thirty miles east of downtown Salt Lake City along I-80 through the mountains, was established in the late 1860s. In 1872 George Hearst laid the foundations of the Hearst media empire by paying $27,000 for a claim which became the Ontario Silver Mine, worth $50 million. These days Park City, together with adjoining Deer Valley, is Utah's largest **ski area**, with the season usually running from mid-November to mid-April. Daily lift passes are $40; equipment rental outlets include *Park City Sport* (☎1-800/523-3922) and *Gart Brothers* (☎1-800/284-4754). *Lewis Bros Stages* (☎649-2256 or 1-800/826-5844) run scheduled shuttles from downtown Salt Lake City ($7) and the airport ($14), and mountain bikes can be rented from *White Pine Touring*, 363 Main St (daily 10am–7pm; ☎649-8710).

Though surrounded by an ever-growing sprawl of new condos, factory outlets and other developments, Park City's restored Main Street still holds much of the flavor of a mountain mining community, albeit now lined with shops and restaurants. The **visitor center** at 528 Main St (May & Oct daily noon–5pm, otherwise Mon–Sat 10am–7pm, Sun noon–6pm; ☎649-6104) doubles as an enjoyable museum of town history, and stands above Park City's original jailhouse.

Accommodation rates double in the ski season; the CVB can provide full listings of resorts and other lodging (☎1-800/453-1360). The *Old Miners' Lodge*, right next to the ski lift at 615 Woodside Ave (☎645-8068 or 1-800/648-8068; summer ③, winter ⑤) is an 1893 lodge restored as a comfortable B&B; the smaller *Chateau Apres*, 1299 Norfolk Ave (☎649-9372; summer ②, winter ③), is a bit more homely. *Evening Star Dining*, 268 Main St (☎649-5686), serves good breakfasts and has some vegetarian entrées on its wide-ranging dinner menu. The *Wasatch Brew Pub* nearby at 250 Main St (☎645-9500) is open until midnight daily.

The Great Salt Lake

The sole point of interest in the barren desert west of Salt Lake City, the **GREAT SALT LAKE** is the last remnant of a 20,000-square-mile inland sea that once stretched into Idaho and Nevada. Its contents have evaporated to such an extent that it's now the second-saltiest body of water in the world, so thick with various minerals as to be all but lifeless – though you can float in it if you don't mind getting coated. Years ago the lake's shores were lined with extravagant resorts, and its waters crossed by steamboats and pleasure cruisers; **Saltair**, the largest of the resorts, burned down in 1970 after years of disuse, but a small replica stands just off I-80 in Great Salt Lake State Park.

Those areas of the ancient sea that now lie west of the lake towards Nevada are used by the US military as a **bombing range** – this is where the flight crews of the *Enola Gay* trained before dropping the A-bomb on Hiroshima – and by thrill-seekers who come together here at the **Bonneville Salt Flats** every August to attempt to set world speed records: rocket-powered cars have raced across the desert at well over 600mph.

On the north side of the lake, the **Golden Spike National Historic Site** commemorates the place where the first transcontinental railroad linked the east and west coasts in 1869. Two competing companies, the *Central Pacific* from Sacramento, California, and the *Union Pacific* out of Omaha, Nebraska, raced across the country laying track in order to win massive US government subsidies; so great was their greed that they completed (and got paid for) over 200 miles of redundant parallel track across the Utah desert before Congress got wise and demanded they join the two lines at Promontory Point. The original junction was bypassed in 1904, and the tracks removed in 1942, so there's not much to see; a well-signposted **visitor center** (daily 8am–6pm; $3), 29 miles west of I-15 via Hwy-83, has some good exhibits and the two original locomotives.

Into the Mountains: Timpanogos Cave and the Alpine Loop

For **hiking information** on the countryside around Salt Lake City, call in at the Salt Lake Ranger District office of the US Forest Service, 6944 S 3000 East St (☎524-5042) at the mouth of Big Cottonwood Canyon. Numerous canyon roads – **Emigration Canyon** (Hwy-65), **Big Cottonwood Canyon** (Hwy-190) and **Little Cottonwood Canyon** (Hwy-210), to name a few – head up from Salt Lake City into the foothills of the **Wasatch Front**. All are beautifully scenic, but perhaps the best way to get a feel for the bountiful wilderness that borders the city is to take the so-called **Alpine Scenic Loop Byway** (Hwy-92), which starts twenty miles south of downtown Salt Lake off I-15.

From I-15, Hwy-92 follows the American Fork River east into the Uinta **National Forest**, reaching **Timpanogos Cave National Monument** ten miles on. Dependent on weather conditions, the cave is normally open, for ranger-guided tours only, between mid-May and September ($5; tickets sold daily 7am–4.30pm between Memorial Day and Labor Day, otherwise 8am–2.30pm; advance reservations highly recommended, call ☎756-5238). The hour-long underground tours start at the mouth of the caves, a moderately steep 1.5-mile hike up from the visitor center; allow three hours in total for the round trip, and be warned that with demand so high, especially on weekends, you may have to wait for up to three hours even before being allowed to set off up the trail. Once underground, the most spectacular of the vast array of dazzling white crystalline formations are the contorted shapes in the Chimes Chamber in the very heart of the mountain; be sure to bring a sweater or jacket, because the temperature is rarely above 50°F.

From here Hwy-92 climbs steeply up behind 11,750ft **Mount Timpanogos**, allowing access to miles of unspoilt **hiking country**. It then drops down from the ridge into **Provo Canyon**, home of the *Sundance* ski resort and film institute, both owned and run by actor Robert *Sundance Kid* Redford, who lives here as well.

The Alpine Loop ends up back on the flatlands 45 miles south of downtown Salt Lake at the tidy little town of **Provo**, whose main feature is **Brigham Young University**, the Mormon-dominated college that has great sports teams – basketball and football especially – and such a squeaky-clean student body you'll feel like you stepped straight back into the Eisenhower years. Grab a bite to eat on campus, or in the town at *Clair's Café*, 154 University Ave (☎373-4077), which has soups, sandwiches and good burgers for fair prices. Provo also has a few inexpensive and moderately priced **motels**.

Northeast Utah

Most of Utah's northeastern corner – due east of Salt Lake City, as Wyoming takes a bite out of its otherwise perfect rectangle – is taken up by the forbidding **Uinta Mountains**, very much of a piece with the rest of the Rockies. However, to the east of the mountains the terrain reverts to the classic Southwestern desert plains, with the small town of **Vernal** serving as the base for explorations of the wildernesses of **Flaming Gorge** and **Dinosaur**.

Dinosaur National Monument

Dinosaur National Monument straddles the border between Utah and Colorado in a remote area only conceivably visitable in your own vehicle. Divided into two separate sections, it was created to preserve a rock stratum in its Utah half, seven miles north of Jensen on Hwy-149 east of Vernal, which has over the years provided brontosaurus skeletons and other astonishing remains to museums around the world. Uniquely, in the **Dinosaur Quarry** building, a tilted layer of sandstone has been painstakingly exposed by paleontologists to display an incredible three-dimensional jigsaw of fossilized dinosaur bones, left in situ for imaginative visitors to piece together.

The other half of the monument is a 25-mile drive north of the fly-blown and unattractive little town of Dinosaur, Colorado, the site of the main **visitor center** (daily, summer 8am–4.30pm, shorter hours in winter). **Harpers Corner** at the end of the road provides a phenomenal view of the goosenecks of the Green and Yampa rivers, approaching their confluence at imposing **Steamboat Rock**.

Flaming Gorge

It took a major controversy in the 1950s to spare the Green and Yampa confluence from submergence by a new dam. **Flaming Gorge**, starting around 25 miles north of Vernal, was not so lucky; the damming of the Red Canyon of the Green River in 1964 has turned it into a National Recreation Area, another "splendid recreational playground" for watersports enthusiasts, anglers and hikers.

Ambivalence about its creation can't obscure its continuing beauty, which can be appreciated from various points on the loop drive which circles the canyon, calling at Green River, Wyoming, at its northern end (see p.630). The **Flaming Gorge** itself is an incandescent wall of red rock named by John Wesley Powell and best seen from the **Antelope Flat** marina-cum-campground on the eastern side. **Red Canyon visitor center** (summer daily 9.30am–5pm) to the west is another good stop, with a dramatic overlook and attractive nearby campground; the actual dam is not all that exciting.

Vernal

Although **VERNAL**, thirty miles west of the Colrado border on US-40 as it heads to Salt Lake City, is the largest community in northeast Utah, and holds a mildly diverting dinosaur museum, for most visitors it's only significant as an overnight stop. Budget **motels** lining Main Street include the *Sage* (no 54 W; 789-1442; ①), and the *Diamond Hills* (no 590 W; 789-1754; ②), both of which have their own adjacent restaurants.

NEVADA

NEVADA is without doubt the most desolate state in the US, consisting largely of endless tracts of bleak empty desert. Its flat sagebrush plains are cut intermittently by angular mountain ranges, and the utter lack of rainfall or fertile soil has ensured its maintenance as untouched wilderness. Apart from the huge acreages given over to mining and to grazing cattle and sheep, much of Nevada is under the control of the **military**, who use it to test aircraft and weapons systems, including Stealth fighters and atomic bombs. Dozens of intriguing small towns are scattered around the state, some showing signs of strong Basque influence (shepherding is big business). Many more are fairly decrepit roadside ghost towns, often little more than a petrol-station-cum-general-store, flanked by a saloon and perhaps a brothel – Nevada is the only US state not to have outlawed **prostitution**, though it is illegal in Las Vegas.

Though millions of people pass through on their way to and from California, there's only one real reason why anyone ever *visits* Nevada, and that is to **gamble**: as soon as you cross the state border, or stop in any town, you'll be attacked by a 24-hour-a-day onslaught of neon signs and gimmicky architecture, each advertising the best odds and biggest jackpots, nowhere more than in the surreal oasis of **Las Vegas**, in the southern corner of the state. Even the smaller and more down-to-earth settlements of **Reno** and **Carson City**, Nevada's capital, both revolve around the casino trade. One spinoff from the casinos' energetic pursuit of passing trade is that rooms and especially food are incredibly cheap, so if nothing else the towns make good places to break a long journey.

The **area code** for the entire state of Nevada is ☎702.

Getting Around Nevada

As there's almost nothing in Nevada outside of Las Vegas and Reno, it's hardly surprising that getting around the state's vast empty spaces is nearly impossible without a car. Las Vegas is on the *Amtrak* route between LA and Salt Lake City, and Reno on the line from San Francisco to Salt Lake City; each has its own airport, but trains and buses do not connect them with each other. About the only other scheduled transportation links Las Vegas with Death Valley and Reno with Lake Tahoe.

Las Vegas

When the bronzed visage of Engelbert Humperdinck – or whichever showbiz grizzly is gracing *Caesar's Palace* at the time – leers out from a Nevada billboard, you know you're approaching **LAS VEGAS**: a flat, sprawling, hot city that's almost entirely devoted to the worship of greed. The first hours in Las Vegas are like entering another world: one where the religion is luck, the language is money, and time is measured by revolutions of a roulette wheel. Once acclimatized, the whole spectacle can be absolutely exhilarating – assuming you haven't pinned your hopes, and your savings, on the pursuit of a fortune. Las Vegas is an unmissable destination, but one that palls for most visitors after a couple of (hectic) days.

Ironically, Nevada was the first state to outlaw **gambling**. Though it was made legal again in 1931, ostensibly to raise taxes for building schools, gaming remained fairly small scale until 1946, when mobster Bugsy Siegel opened the *Flamingo*, the first major combined casino and hotel on what's now **the Strip**. Its instant success cemented Las Vegas' links with organized crime and instigated the system of attracting people to the gaming tables with the bribe of bargain-priced beds, food, drink and entertainment, a policy that still holds today – Las Vegas is one of the **least expensive** places to sleep and eat in the US. Yet, despite the full-frontal glamor that assaults you from all corners, the enduring image is not of high-spending playboys (seldom seen away from their complimentary hotel suites and secluded tables on the Strip), but of ordinary working people standing for hours at a stretch feeding quarters from buckets into slot machines.

If, like most arrivals, you're in Las Vegas solely to gamble, there's not much to say beyond the fact that all the casinos are free, open 24 hours a day, with acres of floor space packed full of ways to lose money: **one-armed bandits**, video **poker, blackjack** (21) with lightning-fast dealers, and loads of **craps, roulette** wheels and much much more. The casinos will just love it if you've come to play a **system**; with the odds stacked against you, your best hope of a large win is to bet your entire stake on one single play, and then stop, win or lose.

In the last few years, Las Vegas has started to wean itself from a dependency on gambling; several of the newer resorts, though still featuring casinos, now compete with Orlando for the family market, and it looks as though movie-related theme parks and fun water attractions may be the wave of the future.

Away from the Strip, and possibly the lower-key downtown, the **rest of Las Vegas** needn't concern you at all. It's either given over to ordinary residential districts or to the business community – mining is the biggest industry after the gigantic tourist trade.

Arriving, Getting Around, and Information

Trains arrive in downtown Las Vegas (westbound in the morning, eastbound in the evening): the station's platform leads directly into the *Union Plaza Hotel*, 1 Main Street. The *Greyhound* terminal (☎382-2640) is at 200 S Main St downtown, and arriving buses also stop on the Strip, outside the *Stardust Hotel*, 3000 N Las Vegas Blvd. **Flights** land at **McCarran Airport**, a mile from the Strip and four from downtown. Many hotels have free buses to collect their guests, otherwise there are frequent minibuses to the Strip ($3) and downtown ($4.50); a cab will cost around $10.

Local buses (*Las Vegas Transit System*; ☎384–3540) run 24 hours per day between the Strip and downtown. The standard single fare on all buses is $1.25, or you can buy ten rides for $8. Given the comparatively small area and lack of places to go beyond the two main districts, you're unlikely to need a taxi. On Friday and Saturday nights especially, the Strip is so clogged with traffic that it's quicker to use I-15 to drive around.

For **information**, pick up the free *What's On in Las Vegas*, *Today in Las Vegas* and *LVT*, which carry details of accommodation, buffets, the latest shows, and assorted discount vouchers. There's also a **visitor center** at 3150 Paradise Rd (Mon–Fri 8am–5pm; ☎733-2323), next to the vast Convention Center, near the Strip. There can be no easier city in which to **change money**: the casinos gladly convert almost any currency, and their walls are festooned with every conceivable ATM machine.

The City

The **Strip** (the 3000 blocks of Las Vegas Blvd) provides the most familiar image of Las Vegas, all flashing neon and spectacle. Here you'll find the largest and most glamorous **casino-hotels** – complete self-contained fantasylands of high camp and genuine excitement. Huge moving walkways sweep you into the casinos, but once you're inside it can be almost impossible to find your way out; the action keeps going day and night, and in this sealed and windowless environment you rapidly lose track of which is which. Even if you do manage to get back onto the streets during the day, the scorching heat is liable to drive you straight back in again; night is the best time to venture out, when the Strip's at its brightest and gaudiest.

The best-known casino still encapsulates what Las Vegas is all about, and makes an ideal first port of call. At **Caesar's Palace**; the moving walkway delivers you past a full-sized replica of Caravaggio's *David* into a vast labyrinth of slots and green baize, where half-naked male employees strut around dressed as Roman centurions and the waitresses are made up and attired to suggest a direct descent from Cleopatra. In the extraordinary Forum of top-class restaurants and stores, the domed roof is lit to provide the illusion of a natural sky which rapidly shifts through the cycles from dawn to dusk. South of *Caesar's Palace*, the sidewalk is thronged for the hourly eruptions of the volcano outside the *Mirage*, and children admire the galleons of *Treasure Island*. The family-orientated **Circus Circus** nearby attempts to pull in the punters by having live circus acts: a trapeze artist here, a fire-eater there, usually performing above dense crowds. At the far end of the Strip, **Excalibur**, with its vast drawbridge, crenellated towers, and relentless pseudo-medieval "pageantry", is also worth experiencing, while the ersatz Polynesia of the **Tropicana** across the road, while not exactly convincing, makes a great setting for some good-quality food and drink. The **Old-Tyme Gambling Museum** (daily 9am–1pm; $1) in the **Stardust Hotel**, 3000 N Las Vegas Blvd, is a well-arranged collection detailing the intimate relationship between gambling and the American West (it was how the early pioneers passed the time, and what got quite a few of them killed), with great displays on the legendary figures of card-playing such as Wild Bill Hickok and Poker Annie – one of the few women to excel in what was a strongly male-dominated pursuit – and a mesmerizing stock of one-armed bandits.

The three miles of **Las Vegas Boulevard** between the Strip and **downtown Las Vegas** are lined by gas stations, fast-food drive-ins, and wedding chapels – getting married being simpler in Nevada than in any other state (no waiting and no blood tests; see Reno, p.751). Downtown itself is a more compact few blocks of less spectacular casinos grouped around so-called "Glitter Gulch", the neon-illuminated junction of Main and Fremont.

One haven of comparative serenity away from the casinos lies two miles east of the Strip: the **Liberace Museum** at 1775 E Tropicana Ave (Mon–Sat 10am–5pm, Sun

1–5pm; $6.50). Popularly remembered as a beaming buffoon who knocked out torpid toe-tappers, the earlier days of Liberace (he died in 1987) make for interesting study. He began his career playing piano in the rough bars of his native Milwaukee; a decade later, in the 1950s, he was being mobbed by screaming adolescents and ruthlessly hounded by the scandal-hungry press. All this is remembered by a yellowing collection of cuttings and family photos, along with the expected electric candelabra, bejewelled quail eggs with inlaid pianos, rhinestone-covered fur coats, glittering cars and more. The music, piped into the scented toilets, may not have improved with age, but the museum is a satisfying attempt to answer one of the seminal questions of our age – "how *does* a great performer top himself on stage?".

Lake Mead and the Hoover Dam

Almost as many people as go to Las Vegas visit **LAKE MEAD**, an artificial expanse of water about thirty miles southeast of the city. As with the similarly incongruous Lake Powell (see p.738) it makes a bizarre spectacle, the blue waters a vivid counterpoint to the surrounding desert, but it gets excruciatingly crowded all year round. You can sail, scuba-dive, water-ski or fish at various points along the five-hundred-mile shoreline; get the details and make bookings through any travel agent before arriving, and bear in mind that accommodation is limited to RV-dominated campgrounds.

Fifteen miles beyond Boulder City on US-93, through the rocky ridges of the Black Mountains, is the 1935 **Hoover Dam**, responsible for creating the lake in 1935. Designed to block the Colorado River and provide low-cost electricity for the cities of the Southwest, it's one of the tallest dams ever built (760ft high), composed of suffi-cient concrete to build a two-lane highway from the West Coast to New York. Informative half-hour **guided tours** (daily summer 8am–6.45pm, otherwise 9am–4.15pm; $1) descend by lift to view the dam's insides. Without your own vehicle, the only way to get to Lake Mead and the dam from Las Vegas is on one of the many daily bus tours; the *Gray Line* (☎384-1234) price of $19.50 for a five-hour tour is fairly typical.

Moving on from Las Vegas

If you're relying on **public transportation**, Las Vegas is a major connection point for **Death Valley** and the **Grand Canyon**. While there are no scheduled services, *LTR Stage Lines* (☎384-1230) run a charter bus to Death Valley; call to check on price and the current frequency of the service, which operates from September to May only.

Buses to the **Grand Canyon** run year-round courtesy of the *Nava-Hopi* line (☎774-5003), whose one daily service costs $25 one-way. That journey takes virtually the entire day, in searing desert heat, so you might consider **flying**, which offers the added bonus of aerial views of Lake Mead and the Canyon itself. *America West* (☎1-800/247-5692), *Scenic Airlines* (☎1-800/634-6801) and *Air Nevada* (☎1-800/634-6377) all operate several flights daily, with a bottom-rate one-way fare of around $50.

Las Vegas Accommodation

Although Las Vegas has some 85,000 motel and hotel rooms (most of them hitched to casinos so you never have to go outside), it's best to book **accommodation** ahead if you're on a tight budget, or arriving on Friday or Saturday – upwards of 200,000 people descend upon the city every weekend. The CVB has a reservation service on ☎1-800/332-5333.

If you're coming from anywhere else in the US, check local newspapers for advertise-ments outlining the latest Vegas accommodation bargains – virtually all hotels and motels offer discounts and food vouchers. Rooms are very inexpensive, but be sure to get the rate confirmed for the duration of your stay – that $25 room you found on Thursday may cost $100 on Friday.

AYH Youth Hostel, 1236 S Las Vegas Blvd (☎382-8119). Halfway between downtown and the Strip, charging members $9, non-members $12, with a $5 key deposit. ①.

Caesar's Palace, 3570 S Las Vegas Blvd (☎731-7110 or 1-800/634-6661). Still the showcase of the Strip hotels; see the description above. Doubles can cost well over $1000. ⑥.

California Hotel, 12 Ogden Ave (☎385-1222 or 1-800/634-6255). One of the most popular mid-range hotels in downtown Vegas – anywhere else in the world it would be considered gigantic – with a small casino and a couple of great restaurants. ③.

Circus Circus, 2880 S Las Vegas Blvd (☎734-0410 or 1-800/634-3450). Strip hotel especially popular with families, with circus acts performing live above the casino floor. ②.

Desert Inn, 3145 Las Vegas Blvd (☎733-4444 or 1-800/634-6906). Complete resort in the heart of the Trip, with one of the most prestigious entertainment line-ups. ⑤.

El Cortez Hotel, 600 E Fremont St (☎385-5200 or 1-800/634-6703). Older and smaller than most, this recently modernized downtown hotel is one of the better bargains. ①.

Excalibur, 3850 S Las Vegas Blvd (☎597-7777 or ☎1-800/937-7777). Arthurian legend built much larger than life, with drawbridges, turrets and nightly jousting matches; staff have to call guests *M'Lord* and *M'Lady*. It opened in 1990 as the largest hotel in the world, with four thousand rooms. ③.

Las Vegas Independent Hostel, 1208 S Las Vegas Blvd (☎385-9955). Cheap and cheerful hostel with bare-bones accommodation, very near the official AYH hostel. They also organize tours of the region's national parks. $10 dorms, some private rooms. ①.

Motel 6, 195 E Tropicana Ave (☎798-0728). The largest branch of this nationwide chain; just off the south end of the Strip. ②.

Nevada Palace, 5255 Boulder Hwy (☎455-8810 or 1-800/634-6283). Small quiet place east of the Strip. ②.

Riviera, 2901 S Las Vegas Blvd (☎734-5110 or 1-800/634-6753). Among the older and larger Strip hotels, with a colossal casino and lots of restaurants. ④.

Tropicana, 3801 S Las Vegas Blvd (☎739-2222 or 1-800/634-4000). The best and least posed of the Strip hotels, at least as far as non-gambling activities go, with swim-up gaming tables around the world's largest indoor–outdoor swimming pool. ③.

Eating, Drinking and Entertainment

Eating is one of the real treats of Las Vegas. All the casinos are so keen to entice visitors onto their premises – and keep them there – that they offer superb-value round-the-clock **buffets**. The process starts off with a low-priced **breakfast**, normally served from 7am until 11am, and costing as little as 99¢ – or even free with a voucher – followed by a $5 **buffet lunch**, served until about 5pm, when it mutates into **dinner** and the price rises by a couple of dollars. If possible, try to avoid eating between 6pm and 9pm, when the lines at the bigger casinos can be endless. Watch out also for special or weekly events, such as the Friday evening *Seafood Extravaganza* at *Frontier's*, 3120 S Las Vegas Blvd.

Each casino has in addition at least one top-quality conventional dining place, and though there are plenty of restaurants away from the Strip, or out in the suburbs, only a small proportion of eccentric tourists bother to venture off in search of them. **Drinks** – beer, wine, spirits and cocktails – are freely available in all the casinos to anyone gambling, and very cheap for anyone else.

Besides gambling, or just watching, the main forms of Las Vegas **entertainment** include credibility-straining "spectaculars" featuring golden-throated warblers and bad comedians, topped off with leggy dancing girls and thumping music. Show seats are $10 on average, but expect to pay (a lot) more if the likes of Frank Sinatra or Dean Martin are topping the bill. Tickets are available from the venues, or can be booked by phone. Full details of what's coming up are in the tourist magazines.

Bally's Big Kitchen, *Bally's Casino*, 3645 S Las Vegas Blvd (☎739-4930). Popularly acknowledged as the best of the buffets; a quite phenomenal spread of fresh seafood, meats and salads, for around $5. The champagne Sterling Brunch, Sun 9am–2.30pm, is magnificent.

Lombardi's, *Caesar's Palace*, 3570 S Las Vegas Blvd (☎735-4663). Patio dining in the Forum at *Caesar's Palace* – or in a secluded interior dining room. Superb, well-priced rural Italian specialties.

Marrakech, 4632 S Maryland Pkwy (☎736-7655). Moroccan delicacies, eaten with the hands while seated on pillows in an enormous mock tent, engulfed by live belly dancers. Set menu only, costing around $25.

Pasta Pirate, *California Hotel*, 12 Ogden Ave (☎385-1222). Excellent seafood and pasta, moderately priced, amid nautical bric-a-brac. The *Redwood Bar and Grill* in the same hotel is equally good for seafood, this time in a traditional English setting.

Sam's Town Uptown Buffet, 5111 Boulder Hwy (☎456-7777). One of the lesser casinos, twenty minutes east of the Strip, but definitely one of the better buffets, plus live country music and dancing with no cover charge.

Crossing Nevada

The bulk of Nevada – the largest but least populated state in the Southwest – is made up of dry, flat plains sliced by knife-edge volcanic mountain ranges. Called the **Great Basin** because its rivers and streams have no outlet to the ocean, the land here does have a certain eerie, even hypnotic, beauty. Its attractions are hard to pinpoint – a few ghost towns, many more odd places with nothing more than a gas-station-cum-general-store and post office – but there is this indefinable, very American sense of the endless frontier, of wide open space, of room to move.

The main route across Nevada, **I-80**, shoots from Salt Lake City to Reno skirting dozens of bizarrely named small towns – Winnemucca, Elko, and Battle Mountain, for example – packed with casinos, bars, brothels, motels, and little else. The other main route, **US-50**, has the reputation of being the loneliest highway in America, with the least traffic and roadside life. Older and slower than I-80, it follows much the same route as did the riders of the Pony Express in the 1860s, though many of the towns along it have faded away, and some have been entirely abandoned, leaving behind whole blocks of uninhabited buildings. US-50 passes by Nevada's sole national park, the recently established **Great Basin National Park** in the eastern mountains, before it links up with I-80 at Reno, and then cuts off to the southwest to circuit magnificent **Lake Tahoe**, covered in the California chapter on p.837. One last main route, **US-95**, links Reno and Las Vegas, passing near Death Valley (see p.790) as well as Nevada's most famous and most evocative ghost town, **Goldfield**.

Great Basin National Park

Just across the border from Utah, **GREAT BASIN NATIONAL PARK** was formed in 1986 when the Lehman Caves National Monument and the Wheeler Peak Scenic Area were amalgamated. It's a distillation of the range of scenery the Nevada desert offers, from angular peaks to high mountain meadows cut by fast-flowing streams. The **Lehman Caves** are some of the most extensive and fascinating limestone caves in the country, not as big as Carlsbad Caverns (see p.683), but if anything more densely packed with intriguing formations. Daily ninety-minute tours ($3) of the caves leave every two hours from the **visitor center** (8am–5pm), five miles west of the hamlet of **Baker** near the mouth of the caves.

From the Lehman Caves, a twelve-mile road climbs the east flank of the bald and usually snow-capped **Wheeler Peak**, and trails lead past alpine lakes and through a grove of gnarled, ancient bristlecone pines to the 13,063ft summit. Few people ever come here, but in winter the mountains and meadows make for excellent off-track cross-country skiing. The nearest real town, **ELY**, an hour's drive away, has two worthwhile museums – the entertaining **Northern Nevada Railway Museum** (daily 9am–4pm; $2) and the **County Museum** (daily 9am–3pm; free) – as well as a dozen motels (try *Motel 6*, 770 Avenue O; ☎289-6671; ②), and a handful of casinos and restaurants.

Elko

One of the few Nevada towns worth aiming for, if you're here at the right time of year, is **ELKO**, a straggling highway town a hundred miles from the Utah border. The self-proclaimed last real cow town in the West is the center of one of the largest open-range cattle-ranching regions in the US, and the fitting home of the annual **Cowboy Poetry Gathering**, held here every January. People get together in a sort of celebration of folk culture, telling stories around campfires, singing about the lonesome life on the range, and keeping alive the dying traditions and tales of the Wild West.

During the 72-hour party of the **National Basque Festival**, each Fourth of July weekend, hulking men throw huge logs at each other, amid a whole lot of carousing and downing platefuls of Basque food. The food is available year-round in restaurants like the *Nevada Dinner House*, two blocks south of the main drag at 351 Silver St (☎738-8485). *Greyhound* and *Amtrak* both stop in Elko, and there are dozens of budget motels, such as the *El Neva*, 736 Idaho St (☎738-7152; ②). Elko's **visitor center** is at 700 Moren Way (☎738-4091 or 1-800/248-3556).

Reno and Around

If you don't make it to Las Vegas, you can get a feel for the non-stop, neon-lit gambler's lifestyle by stopping in **RENO**, on I-80, very near the California border. "The biggest little city in the world", as it likes to call itself, is a somewhat downmarket version of the glitz and glamor of Vegas, with miles of gleaming slot machines and poker tables, surrounded by tacky wedding chapels and quickie divorce courts. While the town itself may not be much to look at, its setting – at the foot of the snow-capped Sierra Nevada, with the Truckee River winding through the center – is superb.

There are three things to do in Reno: gamble, get married, and get divorced. To get **married** you and your intended must be at least eighteen years of age and be able to prove it, swear that you're not already married and appear before a judge at the **Washoe County Court**, at Virginia and Court (daily 8am–midnight; ☎328-3275), to obtain a **marriage licence**, which costs $35. No waiting period or blood test is required. Civil services are performed for an additional $25, $30 during peak periods, at the **Commissioner for Civil Marriages** at 195 S Sierra St (☎328-3400). If you want something a bit more special, wedding chapels all around the city will help you tie the knot; across the street from the courthouse, the *Starlight Chapel* – "No Waiting, Just Drive In" – does the job for a bargain $35, providing a pink chintz parlor full of plastic flowers and heart-shaped seats. If it doesn't work out, you'll have to stay in Nevada for another six weeks before you can get a **divorce**.

Every half hour, free **casino tours** leave from the Town Center Mall, 100 N Sierra St (Mon–Fri 9am–1pm, Sat 9am–noon; bring proof of hotel or motel registration). These take you behind the scenes at several of the town's biggest casinos, and include gambling, food and drink credits for your subsequent use.

Practicalities

Local bus #24 makes the twenty-minute journey from Reno's Cannon International **airport** to the downtown casinos. *Greyhound* **buses** use the terminal at 155 Stevenson St (☎322-2970); *Amtrak* **trains** from Chicago stop in the center of town, on Second St.

The **visitor center**, at 275 N Virginia St (Mon–Fri 9am–4.30pm, Sat & Sun 9am–4pm; ☎1-800/FOR-RENO), should be able to help you find an inexpensive **place to stay**, though rates tend to double at weekends. All the big casinos offer accommodation – the pick of them is the *El Dorado*, at Fourth and Virginia (☎1-800/648-5966; ⑤) – while clean, safe and reliable motels include the *Gatekeeper Inn*, 221 W Fifth St (☎1-800/822-3504; ②), and the *Oxford*, 111 Lake St (☎1-800/648-3044; ②). The *El Dorado* also offers the best **buffet** in Reno, along the lines of those found in Las Vegas (see p.749); the prices at *Circus Circus*, 500 Sierra St (☎1-800/648-5010), are a little lower, but the food isn't as good.

Carson City

US-395 heads south from Reno along the jagged spires of the High Sierra past Mono Lake, Mount Whitney and Death Valley. Just thirty miles south of Reno, **CARSON CITY**, state capital of Nevada, is small by comparison but has a number of elegant buildings, some excellent historical museums and three world-weary casinos, populated mainly by old ladies armed with buckets of nickels which they pour ceaselessly into the one-armed bandits.

Carson City was named after frontier explorer Kit Carson in 1858, and is still redolent with Wild West history. A good introduction is the **Nevada State Museum** at 600 N Carson St (daily 8.30am–4.30pm; $1.50). Housed in a sandstone structure built during the Civil War as the Carson Mint, the museum covers the geology and natural history of the Great Basin desert, from prehistoric times up through the heyday of the 1860s, when the silver mines of the nearby Comstock Lode were at their peak. Amid the many guns and artefacts is the reconstructed **Ghost Town**, from which a tunnel allows entry down into a full-scale model of an **underground mine**, giving some sense of the cramped and constricted conditions in which miners worked.

Greyhound buses stop once a day in each direction between Reno and Los Angeles, at 111 E Telegraph Ave (☎882-3375). Among budget **motels** are the *Westerner* at 555 N Stewart St (☎883-6565; ②), behind the *Nugget* casino, and the *Hardman House Motor Inn* at 917 N Carson St (☎1-800/626-0793; ③). The **visitor center**, on the south side of town at 1900 S Carson St (Mon–Sat 9am–5pm; ☎882-1565 or 1-800/634-8700), can help with practical details and provide maps for self-guided architectural walking and driving **tours** of the town, taking in the State Capitol, the museums, and many of the fine 1870s Victorian wooden houses and churches on the west side.

Virginia City

Much of the wealth on which Carson City – and indeed San Francisco – was built came from the silver mines of the **Comstock Lode**, a solid seam of pure silver discovered underneath Mount Hamilton, fourteen miles east of Carson City off US-50, in 1859. Raucous **VIRGINIA CITY** grew up on the steep slopes above the mines, and a young writer named Samuel Clemens made his way west with his older brother, who'd been appointed acting Secretary to the Governor of the Nevada Territory, to see what all the fuss was about. His descriptions of the wild life of the mining camp, and of the desperately hard work men put in to get at the valuable ore, were published years later under his adopted pseudonym, **Mark Twain**. Though Twain also spent some time in the Gold Rush towns of California's Mother Lode on the other side of the Sierra – which by then were all but abandoned – his accounts of Virginia City life, collected in *Roughing It*, are a hilarious eyewitness account of the hard-drinking life of the frontier miners. There's not much to Virginia City nowadays, since all the old storefronts have been taken over by hot-dog vendors and tacky souvenir stands, but the surrounding landscape of arid mountains still feels remote and undisturbed.

CHAPTER THIRTEEN

CALIFORNIA

P ublicized and idealized all over the world, **CALIFORNIA** really does live up to the myth. More than just a terrestrial paradise of sun, sand, surf and sea, it has high mountain ranges, fast-paced glitzy cities, primeval forests and hot dry deserts. The landscape is imbued with **history**, ranging from rock carvings left by aboriginal Native Americans, to the eerie ghost towns of the **Gold Rush** pioneers.

In some ways, the West Coast is the ultimate "now" society. Anywhere so vulnerable to constant threat of the Big One – the **earthquake** that will one day drop half the state into the Pacific – is bound to have a sense of living for the moment. However, its supposed "superficiality" is largely fictitious. Though home to such reactionary figures as Ronald Reagan and Richard Nixon, it has also been the source of some of the country's most progressive **political movements**. The fierce protests of the Sixties may have died down, but California remains the heart of **liberal** America, at the forefront in issues such as environmental awareness, gay pride and social permissiveness. Economically, too, the region is crucial, whether it's in the long-established **film** industry, the recently ascendant **music** business, or even in the financial markets.

California is too large to be fully explored in a single trip, but in an area so varied it's hard to pick out specific highlights. **Los Angeles** is far and away the biggest and most stimulating city: a maddening collection of freeways, beaches, seedy suburbs, high-gloss neighborhoods and extreme lifestyles. From Los Angeles you can head south to the smaller, up-and-coming city of **San Diego**, with its broad, welcoming beaches and easy access to Mexico; or push inland to the **desert** areas. **Death Valley** is a barren and inhospitable landscape of volcanic craters and windswept sand dunes that in summer becomes the hottest place on earth.

Most people, though, follow the shoreline north up the **central coast**: a gorgeous run which takes in lively small towns like Santa Barbara and Santa Cruz. California's second city, **San Francisco**, at the top end, is about as different from LA as it's possible to get: the oldest, most European-looking city, set on a series of steep hills, its wooden houses tumbling down to water on both sides. It is also well placed for the national parks to the east, such as **Yosemite**, where waterfalls cascade into a sheer glacial valley, and **Sequoia** with its gigantic trees, as well as the ghost towns of the **Gold Country**. **North** of San Francisco the countryside becomes wilder, wetter and greener, approaching Oregon through spectacular and almost deserted volcanic tablelands.

The **climate** in **southern California** consists of endless days of summer sunshine, and warm dry nights – though **LA**'s notorious **smog** is at its worst when the tempera-

ACCOMMODATION PRICE CODES

All accommodation prices in this book have been coded using the symbols below. Note that prices are for the least expensive double rooms in each establishment. For a full explanation see p.35 in *Basics*.

①	up to $30	④	$60–80	⑦	$130–180
②	$30–45	⑤	$80–100	⑧	$180+
③	$45–60	⑥	$100–130		

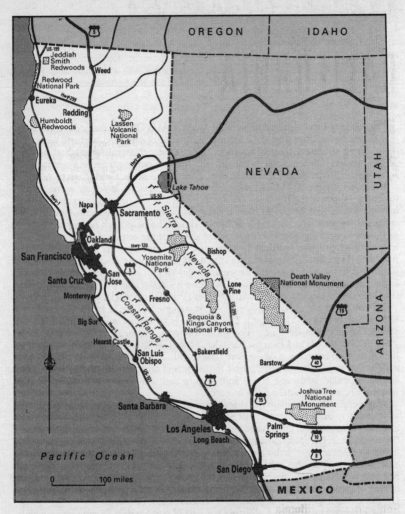

tures are highest, in August and September. All along the **coast** mornings can be hazily overcast, especially in May and June; in exposed **San Francisco** it can be chilly all year, and fog rolls in to ruin many a sunny day. In winter, it can rain for weeks on end, causing massive mudslides that wipe out roads and hillside homes. Most hiking trails in the **mountains** are blocked between November and June by the **snow** which keeps California's ski slopes among the busiest in the nation.

History
Around half a million people – almost half the population of what is now the US – were living in tribal villages along the West Coast when the Spaniard **Juan Cabrillo** first sighted San Diego harbor in 1542, and named **California** for an imaginary island (inhabited by Amazons) from a Spanish novel. **Sir Francis Drake** landed near Point

Reyes north of San Francisco in 1579, where the "white bancks and cliffes" reminded him of Dover. In 1602 **Sebastián Vizcaíno** bestowed most of the place-names that still survive; his exaggerated description of **Monterey** as a perfect harbor led later colonizers to make it the region's military and administrative center. The Spanish occupation began in earnest in 1769, combining military expediency with missionary zeal. Father **Junipero Serra** first established a small mission and *presidio* (fort) at San Diego, before arriving in June 1770 at Monterey. By 1804, a chain of 21 missions, each a long day's walk from the next along the dirt path of *El Camino Real* (The Royal Road), ran from San Diego to San Francisco. The labor of the Indian converts was co-opted; though not all the Indians gave up without a fight, disease ensured that they were soon wiped out.

When Mexico gained its independence in 1821, in theory it also acquired control over California. However, **Americans**, males without exception, were already starting to arrive, despite the immense difficulty of getting to California – three months by sea via Cape Horn, or four months overland in a covered wagon. Though the non-Indian population was a mere ten thousand in 1846, the growing belief that it was the **Manifest Destiny** of the United States to cover the continent from coast to coast soon led to the **Mexican–American War**. Virtually all the fighting took place in Texas; Monterey was captured by the US Navy without a shot being fired, and by January 1847, the Americans controlled the entire West Coast. In 1850, California became the 31st US state.

By chance, a mere nine days before the signing of the treaty that ended the war, flakes of **gold** were discovered in the Sierra Nevada. Prospectors flooded in, in the most madcap migration in history; it took just fifteen years to pick the gold fields clean. The completion of the **transcontinental railroad**, built using Chinese laborers, in 1869, was a major turning point. The crossing from New York now took just five days, and a railroad rate war brought fares down to as little as $1 for a one-way ticket.

California was perceived as immune to the worst effects of the **Great Depression** of the 1930s – thanks in part to the images of prosperity promulgated by its now-established **film industry**. From the Dust Bowl Midwest, entire families of "**Okies**" packed up everything they owned and set off for the farms of the Central Valley. Heavy industry came during **World War II**, in the form of shipyards and airplane factories, and many workers and military personnel stayed on.

As home to the **Beats** in the Fifties and the **Hippies** in the Sixties, and a host of radical political and ecological movements besides, California was at the cutting edge of cultural change. The illusions of the Flower Power days were shattered by Charles Manson, however, and once the anti-war struggle was over, popular culture seemed to withdraw into self-satisfaction. The easy-money boom of the Eighties in turn has now crash-landed in a tangled mess of scandal, and for California the Nineties have kicked off with a stagnant property market, rising unemployment, escalating gang violence and racial tensions in LA, and an appalling death toll from AIDS in San Francisco.

Getting Around California

If you want to explore and enjoy California to the full, you'll be glad of a **car**. A city such as Los Angeles couldn't exist without the automobile, and to drive down the coastal freeways invites irresistible mental images of Beach-Boys-style cruising.

Frequent *Amtrak* **trains** connect **LA** and **San Diego**, with a stop at Fullerton for buses to Disneyland, and one daily service runs up the coast from LA, calling at **Oakland**, the nearest station to San Francisco, and continuing via Sacramento to Seattle. Another line from Oakland runs along the Central Valley, but only connects with LA by bus. **Cross-country** routes leave LA for Florida (via Phoenix, Houston, and New Orleans), and for Chicago (two daily via Flagstaff and Albuquerque, one via Las Vegas, Salt Lake City and Denver). Oakland has its own direct service to Chicago. Foreign visitors can cut fares greatly by using the **Far West Rail Pass** (see p.25). *Greyhound* and *Green Tortoise* (see p.24) **buses** link all the main cities.

For quick hops between the major cities – especially LA and San Francisco – you can't beat **flying**. Services are extremely frequent, and prices competitive – if your plans are flexible enough to take advantage of off-peak deals. Regular scheduled fares are high.

If you plan to do any **long-distance cycling**, cycling from north to south can make all the difference – the wind blows this way in the summer. Be careful if you cycle along Hwy-1 on the coast: it has heavy traffic, tight curves, and is prone to fog.

San Diego

Free from smog and jungle-like freeways, **SAN DIEGO**, set around a gracefully curving bay, represents the acceptable face of southern California. The second biggest city in California may be healthy, affluent and conservative, but it's also amiable, easy-going and far from smug. Though it was the site of the first mission in California, the city only really took off with the arrival of the Santa Fe Railroad in the 1880s, and in terms of trade and significance it has long played second fiddle to Los Angeles. However, during World War II the US Navy made it their Pacific Command Center, and the military continues to dominate the local economy, along now with tourism.

Arrival and Information

Both **trains** and **buses** leave you in the heart of downtown San Diego: *Greyhound* (☎239-9171) at Broadway and First Ave is even more central then *Amtrak*'s Santa Fe Depot. Lindbergh Field **airport** is only two miles out, on bus #2 ($1.50).

Getting around without a car, by day at least, is easy. Seven companies operate an integrated **bus** system; the *Transit Store*, 449 Broadway (Mon–Sat 8.30am–5.30pm; ☎234-1060), has detailed timetables and sells passes. The tram-like **San Diego Trolley** covers the sixteen miles from the Santa Fe Depot to the Mexican border crossing at San Ysidro ($1.75; every 15min). The last trolley back from San Ysidro leaves at 1am, facilitating evenings out south of the border. **Bicycle** rental shops include *Hillcrest Bike Shop*, 141 W Washington St, Hillcrest (☎296-0618).

The **visitor center** is downtown at F St and First Ave (daily 8.30am–5pm; ☎236-1212), and the main **post office** is at 2535 Midway Drive, between downtown and Mission Beach (Mon–Fri 8.30am–5pm, Sat 8.30am–4.40pm; ☎293-5410; zip code 92138).

The City

There's no pressure in San Diego to do anything other than enjoy yourself. The work-hard play-hard ethic may be prevalent, but the accent is strongly on the second part of the equation. Indeed, the city, with its easily managed central area, scenic bay, 42 miles of beaches, and plentiful parks and museums, is hard not to like from the moment you arrive.

Downtown San Diego

Always vibrant and active, **downtown** San Diego is much the best place to start exploring. Since the late 1970s, several blocks of Twenties architecture have been stylishly renovated, while the sleek modern bank buildings symbolize the city's growing economic significance on the Pacific Rim. Downtown is safe by day, but it can be unwelcoming at night, and you should confine your after-dark visits to the restaurants and clubs of the comparatively well-lit and well-policed Gaslamp District.

The area code for San Diego and around is ☎619.

The tall Moorish archways of the **Santa Fe Railroad Depot**, at the western end of **Broadway**, built in 1915, still evoke a sense of grandeur. Broadway slices through the middle of downtown, at its most hectic between Fourth and Fifth avenues. Shoppers, sailors, yuppies, and street bums linger around the fountains outside **Horton Plaza** (Mon–Fri 10am–9pm, Sat 10am–8pm, Sun 11am–6pm), San Diego's major upmarket shopping place. Head for the open-air eating places on its top level; the food may be more expensive than in the streets, but it's fun to sit over a coffee and watch the parade go by. Few of the stores are worth much more than a browse, but don't miss the 21ft-tall **Jessop Clock**, on level one, made for the California State Fair of 1907.

South of Broadway, the sixteen-block **Gaslamp District**, the heart of frontier San Diego, is now filled with smart streets lined with classy cafés, antique stores, art galleries – and gas lamps (albeit powered by electricity). A tad artificial it may be, but its late-nineteenth-century buildings can be intriguing to explore. One of the finest interiors in the city is in *Johnny M's 801*, a seafood restaurant at 801 Fourth Ave. Diners stuff themselves with crabs' legs beneath an epic stained glass dome and above a stunning tiled floor. Also worth a peek is the **Horton Grand** hotel (see p.759), painstakingly rebuilt in Victorian style with original artefacts from one of the raunchiest hotels in the country.

The **Embarcadero**, beyond the Convention Center, leads to the **Maritime Museum** (daily 9am–6pm; $5), where the most interesting of three vintage sailing craft is the *Star of India*, built in 1863 and now the world's oldest still-afloat merchant ship.

Balboa Park and San Diego Zoo

Sumptuous **BALBOA PARK** contains one of the largest groups of **museums** in the US. Yet its real charm is simply itself: its trees, gardens, traffic-free promenades – and a thumping concentration of Spanish colonial-style buildings. Within easy reach of downtown by **buses** #7, #16 or #25, the park is large but fairly easy to **get around** on foot – if you tire, there's a free tram. The $13 **Balboa Park Passport**, which allows admission to any four of the museums, is available from the clearly signposted **information center** (9.30am–4pm; ☎239-0512) inside the House of Hospitality. Most of the museums are closed on Mondays; and almost all are free on the first Tuesday of each month.

The high quality of the **Timkin Art Gallery** (Tues–Sat 10am–4.30pm, Sun 1.30–4.30pm; free), which has impressive works by Rembrandt and El Greco and a stirring collection of Russian icons, makes its stifling formality worth enduring. By contrast, the **San Diego Museum of Art** (Tues–Sun 10am–4.30pm; $5) has few individually striking items, but among its solid stock of European paintings are some exquisitely crafted pieces from China and Japan. Outside, don't miss the free **Sculpture Court and Garden**, with formidable works by Henry Moore and Alexander Calder. The **Museum of Man** (daily 10am–4.30pm; $4), which straddles El Prado, veers from banal crafts demonstrations to excellent Native American displays.

In the much-hyped **Reuben H Fleet Space Theater and Science Center** (daily 9.30am–9.30pm; theater $3.50; science center $2.50), close to the Park Blvd end of El Prado, the child-oriented exhibits are pretty lame, but the Space Theater's dome-shaped tilting screen and 152 loudspeakers can take you on stomach-churning trips into volcanoes, over waterfalls, even through outer space. Across the plaza, the **Natural History Museum** (daily 10am–4.30pm; $5) has a great collection of fossils and pulls no punches in its coverage of threatened species of wildlife. Just behind, in the **Spanish Village Arts and Crafts Center** (daily 11am–4pm; free), some 42 craftspeople practice skills such as painting, sculpture, photography, pottery and glass-working.

The enormous **San Diego Zoo** (daily March–Oct 9am–5pm, otherwise 9am–4pm), immediately north of the main museums, is one of the world's best. Its wide selection of animals – among them rare Chinese pheasants, Mhorr gazelles, and a freak-of-nature two-headed corn snake – are restrained in "psychological cages", without bars. Basic **admission** is $12; a *Deluxe Tour* ticket ($15) includes a bus tour.

Old Town San Diego

In 1769, Spanish settlers chose Presidio Hill as the site of the first of California's missions. They soon began to build homes at the foot of the hill, which was dominated in turn by Mexican officials and then early arrivals from the eastern US. **OLD TOWN SAN DIEGO** is now a state historical park holding a number of original adobe dwellings, plus the inevitable souvenir shops. The stores and restaurants stay open until 10pm or later, but the **best time** to be around is during the afternoon, to enter the more interesting of the adobes on the daily **free walking tour** (2pm). Details can be had from the **visitor center** on San Diego Ave (daily 10am–6pm).

The Spanish-style building now atop Presidio Hill is only a rough approximation of the original mission – moved in 1774 – but its **Junípero Serra Museum** (Tues–Sat 10am–4.30pm, Sun noon–4.30pm; $3) is an intriguing examination of the man who led the Spanish colonization of California. The **Mission Basilica San Diego de Alcalá** itself was relocated six miles north to 10818 San Diego Mission Rd (daily 9am–5pm; $1), to be near a water source and fertile soils – and to be safer from attack by Indians. The present building (on bus #43 from downtown) is still a working parish church, a peaceful complex that gives welcome respite from the nearby freeways. The mood is perhaps enhanced by its general decay. Walk through the dark and echoey church to the garden, where two small crosses mark the graves of Indian neophytes, making this California's oldest cemetery. A small **museum** holds craft objects and historical articles from the mission, including the crucifix held by Junípero Serra at his death in 1834. Despite accusations that the missionary campaign was one of kidnapping, forced baptisms, and virtual slavery, Serra was beatified in 1988, the Pope declaring him a "shining example of Christian virtue and the missionary spirit".

Hillcrest and Mission Bay

North of downtown and on the northwest edge of Balboa Park, **HILLCREST** is an increasingly lively and artsy area at the center of the city's **gay community**. Go there either for something to eat – there's a selection of interesting cafés and restaurants – or simply to stroll around the fine gathering of Victorian homes.

Heading west, you come to **MISSION BAY** and San Diego's most popular tourist attraction. Exhibits and timetabled events at **Sea World** (daily 9am–dusk; $25.95) range from "performances" by killer whales and dolphins, to the eerie sight of the heads of hundreds of moray eels protruding from the hollow rocks of the "Forbidden Reef". All manner of sharks circle menacingly in the Shark House; the Penguin Exhibit is a mock Antarctica, in which hundreds of birds noisily jump around on ice and dive into the water, where they're visible through glass.

Anyone of a nervous disposition, or lacking a physique appropriate to bathing apparel, might find **MISSION BEACH**, just west, too hot to handle. On the other hand, the raver-packed sands, scantily clad torsos, and surfboard-clutching hunks may be precisely what you've come to the West Coast for. Despite first impressions, the city authorities are endeavoring to limit its anarchic hedonism – more families are using the area, but little impact has been made on the beach's freewheeling character.

Point Loma

The **Cabrillo National Monument** at the southern extremity of the hilly and very green peninsula of **POINT LOMA** was where Cabrillo and crew became the first whites to land in California. That's as far as the historical interest goes, for they quickly reboarded their vessel and sailed away. The startling views from this high spot, however, across San Diego Bay to the downtown skyline and right along the coast to Mexico, easily repay the journey here. A mile or two from the monument, a platform makes it easy to view the November-to-March **whale migration**, when scores of gray whales pass by on their way to their breeding grounds off Baja California, Mexico.

Accommodation

Accommodation is plentiful throughout San Diego, at prices to suit all pockets. The best-placed **campground** is *Campland on the Bay*, 2211 Pacific Beach Drive (☎1-800/BAY FUN), linked to downtown by bus #30.

Armed Services YMCA, 500 W Broadway (☎232-1133). Well-equipped budget option between *Amtrak* and *Greyhound*. Dorms for *IYHA* members for $10, also private singles and doubles. ①/②.

Balboa Park Inn, 3402 Park Blvd (☎298-0823). Sizeable gay-oriented B&B inn, in Hillcrest within walking distance of Balboa Park and its museums. ④.

Churchill's Hotel, 827 C St (☎234-5186). Bizarre downtown attempt to recreate a European castle, complete with turrets and moat. ②.

Downtown Inn, 600 G St (☎238-4100). Pleasant modern hotel, with cooking facilities and refrigerators in each room. ②.

Horton Grand, 311 Island Ave (☎1-800/542-1886). Classy modernized century-old hostelry, where the staff dress in Victorian costume. ⑥.

The Maryland Hotel, 630 F St (☎239-9243). Amenable restored hotel, if somewhat lacking in frills, in a good downtown location. ②.

Ocean Villa Motel, 5142 W Point Loma Blvd (☎224-3481). Usefully placed for the sands, with ocean-view rooms. ②.

Point Loma AYH Hostel, 3790 Udal St (☎223-4778). Friendly hostel, six miles from downtown on bus #35 but ideal for the beach. Dorm beds; members $12, others $15. ①.

YWCA, 1012 C St (☎239-0355). Atmospheric Twenties structure with women-only accommodation, in small dorms ($9 plus key deposit) or tidy private rooms. ①/②.

Eating

Wherever you are in San Diego, you'll have few problems finding somewhere to **eat** that offers good food and good value. Everything from crusty coffeeshops to stylish ethnic restaurants are in copious supply, with seafood at its best around Mission Beach.

The Brigantine, 2444 San Diego Ave (☎298-9840). Sumptuous seafood in inventive styles in this award-winning, but not too expensive (especially during the 4–7pm happy hour) restaurant.

California Café, Top Floor, Horton Plaza (☎238-5440). Good California cuisine; great daily specials.

Casa de Bandini, 2660 Calhoun St (☎297-8211). Old Town Mexican lunches, in lovely landmark.

Ichibin, 1449 University Ave (☎299-7203). Few better places exist to enjoy quality Japanese cuisine.

Kung Food, 2949 Fifth Ave (☎298-7302). Succulent vegetarian food, in non-smoking environment.

The Red Onion, 3125 Ocean Front Walk (☎488-9040). Beside the beachside boardwalk, with a riotous atmosphere as huge helpings of Mexican food are washed down with killer margaritas.

Stefano's, 3671 Fifth Ave (☎296-0975). Finely prepared meals, a relaxing atmosphere and decent prices, makes this Hillcrest's top place for Italian food.

Thai Chada, 142 University Ave (☎297-9548). Exquisite gourmet Thai dishes at modest cost, with heaps of care lavished on both food and service.

Nightlife

Though San Diego's money is lavished on classical music and opera, the crowds flock to beachside discos and boozy music venues. It may be narrow in scope, but there is at least plenty going on. For full listings, pick up the free *San Diego Reader*. Most bars and all clubs are very strict about insisting on a signed photo ID.

Blind Melons, 710 Garnet Ave, Pacific Beach (☎483-7844). Earthy, live blues every night.

Bodie's, 528 F St (☎236-8988). Rowdy bar with rock, blues and R&B combos nightly.

Club West Coast, 2028 Hancock St (☎295-3724). Popular gay disco: loud sounds, blinding lights.

Shadows, 4046 30th St (☎563-9051). Enjoyable neighborhood gay and lesbian bar.

Spirit, 1130 Buenos Ave, Mission Bay (☎276-3993). Glam, metal, thrash and grunge bands all get a look-in at this long-running alternative venue. Open every night.

TIJUANA: A TASTE OF MEXICO

You could hardly find a more intriguing day trip out from San Diego than **Tijuana**, just over the border in Mexico. Tijuana may not be the most interesting place in Mexico, but twenty million people every year cross here from the US. Most of them are Californians on day-long shopping expeditions, seeking a change from the local mall. And they find it: blankets, pottery, cigarettes, tequila, dentistry or car repair – everything is lower-priced in Tijuana than in the US, and all of it is hawked with enthusiasm.

Although you can't help but be made aware of the vast economic gulf separating the two countries – you're immediately confronted by beggars crouched in corners and dirty children scuffling for change – Tijuana is, in fact, one of the wealthiest Mexican cities. Things are much safer these days than a decade or so ago, when it really was a rough border town. The main streets and shopping areas are a mile or so from the border in downtown, where the major thoroughfare is Avenida Revolución. Stroll up and down for a while to get the mood and then retire to one of the many bars and watch the throng in the company of a sizeable margarita. At night, the action mostly consists of inebriated North American youths dancing themselves silly in flashy discos.

Heavy traffic, and insurance problems, make crossing into Mexico **by car** a bad idea; from San Diego you can take either the Trolley (p.756) or bus #932. **Border formalities** are minimal: you only need a Mexican Tourist Card (free from consulates in the US or at the border) if you go further into the country. Returning to the US, however, even within a day, immigration procedures are stringent. **Hotels** are cheap, with many low-cost lodgings close to the center. *Hotel del Mar*, Calle 5a 1939 (☎853023), and *Hotel San Jorge*, Avenida Constitución 506 (☎858540), both cost $15 for a double. The comparatively opulent *Hotel Nelson*, Avenida Revolución 503 (☎854303), charges $22 for a basic room. Dollars are accepted as readily as pesos, so there's no need to **change money**.

The Anza-Borrego Desert

Most of eastern San Diego County, which otherwise consists largely of sleepy suburban communities, is taken up by the 600,000-acre **ANZA-BORREGO DESERT**. Some of it can be covered by car, although four-wheel-drive vehicles are necessary for the more obscure – and most interesting – routes. The best **time to come** is in winter, when daytime temperatures stay around the mid-eighties. In the fiercely hot summer, the place is best left to the lizards, but when the desert **blooms**, between March and May, scarlet octillo, orange poppies, white lilies, purple verbena, and other wildflowers make a memorable – and fragrant – sight.

Historical reminders in the desert span Indian tribes, the first white trailfinders and Gold Rush times. In the west, Scissors Crossing, the junction of Hwy-78 and Hwy-2, was once on the **Butterfield Stage Route**, the first regular line of communication between the East and the newly settled West, which began service in 1857. **Box Canyon** is a passage carved through the rock by the Mormons in 1847. Some miles further on, the old adobe rest stop of **Vallecito Stage Station** gives a good indication of the privations of early desert travel. To the south, around Imperial Valley in the least-visited portion of Anza-Borrego, there's a vivid and spectacular clash as grey rock rises from the edges of the red desert floor. Hwy-22 leads east from Borrego Springs past a memorial to Peg Leg Smith, an infamous local spinner of yarns from the Gold Rush days who is celebrated by the **Peg Leg Liars Contest** on the first Saturday in April; anybody can get up before the judges and fib their hearts out.

For details on the many campgrounds in the park, call in at the **visitor center** at 200 Palm Canyon Drive (June–Sept weekends and holidays 10am–3pm, rest of the year daily 9am–5pm; ☎767-5311), a mile or so west of Borrego Springs, the only sizeable town. **Hotels** here tend to be pretty expensive; only *Oasis* at 366 W Palm Drive (☎767-5409; ③) is at all affordable.

LOS ANGELES

The rambling metropolis of **LOS ANGELES** sprawls across a thousand square miles of a great desert basin, knitted together by an intricate network of high-speed freeways between the ocean and the snow-capped mountains. Its colorful melange of shopping malls, palm trees and swimming pools is at once bafflingly strange and startlingly familiar, thanks to the celluloid self-image that it has spread all over the world.

LA is a very young city; just over a century ago, it was a bicultural community of white American immigrants and wealthy Mexican ranchers, with a population of less than fifty thousand. Only on completion of the transcontinental railroads in the 1880s did it really begin to grow. The old ranches were subdivided, and the enduring symbol of the city became the family-sized suburban house (with a swimming pool and two-car garage), set amidst the orange groves in a glorious land of sunshine. The real boom came after World War II in the mushrooming of the aeronautics industry – which, until the recent post-Cold War military cutbacks, accounted for one in four jobs.

The first-time visitor may well find Los Angeles thrilling and threatening in equal proportions; it's a place that picks you up and sweeps you along whether you want it to or not. Sure, it has its fine-art museums and so on, but what people really come here for is to experience the city that has come to epitomize the American Dream – most obviously in the fantasy worlds of **Disneyland** and **Hollywood**, but also in the half-flaunted and half-concealed opulence of **Beverly Hills** and **Malibu**.

Arrival and Information

All roads in southern California seem to lead to LA; plenty of travellers who try to avoid the city end up here anyway. Although LA is capable of bewildering people who've lived in it for years, it's really not *that* intimidating – just don't panic.

By Plane

All European and many domestic **flights** use Los Angeles International Airport – always known as **LAX** – sixteen miles southwest of downtown (☎310/646-5252). Free 24-hour **shuttle buses** (line "C") connect with the LAX Transit Center at Vicksburg Ave and 96th St, where you can pick up **local buses**. Minibuses such as *Airport Shuttle* (☎971-8265), *SuperShuttle* (☎1-800/325-3948) and *Coast Shuttle* (☎310/417-3988) run all over town, delivering you to your door. Fares are generally around $15 (plus tip), with a journey time of between 30 and 45 minutes. **Taxis** from the airport are always expensive: around $25 to downtown, $30 to Hollywood and as much as $70 to Disneyland.

If you're arriving from elsewhere in the US, or Mexico, you might just land at one of the **other airports** in the LA area – at Burbank, Long Beach, Ontario or Newport Beach. RTD buses (☎626-4455) serve them all – see p.764.

By Bus or Train

The main **Greyhound** bus terminal, at 1716 E Seventh St, is in a seedy section of downtown; access is restricted to ticket holders and it's safe enough inside. LA's **other Greyhound stations** handle fewer services: 1409 Vine St, in Hollywood; 645 E Walnut St, Pasadena; 1433 Fifth St, Santa Monica; and 1711 S Manchester Blvd, Anaheim.

Arriving in LA by **train** you'll be greeted with the expansive architecture of Union Station, 800 N Alameda St (☎624-0171), on the north side of downtown.

Information

LA has a number of **visitor centers**. The downtown one is at 695 S Figueroa St (Mon-Fri 8am–5pm, Sat 8.30am–5pm; ☎689-8822); others, all open normal weekday working hours, are in Santa Monica at 1400 Ocean Blvd (☎310/393-7593) and opposite

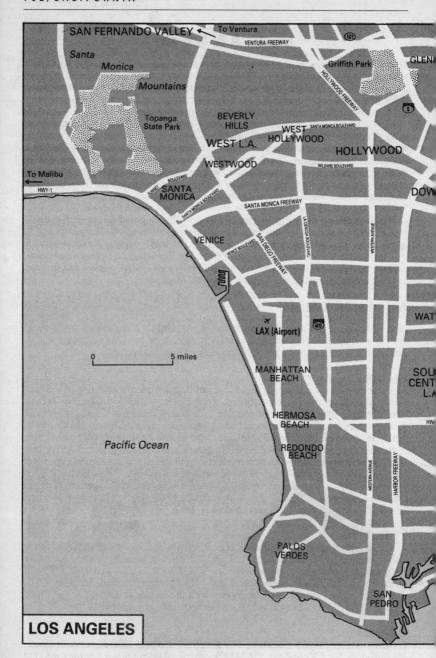

LOS ANGELES

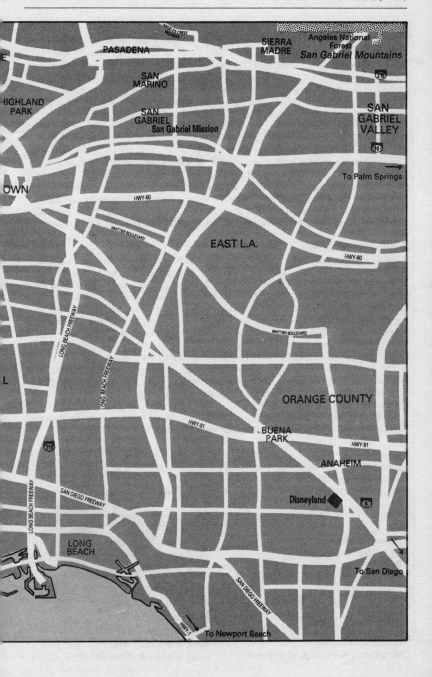

Unless otherwise specified, all LA **telephone numbers** have the area code ☎213.

Disneyland at 800 W Katella Ave (☎714/999-8999). All supply free local **maps**, but you'd do better to spend $1.75 on *Gousha Publications*'s fully indexed *Los Angeles and Hollywood Street Map*, available from machines in visitor centers and hotel lobbies.

For general delivery/poste restante, use the main downtown **post office** at 900 N Alameda (Mon–Fri 8am–3pm; zip code 90086; ☎617-4543), next to Union Station.

Getting Around the City

The sheer scale of LA – its detractors call it "nineteen suburbs in search of a city" – means that it really *is* difficult to **get around** without a **car**. Even though the traffic is often bumper-to-bumper, the freeways are the only way to cover long distances quickly – so if you're not driving yourself, express buses are much the fastest alternative.

Some people are surprised to find sidewalks in LA, let alone pedestrians, but within districts such as downtown or central Hollywood, **walking** is the best way to explore.

Public Transportation

Public transportation in LA is mainly limited to **buses**, mostly run by the *Southern California Rapid Transit District* – **RTD**. For information, phone ☎626-4455 (6am–11.30pm), or call in (Mon–Fri only) at 419 S Main St, 515 S Flower St (level B of Arco Plaza), or 6249 Hollywood Blvd. Buses on the major arteries between downtown and the coast run roughly every fifteen minutes between 5am and 2am; other routes, and the **all-night services** along the major thoroughfares, are less frequent. The standard **single fare** is $1.10; **transfers** cost 25¢ more; **express buses**, and any others using a freeway, are 35¢ extra. A **Monthly Pass** costs $42, or slightly more to include express buses. **Downtown DASH** buses also ply two downtown routes (Mon–Sat; 25¢).

The underground **Metrorail** train system won't be fully operational until the next millenium, but the **Blue Line**, between downtown and Long Beach, and the **Red Line** from downtown west to MacArthur Park, are running; departures are every fifteen minutes and the one-way fare is $1.10.

Taxis don't cruise the streets: among the more reliable companies are *Independent Cab Co* (☎1-800/521-8294) and *United Independent Taxi* (☎1-800/822-TAXI).

Cycling

Cycling in LA may sound perverse, but there are beach bike paths between Santa Monica and Redondo Beach, and from Long Beach to Newport Beach. Enjoyable inland pedals explore Griffith Park, the mansions of Pasadena and along the LA River.

MAJOR LA BUS ROUTES (RTD)

From downtown to:
Santa Monica #22.
Venice #33, #333, #436 (express).
LAX #42, #439 (weekdays only), #607 (rush hours only).
Forest Lawn Cemetery #90, #91.
Exposition Park #40, #42, #81.
Huntingdon Library #79.
Burbank Studios #96.
Long Beach #60, #368, #456 (express).

San Pedro #446 (express), transfer to #146 for Catalina terminal.
Disneyland #460 (express).

To and from downtown:
Along Hollywood Blvd #1.
Along Sunset Blvd #2 .
Along Santa Monica Blvd #4 .
Along Melrose Ave #10 .
Along Wilshire Blvd #20, #21, #22.

The City

With only a finite amount of space between the desert, the mountains, and the ocean, LA has long since filled in the gaps between what were once geographically isolated and small communities. As a result, it's a massive conglomeration of interconnected and not always well-defined districts, not all of which have that much in common.

If LA has a heart, however, it's **downtown**, in the center of the basin. It offers a taste of almost everything you'll find elsewhere around the city, from avant-garde art to the abject dereliction of Skid Row, compressed into an area of small, easily walkable blocks. The area **around downtown** contains some elaborate Victorian suburbs, Twenties Art Deco buildings, and the center of LA's enormous Hispanic population.

A broad corridor runs 25 miles west from downtown to the coast. The first district you come to, **Hollywood**, has streets caked with movie legend – even if the genuine glamor is long gone. Adjoining **West LA** is home to the city's newest money, shown off in Beverly Hills and along Sunset Strip. **Santa Monica and Venice** to the west are the quintessential seafront LA of palm trees, white sands, and laid-back living, while the coastline itself stretches another twenty miles down to **Malibu**.

Suburban **Orange County**, east of the Harbor Area, holds little of interest apart from **Disneyland**. On the far side of the northern hills lie the **San Gabriel and San Fernando Valleys**, distanced from mainstream LA life socially as well as geographically, and the butt of most Angeleno hick jokes.

Downtown LA

Downtown LA embraces LA's every social, economic and ethnic division. It's not the high-rise megalopolis you might expect; only the occasional towering office block punctuates its low and level skyline. During the postwar boom, as businesses spread out across the basin, it seemed to be heading for dilapidation and decay, but a recent revitalization has given it a new life.

The whole area can easily be seen in a day on foot, aided by the odd ride on a 25¢ *DASH* bus. LA's original settlement on the **Northside** is the obvious first stop, before crossing into the brasher and more modern **Westside**, continuing through the chaos along **Broadway**.

GUIDED TOURS

As well as downtown **walking tours**, innumerable **bus tours** introduce the city – though only the "specialists" below show you anything you couldn't see more cheaply for yourself. Costs are $25–40; most will collect you from your hotel.

Walking Tours

Los Angeles Conservancy. Architecture-based downtown treks on Saturday mornings at 10am ($5; ☎623-CITY).

Mainstream Bus Tours

Casablanca Tours, *Hollywood Roosevelt*, 6362 Hollywood Blvd (☎461-0156).

Gray Line Tours and Starline Tours, *Janes House*, 6541 Hollywood Blvd (☎856-5900).

Hollywood Fantasy Tours, 1721 N Highland Ave (☎1-800/782-7287).

Specialist Tours

The California Native, 6701 W 87th Place (☎310/642-1140). One-day trip to the mountain and desert regions on the fringes of LA.

Grave Line Tours, PO Box 931694, Hollywood (☎469-4149). Daily at noon, a Cadillac hearse leaves from Hollywood Blvd and Orchid Ave, pausing at the scene of nigh-on every death, scandal, perverted sex act and drugs orgy that ever tainted Hollywood.

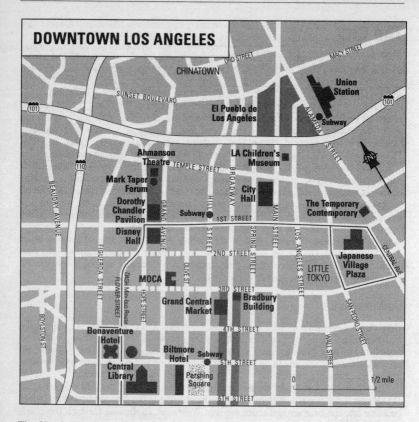

DOWNTOWN LOS ANGELES

The Northside: Olvera Street

To see downtown LA, start at the beginning. **El Pueblo de Los Angeles**, off Alameda Street, was the site of the initial late eighteenth-century Mexican settlement of Los Angeles, and a few evocative early buildings remain in situ. The **plaza church**, the city's oldest, now serves as a sanctuary for Central American refugees. **Olvera Street**, which runs north from the plaza, contrived in part as a pseudo-Mexican village market, is saved only by its lighthearted grouping of food and craft stalls.

The magnificent mission-style **Union Station** nearby is now barely used, though its projected use as a Metrorail terminal may bring back the crowds. Across the Santa Ana Freeway at the **Civic Center**, plodding office buildings surround a lifeless plaza. The one exception is the Art Deco **City Hall**; the city's tallest structure as late as 1960, it has a 360° view from its 28th-storey observation deck . On the south side of the plaza, free tours of the **Los Angeles Times** building (Mon–Fri 11am & 3pm) show how the West Coast's biggest newspaper is put together.

The Westside: Bunker Hill

Until a century ago the area south of the Civic Center, **Bunker Hill**, was LA's most elegant neighborhood, its elaborate mansions and houses connected by funicular rail-road to the growing business district down below. Now it's been subsumed into the amorphous **Financial District**, forever sprouting colossal new fifty-storey towers. The largest and most ambitious of these, the billion-dollar **California Plaza** on Grand Ave, is based around the playfully colorful **MOCA**, designed by showman architect Arata Isozaki as a "small village in the valley of the skyscrapers". The Museum of Contemporary Art (Tues, Wed, Sat & Sun 11am–6pm, Thurs & Fri 11am–8pm; $4, students $2, free Thurs 5–8pm) opened at the end of 1986, funded by a one-percent tax on all new downtown construction. In addition to work by Franz Kline, Mark Rothko, Robert Rauschenberg and Claes Oldenburg and the impressive multimedia memorials of Antoni Tapiès, it houses a compelling collection of paintings and sculpture by the rising stars you're likely to come across in trendy city galleries.

If MOCA's high-brow tone gets too demanding, there's relief in the shallow but amusing **Wells Fargo Museum** (Mon–Fri 9am–4pm; free) at the base of the shiny red towers of the *Wells Fargo Center*, telling the story of the bank of Gold Rush California.

A block away rise the unmistakable shining glass tubes of the **Westin Bonaventure Hotel**. Its lobby doubles as a shopping mall and office complex – a disorientating Escher-style labyrinth of spiralling ramps and balconies that can only be negotiated with frequent recourse to the color-coded map.

Broadway

Though it's hard to picture now, **Broadway** was once LA's most fashionable shopping and entertainment district. Today it's largely taken over by the cash-rich hustle and bustle of Hispanic clothing and jewellery stores, all to a soundtrack of blaring salsa music. Its most vivid taste is to be had amid the pickled pigs' feet and sheeps' brains inside the **Grand Central Market**, on Broadway between Third and Fourth. Right alongside, the whimsical terracotta facade of the 1918 **Million Dollar Theater** mixes buffalo heads with bald eagles. This is one of several Broadway movie palaces still in use; the **Los Angeles Theater** at 615 S Broadway is even more extravagant, built in ninety days for the world premiere of Charlie Chaplin's *City Lights* in 1931.

Around Downtown

The LA sprawl begins as soon as you leave downtown, the diverse environs of which tend to be forgotten quarters, scythed by freeways, and with large distances separating their few points of interest. They are too widely separated for it to make sense to try to see them consecutively; each is ten to thirty minutes by car or bus from the next.

MacArthur Park and Around

Reachable on the new Red Line subway, the dilapidated patches of green and large lake of **MacArthur Park** are the nearest open spaces to the sidewalks of downtown. Half a mile west, the seminal **Bullocks Wilshire** department store is the most complete example of late 1920s Art Deco in LA. Sadly, *Bullocks* was damaged in the 1992 riots and has since closed its doors.

The **Ambassador Hotel**, 3400 Wilshire Blvd, is also rough around the edges these days and perhaps scheduled for demolition. Its *Cocoanut Grove* club flourished from the Twenties to the Forties, and the large ballroom (now closed) featured in the first two versions of *A Star is Born*. The kitchen, however, was the scene of the hotel's most notorious event. **Bobby Kennedy** was fatally shot here on June 5 1968, the day of his greatest political triumph – his victory in the California Democratic Primary.

The so-called "Miracle Mile" (see p.771) continues west from the *Ambassador*. South of Wilshire, along Olympic Blvd between Vermont and Western, **KOREATOWN** is five times larger – and far more genuine and lively – than Chinatown and Little Tokyo combined.

Exposition Park

Across Exposition Boulevard from the USC campus, south of downtown, is the sizeable **Exposition Park**, one of the most appreciated parks in LA. It retains a real sense of community, bolstered by its function as favorite lunchtime picnic place. The free **California Museum of Science and Industry** here, off Figueroa St (daily 10am–5pm), contains enjoyable working models and thousands of pressable buttons – though its displays are uncritical and marred by a bizarrely sited *McDonalds* right in the middle. Just outside, the replica "classic" American diner in the **Hall of Health** (daily 10am–5pm; free) carries displays on what not to eat if you want to stay healthy.

In the neighboring **Hall of Economics and Finance** (daily 10am–5pm; free), you can wreck the American economy with the aid of a few machines. If that seems too lightweight, head for the exhibitions on the history, art and culture of America's black communities in the **California Afro-American Museum** (daily 10am–5pm; free).

The **Los Angeles County Museum of Natural History** (April to Sept Tues–Fri 10am–5pm, Sat & Sun 9am–6pm, rest of the year Tues–Sun 10am–5pm; $5, students $3.50) is the nicest building in the park, with its echoey domes and travertine columns. Its tremendous stock of dinosaur skeletons includes the skull of a Tyrannosaurus Rex, and a Diatryma – a huge flightless bird. Other displays include Mayan pyramid murals and the complete contents of a Mexican tomb (albeit a reconstruction).

South Central LA

South Central LA hardly ranks on the tourist circuit, but it's a large and integral part of the city, whatever wealthy white LA might prefer to think. The population is mostly black with a few pockets of Hispanic and Asian, joined here and there by bottom-of-the-heap, working-class whites. It doesn't look so terribly run-down at first sight, mostly made up of detached bungalows enjoying their own patch of palm-shaded lawn, but just about all its people get an abysmal deal in schooling and work, and have little chance of climbing the social ladder and escaping. If you pass through, what's most striking is the sheer monotony: every block for twenty-odd miles looks much like the last, enlivened periodically by fast-food outlets, dingy supermarkets and uninviting factory sites.

The district of **Watts** achieved notoriety as the scene of the six-day **Watts Riot** of August 1965 which left 36 dead and innumerable buildings in charred ruins, and of the 1975 gun battle which put an end to the Symbionese Liberation Army (SLA), kidnappers of publishing heiress Patti Hearst. It's also the site of the Gaudi-esque **Watts Towers**, which stand alongside railroad tracks at 1765 E 107th St (Sat & Sun 10am–4pm; $2). **Compton** too is renowned worldwide as the home of many of LA's **rappers** – NWA made their reputation with *Straight Outta Compton*. However, outsiders should not attempt to sniff out the local music scene.

THE GANGS OF LOS ANGELES

South Central LA is the heartland of LA's infamous **gangs**, said to number over seventy thousand members. The gangs have existed for forty years, but only recently, with the massive influx of drug money, has violence escalated and automatic weaponry (not least Uzi machine guns) become commonplace. Most fatalities (there are about five hundred a year) are a direct result of drug-trade rivalry, though there are also occasional "drive-by shootings", in which pedestrians are sprayed with bullets from a passing car. Recent clampdowns have made little real headway in tackling the problem.

You're unlikely to see much evidence of the gangs beyond the occasional blue or red scarf (the colors of the Crips and Bloods, the two largest gangs) tied around a street sign to denote "territory"; and fortunately there's even less chance of witnessing inter-gang warfare. As for personal danger, passing through South Central LA by car is safe during the day, but definitely not a good idea after dark.

A BRIEF HISTORY OF HOLLYWOOD

Hollywood started life as a temperance colony in 1887, intended to provide a sober God-fearing alternative to raunchy downtown LA, eight miles away by rough country road. The film industry was drawn here from the East Coast, for the guaranteed sunshine, diverse assortment of natural locations, and to dodge restrictive patent laws. The first studio opened in 1911, and within three years the place was packed with film-makers – such as Cecil B deMille who shared his barn-converted office space with a horse.

The ramshackle industry expanded fast, and eager new arrivals soon swamped the original inhabitants, outraging them with their hedonistic lifestyles. Once movie-making had proved itself to be a financially secure business – with the success of DW Griffith's *The Birth of a Nation* in 1915 – film production became highly specialized. Small companies either went bust or were incorporated into big studios. Hollywood has of course always had its creative side – such as the hard-bitten *film noir* style of the Forties – but big names, big bucks and conservatism are what have kept it alive.

Hollywood

If a single place-name encapsulates the LA dream of glamor, money and overnight success, it's **HOLLYWOOD**. Millions of tourists arrive on pilgrimages; millions more flock here in pursuit of riches and glory. Hollywood is a weird combination of insatiable optimism and total despair. It really *does* blur the edges of fact and fiction, simply because so much *seems* possible – and yet so little, for most people, actually is. Those who do strike it rich here get out as soon as they can, just as they always have; the big film companies, too, long ago relocated well away, leaving Hollywood in isolation, with prostitution, drug dealing and seedy bookstores as the reality behind the fantasy.

Central Hollywood

The myths, magic, fable and fantasy splattered throughout the few short blocks of **Central Hollywood** would put a medieval fairytale to shame. A rich sense of nostalgia pervades the area, giving it an appeal no measure of tourists or souvenir postcard stands can diminish. Although you're much more likely to find a porno theater than spot a real star, the decline which blighted Hollywood from the early Sixties is fast receding. Nevertheless the place still gets hairy after dark, with on-leave marines strutting the sidewalks and adolescents cruising Hollywood Boulevard in customized autos.

The natural place to begin exploring Hollywood Boulevard is the junction of **Hollywood and Vine** – the classic location for budding stars to be "spotted" by big-shot directors and whisked off to fame and fortune. At 6608 Hollywood Blvd, the purple and pink **Frederick's of Hollywood** has been (under-) clothing Hollywood's sex goddesses since 1947, as well as mortal bodies all over the world via mail order. Inside, the **lingerie museum** (free) displays some of the company's best corsets, bras and panties, donated by happy big-name wearers ranging from Lana Turner to Belinda Carlisle.

A little further on, the **Egyptian Theatre** (no 6708) was financed by impresario Sid Grauman, in a modest attempt to recreate the Temple of Thebes. The very first Hollywood premiere (*Robin Hood*) took place here in 1922, but sadly it's now divided into several smaller cinemas. No Hollywood visitor will want to miss the mundane yet magical foot and hand prints in the concrete concourse of the 1927 **Chinese Theatre** at 6925 Hollywood Blvd. Actress Norma Talmadge (supposedly by accident) trod in wet cement while visiting the construction site, and the practice has continued ever since, starting with Mary Pickford and Douglas Fairbanks Sr, at the opening of *King of Kings*. Through the halcyon decades, this was *the* spot for movie first-nights. As for the building, it's an odd western version of a classical Chinese Temple, replete with dodgy Chinese motifs and up-turned dragon tail flanks.

The **Roosevelt Hotel** opposite was movieland's first luxury hotel, its *Cinegrill* restaurant hosting the likes of WC Fields and F Scott Fitzgerald, not to mention hangers-on like Ronald Reagan. In 1929 the first Oscars were presented here, beginning the long tradition of Hollywood rewarding itself in the absence of honors from elsewhere.

Despite the beliefs of some of their loopiest fans, even the biggest Hollywood stars have been mortal; the many LA cemeteries which hold their tombs get at least as many visitors as the city's museums. In the southeast corner of the **Hollywood Memorial Cemetery**, near Santa Monica Blvd and Gower St, a mausoleum contains the resting place of **Rudolph Valentino**, the celebrated screen lover who died aged just 31 in 1926. To this day on each anniversary of his passing (23 August), at least one "Lady in Black" will likely be found mourning. The achingly ostentatious memorial to **Douglas Fairbanks Sr**, who with his wife Mary Pickford did much to introduce social snobbery among the movie-making people, is just outside.

Griffith Park

The gentle greenery and rugged mountain slopes making up vast **Griffith Park**, between Hollywood and the San Fernando Valley (daily 5am–10.30pm, mountain roads close at dusk; free), is a welcome escape from the mind-numbing hubbub of the city. The landmark **Observatory** (daily noon–10pm; free) here has been seen in innumerable Hollywood films, most famously *Rebel without a Cause*, and the surrounding acres add up to the largest municipal park in the country, one of the few places where LA's multitude of racial and social groups at least go through the motions of mixing fairly happily together. Above the landscaped flat sections, the hillsides are rough and wild, marked only by foot and bridle paths, leading into desolate but appealingly unspoilt terrain that gives great views over the LA basin and out to the ocean. One way to explore is on a **rented bike** from *Woody's Bicycle World*, 3157 Los Feliz Blvd (☎661-6665). The park is safe enough by day, but its reputation for after-dark violence is well founded.

The Hollywood Hills

The views from the **Hollywood Hills** take in a bizarre assortment of opulent properties. Around these canyons and slopes, which run from Hollywood itself into Benedict Canyon above Beverly Hills, mansions are so commonplace that only the half-dozen fully blown castles (at least, Hollywood-style castles) really stand out. On Mulholland Drive are Rudolph Valentino's extravagant **Falcon Lair** and Errol Flynn's **Mulholland House**; down Benedict Canyon is the former home of actress Sharon Tate, the last victim of the Manson family. Guided tours (p.765) can point out which is which, but for the most part you can't get close to the most elaborate dwellings anyway, and none is open to the public.

From more or less anywhere in Hollywood, you can see the **Hollywood Sign**, erected as a property advertisement in 1923 (when it spelt "Hollywoodland"; the "land" was removed in 1949). The sign is also famous as a suicide spot, though few have followed the 1932 example of would-be movie star Peg Entwhistle. Hers was no mean feat, the sign being as hard to reach then as it is now: from the end of Beachwood Drive she picked a path slowly upward through the thick bush, to leap to her death from the fifty-foot "H". Attempting to reach it simply isn't worth the bother.

West LA

LA's so-called "Westside" begins immediately beyond Hollywood in **WEST LA**, bordered by the foothills of the Santa Monica Mountains to the north and the Santa Monica freeway to the south. West LA is at the sharp end of all that's new and happening in the city, though tucked away behind the showcase streets, the usual long residential blocks are only marginally less drab than normal.

The LA County Museum of Art

The **Miracle Mile** which stretches from downtown along Wilshire Boulevard was the premier property development of the Thirties. Though the enormous **LA County Museum of Art** or LACMA (Tues–Fri 10am–5pm, weekends until 6pm; $5, students $3.50) is one of the least impressive of its buildings, some of the collections here are among the best in the world. Despite the loss of Armand Hammer's stock of paintings to his own museum in Westwood, it justifies a lengthy visit. The **Fearing Collection** of funereal masks and sculpted guardian figures from Pre-Columbian Mexico is highly impressive, but where the museum really excels is in its specializations, notably the **German Expressionist** prints and drawings and the scrolls and ceramics in the **Pavilion for Japanese Art**.

An astonishing assortment of bones has been recovered from the adjacent **La Brea Tar Pits**. For thousands of years animals who tried to drink from the deceptive layer of water which covers this pool of smelly and still-seeping tar have found themselves stuck fast; it is now surrounded by life-sized models of such victims as mastodons and sabre-tooth tigers. If you're interested, the site's **museum** (Tues–Sun 10am–5pm; $5, students $1.50) will tell you all you want to know.

West Hollywood

Between Fairfax Avenue and Beverly Hills, **West Hollywood** was for many years notorious for after-hours vice clubs and general debauchery. These days it's much more upmarket, home to Los Angeles' prominent – and affluent – gay community. **Melrose Avenue**, LA's trendiest shopping street, runs parallel to the main drag, Santa Monica Boulevard, looking at times like something out of a low-budget 1950s sci-fi feature. Neon and Art Deco abound among a fluorescent rash of designer and secondhand boutiques, exotic antique shops, and avant-garde galleries.

Above West Hollywood, on either side of La Cienega Boulevard, is the roughly two-mile conglomeration of restaurants, plush hotels and nightclubs on Sunset Boulevard known as **Sunset Strip**, which remains one of LA's best areas for nightlife. These establishments first appeared in the early Twenties, along what was then a dusty dirt road linking the Hollywood movie studios with the West LA "homes of the stars". With the rise of TV the Strip declined, only reviving in the Sixties when a scene developed around the landmark *Whisky-a-Go-Go* club, which featured seminal psychedelic rock bands such as Love and Buffalo Springfield.

Greta Garbo was only one of many stars to appreciate the quirky Norman castle that is the **Chateau Marmont Hotel**, towering over the east end of the Sunset Strip at no 8221. Howard Hughes used to rent the entire penthouse so he could keep an eye on the bathing beauties around the pool below, and comedian John Belushi died of a heroin overdose here, in the hotel bungalow he used as his LA home.

Beverly Hills

Though **Beverly Hills** must be one of the world's wealthiest residential areas, the money is discreet rather than vulgar, revealed more by the immaculate shops (for example the high-fashion showcase of **Rodeo Drive**) and squeaky clean streets than ostentatious displays. It's not a particularly welcoming place, especially if your clothes don't match the quietly elegant attire of the residents.

Palatial estates lie hidden behind landscaped security gates in the verdant canyons and foothills above Sunset Boulevard. **Benedict Canyon Drive** climbs past a good number, beginning with the first and most famous: the lavish **PickFair** mansion at 1143 Summit Drive, built for Mary Pickford and Douglas Fairbanks in 1919. Further up, the secret passageways and large private screening room of Harold Lloyd's **Green Acres** survive intact, although the grounds, which contained a waterfall and a nine-hole golf course, have been broken up into smaller lots.

Westwood

West LA's most energetic district, **Westwood**, owes much of its youthful vitality to its proximity to the UCLA campus. Spanish Revival **Westwood Village** has a number of interesting shops and bookstores, and is LA's prime movie-going district. Wilshire Boulevard here exploded in the 1970s with oil-rich high-rise developments; now modest detached houses sit next to twenty-storey condominium towers in which penthouse apartments with private heliports sell for upwards of $12 million. Inside one such tower, on the corner with Westwood Boulevard, is the **Armand Hammer Museum of Art and Culture Center** (Tues–Sun 10am–6pm; $4.50), amassed over seven decades by the flamboyant late boss of Occidental Petroleum. Its Rembrandts and Rubens are less than stunning, but Van Gogh's intense and radiant *Hospital at Saint Remy* is a real jewel. The museum's costliest acquisition is also its most disappointing: the *Codex Hammer*, dreary pages of ramblings about hydraulics from the notebooks of Leonardo da Vinci.

Outside the museum, behind the tiny *Avco* cinema, Hammer's marble tomb in **Westwood Memorial Park** stands near the lipstick-covered plaque that marks the resting place of **Marilyn Monroe**.

Santa Monica, Venice and Malibu

Set along an unbroken twenty-mile strand of clean, white-sand beaches, the small, self-contained communities that line the **Santa Monica Bay** feature some of the best Los Angeles has to offer, with none of the smog or searing heat that can make the rest of the metropolis unbearable. The entire area is well served by public transportation, near (but not too near) the airport, and a wide selection of accommodation makes it a good base for seeing the rest of LA.

Santa Monica

Santa Monica is the oldest and biggest of LA's resort areas, perched on palm-tree-shaded bluffs above the blue Pacific. Once a wild beachfront playground, it's now a self-consciously healthy and liberal community, home to a large expatriate British community of writers and rock stars, ranging from Rod Stewart to Johnny Rotten.

The Santa Monica beachfront grew into a giant funfair city when it was linked to downtown LA by the suburban streetcar system. It was the location for many of the underworld stories of Raymond Chandler, most memorably as "Bay City" in *Farewell My Lovely*, but today Chandler wouldn't recognize the place. The gambling ships and bathing clubs have gone, and Santa Monica is just another elegant seaside town.

Santa Monica reaches nearly three miles inland, but most things of interest are within a few blocks of the beach. The **visitor center** (daily 10am–4pm; ☎310/393-7593) in a kiosk just south of Santa Monica Boulevard, along Ocean Blvd in Palisades Park (the cypress-tree-lined strip along the top of the bluffs), makes a good first stop. Two blocks east of Ocean Blvd, the **Santa Monica Promenade**, a pedestrianized stretch popular with buskers and itinerant evangelists, is the closest LA comes to having an urban energy. On weekend nights this three-block strip hosts a pleasant *passagiata* bringing together Angelenos of all ages and accents, and it's by far the best place to come for *al fresco* dining, downing beers or simply people-watching.

The real focal point of Santa Monica life is down below, on the **beach** and around **Santa Monica pier**, which boasts a giant helter-skelter and a well-restored 1922 wooden **carousel** – featured, along with Paul Newman, in the 1973 movie *The Sting*. The grand beach houses just to the north of the pier were known as Hollywood's "Gold Coast"; the largest, now the **Sand and Sea** beach club, was built as the servants' quarters of a massive 120-room house, now demolished, that belonged to William Randolph Hearst. In the adjacent villa of MGM boss Louis B. Mayer, the Kennedy brothers were later rumored to have had liaisons with Marilyn Monroe.

Venice

Immediately south of Santa Monica, **Venice** was laid out in the marshlands of Ballona Creek in 1905 by developer Abbot Kinney as a romantic twenty-mile network of canals, lined by sham palazzos and waterfront homes. It never really caught on, and the coming of the automobile finished it off altogether. Many of the canals were filled in, and the area fell into disrepair, being taken over by oil wells. Orson Welles' film *A Touch of Evil* starred the then-derelict Venice as a seedy border town.

Kinney was, however, ahead of his time. A fair bit of the original plan survives, and the pseudo-European atmosphere has made Venice one of the coast's trendier spots. Chic cafés and restaurants abound near the beach, and a strong alternative arts scene centers on the *Beyond Baroque* bookstore in the old City Hall at 681 Venice Blvd.

The town's main artery, **Windward Avenue**, runs from the beach into what was the Grand Circle of the canal system. Its original Romanesque **arcade**, around the intersection with Pacific Avenue, is alive with health food shops, used-record stores, and roller-skate rental stands. The few remaining **canals** are just a few blocks south; some with their original quaint little bridges survive.

Venice Beach itself is the reason most people come here. Nowhere else does LA parade itself quite so openly as along the wide pathway of **Venice Boardwalk**, ever packed with jugglers, fire-eaters, roller-skating guitar players or just people-watchers. South of Windward is **Muscle Beach**, a legendary outdoor weightlifting center where serious-looking hunks of muscle pump some serious iron, and high-flying gymnasts swing on the adjacent rings and bars. Spend ten minutes watching and you'll find Narcissus is alive and well, and working on his biceps. Outlets along Washington Street near the pier – such as *Spokes'n'Stuff* (☎310/306-3332) – rent out **bikes**.

At night Venice Beach is taken over by street gangs and drug dealers. Walking on the beach after dark is illegal, and you should be very cautious in the vicinity.

The J Paul Getty Museum

Five miles along the curving Pacific Coast Highway ("PCH") from Santa Monica, a huge French chateau inadvertently marks the easily missed entrance to the **J Paul Getty Museum** at 17985 PCH (Tues–Sun 10am–5pm; free; ☎310/458-2003), a fake Roman villa poised high above the ocean. Drivers must reserve parking space in advance; otherwise take RTD bus #434 from Santa Monica, and ask the driver for a free pass.

Two years after the museum opened in 1974, oil magnate John Paul Getty died, leaving it $1.3 billion. Obliged to spend a set percentage of its endowment – $100+ million – every year, it can outbid anyone to get what it wants. Hence the inflation in international art prices – and allegations of shady behavior among the museum's suppliers.

The quality of the **exhibits** is extraordinary. A formidable array of Getty's major interest, Greek and Roman statuary, includes the only remaining work (an athlete) of Lysippos, sculptor to Alexander the Great; and a feast of ornate French furniture and decorative arts from the reign of Louis XIV, with clocks, chandeliers, tapestries and gilt-edged commodes, fills several overwhelmingly opulent rooms. Although Getty himself was much less interested in painting, a large collection has been amassed since his death, featuring all the major names from the thirteenth century to the present. Photography is represented by the works of Man Ray, Moholy-Nagy, and others.

Malibu

Malibu, at the top of the bay twenty miles north of Santa Monica, is a whole other world, its beach colony houses owned by those famous enough to need privacy and rich enough to afford it. It's not all that impressive on arrival, however, with ramshackle surf shops, fast-food stands and real estate agents scattered along PCH around the graceful **Malibu Pier**. **Surfrider Beach** here was the surfing capital of the world in the Fifties and early Sixties, seen in the *Beach Blanket Bingo* movies of

Annette Funicello and Frankie Avalon (the surf is at its best in late summer). Just beyond is **Malibu Lagoon State Park**, a nature reserve and bird refuge.

Most Malibu residences are tucked away in an insular community in the narrow canyons on the fringes of town. There's very little to see; if you must, you can enter on foot or cycle a mile or so along PCH, on the other side of the hill. You'd do better, though, to visit **Trancas Market**, near the gated entrance to the colony – good both for star-spotting and stocking up on food and drink before a day on the sands.

Much of **Malibu Creek State Park**, at the crest of Malibu Canyon Road along Mulholland Drive, used to belong to *20th Century Fox*, who filmed many Tarzan pictures here, as well as the TV show *M.A.S.H.* The four-thousand-acre park includes a large lake, some waterfalls, and nearly fifteen miles of hiking trails.

Five miles along the coast from Malibu Pier, **Zuma Beach** is the largest and most crowded of the Los Angeles County beaches. Adjacent **Point Dume State Beach**, below the bluffs, is a lot more relaxed, and the rocks at its southern tip, **Pirate's Cove**, are a good place to look out for seals and migrating gray whales in winter.

The South Bay

South of Venice and Marina del Ray, the coast is dominated by the runways of LAX and the oil refineries of El Segundo. Beyond here begins the eight-mile coastal strip of the quieter, more suburban and less pretentious South Bay beach towns: **Manhattan Beach**, **Hermosa Beach** and **Redondo Beach**. Each has a beckoning strip of white sand, and Manhattan and Hermosa especially are well equipped for surfing and beach sports. They're also well connected by regular buses to downtown LA.

Long Beach

Thanks to a billion-dollar clean-up, downtown **Long Beach** is not the seedy stamping ground of off-duty sailors that it was twenty years ago. Pine Avenue is an enjoyable stretch of restored architecture and bargain antique stores, but the only reason you're likely to consider crossing to the far side of LA's massive harbor is to see the **Queen Mary** (daily 10am–6pm; $5). The *Cunard* flagship from the Thirties until the Sixties, the

---

CATALINA ISLAND

The enticing island of **Catalina**, twenty miles offshore, has been in private ownership since 1811, when the Gabrileño Indians were forced to resettle on the mainland. It remains a wilderness, devoted to the conservation of unique species such as the Catalina shrew (so rare that it's only been sighted twice), and tourism has been held largely at bay. Hotels are unobtrusive among the whimsical architecture, and cars are a rarity; the two thousand islanders walk, ride bikes or drive electric mokes. Return **ferry** trips to Catalina run several times daily from San Pedro and Long Beach ($20–28; *Catalina Cruises*, ☎1-800/888-5939, and *Catalina Express*, ☎310/519-1212). From Newport Beach, the *Catalina Passenger Service* (☎714/673-5245) runs a $20 daily round-trip.

The island's one town, **AVALON**, can be fully explored on foot in an hour. Begin at the sumptuous Art Deco **Avalon Casino**, built in the Twenties by William Wrigley Jr (of the Chicago chewing-gum dynasty). The collections at the adjoining **museum** (daily 10.30am–4pm; $1) include Native American artefacts from Catalina's past. On the slopes above, the **Zane Grey Pueblo Hotel** is the former home of the Western author, who visited Catalina to film *The Vanishing American* and liked the place so much he never left.

The **Chamber of Commerce** (☎310/510-1520) has more detailed information of visiting Catalina; mokes and bikes can be rented from the stand on Bay Shore Drive.

Hotel **accommodation** in Avalon is much in demand, and pricey – often upwards of $80: the least expensive is usually the *Atwater* (☎1-800/4-AVALON; ③). The only budget option is the **campground** (☎310/510-0303) on the town's western fringe.

Queen Mary is now a luxury hotel, and guided tours present a sentimentalized version of its days of elegance and refinement. The huge geodesic dome nearby housed Howard Hughes's "Spruce Goose" airplane until it was sold and removed in 1992.

Anaheim: Disneyland and Around

In the early 1950s, Walt Disney conceived a theme park where his already hugely popular cartoon characters – Mickey Mouse, Donald Duck, and the rest – could come to life, to enchant children and make their Uncle Walt even richer. **ANAHEIM** was chosen as the location for **Disneyland** on the basis that these acres of orange groves, thirty miles southeast of downtown, would become LA's next focus of population growth. Which indeed happened; the whole area is now overrun with hotels and restaurants (when Disney opened his next theme park, in Florida – see p.466 – he made sure he owned all of them too), and the boom doesn't look like slowing. If you're not coming to see Disneyland, you may as well give the place a miss: it hasn't an ounce of interest in itself.

Disneyland

1313 Harbor Blvd, Anaheim. Summer daily 9am–midnight, rest of the year Mon–Fri 10am–6pm, Sat & Sun 10am–midnight. $30. 45 minutes by **car** from downtown using the Santa Ana Freeway; for further information, including public transportation details, call ☎714/999-4565.

To make the most of **DISNEYLAND** – the ultimate escapist fantasy, and the blueprint for imitations worldwide – throw yourself right into it. Don't think twice about anything and go on every ride you can. The high admission price includes them all, although during peak periods each can entail queueing for hours. Remember, too, that the emphasis is on family fun; the authorities take a dim view of anything remotely anti-social, and eject those they consider guilty.

Among the best **rides** are two in **Adventureland**: the *Pirates of the Caribbean*, a boat trip through underground caverns, singing along with drunken pirates; and the *Haunted Mansion*, a riotous "doom buggy" tour in the company of the house spooks. **Tomorrowland** is Disney's vision of the future, where the *Space Mountain* roller-coaster zips through the pitch-blackness of outer space, and Michael Jackson dances in 3-D. The *Skyway* cable cars that connect it with the clever but cloyingly sentimental **Fantasyland** are the only spot in the park from which you can see the outside world.

As for **accommodation**, try to visit Disneyland just for the day and spend the night somewhere else. Most of the hotels and motels nearby cost well in excess of $70 per night (see p.779). You're not permitted to bring your own **food** to the park; you can only consume the fast food produced on the premises.

Yorba Linda: the Richard Nixon Library and Birthplace

18001 Yorba Linda Blvd. Mon–Sat 10am–5pm, Sun 11am–5pm. $4.95. ☎714/993-3393.

Mickey Mouse may be its most famous resident, but conservative Orange County's favorite son is former president **Richard Milhous Nixon**, born in 1913 in what's now the freeway-caged **Yorba Linda**, about eight miles northeast of Disneyland. His birthplace is a shrine to a man who forged a career from lies and secrecy, and finally resigned from the world's most powerful job in total disgrace. Oversized gifts from world leaders, amusing campaign memorabilia, and a laugh-a-line collection of obsequious letters written by and to Nixon form the core of the exhibition, but his distinctive persona is best enjoyed in the constantly running archive radio and TV recordings.

Nixon's face leers down in Big Brother fashion from almost every wall, but only inside the **Presidential Auditorium** do you get the chance to ask him a question. Many possibilities spring to mind, but the choice is limited to a small pre-programmed selection. Nixon's gaunt features fill the overlarge screen and provide the stock reply – as endearingly and believably as ever.

The San Gabriel and San Fernando Valleys

The northern limit of LA is defined by two long, wide valleys lying over the hills from the central basin, starting close to one another a few miles north of downtown and spanning outwards in opposite directions – east to the deserts around Palm Springs, west to Ventura on the central coast. You wouldn't miss an awful lot by not visiting the valleys at all, but they do give a picture of life in some of LA's more downbeat suburbs.

The San Gabriel Valley

Spreading east from **Pasadena**, ten miles north of Los Angeles, the **San Gabriel Valley** was settled by farmers and cattle ranchers on the lands of the eighteenth-century Mission San Gabriel. Pasadena itself is as much the home of the grand dames of LA society as it is to the "little old lady from Pasadena" of the Beach Boys song. A luxury resort in the 1880s, it then became a fashionable residential area. Downtown is undergoing a major renovation, modern shopping centers slipping in behind Edward Hopperish 1920s facades, but the historic parts have not been forgotten. Maps and booklets are to be had from the **Convention and Visitors Bureau** at 171 S Los Robles Ave (Mon–Fri 9am–5pm, Sat 10am–4pm; ☎818/795-9311).

The **Norton Simon Museum** at 411 W Colorado Blvd (Thurs–Sun noon–6pm; $5, students $2.50) is not one of LA's better-known museums, but its collection – ranging from Dutch paintings by Rembrandt and Frans Hals to Monet's *Mouth of the Seine at Honfleur* and Picasso's extraordinary *Woman with Book* – is consistently excellent. Your ticket stub entitles you to a free print from the superb museum **bookshop**.

South of Pasadena, in the dull, upper-crust little suburb of San Marino, the **Huntington Library**, off Huntington Drive at 1151 Oxford Road (Tues–Sun 1pm–4.30pm; advance reservations are required on Sun ☎818/405-2141; free, parking $2), contains numerous manuscripts and rare books, such as a Gutenberg Bible and the **Ellesmere Chaucer**, an illuminated manuscript of *The Canterbury Tales* from c.1410. Paintings include Gainsborough's *Blue Boy* and Reynolds' *Mrs Siddons as the Tragic Muse*, and the whole ensemble is set off by acres of beautiful themed **gardens**.

The San Fernando Valley

The **San Fernando Valley**, spreading west, is *the* valley to most Angelenos: a sprawl of tract homes, mini-malls, fast-food drive-ins and auto parts stores. It has more of a middle-American feel than anywhere else in LA, inhabited – at least, in the popular LA imagination – by macho men and bimbo-esque "Valley Girls", speaking their own dialect of "Valley Talk". In the gateway town of **Glendale**, eight miles north of downtown, **Forest Lawn Cemetery** at 1712 S Glendale Ave (daily 9am–5pm; free) was immortalized with biting satire by Evelyn Waugh in *The Loved One*. Among those buried here are Errol Flynn, Walt Disney, Clara Bow, Nat King Cole, Chico Marx, Clark Gable, and Jean Harlow, in a marble-lined room paid for by her fiancé William Powell.

Burbank and the Studios

The name of Hollywood may be synonymous with the movies, but the studios themselves, if they were there at all, moved out of Tinseltown long ago; the nitty-gritty business of actually making films goes on over the hills in otherwise boring **Burbank**.

Studios offering tours include **NBC**, at 3000 W Alameda St (Mon–Sat 10am–4pm; $6) and the technically oriented **Burbank Studios** (Mon–Fri 10am–3pm; $25; ☎818/954-1744). The largest of the old backlots belongs to **Universal Studios**, whose four-hour tours (summer daily 8am–10.30pm, rest of the year Mon–Fri 10am–8pm, Sat & Sun 9.30am–8pm; $26) are more like a trip around an amusement park. You get to witness the fading miracle of the parting of the Red Sea, convincing Wild West shootouts, and the so-called Miami Vice Action Spectacular stunt show.

Los Angeles Accommodation

Finding a **place to stay** in LA is easy; finding somewhere inexpensive and well located is difficult, though not impossible. If you're not driving, choose your base carefully, to avoid lengthy cross-town journeys, or divide your stay between several **districts**. Downtown has the best assortment of budget hotels; Hollywood is more mid-range; and West LA, Santa Monica, Venice and Malibu are predominantly mid-to-upper range.

The nearest **campgrounds** to LA are along the Orange County coast.

Hostels

Hostels are dotted all over the city, though some limit stays to a few nights. Colleges and fraternity houses let out space during summer; details from UCLA's *Pan-Hellenic Sorority Council* (☎310/206-1285) or the *Inter Fraternity Council* (☎310/825-8409).

Airport Hostel, 2221 Lincoln Blvd, Venice (☎310/305-0250). Six-bed dorms, free shuttle bus to LAX. $13.50 per night, $90 per week. ①.

Banana Bungalow, 2775 Cahuenga Blvd (☎851-1129 or 1-800/446-7835). Very new and very large hostel in the Hollywood Hills. Dorms $14, more expensive private doubles. ③/③.

Fullerton Hacienda Hostel (AYH), 1700 N Harbor Blvd (☎714/738-3721). Spacious and comfortable, near Disneyland. 4pm–9.30am. *OCTD* bus #43A stops outside. Members $14, others $17. ①.

Hollywood YMCA, 1553 N Hudson Ave (☎467-4161). Close to Hollywood Blvd. Dorm beds $15 per night. No advance booking. ①.

Huntington Beach Colonial Hostel (AYH), 421 Eighth St, Huntington Beach (☎714/536-3315). Four blocks from the beach, mostly double rooms. 4.30pm–9.30am, with an 11pm curfew. Key rental $1 (plus $20 deposit). $13 per person. ①.

Jim's at the Beach, 17 Brooks Ave, Venice (☎310/399-4018). Beachside dormitory rooms on production of a passport. $15 per night; $90 per week. ①.

Los Angeles International Hostel (AYH), 3601 S Gaffey St, building #613 (☎310/831-8109). In the South bay area, overlooking the ocean. *RTD* bus #232 passes close by, or take *SuperShuttle* from LAX. Open 7–9.30am and 4pm–midnight. Members $10, others $15; private rooms $30. ①/②.

Santa Monica International Hostel, 1436 Second St, Santa Monica (☎310/392-0325). Huge new hostel in well-restored old building, a few strides from the Santa Monica sands. $15 per person. ①.

Hotels, Motels and B&Bs

There are no booking agencies, and visitor centers do not reserve accommodation, so to be sure of a **hotel** or **motel** room you should reserve direct as early as possible (and don't be afraid to haggle – LA's economic slump means it's a buyer's market).

Downtown and Around

Biltmore Hotel, 506 S Grand Ave (☎1-800/421-8000). Classical architecture combined with modern luxury to make your head swim. ⑧.

Figueroa Hotel, 939 S Figueroa St (☎1-800/421-9092). Well-placed mid-range hotel. ②.

Hotel Inter-Continenal, 251 S Olive (☎617-3300 or 1-800/327-0200). Brand-new upscale hotel atop Bunker Hill. ⑧.

Orchid Hotel, 819 S Flower St (☎624-5855). A simple walk to anywhere in downtown. Weekly rates. ②.

Park Plaza, 607 S Park View St (☎384-5281). Sumptuous lobby, ordinary rooms. ③/④.

Terrace Manor, 1353 Alvarado Terrace (☎381-1478). B&B rooms in Victorian house. ④–⑤.

Hollywood

Best Western Hollywood Motel, 6141 Franklin Ave (☎464-5181). Small and pleasant, in the heart of Hollywood. ④.

Holiday Inn Hollywood, 1755 N Highland Ave (☎1-800/465-4329). Expensive and massive, but perfectly placed. ⑤–⑥.

Hollywood Roosevelt, 7000 Hollywood Blvd (☎1-800/423-8262). The first hotel built for the movie greats, lately revamped and reeking with atmosphere – though the rooms are plain. ⑥.

Hotel Hollywood, 5825 Sunset Blvd (☎1-800/445-0021). The best at this price. ④.

West LA

Bevonshire Lodge Motel, 7575 Beverly Blvd (☎936-6154). Well-situated motel. ③.

Chateau Marmont, 8221 Sunset Blvd (☎626-1010). Former haunt of Greta Garbo et al. ⑥–⑧.

Deseret Motel, 10572 Santa Monica Blvd (☎310/474-2035). Faded and ordinary. ③.

Le Reve Hotel, 8822 Cynthia St (☎1-800/424-4443). Gay-friendly hotel a few blocks north of Santa Monica Blvd. Elegant suites in the style of a French provincial inn. ⑤–⑦.

Santa Monica, Venice and Malibu

Cadillac Hotel, 8 Dudley Ave (310/399-8876). Restored 1930s hotel right on Venice Boardwalk. ③.

Hotel Carmel, 201 Broadway (☎310/451-2469). Near Santa Monica beach. ③.

Hotel Santa Monica, 3102 Pico Blvd (☎310/450-5766 or 1-800/231-7679). Reasonable rooms a mile from the beach. ③–④.

Malibu Riviera Motel, 28920 Pacific Coast Hwy (☎310/457-9503). Just outside Malibu. ③.

Near LAX

Airport Courtesy Inn, 901 W Manchester Blvd (☎310/649-0800 or 1-800/231-2508). Free parking and LAX shuttle. ③.

Cockatoo Inn, 4334 Imperial Highway (☎1-800/262-5286). Country-style inn in a faceless suburb just a stone's throw from LAX. Complimentary breakfast. ③.

Howard Johnson, 8620 Airport Blvd (☎310/645-7700). Swimming pool, free LAX shuttle. ④.

The South Bay and Harbor Area

Friendship Inn, 50 Atlantic Ave (☎310/435-8369). A serviceable base for Long Beach. ③.

Hotel Queen Mary, Pier J, Long Beach (☎1-800/421-3732). Cramped cabins. ⑤.

Seahorse Inn, 233 N Sepulveda Blvd (1-800/854-3380). A few blocks from the sands. ③.

Around Disneyland

Apollo Inn, 1741 S West St (☎714/772-9750). Good-value hotel owned by the Stovall family. ④.

The Disneyland Hotel, 1150 W Cerritos Ave (☎714/778-6600). The price does not include admission to the park, although the Disneyland monorail does stop right outside. ⑦–⑧.

Motel 6, 921 S Beach Blvd (☎714/827-9450). The least expensive around. ③.

Place Inn, 1544 S Harbor Blvd (☎714/776-4800). Across from Disneyland. ④.

The San Gabriel and San Fernando Valleys

Belair-Bed & Breakfast, 941 N Frederic Ave (☎818/848-9227). The best value in Burbank. ②.

Econo Lodge, 1203 E Colorado Blvd, Pasadena (☎818/449-3170). Friendly budget chain. ②.

Los Angeles Eating

LA **eating** covers every extreme: whatever you want to eat and however much you want to spend, you're spoiled for choice. Try to take at least a few meals in the more exotic restaurants, if only to watch the city's many self-appointed food snobs going through their paces. If you simply want to load up quickly and inexpensively, the options are almost endless, and include free food available for the price of a drink at happy hours.

Downtown

Bella Cucina, 949 S Figueroa St (☎623-0014). Fabulous pizzas and homemade pastas, with the accent on northern and rural Italian cuisine.

Clifton's Cafeteria, 648 S Broadway (☎485-1726). A cafeteria complete with redwood trees and a waterfall; the food is inexpensive and good too.

El Cholo, 1121 S Western Ave (☎734-2773). One of LA's big first Mexican restaurants and still one of the best, despite the drunken frat-rats from USC.

Ocean Seafood, 750 N Broadway (☎687-3088). Cavernous and often crowded restaurant serving low-priced excellent food.

Shibucho, 333 S Alameda St (☎626-1184). Excellent sushi bar in the heart of Little Tokyo; if possible, go with someone who knows what to order, as no one seems to speak English.

VIP Palace, 3014 Olympic Blvd (☎388-9292). Korean restaurant, strong on spicy barbecued beef.

Hollywood

Addis Ababa, 6263 Leland Way, a block south of Sunset Blvd (☎463-9788). Unpretentious Ethiopian food, served with fresh *injera* bread.

Casita de Campo, 1920 Hyperion Ave (☎662-4255). Great Mexican food, comfortable atmosphere.

French Market Place, 7985 Santa Monica Blvd (☎654-0898). Gay-run, New Orleans-themed restaurant that's at least as much fun as Disneyland.

Gloria's Café, 3603 W Sunset Blvd (☎664-5732). Popular, gay-friendly local hang-out that's a great spot for dinner, especially Cajun food.

Hampton's, 1342 N Highland Ave (☎469-1090). Over fifty styles of gourmet hamburgers.

Musso and Frank's Grill, 6667 Hollywood Blvd (☎467-7788). Since it opened in 1919, all the Hollywood bigwigs have come here – but at $15 for bacon and eggs, you pay for the atmosphere.

Shamshiry, 5229 Hollywood Blvd (☎469-8434). The best of the Iranian restaurants that have been established in West LA since the fall of the Shah, offering kebabs, pilafs and exotic sauces.

Village Coffee Shop, 2695 Beachwood Drive (☎467-5398). A classic laid-back coffeeshop in the hills below the Hollywood sign.

Yukon Mining Co, 7328 Santa Monica Blvd (☎851-8833). Excellent coffeeshop catering to the local gay community and the neighboring senior citizens' home. Open 24 hours.

West LA

Apple Pan, 10801 W Pico Blvd (☎310/475-3585). Grab a spot at the counter and enjoy the best hamburgers in the world, and great pies. Fans of TVs *BH 90210* take note: the *Peach Pit* was shamelessly copied from this landmark restaurant.

The Authentic Café, 7605 Beverly Blvd (☎939-4626). Santa Fe-style desert food; Mexican influenced, mixed in with spicy Chinese and the obligatory designer pizzas. No booze, though.

Carnitas, 4067 Beverly Blvd (☎667-9953). Tasty Mexican food from the Yucatan Peninsula: the dishes are unmistakably inspired by Cuban and Caribbean cooking; lots of seafood, too.

Chung King, 11538 W Pico Blvd (☎310/477-4917). The best neighborhood Chinese restaurant in LA, serving spicy – and lately fashionable – Szechuan food: don't miss out on the *bum-bum* chicken.

Citrus, 6703 Melrose Ave (☎857-0034). Trendy and good upmarket restaurant, serving California cuisine in an outdoor setting indoors. Reservations are essential; lunch for two will be around $50.

Green's Soul Food, 5766 Rodeo Rd (☎295-9111). Ribs, cornbread, chitlins and black-eyed peas – Southern cooking at its best, and with a great jukebox.

The Gumbo Pot, 6333 W Third St in the farmers' market (☎933-0358). Delicious and dead-inexpensive Cajun cooking; try the *gumbo yaya* of chicken, shrimp and sausage, and the fruit-and-potato salad.

Mario's, 1001 Broxton Ave, Westwood (☎310/208-7077). Far and away the best pizza in West LA.

Ships, corner of La Cienega and Olympic Blvd (☎310/652-0401). The best food of any coffeeshop in LA; try the *Ship Shape* hamburger, on sourdough bread, with a chocolate shake. Open 24 hours.

The Source, 8301 Sunset Blvd (☎656-6388). 1970s-style healthy wholefood, right on the Sunset Strip. *Annie Hall* was filmed here.

Santa Monica, Venice and Malibu

Café Montana, 1610 Montana Ave (☎310/829-3990). Good breakfasts and excellent salads and grilled fish in this art gallery-cum-café on the newest strip of upmarket Santa Monica.

Café 50s, 838 Lincoln Blvd, Venice (☎310/399-1955). No doubts about this place: Ritchie Valens on the jukebox, burgers on the tables . . .

Chinois on Main, 2709 Main St (☎310/392-9025). LA's most popular restaurant, serving Chinese-style dishes like fresh fish in garlic and ginger. Very expensive, with lunches from $25.

Freddy's Cantina, 11520 W Pico Blvd (☎310/479-6149). Excellent and authentic Mexican food.

Inn of the Seventh Ray, 128 Old Topanga Rd, just off Topanga Canyon (☎310/455-1311). The ultimate New Age restaurant, serving vegetarian and other wholefoods. Excellent desserts, too.

Lighthouse Buffet, 201 Arizona Ave (☎310/451-2076). All-you-can-eat sushi is a long-accepted concept in LA; indulge to your heart's content for under $8 at lunchtime or $15 in the evening.

Disneyland and Around

Angelo's, 511 S State College Blvd, Anaheim (☎714/533-1401). Straight out of *Happy Days*, drive-in complete with roller-skating car-hops and, incidentally, good burgers. Open until 2am on weekends.

Knott's Berry Farm, 8039 Beach Blvd, Buena Park (☎714/827-1776). Famous for delicious fried chicken long before Disneyland was around – and a fully fledged theme park in its own right.

The San Gabriel and San Fernando Valleys

Casa de Oriente, 2000 W Main St, Alhambra (☎818/282-8833). Dim sum at its best: pork baos, potstickers and dumplings, and delicious sweets.

Dr Hogly-Wogly's Tyler Texas Bar-B-Q, 8136 Sepulveda Blvd, Van Nuys (☎818/780-6701). Queue up for the chicken, sausages, ribs and beans, some of the best in LA.

Merida, 20 E Colorado Blvd, Pasadena (☎818/792-7371). Unusual Mexican restaurant, featuring dishes from the Yucatan Peninsula; try the spicy pork wrapped up and steamed in banana leaves.

Gen Mai-Sushi, 4454 Van Nuys Blvd (☎818/986-7060). Japanese-style vegetarian restaurant with brown rice, sushi and seasonal macrobiotic dishes.

Nightlife and Entertainment

Exploring the jungle of LA's **nightlife** can be great fun. Everyone you meet claims to be either a rock star or in the movies; half of them aren't lying. Even the quietest venue offers a chance to eavesdrop on a bit of vapid *Less Than Zero* dialogue; the wildest ones will take your breath away. In all the pubs, clubs and discos, you'll need to be 21 and will almost certainly be asked for ID.

The best sources of **listings** are *LA Weekly* and the more highbrow "Calendar" section in the *LA Times* at the weekend.

Bars, Pubs and Cafés

LA's **bars and pubs** are rarely the scruffy boozing places found elsewhere in the US, due at least in part to the generally high degree of health consciousness – not to mention the very early (daybreak) starting time of the movie business working day. **Cafés** are a newer phenomenon, but in the past five years have spread all over the Westside.

Al's Bar, 305 S Hewitt St (☎687-3558). At the heart of the Loft District art scene downtown; drink cans of cheap beer in small, smoke-filled rooms, with a pool table and occasional live acts.

Boardners, 1652 N Cherokee Ave, Hollywood (☎462-9621). A likeably unkempt neighborhood bar – a rarity in the heart of Hollywood, but very welcome.

Cat'n'Fiddle, 6530 Sunset Blvd (☎468-3800). Comfortable but boisterous pub with good beers and live music.

King's Road Espresso House, 8361 Beverly Blvd (☎655-9044). This newish sidewalk café is popular day and night with West Hollywood's *nuovo* beatnik crowd.

Musso and Frank's, 6667 Hollywood Blvd (☎467-7788). If you haven't had a drink in this 1940s landmark bar, you haven't been to Hollywood. It also serves food.

The Novel Café, 212 Pier Ave, Santa Monica (☎310/396-8566). Considering the name, and the ever-trendy Venice environs, this is a surprisingly unpretentious café, with good coffees, teas and pastries.

The Power House, 1714 N Highland Ave (☎463-9438). Enjoyable heavy-rockers' watering hole just off Hollywood Blvd; few people get here much before midnight.

Barney's Beanery, 8447 Santa Monica Blvd (☎654-2287). Well-worn pool-hall bar, stocking over two hundred beers. It also serves food.

McGinty's Irish Pub, 2615 Wilshire Blvd, Santa Monica (☎310/828-9839). Friendly, often raucous small pub with dartboards and, frequently, live music.

Clubs and Discos

LA's **clubs** are among the wildest in the country, ranging from absurdly faddish hangouts to industrial noise cellars. The trendier side of the club scene is, as always, hard to pin down; check the *LA Weekly* before setting out. There are further suggestions under "Gay and Lesbian LA".

Cocoanut Teaszer, 8117 Sunset Blvd (☎654-4773). Poseurs, rockers and voyeurs mix uneventfully on the two dancefloors. No cover before 9pm, otherwise $5.

Glam Slam, 333 S Boylston St (☎482-6626). Very glam but not impossibly posey club, owned and inspired by Prince himself – hence the purple dancefloor. Dress nice, but no one turned away, so long as you're 21 or over.

Mayan, 1038 S Hill St (☎746-4287). Get past the doorman and you're in with LA's coolest, eager to shake a leg in gorgeous surrounds. Friday and Saturday; $15. Dress to impress.

Probe, 836 N Highland Ave, Hollywood (☎461-8301). Ultra-trendy but friendly club that hosts top DJs playing whatever's hot: gay disco on Sat, 70s hits on Sun, rest of week everything else.

7969, 7969 Santa Monica Blvd (☎654-0280). West Hollywood's longest running gay & lesbian disco has drag shows on Mon, women-only Tues, English Acid (British Invasion to Happy Mondays) on Wed. Call for details; cover $8, 18 and over only.

Gay and Lesbian Bars and Clubs

Arena, 6655 Santa Monica Blvd (☎462-1742). Many clubs under one huge roof, large dancefloors throbbing to funk, Latin and hi-energy grooves – and sometimes live bands – on Wed, Sat and Sun. Also called **Circus** (☎462-1291), it's mostly men atthe Pink Feather on Tues; gay men and women on Fri.

Detour, 1087 Manzanita, Silverlake (☎664-1189). A friendly and quite inexpensive denim and leather bar.

Jewel's Catch One, 4067 W Pico Blvd (☎734-8849). Sweaty dance barn, packed with gay men Wed, women Thurs, mixed crowd rest of week; $3–7.

Klub Banshee, location varies (☎310/288-1601). Weekend dance club for women, held at various locations around LA.

Le Bar, 2375 Glendale Blvd, Silverlake (☎660-7595). Quiet and welcoming, with a pool table.

Probe, 836 N Highland Ave (☎461-8301). LA's longest-running gay men's disco, playing all the Euro Pop dance hits.

7969, 7969 Santa Monica Blvd (☎654-0280). Formerly called Peanuts, West Hollywood's longest running gay and lesbian disco has drag shows on Mon, women-only Tues for topless girl dancers, *Fetish* and *Fuck!* on Sat. Call for details; 18 and over, cover $5–8.

Rage, 8911 Santa Monica Blvd (☎758-7243). Very flash gay men's club playing the latest hi-NRG hits. Drinks are inexpensive, the cover varies.

Revolver, 8851 Santa Monica Blvd (☎550-8851). Club in which you can watch yourself dancing with yourself on giant video screens hanging above the dancefloor. The definitive West Hollywood gay bar.

S.S. Friendship, 112 West Channel Rd, Pacific Palisades (☎310/454-9080). Welcoming beachfront bar with a mix of gay and straight but mainly local people, from 11am until 2am daily.

GAY AND LESBIAN LA

Although proportionately not as big as that of San Francisco, the **gay scene** in LA is far from invisible, and gay people are out and prominent right across the city. West Hollywood has a gay-led council and has become synonymous with the (affluent, white) gay lifestyle, not just in LA but all over California. The section of West Hollywood on Santa Monica Boulevard between Doheny Blvd and Crescent Heights has many restaurants, shops and bars primarily aimed at gay men. The other overtly gay community is Silverlake, at its most evident along Hyperion Boulevard. We've listed gay accommodation, restaurants, bars and clubs in the relevant sections above.

The city's best known gay and lesbian bookshop is *A Different Light*, 4014 Santa Monica Blvd (☎668-0629). Magazines with good listings sections include *Compass, Dispatch, Edge*, and *Lesbian News*; and the *Gay Community Yellow Pages* (☎469-4454) is a comprehensive annual directory of gay businesses, publications, services and gathering places. **The Gay and Lesbian Community Services Center**, 1213 H Highland Ave (☎993-7400), is the community's prime resource for counselling, health testing and information.

Live Music

LA has a near-overwhelming choice if you're looking for **live music**. Ever since the nihilistic punk bands – Circle Jerks, X, Black Flag – drew the city away from its cocaine-sozzled laid-back West Coast image, LA's **rock music** scene has been excellent. **Country music** is fairly prevalent, at least away from trendy Hollywood, and the valleys are hotbeds of country-folk and swing. **Jazz**, too, is played in a few genuinely authentic downbeat dives, though more commonly found being used to improve the atmosphere of a restaurant. **Salsa** remains immensely popular among LA's Hispanic population, and is found mostly in the bars of East LA; it's worth saying that (aside from the places we've listed) these are very male-oriented, and female visitors may well feel out of place.

anti-club, 4658 Melrose Ave (☎661-3913). The other end of the world from upmarket Melrose, with inexpensive beer and an adventurous booking policy.

The Baked Potato, 3738 Cahuenga Blvd, N Hollywood (☎818/980-1615). A small but near-legendary contemporary jazz spot, where many reputations have been forged; $8.

Birdland West, 105 W Broadway, Long Beach (☎310/436-9341). Very stylish jazz venue with good names. Cover varies.

Casa Rivera, 9001 E Telegraph Rd, Pico Rivera, East LA (☎949-8381). Salsa most nights and *jarocho* music from Veracruz, a sort of festive mariachi, once a week. Cover $3 on Wed, Fri & Sat.

Club Lingerie, 6507 Sunset Blvd (☎466-8557). Long-enduring, stylish venue that's always at the forefront of what's new. Intimate bar, music from rockabilly to jazz to post-industrial thrash; $3–8

Doug Weston's Troubadour, 9081 Santa Monica Blvd (☎310/276-6168). Less heavy metal than it used to be, but still the club for the heaviest riffs and shaggiest manes; $4–12.

The Foothill Club, 1922 Cherry Ave, Signal Hill (☎310/494-5196). A glorious country dance hall from the days when hillbilly was cool. Seven nights a week, doors open at 5pm; no cover.

Golden Sails Hotel, 6285 E Pacific Coast Highway, Long Beach (☎310/498-0091). Has some of the best reggae bands from LA and beyond on Fri and Sat; $5.

Kingston 12, 814 Broadway, Santa Monica (☎310/451-4423). Nightly reggae, nice and small. $10.

Largo, 432 N Fairfax Ave (☎852-1073). Intimate cabaret venue with some of LA's more interesting bands. 18 and over.

Longhorn Saloon, 21211 Sherman Way, Canoga Park (☎818/340-4788). Live country and blues-ish bands every night except Mon. Frequent star-studded jam sessions; $3.

Luminarias, 3500 Ramona Blvd, Monterey Park, East LA (☎268-4177). A hilltop restaurant where the live salsa is reckoned to be as good as the Mexican food; no cover.

McCabe's, 3103 W Pico Blvd, Santa Monica (☎310/828-4403). The back room of LA's premier acoustic guitar shop; long the scene of some excellent and unusual folk and country shows; $5–10.

The Palomino, 6907 Lankershim Blvd, North Hollywood (☎818/764-4010). Long the best place to catch visiting country and western singers, also good for r'n'b and the odd goth gig; $5–10.

Raji's, 6160 Hollywood Blvd (☎469-4552). Back room of an Indian restaurant that makes a good airing place for up-and-coming local rock bands; free–$5.

The Roxy, 9009 Sunset Blvd (☎310/276-2222). The showcase of the rock industry's new signings, intimate and with a great sound system. Also has "pay-to-play" nights for unknown bands; $8–20.

Whisky, 8901 Sunset Blvd (☎310/652-4202). Recently done up after many years as LA's most famous rock'n'roll club, nowadays mainly hard rock; $5–10.

Classical Music, Opera and Dance

Considering its size and stature in the other arts, LA has very few outlets for **classical music**. The *Los Angeles Philharmonic* (☎972-7300), the only major name in the city, perform regularly during the year, and the *Los Angeles Chamber Orchestra* (☎622-7001), appear at assorted venues. San Francisco has more of an **opera** scene (see p.825), although the *Music Center Opera* (☎972-7211) stage productions between October and May, as do Orange County's *Opera Pacific* (☎480-3232 or 714/740-2000), who perform both grand opera and operettas. Prices can be anything from $15 to $80.

The last fifteen years or so have seen an increase in **dance** activity in LA, with major ballet companies like the *Joffrey Ballet* (☎487-8677) relocating on the West Coast after making their name in New York, accompanied by the growth of a number of small modern ensembles and steady visits by companies from around the world.

The Ambassador Auditorium, 300 W Green St, Pasadena (☎818/304-6161 or 1-800/266-2378). Superb acoustics and many international stars.

The Dorothy Chandler Pavilion, in the *Music Center*, 1365 N Grand Ave, Downtown (☎972-7211 or 972-7460). From October until May home to the LA Philharmonic, who perform at 8pm on weeknights and at 2.30pm on Sunday. Also used by the Joffrey Ballet, the Music Center Opera and other top names.

The Hollywood Bowl, 2301 N Highland Ave, Hollywood (☎850-2000). The LA Philharmonic give open-air concerts each Tues–Sat evenings from July to September.

Japan America Theatre, 244 S San Pedro St (☎680-3700). Dance and performance works drawn from Japan and the Far East.

John Anson Ford Theater, 2850 Cahuenga Blvd (☎972-7200). Besides the summer Dance Kaleidoscope, this open-air venue also has one-off productions by local groups.

Orange County Performing Arts Center, 600 Town Center Drive, Costa Mesa (☎714/556-ARTS). Home of the Pacific Symphony Orchestra and Opera Pacific.

The Pacific Amphitheater, 100 Fair Drive, Costa Mesa (☎310/410-1062). A big open-air venue, Orange County's answer to the Hollywood Bowl.

The Shrine Auditorium, 3228 Royal St (☎748-5116), box office at 655 S Hill St (☎749-5123). A bizarre building that hosts regular performances by choral gospel groups and every other Academy Awards ceremony .

Royce Hall, on the UCLA campus (☎310/825-9261 or 310/825-2101). Classical concerts often involving big names throughout the college year.

UCLA Center for the Performing Arts, 10920 Wilshire Blvd (☎310/825-9261). Hosts a wide range of touring companies, and also runs an "Art of Dance" series between September and June which usually has an experimental emphasis.

Comedy Clubs

The Comedy Club, 49 S Pine Ave, Long Beach (☎310/437-5326). Mixed bag of stand-up comics.

Comedy & Magic Club, 1018 Hermosa Ave, Hermosa Beach (☎310/372-1193). Strange couplings of naff magic acts and good-quality comedians.

The Comedy Store, 8433 W Sunset Blvd (☎656-6225). Popular comedy showcase spread over three rooms; you can usually turn up on spec at weekends. Always a good line-up too.

The Ice House, 24 N Mentor Ave, Pasadena (☎818/577-1894). The comedy mainstay of the valley, very established and fairly safe.

Igby's Cabaret, 11637 W Pico Blvd (☎310/477-3553). Fairly new, boasting some surprise big-name turns alongside entertaining hopefuls.

A CALENDAR OF LA'S FESTIVALS

January

1 Tournament of Roses in Pasadena. A parade of floral floats and marching bands along Colorado Boulevard.

February

Early Japanese New Year. Celebrated around Little Tokyo with traditional arts.

First full moon after 21 Chinese New Year. Three days of dragon-float street parades, based in Chinatown.

March

17 St Patrick's Day. A parade through downtown and related events all over the city, with some bars serving green beer.

End The Academy Awards are presented at the Shrine Auditorium.

April

Early The Blessing of the Animals. A long-established Mexican-originated ceremony thanking animals for their services to humans. Pets are blessed in Olvera Street, followed by a parade.

May

5 Cinco de Mayo. Day-long commemoration of the Mexican victory at the battle of Puebla (*not* Mexican Independence Day). A spirited parade in Olvera Street, celebrations with Mexican food, drink and music in most LA parks.

July

Middle Watts Jazz Festival. Two days of free music with the Watts towers as a backdrop.

August

First two weeks Culmination of the South Bay's International Surf Festival, where globally famed surfers compete.

September

4 LA's birthday. A civic ceremony and assorted street entertainment around El Pueblo de Los Angeles to mark the founding of the original pueblo in 1781.

Last two weeks LA County Fair in Pomona, in the San Gabriel Valley. The country's biggest; livestock shows, eating contests and fairground rides.

October

Second weekend LA Street Scene. Free rock music, fringe theater and comedy on the streets of downtown. Usually running at the same time is the West Hollywood Street Festival, a display of handmade arts and crafts and a general slap-on-the-back for LA's newest constituent city.

November

End Hollywood Christmas Parade. The first and best of the many Yuletide events, with a cavalcade of mind-boggling floats.

LA Connection, 13442 Ventura Blvd, Sherman Oaks (☎818/784-1868). An improvisation showcase for highly rated obnoxiousness specialists. Seldom less than memorable.

Theater

We've listed a few picks from LA's very active (and very changeable) **theater** scene; *Theatrix* (☎466-1767) handles reservations and provides details on what's playing at several of the smaller venues. The *LA Weekly* and the LA Times *Calendar* section both have full listings and reviews.

Coronet Theater, 368 N La Cienega Blvd (☎310/276-7461). Home of the LA Public Theater; productions include the odd famous name. Lively bar, patronized by excessively theatrical types.

Gene Dynarski Theater, 5600 Sunset Blvd (☎660-8587). Small-time character actor Dynarski built this likeable little theater himself to rent out to small companies.

Mark Taper Forum, 135 N Grand Ave, downtown (☎972-7392). Theater in the three-quarter round, frequently putting on innovative new plays.

Powerhouse Theater, 3116 Second St, Santa Monica (☎310/392-6529). Experimental shows.

Schubert Theater, ABC Entertainment Center, Century City (☎310/201-1500). The only good thing about Century City is that you can come here to ogle the razzmatazz musicals.

Baseball: the *LA Dodgers* (☎224-1500) play at Dodger Stadium near downtown, seats $6–15; *California Angels* (☎714/937-7200) at Anaheim Stadium in Orange County, seats $6–15.

Basketball: the *LA Lakers* (☎310/419-3100) are at the Forum, in Inglewood, seats (often impossible to get) $15–35.

Hockey: *LA Kings* are also based at the Forum (☎310/419-3182), seats $10–25.

Football: the *LA Rams* (☎714/937-6767) also play at Anaheim Stadium, seats $15–40; *LA Raiders* (☎310/322-5901) in the LA Coliseum, near downtown, seats $15–35.

Pasadena's 102,000-capacity **Rose Bowl**, seven miles northeast of downtown LA, is used for the annual New Year's Day Rose Bowl football game, as well as being the venue for several games in soccer's **1994 World Cup**, including the final on July 17.

Film

Many major feature films are released in LA months (sometimes years) before they play anywhere else in the world. Short seasons of **foreign-language films** often play at the eight *Laemmle Theaters*. If you're looking for a golden-years-of-film **atmosphere**, head for one of the historic downtown movie palaces along Broadway (described on p.769), where the delirious furnishings may captivate your attention longer than the all-action triple-bills. Otherwise, take your pick of **new releases** in one of many mall-based multiplexes, like the Beverly Center *Cineplex* (☎652-7760) or the eighteen-screen Universal City complex (☎818/508-0588).

Bing Theater, at the LA County Art Museum, 5905 Wilshire Blvd (☎857-6010). Afternoon screenings of many neglected Hollywood classics. Matinees cost just $1, evening shows $6.

Chinese Theatre, 6925 Hollywood Blvd (☎464-8111). Landmark Art Deco cinema. Giant screen and six-track stereo sound, but limp MOR films.

El Capitan Theater, Hollywood Blvd at Highland Ave (☎467-7674). Another legendary Hollywood venue, recently restored to full glory.

New Beverly Cinema, 7165 Beverly Blvd (☎938-4038). Imaginative cult double bills.

Nuart Theater, 11272 Santa Monica Blvd (☎310/478-6379). Rare classics, foreign films and documentaries.

Shopping

You can buy virtually anything, anywhere, anytime in LA. The big **department stores** or the thoroughly exclusive **Rodeo Drive** (see p.771) will have it if the ubiquitous run-of-the-mill retailers don't, and if all else fails try LA's massive **malls**, which often resemble self-contained city suburbs as much as shopping precincts. The brand-new **City Walk** mall at Universal Studios distills a dozen LA neighborhoods into cut-out facades fronting all the national chain stores, complete with a sandy beach – safe shopping for the 1990s. Swishest of all is the seven-acre **Beverly Center**, bordered by Beverly Blvd and La Cienega Blvd, and San Vicente Blvd and Third St, where you'll find designer stores, fourteen cinemas – and ample opportunities for star-spotting. West Hollywood, and Melrose Avenue in particular, hold many of the ciy's trendier boutiques, but if you're after a first edition of Shirley MacLaine's autobiography, old movies stills, or a *Buffalo Springfield* album in mint condition, try one of the places listed below.

Books

Acres of Books, 240 Long Beach Blvd, Long Beach (☎310/437-680). LA's largest secondhand collection – well worth a trip down the Blue Line.

Bodhi Tree, 8585 Melrose Ave (☎310/659-1733). New and used New Age, occult and Philip K Dick books.

Book City, 6627 Hollywood Blvd (☎466-2525). An eclectic mix, packed from floor to ceiling.

Book Soup, 8818 W Sunset Blvd (☎310/659-3110). Great selection, right on Sunset Strip.

Bread and Roses, 13812 Ventura Blvd, Sherman Oaks (☎818/986-5376). Store in the heart of the San Fernando Valley, catering to women of all social, racial, ethnic and sociological backgrounds.

Fowler Brothers, at 717 W Seventh St (☎627-7846). LA's oldest, open since 1888, and one of the few small general bookshops to survive.

Hennessey and Ingalls, 1254 Third Street Promenade, Santa Monica (☎310/458-9074). An impressive range of hard-to-find art and architecture books, plus rare posters and catalogues.

Larry Edmunds Book Shop, 6658 Hollywood Blvd (☎463-3273). Stacks of books on every aspect of film and theater, and movie stills and posters.

Midnight Special, 1318 Third Street Promenade, Santa Monica (☎310/393-2923). Excellent for politics and social sciences; open late.

Scene of the Crime, 13636 Ventura Blvd, Sherman Oaks (☎818/981-2583). New and used crime; from hard-boiled private dicks to whodunnits. Done up as an Agatha Christie country mansion.

Sisterhood Bookstore, 1351 Westwood Blvd (☎310/477-7300). Westside landmark. Music, cards, jewellery and of course books, pertaining to the national and international women's movement.

Records

Aron's Records, 1150 N Highland Ave (☎469-4700). Secondhand discs – all styles, all prices, huge stock.

House of Records, 2314 Pico Blvd, Santa Monica (☎310/450-1222). Singles from 1949 onwards.

Moby Disc, 14410 Ventura Blvd, Sherman Oaks (☎818/990-2920). Secondhand and deletions.

Music and Memories, 5057 Lankershim, North Hollywood (☎818/761-9827). Almost entirely devoted to Frank Sinatra, though they also stock singers who sound like Frank.

Poo-Bah Records, 1101 E Walnut Ave, Pasadena (☎818/449-3359). American and imported New Wave.

Rhino Records, 1720 Westwood Blvd (☎310/474-8685). The biggest selection of international independent releases. Also at 328 Santa Monica Blvd in Santa Monica (☎310/394-0842)

Vinyl Fetish, 7305 Melrose Ave (☎935-1300). Besides the punk and post-punk merchandise, a good place to discover what's new on the LA music scene.

THE DESERTS

The **deserts** of Southern California occupy fully a quarter of the state. Untouched but for the three million acres used for military bases, this hot and inhospitable wilderness exerts a powerful fascination. There are two distinct regions: the **Colorado** or **Low Desert** in the south is the most easily reached from LA, containing the opulent artificial oasis of **Palm Springs** and the primeval expanse of **Joshua Tree**; and the **Mojave** or **High Desert**, dominated by **Death Valley**.

Low Desert

Most visitors to the Low Desert have no intention of getting away from it all. They head straight for where it's at – the irrefutable capital of the desert, **Palm Springs**. In these few square miles, overrun with the famous and the star-struck, the average age and average temperature are said to be about the same – a steady 88. Despite its shortcomings, you'll find it hard to avoid: it's the first stopping point east from LA on I-10, at the center of the **Coachella Valley**, part of the most intensively productive agricultural area in the world, growing dates, oranges, lemons and grapefruits in vast quantities.

The sublime landscape of **Joshua Tree National Monument**, well worth a weekend spent taking in the sunsets and the howl of coyotes at twilight, lies one hour's drive east of Palm Springs, three and a half from LA, and is connected by bus from both.

Palm Springs

Sitting in lush farming land, replete with manicured golf courses, condominiums and millionaires, **PALM SPRINGS** does not conform to any typical image of the desert. The massive bulk of Mount San Jacinto glowers over its low-slung buildings, casting an instantaneous and welcome shadow over the town in the late afternoon. Ever since Hollywood stars first came here in the 1930s, the clean dry air and sunshine, just 120 miles east of LA, have made Palm Springs irresistible as a place to bring down stress levels. High-school kids arrive in their thousands for the drunken revelry of **Spring Break**, while others come specifically *not* to get drunk: the **Betty Ford Center** draws a star-studded patient list to its booze- and drug-free environment, attempting to undo a lifetime's behavioral disorders in a $20,000 two-week stay. In addition, Palm Springs has also become one of the US's largest **gay** resorts, with various exclusively gay hotels.

Palm Springs wasn't always like this. Once it was the domain of the **Cahuilla Indians**; they were allocated this land in the 1890s, but exact zoning was never settled until the 1940s, by which time the development of hotels and leisure complexes was well under way. Under an odd checkerboard system, every other square mile of Palm Springs forms part of the **Agua Caliente Indian Reservation**, and high rents have made this the richest tribe in America – over one hundred members of the Cahuilla have individual land-holdings worth $2 million or more.

Arrival and Information

Arriving by **car**, you drive into town on E Palm Canyon Drive. *Greyhound* **buses** (ten daily from LA) come in at 3111 N Indian Ave (☎325-2053). *Desert Stage Lines* (☎367-3581) from the same terminal connect Palm Springs to Twentynine Palms and Joshua Tree. **Trains** link LA with **Indio**, 25 miles away from downtown Palm Springs and connected by *Sun Buses* (6am–6pm; ☎343-3451), which circulate all the local resorts.

The **visitor center** is at 113 S Indian Ave (Mon–Fri 9am–5pm; ☎327-7534).

Downtown Palm Springs

Downtown Palm Springs stretches for about half a mile along Palm Canyon Drive, a wide, bright and modern strip full of expensive boutiques and restaurants. By day, people wear visors and swoon in air-conditioned shopping malls; by night, the youth take over and cruise the main drag in their four-wheel-drives with their stereos blaring.

The luxuriously housed **Desert Museum**, 101 Museum Drive (Tues–Fri 10am–4pm, & Sat 10am–5pm; $3.50), is strong on Native American and Southwestern art, though its only permanent display is the late actor William Holden's collection of Asian and African works. Some surprisingly interesting natural science exhibits focus on the animal and plant life of the desert, demonstrating that it's not all sandstorms and rattlesnakes. There's an anarchic piece of landscape gardening at **Moorten's Botanical Gardens**, 1701 S Palm Canyon Drive (daily 9am–4pm; $2), a bizarre cornucopia of every desert plant and cactus, lumped together in no particular order but interesting for those who won't be venturing beyond town to see them in their natural habitat.

Companies such as *Palm Springs Celebrity Tours*, 174 Palm Canyon Drive (☎325-2682), offer **celebrity tours**. You could do it yourself, with a map of the stars' homes from the visitor center – but you'd miss the sharp anecdotal commentary.

Around Palm Springs

Most visitors to Palm Springs never leave the poolside, but desert enthusiasts still visit to **hike** and **ride** in the **Indian Canyons**, three miles southeast of downtown along S

The **area code** for the California deserts is ☎619.

Palm Canyon Drive. Centuries ago, ancestors of the Cahuilla developed extensive communities here, growing melons, squash, beans and corn. The canyons are about fifteen miles long, and can be toured by car, although it's worth walking at least a few miles; the easiest trails lead past the waterfalls, rocky gorges and palm trees of **Palm Canyon** and **Andreas Canyon**. Some areas are set aside for the specific lunacy of **trailblazing** in jeeps and four-wheel-drives; rent a vehicle from *Dune Off-Road Rentals*, 59755 Hwy-111 (☎325-0376), four miles north of town, for $50 per half-day, or take a **guided jeep adventure** with *Desert Adventures,* 68-733 Perez Rd (☎324-3378), whose excellent half-day tours of the Santa Rosa mountains cost around $25 per hour.

If the desert heat becomes too much to bear, large cable cars grind and sway over eight thousand feet up the **Palm Springs Aerial Tramway**, Tramway Drive, just off Hwy-111 north of Palm Springs (daily 8am–9pm; $153; ☎325-1391), passing through five climatic zones on the way to the top of Mount San Jacinto. There's a **bar** and **restaurant** at the Mountain Station up here. Concrete-paved trails (hardly the hiker's dream) stretch for a couple of miles around, and should sub-alpine ecology not interest you, there's always the option of a snowball fight.

Accommodation

Luxury **hotels** far outnumber the affordable variety in Palm Springs, but prices drop by as much as seventy percent as temperatures rise in summer. The north end of town, along Hwy-111, holds the lower-priced places, virtually all of which have pools. The prices below are **summer rates**; winter rates rise by approximately $10 to $20.

Casa Cody, 175 South Cahuilla Rd (☎320-9346). The one affordable B&B inn. Attractive Southwestern-style buildings in a shady garden. ⑤.

Desert Ho, 120 West Vereda Sur (☎325-5159). Small hotel, a mile or two north of downtown. Nine large rooms around a beautiful pool and gardens, facing Mt San Jacinto. ④.

Ingleside Inn, 200 W Ramon Rd (☎325-0046). An expensive option, but one with real class – as evidenced by a guest list which includes Dali, Garbo and Brando. ⑤.

Motel 6, 595 E Palm Canyon Drive (☎327-2004). Most central of the budget options, 10min walk from downtown with a good pool. ②.

Eating and Drinking

The stifling desert heat suppresses even the healthiest of appetites; most people go all day on nothing, to find themselves suddenly ravenous at dusk. However, Palm Springs has a disappointing selection of **restaurants**; you can find better value, and a whole lot more life, in gay-oriented **Cathedral City** ("Cat City"), ten miles east along Hwy-111.

CC Construction Co, 68–449 Perez Rd, Cathedral City. Seventies-style disco fun at the home of the "jig with a pig" evening; shimmy with a gay cop and mix with a good-natured drag-queen crowd.

Daddy Warbucks, 68–981 E Palm Canyon Drive, Cathedral City. A wild club scene with "whipped cream fighting" on Sunday and talent contests on Wednesday.

El Gallito Café, 68820 Grove St, Cathedral City. Busy Mexican cantina that has the best food for miles and often queues to match – get there around 6pm to avoid the crowds.

Frying Fish, 123 N Palm Canyon Drive. Sushi for around $10 per enormous platter.

Let's Get Juiced, 651 N Palm Canyon Drive. Vegetarian restaurant that has poetry readings, live music and classic movies.

Louise's Pantry, 124 S Palm Canyon Drive. Fifties-looking diner, where none of the waitresses is under sixty and the servings are huge. Especially good for breakfast.

The Saloon, 225 S Indian Ave. The best of Palm Springs' sorry bunch of bars, with a down-to-earth, beer-and-pretzels approach to drinking.

Le Vallauris, 385 West Tahquitz Way (☎325-5059 – reservations only). Excellent Californian/ French cuisine, though the price is around $50 per head. It bills itself as "*the* restaurant where the Stars entertain their friends"; and you may indeed run into one or two once-renowned artistes.

Wheel-Inn Eat, ten miles west on I-10 at the Cabazon exit (marked by two concrete dinosaurs). Humble, 24-hour desert truck stop – so unpretentious they might never have heard of Palm Springs.

Joshua Tree National Monument

In a unique transitional area, where the lower Colorado desert meets the high Mojave northeast of Palm Springs, **JOSHUA TREE NATIONAL MONUMENT** protects 850 square miles of grotesquely gnarled and ragged trees. Each can reach up to forty feet in height, but they have to contend with extreme aridity and rocky soil, and the strain of their struggle to survive is evident. All around lie great heaps of boulders, pushed up by the San Andreas fault, their edges rounded and smoothed by flash floods and winds.

This unearthly landscape is best appreciated at sunrise or sunset, when the desert floor is bathed in red light; at noon it can be a threatening furnace. The name "Joshua Tree" was given by Mormons in the 1850s, who saw the craggy branches of the trees as the arms of Joshua leading them to the promised land.

Be selective in your explorations. As with any desert area, the heat is punishing and an ambitious schedule is impossible. Brief yourself at the visitor centers, and never venture anywhere without a map. On unmarked roads restricted to four-wheel-drive, don't think about taking a normal car – you'll soon grind to a halt, and it could be quite a few panic-stricken hours before anybody finds you. If you're hiking, **stick to the trails**. Joshua Tree is full of abandoned gold mines: watch for loose gravel around openings, undercut edges, never trust ladders or timber, and bear in mind that the rangers rarely check mines for casualties. Even on the simpler trails, allow around an hour per mile.

One of the easiest hiking routes leads 1.5 miles from Canyon Road, six miles from the visitor center at Twentynine Palms, to **Fortynine Palms Oasis**. To the west of the oasis, quartz boulders tower around the *Indian Cove* campground; a trail from the eastern branch of the campground road heads to **Rattlesnake Canyon**, where, after rainfall, the streams and waterfalls break an otherwise eerie silence among the monoliths.

Moving south, follow the trails through **Hidden Valley**, where cattle rustlers used to hide out, to the rain-fed **Barker Dam**, to the east: Joshua Tree's crucial water supply, built by cattlemen around the turn of the century. One negotiable trail climbs past abandoned mining sites, where some buildings and equipment are still intact, to **Lost Horse Mine**, 450 feet up – once worth an average of $20,000 a week.

A brilliant desert panorama of badlands and mountains is to be had from the 5185ft **Key's View** nearby, from where Geology Tour Road leads down to the east through the best of Joshua Tree's **rock formations**.

Practicalities

Hwy-62 from Palm Springs leads to the **park headquarters** ($5 admission) at **Twentynine Palms**. With no hotel accommodation in the monument itself, you may be glad of its good **motels** and restaurants. The best of the lot is the New-Age-style *Twenty-Nine Palms Inn*, 73950 Inn Ave (☎367-3505; ⑤), whose adobe cabins are built on the Oasis of Mara, right on top of the major fault, and which organizes desert hikes with llamas. *Desert Stage Lines* **buses** (☎367-3581) arrive here from Palm Springs. There is another entrance and visitor center at **Cottonwood**, seven miles north of I-10.

Joshua Tree has nine free first-come-first-served **campgrounds**, all in the northwest except for one at Cottonwood. Only two (*Black Rock* and *Cottonwood*) have water.

High Desert

The **Mojave Desert**, known as the High Desert because on average it is two thousand feet above sea level, has no equals when it comes to hardship. Visitors are very thin on the ground, but if you do linger, you'll get the chance to see – and smell – a real desert: a vast, impersonal, extreme environment, sharp with its own peculiar fragrance, and in spring alive with acres of fiery orange poppies and other brightly colored wildflowers.

Barstow

BARSTOW, the one stop-off along the dusty, endless I-15 – served by both *Greyhound* and *Amtrak* en route to Las Vegas – is a lacklustre small town. During the hottest season it seems perpetually empty; everyone hides in their air-conditioned homes from the relentless sun. The one main road is lined with motels – such as *Torches Motel*, 201 W Main St (☎256-3308; ②), near the bus station – and restaurants (good Mexican food can be had at *Rosita's*, 540 W Main St). At the junction of Barstow Rd and I-15, the **California Desert Information Center** (daily 9am–6pm; ☎256-8617) has a good selection of maps, lodging and restaurant guides. You can **camp** in shaded canyons at the contrived **Calico Ghost Town** (daily 9am–5pm; $5), seven miles north along I-15.

Death Valley National Monument

DEATH VALLEY is utterly inhuman: the hottest place on earth and almost entirely devoid of shade, much less water. Its sculpted rock layers form deeply shadowed, eroded crevices at the foot of sharply silhouetted hills, their exotic mineral content turning million-year-old mudflats into rainbows of sunlit phosphorescence. It was named by a party of white settlers who stumbled through in 1849, looking for a short-cut to the Gold Rush towns; they survived despite running out of food and water. For the next 75 years the only people to brave its hardships were miners, whose most successful endeavors were centered on borates, a harsh alkali used in detergent soaps.

Throughout the summer, the air temperature in Death Valley averages 120°F, and the ground can reach near boiling point. Better to come during the spring, when the wildflowers are in bloom, or from October to May when it's generally mild and dry.

The central north–south valley for which the monument is named contains its two main outposts: **Stovepipe Wells** and **Furnace Creek**, where the **visitor center** (daily 8am–9pm in winter, 8am–5pm in summer; ☎786-2331) is located. A $5 entrance fee is payable at the park entrance; the **ranger stations** close to the park boundaries provide free maps and up-to-date information on tours and activities.

Many of the most unusual sights are located south of Furnace Creek. A good first stop, seven miles along Hwy-178/Badwater Rd, is the **Artist's Palette**, an eroded hillside covered in an intensely colored mosaic of reds, golds, blacks and greens. Sixteen miles further south, **Badwater** is an unpalatable but non-poisonous thirty-foot-wide pool of water, loaded with chloride and sulphates, that's the only home of the soft-bodied Death Valley snail. A four-mile hike across the hot valley floor drops down to the **lowest point in the western hemisphere**, 282 feet below sea level.

Zabriskie Point, overlooking Badwater and the Artist's Palette off Hwy-190, four miles south of Furnace Creek, was the inspiration for Antonioni's eponymous 1960s film. The view is best during the early morning, when the pink and gold Panamint Mountains across the valley are highlighted by the rising sun.

Near Stovepipe Wells in the west spread fifteen rippled and contoured square miles of ever-changing **sand dunes**. A ten-mile dirt road west of the campground leads to sheer black-walled **Marble Canyon**, scratched with mysterious ancient petroglyphs.

Practicalities

Death Valley is a long way from anywhere; the only scheduled public transportation is the *LTR Stage Lines* (☎702/384-1230), from **Las Vegas**, 140 miles to the southeast, which leaves roughly every other day from September to May, not at all in summer.

If you plan to **stay**, you must reserve ahead. The **Fred Harvey Consortium** (PO Box 1, Death Valley, CA 92328; ☎786-2345 or 1-800/622-0838) operates two pricey hotels on natural oases at Furnace Creek; the plush *Furnace Creek Inn* (⑧), and the more reasonable *Furnace Creek Ranch* (④), across the road about half a mile north, which has the valley's best-value **restaurants** and a nice bar. Fred Harvey also offer regular three-hour **coach tours** ($21) in winter from the *Furnace Creek Inn*. The *Stovepipe Wells Village* (☎786-2387; ③), is on Hwy-190 about twenty miles northeast of Furnace Creek. **Camping** in one of the many National Park Service campgrounds costs $5 a night, and cannot be reserved. You could also stay **outside Death Valley** altogether, 35 miles past Furnace Creek in **Beatty**, Nevada, in the *El Portal Motel* (☎702/553-2912; ②) on the west side of town, or the *Stagecoach Motel* (☎702/553-2419; ②) on the east side.

Outside the Valley

Hordes of overheated tourists wait patiently to wander through the surreal luxury of **Scotty's Castle**, 45 miles north of the visitor center and well beyond Death Valley itself. It was built in the 1920s as the desert retreat of Chicago insurance broker Albert Johnson, but named after "Death Valley" Scotty, who managed the construction and claimed the house was his own, financed by a hidden gold mine. **Tours** (daily 9am–5pm; $5) take in the ornate wooden ceilings, indoor waterfalls and a remote-controlled player piano; Johnson lost a fortune in the Wall Street Crash and had to abandon plans for swimming pools and elaborate gardens. The house remains as it was when he died in 1948. Scotty himself lived here until 1954, and is buried just behind the house.

Five miles west of Scotty's Castle gapes the half-mile **Ubehebe Crater**, the rust-tinged result of a massive volcanic explosion; half a mile south sits its thousand-year-old younger brother, **Little Hebe**. Beyond the craters the road continues west for another twenty dusty miles to **Racetrack Valley**, a 2.5-mile long mudflat across which giant boulders seem slowly to be racing, leaving faint trails in their wake.

THE CENTRAL COAST

After the hustle of LA and San Francisco, the four hundred miles of coastline in between – the **central coast** – can seem like the land that time forgot. Sparsely populated outside the few medium-sized towns, and lined by clean sandy beaches, it is at its most dramatic at **Big Sur**, where the brooding Santa Lucia mountains rise steeply out of the thundering Pacific surf. The two largest towns are poles apart: **Santa Barbara** in the south is a wealthy resort, **Santa Cruz** in the north is a throwback to the Sixties. In between, languourous **San Luis Obispo** makes a good base for **Hearst Castle**, the hilltop palace of publishing magnate William Randolph "Citizen Kane" Hearst.

Almost all of the towns grew up around Spanish **missions**, each a long day's walk from the next, and enclosed within thick walls to prevent Indian attack. **Monterey**, a hundred miles south of San Francisco, was California's capital under Spain and Mexico, and retains an attractive ensemble of early nineteenth-century architecture.

Amtrak's Coast Starlight **train** runs along the coast up to San Luis Obispo before cutting inland north to San Francisco; *Greyhound* **buses** stop at most of the towns, especially along the main highway, US-101. A better route, if you've got a car, is the smaller Hwy-1, which follows the coast all the way but takes twice as long.

Santa Barbara

The eight-lane coastal freeway that races past oil wells and offshore drilling platforms slows to a leisurely pace a hundred miles north of Los Angeles at **SANTA BARBARA**. This conservative town – home to Ronald Reagan – is beautifully sited, on gently sloping hills above the Pacific. The insistent red-tiled roofs and white stucco walls of its low-rise buildings form a backdrop to some fine Spanish Revival architecture, while the golden beaches are wide and clean, lined by palm trees along a curving bay. However, much of downtown has been replaced by a vast shopping mall, and Santa Barbara seems slowly but surely to be turning into an identikit Southern California town.

The Mission-era feel of Santa Barbara is no accident. Following a devastating earthquake in 1925, the entire town was rebuilt in the image of an apocryphal Spanish Colonial past, with numerous arcades linking shops, cafés and restaurants. **State Street** is the main drag, home to a friendly assortment of diners, bookshops, coffee bars and nightclubs catering for locals rather than visitors. The few remaining, genuine mission-era structures are preserved as the **Presidio de Santa Barbara** (Mon–Fri 10.30am–4.30pm, Sat & Sun noon–4pm; donations), the center of which, the two-hundred-year-old barracks, **El Cuartel**, stand two blocks off State Street on Perdido Street. The second-oldest building in California, this now houses historical exhibits and a scale model of the small Spanish colony. The more recent past is recounted in the nearby **museum** at 136 E de la Guerra St (Tues–Sun noon–5pm; free).

State Street leads half a mile down from the town center to wooden **Stearns Wharf**, built in 1872 and recently restored, with its seafood restaurants, ice cream stands and fish market, while magnificent **beaches** stretch away in either direction.

In the hills above the town is the beautiful **Mission Santa Barbara** (daily 9am–5pm; $2), the so-called "Queen of the Missions", with its colorful twin-towered facade. A small **museum** displays historical artefacts from the mission archives.

Practicalities

Hourly *Greyhound* **buses** from LA and San Francisco stop downtown at 34 W Cabrillo St; **trains** (☎687-6848) call at the old Southern Pacific station at 209 State St, a block west of US-101. The **visitor center** is on East Beach at 1 Santa Barbara St (☎966-9222). A free **shuttle bus** loops around Santa Barbara on weekdays, while the *Santa Barbara Metropolitan Transit District* (☎683-3702) covers the outlying areas.

Dorm beds at the new independent *International Hostel*, 409 State St (☎963-0154; ①), cost $13.50 per night; they run shuttle buses to LA and San Francisco, provide copious local information, and organize a free beer keg party every Monday. Otherwise, **rooms** are generally expensive and hard to find; low-priced options include the characterful old mission-style *Hotel State Street*, 121 State St (☎966-6586; ②), near the beach, and the no-frills *Motel 6*, 443 Corona del Mar (☎564-1392; ②).

Among fine Santa Barbara **restaurants** are the Mexican seafood specialists *Pescado's*, 422 N Milpas St (☎965-3805), and the upscale but not expensive New Mexican *Zia's*, at 532 State St (☎962-5391). Should your appetite for fish be uncontrollable, the *Enterprise Fish Co*, 225 State St (☎962-3313) is also excellent.

Cafés, bars and **clubs** line State Street; *Joseppi's* (no 434; ☎962-5516), is good for jazz, while *Zelo's* (no 630; ☎962-9991), hosts alternative DJs. The *Sojourner Coffee House*, 134 E Canon Perdido (☎965-7922), serves coffee, beer, wine, and a range of vegetarian food, in a friendly, hippyish setting, with live music some nights, while *Earthling Books*, 1137 State St (☎965-0926), has a popular late-night café.

San Luis Obispo

SAN LUIS OBISPO, ten miles northeast of the resort of Avila Beach and halfway between LA and San Francisco, is a few miles inland, but makes the best base for exploring the coast. Still primarily an agricultural market center, it holds more nineteenth-century architecture than any other Californian city, plenty of good restaurants, a couple of pubs, and – outside summer holiday weekends – lots of accommodation.

The compact core of San Luis is eminently walkable, centered around the late eighteenth-century **Mission San Luis Obispo de Tolosa** (daily 9am–5pm; free), a dark and unremarkable church that was the prototype for the now-ubiquitous red-tiled roof, developed to replace the original, flammable thatch in response to Indian arson attacks.

The **area code** for the central coast, from Santa Barbara to Big Sur, is ☎805.

Between the mission and the visitor center, **Mission Plaza**'s terraces step down along San Luis creek, along which footpaths meander, criss-crossed by bridges every hundred feet and overlooked by shops and outdoor restaurants on the south bank. **Higuera Street**, a block south of Mission Plaza, is the main drag, and springs to life on Thursday afternoons for the **Farmers' Market**, when the street is closed to cars and filled with vegetable stalls, mobile barbeques and street-corner musicians.

Practicalities

Greyhound is at 150 South St , while *Amtrak* trains stop at the end of Santa Rosa Street, half a mile south of the business district. The **visitor center** is at 1039 Chorro St (☎781-2777 or 1-800/634-1414). Monterey Street was the site of the world's first (long-gone) **motel** – the *Milestone Mo-tel*. Rates in its modern counterparts are generally low. For a kitsch treat, look in on the shocking pink behemoth that is the *Madonna Inn*, 100 Madonna Way (☎543-3000; ⑤). A waterfall flushes the mens' urinals (which look like whale mouths) and themed rooms range from fairy-tale princesses to cavemen. The English-owned *Adobe Inn*, 1473 Monterey St (☎549-0321; ③), is more conventional.

Higuera Street is the place to **eat**, especially during Thursday's market; *Linnaea's*, at 1110 Garden St off Higuera (☎541-5888) serves salads and healthy light meals, with live music most nights. *Buona Tavola*, 1037 Monterey St (☎545-8000) has a great selection of Italian food and wine.

Hearst Castle

Forty-five miles northwest of San Luis Obispo, the hilltop **HEARST CASTLE** is one of the most extravagant houses in the world. The home where publisher **William Randolph Hearst** held court over such guests as Winston Churchill, Charlie Chaplin, George Bernard Shaw and Charles Lindbergh now brings in over a million visitors a year. Its interior combines walls, floors and ceilings stolen from European churches and castles with Gothic fireplaces and Moorish tiles, and is bursting with Greek vases and medieval tapestries. Work on the 250,000-acre ranch began in 1919, managed by architect Julia Morgan, but was never completed: rooms were torn out as soon as they were finished in order to accommodate yet more bits and pieces of old buildings. The main facade, a twin-towered copy of a Mudejar cathedral, stands at the top of steps which curve up from a swimming pool filled with spring water and lined by a Greek colonnade.

Two-hour guided **tours** (daily summer 8am–5pm, winter 8am–3pm; reserve in summer; $14; ☎927-2020 or 1-800/444-7275) leave from the visitor center on Hwy-1.

W R HEARST – CITIZEN KANE

Often portrayed as a power-mad monster – most memorably by Orson Welles in his thinly veiled *Citizen Kane* – **William Randolph Hearst** seems in retrospect more like a very rich, over-indulged little boy. Born in 1863 as the only son of a multimillionaire mining engineer, he learned his trade in New York working for Joseph Pulitzer, the inventor of "Yellow Journalism". When he published his own *Morning Journal*, Hearst took Pulitzer's advice to heart, fanning the flames of American imperialism to ignite the Spanish-American War of 1898. As he told his correspondents in Cuba: "You provide the pictures, and I'll provide the war". Hearst eventually controlled an empire that during the 1930s sold twenty-five percent of the nation's newspapers – and sixty percent in California.

Despite his war-mongering and nationalism, Hearst was middle-of-the-road politically, a lifelong Democrat who served two terms in the House of Representatives but failed to be elected as Mayor of New York, let alone President. Besides his many newspapers, Hearst owned eleven radio stations and two movie studios, which he used to make his mistress Marion Davies a star. The Depression forced him to sell off most of his holdings, but he continued to exert power and influence until his death in 1951, aged 88.

Big Sur

The ninety wild and undeveloped miles of rocky cliffs of **BIG SUR** form a sublime land-scape at the edge of a continent, where redwood groves line river canyons and the Santa Lucia mountains rise straight out of the blue Pacific. Only the occasional outpost inter-rupts the tortuous exhilarating route of **Hwy-1**, carved out of bedrock cliffs five hundred feet above the ocean, and **public transportation** is limited to the twice-daily *MST* bus from Monterey. Hardly anyone braves the turbulent winters, when violent storms can sweep sections of the highway into the sea. Summer weekends see the roads and camp-grounds packed to overflowing, but a mile or two's walk still gets you away from it all.

The southern coastline of Big Sur is relatively gentle, with sandy beaches hiding below crumbling yellow-ochre cliffs. **Esalen** is named for the Indians who once enjoyed its natural **hot spring**, on a cliff top high above the raging Pacific surf. Since the 1960s, when people came to Big Sur to smoke pot and get back to nature, Esalen has been at the forefront of the "New Age" movement, and the spring is now owned and operated by the *Esalen Institute* (by reservation; $10; ☎667-3047).

Three miles north of Esalen, **Julia Pfeiffer Burns State Park** has some of the best day hikes in the Big Sur area, including a twenty-minute walk along the cliffs from the parking area to see a waterfall crashing down into the sea. As well as a free and basic campground, the lovely old *Deetjen's Big Sur Inn* on Hwy-1 (☎667-2377; ④) has rooms handcrafted from thick redwood planks, and excellent food. There are also good-sized cabins in the *Big Sur Lodge* (☎667-3100; ④).

Further north, at **Nepenthe**, the rooftop *Restaurant Nepenthe* offers affordable whole food and impressive views. Downstairs there's an outdoor sculpture gallery and the *Phoenix* bookstore, including works by Henry Miller, who lived locally until the 1960s. Big Sur's best beach is two miles north, where a barely marked road leads west from Hwy-1 a mile down Sycamore Canyon to **Pfeiffer Beach**, a white-sand beach dominated by a hump of rock whose color varies from brown to red to orange in the changing light.

Two miles north of Pfeiffer Beach, and 65 miles north of Hearst Castle, Hwy-1 drops into the valley of the Big Sur River. In sheltered **Pfeiffer Big Sur State Park**, deep clear swimming holes form in the steep-walled river gorge during late spring and summer, and a hiking trail leads half a mile up a canyon shaded by redwoods to the sixty-foot **Pfeiffer Falls**. The park is the center for information (☎667-2315) on the region's many year-round **campgrounds**. All are available for $14 a night (less if you're on foot or bicycle) on a first-come, first-camped basis; only in Pfeiffer Big Sur State Park itself can you reserve a space, through *MISTIX* (☎1-800/444-7275).

Big Sur Village

The village of **BIG SUR**, just north of Pfeiffer Big Sur State Park, is the most feasible base for seeing Big Sur, with a long strip along Hwy-1 of places to sleep and eat. Accommodation fills up in summer, but a night in one of the rustic **mountain lodges** is well worth experiencing. Those on the river include the *River Inn Resort* (☎625-5255 or 1-800/548-3610; ③–⑦), which has a very good **restaurant**, and the less welcoming *Fernwood* (☎667-2422), which has camping spots ($9–15) and simple cabins (③–④).

The Monterey Peninsula

The rocky headlands of the **Monterey Peninsula**, where gnarled cypress trees amplify the collision between the cliffs and the thundering sea, mark the northern edge of the Big Sur coast, a hundred miles south of San Francisco. The lively harbor town of

The **area code** for the Monterey Peninsula is ☎408.

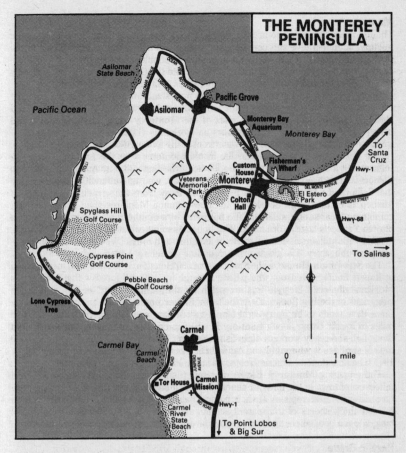

Monterey was the capital of California under the Spanish and Mexicans, and retains many old adobe houses and places of genuine historic appeal alongside some over-stated tourist traps. **Carmel**, on the other hand, three miles to the south, is a contrivedly quaint village of million-dollar holiday homes.

Arrival and Getting Around

If you're coming from the south, both *Greyhound* and *Amtrak* require you to change in the sprawling agricultural town of **Salinas** inland, and take a further 45-minute bus trip to 1042 Del Monte Ave in Monterey. **Getting around** the peninsula itself is surprisingly easy, on *Monterey-Salinas Transit* buses (7am–6pm; ☎899-2555). The most useful routes are bus #4 and #5 (Monterey–Carmel); #21 (Monterey–Salinas); and #1, (Monterey–Pacific Grove); there's also a free shuttle bus from downtown to the Aquarium on Cannery Row. Bus #22 runs to Big Sur twice a day, in summer only.

Another option is to **rent a bike**: the *Doubletree Inn* (☎649-4511) in Monterey, near Pacific House and the Wharf, rents out cruisers, and *Bay Bikes*, 640 Wave St in Cannery Row (☎646-9090), have good-quality mountain bikes; they're also in Carmel (☎625-BIKE) on Lincoln between Fifth and Sixth.

Monterey

Though named by Vizcaino in 1602, **MONTEREY** was not colonized until 1770, as the military, administrative and commercial center of a territory that extended east to the Rockies and north to Canada (with a non-native population of less than seven thousand). With the conjunction of the US takeover and the Gold Rush, Monterey suddenly became a backwater, hardly affected by the waves of immigration which followed.

Impressive vernacular colonial **buildings** now stand unassumingly in the compact town center, within a few blocks of the tourist-thronged waterfront. A loosely organized **Path of History** connects the 35 sites of the **Monterey State Historic Park**, and park rangers lead guided walking tours on weekends (11am & 2pm; $4; ☎649-2836) from the Customs House, near the waterfront at the foot of Alvarado Street.

The best place to get a feel for life in old Monterey is at the **Larkin House**, on Jefferson St a block south of Alvarado, home of the first and only American Consul to California. The New England-born Thomas Larkin, who was influential in persuading the Californians to turn towards the US and away from the erratic government of Mexico, is credited with developing the now-common Monterey style of architecture, combining local adobe walls and the balconies of a Southern plantation home with a puritan Yankee's taste in ornament. The house, the first two-storey adobe in California, is filled with millions of dollars' worth of antiques, and **tours** (Wed–Mon hourly 10am–4pm) are obligatory. The gorgeous surrounding gardens are open all day.

The **Stevenson House**, a short way east at 530 Houston St, is filled with memorabilia of Robert Louis Stevenson, who passed through in 1879 and foresaw that Monterey's Mexican-influenced lifestyle was no match for the "Yankee craft" of the "millionaire vulgarians of the Big Bonanza". At the tacky **Fisherman's Wharf**, the catch-of-the-day these days tends to be overweight families from San Jose. A **bike path** runs the two miles to Pacific Grove, along **Cannery Row** – named after John Steinbeck's portrait of the rough-and-ready workers of its fish canneries. During World War II some 200,000 tons of sardines were caught and canned each year, but the stocks were exhausted by 1945. The abandoned canneries reopened in the 1970s as malls and restaurants.

The engaging **Monterey Bay Aquarium** (daily 10am–6pm; $11, students $7), a mile west of town at the end of Cannery Row, exhibits over five thousand marine creatures in innovative replicas of their natural habitats. Sharks and octopi roam behind two-foot-thick sheets of transparent acrylic, and there's a 300,000-gallon Kelp Forest tank, a touch pool where you can pet your favorite bat rays, and a pool of **sea otters**.

Pacific Grove

PACIFIC GROVE, a quiet little town at the end of the peninsula, began as a campground and Methodist retreat in 1875, and still holds ornate wooden **cottages** from those days. **Ocean View Boulevard** circles the coast around the town, passing the headland of **Lovers Point** – originally called Lovers of Jesus Point – where preachers used to hold sunrise services. Surrounded in early summer by the colorful red and purple cloaks of blooming ice plant, it's one of the peninsula's best **beaches**.

Every year, hundreds of thousands of golden Monarch **butterflies** come to Pacific Grove to escape the winter chill, forming orange and black blankets on the **Butterfly Trees**, on Ridge Road, inland along Lighthouse Ave towards the Point Pinos lighthouse.

Carmel

Set on gently rising headlands above a sculpted rocky shore, **CARMEL** epitomizes parochial snobbery. The chance to catch a rare glimpse of ex-mayor Clint Eastwood may make the sterile shopping mall atmosphere worth bearing for an hour or so, but the real reason to come is the largely untouched nearby coastline. **Carmel Beach** is a tranquil cove of emerald blue water bordered by soft white sand and cypress-covered cliffs; the tides are deceptively strong and dangerous, so be careful if you chance a swim.

Hiking trails at the **Point Lobos State Reserve**, two miles south of Carmel on Hwy-1 ($5), give good views down into deep coves where sea otters may be seen surfing in the waves. The sea here is one of the richest underwater habitats in California, and gray whales are often seen offshore, migrating south in January and returning with young calves in April and early May. Because the point juts so far out into the ocean, chances are good of seeing them from as little as a hundred yards away.

Monterey Peninsula Accommodation

Hotel and **B&B** rates average $120 a night, but **motels** gather along Fremont Street, two miles north of central Monterey. Monterey's **visitor center**, 380 Alvarado St (Mon–Fri 9am–5pm; ☎649-1770), has full listings and can tell you where to find the **youth hostel** (summer only) this year. The nearest **camping** is in Veteran's Memorial Park, site of Steinbeck's fictional *Tortilla Flat*, at the top of Jefferson St in the hills above town.

Asilomar Conference Center, 800 Asilomar Blvd, Pacific Grove (☎372-8016). Rustic, handcrafted cabins and modern lodges in splendid beachfront location. ③.

Bide-a-Wee Motel, 221 Asilomar Ave, Pacific Grove (☎372-2330). Excellent value, no-frills rooms, including a few with kitchenettes. A two-minute walk to the ocean. ③.

Carmel River Inn, Rio Road at Hwy-1, Carmel (☎624-1575). Clean and pleasant motel, on the banks of the Carmel River, near the beach and Carmel Mission. ③.

Motel 6, 2124 Fremont St, Monterey (☎646-8585). Basic, no-frills motel, but in summer you'll have to reserve a room months in advance to avail yourself of their bargain doubles. ②.

Pacific Grove Motel, Lighthouse Ave at Grove Acre (☎372-3218). Basic, small motel in marvellous setting, 100 yards from the sea. Winter ③, summer ④.

Monterey Peninsula Eating

There are many excellent places to eat all over the peninsula. If you're on a tight budget, the best budget eats are on the north side of Monterey along Fremont Street.

Café Fina, Fisherman's Wharf, Monterey (☎372-5200). Pasta dishes, wood-oven pizzas and, of course, grilled fresh fish in the Wharf's most style-conscious setting.

Fishwife Restaurant, 1996 Sunset Drive at Asilomar, Pacific Grove (☎375-7107). Long-standing local favorite, serving great food at reasonable prices in homey, unpretentious surroundings.

La Boheme, Dolores St between Ocean and 7th, Carmel (☎624-7500). Fine dining in a scaled-down replica of a French country hotel. Multi-course, *prix-fixe* meals for $17.50 plus wine and service.

Pepper's Mexicali Café, 170 Forest Ave, Pacific Grove (☎373-6892). Gourmet Mexican seafood Californified into healthy, high-style dishes that won't put too big a hole in your wallet.

Drinking and Nightlife

The clubs on the peninsula feature sedate live and canned music, though things pick up a bit with the world-class Monterey Jazz Festival in September (☎373-3366).

The Club of Monterey, Alvarado and Del Monte St (☎646-9244). Fairly young and upscale crowd at this DJ-dance club; darts and pool tables downstairs. Cover $1–8, with occasional live acts.

The Firehouse, 414 Calle Principal, Monterey (☎649-3016). Characterful cocktail lounge in historic brick fire station. Free live music at the weekend.

Monterey Brewing Company, 700 Cannery Row, Monterey (☎375-3634). Good, micro-brewed lagers and ales, bar food, and nightly live rock or blues bands.

Portofino Café, 620 Lighthouse Ave, Pacific Grove (☎373-7379). Casual café with acoustic folk and jazz musicians on weekend nights; cover under $5.

Santa Cruz

After the overcharged tourism of Monterey, the quiet easy-going community of **SANTA CRUZ**, 75 miles south of San Francisco, comes as a welcome surprise. Although in many ways it's the quintessential Californian coastal town, spread at the foot of thickly wooded mountains beside a clean sandy beach, it has grown a bit too fast for comfort in the last few years, and the destruction wrought by the 1989 earthquake seems to have brought it up short – progress in repairing the damage has been very slow. In the Sixties, the Merry Pranksters turned the local youth on to LSD long before it defined a generation, and the area is still among the most politically and socially progressive in California. It's also surprisingly untouristed. No hotels spoil the miles of wave-beaten coastline; most of the land is agricultural, and roadside stands are more likely to sell apples or sprouts than postcards and souvenirs.

The **Santa Cruz Boardwalk**, the last surviving beachfront amusement park on the West Coast, is the main focus for visitors (summer daily 11am–10pm, winter weekends only; free admission, unlimited rides $16.95). Packed at the weekend with teenagers on the prowl, most of the time it's a friendly funfair, where barefoot hippies mix with mushroom farmers. The star attraction is the **Big Dipper**, a wild wooden roller coaster.

The **beach** next to the Boardwalk is good but can get very rowdy. For more peace and quiet, follow the coast out of town to one of the smaller beaches hidden away at the foot of the cliffs. From **West Cliff Drive**, you'll see some of the biggest waves in California, not least at **Steamer Lane**, beyond the Municipal Pier. The ghosts of surfers past are animated at the **Surfing Museum** (daily noon–4pm; free) in the old lighthouse on the point, were surfboards range from early twelve-foot redwood planks to modern hi-tech multi-finned cutters. A cliff-top cycle path runs two miles to **Natural Bridges State Park**, where waves have cut holes through the coastal cliffs, forming delicate stone arches (though three of its four eponymous bridges have now collapsed).

Practicalities

Greyhound buses from San Francisco stop four times a day at 425 Front St, in the center of town, as do *Peerless Stages* from Oakland and San Jose, and *Green Tortoise*. The **Santa Cruz Visitors Council** is at 701 Front St (Mon–Fri 9am–5pm; ☎425-1234 or 1-800/833-3494). An excellent **public transportation** system centers on the Metro Center at 920 Pacific Ave. The basic fare is $1, and an all-day pass is $2. *Surf City Cycles*, 46 Front St (☎423-9050), rents **bikes** from $25 a day.

Off season, Santa Cruz has plenty of inexpensive places to **stay**. Cheapest of the lot is the *Santa Cruz Hostel*, 511 Broadway (☎423-8304; ①). *Inn Cal*, at 370 Ocean St across the river (☎458-9220; ②), has spartan doubles, and the 1887 *Cliff Crest Inn*, 407 Cliff St (☎427-2609; ⑤), at the top of Beach Hill, is more luxurious. Among several good seafront **restaurants** is the *Miramar*, 45 Municipal Wharf (☎423-4441); *El Paisano*, 605 Beach St at Riverside (☎426-2382), serves great Mexican food. The best **campground** around is at *New Brighton State Beach* (☎475-4850 or 1-800/444-7275 for reservations), three miles south on the edge of the beachfront village of Capitola.

Santa Cruz has the central coast's most diverse nightlife; the music in its unpretentious and unthreatening bars and nightclubs varies from heavy-duty surf-thrash to lilting reggae to the rowdy rock of local resident Neil Young. *The Catalyst*, 1011 Pacific Ave (☎423-1336), is the best bet for catching big-name touring artists and up-and-coming locals, while the *Front Street Pub*, 516 Front St (☎429-8838), offers home-brewed lagers and ales, and live music or comedians most nights.

The Coast North to San Francisco

Twenty-five miles up the coast from Santa Cruz, the beginning of the San Francisco Peninsula is marked by **Pigeon Point Lighthouse** (☎415/879-0633; ①/②), where you can spend the night in the old lighthouse keeper's quarters and soak your bones in a hot tub, cantilevered out over the rocks. Dorm beds cost $11 (plus $2 for non-AYH members) and there are also private doubles. Pigeon Point took its name from the clipper ship, *Carrier Pigeon*, that broke up on the rocks off the point, one of many shipwrecks that led to the construction of the lighthouse in the late nineteenth century.

The cargo of one of these wrecked ships inspired residents of the nearby fishing village of **PESCADERO**, a mile inland, literally to "paint the town", using hundreds of pots of white paint that were washed up on the shore. The two streets of the small village are still lined by white, wooden buildings, and the descendants of the Portuguese whalers who founded the town keep up another, more enticing tradition, celebrating the annual **Festival of the Holy Ghost**, six weeks after Easter, with a lively and highly ritualized parade. Pescadero is well known as one of the best places to **eat** on the entire coast; it has an excellent restaurant, *Duarte's*, 202 Stage Rd (☎415/ 879-0464), serving fish dinners and fresh fruit pies, and *Dinelli's Café*, 1956 Pescadero Creek Rd (☎415/879-0106), with Greek food and tasty fried artichoke hearts.

THE CENTRAL VALLEY

The vast **interior** of California is split down the middle by the Sierra Nevada mountains. The wide **Central Valley** in the west was made super-fertile by irrigation projects during the 1940s, and is now almost totally agricultural. Even if the nightlife begins and ends with the local ice cream parlor, after the big cities of the coast it can all be quite refreshing. However, the real reason to come here is to reach the **national parks** of **Sequoia** and **Kings Canyon** – whose huge trees form the centerpiece of a rich natural landscape – and **Yosemite**, where towering walls of silvery granite are invigorated by cascading waterfalls. No roads penetrate the hundred miles of wilderness to the east, but the entire region is criss-crossed by hiking trails leading up into the pristine alpine back country of the **High Sierra**. Seen from the east side, their Spanish name, *Sierra Nevada* ("snow-capped sawblade"), perfectly describes the sharply serrated ridges that stand high above the deserted **Owens Valley**.

The arrow-straight I-5 barrels straight up from LA to San Francisco. Four daily **trains** and frequent *Greyhound* **buses** run through the valley, with bus connections from Fresno and Merced to Yosemite. Despite its sparse population, the Owens Valley is easy both to reach and to get around, with a daily *Greyhound* service along US-395 between LA and Reno, Nevada, and the *Trailhead Shuttle Service* (☎872-2721) ferrying hikers, bikers and skiers to the main High Sierra trailheads.

Bakersfield

The first town you come to across the rocky peaks north of Los Angeles, looming unappealingly out of a forest of oil derricks, is the flat and featureless **BAKERSFIELD**. This is the unlikely home of one of the liveliest **country music** scenes in the nation, stemming from the arrival during the Depression of midwestern farmers, with their hillbilly instruments and campfire songs. In the mid-Sixties, the gutsy honky-tonk style of Bakersfield artists such as Merle Haggard and Buck Owens challenged the slick commercial output of Nashville, but hopes of luring the major country music record labels to "Nashville West" foundered with the emergence of rivals like Austin, Texas.

Nevertheless, the numerous honky-tonks of Bakersfield are still jumping every Friday and Saturday night. There's never a cover charge, and live sets usually entail one band playing for four or five hours from around 8pm, with a fifteen-minute break every hour. Stetson hats and flowery blouses are the sartorial order of the day, and audiences span generations. Most **venues** are hotel lounges or restaurant backrooms; one not to be missed is the country bar *Trouts*, 805 N Chester Ave (☎805/399-6700). Close by, you might also investigate *Cassidy's*, 4500 Pierce Rd (☎805/631-9206) or *Junction Lounge*, 2620 Pierce Rd (☎805/327-9651). Other worthwhile places lie half an hour's drive across town: *Brandy's Tavern*, 2700 S Union Ave (☎805/831-9853), *Little Bit Country*, 3317 State Rd (☎805/393-8044), and *Porter's House*, 10701 Hwy-78 (☎805/366-6000).

Practicalities

You have to come to Bakersfield from LA by *Amtrak* bus to catch the train through the valley to San Francisco and northern California, and several *Greyhound* routes require changes here too (1820 18th St). The **visitor center** is at 2101 Oak St (Mon–Fri 8am–5pm; ☎805/861-2367). Bargain **overnight stays** are at *EZ-8*, 2604 Pierce Rd (☎1-800/326-6835; ②), and the *Roadrunner Motel*, 2619 Pierce Rd (☎805/323-3727; ②); *Zingo's* at 2625 Pierce Rd (☎805/324-3640) is a 24-hour truckstop where frilly-aproned waitresses deliver plates of diner staples.

Sequoia and Kings Canyon

The southernmost of the Sierra Nevada national parks, preserving ancient forests of giant sequoia trees, are **SEQUOIA** and **KINGS CANYON**. As you might expect, **Sequoia National Park** contains the thickest concentration – and the biggest specimens – of sequoias to be found anywhere, tending (literally) to overshadow its assortment of meadows, peaks, canyons and caves. **Kings Canyon National Park** has few big trees but compensates with a gaping canyon gored out of the rock by the Kings River as it cascades down from the High Sierra. The few established sights (like the drive-through Auto Log) of both parks are near the main roads, leaving the vast majority of the landscape untrammelled and unspoilt, but well within reach for willing hikers.

Arrival and Information

No **public transportation** of any kind serves the parks, but by **car** things are simple: the closest large town is **Visalia**, just under fifty miles distant on Hwy-198, or a slightly longer drive uses Hwy-180 from Fresno. On payment of a **fee** of $5 per car, or $3 per person for those on foot or bike, you'll be given a copy of *Sequoia Bark*, detailing **guided hikes** and other activities. The two parks are separate but jointly run; **park headquarters** is on ☎565-3134, and **weather** and **road information** on ☎565-3351.

Sequoia National Park

While trees are seldom scarce in Sequoia National Park – where the giant sequoias can't grow there are thick swathes of pine and fir – the scenery varies. Paths lead through forests and meadows; longer treks rise above the treeline to the barren peaks of the High Sierras. Soon after entering the park, Hwy-180 becomes the **Generals' Highway** and climbs swiftly into the dense woods of the aptly labelled **Giant Forest**. **Giant Forest Village**, near the junction with Crescent Meadow Road, makes a good base for explorations. Six miles along a marked trail from the village (or a 15-min walk off Crescent Meadow Rd), the granite monolith of **Moro Rock** streaks wildly upward from the green hillside. Views from its remarkably level top can stretch 150 miles. A masonry staircase makes it easy to climb the rock, although the altitude can be a strain.

Continuing along Crescent Meadow Road you pass the **Auto Log**, chiselled flat for motorists to drive on to it, and go under the **Tunnel Log**, which fell across the road in 1937 and had a vehicle-sized hole cut through it. Further on, **Crescent Meadow** is, like other grassy fields in the area, more accurately a marsh, and too wet for the sequoias which form an impressive boundary around. A perimeter trail leads to **Log Meadow**. Hale Tharp, searching for a summer grazing ground for his sheep, was led here by Indians in 1856. He was not only the first white man to see the giant sequoias but the first to live in one – the hollowed-out **Tharp's Log**. Just north of Giant Forest

---

The **area code** for the national parks of the central valley is ☎209.

on the Generals' Highway is the biggest sequoia of them all, the three-thousand-year-old, 275ft **General Sherman Tree**. While it's certainly a thrill to be face-to-bark with what is held to be the largest living thing on the planet, its extraordinary dimensions are hard to grasp alongside the almost equally monstrous sequoias around.

Whatever your plans, you should stop at **Lodgepole Village**, at the end of Tokopah Valley four miles from Giant Forest Village, for the geological displays and film shows at the **visitor center** (daily 8am–5pm). You can explore the glacial canyon on the **Tokopah Valley Trail**, which leads to the base of Tokopah Falls, beneath the 1600ft **Watchtower** cliff. The top of the Watchtower, with its great view of the valley, are accessible by way of the fatiguing but straightforward seven-mile **Lakes Trail**.

Kings Canyon National Park

Kings Canyon National Park is wilder and less visited than Sequoia, with a maze-like collection of canyons and a sprinkling of isolated lakes – the perfect environment for careful self-guided exploration. To reach the canyon proper, you have to pass through **Grant Grove**, where there's a useful **visitor center** (daily 8am–5pm) and the General Grant and Robert E Lee giant sequoias, as well as the massive stump of another which was taken to the 1875 World's Fair in Philadelphia to convince cynical easterners that such enormous trees really existed. A mile from Grant Grove, the **Big Stump Area** is named after the big stumps which litter the place – remnants from the first logging of sequoias carried out during the 1880s. A mile-long nature trail leads through this scene of devastation. It's hardly an enjoyable experience, even if you can spot the ageing remains of flumes used to transport logs to the valley.

Kings Canyon Highway, Hwy-180, descends from Grant Grove into the steep-sided Kings Canyon, cut by the furious gushings of various forks of the Kings River. Whether or not this is the deepest canyon in the US, as some would have it, its wall sections of granite and gleaming blue marble and the yellow pockmarks of yucca plants are magnificent. It's extremely perilous to wade into the river: people have been swept away even when paddling close to the bank in a seemingly placid section.

Once into the National Park proper, the canyon sheds its V-shape and gains a floor. **Cedar Grove Village** here is named for its proliferation of incense cedars. There's a **ranger station** across the river (Mon–Thurs 7am–3pm, Fri & Sat 7am–5pm). Apart from the scenery, you should look out for the **flowers**: Leopard lilies, shooting stars, violets, lupines and others, and a variety of birdlife. The longer hikes through the creeks, many seven or eight miles long, are fairly strenuous. An easy alternative, however, is to pootle around the beckoning green carpet of **Zumwalt Meadow**, four miles from Cedar Grove Village and a short walk from the road, beneath the forbidding grey walls of Grand Sentinel and North Dome.

Just a mile further, Kings Canyon Road comes to an end at **Copper Creek**. Thirty years ago it was sensibly decided not to allow vehicles to penetrate further. Instead the multitude of canyons and peaks which constitute the Kings River Sierra are networked by **hiking paths**, almost all best enjoyed armed with a tent and some provisions.

Accommodation and Eating in the Parks

The least expensive **rooms** are in the motels near the park entrances; *Snowline Lodge*, on Hwy-180 (☎336-2300; ③), and the *Badger Creek Ranch Resort*, beside Hwy-245 (☎337-2340; ③). Inside the parks, all facilities are managed by *Guest Services Inc* (☎561-3314), with cabins at Giant Forest Village, Grant Grove and Cedar Grove. Space is at a premium during the high season (May–Oct), but you can usually pick up cancellations on the day. Summer prices range from $30 for basic cabins, to $90 for a deluxe version. In winter the cheaper cabins are too cold; a mid-range one costs around $40.

Recorded **camping** information for both parks is on ☎565-3351. In **Sequoia**, the busiest campground is *Lodgepole* (only bookable through *MISTIX*; ☎1-800/365-2267); Mineral King offers the basic *Atwell Mill* and *Cold Springs*. In **Kings Canyon**, the *Sunset*, *Azalea* and *Crystal Springs* campgrounds are all close to Grant Grove, and *Canyon View*, *Moraine*, *Sheep Creek* and *Sentinel* are dotted around Cedar Grove. At artificial Hume Lake, five miles north of Grant Grove, there's the large *Princess* campground. For **backcountry** camping, get a free permit from a visitor center or ranger station.

There are **food** markets and cafeterias in the various villages, but the only fully fledged **restaurant** is *Giant Forest Lodge Dining Room* at Giant Forest Village, which provides a fitting culinary reward for a hard day's hiking.

The Sierra National Forest

The entire gaping tract of land between Kings Canyon and Yosemite is taken up by the less-visited **SIERRA NATIONAL FOREST**. If you want to hike and camp in complete solitude, this is the place to do it. But don't try lone exploration without thorough planning, and don't expect a convenient bus to pick you up when you're tired. Public transportation is virtually nonexistent. For practical information in advance call in at the **forest information office**, 1130 O St, in **Fresno** (Mon–Fri 8.30am–4pm; ☎487-5155).

Of the forest's two main regions, the **Pineridge** district, forty miles east from Fresno using Hwy-168, is the best for adventurous hiking. The most isolated alpine landscapes are around Kaiser Pass, where the campgrounds are all free, and there are rooms at the *Vermillion Valley Resort* close to Edison Lake. The sheer challenge posed by the rugged, unspoilt terrain of the adjoining **John Muir Wilderness**, with some of the starkest peaks and lushest alpine meadows of the High Sierra, can make the national parks look like holiday camps. Buses run to the trailheads from the resort; if you want to do some serious hiking, or even just spend the night camped out under the stars, you need a free permit from the **ranger station** (daily 8am–4.30pm, ☎841-3311) along Hwy-168, a mile south of Shaver Lake. Bad weather can strike even in late spring or early autumn, and the road and trails are often closed.

Further north, pine-fringed **Bass Lake** in the **Mariposa** district, just off Hwy-41 between Fresno and Yosemite, is the biggest tourist attraction in the forest. A stamping ground for Hell's Angels in the Sixties, it's now simply a good base for hiking and camping; you can get details from the **Mariposa Ranger District Office** in **Oakhurst** seven miles south (daily 8am–4.30pm; ☎683-4665). As an alternative to the fully equipped **campgrounds** around the lake, for which reservations are essential in summer (made via *MISTIX*), there are four-berth rooms at *Ducey's Bass Lake Lodge* on road 342 on its northern side (☎642-3131; ②), or *Miller's Landing* on road 222 to the south (☎642-3633; ②). Again, booking ahead is vital.

Yosemite National Park

More gushing adjectives have been thrown at **YOSEMITE NATIONAL PARK** than at any other part of California. However excessive the hyperbole may seem, the instant you turn the corner which reveals **Yosemite Valley** you realize it's actually an understatement – this is one of the world's most dramatic geological spectacles. Just seven miles long and at most one mile across, it's walled by near-vertical mile-high cliffs, streaked by cascading waterfalls and topped by domes and pinnacles which form a jagged silhouette against the sky. At ground level, grassy meadows are framed by oak, cedar and fir trees; deer, coyotes, and even black bears are not uncommon. Tourists are even more common, but the park is big enough to endure the crowds: you can visit

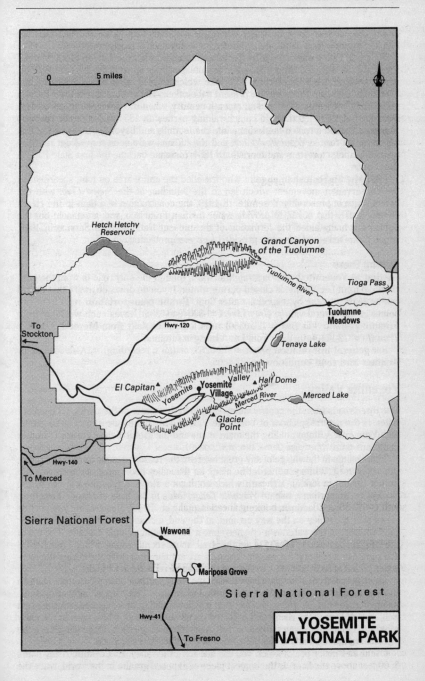

0   5 miles

Hetch Hetchy
Reservoir

Grand Canyon
of the Tuolumne

Tuolumne River

Tioga Pass

To
Stockton

Hwy-120

Tuolumne
Meadows

Tenaya Lake

El Capitan

Yosemite

Yosemite
Village

Half Dome

Merced River

Merced Lake

Glacier
Point

Hwy-140

To Merced

Sierra National Forest

Wawona

Mariposa Grove

Sierra National Forest

Hwy-41

To Fresno

**YOSEMITE
NATIONAL PARK**

at any time of year, even in winter when the waterfalls turn to ice and the trails are blocked by snow, and out of high summer the valley itself is rarely crammed.

Yosemite Valley was created by glaciers gouging through the canyon of the Merced River; the ice scraped away the softer granite but only scarred the harder sections, which became the present cliffs. The lake which formed when the glaciers melted eventually silted up to create the present valley floor. Native Americans lived here in comparative peace until the mid-nineteenth century, when the threatening approach of Gold Rush settlers led them to launch raiding parties. In 1851 Major James Savage's Mariposa Battalion trailed the Indians into the foothills and beyond, becoming the first whites to set foot in Yosemite Valley, and the Indians were soon moved out to make way for farmers, foresters and tourists. In 1864 Yosemite became the first State Park in the country.

John Muir, a Scottish immigrant who travelled the entire area on foot, spearheaded the conservation movement which led to the founding of the *Sierra Club*, with the express aim of preserving Yosemite. In 1913, the construction of a dam in the Hetch Hetchy Valley just north, to provide water for San Francisco, was a setback; but the publicity actually aided the formation of the present National Park Service in 1916, which promised – and has since provided – greater protection.

Getting There
Getting to Yosemite by car is straightforward, though the only road in from the east, Hwy-120 from Lee Vining, is closed during winter. If you do drive, be aware that **petrol** can be hard to come by, especially after 6pm. **Public transportation** runs from two points in the central valley. *Gray Line* (☎1-800/640-6306) leaves each weekday from **Fresno**; *Yosemite Via Bus* (☎722-0366) runs four times daily from **Merced**. *Yosemite Transit* (☎372-1240) run daily from **Lee Vining** in summer.

For **general information** phone ☎372-0265, or (for a recording) ☎372-0264; and for **weather and road conditions** ☎372-4605.

Yosemite Valley

The three roads from the central valley end up in the center of the park's 1200 square miles, in the natural splendor of **Yosemite Valley**. This is the busiest part of Yosemite, with **Yosemite Village** holding the main shops and the useful **visitor center** (summer daily 9am–6pm, otherwise 9am–5pm; ☎372-0299).

There's little in the village of any great interest; the reason to come here is to explore the valley itself. While you'll never be alone on the valley floor, most of the crowds can be left behind by taking any path which contains a slope. A 3.5-mile walk from the *Sunnyside* campground, behind *Yosemite Lodge*, leads to the base of **Upper Yosemite Falls**. This almost continuous ascent is very sapping on the leg muscles, but you get fine views over the valley on the way up, and, at the end, a chance to appreciate the power (and volume) of the water as it crashes almost 1500 feet in a single cascade. The top of the falls can be reached by way of another trail, about six miles long, which branches off at a signposted point on the way up. The falls are at their most dramatic during the melt-water period of April and May; by August they can be reduced to a trickle.

An easy trail from *Yosemite Lodge* passes the disappointing Lower Yosemite Falls on the way to **Mirror Lake**, a mile from shuttle bus stop 17. This compellingly calm lake – its meditative stillness due to the fact that it's slowly silting up – lies beneath the great bulk of Half Dome, the rising cliff reflected on its surface, and is best seen in the early morning, before too many tourists arrive. Also within easy reach of the village are the sensual **Bridalveil Falls**, a slender ribbon at the valley's western end.

Of the two major peaks which you can see from the valley, **El Capitan**, rising some 3500 feet above the floor, is the biggest piece of exposed granite in the world, twice the size of the Rock of Gibraltar. A sense of its dimensions can be gleaned by the fact that rock-climbers fast become invisible to the naked eye from ground level. The best time for attempting an assault is early summer or autumn; during the height of summer the heat of the rock face can reach 100° F. **Half Dome**, the sheerest cliff in North America, is only seven percent off the vertical. You can hike up by way of a steel staircase hooked on to its curving back from the far end of Little Yosemite Valley; if you plan a one-day assault, you'll need to start at the crack of dawn.

The most spectacular views of Yosemite Valley are from **Glacier Point**, the top of a 3200ft almost sheer cliff, 32 miles by road from the valley. It's possible to get there on foot using the very steep four-mile track from the western end of the valley, beside Hwy-41, though the lazy prefer to take the bus up (details below) and the trail down. The valley floor lies directly beneath the viewing point, and there are tremendous views across to Half Dome and the distant snow-capped summits of the High Sierra.

Practicalities

Prices within Yosemite are uniformly higher than outside the park, but not unaffordable. Of the **hotels** in the valley, *Yosemite Lodge* has cabins (②) and rooms (④); you may get substantial reductions by waiting for cancellations. *Curry Village*, a mile from Yosemite Village, has similarly priced rooms but also offers fixed tents and cabins (①). For hotel information, call ☎252-4848.

Camping in the valley is only permitted in campgrounds, such as *Sunnyside Walk-In*, just west of *Yosemite Lodge*, which is popular with rock-climbers and has a bohemian reputation, and the calmer *Backpacker's Camp*. You must book ahead in summer, via *MISTIX* (☎1-800/365-2267); general information is on ☎372-4845.

As for **food**, there are stores, diners and snack bars in Yosemite Village, the best of which is *Degnan's Deli*, where massive sandwiches cost around $4. The *Mountain Room Broiler* at *Yosemite Lodge* is good but fairly pricey, while the baronial *Ahwahnee Dining Room* (☎372-1489) has the best (and most expensive) food in Yosemite. *Yosemite Lodge* also has the valley's liveliest **bar**.

Free **shuttle buses** loop around the valley in summer (7.30am–10pm). **Cars** spoil everybody's fun; if you drive in for the day, park at Curry Village. A number of **bicycle paths** cross the valley floor but **bike rental** is limited to outlets at *Yosemite Lodge* and *Curry Village*. There are also **guided tours** (☎372-1240), **hikes**, and **horseback trips**.

Outside the Valley

The **Mariposa Grove**, three miles east of Hwy-41 on a small road which cuts off just past the park's southern entrance, is the biggest and best of Yosemite's groves of **giant sequoia** trees. To get to the towering growths, walk the 2.5-mile loop trail from the parking lot at the end of the road, which is also served by a free tram from the entrance. The most renowned of the grouping, well marked along the route, is the **Grizzly Giant**, thought to be 2700 years old.

On the eastern edge of the park, the alpine **Tuolumne Meadows** have an atmosphere quite different from the valley; here, at 8500 feet, you almost seem to be level with the tops of the surrounding snow-covered mountains. The air always has a fresh, crisp bite, and early summer reveals a plethora of colorful wild blossoms. It's a better starting point than the valley for backcountry hiking into the High Sierras, where seven hundred-odd miles of trails, both long and short, criss-cross their way along the Sierra Nevada ridge. To use any of the primitive **backcountry campgrounds**, you must get a **wilderness permit**, available by post from the Wilderness Office, Box 577, Yosemite National Park, CA 95389, or from the nearest visitor center no more than 24 hours in advance. Canvas **tent cabins** are available in Tuolomne in summer only for around $35.

The High Sierra and Owens Valley

The towering **eastern** peaks of the **High Sierra** drop abruptly to the empty landscape of the **Owens Valley** far below. Almost the entire range is wilderness: well-maintained roads lead to trailheads at over ten thousand feet, providing access to the stark terrain of spires, glaciers and clear mountain lakes. US-395 is the lifeline of the area, travelled daily by *Greyhound* and with plenty of budget motels. *Backpacker Shuttle Service* runs to trailheads in the Eastern Sierra ($10 per person, $20 minimum per trip; ☎872-2721).

Mount Whitney

Rising out of the northern Mojave Desert, the Sierra Nevada Mountains announce themselves with a bang two hundred miles north of Los Angeles at 14,494ft **MOUNT WHITNEY**, the highest point in the continental US. A silver-grey knifelike ridge of pinnacles forms a nearly sheer wall of granite, dominating the small roadside town of **Lone Pine** eleven thousand feet below. **Motels** here include *Trails Motel* at 633 S Main St (☎1-800/524-9999; ②), and the *Frontier Best Western*, 1008 S Main St (☎1-800/231-4047; ②). The *Sportsman Café*, 206 S Main St (☎876-5454), and the *Sierra Cantina*, 123 N Main St (☎876-5740), are decent places to **eat**. For more information, contact the **Chamber of Commerce** at 126 S Main St (Mon–Sat 9am–5pm; ☎876-4444).

Many early Westerns, and the epic *Gunga Din*, were filmed in the **Alabama Hills** to the west, a rugged expanse of bizarrely eroded sedimentary rock. Some of the oddest formations are linked by the **Picture Rocks Circle**, a dirt road that loops around from Whitney Portal Road, passing rocks shaped like bullfrogs, walruses and baboons. There is a free **campground** at Tuttle Creek, on the south edge of the hills.

Two thousand eager mountaineers make the strenuous 21-mile round-trip climb to the summit of Mount Whitney each summer. Ascents start at dawn from the non-reservable **campground** (reachable on a shuttle bus) at the end of twisting Whitney Portal Road. The trail cuts up past alpine lakes to boulder-strewn Trail Crest Pass, the southern end of the 220-mile John Muir Trail to Yosemite, then climbs along the top of vertical cliffs. At the rounded summit, a stone cabin serves as an emergency shelter.

Big Pine and the White Mountains

Nearly fifty miles north, hikes lead from the end of Glacier Lodge Road, ten miles west of nondescript **BIG PINE**, up to the **Palisades Glacier**, the southernmost glacier in the northern hemisphere. Along the opposite wall of the five-mile-wide Owens Valley, the bald, dry and inhospitable **White Mountains** are home to the gnarled **Bristlecone Pines**, the oldest living things on earth. Standing on the lower slopes, and often covered in snow until mid-June, some of these gnarled trees have been alive for over four thousand years. Battered and beaten by the harsh environment into contorted but beautiful shapes, even when dead they hang on without decaying for upwards of another thousand-odd years, slowly being eroded by wind-driven ice and sand.

Schulmann Grove, named for Dr Edmund Schulmann who discovered the trees in the mid-Fifties, is the most accessible collection, at the end of the paved road that twists up from Hwy-168. The mile-long Discovery Trail passes by some photogenic examples; another, longer, trail loops past the oldest tree, the 4700-year-old Methuselah. **Patriarch Grove**, eleven miles further, along a dusty dirt road that gives spectacular views of the Sierra Nevada to the west and the Great Basin ranges of the deserts to the east, contains the largest Bristlecone Pine, also over four thousand years old.

The **area code** for the High Sierra and Owens Valley is ☎619.

A couple of **motels** can be found along US-395 in Big Pine – the *Big Pine Motel* (☎938-2282; ②), and the *Starlight Motel* (☎938-2011; ②).

The Bishop Area

BISHOP, to a Californian, means outdoor pursuits. The largest town (population 3500) in the Owens Valley, it's an excellent base for rock-climbing, hang-gliding, cross-country skiing or even fly-fishing. It's also easy to get to; besides *Greyhound* buses, two scheduled airlines serve the city daily from Los Angeles: *Alpha Air* (☎1-800/421-9353) and *United Express*, both for around $120–150 round-trip. Motels and bargain restaurants can be found within a block of US-395 (Main Street in the town), such as the *El Rancho*, 274 W Lagoon St (☎872-9251; ②); and the *Thunderbird*, 190 W Pine St (☎873-4215; ②). The **visitor center** at 690 N Main St (Mon–Fri 9am–5pm, Sat & Sun 10am–4pm; ☎873-8405) can provide details of the many **adventure travel specialists** based in town.

For information on **hiking** and **camping**, contact the ranger station at 798 N Main St (☎873-2500). One appealing destination is the **Devil's Postpile National Monument**, 25 miles northwest beyond the ski resort of **Mammoth Lakes**. A collection of slender, blue-grey basaltic columns, some as tall as sixty feet, the Postpile was formed as lava from a volcanic eruption cooled and fractured into multi-sided forms. The real highlight is **Rainbow Falls**, reached by a two-mile hike along the San Joaquin River.

Mono Lake and Lee Vining

The blue expanse of **Mono Lake** sits in the midst of a volcanic, desert tableland at the north end of the valley. It looks like a science-fiction landscape, with two large islands, one light colored, the other shiny black, surrounded by salty, alkaline water. Strange sandcastle-like **tufa** formations have been exposed over the fifty years since the City of Los Angeles extended an aqueduct into the Mono Basin through an eleven-mile tunnel, dropping the **water level** by over forty feet and creating the biggest environmental controversy in California. Mono Lake is the primary nesting ground for the state's seagull population – twenty percent of the world total – and a prime stopover point for thousands of migratory geese, ducks and swans. As the levels drop, the islands in the middle of the lake, where the seagulls lay their eggs, become peninsulas, and the colonies fall prey to coyotes and other mainland predators. The landlocked water is becoming increasingly alkaline, threatening its unique eco-system.

For more details about Mono Lake and the fight for its survival, stop by the **visitor center** (daily 9am–5pm; ☎647-3044), between the lake and the small town of **LEE VINING** on US-395. *Greyhound* buses from the south stop here daily at 1.50am, while the bus from Reno in the north comes in at the more reasonable 11am. There are a couple of **motels** along US-395: *El Mono Motel* (☎647-6310; ②) and *Murphey's* (☎647-6316; ②). **Eat** at *Nicely's Restaurant* (☎647-6477), a Fifties vinyl palace that opens at 6am. In summer, *Yosemite Transit* buses leave from the parking lot each morning for the trip into the park, costing $20.25 round-trip. **Campgrounds** line Lee Vining Creek off the Tioga Pass Road, Hwy-120; stop by the **ranger station** (☎647-6525) one mile west of Lee Vining, for details, and wilderness permits for backcountry camping.

Northeast of Lee Vining, in a remote, high desert valley, stands a well-preserved and evocative relic of the gold-mining 1870s. **BODIE** is perhaps the best **ghost town** in the US, far enough out of the way to be relatively tourist-free. With thirty saloons and dance halls and a population of ten thousand, it was once the raunchiest and most lawless mining camp in the west; over 150 wooden buildings survive in a state of arrested decay around the intact town center, littered with old bottles and bits of machinery and old stagecoaches. The ruins of the mines themselves, in the hills east of town, are unfortunately off limits to visitors due to their dangerously run-down state.

SAN FRANCISCO

SAN FRANCISCO proper occupies just 48 hilly square miles at the tip of a slender peninsula, almost perfectly centered along the California coast. Arguably the most beautiful, certainly the most liberal city in the US, it remains true to itself: a funky, individualistic, surprisingly small city whose people pride themselves on being the cultured counterparts to their cousins in LA – the last bastion of civilization on the lunatic fringe of America. It's a compact and approachable place, where downtown streets rise on impossible gradients to reveal stunning views of the city, the bay and beyond, and blanket fogs roll in unexpectedly to envelop the city in mist. This is not the California of monotonous blue skies and slothful warmth – the temperatures rarely exceed the seventies, and even during summer can drop much lower.

The original inhabitants of this area, the **Ohlone Indians**, were all but wiped out within a few years of the establishment in 1776 of the **Mission Dolores**, the sixth in the chain of Spanish Catholic missions that ran the length of California. Two years after the Americans replaced the Mexicans in 1846, the discovery of gold in the Sierra foothills precipitated the rip-roaring **Gold Rush**. Within a year fifty thousand pioneers had travelled west, turning San Francisco from a muddy village into a thriving supply center and transit town. By the time the **Transcontinental Railroad** was completed in 1869, San Francisco was a lawless, rowdy boom town of bordellos and drinking dens.

Though a massive earthquake, followed by three days of fire, wiped out most of the city in 1906, recovery was rapid. In the decades which followed, writers like Dashiell Hammett and Jack London lived and worked here, as did Diego Rivera and other WPA-sponsored artists. Many of the city's landmarks, including Coit Tower and both the Golden Gate and Bay bridges, were built in the 1920s and 1930s. By World War II San Francisco had been eclipsed by Los Angeles as the main West Coast city, but it achieved a new cultural eminence with the emergence of the Beats in the Fifties and the hippy era of the Sixties, when the fusion of music, protest, rebellion and, of course, drugs that characterized 1967's "Summer of Love" took over the Haight-Ashbury district.

In a conservative America, San Francisco's reputation as a liberal oasis continues to grow. As gay capital of the world it is handling a massive AIDS crisis with intelligence and dignity. Freedom is the key word, but with responsibility, and for all its failings San Francisco remains one of the least prejudiced and most proudly distinct cities on earth.

Arrival and Information

All international and most domestic flights arrive at **San Francisco International Airport** (SFO), about fifteen miles south of the city. *San Mateo County Transit* (*SamTrans*) **buses** ($1.25) leave every half hour from the lower level of the airport; the #7F express takes around 25 minutes to reach the Transbay Terminal downtown, while the slower #7B stops everywhere and takes nearly an hour. On both, you're only allowed as much luggage as you can carry on your lap. The *San Francisco Airporter* bus ($6) picks up outside each baggage claim area every fifteen minutes and travels to the downtown hotels. The blue **Supershuttle** and the **Yellow Airport Shuttle** minibuses depart every five minutes from the upper level of the loop road and take passengers to any city-center destination for around $15 a head. Be ruthless – competition for these is fierce and queues nonexistent. **Taxis** from the airport cost a hefty $30 to $35 (plus tip) for any downtown location, more for East Bay and Marin County. If you're planning to drive, the usual **car rental** agencies operate free shuttle buses to their depots.

> The **area code** for San Francisco is ☎415;
> for the East Bay it's ☎510, and for San Jose it's ☎408.

Several domestic airlines (*America West, Southwest* and *Continental* are three) fly into **Oakland International Airport** (OAK; see p.829 for details), across the bay. This is actually closer to downtown San Francisco than SFO, and is efficiently connected with the city by the $2 *AirBART* shuttle bus from the Coliseum *BART* station.

By Bus and Train

All San Francisco's **Greyhound** services use the **Transbay Terminal** at 425 Mission St (☎495-15569), south of Market St, near the Embarcadero *BART* station; the old Seventh Street Terminal was closed by the 1989 earthquake. **Green Tortoise** buses (☎285-2441) disembark behind the Transbay Terminal on First and Natoma. **Amtrak** trains stop across the bay in **Richmond** (with easy *BART* transfers) and continue to Oakland, from where free shuttle buses run across the Bay Bridge to the Transbay Terminal.

Information

The **San Francisco Visitor Information Center**, in Hallidie Plaza at the end of the cable car line on Market Street (Mon–Sat 9am–5pm, Sun 9am–3pm; ☎974-6900), has free maps of the city and the Bay Area, and can help with lodging and travel plans. Their free *San Francisco Book* is a comprehensive guide to accommodation, entertainment, exhibitions and stores.

Most public buildings have been modified for **disabled access**, all *BART* stations are wheelchair accessible, and most buses have lowering platforms for wheelchairs – and, usually, understanding drivers. The *Mayor's Council on Disabilities* puts out an annual guide for disabled visitors (Box 1595, San Francisco, CA; ☎554-6141).

San Francisco's main **post office**, with telephone and general delivery facilities, is at Seventh and Mission (Mon–Fri 9am–5.30pm, Sat 9am–1pm; zip code 94101).

Getting Around the City

Getting around San Francisco is simple. The city center is small enough to walk around, and if the hills get a bit too breathtaking, there are always the famous cable cars (see p.813). Public transportation is inexpensive, efficient and easy to use, both in the city and the surrounding Bay Area. Cycling and – outside the city center – mountain biking are good options too, though you'll need stout legs to tackle the hills.

Muni

The city's public transportation is run by the **San Francisco Municipal Railway**, or *Muni* (☎673-6864). A comprehensive network of **buses**, **trolley buses** and **cable cars** run up and over the city's hills, while the underground **trains** become **streetcars** when they emerge from the downtown metro system to split off and serve the suburbs. On buses and trains the flat **fare** (correct change only) is 85¢, $2 on cable cars; with each ticket you buy, ask for a **free transfer** – good for another two rides on a train or bus, and a fifty percent reduction on cable cars if used within ninety minutes.

If you're staying more than a week or so, a **Fast Pass** costs $28 and is valid for unlimited travel on the *Muni* system and *BART* stations (see below) within the city limits for a full calendar month.

Muni trains run **throughout the night** on a limited service, except those on the M-Ocean View line, which stop around midnight. Buses run all night, but services are greatly reduced after midnight. For **more information** pick up the handy *Muni* map ($1.50) from the Visitor Information Center or bookstores.

Other Transportation Services

Various other public transportation networks serve San Francisco and the Bay Area. Along Market Street downtown, *Muni* shares the station concourses with **BART**, the

Bay Area Rapid Transit system, which runs to the East Bay and outer suburbs. The **CalTrain** commuter railway (depot at Fourth and Townsend, South of Market, or SoMA) links San Francisco along the Peninsula south to San Jose. **Golden Gate Ferry** boats leave from the Embarcadero, crossing the bay past Alcatraz to Marin County.

Taxis do not ply the streets. Phoning around, try *Veterans* (☎552-1300) or *Yellowcab* (☎626-2345). Fares are roughly $3 for the first mile, $1.50 per mile thereafter.

If you fancy **cycling**, *Park Cyclery*, 1865 Haight St (☎221-3777), rent touring bikes for $18 per day, and mountain bikes for $25 per day; *Presidio Bicycles*, 5335 Geary Blvd (☎752-2453) are similar.

Organized Tours

One way to orientate yourself is an **organized tour**. *Gray Line Tours* (☎558-9400), for example, take you around the city in three fairly tedious hours for around $25 a head. Considerably more exciting are the two-hour **bay cruises** operated by the *Blue & Gold Fleet* ($17; ☎781-7877) from piers 39 and 40 – though in any case everything may be shrouded in fog. Excruciatingly expensive but spectacular **aerial tours** of the city and Bay Area in light aircraft are available from several operators, such as *Airship Industries Skycruise* (☎568-4101), who offer one-hour airship cruises for $150.

The best of the **walking tours** include *AM Walks* (1433 Clay St; $12; ☎928-5965), a witty, anecdotal early-morning trek; *Cruisin' the Castro* (375 Lexington St; $25; ☎550-8110), a fascinating tour of the gay community; and *Helen's Walk Tour* ($20; ☎524-4544), which leads you around the murals of the Mission.

The City

San Francisco is a city of hills. Becoming familiar with these is not just a good way to get your bearings; it will also give you a real insight into the city's class distinctions. As a general rule, geographical elevation means wealth – the higher you live, the better off you are. Commercial square-footage is surprisingly small and mostly confined to the downtown area, and the rest of the city is made up of distinct, primarily residential neighborhoods, easily explored on foot. Armed with a good map you could plough through most of it in a day, but the best way to get to know San Francisco is to dawdle.

SAN FRANCISCO PUBLIC TRANSPORTATION

Useful Bus Routes

#5 From the Transbay Terminal, west alongside Golden Gate Park to the ocean.

#7 From the Ferry Terminal (Market St) along Haight St to the ocean.

#15 From Third St (SoMa) to Pier 39, Fisherman's Wharf, via the Financial District and North Beach.

#20 (Golden Gate Transit) From Civic Center to the Golden Gate Bridge.

#38 from Geary St via Civic Center, west to the ocean along Geary Blvd.

#30 From the CalTrain depot in SoMa, north to Fisherman's Wharf via North Beach and the Financial District.

Muni Train Lines

Muni J-CHURCH LINE From downtown to Mission and East Castro.

Muni K-INGLESIDE LINE From downtown to Balboa Park.

Muni L-TARAVAL LINE From downtown west to the zoo and Ocean Beach.

Muni M-OCEAN VIEW From downtown west to Ocean Beach.

Muni N-JUDAH LINE From downtown west to Ocean Beach, via the Haight.

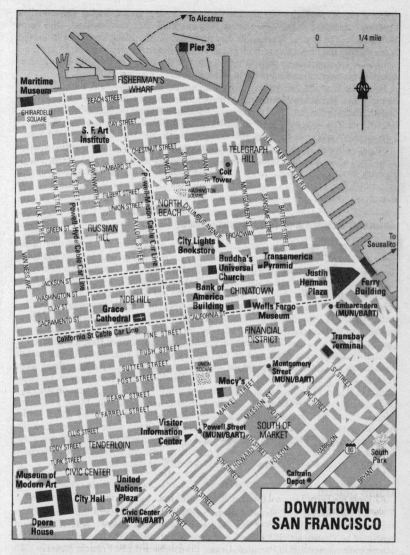

To Alcatraz

■ Pier 39

0   1/4 mile

Maritime
Museum
FISHERMAN'S
WHARF
BEACH STREET
GHIRARDELLI
SQUARE
BAY STREET
S. F. Art
Institute
CHESTNUT STREET
TELEGRAPH
HILL
LOMBARD ST
Coit
Tower
FILBERT STREET
WASHINGTON
SQUARE
UNION STREET
NORTH
BEACH
GREEN ST
RUSSIAN
HILL
City Lights
Bookstore
BROADWAY
Transamerica
Pyramid
JACKSON ST
Buddha's
Universal
Church
Justin
Herman
Plaza
Ferry
Building
WASHINGTON ST
CLAY ST
NOB HILL
Bank of
America
Building
CHINATOWN
Wells Fargo
Museum
Embarcadero
(MUNI/BART)
SACRAMENTO ST
Grace
Cathedral
CALIFORNIA ST
California St Cable Car Line
FINANCIAL
DISTRICT
Transbay
Terminal
PINE STREET
RUSH STREET
SUTTER STREET
UNION
SQUARE
Montgomery
Street
(MUNI/BART)
POST STREET
GEARY STREET
Macy's
O'FARRELL STREET
ELLIS STREET
TENDERLOIN
Visitor
Information
Center
Powell Street
(MUNI/BART)
SOUTH OF
MARKET
EDDY STREET
TURK STREET
CIVIC CENTER
Museum of
Modern Art
United
Nations
Plaza
Caltrain
Depot
South
Park
City Hall
Civic Center
(MUNI/BART)
Opera
House

HYDE STREET
LEAVENWORTH ST
POLK STREET
LARKIN STREET
VAN NESS AVE
Powell-Hyde Cable Car Line
POWELL ST
STOCKTON ST
GRANT AVE
COLUMBUS AVENUE
Powell-Mason Cable Car Line
TAYLOR STREET
MONTGOMERY ST
SANSOME STREET
BATTERY STREET
THE EMBARCADERO

To
Sausalito

MARKET STREET
MISSION ST
1ST STREET
2ND STREET
3RD ST
4TH STREET
5TH STREET
HOWARD STREET
6TH STREET
FOLSOM
HARRISON
BRYANT
7TH STREET
80

DOWNTOWN
SAN FRANCISCO

Downtown: the Financial District

The top right-hand corner of the peninsula, bordered by I-80 to the south, US-101 to the
west, and the water, makes up **downtown San Francisco**. North of the city's main
artery, **Market Street**, the glass and steel skyscrapers of the **Financial District** have
sprung up in the last twenty years to form its only real high-rise district. Sharp-suited
workers clog the streets in well-mannered rush-hour droves, racing between their
offices and the Montgomery *BART/Muni* station on Market Street.

Once cut off from the rest of San Francisco by the double-decker Embarcadero Freeway – damaged in the 1989 earthquake, and finally torn down in 1991 – the **Ferry Building**, at the foot of Market St, was modelled on the cathedral tower in Seville, Spain. Before the bridges were built in the Thirties it was the arrival point for fifty thousand cross-bay commuters daily. A few ferries still dock here (see p.810), but the characterless office units inside do little to suggest its former importance.

From the vast and unimaginative **Embarcadero Center** across the way, it's a few blocks down Market to **Montgomery Street**, where the grand pillared entrances and banking halls of the post-1906 earthquake building era jostle for attention with a mixed bag of modern towers. For a hands-on grasp of modern finance, the **World** of **Economics Gallery** in the **Federal Reserve Bank**, 101 Market St (Mon–Fri 10am–4pm), is unbeatable: computer games allow you to engineer your own stock-market disasters, while exhibits detail recent scandals and triumphs. The **Wells Fargo History Room**, 420 Montgomery St (Mon–Fri 10am–5pm), traces the far-from-slick origins of San Francisco's big money, right from the days of the Gold Rush, with mining equipment, gold nuggets, photographs and even an old wagon.

Jackson Square and the Barbary Coast

A century or so ago, the eastern flank of the Financial District formed part of the **Barbary Coast**, a rough and tumble waterfront district packed with saloons and brothels where hapless young males were given *Mickey Finns* and shanghaied into involuntary servitude on merchant ships. Its wicked reputation made it off limits for military personnel up until World War II, and many of the old dives died an inevitable death. During the 1930s, the Barbary Coast became a low-rent district, attracting writers and artists such as Diego Rivera, who had a studio on Gold Street at the height of his fame as the "communist painter sought after by the world's biggest capitalists". Most of these old structures have been preserved as the **Jackson Square Historic District**.

The **Transamerica Pyramid** at the foot of diagonal Columbus Avenue is San Francisco's most unmistakable (some would say unfortunate) landmark. There was a rumpus when this went up, and it earned the name "Pereira's Prick" after its LA-based architect William Pereira. It's now a symbol of San Francisco, prominent on the city's promotional literature. Rudyard Kipling, Robert Louis Stevenson, Mark Twain and William Randolph Hearst all rented office space in the *Montgomery Block*, which originally stood on this site, and regularly hung around the notorious *Bank Exchange* bar within. Legend also has it that Sun Yat-Sen – whose statue is in Chinatown, three blocks away – wrote the Chinese constitution and orchestrated the successful overthrow of the Manchu Dynasty from his second-floor office here.

Union Square

West of Kearny Street, around **Union Square**, the skyscrapers thin out and are replaced by the bright lights of San Francisco's **shopping district**: several spreading blocks of boutiques, speciality shops and department stores. The square witnessed the attempted assassination of President Gerald Ford outside the **St Francis Hotel** in 1975, and was also the location of Francis Ford Coppola's paranoid film, *The Conversation*, where Gene Hackman spied on strolling lovers. Many of **Dashiell Hammett's** detective stories, such as *The Maltese Falcon*, are set partly in the *St Francis*, in which he worked during the Twenties as a Pinkerton detective.

On Geary Street, on the south side of the square, the optimistically named **Theater District** is a pint-sized Broadway of restaurants, tourist hotels and serious and "adult" theaters – like New York's Broadway or London's Soho, the Theater District of San Francisco shares space with the less rarified institutions of porn and prostitution.

THE CABLE CARS

It was the invention of the **cable car** that made high-society life on San Francisco's hills possible and practical. Since 1873, these little trolleys have been an integral part of life in the city. At their peak, just before the 1906 earthquake, over six hundred cable cars travelled 110 miles of track throughout the city; by 1955, when usage had dwindled, nostalgic citizens voted to preserve the last seventeen miles as a moving historic landmark.

Today there are three lines. Two run from Powell Street to Fisherman's Wharf; the steepest and best climbs Nob Hill along California Street from the Embarcadero. The cars fasten on to a moving two-inch cable which runs beneath the streets, gripping on the ascent then releasing at the top and gliding down the other side. You can see the huge motors which power these cables in the **Cable Car Barn**, at Washington and Mason streets (daily 10am–5pm; free).

On the eastern side of the square, **Maiden Lane** is a chic little urban walkway that before the 1906 earthquake and fire was one of the city's roughest areas, where homicides averaged around ten a month. Nowadays, aside from some prohibitively expensive boutiques, its main feature is San Francisco's only **Frank Lloyd Wright** building, the pricey little **Circle Gallery** that was a try-out for the Guggenheim in New York.

Nob Hill

From Nob Hill, looking down upon the business wards of the city, we can decry a building with a little belfry, and that is the stock exchange, the heart of San Francisco; a great pump we might call it, continually pumping up the savings of the lower quarter to the pockets of the millionaires on the hill.

Robert Louis Stevenson

If the Financial District is representative of new money in the city, the posh hotels and masonic institutions of **Nob Hill**, just above, exemplify San Francisco's old wealth; it is, as Joan Didion wrote, "the symbolic nexus of all old California money and power". Once you've made the stiff climb up (or taken the cable car), there are very few real sights as such, but nosing around is pleasant enough, taking in the aura of luxury, and enjoying the views over the city and beyond.

This area became known as Nob Hill after the robber-baron industrialists who came to live here while running the Central Pacific Railroad. **Grace Cathedral** here is one of the biggest hunks of sham-Gothic architecture in the US. Construction began soon after the 1906 earthquake, but most of it was built, of faintly disguised reinforced concrete, in the early Sixties. The entrance is adorned with faithful replicas of the fifteenth-century Ghiberti doors of the Florence Baptistry.

Chinatown

Twenty-four square blocks of seeming chaos smack in the middle of San Francisco make up **Chinatown**. Dense, noisy, and colorful, the second-largest Chinese community outside Asia is almost entirely autonomous, with its own schools, banks and newspapers. It has its roots in the migration of Chinese laborers to the city after the completion of the Transcontinental Railroad. The city didn't extend much of a welcome: they were met by a tide of vicious racial attacks. Nowadays they have been joined by Vietnamese, Koreans, Thais and Laotians: by day the area seethes with activity, by night it's a blaze of neon. Overcrowding is compounded by a brisk tourist trade – sadly, however, Chinatown boasts some of the tackiest stores and facades in the city.

Gold ornamented portals and brightly painted balconies sit above the souvenir shops and restaurants of narrow **Grant Avenue**. Plastic Buddhas, floppy hats and chopsticks assault the eye from every doorway. This was once Dupont Street, a wicked ensemble of opium dens, bordellos and gambling huts policed, not to say terrorized, by Tong hatchet men. These days there's little trace of them on the streets, but the Mafia-style mob continues to operate, battling for a slice of the lucrative West Coast drug trade.

Parallel to Grant Avenue, **Stockton Street** is crammed with exotic fish and produce markets, bakeries and spice stores. The **Chinese Historical Society of America** at 17 Waverly Place (daily 9am–4pm; donations) has a small but worthy collection of photographs, paintings and artefacts. Also in Waverly Place, three opulent but skilfully hidden **temples** (numbers 109, 125 and 146), their interiors a riot of black, gold and vermillion, are still in use and open to visitors.

The best of Chinatown's very few **bars** is the dimly lit **Li Po's** at 916 Grant Ave, a retreat from the confusion of the surrounding streets. Some of the more than one hundred restaurants (see p.821 for recommendations) are historical landmarks in themselves. **Sam Wo's**, at 813 Washington St, is a cheap and churlish ex-haunt of the Beats where Gary Snyder taught Jack Kerouac to eat with chopsticks and had them both thrown out for his loud and passionate interpretation of Zen poetry.

One block further west, **Portsmouth Square** was the original center of the city. Sam Brannan announced the discovery of gold here, transforming San Francisco from a sleepy Spanish pueblo into a rowdy frontier city.

North Beach

Resting in the hollow between Russian and Telegraph hills, and split by Columbus Avenue, **North Beach** likes to think of itself as the happening district of San Francisco. It has been a focal point for anyone vaguely alternative ever since the **City Lights Bookstore** opened in 1953. The first paperback bookstore in the US stands amid the flashing neon and sleazy clubs of Columbus Avenue at Broadway, open until midnight seven days a week, and is still owned by poet and novelist Lawrence Ferlinghetti. The **Beat Generation** made this the literary capital of California, achieving overnight notoriety when charges of obscenity were levelled at Allen Ginsberg's poem *Howl* in 1957. It was the hedonistic antics of the Beats, as much as their literary merits, which struck a chord, and North Beach came to symbolize a wild and subversive lifestyle. The road-trips and riotous partying, the drug-taking and embrace of eastern religions were emulated nationwide; tourists poured into North Beach for "Beatnik Tours".

Next to the bookstore, **Vesuvio's**, an old North Beach bar where the likes of Dylan Thomas and Kerouac would get loaded, remains a haven for the lesser-knowns to pontificate on the state of the arts. At the crossroads of **Columbus and Broadway**, poetry meets porn in a raucous assembly of strip joints, rock venues and drag queens. Most famous, the now-derelict *Condor Club* is where Carol Doda's revealing of her silicone-implanted breasts started the topless waitress phenomenon. Her nipples are immortalized in neon above the door as a tribute to years of mammary fascination.

As you continue north on Columbus Avenue, you enter the heart of the old **Italian neighborhood**, an enclave of narrow streets and leafy enclosures. Explorations lead to small landmarks like the **Café Trieste**, where the jukebox blasts out opera classics to a heavy-duty art crowd, toying with capuccinos and browsing slim volumes of poetry.

To the west of Columbus, **Russian Hill** was named for Russian sailors who died here in the early 1800s. There's always a tailback of cars waiting to drive down the tight curves of **Lombard Street**. Surrounded by palatial dwellings and herbaceous borders, Lombard is an especially thrilling drive at night, when the tourists leave and the city lights twinkle below. Even if you're without a car the journey up here is worth it for a visit to the **San Francisco Art Institute**, 800 Chestnut St (Tues–Sat 10am–5pm; free), the oldest art school in the west, where the **Diego Rivera Gallery** has an outstanding mural done by the painter in 1931.

ALCATRAZ

Before the rocky islet of **Alcatraz** became America's most dreaded **high-security prison**, in 1934, it had been home to little more than the odd pelican (*alcatraz* in Spanish). Surrounded by the freezing, impassable water of San Francisco Bay, it made an ideal place to hold the nation's most wanted criminals – men such as Al Capone and Machine Gun Kelly. The conditions were inhumane: inmates were kept in solitary confinement, in cells no larger than nine by five feet, most without light. They were not allowed to eat together, read newspapers, play cards or even talk; relatives could visit for only two hours each month. Escape really was impossible. Nine men managed to get off the rock, but there is no evidence that any of them made it to the mainland.

Due to its massive running costs, the jail finally closed in 1963. The island remained abandoned until 1969, when a group of Native Americans staged an occupation as part of a peaceful attempt to claim the island for their people, citing treaties which designated all federal land not in use as automatically reverting to their ownership. Using all the bureaucratic trickery it could muster, the government finally ousted them in 1971, claiming the operative lighthouse qualified it as active.

At least 750,000 tourists each year take the excellent hour-long, self-guided audio **tours** of the abandoned prison, which include some sharp anecdotal commentary and possibly even the chance to spend a minute (it feels like forever) locked in a darkened cell.

Boats to Alcatraz leave from pier 41 (hourly from 9.15am, last boat back at 6pm; $8.15).

Fisherman's Wharf

San Francisco rarely goes out of its way to please the tourist, but with **Fisherman's Wharf**, and the nearby waterfront district, it makes a rare exception. An inventive use of statistics allows the area to proclaim itself the most-visited tourist attraction in the entire country; in fact this crowded and hideous ensemble of waterfront kitsch and fast-food stands makes a sad and rather misleading introduction to the city. It may be hard to believe, but this was once a genuine fishing port; the few fishing vessels that can still afford the exorbitant mooring charges are usually finished by early morning and get out before the tourists arrive. The shops and bars here are among the most overpriced in the city, and crowd-weary families do little to add to the ambience.

Two-hour **bay cruises** depart several times a day from piers 39 and 40 (see p.810).

The Tenderloin, Civic Center and South of Market

While parts of San Francisco may almost match the image of an urban utopia, the adjoining districts of **the Tenderloin**, **Civic Center** and **South of Market** (aka SoMa) reveal the harsh realities. With not a pretty tree-lined street nor a stunning view to be seen, these areas are a gritty reminder that not everybody has it so easy.

The majestic federal and municipal buildings of **Civic Center**, squashed between the Tenderloin and SoMa, can't help but look strangely out of sync, both with their immediate neighbors and with San Francisco as a whole. Their grand Beaux Arts style is at odds with the quirky wooden architecture of the rest of the city. At night, when the ritzy **War Memorial Opera House** and the giant aquarium-like **Louise M Davies Symphony Hall** swarm with well-heeled patrons of the ballet, opera and symphony hall, it all looks distinctly more impressive than by day.

It was at the huge, green-domed **City Hall**, on the northern edge of the dismal **United Nations Plaza**, that Mayor George Moscone and gay supervisor Harvey Milk were assassinated in 1978 (see below). Major works at the **Museum of Modern Art** (Tues–Sun 10am–4pm; $4.50), directly behind, include paintings by Jackson Pollock, Frida Kahlo and Diego Rivera. Dali, Matisse and Picasso are also represented, if not at their peak, and there's a good selection of twentieth-century photography.

Although traditionally one of San Francisco's least desirable neighborhoods, **SoMa**, the district south of Market, enjoyed a renaissance in the 1980s. It's reminiscent in a way of New York's SoHo several years ago; many of its abandoned warehouses have been converted into studio spaces and art galleries, and the neighborhood is now home to artists, musicians, hep-cat entertainers and trendy restaurants. This may well, however, be short-lived: SoMa is a prime piece of central real estate, and it's only a matter of time before the bulldozers move in and the artists move out. Indeed, the new home of the SF Museum of Modern Art opens here in January 1994.

Above all, SoMa is the nucleus of **clubland**, where the city's wildlife is at its best. Folsom Street was a major gay strip, the center for much lewder goings-on than the Castro; in recent years the mix has become pretty diverse, though never tame.

The Mission

Low-rent, hip, colorful, and occasionally dangerous, **The Mission** is easily San Francisco's funkiest neighborhood. A mile or so south of downtown, it is also the warmest, avoiding the summer fogs. As the traditional first stop for immigrants, the Mission serves as a microcosm of the city's history. It takes its name from the old **Mission Dolores**, at 16th and Dolores (daily 10am–4pm; $2), the most ancient building to survive the 1906 earthquake and fire. Founded in 1776, it was the sixth in a series of missions built as Spain staked its claim to California; the graves of the Indians it tried to "civilize" can be seen in the cemetery next door, along with those of white pioneers.

The heart of the Mission lies in the restaurants, thrift stores, cafés and bookstores around 16th and Valencia. At the **Levi Stauss & Co** factory at 250 Valencia St (Mon–Fri 10am–5pm; free), you can see how the world's most famous jeans are made. What really sets the Mission apart from other neighborhoods, however, are its **murals** – there are over two hundred in all. A brilliant tribute to local hero **Carlos Santana** adorns three buildings where 22nd St meets South Van Ness, while every possible surface on **Balmy Alley** between Folsom and Harrison off 24th St (the axis of Latino shopping, with Nicaraguan, Salvadorean, Costa Rican, Mexican and other Latin American stores and restaurants) has been covered with murals depicting the political agonies of Central America.

The Castro

San Francisco's most progressive, if no longer most celebratory, neighborhood has to be **the Castro**. As the city's avowed Gay Capital, it's the best barometer for the state of the AIDS-devastated gay scene. Some people insist that this is still the wildest place in town, others reckon it's a shadow of its former self; all agree that things are not the same as ten or even five years ago, when a walk down the Castro would have had you gaping at the revelry. Most of the same bars and hangouts still stand, but these days they're host to an altogether different, younger and more conservative breed. A visit to the district (inevitably somewhat voyeuristic) is a must if you're to get any idea of just what San Francisco is all about, though in terms of visible street life the few blocks from Market to 20th Street contain about all there is to see.

Harvey Milk Plaza, by the Castro MUNI station, is dedicated to the assassinated gay supervisor (or councillor), who owned a camera store in the Castro. The man who shot Milk and Mayor George Moscone, Dan White, was a disgruntled ex-supervisor who resigned in protest at their liberal policies. At the trial, his plea of temporary insanity caused by harmful additives in his fast food – the "Twinkie defence" – won him a sentence of five years' imprisonment for manslaughter. The gay community reacted angrily; the riots that followed were among the most violent San Francisco has ever witnessed, with protesters marching into City Hall, burning police cars as they went.

Before heading down the hill into the heart of the Castro, take a short walk to the headquarters of the **Names Project** at 2362 Market St (daily 10am–7pm). This sponsored the creation of "**The Quilt**" – a gargantuan blanket in which each panel measures six feet by three feet (the size of a grave site) and bears the name of a man lost to AIDS. Made by lovers, friends and families, the panels are stitched together and regularly tour the country and the world; it has been spread on the Mall in Washington DC several times to dramatize the epidemic. Inside the showroom, you can see thousands of panels stored on shelves, and a few are hung up for display.

The junction of **Castro and 18th Street,** known as the "gayest four corners of the earth", marks the Castro's center, cluttered with bookstores, clothing stores, cafés and bars. The side streets offer a slightly more exclusive fare of exotic delicatessens, fine wines and fancy florists, and enticingly leafy residential territory.

The zenith of the Castro's social calendar is **Halloween,** when six-foot beauties bedecked in jewels and ball gowns strut noisily through the streets. Those not in their finery strip down and take their carefully worked-on pectorals out for a stroll. The police block certain roads off, and turn a blind eye to minor indiscretions.

Haight Ashbury

The fame of **Haight Ashbury,** two miles west of downtown San Francisco, far outstrips its size. No more than eight blocks in length, centered around the junction of Haight and Ashbury streets, "The Haight" was a respectable Victorian neighborhood-turned-slum until it transmogrified into the epitome of cool during the Sixties. Since then it's become gentrified, but it retains a collection of radical bookstores, laid-back cafés, record stores and secondhand clothing emporia, and a smattering of residents still fly a slightly limp freak flag.

All there is to do in the Haight today is to stroll around what is still one of the best areas in town to **shop.** It shouldn't take more than a couple of hours to update your record collection, dress yourself up and blow money on books and beer. The eastern end of Haight Street, around the crossing with Fillmore Street, is the funkiest corner of the district. Known as the **Lower Haight,** and the center of black San Francisco for decades, it is now emerging as the major stomping ground for the sort of fashion victims usually spotted South of Market. Some of the city's best bars and meeting places are here, as well as a growing mix of ethnic restaurants.

THE HIPPIES

During the heady days of the massive "be-in" in Golden Gate Park in 1966 and the so-called "Summer of Love" the following year, no less than 75,000 pilgrims turned the busy little intersection of Haight Ashbury into the mecca of alternative culture.

Where Beat philosophy had emphasized self-indulgence, the **hippies,** on the face of it at least, stressed such concepts as "universal truth" and "cosmic awareness". Characters like Ken Kesey and his Merry Pranksters set a precedent of wild living and challenging authority. The use of drugs was seen as an integral – and positive – part of the movement. LSD, especially, which was not then illegal, was claimed as an avant-garde art form, pumped out in private laboratories and distributed by Timothy Leary and his supporters with a prescription – "Turn on, tune in, drop out" – that galvanized a generation into inactivity. Life in the Haight took on a theatrical quality: Pop Art found mass appeal, light shows became legion, and dress flamboyant. The psychedelic music scene, spearheaded by the Grateful Dead, Jefferson Airplane and Janis Joplin, became a genuine force nationwide, and it wasn't long before kids from all over America started turning up in Haight Ashbury for the free food, free drugs . . . and free love. Money became a dirty word, the hip became "heads", and the rest of the world were "straights".

Golden Gate Park

In a city which is hardly short of green space, **Golden Gate Park** stands out as not just the largest, but also the most beautiful, and the safest, of its parks. Spreading three miles or so west from the Haight as far as the Pacific, it was constructed on what was then an area of wild sand dunes, buffeted by the spray from the ocean. Despite the throngs of joggers, polo players, roller skaters, cyclists and strollers, it never gets overcrowded and you can always find a spot to be alone.

Of the park's several museums, the **M H de Young Museum** (Wed–Sun 10am–5pm; $4, first Wed of each month and Sat mornings free) has a large and diverse range of painting and sculpture, while the **Asian Art Museum** (same times) is drearily exhaustive. The **California Academy of Sciences** (daily 10am–5pm; $4) opposite is a good place to amuse restless children, with its thirty-foot dinosaur skeleton and life-size replicas of humans throughout the ages. Over 14,500 specimens of aquatic life can be viewed in its **Steinhart Aquarium** (daily 10am–5pm; $3); the best are the alligators and other reptiles lurking in a simulated swamp. Slightly to the west is the **Japanese Tea Garden** (daily 8am–6pm; $2 admission charged 9am–5pm), dominated by a massive bronze Buddha. Bridges, footpaths, pools filled with carp, bonsai and cherry trees lend a peaceful feel. Busloads of tourists pour in; by far the best idea is to get here around 8am, for a breakfast of tea and fortune cookies in the tea house.

The Golden Gate Bridge and the Beaches

The orange towers of the **Golden Gate Bridge**, perhaps the best-loved symbol of San Francisco, are visible from almost every high point in the city. The bridge, which spans 4200 feet, had taken only 52 months to design and build when it was opened in 1937. Some quarter of a million people turned up for a sunrise party to celebrate its fiftieth anniversary in 1987; the winds were strong and the bridge buckled, but fortunately did not break. **Driving** across is a real thrill, racing under the towers, while the half-hour **walk** across allows you to take in its enormous size and absorb the views.

The **Fort Point National Historic Site** beneath the bridge gives a good sense of the place as the westernmost outpost of the nation. This brick fortress, built in the 1850s, has a dramatic site, the surf pounding away beneath the great span of the bridge high above – a view made famous by Kim Novak's suicide attempt in Alfred Hitchcock's *Vertigo*. A small **museum** (daily 9am–4pm; free) inside the fort shows some rusty old cannons and firearms.

San Francisco's best waters are to be found at the **beaches** at the tip of the peninsula, but beach culture doesn't exist here the way it does in southern California. Dangerous riptides and very cold water make it impossible to swim with any confidence, and nude sunbathing is about as adventurous as things get.

Inland, **Lincoln Park** is primarily a golf course, though it does have some striking trails. When open, the isolated, white-pillared **California Palace of the Legion of Honor** – it closed for a possible maximum of two years from March 1992 for renovation – is arguably San Francisco's best museum, as well as being its most beautifully located. Until a few years ago, the collection was mainly French and not particularly strong, but several new additions enabled it to emerge as the city's best assemblage of fine art. The **Renaissance** is represented with the works of Titian and El Greco, hung in high-ceilinged, well-lit, spacious marble halls. Some great canvases by Rembrandt and Hals, as well as Rubens' magnificent *Tribute Money*, are highlights of the seventeenth-century Dutch and Flemish collection. The **Impressionist** and **Post-Impressionist** galleries contain works by Courbet, Manet, Monet, Renoir, Degas and Cezanne. One enormous hall is filled with **Rodin** sculptures – bronze, porcelain and stone pieces including *The Athlete, Fugit Amor,* and a small cast of *The Kiss*.

San Francisco Accommodation

Visitors are San Francisco's number one business, and the city isn't short on lodging. The **hotels and motels** have a good reputation for comfort and cleanliness. Hotels in the slightly seedy areas of South of Market and the Tenderloin start at around $30 per night or $120 a week, without a private bath or even toilet. In the glitzier areas around Union Square and Nob Hill it's hard to find a place for under $150 a night.

For **B&Bs**, consult the list below, or contact a specialist agency such as *Bed and Breakfast International* (1181-B Solano Ave, Albany, CA 94706; ☎525-4569) or *Bed and Breakfast San Francisco* (Box 349, San Francisco, CA 94101; ☎931-3083). British visitors can reserve rooms through **Colby International** (☎051/220-5848; see p.86).

Both *Central Reservations of Hotel Group of America* at 693 Sutter St (☎202-8700), or *Golden Gate Lodging Reservations* at 1030 Franklin St (☎771-6915), will, for a small fee, find you a room from around $80 a double. If all else fails and you've got a car, **motels** are legion along the highways and bigger roads throughout the Bay Area, at a standard rate of $35 to $45 a night. In all cases, bear in mind that all quoted room rates are subject to an **eleven percent room tax**.

Camping isn't really an option in San Francisco itself.

Hostels and YMCAs

AYH Hostel at Union Square, 312 Mason St (☎788-5604). Large new downtown hostel with dorm beds for $14 a night. AYH members only; day memberships cost $5. ①.

European Guest House, 761 Minna St (☎861-6634). Dormitory-style accommodation with communal kitchen. No curfew; safe locker facilities. $12 per person per night. ①.

Interclub/Globe Hostel, 10 Hallam Place (☎431-0540). Lively, recently redecorated South-of-Market hostel with young clientele and no curfew. $15 per person, per night; doubles $25. ①.

San Francisco International Guest House, 2976 23rd St (☎641-1411). Very popular with European travellers, this Mission District Victorian has four-to-a-room dorms and a few private rooms. $14 per person, 5-day minimum stay, no curfew. ①.

San Francisco International Hostel, Building 240, Fort Mason (☎771-7277). On the waterfront between the Golden Gate Bridge and Fisherman's Wharf. Annoying 11pm curfew, but one of the most comfortable and convenient hostels around. 150 beds, free parking. $13 per person. ①.

San Francisco State University, 800 Font Blvd (☎338-2721). Year-round dorms and summer-only suites on college campus, near SF Zoo. Dorm beds with meals $25 a night, private rooms. ①–④.

YMCA Central Branch, 220 Golden Gate Ave (☎885-0460). Good central single and double rooms, two blocks from Civic Center. Rates include free breakfast and use of gym, pool, and sauna. ②.

Hotels, Motels and B&Bs

Adelaide Inn, 5 Isadora Duncan Court, between Geary and Post (☎441-2261). Small downtown B&B hotel with shared bathroom facilities. ②–③.

Bay Bridge Inn, 966 Harrison St (☎397-0657). Basic and somewhat noisy, but perfectly placed for late nights in SoMa's clubland. ③.

Beresford Arms Hotel, 701 Post St (☎673-2600). Luxury B&B in the heart of town. ⑤.

Edward II, 3155 Scott St (☎922-3000). Large and comfortable inn-style Northern Waterfront accommodation with free breakfast and afternoon sherry. ④–⑤.

Fairmont Hotel, 950 Mason St (☎772-5000). Most famous of the top-notch hotels, an over-ornate palace with seven restaurants, ten lounges and fantastic views from the rooms. ⑦.

Gates Hotel, 140 Ellis St (☎781-0430). Absolute bargain downtown location. ②.

Grant Plaza Hotel, 465 Grant Ave (☎434-3883). Clean, newly renovated Chinatown hotel. ③.

Hyde Plaza Hotel, 835 Hyde St (☎885-2987). Unbelievably inexpensive accomodation on the Tenderloin/Nob Hill border. Small, clean and comfortable rooms with shared bath. ①–②.

The Mansion, 2220 Sacramento St (☎929-9444). Luxury-swaddled Victorian mansion, perched high up in the fancy reaches of Pacific Heights. ⑥–⑧.

Marina Motel, 2576 Lombard St (☎921-9406). Least pricey of northern waterfront motels. ③–④.

Hotel Mark Twain, 345 Taylor St (☎673-2332). Elegantly decorated colonial-style hotel in the middle of the Theater District. ⑤.

Pensione San Francisco, 1668 Market St (☎864-1271). A good base near the Civic Center, walkably close to SoMa and the Castro. ②–③.

La Quinta Inn, 20 Airport Blvd (☎583-2223). Overnight laundry service and a pool make this a comfortable stopover near the airport. Free shuttle service to the airport. ④.

The Red Victorian Bed and Breakfast, 1665 Haight St (☎864-1978). Bang in the middle of the Haight Ashbury. Lively New Agey B&B, with hippy art gallery; a real relic of the Sixties. ④–⑤.

San Remo Hotel, 2237 Mason St (☎776-8688 or ☎1-800/352-7366). Pleasant, old-fashioned rooms (sharing bathrooms) in nice North Beach house. Friendly staff, good bar and restaurant. ④–⑤.

Stanyan Park Hotel, 750 Stanyan St (☎751-1000). Gorgeous small Victorian hotel in a great setting across from Golden Gate Park, with friendly staff and free continental breakfast. ⑤.

Super 8 Lodge, 111 Mitchell Ave, South San Francisco (☎877-0770). Plain, motel-style accommodations near the airport. Free laundry service, breakfast and airport shuttle. ③.

Hotel Triton, 342 Grant Ave (☎394-0500 or 1-800/433-6611). Very stylish, very comfortable and very central hotel, across from the Chinatown Gateway, two blocks from Union Square. ⑥–⑦.

UN Plaza Hotel, Seventh and Market St (☎626-4600). Good location just opposite the Civic Center. Glitzy lobby and large, comfy rooms. ④.

Washington Square Inn, 1660 Stockton St (☎981-4220). Cozy B&B bang on North Beach's lovely main square. Non-smokers only. ④–⑤.

Westin St Francis, 335 Powell St (☎397-7000 or ☎1-800/228-3000). Truly grand hotel with a sumptuous lobby, five restaurants, an elegant bar but disappointingly plain rooms. ⑦.

York Hotel, 940 Sutter St (☎885-6800 or ☎1-800/227-3608). Quiet, older hotel on the western edge of downtown; movie locations for the dramatic stairway scenes in *Vertigo*. ⑥.

Gay Men's Accommodation

Casa Loma Hotel, 600 Fillmore St (☎552-7100). Mid-sized, friendly hotel with sauna, jacuzzi, sun deck and a lively bar. ②.

Gough Hayes Hotel, 417 Gough St (☎431-9131). Informal favorite in San Francisco, no private toilets but 24hr sauna and sun deck. ④.

Inn on Castro, 321 Castro St (☎861-0321). Luxury B&B; well worth the price for the large rooms and good breakfasts. About two minutes' walk from the Castro. ⑥.

Queen Anne Hotel, 1590 Sutter St (☎262-2663). Very much a gay hotel with overdone decor, full valet service and complimentary afternoon tea and sherry. ⑥.

24 Henry, 24 Henry St (☎864-5686). Quiet, intimate guest house near the heart of the Castro. ④.

Women's Accommodation

Bock's Bed & Breakfast, 1448 Willard St. Secure and friendly hotel for women. ③.

The Langtry, 637 Steiner St (☎863-0538). Nineteenth-century mansion. Each room is dedicated to a famous woman in history. Fabulous but far from inexpensive. ⑤.

Mary Elizabeth Inn, 1040 Bush St (☎673-6768). Run by the United Methodist Church; a safe but unexciting place to stay. ③–④.

Women's Hotel, 642 Jones St (☎775-1711). Comfortable, secure building, unfortunately situated in the unpleasant Tenderloin district. Weekly rates only: singles $100 per week, doubles $120.

San Francisco Eating

With over four thousand restaurants crammed on to the small peninsula, and scores of bars and cafés which are open all day (and many all night), **eating** in San Francisco is never difficult. As well as ethnic cuisines of all kinds – watch out for **Mexican** food in the Mission, the **Italian** places in North Beach, and of course the **Chinese** restaurants in Chinatown – health-conscious San Francisco also has a wide range of **vegetarian** and **wholefood** restaurants. With the vineyards of Napa and Sonoma Valley on the city's doorstep, quality **wines** have a high profile in most San Francisco restaurants.

Budget Eating: Breakfasts and Burgers

Hamburger Mary's Organic Grill, 1582 Folsom St (☎626-5767). Rowdy restaurant, where punky waiting staff serve up burgers, sandwiches and several vegetarian options for less than $8.

Limbo, 299 Ninth St (☎255-9945). Super cheap, ultra-trendy. Wholefood and burgers from $4.50.

Orphan Andy's, 3991 17th St (☎864-9795). Favorite hang-out in the Castro for filling burgers, omelettes and breakfasts.

Sparky's Diner, 240 Church St (☎621-6001). Inexpensive 24hr diner. Burgers, pastas and pizzas and delicious breakfasts, particularly a marvellous eggs florentine. Beer and wine as well.

Spaghetti Western, 576 Haight St (☎864-8461). Best breakfasts in town and a lively Lower-Haight crowd to look at while you chow down.

American, Californian, Italian and French

Bix, 56 Gold St (☎433-6300). Jackson Square restaurant kitted out like an ocean liner, with torch singer, sax player and pianist. The food is great – straightforward, classic dishes. Book early. Dinner for two will be around $50, but if you're into elegant dining experiences you should definitely go.

Café Landais, 489 Third St (☎495-6944). SoMa bistro that's about the least expensive place for French food in town. Popular with connoisseurs on a budget.

Capp's Corner, 1600 Powell St (☎989-2589). Funky, family-style Italian restaurant in North Beach, with a fashionable clientele who line up for the big portions.

Cypress Club, 500 Jackson St (☎296-85555). Jackson Square hot spot. Delicately presented, inventive California cuisine served up in one of SF's most stylish dining rooms – a cross between a *Ritz Carlton* and a Bedouin tent.

Ernie's, 847 Montgomery St (☎397-5969). A lovely Victorian interior and a *haute cuisine* menu made famous by Hitchcock's *Vertigo* – it figured in some of the crucial scenes.

Little Joe's, 523 Broadway (☎433-4343). Always a queue for tables, but worth it for the low-cost, enormous portions of well-cooked food in this North Beach institution.

Lulu's, 816 Folsom St (☎495-5775). The latest in chic mastication; excellent international/ Californian food, cooked in open kitchens by headphone-wearing chefs, and served, annoyingly, "family style" – everything is put in the middle to share. The restaurant that everybody is talking about. Until the next one comes along . . .

Miss Pearl's Jam House, 601 Eddy St (☎775-5267). The cuisine may be Caribbean but the experience is definitely Californian. Run in conjunction with the *Phoenix* motel; poolside tables with nightly live reggae and down-home atmosphere. Outstanding – and not bank-breaking – fish dishes.

Trader Vic's, 20 Cosmo Place (☎776-2232). A San Francisco "society" institution. Ostensibly Polynesian/Indian, but ethnicity stops at the dinner plate. Dining moneyed-American style.

Washington Square Bar & Grill, 1707 Powell St (☎982-8123). Stylish grill – *the* place to see San Francisco society power-lunching. Food cooked to rich and heavy perfection; perhaps $15 a head.

Zuni Café, 1658 Market St (☎552-2522). The chic place to be and be seen, with Californian nouvelle cuisine portions as minimal as the elegant decor for around $30 a head with wine.

Asian and Middle Eastern

Bangkok 16, 3214 16th St (☎431-5838). Moderately priced Thai restaurant in the Mission, with a great selection for vegetarians – and for meat-eaters they do a mean lamb saté.

Brandy Ho's Original Hunan, 217 Columbus Ave (☎788-7527). Excellent Hunan restaurant.

China Moon Café, 639 Post St (☎775-4789). Cantonese cuisine, excellent budget dim sum lunches.

Elka's, 1611 Post St (☎922-7788). The latest word in seafood with a Japanese twist. State-of-the-art fish by celebrity chef Elka Gilmore. Take a bankroll.

Empress of China, 838 Grant Ave (☎434-1345). The poshest Chinese place in town. An incredible selection of dishes, amazing views over North Beach. At least $18 for a main course.

Gaylord, Ghirardelli Square, 900 North Point, Fisherman's Wharf (☎771-8822). The best of San Francisco's very few Indian restaurants. Expect to pay around $15 for a main course.

Mamounia, 441 Balboa St (☎752-6566). Eat Moroccan food with your fingers and pay for it through the nose.

Manora's Thai Cuisine, 1600 Folsom St (☎861-6224). Massively popular, and you may have to wait, but it's worth it for light, spicy and fragrant Thai dishes at around $7 each.

Moshi Moshi, 2092 Third St (☎861-8285). Out-of-the-way gem of a Japanese restaurant in SoMa. Excellent sushi and seafood, moderately priced.

Mun's, 401 Balboa St (☎668-6007). Inexpensive and simple Korean food in the Western Addition.

New Asia, 772 Pacific Ave (☎391-6666). Amazing place for such a cramped neighborhood. Some of the most authentic dim sum in town.

Pasha's, 1516 Broadway (☎885-4477). An extraordinary dining experience. Morrocan and Middle Eastern cuisine served while you sit on the floor. Belly dancers gyrate past your table, proffering their cleavage for you to insert dollar bills.

Silver Moon, 2301 Clement St (☎386-7852). Light Japanese seafood and vegetarian dishes.

Thep Phanom Restaurant, 400 Waller St (☎431-2526). Delicate decor and beautifully prepared Thai dishes in the Lower Haight. Only $7 for a main course, but expect to queue.

Yoshida-Ya, 2909 Webster St (☎346-3431). Genuine sushi bar; kick off your shoes and eat at low tables on futoned floors. Expect to pay around $20 a head, with a few drinks.

Mexican and Hispanic

El Cubane, 1432 Valencia St (☎824-6655). Big portions of Cuban food. Tues–Fri lunches for $4.50.

El Tapatio, 475 Francisco St (☎981-3018). Not as inexpensive as the Mission's Mexican restaurants, but the food in this North Beach eatery is notably better – and the margaritas larger.

El Tazumal, 3522 20th St (☎550-0935). Interesting Salvadorean place, small but lively. Tripe, tongue and spicy rice dishes for around $6 for a lunch and up to $10 for a dinner.

Las Guitarras, 3200 24th St (☎285-2684). Noisy Mexican favored by the locals. Don't expect a fine dining experience, but you can count on a good hearty dinner.

Mom's Cooking, 1192 Geneva St (☎586-7000). Small and crowded, on the fringes of the Mission. You may have to queue for the super-inexpensive fresh Mexican food.

Vegetarian and Wholefood

Amazing Grace, 216 Church St (☎626-6411). Highly rated vegetarian food for around $5 a dish.

Greens, Building A, Fort Mason Center, Fort Mason (☎771-6222). The city's only Zen Buddhist restaurant. Delicious macrobiotic and vegetarian food. Book in advance; $30 for a five-course dinner.

Marty's, 508 Natoma St (☎621-0751). Stuck down a little alley, this isn't the sort of place you'd stumble over, but if you're into macrobiotic food, you should definitely make the effort. Thurs–Sun only.

Nightlife and Entertainment

Compared to many US cities, where you need money and attitude in equal amounts, San Francisco's **nightlife** scene demands little of either. This is no 24-hour city, and the approach to socializing is often surprisingly low-key, with little of the pandering to fads and fashions that goes on in New York or LA. For $30 you can get a decent night out, including cover charge, a few drinks and maybe even a taxi home.

The Sunday *Chronicle*'s "Pink Pages" supplement, along with the free weekly *Bay Guardian* or the *San Francisco Weekly*, are the best sources of **listings**. *BASS* (☎893-2277) and *Ticketron* (☎392-7469) are the major **ticket** agencies.

Bars

Since its lawless, boomtown days, San Francisco has been a **drinking** town. Even as the rest of California cleans up its act, San Franciscans continue to indulge; the city's bars vary from seedy late-night dives to rooftop piano lounges touting glittering views.

Bouncers Bar, 64 Townsend St. Old waterfront hangout. Free live music and a very earthy crowd.

Brainwash, 1122 Folsom St. Great idea – café/bar and laundromat where you can have breakfast and a beer while you do your washing. Popular with the young and novelty-conscious.

Jimmy's West Point, 669 Haight St. The joint is jumping most nights at this black neighborhood bar, where Philadelphia soul and Motown blare out relentlessly from the jukebox.

Perry's, 1944 Union St. Sophisticated meat market, featured in Armistead Maupin's *Tales of the City* as the quintessential breeder bar.

The Rat and the Raven, 4054 24th St. Friendly, hard-drinking neighborhood bar with pool, darts, and one of the best country music jukeboxes in town.

Rockin Robin's, 133 Beale St. Fifties rock and roll, and lots of boys in leather. Mon–Fri only.

Tropical Haight, 582 Haight St. Best decorated (tropical-themed) bar in the district.

The Uptown, 200 Capp St. Best of the Mission's neighborhood bars, embracing an eclectic crowd who shoot pool, drink like fiends and fall around on the scruffy, leatherette upholstery.

Vesuvio's, 255 Columbus Ave. Legendary North Beach Beat haunt in the Fifties, next to *City Lights Bookstore*. Still caters to an arty but friendly crowd who prop up the bar into the small hours.

Gay and Lesbian Bars

San Francisco's **gay or lesbian bars** are many and varied, ranging from cozy cocktail bars to full no-holds-barred leather-and-chain hangouts. The scene may no longer be quite as wild as its reputation would have you believe, but at its best it can still be hard to beat.

Café Flore, 2298 Market St. Very much the in spot before dark. Attractive café with leafy outdoor area and no shortage of people sizing each other up.

Castro Station, 456 Castro St. Noisy disco bar that packs 'em in even in the middle of the day. Very much the die-hard scene of the Seventies, with a fair number still in leather gear.

Eagle, 12th & Harrison St. Legendary SoMa biker bar. Not for wimps.

Empress Lily, 4 Valencia at Market. Formerly an old, little frequented drive known as the *Travel Lounge*, this bar has had a big revival of its fortunes since the gay community got hold of it and turned it into one of the liveliest drag venues for miles. Draws a good, mixed crowd.

Midnight Sun, 4067 18th St. Young, white boys dressed to the nines and cruising like maniacs in this noisy Castro video bar.

Rawhide, 280 Seventh St. If men in chaps are your scene, go no further than this dimly lit SoMa bar/dance club that plays country and western and bluegrass favorites.

Live Music: Rock, Jazz and Folk

San Francisco's **music scene** reflects the character of the city: laid-back, eclectic, and not a little nostalgic. The options for catching live music are wide and the scene is definitely on the up and up, with the city spawning some good young bands. The best of the music press, the free *BAM* (*Bay Area Music*), is available in most record stores, and carries exhaustive listings of events in the city and Bay Area.

Bahia Tropical, 1600 Market St (☎861-8657). Expensive, yuppie hangout and supper club with good Brazilian and samba bands. Cover $8.

Bajone's, 3140 Mission St (☎648-6641). Excellent nightly Latin jazz. Casual, unpretentious and genuine, with an unusual – and refreshing – age mix for San Francisco. $6 cover at weekends.

Full Moon Saloon, 1725 Haight St (☎775-6190). Pot luck – expect anything from reggae and funk to bluegrass. Consistently lively punters and good fun. No cover.

I-Beam, 1748 Haight St (☎668-6023). Haight-Ashbury's most famous venue. No place to see bands on the cheap, although midweek you can generally get in for around $6–10.

Jack's, 1601 Fillmore St (☎567-3227). Small, intimate bar. Jazz and blues nightly. No cover.

Nightbreak, 1821 Haight St (☎221-9008). Slightly shabby, small Haight venue. New wave and goth bands play to a matching crowd. Very dark, very loud, very crowded. A small cover at weekends.

Pasand Lounge, 1875 Union St (☎922-4498). Unusual club where you can come to eat Indian food and listen to very mellow jazz in the comfortable lounge. Open Wed–Sat. They sometimes make a small cover charge.

The Rite Spot Café, 2099 Folsom St (☎552-6066). Informal, café-style club with jazz and r'n'b bands. Snacks, drinks and coffee until 1am. Open Mon–Sat, small cover at weekends.

San Francisco is still the undoubted **gay capital of the world**, but the gay scene hasn't had much to celebrate in the last few years and there's been a definite move from the outrageous to the mainstream. The increasing number of gay activists in public office have become more conservative in approach, if not in policy. However, gay parties, parades and street fairs still swing better than most. If you're here in June, you'll coincide with the Gay and Lesbian Film Festival, Gay Pride Week, the Gay Freedom Day Parade and any number of conferences. Come October, the street fairs are in full swing and Halloween still sees some of the most outrageous carrying on.

Although the 1980s saw the flowering of a **lesbian** culture to rival the male 1970s upsurge, the bars for women have all closed down, and now nightlife revolves around a handful of women's club nights. Lesbian culture is more in evidence in the bookstores.

The Sentinel, Coming Up, The Bay Area Reporter and *Gay Times* are all free **publications**, listing events, services, clubs and bars. *On Our Backs* and *Bad Attitude* are of particular use to lesbians. Gay men could not do better than to purchase a copy of *Betty and Pansy's Severe Queer Review* ($7.95), available from gay bookstores – as is *The Gay Book*, a telephone-cum-resource book. The *AIDS Hotline* (☎863-2437) and the *Lesbian/Gay Switchboard* (☎841-6224) provide 24-hour counselling and advice. The *Gay Men's Group*, 450 Stanyan St (☎750-5661), is good for contacts and advice on places to go.

You'll find gay **accommodation** and **bars** on pp.820 and 823 respectively.

Roland's, 2513 Van Ness Ave (☎567-1063). Classic and Latin jazz in a dark, smoky atmosphere, for serious fans. Open Tues–Sun. Small cover at weekends.

The Saloon, 1232 Grant St (☎397-3751). Always packed, North Beach's best spot for r'n'b. Free.

The Stone, 412 Broadway (☎391-8282). Solid venue with consistently good billing of rock and new wave bands. Open until 6am Fri and Sat for a very danceable rock disco. Cover around $8.

Tar & Feathers, 2140 Union St (☎563-2612). Young, casual, country and western. The Marina's place to go for a few beers and a singalong when you can't face the singles bars.

The Tonga Room, basement of the *Fairmont*, 950 Mason St (☎772-5000). A must for fans of the ludicrous or just the very drunk. It's decked out like a Polynesian village, complete with a pond and simulated rain storms, and a grass-skirted band plays terrible jazz and pop covers on a raft in the middle of the water. Worth every penny of the cover charge and outrageously priced cocktails. Cover $4.

Clubbing

Trading on an ageing reputation, the city's **nightclubs** continue to trail vapidly behind those of other large American cities. That said, the compensations are manifold – no long queues, high cover charges, ridiculously priced drinks or feverish posing. The greatest concentration of clubs is in **SoMa**, especially around 11th Street and Folsom.

Caesar's Latin Palace, 3140 Mission St (☎826-1179). A big laugh: relive Seventies discomania with Latin, jazz and disco rock. Naff enough to have achieved cult status. $7 cover.

Covered Wagon Saloon, 917 Folsom St (☎974-5906). One of the better SoMa places, especially on Thurs for the *Love Shack* hi-tech psychedelic night, and on Sat for hip-hop. Cover $5–8.

Crystal Pistol, 842 Valencia St (☎695-7887). One of the newer gay men's clubs, enjoying a very healthy patronage. Good dancing and a young, well-turned-out set.

DNA Lounge, 375 11th St (☎626-1409). The music changes nightly, but the young hipsters are the same. Large dance floor downstairs, comfy sofas in the mezzanine. Cover $8. Tues–Sun 9pm–4am.

DV8, 540 Howard St (☎777-1419). Huge, ornate and fashionable, about the only club in town worth dressing up for. High-energy funk and house music. Open Wed–Sat. Cover $12.

El Rio, 3158 Mission St (☎282-3325). Latin, jazz and samba are the specialty here, with live bands on Sunday, dancing to modern funk on Friday, and comedy cabaret on Wednesday in a friendly, anything-goes atmosphere. Open seven nights 3pm–2am, until 6am at weekends. No cover.

The Endup, Harrison and Sixth St (☎495-9550). A mostly gay crowd. Good for the hard-core party animal – especially on "wet jockstrap night". Open from 6am Sat until 2am Mon. Small cover.

Esta Noche, 3079 16th St (☎861-5757). Gay discomania Latin-style. Young men and their pursuers dance to a hi-NRG disco beat reminiscent of the 1970s.

Kennel Club, 628 Divisadero (☎931-9858). Best known for the gay-oriented *Box* club on Thurs & Sat, and Friday's enjoyable *Club Q* for women. Roomy interior and enormous circular bar. Cover $8.

The New Martini Empire, 1015 Folsom St (☎626-2899). Club with an international bent where you'll be able to hear Brazilian, salsa, Arabic, African and Soca. Open Fri–Sun. Cover $5.

Nightbreak, 1821 Haight St (☎221-9008). Small Haight club where the slogan is "All the funk that's fit to pump" – house, hip-hop and funk most nights, except for Wed when it becomes "Female Trouble", lesbian dance night. Small cover at weekends.

Paula's Clubhouse, 3160 16th St (☎621-1617). Not to be missed; bar/club with broad cross section of music styles and clientele. Reggae Wed, live music Fri, house music Sat. $4 cover at weekends.

Rock & Bowl, 1855 Haight St (☎752-2366). Try this one for a change – a bowling alley that turns up the music at weekends so that you can dance while you bowl.

The Stud, 399 Ninth St (☎863-6623). An oldie but a goodie. A favorite dancing spot with a mixed but mostly gay crowd. Energetic, uninhibited dancing and good times. No cover.

Townsend, 177 Townsend St (☎974-6020). A must for house fans, this place really cranks up the bass and keeps it blaring. Thurs–Sat. Cover $5.

Classical Music, Opera and Dance

Though the San Francisco arts scene has a reputation for provincialism, this is the only city on the West Coast to boast its own professional **symphony**, **ballet** and **opera** companies. These companies rely entirely on private contributions for their survival and low-priced tickets are rare, if not nonexistent. Look out also in summer for the **free concerts in Stern Grove** (at 19th Ave and Sloat Blvd) where the symphony, opera and ballet give open-air performances for ten successive Sundays (starting in June).

Louise M Davies Symphony Hall, 201 Van Ness Ave (☎431-5400). Permanent home of the San Francisco Symphony. A year-round season of classical music and sometimes performances by other, often offbeat musical and touring groups. The least expensive seats go for around $20.

War Memorial Opera House, 401 Van Ness Ave (☎864-3330). The very opulent venue for both the San Francisco Opera Association, whose main thirteen-week season opens with great pomp at the end of September. In general, tickets for the June–July summer season are easier to come by. Expect to pay upwards of $40. The San Francisco Ballet (☎893-2277), which has gone from strength to strength since the appointment of Icelandic Helgi Tomasson as artistic director in 1985, appears here Jan–June.

Theater

The majority of the **theaters** in downtown's Theater District are not especially innovative, but tickets are reasonably inexpensive – up to $20 a seat – and there's usually good availability. The *STBS* ticket booth in Union Square (Mon–Sat 11am–6pm; ☎433-7717) regularly has last-minute tickets for up to thirty percent off the price.

American Conservatory Theater, *Geary Theater*, 450 Geary St (☎749-2228). After its destruction by the 1989 earthquake, the ACT is now better than ever. The city's best serious theater venue.

Golden Gate Theater, 1 Taylor St (☎474-3800). San Francisco's most elegant theater, with marble flooring, rococo ceilings and gilt trimmings. A pity the programme doesn't live up to the surroundings – generally a mainstream diet of Broadway musicals.

Lorraine Hansberry Theater, 620 Sutter St (☎474-8800). Radical young group of black performers. Traditional theater as well as contemporary political pieces and jazz/blues musical reviews.

The Magic Theater, Fort Mason Center, Building D (☎441-8822). Specializes in contemporary American playwrights and emerging new talent: Sam Shepard premieres his work here.

Theater Artaud, 450 Florida St (☎621-7797). Very modern theater in a converted warehouse that tackles the obscure and abstract: always something interesting.

Theater Rhinoceros, 2926 16th St (☎861-5079). San Francisco's only uniquely gay theater group. Lighter, humorous productions as well as those that confront gay issues.

Theater on the Square, 450 Post St (☎433-9500). Converted Gothic theater with drama, musicals, comedy and mainstream theater pieces. San Francisco's main fringe venue.

WOMEN'S SAN FRANCISCO

The flip side of San Francisco's gay revolution has in some women's circles led to a separatist culture, and women's resources and services are sometimes lumped together under the lesbian category. While this may be no bad thing, it can be hard to tell which organizations exist irrespective of sexuality. Don't let this stop you checking out anything that sounds interesting; nobody is going to refuse you entry or help if you're not a lesbian.

Contacts and Resources

Bay Area Resource Center, 318 Leavenworth St (☎474-2400). Services, info and clothing.

Rape Crisis Line (☎647-7273). 24-hr switchboard.

Women's Building, 3543 18th St (☎431-1180). Central stop in the Mission for women's art and political events. A very good place to get information – the women who staff the building are happy to deal with the most obscure of enquiries.

Women's Health Center No.1, 3850 17th St (☎558-3908). Free contraception, AIDS testing, pregnancy testing and a well-woman clinic.

Women's Needs Center, 1825 Haight St (☎221-7371). Low-cost health care and referral service.

Women's Yellow Pages, 270 Napoleon St (☎821-1357). Call for a copy of this invaluable directory, with everything from where to stay to where to get your legs waxed.

Comedy Clubs

El Rio, 3158 Mission St (☎282-3325). Wed night comedy shows, with a riskier choice of performers than the established clubs. Very alternative, and, more often than not, extremely funny.

Josie's Cabaret and Juice Joint, 3583 16th St (☎861-7933). Good all-rounder offering a mixed menu of cabaret, comedy, live music and dancing. The bill changes weekly.

The Improv, 401 Mason St (☎441-7787). The chain store of the comedy world. Some good established talent and up-and-coming acts. Mon is the least expensive and best night to go.

Morty's, 1024 Kearny St (☎986-6678). Old North Beach club that evokes the Lenny Bruce era, even if none of the acts is quite as good as he was.

The Punch Line, 444 Battery St (☎397-7553). Frontrunner of the city's "polished" cabaret venues. Intimate, smoky feel; ideal for downing expensive cocktails and laughing your head off. The club usually hosts the bigger names in the world of stand-up, and is always packed.

Shops and Galleries

San Francisco does have the large-scale shopping facilities you'd expect in a major city, with the usual international names prominent in its downtown shop windows. However, most places are low-key and unpretentious. Not only does this mean slightly lower prices, but it also makes shopping a more pleasant, stress-free activity all round.

If you want to run the gauntlet of designer labels, or just watch the style brigades in all their consumer fury, **Union Square** is the place to aim for. Heart of the city's shopping territory, it has a good selection of big-name and chic stores – expense account stuff admittedly, but good for browsing, especially in the many art galleries.

Clothes

Aardvarks Odd Ark, 1501 Haight St (☎621-3141). Large secondhand clothing store in Haight Ashbury: stocks some junk, but also some priceless pieces and an infinite supply of perfectly faded Levis.

Mascara Club, 1408 Haight St (☎863-2837). Vintage clothing in the heart of Haight Ashbury, heavy on the psychedelic and more recently Wild Western garments.

Past Tense, 665 Valencia St (☎621-2987). Mission district store selling Thirties to Sixties collectable vintage clothing. One of the smarter secondhand stores.

Purple Heart, 1855 Mission St (☎621-2581). Top quality junk and kitsch.

San Francisco Symphony Thrift Store, 2223 Fillmore St (☎563-3123). Top-rate vintage clothing store in Pacific Heights, with flamboyant and original pieces going for top dollar.

Worn Out West, 1850 Castro St (☎431-6020). Gay secondhand cowboy gear store – a trip for browsing, but if you're serious about getting some Wild West kit, this is about the lowest-priced place in town to pick out a good pair of boots, stylish western shirts and chaps.

Books

Around the World, 1346 Polk St (☎474-5568). Musty, dusty and a bit of a mess, this is a great place for hours of poring over first editions, rare books and records.

The Booksmith, 1644 Haight St (☎863-8688). Good general Haight Ashbury bookstore with an excellent stock of political and foreign periodicals.

City Lights Bookstore, 261 Columbus Ave (☎362-8193). America's first paperback bookstore, and still San Francisco's best. The range of titles includes their own publications.

A Different Light, 489 Castro St (☎431-0891). Well-stocked and diverse gay bookstore.

Modern Times, 968 Valencia St (☎282-9246). Largely radical feminist publications, but a hefty stock of Latin American literature and progressive political publications.

Rand McNally, 595 Market St at Second St (☎777-3131). Brand new store selling travel guides, maps and paraphernalia for the person on the move.

Small Press Traffic, 3599 24th St (☎285-8394). Don't be misled by the unprepossessing Mission storefront: this is San Francisco's prime outlet for independent, contemporary fiction and poetry, with an astounding range.

Tillman Place Bookstore, 8 Tillman Place, off Grant Ave, near Union Square (☎392-4668). Downtown's premier general bookstore, with a beautifully elegant feel.

Records

Aquarius Music, 3961 24th St (☎647-2272). Small neighborhood store with friendly, knowledgeable staff. Admirably reluctant to stock CDs. Emphasis on indie rock, jazz and blues.

Discoteca Habana, 24th and Harrison St (no phone). Caribbean and samba recordings.

Embarcadero Discs and Tapes, 2 Embarcadero Center, the Embarcadero (☎956-2204). Not a piece of vinyl in sight – up-to-the-minute CDs and tapes.

Jack's Record Cellar, 254 Scott St (☎431-3047). The city's best source for American roots music – r'n'b, jazz, country and rock & roll.

Reckless Records, 1401 Haight St (☎431-3434). If you can't complete your Sixties collection here, you never will.

SPORTS IN SAN FRANCISCO

While the city is still reeling from the departure of 49ers quarterback Joe Montana, San Francisco's dedication to its **professional sports** teams can verge on the obsessive. Tickets for the big events can sell out, but it's usually possible to show up on the day, and it needn't cost all that much: an outfield seat to watch baseball from the "bleachers" goes for around $7, with seats closer-in topping the scale at around $15. Advance tickets for all Bay Area sports events are available through the BASS charge-by-phone ticket service (☎510/762-BASS), or through the teams themselves.

Baseball: The **Oakland A's** play at the usually sunny Oakland Coliseum (☎510/638-0500), the **San Francisco Giants** at often cold and foggy Candlestick Park south of the city (☎467-8000).

Football: The **San Francisco 49ers**, many-time Super Bowl champions, also play at Candlestick Park, where you may have to pay as much as $100 (☎468-2249).

Basketball: The **Golden State Warriors** play at Oakland Arena (☎638-6000).

Ice hockey: The **San Jose Sharks** (☎408/287-4275), the Bay Area's newest sports team, play at their own arena in the South Bay.

Stanford Stadium, scene of six matches in soccer's **1994 World Cup**, is on the campus of Stanford University, 27 miles south of San Francisco and not far north of San Jose.

Record Finder, Noe and Market St (☎431-4443). One of the best independents, with a range as broad as it's absorbing. Take a wad and keep spending.

Record House, 1550 California St (☎474-0259). Nob Hill archive library of over 25,000 Broadway and Hollywood soundtracks. Great record-finding service.

Record Rack, 3987 18th St (☎552-4990). Castro 12" single emporium with a few albums, but the accent is definitely on stuff you can dance to.

Recycled Records, 1377 Haight St (☎626-4075). Good all-round new and used store for records, tapes and CDs, as well as a good selection of music publications.

Rooky Ricardo's, 448 Haight St (☎864-7526). Secondhand soul and funk, some albums but mostly 45s. Brilliant.

Rough Trade, 1529 Haight St (☎621-4395). Because of its London connections, this is the first place in town to get imports. Good reggae and indie rock.

Star Records, 551 Hayes St (☎552-3017). Secondhand rap, soul, jazz, gospel and reggae specialist, out in Western Addition. Any track ever cut by a black artist, you'll find here.

Art Galleries

American Indian Contemporary Arts, 685 Market St (☎495-7600). The only non-profit gallery in the country run by contemporary Native American artists.

Artspace, Ninth and Folsom St (☎626-9100). Adventurous, avant-garde gallery that often exhibits video installations.

Atelier Dore, 771 Bush St (☎391-2423). Salon-style gallery. Historical genre paintings from California, as well as nineteenth- and twentieth-century black American painters.

Joseph Chowning Art Gallery, 1717 17th St (☎626-7496). Humorous and bizarre art.

Contemporary Realists Gallery, 506 Hayes St (☎863-6556). One of the more interesting galleries and the first California gallery dedicated to promoting current realist drawing.

Crown Point Press, 871 Folsom St (☎974-6273). With a showcase that changes monthly, you never know what to expect from one of SoMa's most eclectic galleries.

SF MOMA Rental Gallery, Building A, Fort Mason (☎441-4777). Large exhibition space of over 500 artists trying to break into the commercial art world.

Smile, A Gallery With Tongue In Chic, 1750 Union St (☎771-1909). From the whimsical to the very serious, this gallery is one of very few into it just for fun. They'll exhibit anything.

The Bay Area

Of the six million people who make their home in the vicinity of San Francisco, only a lucky one in every eight lives in the city itself. Everyone else is spread around the **Bay Area**, either down the peninsula or across one of the two impressive bridges that span the chilly waters of the exquisite natural harbor. In the **East Bay** are industrial Oakland and intellectual Berkeley. To the south lies the gloating new wealth of the **Peninsula**, known as "Silicon Valley" for its multibillion-dollar computer industries. Across the Golden Gate Bridge to the north is the woody, leafy landscape and rugged coastline of **Marin County**, the Bay Area's richest suburb.

The East Bay

The largest and most-travelled bridge in the US, the **Bay Bridge** heads east from San Francisco, part graceful suspension bridge and part heavy-duty steel truss. Now recovered from its partial collapse during the 1989 earthquake, the Bay Bridge works a whole lot harder for a lot less respect than the more famous (and better-loved) Golden Gate: a hundred million vehicles cross it each year. The heart of the East Bay is

The **area code** for the Bay Area is ☎510.

Oakland, a hard-working, blue-collar city that was badly scarred by the firestorm of October 1991. Just north is the image-conscious university town of **Berkeley;** the two communities all but merge into one city, with the hills above them topped by a twenty-mile string of forested **regional parks.**

Arrival, Getting Around and Information

Flights direct to the East Bay touch down at **Oakland Airport,** just outside town. The *AirBART Shuttle* van (every 15min; $2) connects to the Coliseum *BART* station, and there are also door-to-door shuttle buses such as *Bayporter* ($15; ☎415/467-1800). The **Greyhound** station is in a dodgy part of northern Oakland on San Pablo Ave at 21st St. **Amtrak** terminates at 16th and Wood in West Oakland, but a better option is to get off at Richmond and change onto the ultra-modern **BART** trains. Three of these underground lines link San Francisco with the East Bay (Mon–Sat 6am–midnight, Sun 9am–midnight; fares 80¢–$3), heading their separate ways from downtown Oakland. *AC Transit* (☎839-2882) buses cover the entire East Bay area, with a more limited service running to Oakland and Berkeley from the Transbay Terminal in San Francisco.

There are **visitor centers** at 1000 Broadway near the 12th Street *BART* station in downtown Oakland (Mon–Fri 8.30am–5pm; ☎839-9000), and in Berkeley at 1834 University Ave (Mon–Fri 9am–4pm; ☎549-7040).

Oakland

OAKLAND, the workhorse of the Bay Area, is one of the largest ports on the West Coast. It has also been the breeding ground of revolutionary **political movements.** In the Sixties, the city's fifty percent black population found a voice through the militant Black Panthers, and in the Seventies the Symbionese Liberation Army, kidnappers of heiress Patty Hearst, obtained a ransom of free food for the city's poor. It's not all hard graft: the climate is often sunny and mild when San Francisco is cold and dreary, and there's great hiking in the redwood- and eucalyptus-covered hills above the city.

Half a mile down Broadway from the recently spruced-up downtown – or direct by ferry from San Francisco – **Jack London Square** is Oakland's sole concession to the tourist trade. Stretching along the waterfront, this aseptic complex of boutiques and eateries is named for the writer, who grew up here as an orphaned delinquent, but is about as far from the spirit of the man as it's possible to get. **Gertrude Stein,** who was born in Oakland at around the same time as the macho and adventurous London, is barely commemorated – perhaps because she wrote "what was the use of me having come from Oakland, it was not natural for me to have come from there yes write about it if I like or anything if I like but not there, *there is no there there*" – a quote which has haunted Oakland ever since.

Joaquin Miller Park, the most easily accessible of Oakland's hilltop parks, stands above East Oakland. It was once home to the "Poet of the Sierras", Joaquin Miller, who made his name playing the eccentric frontier American in the salons of 1870s London. His poems weren't exactly acclaimed (his greatest poetic achievement was rhyming "teeth" with "Goethe"), but his prose account of the time he spent with the Modoc Indians near Mount Shasta (see p.843) remains invaluable. His house, a small white cabin called **The Abbey,** still survives, as do the thousands of trees he planted.

Berkeley

BERKELEY (pronounced as for Busby) is dominated by the **University of California,** whose grand buildings and thirty thousand students give off an energy that spills south down raucous **Telegraph Avenue.** The very name of Berkeley conjures up images of dissent. Among the sites of the almost-daily pitched battles of the Sixties and early Seventies, part of the broad campus revolt against the Vietnam War, was the now-seedy **People's Park.** Organized resistance to the university authorities' misguided plans to develop the site into student dormitories brought out the troops, who shot an onlooker dead by mistake. Even in the 1990s, when the university began to build volleyball courts in the middle of People's Park, violent demonstrations returned to the streets once again, and a 19-year-old woman was shot to death after trying to stab the Chancellor.

Telegraph Avenue holds most of the student hangouts, and several excellent bookstores. Older students congregate in **Northside**, popping down from their woodsy hillside homes to partake of goodies from "Gourmet Ghetto" – the restaurants, delis and bakeries on Shattuck Avenue. Along the bay itself, at the **Berkeley Marina**, you can rent windsurfing boards and sail boats or just watch the sun set behind the Golden Gate.

East Bay Accommodation

The East Bay's **motels** and **hotels**, at around $35 a night, are slightly better value for money than their San Francisco equivalents.

Berkeley YMCA, 2001 Allston Way at Milvia St, a block from Berkeley *BART* (☎848-6800). Berkeley's best bargain accommodation; rates include use of gym and pool. ①.

Golden Bear Motel, 1620 San Pablo Ave, West Berkeley (☎525-6770). The most pleasant of the many motels in the "flatlands" of West Berkeley, though somewhat out of the way. ②–③.

Waterfront Plaza Hotel, 21 Jack London Square, Oakland (☎836-3800). Plush, modern hotel moored on the best stretch of the Oakland waterfront. ⑤.

London Lodge, 700 Broadway, downtown Oakland (☎451-6316). Spacious rooms, some of which have kitchens, make this a good option for families or groups. ③–④.

Shattuck Hotel, 2086 Allston Way, Berkeley (☎845-7300). Comfortable, central rooms in well-restored older hotel. ⑤.

Eating

As befits the birthplace of California Cuisine, the Bay Area offers a choice of good **restaurants**. Berkeley is both an upmarket diner's paradise and a student town where you can eat inexpensively and well, especially along and around Telegraph Avenue.

Alvita's Restaurant, 3522 Foothill Blvd, East Oakland (☎536-7880). Arguably the best Mexican restaurant in the Bay Area, with great *chiles rellenos, carnitas* and a range of seafood dishes.

Cha-Am, 1543 Shattuck Ave, North Berkeley (☎848-9664). Climb the stairs up to this unlikely, always crowded small restaurant for deliciously spicy Thai food at bargain prices.

Cheeseboard Pizza, 1512 Shattuck Ave (☎549-3055). Incredibly good designer pizza at incredibly low prices: $1.50 a slice.

Chez Panisse, 1517 Shattuck Ave, North Berkeley (☎548-5525). The first and still the best of the California Cuisineries – although at $50 a head *prix-fixe* (plus wine) you may prefer to try the comparatively inexpensive *Café* upstairs, especially if you don't have the obligatory three-months-in-advance reservation.

Gulf Coast Oyster Bar & Specialty Co, 736 Washington St, downtown Oakland (☎839-6950). Popular and reasonably priced Cajun-flavored seafood restaurant.

Jade Villa, 800 Broadway, downtown Oakland (☎839-1688). For dim sum lunches or traditional Cantonese meals, this is one of the best places to go in Oakland's thriving Chinatown.

Juan's Place, 941 Carlton St, West Berkeley (☎845-6904). The original Berkeley Mexican restaurant, with great food (tons of it) and an interesting mix of people.

Tambo Café, 1981 Shattuck Ave near University Ave, Berkeley (☎841-6884). Brilliant, reasonably priced Peruvian food – including marvellous *ceviche* – served up fresh and fast.

Cafés and Bars

The many bohemian **cafés** of Berkeley are full from dawn to near midnight of earnest characters wearing their intellects on their sleeves; if you're not after a caffeine fix, you can generally get a glass of beer or wine. For serious drinking you're better off in one of the many **bars**, particularly in rough-hewn Oakland. Grittier versions of what you'd find in San Francisco, they're mostly blue-collar, convivial, and almost always less expensive.

Café Mediterranean, 2475 Telegraph Ave, Berkeley (☎841-5634). Berkeley's oldest café, straight out of the Beat generation archives: beards and berets optional, books *de rigueur*.

Heinhold's First and Last Chance Saloon, Jack London Square, Oakland (☎839-6761). Authentic waterfront bar that's hardly changed since the turn of the century, when Jack London himself drank here.

Larry Blake's, 2367 Telegraph Ave, Berkeley (☎848-0886). Upstairs there's a small bar, downstairs there's an r'n'b club and large bar; in between the two there's a good-value restaurant.

Mama Bear's, 6536 Telegraph Ave, North Oakland (☎428-9684). Women's bookstore, doubling as a café and meeting place. Open daily 10am–7pm, later for regular readings by lesbian and feminist writers.

The White Horse, 6560 Telegraph Ave at 66th St, North Oakland (☎652-3820). Smallish, friendly mixed bar, with nightly dancing.

Live Music Venues

Nightlife is where the East Bay really comes into its own. **Discos** are virtually nonexistent; however, dance music – from the likes of Oakland's own Hammer, En Vogue and Digital Underground – is thriving, and **live music venues** range from smoky jazz cafés to sweaty r'n'b dives.

Berkeley's **Pacific Film Archives** at 2621 Durant Ave (☎642-1412), perhaps the best **cinema** in California, puts on contemporary international films, plus old favorites. The free *East Bay Express* has the most comprehensive listings of **what's on**.

Ashkenaz, 1317 San Pablo Ave, Berkeley (☎525-5054). World music and dance café. Acts range from modern Afrobeat to the best of the Balkans. Kids and under-21s welcome. Cover $5–8.

Caribee Dance Center, 1408 Webster St, downtown Oakland (☎835-4006). For reggae, rockers, calypso, soca, dub, salsa or lambada, this new place is hard to beat. Cover $3–8.

Eli's Mile High Club, 3629 Martin Luther King Jr Way, North Oakland (☎655-6661). The best of the Bay Area blues clubs. Cover $5–8.

Gilman Street Project, 924 Gilman St, West Berkeley (☎525-9926). On the outer edge of the hard-core punk scene. No booze, all ages, cover $3–6.

Kimball's East, 5800 Shellmound, off Powell St, Emeryville (☎658-2555). The prime jazz and blues venue in the entire Bay Area, hosting big-name players in an intimate setting. Cover $12–20.

The Peninsula

The city of San Francisco sits at the tip of a five-mile-wide **peninsula**. Home of old money and new technology, this stretches for fifty miles of relentless suburbia south from San Francisco along the bay to wind up in the futuristic roadside landscape of the so-called "Silicon Valley" near **San Jose**.

There was a time when the region was covered with orange groves and fig trees, but the continuing computer boom – spurred by Stanford University in **Palo Alto** – has put paid to that. Surprisingly, most of the land along the **coast** – separated from the bayfront sprawl by a ridge of redwood-covered peaks – remains rural and undeveloped; it also contains some of the best **beaches** in the Bay Area, well worth a day trip from San Francisco.

San Jose

But for the odd Burt Bacharach song, **SAN JOSE**, the fastest-growing city in California, is not strong on identity – though in area and population it's close on twice the size of San Francisco. Sitting at the southern end of the Peninsula, San Jose has in the past 25 years emerged as the civic heart of Silicon Valley, surrounded by miles of faceless high-tech industrial parks where the next generations of computers are designed and crafted. Ironically, it's also one of the oldest settlements in California, though the only sign of that is the eighteenth-century **Mission Santa Clara de Asis**, on the pleasant campus of the Jesuit-run University of Santa Clara.

The **Winchester Mystery House**, 525 S Winchester Blvd, just off I-280 near Hwy-17 (daily 9.30am–4.30pm; $15.95), has to be seen to be believed. Sarah Winchester, heiress to the Winchester rifle fortune, was convinced upon her husband's death that he had been taken by the spirits of men killed with Winchester rifles, and believed that unless a room was built for each of the spirits and the sound of hammers never ceased, the same fate would befall her. Work on the mansion went on 24 hours a day for the next thirty years – stairs lead nowhere, windows open on to solid brick.

San Jose's **visitor center** is at 333 W San Carlos St (Mon–Sat 9am–5pm; ☎408/295-9600 or ☎1-800/SAN-JOSE). Downtown **accommodation** options include the *Valley Inn*, 2155 The Alameda (☎408/241-8500; ③), and the slightly more expensive *Best Western Inn*, 455 S Second St (☎408/298-3500; ③). Good old-fashioned American **food** can be had at *Original Joe's*, 301 S First St (☎408/292-7030). Grab a stool at the counter or settle into one of the comfy booths and enjoy a burger and fries or a plate of pasta at this San Jose institution, where $10 goes a long way.

The Coast

The **coastline** of the peninsula south from San Francisco is more appealing than inland: relatively undeveloped, with very few buildings, let alone towns, along the 75 miles of coves and beaches that extend down to the resort city of Santa Cruz. However, not until fifteen miles south of **Daly City** do you finally escape the suburban sprawl, at the clothing-optional sands of **Gray Whale Cove State Beach** (daily dawn–dusk; $5 to park). Despite the name it's not an especially great place to look for migrating gray whales, but there is a stairway from the bus stop down to a fine strand. Two miles south, the red-roofed buildings of the 1875 **Montara Lighthouse**, set among the wind-swept Monterey pine trees at the top of a steep cliff, have been converted into a **youth hostel** (☎728-7177), where dorm beds cost $13.

Marin County

Across the Golden Gate from San Francisco, **Marin County** (pronounced *Ma-RINN*) is an unabashed introduction to Californian self-indulgence: an elitist pleasure zone of conspicuous luxury and abundant natural beauty, with sunshine, sandy beaches, high mountains and thick redwood forests. Often ranked as the wealthiest county in the US, Marin has drawn a sizeable contingent of wealthy young professionals to live in its swanky waterside towns – though many of the cocaine-and-hot-tub devotees who populated the place in the 1970s have traded in their drug habits for mountain bikes.

The modern **ferries** across the bay from San Francisco can make a great start to a day out. Boats to the chic bayside settlement of **Sausalito** leave from the Embarcadero (*Golden Gate Transit*; 5.30am–8pm, half-hourly at busy periods, every two hours at weekends; $3.50 each way; ☎322-6600) or Pier 43 1/2 at Fisherman's Wharf (*Red and White Ferries*; $9 round trip; ☎546-2805).

Across the Golden Gate: The Marin Headlands

The largely undeveloped **Marin Headlands**, across the Golden Gate from San Francisco, afford some of the most impressive views of the bridge and the city behind. The coastline is much more rugged than it is on the San Francisco side, and it makes a great place for an aimless cliff-top scramble, in among the concrete remains of old forts and gun emplacements. At the end of the road, there's a wide sandy **beach** in between the chilly ocean and **Rodeo Lagoon**, a rush-filled seabird nesting area. The largest of the old army officers' quarters in the adjacent Fort Barry, half a mile to the east, has

---

The **area code** for the Peninsula and Marin County is ☎415; for San Jose it's ☎408.

been converted into the spacious and homely **Golden Gate Youth Hostel** (closed 9.30am–4.30pm; ☎331-2777), an excellent base for more extended explorations of the inland ridges and valleys.

Sausalito

Pretty, smug little **SAUSALITO**, along the bay below US-101, was once a gritty community of fishermen and sea traders, full of bars and bordellos. Now exclusive restaurants and pricey boutiques line its picturesque waterfront promenade, and expensive, quirky houses climb the overgrown cliffs above Bridgeway Avenue, the main road and bus route through town. Ferries from San Francisco arrive next to the Sausalito Yacht Club in the town center.

Casa Madrona at 801 Bridgeway Ave (☎332-0502; ⑥), a deluxe hideaway in the hills above the bay, is also a delectable seafood restaurant, with a great view of the harbor. Less expensive food can be found near the waterfront; *Greater Gatsby's*, 39 Caledonia St (☎332-4500) at the north end of town, is an inexpensive pizza parlor, while the *Bridgeway Café*, 633 Bridgeway Ave (☎332-3426), does nice teas and sandwiches. The *no name bar*, 757 Bridgeway Ave (☎332-1392), is a thriving ex-haunt of the Beats which still hosts poetry readings and evening jam sessions.

Mount Tamalpais and Muir Woods

Mount Tamalpais dominates the skyline of the Marin peninsula, hulking over the cool canyons of the rest of the county in a crisp yet voluptuous silhouette, and dividing the county into two distinct parts: the wild western slopes above the Pacific coast and the increasingly suburban communities along the calmer bay frontage. Panoramic Highway branches off from Hwy-1 along the crest through the center of **Mount Tamalpais State Park**, which has some thirty miles of hiking trails and many campgrounds. Most of the redwood trees which once covered its slopes have long since been chopped down to build San Francisco's Victorian houses; one towering grove does remain, however, protected as the **Muir Woods National Monument** (daily 8am–sunset; free). It's a tranquil and majestic spot, with sunlight filtering three hundred feet down from the treetops to the laurel- and fern-covered canyon below. Being so close to San Francisco, Muir Woods is a popular target, and the trails nearest the car park have been paved and are often packed with coach-tour hordes.

Mill Valley

From the East Peak of Mount Tamalpais, a quick two-mile downhill hike follows the Temelpa Trail through velvety shrubs of chaparral, to the town of **MILL VALLEY**, the oldest and most enticing of the inland towns of Marin County. This was originally a logging center, from which the destruction of the surrounding redwoods was organized, but for many years the town has made a healthy living out of tourism.

The town centers today around the *Book Depot and Café* (daily 7am–10pm), a popular bookstore, café and meeting place at 87 Throckmorton Ave; there's also a small **visitor center** next door (☎388-9700). The *Dipsea Café*, 1 El Paseo (☎381-0298), serves hearty diner food, especially good for carbo-loading breakfasts; *Piazza D'Angelo*, across the plaza at 22 Miller Ave (☎388-2000), has very good pizzas and pastas. *Sweetwater* at 153 Throckmorton Ave (☎388-3820) is a comfortable saloon which doubles as Marin's prime live music venue, with gigs ranging from jazz and blues all-stars to Jefferson Airplane survivors.

Point Reyes National Seashore

The westernmost tip of Marin County comes at the end of the **Point Reyes National Seashore**, a near-island of wilderness surrounded on three sides by over fifty miles of isolated coastline – pine forests and sunny meadows bordered by rocky cliffs and sandy, windswept beaches. This wing-shaped landmass is a rogue piece of the earth's crust that has been drifting steadily northwards along the San Andreas Fault, having started some six million years ago as a suburb of Los Angeles. When the great earth-quake of 1906 shattered San Francisco, the land here, at the epicenter, shifted over sixteen feet in an instant, though damage was confined to a few skewed cattle fences.

The **visitor center** (daily 9am–5pm; ☎663-1092), two miles southwest of Point Reyes Station, has engaging displays on local geology and natural history, plus details of hiking trails. Just north, Limantour Road heads six miles west to the **Point Reyes Youth Hostel** (closed 9.30am–4.30pm; ☎663-8811; ①) in an old ranch house, where dorm beds cost $13. Nearby **Limantour Beach** is good for swimming.

Eight miles west of the hamlet of Inverness, a turning leads down to **Drake's Beach**, the presumed landing spot of Sir Francis Drake in 1579. Appropriately, the coastline resembles the southern coast of England – cold, wet and windy, with chalk-white cliffs rising above the wide sandy beach. The road continues west another four miles to the very tip of Point Reyes. A precariously sited **lighthouse** stands firm against the crashing surf, and the bluffs are excellent for watching sea lions and, in winter, migrating **gray whales**.

THE GOLD COUNTRY

The single most enduring image of California, after surfers and movie stars, is that of the rough and ready 49ers, who came from all over the world to get rich in the **Gold Country** of the Sierra Nevada, 150 miles east of San Francisco. The area ranges from the foothills near Yosemite two hundred miles north to the deep gorge of the Yuba River, with **Sacramento** as its largest city. Many of the mining camps that sprung up around the Gold Country vanished as quickly as they appeared, but about half still survive. Some are bustling resorts, standing on the banks of white-water rivers in the midst of thick pine forests; others just eerie ghost towns, all but abandoned on the grassy rolling hills. Most of the mountainous forest along the Sierra crest is preserved as near-pristine wilderness, with excellent hiking, camping and backpacking. There's great skiing in winter, around the mountainous rim of **Lake Tahoe** on the border between California and Nevada, aglow under the bright lights of the nightclubs and casinos that line its southeastern shore.

Sacramento

California's state capital, **SACRAMENTO**, in the flatlands of the Central Valley, was founded in 1839 by the Swiss **John Sutter**. He worked hard for ten years to build a busy trading center and cattle ranch, only to be thwarted by the discovery of gold at a nearby sawmill in 1848. His workers quit their jobs to go prospecting, and thousands more flocked to the gold fields of the **Central Mother Lode** without any respect for Sutter's claims to the land. Sacramento became the main supply point for the miners, and remained important as the western headquarters of the transcontinental railway. Flashy office towers and hotel complexes have now sprung from its rather suburban streetscape, enlivening the flat grid of leafy, tree-lined blocks, and going some way toward resurrecting the rowdy, free-for-all spirit of the city's Gold Rush past.

It's not especially prominent on most travellers' itineraries. There's not a great deal to see, though the wharves, warehouses, saloons and stores of the historic core along the **riverfront** have been restored and converted into the stores and restaurants of **Old Sacramento**. On the northern edge of the old town, the **California State Railroad Museum** (daily 10am–5pm; $5) brings together a range of lavishly restored 1860s locomotives, with "cow-catcher" front grilles and bulbous smokestacks. The old passenger station and freight depot a block south now serve as the summer depot for a refurbished **steam train** ($4) making a seven-mile, 45-minute round trip along the river.

Further east, and isolated from downtown, the dome of the **state capitol** stands proudly in a spacious green park two blocks south of K Street Mall. Recently restored to its original elegance, and still the seat of state government, the luxurious building brims over with finely crafted details. Although you're free to walk around, you'll see a lot more if you take one of the free hourly **tours** (daily 9am–5pm).

Sutter's Fort (daily 10am–5pm; $2), on the east side of town at 27th and L streets, is a recreation of Sacramento's original settlement. An adobe house displays relics from the Gold Rush, and on summer weekends volunteers dress up and act out scenes from the 1850s. The adjacent **Indian Museum** (daily 10am–5pm; $2) on K Street displays tools, handicrafts and ceremonial objects of local Native Americans.

Practicalities

Trains come in at Fourth and I streets, near Old Sacramento, and an almost continuous stream of *Greyhound* **buses** (☎444-6800) arrive at 1107 L St. The **airport** is twelve miles northwest: *Air Commuter* vans (☎424-9640; $9) run downtown.

Sacramento's **visitor center** is at 1421 K St (Mon–Fri 8am– 5pm; ☎264-7777). As well as the *Gold Rush Home* **AYH Hostel**, at 1421 Tiverton Ave (☎421-5954; ①), there are plenty of places to stay within walking distance of the city center. The least expensive is the *Central Motel*, 818 16th St (☎446-6006; ②), while *Abigail's*, 2120 G St (☎1-800/858-1586; ⑤), is an attractive B&B half a mile from the state capitol. *Annabelle's*, at 200 J St (☎448-6239), is a bustling Old Sacramento Italian restaurant, and *Rubicon Brewing Company*, 2004 Capitol Ave (☎448-7032), offers good Mexican bar food washed down by the flavorful house-brewed *Amber Ale*, with live jazz at weekends.

The Mines

In the romantic landscape of the **Gold Country**, overshadowed by the ten-thousand-foot granite peaks of the Sierra Nevada, fast-flowing rivers cascade through steeply walled canyons. In autumn, the flaming reds and golds of poplars and sugar maples on the slopes stand out against an evergreen background of pine and fir. The camps of the **southern mines** of the Gold Country were the liveliest and most uproarious of all the Gold Rush settlements, and inspired most of the popular images of the era: Wild West towns full of gambling halls, saloons and gunfights in the streets. Freebooting prospectors in these "placer" mines sometimes picked nuggets of gold out of the streams and rivers; further **north**, the diggings were far richer and more successful, but the gold was (and is) buried deep underground, and had to be pounded out of hardrock ore.

Sonora, Columbia and Jamestown

The center of the southern mining district is **SONORA**, set on steep ravines roughly a hundred miles east of San Francisco. This friendly and animated logging town is more than just another tourist trap, with its appealing false-fronted buildings and Victorian houses on the main **Washington Street**. The *Tuolumne County Visitors Bureau*, 16 W Stockton Rd (☎1-800/446-1333), a block from Washington Street, is the best source of **information**.

The **area code** for Sacramento, Lake Tahoe, and the northern Gold Country is ☎916; for the southern Gold Country, it's ☎209.

Sonora's one-time arch-rival, **COLUMBIA**, three miles north on Parrots Ferry Road, is now a ghost town, with a carefully restored Main Street that gives an excellent – if slightly contrived – idea of what Gold Rush life might have been like. In 1854 it was California's second largest city, and it missed becoming the state capital by two votes – just as well, since by 1870 the gold had run out and the town was abandoned.

Most of the saccharine-sweet village of **JAMESTOWN**, three miles south of Sonora, was burned down in 1966. Prior to that it was the location for *High Noon*, the train from which is now the biggest attraction of **Railton 1897 State Park**, a block east of Main St – a collection of old steam trains that's open summer weekends, and offers half-day trips on restored local railroads.

Practicalities

The nicest **place to stay** in Sonora is the *Ryan House*, 153 S Shepherd St (☎533-3445; ④), a very comfortable and welcoming B&B; motels on Hwy-49 include the *Miner's Motel* (☎532-7850; ②). Main Street Jamestown is lined by balconied old Gold Rush hotels such as the *National* (☎984-3446; ③) and the *Royal* (☎984-5271; ③), and also holds a few good **places to eat**, like the excellent *Michaelangelo* (no 18228; ☎984-4830).

Grass Valley and Nevada City

The compact communities of **GRASS VALLEY** and **NEVADA CITY**, four miles apart in the Sierra Nevada mountains, were the most prosperous and substantial of the gold mining towns. Since the Sixties, artists and craftspeople have settled in the elaborate Victorian homes of the surrounding hills and gorges. In Grass Valley, the **North Star Mining Museum** (daily, April–Oct 11am–5pm, irregular hours rest of year; donations) at the south end of Mill Street is housed in what used to be the power station for the North Star Mine. Its giant water-driven **Pelton wheel**, fitted with a hundred or so iron buckets, once powered the drills and hoists of the mine. Dioramas show the day-to-day working life of the miners, three-quarters of whom had emigrated here from the depressed tin mines of Cornwall (bringing the Cornish pasty with them).

The last mine in California to shut down was its richest, the **Empire Mine**, now preserved as a state park in the pine forests a mile east of Grass Valley (daily 9am–5pm; $2). It closed in 1956, after more than six million ounces of gold had been recovered, when the cost of getting the gold out of the ground exceeded $35 an ounce, the government-controlled price at the time. Most of the machinery has been dismantled, but there's a small but very informative **museum** at the entrance.

As well as the usual information, the Grass Valley **tourist office** at 248 Mill St (Mon–Sat 10am–5pm; ☎273-4667) contains mementoes of Lola Montez, an Irish entertainer and former mistress of Ludwig of Bavaria who retired here after touring America with her provocative "Spider Dance" (and kept a grizzly bear in her front yard).

It's hard to pick out specific highlights of **Nevada City**; it's really the town as a whole that's worth seeing. The newly restored **Old Firehouse**, a lacy, balconied and bell-towered piece of gingerbread, houses a small **museum** (daily 11am–4pm; donations) of local social history.

Greyhound stops four times a day at 123 Bank St in Grass Valley from Sacramento via Auburn (☎1-800/231-2222), and the *Gold Country Stage* connects the two towns every half hour (daily 8am–5pm; $1 a trip, $2 for a day pass; ☎265-1411).

Grass Valley and Nevada City Accommodation

Accommodation in the revamped old Gold Rush hotels doesn't come cheap, but if you can afford to splash out on a B&B, Nevada City has some excellent options.

Airway Motel, 575 E Broad St, Nevada City (☎265-2233). Quiet, 1940s motel with swimming pool, ten minute's walk from center of town. ②.

Annie Horan's, 415 W Main St, Grass Valley (☎272-2418). Sumptuous small home with antiques galore. ④.

Downey House, 517 W Broad St, Nevada City (☎265-2815). Pretty 1870s Victorian home at the top of Broad Street looking out over the town and surrounding forest. ④.

Holbrooke Hotel, 212 W Main St, Grass Valley (☎273-1353 or ☎1-800/933-7077). Historic hotel, once visited by Mark Twain, and right in the center of town. ④.

Eating and Drinking

Both Grass Valley and Nevada City have good places to eat and drink, as well as many bars and saloons, where you'll often be treated to free live music.

Gold Exchange Saloon, 158 Mill St, Grass Valley (☎272-5509). Lively, unpretentious beer bar and saloon, great for quenching a thirst after a day's hiking, biking or prospecting.

The Live Wire, 11990 Plaza Drive, Grass Valley (☎477-0855). The Gold Country's main live venue. Headbanging metal music most nights, occasional bigger-name rockers and cabaret performers.

Main Street Café, 213 W Main St, Grass Valley (☎477-6000). Casual but refined restaurant. An eclectic menu, from pastas to Cajun specialities. Recommended for grilled meats and fresh fish.

Marshall's Pasties, 203A Mill St, Grass Valley (☎272-2844). Mind-boggling fresh pasties.

Lake Tahoe

One of the highest, largest, deepest, cleanest and coldest lakes in the world, **Lake Tahoe** is perched high above the Gold Country in an alpine bowl of forested granite peaks. Longer than the English Channel is wide, and more than a thousand feet deep, it's so cold that perfectly preserved cowboys who drowned over a century ago have been recovered from its depths. The sandy beaches around the shores attract thousands of families in summer, and in winter the snow-covered slopes of the nearby peaks are packed with skiers. The eastern third of the lake lies in Nevada, and gleams with the neon signs of flashy casinos; they offer cheap food, tawdry entertainment, and of course gambling, but not, unusually for Nevada, cheap rooms.

The prettiest part of the lake by far is along the southwest shore, at **Emerald Bay State Park**, ten miles from South Lake Tahoe, which has many good shoreline **campgrounds**. A mile from the parking lot, **Vikingsholm** is an unlikely reproduction Viking castle (summer daily 10am–4pm; $2). In **D L Bliss State Park**, two miles north, the 15,000-square-foot **Ehrman Mansion** (daily 11am–4pm; free) is decorated in Thirties-era furnishings; the extensive lakefront grounds were seen in *Godfather II*.

The rest of the 75-mile **drive** around the lake can be a bit of a disappointment; a better way to see it is to take a **paddle-wheel boat cruise** on either the *Tahoe Queen* from South Lake Tahoe (daily 11am, 1.30pm and 3.55pm; $14; ☎1-800/23-TAHOE) or the *MS Dixie*, from Zephyr Cove (daily at 11am & 2.15pm; $12; ☎702/588-3508).

Practicalities

Ten daily *Greyhound* buses from San Francisco and Sacramento stop at the Nevada casinos before returning to the **depot** (☎544-2241) at 1099 Park Ave in South Lake Tahoe. Local **buses** serve the communities of Tahoe City and South Lake Tahoe; in the latter, you can rent **bicycles** from the *Tahoe Cyclery* (☎541-2726).

Both South Lake Tahoe and Tahoe City have dozens of bargain **motels**, though weekday rates from $30 can easily double at weekends, or in summer. Try the huge *Motel 6* at 2375 Lake Tahoe Blvd, South Lake Tahoe (☎542-1400; ②), or the *Falcon Motor Lodge* on Hwy-28 in King's Beach on the north shore of the lake (☎546-2583; ②). *Bobby's Café*, Hwy-267 at Hwy-28, King's Beach (☎546-2329), is an excellent and inexpensive North Shore diner. If you get stuck for a room, the South Lake Tahoe Visitors Authority (☎1-800/288-2463) runs a free **reservation service**.

Truckee and Donner Lake

Twenty-five miles north of Lake Tahoe, **Donner Lake**, surrounded by alpine cliffs of silver-grey granite, was the site of a gruesome tragedy in 1846, when the **Donner Party**, heading for the Gold Rush, found their route blocked by early snowfall. They stopped and built crude shelters, hoping that the snow would melt; it didn't. Fifteen of their number braved the mountains in search of help from Sutter's Fort in Sacramento; only two men and five women made it, surviving by eating the bodies of the men who died. A rescue party set off immediately, only to find more of the same: thirty or so half-crazed survivors, living off the meat of their fellow travellers. The horrific tale is recounted in the small **Emigrant Trail Museum** (daily 10am–4pm; $2), just off Donner Pass Road.

The small town of **Truckee**, three miles east, is a refreshing change from the tourist-dependent towns around Lake Tahoe, and lies on the main *Greyhound* (☎587-3822) and *Amtrak* routes. Its *Star Hotel/AYH Youth Hostel* at 10015 W River St (☎587-3007; ①/②), south of the river and the railroad tracks, has dormitory beds for $12 and private doubles. *Coffee And*, on Commercial Row (☎587-3123), is a good **place to eat**, while the *Bar of America* (☎587-3110) and *The Passage* (☎587-7619) at the east end of Commercial Row both have free **live music** most nights.

NORTHERN CALIFORNIA

The massive and eerily silent volcanic lands of **northern California** have more in common with Oregon and Washington than with the rest of the state. Its small settlements live by logging, fishing and farming, though locals have been joined in recent years by New Ageists and ex-hippies. Once you're past the atypically lush valleys of the **wine country**, the **coast** stretches for four hundred miles of rugged bluffs and forests. Trees are the big attraction, thousands of years old and hundreds of feet high, dominating a landscape swathed in swirling mists. The **Redwood National Park** teems with campers and hikers in summer, but out of season it can be idyllic. The remote wildernesses of the **interior** can be enchanting, especially around the **Shasta Cascade** and **Lassen Volcanic National Park**.

Public transportation is, not surprisingly, scarce, though *Greyhound* buses run from San Francisco and Sacramento up and down I-5 and US-101.

The Wine Country

The warm and sunny hills of **Napa** and **Sonoma valleys**, an hour north of San Francisco, are by reputation if not statistically at the center of the American wine industry; their 29,000 grape-acres turn out vintages to satisfy a snobbery every bit as rampant as in Europe. In summer, cars jam Hwy-29 through its heart, as visitors embark on a day's free drinking, thinly disguised as an avid interest in wine.

The Napa Valley

A 35-mile strip of gently landscaped hillsides, the **Napa Valley** looks like something you'd expect in rural England rather than beside the Pacific. Of the large wineries at its southern end, **Robert Mondavi**, at 7801 St Helena Hwy at Oakville (daily 9am–5pm; free), offers the most informative and least hard-sell tours and tastings.

A little way up the valley at the pretty village of **St Helena**, the **Christian Brothers Vineyard**, 2555 Main St (daily 10am–4pm; ☎963-0765), was the world's largest winery when erected in 1889, and turns out some of the best sparkling wines and champagnes in the valley. The **Berringer Brothers Winery** (daily 9.30am–4pm; closed Aug), modelled on a German Gothic mansion, has graced the cover of many a wine maga-zine. Spacious lawns and a grand tasting room, heavy on the dark wood, make for quite a regal experience.

Homely **Calistoga**, at the very tip of the valley, is well known for its mud baths, whirlpools and mineral water. The **Chateau Montelena**, 1429 Tubbs Lane, just north of town, is one of the valley's oldest and smallest wineries, with an impressive medieval facade. A mile further up the road, the **Old Faithful Geyser** (daily 9am–5pm; $3) spurts boiling water sixty feet into the air at fifty-minute intervals. The water source was discovered while drilling for oil here in the 1920s, when search equipment struck a force estimated to be up to a thousand pounds per square foot.

Practicalities

Daily *Gray Line* **bus tours** (☎558-9400) are the only option for San Francisco-based trav-ellers who can't tour the Wine Country by car. **Napa** itself is somewhat bland and not at all budget-oriented , but it does have a *Motel 6* at 3380 Solano Ave (☎226-1811; ③). The expensive, dinner-only *La Boucane*, 1778 Second St (☎253-1177), dishes up mouth-watering chunks of tender meat in imaginative sauces, and perfect fish.

In **Calistoga**, *Dr Wilkinson's Hot Springs*, 1507 Lincoln Ave (☎942-4102; ⑥), is a legen-dary health spa and hotel; less expensive lodgings (and spa facilities) lining the main drag, Lincoln Ave, include the quiet, modern *Comfort Inn* (no 1865; ☎942-9400; ④). The *Calistoga Wine Way Inn*, 1019 Foothill Blvd (☎942-0680 or 1-800/572-0679; ⑤), is a small and friendly B&B, with a lovely garden and antique-filled rooms, a short walk from the center of town. Good-sized portions of California cuisine at the *All Seasons* bistro, 1400 Lincoln Ave (☎942-9111), are accompanied by a massive wine list; the *Calistoga Inn*, 1250 Lincoln Ave (☎942-4101) serves very good seafood, including spicey Cajun prawns and crispy crab cakes.

The Sonoma Valley

On looks alone the crescent-shaped **Sonoma Valley** beats Napa hands down. This alto-gether more rustic valley curves between oak-covered mountain ranges from the Spanish colonial town of **SONOMA** a few miles north along Hwy-12 to Glen Ellen. It's far smaller than Napa, and most of its wineries are informal, family-run businesses, where a charge for tasting is still frowned upon and visitors are few.

The restored **Mission San Francisco Solano de Sonoma** (daily 10am–5pm; $1), just north of the spacious plaza in Sonoma, was the last and northernmost of the California missions, and the only one established in northern California by the nervous Mexican rulers, who were fearful of expansionist Russian fur-traders. Sonoma's winer-ies are concentrated a mile east, within walking distance, and include the grand old **Buena Vista Winery**, 18000 Old Winery Rd (tasting daily 10am–5pm; tours daily 2pm, also 11.30am Sat & Sun), which has champagne cellars, tunnels of oak caskets and a high-ceilinged tasting room.

Practicalities

On weekdays, *Sonoma County Transit* (☎527-7665) buses link the town to Napa, and Santa Rosa in the north. **Accommodation** is pricey, though the *Sonoma Hotel*, 110 West Spain St (☎996-2996; ④), has antique crammed doubles, as well as a good bar and *Regina's* Italian-American restaurant. *La Casa*, 121 E Spain St (☎996-3406) is a friendly, festive and inexpensive Mexican restaurant across from the Mission. For something more unusual, try *Little Switzerland* just west of town on Grove St and Riverside Drive (☎938-9990). This former bordello has evolved into a cabaret with accordion and drums, serving bratwurst and goulash dinners – a full bar helps it all go down easier, but all the same, it's quite mad.

The Northern Coast

Rugged in the extreme, often foggy, always dangerous and thunderously dramatic, the **northern coast** is leagues away from the gentle, sun-drenched beaches of southern California. Sunbathing is right out, as is swimming; instead, don your hiking boots, wrap up warm and get out into the enormous forests.

The Sonoma Coast and Russian River

Despite the weekend influx from San Francisco, the villages of the **Sonoma Coast** and **Russian River Valley** seem all but asleep for most of the year. From tiny **Bodega Bay**, where Hitchcock filmed *The Birds*, a great thirteen-mile hike leads along the rugged cliffs to busy **Goat Rock Beach**, where the Russian River joins the ocean.

About ten miles up the warm and pastoral **Russian River Valley**, **Guerneville** is an (unofficial) gay resort. It offers plenty of **places to stay** – though none of them inexpensive. *The Fern Grove Inn*, 16650 River Rd (☎869-9083; ⑥), offers luxurious cottages, while the **campground** at *Johnson's Resort* on First St also has cabins, as well as a lively nightlife (☎869-2022; ③). The *Rainbow Cattle Company* on Main St and *Molly Brown's Saloon* on Old Cazadero Rd are good for eating, drinking, and dancing in cowboy company. The **Armstrong Redwoods State Reserve**, two miles north, contains 750 very dense acres of enormous redwoods, interspersed by trails – horse riding is particularly recommended. Guided expeditions run by the *Armstrong Woods Pack Station* (☎887-2939) vary in length from half a day ($35) to three-day pack trips ($350).

Monte Rio, five miles back down the river, is a lovely old resort town, at the entrance to the 2500-acre **Bohemian Grove**, where the richest and most powerful men in the country gather in privacy each July for a week of (supposedly male-only) high jinks.

The Mendocino Coast

Another hundred miles up the coast, **Mendocino** is weathered and almost cute, with a low-key, raffish charm and a plethora of art galleries, gift stores and boutique-delicatessens. Just south of town, hiking and cycling trails weave through the unusual **Van Damme State Park**, on Hwy-1 (☎937-5804; $3), where the ancient trees of the **Pygmy Forest** are stunted to waist height because of poor draining and soil chemicals.

The *Mendocino Village Inn*, 44860 Main St (☎937-0246; ④) is a welcoming B&B, stuffed with antique furniture, where your muesli comes with added Vivaldi; the friendly *Joshua Grindle Inn*, 4480 Little Lake Rd (☎937-4143; ③), is a little less expensive. *Mendocino Coast Reservations* (937-5033) are a general B&B booking service, but they have nothing under $100 per night. The town's oldest bar is *Dick's Place* on Main Street, with all the robust conviviality you'd expect from a spit-and-sawdust saloon. Of the town's **restaurants**, the *Wellspring* at 955 Ukiah St is good for seafood.

BIGFOOT COUNTRY

Willow Creek, forty miles east of Arcata, is the gateway to "Bigfoot Country". Reports of giant 350- to 800-pound humanoids wandering the forests of northwestern California have circulated since the late nineteenth century, fuelled by long-established Indian legends, but weren't taken seriously until 1958, when a road maintenance crew found giant footprints. Thanks to their photos, the Bigfoot story went worldwide. Since then, there have been over forty separate sightings of Bigfoot prints. At the crossroads in Willow Creek is a huge wooden replica of the man-ape, with slanted forehead, flared nostrils and short ears, an identikit of the creature who in recent years has added kidnapping to his list of alleged activities. A small visitor center here has details of Bigfoot's escapades, as well as information on the adjacent Hoopa Valley Indian Reservation, which has often been the site of violent confrontation between Native Americans and whites over fishing territory.

Five miles north in the tiny village of **CASPAR**, an excellent **health spa** offers open-air hot tubs for $7 per hour. Caspar also has the best **bar** in the area, the *Caspar Inn*, which has a nightly billing of rock, jazz and rhythm and blues.

The Humboldt Coast

Humboldt is by far the most beautiful of the coastal counties: almost entirely forest-land, overwhelmingly peaceful in places, in others plain eerie. The impassable cliffs of **Kings Range** prevent even the sinuous Hwy-1 from reaching the "Lost Coast" of its southern reaches. To get there you have to travel US-101 through deepest redwood territory as far as **Garberville**, a one-street town with a few good bars, at the center of the "Emerald Triangle" which produces the majority of California's largest cash crop, marijuana. Every August, the town hosts a **Reggae on the River** festival.

Most of the town's **accommodation** is overpriced; the scruffy *Johnston Motel*, 839 Redwood Drive (☎923-3327; ②), has the lowest rates. Garberville's **restaurants** and **bars**, such as *The Cellar*, at 728 Redwood Drive, turn out some great live bluegrass. The Italian food at *Sicilio's*, 445 Conger Lane, is inexpensive and reliable.

Redwood country begins in earnest a few miles north, at the **Humboldt Redwoods State Park**. The serpentine **Avenue of the Giants** weaves for 33 miles through trees which block all but a few strands of sunlight. This is the habitat of *sequoia sempervirens*, a coastal redwood with ancestors dating back to the dinosaurs. Some are over 350ft tall. The three **campgrounds** fill quickly in summer; you must book (☎946-2436).

Tiny **Samoa**, a few minutes by car from **Eureka**, holds the last remaining cookhouse in the west. Lumbermen came to the **Samoa Cookhouse** to eat gargantuan meals after a day of felling redwoods; the oilskin tablecloths and burly workers have gone, but the lumber-camp style remains, with long tables and colossal portions of red meat.

Arcata, twelve miles across the bay from Eureka, is a small college town with an earthy, mellow pace, a few raunchy bars, and some excellent white-sanded and wind-swept beaches to the north. Three blocks from the *Greyhound* station on Tenth St, the *Arcata Crew House Hostel*, 1390 I St (May–Sept only; ☎822-9995; ①), has $10.50 dorms; not far away is the *Fairwinds Motel*, 1674 G St (☎822-4824; ②). The working *Humboldt Brewery*, 856 Tenth St, has its own bar and low-priced restaurant.

The Redwood National Park

Thirty miles north of Arcata, the small town of **Orick** marks the southern limit, and busiest section, of the enormous **REDWOOD NATIONAL PARK**. **Tall Trees Grove** here is home of the world's tallest tree – a mighty 367-footer. Many visitors hike to it on the 8.5-mile trail from the **ranger station** (daily 8am–5pm; ☎488-3461), but if you're unsure of your footing in the dense undergrowth, there's also a **shuttle bus** ($3).

The varied **Prairie Creek** area further north is the only place in the park where you can take **ranger tours** of the wild and damp profusion. These leave from the ranger station on US-101 (daily, summer 8am–6pm, winter 8am–5pm, ☎488-2171), beside the meadows of **Elk Prairie**, which is roamed by Roosevelt elk and even bears. A line of **restaurants** along US-101 as you approach Prairie Creek have the bad taste to serve wild boar roasts, elk steaks and the like, as well as more traditional dishes. One mile north, a magnificent redwood, more than a 300ft tall, overlooks the road.

Spectacular coastal views can be had from trails in the **Klamath** area, especially the **Klamath Overlook**, on Requa Road about three quarters of a mile down to the sea. You can drive through, jump over, or lumber under all the sculpted **Trees of Mystery** (daily 8am–6pm; $6), except the impressive **Cathedral Tree**, where nine trees have grown from one root structure to form a spooky circle. The **Redwood Hostel** (☎482-8265; ①) on US-101 has dorms at around $17 per night.

The park headquarters are in **Crescent City** at 1111 Second St (☎464-6101), but you can pick up information all over the park. There are **campgrounds** everywhere; three that have showers and water are *Prairie Creek* on US-101; *Mill Creek*, eight miles south of Crescent City; and *Jedediah Smith*, five miles north of Crescent City on Smith River. If you must come in summer, make reservations on ☎452-1950; and if things get really desperate, head up US-101 and look for **motels** around Crescent City.

The Northern Interior

The remote **northern interior** of California, cut off from the coast by the **Shasta Cascade** range and dominated by forests, lakes, and mountains, is largely uninhabited too, and infrequently visited. I-5 leads through the heart of this near wilderness, forging straight through the unspectacular farmland of **Sacramento Valley** to **Redding** – the regions' only buses follow this route. Redding isn't much of a place in itself, but it's a good base for the **Whiskeytown-Shasta-Trinity area** and the more demanding **Lassen National Volcanic Park**. The volcanic **Lava Beds** at the very northeastern tip of the state are for most of the year inaccessible.

Redding and Shasta
REDDING itself is basically a railway center, a characterless assembly of low-cost lodgings and little else whose streets only really brighten during midsummer when the tourists hit town. Its **motels** are concentrated along Market Street (Hwy-273) and Pine Street, four blocks from the *Greyhound* station (☎241-2643); *Budget Lodge*, 1055 Market St (☎243-4231; ②), is a typical inexpensive option; down the road a little, the *Redding Lodge*, 1135 Market St (☎243-5141; ③), is slightly more luxurious.

SHASTA, ten miles west of Redding, is altogether more appealing. These half-ruined brick buildings were once a booming gold-mining town, literally at the end of the road from San Francisco and on the very edge of the wilderness. The **courthouse** has been turned into a museum (daily 10am–3pm; $2), full of mining paraphernalia; the gallows and prison cells are a grim reminder of the once daily executions.

Precipitous Hwy-299 climbs from Shasta into the **Whiskeytown-Shasta-Trinity National Recreation Area**, where the artificial beaches, forests and camping facilities at three lakes – Clair Eagle, Whiskeytown and Shasta – meet the needs of water-skiers, sailors and wilderness hikers. Sadly, during summer it's completely congested, and severe drought in the last few years has led to receding water levels, evidenced by the red band of hitherto unexposed rock just above the surface of the water. An extensive system of tunnels, dams and aqueducts directs the plentiful waters of the Sacramento River to California's central valley to irrigate cash crops. The lakes are pretty enough, but residents complain they're not a patch on the wild waters that used to flow from the mountains before the Central Valley Project came along in the 1960s.

Roughly sixty miles north of Redding, a scenic road branches off I-5 and pushes eight thousand feet up the slopes to the tiny town that describes itself as "the best kept secret in California": **MOUNT SHASTA CITY**, hard under the enormous bulk of the 14,162ft **Mount Shasta**. Still considered active despite not having erupted for two hundred years, this lone peak dominates the landscape for a hundred miles around. If you want to climb to the summit, or simply to explore the flanks of the mountain along the many trails, you must register (before and after) with the Mount Shasta Ranger District Office, 204 W Alma in town (☎926-3781). It's a rewarding journey, and easily done by *Greyhound* (305 N Mt Shasta Blvd; ☎926-3797), which connects the town with Redding in the south and Oregon in the north.

Budget **accommodation** can be found in Mount Shasta at the *Mountain View Lodge*, 305 McCloud Rd (☎926-4704; ②), and the *Das Alpenhaus Motel*, 504 Mount Shasta Blvd (☎926-4617; ②); nicer options include the *McCloud Guest House*, 606 W Colombero Drive (☎964-3160; ④), set in the former headquarters of the old logging company. The picturesque *Lake Siskiyou Campground* (☎926-2618) is in a wood four miles west of town. *Bellissimo's*, at 204 E Lake St, serves delicious well-priced **meals**, while the excellent Italian *Mike and Tony's*, 501 Mount Shasta Blvd, is a bit more expensive.

Lassen National Volcanic Park

Around forty miles directly east from Redding are the pine forests, crystal-green lakes and boiling thermal pools of the **Lassen National Volcanic Park**. A forbidding climate, which brings up to fifty feet of snowfall each year, keeps the area pretty much uninhabited outside the brief June-to-October season. **Mount Lassen** itself last erupted in 1915, when the peak blew an enormous mushroom cloud some seven miles skyward, tearing the summit into chunks that landed as far away as Reno; scientists predict that it is the likeliest of all the West Coast volcanoes to blow again.

The thirty-mile tour of the park along Hwy-89 from **Manzanita Lake** in the north should take no more than a few hours. The explosion of seventy years ago denuded the **devastated area**, ripping out every tree and patch of grass. Slowly the earth is recovering a green blanket, but the most vivid impression is one of complete destruction. Marking the halfway point, **Summit Lake** is a busy camping area set around a beautiful icy lake, close to which are the park's most manageable hiking trails. From a parking area to the south (eight thousand feet up), the steep five-mile ascent to Lassen Peak begins. Experienced hikers can do it in four hours, but wilderness seekers will have a better time pushing east to the steep trails of the **Juniper Lake** area.

Continuing south along Hwy-89, Lassen's indisputable show-stealers are **Bumpass Hell** and **Emerald Lake**, the former (named after a man who lost a leg trying to cross it) a steaming valley of active pools and vents which bubble away at a low rumble all around. The trails are sturdy and easy to manage, but *never* venture off them. The crusts over the thermal features are often brittle, and breaking through could plunge you into very hot water. Before leaving the park at **Mineral**, make an effort to stop at **Sulphur Works**, an acrid cauldron of steam vents. A magnificent but gruelling trail leads for a mile around the site to the avalanche-prone summit at **Diamond Peak**, and great views over the entire park and forestland beyond.

Visitor centers at Manzanita and Mineral (daily 8.30am–4.30pm; ☎335-4266) have free maps and information on the park.

Lava Beds National Monument

Lava Beds National Monument (May–Sept only), in the far northeastern corner of the state, is the most remote and forgotten of California's parks. The history of these volcanic caves and huge black lava flows is as violent as the natural forces that created them. Before the Gold Rush the area was home to the **Modoc** Indians, but repeated and bloody confrontations with miners led the government to order them into a reservation shared with another, traditionally enemy, tribe. After only a few months the Modocs drifted back to the isolation of the lava beds, and in 1872 the Army was sent in. Fifty-two Modoc warriors, under the leadership of "Captain Jack", held back an army twenty times the size of theirs for five months from a natural fortress of caves now known as **Captain Jack's Stronghold** at the northern tip of the park. On the outside the stronghold looks like nothing special, but a trail into the darkness reveals a subterranean labyrinth of passageways. You're allowed to explore the caves alone, but that takes considerable nerve, and most opt for the ranger-led tours which leave daily at 2pm from the **visitor center** near the entrance (daily 8.30am–5.30pm; ☎667-2283).

This entrance is in the southeastern corner of the park along Hwy-139, 160 miles from Redding. The town of **TULELAKE** 25 miles north is your last chance to buy supplies – there's nothing in the park itself – and has several roadside budget **motels** and a few budget restaurants. Both the *Park Motel* (☎667-2913; ②) and the *Ellis Motel* (☎667-5242; ②) have low-cost rooms.

CHAPTER FOURTEEN

THE PACIFIC NORTHWEST

The two northern Pacific states of **WASHINGTON** and **OREGON** are similar in both topography and climate. Significantly cooler than California to the south – and hence spared most of the damaging effects of over-tourism – both are split in half by the great north–south spine of the **Cascade Mountains**, with their western portions far more inviting and exciting to visit.

To the **west**, the ocean rains, if not quite as unceasing as local folklore might suggest, have created a verdant and rugged landscape, thick with woodlands that on the **Olympic Peninsula** become mini-rainforests. This fertile land is where the population is most heavily concentrated, although the principal cities are not along the exposed coast itself, which remains remarkably pristine, scattered with remote driftwood-strewn beaches. Both **Seattle** and **Portland** lie roughly fifty miles from the open Pacific, along I-5 which runs from Canada to California. Seattle, the commercial and cultural capital of the Northwest, is nonetheless a major port, perched on the edge of the beautiful island-strewn **Puget Sound**, with a busy network of local and long-distance ferries among the container traffic. Portland lies in the rich farmlands of the Willamette valley, long the historic heartland of Oregon.

Across the Cascades, the **east** is far drier and less hospitable, sometimes verging on desert. Of the towns, only **Spokane** is of any appreciable size, though the wide-skied empty landscapes of the east have a striking beauty all their own, at its most severe along the Columbia River Gorge between Boardman and The Dalles. There are advantages in approaching the Cascades from the east too – a regular ferry service leaves Chelan to travel deep into the mountains. The scarred territory well to the south of Seattle around Mount St Helens, which erupted to devastating effect in 1980, remains of outstanding interest.

History

The first inhabitants of the Americas are believed to have reached the continent across a land bridge over what is now the Bering Strait between Siberia and Alaska. Thus the Pacific Northwest could well have been the earliest populated area of the lower 48 states. Little evidence remains of the Native American presence, though artefacts unearthed from the perfectly preserved five-hundred-year-old settlement at **Makah Bay** provide a great opportunity to appreciate how the local Indians once lived.

Not until late in the eighteenth century was there a significant white presence in the region, and that was very much confined to trading and exploration along the coast

---

ACCOMMODATION PRICE CODES

All accommodation prices in this book have been coded using the symbols below. Note that prices are for the least expensive double rooms in each establishment. For a full explanation see p.35 in *Basics*.

①	up to $30	④	$60–80	⑦	$130–180
②	$30–45	⑤	$80–100	⑧	$180+
③	$45–60	⑥	$100–130		

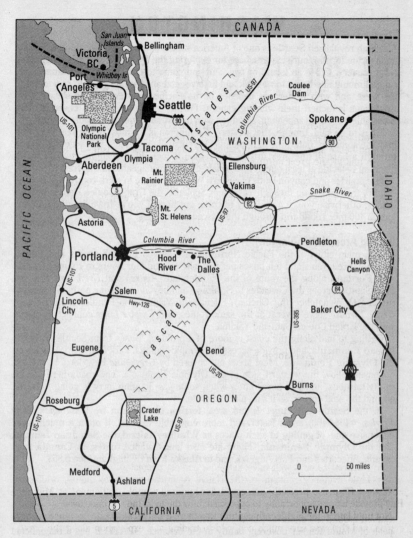

rather than permanent settlement. Russian trappers began to make their way down from the north, while European sea captains such as Cook and Vancouver came in search of the **Northwest Passage**. A brief period of hectic competition, in which entrepreneurs of many nationalities vied for fur-trading profits, only came to an end when the whole coast was all but "trapped out". Lewis and Clark, who came hurtling along the Columbia River Gorge in 1804, were the first whites to cross the interior of the continent, and within forty years settlers were streaming in along the Oregon Trail. During the forty years after that, the railroads reached Portland and Seattle, Chief Joseph of the Nez Percé made his last despairing bid on behalf of the displaced Native Americans (see p.659) and both Oregon and Washington achieved statehood.

WASHINGTON

Although revitalized **Seattle** is one of America's most popular cities in which to live, its main virtue for the tourist is as a base for exploring the **Puget Sound** and its glorious rural scenery. Cross an island or two, and you come to the **Olympic Peninsula**, its rugged mountains home to rare elk and lush vegetation that merges into rain forest to the west, and with wilderness beaches on its Pacific edge unchanged since Native Americans launched their whaling canoes. Further south, the **lower coast** is more accessible but not as appealing, splodged with industrial towns and holiday resorts.

It has to be said, though, that western Washington is for most of the year very wet: only the summers (late June to September) are usually warm and blue-skied. But even through a haze of fine grey drizzle, the region is incredibly beautiful, and it's worth planning to tackle at least one of its well laid-out and manageable hiking trails.

The prairies and canyon-lands of eastern Washington are in stark contrast. If a cross-country trek takes you through Yakima or Spokane, the Grand Coulee Dam is worth a detour; otherwise you're only likely to come out here if you're travelling the Cascade loop, a 400-mile round trip through the Cascade mountains.

Getting Around Washington

All the main cities of the Pacific Northwest are served by both **trains** and **buses**. Roughly three trains and ten buses per day take around four hours to connect **Seattle** with **Portland** along the route of the I-5 interstate. *Amtrak* and *Greyhound* run east from **Seattle** across the Cascades to **Spokane** and beyond, with one of the *Greyhounds* running to Wenatchee (for Chelan), Ellensburg, Yakima and Pendleton on the way; *Green Tortoise* serve several of the same routes, and *Empire Lines* connect **Spokane** with the Grand Coulee Dam and Yakima.

Getting to and along the coast is more of a problem. Buses from Seattle cross the **Kitsap Peninsula**, and provide access to Olympic National Park from Port Angeles on the **Olympic Peninsula**. Most areas not covered by *Greyhound* have local buses, but no buses follow the western side of the Olympic Peninsula. The roads here can be pretty tortuous, and you never know when some vast logging lorry is going to hurtle around the next corner, so it's no place to cycle.

In the Seattle and Puget Sound area, **ferries** (mostly run by *Washington State Ferries*; ☎464-6400) are a faster and more enjoyable method, if often a much more expensive one, of getting to such places as **Whidbey Island**, the **San Juan Islands**, and the **Olympic Peninsula**. There are also long-distance routes, to **Canada** from Seattle, Anacortes and Port Angeles, and to **Alaska** from Bellingham; see p.853.

Seattle

Curved around the shore of Elliott Bay, with Lake Washington behind and the snowy peak of Mount Rainier hovering faintly in the distance, **SEATTLE** has a magnificent setting. Its insistently modern skyline of glass skyscrapers gleams across the bay, emblem of two decades of vigorous urban renewal. In many ways it feels like a new city, groping for a balance between the smart high-rises and a downbeat streetlife that reflects its tough past, its old center now restored as a colorful historic district.

Seattle's **beginnings** were inauspiciously muddy. Flooded out of its first location on the flat little peninsula of **Alki Point**, the town shifted in the 1850s to what's now Pioneer Square, renaming itself after a local Native American chief. This was soggy ground, and the small logging community built its houses on stilts. As the surrounding forest was gradually felled and the wood shipped out, Seattle grew slowly until the Klondike Gold Rush of 1897 put it firmly on the national map. World War I boosted shipbuilding, and the city was soon a large industrial center. Trade unions grew strong, based on the shipworkers, and the *Industrial Workers of the World*, or "Wobblies", co-ordinated the USA's first general strike here on February 6, 1919.

Since the turn of the century, the **Boeing** airline corporation has been crucial to the city's well-being, booming during World War II and employing one in five of Seattle's workforce by the 1960s. The obvious prosperity Boeing and more recent success stories such as computer software giant Microsoft have brought the city jars with a large and visible community of teenage runaways and homeless people on the streets.

Arrival, Information and Getting Around

Flights land at Seattle/Tacoma's **Sea-Tac Airport** at 18612 Pacific Hwy S (☎433-5217), fourteen miles south of downtown. There's a **visitor information kiosk** (daily, summer 9.30am–7.30pm, winter 8.30am–1pm) in front of the baggage carousel. Outside, the *Gray Line Airport Express* **bus** ($7) leaves every half hour for the thirty-minute journey downtown, dropping off at major hotels. The *Metro* express city bus #194 ($1.10) takes 25 minutes to reach downtown's Transit Tunnel. Hwy-99, the Pacific Highway, leads into town.

The **Amtrak** station at Third and Jackson, just south of downtown, and **Greyhound**, at Eighth and Stewart to the east (☎624-3456), are both an easy bus ride from down-town. *Green Tortoise* drops off and picks up at Ninth and Stewart (☎324-RIDE).

For **information**, walk a couple of blocks towards downtown (the less rundown-looking direction) from *Greyhound*, to the **visitor center**, inside the Washington State Convention Center at Seventh and Pike (Mon–Fri 8.30am–5pm; ☎461-5840). The main **post office** is at Union St and Third Ave downtown (Mon–Fri 8am–5.30pm; ☎442-6255; zip code 98101).

City Transportation

It's best to **get around** either on foot or on the free downtown **buses**. Cross out of the free zone, and you pay as you get off; come back in and you pay as you enter. Single fares vary between 85¢ and $1.60, and tickets are valid for an hour. **Day passes** ($1.70; bought from the driver) are available on weekends and holidays: discount ticket books (for 10 and 20 rides) can be purchased at the **Metro Customer Assistance Offices** at the Metro Transit Tunnel, Westlake Mall, Fifth Ave and Vine (☎553-3000), and can be used on the overhead **monorail** (otherwise 80¢) between downtown and the Seattle Center, and on the waterfront **streetcar** (85¢ off-peak; $1.10 peak).

Washington State **ferries** run to Bainbridge Island and Bremerton; tickets from Pier 52, Colman Dock (☎464-6400). *Gray Line* (☎623-4252) organize guided half-day **bus tours** ($18), and are among several operators of **boat tours**, of which the best is the *Water Sightseeing* tour from Pier 57 (2hr 30min; $19).

The City

Downtown Seattle's main attractions are the busy stalls and cafés of **Pike Place Market** and the restored nineteenth-century **Pioneer Square**, lined with taverns. A stroll along **the waterfront** lets you enjoy fabulous views of Elliott Bay. At the **Seattle Center** in the north, the **Space Needle** presides over a collection of theaters and museums. A couple of outlying districts are often livelier than downtown: **Capitol Hill**'s cafés and bars form the heart of the city's gay scene, and the **University District** is a studenty area of cheap cafés and uptempo nightlife.

> The **area code** for Seattle and western Washington is ☎206.

Pike Place Market and the Waterfront

Farmers first brought their produce to **Pike Place Market** in 1907, lowering food prices by selling straight from the barrow. The market prospered during the Depression, but by the 1960s it was shabby and neglected, and the authorities decided to flatten the area altogether. Following vigorous protests, Seattlites voted overwhelmingly to preserve this as the affordable domain of the elderly and poor. The restoration has been highly successful; the whole place, stretched over several city blocks, bustles with energy, and a real attempt has been made to stay true to its roots, even if upscale restaurants are inevitably creeping in. Street entertainers play to busy crowds, smells of coffee drift from the cafés, and stalls are piled high with lobsters, crabs, salmon, vegetables and fruit. Further into the long market building, handmade jewellery, woodcarvings and silk-screen prints are on sale, while close by small shops stock a massive range of ethnic foods.

Also nearby, the **Seattle Art Museum** at 100 University and First (Tues, Wed, Fri & Sat 10am–5pm, Thurs 10am–9pm, Sun noon–5pm; $5), has recently moved into its new Robert Venturi-designed building on First Ave, a lavish setting for some pretty ropey modern art, redeemed by eclectic collections of African, Pacific and native American art.

Stairs in the market lead down to the **Hillclimb**, and to the **Waterfront** below. No longer deep enough for ocean-going ships, much of this has become cluttered with tourist shops while the port's real business goes on to the north and south. Almost opposite the Hillclimb, **Pier 59**, an old wooden jetty which once served the tall ships, now houses the underwater viewing dome of the **Aquarium** (daily, summer 10am–7pm, winter 10am–5pm; $6.50). A combined ticket ($10–80) also admits to the 3-D **Omnidome** next door (daily 10am–10pm), where films on the huge screen include one on the eruption of Mount St Helens. On Pier 54 to the south, the most famous of the waterfront's fish-and-chips stands, *Ivar's Acres of Clams*, has its own special stop (*"Clam Central Station"*) on the restored vintage **waterfront streetcar**. **Colman Dock** at Pier 52 is the terminal for the *Washington State Ferries* (see p.853).

Pioneer Square and Around

A few blocks inland from the ferry terminal, the **Pioneer Square** area, Seattle's oldest section, also had a close brush with the demolition balls of the 1960s. The restoration work is a little glossier here, with bookshops and galleries adding a veneer of sophistication to the old red brick, wrought iron and shady trees. Things get a bit more raucous at night, when rock music booms out from assorted taverns – though the area is peopled by persistent, sometimes agressive, panhandlers. Locals – unless they're in groups – make most night-time journeys around downtown by cab.

By far the most amusing way to find out about the city's seamy past is on an **Underground Tour** from *Doc Maynard's* tavern, 610 First Ave ($6.50; ☎682-1511). This area was rebuilt after a disastrous fire in 1889 with the street level raised by one storey, so what used to be the ground floors of its brick buildings are now underground, linked by subterranean passageways. A couple of blocks from *Doc Maynard's*, at 117 South Main St, the free **Klondike Gold Rush National Historical Park** (daily 9am–5pm) is not a park at all, but a small museum. It celebrates the days when, thanks to a formidable campaign to promote Seattle as the gateway to Alaskan gold, prospectors streamed in, and traders (and con artists) made their fortunes. The dog population fared less well, as many a hapless mutt was harnessed to a sledge while gold-seekers practised "mushing" up and down Seattle's streets before facing Alaskan snow (see Jack London's novel *The Call of the Wild*). Charlie Chaplin's *The Gold Rush* – shown free here on weekend afternoons – sends up the whole gold fever.

The large cobblestoned square of **Occidental Park**, with its crowds of homeless alcoholics, holds four recently erected totem poles carved with grotesque creatures from Northwest Native American legends.

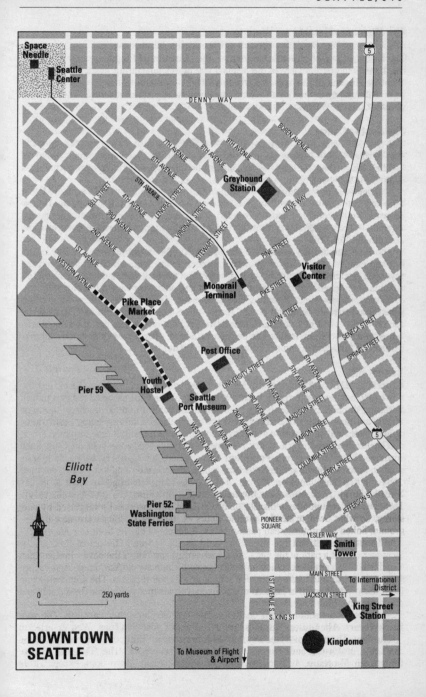

Space
Needle

Seattle
Center

DENNY WAY

7TH AVENUE
6TH AVENUE
9TH AVENUE
BOREN AVENUE

8TH AVENUE

5TH AVENUE

Greyhound
Station

OLIVE WAY

Bell Street
4TH AVENUE
LENORA STREET

3RD AVENUE

VIRGINIA STREET

Pine Street

2ND AVENUE

STEWART STREET

Visitor
Center

1ST AVENUE

WESTERN AVENUE

PIKE STREET

Monorail
Terminal

Pike Place
Market

UNION STREET

SENECA STREET

SPRING STREET

Post Office

UNIVERSITY STREET

6TH AVENUE

5TH AVENUE

4TH AVENUE

Pier 59

Youth
Hostel

Seattle
Port Museum

3RD AVENUE

2ND AVENUE

1ST AVENUE

MADISON STREET

MARION STREET

WESTERN AVENUE

ALASKAN WAY VIADUCT

COLUMBIA STREET

CHERRY STREET

*Elliott
Bay*

JEFFERSON ST

Pier 52:
Washington
State Ferries

PIONEER
SQUARE

YESLER WAY

Smith
Tower

N

MAIN STREET

To International
District →

0   250 yards

1ST AVENUE S.

JACKSON STREET

King Street
Station

S. KING ST

**DOWNTOWN
SEATTLE**

To Museum of Flight
& Airport ▼

Kingdome

The Museum of Flight

9404 E Marginal Way (daily 10am–5pm; $5). 20min bus ride south of downtown.

The best and biggest of Seattle's museums, the **Museum of Flight**, is partly housed in the 1909 "Red Barn" that was the original *Boeing* manufacturing plant. Displays lead from the dreams of the ancients, via the Wright brothers, to the growth of Boeing itself, culminating in the Great Gallery, hung with twenty full-sized aircraft and a replica of John Glenn's 1962 Mercury space capsule.

The Seattle Center

The Seattle Center dates from the 1962 World's Fair, whose theme was "Century 21" (hence the spindly flying-saucer-tipped Space Needle tower, now the symbol of Seattle). Since then the site has become a sort of culture park, collecting the city's symphony, ballet and opera, a museum and a small amusement park.

The center is best reached by the **monorail**, which runs from the Westlake Mall at Fifth and Pine downtown (80¢ one-way) and crosses the area now known as the **Denny Regrade** on thin concrete stilts. Considering an entire hill was bulldozed to create the Regrade, there's not much to show for it, beyond a few tough taverns in **Belltown**, the area around Bell Street.

The monorail drops you close to the **Space Needle**, which now feels oddly dated, but still exudes a fair amount of glamor, especially at night, when it's lit up and the revolving restaurant is in full swing. The view from the observation deck, where there's a bar, is unmatched (daily, summer 8am–midnight, otherwise 9am–midnight; $6).

Nearby, the excellent **Pacific Science Center** (daily, summer 10am–6pm, otherwise Mon–Fri 10am–5pm, Sat & Sun 10am–6pm; $4) is easily recognized by its white arches. This is full of bright and innovative exhibits on science-based topics, sometimes linked to cultural issues; the permanent *Sea Monster House* exhibit, for example, recreates a turn-of-the-century Native American home.

Capitol Hill

CAPITOL HILL, a fifteen-minute bus ride east of downtown, has been the closest the city has to an alternative center since young gays, hippies and assorted radicals moved in during the Sixties and Seventies. The shops and cafés around **Broadway**, the main street, are now pretty mainstream, but the concentration of easy-going restaurants, coffeehouses and bars provide good day-time café-sitting and night-time drinking.

The northern end of the district is quietly wealthy. Mansions built on Gold Rush fortunes sit sedately around **Volunteer Park**, where the **Conservatory**'s hothouses contain flowers, shrubs and orchids from jungle, desert, and rain forest (daily, summer 10am–7pm, winter 10am–4pm; free). Ten blocks east, **Washington Park** stretches away to the north, encompassing the **Arboretum**, where the trees are especially beautiful in fall. At the south end of the park, the immaculate **Japanese Gardens** flash banks of pink flowers beside neat little pools (March–Nov, daily 10am to around 5pm; $2).

The University District

Across Union Bay from the park, the **University** (or "U") **District** is livelier than Capitol Hill: a busy hotchpotch of coffeehouses, cinemas, clothes, book- and record stores, catering to the University of Washington's 34,600 students. The area centers on University Way, known as "**the Ave**" and lined with inexpensive ethnic restaurants and the cavernous *University Bookstore*.

A couple of museums stand on the sedate nineteenth-century **campus**. The pale brick **Henry Art Gallery**, at 15th Ave NE and NE 41st St (Tues, Wed & Fri–Sun 11am–5pm, Thurs 11am–9pm; $3), houses American and European paintings from the last two centuries, and mounts small, innovative shows. The **Thomas Burke Memorial Museum**, at 17th Ave and NE 45th St (daily 10am–5pm, except Thurs

10am–8pm; $3), has carved totem poles, painted wooden masks from the Northwest coast, plaited fiber fans from Polynesia and sorcery charms from New Guinea.

Ballard and the Ship Canal

The "U" district and Seattle's other northern neighborhoods are sliced off from the rest of town by water; the **Lake Washington Ship Canal** connects Lake Union with the sea to the west and Lake Washington to the east. The procession of boats passing through the locks near the mouth of the canal makes pleasant viewing (bus #17 from downtown). Migrating salmon bypass the locks via a **fish ladder**, laid out with viewing windows. In peak season (late summer for salmon, autumn and early winter for trout) the water is full of enormous leaping fish.

Behind the locks is Salmon Bay, with **Fisherman's Terminal** on its south side crowded with Seattle's fishing fleet and selling freshly caught fish. On the northern side of Salmon Bay, **BALLARD** (reachable by several buses from downtown) was settled by Scandinavian fishermen, whose history is outlined at the **Nordic Heritage Museum**, 3014 NW 67th St (Tues–Sat 10am–4pm, Sun noon–4pm; $3). Bar a couple of nightspots, there's little else to see.

Accommodation

While there's no shortage of **hotel** space in Seattle, it can be difficult to find the middle ground between smart, expense-account-type places and seedy dives. Two specialist **B&B agencies** are *Pacific B&B* (701 NW 60th St; ☎784-0539), who can find rooms for $45 and upwards, and the statewide *Washington Bed and Breakfast Guild* (2442 NW Market St, #355, Seattle, WA 98107; ☎385-6753).

College Inn, at 4000 NE University Way in the U District (☎633-4441). Popular, friendly B&B. ④.

Gaslight Inn, 1727 15th Ave (☎325-3654). Capitol Hill landmark home converted into attractive B&B, with its own swimming pool. ③.

Green Tortoise Backpacker's Guesthouse, 715 Second Ave N (☎322-1222). New uptown hostel, partly owned by the alternative bus company, three blocks from Space Needle and Seattle Center. Bus #15 or #18 from *Amtrak*, #1, #2 or #13 from *Greyhound*. $10 dorms, also private doubles. ①/②.

Mercer Island Travelodge, 7645 Sunset Hwy (☎232-8000). Simple, comfortable rooms just off I-90 on Mercer Island, a leafy low-key island-suburb not far from downtown. ③.

Pacific Plaza, 400 Spring St (☎623-3900 or 1-800/426-1165). Newly renovated but still quite basic 1920s hotel, halfway between Pike Place Market and Pioneer Square. ④.

Seattle International Youth Hostel, 84 Union St, behind Pike Place Market (☎622-5443). Comfortable, modern and well equipped. Dorms for $14 (AYH members) or $17 (non-members, permitted Oct–May only) a night, although there's a midnight curfew and you'll need a sheet sleeping bag. Closed 10am–5pm. Reservations advised in summer. ①.

St Regis Hotel, 116 Stewart St (☎448-6366). Scruffy but well located budget downtown hotel. Take care in this area after dark. ②.

Woodmark Hotel at Carillon Point (☎822-3700 or 1-800/822-3700). Handsome hotel with most rooms facing over Lake Washington. A few minutes' east of downtown in prosperous Kirkland. ⑦.

YMCA, 909 Fourth Ave (☎382-5000). Clean, safe and open to men and women. Dorms $17, plus private singles and doubles. ①/②.

YWCA, 1118 Fifth Ave (☎461-4888). Large clean women-only singles and doubles. ②.

Eating

You won't have to spend a fortune in Seattle's elegant French restaurants to **eat** well: between the coffeeshops of Capitol Hill, the ethnic restaurants of the University District, and above all Pike Place Market there are some excellent pickings. **Seafood** is the specialty, ranging from salmon and crab to fish and chips or clam chowder. Most social interaction in the city seems to be fuelled with copious quantities of espresso **coffee**.

Athenian Inn, Pike Place Market (☎624-7166). Popular local café with a great view over the piers, plus good value ultra-fresh seafood and dozens of beers. Closes 6.15pm.

Byzantion, 601 Broadway E (☎325-7580). Well-priced Greek meals in elegant Capitol Hill setting.

Cause Celebre, Mercer St and E Fifteenth Ave (☎323-1888). First-class wholefood, cheerful service.

Chile Pepper, 5000 University Way (☎526-5004). Good cheap Mexican food.

Deluxe Bar and Grill, 625 Broadway E (☎324-9697). Casual Capitol Hill restaurant serving nachos, salads and pasta, at outdoor tables.

Kokeb, 926 12th Ave (☎322-0485). Low-priced and spicy Ethiopian food on Capitol Hill.

Last Exit on Brooklyn, 3930 Brooklyn Ave at NE 40th St (☎545-9873). Warm, late-opening University District coffeehouse; classic student hangout.

Mikado, 514 S Jackson St, International District (☎622-5206). Classy Japanese restaurant with a good sushi bar.

The Unicorn, 4550 University Way (☎634-1115). British-style pub, with Cornish pasties, steak-and-kidney pies and British beer.

Nightlife

Seattle's **nightlife** doesn't quite live up to expectations aroused by the city's recent musical notoriety, but it's not bad for a convivial atmosphere and a beer or two. **Taverns** in Washington sell beer and wine but not spirits, while **bars** sell everything but must be attached to a restaurant; the tavern scene is at its most accessible (and touristy) in **Pioneer Square** downtown, where bars such as *Doc Maynard's, Old*

GRUNGE

Each time a new musical sound emerges, the media like to credit a particular city with its creation. Detroit, Philadelphia, Memphis and LA have each had their turn, and **Seattle** is now revered as the cradle of the punk-metal mix-up, **grunge**. Though cities such as Minneapolis (Hüsker Dü) and Boston (Dinosaur Jr) have produced arguably finer and more innovative music in recent years, neither has enjoyed the hype of Seattle.

The root of all the fuss lies with **Sub Pop Records**. From its humble inception in 1986, this indie label stuck to a strategy similar to Motown's, drawing on a pool of regional talent and forging a corporate identity by relying heavily on one producer, **Jack Endino**. Flying in the face of CD-obsessed music industry trends, Sub Pop set up a Single of the Month Club, releasing what are now collectors' items on seven-inch vinyl, and bringing the world's attention to bands such as **Mudhoney**, **Soundgarden** and **Nirvana**, from the nearby lumber town of Aberdeen, who debuted in 1988 with the *Love Buzz* single. Following up with the excellent *Bleach* album and the single, *Sliver*, they became the object of every major label's desires. The trio signed with DGC in 1991, recorded the quasi-anthemic **Nevermind** (*Smells Like Teen Spirit, In Bloom, Lithium*), and the rest is history. DGC would have been satisfied if the album had netted sales of 100,000, but grunge rock's time had come and Nevermind shifted close to five million units.

The floodgates were open. Mudhoney, Soundgarden and others picked up lucrative contracts, but a non-Sub Pop outfit were next to strike it big. **Pearl Jam**, a composite of young journeymen rockers, released *Ten*, which outsold G'n'R, Van Halen and the other dinosaurs to become the nation's top-selling hard rock album in 1992. Hollywood also leapt into the action with the 1992 movie *Singles*, featuring a great performance by **Matt Dillon** as lead singer of the fictional band Citizen Dick. Meanwhile more local hopefuls – such as Screaming Trees, Hole, Afghan Whigs and Alice in Chains – wait in the wings.

Few of the big names spend much time here nowadays, but hundreds of bands have moved here from all over the US, figuring that the record company personnel in the city looking for the new Nirvana will catapult them into overnight stardom. A lot of bands are playing Seattle's clubs and pubs; one or two might evolve into a group of Nirvana's stature, but an even greater number display the musical imagination and prowess of Beavis and Butt-Head: a night out in the city is very much a hit-and-miss affair. Nevermind.

Timer's Café and the *Central Tavern* often host bands. Look out for "joint cover nights", when you can get into five or six venues for as many dollars. Seattle's lively and well-organized **gay scene** is focused around the Capitol Hill district.

For what's on **listings**, *The Weekly*, 75¢ from boxes on the streets, is good for reviews and theater, cinema and arts listings, and the Friday editions of *The Seattle Times* and *Seattle Post Intelligencer* supply live-music details.

Backstage Club, 2208 NW Market St, Ballard (☎781-2805). Quality jazz, rock, reggae or folk acts.

Beso del Sol, 4468 Stone Way N, Wallingford (☎547-8087). Latin salsa every Fri & Sat in Fremont.

Colourbox, 113 First St (☎340-4101). Downtown club, often featuring half-decent grunge bands.

Comet Tavern, 922 E Pike St (☎323-9853). Counter-cultural Capitol Hill drinking place. Smoky pool tables.

Crocodile Café, 2200 Second Ave (☎441-5611). All sorts of stuff; jazz and rock to poetry readings.

Murphy's Pub, 1928 N 45th St (☎634-2110). Massive beer list and live folk music, often Irish, for no cover.

Neighbours, 1509 Broadway, Capitol Hill (☎324-5358). High-octane gay dance scene.

New Melody Tavern, 5213 NW Ballard Ave (☎782-3480). Barn-like place, lacking atmosphere, but puts on classy jazz, bluegrass and folk.

Off-Ramp Music Café, 109 Eastlake Ave E (☎628-0232). Live alternative bands Mon–Thurs; womens' discos Fri–Sun.

Rockcandy, 1812 Yale St (☎623-0470). Premier club venue for alternative bands.

Wild Rose Tavern, 1021 E Pike St (☎324-9210). A popular venue for gay women, with decent food and often live music or entertainment.

Dance, Classical Music, Opera, Theater and Film

The **Seattle Center** is the base for the city's cultural institutions: the *Pacific Northwest Ballet* (☎628-0888), the *Seattle Symphony Orchestra* (☎441-9411) and the *Seattle Opera* (☎389-7676) take it in turns to use its Opera House. Tickets ($10–55) tend to sell out in advance, especially for the opera, but there are sometimes reduced last-minute returns.

Theater is Seattle's strongest suit. The longest-established small company is the *Seattle Repertory Company* (☎443-2222) at the Seattle Center. For more offbeat and adventurous productions, try *A Contemporary Theater* (ACT), 100 W Roy St near the Seattle Center at First Ave West. Seattle's most politically right-on company is *The Group*, based at 306 Harrison St (☎441-1299), also in the Seattle Center, while the *Alice B Theatre* at 1100 E Pike St (☎322-5423) is a thriving gay and lesbian company.

August's **Seafair** is Seattle's answer to Mardi Gras, complete with pirates, parades and the gay-inspired "Unofficial Seafair Tacky Tourist Queen City Cruise" through the Ship Canal. In May, the **Seattle International Film Festival** centers on independent venues such as the Art Deco *Egyptian*, in an old Masonic Temple at 801 E Pine St (☎323-4978), and the *Market Theater*, on Lower Post Alley near Pike Place Market (☎382-1171).

ONWARDS TO CANADA AND ALASKA

VICTORIA on Vancouver Island in Canada is just two and a half hours by the high-speed **passenger-only** *Victoria Clipper* from Seattle's Pier 69 (summer 3–4 daily, winter once daily; $49 one-way, $79 round-trip; ☎448-5000 or 1-800/888-2535). The nearest **car and passenger** ferry service from Washington State to Vancouver Island leaves Anacortes daily for Sidney, Canada, calling in at the San Juan Islands on the way. For details contact *Washington State Ferries* (☎464-6400).

The much more expensive **Alaska Marine Highway** is a weekend-long ferry ride that winds between islands and a fjord-lined coast from **Bellingham**, 90 miles north of Seattle to **SKAGWAY**, Alaska. *Alaska Marine Highways* have an office in Seattle at 355 Harris (☎676-8445). For more details see p.885.

Around Seattle: Bainbridge Island

For a brief escape from Seattle, **BAINBRIDGE ISLAND**, a serene half-hour ferry ride across Elliott Bay, is well worth the trip. *Washington State Ferries* leave every hour from Pier 52 ($3.30 return for foot passengers, $13.50 car; avoid rush hours), landing in the town of **Bainbridge Island** (formerly Winslow) – which is so small that once you've admired the harbor and had lunch, you'll probably be ready to head back. This green and rural island is mostly private land; if you want to pitch a tent, there's **camping** at the far end in Fay Bainbridge State Park.

The Puget Sound

The broad and deep **Puget Sound** hooks far into Washington, a clutter of tiny islands and ragged peninsulas teeming with yachts, ocean-going ships, fishing trawlers, and even nuclear submarines. At first, the dense forest deterred homesteaders, but soon small logging communities sprang up, and the sound became a vital waterway. As more and more settlers arrived, the demand for land grew, and in the 1850s treaties confining Indians to reservations were put before tribal leaders. Some signed, including Chief Seattle of the Suquamish; but others refused, and accusations of forgery flew. A legacy of injustice was created, with which modern courts still struggle.

The southern end of the sound is increasingly urban. There's little to attract visitors to polluted **Tacoma** or the small state capital of **Olympia**, but mountains, forests and lakes are all around. Popular weekend escapes include the rural parts of **Whidbey Island**, and the beautiful **San Juan Islands** further north.

Tacoma and Vashon Island

It's hard to avoid passing through **TACOMA**, on the main Seattle–Portland route, but there's no great reason to prolong your exposure to the smell and dirt of its industry, or its strong military presence. Downtown Tacoma is generally considered unsafe at night, and its **hotels** tend either to be too smart or too grim; keep going the few miles north to *Motel 6* at 5201 20th St in Fife (☎922-1270; ②), or **camp** at **Dash Point State Park**, 5700 SW Dash Point Rd, Federal Way, five miles northeast of Tacoma with wide beaches and hiking trails. The *Antique Sandwich Shop*, 5102 N Pearl St (☎752-4069), near the large Point Defiance Park, is an offbeat café which often has live folk or classical music in the evenings.

Hourly ferries from Tacoma take fifteen minutes to reach the pleasant, cycleable **Vashon Island**. Housed partly in a hand-built log cabin and partly in tepees, the *AYH Hostel* here, at 12119 SW Cove Rd (members $8, non-members $11; ☎463-2592) is a mile and a half from the Seattle–Vashon ferry dock at the north end of the island. Ring ahead to make a reservation and arrange a free pick-up at the jetty.

Olympia and Around

Just a muddy little logging community when picked as Washington's territorial capital in 1853, **OLYMPIA** has never really grown into the metropolis its founders hoped for. A handsome but top-heavy load of weighty architecture eclipses its rather small center; you can but wonder at the sheer energy of the pioneers, who plotted something along the lines of St Paul's Cathedral in what was then a backwoods.

Eight blocks south of the imposing Romanesque **Legislative Building** (Mon–Fri 9am–5pm; free), the small **Washington State Capital Museum**, 211 W 21st Ave (Tues–Fri 10am–4pm, Sat & Sun noon–4pm; donation), juxtaposes a restored well-to-do dining room with displays of Native American basketwork and local natural history. In the other direction, the **town center** offers a few streets of stores and restaurants, presided over by the chateau-like **Old Capitol** at Seventh Ave between Washington and Franklin, its turreted roofs and arched windows facing a green town square. The *Urban Onion*, 116 Legion Way SE (☎943-9242; closed Sun), across the square from the Old Capitol, serves its own herb and onion bread, while the *Spar*, a few blocks away at 114 Fourth Ave E (☎357-6444) is a Thirties diner with a long, curved counter.

A short drive south of Olympia, tiny **TUMWATER** was Washington's first pioneer community, settled in 1845 by a group which included Bing Crosby's grandparents. Its name comes from the tumbling water of the Deschutes River, which now goes into the making of Olympia beer at the **Pabst (Olympia) Brewing Company**, by the Tumwater turning (exit 103) off I-5 (tours and tastings daily 8am–4.30pm; free). Smelling strongly of hops, the brewery overlooks **Tumwater Falls**, now enclosed in a park but once a rich salmon-fishing site for the Nisqually tribe.

Practicalities

Greyhound is at Capitol Way and Seventh Ave (☎357-5541), about five blocks north of the Capitol Campus; the *Amtrak* station is about eight miles southeast and not on the bus route. *Intercity Transit* (☎786-1881) runs **local buses**.

Olympia's **visitor center** (Mon–Fri 9am–5pm; ☎586-3460) is on the State Capitol Campus near the Legislative Building. In-town **accommodation** is geared towards business visitors; budget options include Tumwater's *Motel 6*, 400 W Lee St (☎754-7320; ②), or the *Holly Motel*, 2816 Martin Way (☎943-3000; ②), east of town at exit 109 off I-5. There's **camping** at forested **Millersylvania State Park**, 12245 Tilley Rd south of Olympia, two miles east of I-5 (exit 99).

Whidbey Island

With sheer cliffs and craggy outcrops, rocky beaches and prairie countryside, **WHIDBEY ISLAND** is a favorite retreat for Puget Sound's city-dwellers. In its north is a large naval base, but in the southern and central parts, narrow country roads wind through farmland and small villages. The quickest route from Seattle is to head north to Mukilteo and catch the ferry to Whidbey's southern tip (every half-hour; round-trip $2.15 per person, $9 with a car). By *Greyhound*, take the daily (Mon–Fri) bus from Seattle to Port Townsend (see p.858) and get the hourly ferry from there to Keystone, in the middle of the island (round-trip $3.30 per person, $13.30 with a car). Whidbey's own (sketchy) bus system, *Island Transit* (☎321-6688), runs the length of the island.

The Mukilteo ferry lands at the small town of Clinton, but **LANGLEY** further around the east coast makes a better first stop, its short high street of old-west wooden storefronts set on a bluff overlooking the water. The **visitor center** (☎221-6765) in the small arcade at 124 Second St carries information. If you're here in the evening, the *Dog House Tavern* (☎221-9996) is a convivial gathering place and restaurant.

The middle part of the island is a National Historic Reserve called **Ebey's Landing**, where charming **COUPEVILLE**, with its nineteenth-century sea captains' houses, is of most appeal – and certainly preferable to Oak Harbor, Whidbey's largest town and the site of most of its motels. Northwards, at **Deception Pass State Park**, a steel bridge arches gracefully over the narrow gorge between Whidbey and Fidalgo Island, connecting-point for the San Juans beyond. Seals sometimes bask on the rocks below, though mist can make the pass obscure.

On the edge of Coupeville, you'll find the *Tyee Motel*, 405 S Main St by Hwy-20 (☎678-6616; ②); the local Chamber of Commerce, 5 South Main St (☎678-5434), has lists of local **B&Bs**. The *Captain Whidbey Inn*, two miles west of Coupeville on Penn Cove, is a lovely hotel, serving superb food (☎678-4097 or 1-800/366-4097; ⑤). Whidbey's four state parks all offer **camping**.

The San Juan Islands

North and west of Whidbey Island, midway between the Washington coast and Canada, the beautiful **San Juan Islands** scatter across the northern reaches of the Puget Sound, and entirely upstage the rest of the inlet. Every summer brings more visitors than the islands can really accommodate, especially on the largest, San Juan and Orcas. You'll need to book somewhere to stay in advance, though even in July and August peaceful corners can easily be found.

Getting There

Washington State Ferries run a dozen boats per day, more in summer, to the islands from the harbor a couple of miles west of **ANACORTES** – a gritty port and fishing town at the end of Hwy-20. The ferry only stops at four of the 172 islands, but the slow cruise through the archipelago is a delight. Motorists should get to the port early; pedestrians and cyclists have less hassle. Summer fares are up to $40 round-trip for a car and driver, $10 for foot passengers to San Juan island. One ferry a day (more in summer) goes on to Sidney in British Columbia. Fares are collected on westbound sailings only.

If you want to catch an early ferry (the first one leaves before 6am) from Anacortes you may well decide to spend the night. The *Islands Motel*, 3401 Commercial Ave (☎293-4644; ③), is one of several roadside **motels**, while the grand old *Majestic*, 419 Commercial Ave (☎293-3355 or 1-800/950-3323; ④), also has the best **restaurant** (and bar) in Anacortes. **Gas** on the islands is considerably more expensive than on the mainland, so drivers will save by filling up in Anacortes first.

San Juan Island

SAN JUAN, the ferry's last stop, is the only island where the ferry drops you in a town. Though small, **FRIDAY HARBOR** is the largest town in the archipelago and the best place to rent the necessary transportation. The *Inn at Friday Harbor*, 410 Spring St, rents out **cars and mopeds** (and runs tours), while **bikes** can be had from *Island Bicycles* at 380 Argyle St. Ask for advice on cycling routes – and maps, essential on such twisting and badly marked roads – at the **information center** (daily 8am–4.30pm, longer hours in summer), nearby at First and Spring.

Friday Harbor's cafés, shops and waterfront make for pleasant wandering. There's a **Whale Museum** on First Street, but to see the real thing, head past the coves and bays on the island's west side to **Limekiln Point State Park**. Orcas come here in summer to feed on migrating salmon, and there's usually at least one sighting a day.

Camping is an obvious way to stay on San Juan island; there's a very pleasant cyclists-only camp, the *Pedal Inn* at 1300 False Bay Drive, and *Lakedale Campground* is six miles from the ferry on Roche Harbor Road and reachable by bus. In Friday Harbor, the *Elite Hotel* on First St (☎378-5555; ①/②) is the island's best budget deal (where it's essential to book ahead, especially in July and August), with dorm beds from $15, and shared rooms; no kitchen but no curfew. The friendly and easy-going *Island Lodge* (☎378-2000 or 1-800/822-4753; ③) is a mile out of town on Guard St.

Of Friday Harbor's plentiful places to **eat**, *Cannery House* (lunch only; ☎378-2500) at the top of First St offers a wonderful view and Mexican-style food; the *Electric Company*, 175 First St (☎378-4118), has live music at weekends. The *San Juan Donut Shop*, 209 Spring St (☎378-2271), serves hefty breakfasts from 5am.

Orcas Island

Horseshoe-shaped **ORCAS ISLAND** is quieter than San Juan, its several holiday resorts tucked away in distant coves. Tiny **ORCAS** itself, where the ferry lands, holds little beyond the grand Victorian **Orcas Hotel** (☎376-4300; ④). You can rent **mopeds** and **bikes** from the café above the ferry dock.

Most visitors head ten miles north through the farmlands to the main town, **EASTSOUND**, where the **visitor information** kiosk on North Beach Road, just past Eastsound Square, can provide maps. Its handful of stores and restaurants include *Doty's Café* (☎376-2593), a homey diner a block inland from the waterfront, and the more upscale *Outlook Inn* (☎376-2200), west of the center. Two miles west, at the end of W Beach Road, the *Beach Haven Resort* (☎376-2280; ④) is a great place to stay, its fifty-year-old beachfront log cabins lined up along a densely wooded, sunset-facing cove; in summer they are only available by the week.

The island's real highlight is a little further on at **Moran State Park**, where miles of hiking trails wind through dense forest and open fields to freshwater lakes, as well as up to the summit of **Mount Constitution**. Its four **campgrounds** fill up early in summer.

The lovely **Doe Bay Village Resort (AYH)**, Star Rte 86 (☎376-2291; dorms ①, cabins ②, cottages ③), is tucked round to the east on a secluded bay. Its excellent facilities, including an open-air **spa**, are open to day visitors ($5).

Lopez Island

The archipelago's most tranquil spot of all must be modest **LOPEZ ISLAND**, whose rolling hills also make it the most enjoyable place to cycle. The delightful *Islander Lopez* resort-hotel (☎468-2233; ④) sits on the edge of Lopez Village, about four miles from the ferry dock, and not far from the excellent *Bay Café Restaurant* (closed Mon).

Bellingham and Mount Baker

I-5 speeds north past the Puget Sound along the mainland towards Canada, cutting past forests, lakes and, eventually, distant Mount Baker. Long, sprawling **BELLINGHAM** – rapidly expanding thanks to its new role as the southern terminus of *Alaska Marine Highways* (see p.853 and p.858) – is the first sizeable town you come to. **Motels** around exit 252 off I-5 include *Mac's*, at Samish and Maple (☎734-7570; ②), and *Motel 6* (☎671-4494; ②) at 3701 Byron Ave, which crosses Samish Way. Women can stay at the *YWCA*, 1026 N Forest St (☎734-4820; ①), not far from the *Greyhound* station at 1329 N State St (☎733-5251) and the **local bus** terminal, which serves the widely separated terminals of the Alaska service and the *Victoria Star* foot passenger ferries to Victoria, BC, which leave daily from 355 Harris Ave (mid-May to early Oct only; ☎1-800/443-4552).

Bellingham's most appealing section is the restored railroad community of **Fairhaven Village**, a pleasant drive or bus ride around the bay, and the best place to find **food and drink**. *Tony's* at 1101 Harris Ave (☎733-6319) is a lovely coffeeshop, sometimes hosting live music, while across the road, *Bullie's* (☎734-2855) has an extraordinary list of beers.

Parks surrounding the city are laid out with hiking trails, and beyond them to the east are the foothills of **MOUNT BAKER**, 56 miles along Hwy-542. Lummi tribal mythology has this as a sort of Ararat, surviving the Great Flood to provide sanctuary for a Native American Noah in his giant canoe, but it's better known today for its **skiing**, with a seven-month season from early November until May, and the best early snow in the Northwest (ski information on ☎734-6771). Good local **camping** includes **Larrabee State Park**, seven miles south of Bellingham on Hwy-11, as well as the many campgrounds along the highway to Mount Baker.

The Olympic Peninsula

The broad mass of the **Olympic Peninsula** projects across the Puget Sound, sheltering Seattle from the open sea. Small logging communities are sprinkled around its edges, but at the core the Olympic mountains thrust upwards, shredding rain clouds as they drift in from the Pacific and drenching the surrounding area. In the western river valleys, the dense vegetation thickens into rain forest, and the forests and lonely Pacific beaches provide cover for a huge variety of wildlife and seabirds.

Port Townsend

With its brightly painted Victorian mansions, convivial cafés and vigorous cultural scene, **PORT TOWNSEND** has always had aspirations beyond its small-time logging roots. A would-be San Francisco since the nineteenth century, Gothic mansions sprang up above the flourishing port in the 1890s, when confident predictions of a railroad terminus lured in the rich. Unfortunately for the investors, the trains never arrived, and the town was left with a glut of stylish residences and a very small business district.

Port Townsend's physical split – half on a bluff, half at sea level – reflects nineteenth-century social divisions, when wealthy merchants built their houses uptown, well above the noise and brawl of the port. The downtown area is at the base of the hill, its shops and pleasant cafés centering on **Water Street** – lined with proud 1890s brick-and stonework. In recent times the old mansions have been restored, and the town has mellowed into an artsy community with hippy undertones and a fair amount of charm.

During the enjoyable annual **music festivals** at **Fort Worden**, two miles north – *Jazz Port Townsend* towards the end of July, the *Hot Jazz* festival in February and *American Fiddler Tunes* in early July – you should book accommodation well ahead. The well-preserved nineteenth-century fort itself, the set for *An Officer and a Gentleman*, makes rather dull viewing.

Practicalities

Pick up a map and information in Port Townsend at the helpful **visitor center**, 2437 Sims Way (☎385-2722), west on Hwy-20. The *AYH* youth hostel at **Fort Worden** (March–Oct only; ☎385-0655; ①) offers the cheapest beds; there's also a campground. Another youth hostel (May–Sept only; ☎385-1288; ①) and campground are twenty miles west at **Fort Flagler**, on the tip of rural Marrowstone Island – usually pretty empty, probably because of the lack of public transit. Otherwise, there are plenty of plush B&Bs, as well as the *Port Townsend Motel*, 2020 Washington St (☎385-2211; ③).

Port Townsend is the peninsula's best place to **eat** and **drink**; try the *Salal Café*, 634 Water St (☎385-6532), or *Bread and Roses*, 230 Quincy St (☎385-1044). The *Fountain Café*, 920 Washington St (☎385-1364), serves more substantial seafood and pasta. *Russell's Back Alley Tavern*, down an alley off Water and Tyler (☎385-2914), has live music Wednesday to Sunday evenings.

Port Angeles

Originally named "Puerto de Nuestra Senora de los Angeles" by the Spanish in 1791 (the post office later insisted one Los Angeles was enough), **PORT ANGELES** is the peninsula's main town and the most popular point of entry into the Olympic National Park. Though its setting is lovely, it's very much a working town, the main strip of motels and restaurants making few concessions to quaintness. Timber is Port Angeles' real business, but the harbor has its own harsh beauty: industrial chimneys are back-dropped by mountains, and out in the bay, cormorants fly over the fishing boats.

The two parallel one-way main drags, First Street and Front Street, are cluttered with **motels** (book ahead on summer weekends): the rooms at *Aggies*, 602 E Front St (☎457-0471; ③), are palatially large, though *Dan Dee Motel*, 132 E Laurisden Blvd (☎457-5404; ②), has lower rates. To get to any of the excellent **campgrounds** in Olympic National Park, you need your own vehicle: six miles south of Port Angeles along Hurricane Ridge Road, the *Heart o' the Hills* is one of the best. For breakfast or lunch, try the tiny *First*

Street Haven café, 107 E First St (☎457-0352); for dinner, the *Greenery Restaurant*, 117-B E First St (☎457-4112), practically opposite, has low prices and tasty homemade pasta.

Port Angeles has the peninsula's best **transit connections**: *Greyhound*, at 215 N Laurel St (☎452-7611), run daily to Seattle, while *Clallam Transit* buses (☎1-800/858-3747) go part-way to Port Townsend, into the national park and west around the peninsula to Neah Bay and Forks. *Black Ball Transport* (☎457-4491) run **ferries** to Victoria in Canada for a bargain $6.25 walk-on one-way fare, $25 with car. The **visitor center** is at 121 East Railroad St, near the ferry terminal (summer daily 7am–10pm, winter Mon–Fri 10am–4pm; ☎452-2363).

Olympic National Park

Theodore Roosevelt created **Olympic National Park** in 1909, partly to ensure the survival of the rare Roosevelt elk; it now has the largest remaining herd in the US. Much of the peninsula is protected land, and large areas of national forest surround the national park. Some logging is allowed; the timber trade brought settlers here in the first place, almost every town has a sawmill, and logging is still crucial for local jobs. However, the opportunities for spectacular camping, hiking and wildlife-watching are attracting more and more visitors, and ecologists now reluctantly favor tourism as the lesser environmental evil.

The **visitor center**, just outside Port Angeles, at the top of Race St en route to Hurricane Ridge (summer 8am–8pm, winter 8am–4pm; ☎452-4501), is an excellent source of maps and hiking information. The weather can be dodgy so carry raingear; there's a fair amount of snow even as late as June.

No roads cross the park, but many run into it, so you'll probably end up making several forays into different sections around the peninsula's western rim. *Gray Line* (☎1-800/426-7532) run excursions in summer, while in winter *Clallam Transit* buses climb seventeen miles of precipices to **Hurricane Ridge** for cross-country skiing. A **lodge** on the ridge (May–Oct; ☎928-3211; ④) has tourist facilities and information, and **trails** lead off – through masses of wild flowers in summer – to isolated spots.

Neah Bay and the Makah Indians

A perfectly preserved ancient settlement of the sea-going **Makah Indians** – buried for five hundred years, Pompeii-like, by a mudslide – was revealed at Lake Ozette by tidal erosion in 1970. The first witnesses encountered bizarre scenes of instantaneous ageing – green alder leaves, lying where they fell centuries ago, shrivelled as soon as they were exposed. Eleven years of excavation have uncovered thousands of artefacts: harpoons, intricately carved seal clubs, watertight boxes made without the use of metal, bowls, toys – all belonging to a period before trade with Europeans. The site itself has been re-buried, but the finds are displayed at the **Makah Cultural and Research Center** (summer daily 10am–5pm, otherwise Wed–Sun 10am–5pm; $4) in the small and run-down village of **NEAH BAY**, the home of the few remaining Makah.

There are a couple of **motels**: the *Thunderbird* (☎645-2450; ③), and the slightly cheaper *Tyee Motel* (☎645-2223; ③), but *Hilden's Motel* (☎645-2306; ③), east of Neah Bay at Bullman Beach, is better. The village's two cafés are friendly, but the food isn't great: the *Breakwater Inn* on Hwy-112 near Seiku (☎963-2428) is a good alternative.

The Peninsula's Ocean Beaches

The wild, lonely Pacific **beaches** that start near Neah Bay and stretch down the Olympic Peninsula's west side still look exactly as they did before the pioneers got here: black rocks point out of a grey sea, populated mostly by seabirds. With their strong currents and dramatic tides, these beaches are not suitable for swimming, but the hiking can be magnificent. Even if you have your own vehicle, you can expect to do a lot of walking – the roads tend to be rough, and many peter out altogether.

Cape Flattery at the northern corner of the Makah Reservation is comparatively accessible, by an unpaved road, from Neah Bay. A short hike leads to the cape which once "flattered" Captain Cook with the hope of finding a harbor and is the USA's north-westernmost point, excluding Alaska. Below the cape, the waves have worn caves into the sheer rock of the cliff face, while opposite on **Tatoosh Island**, coastguards run a remote lighthouse. **Beaches** at the south of the cape include **Hobuck** and the crescent-shaped **Shi-Shi**.

The Rain Forests

Incredible though it seems in cool Washington, the river valleys of the western peninsula produce an environment akin to a jungle, as the Olympic rain combines with river-water from the mountains to feed the hyper-fertility associated with much warmer climates. Temperate rain forests are rare, but the peninsula's mild climate and more than twelve feet of annual watering have produced giant trees; mosses cling to the bark and hang in pendants from the branches, filtering the sunlight – while below, three hundred species of plants fight for space, crowding the ground with ferns, mushrooms and more mosses. The only way to get through the forest is on the cleared **trails**, which tend to get slippery as moss grows back again – bring footwear that grips.

The Hoh River Rain Forest

The most popular of the rain forest areas, the **Hoh River Rain Forest**, has the only large **visitor center** (daily 9am–5pm), nineteen miles along Upper Hoh River Road, which leaves US-101 twelve miles south of Forks. Two short trails explore the rain forest; the three-quarter mile Hall of Mosses Trail, and the slightly longer Spruce Trail, which reaches the Hoh River on a circuit through the forest. More energetic hikers can follow the 36-mile Hoh River Trail right up to the base of 8000-foot Mt Olympus. Climbing the ice-covered peak is a major undertaking; if you just want to camp out along the route, check in with the rangers and get a free **Backcountry Permit**. Cougars and other beasts are still very much present in the park.

Kalaloch and the Queets River Rain Forest

US-101 runs right along the coast beyond the Hoh River, passing a continous strand of windswept beaches. One of the prettiest spots, **KALALOCH**, has a couple of camp-grounds and the very pleasant *Kalaloch Lodge* (☎962-2271; ④), which has a good restaurant and large ocean-view rooms. A **ranger station** on the south edge of the short built-up strip has lots of information and suggestions for hiking trips.

South of Kalaloch, US-101 cuts inland around the Quinault Indian Reservation, while the Queets River, and a 25-mile-long dirt road, head inland to the **Queets River Rain Forest**, the least visited of the three main rain forest areas. The luxuriant flora and fauna along the well-marked path includes the **world's tallest Douglas Fir** tree – 220 feet tall and 45 feet in circumference.

Lake Quinault and the Quinault Rain Forest

The most accessible, and beautiful, of all the rain forests is the **Quinault Rain Forest**, around the shores of Lake Quinault. The lake itself was already a popular resort area when Teddy Roosevelt visited in the 1900s and decided to proclaim it part of an expanded Olympic National Park. Thick and impressive groves fan off from the road, but in places it feels a bit overdeveloped. Motels, cafés and lodges such as the rustic *Quinault Lodge* (☎288-2571 or 1-800/562-6672; ⑤) line the southern shore.

One good short hike starts from the ranger station just north of the lodge, climbing up and along a small stream through some textbook rain forest vegetation. A huge expanse of dense overgrowth covers the eastern shore of the lake, around which winds a narrow but definitely passable road, perfect for a mountain bike tour. The best **camping** is on the northeast shore, at the **July Creek Campground**.

Forks

Most of the best options for **accommodation** within reach of the park area are in and around **FORKS**, on US-101 to the west. The *Miller Tree Inn* (☎374-6806; ③), is a relaxed B&B five hundred yards east of the town's only set of stop lights; *Olympic Suites* (☎374-5400 or 1-800/262-3433; ③) is on the north side of town.

Washington's Lower Coast

As you head south along the Washington coast from Lake Quinault, the roads improve but the scenery gradually grows tamer. Wilderness beaches give way to holiday resorts, dense virgin forest to privately owned timber land, thinned by logging and replanting and punctuated by completely bald patches of "clear-cutting".

Once clear of the awkward loop around the **Quinault Indian Reservation** – plans to build a coastal highway have been consistently vetoed by the Quinaults to preserve their seclusion – the main highway skips down to industrial **Aberdeen** in the bay of Gray's Harbor (and only notable as the hometown of Nirvana). Hwy-109 sneaks back from here up the coast, ending abruptly at **TAHOLAH** at the reservation's center.

The next indentation is muddy **Willapa Bay**, ringed by oyster beds and wildlife sanctuaries. At the base of **Long Beach Peninsula**, **Cape Disappointment** hooks into the mouth of the wide Columbia River, the boundary with Oregon. Before the US-101 toll bridge, and just past tiny **Chinook**, turn-of-the-century **Fort Columbia** (grounds open: summer daily 8am-dusk, winter closed Mon & Tues) houses an Interpretive Center portraying early military life, as well as displays on the local Chinook Indians. The least expensive place to stay is in the fort's old hospital, now a summer-only *AYH* youth hostel (☎777-8755; ①).

The Cascade Mountains

The serene beauty of the snow-capped and pine-covered **Cascade Mountains** conceals awesome volcanic power – as proved by the 1980 explosion of **Mount St Helens**. But away from the grey scar left by the blast, the Cascades offer mile upon mile of forested wilderness, sheltering all kinds of wildlife and traversed by a skein of beautiful trails – which, for all but a few summer months, you'll need snowshoes to follow. Deservedly the most popular access point is **Mount Rainier**, set in its own national park and accessible from Tacoma or Seattle. Further afield, the **North Cascades** demand more time; Hwy-20, the high mountain road that crosses them, is by far the most spectacular route to the east.

The North Cascades and the Cascade Loop

When Hwy-20 opened up the rugged **North Cascades** to an admiring public in 1972, the towns of the eastern foothills got together and came up with the **Cascade Loop**, a 400-mile round trip that channeled tourist traffic their way, along Hwys 20, 97 and 2. The complete trip is only feasible during the summer, as snow otherwise closes the mountain passes and completely covers the hiking trails. With the possible exception of Chelan, the towns themselves are best taken simply as bases between trips into the gorgeous scenery, for all their efforts to attract visitors. **Winthrop**, for example, on the north side of the Loop, has dressed itself up in Wild West regalia (befitting its status as the original setting for Owen Wister's *The Virginian*).

Leavenworth, on the other hand – on the south side of the Loop and served by *Greyhound* from Seattle – has turned Bavarian. Bikes are for rent from *Leavenworth Ski & Sport Center* (☎548-7864), and you can pitch a tent at the **campgrounds** eight miles down Icicle Creek Road. In town, the *Edelweiss* on Front St (☎548-7015; ①/②) is a **hotel** with one especially cheap double room. The **ranger station** just off US-2 provides trail guides and hiking information. *Greyhound* continues to the apple-growing center of **Wenatchee**, where a strip of budget **motels** lines N Wenatchee Ave.

Wenatchee is connected by free *Link* (☎1-800/851-LINK) buses to the trim resort of **CHELAN**. Here, the excellent *Campbell's Resort* (☎1-800/553-8225; ⑤) overlooks the lake, with a good restaurant, *Goochi's*, close by at 104 E Woodin Ave (☎682-2436). From the Boat Dock, a mile south, a **ferry**, the *Lady of the Lake* (☎682-2224), sails slowly up long thin **Lake Chelan**, leaving daily in summer at 8.30am and returning early evening ($21). It's a delightful cruise, stopping briefly at the lake's mountainous western tip in **STEHEKIN**, an isolated village otherwise accessible only by air-taxi ($50 each way from Chelan; ☎682-5555). Stehekin is an ideal base for exploring the North Cascades; you can rent bikes and canoes from the *North Cascades Lodge* (reserve well ahead; ☎682-4711; ③), which also runs a shuttle bus deeper into the mountains. For camping and hiking information (and, for some of the trails, a wilderness permit), visit the **ranger station** in Stehekin, or the helpful **Chelan ranger station**, 428 W Woodin Ave, at the south end of town by the lake (summer daily 8am–4.30pm, otherwise Mon–Sat 8am–4.30pm). The **National Park Headquarters** is back in **Sedro Woolley**, twenty miles east of Anacortes, at 800 State St (Mon–Fri 8am–4.30pm).

The southern portion of the Cascade Loop – along US-2 – cross the mountains over Steven's Pass, but the principal east–west highway, I-90, lies further to the south, connecting Seattle with the fertile Yakima Valley. Near I-90, you can see **Snoqualmie Falls** – as seen in David Lynch's *Twin Peaks* – and **Roslyn**, an isolated, but interesting, former coal-mining town possibly familiar from *Northern Exposure*.

Mount Rainier National Park

Set in its own National Park, **MOUNT RAINIER** is the tallest and most accessible of the state's Cascade peaks. Recurrent jokes characterize its name as a description of its weather: often very wet, with heavy snowfalls during the long winter season. Not until late June or July does the snow line creep up the slopes, unblocking roads and revealing a web of hiking trails. But in summer, when the deer, mountain goats and marmots reappear, and meadows sprout alpine flowers, the mountain makes for some perfect – and not always tough – hiking.

Admission to the national park is $5 per car, $2 per hiker or cyclist. Its four entrances all lead to distinct sections, though in summer you can drive between the **Nisqually entrance** in the southwest corner and the smaller entrance to the southeast.

Only the Nisqually section is kept open year-round (for cross-country skiing; the others open around May). It's the only part you can see by public transit – confined to pricey day trips with *Gray Line* from Seattle (May–Oct only; ☎626-5208). The park road passes through **LONGMIRE**, around sixty miles southeast of Tacoma on Hwy-7, then Hwy-706, where there's a **hiker information center**. You can rent skis in winter, and stay year-round at the *National Park Inn* (☎569-2411; ④). Alternatively, further up the mountain, beyond waterfalls of melted glacier snow, **PARADISE** holds the huge wooden *Paradise Inn* (☎569-2411; ④), and another, larger **visitor center**.

Several hiking routes begin in Paradise, which is also the starting point for the highly serious undertaking of **climbing the peak**. Unless you're very experienced

THE ERUPTION OF MOUNT ST HELENS

From its first rumblings in March 1980, Mount St Helens became a big tourist attraction. Residents and loggers working the forests were evacuated and roads were closed, but by April the entrances to the restricted zone around the steaming peak were jammed with reporters and sightseers. Impatient residents were soon demanding to be let back to their homes. Even the official line became blurred when Harry Truman, a local pensioner who refused to move out, became a national celebrity and was, incredibly, congratulated on his "common sense" by Washington's governor.

A convoy of homeowners was waiting at the barriers, about to go and collect their possessions, when the explosion finally came on May 18 – not upwards but sideways, ripping a great chunk out of the mountainside. An avalanche of debris slid into Spirit Lake, raising it by two hundred feet and turning it into a steaming cauldron of mud. Heavy clouds of ash suffocated loggers on a nearby slope, and drifted east to smother the town of Yakima several feet deep.

Fifty-seven people died on the mountain: a few were there officially, but most, like Harry Truman, had ignored the warnings. The wildlife population was harder hit: about a million and a half animals – deer, elk, mountain goats, cougar and bear – were killed, and thousands of fish were boiled alive in sediment-filled rivers. There were dire economic effects, too, as falling ash devastated the land, and millions of feet of timber were lost.

(and even then, you have to register with rangers), do it with *Rainier Mountaineering Inc* in Paradise (☎569-2227), who offer three-day courses – one day's practice, then the two-day climb – and rent out equipment for around $275.

Other Entrances

During summer it's possible to drive from Paradise along rugged Stephen's Canyon Road to the park's southeastern corner. Here, the **Ohanapecosh visitor center** is set in deep forest, near the trout-packed Ohanapecosh River. Two further entrances are accessible from Seattle and the west: the **White River entrance** on Hwy-410 in the northeastern corner leads to the Sunrise visitor center and wonderful views of Emmons Glacier and the mountain's crest; the **Carbon River entrance** on Hwy-165 in the northwest is the least used, and has no visitor center. There are campgrounds near each entrance; for overnight backpacking you'll need a wilderness permit (free from any ranger or visitor center).

Mount St Helens

The Klickitat Indians who called **MOUNT ST HELENS** *Tahonelatclah* ("Fire Mountain") knew what they were talking about. A perfect snow-capped peak, long popular with scout camps and climbing expeditions, Mount St Helens suddenly exploded in May 1980, leaving a charred area of almost total destruction. The force of the explosion flattened the forests for miles around; heavy clouds of ash choked an even larger area; and a massive lateral blast threw an avalanche of debris down the Toutle River Valley.

Slowly but surely, the forests are starting to grow again, and the ash is being re-inhabited, but the scarred landscape bears witness to the awesome force of the eruption. In the meantime, Mt St Helens has become a major attraction, with most tourists heading for the brand new visitor center, immediately northwest of the mountain and reached by taking Hwy-504 off I-5 roughly halfway between Olympia and Portland. Several excellent walking trails begin nearby; an especially long one circles the entire mountain, but unless you're indifferent to clouds of dust or ash a morning or afternoon walk is really enough.

Mt St Helens makes a feasible day trip (of around 200 miles) from Portland; there's no obvious base, though if you want to avoid a long haul there's a *Motel 6* at 106 Minor Rd, Kelso – exit 39 off I-5 (☎425-3229; ②), and plenty of **campgrounds** in the National Forest surrounding the blast area. To reach any of theses, you have to retrace your steps along Hwy-504 and approach the mountain along any of the three other access roads – the most popular of which comes from the northeast, turning down Hwys 26/99 off Hwy-12 to reach the Windy Ridge vantage point (road closed in winter). From I-5, the most convenient campground is south of the mountain at **Merrill Lake**, on forest road 8100; head north off Hwy-503 at Cougar.

The **Coldwater Ridge visitor center** has exhibits, interpretive programmes and a free film detailing the eruption. Reconstruction work is gradually pushing Hwy-504 back towards the mountain, and another visitor center at **Johnson Ridge** is scheduled to open in 1996. Both the main access roads are clogged by cars in summer, a steady crawl around hairpin bends through dark green forests, until bald, spikey trees signal a sudden change: thousands of grey tree-skeletons lie in combed-looking rows, knocked flat in different directions as the blast waves bounced off the hillsides. The waste is staggering: the trees were deliberately left to rot, as decaying wood helps to regenerate the soil and provides cover for small animals and insects. Beside Hwy-26, the wrecked car of a couple who ducked the entry restrictions has been left where it was blown by the blast, the rusty roof crushed in.

Eastern Washington

Big, dry and empty, eastern Washington has more in common with neighboring Idaho than with the green western side of the state. Faded olive-colored sagebrush covers mile upon mile, and huge reddish rocks loom over the prairies – the powerful landscape of a thousand westerns. The towns, though, are no-nonsense agricultural and commercial centers, and only **Spokane** has any degree of cultural life. The **Grand Coulee Dam** is an engineering marvel with emotive echoes of the Depression, while at **Walla Walla**, near the border with Oregon, are the remains of the home of Marcus Whitman, massacred by Cayuse Indians.

Ellensburg

If you're travelling east beyond the mountains by *Greyhound* along I-90, your first major stop will be **ELLENSBURG**, a dusty little town with a red-brick core. On Labor Day weekend (early Sept), the **Ellensburg Rodeo** fills the town with Stetsoned cowboys (and cowgirls) who rope steers, ride bulls and sit on bucking broncos, accompanied by much pageantry. For tickets, call the Rodeo Ticket Office (☎1-800/637-2444).

Greyhound (☎925-1177) and *Empire Lines* stop at Oakanogan and Eighth. The **visitor center**, a short walk away at 436 N Sprague St (Mon–Fri 8am–5pm; ☎925-3137), can provide a downtown map and advice on **accommodation**. The Art Deco *Valley Café*, 105 W Third St (☎925-3050), is by far the nicest place to **eat** in town.

Yakima

YAKIMA, to the south, is not about to win any beauty contests either: the railroad yard, busy with freight trains, is its real center of gravity. The attractions are few, though it is a base for exploring the wineries scattered through the Yakima Valley to the east. That part of downtown that hasn't been scooped into the main mall is enlivened by the brightly painted train carriages of **Track 29** at Yakima Ave and Front St,

The **area code** for eastern Washington is ☎509.

which house a small collection of shops and food stalls. Opposite, **Yesterday's Village and Farmer's Market** is trying to turn the old Fruit Exchange building into a nostalgic antiques-and-crafts mall.

Wine tour maps and local information can be had from the **visitor center**, 10 N Eighth St at E Yakima Ave (Mon–Fri 8am–5pm; ☎575-1300). *Greyhound* stop nearby at 602 E Yakima Ave (☎457-5131), sharing the depot with *Empire Lines*. Motels and diner-style restaurants abound along N First St, and the central **YWCA**, at 15 N Naches Ave (☎248-7796; ①), has dorm beds for women from $8. The *Brewery Pub*, 32 N Front St (☎575-2922), serves *Grants* ales from the brewery next door and pub-type **food** in a friendly atmosphere.

Walla Walla: the Whitman Mission

WALLA WALLA, about 120 miles southeast of Yakima along I-82 and US-12, is an uneventful college and agricultural town, known best for its mild onions, eaten raw like apples. There's little to see now, but this was the place where the missionary **Dr Marcus Whitman** arrived from the East Coast in 1836. He made little headway in his bid to convert the Cayuse from their nomadic ways into crop-growing Christian citizens, and soon turned his attention to white settlers. In 1843, Whitman guided the first wagon-train across the Oregon Trail: his mission became a refuge for sick and orphaned travellers. The Cayuse eyed the ever-increasing emigrants warily, and when measles spread among the tribe, suspicions grew that they were being poisoned, particularly as Dr Whitman could help (some) whites but few of the Indians – who had no natural immunity to the epidemic. Half the tribe died. Whitman must have known the tribal tradition that medicine-men were directly liable for the deaths of their patients, but continued to take on even hopeless cases. In November 1847 a band of Cayuse murdered Whitman, his wife Narcissa and several others. Fifty more, mostly children, were taken captive, and although they were later released, angry settlers raised volunteer bands against the Cayuse. When the story hit the newspapers back east, it generated such a tide of fear about Indian uprisings that the government finally declared the Oregon land (then including Washington) a US territory, which meant the army could be sent in to protect the settlers – with drastic implications for the Indians.

The site where the **Whitman Mission** was burnt down (summer daily 8am–8pm, rest of the year 8am–4.30pm; $2), seven miles west off US-12, is bare but effective. Simple marks on the ground illustrate its one-time layout, and a visitor center shows a film on Whitman's life.

Greyhound stops at 315 Second St (☎525-9313), a couple of blocks from the **visitor center**, Sumach and Colville (Mon–Fri 9am–5pm). The *Whitman Motor Inn*, 107 N Second Ave (☎525-2200; ③), has an excellent restaurant, while the *Tapadera Budget Inn*, 211 N Second Ave (☎1-800/722-8277; ②), offers lower rates. For women, the central *YWCA* at First and Birch (☎525-2570; ①) has single rooms from $15 a night.

Spokane

The wide open spaces and plain little towns of eastern Washington don't really prepare you for **SPOKANE**. Just a few miles from the Idaho border, it's the region's only real city, and its scattering of grandiose late nineteenth-century buildings – built on the spoils of the Coeur d'Alene silver mines, just across the state divide – sport some unexpectedly elegant touches. But its heyday came and went, and shades of the down-at-heel freight town it became haunt the modern city. It's not a place to linger long, but its pleasant parks and unusual architecture can easily fill a day or so.

In summer at least, the town's focal point is **Riverfront Park**. Set beside the Spokane River, this was originally planned by Frederick Olmsted of Central Park fame, though it was not laid out as specified until just before the 1974 World's Fair. Bisecting the park, the river tumbles down a series of rocky shelves known as **Spokane Falls**, once a fishing site for the Spokanee Indians and later the home of the first pioneers. The **Gondola Skyride** cable cars (summer daily 11am–9pm; $3) run across the river from the west end of the park.

Most of the relics of Spokane's early grandeur are several blocks southwest on W Riverside Ave, where neo-Classical facades cluster around Jefferson St. Further west, the florid **Grace Campbell House**, 2316 First Ave (Tues–Sat 10am–5pm, Sun 1–5pm), forms part of the **Cheney Cowles Museum** ($3), which features a fine collection of prehistoric artwork from Central and South America – weavings, images, odd little dolls – as well as some small tableaux showing excruciating initiation ceremonies, where the candidates are suspended from hooks embedded in their chests.

Practicalities

Greyhound (☎624-5251) and *Empire Lines* (☎624-4116) **buses** share a depot at 1125 W Sprague Ave, a couple of blocks from the **visitor center**, 926 W Sprague Ave (Mon–Fri 8.30am–5pm; ☎747-3230). *Amtrak* trains pull in at W First and Bernard St. **Accommodation** options range from the *Brown Squirrel AYH Hostel*, a few blocks south of the city center at 930 S Lincoln and Ninth (☎838-5968; ①), through *Motel 6*, near the airport in the west at 1508 S Rustle St (☎459-6120; ②), to the more central *Shilo Inn* at E 923 Third Ave (☎535-9000; ③). There's **camping** in *Riverside State Park* (☎456-3964), six miles northwest off Hwy-291.

Auntie's Bookstore and Café, at 313 W Riverside Ave downtown (☎838-0206), offers soups, salads, and good filling lunches, and there's great Greek food nearby at Niko's, 725 W Riverside Ave (☎624-7444). *Knights Diner*, 2909 N Market St, is a beautiful old train carriage in which an astoundingly dexterous chef dishes out large platefuls.

The Grand Coulee Dam and Around

The huge **Grand Coulee Dam** – the largest concrete structure in the world – is around eighty miles west of Spokane. When work began in 1933, it was as much a political icon as an engineering feat. Probably the most ambitious scheme of the New Deal, this symbol of hope provided jobs for hundreds of workers from all over the country, notably the dustbowl regions further east. Folk singer Woody Guthrie, who worked on the Bonneville Dam lower down the river, was commissioned to write some twenty songs about the Columbia project. These were originally played at local rallies, held to raise investment money and combat propaganda from the private power companies who wanted to keep power production in their own hands. Glowing with optimism, the songs underline the promise the dam held for impoverished working people.

Grand Coulee Dam is now the world's biggest producer of hydro-electricity, and has certainly controlled flooding lower down the Columbia. But the power-guzzling demands of industry switched attention and resources from irrigation, and Guthrie's vision of "green pastures of plenty from dry desert ground" has been much slower to get underway – even now, only half the area originally planned has been irrigated.

The whole story is detailed in the **visitor center**, Hwy-155 on the west side of the dam, which also runs tours of the dam and its generating plants (summer daily 8am–10pm, rest of the year daily 8.30am–5pm). The **dam itself** is initially something of an anti-climax; It just doesn't look that big, a trick of the huge-scale scenery that surrounds it.

The twin neighboring towns of **COULEE DAM** and **GRAND COULEE** have a few motels and fairly dire restaurants. More appealingly, more than thirty **campgrounds** are scattered around the long, spindly reservoir of Lake Roosevelt, becoming more woody and secluded as you get further north. *Empire Lines* run a daily service from Spokane to Grand Coulee.

OREGON

For nineteenth-century pioneers, driving in covered wagons over the mountains and deserts of the Oregon Trail, **Willamette Valley** was the promised land. Rich and fertile, it became the home of Oregon's first settlements and towns, and the valley is still the heart of the state's social, political and cultural existence, its citizens proud of their traditions and keen to keep the worst excesses of urban life at bay. **Portland**, the biggest city, has a homely European feel; **Salem**, the state capital, is not much more than an overgrown village; and **Eugene**, at the foot of the valley, with its jogging tracks and spruce, modern center must be one of the country's most liveable cities.

Just east of Portland, waterfalls cascade down mossy cliffs along the **Columbia River Gorge**, south of which the twisting path of an old pioneer road leads through more gorgeous scenery around **Mount Hood**. Several highways link the Willamette Valley to the rugged **coast**, where wide expanses of sand are broken by jagged, black monoliths; white lighthouses look out from stark headlands; and rough cliffs conceal small, sheltered coves. With its sand dunes, dense forests, and sheer variety, the coast is every bit as appealing as its Californian counterpart, albeit not as warm. Along it, a couple of working ports and several small resorts are busy in summer, half-deserted and lashed by waves and wind out of season.

Eastern Oregon was only settled on any scale once the prime land in the west was already taken, and the process involved not only ferocious Indian campaigns but also the bitterly violent "range wars" between sheep-farmers and terrorist "sheep-shooters" associations of cattle-ranchers. Sheep and cows now graze in peace, and some small towns still celebrate their cowboy roots with annual rodeos.

Getting Around Oregon

Portland is well connected by train and bus along the line of highway I-5, to **Seattle** in the north (three trains, ten buses daily), and California to the south. *Amtrak* and *Greyhound* also follow the line of I-84 east from **Portland** as far as Pendleton and then south towards Boise in Idaho. Bus routes radiate from Portland out to **Spokane** in Washington, across **southern** and **central Oregon**, to the coast, and south to California.

Though not all the **coast** is served by buses – there's nothing, for example, between Tillamook and Lincoln City – it's excellent for cycling, if a bit windy. If you want to get any distance off the beaten track – and certainly if you plan to **hike** – having your own vehicle can make all the difference. **Hitching** in Oregon is illegal.

Portland

Small, friendly **PORTLAND** is not the most obvious tourist destination. It has museums, galleries and parks, a colorful weekend market and any number of cheerful coffeehouses, bars and plenty of jazz music; and as a base for exploring the surrounding countryside, it's hard to beat. But there are no really major sights, and only a patchy nightlife – though its fans say that's half the appeal.

The city was named after Portland, Maine, after a coin toss between its two East Coast founders in 1845 ("Boston" was the other option). Its location on a deep part of the Willamette River, near fertile valleys, made it a perfect trading port, and it grew fast, gentrifying quickly and replacing its clapboard houses with ornate Florentine facades and Gothic towers and gables. Through the nineteenth century – until the new

---

The **area code** for the entire state of Oregon is ☎503.

ports in the Puget Sound gained ascendancy – it was a raunchy, bawdy place, notorious for gambling, prostitution and opium dens.

Now Portland is scrupulously salvaging what's left of its past, while risking the odd splash of Post-Modernist architectural color (one splash, in fact, but it is an odd one). City planners in the Seventies faced a downtown in tatters, its historic buildings decayed or sacrificed to parking lots and expressways. There's been much assiduous gap-filling since, and today, overlooked by extensive parkland on the green west hills, Portland is almost a very attractive city.

Arriving, Information and Getting Around

Portland International Airport is in the far northeast of the city. Two buses into town leave from right outside the doors; the express *RAZ* ($7) drops off regularly at major hotels, and the cheaper local *Tri-Met* bus (#12; $1.25) runs to SW Sixth Ave and Main St downtown. *Greyhound*, at 550 NW Sixth Ave (☎243-2323), and *Amtrak*, 800 NW Sixth Ave, are either in or very close to the local bus system's downtown free-ride zone. *Green Tortoise* (☎225-0310), call at the *University Deli* café at 616 SW College St.

Max, Portland's light railroad, shunts tourists around downtown and the old town, then carries commuters over the river to the suburbs. The **bus system** is based at the downtown "transit malls" along Fifth Avenue (southbound) and Sixth Avenue (northbound). Each bus shelter has a small symbol – brown beaver, blue snowflake, purple rain – as a route code. The **Tri-Met Customer Assistance Office** on Pioneer Square (Mon–Fri 9am–5pm; ☎238-7433) can sort you out if you find it confusing. Buses are free in the downtown zone, or otherwise 95¢ to $1.25 (all-day passes cost $3.25).

You can see much of the city on foot: the friendly **visitor center**, in the World Trade Center, 26 SW Salmon St (Mon–Fri 8.30am–5pm; ☎222-2223), provides maps and information. Portland's **post office** is at 715 NW Hoyt St (Mon–Fri 8.30am–8pm, Sat 8.30am–5pm; ☎223-6906; zip code 97209).

The City

Portland is a compact city, divided in half by the Willamette River. The downtown area, where you'll probably spend most time, is on the west bank; the east is mostly residential. When the sun shines, **Pioneer Courthouse Square** is downtown Portland's focal point, filled with music and people. Red-bricked and lined with curving steps, it's a compact mix of gleaming new offices and old plasterwork, punctuated by small grassy parks. This is where to find the malls, theaters and the main museums.

A block up from the transit malls along Fifth and Sixth avenues, **Broadway** pulls together Portland's mix of early grandeur and new wealth, prestigious hotels sharing space with great white movie palaces. One such, the grand *Portland*, has been restored as part of the **Portland Center for the Performing Arts**. Across the park, next to the columned front of the **Masonic Temple**, is the long, low facade of **Portland Art Museum** (Tues–Sat 11am–5pm, Sun 1–5pm; $4, free first Thurs each month 4–9pm). The collection is wide ranging and well laid out, with haunting Northwest Indian masks, squat Mexican statues, ancient Chinese figures – and one of Monet's *Waterlilies*. Opposite the museum, beside an old, ivy-covered church, the **Oregon Historical Center** (Mon–Sat 10am–5pm, Sun noon–5pm; $3.50) has fascinating displays on Oregon's covered-wagon past, and an excellent little bookstore.

The junction of Madison and Fifth holds Portland's one sight of national, if not world, renown – Michael Graves' **Portland Building**, a concoction of concrete, tile and glass, adorned with rosettes and pink and blue tiling. It's quite possible to walk straight past without realizing this is anything special; in fact it was the USA's first post-modern building. On closer examination it's certainly eclectic: an uninhibited (some say flippant) re-

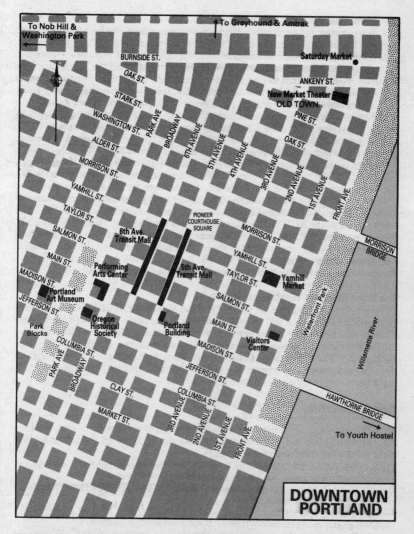

To Nob Hill &
Washington Park

To Greyhound & Amtrak

BURNSIDE ST.

Saturday Market

OAK ST.

ANKENY ST.

STARK ST.

New Market Theater
OLD TOWN

WASHINGTON ST.

PINE ST.

PARK AVE

BROADWAY

6TH AVENUE

5TH AVENUE

4TH AVENUE

3RD AVENUE

2ND AVENUE

1ST AVENUE

FRONT AVE

ALDER ST.

OAK ST.

MORRISON ST.

YAMHILL ST.

TAYLOR ST.

SALMON ST.

PIONEER
COURTHOUSE
SQUARE

6th Ave.
Transit Mall

MORRISON ST.

MAIN ST.

YAMHILL ST.

MORRISON
BRIDGE

MADISON ST

Performing
Arts Center

5th Ave.
Transit Mall

TAYLOR ST.

Yamhill
Market

Portland
Art Museum

SALMON ST.

JEFFERSON ST.

Park
Blocks

Oregon
Historical
Society

Portland
Building

MAIN ST.

Waterfront Park

Willamette River

COLUMBIA ST.

Visitors
Center

PARK AVE

MADISON ST.

BROADWAY

JEFFERSON ST.

CLAY ST.

COLUMBIA ST.

HAWTHORNE BRIDGE

MARKET ST.

3RD AVENUE

2ND AVENUE

1ST AVENUE

FRONT AVE

To Youth Hostel

**DOWNTOWN
PORTLAND**

working of classical and other motifs that outraged conservatives and delighted the
avant-garde. Portland relished the controversy, going so far as to hoist an enormous
kneeling copper figure of *Portlandia* above the main entrance.

A few blocks further east, the **riverfront** has been rescued from over a century of
burial beneath wharves, warehouses, and, more recently, an express highway, and is
now lined by the mile-long **Waterfront Park**. Just behind the park, the modern, grey
and glassy **World Trade Center** looms over the gushing fountains of the Salmon
Street Springs. A couple of blocks over, the small **Yamhill Historic District** is lined
with 1890s buildings. **Yamhill Marketplace** (actually built in 1982) has a couple of
produce stalls, though most of its stands now serve hot food.

Old Town, Chinatown and Nob Hill

Old Town, seven rather desolate blocks north, was where Portland was originally founded. The area tended to flood, and when the railway came in 1883 the town center shifted away; its big, ornate buildings became warehouses and it plummeted down the social scale, though a few bistros and boutiques now stand amid the dereliction. The **Saturday Market** (March to Christmas Sat 10am–5pm, Sun 11am–4.30pm) packs the area around Burnside Bridge with arts and crafts stalls, street musicians, spicy foods and lively crowds. Across an angular plaza from the **Skidmore Fountain**, a colonnade stretches from the side of the **New Market Theater**, a restored theater-cum-vegetable market that is now full of cafés. Close by, the **American Advertising Museum**, 9 NW Second Ave (Wed–Fri 11am–5pm, Sat–Sun noon–5pm; $3), gives a fascinating account of the rise of advertising, from printed posters to tapes of old radio and TV ads.

Away from the river, up Burnside, the oriental gate at Fourth Avenue marks what's left of **CHINATOWN**. This was once the second largest Chinese community in the US, but white unemployment in the 1880s led, as elsewhere, to racist attacks, and most Chinese workers were forced to leave. The further west you go, the sleazier Burnside becomes, though it's worth pushing on to the labyrinthine *Powell's Bookstore* at no 1005. A bus ride away, the **NOB HILL** district (or "North West Section") focuses around NW 23rd Avenue and NW 21st Avenue: the name was borrowed from San Francisco by a grocer who hoped the area would become as fashionable as the Nob Hill back home. It did, almost, and a few multicolored wooden mansions add a San Franciscan tinge – though the main interest up here is the neighborhood's cafés and restaurants.

The West Hills and Washington Park

Directly behind Nob Hill are the wooded bluffs of elegant **WEST HILLS**. A special bus (#63) winds to the green and leafy **Washington Park**, home to a **zoo** (daily 9.30am–7.30pm; $3). In summer, there are free evening concerts for visitors; **Zoo Jazz** on Wednesdays and **Zoo Grass** (bluegrass) on Thursdays (further details on ☎226-1561). Nearby, the **World Forestry Center** (daily 10am–5pm: $2) goes in for hands-on displays, with schoolkids romping up and down, charging around the seventy-foot "talking" tree.

Accommodation

Though inexpensive old **hotels** are scattered throughout the downtown area, most are fairly shabby, inside and out. Dozens of **motels** can be found off the interstates and along Sandy Boulevard east of downtown.

Clinkerbrick House, 2311 NE Schuyler St (☎281-2533). This peaceful Dutch Colonial B&B inn, some way out from the center, has a lovely garden and comfortable rooms. ④.

General Hooker's House, 125 SW Hooker St (☎222-4435). Small and relaxed B&B inn, offering evening cocktails on the roofdeck. ③.

Heathman Hotel, 1009 SW Broadway (☎241-4100 or 1-800/551-0011). Restored downtown landmark, with elegant eucalyptus-panelled interior. It would be a standout anywhere. ⑥.

Mallory Hotel, 729 SW 15th Ave at Yamhill (☎223-6311 or 1-800/228-8657). Old, well worn, and comfortable – if slightly spartan. Just a few blocks from Pioneer Square. ③.

Portland International AYH Hostel, 3031 SE Hawthorne Blvd (☎236-3380). Cheery old Victorian house, across the river in a lively neighborhood. Dorm beds cost $10 for AYH members, $13 non-members. ①.

Riverside Inn, 50 SW Morrison St (☎221-0711). For a river view at a reasonable price, this is the best bet. Overlooking the riverfront promenade, and near the Old Town district, with fairly plain rooms. ⑤.

Travelodge, 949 E Burnside St (☎234-8411). Standard motel, half a mile east of Pioneer Square. ②.

YWCA, 1111 SW Tenth Ave (☎223-6281). Clean and central women-only doubles – right next to the downtown arts center – but its very few rooms are often booked solid months in advance. ②.

Eating

Friendly and unpretentious are the two words that best describe Portland's **eating** options, most of which are concentrated in the downtown area, with quite a few in Nob Hill to the northwest and a handful on the less-touristed east side of the river, on and around Hawthorne Boulevard. At the *Metro on Broadway*, 911 SW Broadway, a dozen low-priced stands offer food from around the world under one roof.

Brasserie Montmartre, 626 SW Park Ave (☎224-5552). Pseudo-Left Bank bistro. Free live jazz and good food. Not exactly cheap, but the only place to get fresh pasta with pesto and scallops at 2am.

Cisco and Pancho's, 107 NW Fifth Ave (☎223-5048). Lively, inexpensive Tex-Mex restaurant with free live jazz or blues most evenings.

Dan and Louis Oyster Bar, 208 SW Ankeny St (☎227-5906). Good cheap Old Town seafood.

Jake's Famous Crawfish, 401 SW 12th Ave (☎226-1419). Portland's prime spot for fresh seafood, though at weekends it's packed. The daily fish specials are excellent and not exorbitantly priced.

McCormick and Schmick's, 235 SW First Ave (☎224-7522). Excellent fish restaurant, with a variety of ultra-fresh nightly specials, and a lively oyster bar.

Old Wives' Tales, 1300 E Burnside (☎238-0470). Feminist café with great breakfasts, sandwiches and innovative vegetarian dishes.

Vat and Tonsure, 822 SW Park Ave (☎227-1845). Unreconstructed Beat Generation hangout, energized by good-sized portions of bistro-style food, copious amounts of wine, and reasonable prices.

Drinking and Nightlife

Portland's streets can seem pretty quiet at night, but there's a lot more going on here than you might think. **Coffeehouses** and dozens of **bars** form the fulcrum of a lively scene, and the city is a beer-drinker's heaven, with dozens of local micro-breweries. For **music**, the place to head is downtown, on- and off-Broadway.

The Downtowner and *Willamette Week*, and the younger and livelier *PDXS*, available free on most street corners, carry up-to-the-minute listings of what's on and where.

Bars, Pubs and Coffeehouses

B Moloch's, 901 SW Salmon St (☎221-5700). Downtown brew-pub, with beer ranging from *Widmer's* weisen lagers to *Deschutes'* Black Butte Porters, and good-value designer pizzas. Huge and very popular, but worth waiting for.

Dublin Pub, 6821 SW Beaverton Hillsdale Hwy (☎297-2889). Traditional Irish pub, with regular live folk music, including bagpipes, and well-kept pints of Guinness. A short walk from the youth hostel.

Papa Hayden's, 701 NW 23rd Ave (☎228-7317). Chic, upscale ice-cream café that brews up some good coffees to wash down sugar-shock-inducing desserts, such as a world-class chocolate mousse.

Produce Row Café, 204 SE Oak St (☎232-8355). Just across the river amongst the still-working fruit-and-vegetable warehouses, with about a million different beers and gigantic sandwiches to help soak it up. Pool tables and a varied crowd keep things interesting.

Rimsky Korsakoffee House, 707 SE 12th Ave (☎232-2640). Looks like someone's house from the outside, but inside live chamber music enlivens a very pleasant if slightly cliquish café.

Music Venues

Café Vivo, 555 SW Oak Ave (☎228-8486). Lively jazz and blues venue.

East Avenue Tavern, 727 E Burnside St (☎236-6900). Located about half a mile east of the river, with nightly Irish, folk or bluegrass music.

Key Largo, 31 NW First Ave (☎223-9919). Tropical decor, steamy dancefloor, and the hottest blues bands. Cover at weekends only.

Melody Ballroom, 615 SW Alder (☎232-2759). Cavernous old dancehall, a prime venue for up-and-coming pop bands and touring indie stars.

Satyricon, 125 NW Sixth Ave (☎243-2380). Somewhat forbidding post-punk club in a seedy neighborhood, mixing live bands and various oddball acts. Cover free–$5, and good bar food.

Parchman Farm, 1204 SE Clay St (☎235-7831). Intimate club; good pizzas, great jazz, no cover.

The City, 13 NW 13th Ave (☎224-2489). Portland's largest and liveliest gay nightclub, with huge dancefloors and occasional live acts. Thurs–Sun only, till 4am Fri and Sat; cover $2–6.

Red Sea, 318 SW Third Ave (☎241-5450). Small dancefloor in the back of an Ethiopian restaurant, grooving most nights to DJ'ed reggae and rockers tunes. No cover, strong drinks.

Classical Music, Theater and Cinema

Portland's **arts scene** centers on the *Portland Center for the Performing Arts* on Broadway (☎248-4496). One of its two small auditoria, the cherrywood-panelled *Intermediate Theater*, is the main venue for the local chamber orchestra and ballet companies; the other, the high-tech *Winningstad Theater*, is used by the *New Rose Theater*, who perform everything from the classics to sharp-eyed new works. For what's on and ticket information, call the **events hotline** on ☎233-3333.

The **Oregon Symphony Orchestra** perform between September and April at the opulent *Arlene Schnitzer Concert Hall* next door (☎228-1353); tickets range from $15 to $40 for evening performances, but you can catch a Sunday afternoon concert for as little as $7. A few blocks away at SW Third Ave and Clay St, the *Civic Auditorium* (☎248-4496) is a venue for big musical extravaganzas, operas and the *Oregon Shakespeare Festival* (Oct–Feb).

Free concerts are held in Pioneer Square, Waterfront Park, and at the zoo in the summer, as well as year-round at the *Old Church*, Eleventh Ave and Clay St downtown, every Wednesday at noon.

Around Portland: Columbia River Gorge and Mount Hood

The **Columbia River Gorge**, to the east of Portland, was scoured deep and narrow by huge glaciers and rocks during the Ice Age. Now it's covered with green fir and maple trees, which turn fabulous shades of gold and red in the fall, and narrow white waterfalls cascade down its sides. The most dramatic part of the Gorge, between Troutdale and Hood River, lies in the shadow of snow-tipped Mt Hood. It's best seen by **car**, allowing plenty of time – whatever the tourist leaflets say, it's much better not to attempt the gorge and Mount Hood in one day. A nice **Mount Hood Loop** takes in both areas, but leaves no time for walking. *Greyhound* stop at **Cascade Locks**, and more scenic – but brief – day **tours** are run from Portland during the summer by *Gray Line* ($50; ☎226-6755).

Early British explorers such as Drake and Cook accidentally missed the Columbia River. It was left to the American trader Robert Gray to cross the sand bar at its mouth in 1792 and sail into Oregon's interior. More interested in buying furs than making maps, he didn't follow the river very far, and its first non-native explorers in fact came down the Columbia the other way – a tired Lewis and Clark, on the last stage of their 1804 trek. Forty years later, the gorge became the final leg of the Oregon Trail, negotiated by pioneer families on precarious rafts.

Mount Hood is the tallest of the Oregon Cascades. The highest point on the loop road, **Barlow Pass**, is named after Samuel Barlow, a wagon-train leader who blazed the first trail around the gorge. Much of the **Barlow Road** is still followed by Hwy-26, including the steep ridges where wagons frequently skidded out of control and plummeted downhill. You can still see deep gashes on some of the trees where ropes were fastened to check the wagons' descent.

Shortly after Hwy-35 meets Hwy-26, a turning up the mountain leads to the solid stone **Timberline Lodge** (☎272-3311; ④), a New Deal scheme which is now a year-round ski resort, good for hiking in summer. Out of season, the deserted roads around here can feel downright eerie, especially if you know that *Timberline* was the set for *The Shining*.

South through the Willamette Valley

South of Portland, I-5 threads towards the Californian border along a series of inland valleys, bypassing historic **Oregon City**, the first state capital, at the end of the Oregon Trail. Today, the split-level town consists of a short modern main street, connected by steps, steep streets and a cliff-face elevator to an uptown area of old wooden houses set on a bluff.

Salem

The build-up of motels and fast-food chains that ushers you into **SALEM** is deceptive for what is in fact a small and rather staid little town, content dutifully to point visitors around its quota of attractions, but not expecting them to linger. Its showpiece is the 1869 **Reed Opera House**, now a mall full of antique shops. A short walk from the downtown shopping area the tall, white, Vermont-marble **capitol building** is topped with a large gold-leaf pioneer, axe in hand, eyes towards the West. Next to the capitol, tree-lined **Willamette University** is the oldest university in the West.

Greyhound is at 450 Church St NE (☎362-2428), *Green Tortoise* drops off at the Bingo truckstop, exit 263 from I-5, and *Amtrak* is at 13th and Oak. Space is tight at both the women-only *YWCA*, 768 State St (☎581-9922; ①), next to the university, which charges around $18 a day, and the *YMCA*, 685 Court St (☎581-9622; ①), two blocks away, but there are plenty of **motels**, including the *City Center Motel*, 510 Liberty St SE (☎364-0121; ②). **Camping** options are limited to the *KOA* site, 3700 hagers Grove Rd SE (☎581-6736), on the outskirts of town; 26 miles east of Salem, **Silver Falls State Park**, 20024 Silver Falls Highway (☎873-8681), has a much more attractive location.

The area around the university is not the busy **food** scene you might expect, and you're better off downtown, where the *Court Street Daily Lunch*, 347 Court St at Liberty, is a classic 1960s diner, where the food is both good and inexpensive; close by, the more up-to-date *Governor's Cup*, 471 Court St(☎581-9675), serves substantial meals.

Eugene

EUGENE dominates the lower end of the Willamette Valley – a lively social mix of students and professionals, loggers and hippies. Oregon's second largest center, it has been a cultural focus since the days of the travelling theater groups last century. Now, beyond the standard downtown shopping malls, Eugene's markets make colorful wandering, and there are plenty of ethnic restaurants. The **University of Oregon** campus in the city's southeast corner lends a youthful feel. Its **Museum of Art** (Wed–Sun noon–5pm; free) has a strong Asian collection.

Though short on sights as such, Eugene offers two big markets, especially the weekly **Saturday Market** (Eighth and Oak between April and Christmas), which is something of a carnival, with live music and street performers. Tie-dye and wholefoods set the tone, but rastas, skateboarders, punks and students join in. **Fifth Street Market** to the north is more touristy, though still lively, set in a converted chicken-processing plant and selling arts, crafts, and clothes, as well as a huge variety of ethnic food, from Chinese to Mexican to fish and chips.

Eugene is also a **sports** capital. Trails and paths abound for runners and cyclists, both in the city center and along leafy river banks; bikes can be rented from *Pedal Power*, 545 Sixth St (☎687-1775).

Greyhound are at Tenth and Pearl (☎344-6265), *Amtrak* pull in at Fourth and Willamette, and *Green Tortoise* stop at 15th and Kincaid (☎937-3603). There's a **visitor center** downtown at 305 W Seventh Ave (Mon–Fri 8.30am–5pm; ☎484-5307). Hotels and motels line Franklin Blvd, across from the university: *Eugene Motor Lodge Motel* is more central at 476 E Broadway (☎344-5233; ②), as is the best hotel in town, the *Eugene Hilton*, overlooking the town at 66 E Sixth Ave (☎342-2000; ⑥).

With over fifteen thousand students to feed, Eugene has plenty of places to eat. *Café Zenon*, 898 Pearl St (☎343-3005), is an eclectic but pricey bistro; the cheaper *Keystone Café*, 395 W Fifth St (☎342-2075), serves high-quality American and Mexican food. In the town center, the *Electric Station*, 27 E Fifth St (☎485-4444), sells superb and filling meals. The **WOW Hall**, 291 W Eighth St (☎687-2746), once a meeting hall for the "Wobblies", is an informal venue for up-and-coming bands.

The **Oregon Country Fair**, a big hippy-flavored festival of music, arts, food and dancing, is held twenty minutes west on US-26 in **Veneta** on the second weekend in July ($10 per day). Traffic then is heavy, and even if you have a car it's easier to take the local *LTD* buses, which run every half-hour during the fair for 75¢.

South to California

South of Eugene along I-5, almost to the California border, **GRANTS PASS** lies on the Rogue River, which tumbles vigorously from the Cascades. It earns its living mainly from taking visitors **whitewater rafting**. Half a day will cost around $40, a full day $50 – the **visitor center**, just off I-5 at 1501 NE Sixth St (☎1-800/547-5927 or 476-7717) can provide brochures from more than two dozen *licensed* (and so safer) river guides.

The Oregon Caves

Some thirty miles southwest of Grants Pass, a turning off Hwy-199 at the small town of **Cave Junction** leads to the **Oregon Caves**, Oregon's only national monument, tucked in a wooded canyon at the end of a narrow, twisting road. It's actually one enormous cave, with smaller passages leading off. The dripping marble walls are covered with elaborate stalactites and stalagmites. Organized (and very cold) tours of the caves run all year round (75min; $6; ☎592-3400).

Eight miles from Cave Junction, the **Fordson Home Hostel**, 250 Robinson Rd (☎592-3203; ①), offers a cheap bed ($8), camping and $2 discount off entry to the caves for non-Americans. There's plenty of other **camping** around, including two US Forest Service campgrounds near the caves, and the *Gold Leaf Resort*, 7901 Caves Highway (☎592-3406; ③), has motel rooms.

Ashland and the Shakespeare Festival

Throughout Oregon, small **ASHLAND** is identified with William Shakespeare; a real anomaly among the timber and dairy-farming towns. For fifty years, the **Oregon Shakespeare Festival** has been held here between February and October, packing audiences into the half-timbered **Elizabethan Theater**. It may all be phony, but Ashland is no more tacky than Shakespeare's real birthplace, and in some ways has the distinct edge. Its setting, between the Cascade and the Siskiyou mountains, is magnificent; there's good skiing in the winter and river-rafting in summer, performance standards are high, and there's some excellent contemporary fringe theater – not to mention pleasant cafés and a young, friendly atmosphere when the nearby college is in session.

Shakespeare is performed at the *Elizabethan* and *Angus Bowmer* theaters, both in **Lithia Park**, while the smaller *Black Swan*, off Pioneer St, stages contemporary plays (☎482-2111; $10–18, sometimes half-price on the day; standing at the *Elizabethan* for $5). Contemporary drama comes cheaper ($5–10): try the *Actors' Workshop Theater*, 295 E Main St (☎482-9659; tickets from *Blue Dragon* bookstore), the *Oregon Cabaret Theater*, in a renovated pink church at First and Hagerdine (☎488-1926), or the *New Playwright's Theater*, 31 Water St (☎482-9286).

The **visitor center** is at 110 E Main St; *Greyhound* stop at 91 Oak St (☎482-2516). For **accommodation**, there's the Ashland *AYH Youth Hostel*, 150 N Main St (☎482-9217 – book ahead; ①), while **motels** along Main Street include the *Manor Motel* (no 476 N; ☎482-2246; ②). Numerous B&Bs in town charge up to $150.

Good places to eat and drink range from the *Ashland Bakery Café*, 28 E Main St (☎482-2117), to more upscale haunts like *Alex's Plaza Restaurant,* 35 N Main St; the *Rogue River Brewery*, off N Main St at 31-B Water St (☎488-5061), has a dozen of Oregon's best micro-brewed beers as well as pizzas and nightly live music.

The Oregon Coast

Although the **Oregon coast** is as beautiful as any in the West, the Californian sun (summer temperatures here stay in the sixties and seventies) draws off the tan-seeking masses, leaving Oregonians to hike and clam-dig along their own four hundred miles, most of it public land. State park after state park lines the shore, scattering campgrounds thickly; hostels appear at strategic intervals, while extensive and often isolated beaches offer a multitude of free activities, from beach-combing for Polynesian glass floats and sea-carved driftwood, to shell-fishing, whale-watching, or, in winter, storm-watching. This isn't to say that Oregon has escaped commercialism: small fishing towns, hard-hit by decline, are jumping onto the tourism bandwagon as fast as they can, and it's a lucky traveller who finds a budget room without booking ahead in July and August.

The coast is almost perfect for cycling (pick up the *Coast Bike Route Map* from the tourist board). US-101 follows the coast right down to the Californian border, and you can escape onto the many smaller "scenic loop" roads.

Astoria

ASTORIA, at the mouth of the Columbia River, was founded by John Jacob Astor in 1811, in the hope of establishing his own fur-trading empire. In fact "Fort Astoria" survived eighteen months, before selling out to the British: Washington Irving tells the saga in his novel *Astoria*. A small replica of the old fort stands at Fifteenth and Exchange, but nowadays Astoria is really a working port, with enough history to attract a few tourists, but little of the razzmatazz of the communities further south.

The road into Astoria runs parallel with the waterfront – crammed with saloons and brothels in the nineteenth century, many equipped with built-in trap doors for shanghai-ing drunken customers, who might wake up halfway across the Pacific. It all got so out of hand at one point that workers on quayside canneries carried guns to get themselves safely to the night shift. Things are much tamer now, but exhibits from Astoria's seafaring past are on display at the huge **Columbia River Maritime Museum**, at 17th and Marine Drive (daily 9.30am–5pm; $5).

From Marine Drive, numbered streets climb towards the elegant uptown area. On top of Coxcomb Hill, the **Astoria Column** is coated with a faded mural depicting the town's early history, and offers a superb view. The concrete replica of an Indian burial canoe near the base of the column is a memorial to Chief Comcomly of the Chinook. He was on amiable terms with the first settlers, one of whom married his daughter, until he caught his son-in-law hoeing potatoes (woman's work in the chief's opinion). Comcomly's son, on the other hand, is said to have proposed to **Jane Barnes**, a barmaid from Portsmouth who arrived on an English ship in 1814 to become, Astorians claim, the first white woman in the Northwest. Jane turned him down, which wrought havoc with local race relations but is commemorated each year by **Jane Barnes Day**, held in the second week of May.

South and west of town, you can visit Lewis and Clark's reconstructed 1808 winter base at **Fort Clatsop** (daily, summer 8am–6pm, winter 8am–5pm; free) before continuing to **Fort Stevens State Park** off US-101, with its trails, camping and miles of beaches. Fortifications were first put up at Fort Stevens to guard against Confederate raiders during the Civil War, though **Battery Russell** was part of World War II defences. It did get shelled one night by a passing Japanese submarine, which makes it, incredibly, the only military installation on the mainland US to have been fired on by a foreign power since 1812.

The *Greyhound* station is at 364 Ninth St (☎325-5641), connected daily with Portland. The **visitor center** is in the south at 111 W Marine Drive (June–Aug Mon–Sat 8am–6pm, Sun 9am–5pm; winter Mon–Fri 8am–5pm, Sat & Sun 11am–4pm). You can **camp** at *Fort Stevens State Park* (see above), or stay in one of the inexpensive but grim **motels** along West Marine Drive, such as the *Lamplighter* (no 131; ☎325-4051; ②), or the *Rivershore* (no 59; ☎325-2921; ②). **Bed and breakfast** at *Franklin St Station*, 1140 Franklin St (☎325-4314; ④), is far more agreeable. There's a **youth hostel** across the Columbia River in *Fort Columbia State Park* (see p.861). For **eating**, the *Feed Store*, Pier 11 at the foot of 11th St (☎325-0279), serves excellent seafood and steaks; close by, the *Columbian Café*, 1114 Marine Drive (☎325-2233), has tasty vegetarian food.

Seaside

Seventeen miles down the coast from Astoria, **SEASIDE** is an endearingly tacky holiday resort, with a long sandy **beach** and a few places to stay. The *Riverside Inn*, 430 S Holladay Drive (☎738-8254; ④), officially a B&B, is a good cut above the average motel: the *Mariner-Holladay Motel*, 429 S Holladay Drive (☎738-3690; ②) next door, is less expensive. Seaside is on the *North Coast Transit* bus line (Mon–Fri only; ☎738-7083) from Astoria south to Cannon Beach.

Cannon Beach

Nine miles south from Seaside, the more upmarket **CANNON BEACH**, is home of a **sandcastle competition** held each May. Past subjects have included dinosaurs, sphinxes, even a Crucifixion. **Accommodation** is tight, especially during the competition. The *Mcbee Motel* is close to the beach at 888 S Hemlock St (☎436-2569; ②), while the plush *Hallmark Resort* is right on the seafront at 1400 S Hemlock St (☎436-1566; ⑤). For **food**, N Hemlock St is the best bet. *Lazy Susan Café* (no 126; ☎436-2816), next to the *Coaster Theater*, does excellent health food, and the *Bistro* (no 263; ☎436-2661), has tasty seafood and the town's best bar.

Lincoln City

There's no avoiding **LINCOLN CITY** if you're driving; probably the ugliest town on the coast, it sprawls along the highway for seven congested, motel-lined miles. **Greyhound** buses, 316 SE US-101 (☎994-8418), run to Portland and south. The **visitor center** is on US-101 at 40th (Mon–Fri 9am–5pm; ☎1-800/452-2151). **Motels** include the clean *City Center*, 1014 NE US-101 (☎994-2612; ②), and the *Shilo Inn*, 1501 NW 40th St (☎994/3655; ③).

Newport

NEWPORT, 26 miles further on, is another fishing town laboring to turn itself into a resort – this time a surprisingly chic one, with the smart new *Mariner Square* development right opposite the dented metal walls of the old canneries. The place has an artsy undertone, manifest in a new Performing Arts Center and two small art museums on long, uncrowded **Nye Beach**.

The highlight of its good budget **accommodation** is the *Sylvia Beach Hotel*, 267 NW Cliff (☎265-9231; ①/④), which aims to encourage would-be writers, with a cosy attic library, various small rooms decorated in the styles of assorted writers, and dorm beds at $20 per night, including breakfasts. The *Penny Saver*, 710 N Coast Hwy (☎265-6631; ②), is a good **motel**. Complete motel and **campground** listings are available from the **Chamber of Commerce**, 555 SW Coast Highway (summer Mon–Fri 8.30am–5pm, Sat & Sun 10am–4pm; winter Mon–Fri 8.30am–5pm). For **food**, the *Whale's Tale* on Bay

Blvd (☎265-8660) has a good, varied menu and live music at weekends. Nearby is the pleasant *Canyon Way Restaurant and Bookstore*, 1216 SW Canyon Way (☎265-8319); at Nye Beach, the *Chowder Bowl*, 728 NW Beach Drive (☎265-7477), is good value, as is the Italian *Don Petrie's*, 613 NW Third St (☎265-3663). *Greyhound* is at 956 SW Tenth St (☎265-2253).

Bandon

Further along the coast at the mouth of the Coquille River, 24 miles south of industrial Coos Bay, easy-going **BANDON** combines old town restoration with a strong New Age presence, becoming something of an arts and crafts center in the process. It was originally a Native American settlement, which was swamped by the onset of the Gold Rush. This century began rather ominously, when townsfolk dynamited Tupper Rock, a sacred tribal site, to build the sea wall, and the town was cursed to burn down three times: it's happened twice so far, in 1914 and 1936, and the superstitious are still waiting.

Bandon's main attraction today is the unusual rock formations along its rugged **beach**. Magnificent in stormy weather, the prolific quantities of shellfish make this a prime venue for seashell collectors, while **crabbers** gather at the town dock and **clammers** dig away along the banks of the estuary. Bandon's history is on display at the **Coquille Museum**, in the Coast Guard building overlooking the river mouth (Tues–Sat noon–4pm).

The best place to **stay**, right in the town center at 370 First St, is the *Sea Star Guest House* (☎347-9632; ④). Just in front of that is the associated *Sea Star Hostel*, 375 Second St (☎347-9632; ①), which has a friendly café downstairs. The **visitor center** (daily 9am–4.30pm; ☎347-9616) is across the road. The **food** at *Andrea's Old Town Café*, two blocks away on Baltimore St (☎347-2111), is great, and good value for money. There's **camping** just north of town at **Bullards Beach State Park**, where a lighthouse stands guard over miles of windswept wilderness.

South to California

Towns are fewer and further between as you travel south along US-101, which passes dozens of secluded **beaches**. Ugly little **GOLD BEACH**, where the wild **Rogue River** reaches the sea, is largely devoted to whitewater rafting expeditions, up canyons and through roaring rapids into the depths of the **Siskiyou National Forest**. The **visitor center**, 1225 S Ellensburg St (Mon–Fri 9am–4.30pm; ☎247-7526), has all the details.

Central and Eastern Oregon

Once you cross the Cascades, Oregon, like Washington, grows warmer, drier, and wilder; green valleys give way to scrubby sageland, bare hills and stark rock formations, fringed with juniper and broken up by the occasional tract of pine forest. The landscape is volcanic and often alien, with cracked lava flows, abrupt cone-like hills, and high craters such as lovely **Crater Lake** in the south. The **east**, though seldom visited, can be surprisingly beautiful, with the **John Day Fossil Beds** along US-26, and the remote, snow-capped Wallowa Mountains overlooking the long, deep slash of **Hells Canyon**.

Bend and Around

BEND is a useful base for visiting Central Oregon, giving access both to Cascade grandeur and the eerie landscape of Oregon's Lava Lands. It's a pleasant enough little town, eagerly benefitting from the recent explosion of interest in outdoor pursuits.

The *Greyhound* from Portland arrives a mile east of the town center at 1068 NW Bond St (☎382-2151). **Local buses** run to nearby towns. You can pick up **information** at the **welcome center** on US-97 just north of town (☎1-800/800-8334 or 382-8334).

Budget **motels** – often full – line Third Street (US-97); try the pleasant *Dunes Motel* (no 1515 NE; ☎382-6811; ②). There's summer **camping** in *Tumalo State Park*, five miles along US-20 northwest. For **eating**, Bend has several pricey little bistros such as the *Old Bend Blacksmith Shop and Broiler*, 211 Greenwood Ave (☎388-1994); less expensive meals can be found at *D&D Bar and Grill*, 927 NW Bond St and, opposite, *Arvard's Lounge and Café*, 928 NW Bond St (☎388-0990). *Deschutes Brewery and Public House*, nearby at 1044 Bond St (☎382-9242), is a **brew-pub** with a very good selection of micro-brewed ales and stouts, and also serves exceptionally fresh food.

Mount Bachelor and the Cascades Lake Highway

The largest ski resort in the Northwest is at **Mount Bachelor**, 22 miles southwest of Bend, its Olympic-standard facilities open from mid-November to as late as July, snow-fall permitting. Mount Bachelor is also the first stop on the **Cascade Lakes Highway**, known as "Century Drive" – a hundred-mile mountain loop road which gives access to trailheads into the **Three Sisters**, or further south, the **Diamond Peak** wilderness areas, and a sprinkling of campgrounds. Get details at the **Deschutes National Forest Office**, 1645 East Hwy-20 (☎388-2715), or the Lava Lands visitor center (see below).

The Lava Lands

The **Lava Lands** cover a huge area of central Oregon, though the greatest concentration of weird lava formations – neat conical buttes, caves and the frozen forms of trees – is in the Bend area. They date back seven thousand years to the explosions of mounts Newberry and Mazama, which dumped enormous quantities of ash and pumice across the region. The **Lava Lands visitor center** (daily in summer; ☎593-2421) is an excellent source of maps and information on hiking trails; it's eleven miles south of Bend on Hwy-97, near the spectacular dark cinder cone of **Lava Butte**.

A mile south, off US-97, the **Lava River Cave** (summer daily 8.30am–6pm; $2, plus $1 for a lamp), is a subterranean passage into the volcanic underworld. Most of the lava which created the cave eventually cooled and hardened around the still-molten center of the flow. When this drained away, it left an empty lava tube, over a mile long, discovered only when part of the roof fell in. There are all kinds of formations along the chilly cave, but even if you have a lantern it's hard to see much beyond the next few steps.

Crater Lake and Klamath Falls

The Northwest's best-looking volcanic crater, now preserved as Oregon's only National Park, is just over a hundred miles south of Bend. The shell of Mount Mazama holds the blue, deep and resoundingly beautiful **Crater Lake**. The explosion which created the lake was 42 times greater than the Mount St Helens blast; the two islands you see in it are the tips of two mini-volcanoes which began to grow again within the hollowed mountaintop. In its snow-covered isolation, the lake is awe-inspiring; in summer too it's spectacular, when wildflowers bloom and wildlife emerges from hibernation.

You need a car to get here, though only the southern of the two approach roads (off Hwy-62, which leads off US-97) is kept open year-round. The northern acess road (off Hwy-138) is closed from mid-October to July, as is the "Rim Drive" around the crater's edge. At tiny **Rim Village**, the National Park maintains a summer-only **visitor center**, and close by a steep one-mile trail leads down to the lakeshore, from where regular boat trips tour the lake (June–Sept daily 10am–4pm; $10; details on ☎594-2511). *Crater Lake Lodge*, the best place to stay, is closed for refurbishment until 1995, but there are two campgrounds inside the park, one of which – **Mazama** – is eight miles south of the rim, not far from *Mazama Village Motel* (☎594-2511; ③).

The logging and agricultural town of **KLAMATH FALLS**, sixty-odd miles away on the enormous Upper Klamath Lake, is a nexus for public transit; *Greyhound* arrives from Portland and Eugene at 1200 Klamath Ave (☎882-4616), and *Amtrak*, 1600 Oak St, also crosses the mountains. While the town has few actual sights, you can at least be sure of a cheap **room** and some sort of a **meal**. The **visitor center**, 125 N Eighth St (Mon–Fri 8.30am–5pm; ☎884-5193), has maps and listings, while among several budget motels the clean *Maverick Motel*, 1220 Main St (☎884-7735; ②), stands out.

East on US-26: the John Day Fossil Beds

Hwy-140 continues on from Klamath Falls into southeast Oregon, but it's a numbingly boring journey. If instead you follow US-97, then Hwy-126/26 from Bend, you'll emerge from a brief green passage through the **Ochoco National Forest** into a bare, sun-scorched landscape of ochers and beige. Many features of the area are named after John Day, a fur-trapper from the Astoria colony, who early in the nineteenth century fell victim to local Indians and was later discovered wandering robbed, lost and naked. Of especial importance are the **John Day Fossil Beds**, a little way north of US-26, which hold some of the most revealing fossil formations in the US. These were preserved in a layer of volcanic ash as the Cascades sputtered into being, just after the extinction of the dinosaurs.

The **Painted Hills** unit, down a side road six miles west of one-horse Mitchell, is the most accessible of the three widely separated fossil-bed sites. Striped in shades of rust and brown, the hills look like sandcastle mounds, the smooth surface quilted with rivulets worn by draining water. Back on US-26, just before the **Sheep Rock** unit – where you'll find the main visitor center (Mon–Fri 8am–4.30pm; ☎575-0521) – a turning leads to the area known as **Blue Basin**, a natural amphitheater where a trail leads past perspex-covered fossil exhibits, including a tortoise that hurtled to its death millions of years ago, and a saber-toothed cat.

John Day Town and Baker

Small, dry **JOHN DAY** is, despite its size, the largest town along US-26, with a handful of motels and restaurants and the fascinating **Kam Wah Chung & Co Museum**, next to the City Park (summer only Mon–Thurs 9am–noon & 1–5pm, Sat & Sun 1–5pm; $1.50), once the home of a famed Chinese herbalist.

The road leads after eighty miles to more substantial **BAKER** – more properly Baker City – which is well equipped with motels. The mundane *Super 8*, near I-84 at 250 Campbell St (☎523-8282; ③), is the best value, and the area is sprinkled with campgrounds; details from the **Chamber of Commerce**, 490 Campbell St (☎523-5855). *Greyhound*, 515 Campbell St (☎523-5011), and *Amtrak*, 2803 Broadway, both run to Portland. You'll find **restaurants** around Main Street.

La Grande and Around

The **Grande Ronde Valley**, north of Baker on I-84 through cattle-grazing rangeland, is large, round, flat and rimmed by mountains. Now mostly drained to become farmland, this was once a marsh, fatally boggy to pioneer wagons, forcing the Oregon Trail to keep to the higher but tougher ground around the hills as it headed northwest towards the Blue Mountains.

The hub of the valley is **LA GRANDE**, a simple lumber-and-railroad town linked with Portland by *Greyhound* (2108 Cove Ave) and *Amtrak*. The **visitor center** at 2111

Adams Ave (US-30), near the railroad station (Mon–Fri 8.30am–5pm; ☎963-8588), has maps and information. **Motels** nearby include the *Broken Arrow Lodge*, 2215 East Adams Ave (☎963-7116; ②); more pleasantly, you could splash out on B&B at the luxurious *Stange Manor* at 1612 Walnut St (☎963-2400; ④). There's **camping** at Morgan Lake, two miles west down B Avenue. **Restaurants** also line up on Adams Avenue; *Mamacita's* at 110 Depot St (☎963-6223) is best for Mexican food.

Pendleton

From La Grande, I-84 follows the Oregon Trail northwest to **PENDLETON**. Stetsons and pick-up trucks proliferate in this quintessential Western town, befitting its status as home of the immensely popular annual four-day **Pendleton Round-Up** in mid-September, which combines traditional rodeo with extravagant pageantry; tickets from the Round-Up Association, PO Box 609, Pendleton, OR 97801 ($6–15 per rodeo session; ☎276-2553, or 1-800/45-RODEO inside Oregon).

The hugely enjoyable **Pendleton Underground**, 370 SW First St (Mon–Sat 8am–5pm; $5), is basically a tour of the town's extensive network of subterranean passageways, used during Prohibition as saloons, card rooms and brothels, and as housing for the area's much-abused Chinese population.

The **Chamber of Commerce** in Pendleton is at 25 SE Dorion Ave (Mon–Fri 9am–5pm; ☎276-7411), a short walk from *Greyhound*, as is the basic *Longhorn Motel*, 411 SW Dorion Ave (☎276-7531; ①). For something more comfortable, sample the kitsch extravagance of the *Red Lion Inn*, a mile or so out of town beside I-84 at 304 SE Nye Ave (☎276-6111; ⑤). Book early at round-up time.

Joseph and the Wallowa Mountains

The **Wallowa Mountains**, reached by leaving I-84 at La Grande and heading east on Hwy-82, make up one of eastern Oregon's loveliest and least-discovered areas. Set at the northern tip of glacially carved Wallowa Lake, the mountains rearing behind, the tiny

---

ANTELOPE AND THE BHAGWAN

In 1981, followers of the Indian guru Bhagwan Shree Rajneesh bought a ranch near **ANTELOPE** (77 miles north of Bend), and converted it into an agricultural commune. Bhagwan's red-dressed followers were a middle-class and apparently idealistic lot. Their mish-mash of eastern philosophy and western therapies initially raised sympathetic interest across Oregon – and eyebrows in conservative Antelope. Despite the commune's agricultural success in this relatively depressed region, relations disintegrated fast, especially when Rajneeshis took over the town council – and "peace patrols" appeared, clutching semi-automatic weapons.

The Rajneeshis' hold on the community was fairly short-lived. Just before the local elections, they began to bus in street people from across the US and register them to vote. Many vagrants turned up in neighboring towns (without the promised ticket home), saying they'd been conned, drugged or both. Worse, an outbreak of salmonella poisoning turned out to have been a Rajneeshi strategy for laying low the voting opposition. When the law eventually moved in on the commune – by now an armed fortress – they discovered medical terrorism (more poisoning, the misdiagnosis of AIDS) had been used on Rajneeshis themselves in an internal power struggle. The culprits were jailed and commune members dispersed. The Bagwhan meanwhile, after a bungled attempt to flee the country, was deported to India (where he died soon afterwards), and his fleet of Rolls Royces sold off, along with the ranch. By 1986, the embattled Antelope was quiet again, and a plaque on a new memorial flagpole in the town center is dedicated to the triumph of the Antelope community over the "Rajneesh invasion".

town of **JOSEPH** is a perfect spot to spend the night. It has a handful of **motels**, but with just a little more money, the friendly *Bed, Bread and Trail* **B&B inn**, 700 S Main St (☎432-9765; ③), offers a big morning feed. The sad story of the Nez Percé Indians (see p.659) is detailed alongside an attic-like collection of pioneer bits and pieces at the small **Wallowa County Museum** on Joseph's Main St (officially daily in summer 10am–5pm, but in practice less often; donation requested).

A mile or so south of Joseph, mountain-rimmed **Wallowa Lake** is supposedly inhabited by an Indian version of the Loch Ness monster. At its far end, the **state park** has **camping**, and the **Wallowa Lake Tramway** cable-car sets off up into the mountains, where short trails lead to magnificent overlooks (summer daily 10am–4pm, May 16–June 7 weekends only; $10). Much of the mountain scenery behind Joseph belongs to the **Eagle Cap Wilderness** area, whose lakes, streams and peaks are accessible only along trails (no roads). Backcountry hiking and camping here really is remote – contact the **Forest Service station** by Hwy-82 in Enterprise (☎426-3151) for details.

Hells Canyon

East of Joseph, along the Idaho border, the Snake River has gouged the deepest canyon on the continent, a thousand feet deeper than the Grand Canyon, with the Seven Devils mountains rising behind and the river glimmering in its depths. **Hells Canyon** is what's known as a low-relief canyon, edged by a series of gradually ascending false peaks – so it doesn't have the overwhelming impact of the steep-walled Grand Canyon. Since time immemorial, this has been a winter sanctuary for wildlife and Indians, and stone tools and rock carvings have been found at old Nez Percé village sites. For more on the area, which extends into Idaho, see p.658.

The Nez Percé are long gone, but the canyon is now preserved as the **Hells Canyon National Recreation Area**: deer, otters, mink, black bears, mountain lions and elk live here, along with rattlesnakes and black widow spiders. Mechanical vehicles are banned above water-level in much of the canyon (boats along the Snake are allowed), so you can only explore on foot or horseback. Roads through the rest of the recreation area tend to be rough and slippery, and many are closed by snow for much of the year: check with the **rangers** in Enterprise (☎426-3151) or Baker (☎523-6391) before you set out.

Of the two ways to reach the canyon from Oregon, the first – from Joseph – follows Hwy-350 and then Hwys 4240/315, leading to the ultimate view at **Hat Point**, where there's a campground and look-out tower. The second approach is to the south end of the canyon, along Hwy-86 east from Baker City. On the way, tiny tin-roofed **HALFWAY** makes a good stop-off, with rooms at *Halfway Motel*, 170 S Main St (☎742-5722; ②), and the lovely, rural B&B *Clear Creek Farm* (☎742-2233/2238; call for directions from the town; ③).

Hwy-86 winds towards the canyon from Halfway, meeting the Snake River at Oxbow Dam, where a rough Forest Service road leads on to Hells Canyon Dam, the launching-point for **jet boat** and **raft trips** through the canyon. *Hells Canyon Adventures Inc* (☎1-800/422-3568) run sightseeing tours in summer, costing from $30 per person. Skimming over whitewater rapids, the boats take you between the deceptively low, bare hills, past rocks faintly colored with ancient Indian rock carvings, to an old pioneer homestead. They also operate a "drop-off" service, taking you to hiking trails along the canyon and picking you up either later in the day or the week (fee from $25 per person).

CHAPTER FIFTEEN

ALASKA

No other region in North America possesses the mythical aura of **ALASKA**; the name itself – a derivation of Alayeska, an Athabascan word meaning "great land of the west" – fires the imagination of many a traveller. Few who see this land of gargantuan ice fields, sweeping tundra, glacially excavated valleys, lush rain forests, deep fjords and active volcanoes leave disappointed. **Wildlife** may be under threat elsewhere, but here it is abundant, with grizzly bears standing twelve feet tall, moose stopping traffic in downtown Anchorage, wolves howling in the still of the night, bald eagles soaring above the trees and fifty-plus-pound salmon leaping upstream.

The sheer size of Alaska is hard to comprehend: America's **northernmost, westernmost** and, because the Aleutians stretch across the 180th meridian, its **easternmost** state would, if superimposed onto the Lower 48 (the rest of the continental United States) stretch from the Atlantic to the Pacific. This vast expanse covers more than double the area of Texas, and its coastline is longer than the rest of the US combined. All but three of the nation's highest peaks are found within its boundaries and one glacier alone is larger than Switzerland.

A mere 570,000 people live in this huge state, of whom only one-fifth were actually born here. Forty percent live in Anchorage. As a rule of thumb, the more winters you have endured, the more Alaskan you are, and recent arrivals are known by the mildly abusive nickname of *cheechako*. Often referred to as the **"Last Frontier"**, Alaska in many ways mirrors the American West of the nineteenth century: an endless, undeveloped space in which to stake one's claim and set up a life without interference. Or at least that's how many Alaskans would like it to be. Throughout this century tens of thousands have been lured by the promise of wealth, first by gold and then by fishing, logging and, most recently, oil. However, Alaska's 86,000 **Native peoples**, who don't have the option of returning to the Lower 48 if things don't work out, have been left behind in the state's economic boom.

Travelling around Alaska still demands a spirit of adventure. You need to have an enthusiasm for striking out on your own, and to be prepared to rough it. If you plan to camp, you'll need the best possible gear. Binoculars are an absolute must, as, rather more mundanely, is bug spray; the **mosquito** is referred to as the "Alaska state bird", and only a repellent with 100 percent DEET keeps them off. On top of that, of course, there's the climate, though Alaska is far from the popular misconception of being one big icebox. While winter temperatures of -40°F in Fairbanks are pretty commonplace and northern towns like Barrow see no sunlight for 84 days each year, its most

---

ACCOMMODATION PRICE CODES

All accommodation prices in this book have been coded using the symbols below. Note that prices are for the least expensive double rooms in each establishment.
For a full explanation see p.35 in *Basics*.

①	up to $30	④	$60–80	⑦	$130–180
②	$30–45	⑤	$80–100	⑧	$180+
③	$45–60	⑥	$100–130		

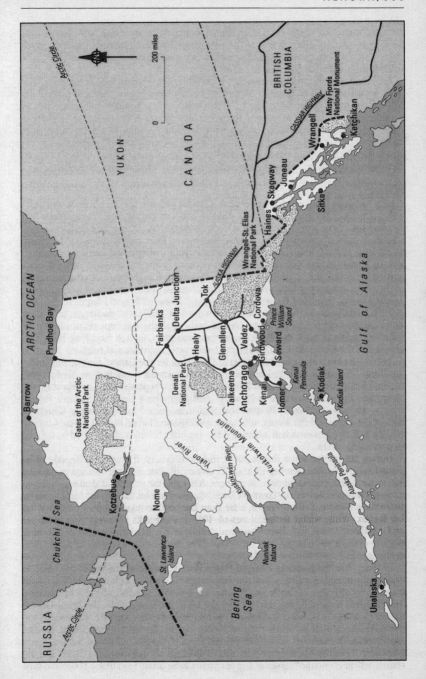

touristed areas, the southeast and the Kenai Peninsula, enjoy a maritime climate (45–65°F in summer) similar to that of the rest of the Pacific Northwest, meaning much more rain (in some towns 180-plus inches per year) than snow. Remarkably, the Interior in summer often gets as hot as 80°F.

Experiencing Alaska on a low budget is possible, but requires a lot of planning. The peak period of mid-June through August sees crazy room prices; May and particularly September, when tariffs are relaxed and the weather only slightly chillier, are just as good times to go. Except for around thirty **hostels**, mostly in the major towns, there is little budget **accommodation**; **transport**, thanks to the long distances, is far from cheap; and **eating and drinking** are about twenty percent more expensive than in the Lower 48. **Winter**, when hotels drop their prices by as much as half, is becoming an increasingly popular time to visit, particularly for the dazzling **aurora borealis**.

History

Alaska has been inhabited for longer than anywhere else in the Americas; it was here, across the land bridge that spanned what is now the Bering Sea, that humans first reached the "New World", possibly as early as 40,000 BC. These first settlers can be classified into four groups, which until whites arrived lived within well-defined regions. The **Aleut**, in the inhospitable Aleutian islands, built underground homes and hunted sea mammals such as walrus for food and clothing, while the nomadic **Athabascans** herded caribou in the Interior. The warrior **Tlingit** lived in the warmer coastal regions of the southeast, where food was plentiful, in contrast to the **Inuit** (also known as the **Eskimos**) who inhabited the northwestern coast, living off fish and larger marine life. Their famous **igloo** ice houses were seldom used as permanent dwellings, but rather as temporary lodging during hunts. Descendants of all these groups remain in Alaska today; a few live in much the same way as their ancestors, though most have been integrated into the European way through conquest, rape, marriage and religion.

In 1741, a Dutch explorer, **Vitus Bering**, working for the Czar of Russia, sailed into the Prince William Sound, and became the first Caucasian to set foot on Alaskan soil. He died before he could return to Russia, but his crew reported huge numbers of **sea otters** and **fur seals** – whose pelts were ideal for making hats – in Alaska's coastal waters. Russians, and later, Britons and Spaniards, joined in the ensuing slaughter, both of the otters and the Aleuts, who were enslaved and forced to hunt for the fur traders. By 1799 the Russians had decimated the sea otter colonies and pressed as far east as present-day Sitka.

During the 1860s, when Russia hit economic difficulty, it proposed the sale of its lands to America. On October 18 1867, Secretary of State William Seward purchased Alaska for $7,200,000 – less than 2¢ per acre. Although the unpopular deal was referred to as **"Seward's Folly"** or "Seward's Icebox", Alaska soon turned out to be a literal **gold mine**. Gold was discovered in 1880 at Juneau, eighteen years later near Nome on the Bering Strait, and subsequently outside Fairbanks in 1902. With logging companies and commercial fishing operations also descending upon Alaska, the government began to take a more active interest in its affairs. In 1912 the Territory of Alaska was set up, and in 1959 it became the 49th state.

In 1942, after the Japanese bombed Dutch Harbor and occupied two of the Aleutian islands, the huge US **military build-up** that was to last all through the Cold War began with the construction of the Alaska Highway to link the state with the rest of America. Alaska's next boom followed the discovery of **oil** at Prudhoe Bay on the Arctic Ocean, and fortune-seekers headed to Alaska in the mid-Seventies to construct and work on the **trans-Alaska pipeline** which runs to Valdez on the Prince William Sound. Today, despite price fluctuations, Alaska still derives about 85 percent of its wealth from oil and gas; indeed, each resident receives an annual dividend cheque of around $1000. But the state is still in economic transition and continues to be prone to extreme boom-and-bust cycles. The once lucrative fishing and lumber industries are fast giving way to tourism as the state's second most important source of income, and the ethical question of how best to use Alaskan lands in the future has led to bitter controversy.

Getting to Alaska

Alaska is a long way from the rest of the United States, and whichever way you get there is going to be **expensive**. Once you accept that, however, there is no question as to which is the most **enjoyable** method – the memorable sea trip on the Alaska Marine Highway.

By Air

Anchorage is no longer the major air crossroads it once was, but it's still easy to **fly** to Alaska. It is, however, very expensive. Most but not all flights from the Lower 48 are routed through Seattle. The best service from the West Coast is operated by *Alaska Airlines*, whose money-saving package enables you to fly to towns like Juneau, Sitka, Cordova and Fairbanks at little extra cost. Round-trip fares from Seattle are around $450.

By Sea – The Alaska Marine Highway

The ferries of the state-run *Alaska Marine Highway* cover many areas otherwise only reachable by air, operating two separate and unconnected systems. The most popular route, in the southeast, runs for more than a thousand miles from Bellingham, WA, just north of Seattle, through a wonderland of pristine waters, towering glaciers and untouched forests to Skagway at the top of the **Inside Passage**. Stops on the principal route are Ketchikan, Wrangell, Petersburg, Juneau, Haines and Skagway, though many other communities, including Sitka, are served by smaller ferries in the fleet. The whole trip takes two and a half days and costs $245 for walk-on passengers, plus $656 for a small car. It is possible to sleep – and even to pitch a tent – on the "solarium", a covered, heated, upper deck. The **Southwest** ferry system, which charges slightly higher fares, connects the Kenai Peninsula and the Prince William Sound to the Aleutians.

For information on either route, contact the **Alaska Marine Highway**, PO Box R, Juneau, AK 99811 (☎1-800/642-0066 or 465-3941). Book ahead in summer; standby space is available, but such passengers risk being off-loaded at each port of call.

By Road

For many people, the drive up to Alaska through Canada is one of the major highlights of a visit to the state. Originally built by the military in just eight months, the **Alaska Highway**, which can be accessed from Washington, Idaho and Montana, used to consist of 1520 fearsome miles of dirt, gravel, steep descents and thick mud. These days all but a small section of the route is paved, with sufficient service stations, campgrounds and hotels along the way, but it remains as beautiful as ever, and still demands a spirit of adventure from drivers who attempt it.

The unwieldy *Milepost* (*Vernon Publications*; $17.95), provides mile-by-mile information on the Alaska Highway and all roads within Alaska, but almost exclusively plugs its advertisers – unless you're travelling the Alaska Highway, it's a rather bulky luxury.

No direct **buses** run to Alaska, though for around $350 total you can hop on a *Greyhound* in Seattle, and after a few transfers, reach Whitehorse in the Yukon, from where local companies such as *Alaska Direct* and the pricier *Alaskon Express* continue to Haines or Skagway in the southeast, or on the longer haul to Fairbanks and Anchorage. *Green Tortoise* (see p.24) run trips each summer from San Francisco.

The **area code** for the entire state of Alaska is ☎907.

Getting Around Alaska

Getting around Alaska on the cheap can be tough; **public transportion** is limited, and many areas are only accessible by boat or plane, which is quick and convenient, but invariably pricey. **Hitching** is hard work, simply due to the lack of traffic, but, with enough time, it can be done, and is more acceptable, and safer, here than elsewhere.

Anchorage is very much the hub of Alaska; from it, **buses** run to Haines and Skagway via Whitehorse, Yukon (see above), Denali, Fairbanks, Valdez (*Caribou Express*) and the Kenai Peninsula (*Seward & Homer Bus Lines*). The "big city" is also the base for tour operators such as *Gray Line of Alaska*.

The **Alaska Railroad**, constructed between 1915 and 1923 to transport supplies to the mines in the Interior, runs nearly five hundred miles north from Seward on the Kenai Peninsula to Fairbanks. Another service from Anchorage to Whittier connects with ferries to Valdez.

Visitors intending to **drive** around Alaska should bring an **emergency kit**, particularly essential in winter, as traffic can be sparse even on major routes. Conditions on the roads can change rapidly – for information, call ☎243-7675. Avalanches are a serious threat, as are collisions with wild animals, especially moose. Drivers on gravel roads are advised to keep speeds low, as rocks often fly up to shatter windscreens.

Travel by **plane** is not always more expensive than other methods, especially if you can map out your itinerary in advance with the state's largest operator *Alaska Airlines* who fly to most major communities and use subcontractors such as *ERA Aviation* to get to Bush towns in the Interior, or *LAB* to communities in the southeast. The other major inter state carrier, *Mark Air*, offers particularly good connections to the west. For short-haul flights, **chartering a plane** can be an inexpensive alternative for groups. A

ALASKAN TRANSPORTATION AND TOUR OPERATORS

Air Excursions	☎907/789-5591	Kenai Coastal Tours	☎1-800/770-9119
Alaska Airlines	☎1-800/426-0333	Ketchikan Air	☎907/225-6608
Alaska Car Rental	☎907/225-5000	LAB	☎907/766-2222
Alaska Direct Bus Line	☎1-800/770-6652	Mark Air	☎1-800/426-6784
Alaska Marine Highway	☎1-800/642-0066	Mt McKinley Alaska Tours	☎1-800/327-7651
Alaska Railroad	☎1-800/544-0522	Northern Alaska	☎907/454-8600
Alaskon Express	☎1-800/544-2206	Tour Company	
Backcountry Connections	☎1-800/478-5292	Princess Tours	☎907/276-7711
Caribou Express	☎907/278-5776	Seward & Homer	☎907/278-0800
Central Charters	☎1-800/478-7847	Bus Lines	
Denali Air	☎907/683-2261	Southcentral Air	☎907/235-6172
Denali Express	☎907/274-8539	Taquan Air	☎1-800/348-1330
ERA Aviation	☎1-800/843-1947	Wrangell Mountain Air	☎1-800/478-1160
Frontier Flying Service	☎907/474-0014	White Pass and	☎1-800/343-7373
Gray Line of Alaska	☎907/277-5581	Yukon Railway	☎1-800/478-7373
			in western Canada

lot of nonsense has been written about **bush planes**, which serve remote communities. Sure they can be scary at times: Alaskan weather does throw up problems and accidents can happen, but remember that the pilot wants to crash just as much as you do. A trip on a light aircraft can be the crowning glory of an Alaskan vacation.

The **Alaska Marine Highway** is a practical way to explore the southeast and the Prince William Sound/Kenai Peninsula. The only weak link in the setup is that there's no connecting service between the southeastern and southwestern systems; but if you take a short flight from Juneau to Cordova, you can get back on the ferry.

Southeast Alaska

Southeast Alaska – also known as the **Inside Passage** – may lack the vast openness of the Interior, but its narrow fjords, steep mountains, glaciers and thick conifer forests are awesome in their own right. All of its communities have their economic base in lumber, fishing and tourism and are set amid magnificent scenery. The state's southernmost town, **Ketchikan**, rich in Native heritage, makes a pretty introduction, tiny **Wrangell** emits a pioneer air, while **Petersburg** and **Sitka** retain the respective influence of Norway and Russia. Further north are swanky **Juneau**, the capital, **Haines**, with its mix of old-timers and recent arty recruits, and **Skagway**, at the northern end of the Inside Passage and thoroughly redolent of the old gold-mining days.

Although this six-hundred-mile panhandle, looking out toward over a thousand rugged islands, can take months to explore, it holds surprisingly few "sights". With the exception of the **Mendenhall Glacier**, many of the most beautiful spots are expensive jaunts – none more so than **Glacier Bay National Park**.

The region's first settlers, the **Tlingit** (*Clink-it*), were joined somewhat violently by Russian expansionists at the end of the eighteenth century. A steady stream of freelance profiteers, keen on tapping the region's gold, fur, fish and lumber soon followed, and today its small communities resound with tales of endurance, folly and cruelty.

By far the best way to travel is on **Marine Highway ferries**, though at some stage it's worth taking a **floatplane** ride. No roads connect the major towns; access by car is limited to Haines and Skagway, but only after long drives through British Columbia. For a true outdoor adventure, you can rent a **cabin** in the Tongass National Forest – which encompasses most of southeast Alaska – for around $20 per night; get details from the US Forest Service in Juneau (see p.889) or Ketchikan (see below).

Ketchikan

KETCHIKAN, the sole community on Revillagigedo Island, five hundred miles north of Bellingham, likes to be known as Alaska's "first city". As the first port of call for many cruise ships, its historic downtown, wedged between the waters of the Tongass Narrows and forested Deer Mountain, becomes saturated in summer with elderly tourists. But beyond the trinket shopping it can be a delight, built into steep hills and partly propped on wooden pilings, with boardwalks and wooden staircases common thoroughfares. High points include the totem poles dotted everywhere, and a chance to view bald eagles and, if you're daft enough, bears, in the town dump.

White settlers reached Ketchikan in the early 1880s. By 1886 the first of dozens of canneries had opened in what was soon to be the "salmon capital of the world". Tall forests of cedar, hemlock and spruce, which had provided timber for Tlingit homes and totems, also fed the town's sawmills. Though the timber and fishing industries have declined, the largest employer remains the massive pulp mill eight miles north.

The state's fourth largest city is a strong contender to be the nation's **wettest**; annual precipitation averages 165 inches. The tourist board shrugs it off as "liquid sunshine".

Arrival and Information

Alaska Marine Highway ferries (☎225-6181) dock two miles north of downtown on Tongass Highway; city buses stop here every hour until 6.45pm. The **airport**, served by *Alaska Airlines*, is a five-minute ferry ride ($4) across the Narrows. The **visitor center** stands downtown at 131 Front St (daily 8am–5pm; ☎225-6166). Close by, on Federal Street, is the **US Forest Service Information Center** (☎225-2148).

An incredible number of companies run excursions to the farther-flung sites: choose from expensive taxis, generic minibuses, kitsch trolleys or a luxury option in the shape of an immaculate red and white '55 Chevy (*Classic Tours*; from $35; ☎225-3091).

The prime way to see the area is by **floatplane**. *Ketchikan Air* and *Taquan Air* (both on Tongass Ave; see p.886), provide flight-seeing excursions and scheduled flights to Prince of Wales Island. *Southern Exposure*, 507 Stedman St (☎225-6044), rents kayaks and organizes paddling in the Narrows – six hours costs $60.

The Town

The bulk of Ketchikan's historic buildings lies on **Creek Street**, a rickety-looking board-walk along Ketchikan Creek. This was a red light district until 1953; now all the former houses of ill-repute are given over to gift shops and cafés. **Dolly's House**, 24 Creek St, once the home and workplace of Dolly Arthur, the town's most famous madam, is now a small museum stuffed with saucy memorabilia (hours vary; $2; ☎225-6329).

While most of the totem poles you see around town are replicas, the **Totem Heritage Center** on Deermount St exhibits 33 genuine nineteenth-century examples, recovered from abandoned Native villages (Mon–Sat 8am–5pm, Sun 9am–4pm; $2, free Sun noon–4pm). Fourteen of the best replica totem poles and a rebuilt tribal house stand in **Totem Bight State Park**, breathtakingly set on a forested strip of coast over-looking the Narrows, ten miles north of town on the Tongass Highway. The Tlingit-run **Saxman Totem Park**, three miles south of town, displays the world's largest standing collection of poles. Admission, including a chance to see sculptors at work, is free, but **guided tours** can help to decipher the images (daily 8.30am–5pm; $2).

A *Marine Highway* ferry (almost daily during summer) connects Ketchikan with **Prince of Wales Island**, less than fifty miles west, where 650 miles of dirt roads make for superb explorations by 4WD or mountain bike. There's nowhere to stay in **Hollis**, the ferry terminal, some forty miles east of the main town of **Craig**; if you don't have transportation, ask about the current status of the shuttle van service before setting off.

Misty Fjords National Monument

Twenty-two miles east of Ketchikan on the mainland, the awe-inspiring **Misty Fjords National Monument** consists of 2.3 million acres of deep fjords flanked by sheer 3000-feet glacially scoured walls topped by dense rain forest. As befits its name, the Monument is at its most atmospheric when swathed in low-lying mists. No roads lead here, but various operators run floatplane or boat trips. Fly-in/cruise-out tours with *Outdoor Alaska*, 215 Main St, Ketchikan (☎225-6044), cost $135; they also rent sea kayaks. Fourteen rustic cabins are rented by the Forest Service (☎225-2143; ①).

Ketchikan Accommodation

Hotels in Ketchikan vary widely, while *Ketchikan B&B* (☎225-8550) arranges accommodation from around $50. The closest **campground** to town is in the attractive Ward Lake Recreation Area, five miles northwest of the ferry terminal.

Alaska Rainforest Inn, 2311 Hemlock St (☎225-9500). A mile from the ferry terminal with bunks, or rooms which sleep four. Gets a bit rowdy sometimes. ① and ③.

Great Alaska Cedarworks B&B, 1527 Pond Reef Rd, AK 99901 (☎247-8287). Exceptional value; one of Alaska's very best B&Bs. Two beautiful self-contained waterside cabins, great hosts and fresh-baked breads. Unfortunately, it's eleven miles north of town and only really accessible by car. ③.

Ketchikan Youth Hostel (AYH), in the United Methodist Church, 400 Main St (☎225-3319). Very basic hostel with beds for $7, May–Sept only. ①.

The New York Hotel, 207 Stedman St (☎225-0246). Nicely restored eight-room hotel overlooking the small boat harbor. ⑤.

Eating and Drinking in Ketchikan

Inexpensive **food** in Ketchikan tends to be rather good. It's also renowned as a wild "party town", its bars teeming with commercial fishers and cannery workers eager to forget the sight and smell of raw fish.

Annabelle's Keg & Chowder House, 326 Front St (☎225-6009). Classy but relaxed atmosphere.

Chico's, 435 Dock St (☎225-2833). Great Mexican food and pizza, dinners starting at $8.50.

Diaz Chinese Restaurant, 335 Stedman St (☎225-2257). Good-value, tasty Filipino dishes.

Potlatch Bar, 126 Thomas St (☎225-4855). Lively, no-frills pub overlooking the small boat harbor.

Roller Bay Café, 1287 Tongass Ave (☎225-0696). Cocktails and seafood on the waterfront.

Wrangell and Petersburg

WRANGELL, the second stop on the Marine Highway System and with a population of just 2630 altogether quieter than Ketchikan, has a distinctly old-fashioned feel. Right in the busy harbor, accessible by a short boardwalk, **Chief Shakes Island** holds an excellent collection of totem poles and a replica tribal house filled with Tlingit blankets. The ancient rock carvings at **Petroglyph Beach**, a mile north of town on Evergreen Road, which date back as far as 7500 years, are only obscured during high tide.

Ferries dock right in town and usually stop over long enough to allow explorations of Chief Shakes Island. The nearest **campground** is at **City Park**, two miles south on Zimovia Highway. Of **motels** , the comfortable *Thunderbird* at 110 Front St (☎874-3322; ③), is the least expensive option. The First Presbyterian Church sometimes runs a summer-only **hostel** in town (☎874-3534; ①). The **visitor center** (☎874-3901) occupies the A-frame building on Outer Drive facing the harbor.

One of the highlights of an Inland Passage ferry ride is sitting up front watching the boat grope its way through the 46 tight turns of the 22-mile-long **Wrangell Narrows**. At times it feels like you can reach out and touch the steep-walled shore, and the whole deal is even more spectacular at night when the channel is floodlit. At the north end of the narrows, the pretty fishing town of **PETERSBURG** is invariably referred to as "Alaska's Little Norway". The best times to come are during the summer halibut season, when the largest fleet in the nation takes to sea, and the annual **Little Norway Festival** (held the weekend nearest Norwegian Independence Day, May 17). In the absence of budget **accommodation**, choices include the 24-room *Scandia House*, 110 N Nordic Drive (☎772-4281 or 1-800/722-5006; ④), and *Jewell's By The Sea B&B*, 806 Nordic Drive (☎772-3620; ④). As for **food**, *Harbor Lights Pizza*, 16 Sing Lee Alley (☎772-3424) and the nearby healthfood deli *Helse* (☎772-3444), come recommended. The **visitor center** is at First and Fram (Mon–Fri 9am–5pm; ☎772-3646).

Juneau

The sophisticated and vibrant city of **JUNEAU** is unlike any other state capital in the nation. Only accessible by sea or air, it is exceptionally picturesque, hard against the **Gastineau Channel**, with steep, narrow roads clawing up into the rain forested hills behind. Gold features heavily in its history. In 1880, two prospectors – one of them Joe Juneau – made **Alaska's first gold strike** in the rain forest along the banks of the Gastineau Channel. Named Gold Creek, the camp grew rapidly. Until the last mine was shut down in 1944, this was the world's largest producer of low-grade ore – all the flat land in Juneau, stretching from downtown to the airport is landfill from mine tailings.

Arrival, Information and City Transit

The **Marine Highway ferry terminal** (☎789-7453) is fourteen miles northwest of downtown at Auke Bay. Because the daily ferries often arrive at unearthly hours, getting into town can be a problem. A *Mendenhall Glacier Transport* bus (☎789-5460) usually leaves the terminal about fifteen minutes after the ferry arrives, dropping off at the airport and the downtown hotels ($5). Alternatively, you could walk a mile and a half along the road towards town and catch the *Capital Transit* (☎789-6901) bus #3 at Mendenhall Loop Road, which costs $1 and runs every hour from 7am. The ferry dock is not to be confused with the cruise-ship terminal, right downtown. Daily *Alaska* and *Delta* flights land at Juneau's **airport** (☎789-7281), nine miles out towards the ferry terminal; buses from the adjacent Nugget Mall go downtown.

The **Davis Log Cabin**, 134 Third St, carries information about Juneau and the surrounding area (June–Sept Mon–Fri 8am–5pm, Sat & Sun 10am–5pm; Oct–May Mon–Fri 8am–5pm; ☎586-2284), and there's an **information booth** at Marine Park on the waterfront, by the cruise-ship dock (May–Sept daily 9am–6pm).

Popular hikes from **Juneau** include the steep Perseverance Trail and, over the bridge on Douglas Island, the Treadwell Mine Historic Trail. *D M Bicycles* (☎586-2277), at 217 S Franklin St, rents out **mountain bikes** and offers customized area tours. Next door, *Alaska Discovery* (☎463-5560) organizes sea-kayaking trips amid wondrous scenery. *Alaska Rainforest Tours* (☎463-3466), run all manner of local and regional tours .

Downtown Juneau

From the kiosk in Marine Park, it takes an hour and a half to follow the self-guided Juneau walking tour. Many original buildings stand in the **South Franklin Street Historic District** – Juneau never suffered the fires that destroyed many other gold towns in Alaska. The onion-domed **St Nicholas Russian Orthodox Church**, on Fifth and Gold, contains icons and religious treasures, while the excellent **Alaska State Museum**, 395 Whittier St, covers Native culture, the Russian heritage and the first gold strikes. Its pride and joy is the log book in which Bering reported his first sighting of Alaska (Mon–Fri 9am–6pm, Sat & Sun 10am–6pm; $2). The smaller **City Museum** at Fourth and Main displays relics from the mining era (summer Mon–Fri 9am–5pm, Sat & Sun 11am–5pm; $1).

One of the best day trips out of Juneau is up the narrow, twisting **Tracy Arm Fjord**. Day-long boat trips cost $125; fly-in/cruise-out experiences cost $199. Many feel this to be a better deal than the Glacier Bay trip; book on ☎463-5510 or 1-800/451-5952.

Mendenhall Glacier Area

There are certainly bigger and more spectacular glaciers in Alaska, but the twelve–mile-long, one-and-a-half-mile-wide **Mendenhall Glacier**, thirteen miles from downtown, is easily the most accessible. Should your knowledge of cirques and striations be a little rusty, the **visitor center** (on a point this receding glacier occupied as recently as 1940) has all you need to know (daily 8.30am–6pm; ☎789-0097). Hiking trails include the **West Glacier Trail**, on which, with some caution, you can explore the ice caves.

Capital Transit buses leave for the Mendenhall hourly (Mon–Sat) from downtown; get off at Glacier Spur Road for the visitor center, or Montana Creek Road for the West Glacier trail. *Alaska Travel Adventures* run four-hour float trips on the Mendenhall River ($75; ☎789-0052); *Temsco Helicopters* land on the glacier itself ($135; ☎789-9501).

Accommodation

There are plenty of motels near downtown, though it's worth trying one of Juneau's many good **B&Bs**; the *Alaska B&B Association*, 3444 Nowell St (☎586-2959), reserves rooms for $50 and up. *Mendenhall Lake Campground*, accessible by buses #3 or #4 and a short hike, is spectacularly situated near the glacier, but gets cold even in summer.

Alaskan Hotel and Bar, 167 S Franklin St (☎586-1000 or 1-800/327-9374). Pleasant old hotel in the heart of downtown, with a fine bar. Twelve doubles with shared or private bath. ③.

Crondahl's B&B, 626 Fifth St (☎586-1464). Two rooms and a gourmet breakfast are on offer at this cosy home high on the hill in downtown Juneau. ③.

Driftwood Lodge Motel, 435 Willoughby Ave (☎586-2280). One block from the waterfront, with rooms including kitchenettes. Transportation to and from the airport and ferry terminal. ④.

Eagle's Nest B&B, N Douglas Hwy (☎586-6378). Spend a night with Higgins the mega-cool dachshund in this cosy retreat eight miles from town on Douglas Island. TV, VCR and a DIY breakfast. ④.

Juneau International AYH Hostel, 614 Harris St (☎586-9559). Clean and comfortable, in an old home near downtown, with dorm beds for $10. ①.

Pearson's Pond Luxury B&B, 4541 Sawa Circle (☎789-3772). Spacious modern home close to Mendenhall Glacier (and a bus stop). Self-serve breakfast, plus outdoor spa, bicycles, rowboat, VCR, computer, and discount excursions. Smoking is viewed as a heinous crime. ⑤.

Eating and Drinking

Downtown's excellent places to eat fill up very quick when cruise ships are in town.

Alaskan Hotel and Bar, 167 S Franklin St (☎586-1000). Great old bar, with occasional live music.

Armadillo Tex-Mex Cafe, 431 S Franklin St (☎586-1880). Huge plates of nachos start at $5.50, or try the Enchiladas Azteca, served with beans, rice and guacamole for $10.

Fiddlehead Restaurant and Bakery, 429 Willoughby Ave (☎586-3150). Known throughout the state for wholesome food. Their bread has become so popular they charge a dollar a slice, but don't let that put you off – most entrees are well under $10 and this is Juneau's finest place to eat.

Heritage Coffee and Café, 174 S Franklin St (☎586-1088). Excellent coffee, huge sandwiches.

Luna's, 210 Seward St (☎586-6990). The locals' favorite Italian restaurant. Great calzone.

Red Dog Saloon, S Franklin St (☎463-3658). Touristy bar opposite the cruise-ship terminal with a carefully fabricated olde worlde ambience. At night there's a much younger crowd and live music.

Glacier Bay National Park

When Capt George Vancouver sailed through Icy Strait in 1794, **Glacier Bay** was no more than a dent in the ice-packed coastline. Since then the Grand Pacific Glacier has receded 65 miles, to reveal a tranquil "land that time forgot" of deep fjords lined by rock walls and fed by fifteen other receding tidewater glaciers. The flora of the bay ranges from mature spruce forests to delicate plant life, while brown and black bear, moose, mountain goats, sea otters, humpback whales, porpoise, harbor seals and a colorful array of birds have made the area their home. Most if not all of them can be seen on a day cruise through Glacier Bay (the only way to access the area). The most spectacular moment comes when the boat, having negotiated its way through three miles of icebergs, comes face to face with the massive wall of the Grand Pacific Glacier.

The only way to get to Glacier Bay is to fly into **Gustavus Airport**. Local airlines make daily trips from Juneau for around $120 round-trip, and a little more expensively from Skagway and Haines. Larger *Alaska Airlines* planes also touch down once a day, from Juneau and Anchorage. If you **charter** a plane, *Air Excursions* (see p.886) do the round trip from Juneau for $220 for up to four people. Park buses from the airport to the park headquarters in Bartlett Cove cost $8; otherwise it's a lonesome ten-mile walk, while the cruise itself – the reason for coming here – costs $148.

Accommodation within the park ranges from a pleasant free campground, through $28 dorm beds (①) to tasteful rooms at the *Glacier Bay Lodge* (⑦). The concession company, *Glacier Bay Tours* (☎1-800/451-5952), handle bookings for park accommodation, cruises and also offer a bewildering number of packages. If you want a roof over your head the best bet lies in **GUSTAVUS**, a little hamlet occupying a sand spit that tapers its way into Icy Strait, where *A Puffin B&B* (☎697-2258 or 1-800/478-2258 in AK; ④), features half a dozen modern cabins in a forest clearing.

Sitka

Protected from the Pacific Ocean by dainty tree-blanketed islands, **SITKA** ranks as not just one of Alaska's prettiest towns, but also one of its most historic. Fuji-like **Mount Edgecumbe volcano** ascends menacingly across Sitka Sound from the spot where Russian colonists established a fort in 1799. Three years later Tlingit warriors killed virtually all the imperialist troops and their Aleut slaves, but were cannoned into submission in 1804, after which the Russians reconstructed the town, named it **Novaya Archangelsk** (New Archangel) and established it as capital of Alaska – a role it retained beyond the 1867 transfer of ownership to the US, until federal powers passed control to Juneau in 1906. Sitka today earns its keep from logging, commercial fishing and tourism; it's all too keen to pander to a taste for tacky Russianesque trivia (dancers, singers, people dressed in silly clothes, etc), but has a wealth of great outdoor opportunities. Sitka also commands a fine reputation for its festivals, especially the chamber-orientated **Summer Music Festival** each June. Redneck culture is celebrated in late June with the **All-Alaska Logging Championships**.

Arrival, Information and Getting Around

Marine Highway **ferries** pass through five times per week, dropping anchor seven miles out on Halibut Point Rd (☎747-3300). Old school buses operated by *Sitka Tours* (☎747-8443) will take you downtown for $3; they also do short "stopover tours" ($8). *Alaska Airlines* offer daily service on the Seattle–Juneau–Anchorage route from the **airport** on Japonski Island, just under two miles from downtown, across O'Connell Bridge. Round-trip tickets from Juneau cost under $100 if you include a Saturday night in your stay, and the flight in and out makes for spectacular sightseeing. The **CVB** office is in the Centennial Building, 330 Harbor Drive (daily 8am–5pm; ☎747-8279).

The Town

Getting a grasp of Sitka's Russian past doesn't take much time. The best place to start is from the vantage point of **Castle Hill**, a rocky knob where Alaska was officially transferred to the US on October 18, 1867; a plaque marks the spot. A two-minute stroll to the heart of downtown leads to **St Michael's Cathedral** on Lincoln Street. A fine piece of rural Russian church architecture, completed in 1848 and rebuilt after a disastrous fire in 1966, it displays priceless original icons (open when cruise ships are in town; $1). Free tours take in the restored chapel, school room and living quarters of the large mustard-colored **Russian Bishop's House**, by the harbor – a log structure that is the oldest standing building in Alaska (daily 8.30am–4.30pm).

Four blocks further along at 104 College Drive, the **Sheldon Jackson Museum** (summer daily 8am–5pm, otherwise Tues–Sat 10am–4pm; $2, free on Sat) houses the most extensive accumulation of Native artefacts in the state. All of the tools, utensils and craft objects from Aleut, Athabascan, Tlingit and especially Eskimo/Inuit peoples were collected by the Rev Dr Sheldon Jackson on his wide-ranging travels throughout Alaska as a missionary and the territory's first General Agent of Education.

At the end of Lincoln Street, in a verdant copse between ocean and creek, **Sitka National Historic Park** embraces both the town's Tlingit heritage and its days of Russian rule. When Tsarist troops attacked a Tlingit fort on this site in 1804, the Natives withheld bombardment for six days, but after running out of gunpowder, decided to exit the fort silently at night. The next day Russians stormed the stockades only to find them empty except for a few dead children, whom they alleged were murdered to accomplish the retreat in complete silence. Nothing remains of the fort, but the evocative air is enhanced by several vividly painted replica **totem poles**. A **visitor center** features good interpretive displays on what is commonly called the "Battle of Sitka", as well as hosting Native craft workshops (daily 8am–5pm; free).

Sitka's **trail system** ranges from shoreside strolls to a difficult switchback path up Mount Verstovia. Three of the nineteen Forest Service cabins (☎747-6671) in the area are reachable by trail, but are twenty to forty miles from town, making it easier to pedal there; mountain bike rental costs $20 per day from *J & D*, 203 Lincoln St (☎747-8279).

Accommodation

Sitka has southeast Alaska's best range of **accommodation**, with a fine hotel, two dorm-style lodgings and twenty B&Bs. If you're looking for something a bit different, *Burgess Bauder's Lighthouse* (☎747-3056; ⑦), accessible only by boat, sleeps eight. The rustic Starrigavan campground ($5), a mile north of the ferry is the best bet for campers.

Karras B&B, 203 Kogwanton St (☎747-3978). Stunning view of the sea, great breakfasts. ③.

Sheldon Jackson College, Lincoln St campus (☎747-5220). Immaculately clean $25 dorms. ①.

Sitka AYH Hostel, 303 Kimshan St (☎747-8356). Spartan $6 hostel, a mile from downtown. ①.

Sitka Hotel, 118 Lincoln St (☎747-6241). Safe, clean and basic rooms downtown. ③.

Sitka House B&B, 325 Seward St (☎747-4937). Two rooms in a beautiful downtown home with breakfasts, such as baked crab, in the patio. ③.

Westmark Shee Atika, 330 Seward St (☎747-6241 or 1-800/544-0970). Fine hotel tastefully decked out with Native paintings and trimmings. ⑥.

Eating

Sitka's **restaurants** aren't exactly going to set gourmet tongues wagging, though there are several unusual places to dine out. For evening drinks, join the crowds in the *Westmark Shee Atika*'s bar, or the down-to-earth *Pioneer Bar* on colorful Katlian St.

Back Door Café, behind *Old Harbor Books*, 201 Lincoln St (☎747-8856). Great coffee, plus tasty sandwiches and pastries. Daytime only.

Bayview Restaurant, upstairs at 407 Lincoln St (☎747-5440). Gourmet burgers, Russian special-ties, chowders and entrees including white salmon. Reasonably-priced. Open 7am–7.30pm.

Marina, 205 Harbor Drive (☎747-8840). Decent pizza and Mex food. Open until 11pm.

Nugget Restaurant, Sitka Airport Terminal (☎966-2480). One of the most popular airport cafés in North America. The pies – great creamy fruit-filled slabs of gastric ecstasy – are a must.

Sheldon Jackson College Cafeteria, Lincoln St (☎747-2506). All-you-can-eat buffet meals: break-fast (7–8am; $4.50), lunch (11.30am–1pm; $5.50), dinner (5–6.30pm; $8).

Haines

Although it lacks the fascinating history of other southeastern communities, **HAINES**, at the northern end of the Lynn Canal fjord on a peninsula between the Chilkat and the Chilkoot inlets, is a real "Alaskan experience". When the weather is clear, it is nothing short of spectacular, with snow-covered **Mount Ripinsky** rising up behind, the **Chilkoot and Chilkat mountains** hemming it in on either side, and glaciers spilling out into the deep fjord. The community itself is an interesting mix of unreconstructed rednecks and urban escapees from the Lower 48.

The Tlingit fished and traded here for years before 1881, when the first missionaries arrived and renamed the settlement for a prominent Presbyterian, Mrs F Haines. Today Haines survives on timber and fishing, and though few cruise ships stop here it's becoming a popular tourist spot, which in mid-August hosts the cookouts, crafts, pig-racing and log-rolling of the **Southeast Alaska Fair**. The fairgrounds also hold *Dalton City*, a small pioneer theme park notable only in that its buildings came from the movie sets of Jack London's *White Fang* which was filmed in the Haines area in 1989.

Arrival, Information and Getting Around

Haines' **Marine Highway terminal** (☎766-2111) is about four miles west of town. The *Haines Streetcar* shuttle service (☎766-2819; $6) meets all ferry arrivals, as do local taxis. *Alaska Direct* and *Alaskon Express* buses leaves Haines three times a week in the summer for the 150-mile trip to Haines Junction in Canada, Anchorage and Fairbanks. The fifteen-mile trip to Skagway on the *Haines Water Taxi* (359 miles by road) is more like a scenic cruise than a ferry ride ($29 round-trip, $19 one-way, bikes $5; ☎766-3395).

The **visitor center**, at Second and Willard (☎766-2234; ☎1-800/478-2268 in AK, BC & YK; ☎1-800/458-3579 in the US), has all kinds of maps and information.

The Town

Apart from its well-respected art galleries and craft shops, concentrated around the visitor center, downtown Haines holds little interest. Instead, an exciting agenda of outdoor pursuits makes it a must on an Inside Passage itinerary. Two great wild **state parks** – Chilkoot Lake and Chilkat – are a mere half-hour cycle ride to the north and south of town, respectively. Chilkat in particular has some great trails and vistas, while from town, well-tramped treks lead to the summits of Mount Riley, and the much more difficult Mount Ripinsky. Haines is also a popular starting point for **rafting trips**: *Chilkat Guides* (☎766-2491), on Beach Road below Fort Seward, organizes four-hour float trips ($70) down the Chilkat River (great for viewing eagles and other wildlife).

Each autumn, the world's largest gathering of **bald eagles** flocks to the banks of the Chilkat River to feed on an unusually late chum salmon run (delayed by a hot spring that keeps the river from freezing). By November up to four thousand of the rare birds – as many as two dozen in one tree – are gathered along a five-mile sand bar at the **Chilkat Bald Eagle Reserve**, nine miles north of town on the Haines Highway.

In response to the general lawlessness of the gold rush era, and territorial disputes with Canada, **Fort William H Seward** was established in Haines in 1903. Half a mile west of downtown, it now buzzes with fairgrounds, a reconstructed Totem Village as well as replicas of a Tlingit tribal house and a trapper's cabin. During the summer, the Chilkat Dancers perform in traditional costumes at the **Chilkat Center for the Arts**, in Fort Seward's recreational center ($7; ☎766-2160).

Accommodation

As well as the usual mid-range **accommodation**, Haines has several campgrounds, such as the spotless Haines Hitchup Park, half a mile west on Main (☎766-2882),and Portage Cove, on a great beach less than a mile from Fort Seward on S Front Street.

Bear Creek Camp and Hostel, two miles south on Small Tract Rd (☎766-2259). Utterly rustic lodgings; dorm beds ($12), four-person cabins ($30), including free pickup from the ferry. ①.

Hotel Haslingland and Officers Inn B&B, Fort Seward (☎766-2000; 1-800/478-2525 in US; 1-800/542-6363 in Canada). Choice of grand old hotel or B&B in the center of the old barracks. ④.

Mountain View Motel, Fort Seward (☎766-2900). Comfortable doubles. ④.

River House B&B, Mile 1 Mud Bay Rd (PO Box 1009, AK 99827; ☎766-2060). Beautiful large cottage, one mile south of town where the Chilkat River meets the sea. ⑤.

Eating and Drinking

Haines' most exciting **bars** and **restaurants** can be found in the Fort Seward area. In the evening, kayakers, cyclists and hikers frequent the friendly bar at the *Haslingland Hotel* (☎766-2000); locals stick to the more raucous joints downtown.

Bamboo Room, on Second near Main (☎766-9101). Breakfasts such as jalapeno-filled Spanish omelettes cost about $4. It's also a favorite late-night drinking hole for locals.

Chilkat Restaurant and Bakery, Fifth and Main (☎766-2920). Reasonably priced, freshly made breads, breakfasts and lunches.

Dejon Delights, Portage St, Fort Seward (☎766-2505). Take away the best smoked or pickled salmon in the state and fresh bread for the price of burger and fries.

Fort Chilkoot Potlatch, Parade Grounds, Fort Seward (☎766-2003). All-you-can-eat salmon bake on summer evenings between 5pm & 8pm.

Skagway

SKAGWAY, the northernmost stop on the Marine Highway, sprang up overnight in 1897, as a trading post serving **Klondike gold rush** pioneers about to set off on the five-hundred-mile ordeal. It was also the last stop before the harrowing White Pass Trail, known as the "Dead Horse Trail", on which over three thousand horses perished during the winter of 1897–98 from severe weather, rugged ground and exhaustion. Having grown from one cabin to a town of twenty thousand in three months, Skagway, rife with disease and desperado violence, was reported to be "hell on earth". It boasted over seventy bars and hundreds of prostitutes, and was controlled by organized criminals, including the notorious Jefferson Soapy Smith, renowned for cheating hapless prospectors out of their gold (see also p.605). One of his scams was to operate a bogus telegraph office through which he concocted false messages from loved ones in the Lower 48 urgently demanding money, which "Soapy", of course, took responsibility for sending. He finally met a nasty end in 1899 after a shoot-out with Frank Reid, head of a vigilante group.

By 1899, the gold rush was over, but the completion in 1900 of the **White Pass and Yukon Railway** from Skagway to Whitehorse, the Yukon capital, ensured Skagway's survival. The 712 residents have gone to great lengths to maintain the original appearance of their town, much of which lies in the **Klondike Gold Rush National Historic Park**, but the cynical visitor might say they've overdone it. Skagway's charm is also its curse, and in the summer it gets packed out, with as many as three cruise ships calling in each day. However, from mid-September to early May most places in town are closed, and it becomes far more sedate, indeed almost eerie.

Arrival, Information and Getting Around

Marine Highway ferries (☎983-2941) arrive daily a few minutes southwest of the main thoroughfare, Broadway Street. The train station (☎983-2217), a block off Broadway St on Second Ave, offers daily rail service to Whitehorse and the White Pass Summit. *Alaska Direct* buses travel daily in summer to Whitehorse, Yukon ($38), from where thrice weekly trips run to Anchorage ($145) and Fairbanks ($125); *Alaskon Express* offer a similar service from the *Westmark Inn* on Third Ave (☎983-2241). *Haines Water Taxi* ($29 round-trip, $18 one-way, bikes $5; ☎983-2083), is the easiest way to get to Haines.

Skagway is very compact, and most of the sights can be seen easily on foot. The National Park Service **visitor center**, between Second Ave and Broadway St, holds talks, leads walking tours, and has historical displays and an impressive movie about the gold rush, as well as maps and information on the Chilkoot Trail (daily June–Aug 8am–8pm, May & Sept 8am–6pm; ☎983-2921). Skagway's **visitor center** is in the Arctic Brotherhood Hall, detailed below (summer, Mon–Fri 9am–6pm; ☎983-2854).

The Town

The facade of the remarkable **Arctic Brotherhood Hall**, on Broadway St between Second and Third, built in 1899 by gold miners who paid their dues in nuggets, is decorated with over twenty thousand pieces of driftwood. You can see antiques from the gold rush days at the small **Trail of 98 Museum**, on Seventh Ave, just off Broadway St (daily 8am–8pm; $2). A block away, at the corner of Sixth and Broadway, the *Days of 98 Show* is a reasonably entertaining historical musical about Soapy Smith ($14).

About one and a half miles north of town, the **Gold Rush Cemetery** is the final resting place of many of the stampeders. Among them are Soapy Smith and Frank Reid, who according to his gravestone "gave his life for the honor of Skagway"; a local prostitute, on the other hand, is remembered for "giving her honor for the life of Skagway".

If you've had enough of Soapy and his cronies, you may feel like **hiking**; one of the best short trails leads from the cemetery to the three-hundred-foot-high Reid Falls. The useful *Skagway Trail Map*, available from the CVB, details other walks in the area including those in the Dewey Lakes system, which pass pretty subalpine lakes and tumbling waterfalls, and the more difficult scramble uphill to Denver Glacier. *Sockeye Cycles*, Fifth Ave off Broadway (☎983-2851) rent out well-maintained **mountain bikes**.

The lazy way to take in the scenery is on the **White Pass and Yukon Railway** (mid-May–late Sept; see p.886) which follows the gushing Skagway River upstream past waterfalls, ice-packed gorges and over a thousand-foot-high wooden trestle bridge, stopping at the Canadian border ($75) or on to Lake Bennett, BC ($105). It's not inexpensive, but there's no shortage of takers; if you decide to go, get there early and grab a seat on the left-hand side. The company also offers a through bus service to Whitehorse after a train ride to Fraser, BC ($99).

The Chilkoot Trail

Alaska's most famous and popular trail, the 33-mile **Chilkoot Trail**, is one huge "wilderness museum". Following the exact footsteps of the original Klondike prospectors, it is strewn with haunting reminders of the past, including old mining dredges and gold-rush ghost towns. Starting in **Dyea**, nine miles from Skagway, and ending in **Bennett** in Canada, the trail climbs through rainforest to tundra with fast-flowing streams and waterfalls in evidence for much of the way.

The three- to five-day hike can be strenuous, especially the final ascent up steep scree from Sheep Camp (1000ft) to Chilkoot Pass (3550ft). You must be self-sufficient for food, fuel and shelter, and be prepared for foul weather. Campgrounds line the trail, as well as emergency shelters with stoves and firewood. There are also ranger stations at Dyea, Sheep Camp and Lindeman City. Dyea is accessible by road, and the *White Pass and Yukon Railway* has a service for hikers returning to Skagway for $69.

Before setting off, you must register at the NPS visitor center at Second and Broadway, where rangers can provide information on weather conditions and current bus and train schedules for the trip back to Skagway. You must also make prior arrangements with Canadian customs; phone them on ☎403/821-4111.

Accommodation

In such a touristy little town, prices run a little higher, with places booked up in advance. There's a pleasantly secluded campground ($7) at Fourteenth and Broadway.

Golden North Hotel, Broadway St (☎983-2294). Skagway's most famous hotel, built in 1898. All rooms are decorated with gold-rush antiques and have large cast-iron bathtubs. ④.

Skagway International Hostel, Third and Main (☎983-2181). Homely and welcoming, one of the finest hostels in the state, despite its strict 10.30pm curfew. $10 per night. ①.

Skagway Inn B&B, Seventh and Broadway (☎983-2289). Turn-of-the-century ambience and fresh-baked breakfasts in one of Alaska's very best small inns, with very reasonable rates. ④.

Wind Valley Lodge, 22nd and State (☎983-2236). Clean, modern motel less than a mile from downtown. Lacks the charm of the *Golden North Hotel* or *Skagway Inn*, but a good option if they are full. ④.

Eating and Drinking

Most of Skagway's **bars** and its predominantly bland **restaurants**, lie in the touristy area on Broadway St between Second and Seventh. The best snacks, in the form of smoked salmon, are on offer at *Dejon Delights* next to the popcorn wagon on Broadway.

Dee's Restaurant, Second Ave, off Broadway (☎983-2200). Salmon and halibut bakes, burgers and decent salads, with indoor and outdoor seating.

Northern Lights, Broadway, between Fourth and Fifth avenues (☎983-2225). Good Italian food, with pizza from $10 and pasta from $8, in a pleasant setting.

Red Onion Saloon, Second and Broadway (☎983-2222). Best bar in town. Live music, excellent pizza, and Alaskan Amber on tap.

Sweet Tooth Café, Third and Broadway (☎983-2405). Skagway's top traditional American-style café, serving breakfast, burgers and ice cream.

Anchorage

Wedged between the two arms of the Upper Cook Inlet and the imposing Chugach Mountains to the east, **ANCHORAGE** is home to over forty percent of Alaska's population, and serves as the transportation center for the whole state. This sprawling conurbation on the edge of one of the world's great wildernesses often gets a bad press from those who live elsewhere in Alaska – many call it *Los Anchorage* – but it has its attractions, and with its beautiful setting can make a pleasant one- or two-day stopover.

By the time Captain James Cook came up what is now the Cook Inlet in 1778, in search of a Northwest Passage to the Atlantic, Russian fur-trappers had already started to settle the area, trading copper and iron for fish and furs with the Indians. Though Cook was sure that the inlet was not the Passage, he sent boats out in a southeasterly direction to investigate. When they were forced to turn back by the severe tides, Cook named this gloriously scenic stretch the **Turnagain Arm**.

Anchorage itself began life in 1915 as a small tent city for construction workers on the Alaska Railroad. During the Thirties, hopefuls fleeing the Depression came pouring in from the Lower 48, and World War II – and the construction of the Alaska Highway – further boosted the city's size and importance. The opening of the airport established Anchorage – equidistant between New York and Tokyo – as the "Crossroads of the World", and statehood in 1959 brought in yet more optimistic adventurers.

Arrival, Information and Getting Around

Anchorage International Airport lies seven miles west of town, served, in the early morning and late afternoon only, by the *People Mover* bus (see below). If you arrive at an inconvenient time you can take a taxi (around $15 to downtown) or a hotel courtesy van. The *Dynair Charter* shuttle service (☎243-3310) costs $6.50 to downtown. The train station is on the edge of town at 411 W First Ave.

Most of the major sights downtown are easily reached on foot, but the best way to get around is by bike. *Anchorage Coastal Bicycle Rentals*, 414 K St (☎279-1999) have good machines. *People Mover* buses cover the city and the surrounding area – known together as the "bowl" – between 5am and midnight, for a $1 flat fare. However, they can be very infrequent. Schedules cost $1 from the Transit Center office on Sixth and G (Mon–Fri 9am–5pm), or call *Rideline* on ☎343-6543. Numerous tours range from downtown trolley rides to flights to Nome; shop around before taking the plunge.

Information

The main information office downtown is the **Log Cabin Visitor Center**, at Fourth and F (daily May–Sept 7.30am–7pm, Oct–April 8.30am–6pm; ☎274-3531), which has details of a pleasant and easy self-guided downtown walking tour. For a recorded message detailing events in town, call the *All About Anchorage* hotline (☎276-3200).

Diagonally across the street from the Log Cabin, the **Alaska Public Lands Information Center** has natural history information, maps, and brochures. They help plan trips into the Interior, and make reservations both for accommodation and the shuttle bus to Denali National Park – important in summer (daily 9am–7pm; ☎271-2737).

The City

Travellers eager to rush off into the "real" Alaska tend to overlook cosmopolitan Anchorage – a blend of old and new, urban blight and rural parks, as a destination. There is, however, plenty to see in town, and it's worth spending some time here experiencing big-city Alaska, as uncompromisingly "real" as the rest of the state. The city is laid out on a grid; numbered avenues run east–west, lettered streets north–south.

The **Anchorage Museum of History and Art**, 121 W Seventh Ave, includes a massive oil painting of Mount McKinley by Sydney Laurence, and dioramas of Alaskan history (daily 9am–6pm; $4). **The Imaginarium**, 725 Fifth Ave, is exciting, especially for the young at heart, with hands-on displays to tell you whatever you need to know about glaciers, the Northern Lights, polar bears and the private life of the dopey-looking moose (Mon–Sat 11am–6pm; $5). At the **Alaska Experience Center**, Sixth and G, forty minutes of Alaska's best scenery, shot from choppers, planes, trains and rafts, is beamed onto a 180° wraparound screen ($6). The center's **Earthquake Theater** ($5) shows a sensible film on the 1964 disaster and then sets off your chair to simulate a 4.6 tremor (summer; daily 9am–9pm).

As well as some of the most garish T-shirt designs on the planet, Anchorage is also home to very good **shopping**. The not-for-profit gift store in the *Alaska Native Medical Center*, on Third Ave and Gambell St, has a fine selection of authentic native crafts for sale, including jackets and moccasins (Mon–Fri 10am–2pm). For a non-garish shirt, head for the gift shop in the *4th Avenue Theatre*, 630 W Fourth Ave.

Originally a firebreak for the town site, downtown's **Delaney Park**, running parallel to Ninth Avenue from A to P streets, also served as an airstrip and golf course. Today it's a popular spot to play baseball, tennis, soccer and basketball, or simply to hang out. West of the city the almost eerie tranquillity of **Earthquake Park**, at the end of Northern Lights Boulevard, offers restorative views of the mountains, and an interpretive display provides an inkling of the havoc wrought by the **earthquake** of Good Friday 1964, which devastated much of downtown, and at 9.2 on the Richter scale remains North America's strongest-ever **earthquake**.

Just fifteen minutes' drive north from Anchorage, the mountains and lakes of the 495,000-acre **Chugach State Park** make for great moose-spotting territory. Challenging trails traversing the park include an often treacherous scramble to the summit of the 4500-foot Flattop Mountain, a spectacular vantage point from which to view the city and Cook Inlet. Half-day rafting trips in the adjacent Eagle River Valley are operated by *Eagle River Raft Trips* ($40; ☎333-3001).

Accommodation

Inexpensive **accommodation** in Anchorage can be hard to find, especially in summer, and many places are reserved months in advance. Downtown, the hotels are nearly all prohibitively expensive from June to September, though at other times they reduce their price by as much as half. The most convenient campgrounds are *Lion's Campground*, half a mile south on Boniface Hwy from the Glenn Hwy and, a little further out, Centennial Park, five miles north on Glenn Hwy. Free B&B reservation services include *Stay With A Friend* (☎258-4036), *AAAB&B* (☎346-2533), and *Alaska Sourdough B&B Association* (☎563-6244).

Alaskan Samovar Inn, 720 Gambell St (☎277-1511). No-nonsense mid-priced motel. ④.

Anchorage Hotel, 330 E St (☎277-4483 or 1-800/544-0988). Small historic hotel that survived the earthquake. ⑦.

Anchorage International Hostel, 700 H St (☎276-3635). Welcoming, cosy, and very central, a block south of the Transit Center, the only gripes being the afternoon lockout and midnight curfew. Dorm beds are $10 for members, $13 for nonmembers – reserve well ahead in the summer. The managers also run a hostel at 2845 W 42nd St in the Spenard district (☎248-4691). ①.

Comfort Inn Heritage Suites, 111 W Warehouse Ave (☎277-6887). New hotel next to the train station and overlooking the combat fishing zone of Ship Creek. ⑥.

Inlet Inn, 539 H St (☎277-5541). Spotless small motel right downtown. ④.

Sixth and B B&B, 145 W Sixth Ave (☎279-5292). Downtown Thirties home. Free bicycles. ④.

Snowline B&B, 11101 Snowline Drive (☎346-1631). Tucked into a quiet hillside area, twenty minutes from downtown. Continental breakfast served on outside deck. ④.

Eating

Anchorage is home to countless fast-food joints and snack bars, with plenty of small, reasonably priced cafés downtown. The best of its **restaurants**, however, are along L Street overlooking the Inlet. Cheaper ethnic food is also excellent.

Cyrano's Bookstore and Café, 413 D St (☎274-2599). Sandwiches, soups, occasional live entertainment, free papers and taped classical music in a lively bookstore (open until 2am on Saturday).

Downtown Deli, 525 W Fourth Ave (☎274-0027). Old Anchorage institution; not particularly cheap for a deli (entrees start at $7), but serving bagels, pastrami and lox to rival New York's best.

Dynasty, 420 G St (☎279-4745). First-class mandarin and Szechuan dishes for around ten bucks.

Legal Pizza, 1034 W Fourth Ave (☎274-0686). Decent pizza and pasta, plus live acoustic acts.

Maharaja's, 328 G St (☎272-2233). Excellent Indian cuisine, with an all-you-can-eat lunch buffet, though quite pricey in the evening.

Simon and Seaforts, 420 L St (☎274-3502). One of the best of the mid-priced restaurants, with gorgeous views over the Inlet and wondrous seafood from around $15. Reservations recommended.

Thai Cuisine, 444 H St (☎277-8424). The best of Anchorage's many oriental restaurants.

Entertainment and Nightlife

Good bars abound in downtown Anchorage, and the atmosphere varies as much as the clientele. Late at night, the main drag of **Fourth Avenue** can seem like a surreal slalom course as you swerve to avoid the terminally drunk. The other sleazy area – **Spenard**, on Spenard Rd between Northern Lights Blvd and International Airport Rd – can be fun as long as you're careful, though new hotels in the locality mean more tourists are making tracks to the better bars and clubs. Women travellers may not find the "Bohemian" side of macho Anchorage quite as endearing as many locals seem to think it is, with numerous innocent-looking bars turning out to be strip joints.

Not much can lure Alaskans indoors during the summer, so there are few summer performances, but for the rest of the year, the *Center for Performing Arts* (☎263-2787) has a huge variety of shows, plays, opera and concerts. *Cyrano's Cinema*, part of the restaurant and bookstore at 413 D St (see above), shows foreign and classic movies ($4; ☎274-0064). A giant screen in the glorious Art Deco *4th Avenue Theatre*, 630 W Fourth Ave (free; ☎257-5650) shows Alaskana films throughout the day and a classic movie each night at 11pm.

Chilkoot Charlie's, 2435 Spenard Rd (☎272-1010). Anchorage's busiest bar; a huge, sawdust-on-the-floor, wild-time kind of place. Six bars, live music, and a diverse lot of customers. Standard bar food, and lunchtime specials. "We screw the other guy and pass the savings on to you!".

Darwin's Theory, 426 G St (☎277-5322). Good, friendly downtown bar with appealing prices.

Downbeat, 3230 Seward Hwy (☎274-2328). Students' hangout underneath a restaurant, with unusually good music for this part of the world.

Jens's, 36th Ave and Arctic St (☎561-5367). Trendy, arty café-bar, south of downtown.

South of Anchorage

All that stands on the original site of **GIRDWOOD**, 37 miles south of Anchorage and destroyed by the 1964 earthquake, is an ordinary strip mall. The village now lies two miles inland in the shade of the **Alyeska Ski Resort**, Alaska's largest winter sports complex and the lowest-elevation ski resort in the world – Mount Alyeska's 3160-foot summit rises from just 270 feet above sea level. Until 1993 *Alyeska* resembled one of the small municipal resorts in the Rockies, but a huge investment from its Japanese owners has given it many new downhill runs, a first-class hotel and an extensive night-skiing operation. In summer, this is prime mountain biking terrain, and *Alyeska*'s new aerial tram ($15) provides access to a stunning view of Turnagain Arm, and **hiking trails**.

Rooms and packages at the resort's superb *Prince Hotel* (☎783-2222; winter ⑨; summer ⑥), are complemented by assiduous service and half a dozen good restaurants. *Alyeska AYH Hostel*, right on Timberline and right again on Alpina (☎783-2099; ①), has six beds for $9 in the loft of a cozy lodge. The best inexpensive **food** is at the innocuous-looking *Lyon's Cafe and Bakery* (☎783-2000), on the strip mall next to *7-Eleven*. Locals salivate when they talk about the Cajun food at the *Double Musky Inn* (☎783-2822) on Crow Creek Rd; budget on $30 a head. *Max's Bar* next door is lively at night.

Eleven miles south of Girdwood, a five-mile road leads to **PORTAGE GLACIER**, popular with tour buses not as the Alaska's most stupendous glacier, but for its proximity to Anchorage. Frustratingly, you can't see the glacier from the parking lot; if you want to get face to face with it you'll have to pay *Gray Line* $20 for a place on a cruise boat. At the fascinating **visitor center** (May–Sept 9am–7pm; ☎783-2326), made memorable by its mock-up walk-through ice cave, an observation deck looks out onto iceberg-packed Portage Lake. Rangers lead hikes to search for tiny wriggly brown **ice worms** in the smaller Byron Glacier every Tuesday and Friday in summer at 7pm. Two USFS **campgrounds** ($6) can be found a mile from the visitor center.

The Kenai Peninsula

Beyond Portage, Seward Highway skirts the south shore of Turnagain Arm and enters the **Kenai Peninsula**, "Anchorage's playground". At over nine thousand square miles, the peninsula is larger than many states in the Lower 48, and offers an endless diversity of activities and scenery. Most of the major communities are accessible by public transportation, including **Homer**, at the end of the highway. Cruises leave this artsy little town to glorious **Kachemak Bay State Park**, while on the east coast, **Seward** is the base for boat trips into the inspirational **Kenai Fjords National Park**.

Throughout the peninsula, trails branch off all along the highway to provide excellent hiking in the **Kenai Mountains**; the four-day **Resurrection Trail** begins at the wonderful gold-mining village of **Hope**, and comes out on the Sterling Highway near the rafting center of **Cooper's Landing**.

Most Alaskans who come to the Kenai Peninsula do so to **fish**. Cast aside preconceptions of this as a tranquil activity – "combat fishing", when thousands of anglers stand elbow to elbow along the Kenai, Russian and Kasilof rivers, is intense stuff, and it takes strength and know-how to pull in a thirty-pound king salmon. **Campgrounds** along the rivers fill up fast, but in July and August hungry bears join in the fun and games, so that most people opt to stay elsewhere. Frequently changing regulations limit fishing; call the Department of Fish and Game in Juneau (☎344-0541) before you set out.

Seward

SEWARD, 127 miles south of Anchorage, sprang to life in 1903 after engineers declared this ice-free port the ideal starting point for railroad tracks to the Interior. Since then it has been an important freight terminal, but tourism – particularly cruises into **Kenai Fjords National Park** – is now its most conspicuous business.

Seward fronts onto a classic view of the Gulf of Alaska, and is ringed by glaciers and mountains. In 1909 two pioneers bet each other to run up and down 3022-foot **Mount Marathon**; this masochistic dare has developed into an annual Fourth of July race (current record 43 minutes 23 seconds). Most athletes accomplish the descent in ten minutes by launching themselves down the sleep slope on their butts. A good hiking trail leads to the top for a glorious view, but unlike the runners, you should allow on four hours to complete the trip. Other than that, Seward's main activities are enjoying the scenery, mingling in the busy small boat harbor, and drinking in the downtown bars.

Kenai Fjords National Park

Beginning just south of Seward, **KENAI FJORDS NATIONAL PARK** is a magnificent 670,000-acre region of peaks, glaciers and craggy coastline. Its towering mountains are mantled by the prodigious seven-hundred-square-mile Harding Icefield, whose retreating glaciers have cut out the dramatic fjords for which the park is named.

Eight tidewater glaciers "calve" icebergs into the sea with thunderous booms, and the fjords also hold a wealth of **marine wildlife** – sea otters, porpoises, harbor seals, stellar sea lions plus gray, humpback, killer and minke whales – as well as the **seabird rookeries** on the cliffs of the Chiswell Islands. The best of the full-day **cruises** from Seward – if marginally the most expensive – is conducted aboard the new boats of *Kenai Coastal Tours* ($99 including lunch; see p.886).

Exit Glacier, down a rough dirt road which starts at Mile 3.7 Seward Hwy, is the one section of the park you can see without spending lots of money. From the ranger station at the end of the track, a half-mile stroll leads to the still-active glacier, though if you want a more strenuous day you can walk a very steep, slippery three-mile trail to the edge of the Harding Icefield. The effort is rewarded with an adjective-defying vantage point out over isolated mountain peaks – **nunataks** – interrupting the almost completely flat virgin-white surface of the ice field.

The park's **visitor center**, in Seward's small boat harbor, offers maps, film shows and hiking details (summer daily 8am–7pm, winter Mon–Fri 8am–5pm; ☎224-3175).

Practicalities

Alaska Railroad trains wind their way through wild rocky terrain on a daily four-hour journey from Anchorage, arriving at the depot (☎224-5550) next to the tour boats. **Marine Highway ferries** between Valdez and Kodiak dock downtown (☎224-5485). *Seward & Homer Bus Lines* charge $32 for a one-way ride from Anchorage.

Seward's two hubs of activity, the small boat harbor and downtown, are joined by the mile-long Fourth Avenue; if you don't feel like walking, jump on the local **trolley** ($1; ☎224-3133) which also goes out as far as Exit Glacier Road. The main **visitor center** is at Mile 2, Seward Hwy (summer only, daily 8am–5pm; 224-8051). You can also get information at the old railroad car on Third and Jefferson, though opening times can be erratic. The US Forest Service office at Fourth and Jefferson (☎224-3374) provides details on trails, campsites and cabins in the Chugach National Forest.

A couple of old downtown **hotels** offer good value for money: the clean *New Seward Hotel*, 217 Fifth Ave (☎224-8001; ④), and the historic *Van Gilder Hotel*, 308 Adams St (☎224-3079; ④/⑤). Out on Exit Glacier Road, the thoroughly relaxing *Le Barn Appetite B&B* (☎224-8706), has rooms in a big rustic barn, and a superb café serving fresh crepes, quiches and deli sandwiches. The one **hostel** – the *Snow River AYH*, Box 425, Seward AK 99664 – is way out at Mile 16 Seward Highway and has no phone.

Cafés and **restaurants** in Seward are fairly reasonably priced. *Ray's Waterfront Bar and Grill*, by the harbor (☎224-3012), provides stunning views and big steak and seafood dinners for around $20 per person. *Breeze Inn* (☎224-5237), across the street, has tasty bar meals. Good food downtown can be found at the *Harbor Dinner Club* on Fifth Ave (☎224-3012), while *Niko's*, 133 Fourth Ave, do inexpensive burritos and pizza.

Homer

At the end of the Sterling Highway, **HOMER**, 226 miles from Anchorage, is the Kenai Peninsula's southernmost town to be accessible by road. It commands a truly magnificent setting, tucked beneath gently sloping verdant bluffs with a five-mile finger of land – **The Spit** – slinking out into the dark waters of Kachemak Bay, into which flow crystal-blue glaciers, framed by dense black forest. It's so appealing that you can forgive the tourist board for billing it the "Shangri-La of Alaska", while its activities and lively nightlife make this a place to scrap your itinerary and linger a few days.

Russians, drawn by the abundance of coal, were the first whites to reach the area, and by the mid-1800s, several American companies had followed suit. In 1896, **Homer Pennock**, a gold-seeker from Michigan (who dreamed of riding back home on a golden chariot), set up the community that still bears his name. For some years, every summer, young people from the Lower 48 have arrived here in droves to work on the halibut boats or in the cannery, though this tradition may disappear with the recent decline in the price and quantity of salmon in Alaska.

Homer's other main industry, **tourism**, is under no such threat. Due to its dramatic surroundings and "mild" winters (temperatures average 20–30° F), visitors flock to this pretty fishing village. The resident population, younger and more mixed than elsewhere in the state, support a thriving arts community.

Arrival, Information and Getting Around

The *Alaska Marine Highway* office (Mon–Fri 9am–1pm; ☎235-8849) stands at the end of the Spit; **ferries** usually go to to Seldovia, Kodiak and Seward, once a week and to the Aleutian Islands around eight times during the summer. *Seward & Homer Bus Lines* run a daily service from Anchorage via Kenai/Soldotna for under $70 round-trip. *ERA*, *Southcentral Air* and *Mark Air* operate regular flights to Anchorage for around $75 one-way, from the **airport** two miles east of town on Kachemak Way.

Although small, Homer is quite spread out, and lacks public transit. Most hotels, restaurants and shops are in town, while almost all of the tour operators can be found along the twee boardwalks of the Spit. Getting a ride between the two seldom poses a problem, and you can rent mountain bikes from *Quiet Sports*, 141 W Pioneer Ave (☎235-8620). The main **visitor center** is on the Spit (summer daily 9am–9pm; ☎235-5300). KBBI (890 AM) broadcast a "Bush Line", useful for offering or requesting rides.

The Town

The downtown **Pratt Museum**, 3779 Bartlett St, features high-quality works by local craftspeople, as well as Inuit and Indian artefacts, aquariums and historic Homer oddities (daily 10am–6pm; $3). Many of Homer's most popular activities, however, revolve around the **Spit**. A large proportion of the Alaskans who visit each summer come for the excellent **halibut fishing** in the "Halibut Capital of the World". A full day's excursion with any of dozens of charter companies costs from $125. If you don't mind joining the crowds, it's cheaper and simpler to visit the **Fishing Hole**, a tiny bight on the Spit, which is stocked with salmon and offers good fishing from mid-May to mid-September.

Skyline Drive, which runs along the top of a bluff above the town, offers glorious views of glaciers spilling into Kachemak Bay; the twenty-odd miles of the dead-end **East End Road** provide similarly good views.

Kachemak State Park

The prime tourist attraction in the Homer area is exploring the 250,000 acres of forested mountains, glaciers, pristine fjords and inlets that comprise **Kachemak Bay State Park**, directly across the bay from Homer. Bird species here include puffin, auklets, kittiwakes and storm petrels, and marine creatures such as seals, sea otters and whales are also plentiful. *Rainbow Tours* (☎235-7272) operate two-hour sightseeing cruises to **Gull Island** – a 15,000-strong rookery. However, a longer stay reaps its rewards. The area's best trails, most of them manageable in a day, originate from the gorgeous hamlet of **Halibut Cove**. The most-travelled route, up to **Grewingk Glacier**, is an easy three-and-a-half-mile trek above the spruce and cottonwood forest to the foot of the glacier, from where you get splendid views of the bay.

The *Danny J* ferry (☎235-7847) makes two daily trips to Halibut Cove, on the south shore of the bay, via Gull Island rookery, for around $35 round-trip, while *Central Charters* (see p.886) run several excursions. Pick up maps and information from the **Alaska National Marine Wildlife Refuge**, 202 Pioneer Ave in Homer (☎235-6546).

Accommodation

Homer's good-value **hotels** and **B&Bs** can be fully booked in midsummer; the visitor center can help. There's **camping** in town, across the bay, or on the Spit.

Driftwood Inn, 135 W Bunnel Ave (☎235-0019 or 1-800/478-8019). Homer's most pleasant motel, near downtown on the edge of the bay. Barbecue and shellfish cookouts, and a good bar opposite. ④.

Heritage Hotel, 147 E Pioneer Ave (☎235-7787 or 1-800/478-7789 in AK). Central log-built hotel; rooms without baths in the original wing, or in the extension with full facilities. ③/⑤.

Ocean Shores Motel, 3500 Crittenden Ave (☎235-7775). Attractive colony of lodges, cabins and huts spread over a four-acre seafront site, just off downtown. ③.

Pioneer B&B, 243 Pioneer Ave (☎235-5670). Central self-contained rooms, lots of amenities. ④.

Seaside Farm, 58335 East End Rd (☎235-7850). Lively atmosphere and a great place to meet back-packers. Clean dorms $12 a night, tent sites $6, with discount for long stays. You can also work off part of the cost by doing some work on the farm. Five miles out of town but lifts are no problem. ①.

Eating and Drinking

Downtown Homer offers some of the best meal deals for budget travellers in Alaska: all-you-can-eat specials are the order of the day. For nightlife, head for the colorful bars, or to the relaxed *Pier One Theatre* (☎235-7333), next to the fishing hole on the Spit (May–Sept only), where Tom Bodett, the voice behind those catchy *Motel 6* commercials, usually records his radio show once a week.

Café Cups, 162 W Pioneer Ave (☎235-8330). Good coffee and innovative cuisine.

Fresh Sourdough Express Bakery and Café, 1316 Ocean Drive (☎235-7571). Tasty breads and pastries, plus all-you-can-eat breakfast for $10.

Lands End Resort, at the end of the Spit (☎235-2500). Plush and pricey restaurant offering an absolutely wonderful view of the bay. Breakfast is a must.

Sawlty Dog Saloon, the Spit (☎235-9990). It's hard to miss this Homer landmark; a log-built bar with a lighthouse tower, at the end of the Spit. Rowdy, raucous and fun.

Smoky Bay Co-op Natural Food Store, Pioneer Ave and Bartlett St (☎235-7242). Wholefood shop and café with great lunches from $5.

Young's, 565 E Pioneer Ave (☎235-4002). One of the best and least expensive all-you-can-eat Chinese (with a Japanese twist) buffets that you're likely to find anywhere.

Kodiak Island

Known as the "Emerald Isle" for the thick spruce forests in the north and an interior carpeted by wild grasses studded with marshes, lumpy knolls and reeded lakes, **KODIAK ISLAND** offers some of Alaska's most uncommon and pleasing landscapes. The dominant landmass in a small Gulf of Alaska archipelago some hundred miles south of the Kenai Peninsula, this is the second largest island in the US (after Hawaii's Big Island). Despite its size, no point lies more than fifteen miles from the ocean.

The island is renowned as the home of the **Kodiak bear**, a sub-species of the brown/grizzly which weighs up to 1500 pounds. Streams chock full of spawning salmon allow these monsters to thrive in the **Kodiak National Wildlife Refuge**, covering the southwestern two-thirds of the island. Roughly ten bears inhabit each square mile around Red and Fraser Lakes, and bear-watching trips are big business. In addition to *Ursus*, the Emerald Isle provides favorable habitat for **bald eagles**, and as many as two million sea birds nest along the fjords, bights and bays. Accommodation in nine **wilderness cabins** ($20 a night), dotted throughout the island, is drawn by lottery each year; details from Kodiak NWR, 1390 Buskin River Rd, Kodiak AK 99615 (☎487-2600).

The **Japanese Current** sponsors a mild maritime climate along with plenty of rain and fog, creating poor flying conditions and the distinct possibility that your stay could be extended by a day or two. If you want to avoid peak season prices, May and June are notoriously wet but September weather is usually fairly reliable.

Kodiak

All but two thousand of the island's 15,000 human population live in and around its only major town, the likeable and busy fishing port of **KODIAK** on the northwestern tip. Before Russian explorers established a community here in 1792, Aleuts and Konyag had fished the area for millennia. After Alaska was transferred to the US, Kodiak survived as a center for trappers, whale-hunters and salmon-fishers, and in 1939 was just another sleepy Alaskan village when a massive war base was established and the population rocketed to around 50,000. However, most of Kodiak's wealth comes from fishing the rich waters of the Gulf, and the town maintains a fleet of over 2750 fishing vessels. Tourism definitely plays second fiddle; few cruise ships stop, but this bustling little town has a splendid range of activities, good B&Bs and a lively nightlife.

Arrival, Getting Around and Information

Marine Highway **ferries** on the Seward–Homer route dock once weekly at Center Ave and Marine Way downtown (☎486-3800), taking twelve hours from Homer. Both *Mark Air* and *ERA Aviation* operate daily 45-min flights from Anchorage (costing around $300 round-trip). *Airporter* vans (☎486-7583) take you the four miles to downtown for $5. *Kodiak Tours* (☎486-5989 or 486-6635) charge $10 for a two-hour "stopover" tour.

Except for Port Lions, which is served by ferry, the most practical way to explore the island is to **fly**; *Uyak Air*'s Kodiak trips(☎486-3407), which guarantee close-up views of bears or your money back, have never had to refund the $300-plus fee.

The helpful **visitor center** is next to the ferry dock at Center Ave and Marine Way (Mon–Fri 8.30am–5pm and when the ferry is in dock; ☎486-4782).

The Town and Around

Downtown Kodiak is usually lively, with plenty of comings and goings in the small boat harbor and adjacent bars and cafés on Marine Way. The small **Baranov Museum**, in an old Russian house opposite the dock, holds Aleut, Russian and American pioneer artefacts such as some impressive whale bones (summer Mon–Fri 10am–4pm, Sat & Sun noon–4pm; winter Mon–Fri 11am–3pm, Sat & Sun noon–3pm; $1).

Etched out of lush rain forest, less than four miles south, **Fort Abercrombie State Historical Park** is a great place to do some sea bird- and **whale-watching**, camp or take a shoreline hike: a meadow on the north end provides a dazzling blaze of color in summer. Other moderately easy **hiking trails** originating near town go to the top of Pillar Mountain and Termination Point. However most trails are unmaintained and can be confusing; get precise details from the visitor center or the rangers at Fort Abercrombie. The undulating and unpaved **Chiniak Highway** runs for 48 miles to Cape Greville and the Road's End Cafe, sweeping through tightly bunched spruce and passing many abandoned World War II defences plus prime bay vistas of Chiniak Bay.

The **Kodiak National Wildlife Refuge Visitor Center**, just past the airport at 1390 Buskin River Rd (Mon–Fri 8am–4.30pm, Sat & Sun noon–4.30pm; ☎487-2600), stocks a wealth of information on bears and the backcountry.

Accommodation

Most **lodging** in Kodiak is expensive, but the hotels and B&Bs are generally very good. The best place to **camp** is in Fort Abercrombie State Park, for $6.

Buskin River Inn, 1395 Airport Way (☎487-2700 or 1-800/544-2202). Good independent hotel next to the airport, four miles out. Excellent dining, a good bar and sightseeing packages. ⑤.

Kalsin Bay Inn, Mile 30 Chiniak Hwy (☎486-2659). Small rustic hotel, with a bar, restaurant and pebbly beach, thirty miles from downtown. Reservations advisable. ③.

Kodiak B&B, 308 Hope St (☎486-5367). Overlooking the harbor, with fresh-fish breakfasts. ④.

Shelikof Lodge, 211 Thorsheim Ave (☎486-4141). Basic but clean motel rooms downtown. Much better, and not that more expensive than the nearby *Kodiak Star*. ④.

Wintel's B&B, (☎486-6935). Kodiak's premier B&B. Big yet cosy home overlooking the channel, a 20-min walk from downtown. Complimentary fruit basket and a great breakfast. ④.

Eating and Drinking

Food in Kodiak is generally good, and not overpriced. Junk food addicts should be aware that the town has the only *McDonalds* to serve **"Salmon McNuggets"**. Cynics might like to know that they don't taste a lot different from the chicken variety.

Beryl's Sweet Shop, 202 Center Ave (☎486-3323). Known for its great shakes and ice cream, but also serves good stews, sandwiches and snacks.

Buskin River Inn Restaurant, 1395 Airport Way (☎487-2700). Where the locals go for top-class seafood and steak. Inventive dishes (average $15), big desserts and a long wine list.

Henry's Sports Bar & Café, Marine Way Mall (☎486-2625). Downtown entertainment hub, open from 11am until the fun runs out. Two other bars – the *Mecca* and the *Village* – also put on music.

King's Diner, 1941 Mill Bay Rd (☎486-4100). No-nonsense café popular with locals for its huge portions. Two miles south of downtown.

Road's End, Mile 42 Chiniak Hwy (☎486-2885). Great seafood and steak dinners, snacks and desserts right at the end of the road. Also has some rooms upstairs (③).

The Prince William Sound

Prince William Sound, a largely unspoiled wilderness of steep fjords and mountains, glaciers and rain forest, rests calmly at the head of the Gulf of Alaska. Sheltered by the Chugach Mountains in the north and east, and the Kenai Peninsula in the west, and with its sparkling blue waters populated by copious numbers of whales, porpoise, sea otters and seals, the Sound has a relatively low-key tourist industry. The only significant settlements, spectacular **Valdez**, at the end of the trans-Alaska oil pipeline, and **Cordova**, a modest and untouristy fishing community, are the respective bases from which to see the **Columbia** and **Childs glaciers**. Just behind the Chugach peaks, lies the vast and relatively untramped world of **Wrangell-St Elias National Park**.

The region's first settlers, the Chugach Eskimos, were edged out by the more aggressive Tlingit, who in turn were displaced first by Russian trappers in search of sea otter pelts, and then by American gold prospectors and fishers. The whole glorious show was very nearly spoiled for ever on Good Friday 1989, when the **Exxon Valdez** spilt its cargo of crude oil. Although the long-term effects have yet to be fully determined, the spill fortunately affected just twenty percent or so of the Prince William Sound, and so far as the tourist eye is concerned there's no visible damage.

Valdez

VALDEZ, 187 miles from Anchorage and the northernmost ice-free port in the Western hemisphere, lies at the head of a fjord that reaches inland twelve miles from Prince William Sound. Known as "Little Switzerland" for its stunning backdrop of steep mountains, glaciers, waterfalls and an annual snowfall of over five hundred inches, Valdez (pronounced *Valdeez*) offers great hiking, fishing and wildlife viewing.

The 1890s **gold rush** transformed Valdez from a remote whaling station into a flourishing settlement, when thousands of prospectors arrived to head up the Valdez Trail to the mines in the Yukon and Alaskan Interior. They arrived to find that no trail existed and that the roughly mapped-out "all-American route" crossed the deadly Valdez and Klutina glaciers. Only an estimated three hundred of the 3500 miners who set out completed the journey – many died from frostbite, exhaustion and falling into steep crevasses. The gold boom passed as miners found alternative routes, and Valdez came to depend on fish canneries, logging companies and occasional military use for its economic survival. Nature conspired to finish it off on Good Friday 1964: the epicenter of North America's largest **earthquake** (see p.898) was just 45 miles away. Shock waves turned the ground to quivering jelly, breaking roads, toppling buildings, and killing 33 residents. A tidal wave completed the devastation. However, the citizens of Valdez refused to be intimidated, and moved around sixty buildings to the more stable present site four miles away, where the "new" Valdez struggled on.

The town's fortunes rose again during the 1970s, when **oil** was found beneath Prudhoe Bay, and Valdez became the southern terminus of the 800-mile **trans-Alaska pipeline**, which carries one and a half million barrels of oil per day. Although winds and tides ensured that no oil from the *Exxon Valdez* made it into the port of Valdez, the spill ironically triggered an economic boom for the city as it was the most accessible site from which to direct the massive **cleanup**. The operation, which lasted into 1991, cost Exxon and the government over one hundred billion dollars. Eleven thousand workers in over one thousand boats and three hundred planes scoured the beaches.

Arrival and Information

One of the most exciting things about Valdez is getting here; both car and ferry rides are unforgettable. The turn-off at Glenallen takes you onto the scenic **Richardson Highway** and the remaining 115 miles hold totally epic scenery: restful alpine meadows, angry-looking waterfalls, mountain **glaciers** and the icy summit of **Thompson Pass**.

Caribou Express **buses** from Anchorage (daily in summer, otherwise Mon, Wed & Fri), charge $80 one-way. *Alaskon Express* ply the route four times a week in high season for $95, while *Gray Line*'s frequent cruise ship shuttles to the big city cost around $60 (☎835-2357). Many visitors arrive on the **Alaska Marine Highway** from either Whittier or Seward at the city dock at the end of Hazelet Ave (☎835-4436). If the weather is clear, the ride offers superb views of the Columbia Glacier. The **airport**, with two or three daily flights to Anchorage provided by *ERA/Alaska Airlines* and *Mark Air*, lies five miles north; **taxis** (☎835-2500) are the only way to get downtown.

The **visitor center**, at Chenega and Fairbanks, offers a left-luggage service (daily 8am–8pm; ☎835-2330 or 1-800/770-5954).

The Town

Detailed displays on the town's checkered history in the small but excellent **Valdez Museum**, 217 Egan Drive (summer daily 9am–7pm; $2), cover the gold rush, whaling, the earthquake and a rather cheeky account of the oil spill. In addition to the barbed comments about the success of the cleanup, look out for the chunk of the *Exxon Valdez* hull in which numerous serrations were cut to make souvenirs in the shape of the ill-fated tanker, and a vial of crude oil – "Do your part to help clean up the spillage!".

Although you only get to see what the company want you to, a nose around the **Alyeska pipeline terminal**, eight miles north, is recommended. Crude oil arrives at the terminal after an 800-mile, five-day journey through the 48-inch-diameter pipeline from Prudhoe Bay, to be stored in eighteen huge tanks before being loaded onto ships. Constructed at a cost of $1.4 billion, it's the largest and most expensive facility of its kind in the world. Free tours leave several times per day from the **visitor center** (☎835-2686) at the airport; *Gray Line* buses can bring you from downtown for around $10.

The Columbia Glacier

Over four miles wide at its face, and towering three hundred feet above the sea, **Columbia Glacier** is particularly spectacular when huge blocks of ice crash into the water. *Alaska Marine Highway* ferries represent the cheapest way to see this calving giant, but local cruise operators tread their way through an iceberg field to achieve a closer look. Experienced operators like *Stan Stephens* (☎835-4730 or 1-800/992-1297) point out such sights as Bligh Reef where the *Exxon Valdez* ran aground, as well as the channel the ship should have been on – there's quite a difference. Choose from an eight-hour cruise, which includes a salmon bake, for $92, and a six-hour cruise at $65.

Accommodation

Valdez has very little inexpensive **accommodation**, and what there is gets snapped up pretty quickly. A freephone outside the visitor center connects with some of the fifty-plus **B&Bs**, while *"One Call Does It All"* (☎835-4988 or 1-800/242-4988) or *PWS Central Reservations* (☎835-3717 or 1-800/425-2752) can book accommodation in advance. If you want to **camp**, the Valdez Glacier Campground, seven miles from town past the airport, is somewhat impractical for those without transport, while the small Bear Paw campground (☎835-2372), close to the ferry terminal, gets booked up very quickly.

Casa de La Bellezza B&B, 333 Oumalik St (☎835-4489). Comfortable oak-floored home with a grand view of the mountains from the rear deck. Alasko-Italian breakfast and evening snacks. ④.

Cooper's Cottage B&B, 325 Mendelta St (☎835-4810). Close to the *Casa*, also a few minutes' walk to the waterfront. Courtesy mountain bikes and continental breakfast. Strongly non-smoking. ④.

Downtown B&B, 113 Galena Drive (☎835-2791 or 1-800-478-2791). Don't be fooled by the name – it's more like a small motel – but it enjoys a good location, one block from the waterfront. ④.

Totem Inn, Richardson Hwy and Meals Ave (☎835-4443). Comfortable if unexciting hotel, costing a few dollars less than the others. A big log fire and a reasonably priced restaurant. ⑤.

Eating

Don't schedule a gourmet night out while in Valdez. Considering its size and wealth the town's dining options are disappointing.

Alaska Halibut House, Meals and Fairbanks (☎835-2788). Fast food, but for the most part, fresh (fried) local seafood: catch of the day and fries, $4. Also burgers and salad bar.

Mike's Pizza Palace, 210 N Harbor Drive (☎635-2368). Best place in town for steak, seafood and entrees with a Greek twist and pizza. Great view of the harbor from the bar.

Oscar's, N Harbor Drive (☎835-4700). Hybrid place next to Mike's, which can't seem to make up its mind whether it's a diner, fast-food-joint, coffeeshop or ice-cream parlor.

The Pipeline Club, at the *Valdez Motel*, 136 Egan Drive (☎835-4332). Reasonable steak and seafood dinners; Captain Hazelwood of the *Exxon Valdez* was drinking in the bar on the fateful night.

Cordova

Far quieter than Valdez, and only accessible by sea or air, **CORDOVA** is an unpretentious fishing community set in forests and mountains on the southeastern edge of the Sound. In 1906, the Irish engineer, **Michael J Heney** (who made a name for himself by building the White Pass and Yukon Railway over "impassable" terrain out of Skagway), chose Cordova as the port from which to ship the copper mined in Kennicott, a hundred miles northeast. The government labelled it a foolhardy idea (his proposed Copper River and Northwestern Railroad – the CR&NW– was ridiculed as "Can't Run & Never Will") and commissioned a syndicate headed by Guggenheim to lay tracks over an easier but longer route to Katalla, near Valdez. Heney, who had rejected Katalla as being prone to winter storms, and gambled on trying to cut a path through two active glaciers, was vindicated when a huge gale wrecked the Katalla pier. His crew won the race, but only after completing the elaborate **"Million Dollar Bridge"** across the glacier-walled Copper River in 1911.

Ironically after such effort, the mines became exhausted just 27 years later. Cordova shifted its dependency to fishing, but this means of livelihood was also dealt a potentially fatal blow in 1989 with the sinking of the *Exxon Valdez*. For the next two seasons, the community reeled from the effects of the **oil spill**. Fortunately, it now seems that most of the salmon and halibut have survived, though fishers still bear a grudge against the oil companies – just read their bumper stickers.

Today the "Million Dollar Bridge", heavily battered by the 1964 earthquake, cuts a lonely figure at the end of the Copper River Highway, a gravel road that traverses the wondrous **Copper River Delta**, a major homing ground for America's migratory birds. Right next to the bridge is the incredibly active **Childs Glacier**. The delta and glacier rank as two of Alaska's very best sights – relatively few tourists get to see them, but if current plans to overhaul the bridge and build a road over the old railroad tracks to Chitina are realized, you can be guaranteed that this desolate area will be mobbed out.

Arrival, Getting Around and Information

There is no road access to Cordova; **flights** land at the airport twelve miles from town on the Copper River Highway. *Alaska Airlines* offer services from Anchorage, Sitka and Juneau; *Mark Air Express* from Anchorage and Valdez. Fares are lowest if you include a Saturday in your stay. A bus between the airport and downtown costs $9 one-way.

Most people get to Cordova on the Alaska Marine Highway's MV Bartlett **ferry** which plies the Whittier–Valdez–Cordova route three times a week. A 6am arrival and a late-night departure means you can see everything including the delta and the Childs Glacier in a day, and save money by sleeping on the boat. The ferry dock lies a mile from downtown (☎424-7333).

The tiny **Chamber of Commerce** office on First St between Adams and Browning is open fairly irregular hours (☎424-7260); when it's shut, head for the museum (see below) which keeps a rack full of information.

The Town

There are few sights in untouristy Cordova; the **small boat harbor** is the core of the town's activity, particularly when the fleet is in, from May until September. The **Cordova Historical Museum** on First and Adams has quirky exhibits on local history, including the evolution of the little ice worm who lives in the glaciers, and the funky annual festival that celebrates its existence (Tues–Sat 1–5pm; free).

Copper River Delta

A superb 48-mile drive along the mostly unpaved Copper River Highway leads through the incredible wetlands of the **Copper River Delta**, a fascinating tapestry of marshes, sluggish streams, glacial sloughs and shallow ponds all backed by the heavy-shouldered Chugach Mountains. This is also one of the continent's best sites for bird-watching. Common mammals include moose, beaver and mountain goat, while bears can often be seen feasting upon berries or fishing out salmon in summer. In all, it's a wonderful – and tranquil – site for fishing, bird-watching, or **hiking** along many of the excellent trails such as the difficult trek up to Crater Lake.

A visit to Cordova simply has to incorporate a trip along the entire length of the Copper River Highway to **Childs Glacier**. By far the best way to experience it is in your own vehicle: *Imperial Car Hire* (Mon–Sat ☎424-5982; Sun ☎424-7440), rent out eight-seater minivans with unlimited mileage for $60, if picked up at the airport, or $70 from town. Alternatively, *Footloose Tours* (☎424-7175) run a five-hour narrated van ride through the delta to the glacier for $38 including lunch, and rent out **mountain bikes**. Both Chitina (☎424-3524) and Cordova (☎424-3289) **air services** can take you out to far-flung cabins or fishing holes.

Accommodation

Most of Cordova's **hotels** get fully booked in summer, but **B&Bs** are a good option. There are also **forest cabins** ($20 per night) throughout the Copper River Delta, administered by the Forest Service (☎424-7661). Official **campgrounds** line the beautiful Copper River Highway, but real back-to-nature types prefer "Hippy Cove", two miles north of town on Orca Road, where the seasonal workers hang out.

Alaskan Hotel and Bar, First St (☎424-3288). Clean simple rooms above a popular bar. Caters mostly for long stays; reserve ahead. ④.

Harborview B&B, Observation Ave (☎424-5356). Good range of big downtown rooms that come equipped with shower, TV, microwave, fridge and DIY breakfast. Well recommended. ③/④.

Oystercatcher B&B, Third St and Council Ave (☎424-5154). Old B&B with rooms and hearty cooked breakfasts. ③.

Reluctant Fisherman, 407 Railroad Ave (☎424-3272). Tastefully decorated rooms overlooking the small boat harbor. ⑤.

Eating and Nightlife

There are plenty of cheap places to eat in town, as well as, for such an isolated community, some fairly good ones. Cordova is pretty quiet at night, with bars catering mostly to locals. The bar in the *Alaskan Hotel* is a favorite, as is the pricier *Reluctant Fisherman* (see below). Cordova's annual **Iceworm Festival** in the first week of February is an excuse for much drinking and revelry.

Ambrosia Pizza, First and Council (☎424-7175). Cozy setting and huge portions of lasagne, ravioli and whopping pizzas.

Killer Whale Café, First St (☎424-7733). Popular backpackers' haunt over the *Orca Bookshop*, serving soup, sandwiches and muffins at reasonable prices, and with great views over the harbor.

Reluctant Fisherman, 407 Railroad Ave (☎424-7446). Great views and lunch specials (try Chef Ted's salmon chilli). The superb seafood in the evening is a bit more expensive but good.

Wrangell-St Elias National Park

As Denali becomes more crowded, a greater number of people are making the trip to more out-of-the way **Wrangell-St Elias National Park** in the extreme southeast corner of the Interior. Just over the (inaccessible) peaks from Valdez and Cordova, the park is where four of the continent's great mountain ranges – the Wrangell, St Elias, Chugach and Alaskan – cramp up against each other. Most of the eastern border is shared with the adjoining Kluane National Park in Canada. The usually unsensational-ist National Park Service literature breaks ranks by saying, "Incredible. You have to see Wrangell-St Elias . . . to believe it – and even then you won't be so sure".

Everything in Wrangell-St Elias is writ large: peak after peak (including nine of the sixteen highest in the US), glacier after enormous glacier, canyon after dizzying canyon – all laced together by braided rivers, massive moraines and idyllic lakes, with the volcanic monster of Mount Wrangell still steaming on in the background. Vegetation struggles to take hold in much of the park, though does enough to support mountain goats, Dall sheep, bears and moose throughout its environs, while the silty lowlands are traversed by three sizeable herd of caribou and numerous bison.

Wrangell-St Elias, created in 1980, is very much in the stage of development with a lot of the land still privately owned. The first whites in the area came in search of gold but instead hit upon one of the continent's richest copper deposits. The mines closed after thirty frantic years of production in 1938 and today **Kennicott**, with over thirty big disused buildings, looks like a ghost town, save for an elaborate tourist lodge. A local guide will take you on a ninety-minute tour of the buildings for $15.

McCarthy, the main social hub and base for outfitters, lies at the end of the entrance road. It's nothing more than a scattered little hamlet, though most visitors spend a good deal of time here. Wrangell-St Elias is a trail-less park so in theory you can head off near enough anywhere, but *St Elias Alpine Guides* (☎277-6867) offer a number of hikes, ice climbing, mountain bike rides, raft trips and even glacier skiing.

Practicalities

Getting here is half the fun. From Glenallen, travel 32 miles along the Edgerton Highway to Chitina, the start of the rough dirt McCarthy Road through the park. This 58-mile track along an old railway line (rail spikes still stick out so be wary of punctures), hemmed in by trees which obscure the beautiful scenery, takes at least three hours. Apart from negotiating the rickety bridge high over the Kuskulana river at mile 17, the drive is so tedious you start to look on it as some kind of fond achievement by the time you hit the Kennicott River. This is where you leave the car behind and cross the water on a hand-pulled tram – try to remember to bring gloves. From here a short walk up the hill brings you to the hamlet of McCarthy, from where a shuttle bus runs along the rough five-mile dirt road to Kennicott.

Hitching along the park road can be a hit-or-miss affair; if you haven't got a vehicle you take a *Backcountry Connections* van (see p.886; $60) from Glenallen, which is on the main Anchorage–Valdez bus route. Alternatively you can enjoy a great flight into McCarthy from Glenallen or Chitina with *Wrangell Mountain Air* (see p.886).

Due to their remoteness, neither McCarthy nor Kennicott are cheap **places to stay**. The only option for budget travellers is **camping**, which is free, but check current protocol on sites. The *Johnson Hotel/McCarthy Lodge* (☎333-5402; ⑤), evoking the atmosphere of its 1916 construction date, is very pleasant; the only other option, the *Kennecott Glacier Lodge* (☎1-800/478-2350; ⑦) is much fancier. Both offer more affordable shoulder season specials.

The park **visitor center** is just north of **Copper Center** at Mile 105.5 Old Richardson Hwy (June–early Sept daily 8am–6pm; otherwise Mon–Fri 8am–5pm; ☎822-5235).

INTERIOR ALASKA

Falling roughly within a triangle outlined by the Glenn, Parks and Alaska Highways, **Interior Alaska** cannot fail to live up to expectations of the Great Land. For the most part it's a rolling plateau in between the Alaska and Brooks ranges, crisscrossed by river valleys, punctuated by glaciers and with views of imposing peaks, including Mount McKinley, the nation's highest, ever present. People are hugely outnumbered by game: moose, Dall sheep, grizzly bears and herds of caribou sweep over seemingly endless swathes of taiga and tundra.

Tourists speeding north from Anchorage to Denali tend to overlook the magnificent glacially contorted **Mat-Su Valley**, which starts at Mile 35.3 of the Glenn Hwy, where the Parks Hwy shoots out west for seven miles to busy **Wasilla**; antiquated **Palmer** lies seven miles further north on the Glenn. Between the two, the scenic summer-only Fishhook–Willow Road runs high over 3886-foot **Hatcher Pass** through the Talkeetna Mountains, twisting and weaving for fifty mostly unpaved miles through high tundra, passing old mine workings and vast memorable vistas along the way.

The jewel of the Interior is **Denali National Park**, some one hundred miles south of **Fairbanks**, the jumping-off point for the roadless and even wilder **Alaskan Bush**. Weather can vary enormously from day to day with even more severe seasonal variations: in winter, temperatures can drop to -50°F for days at a time, while summer days reach a sweltering 90°F. However, the major problem during the warmer months is huge mosquitoes – with attitude. Don't leave without the insect repellent.

Talkeetna

At mile 98.7 on the Parks Highway comes the fourteen-mile turn-off to **TALKEETNA**, the center for climbers attempting **Mount McKinley**, and altogether a very pleasant little village. Its dirt roads, log cabins and small-town-Alaska feel, combined with an international flavor as mountaineers from all over the world gather to prepare for their assaults on McKinley, make for an unusual if not downright essential stop. Rumor has it that this eclectic hamlet was the model for Cicely in *Northern Exposure*, but to its credit Talkeetna doesn't use this as tour bus bait.

The major summer celebration – the **Moose Dropping Festival** – falls on the second weekend of July; little brown balls can be purchased (with a heavy coat of varnish), for use as earrings, necklaces and so on, throughout the town. In addition to these highly desirable lumps of Alaskana, the festival features dancing, drinking and a moose-dropping throwing competition.

Trains en route between Anchorage and Denali stop in the center of Talkeetna once a day. Hitching the fourteen miles to and from the Parks Highway rarely poses few problems. The **information booth** is infrequently staffed, but the people in the museum or the filling station should be able to help you out.

MOUNT MCKINLEY/DENALI

Long before whites reached Alaska, Athabascan Natives referred to **Mount McKinley** as **Denali**, "the Great One". Although an early adventurer renamed the mountain after the governor of Ohio who later became the 25th US president, Alaskans have never really taken to the name, and still refer to both the mountain and the park by their original title. Whatever you choose to call it, North America's tallest mountain rises from two-thousand-foot lowlands to a height of 20,320 feet, and on a clear day its white glow, in sharp contrast to the warm colors all around, makes for a transcendent experience.

The ice-covered giant dominates life in the village of **Talkeetna**, 153 road miles south of the park entrance, during the climbing season of mid-April to mid-July. Only 45 percent of the one thousand mountaineers who annually tackle McKinley, "the coldest mountain in the world" – and the highest, from base to peak (Everest et al start off from a high plateau) – succeed in the ascent, thanks largely to its extreme weather conditions. Fast-swirling ice storms can trap climbers for days, and almost every season sees at least one fatality: 1992 was one of the worst years on record with eleven fatalities.

Several companies based in Talkeetna will whisk you on a 120-mile, ninety-minute "Circle McKinley" tour over moose-grazing lowlands, past ugly moraines, alongside dazzlingly blue glaciers and (weather permitting) the 20,320-foot peak, for $150 or so. *K2 Aviation* (☎733-2291), the choice of most climbing expeditions, offers the widest range of options, including a glacier landing at base camp in planes fitted with skis.

Talkeetna teems with good **accommodation**. Dating back to 1917, the *Talkeetna Roadhouse* (☎733-1351; ③), bolsters its old-style atmosphere with some great home-cooking and neat, tidy rooms with shared baths. The *Swiss Alaskan Inn* (☎733-2424; ④) is the swish option, but good value, while excellent B&Bs serving huge morning meals include *River Beauty* (☎733-2741; ④), and *Belle's Cabin* (☎733-2414; ④). Perhaps the most salubrious dorm space in the state, the *K2 Bunkhouse* (☎733-2291; ①), lies off Main Street. Run by *K2 Aviation*, it costs $12 a night; priority is given to climbers so it's usually chock-full from April to mid-August. Good places to **eat** include the *McKinley Deli*, which serves good pizza, and *Latitude 62* (☎733-2262), for steak and seafood dinners; **drink** in the wonderfully ancient *Fairfield Inn* on Main Street (☎733-2423; ②).

Denali National Park

The six-million-acre wildlife reserve of **DENALI NATIONAL PARK**, 237 miles north of Anchorage, is named after the Athabascan word for its most famous denizen, **Mount McKinley**. However, the mountain is far from being the park's only attraction. In fact it's frequently surrounded by a thick blanket of cloud, and only around one quarter of visitors actually get to see the snow-covered massif. Don't let this put you off, as a ride through Denali on a shuttle bus guarantees a chance to glimpse a vast world of tundra and taiga, glaciers and U-shaped valleys, reflective lakes and other huge mountains in the Alaskan range. Best of all is the park's vast wildlife population – most visitors return with tales of sighting grizzlies, caribou, moose and Dall sheep.

Visiting Alaska without seeing Denali is unthinkable for most travellers, and therein lies the park's only problem. In the height of summer, the visitor center and the service hotels out on Parks Highway are clogged with RVs, tour buses, screaming brats and the like. Things pick up in the park itself, and backcountry hiking remains a wonderful lonesome experience, though it's probably best if you try to get here early in the season when there are less people and mosquitoes.

Getting There

Driving to the Denali Park entrance (Mile 237.3 Parks Hwy) takes about five hours from Anchorage, or three from Fairbanks. **Hitching** along the Parks Highway is quite easy, especially during the summer when there are more than twenty hours of daylight. Alternatively, the easy and comfortable trains of the **Alaska Railroad** leave Anchorage daily in summer at 8.30am; the trip to the station at Denali, one and a half miles inside the park entrance, takes around eight hours and costs $90 one-way. The 8.30am departure from Fairbanks arrives at 12.30pm ($50). It's also possible to buy a through ticket from Anchorage to Fairbanks, and stop off in the park along the way, for $140. The luxurious way to arrive is in one of the (expensive) glass-domed railroad cars operated from Anchorage by *Princess Tours* (see p.886), and *Gray Line*.

Alaska Direct Busline stops at Denali on the way between Anchorage and Fairbanks; fares from the two cities are $55 and $35 respectively. Several companies offer all-in sightseeing tours to the park: *Mt McKinley Alaska Tours* (see p.886) offer some of the best prices. *Denali Express* (see p.886) operate a van service to Denali, charging $85 from Anchorage, and an additional $25 to continue onto Fairbanks.

Sightseeing, Hiking and Other Activities

Bar a few tour companies and RVs with special permits, the only vehicles allowed on Denali's narrow unpaved 97-mile road are yellow **shuttle buses**, a policy that ensures that the native flora and fauna remain, for the most part, undisturbed. Travel on the buses is "free" once you pay a $3 park entrance fee which is good for a week, but, and it's a big but, you may have to wait up to three days to get on one. Tickets are available up to two days in advance from the **Visitors Access Center (VAC)**, just inside the park entrance (late May–mid-Sept daily 5.45am–8pm; ☎683-1266, or 452-PARK for recorded information). The VAC also stocks a wide range of literature, and each vistor receives a copy of the *Denali Alpenglow* paper; ranger-led activities include short hikes and the popular sled dog demonstration held daily at 10am, 2pm and 4pm.

Shuttle buses run to either the **Eielson Visitor Center** at mile 66 where rangers lead one-hour tundra tours each day at 1.30pm, or to the aptly named **Wonder Lake** at mile 84; round trips take around eight and ten hours respectively. You can of course jump off the bus at any point along the route for a hike and return to the road and flag down the next bus to the VAC. Though the shuttle bus drivers do not perform guided tours, with up to forty pairs of watchful eyes on board, you're almost guaranteed to see the big game; a recent park questionnaire revealed that 95 percent of visitors saw **bear**, **caribou** and **Dall sheep**, 82 percent **moose** and over one-fifth, **wolves**. Other regularly sighted creatures include porcupine, snowshoe hare and arctic foxes, while over 160 bird species populate the park.

Backcountry hiking represents the best way to appreciate Denali's scenery and its inhabitants. The park is divided into 43 zones and only a designated number of hikers are allowed into each section at a time. Free permits are available, one day in advance, from the VAC's Backcountry Desk (daily 8am–8pm), who will also issue you with bear-resistant food containers. The idea is to disassociate human smells and food, thus sparing bears from becoming dependent on hikers, and hikers from becoming food for bears. It's also more than a good idea to view the five backcountry simulator programmes in the VAC before you set out across fast-flowing rivers and within sniffing distance of the grizzlies. Special camper buses – reserved for those with campground or backcountry permits – head into the park; riders are free to get off in their assigned section and start hiking. There are no trails across the tundra; just choose a good landmark and head towards it. It's not a bad idea to reconnoitre the park on a full-day bus trip in order to choose where you might like to hike on subsequent days. If there's room, buses also carry bikes; cyclists can be dropped off wherever they like, but are obliged to keep to the roads.

Just outside the park entrance, several **rafting** companies take two-hour trips down the Nenana River: all offer a gentle "scenic float", and an eleven-mile "Canyon Run" through Class III and IV rapids. *Denali Raft Adventures* (☎683-2234) usually offer the best prices; around $38 a trip. For close-up views of Mount McKinley, **flight-seeing** tours cost about $120 per hour. *Denali Air* (see p.886) have an office at the Denali National Park Hotel, though a better perspective is achieved by taking a flight from Talkeetna (see p.911).

In **winter**, Denali transforms itself into a ghostly snow-covered world. Motorized vehicles are banned and transport, even for park personnel is by snowshoe, skis or dog sled in temperatures often below –40°F.

Accommodation

The only **hotel** inside the park – the *Denali Park* – is usually booked up well in advance. Most unimaginative souls head for the busy summer-only gaggle of hotels and cabins two miles north of the park entrance at Mile 239 Parks Hwy. You can do better than this: ten miles further up the road the little coal-mining town of **HEALY** boasts a number of good **B&Bs** and a roadhouse-style hotel. If you get horribly stuck try *Denali Hotel and B&B Hotline* (☎1-800/345-6020 or 683-1422 locally).

Camping is the best way to experience Denali up close, with most of the park's eight campgrounds open from May through September. The best sites are at **Wonder Lake**, where on a good day McKinley is reflected in the water; failing that, **Igloo Creek** is good for spotting Dall sheep. Try to book at one of the Alaska Public Lands Information Centers (APLIC) in Tok, Anchorage or Fairbanks; they accept reservations up to three weeks in advance and will also keep you a place on one of the special buses reserved for campers. If you fail to do so, you risk turning up in Denali and finding all buses and campgrounds booked for at least a day, meaning an expensive and irritating time in the parasitic little seasonal town outside the park. Otherwise, all sites (except Morino where you can self-register) are bookable at the main visitor center, though you may have to wait for up to three days to get a spot.

The closest private campground outside park boundaries is *Lynx Creek* (☎683-1240), in the noisy hubbub of shops and motels, two miles north of the park entrance at Mile 238.7 Parks Hwy; *Denali Grizzly Bear Cabins and Campground* (☎683-2696) enjoys a more pleasing location, south of the park at Mile 231.1.

Denali Grizzly Bear Cabins, Mile 231 Parks Hwy (☎683-2696). Rustic and tent cabins overlooking the Nenana River. Basic models come without bedding, others have heat and sheets. ①–④.

Denali Hostel, Otto Lake Rd (☎683-1295). Nice enough hostel some ten miles north of the park, but the $24 fee sticks in the throat. ①.

Denali Park Hotel, opposite the train station (☎276-7234). The only hotel inside the park. Open mid-May to early Sept; reservations essential. The rooms are pretty standard, but above all you're paying for convenience. The operators, *ARA Services*, offer two nights for the price of one before mid-June and also run the similarly priced *McKinley Village Lodge*, Mile 224 Parks Hwy along with the more expensive *McKinley Chalet Lodge*, Mile 239 Parks Hwy. ⑥.

Dome Home B&B, just off Mile 248.8 Parks Hwy, Healy (☎683-1239). Four-level geodesic dome with good rooms and big "Alaskan" breakfast. ④.

Happy Wanderer Hostel, Mile 239 Parks Hwy (☎683-1295). Eight beds with kitchen facilities in a mobile home. Very basic, but close to the park. $17 a night. ①.

Healy Heights B&B, Mile 248 Parks Hwy, Healy (☎683-2639). Very comfortable rustic home. Hearty breakfast and very informative owners. ④.

Historic Healy Hotel, Mile 248.8 Parks Hwy, Healy (☎683-2242). Nice, clean simple rooms in an old railroad employees' hotel. ⑤.

McKinley–Denali Cabins, Mile 239 Parks Hwy (☎683-2733). Inexpensive heated canvas cabins in the hectic touristy jumble two miles north of the park entrance. ③.

Fairbanks

FAIRBANKS, 358 miles north of Anchorage, is at the end of the Alaska Highway route from Canada and definitely at the end of the road for most tourists. Its central location makes it the focal point for the tiny villages scattered around the surrounding wilderness, and a staging post for North Slope villages such as **Barrow** and the oil community of **Prudhoe Bay**. These northern areas are accessible by air, and the **Dalton Highway**, also known as the Haul Road in honor of its fast, stop-at-nothing trucks.

The town was founded accidentally when, in 1901, a steamship carrying E T Barnette, a merchant with all his wares on board, ran aground in the shallows of the Chena River. Unable to transport the supplies he was carrying, Barnette set up shop in the wilderness and catered to the few trappers and prospectors trying their luck in the area. The following year, with the beginnings of the **gold rush**, a tent city sprang up on the site, and Barnette made a mint.

In 1908, at the height of the gold stampede, Fairbanks had a population of 18,500. Due to the difficulty in retrieving gold from the frozen bedrock, most independent miners gave up, and by 1920 the population had dwindled to only 1100. The community sputtered along until World War II when several huge **military bases** were built to thwart possible Japanese attacks. Many bases remained after the war (and still do today), and the town received another major boost in the mid-Seventies when it became the transport center for the **trans-Alaska oil pipeline** project: construction and other oil-related activities brought a rush of workers seeking wages of up to $1500 per week and the population reached an all-time high. The city's economy dropped dramatically with the oil crash, and unemployment hit twenty percent before government spending put the city back on track.

Fairbanks may be flat and somewhat bland, but it's a good base for exploring a hinterland that includes gold-mining areas, hot springs and bush communities, and is surrounded by beautifully wooded rolling hills, accented by the distant Alaskan and Brooks ranges. Tourism is becoming an increasingly important earner. The spectacular **aurora borealis** is a major winter attraction, as is the **Ice Festival** in mid-March, when the North American Open Sled Dog Championships take place on the frozen downtown streets. The Festival is perhaps most famous for its ice-sculpting competition; the impressive design and detail which goes into these large works makes it well worth braving the evil subzero temperatures.

Summer visitors should try to catch the three-day **World Eskimo–Indian Olympics** in mid-July. Competitors from around the state compete in the standard dance, art and sports competitions, as well as some unusual ones like ear-pulling, knuckle hop, high kick and the blanket toss, where age and wisdom often defeat youth and strength.

Fairbanks inflicts remarkable extremes of climate. Temperatures of –40°F are not uncommon, but the thermometer can rise to over 90°F in summer. Because the city sits just 188 miles south of the Arctic Circle, above which the sun neither sets during the summer nor rises during the winter equinoxes, Fairbanks also has very long days. The shortest day of the year has less than three hours of sunlight, the longest has over 21. Both can be disconcerting, and residents suffer from a high rate of depression. In summer, midnight baseball games under natural light are great fun, but stumbling out of a bar at 2am into bright sunshine can be really perturbing.

Arrival, Getting Around and Information

Fairbanks International Airport lies about four miles southwest of downtown; there are no buses and a taxi to the center will cost around $10. Carriers offering daily flights from Anchorage include *Mark Air, Alaska Airlines, Delta*, and *United*. The city acts as a gateway for flights into the Bush; *Frontier Flying Service* (see p.886) operate a reliable service, weather permitting of course.

By **road**, Fairbanks is 653 miles from Haines via the Alaska Highway, and 348 miles north of Anchorage along the scenic and seldom-crowded Parks Highway. **Alaska Railroad trains**, stopping downtown at 280 N Cushman Rd, offer the most relaxing and scenic way of travelling between Anchorage and Fairbanks, for $130 round-trip (daily in summer) or $245 for a fly/rail package with *Mark Air. Alaska Direct* ($65) offer the least expensive **bus** fares from Anchorage, and make a stop at Denali. *Alaskon Express* make the trip four times a week from Haines ($179) and Skagway ($205) via Whitehorse, Canada. The two-day bus trip stops overnight at Beaver Creek in the Yukon, where you make your own sleeping arrangements (motel rooms ③ and up; camping $18).

Sprawling Fairbanks belies its meager population of 40,000; having a vehicle is a good idea. Two bus lines provide a reasonable service, but routes and schedules change frequently; call ☎459-1011 for information or collect a schedule from Transit Park between Fifth and Sixth avenues. *G O Shuttle Service* (☎474-3847) stops at all the major attractions and lets you explore them at your own pace for $20. They also run a night service to the *Howling Dog and Fox Roadhouse* (see "Drinking") for $15. Several other companies can whisk you off into the Bush and Alaska's far west. The *Northern Alaska Tour Company* (see p.886) are the specialists for the Arctic Circle and Prudhoe Bay, while *Gray Line* operate tours to Denali, Barrow and the Yukon.

Numbered avenues in Fairbanks run parallel to the Chena River, getting higher as you head south. The **visitor center**, 550 First Ave (daily 8am–5pm; ☎456-5774), stores a vast amount of information on lodging and activities. For information on area parks, including Denali, the useful **Alaska Public Land Information Center** (APLIC) is at 250 N Cushman St (☎451-7352).

The Town

Downtown Fairbanks shouldn't take up much of your time. Besides the CVB and APLIC visitor centers, the only real stop of interest is the small **Dog Mushing Museum** in the Courthouse Building at Second and Cushman. Celebrating sled dog racing through videos, memorabilia and trophies, it concentrates on the north country's other great mushing event, the **Yukon Quest** – a gruelling thousand-mile marathon from Fairbanks to Whitehorse, Yukon (summer Mon–Fri 9am–6pm, Sat & Sun 9am–5pm; otherwise times vary; $2).

A couple of miles west on Airport Way, the forty-acre **Alaskaland** complex on the banks of the Chena River celebrates Alaskan history in a very touristy, but friendly way, and admission is free. Two reasonable free museums cover Athabascan culture and early pioneers and the **Crooked Creek and Whiskey Island Railroad** encircles the entire park. A carousel, playgrounds and crazy golf course account for the rest of the space. Numerous free shuttle buses head out from the major hotels in town, and there is sometimes a bus from the visitor center.

The **University of Alaska–Fairbanks (UAF) Museum**, occupying a corner of the attractive campus on the northeastern edge of town houses some of the best examples of Native artefacts and pioneer relics, as well as natural and human history displays, in Alaska (summer daily 9am–7pm, otherwise times vary; $4).

Accommodation

The dozens of **motels** and **hotels** in downtown Fairbanks, tend either to be quite pricey or pretty dodgy. **B&Bs** are plentiful, with rooms from $50; the *Fairbanks B&B Registry* (☎452-4957) has details, though the visitor center offers free phone calls and all the brochures. Thankfully there are plenty of **hostels**, all on a good bus route.

For **campers**, the *Norlite Campground*, 1660 Peger Rd (☎474-0206 or 1-800/478-0206), carries on the kitschy theme of neighboring Alaskaland.

Alaska Motel, 1546 Cushman St (☎456-6393). The safest pick of the budget motels downtown. ③.

A Taste of Alaska Lodge, Eberhardt Rd, Mile 5.3 Chena Hot Springs Rd (☎488-7855). Somewhere in between a B&B and a small country lodge. Sumptuous decor and a good view of McKinley. ⑤.

Billie's Backpackers Hostel, 2895 Mack Rd (☎479-2034). Welcoming and enthusiastically run hostel. Free pickup from train station or airport, volleyball court, tent space ($7) and an all-you-can-eat evening cookout for $5. In a nice area and handy for buses to town and UAF. Bunks $14. ①.

College Bunkhouse, 1541 Westwood Way (☎479-2627). A few doors up from *Billies* but with a slightly different atmosphere. The owner of the *Bunkhouse* is a scream and a compulsive smoker: "Yeah. We do have a no-smoking section. It's outside." ①.

Cripple Creek Resort Hotel, Ester, 5 miles south of Fairbanks (☎479-2500). The resort – a kind of adult hillbilly theme park – may not be to everyone's taste, but the rooms are good value. Bath shared between two rooms. ③.

Fairbanks AYH Hostel, 1641 Willow St (☎456-4159). Really good rooms in the manager's comfortable home (it can be a bit avuncular). Beds $12, nice tent sites for $6. Reservations essential. ①.

Fox Creek B&B, Mile 1.1 Elliot Hwy, Fox (☎457-5494). 12 miles north of downtown. Quiet and extremely comfortable, with big cooked breakfasts. Near the *Howling Dog Saloon* (see below). ③.

Pioneer B&B, 119 Second Ave (☎452-4628). 1906 log cabin on the edge of downtown. One of the rooms accommodates four people, making for exceptional value. ④.

Eating

Apart from fast-food joints, inexpensive food is difficult to find in Fairbanks, although there are a number of good spots to **eat**, and **drink**, out near the university.

Café de Paris, 801 Pioneer Rd (☎456-1669). Crepes and sandwiches in an old cottage near the train station. Pricey but good. Mon–Sat 10am-3pm.

Golden Exchange Bar and Grill, 500 First Ave (☎452-1978). Great (if expensive) dinners.

Souvlaki, 112 N Turner St (☎452-5393). Good value East Mediterranean dishes including spinach pie and other vegetarian options. Next to the train station.

Two Rivers Lodge, Mile 16, Chena Hot Springs Rd (☎488-6815). A fair way out of town, but it's a pleasant drive and you'll be well rewarded with inventive steak and seafood dishes from a huge menu. They also run a shuttle service from town. Budget on around $30 a head.

Whole Earth Grocery and Deli, 3649 College Rd (☎479-2062). Healthy eating near the university.

Nightlife

Fairbanks has its decent nightspots, though none of them lies in the hard-drinking downtown district.

Hot Licks, 3549 College Rd (☎479-7813). Ice cream and espresso bar that stays open until midnight and features live jazz several nights a week.

Howling Dog Saloon, junction of Eliot and Steese Hwys, Fox (☎457-8780). An inconvenient eleven miles north of town, but perhaps the best bar in the entire North Country. Unassuming, untouristy, unpretentious and fun. Live rock and r'n'b bands and the ideal place to play volleyball under the midnight sun. A c'n'w dance hall, the *Fox Roadhouse* (☎457-8780), stands right across the street.

Pike's Landing, 4.5 Mile, Airport Rd (5479-7113). Large and hugely popular bar/restaurant serving good light meals and cocktails on a sun deck overlooking the Chena River.

Pump House, 1.3 Chena Pump Rd (☎479-8452). Even more popular than Pike's Landing. The restaurant draws in tourists for surf'n'turf dinners, while a young crowd packs out the bar at night.

Outside Fairbanks: Two Hot Springs

Chena Hot Springs, the most accessible and developed resort, stands in a clearing, sixty miles east of Fairbanks at the end of the Chena River State Recreation Area – a wonderfully bucolic swathe of **muskeg** (grassy swamp land) and forest traversed with good hiking trails and teeming with moose. Rooms at the fully equipped resort range from good-value rustic trapper cabins to luxury doubles (☎452-7867; ②–⑥), and camping costs $8. Walking in the area is especially enjoyable after a soak in the steaming natural spring waters; if you're not staying at the resort, it costs $8 per day to use the indoor pool and hot tubs. The resort also rents out canoes and mountain bikes as well as offering rafting trips.

The traditional favorite for folks from Fairbanks has been the more rustic **Circle Hot Springs**, 130 miles northeast of the city along scenic Steese Highway. It's a long drive but you pass through some pristine scenery, alongside the Chatanika River and over the 3624-feet Eagle Summit. To get to the resort, take a right at the mining village of **Central** and carry on for eight miles. In addition to taking a dip, you can go on a boat

---

THE NORTHERN LIGHTS

The **aurora borealis**, or "Northern Lights", an ethereal display of light in the uppermost atmosphere, give their brightest and most colorful displays in the sky above Fairbanks. For up to one hundred winter nights, the sky appears to shimmer with dancing curtains of color, ranging from luminescent monotones – most commonly green or dark red – to fantastic veils that run the full spectrum. The display becomes more animated as it proceeds, twisting and turning in patterns called "rayed bands", and as a finale a corona sometimes appears in which rays seem to flare in all directions from a central point.

Named after the Roman goddess of dawn, the aurora was long thought to be produced by sunlight reflected from polar snow and ice, or refracted light produced in the manner of a rainbow. Research still continues into the phenomenon, but it seems the aurora is caused by **radiation** emitted as light from atoms in the upper atmosphere as they are hit by fast-moving electrons and protons. The **sun** also appears to have an influence: auroras become more distinctive and are spread over a larger area two days after intense solar activity, the time it takes the "solar wind" to arrive.

The "Northern Lights", at their most dazzling from December to March when nights are longest and the sky darkest, can usually be seen even as far south as Juneau.

ride or pan for gold, and the area is laced with good hiking, skiing and snowmobiling trails. Accommodations range from dorm beds for $20 right up to deluxe rooms for around $100 (☎520-5113; ①–⑤).

Don't confuse the resort with the town of **CIRCLE** – à 34-mile drive over very rough roads from Central. The name was given by prospectors, who in 1893 thought they were establishing a community on the Arctic Circle; it's actually fifty miles south. Today Circle is a classic end-of-the-road community numbering seventy souls with a reputation for heavy boozing. It all adds up to a rather essential side trip.

The Dalton Highway

Built in the 1970s, to service the **trans-Alaska pipeline**, the gravel-surfaced **Dalton Highway**, or North Slope Haul Road, begins north of Fairbanks and slips and slides for 341 miles, beyond the Arctic Circle to the oil facility of Prudhoe Bay on Alaska's north coast. This long, lonesome and risky road begins 73 miles north of Fairbanks. Just beyond the city limits you start to get glimpses of the pipeline snaking up hills and in and out of the ground. At 188 miles north of Fairbanks a rather snappy little sign, an observation platform, a scrap of red carpet and a picnic area alert you to the fact that you've just crossed **the Arctic Circle**.

Twenty miles inside the circle, **Disaster Creek**, in the shade of the still largely unmapped and unexplored **Brooks Range** and the **Gates of the Arctic National Park**, marks the end of the road, at least for the moment: plans to open the rest of the route have been delayed due to oil company claims that the heavy truck traffic would cause accidents. **Prudhoe Bay**, at the end of the highway and nothing more than a collection of oil tanks and trailer homes, is closed to the public, and unless you can get hold of a press pass or pay $60 for a tour and some oil company propaganda, the journey comes to an end, ten miles from the coast at dead-boring **Deadhorse**.

Permits to travel north are available from the Dept of Transport, 2301 Peger Rd, Fairbanks (☎451-2209). Many people ignore the regulations, but do bear in mind that most rental companies forbid you to take their cars on this road. In any case it's a treacherous journey. Trucks speeding along the slippery gravel track kick up frightening clouds of dust or mud which reduce visibility to absolute zero; potholes beat the hell out of the car and services, gas and repairs are practically nonexistent. You shouldn't even think about coming here unless you've got a sturdy 4WD, a CB radio, a trunkload of supplies and have done some careful planning.

Even driving the relatively short stretch to the Arctic Circle poses its problems with trucks. Nevertheless going to the Arctic Circle commands an irresistible pull no matter how pointless it is to drive almost two hundred miles to see a roadsign. By far the best way to do it is with the **Northern Alaska Tour Company** (see p.886) who'll drive you up in a minibus, supply commentary and video films (but no lunch), and fly you back down to Fairbanks for around $150 (you can save $50 by taking the minibus back, but that makes for a long, long day). The company also run a two-day tour to Prudhoe Bay for $450.

CHAPTER SIXTEEN

HAWAII

The islands of **HAWAII**, with their **volcanoes**, palm-fringed **beaches**, verdant **valleys**, glorious **rainbows**, and awesome **sea cliffs**, hold some of the most spectacularly beautiful scenery on earth, constantly presenting the chance to hike into pristine wilderness, or to camp on the seashore or mountainside. However, despite their isolation, two thousand miles out in the Pacific, they belong very definitely to the United States – if you expect your South Seas idyll to be completely unspoiled, forget it. This is where Americans come on honeymoon, and frequent-fliers cash in their mileage, and the fantasy of a dream holiday in Paradise remains firmly rooted in the creature comforts of home. With six million tourists per year – including over a million Japanese, said to spend an average of $600 each per day – the islands can seem like a gigantic theme park. Worldwide recession, and the sobering impact of Hurricane Iniki on Kauai in September 1992, may have combined to slow resort development, but you can't help but be aware of how much of what was unique has gone.

Honolulu, by far the largest city of the fiftieth state, and with its resort annexe of **Waikiki** the main tourist center, is on **Oahu**. The biggest island, **Hawaii** itself, is known as the **Big Island**, in a vain attempt to avoid confusion. **Maui** and **Kauai** also attract mass tourism, while smaller **Molokai** is gearing itself up. The islands share a similar topography and **climate**. Ocean winds from the northeast shed their rain on that, **windward**, coast, keeping it wet and green; the southwest or **leeward** coasts can be almost barren, and so make ideal locations for big resorts. Rainfall is heaviest from December to March, but temperatures remain consistent at between 70°F and 85°F.

Thanks to the usual American vacation patterns, Christmas and mid-summer are far more expensive times to visit than the "off-seasons" of September to December and April to May, with top-range accommodations charging as much as fifty percent extra.

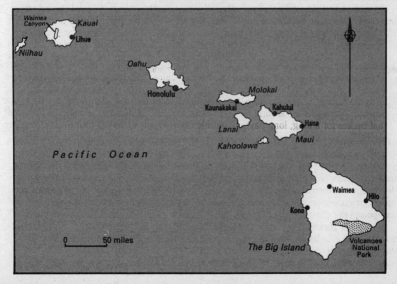

A visit to Hawaii doesn't have to cost a fortune, however; there are plenty of **budget** facilities if you know where to look. The one major expense you really can't avoid, except possibly on Oahu, is **car** rental – rates are very reasonable, but gas is pricey.

History

Each of the Hawaiian islands in turn was forced up like a vast mass of candle drippings by submarine volcanic action, all fuelled by the same "hot spot" below the seabed, which has remained stationary as the Pacific plate drifted above. The oldest islands are now mere atolls way off to the northwest; the process is continuing at Kilauea on the Big Island, with lava exploding into the sea to add new land day by day.

Until less than two thousand years ago, these unknown specks in the ocean were populated only by the mutated descendants of what few organisms had been carried here by wind or wave. Though carbon dating suggests that *someone* was here in the second century AD – possibly the legendary dwarf-like *menehune* – the first known human inhabitants were the **Polynesians**, who arrived in two separate migrations; one from the Marquesas in the eighth century, and another from Tahiti four or five hundred years later. (Though justly famous for their navigational skills, they only undertook such long-distance canoe voyages in exceptional circumstances.)

The first European to cross the Pacific, Magellan, saw not a single island; no western ship chanced upon Hawaii until **Captain Cook** arrived at Kauai in January 1778. He was amazed to find a civilization sharing a culture – and language – with the peoples of the South Pacific. The Hawaiians too were amazed, having long since lost contact with the outside world. Cook himself was killed in Hawaii in 1779 (see p.936), but he had started an irreversible process of change. The first Polynesians had brought the plants and animals necessary to create a self-sufficient way of life. Westerners took things further, and in reshaping the islands to suit their economic and agricultural needs decimated most of the indigenous flora and fauna – as well as the Hawaiians themselves. Cook's men estimated that there were a million islanders; the figure today is roughly the same, but a mere eight thousand **pure-blood Hawaiians** are left. The geographical distribution has changed too; it's striking how often the accounts of the early explorers describe being greeted by vast numbers of canoes in areas which are now virtually uninhabited.

As well as bringing venereal and other diseases, Cook's voyage opened the fur trade between the Pacific northwest and China. Passing ships regularly traded arms to the Hawaiians, and within a few years, chief **Kamehameha** of the Big Island, with the help of westerners and their cannons, became the first king to unite all the islands.

In a sense, ancient Hawaii had no economy, not even barter; the abundant fruits of earth and sea were simply shared out. The sudden advent of capitalism was devastating. When the fur traders realized that Hawaiian **sandalwood** fetched enormous prices in China, the mass of the population abandoned taro-farming and fishing to become wage-slaves. The great forests were almost entirely denuded by the end of the 1820s, at which point a replacement industry appeared – **whaling** (see p.941).

With the dislocation of traditional ways, Hawaiian **religion** fell apart. After the death of Kamehameha in May 1819, the female regent Kaahumanu set out to break the **kapu** (*tabu*) system which held society together. Her public defiance of the injunctions forbidding women to eat alongside men, or to eat bananas or pork, threw the islands into moral anarchy – just as the first Puritan **missionaries** arrived from New England, determined to turn Hawaii into the Promised Land. Their wholehearted capitalism and harsh strictures on the easy-going Hawaiian lifestyle might have been calculated to compound the chaos. White advisers and ministers soon dominated the government.

In the old Hawaii there was no private land; all was held in trust by the chief, who apportioned it to individuals at his continued pleasure only. After a misunderstanding with the British consul almost resulted in the islands' permanent cession to Britain, the king was requested to "clarify" the situation. In 1848 all the land was parcelled out, to native Hawaiians only, but within two years the *haole* (non-Hawaiians) too were allowed to buy and sell land. The jibe that the missionaries "came to Hawaii to do good – and they done good" stems from the speed with which they amassed vast acreages; their children became Hawaii's wealthiest and most powerful class.

While the Civil War severely disrupted whaling, it triggered a Hawaiian **sugar** boom, to replace southern sugar in the markets of the north. From then on, the machinations of the sugar industry to get favorable prices on the mainland moved Hawaii inexorably towards **annexation** by the US. In 1887 an all-white (and armed) group of "concerned businessmen" forced King David Kalakaua to surrender power to an assembly elected by property owners (of any nationality) rather than citizens. When after his death his sister Liliuokalani announced her desire to proclaim a new constitution, the businessmen called in the US warship *Boston*, then in Honolulu, and declared a provisional government. US President Grover Cleveland (a Democrat) responded that "Hawaii was taken possession of by the United States forces without the consent or wish of the government of the islands. . . . (It) was **wholly without justification** . . . not merely a wrong but a **disgrace**." With phenomenal cheek, the provisional government rejected his demand for the restoration of the monarchy by saying the US should not "interfere in the internal affairs of their sovereign nation". They found defenders in the Republican US Congress, and declared themselves a republic on July 4 1894.

A Republican president, McKinley, came to office in Washington in 1897, arguing that "annexation is not a change. It is a consummation." The strategic value of Pearl Harbor was emphasized by the Spanish-American War in the Philippines; and on August 12 1898 Hawaii was formally annexed as a territory of the United States. At this point there was no question of Hawaii becoming a state; the whites were outnumbered ten to one, and had no desire to afford the natives the protection of US labor laws, let alone to give them the vote (one leader, Sanford Dole, said that natives couldn't expect to vote "simply because they were grown up"). Furthermore, as the proportion of Hawaiians of Japanese descent (*nisei*) increased (to 25 percent by 1936), Congress feared the prospect of a state whose people might consider their primary allegiance to be to Japan.

Consequently, Hawaii was for the first half of this century the virtual fiefdom of the so-called **Big Five**, conglomerations started by the missionary families and rooted in their massive land holdings (still-familiar names include *Castle & Cooke* – now *Dole* – and *Alexander & Baldwin*). By controlling agriculture (owning 96 percent of the sugar crop), they also dominated transport, banks, utilities, insurance – and government.

The inevitable integration of Hawaii into the American mainstream was hastened by its crucial role in the war against Japan – with the clear support of the *nisei* – and the expansion of tourism thereafter. The islands finally became the fiftieth of the United States in 1959, after a plebiscite showed a 17-to-1 majority in favor. The only group to oppose statehood was the few remaining native Hawaiians. Since then support has grown for **Hawaiian sovereignty**, on the basis that those of Hawaiian descent should gain at least the rights already held by Native American nations on the mainland.

Modern Hawaii

Roughly sixty percent of the million-plus modern Hawaiians were born here. Around one third are Caucasian (many of them US military personnel), one third Japanese, and one sixth Filipino, with 200,000 claiming at least some Hawaiian ancestry. Except for sugar and pineapples, the economy has shifted away from agriculture, with many of those green fields that survive doing so mainly because they're prettier than building sites. In Maui, they have to import agricultural laborers from Mexico, as the locals prefer more lucrative employment in hotels and tourism. The need to import virtually all the basics of life has resulted in an extraordinarily high **cost of living** (the *Paradise Tax*, as they call it). In particular, the cost of housing is so high that many islanders find themselves either obliged to work at two jobs, or simply to sleep on the beaches.

Visitors in search of the **ancient Hawaii** will find that few vestiges remain, often as decoration in the big hotels. What is presented as "historic" usually post-dates the missionary impact. The "old towns" are pure nineteenth-century Americana, with false-front stores and raised wooden boardwalks. The ruins of temples (*heiaus*) to the old gods still stand in some places – notably on the Big Island – and committed campaigners work to revive traditional philosophies, but the closest Hawaii comes to a state religion now appears to be Elvis-worship. The two biggest **festivals** are the Big Island's week-long "**Merrie Monarch Festival**", honoring King David Kalakaua (April 11–17), and Oahu's "**King Kamehameha**" events (around June 11–12). Authentic **hula** dancing is a powerful art form, but you're far more likely to encounter it bastardized in some kind of "Polynesian spectacular" – perhaps a **luau** or "traditional feast". Primarily tourist money-spinners, *luaus* provide an opportunity to sample Hawaiian **foods** such as *kalua* pig, baked underground, and local fish such as *ono*, *ahi*, *mahi-mahi* and *lomi-lomi* (raw salmon). *Poi* – a paste made from mashed taro root – remains a staple of the diet, much as it was when one of Captain Cook's men described it as "a disagreeable mess".

The Hawaiian **language** endures in place names and music. At first glance it looks unpronounceable – especially as it is written using a mere twelve letters (the five vowels, plus *h*, *k*, *l*, *m*, *n*, *p* and *w*). Usually, each letter is enunciated individually – apostrophes indicate a pause for breath. Long words often break down into repeated sounds, such as "*meha-meha*" in "Kamehameha". Hawaii itself is more correctly written (and pronounced) *Hawai'i*, but for visual clarity we've omitted the apostrophes in this book.

Getting To and Around Hawaii

Honolulu, just under six hours by plane from the US West Coast, is one of the world's busiest centers for air traffic; return fares from **LA**, **San Francisco** and **Seattle** start at around $300. There are also direct flights from the mainland to Maui and the Big Island. Many flights to the US from **Australia** – such as all on *Continental* – include free stopovers in Hawaii. **European** travellers should buy all-inclusive tickets from Europe.

Hawaiian Air (Oahu ☎537-5100; US ☎1-800/367-5320; Britain ☎0293/774412), and *Aloha Air* (Oahu ☎484-1111; US ☎1-800/367-5260) and its subsidiary *Island Air* (Oahu ☎484-2222; US ☎1-800/323-3345), connect the major islands, usually several times daily, for a standard single fare of around $65 (reductions for early morning and late night, and multiple tickets). *Air Molokai* flies between Oahu, Maui and Molokai (☎871-5990).

All the airports have car rental outlets; with the exception of Oahu, **bus** services on the islands barely exist. Several companies run **bicycle tours**, including *Island Bicycle Adventures* (PO Box 458, Volcano HI 96785; ☎967-8603, or ☎1-800/233-2226 in the US).

The **area code** for all Hawaii is ☎808.

OAHU

Three quarters of Hawaii's population live on **OAHU**, which has monopolized the islands' trade and tourism since the first white sailors realized **Pearl Harbor** to be the finest deep-water harbor in all the Pacific. Over eighty percent of visitors to Hawaii still arrive in **Honolulu** – albeit by air now rather than by sea – and most remain for their entire vacation. Oahu effectively confines tourists to the tower-block enclave of **Waikiki**, just east of downtown Honolulu; there are few rooms anywhere else. In much the same way, the **military** are closeted away in relatively inconspicuous camps. On any one day, the numbers of military personnel and tourists on Oahu are roughly the same.

Overcrowding and rampant development mean Oahu can't be recommended over the **Neighbor Islands** (as the other Hawaiian islands are known), but it can still give a real flavor of Hawaii. There are some excellent **beaches**, with those on the north shore a haven for **surfers** and campers, and the cliffs of the **windward** side are awesome.

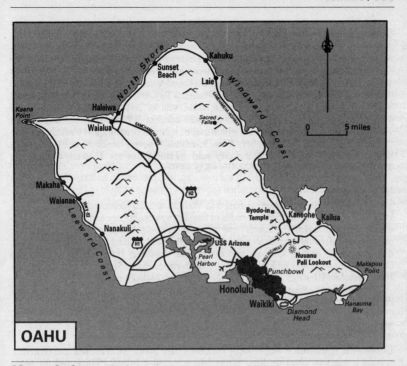

OAHU

Honolulu

Until the Europeans came, **HONOLULU** was insignificant; soon so many foreign ships were using adjacent Pearl Harbor that it had become King Kamehameha's capital, and it remains the economic center of the island. The city covers a long (if narrow) strip of southern Oahu, but **downtown** is a manageable size, and a lot quieter than its glamorous image might suggest. The tourist hotels, and a lot of Honolulu's hustle, are concentrated among the skyscrapers of very distinct **Waikiki**, a couple of miles east.

The setting is beautiful, right on the Pacific and backed by dramatic *pali* (cliffs) and the extinct volcanoes of **Punchbowl** (a military cemetery) and **Diamond Head**; but then beauty is not so rare a commodity on Hawaii, and you can see this sort of scenery in plenty of other places without a city slapped down in the middle of it. What attracts most visitors to stay in Honolulu, and especially Waikiki, is the sheer **hedonism** of shopping, eating and generally hanging out in the sun. Hawaii's broad ethnic mix, and Honolulu's status as a major world crossroads, make it a cosmopolitan place where something is always happening (and everything is for sale). It's also the center of an exemplary **public transit** system, facilitating explorations of the whole island.

Arrival and Information

The runways of Honolulu's **International Airport**, just west of downtown, extend out to sea on a coral reef. **Car rental** outlets abound, but a car is not especially desirable in Honolulu, what with city traffic and hefty parking fees in Waikiki. The nine-mile – not at all scenic – drive to Waikiki takes anything from 25 to 75 minutes. A **taxi** (*SIDA*, ☎836-0011) will cost around $20, while the *Airport Motor Coach* shuttle costs $6 each way.

Getting Around – *TheBus*

A network of over sixty **bus** routes, officially named *TheBus*, covers the whole of Oahu. All journeys, however long, cost 60¢ – exact change only – with free transfers onto any connecting route if you ask as you board (enquiries ☎848-5555; customer service ☎848-4500). The most popular routes with Waikiki-based tourists are **#8** to Ala Moana, **#2** to downtown, **#20** to Pearl Harbor, **#22** to Hanauma Bay, and the bargain "**Circle Island**" buses which take four hours to tour the island, still for just 60¢: **#52** (clockwise) and **#55** (counterclockwise). Routes #19 and #20 connect Waikiki with the airport, but *TheBus* doesn't allow big suitcases, which makes it impractical for most travellers.

In Waikiki, *Aloha Funway* offers **bicycle rental** at seven locations, at $19.95 for 24 hours. Among companies running **city and island tours** are *Polynesian Adventure Tours* (full day $45–60, half-day $22–25; ☎833-3000).

Information

The **Hawaii Visitors Bureau** is based in Waikiki at 2270 Kalakaua Ave (☎923-1811), but you're unlikely to need them; racks of free listings magazines and leaflets are everywhere you turn, and all the hotels have information desks. Kiosks around Kalakaua Ave offer greatly discounted rates for the various "**activities**" – island tours, helicopter rides, dinner cruises, surfing lessons, and so on. For **disabled information**, contact the *Commission on Persons with Disabilities*, 5 Waterfront Plaza, Suite 210, 500 Ala Moana Blvd, Honolulu HI 96813. *Handicabs of the Pacific* (☎524-3866) run taxis for the disabled.

The main **post offices** are at 330 Saratoga Rd, Waikiki (☎941-1062) and 3600 Aolele St, Honolulu (☎423-3930; zip code 96813).

The City

Downtown Honolulu is surprisingly small, set back a little from the sea and centering around a spacious plaza on King Street which includes **Iolani Palace** and the **state capitol**. The palace was built for King David Kalakaua in 1882, and apart from its *koa*-wood floors contains little that is distinctively Hawaiian (Wed–Sat 9am–2.15pm; $4). Across the road is a colorful statue of Kamehameha I.

To reach the nearby ocean, pedestrians have to negotiate fearsome traffic. Although the sea may be turquoise, the shorefront is concrete, not beach, and you can't wander along it for any distance. Free elevators go to the top (tenth) floor of the **Aloha Tower** on pier 9, which as the city's tallest building once greeted all new arrivals to Honolulu. The view is little short of ugly, but is good for orientation. East towards Diamond Head is the new black glass of Restaurant Row, loomed over by the two stereo-speakers of the Waterfront Towers condominiums. To the west (where planes swoop down to land at the airport) is Pearl Harbor; a giant pineapple in the distance marks the *Dole* factory.

The **Hawaii Maritime Center** (daily 9am–5pm; $7), almost at the foot of Aloha Tower, documents Hawaii's seafaring past in superb detail, from ancient migrations through white contact, nineteenth-century trade and twentieth-century cruises. A stunning film from 1922 (with Clara Bow in a bit part) shows the true-life drama of whaling, and there's a wall of gigantic historic surfboards. In the adjacent dock are the fully rigged four-master *Falls of Clyde* and the replica Polynesian canoe *Hokulea*, which has three times crossed the Pacific using traditional methods of navigation.

Chinatown

TheBus #2 from Waikiki drops you at Hotel and Bishop, outside the gleaming hi-tech Executive Center in downtown Honolulu. Just five minutes' walk away down Hotel Street, the fading green clapboard storefronts of **Chinatown** seem like another world. Traditionally the city's red-light district, the narrow streets leading down to the Nuuanu Stream are still characterized by pool halls, massage parlors and heavy-duty bars.

The **Chinatown Visitor Center**, 1250 Mauna Kea (Mon–Fri 10am–1pm; ☎521-3045), part of the Chinatown Cultural Plaza Shopping Center, offers two different walking tours for $2 each. Exhibits trace the area's history since the first Chinese arrived in 1788, covering its near-destruction in January 1900, when an attempt to burn out a plague epidemic went hideously wrong. The center also gives contemporary information on shops and restaurants. The oriental food specialties at **Oahu Market**, on N King and Kekaulike, make for fascinating browsing.

Bishop Museum

The anthropological collection at the **Bishop Museum**, back from the ocean at 1525 Bernice St (daily 9am–5pm; $7.95), demonstrates the reality of Polynesian culture, as opposed to the fakery of Waikiki. Three floors of one of Hawaii's oldest houses display magnificent feather cloaks and Japanese samurai armor, and a full-size sperm whale hangs in the central well. There are also excellent special exhibitions for kids, and a planetarium. *TheBus* #2 from Waikiki stops two blocks away on Kapalama St.

Pearl Harbor

Almost the whole of **Pearl Harbor**, the principal base for the US Pacific fleet, is off limits to visitors. However, the surprise Japanese attack of December 7 1941, which an official US inquiry called "the greatest military and naval disaster in our nation's history", is commemorated by a simple white memorial set above the wreck of the battleship **USS Arizona**, still discernible in the clear blue waters. More than 1100 of its crew – who had earned the right to sleep in late that Sunday morning by coming second in a military band competition – are entombed there.

Free tours to the ship operate between 8am and 3pm each day, but it can be two or three hours after you pick up your numbered ticket at the visitor center (daily 7.30am–5pm) before you are called to board the ferry across the bay. Many of the 1.5 million annual visitors are Japanese; an even-handed 20-minute film pays tribute to "one of the most brilliantly planned and executed attacks in naval history", and books and charts are on sale telling the Japanese side of the story. The USS Arizona memorial was partly financed by Elvis Presley's 1961 Honolulu concert, his first show after leaving the Army.

Pearl Harbor is just over one hour from Waikiki, beyond the airport, on *TheBus* #20.

Punchbowl

High above Honolulu, lush lawns growing in the caldera of an extinct volcano are the emotive setting for the **National Memorial Cemetery of the Pacific** (summer daily 8am–6.30pm; winter 8am–5.30pm), in which are buried the dead of all US Pacific wars, including Vietnam. Hawaiian shuttle astronaut Ellison Onizuka is also here. The site is said to have been an ancient sacrificial temple, and is on *TheBus* route #15 from town.

Waikiki

Built on a reclaimed swamp, **Waikiki** is very nearly an island, all but separate from Honolulu between the sea and the Ala Wai canal (which provides the drainage to make its incredible high-rise profusion possible). Once home to King Kamehameha I, the site may be venerable, but these days its *raison d'être* is rampant commercialism. You could, just about, survive here with very little money, buying snacks from the omnipresent *ABC* convenience stores, but there would be no point – there's nothing to see, and the only thing to do apart from surf and sunbathe is to buy, anything and everything.

Time in Waikiki is spent strolling seafront **Kalakaua Avenue**, resisting or succumbing to temptation as you see fit. The most striking thing about the parallel **Waikiki Beach** is quite how narrow it is, a thin but somehow attractive strip of shipped-in sand. Compared to other Hawaiian beaches, it's overcrowded and small, but then it serves a different function; no-one is trying to "get away from it all", they're there to be seen.

Diamond Head

Waikiki's most famous landmark is the pinnacle of **Diamond Head**, just to the east. Named for the erroneous belief of a party of English sailors that they'd found diamonds on its slopes, it's another extinct volcano. The lawns of the crater interior are oddly bland, almost suburban in fact, but a straightforward hiking trail leads up to a panorama of the whole coast, and passes through a few of an enormous network of tunnels built by the military during World War II. *TheBus* #14 stops on the road nearby.

Hanauma Bay

A few miles further on, the magnificent crescent-shaped **Hanauma Bay**, formed when the wall of a crater collapsed to let in the sea, is renowned as Oahu's best place to **snorkel**. It makes a nice excursion, and the sea is full of brightly colored fish; but overuse has killed off most of the coral near the shore, and the feeding of fish with food sold at the bay has led to a decline in the range of species. Tour parties were banned in 1991, and attempts are made to educate visitors about the fragile ecology of the shallow bay. Patches of living coral, and bigger fish, can be seen if you swim out to the deeper waters beyond the inner reef, but the currents can be strong, and you invite coral cuts that can take weeks to heal. Snorkelling equipment is available for $6 rental (bring a deposit). The beach is closed on Wednesday mornings.

TheBus #22 ("The Beach Bus") runs by the bay every forty minutes.

Accommodation

Waikiki accommodations cover a wide range, and the highest rates will bring absolute luxury, but it's possible to pay much less.

Aston Island Colony, 445 Seaside Ave (☎923-2345; details on others in the chain ☎1-800/922-7866). Good rooms with and without kitchenettes. ④–⑤.

Big Surf Hotel, 1690 Ala Moana Blvd (☎946-6525). Compact hotel offering clean basic rooms with minimal extra frills and facilities. ②.

Driftwood Hotel, 1696 Ala Moana Blvd (☎1-800/669-7710). 70-room hotel near Ala Moana mall, with generally good facilities. ②.

Hale Aloha AYH Hostel, 2417 Prince Edward St (☎926-8313). $15 dorm beds, members only, plus a few doubles. Three-day stay guaranteed, seven-day maximum. ①/②.

Honolulu International AYH Hostel, 2323-A Seaview Ave (☎946-0591). Well back from the sea, near the University in Manoa Valley. $9 members, $12 non-members. ①.

InterClub Hostel Waikiki, 2413 Kuhio Ave (☎924-2636). Friendly small hotel, no reservations. Five to eight people share each of 12 dorms for $16 each. ①.

Outrigger, numerous locations around Waikiki, mostly skyscrapers (reservations ☎1-800/462-6262). Choices include rooms with kitchenettes at the *Ala Wai Terrace*, 1547 Ala Wai Blvd (③); or a little more luxury at the *Waikiki Surf*, 2200 Kuhio Ave (④); most of the others will have rooms for under $75. On request, a free *Dollar* rental car is provided for every day of your stay. ③–⑧.

Waikiki Joy, 320 Lewers St (☎923-2300). Small-scale "boutique hotel", offering friendly and personalized top-of-the-range accommodation. ⑤.

ACCOMMODATION PRICE CODES

All accommodation prices in this book have been coded using the symbols below. Note that prices are for the least expensive double rooms in each establishment.

For a full explanation see p.35 in *Basics*.

①	up to $30	④	$60–80	⑦	$130–180
②	$30–45	⑤	$80–100	⑧	$180+
③	$45–60	⑥	$100–130		

Waikiki Prince, 2432 Prince Edward St (☎922-1544). Small, basic but perfectly adequate budget hotel near the beach. ③.

Eating

Honolulu offers so many **food** possibilities that recommendations are inevitably highly personal. Check out **Restaurant Row** near the Harbor for classy dining, or Waikiki's Kuhio Avenue for **snacks** and franchise fast-foods. The assorted ethnic kitchens in **Makai Market** in the Ala Moana Center are hard to beat; lunches at the **International Food Court** in Waikiki's International Market Place are a little overrated and over-priced, but they're accompanied by live Polynesian music and dance.

Once-in-a-lifetime opportunities include a **dinner cruise** – the *Ali'i Kai Catamaran* leaves Pier 5 at 5.30pm daily (hotel pick-up if necessary; ☎524-6694) – or a **luau** – the biggest "Polynesian feast" is *Paradise Cove* ($45; ☎973-5828), with hundreds of people daily being bussed 30 miles (sing-alongs compulsory) to eat indifferent food, get drunk, and make fools of themselves.

Columbia Inn, 645 Kapiolani Blvd, Waikiki (☎531-3747). Long-standing traditional diner, 6am–1am. Late-night snacks and good full meals for $7–15. The shrimp tempura is recommended.

Duke's, 2335 Kalakaua Ave, #116, Waikiki (☎922-2268). Clone of the Waikiki *Hard Rock Café*, with a great view. Good-value breakfasts, also lunch and dinner.

El Burrito, 550 Piikoi Ave, Waikiki (☎533-3457). Genuine Mexican diner (as opposed to Tex-Mex) near Ala Moana mall, serving 11am–8pm.

Leonard's Bakery, 933 Kapahulu Ave, Waikiki (☎737-5591). Long-standing and delicious bakery, renowned for its Portuguese desserts.

Mekong Thai I, 1295 S Beretania St (☎523-0014), and **Mekong II**, 1726 S King St (☎941-6184), both Honolulu. Excellent evening-only Thai specialties; red and green curries and garlic shrimp.

New Orleans Bistro, 2139 Kuhio Ave, Waikiki (☎926-4444). Pricey and so-so Cajun and Creole dishes – crawfish and even alligator – but there's live jazz every night until 2am.

Perry's Smorgy, 2380 Kuhio Ave, Waikiki (☎926-0184). All-you-can-eat buffets, indoor and al fresco (with hordes of scavenging birds). $4.45 breakfast (7–10.30am), $5.95 lunch (11am–2.30pm), $7.95 dinner (5–9pm). Also at the *Coral Seas Hotel*, 250 Lewers St.

Roy's Park Bistro, 1956 Ala Moana Blvd in *Park Plaza Waikiki Hotel* (☎944-4624). Much-acclaimed restaurant serving all meals. Mediterranean lamb a specialty.

Ruffage Natural Foods, 2443 Kuhio Ave, Waikiki (☎922-2042). Tiny grocery and patio dining, with cheap vegetable and tofu dishes. Sushi bar open until 10pm.

Sheraton Moana Surfrider, 2365 Kalakaua Ave, Waikiki (☎922-3111). Historic hotel offering beach barbecue for $20, and afternoon entertainment on the *lanai* for one-drink minimum. Fabulous ocean views, especially at sunset.

Woodland's, 1289 S King St, Honolulu (☎526-2239). Bargain Northern Chinese and Peking dishes.

Yanagi Sushi, 762 Kapiolani Blvd, Waikiki (☎537-1525). Authentic and popular sushi bar and Japanese restaurant; a full dinner will cost upwards of $18.

Yuen's Garden, 2140 S Beretania St, Honolulu (☎526-2239). Hong-Kong-style seafood dinners.

Entertainment and Nightlife

Various free magazines will make sure you get details of musical and other attractions during your visit. The **bars** of Chinatown are the most raucous in town, but way too hair-raising for most tastes. Otherwise the clubs and discos are pretty mainstream.

Anna Banannas, 2440 S Beretania St (☎946-5190). Reasonable bar, live music Wed–Sun 9.30pm.

Hula's Bar and Lei Stand, 2103 Kuhio Ave (☎923-0669). Waikiki's most popular gay venue.

Garbo's, 2260 Kuhio Ave, 2nd floor (☎922-1405). Women's bar and disco; *Fusion*, above it on the 3rd floor (☎955-7798), caters for a mixed crowd.

Studebakers, Restaurant Row (☎526-9888). Fifties-style nightspot, age 24 or over, with free buffet.

Wave Waikiki, 1877 Kalakua Ave (☎941-0424). Loud heavy rock, live and on record, 10pm–4am.

Windward Oahu

Much the most spectacular moment of a tour of Oahu comes as you cross the Koolau Mountains on the **Pali Highway** (Hwy-61) to see the sheer green cliffs of the windward side of the island, swirling with mists. The highest spot, just four miles out of Honolulu heading northeast, is the **Nuuanu Pali Lookout**. King Kamehameha finalized his conquest of Oahu here in 1795, forcing hundreds of enemy warriors over the edge of the cliffs; Mark Twain saw the battlefield seventy years later, littered with skulls.

The wide highway is barely adequate for its role as a major commuter thoroughfare connecting Honolulu with **Kailua** and **Kaneohe**, and a new tunnel is being dug which will inevitably bring further "development" to the windward side. Apart from the inaccessible cliffs a few miles inland, there's little worth seeing. **Sea Life Park** at Makapuu Point (Thurs, Fri & Sun 10am–10pm, otherwise 10am–5pm; $14.95), for example, is a dismal and heavily commercial theme park. The replica Japanese Buddhist **Byodo-In Temple** off Hwy-83, however, should not be missed (8.30am–4.30pm; $2).

SEA, SURF AND SAFETY

Drownings in Hawaii are all too common. In many places the waves come sweeping in from 2000 miles of open ocean, onto beaches – magnificent to look at – unprotected by any reef. Not all beaches have lifeguards and warning flags; unattended beaches are not necessarily safe. Look for other bathers, but whatever your experience elsewhere don't assume you'll be able to cope with the same conditions as the local kids. Don't rush into the water, watch the sea carefully before going in, and never take your eyes off it thereafter. Fierce **rogue waves** can appear from the blue to drag waders – or even those walking along the shore – far out to sea in seconds, and powerful **undertows** may not be detectable until too late. If you do get swept out, wait until the big waves die down, even if it takes hours. Never attempt to swim where waves are breaking right on the reef.

Sea creatures to avoid include *wana* – black spiky **sea urchins** – Portuguese Men of War **jellyfish**, and **coral** in general, which can give painful infected cuts. **Shark attacks** are much rarer than popular imagination suggests; those which do occur are usually due to "misunderstandings", such as spear-fishers inadvertently keeping sharks from their catch, or surfers idling on their boards looking a bit too much like turtles from below.

Assuming that you're self-destructive enough to want a **tan**, take exposure to the harsh tropical **sun** in moderation; a mere twenty minutes is the safe recommendation for the first day. Even on overcast days your skin still absorbs most of the harmful UV rays.

Ocean Fun

The nation that invented **surfing** – long before the whites came – remains its greatest arena. The sport was popularized earlier this century by Olympic swimmer Duke Kahanamoku, using a twenty-foot board; these days most are around six-foot. Smaller **boogie boards**, which you don't stand on, make an exhilarating initiation. **Windsurfing** too is rapidly growing, using the same favorite beaches, usually on the north shore of each island. **Snorkelling** and **diving** are top-quality, although Hawaii's **coral** has fewer brilliant hues than in warmer equatorial waters – and in places it's just plain dead. Two-day diving courses cost around $300. **Snuba**, basically snorkelling with a longer tube, is less demanding. For the sedentary, **submarines** are in action on Oahu and Hawaii.

Snorkel sets are widely available for around $5 per day (or buy your own). A week's rental at the excellent **Snorkel Bob's** outlets costs $15. "Snorkel Bob" also writes entertaining handbooks to having a good time on each island, and can be found at:

Oahu: 702 Kapahiulu Ave, Honolulu (☎735-7944), on the road out to Hanauma Bay.

Big Island: 75-3831 Kahakai St, Kailua-Kona (☎329-0770).

Maui: Lahaina, at *Napili Village Hotel* (☎669-9603) and 161 Lahainaluna Rd #3 (☎661-4421); also 34 Keala Place, Kihei (☎879-7449).

Kauai: 4480 Auhukini Rd, Lihue (☎245-9433).

Oahu's leading paying attraction, with one million annual visitors, is the **Polynesian Cultural Center** at Laie (Mon–Sat 12.30–9pm; $25). This haphazard mixture of real and bogus Polynesia – in which the history is firmly on the bogus side – is owned by the Mormons, and staffed by students at Brigham Young University right behind it. The imposing white Mormon Temple nearby was the first to be built outside the continental United States. *TheBus* #52 takes roughly two hours to get this far.

At **Amorient Aqua Park** a little further on in Kahuku (☎293-8661), delicious fresh (cooked) shrimps are on sale for immediate consumption at the picnic tables.

All the windward beaches are public, but use proper paths to reach them.

North Shore Oahu

The **surfing beaches** of northern Oahu are famous the world over, but they're barely equipped for tourists. **Waimea, Sunset** and **Ekuhai** beach parks (the latter is home of the Banzai Pipeline) are all laid-back roadside stretches of sand, where you can usually find a quiet spot to yourself. Sunset is best for savoring the atmosphere, though surfers can be an exclusive bunch. The tame summer waves may make you wonder what all the fuss is about; if you see them at full tilt in the winter you'll have no doubts.

HALEIWA is the main surfers' hang-out, combining alternative shops and cafés with upfront tourist traps. The *Backpacker's Vacation Inn*, at 59-788 Kamehameha Hwy by Waimea Bay (☎638-7838; ①/②), has dorm beds for $16 a night as well as private rooms. At 66-443 Kam Hwy is the *Paradise Café* (☎637-4540), serving breakfast and lunch for about $5, and the *Celestial Natural Foods* store. The friendly *Coffee Gallery* at 66-250 Kamehameha Hwy (☎637-5571) is open each day from dawn until 9.30pm, serving health food and featuring occasional live music.

At Waimea Bay, **Waimea Falls Park** is a commercial exploitation of what is nonetheless a beautiful valley, replete with waterfalls and river, charging adults $15. The only resort on this side of the island is the *Hilton at Turtle Bay* (☎1-800/445-8667; ⑥), but it's possible to find rentals with *Countryside Cabins* (☎237-8169; ④).

Leeward Oahu

The leeward (Waianae) coast of Oahu, customarily dismissed as "arid", is only so by Hawaiian standards. It certainly has its share of fine beaches, the best being **Makaha Beach Park** (served by *TheBus* #51). However, the traditionally minded inhabitants of towns such as **Nanakuli** are not disposed to welcome the encroachment of hotels and golf courses, and visitors tend to be treated with a degree of suspicion. The further north you go the stronger the military presence becomes, with soldiers in camouflage blending into the green valleys. You are not encouraged to attempt an island circuit; the last stretch of road, through a military reservation, is deliberately left unpaved.

THE BIG ISLAND

The **Big Island** of **HAWAII** is indeed big – it could accommodate all the other islands with room to spare. With a population of only 120,000, half what it was in Captain Cook's day, and a comparatively low level of tourism, there's far more space than on Oahu or Maui. The development that will surely come may put an end to that, but for the moment there are sleepy old towns all over the island, unchanged for a century. The few resorts are in the least beautiful areas, built on the barren lava flows of the **Kona** coast to catch maximum sunshine.

What's more, the Big Island is still growing. The southern shore is inching ever further out to sea, thanks to the **Kilauea** volcano, still wiping out roads and even towns and spewing out pristine beaches of jet-black sand. **Hawaii Volcanoes National Park**, which includes **Mauna Loa** as well as Kilauea (though not **Mauna Kea**, higher than either at 13,796 feet), is absolutely compelling; you can explore steaming craters and cinder cones, venture into the rainforest, and at times approach within feet of the eruption itself. The summits of Mauna Loa and Mauna Kea have the clearest air on earth – and astronomical observatories to take advantage of it – but down below, when the tradewinds drop, the island is prone to a choking sulfurous haze known as "**vog**".

As befits the birthplace of **King Kamehameha**, the base from which he became the first man to rule all the Hawaiian islands, more of the ancient Hawaii survives on the Big Island than anywhere else. **Puuhonua O Honaunau** National Historical Park preserves a temple complex which served as a "place of refuge" for *kapu*-breakers and defeated warriors, just a few miles from the site of Captain Cook's death, and there are further temples and *heiaus* north along the Kohala coast. **Waipio Valley**, where Kamehameha spent his youth, remains as lush and green as ever, all the more magical for the knowledge that six further impenetrable valleys lie beyond it.

Flights to Hawaii arrive at **Hilo** on the rainy east coast, or the much less genuine but unoffensive resort of **Kona** (also known as Kailua). If you don't rent a **car**, you may not get to the interesting sites; occasional buses link Hilo and Kona, and organized bus tours go to specific attractions, but public transit is all but non-existent.

Windward Hawaii

Almost all the rain that falls on the slopes of Mauna Kea flows down to the sea on the eastern side of the Big Island. Numerous streams and waterfalls nourish dense jungle-like vegetation; the main road north along the coast from Hilo is alive with colorful orchids, and most of the state's commercial tropical gardens are in this area. Hilo is the only sizeable base for travellers, though several places have small hotels.

Hilo

Although it's the Big Island's capital, and largest town, just 45,000 people live in **HILO**, which remains endearing and unpressured. Despite the construction of the only airport on the island which can accept jumbo jets direct from the mainland, mass tourism has never taken off. Quite simply, it rains too much. However, the rain falls mostly at night, and America's wettest city blazes with wild orchids and tropical plants.

Historically, Hilo's role as the island's main port gave it an unusually radical labor force. From the Thirties onwards, Hilo's workers spearheaded successive campaigns against the "Big Five". Fifty were injured, though none died, in the "Hilo Massacre" of August 1 1938, when strikers were attacked by armed police, and strikes in 1946 and 1949 helped to end the long-term Republican domination of state politics.

Hilo has always been at the mercy of the twin natural forces of fire and water. Cataclysmic tidal waves killed 96 people in April 1946, and a further 61 in May 1960. Countless lava flows have also threatened to engulf it; in 1881 Princess Ruth (see p.935) summoned up all her *mana*, watched by missionaries and journalists, to halt one on the edge of town, while in 1984 another flow stopped eight miles short.

Arrival

Downtown Hilo is compact and very walkable, around the junction of the seafront Kamehameha Avenue and Waianuenue Avenue, which heads towards the Saddle Road across the island. However, the urban area extends for several miles, and the **airport**

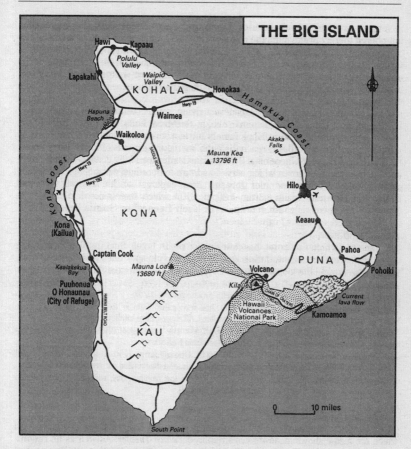

THE BIG ISLAND

at **General Lyman Field** (☎935-4782), on the eastern outskirts, is well beyond walking distance. If you're not renting a car at the airport, a taxi into town will cost around $5.

The **Hawaii Visitors Bureau** is at 250 Keawe St (Mon–Fri 8am–noon & 1–4.30pm; ☎961-5797). Hilo's *Mass Transportation Agency* (25 Aupuni St; ☎935-8241) operates a very small-scale **city bus** service (only two per day), as well as scheduled buses across to Kona from the Mooheau Bus Terminal on Kamehameha Avenue.

Exploring Hilo

There is a simple and tragic reason why **downtown Hilo** looks so appealingly low-key, with its modest streets and wooden stores: all the buildings which stood on the seaward side of Kamehameha Avenue were destroyed by the two *tsunami*. After 1960, no attempt was made to rebuild the "little Tokyo" that had housed Hilo's predominantly Japanese population, and the seafront is now occupied by a succession of pleasant gardens. Besides plenty of conventional shopping, Hilo has a seafront **market** on Wednesday and Saturday mornings. If you want to **swim**, follow Kamehameha Avenue for four miles beyond Banyan Drive to tiny **Richardson's Beach**.

The focus of the two-part **Lyman Museum** at 276 Haili St (Mon–Sat 9am–5pm; $3.50) is the original 1830s **Mission House**, furnished in dark *koa* wood, which belonged to Calvinist missionaries David and Sarah Lyman. Their congregation numbered merely twenty until the charismatic Titus Coan arrived in 1835, and aided by a fortuitous tidal wave in 1837, started a Revival – complete with speaking in tongues – which baptized thousands of ordinary Hawaiians but antagonized his superiors. The museum next door starts with a fascinating set of **ancient weapons** and then documents Hawaii's various **ethnic groups**, including the Portuguese shipped in 1878 from the overpopulated but similarly volcanic Azores, who brought the *braginha* which became the ukelele, and the first Japanese arriving from Hiroshima, Hilo's sister city.

A couple of miles up Waianuenue Ave, at **Rainbow Falls**, just to the right of the road, a spectacular wide waterfall plummets 100 feet across the mouth of a huge cavern. Continue another two miles to reach the bubbling natural jacuzzis of the **Boiling Pots**.

The **Hilo Tropical Gardens** at 1477 Kalanianaole Ave (daily 8.30am–5.30pm; free) are the best of the commercial gardens. To admire extraordinary plants in a less formal setting, take a self-guided tour through the rainforest of the **Hawaii Tropical Botanical Gardens** (daily 8.30am–4.30pm; $10), which sweep down to the sea at Onomea Bay, seven miles out of town on the lovely **Peepeekeo Scenic Drive**.

Accommodation

Hilo, and the whole east coast, has fewer major resort hotels than usual in Hawaii, but there are several **accommodation** possibilities; the cheaper ones tend to be in town rather than around the loop of **Banyan Drive** on the seafront near the airport.

Arnott's Lodge and Hostel, 98 Apapane Rd (☎969-7097 or 1-800/953-7773 in-state). 10 units with shared baths and kitchen. Bunks $15, also semi-private rooms. ①/②.

Dolphin Bay Hotel, 333 Iliahi St (☎935-1466). Just across the Wailuku River from the town center. A very friendly place, popular with budget travellers. All rooms have kitchens. ③.

Hawaii Naniloa Hotel, 93 Banyan Drive (☎969-3333). The grandest of Hilo's options, with luxury rooms and superb views across the bay towards Mauna Kea. ⑤.

Hilo Seaside, 126 Banyan Drive (☎1-800/367-7000). One of four properties in the Hawaiian-owned *Sand & Seaside* chain. Rooms with and without kitchens, and discounted car rental. ③/⑤.

Wild Ginger Hotel, 100 Puueo St (☎935-5556). Near the *Dolphin Bay*, renovated (and painted shocking pink) in 1993. Rates include breakfast buffet. ②.

Eating and Nightlife

Most of Hilo's (eminently missable) **nightlife** is in the Banyan Drive hotels, though there are a few shows at downtown's restored *Palace Theater*. As well as its **restaurants**, early risers will enjoy the 7am daily **Suisan Fish Auction**, at Banyan and Lihiwai, where you can buy from the night's catch of marlin and other big fish.

Fiascos, 200 Kanoelehua Ave (☎935-7666). All-American but adventurous menu, salad bar. $6–10.

Ken's Pancakes, 1730 Kamehameha Ave (☎935-8711). Hilo landmark for 20 years, open 24 hours.

Leahu's Bay City Grill, 90 Kamehameha Ave (☎935-8055). Seafood and steaks, lunch and dinner. Entertainment Fri–Sat with $3 cover; country music Wed.

Nihon Cultural Center, 123 Lihiwai St (☎969-1133). Next to the Fish Auction and Liliuokalani Gardens. Full Japanese meals and sushi too, with exquisite fresh fish and magnificent views. $5–15.

Roussels, 60 Keawe St (☎935-5111). French Creole; formal but good, $13–22. Occasional live jazz.

North from Hilo

The **Belt Road** (Hwy-19) follows the **Hamakua coast** north of Hilo, clinging to the hillsides and crossing ravines on slender bridges. At first the fields are crammed into narrow rain-carved "gulches"; further north the land spreads out and there's room for larger sugar plantations. For an easy glimpse into the interior, head into the mountains after 15 miles to the 450ft **Akaka Falls**. A short loop trail through the forest, festooned with wild orchids, offers views of Akaka and other jungle-like tropical waterfalls.

Waipio Valley

Hwy-240, which turns north off the Belt Road at **HONOKAA**, comes to an abrupt end after nine miles at the edge of **WAIPIO VALLEY**. As the southernmost of six successive sheer-walled valleys, this is the only one accessible by land – and it's as close as Hawaii comes to the classic South Seas image of an isolated and self-sufficient valley, dense with fruit trees and laced by footpaths leading down to the sea. Just off the black-sand beach (greyish in fact) of his boyhood home, Kamehameha the Great fought Kahekili of Oahu in the inconclusive but bloody "Battle of the Red-Mouthed Gun" of 1791, in which for the first time Hawaiian fleets were equipped with cannons, operated by foreign gunners. Spectacular waterfalls cascade down the valley's flanks, but recurrent tidal waves have ensured that only a few taro farmers now live here. A more recent threat has come from Japanese developers, who plan to build two golf courses.

It's perfectly possible to walk down the steep track into Waipio, but most visitors take tours, either in the four-wheel-drive vehicles of the *Waipio Valley Shuttle* (daily 8am–4pm; $30; ☎775-7121), based at the *Waipio Valley Art Works* in Kukuihaele a mile from the end of the road, in horse-drawn wagons ($40; ☎775-9518), or on horseback ($65; ☎775-7291). It's possible to **camp** discreetly on the beach, for which officially you need a permit from the Hamakua Sugar Company (☎776-1211), or at **Kalopa State Beach** (☎775-7114), back on the Belt Road. Rough-and-tumble Honokaa itself – scene of a **Western Week** each May, featuring rodeo – has rooms at the *Hotel Honokaa Club* (PO Box 185; ☎775-0678; ②), and the *Waipio Wayside B&B* (☎775-0275; ③).

Kohala

On the green slopes of **Kohala Mountain**, at the northern tip of the Big Island, old-style plantation towns such as **HAWI** survive virtually unchanged; it's run-down in an appealing sort of way, the all-purpose general stores still floored with creaking planks. In **KAPAAU**, the birthplace of Kamehameha (who was brought up in Waipio Valley, hidden from his enemies) is marked by his statue. Identical to that in Honolulu, this is in fact the original, lost at sea near the Falklands, and then miraculously recovered after the insurance money had paid for a new one. The *Deli Cafe* opposite (☎889-5822) does basic snacks, with vegetarian options.

Pololu Valley at road's end is the last of the chain of inaccessible valleys which begins with Waipio, and for the moment is every bit as pristine, with a black sand beach. The fear of *tsunami* which led the Hawaiians to abandon these once densely populated valleys is probably their best defence against the rapacity of the developers.

An illuminating insight into the ancient way of life can be had at **Lapakahi State Historical Park**, a partly reconstructed 600-year-old village (daily 8am–4pm; free). The waters off its small beach are a marine conservation area, great for snorkellers.

Waimea and Inland Hawaii

Inland Hawaii comes as a surprise; pastoral meadows roll over gentle hills where once stood forests of sandalwood. This is cattle-ranching country, most of it – ten percent of the island – owned by the United States' largest private ranch, the **Parker Ranch**.

WAIMEA (also known as **Kamuela**) is not the company town it once was – the Parker Ranch now employs just one hundred of its eight thousand inhabitants – but more of a sophisticated country-town resort, which retains traces of its cowboy past. Though you can no longer tour the ranch itself, there's an interesting **visitor center** (Mon–Sat 9am–4pm; $5) in town, with a good section on surfer Duke Kahanamoku; the nearby **Kamuela Museum** is enjoyably eclectic and eccentric (daily 8am–4pm; $5).

Waimea Practicalities

B&B is booming in Waimea; in fact there's little else. Barbara Campbell runs her own *Waimea Gardens Cottage* (☎885-4550; ⑤), and also coordinates *Hawaii's Best B&Bs* (PO Box 563, Kamuela 96743), a selection of Big Island properties costing from $70 to $100 per night. Outbuildings at the *Historic Hale Kea Ranch* (☎885-6094; ⑤), on the main road out, serve as B&B accommodation; the main building holds a restaurant, and is open for free tours daily. *Merriman's* in Opelo Plaza (☎885-6822) wins awards for its innovative cuisine, but entrees begin $20; *Yuni's Korean BBQ* in Lanihao Center (☎329-3167) is popular with locals. The only place to get breakfast is *Auntie Alice's* in the Parker Ranch Shopping Center (☎889-0206), which is also good for cheap snacks.

The Saddle Road

The fifty-mile **Saddle Road** cuts across the Big Island, from Hilo to Kona between Mauna Kea and Mauna Loa. Even locals call it "dangerous", especially at night, as there are no facilities, and it's a winding, foggy drive. If you do choose to chance it (in the daytime), you get some great views of the volcanoes – and a good deal of mist even then.

The Kona Coast

Hawaii's leeward **Kona coast** divides into two distinct areas. To the north of its only sizeable community, **Kona**, a long bleak slope of barren lava trails from dormant Mauna Kea down to the sea. Thanks to the relentless sun on its magnificent beaches, luxury hotels dot the shoreline, incongruous green patches in the wasteland. Southwards, the hillsides are more fertile, and although the condos are spreading, you can still get a real feel of the old Hawaii, in the land where Captain Cook met his end.

North Kona

The best of the spectacular sandy beaches north of Kona – safe for summer swimming, though with tempestuous winter surf – is the long crescent of **Hapuna Beach** (where the state park rents cabins; ☎882-1095). Each of the extraordinary **hotels** in the three resort areas – Waikoloa, Mauna Kea and Mauna Lani – is a self-contained oasis in this inhospitable lava desert. The *Hyatt Regency* (☎885-1234; ⑧), which consumes four percent of all the island's energy, is ludicrously ostentatious, its rooms reached by electric boats or monorail. The *Royal Waikoloan* (☎885-6709; ⑦) is half the price – for what that's worth – and has two good restaurants as well as its own field of petroglyphs.

Kona (Kailua)

Although the Big Island's main resort is officially called Kailua, and its postal address is "Kailua-Kona", confusingly enough everyone refers to it simply as **KONA**. It's reasonably attractive, and has played its part in Hawaiian history, but its summer-holiday seafront of fast-food restaurants and souvenir shops could be anywhere; and the wind-borne "vog" means that the atmosphere can be as bad as in Los Angeles or London.

Arrival and Information

Open-plan **Keahole Airport**, on a field of black lava nine miles north of Kona, has the usual car rental places; otherwise a shared *Gray Line Limousine* into town costs around $12, and a cab $30. Once in Kona, a regular **shuttle bus** runs the six-mile length of Alii Drive every ninety minutes (7.45am–9.15pm; $1). One daily bus follows Highway 11 round to Hilo, leaving Kona just before 6am and returning in the evening.

The **Hawaiian Visitors Bureau** is in Kona Plaza on Alii Drive (Mon–Fri 8am–noon & 1–4.30pm; ☎329-7787), as is the well-stocked *Middle Earth* bookstore. **Bicycles** can be rented from *Hawaiian Pedals* in the Kona Inn Shopping Village (☎329-2294), which recommends the Old Highway through Holualoa.

The Town

Hulihee Palace (daily 9am–4pm; $4) stands square-on to the ocean in the middle of Kona. Built as the governor's residence in 1838, it's not all that imposing from the outside. Within, it's notable for massive *koa*-wood furnishings, made to fit the considerable girth of the various members of the Hawaiian royal family who later lived here, such as the redoubtable four-hundred-pound Princess Ruth. The 1836 **Mokuaikaua Church** opposite was the first in Hawaii, and acts in part as a museum of the early days of Hawaiian Christianity, setting out to debunk the popular notion of the missionaries as having been primarily concerned with feathering their own nests. A peculiar "sausage-tree" from Mozambique stands in the grounds. Nearby, the *King Kamehameha Hotel* (see below) dominates the northern end of the bay. King Kamehameha's funeral rites were performed in the **Ahuena Heiau** which juts into the sea in front of its beach.

Some of the world's best fishing and snorkelling or scuba spots are approached by sea from Kona. Two-hour tours on *Atlantis Submarines* descend one hundred feet to a coral reef, accompanied by the *Star Wars* theme, to see a frenzy of feeding fish and the occasional lurking shark ($79, under-12s half-price; ☎329-6626). The catamaran *Fair Wind* ($50; ☎322-2788) goes to Kealakekua Bay, for snorkelling and a bit of snuba (lesson and 40-minute dive, $40). To fish for the big ones, the *Kona Charter Skippers Assn* can accommodate all size parties (☎1-800/367-8047 ext 360 in US, or 329-3600; half-day $65, all-day $100 and up).

South Kona Accommodation

Alii Drive is lined for about five miles south from Kona with hotels and condos, but none offers much by way of cheap accommodation. The listings below therefore include a couple of places a bit further along the coast.

Aston Royal Sea Cliff Resort, 75-6040 Alii Drive (☎1-800/922-7866). Upscale condo rooms. ⑤.

Hotel King Kamehameha, 75-5660 Palani Rd (☎329-2911 or ☎1-800/733-7777). Kona's grandest hotel; Hunter S Thompson abandoned a monstrous demented dog in one of the plushest suites. The *heiau* (altar) is the backdrop to a *luau* (Tues, Thurs & Sun; $45), at which the baked pig is supplemented with raw fish, Hawaiian and Japanese dishes, and Polynesian entertainment. ⑥.

Kona Seaside, 75-5646 Palani Rd (☎822-4951 or 1-800/367-7000). One of the *Sand & Seaside* chain. Rooms with and without kitchens, and discounted car rental. ③/⑤.

Kona Tiki Hotel, at 1-mile marker on Alii Drive (PO Box 1567; ☎329-1425). Old and well-maintained inn between the main road and the sea. No phones or TV, but free breakfast. ③.

Manago Hotel, on Hwy-11 in Captain Cook (PO Box 145, Captain Cook; ☎323-2642). Hawaii's best value. Very comfortable ocean-view rooms, in flower-filled Japanese gardens; cheaper ones have shared bathrooms. Discounted weekly rates. Run by the same friendly family since 1917. Good Japanese/American restaurant (closed Mon). Reserve three months ahead. ①/②.

Patey's Place, 75-195 Ala Ona Ona (☎326-7018 or 1-800/972-7408). $16 beds in 4-person dorms, and some private rooms with shared bath. ①/③.

Eating and Drinking

Competition ensures that the bars and restaurants of central Kona – especially those along the seafront – are well priced, though the relentless holiday atmosphere means the place can seem a bit unreal.

Banana Bay, at the *Kona Bay Hotel*, 75-5739 Alii Drive (☎329-1393). $4.95 breakfast buffet in central Kona hotel.

Huggo's, on the beach at 76-6828 Kuhakai St (☎329-1493). Lunch and dinner only; burgers, salads and sandwiches, plus live evening entertainment.

THE DEATH OF CAPTAIN COOK

Captain James Cook sailed into Kealakekua Bay on January 17 1779 at a singularly auspicious moment. The *makahiki* festival, at the temple of the god **Lono**, was at its height; Lono's return, circling Hawaii on a floating island of tall trees, had long been prophesied. As the billowing sails of the *Resolution* (originally a "Whitby cat", built to transport coal from Newcastle down the English coast) hove into view, they looked just like the cloth-draped sticks which were Lono's emblems. Cook and his men were welcomed as honored guests, and fed and feted for three long weeks before they set off once more across the ocean, having dismantled the temple for firewood.

A week later they returned, forced back by a storm which left their ship in tatters – and this time the islanders were not so hospitable, far from keen to part with further scarce resources. On February 14, Cook led a landing party of nine men in an attempt to kidnap the local chief and effect the return of a stolen small boat. In an undignified scuffle, surrounded by thousands of hostile warriors including the future Kamehameha the Great, he was stabbed and died at the water's edge, unable as a non-swimmer to reach safety. His body was treated as appropriate for a dead chief; the skull and leg bones were kept, and the rest cremated (though his heart was eaten by children who mistook it for a dog's). His crew, however, were far from mollified by the eventual return of just a few charred bones.

Whether the Hawaiians believed Cook to be Lono is debatable, despite the various coincidences; they were certainly puzzled and cautious, testing Cook to see just what sort of creature he might be. That he failed such tests, for example by groaning when struck a severe blow instead of maintaining a godlike tranquillity, is hardly surprising.

Jennifer's Korean BBQ, Luhia St, Kailua-Kona (☎326-1155). Lunch and dinner from $6. Not a buffet, but you do cook it yourself.

Kona Amigos, Alii Drive (☎326-2840). Restaurant (until 10pm) and bar (until midnight) in Kona Square opposite the *King Kamehameha*. Mexican/Hawaiian cuisine; *mahi-mahi fajitas* for $7.

Ocean View Inn, Alii Drive (☎329-9998). Very cheap Hawaiian and Oriental food overlooking the sea; traditional fish dishes. Closed Mon.

Sibu Café, Alii Drive (☎329-1112). Good Indonesian specialties, but no rice table.

Kealakekua Bay

Kealakekua Bay, a dozen miles south of Kona, was where Captain Cook was killed on his second voyage to Hawaii (see box). One of ancient Hawaii's major population centers, it's now barely inhabited, and the white **obelisk** on the death site – legally a small piece of England – is all but inaccessible. You can only get to within a mile of it by car, to the beach at **Napoopoo** across the bay, though you'll glimpse it from the road on the way down. The bay itself is the best place on the Big Island for **snorkelling**, even if there are sharks further out. It's also possible to hike down to the monument from the town of **CAPTAIN COOK**; in fact this is the track to follow to reach the sea if you're staying at the *Manago Hotel* (see previous page).

South Kona is the prime source of **Kona coffee**, which sells here for around $13 a pound (including shipping). You can tour the restored **Old Hawaiian Coffee Plantation**, reached via a one-track rutted road 400 yards from marker 105 outside Captain Cook, and buy the produce of its 5000 coffee trees and macadamia nut trees.

Puuhonua O Honaunau – "The City of Refuge"

Puuhonua O Honaunau National Historical Park (daily 7.30am–5.30pm; $2), four miles on from Kealakekua, is the single most evocative historical site in all the Hawaiian islands, jutting into the Pacific on a small peninsula of jagged black lava. The grounds include a palace, with fishpond and private canoe landing, and three *heiaus*, guarded by large carved effigies of gods – reproductions, but still eerie in their original setting. An ancient "**place of refuge**" lies firmly protected behind the mortarless masonry of the sixteenth-century **Great Wall**. Those who broke ancient Hawaii's intricate system of *kapu* (*tabu*) – perhaps by treading on the shadow of a chief, or fishing in the wrong season – could expect summary execution . . . unless they fled to the sanctuary of such a place as this. As chiefs lived on the surrounding land, transgressors had to swim through the shark-infested seas. If successful, they might be absolved and released overnight. In times of war, non-combatants came here to sit out the conflict.

Hawaii Volcanoes National Park

The southern and smaller two of the Big Island's volcanoes, **Mauna Loa** and **Kilauea**, jointly constitute **HAWAII VOLCANOES NATIONAL PARK**, thirty miles from Hilo and eighty from Kona. It's possibly the most dramatic of all the US national parks; as well as two active volcanoes, of which at least one is likely to be erupting, it includes desert, arctic tundra, and the Wao Kele O Puna rainforest (where a much-opposed pilot project is drilling for geothermal energy).

Evidence is everywhere of the awesome power of the volcanoes to create and destroy; no map can keep up with the latest whims of the lava flow. Whole towns have been engulfed, and what were once prized beachfront properties lie buried hundreds of yards back from the sea. No one knows quite where they are – there's nowhere for surveyors to get their bearings. There are no towns left on the southern coast. The Hawaiians abandoned their villages 150 years ago, after a succession of terrible tidal waves; now the Americans too have been driven out.

Kilauea Caldera

The headquarters of the park ($5 admission) is on the rim of Kilauea Caldera. Both the **visitor center** (daily 7.45am–5pm; ☎967-7311) and the fascinating **Jaggar Museum** of geology (daily 8.30am–5pm) on the 11-mile **Crater Rim Drive** offer basic orientation.

Kilauea is said to be the home of the volcano goddess **Pele**, who has followed the "hot spot" from island to island. In 1824 Queen Kapiolani, a recent convert to Christianity, defied her by descending into the crater, reading aloud from her Bible, eating the *tabu* red ohelo berries, and throwing stones into the pit. When Mark Twain came here, he saw a dazzling lake of liquid fire; since a huge explosion in 1924 it's been shallower and quieter, a black dusty expanse dotted with hissing steam vents. The three-mile **Halemaumau Trail** leads across the crater floor, now (mostly) solid.

The **Devastation Trail** is a boardwalk laid across the scene of a 1959 eruption; scientists are monitoring how long vegetation takes to re-establish itself. Most of what you see is new growth – fresh lava is full of nutrients, and rainwater and seeds soon collect in the recesses – but a few older trees survived partial submersion in ash by growing "aerial roots" some way up their trunks. Around the cinder cone of **Puu Puai**, the land is utterly barren, scattered with bleached dead branches.

A short drive from *Volcano House*, and across the road from the crater, is a rainforest. A ten-minute walk takes you through **Thurston Lava Tube**, created when the surface of a lava stream, exposed to the air, hardened. Just below, the now-protected lava was able to keep flowing 28 miles to the sea with only a slight loss of temperature. It's now a damp empty tunnel, an illuminated segment of which is open. Gigantic ferns grow over the top, and a few roots have worked their way through cracks in the rock to dangle from the ceiling. Outside, the native red-billed *iiwi* bird can always be heard, if not seen.

Stretching away southwest of Kilauea, the **Kau Desert** receives plenty of rainfall – but it's a natural sulfurous acid rain, composed of volcanic fumes carried by the trade-winds, and far too noxious to support life.

Chain of Craters Road

The twenty-mile dead-end **Chain of Craters Road** winds down to the sea from Crater Rim Drive, sweeping around a succession of cones and vents where an occasional dead white tree trunk or flowering shrub pokes up. Fresh sheets of lava constantly ooze down the slopes to cover the road. When they build the road again on top of the new flow, more lava covers it. From high on the hillside it looks like a stream of black tarmac, an ever-widening highway down to the endless blue ocean.

The **black sand beach** at **KAMOAMOA** was created literally overnight in January 1988 by the explosive impact of lava striking the sea; there it was the next morning, two miles long and absolutely jet black, made up of rounded glass-like fragments.

Approaching the Eruption

For several years, though the exact site varied, it was possible to walk across the congealed lava blocking Chain of Craters Road and see molten rock gush from the earth – sometimes directly into the sea. A **Volcano Update** information line (☎967-7977) has the latest details (for information on tours run by park rangers, ring ☎967-7311).

A wooden shack on wheels – of necessity, periodically shifted – at the end of the road hands out warnings that new lava is unstable and may collapse at any time, and that it's best to avoid clouds of hydrochloric acid. There's no set path to follow, you just pick your way through a disarray of broken slabs. Every surface is like sandpaper, a fall can shred your skin, and the ground can be searingly hot. It's essential to carry water.

Pele was the most capricious of Hawaiian deities; chiefs and priests tested their spiritual strength (*mana*) by controlling her outbursts. Sacred sites too could possess *mana*; and sure enough one of Hawaii's oldest temples is the only human structure to survive in this wasteland. A few miles away, the **Star of the Sea** church stands forlorn beside Hwy-30, moved bodily from doomed Kalapana before its *mana* could be put to the test. **Wahaula Heiau** ("the Temple of the Red-mouthed God") stayed put, relying on an impeccable five-century record of human sacrifice to Pele. Perhaps it's not so surprising that the lava flowed to either side of its stone walls, built on high ground; the chill wind that swirls around the sacrificial platform suggests deeper forces at play.

When the lava is flowing, self-confident – or stupid – hikers continue past the rough noticeboards reading "EXTREME DANGER: Do not go beyond this point", to approach the conflagration, even prodding with sticks at the eggshell crust. Many stay out all night to marvel at the glowing orange rivers of molten rock, somehow considering themselves impregnable. Nature seems to concur; there has yet to be a serious injury, after years of such nocturnal hikes. If you try it, be sure to carry a flashlight for the long walk back across the treacherous lava.

Accommodation and Eating

The National Park operates two **campgrounds** on a first-come first-served basis, as well as a dozen cabins that can be reserved a month or more in advance, for $24 a night. Otherwise, the small and inconspicuous town of **VOLCANO** just before the park entrance on the Hilo side provides the best places to **stay** in the vicinity, with B&Bs such as *My Island*, run by local expert Gordon Morse (PO Box 100; ☎967-7216; ③) and *Volcano* at 19-3950 Keonelehua St (☎967-7779; ③). The famous *Volcano House* on the very edge of the crater within the park (PO Box 53; ☎967-7321; ⑦) – not the same building as Mark Twain stayed in – has spectacular views, but except for its **campground** it's expensive, especially if you want a room overlooking the crater, and generally unsatisfactory; *Kilauea Lodge* is cheaper (☎967-7366; ⑤). Neither is *Volcano House* a good place to **eat**; the restaurant at *Volcano Golf & Country Club* (☎967-7331), two miles from the park entrance on the Kona side, is much better value, and various stores in Kiluaea sell provisions. Note that there are no facilities of any kind – no food, no gas – along Chain of Craters Road or down by the ocean.

Pahoa and the Southeast

The southeastern corner of the Big Island is off the usual tourist trail. **PAHOA** in particular has gone its own sweet way, its distinctive blend of lawless cowboy town and hippy hang-out probably due to its alleged role as the island's main marijuana-growing area. Businesses along the rudimentary boardwalks include a New Age bookstore and café, the *Naung Mai Thai Kitchen* (☎965-8186) serving plenty of vegetarian options, and *Luquin's* Mexican restaurant (☎965-9990). The *Bamboo House* is a small and friendly B&B (enquire at *Pahoa Natural Groceries* or ring ☎965-8322; ③).

At **Pohoiki**, seven miles southeast, a jagged expanse of black rocks and sand is pummelled by ferocious surf. Following the coast south from here you rejoin Hwy-130 from Pahoa shortly before it is blocked by lava flows from Kilauea.

MAUI

The island of **MAUI**, the second largest in the Hawaiian chain, is Oahu's fastest-growing rival, attracting roughly a third of all visitors to Hawaii. Opponents of plans to extend Kahului Airport to accommodate jumbo jets fear things are going too far. What were remote unspoiled beaches twenty years ago, around **Kaanapali** and **Kihei** for example, have been swamped by ugly sprawling resorts, and **Lahaina**, once "whaling capital of the world", is now just another tourist trap. Traffic clogs the roads, and most towns consist of little more than a succession of malls.

On the other hand, the crowds come to Maui for the good reason that it's still beautiful. This is probably the best equipped of all the islands for **activity** holidays – whale-watching, windsurfing, diving, sailing, snorkelling, cycling. Temperatures along the coast can be searing, especially at Lahaina, but it's always possible to get somewhere cooler. **Upcountry Maui**, on the slopes of the mighty **Haleakala** volcano, is a delight, well away from the bustle; **Makawao** and **Paia** here make good alternative hang-outs, if short on accommodation. The tortuous road out west to **Hana** does not quite merit its legendary status, but with its waterfalls and ravines it outclasses anything on Oahu.

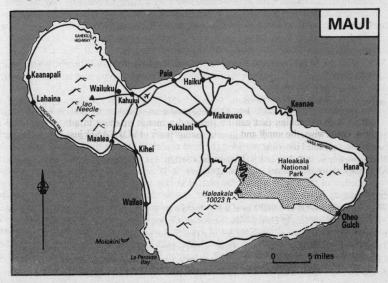

Kahului and Wailuku

Half of Maui's 91,000 inhabitants – the workers who keep this fantasy island going – live in the twin towns of **KAHULUI** and **WAILUKU**, to the north of the "neck" connecting its two mountainous sections. The land here can be so flat you fear the waves will wash right over it. Kahului is the main commercial center; Wailuku, if not aesthetically pleasing, is unusual for Maui in feeling like a genuine community, and with its cheap hotels and restaurants – and the stunning **Iao Needle** nearby – it makes a good central base.

Arrival and Information

Virtually all visitors to Maui arrive at **Kahului Airport**, which is well placed for all the major destinations and has an information booth. In the absence of anything other than extremely local bus services, a rental car from the airport is almost essential; a taxi into Wailuku costs around $8, to Lahaina more like $30. **Bicycles** – scarcely cheaper than cars – can be rented from *The Island Biker* in Kahului Shopping Center (☎877-7744).

The **Maui Visitors Bureau** is at 250 Alamaha Bay N16 (Mon–Fri 10am–4.30pm; ☎871-8691).

Exploring Kahului and Wailuku

There's no sightseeing to speak of in either Kahului or Wailuku, though you may well become familiar with both while shopping for food and other necessities, better value here than elsewhere on the island. **Market Street** in Wailuku contains several interesting curio and souvenir shops, and commands a view across to Haleakala.

Wailuku's Main Street heads straight into the West Maui Mountains, stopping three miles in at **Iao Needle**, a stunning 1200ft pinnacle of green-clad lava. It stands, head usually in the clouds, at the intersection of two lush valleys; you can't climb the needle itself, but hiking trails lead off in all directions, and as very few visitors follow them for any distance you can soon be alone in the wilderness. King Kamehameha won control of Maui here in 1790, in a battle determined by a cannonade directed by two captured European gunners. On the road up, a natural rock formation has become known for fairly – but not very – obvious reasons as the **John F Kennedy Profile**.

Accommodation

As most of the Maui resorts are long oceanfront strips of expensive hotels, where you have to drive just to get to a shop or restaurant, there's a lot to be said for a cheap and simple room in Wailuku.

Banana Bungalow, 310 N Market St, Wailuku (☎244-5090 or 1-800/846-7835 from the US). Extremely convivial budget hotel with Maui's cheapest accommodation. $15 for a dorm bed, also some bare, basic doubles. Informal meals, organized trips, cut-price car rental. ①/②.

Maui Seaside Hotel, 100 W Kaahumanu at harbor (☎877-3311 or 1-800/367-7000). Good-value rooms and discounted car rental. ③.

Northshore Inn, 2080 Vineyard St, Wailuku (☎242-8999). $16.50 dorms, plus some private rooms. Much the same communal feel as *Banana Bungalow*. ①/③.

Eating

Wailuku has several of Maui's best-value restaurants, some near *Banana Bungalow* on Market Street, others in Lower Main Street as it loops down towards Kahului Harbor.

Siam Thai, 123 N Market St (☎244-3817). Fiery Thai curries and lots of vegetarian choices, $6–8.

Tasty Crust, 1770 Mill St (☎244-0845). Basic home-cooking, especially good value for breakfast.

Chum's, 1900 Main St (☎244-1000). Family restaurant, good for breakfast and dinner.

Tokyo Tei, 1063 Lower Main St (☎242-9630). Very popular for the cheapest Japanese food around.

West Maui

It's easy to state the disadvantages of staying on Maui's **west coast**: the prices are higher, it's well away from the best beaches and sights of the island, and the long drive around is made worse by the volume of traffic. Holiday-makers come for the guarantee of sun, then spend their days in expensive air-conditioned hotels and shopping centers of the two main resorts, **Lahaina** and **Kaanapali** (an *Amfac* development). One real plus is that development has sensibly been restricted to the *makai* (oceanward) side of the Honoapiilani Highway, leaving the inland hills and valleys largely untouched except by drifting rainbows.

Lahaina

The square at the heart of modern **LAHAINA** is all but filled by a magnificent **banyan tree**, its branches pushing pack into the earth to become sturdy additional trunks. Just in front, in the small boat harbor, the replica square-rigged *Carthaginian* houses a **maritime museum** (Mon–Sat 9am–4.30pm, Sun 11am–4pm; $3). **Pioneer Inn** nearby is Lahaina's main social center, well worth wandering into for a beer, if not exactly quiet.

Otherwise, a walk up Front Street and back down Wainee Street just about covers what Lahaina has to offer; but it may well take you some time, as the concentration of tourist shops, fast-food places and so on is phenomenal. The one respite is the view out to sea, towards the island of Lanai. These cramped streets make **parking** a terrible business, incidentally; the only free public parking is at Front and Prison streets.

WHALE-HUNTING AND WHALE-WATCHING

The first **whaling ships** arrived in Hawaii in 1820, the same year as the missionaries – and had an equally dramatic impact. With the ports of Japan closed to outsiders, Hawaii swiftly became the center of the industry. Any Pacific port of call would have seemed a godsend to the whalers, who were away from New England for three years at a time, and paid so badly that most were either fugitives from justice or just plain mad (see p.170). Hawaii was such a paradise that up to fifty percent of each crew would desert, to be replaced by native Hawaiians, born seafarers eager to see the world. Soon King Kamehameha IV had established his own whaling fleet, and the economy adapted to meet the sailors' needs. The Big Island turned to raising cattle, and Maui began to grow vegetables.

Until the 1840s, Honolulu, which permitted drinking, was the whalemen's favorite port. Then potatoes and prostitution lured them to **Lahaina** as well, which by 1857 stretched for several miles. The sea was calm enough for ships to dock along the open roadstead, and a grassy marketplace stood beside a central canal. Both Lahaina and Honolulu were notorious for such diseases as syphilis, influenza, measles, typhoid and smallpox.

At the peak of the trade, almost six hundred whaling vessels docked in Honolulu in a single year. Decline came with the Civil War – when many ships were bought up in order to be sunk as a blockade of Confederate ports – and an 1871 disaster, when 31 vessels lingered in the Arctic too long, became frozen in, and had to be abandoned.

Whale-watching

Ironically, the waters just off western Maui are now one of the world's best areas for whale-watching and research. Between January and March each year, and for up to a month either side of that, **humpback whales** use the ocean channels here as both sanctuary and playground. They did not do so in the nineteenth century, although they would have been safe enough, as humpbacks were not then hunted. When caught with the old technology, they sank uselessly to the bottom of the sea.

The whales are often clearly visible from the shore, but specific whale-watching trips can take you much nearcr (with money-back guarantees if you don't see one). Operators include *Pacific Whale Foundation* ($29; ☎879-8811) and *Maui Princess* ($31; ☎661-8397).

Accommódation

If you have the money to spend on resort-style accommodation, Lahaina and the coast northwards have some good options; otherwise the availability of rooms at the historic *Pioneer Inn* may well determine whether you come here at all.

Maui Islander, 600 Wainee St (☎667-9766). Very central low-key top-range accommodation. ⑤.

Pioneer Inn, 658 Wharf St (☎661-3636). Characterful and very lively old hotel, right in the thick of things. The cheaper rooms are in the old building (above the bar). ②/④.

Tony's Place, 13 Kauaula Rd (☎661-8040). Simple but comfortable B&B near the beach. ④.

Food and Nightlife

Lahaina's harborside malls contain a tremendous selection of restaurants, national and local chain outlets (*Chili's*, *Hard Rock Café*, *Pacific Café*), and takeaways, not all of them good by any means but covering a wider spectrum than the hotels.

Carola's Village Pizzeria, 505 Front St (☎661-8112). Notable for its *Studio 505* club (☎661-1606).

Golden Palace, Lahaina Shopping Center (☎661-3126). Good-value Chinese with varied menu. $8.

Kimo's, 845 Front St (661-4811). Polynesian atmosphere, so-so dinners from about $18.

Moose McGillycuddy's, 844 Front St (☎667-7758). Breakfast $3–4 for twenty different omelettes. American menu, lunch and dinner, live entertainment (9.30pm–2am; $2 cover).

Musashi, Lahaina Square, Wainee St (☎667-6207). Sushi until 9pm, and full Japanese menu.

Kaanapali

KAANAPALI, just a few miles north but reliably cooler, was never a town; fields of sugarcane were replaced in the Sixties by high-rise hotels and condos, each no doubt comfortable enough but soulless en masse. Besides several reasonable **beaches** – swimming and snorkelling are best at **Black Rock**, in front of the *Sheraton* – the main attraction is the **whaling museum** in the Whalers Village mall (daily 9.30am–10pm). Grisly but fascinating exhibits include a cast-iron "try pot", used for reducing whale blubber at sea; such pots gave rise to the stereotyped but not entirely untrue image of cannibals cooking missionaries in big black cauldrons.

A free shuttle bus connects Kaanapali with Lahaina, and a trolley operates within the resort. The warnings of the rental car companies concerning the **Kahekili Highway**, which looks on the map like a good route to continue around northwest Maui and back to Wailuku, should be taken seriously; it's an exceptionally dangerous drive.

Kihei and Wailea

Maui's other main resort area is south of Kahului, across the isthmus. The long strip of hotels, malls and condos begins at **KIHEI**, with the road heavily built up to both sides, but thins out beyond the manicured lawns of **WAILEA** near some superb beaches. **Palliea Beach** is ideal for families; **Little Beach**, reached by a trail from cactus-lined Makena (or Big) Beach, is famous for (illegal) nudism. A very rough one-lane track, with minimal visibility, peters out altogether just before **La Perouse Bay**. Once a significant population center, the beach here is good for snorkelling, and **dolphins** regularly come to play with swimmers, though you're forbidden to encourage them.

None of the **accommodation** is cheap; condo options include *Wailana Sands*, 25 Wailane Place (☎879-2026; ③), and the newer *Aston Kamaole Sands*, 2965 S Kihei Rd (☎874-8700 or 1-800/922-7866; ⑤). For **snacks**, the 24-hour *Paradise Fruit* stand in Rainbow Mall at 1913 S Kihei Rd (☎879-1723) serves fresh juices, shakes and sandwiches. *Royal Thai Cuisine* in Azeka Shopping Center, 1280 S Kihei Rd (☎874-0813), is a good-value Thai restaurant, *Mauilu*, 575 S Kihei Rd (☎879-5881), is a breakfast favorite, and *Chums*, 2439 S Kihei Rd #201A (☎874-9000), serves *kalua* pork for $6.50.

Upcountry Maui

Not always is Hawaii a land tarnished by civilization. Central Maui, in the last century "a dreary expanse of sand and shifting sandhills, with a dismal growth . . . of thornless thistles", is now a pastoral idyll, thanks to an ingenious system of irrigation channels.

The highway to the top of **Haleakala** rises higher, faster, than any road on earth, starting in the rich meadows where Jimi Hendrix's *Rainbow Bridge* concert was filmed. Beyond the exclusive homes and white clapboard churches, it climbs past purple-blossoming jacaranda, firs and eucalyptus to reach open ranching land and then ascends in huge curves to the volcanic desert and the crater itself.

Haleakala

Though **HALEAKALA** – "the House of the Sun" – is the world's largest dormant volcano, you may not appreciate its full ten thousand feet until you're at the top. Shield volcanoes are not as dramatic as the classic cones, and the summit is often obscured by cloud. That it hasn't erupted for two hundred years doesn't necessarily mean it won't ever again – in 1979, for example, Haleakala was thought more likely to explode than Mount St Helens (see p.863).

The higher reaches of the mountain are a **national park**, kept open non-stop (admission $4). Manhattan would fit comfortably into the awe-inspiring **crater**, almost eight miles across, which was for the ancient Hawaiians a site of deep spiritual power. The most popular time to come is for the **sunrise**; the **visitor center** at the top operates from just before dawn until 3pm (weather ☎572-7749; information ☎572-9306). Hiking trails of varying difficulty cross the crater floor, where **camping** is permitted in three remote cabins, awarded by lottery two months in advance, that require a hike of four to ten miles and $15 fee per night. In addition, 15 to 25 free tent sites are available every day (first-come, first-served). Details from the National Park Service, Prince Kuhio Federal Bldg #6305, 300 Ala Moana Blvd, Honolulu HI 96813 (☎541-2693), or Haleakela National Park, PO Box 369, Makawai HI 96768.

On the way up or down, stop to eat and admire the view at *Kula's*, 3200 feet up (☎878-1535). Homemade granola breakfasts are $5; they also serve lunch and dinner.

MAUI ACTIVITIES

Promotional hand-outs, and free newspapers such as *Maui Beach Press*, will familiarize you with a wide range of possible tours and activities. Agencies throughout the island, especially along Front Street in Lahaina, offer cut-price deals well below advertised rates.

Molokini

Maui's best-known **snorkelling** and **diving** spot is the tiny crescent of Molokini, all that's left poking above the sea of a once-great volcano. There's no beach, or landfall of any kind, but you do see a lot of fish, including deep-water species. Countless cruises leave early each morning (to avoid the worst of the heat) from Maalea Harbor. Vessels range from the Kihei-based 16-passenger racing yacht *Suntan Special* ($59; ☎874-0332) up to the 150-seater *Prince Kuhio* ($65; ☎242-8777). Official rates vary from $40 to $70.

Downhill Cycle Rides

One of Maui's more unusual opportunities is to be taken by van to see the dawn on top of Haleakala, and then to roll on a bicycle 39 miles down to Paia by the sea – without pedalling once. Even Dan Quayle managed it, accompanied by six uzi-toting Secret Service men on mountain bikes. Serious cyclists may find the slow pace of the trip frustrating; complete novices or the unfit shouldn't try; the in-betweens think it's great.

Companies running trips for around $100 (including pick-ups) include *Cruiser Bob's Downhill*, in Paia (☎667-7717), and *Maui Downhill* in Kahului (☎871-2155).

Makawao and Paia

Coming down from Haleakala, Hwy-365 leads north to two laid-back little country towns, populated mainly by Californian veterans of the Sixties: **MAKAWAO**, five miles up from the ocean, and **PAIA**, Maui's first plantation town, near the surfing beach of **Hookipa**. Neither has much accommodation, but advertisements at Paia's wholefood store *Mana Foods*, 49 Baldwin Ave (☎579-8078), offer rooms for around $25. In the center of Makawa, the friendly Italian restaurant *Casanova's*, 1188 Makawao Ave (☎572-0220), puts on live music at night, thanks to the local community of rock exiles. Fresh fish is the specialty in Paia, at *Paia Fishmarket*, 101 Hana Hwy (☎579-8030), and the more expensive but greatly recommended *Mama's Fish House*, 799 Poho Place (☎579-8488), set next to the sea a mile along the Hana Highway. Vegetarians will be glad of *The Vegan*, at 115 Baldwin Ave, Paia (closed Mon; ☎579-9144).

The Road to Hana

The rains which fall on Haleakala cascade down Maui's long windward flank, covering it in thick jungle-like vegetation. Convicts in the Twenties hacked out a road along the coast which has become a major tourist attraction in its own right, twisting tortuously in and out of gorges, past innumerable waterfalls, and over more than fifty tiny one-lane bridges. All year round, and especially in June, the route is ablaze with color, from orchids up to rainbow eucalyptus and African tulip trees with their orange blossom.

The usual day's excursion is roughly fifty miles (three hours) each way from Paia, to Oheo Gulch just past Hana. Don't attempt it if it's raining; in good weather, this road of hairpin turns, while not too difficult, is not recommended for the potentially carsick. Drivers can miss much of the scenery, and may prefer to take an **organized tour** with *No Ka Oi Scenic Tours* (☎871-9008) or *Polynesian Adventure Tours* (☎877-4242).

Keanae

Halfway along the Hana Highway, a side road down to the peninsula of **KEANAE** brings you to a small Hawaiian village with taro fields and a fine old church. Banana trees and birds of paradise grow in abundance, and the ocean surf crashes onto sharp headlands of black *aa* lava. YMCA **Camp Keanae**, on the highway just before the turning, is a **youth hostel** (once a prison) with dorm beds at $8 per night, for a maximum of three days. Book ahead via Maui YMCA (95 Mahalini St, Wailuku HI 96793; ☎244-3253).

Hana

The former sugar town of **HANA** itself might seem a disappointment at the end of the road; really it's a pleasant enough little community that isn't especially interested in attracting tourists. *Hasegawa's General Store* is a friendly place to pick up supplies, and a delightful **red sand beach** can be reached by a trail from the end of Uakea Road.

Rooms at the deluxe *Hotel Hana-Maui* (☎248-8211; ⑧) *start* at $295; the Japanese-style *Heavenly Hana Inn* (☎248-8442; ⑤) out towards the tiny airport is better value.

Beyond Hana

A mile or two past Hana, a dirt track leads to the banyan-shaded oceanside cemetery of **Palapala Hoomau** church, where **Charles Lindbergh** was buried in 1974. The first man to fly the Atlantic, who retired to Maui for privacy, was a notorious Nazi sympathizer who once told the *Reader's Digest* that aviation is "one of those priceless possessions which permit the White Race to live at all in a sea of Yellow, Black, and Brown".

The gorgeous scenery of **Oheo Gulch**, part of Haleakala National Park, is ten miles out of Hana. Waterfalls tumble down the hillside to oceanfront meadows. If you hike up, you soon escape the crowds and reach cool rock pools which are ideal for swimming; most visitors stroll down to an attractive spot the tour operators persist in calling the **Seven Sacred Pools** – a groundless label which in its time has been attached to other features along the way, and is discouraged by Hawaiians.

If you're congenitally averse to going back the same way you came, in normal conditions (but *not* rain) it is possible with four-wheel drive to follow the road right around southern Maui, although it has several rocky and unpaved stretches and rental car insurance is invalid. At first the countryside is lovely, dotted with exclusive homes whose owners would prefer this not to become a standard tourist loop. Beyond a small black sand beach, the 1859 church at Huailoha, and the last-chance store at Kaupo, the road climbs thirty miles up bleak lava fields and rounds the corner to give spectacular views out to the island of **Kahoolawe** (a naval bombing range until 1990, which has now been returned for restoration to the Hawaiians). You're now back in upcountry Maui, and soon come to the **Tedeschi Winery** (daily 9am–5pm), Hawaii's only vineyard.

MOLOKAI

Halfway between Oahu and Maui, little **MOLOKAI** is the least touristed of the major Hawaiian islands. It doesn't have a single traffic light or elevator; a brief visit is a chance to feel how Hawaii must have been fifty years ago. The capital, **Kaunakakai**, is one dusty street of wooden falsefront stores, the scenery of **Kalaupapa Peninsula** and **Halawa Valley** is unspoiled, and gigantic **Papahoku Beach** is usually deserted. The downside is that agriculture is on the decline, and Molokai has the highest unemployment in the United States; some islanders have to commute to factory jobs in Maui.

Eastern Molokai

Halawa Valley is perhaps the finest of all Hawaii's "lost valleys", an absolute gem a laborious hour's drive east of Kaunakakai. The first view from the **overlook** is staggeringly beautiful, with Moaula Falls high in the distance half-hidden by clouds, and the rich green valley with its black sand beach below. You can continue down to the beach, where the shore is taken up with lush meadows filled with bright wildflowers, or hike for an hour up to the foot of the falls. The pool there is supposedly home to a giant lizard.

The highest **sea cliffs** in the world, four thousand feet high, are further around the northern coast. The best way to see them is by air – scheduled flights south from Molokai pass over them, as do helicopter trips.

Kalaupapa Peninsula

King Kamehameha IV set aside the flat peninsula of **Kalaupapa** in northern Molokai, created by a lava flow at the base of a colossal cliff, as a **leper colony**. Sufferers from all the islands were sent here to live out their days, separated forever from their homes and families, and without help until 1873, when the Belgian priest **Father Damien** began to improve their conditions. Robert Louis Stevenson sprang to his defence when his reputation was maligned; he eventually succumbed to the disease himself and is a likely candidate for sainthood. In the 1940s, when new drugs made leprosy (Hansen's Disease) no longer contagious, the need for isolation ended, but many patients remain. To set up a tour – you can hike ($30) or fly ($80) – call the Kalaupapa Settlement (☎567-6613). A deeply grooved path climbs from the overlook to a not-very **Phallic Rock**.

Western Molokai

The few resort hotels at the west end of Molokai are a surreal testament to the wonders a bit of water can work in a volcanic wasteland. They can't be claimed to have any character; on the other hand, **Papahoku Beach** is phenomenal. Stretching for miles of empty white sand and magnificent pounding surf, it's so massive that unscrupulous developers were able to cart much of it off to Waikiki before anyone realized.

Mauna Loa on the road down used to be a *Dole* pineapple town, and in antiquity was the birthplace of *hula*. This enclave amid the fields is now a sleepy sort of alternative arts community. There's a nice *General Store*, and the *Big Wind Kite Factory* makes kites and sells artefacts from Bali and Nepal alongside Molokai "Red Dirt" T-shirts. At the top end of town you can walk out to the old cemetery along a path of that red dirt.

Molokai Practicalities

Molokai's **airport** is in the center of the island, with rental cars and taxis but no public transport. The *Maui Princess* ferry ($25 one-way; ☎553-5736 on Molokai; ☎661-8397 on Maui) sails twice daily between Kaunakakai and Lahaina on Maui.

Rooms in **Kaunakakai** can be had at the stylish *Pau Hana Inn* (☎1-800/423-MOLO or ☎553-5347; ③), with its spreading banyan tree and low-slung buildings, or for a little more at the bizarre but comfortable *Hotel Molokai* (same phone; ③). B&Bs in superb settings along the road to Halawa, **east** of Kaunakakai, include the *Kamalo Plantation* after 10.5 miles (☎558-8236; ④), and the *Honomuni House* after 18 miles (☎558-8383; ④). In the **west**, there's the *Kaluakoi Hotel* (☎1-800/777-1700; ⑤), and *Paniolo Hale* (☎1-800/367-2984 or 552-2731; ⑤), more human in scale and less antiseptic.

Kaunakakai has good **food** at the *Pau Hana Inn* and the rough-and-ready *Mid-Nite Inn* (☎553-5302) on the main street. *Outpost Natural Foods* (☎553-3377) behind the *Chevron* garage does wholefood snacks and smoothies. The wooden-verandahed *JoJo's Cafe* is a nice place to eat in **Mauna Loa** (☎552-2803; closed Wed & Sun).

KAUAI

Although no point on the tiny island of **KAUAI** is as much as eleven miles from the sea, the variety of its landscapes is quite incredible. This is the oldest of the major islands, and erosion has had that many more million years to sculpt it into fantastic shapes. The mist-shrouded extinct volcano **Mount Waialeale** at its heart is the world's wettest spot, draining into a high land-locked swamp, full of unique plants and animals. Nearby is the chasm of **Waimea Canyon**, while the north shore holds the vertiginous green cliffs of the awe-inspiring **Na Pali** coast, familiar to millions from films such as *Jurassic Park* but the sole preserve of adventurous **hikers**. Kauai is a place to be active, on sea and land; and if you only go on one **helicopter** flight in your life, do it here.

On September 11 1992, **Hurricane Iniki** (*"9-1-1"*) slammed into Kauai; along with 300,000 tons of debris, it created a unique opportunity for the island and its tourism industry to rebuild from the ground up. The windswept trees and foliage recovered within a few months, but settlement of insurance claims and rebuilding of the resorts continues. Most budget properties, on the east shore, escaped major damage.

Lihue

Flights to Kauai arrive at the capital, **LIHUE**, where lovely little Nawiliwili Harbor welcomes *American Hawaii* boat passengers from other islands. It's roughly at the midpoint of the circle-island highway (prevented from completing a loop by the Na Pali cliffs), and has the few cheap hotels around, but as a base it's pretty undistinguished. The population is just five thousand, and downtown consists of a few tired plantation-town streets, well back from the sea and surrounded by anonymous malls.

The small **Kauai Museum** at 4428 Rice St (Mon–Fri 9am–4.30pm, Sat 9am–1pm; $3) traces the island's history from the mythical *menehune* through Captain Cook's landfall

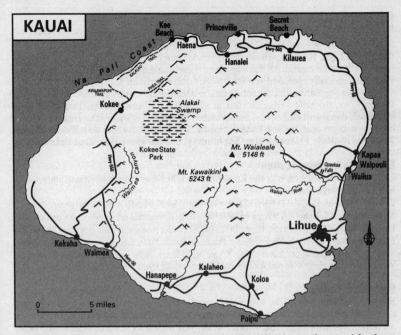

KAUAI

Na Pali Coast

Kee Beach • Haena • Princeville • Secret Beach

KALALAU TRAIL

Hwy-560 • Hanalei • Kilauea

AWAAWAPUHI TRAIL • PIHEA TRAIL

Kokee

Alakai Swamp

Kokee State Park

Mt. Waialeale ▲ 5148 ft

Hwy-56

Kapaa • Waipouli

Opaekaa Falls • Wailua

Mt. Kawaikini ▲ 5243 ft

Waimea Canyon

Wailua River

Hwy-550

Lihue

Kekaha • Waimea

Hwy-50

Hanapepe • Kalaheo • Koloa

0   5 miles

Poipu

in January 1778 and on to its sugar-growing heyday. Kauai was the one island not conquered by Kamehameha the Great; he spent six years amassing a fleet which never sailed, and settled in the end for accepting economic tribute.

Arrival and Information

Lihue's **airport** is only two miles from downtown ($5 by **taxi**; Wailua or Kapaa cost more like $15). Along with the usual **car** rental outlets, it has **helicopters** – *South Sea Helicopters* (☎245-7781) is typical in offering basic tours from $130. Shopping around in the malls, and checking freesheets like *Kauai Beach Press*, you'll find discounts. The **Hawaii Visitors Bureau** is in town at 3016 Umi St (Mon–Fri 8am–4.30pm; ☎245-3971).

Accommodation

Since Iniki, Lihue's range of budget rooms is not what it was.

Aston Kauai Beach Villas, 4330 Kauai Beach Drive (☎245-7711 or 1-800/922-7866). Condo studios at the harbor. ⑥.

Garden Island Inn, 3445 Wilcox Rd, Kalapaki Beach (☎1-800/648-0154). Near the harbor beach, refurbished after losing its roof to Iniki. ③.

Hale Lihue Motel, 2931 Kalena St (☎245-3151). Central, well-kept motel. Two-night minimum. ②.

Weston Kauai, Nawiliwili Harbor (☎1-800/228-3000). Big resort, reopened March 1994. ⑧.

Eating

The ethnic mix in Lihue means its restaurants offer a wide range of cuisines and prices.

Dani's, 4201 Rice St (☎245-4991). Mon–Sat only, 5am–1.30pm. Good-value breakfasts and lunches.

Hamura Saimin, 2956 Kress St (☎245-3271). Family-run communal Japanese food counter, open very late. Standard bowls of *saimin* (noodles) under $3, shrimp $3.75.

Kiibo, 2991 Umi St (☎245-2650). Sushi, tempura, teriyaki lunches and dinners.

East Kauai

Most Kauaians live between Lihue and the overlapping communities of **WAILUA**, **WAIPOULI** and **KAPAA**, whose malls, condos and hotels blend into each other a few miles north of the capital. All the way along there's an exposed thin strip of beach; only Wailua is especially nice, and you have to go further north for snorkelling.

The most popular tourist attraction on the island is the excursion from Wailua up the Wailua River, the only navigable river in all Hawaii, to **Fern Grotto**. This large, fern-bedecked, damp and dull cave – immortalized by Elvis Presley in *Blue Hawaii* – draws crowds in large open-topped barges, run by *Smith's* (☎822-4111) and *Waialeale Boat Tours* (☎822-4908). Following Hwy-580 brings you to the spectacular **Opaekaa Falls**.

East Coast Accommodation

Most east-coast hotels are in the luxury bracket, but there are many possibilities on a more manageable scale.

Hotel Coral Reef, 1516 Kuhio Hwy, Kapaa(☎822-4481). Small friendly hotel on the ocean. ④.

Kauai Sands, 420 Paploa Rd, Wailua (☎1-800/367-7000). Reasonable prices, discounts on cars. ③.

Lampy's B&B, 6078 Kolopua St, Kapaa (☎822-0478). Private rooms and bath, past *Coco Palms*. ③.

Plantation Hale, 484 Kuhio Hwy, Coconut Plantation (☎822-4941). Luxury beach-side condos. ⑥.

Royal Drive Cottages, 147 Royal Drive, Kapaa (☎822-2321). Fully equipped cottages beyond the Wailua Falls. Knowledgeable and friendly host. Discounts for longer stays. ⑤.

East Coast Eating

Kapaa is the only one of the towns with anything like a center; you can window-shop for restaurants along its street of wooden stores fronted by a beach park.

A Pacific Cafe, Kauai Village, Kapaa (☎822–0013). Very popular for its exotic, eclectic (and expensive) Pacific cuisine. Dinner only.

Perry's Smorgy, *Kauai Beachboy Hotel*, Coconut Plantation (☎822-3111). As on the other islands, all-you-can-eat buffets at $4.45 breakfast, $5.95 lunch, $7.95 dinner.

The King And I, Waipouli Plaza (☎822–1642). Great Thai restaurant, with vegetarian specialties.

North Kauai

That part of northern Kauai which is unique and unspoiled seems to be diminishing all the time. The astonishing valleys of the **Na Pali coast** itself must surely remain inviolate – though accessible enough by canoe to sustain large Hawaiian populations, their awesome walls shield them from any attempt to build roads in. But the bulldozers are inching ever closer. Iniki managed to slow the growth of the resort of **Princeville**, which began life as a sugar plantation in 1860 and, since its reopening in late 1993, appears once more bent on ruining a considerable area of oceanfront.

Long golden **Secret Beach**, hidden away from the road up from Kapaa, is Kauai's best-looking beach, though swimming is usually unsafe. It's an unofficial center for campers and nudists, though land-owners are cracking down on long-term stays. Driving up Hwy-56 from the south, pass **Kilauea** and then turn right at Kalihiwai. Take the second right, which is a dirt track leading to a parking area. The beach is a ten-minute walk down through the woods. At the far end there's a waterfall of beautiful fresh mountain water, and there are often spinner dolphins just offshore, especially around the picturesque 1913 Kilauea **lighthouse**. The cliffs above are a bird sanctuary.

Hanalei

For the moment, major development stops beyond Princeville, mainly because the road then crosses seven successive one-lane bridges. The first is over the Hanalei River, where the valley stretching away inland is a National Wildlife Refuge. Here endangered Hawaiian ducks, coots and stilts are protected by the preservation of their major habitats – natural wetlands and taro ponds. As a result, this is a rare chance to see a Hawaiian landscape relatively unchanged since ancient times.

The small town of **HANALEI**, set around a magnificent bay, has some low-key apartments for rent, but the area has little formal accommodation. All the roadside beaches from here on, such as **Tunnel Reef** with its sudden deep waters, are good for snorkelling; at **HAENA**, the beachfront *Camp Naue* YMCA has $12 dorm beds and $10 camping spaces (Mon–Fri ☎246-9090, Sat & Sun ☎826-6419). Of Hanalei's **restaurants**, the *Tahiti Nui* (☎826-7320) is particularly nice, with its authentic Tahitian decor, rattan screens and old prints, while the *Snack Shop and Bakery* in Ching Young Village does reasonable breakfasts and homemade pastries (☎826-6841).

The Na Pali Coast

The lush valleys of the **Na Pali coast**, separated by knife-edge ridges of rock often thousands of feet high but just a few feet thick, make Kauai one of the great hiking destinations of the world. Although many of the best views (other than from a helicopter) are from the trails in Kokee State Park (see overleaf) or boat trips out at sea, the **Kalalau Trail** along the shore is unforgettable. The full eleven miles to Kalalau Valley is arduous, and gets progressively more dangerous; in places you have to scramble along a precipitous (and shadeless) wall of crumbly red rock.

However, the first two miles of the trail, to **Hanakapiai Beach**, are probably the most beautiful. They're steep but straightforward, passing through patches of dense vegetation where you clamber over the gnarled root systems of the baffling *hala* (or pandanus) tree. Creepers and vines hang down, and it's all pretty exposed to the sun. From the beach, a further hour's hike (off the main trail), which requires a lot of climbing up little rock faces and over fallen trees, leads inland to the natural amphitheater of the towering **Hanakapiai Falls**. An absolute minimum to get to the falls and back from the trailhead at Kee Beach would be four and a half hours. Hikers and campers doing anything more than a day-hike must obtain (free) permits from the State Parks Office (3060 Eiwa St, Lihue; Mon–Fri 8am–4.15pm; ☎245–4444). There are a lot of accidents and drownings along the way, and they need a record of who may be missing.

Stores in Hanalei's small **Ching Young Village** mall specialize in equipping hiking and other expeditions. *Captain Zodiac* (☎826–9371 or ☎926-9192) offers exhilarating motorized rubber **raft trips** up the coast ($50–105), racing at top speed into caves, through tunnels, and under waterfalls – and you get a snorkelling stop too. If you have a camping permit, their 6.15am boat will drop you off at the far end of the trail for $60 one-way or $110 return. The catamaran *Kahanu* also runs half-day Na Pali snorkelling trips ($75; ☎826-4596). *Jungle Bob's* (☎826–6664) has books, maps and first-hand trail information, renting tents and backpacks. Next door, *Pedal'n'Paddle* (☎826-9069) rents out bikes ($20), as well as canoes and kayaks ($35–55) for use on the rivers and inland waterways.

South Kauai

POIPU, the southernmost point on Kauai and the island's principal beach resort, was hard hit by Iniki. Only the local beach is currently accessible, until the resorts rebuild; there's good surf and snorkelling in the area, seven-foot monk seals come ashore to sunbathe, and sea turtles can be seen close up offshore, but there's no real point basing yourself here. For good-value food, nearby **Kalaheo** has the *Brick Oven* pizzeria (closed Mon; ☎332-8561) and the popular *Kalaheo Steak House*, 4444 Papalina St (☎332-9780).

West Kauai

Two of the major scenic attractions in all Hawaii, the gorge of **Waimea Canyon** and **Kokee State Park** with its views of the Na Pali cliffs to one side and the sodden Alakai Swamp to the other, can only be reached from the west coast of Kauai. The coast itself, however, is nondescript. **WAIMEA**, the largest town, is just one short street at the foot of the poorly marked road up to the canyon. In the small shopping plaza is one of the island's three *Kauai Kitchens*, selling a good full lunch for $6. The statue of **Captain Cook**, which commemorates his "discovery" of Hawaii here on January 20 1778, is an exact replica of one in Cook's home town of Whitby, England. A little way upstream along the Waimea River, the uninspiring **Menehune Ditch** is said to be the remains of an aqueduct built by the mythical *menehune*. *Waimea Plantation Cottages* (☎338-1625; ④) are exactly what they sound like: self-contained cottages for rent.

Waimea Canyon and Kokee State Park

It's not unreasonable to call **Waimea Canyon** the "Grand Canyon of the Pacific". It may not be quite as deep, at three thousand feet, but the colors – all shades of green against the bare red earth – and the way it all manages to fit into such a tiny island, are absolutely breathtaking. The road from Waimea climbs beside the widening gorge, until after eight miles the mile-wide canyon can be seen in all its splendor. Each of the roadside lookouts is worth stopping for. Erosion by torrential rains created this landscape, but the process began when a massive geological fault almost split Kauai in two.

Explore Kokee Park as early in the day as possible; by late morning the valleys may fill with mist and cloud. Trails head off to both sides of the highway. Although the ranger station at **KOKEE**, the park headquarters, is often unstaffed, you can pick up detailed information from the small but informative **Kokee Museum** nearby, where displays center on the indigenous wildlife. Kauai is the only island where mongooses have not killed off most native **birds**, and at this height mosquitoes are no threat either, so some of the world's rarest species (such as the *o'o a'a*) survive here and nowhere else.

Kokee Lodge Housekeeping Cabins are rented by the day (PO Box 819, Waimea, Kauai, HI 96796; ☎335-6061; ③), and there's free **camping**, with permits from the parks office in Lihue (see previous page). *Kokee Lodge* has lunch specials for $7.

Awaawapuhi Trail

The **Awaawapuhi Trail** drops steeply from the road beyond Kokee, passing through three miles of dense forest before abruptly emerging at a staggering view of a valley open only to the ocean, tucked between the Na Pali cliffs. The sheer razorback ridges are almost vertical, even if they are somehow covered with clinging vegetation.

Kalalau Lookout and Pihea Trail

A few miles further up, **Kalalau Lookout** stands over the valley where the Kalalau Trail ends (see previous page) – though to attempt a descent would be certain suicide. The **Pihea Trail** follows the course of a lunatic attempt to extend the road beyond its current end. At times it narrows to a few feet, with precipitous drops to either side. Visibility can drop to nothing, as the clouds siphon across the ridges. Inland lies the **Alakai Swamp**, where the heaviest rainfall on earth collects in the volcanic rock. You can hike in, but that involves wading thigh-deep through patches of cloying sticky black swamp mud, and potentially damaging a unique environment. Better to remain here above, listening to the shrills and whistles and buzzes of a jungle without mammals or snakes, and watching the darting flashes of color. Giant ferns dangle above the trail, and orchids gleam from the undergrowth, while the trees – especially in June – erupt into brilliant flowering displays.

PART THREE

THE

CONTEXTS

A CHRONOLOGICAL INDEX

Throughout this book, we've covered the history of the various colonies, states and communities of North America in as much detail as space will allow. The chronology below is designed as a readily accessible means of drawing together the many disparate historical and cultural trends that have contributed towards the development of the modern United States. Most of the topics and incidents mentioned are covered in more detail at the relevant point in the book; we've provided page references as appropriate.

BC	30,000 BC Aleuts, Inuits and Athabascans cross frozen straits from Asia to America → p.882.		
	6000 BC With the giant bison and other oversized mammals hunted to extinction, nomadic peoples start to settle in agricultural communities.		
	1000 BC First terraced villages in New Mexico.	800 BC Adena construct Great Serpent Mound in Ohio Valley → p.219.	
AD	0–250 The peoples of the Ohio Valley establish trading links throughout the continent.		
	1–550 Anasazi Basketmakers on the Colorado → p.675.	500 Caddo build city of Cahokia around what is now St Louis.	
	700 Pueblo culture begins to develop in the Southwest → p.675.		
	750 Polynesian voyagers from the Marquesas arrive in Hawaii → p.920.		
1000	1000 Norse sailors touch on northeast coast; repelled by Algonquin → p.147.	1000 Creation of Creek settlement at Ocmulgee → p.383.	
	1100–1500 Navajo and Apache migrate from western Canada to the Southwest.	1066 Eruption of Sunset Crater in Arizona leads to rapid agricultural development → p.701.	
	Second wave of Polynesian settlers reach Hawaii from Tahiti → p.920.	1100–1276 "Golden Age" of Anasazi in Southwest → p.675; construction of Cliff Palace in Mesa Verde → p.626, and White House in Canyon de Chelly → p.708.	
	1200 Southeastern Creek build city of Etowah in Georgia.	1170 Hopi establish Old Oraibi, → p.711. Acoma Pueblo founded → p.681.	
	1492 First voyage of Christopher Columbus.	1276–99 Great Drought disperses Anasazi → p.675.	
	1497 John Cabot touches on Labrador → p.147.		

1500	1521 Ponce de León lands in Florida → p.441. 1524 Verrazano sails up the Hudson River → p.101. 1540 Francisco Vásquez de Coronado treks north from Mexico in search of cities of gold, and comes across the Grand Canyon → p.661. 1541 De Soto reaches the mouth of the Mississippi. 1565 First permanent white settlement founded by Spain in St Augustine, FL → p.461. 1579 Sir Francis Drake claims California for England → p.754. 1585 Sir Walter Raleigh lands on Roanoke Island and founds first British settlement, which vanishes mysteriously a few years later → p.355.	1550s The League of the Iroquois extends from Massachusetts to Ohio, and Canada to Kentucky. 1586 Sir Francis Drake destroys St Augustine → pp.441, 461.	1542 De la Vega, member of De Soto's Florida expedition, publishes first comprehensive description of the new land. 1589 Richard Hakluyt prints anthology of travellers' impressions of America.
1600	1604 French establish colony at Mount Desert Island, Maine → p.209. 1607 Colony of Virginia founded at Jamestown; Captain John Smith encounters the Powhatan → p.311. 1609 Spanish establish Santa Fe as northern capital of their colonial empire → p.671. 1620 Pilgrims land at Plymouth → pp.147, 163. 1626 Dutch found New Amsterdam → p.99. 1630 Boston founded as Puritan "City Upon A Hill" → p.148. 1636 New England colonists massacre the Pequot of southern Connecticut. 1638 Swedes settle in Delaware. 1664 British take control of New Amsterdam and rename it New York → p.101. 1673 Marquette and Joliet get to the northern reaches of the Mississippi River.	1619 First black slaves introduced in Virginia → p.305. 1600s The introduction of horses by the Spanish enables the development of the culture of the Plains Indians → p.512. 1639 Harvard College founded → p.157. 1675 "King Phillip" leads Wampanoag in final doomed resistance to white presence in New England → p.147.	 1643 Roger Williams publishes guide to the languages and customs of Native Americans in New England → p.173.

	1680 Pueblo Indians temporarily drive Spanish out of much of the Southwest → p.669. 1682 William Penn founds Pennsylvania as Quaker Colony → p.116.	1692 Salem witchtrials → p.161.	
1700	1718 New Orleans founded by the French → p.485. 1733 Georgia settled at Savannah → p.384. 1741 Vitus Bering lands in Alaska, presaging large-scale presence of Russian fur-traders in the region → p.884. 1755 French Acadians ("Cajuns"), expelled from Nova Scotia in Canada, settle in Louisiana → p.500. 1763 British victory in French and Indian War confirms their control of eastern continent → p.131. 1763 Spain cedes Florida to Britain → p.461. 1764 French hand Louisiana over to Spanish → p.485. 1770 Spanish establish first of trail of Catholic missions along the California coast → p.754. 1773 Growing protest at burden of English taxation finds expression in the Boston Tea Party → p.155. 1775 First shots of Revolutionary War fired at Concord and Lexington → p.157. 1776 Declaration of Independence signed → p.118. 1778 Captain Cook encounters Hawaiian islands → p.920. 1781 Cornwallis surrenders on behalf of Britain at Yorktown → p.315. 1781 Florida returns to Spanish control → p.441.	1760 Pontiac of the Ottowa joins forces with French in resisting English expansion into Great Lakes area. 1779 Captain Cook dies in Hawaii → p.936. 1787–88 Draft constitution enshrines distinction between federal government and states' rights, allowing each state to adopt its own stand on slavery. → pp.99, 116.	1782 Publication of de Crèvecoeur's *Letters from an American Farmer* → pp.170, 968.

	1789 First meeting of US Congress; George Washington becomes President → p.287. 1791 First ten amendments to constitution ratified as the Bill of Rights. 1793 Eli Whitney's invention of the cotton gin → p.184, and Samuel Slater's water-powered textile mill → p.176, mark beginning of industrialization.	1789 Olaudah Equíano (Gustavus Vassa) publishes first-hand account of his kidnapping into slavery and life as a slave → p.965.
1800	1800 Washington DC built as national capital → p.289. 1801 Louisiana ceded by Spanish to French → p.486. 1803 The Louisiana Purchase: President Jefferson buys the Louisiana territory from France for $15 million → pp.486, 559, 601. 1804–1806 Lewis and Clark expedition from St Louis to Oregon to map out new territory → pp.319, 563, 565, 601, 632, 647, 649, 653, 845. 872. 1815 Andrew Jackson's victory at the Battle of New Orleans ends the "1812 War" with Britain for control of the seas → pp.487, 491. 1819 Spain cedes Florida to the US → p.441. 1825 Erie Canal opens crucial trade route between New York and Great Lakes → pp.102, 111. 1835 Texan Revolution → p.512; Battle of the Alamo → p.521. 1836–1845 Texas an independent Republic → pp.512–513. 1846–48 War between the US and Mexico results in the cession of California and much of the Southwest to the United States → pp.661, 664, 755. 1848 Mormons arrive in Utah → p.722.	1802 West Point Military Academy formed → p.102. 1808 Importation of slaves prohibited by Congress. 1820 The Missouri Compromise permits slavery to continue in the southern states → p.202. 1838 Cherokee Indians forced onto Trail of Tears → p.417.	1820s Sequoyah develops written Cherokee language and publishes the *Cherokee Phoenix* newspaper → p.417. 1832 Frances Trollope publishes *Domestic Manners of the Americans.* 1835 De Tocqueville's *Democracy in America* appears. 1839 Abner Doubleday pioneers baseball at Cooperstown, New York → p.110. 1839 Edgar Allen Poe publishes *The Fall of the House of Usher.* 1842 Charles Dickens makes extensive lecture tour and publishes *American Notes.*

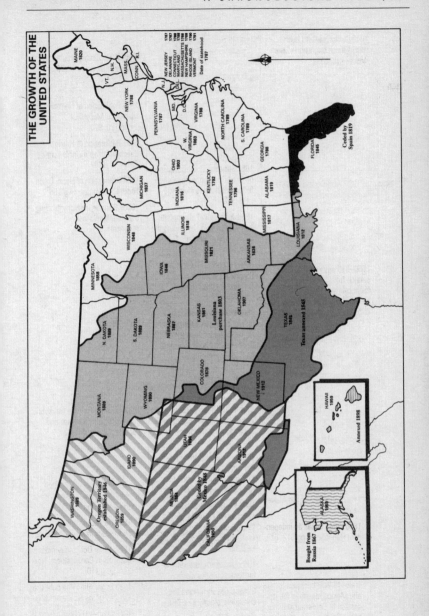

THE GROWTH OF THE UNITED STATES

	1849 California Gold Rush sparks mass migration to the West → p.755.	1848 Walt Whitman publishes *Leaves of Grass* → p.976.
1850		1851 Publication of Herman Melville's *Moby Dick* → pp.170, 970.
		1852 Publication of Harriet Beecher Stowe's *Uncle Tom's Cabin* → p.207.
	1857 Supreme Court decision on Dred Scott appears to give federal backing to slavery → p.563.	1854 Publication of Henry David Thoreau's *Walden* → p.158.
	1859 John Brown attempts to incite slave revolt by raiding the US Arsenal at Harper's Ferry → p.324.	1850s German immigrants bring the "hamburg steak" to America.
1860–61 Pony Express mail service from Missouri to California survives for 18 months before being driven out of business by the telegraph → p.569.	1860 Following election of President Lincoln, South Carolina secedes from US → p.365.	
	1861 Eleven southern states join to form the Confederate States of America → p.422. Confederate forces attack US garrison at Fort Sumter → p.368; the first shots of the Civil War → pp.305, 350.	
	1863 After a run of Confederate successes, Union victories at Vicksburg and Gettysburg mark a turning point in war → pp. 430, 129.	1862 Anthony Trollope follows in his mother's footsteps and publishes *North America*.
	1864 Navajo rounded up in Canyon de Chelly, Arizona by Kit Carson and deported to New Mexico → p.709.	
	1864–65 General Sherman marches his Union troops through Georgia, destroying southern economy and morale → p.377.	
	1865 Thirteenth amendment formally abolishes slavery.	
	General Lee surrenders the Confederate army → p.351.	
	President Lincoln assassinated five days after war ends.	
	Ku Klux Klan formed by ex-Confederate soldiers → p.351.	

1867 US purchases Alaska from Russia → p.884. 1869 Transcontinental Railroad opens → p.755.	1867 Reconstruction imposed on southern states by often corrupt Northern Republican "carpetbaggers" → p.351. 1869 Wyoming grants all women the vote → p.628. 1873 Jesse James Gang stages first ever train robbery → p.569.	1869 First inter-collegiate football game. 1870 Atlantic City's Boardwalk opens → p.140.
1875	1876 Custer's Seventh Cavalry wiped out at Little Bighorn by Sioux and Cheyenne under the leadership of Sitting Bull; US Army responds by stepping up campaign to drive the Plains Indians onto reservations → p.645. 1877 Crazy Horse murdered, Oglala Sioux deported to Missouri → p.585. 1878 Billy the Kid comes to prominence in Lincoln County Wars → p.685. 1881 Gunfight at the OK Corral → p.694. 1890 Ghost Dance cult sweeps Native Americans; massacre at Wounded Knee → p.589.	1875 First Kentucky Derby → p.394. 1876 Publication of Mark Twain's *Tom Sawyer* → p.560. 1882 Oscar Wilde lectures Colorado miners on etiquette. 1883 Buffalo Bill's Wild West Show starts touring → p.635. 1886 Statue of Liberty unveiled → p.62. 1891 Tchaikovsky conducts on opening night of New York's Carnegie Hall → p.73. 1892 *Coca-Cola* company established in Atlanta → p.376. 1896 Basketball invented in Massachusetts → p.172.
	1897 Alaskan Gold Rush → pp.889, 895, 906, 914 1898 Hawaii annexed as a territory of the USA → p.921. 1899 Spain cedes Puerto Rico, Guam and the Philippines to the USA.	
1900		1902 "Jazz" music heard for the first time in the red-light district of New Orleans → p.497. 1903 Henry Ford founds *Ford Motor Company* → p.234.

		1905 Industrial Workers of the World (the "Wobblies") hold first convention in Chicago → p.647. 1906 San Francisco earthquake kills 100 people → p.808.	1903 Wilbur and Orville Wright make first ever powered flight → p.354. 1906 William S Kellogg invents corn flakes in Battle Creek MI as a therapy for mental patients. 1906 Upton Sinclair's _The Jungle_ exposes conditions in Chicago's Stockyards → p.260. 1911 First Indianapolis 500 motor race → p.246.
	1914 Opening of Panama Canal.	1915 Ku Klux Klan claims a million members. 1917 President Wilson abandons isolationism; US enters World War I. 1920 The 18th Amendment to the Constitution, forbidding the "manufacture, sale, or transportation of intoxicating liqueurs" introduces total Prohibition to the US. The 19th Amendment grants all US women the vote.	1915 D W Griffith's melodrama _Birth Of A Nation_ has sympathetic portrayal of the Ku Klux Klan. 1920 Boston Red Sox sign Babe Ruth for a record $125,000. 1922 The Will Hays Code imposes rigorous censorship on on-screen lewdness.
1925		1927 Sacco and Vanzetti executed in Boston → p.148. Charles Lindbergh makes first flight across the Atlantic → p.296. 1929 Al Capone's St Valentine's Day Massacre in Chicago. Wall Street Crash. 1934 FBI shoot John Dillinger, Public Enemy No. 1, in Chicago → p.259. 1930s Depression hits US; President Franklin Roosevelt instigates New Deal programme → p.351. 1933 Prohibition ends. 1935 Amelia Earhart makes first flight from Hawaii to California.	1925 First presentation of _Grand Ole Opry_ show on Nashville radio → p.410. 1927 Hollywood's transition to sound; Al Jolson stars in _The Jazz Singer_. 1928 Walt Disney produces first Mickey Mouse film, _Steamboat Willie_. 1931 Empire State Building constructed → p.70. 1936 Robert Johnson records _Crossroads Blues_ → p.427. 1939 John Steinbeck's _The Grapes of Wrath_ published → p.553.

			1939 *Gone With the Wind* stars Vivien Leigh and Clark Gable → pp.376, 506.
			John Ford's *Stagecoach* stars John Wayne → p.714.
			1940 First *Kentucky Fried Chicken* diner opens → p.392.
		1941 Japanese attack Pearl Harbor; US enters World War II → p.925.	1941 Opening of Orson Welles' *Citizen Kane* → p.793.
			1941 Dedication of Mount Rushmore → p.592.
			1941 Glenn Miller records *Chattanooga Choo-Choo* → p.416.
			Jackie Robinson becomes first black player in Major League baseball.
	1946 Philippines granted independence; Guam and Puerto Rico maintained as protectorates.	1945 First atomic bomb detonated in New Mexico → p.685.	1943 Frank Sinatra drives bobby-soxers wild at New York's *Paramount Theater*.
			1946 Bugsy Siegel opens the *Flamingo*, Las Vegas' first resort casino → p.746.
1950		1950 Senator Joseph McCarthy spurs the House Un-American Activities' Committee into investigating supposed Communist infiltration in all walks of American life, including Hollywood.	1951 Ronald Reagan co-stars in *Bedtime for Bonzo*.
			1954 Elvis records *That's All Right Mama* in Sun Studios, Memphis → p.402.
		1954 Supreme Court outlaws segregation in schools (Brown vs. Topeka).	1954 Marlon Brando stars in *On The Waterfront*.
		1955 Black protesters boycott segregated buses in Montgomery, Alabama → p.422.	1955 James Dean stars in *Rebel Without A Cause*.
			Disneyland opens in Anaheim, California → p.775.
	1958 NASA set up. First US space satellite put into orbit.	1957 Riots engulf Little Rock High School, Arkansas, after enrolment of nine black students → p.435.	1957 The publication of Allen Ginsberg's *Howl* and Jack Kerouac's *On The Road* kicks off the so-called Beat Generation.
	1959 Alaska and Hawaii granted statehood → pp.884, 921.		1959 Buddy Holly, Ritchie Valens and the Big Bopper die in plane crash → p.542.
			Berry Gordy Jr sets up *Motown Records* → p.233.
			Marilyn Monroe stars in *Some Like It Hot*.

		1961 President John Kennedy instigates abortive invasion of Cuba at Bay of Pigs → p.447.	1961 Andy Warhol screen-prints cans of *Campbell's Soup*.
		1962 Riots on University of Mississippi campus protesting against enrolment of the first black student → p.429.	1962 James Brown records *Live At The Apollo* → p.81.
		1963 March on Washington culminates in Dr Martin Luther King Jr's "I have a dream" speech → p.295.	
		1963 Assassination of President Kennedy → p.535.	
		1964 President Johnson deepens American commitment in Vietnam.	
		1965 Malcolm X assassinated in Harlem → pp.91, 974.	1965 Timothy Leary, Ken Kesey and the Merry Pranksters, the Grateful Dead and the Hell's Angels all active in San Francisco → p.817.
		1965 President Johnson steers through passage of Voting Rights Act; 250,000 new black voters register before the end of the year.	Bob Dylan records *Highway 61 Revisited* → p.283.
		1965 25,000 march from Selma to Montgomery, Alabama → p.423.	
		1965 Six-day riot in Watts, Los Angeles, leaves 36 dead → p.768.	
		1967 Over 200,000 Americans involved in anti-Vietnam demos in San Francisco and New York. Norman Mailer and Joan Baez among those arrested at anti-war demo outside the Pentagon. Muhammad Ali stripped of World Heavyweight Boxing Championship following his refusal to be drafted.	1967 "Summer of Love" in San Francisco's Haight-Ashbury district → p.817. Green Bay Packers win first Superbowl.
		1968 Assassination of Dr Martin Luther King Jr in Memphis → p.403.	
		1968 Random police brutality scars Democratic Convention in Chicago → p.250.	
		1968 Tommy Smith and John Carlos give Black Power salute at Mexico Olympics.	
	1969 Neil Armstrong and Buzz Aldrin make one giant leap for mankind on the moon.	1969 Sharon Tate brutally murdered in Hollywood; Charles Manson's "Family" held responsible.	1969 Woodstock Festival held in upstate New York → p.103.

		1969 Gay men battle police on streets of New York City → p.68.	
		1969 Native Americans occupy Alcatraz → p.815.	
		1970 Six students shot dead during anti-war demonstrations at Kent State University, Ohio, and Jackson State, Mississippi.	
		1970–72 As US involvement in Vietnam draws to an end, President Nixon illegally authorizes bombing of Cambodia and Laos.	
		1972 Break-in at Democrat headquarters in Watergate building linked to Richard Nixon's re-election organization, CREEP.	1972 Francis Ford Coppola's The Godfather opens.
		1974 President Nixon is obliged to become the first president ever to resign.	1974 Symbionese Liberation Army kidnap Patty Hearst; demand that food be distributed among the poor of San Francisco → p.829.
1975			1977 George Lucas produces Star Wars.
			1977 John Travolta stars in Saturday Night Fever.
			1977 Elvis dies in Graceland → p.403.
			1977 Roots attracts nightly TV audience of 80 million.
		1978 Gay Supervisor Harvey Milk and Mayor George Moscone shot in San Francisco → p.816.	1979 Sugarhill Gang release Rappers' Delight.
		1979 Nuclear leak at Three Mile Island in Pennsylvania.	
		1980 Continuing detention of US hostages in Iran scuppers President Carter's chances of re-election and paves way for Ronald Reagan.	1982 Alice Walker publishes The Color Purple → p.971.
	1983 Development of Star Wars space-defence programme announced → p.613.	1983 US Marines land in Grenada.	1982 Release of Michael Jackson's Thriller video spurs growth of MTV.
		1984 Democrats adopt Geraldine Ferraro as first female candidate for US vice-president.	1984 Bruce Springsteen records Born In The USA.
	1986 Space shuttle Challenger explodes on take-off.		1984 Arnold Schwarzenegger is the Terminator.
			1984 Madonna's Like A Virgin hits number 1.

		1986 US Air Force bombs Libya. Irangate scandal reveals that Ollie North set up arms-for-hostages deals with the Iranians.	
		1987 "The Quilt" spread on the Mall in Washington DC as memorial to AIDS fatalities → p.817.	1987 God threatens to call Oral Roberts home → p.554.
		1988 Early campaign successes make Jesse Jackson the first-ever black front-runner for the presidency.	
		1989 US troops blast Noriega out of Panama with rock'n'roll.	
			1990 Donald Trump's Taj Mahal casino opens in Atlantic City → p.141.
		1991 US Army leads allied forces in Operation Desert Storm in Middle East.	
		1992 LA erupts in riots.	
		1992 Hurricane Andrew hits Florida and the Gulf of Mexico → p.443; Hurricane Iniki hits Kauai → p.946.	
		1992 Bill Clinton elected President → p.435.	
		1993 Shootings of foreign visitors dent Florida tourism → p.441.	1993 Seattle's grunge scene hits rock mainstream with new albums from Nirvana and Pearl Jam → p.852.
		1993 Midwest devastated by record flooding → pp.565, 567.	1993 Last episode of *Cheers*.

BOOKS

It would be futile to attempt to provide a comprehensive overview of American literature in the limited space available. The following bibliography is, therefore, a personal selection of those books which proved most useful or enjoyable during the preparation of this guide.

HISTORY AND SOCIETY

James Baldwin, *No Name On The Street, The Fire Next Time, Evidence Of Things Not Seen*, and many others. The most brilliant prose stylist of twentieth-century America. Stunningly incisive accounts of the black experience in the cities of the USA, although Baldwin was such a powerful polemicist that he was occasionally swept away by his own rhetoric.

John W Blassingame, *Black New Orleans 1860–1880*. Comprehensive and impressively detailed history of urban blacks during Reconstruction.

Hugh Brogan, *Penguin History of the USA*. Good, up-to-date and very complete history of the United States.

Dee Brown, *Bury My Heart At Wounded Knee*. Twenty years on from its first publication, this remains the best narrative of the impact of white settlement and expansion on Native Americans across the continent.

Peter Carroll and David Noble, *The Free and the Unfree: A New History of the USA*. A good interpretive history of American political development, focusing on the wide gap between those who hold power and those who are disadvantaged on grounds of race, sex or class.

Alston Chase, *Playing God In Yellowstone*. Taking Yellowstone as his example, the icono-clastic Chase explores the truth behind the National Park Service's rhetoric.

Alistair Cooke, *America Observed*. Incisive, illuminating comments on American life, by the broadcaster and chief American correspondent for the *Manchester Guardian* from 1946 to 1972.

Mike Davis, *City of Quartz*. City politics, neighborhood gangs, unions, film noir and religion are drawn together in this award-winning, leftist, hyperbolic history of Los Angeles.

Joan Didion, *The White Album, Slouching Toward Bethlehem, Miami and others*. Essays on the American way of life, drawing heavily on the late Sixties. A respected social commentator, Didion spoils the act at times by dropping too many names.

Frederick Douglass et al, *The Classic Slave Narratives*. Compilation of ex-slaves' autobiographies, ranging from Olaudah Equíano's kidnapping in Africa and global wanderings to Frederick Douglass' eloquent denunciation of slavery. Includes Harriet Jacobs' story of her escape from Edenton, North Carolina – see p.353.

Michael Kioni Dudley, *A Hawaiian Nation*. Immensely readable, if short, two-volume account of Hawaiian history and theology, which culminates in the well-argued *Call For Hawaiian Sovereignty*.

Brian Fagan, *Ancient North America*. Archeological history of America's native peoples, from the first hunters to cross the Bering Strait up to European contact.

Frances Fitzgerald *Cities on a Hill*. Intelligent, sympathetic exploration of four of the odder corners of American culture, including San Francisco's gay Castro district and the Rajneeshi community in eastern Oregon – see p.880.

Shelby Foote, *The Civil War: A Narrative*. Epic three-volume account containing anything you could possibly want to know about the War Between The States.

Stephen Jay Gould, *Bully for Brontosaurus*. Gould's best-known collection of essays weaves together natural history and contemporary Americana in a most readable form.

U S Grant, *Personal Memoirs*. Encouraged by Mark Twain, the Union general and subsequent president wrote his autobiography just before his death, in a (successful) bid to recoup his horrendous debts. At first the book feels oddly downbeat, but the man's down-to-earth modesty grows on you.

James R Grossman, *Land of Hope*. Scholarly yet moving account of the exodus of Southern blacks to northern cities, specifically Chicago, during the early twentieth century. Though it focuses on the broader social and economic issues, it also manages to bring to life the individual stories involved.

Frederick Hoxie (ed), *Indians in American History*. Eye-opening collection of essays focusing on the role of Native Americans in US history, and presenting them as active and aware (if hopelessly out-gunned) players rather than passive victims. Filled with illustrations and extensive quotes from journals and contemporary accounts of Native Americans from across the US.

J B Jackson, *American Space*. Engagingly written work which traces the transition of America from a rural to an urban and industrialized nation in the crucial decade immediately after the Civil War.

Charles Jencks, *The New Moderns*. Occasionally impenetrable, always opinionated academic study of neo-modernist architecture as designed by Philip Johnson, Peter Eisenman and Richard Meier. Interviews and lots of glossy photographs lighten the tone.

Roger G Kennedy, *Rediscovering America*. Collected essays by one of America's most readable historians, appointed by Clinton to run the National Park Service. Kennedy looks behind the gloss of conventional tellings to reveal something of the real story of how America came to be.

Jill Ker Conway (ed), *Written by Herself*. Splendid anthology of womens' autobiographies from the mid-1800s to the present, including sections on African Americans, scientists, pioneer women and artists.

Meriwether Lewis and William Clark, *The Original Journals of the Lewis and Clark Expedition, 1804–1806*. Eight volumes of meticulous jottings by the Northwest's first inland explorers, scrupulously following President Jefferson's orders to record every detail of flora, fauna and native inhabitant.

Ed Marston (editor), *Reopening The Western Frontier*. Assorted contributors to *High Country News* reflect on possible futures for what was once the Wild West.

James M McPherson, *Battle Cry Of Freedom*. Extremely readable history of the Civil War which integrates and explains the complex social, economic, political and military factors into one concise volume. Highly recommended.

James Mooney, *The Ghost Dance Religion and The Sioux Outbreak of 1890*. An extraordinary Bureau of Ethnology report, first published in 1890 but still available in paperback. Mooney persuaded his Washington superiors to allow him to roam the West in search of first-hand evidence, and even interviewed Wovoka, the Ghost Dance prophet, in person.

Marc Reisner, *Cadillac Desert*. Compendious but compulsive account of the environmental and political impact on the West of this century's mania for dam-building and large-scale irrigation projects.

Hunter S Thompson, *The Great Shark Hunt* and *Songs of the Doomed*. Accessible and varied collections of the maverick Dr Gonzo's journalistic rantings on contemporary American life and politics. Spiced up by tales of his own anarchic love of good times, guns and gambling.

Mark Twain, *Roughing It, Life on the Mississippi*, and many others. Mark Twain was by far the funniest and most vivid chronicler of nineteenth-century America. *Roughing It*, which covers his early wanderings across the continent, all the way to Hawaii, is absolutely compelling.

John Unruh, *The Plains Across*. A history of the wagon trains, drawing heavily on pioneer journals.

Geoffrey C Ward, with Ric and Ken Burns, *The Civil War*. Marvellous illustrated history of the Civil War, designed to accompany the TV series and using hundreds of the same photographs.

Juan Williams, *Eyes On The Prize*. Informative and detailed accompaniment to the excellent TV series, covering the Civil Rights years from the early Fifties up to 1966, with lots of rare and some very familiar photos.

Edmund Wilson, *Patriotic Gore*. Fascinating eight-hundred-page survey of the literature of the American Civil War, which in its own right serves as an immensely readable narrative of the conflict.

BIOGRAPHY AND ORAL HISTORY

Maya Angelou, *I Know Why The Caged Bird Sings*. First volume of an autobiographical sequence which provides an ultimately uplifting account of how a black girl transcended her traumatic childhood in 1930s Arkansas.

William F Cody, *The Life Of Hon William F Cody, Known As Buffalo Bill*. Larger than life autobiography of one of the great characters of the Wild West. Particularly treasurable for the moment when he refers to himself more formally as "Bison William".

Ben Hamper, *Rivethead*. With a great introduction by Michael Moore (director of *Roger & Me*), Rivethead tells you what it's like to work on the assembly lines of General Motors in Flint, Michigan, and provides an often hilarious tirade against the fat cats of GM.

Henry Hampton and Steve Fayer, *Voices of Freedom*. Hugely impressive oral history of the Civil Rights movement, heavily drawn from the TV series.

Joyce Johnson, *Minor Characters*. Johnson, Jack Kerouac's girlfriend and "muse", tells her own story and those of the other women in the 1950s East Village scene, revealing the stiflingly reactionary male elitism of the Beats.

Malcolm X, with Alex Haley, *The Autobiography of Malcolm X*. Searingly honest and moving account of a progress from street hoodlum to political leadership. Written on the hoof over a period of years, it traces the development of Malcolm X's thought before, during and after his split from the Nation of Islam. The conclusion, when he talks about his impending assassination, is painful in the extreme.

Muhammad Ali, *The Greatest*. Powerful and entertaining autobiography of the Louisville boy who grew up to become world heavyweight boxing champion. The most memorable parts deal with his fight against the Vietnam draft and the subsequent stripping away of his world championship status.

John Neihardt, *Black Elk Speaks*. Oglala Sioux healer relates his life and times to the "Nebraskan poet laureate".

Tony Parker, *A Place Called Bird*. Fascinating oral history based on interviews with the inhabitants of a tiny town in the very center of Kansas, the heartland of the Midwest.

Ishbel Ross, *Rebel Rose*. Evocative rebel-yelling biography of Rose Greenhow, glamorous Washington socialite and remarkably brave Confederate spy. Works equally well as an exciting tale of political espionage and an impeccably detailed historical document.

Quinta Scott and Susan Croce Kelly, *Route 66*. Moving oral histories and monochrome photographs trace the life span of the now abandoned 2000-mile highway immortalized in film, novels and song.

Ralph Steadman, *Scar Strangled Banner*. Warped, cynical and crazy underview of America, full of sketches and hacked-about photos, from sometime Hunter S Thompson collaborator and illustrator.

Joanna L Stratton, *Pioneer Women*. Original memoirs by women – mothers, teachers, homesteaders and circuit riders – who ventured across the Plains from 1854 to 1890. Lively, superbly detailed accounts, with chapters on journeys, homebuilding, daily domestic life, the church, the cowtown, temperance and suffrage.

Studs Terkel, *American Dreams Lost and Found*. Interviews with ordinary American citizens. As illuminating a guide to US life as you could hope for.

Frank Waters, *Book Of The Hopi*. Extraordinary insight into the traditions and beliefs of the Hopi, prepared through years of interviews and approved by tribal elders.

ENTERTAINMENT AND CULTURE

Kenneth Anger, *Hollywood Babylon*. A vicious yet high-spirited romp through Tinseltown's greatest scandals, amply illustrated with gory and repulsive photographs, and always inclined to bend the facts for the sake of a good story. A shoddily researched second volume covers more recent times.

Thomas A Bass, *The Newtonian Casino*. Daydreaming gamblers will love this account of the attempt by a bunch of Californian college dropouts, with computers hidden in their shoes, to beat the casinos in Las Vegas.

Thomas Boswell, *How Life Imitates The World Series and Time Begins On Opening Day*. Boswell elevates baseball into something higher than a mere sport. Full of perceptive insights and amusing anecdotes.

Peter Guralnick, *Lost Highways, Feel Like Going Home*, and *Sweet Soul Music*. Thoroughly researched personal histories of black popular music, packed with obsessive detail on all the great names.

Charlotte Greig, *Will You Still Love Me Tomorrow?* Enthusiastic feminist appraisal of (predominantly American) girl groups from the Fifties (the Chantels and the Crystals) through to contemporary rap stars like Salt'n'Pepa. Lots of photos and personal recollections make it a great read.

Gerri Hershey, *Nowhere To Run: The History of Soul Music*. Definitive rundown on the evolution of soul music from the gospel heyday of the Forties through the Memphis, Motown and Philly scenes to the sounds of the early Eighties. Strong on social commentary and political background and studded with anecdotes and interviews.

Bill Malone, *Country Music, USA: A Fifty Year History*. An academic but thoroughly engrossing study of the roots and development of country music up to 1968.

Greil Marcus, *Dead Elvis*. Vastly entertaining overview of the many Elvis myths, if a little hastily put together from previously published articles. Marcus' *Mystery Train* is an intelligent and absorbing overview of American popular music, from Robert Johnson to Elvis Presley and Randy Newman.

Robert Palmer, *Deep Blues*. Readable history of the development and personalities of the Delta Blues.

Randall Reise, *Nashville Babylon*. Thrashes the squeaky clean image of the country music scene. Cocaine, whiskey, infidelity, murder, rape, and other skeletons are dug up from the cupboards of some unlikely characters.

John Williams, *Into The Badlands*. Williams' interviews with a batch of America's very best crime writers build a picture of the underbelly of US society from the Montana mountainsides of James Crumley to the mean streets of Elmore Leonard's Detroit. He lapses into sexism, however, when dealing with Chicago's Sara Paretsky, who "is learning as she goes along".

TRAVEL WRITING

Edward Abbey, *The Journey Home*. Hilarious accounts of whitewater rafting and desert hiking trips alternate with essays, by the man who inspired the radical environmentalist movement Earth First! All of Abbey's many books, especially *Desert Solitaire*, a journal of time spent as a ranger in Arches National Park, make great travelling companions.

James Agee and Walker Evans, *Let Us Now Praise Famous Men*. A deeply personal but also richly evocative journal of travels through the rural lands of the Depression-era Deep South, complemented by Evans' powerful photographs.

Stephen Brook, *New York Days, New York Nights*. An Englishman's drily witty impressions of the Big Apple, with chapters on every aspect of the place from flotation chambers to Jewish restaurants. Brook's *Honky Tonk Gelato* (also in Picador) treats Texas in a similar, if sometimes patronizing, vein.

Bill Bryson, *The Lost Continent*. Using his boyhood home of Des Moines in Iowa as a benchmark, the author travels the length and breadth of America to find the perfect small town. At times hilarious but marred by some very smug, self-indulgent comments.

J Hector St-John de Crèvecoeur, *Letters from an American Farmer and Sketches of Eighteenth-Century America*. First published in 1782, a remarkable account of the complexities of Revolutionary America.

Ian Frazier, *Great Plains*. An immaculately researched and well-written travelogue containing a wealth of information on the people of the American prairielands from Native Americans to the soldiers who staff the region's many nuclear installations.

Bill Kaysing, *Great Hot Springs of the West*. If you like the idea of soaking your bones in pools of naturally hot water in some of America's most beautiful locales, this fact-packed guidebook will point you in the right direction.

Jack Kerouac, *On The Road*. Definitive account of transcontinental Beatnik wanderings which now reads as a curiously dated period piece. Not as incoherent as you might expect.

James A MacMahon (ed), *Audobon Society Nature Guides*. Attractively produced, fully illustrated and easy to use guides to the flora and fauna of seven different US regional ecosystems, covering the entire country from coast to coast and from grasslands to glaciers.

Virginia and Lee McAlester, *A Field Guide to American Houses*. Well-illustrated and engagingly readable guide to America's rich variety of domestic architecture, from pre-colonial to post-modern.

John McPhee, *Encounters with the Arch Druid*. In three interlinked narratives, environmental activist and Friends of the Earth founder David Brower confronts developers, miners and dam builders, while trying to protect three different American wilderness areas – the Atlantic shoreline, the Grand Canyon, and the Cascades of the Pacific Northwest.

William Least Heat Moon, *Blue Highways*. Account of a mammoth loop tour of the US by backroads, in which the author interviews ordinary people in ordinary places. A good overview of rural America, with lots of interesting details on Native Americans. His next book, *Prairyerth*, opted for the microcosmic approach, taking six hundred loving pages over the story of Chase County, Kansas.

Jonathan Raban, *Old Glory*. A somewhat pompous though always interesting account of Raban's journey on a small craft down the Mississippi River from the headwaters in Minnesota to the bayous of Louisiana.

Bernard A Weisberger (ed), *The WPA Guide to America*. Prepared during the New Deal as part of a make-work programme for writers, these guides paint a fairly comprehensive portrait of 1930s and earlier America. Also available are state by state guides, most of them out of print but easily found in US libraries and secondhand bookshops.

Edmund White, *States of Desire: Travels in Gay America*. A revealing account of life in gay communities across the country, focusing heavily on San Francisco and New York.

FICTION

Nelson Algren, *A Walk on the Wild Side*. Bleak novel charting the decline of a youth who flees his Tex-Mex border town after raping a girl and embarks upon a hobo life, ending up in the sleazy red-light district of New Orleans.

Paul Auster, *New York Trilogy*. Three Borgesian investigations into the mystery and madness of contemporary New York. Using the conventions of the detective novel, Auster unfolds a disturbed and disturbing picture of the city.

Tom Bodett, *The End Of The Road*. First novel by broadcaster from Homer, Alaska, who shot to fame as the voice on *Motel 6* radio commercials. Funny, witty and certainly better than his often shallow collections of essays (viz. *As Far As You Can Go Without A Passport*), but for the best value invest in some of his taped books.

James Lee Burke, *Black Cherry Blues*. Cajun cop Dave Robicheaux sets out to expose alliances between government and organized crime in the beautiful environs of Louisiana and Montana. A detective book that has it all.

George Washington Cable, *The Grandissimes*. Romantic saga of Creole family feuds, written at the turn of the century but set during the Louisiana Purchase. Superb evocation of steamy Louisiana, elite Creole lifestyle and the resistance of New Orleans to its Americanization. Apparently shocking at the time for its sympathetic portrayal of blacks.

Willa Cather, *Death Comes for the Archbishop*. Melodramatic title for a sober but very emotive fictionalized biography of the first archbishop of Santa Fe. *The Professor's House* has a similar feel for the history of the Southwest, reaching back to the Anasazi, while her Nebraska novels, such as the stunning *My Antonia*, provide a great sense of pioneer hardships on the Plains.

Nick Cave, *And The Ass Saw The Angel*. Rock singer Cave creates the ultimate outsider and subjects him to more misery, abuse and hardship than you'll find in the collected works of Faulkner and McCullers. An intense, well-executed jibe at moral excesses in the Deep South and a superb pastiche of the heavy-weight southern novel.

Michael Chabon, *The Mysteries of Pittsburgh*. A just-graduated gangster's son learns about life during a sweltering Pittsburgh summer.

Kate Chopin, *The Awakening*. Subversive story of a bourgeois married woman whose fight for independence ends in tragedy. Swampy turn-of-the-century Louisiana is portrayed as both a sensual hotbed for her sexual awakening and as her eventual nemesis.

James Crumley, *The Wrong Case*. The lack of an intricate plot is more than compensated for by accounts of Montana scenery and the hapless detective Milo Milodragonovic, a man with a drink problem and a knack for doing things the hard way. An enjoyable, easy read.

John Dos Passos, *USA*. Hugely ambitious novel (originally a trilogy) which grapples with the US in the early decades of this century from every possible angle. Gripping human stories with a strong political and historical perspective.

Louise Erdrich, *The Beet Queen*. Slightly offbeat tale of passion and obsession amongst poor white North Dakota folk – particularly women – set against the backdrop of an economy and culture changing with the introduction of sugar beet as a crop in the 1940s. Erdrich's *Love Medicine* describes two Native American families on a North Dakota reservation, the strong women who hold them together, and the tensions between tradition and "progress".

William Faulkner, *The Reivers*. The last and most humorous work of this celebrated southern author. *The Sound and the Fury*, a fascinating study of prejudice, set like most of his books in the fictional Yoknatapawpha County in Mississippi, is a much more difficult read.

A B Guthrie Jr, *Big Sky*. When first published in the Thirties it shattered the credibility of the mythical west peddled by Hollywood. Realistic historical fiction at its very best, following desperate mountain man and fugitive Boone Caudill whose idyllic life in Montana was ended by the arrival of white settlers.

Carl Hiaasen, *Double Whammy*. Hiaasen is the most humorous crime writer on the scene. This one sees rednecks/bass fishermen and religious sects caught up in a fast-moving and hilarious plot.

George V Higgins, *Penance for Jerry Kennedy*. Crime thriller written almost entirely in the dialogue of Boston lowlifes and crooked lawmen.

Tony Hillerman, *The Dark Wind* and many others. The adventures of Jim Chee of the Navajo Tribal Police on the reservations of northern Arizona, forever dabbling in dark and mysterious forces churned up from the Anasazi past.

Chester Himes, *Cotton Comes to Harlem*, *Blind Man with a Pistol*, and many others. Action-packed and uproariously violent novels set in New York's Harlem, starring the much-feared detectives Coffin Ed Johnson and Grave Digger Jones.

Zora Neale Hurston, *Spunk*. Short stories celebrating black culture and experience from around the country, by a writer from Florida who became one of the bright stars of the Harlem cultural renaissance in the 1920s.

Garrison Keillor, *Lake Wobegon Days*. Wry, witty tales about a mythical Minnesota small town. Pokes fun at the rural Midwest with an affectionate finger.

Harper Lee, *To Kill A Mockingbird*. Classic tale of racial conflict and society's view of an outsider, Boo Radley, as seen through the eyes of children.

Elmore Leonard, *Freaky Deaky*. One of the funniest of Leonard's tough, brutal thrillers. Set in Detroit, it follows two former Sixties radicals who turn to crime.

Jack London, *The Call of the Wild and Other Stories*. London's classic tale, of a family pet discovering the ways of the wilderness while forced to pull sleds across Alaska's gold rush trails, is still essential reading before a trip to the far north.

Norman MacLean, *A River Runs Through It*. Unputdownable – the best ever novel about fly-fishing, set in beautiful Montana lake country.

Armistead Maupin, *Tales Of The City*. Long-running saga comprised of sympathetic and entertaining human tales of life in San Francisco, that also work surprisingly well as suspenseful stand-alone novels. The fact that many of its key characters are gay meant that over the years the series became a chronicle of the impact of AIDS on the city.

Carson McCullers, *Member of the Wedding*. McCullers is unrivalled in her sensitive treatment of misfits, in this case the attitude of a small southern community to a deaf mute.

Herman Melville, *Moby Dick*. Compendious and compelling account of nineteenth-century whaling, packed with details on American life from New England to the Pacific.

Margaret Mitchell, *Gone With The Wind*. Worth a read even if you know the lines of Scarlett and Rhett off by heart.

Toni Morrison, *Beloved*. Exquisitely written ghost story by the Nobel-Prize-winning novelist, which traces the painful lives of a group of freed slaves after Reconstruction, and the obsession a mother develops after murdering her baby daughter to spare her a life of slavery.

Flannery O'Connor, *A Good Man is Hard to Find*. Short stories, featuring strong, obsessive characters, that explore religious tensions and racial conflicts in the Deep South.

Grace Paley, *The Little Disturbances of Man*. Shrewd love-hate stories set in the immigrant Jewish communities of New York.

Anne Rice, *Interview with the Vampire*. One of a series of sensual, chilling vampire novels set in Louisiana.

J D Salinger, *The Catcher in the Rye*. Classic novel of adolescence, tracing Holden Caulfield's sardonic journey through the streets of New York.

Mari Sandoz, *Old Jules*. Written in 1935, this fictionalized biography gives a wonderful insight to the life of the author's pioneer Swiss father on the Nebraskan plains. Sandoz's other major work *Crazy Horse* contains great historical overviews but is spoilt somewhat by her insistence on narrating it through Sioux eyes.

John Steinbeck, *The Grapes of Wrath*. The classic account of a migrant family forsaking the Midwest for the Promised Land. Steinbeck's lighthearted but crisply observed novella *Cannery Row* captures daily life on the prewar Monterey waterfront, and the epic *East of Eden* (Pan) updates and re-sets the Bible in the Salinas Valley and details three generations of familial feuding.

Peter Taylor, *Summons To Memphis*. Warm tale of a wealthy Tennessee family who make a downmarket move from Nashville to Memphis during the Thirties.

John Kennedy Toole, *A Confederacy of Dunces*. Anarchic black tragicomedy in which the pompous and repulsive antihero Ignatius O Reilly wreaks havoc through an insalubrious and surreal New Orleans.

Alice Walker, *In Love and Trouble*. Moving and powerful stories of black women in the South, from the author of the much-acclaimed *The Color Purple*.

Eudora Welty, *The Ponder Heart*. Quirky, humorous evocation of life in a backwater Mississippi town. Her most critically acclaimed work, *The Optimist's Daughter*, explores the tensions between a judge's daughter and her stepmother.

Richard Wright, *Native Son*. A harrowing story about Bigger Thomas, a black chauffeur who accidently kills his employer's daughter. The story develops his relationship with his lawyer, the closest he has ever come to being on an equal footing with a white.

BIOGRAPHIES

The following are some of the many personalities from American history whose names recur throughout this book. You can find detailed page references for all of them in the main index, which begins on p.977.

Susan B Anthony (1820–1906). Pioneer suffragette and president of the US suffragist society from 1892 to 1900, Anthony began her campaigning career in the temperance movement. She was also a committed abolitionist, published the New York liberal paper *The Revolution* (1868–70), and advocated equal pay for women, as well as donning bloomers to protest against the constrictive nature of women's clothing.

Louis Armstrong (1900–1971). New Orleans-based jazz trumpeter, known as Satchmo (from "satchel mouth"). Credited with devising the scat style of improvisational singing, and for his individualistic style which foregrounded the solo performance above that of the band. Well known for his humor and affability, Armstrong also appeared in a number of Hollywood films.

Benedict Arnold (1741–1801). Revolutionary commander who shifted his allegiance to the British in 1779, but soon lost popularity with loyalists for leaving his British contact, Major John Andre, to be captured and hanged as a spy.

Chuck Berry (born 1926). Rock'n'roll pioneer born in (*Johnny B*) Goode Street, St Louis. Consummate lyricist, red-hot guitarist, and sharp businessman.

Billy the Kid (1859–1881). The subject of innumerable Wild-West legends, former busboy William Bonney made his name in the Lincoln County Wars in New Mexico. His brief and bloody career ended at the hands of Pat Garrett.

Daniel Boone (1735–1820). Legendary hunter, trapper and explorer. One of the first whites to cross the Appalachians and stake out Kentucky for settlement.

John Brown (1800–1859). Fervent white abolitionist who, as part of a grand plan to set up a free state for escaped slaves, seized the US Armory at Harpers Ferry. After a short battle, Brown was captured, tried and hanged for treason.

Calamity Jane (1852–1903). Bawdy frontierswoman, cook, dancer, prostitute and camp follower, who in 1876 took up as bullwhacker for the gold rush camps in South Dakota. "Calam" travelled with Wild West shows but was fired for boozing and brawling.

Al Capone (1899–1947). Bootlegger and gangster who controlled the Chicago underworld during the 1920s, and later died in Florida of syphilis.

Andrew Carnegie (1835–1919). Scots-born industrialist and philanthropist, responsible for major innovations in the steel industry. By the close of the nineteenth century, when US steel production outdid that in Britain, most of it came from Carnegie's "vertically integrated" company – which owned the coal fields and the ships and railroads for transportation of the supplies to the mills.

Kit Carson (1809–1868). Carson, who moved to Taos in 1826 and became a guide on the Santa Fe Trail and "mountain man", was later instrumental in rounding up the Navajo from Canyon de Chelly.

William "Buffalo Bill" Cody (1846–1917). Pony Express rider and Indian scout immortalized by the dime novels of Ned Buntline. His Wild West show toured all over the world.

Francisco Vázquez de Coronado (1510–1554). Spanish explorer who travelled through the Southwest as far as Kansas in search of cities of gold. When he eventually threw in the towel in 1542 and returned to Mexico, he faced a series of indictments for his lack of success.

Crazy Horse Ta-Sunko-Witko (1842?–1877). Oglala Sioux leader, and one of the most able and determined Native American warriors. Prominent in the Fetterman Massacre, Battle of the Rosebud and Custer's Last Stand. Murdered at Fort Robinson, Nebraska.

Davy Crockett (1786–1836). Frontiersman, Indian fighter and Tennessee politician, who perished at the Alamo with all the other American volunteers. Popularly represented as a backwoods boy in a raccoon hat, with no education but the gift of the gab, Crockett was, in fact, less unconventional than his legend suggests.

George Armstrong Custer (1839–1876). Legendary US Cavalry general whose first big mistake – leading over two hundred troops into an ambush at Little Bighorn – was his last.

John Dillinger (1902–1934). Bankrobber whose criminal activities earned him the title of Public Enemy Number One. After being set up by the legendary "Lady in Red", Dillinger was killed by FBI agents outside a Chicago movie theater.

Walt Disney (1901–1966). Inventor of Mickey Mouse, Donald Duck and Disneyland, Disney was also Hollywood's Last Tycoon, singlehandedly controlling a vast media and entertainment empire.

Frederick Douglass (1817?–1895). Escaped slave who rose to prominence as a writer and orator in the abolitionist movement.

W E B Du Bois, (1868–1963). Black intellectual and civil rights activist best known for his debates with Booker T Washington (see below) in the early part of this century, and his role in forming the National Association for the Advancement of Colored People. A long-time campaigner for the independence of African colonies, he joined the Communist Party in 1961 and emigrated to Ghana where he renounced his US citizenship.

Bob Dylan (born 1941). North-country Minnesota boy who redefined himself first as Woody-Guthrie-style folkie and later as enigmatic rock star. The endearing elliptical games of his youth have long since grown wearisome in a man of 50, but he can still write songs to equal his best.

Amelia Earheart (1897–1937). Pioneer aviatrix, the first woman to fly solo across the Atlantic (in 1932), and the first person ever to fly the perilous route from Hawaii to California (1935). Both she and her navigator vanished without trace on an attempted round-the-world flight, and were last contacted just near the international date line.

Thomas Edison (1847–1931). Mercurial inventor and entrepreneur who developed the light bulb, motion pictures and phonograph records. He also founded General Electric, still one of the largest US corporations.

Thomas Stearns Eliot (1888–1965). Born beside the Mississippi in St Louis, Eliot reversed the usual American pattern and moved east, first to Harvard and then England, where he was awarded the Nobel Prize for Literature for a body of poetry including *The Waste Land* and *The Four Quartets*.

Henry Ford (1863–1947). Michigan farmer's son and industrial genius who pioneered assembly-line production in his car factories. A vehement right-winger, particularly on trade union and racial issues.

Benjamin Franklin (1706–1790). Printer, inventor, diplomat and politician, responsible amongst other things for publishing *Poor Richard's Almanac* (a litany of mottos advocating prudence and honesty), setting up America's first public library, the invention of bifocal glasses and early experiments with electricity. Franklin also helped draft the Declaration of Independence, and went to France to seek aid for the revolutionary cause.

Geronimo (1829–1909). Brilliant Chiricahua Apache leader who battled the US Army in Arizona and New Mexico throughout the 1880s. Despite US promises, after surrendering he and his people were deported to Florida.

Ulysses Simpson Grant (1822–1885). At the start of the 1860s, the 38-year-old Ulysses Grant was finding it difficult to hold down a part-time job in his brother's saddle shop; within ten years he had led the Union armies to victory in the Civil War, and become president of the US.

William Randolph Hearst (1863–1951). Publishing magnate and role model for *Citizen Kane*, whose inflammatory "yellow journalism" kindled public support for the Spanish-America War.

Billie Holiday (1915–1959). Definitive song stylist – not quite blues, not quite jazz – who made her greatest recordings with Lester Young and Duke Ellington.

Buddy Holly (1936–1959). Bespectacled kid from Lubbock, Texas, who died at 22 but was the first and the greatest of rock's singer-songwriters.

Henry Hudson (1565–1611). English explorer whose expedition for the Dutch East India Company to find a route from Europe to Asia through the Arctic led to the discovery of the Hudson River in 1609 – which he mistakenly believed would lead to the Pacific – and formed the basis for Dutch colonization in the New World.

Howard Hughes (1905–1976). Business magnate and Hollywood film producer (*Hell's Angels*, 1930; *Scarface*, 1932), who became increasingly eccentric after an aircraft crash in 1946. Twenty years later, he sold his majority holding in *TWA* for $500,000,000 and lived from then on in complete seclusion in sealed-off hotel suites.

Andrew Jackson (1767–1845). Military general who was a major light in the Revolutionary War. His defeat of the British in New Orleans in 1815 led to huge popular support, and he was elected seventh US president (Democrat) in 1829. The first president from west of the Appalachians, Jackson had much grass-roots support in Tennessee, and his election is seen as the first truly democratic choice in the nation's history.

Rev Jesse Jackson (born 1941). Black religious and political leader whose Rainbow Coalition has come to represent the most viable progressive alternative to the centrist Democratic Party.

Thomas Jefferson (1743–1838). Author of the Declaration of Independence, third US president, and slave-owner, Jefferson was a strong advocate of freedom of the press and of religion, as well as being an accomplished architect.

Lyndon Baines Johnson (1908–1973). Brash Texan Democrat sworn in as president two hours after John Kennedy's assassination in 1963. Johnson pushed through liberal civil rights and social welfare bills, but his failure to deal with the increasingly horrific mess of Vietnam left him obliged not to seek re-election in 1968.

Robert Johnson (1911?–1938). Seminal Delta bluesman, whose songs were imbued with such a brooding aura that he was rumored to have sold his soul to the Devil. The clearest, earliest fore-runner of rock'n'roll.

Kamehameha the Great (1760?–1819). The first man to unite the Hawaiian islands – by terror, force of personality, and shrewd exploitation of European expertise.

Helen Keller (1880–1968). Despite being struck blind and deaf by scarlet fever as an infant, Keller's writings and activism made her an inspirational early leader in the movement for equal rights for disabled people.

John Fitzgerald Kennedy (1917–1963). When elected in 1960, Kennedy was the youngest ever, and the first Catholic, president. His liberal domestic policies (known as "new frontier" programmes) and success in securing the nuclear test ban treaty with the USSR and Britain won him huge popularity, as did his superficially glamorous life with wife Jackie. His assassination in Dallas, on November 22 1963, might be said to mark the beginning of a long period of disillusionment and hopelessness in the American psyche.

Dr Martin Luther King Jr (1929–1968). Baptist minister who was the main black spokesperson during the Civil Rights years, and was awarded the Nobel Peace Prize after his "I have a dream" speech. Remembered by a public holiday in most states, and a street name in most major cities.

General Marie Joseph Paul Yves Roch Gilbert du Motier Lafayette (1757–1834). French aristocrat, known as "the hero of two worlds" for supporting the Americans in the Revolutionary War, who went on to fight with the revolutionary bourgeoisie in France. A great friend of George Washington, Lafayette advocated religious tolerance and the abolition of slavery.

Robert Edward Lee (1807–1870). Confederate Civil War general, considered one of the outstanding military strategists of all time. Enjoyed early success by whipping the vastly superior Union forces under the incompetent McClellan, but crashed to defeat at Gettysburg.

Meriwether Lewis (1774–1809) and **William Clark** (1770–1838). Jointly famed as leaders of the first exploratory expedition west from the Mississippi to the Pacific in 1804–1805. Lewis' journals and Clark's drawings are invaluable documents of pre-conquest western US.

Abraham Lincoln (1809–1865). To northerners at least, the most revered of all US presidents. The son of a Kentucky backwoodsman, he taught himself law and later entered Illinois politics, beating better-known opponents for the 1860 Democratic presidential nomination. He led the Union through the Civil War, but was shot five days after the Confederate surrender.

Charles Lindbergh (1902–1974). In 1927, Lindbergh became the first person to complete a solo flight across the Atlantic, in the *Spirit of St Louis*, named for his home town. Ticker-tape parades feted him across the continent, and the "Lindy Hop" was named for him. The kidnapping and murder of his infant son was one of the most notorious crimes of the Thirties, but his pronounced Nazi sympathies lost him public support.

Huey Long (1893–1935). Flamboyant, populist governor of Louisiana known as the "Kingfish". His radical social welfare policies and tax reforms boosted the morale of poor rural whites during the Depression, and as senator, in the last three years of his life, he claimed his "Share the Wealth" programme would make "every man a king". However, his corrupt and intimidating style of government made him plenty of enemies, and he was eventually assassinated in still-mysterious circumstances in Baton Rouge.

Joe Louis (1914–1981). Black Detroit heavyweight boxer who took the world championship from Mussolini-sidekick Primo Carnera in 1937 and retained it for twelve years.

Malcolm X (1925–1965). Successful burglar who came into contact in prison with the teachings of Elijah Muhammad's Nation of Islam, rose to become its leading minister and spokesperson, and then broke with the organization after a trip to Mecca and tour of Africa. Malcolm occasionally worked with Dr Martin Luther King Jr during his Civil Rights campaigns, and for many people his militant approach remains more persuasive than Dr King's.

Joseph McCarthy (1909–1957). Republican Senator for Wisconsin, notorious for his hysterical and unproven charges of Communist subversion in high government circles. President Truman called him a "pathological character assassin" and his career was ended when the Senate censured him for unconstitutional behavior.

J Pierpoint Morgan (1837–1913). The quintessential New York financier, Morgan achieved sufficient wealth to buy out Andrew Carnegie and served as a broker between world governments.

Muhammad Ali (born 1941). Heavyweight boxer who upon winning the world title from Sonny Liston in 1964 announced that he was a member of the Nation of Islam. Within three years his anti-war stance – "no Vietcong ever called me nigger" – had cast him into the wilderness, but eventually America took him to its bosom once more.

Carry Nation (1846–1911). Temperance activist and suffragette whose tendency to take an axe to saloons after storming in, singing hymns and bellowing Biblical insults, won her no popularity with the official temperance movement (although she made lots of money on lecture tours). Frequently imprisoned, she paid her fines from souvenir axe sales.

Richard Nixon (born 1913). From his earliest days as Eisenhower's vice-president – a position obtained with the help of his maudlin "Checkers" speech, about his little puppy dog – Nixon was the man American liberals most loved to hate. That he emerged from the turmoil of 1968 as America's president made a mockery of the idea that the Sixties would turn out to be a progressive decade. The seemingly relentless progress of his latest rehabilitation, following the disgrace of Watergate, has much to do with an enduring and perverse media fondness for him.

Annie Oakley (1860–1926). Performer with Buffalo Bill's Wild West show. Nicknamed "Little Miss Sure Shot", she once shot the cigar from the mouth of Kaiser Wilhelm.

Georgia O'Keeffe (1887–1986). Prolific painter whose stark, brightly colored abstractions of flowers and the Southwest desert won her acclaim as one of the greatest modern US artists.

Dolly Parton (born 1946). Country singer, movie star, perennial talk-show guest and part-owner of a theme park.

William Penn (1644–1718). British Quaker, often imprisoned in England for his beliefs. He gradually softened towards other doctrines, and campaigned strongly against any form of persecution, eventually establishing the colony of Pennsylvania as a refuge for religious minorities.

John Wesley Powell (1834–1902). After losing an arm in the Civil War, Powell headed west to lead the first group of white men through the rivers and canyons of the Colorado Plateau.

Elvis Presley (1935–1977). Poor white boy from Tupelo, Mississippi, who moved to Memphis and became the first and the greatest white rock'n'roll star. Whether you blame Colonel Tom Parker or Elvis himself, within a couple of years he was throwing away his magnificent voice on empty show-tunes, and embarking on the long road to Hamburger Heaven.

Paul Revere (1735–1818). Silversmith and unofficial political leader of the mechanic class in Boston in the period leading up to the Revolutionary War. As principal rider for Boston's Committee of Safety, in April 1775 he made the famed horseback journey from Boston to Concord to warn the rebels that the British were coming; thus started the War of Independence.

John D Rockefeller (1839–1937). Petroleum magnate whose *Standard Oil* company dominated the US and international markets from the 1880s to 1911, when the government dissolved his monopoly. Also a great philanthropist, in his later years he gave away his money – over half a billion dollars.

Franklin Delano Roosevelt (1882–1945). Four-term Democratic president, crippled by polio in 1920, who steered the country through the Depression with the closest the US has ever come to having socialist policies: his "New Deal" provided work for the unemployed and enforced collective bargaining with unions. His wartime leadership was often criticized, especially, with hindsight, his appeasement of Stalin.

Theodore (Teddy) Roosevelt (1858–1919). Explorer, writer, soldier and Republican president from 1901 to 1909. His "square deal" policies, which included "trust busting" and government arbitration in wage disputes, were seen to serve the public interest over Big Business, and he won the Nobel Peace Prize in 1906 for mediating an end to the Russo-Japanese War. In 1912 he founded the Progressive Party and ran (unsuccessfully) for president as an independent, advocating a strong social service state.

Dred Scott (1795?–1858). Black slave who made constitutional history as the plaintiff in a widely publicized but unsuccessful test case, in which he sought his freedom on the grounds that his master had taken him to live in a free state. The ruling effectively allowed slavery in US territories and was a leading factor in the build-up to the Civil War.

William Tecumseh Sherman (1820–1891). The Union general who burned Atlanta and boasted about it in his memoirs, and invented the blitzkrieg by laying waste to Georgia. The bane of his later life was to be greeted at all official functions with *Marching through Georgia*, a song he detested. His son, a Jesuit priest, had to be forcibly persuaded from attempting his own march thirty years later.

Frank Sinatra (born 1915). Italian boy from Hoboken, NJ, who made his name thrilling bobby-soxers with New York's Tommy Dorsey Band in the early Forties and has barely let up since. One of the few singers to turn into a decent movie actor.

Sitting Bull Tatanka Iyotake (1834–1890). Chief of the Dakota Sioux and leader of the Native American forces at the Battle of Little Bighorn. Pursued by the army, he escaped to Canada but surrendered in 1881. He was killed by police in the attempt to suppress the 1890 Ghost Dance movement.

Bruce Springsteen (born 1949). New Jersey singer-songwriter known as "the Boss". His energetic and poignant articulations of white, male, working-class America are often dismissed as machismo; President Reagan missed the point completely in the 1980s and announced his approval of Springsteen's *Born in the USA*, mistaking its ironic blue-collar disillusionment for reactionary blue-eyed patriotism.

Harriet Beecher Stowe (1811–1896). Though she had little first-hand experience of the South, Stowe's *Uncle Tom's Cabin* aroused the world in fierce opposition to slavery. Abraham Lincoln greeted her with the words "so this is the little lady that made this great big war".

Peter (Petrus) Stuyvesant (1592–1672). Early governor of all Dutch colonies in North America, known as "Peg-leg Pete" for his wooden leg. He arrived in New Amsterdam (now New York) in 1647, doubling the colony's size and population, but was so unpopular, ignoring all appeals for self-government, that in 1664 he was forced to surrender the colony to the British. His farm, the Bowerie, gave the district in New York City its name.

Harriet Tubman (1820–1913). Escaped from slavery in Maryland in 1849 to become the leading abolitionist voice in the pre-Civil War years. Led hundreds of slaves to freedom on the Underground Railroad and served as a nurse and spy for Union forces during the war.

Nat Turner (1800–1831). Black preacher who led five other Virginia slaves on a murderous rampage, killing over fifty whites, mostly with knives and axes, in a single day. In reaction, whites murdered hundreds of blacks and enacted an even more repressive regime.

Mark Twain (1835–1910). The great humorist and novelist, whose works provide the most vivid imaginable account of pioneer days across the continent, was also a powerful polemicist for liberal causes, and pioneered white-suit chic long before Tom Wolfe. He pursued his desire to typeset his own books, and break free from the evil machinations of self-important publishers, almost to the point of bankruptcy.

George Wallace (born 1919). Segregationist three-times Alabama governor; received 13 percent of the popular vote in the 1968 presidential election and looked set to increase his tally in the 1972 race before he was shot and paralyzed. Towards the end of his political career he eschewed his previous racist policies and was re-elected governor in 1982.

Booker Taliaferro Washington (1856–1915). Controversial self-taught black educationalist who founded Tuskegee University. His 1901 book *Up From Slavery* proposed that blacks should abandon campaigns for voting rights and instead gain skills to work for economic gains.

John Wayne (1907–1979). Alias "the Duke": movie macho man, legendary boozer, Reagan role model and right-wing crank.

Walt Whitman (1819–1892). Writer and poet whose *Leaves of Grass*, first published in 1848, is among the most original and passionate works of American literature.

Hank Williams (1923–1953). Country music legend whose compositions (*I Saw The Light*, *Jambalaya*, etc) are still Nashville standards. A drink- and drug-sodden lifestyle accounted for his premature death.

Frank Lloyd Wright (1867–1959). Prolific architect who came to prominence around 1900 with a series of prototypical suburban houses and went on to design such landmarks as New York's Guggenheim Museum.

Wilbur (1867–1912) and **Orville** (1871–1948) **Wright**. Bicycle shop proprietors from Dayton, Ohio, who went on to greater things at Kitty Hawk, North Carolina, when they made the world's first ever powered flight on December 17 1903 – it lasted twelve seconds.

Brigham Young (1801–1877). The son of near-illiterate Vermont farmers, Young led the Mormons to Utah following the assassination of Joseph Smith in 1844. More of a pragmatist than a theologian, he confronted the full force of the US to establish a permanent home for his people.

INDEX

ROUGH GUIDE FAVORITES	
Sports	
Cheyenne Frontier Days, WY	→ p.601
Daytona Beach, FL	→ p.460
Fenway Park, Boston, MA	→ p.161
Indianapolis Speedway, IN	→ p.246
Kentucky Derby, Louisville, KY	→ p.394
Rose Bowl, Pasadena, CA	→ p.785
Wrigley Field, Chicago, IL	→ p.259

ROUGH GUIDE FAVORITES		
Ski Resorts		
Alyeska, AK	→ p.899	
Aspen, CO	→ p.618	
Crested Butte, CO	→ p.621	
Jackson, WY	→ p.642	
Mammoth Lakes, CA	→ p.807	
Park City, UT	→ p.743	
Stowe, VT	→ p.199	
Summit County, CO	→ p.615	
Sun Valley, ID	→ p.655	

ROUGH GUIDE FAVORITES Scenic Drives	
Blue Ridge Parkway, VA	→ p.322
Going-to-the-Sun Road, MT	→ p.652
Hatcher Pass, AK	→ p.911
Lake Superior South Shore, MI	→ p.242
Moqui Dugway, UT	→ p.736
Red Mountain Pass, CO	→ p.625
River Road, TX	→ p.546
The Road to Hana, HI	→ p.944
The Sandhills, NE	→ p.583
Sawtooth National Recreation Area, ID	→ p.656
St Charles Street Car, LA	→ p.488
Wapiti Valley, WY	→ p.635

DIRECT ORDERS IN THE USA

Title	ISBN	Price
Able to Travel	1858281105	$19.95
Australia	1858280354	$18.95
Berlin	1858280338	$13.99
Brittany & Normandy	1858280192	$14.95
Bulgaria	1858280478	$14.99
Canada	185828001X	$14.95
Crete	1858280494	$14.95
Cyprus	185828032X	$13.99
Czech & Slovak Republics	185828029X	$14.95
Egypt	1858280753	$17.95
England	1858280788	$16.95
Europe	185828077X	$18.95
Florida	1858280109	$14.95
France	1858280508	$16.95
Germany	1858280257	$17.95
Greece	1858280206	$16.95
Guatemala & Belize	1858280451	$14.95
Holland, Belgium & Luxembourg	1858280877	$15.95
Hong Kong & Macau	1858280664	$13.95
Hungary	1858280214	$13.95
Italy	1858280311	$17.95
Kenya	1858280435	$15.95
Mediterranean Wildlife	1858280699	$15.95
Morocco	1858280400	$16.95
Nepal	185828046X	$13.95
New York	1858280583	$13.95
Paris	1858280389	$13.95
Poland	1858280346	$16.95
Prague	185828015X	$14.95
Provence & the Côte d'Azur	1858280230	$14.95
St Petersburg	1858280303	$14.95
Scandinavia	1858280397	$16.99
Sicily	1858280370	$14.99
Thailand	1858280168	$15.95
Tunisia	1858280656	$15.95
USA	185828080X	$18.95
Venice	1858280362	$13.99
Women Travel	1858280710	$12.95
Zimbabwe & Botswana	1858280419	$16.95

Rough Guides are available from all good bookstores, but can be obtained directly in the USA and Worldwide (except the UK*) from Penguin:

Charge your order by Master Card or Visa (US$15.00 minimum order): call 1-800-255-6476; or send orders, with complete name, address and zip code, and list price, plus $2.00 shipping and handling per order to: Consumer Sales, Penguin USA, PO Box 999 – Dept #17109, Bergenfield, NJ 07621. No COD. Prepay foreign orders by international money order, a cheque drawn on a US bank, or US currency. No postage stamps are accepted. All orders are subject to stock availability at the time they are processed. Refunds will be made for books not available at that time. Please allow a minimum of four weeks for delivery.

The availability and published prices quoted are correct at the time of going to press but are subject to alteration without prior notice. Titles currently not available outside the UK will be available by January 1995. Call to check.

* For UK orders, see separate price list.

DIRECT ORDERS IN THE UK

Title	ISBN	Price
Amsterdam	1858280184	£6.99
Australia	1858280354	£12.99
Barcelona & Catalunya	1858280486	£7.99
Berlin	1858280338	£8.99
Brazil	0747101272	£7.95
Brittany & Normandy	1858280192	£7.99
Bulgaria	1858280478	£8.99
California	1858280575	£9.99
Canada	185828001X	£10.99
Crete	1858280494	£6.99
Cyprus	185828032X	£8.99
Czech & Slovak Republics	185828029X	£8.99
Egypt	1858280753	£10.99
England	1858280788	£9.99
Europe	185828077X	£14.99
Florida	1858280109	£8.99
France	1858280508	£9.99
Germany	1858280257	£11.99
Greece	1858280206	£9.99
Guatemala & Belize	1858280451	£9.99
Holland, Belgium & Luxembourg	1858280036	£8.99
Hong Kong & Macau	1858280664	£8.99
Hungary	1858280214	£7.99
Ireland	1858280516	£8.99
Italy	1858280311	£12.99
Kenya	1858280435	£9.99
Mediterranean Wildlife	0747100993	£7.95
Morocco	1858280400	£9.99
Nepal	185828046X	£8.99
New York	1858280583	£8.99
Nothing Ventured	0747102082	£7.99
Paris	1858280389	£7.99
Peru	0747102546	£7.95
Poland	1858280346	£9.99
Portugal	1858280222	£7.99
Prague	185828015X	£7.99
Provence & the Côte d'Azur	1858280230	£8.99
Pyrenees	1858280524	£7.99
St Petersburg	1858280303	£8.99
San Francisco	0747102589	£5.99
Scandinavia	1858280397	£10.99
Sicily	1858280370	£8.99
Spain	1858280079	£8.99
Thailand	1858280168	£8.99
Tunisia	1858280656	£8.99
Turkey	1858280133	£8.99
Tuscany & Umbria	1858280559	£8.99
USA	185828080X	£12.99
Venice	1858280362	£8.99
West Africa	1858280141	£12.99
Women Travel	1858280710	£7.99
Zimbabwe & Botswana	1858280419	£10.99

Rough Guides are available from all good bookstores, but can be obtained directly in the UK* from Penguin by contacting:

Penguin Direct, Penguin Books Ltd, Bath Road, Harmondsworth, West Drayton, Middlesex UB7 0DA; or telephone our credit line on 081-899 4036 (9am–5pm) and ask for Penguin Direct. Visa, Access and Amex accepted. Delivery will normally be within 14 working days. Penguin Direct ordering facilities are only available in the UK.

The availability and published prices quoted are correct at the time of going to press but are subject to alteration without prior notice.

For USA and international orders, see separate price list.

Hertz the freedom to Travel

You are
A STUDENT

You travel
THE WORLD

You want
TO SAVE MONEY

Here's how

The International
Student Identity Card

Available at Student Travel Offices Worldwide.

Entitles you to discounts and special services worldwide.

USA

THE ROUGH GUIDE

Rough Guide credits

Series Editor:	Mark Ellingham
Editorial:	Martin Dunford, John Fisher, Greg Ward, Jonathan Buckley, Jules Brown, Graham Parker, Samantha Cook, Jo Mead
Production:	Susanne Hillen, Andy Hilliard, Gail Jammy, Vivien Antwi, Melissa Flack, Alan Spicer
Finance:	Celia Crowley, Simon Carloss
Publicity:	Richard Trillo

All four authors would like to thank everyone at Rough Guides for their continued support, help and encouragement; Andrew Gilchrist, Andrew Neather and Wendy Ferguson for their contributions to the first edition; for their original text, and prompt and detailed updates, Mick Sinclair (Florida, California and parts of Nevada), Deborah Bosley (California), and Jack Holland and Martin Dunford (New York); Marjorie Jensen in Hawaii and Phil Lee in the Northwest; Stefan Loose in Berlin; Micromap Ltd, for map revisions; and Margaret Doyle, Gareth Nash, and Susanne Hillen for expert proof-reading to a tight schedule.

Greg: Thanks to everybody in the office for the daily round of drama and excitement; to Nancy Everist, Sharon Maloof, Paul Vargas and Rosemary Drexel in New Mexico; to Jeri Cartwright, David Porter and Stacey Kouris in Salt Lake City; to David Nicholson and the Rev Al Green; to my parents; and especially Robert, Jules, and Sam for lots of fun on the road, and keeping me going at home too.

Sam: In the USA, special mention to Lorene Lambert, Mark Forrester, June Norman, Al Elmore, Cristina Castro, Teresa Watts, Pawel Kwiatkowski, Carole Mumford, and Jenny Stacey. Back home, big thanks to Jim Cook, Nat Payne, Leslie Faizi, Ally Scott, Mark Graindorge, Sophie Perkins and Margaret O'Brien. Thanks also to all the team, especially Greg for being a great editor and splendid travelling companion, but above all, this is, again, for Pam Cook.

Tim: Bottomless gratitude to Sharon Gaiptman, Linda Mickel and Arna & Jeff in Alaska, and everyone else who helped out in the "Great Land". Also to everyone in Colorado: Kristy Summers, Paula Sheridan, Jim Felton, Darcey Campbell and Gina Croft. Hello again to Jim Karas, Nancy Milton, Mary Ethel Emmanuel, Jim Williams. and to Bruce and Joe in Hot Springs, SD. More thanks due to Greg Ward and Pat Richardson. Personal thanks and gratitude to Daniel Jerome, John Breslin and Tony Clare for support during an itinerant year, and of course, to JILL !

Jamie: Once again, thanks to Hilary Delamere, Jules Brown, Greg Ward, Ian and Jane (and Sam and Mully) in the UK, and Danny, Maayan (and Leore) Klein in New York, Mom in DC, Randy Terry and James T Gibson in Chicago, Greg, Syvilla and Kyle Rachal in LA, and, more than ever, to Catherine, Brando and Judah.

The publishers and authors have done their best to ensure the accuracy and currency of all the information in *The Rough Guide to the USA*; however, they can accept no responsibility for any loss, injury or inconvenience sustained by any traveller as a result of information or advice contained in the guide.

This second edition published 1994 by Rough Guides Ltd, 1 Mercer Street, London WC2H 9QJ.

Distributed by the Penguin Group:

Penguin Books Ltd, 27 Wrights Lane, London W8 5TZ.
Penguin Books USA Inc., 375 Hudson Street, New York 10014, USA.
Penguin Books Australia Ltd, 487 Maroondah Highway, PO Box 257, Ringwood, Victoria 3134, Australia.
Penguin Books Canada Ltd, 10 Alcorn Avenue, Toronto, Ontario M4V 1E4, Canada.
Penguin Books (NZ) Ltd, 182–190 Wairau Road, Auckland 10, New Zealand.

Originally published in the UK by Harrap Columbus Ltd, 1992.
Previous edition published in the United States and Canada as *The Real Guide USA*.
Typeset in Linotron Univers and Century Old Style to an original design by Andrew Oliver.
Printed in the UK by Cox & Wyman Ltd, Reading, Berks.

Incidental illustrations in Parts One and Three by Ed Briant.

Front cover photo: Bryce Canyon, Utah. Back cover photo: Grand Junction, Colorado.

© Samantha Cook, Jamie Jensen, Tim Perry and Greg Ward 1992, 1994.

No part of this book may be reproduced in any form without permission from the publisher except for the quotation of brief passages in reviews.

1024pp. includes index
A catalogue record for this book is available from the British Library.
ISBN 1-85828-080-X